W9-CDD-523

Cost Accounting

Charles T. Horngren Series in Accounting

Auditing and Assurance Services: An integrated Approach, 12th ed. *Arens/Elder/Beasley*
Governmental and Nonprofit Accounting: Theory and Practice, 9th ed. *Freeman/Shoulders/Allison/Patton/Smith*
Financial Accounting, 7th ed. *Harrison/Horngren*
Cases in Financial Reporting, 5th ed. *Hirst/McAnally*
Cost Accounting: A Managerial Emphasis, 13th ed. *Horngren/Datar/Foster/Rajan/Ittner*
Accounting, 7th ed. *Horngren/Harrison*
Introduction to Financial Accounting, 9th ed. *Horngren/Sundem/Elliot*
Introduction to Management Accounting, 14th ed. *Horngren/Sundem/Stratton*

Cost Accounting

A Managerial Emphasis

Thirteenth Edition

Charles T. Horngren
Stanford University

Srikant M. Datar
Harvard University

George Foster
Stanford University

Madhav V. Rajan
Stanford University

Christopher Ittner
University of Pennsylvania

Upper Saddle River, NJ 07458

Library of Congress Cataloging-in-Publication Data

Cost accounting : a managerial emphasis / Charles T. Horngren ... [et al.].— Thirteenth ed.
p. cm.
Includes bibliographical references and index.
ISBN-13: 978-0-13-612663-8 (casebound)
ISBN-10: 0-13-612663-4 (casebound)
1. Cost accounting. I. Horngren, Charles T., 1926–
HF5686.C8H59 2008
658.15'11—dc22
2008001681

AVP/Editor-in-Chief: Eric Svendsen
Editorial Assistant: Mauricio Escoto
Senior Marketing Manager: Jodi Bassett
Associate Director, Production Editorial: Judy Leale
Production Project Manager: Kerri Tomasso
AV Project Manager: Rhonda Aversa
Permissions Coordinator: Charles Morris
Senior Operations Supervisor: Arnold Vila
Operations Specialist: Michelle Klein
Interior Design: Judy Allen
Senior Art Director: Steve Frim
Cover Design: Steven Frim
Cover Photo: Digital Vision: Photographer: Jeremy Woodhouse
Composition/Full-Service Project Management: GEX Publishing Services
Printer/Binder: Quebecor World Color/Versailles
Typeface: Sabon 10/12

Credits and acknowledgments borrowed from other sources and reproduced, with permission, in this textbook appear on appropriate page within text.

Photo Credits: page 3 © Lee Snider / CORBIS All Rights Reserved; **page 15** Getty Images/Digital Vision; **page 27** AP Wide World Photos; **page 33** Michael Newman/PhotoEdit; **page 61** Melissa Zavadil; **page 77** Boeing Satellite Systems, Inc.; **page 97** David Young Wolff/PhotoEdit Inc.; **page 106** U.S. Air Force; **page 137** Comstock Production Department/ Alamy Images; **page 159** Corbis/SABA Press Photos, Inc.; **page 181** Spencer Grant/PhotoEdit Inc.; **page 196** Rusty Jarrett/Getty Images; Inc. **page 225** Stephen Chernin/NewsCom; **page 237** © image100/Corbis; **page 261** Mary Altaffer/AP World Wide Photos; **page 273** RobertMaass/CORBIS–NY; **page 299** AP World Wide Photos; **page 310** Brownie Harris/Corbis/Stock Market; **page 337** Scott Olson/Getty Images/Newscom; **page 354** Anthony Johnson © Dorling Kindersley; **page 387** Union Pacific Historical Collection; **page 398** © Sherwin Crasto / Reuters / Corbis; **page 429** Parker Hannifin Corporate Headquarters; **page 437** Michael Newman/PhotoEdit Inc.; **page 463** Courtesy of Clevelandskyscrapers.com; **page 483** Yonathan Weitzman/Reuters/ Landov LLC; **page 501** Getty Images Inc.; **page 515** Bill Aron/PhotoEdit Inc.; **page 541** Paramount/ Picture Desk, Inc./Kobal Collection; **page 559** Andre Jenny/Alamy Images; **page 573** Dennis Hallinan/Alamy Images; **page 587** Peter Frischmuth/Argus/Peter Arnold, Inc.; **page 601** © Jasper Juinen/ CORBIS All Rights Reserved; **page 624** Adidas—Salomon AG; **page 639** © Gideon Mendel/CORBIS-NY All Rights Reserved; **page 653** Al Behrman/AP Wide World Photos; **page 665** © David Butow/CORBIS-NY All Rights Reserved; **page 678** Harry How/Getty Images Inc.; **page 699** © FK Photo/CORBIS-NY All Rights Reserved; **page 712** Photos.com; **page 733** © Mike Kepka/CORBIS-NY All Rights Reserved; **page 751** Mason Morfit/Getty Images, Inc.—Taxi; **page 769** Symantec Corporation; **page 785** Bruce Hands/Getty Images, Inc.—Stone Allstock; **page 799** AP Wide World Photos; **page 818** AP Wide World Photos.

Pearson Education LTD., London
Pearson Education Singapore, Pte. Ltd.
Pearson Education, Canada, Inc.
Pearson Education–Japan
Pearson Education Australia PTY, Ltd.
Pearson Education North Asia Ltd.
Pearson Educación de Mexico, S.A. de C.V.
Pearson Education Malaysia, Pte. Ltd.

10 9 8 7 6 5 4
ISBN-13: 978-0-13-612663-8
ISBN-10: 0-13-612663-4

To Our Families
Joan, Scott, Mary, Susie, Cathy (CH)
Swati, Radhika, Gayatri, Sidharth (SD)
The Foster Family (GF)
Gayathri, Sanjana, Anupama (MVR)
Caroline, Cameron, Kyle (CI)

About the Authors

Charles T. Horngren is the Edmund W. Littlefield Professor of Accounting, Emeritus, at Stanford University. A Graduate of Marquette University, he received his MBA from Harvard University and his Ph.D. from the University of Chicago. He is also the recipient of honorary doctorates from Marquette University and DePaul University.

A Certified Public Accountant, Horngren served on the Accounting Principles Board for six years, the Financial Accounting Standards Board Advisory Council for five years, and the Council of the American Institute of Certified Public Accountants for three years. For six years, he served as a trustee of the Financial Accounting Foundation, which oversees the Financial Accounting Standards Board and the Government Accounting Standards Board. Horngren is a member of the Accounting Hall of Fame.

A member of the American Accounting Association, Horngren has been its President and its Director of Research. He received its first Outstanding Accounting Educator Award. The California Certified Public Accountants Foundation gave Horngren its Faculty Excellence Award and its Distinguished Professor Award. He is the first person to have received both awards.

The American Institute of Certified Public Accountants presented its first Outstanding Educator Award to Horngren.

Horngren was named Accountant of the Year, Education, by the national professional accounting fraternity, Beta Alpha Psi.

Professor Horngren is also a member of the Institute of Management Accountants, from whom he received its Distinguished Service Award. He was also a member of the Institutes' Board of Regents, which administers the Certified Management Accountant examinations.

Horngren is the author of other accounting books published by Prentice Hall: *Introduction to Management Accounting*, 13th ed. (2005, with Sundem and Stratton); *Introduction to Financial Accounting*, 9th ed. (2005, with Sundem and Elliott); *Accounting*, 6th ed. (2005, with Harrison and Bamber); and *Financial Accounting*, 6th ed. (2005, with Harrison).

Horngren is the Consulting Editor for the Charles T. Horngren Series in Accounting.

Srikant M. Datar is the Arthur Lowes Dickinson Professor of Business Administration and Senior Associate Dean at Harvard University. A graduate with distinction from the University of Bombay, he received gold medals upon graduation from the Indian Institute of Management, Ahmedabad, and the Institute of Cost and Works Accountants of India. A Chartered Accountant, he holds two masters degrees and a Ph.D. from Stanford University.

Cited by his students as a dedicated and innovative teacher, Datar received the George Leland Bach Award for Excellence in the Classroom at Carnegie Mellon University and the Distinguished Teaching Award at Stanford University.

Datar has published his research in leading accounting, marketing, and operations management journals, including *The Accounting Review, Contemporary Accounting Research, Journal of Accounting, Auditing and Finance, Journal of Accounting and Economics, Journal of Accounting Research*, and *Management Science*. He has also served on the editorial board of several journals and presented his research to corporate executives and academic audiences in North America, South America, Asia, Africa, Australia, and Europe.

Datar is a member of the board of directors of Novartis A.G., ICF International, and KPIT Cummins Infosystems Ltd. and has worked with many organizations, including

Apple Computer, AT&T, Boeing, Du Pont, Ford, General Motors, Hewlett-Packard, Kodak, Morgan Stanley, PepsiCo, Stryker, TRW, Visa, and the World Bank. He is a member of the American Accounting Association and the Institute of Management Accountants.

George Foster is the Paul L. and Phyllis Wattis Professor of Management at Stanford University. He graduated with a university medal from the University of Sydney and has a Ph.D. from Stanford University. He has been awarded honorary doctorates from the University of Ghent, Belgium, and from the University of Vaasa, Finland. He has received the Outstanding Educator Award from the American Accounting Association. Foster has received the Distinguished Teaching Award at Stanford University and the Faculty Excellence Award from the California Society of Certified Public Accountants. He has been a Visiting Professor to Mexico for the American Accounting Association. Research awards Foster has received include the Competitive Manuscript Competition Award of the American Accounting Association, the Notable Contribution to Accounting Literature Award of the American Institute of Certified Public Accountants, and the Citation for Meritorious Contribution to Accounting Literature Award of the Australian Society of Accountants.

He is the author of *Financial Statement Analysis*, published by Prentice Hall. He is co-author of *Activity-Based Management Consortium Study (APQC and CAM-I)* and *Marketing, Cost Management and Management Accounting (CAM-I)*. He is also co-author of two monographs published by the American Accounting Association—*Security Analyst Multi-Year Earnings Forecasts and The Capital Market and Market Microstructure and Capital Market Information Content Research*. Journals publishing his articles include *Abacus, The Accounting Review, Harvard Business Review, Journal of Accounting and Economics, Journal of Accounting Research, Journal of Cost Management, Journal of Management Accounting Research, Management Accounting*, and *Review of Accounting Studies*.

Foster works actively with many companies, including Apple Computer, ARCO, BHP, Digital Equipment Corp., Exxon, Frito-Lay Corp., Hewlett-Packard, McDonald's Corp., Octel Communications, PepsiCo, Santa Fe Corp., and Wells Fargo. He also has worked closely with Computer Aided Manufacturing-International (CAM-I) in the development of a framework for modern cost management practices. Foster has presented seminars on new developments in cost accounting in North and South America, Asia, Australia, and Europe.

Madhav V. Rajan is the Gregor G. Peterson Professor of Accounting and area coordinator for Accounting at the Graduate School of Business, Stanford University. He is also Professor of Law (by courtesy) at Stanford Law School.

Rajan received his undergraduate degree in Commerce from the University of Madras, India, and his MS in Accounting, MBA, and Ph.D degrees from the Graduate School of Industrial Administration at Carnegie Mellon University. In 1990, his dissertation won the Alexander Henderson Award for Excellence in Economic Theory.

Rajan's primary area of research interest is the economics-based analysis of management accounting issues, especially as they relate to internal control cost allocation, capital budgeting quality management, supply chain, and performance systems in firms. He has published his research in leading accounting and operations management journals including *The Accounting Review, Review of Financial Studies, Journal of Accounting Research*, and *Management Science*. In 2004, he received the Notable Contribution to Management Accounting Literature award.

Rajan has served as an editor of *The Accounting Review* for the past six years. He is an associate editor for both the Accounting and Operations areas for *Management Science*, and for the *Journal of Accounting, Auditing and Finance*. He is a member of the Management Accounting section of the American Accounting Association and has twice been a plenary speaker at the AAA Management Accounting Conference.

Rajan has won several teaching awards at Wharton and Stanford, including the David W. Hauck Award, the highest undergraduate teaching honor at Wharton. Rajan teaches in a variety of executive education programs including the Stanford Executive Program, the National Football League for Managers, and the National Basketball Players Association Program.

Christopher D. Ittner is the Ernst & Young Professor of Accounting at The Wharton School of the University of Pennsylvania. A graduate of California State University, Long Beach, he received his MBA from UCLA and a Doctorate in Business Administration from Harvard University.

Ittner has received a number of teaching awards from Wharton students, and teaches management accounting courses for doctoral students from throughout the United States and Europe.

His research has been published in leading accounting, marketing, and operations management journals, including *The Accounting Review*, *Journal of Accounting and Economics*, *Journal of Accounting Research*, *Management Science*, and *Operation Research*. Awards for his research include the American Accounting Association's Notable Contribution to Management Accounting Literature and Outstanding Dissertation in Management Accounting. He is also co-author of the book *Linking Quality to Profits: Quality-Based Cost Management (ASQC and IMA)*. Ittner is an Associate Editor of *Accounting, Organizations and Society* and *Management Science* and serves on the editorial boards of a number of other accounting and operations management journals.

Ittner is a founding board member of the Performance Measurement Association and a member of the American Accounting Association, Institute of Management Science, and Production and Operations Management Society. He has worked with a large number of companies on cost accounting and performance measurement issues, including Capital One, EDS, Ernst & Young, General Motors, and Sunoco.

Brief Contents

Contents

Preface

Studying Cost Accounting is one of the best business investments a student can make. Why? Because success in any organization—from the smallest corner store to the largest multinational corporation—requires the use of cost accounting concepts and practices. Cost accounting provides key data to managers for planning and controlling, as well as costing products, services, and customers. The central focus of this book is how cost accounting helps managers make better decisions. Cost accountants are increasingly becoming integral members of decision-making teams instead of just data providers. To link to this decision-making emphasis, the "different costs for different purposes" theme is used throughout this book. By focusing on basic concepts, analyses, uses, and procedures instead of procedures alone, we recognize cost accounting as a managerial tool for business strategy and implementation. We also prepare students for the rewards and challenges facing them in the professional cost accounting world both today and tomorrow. In this edition, for example, we emphasize both the development of analytical skills such as Excel to leverage available information technology and also the values and behaviors that make cost accountants effective in the workplace.

Hallmark Features of Horngren/Datar/Foster/Rajan/Ittner: *Cost Accounting*

- Exceptionally strong emphasis on managerial uses of cost information
- Clarity and understandability of the text
- Excellent balance in integrating modern topics with existing content
- Emphasis on human behavior aspects
- Extensive use of real-world examples
- Ability to teach chapters in different sequences
- Excellent quantity, quality, and range of assignment material

The first thirteen chapters provide the essence of a one-term (quarter or semester) course. There is ample text and assignment material in the book's twenty-three chapters for a two-term course. This book can be used immediately after the student has had an introductory course in financial accounting. Alternatively, this book can build on an introductory course in managerial accounting.

Deciding on the sequence of chapters in a textbook is a challenge. Every instructor has a favorite way of organizing his or her course. Hence, we present a modular, flexible organization that permits a course to be custom tailored. *This organization facilitates diverse approaches to teaching and learning.*

As an example of the book's flexibility, consider our treatment of process costing. Process costing is described in Chapters 17 and 18. Instructors interested in filling out a student's perspective of costing systems can move directly from job-order costing described in Chapter 4 to Chapter 17 without interruption in the flow of material. Other instructors may want their students to delve into activity-based costing and budgeting and more decision-oriented topics early in the course. These instructors may prefer to postpone discussion of process costing.

New to This Edition

A New Framework for Decision Making

Chapter 1 introduces a five-step decision-making process that managers use when making decisions. These steps are (1) identify the problem and uncertainties, for example, whether a newspaper should increase its advertising rates and the effect this decision will have on advertising demand; (2) obtain information, for example, by reviewing the effects on demand of past increases in advertising rates or doing market research on advertising rates charged by competing newspapers; (3) make predictions about the future, for example, how demand will be affected by different potential increases in advertising rates; (4) make decisions by choosing among alternatives, such as choosing a new advertising rate, and (5) implement the decision, evaluate performance, and learn—for example, by informing potential advertisers about the new rates and comparing what actually happened against the plans. Almost all subsequent chapters use the five-step decision-making process to describe the relevant management accounting concepts in the context of management decisions. The framework helps students see how the demand for various types of management accounting information is a response to the decision-making needs of managers.

New Cutting Edge Topics

The pace of change in organizations continues to be rapid. The thirteenth edition of *Cost Accounting* reflects changes occurring in the role of cost accounting in organizations.

- The chapter on budgeting has been completely rewritten within a simple activity-based framework to illustrate modern budgeting practices in companies.
- Capacity management issues are discussed throughout the book because managing capacity is key to improving performance in many organizations.
- We introduce customer preference maps and strategy maps to describe how companies are strengthening links between the development of their strategy and the measures on the balanced scorecard.
- Value streams and lean accounting describes how companies are simplifying their costing systems.

Opening Vignettes

Each chapter opens with a vignette on a real company situation. The vignettes engage the reader in a business situation, or dilemma, illustrating why and how the concepts in the chapter are relevant in business. For example, Chapter 1 describes how Xerox uses cost accounting information to make decisions relating to strategy formulation, research and development, budgeting and pricing. Chapter 2 discusses how GM has met the challenge of cutting costs during tough times. Chapter 3 explains a recent dilemma faced by the jeweler Tiffany & Co.—whether to increase the prices on one of its best-selling jewelry lines recognizing that it will likely lower the quantity of jewelry sold. Chapter 5 shows how Scotland Yard uses activity-based costing to reduce paperwork and improve operations. Chapter 10 describes how Boeing, in undertaking a new contract, meets the challenge of examining unfamiliar categories of costs. Chapter 11 shows how Delta Airlines decides which costs and benefits are relevant when making pricing decisions for tickets. Chapter 13 discusses how the bank holding company Keycorp has successfully used the balanced scorecard approach to earn record profits. Chapter 14 shows how Best Buy boosts profits by analyzing its customers and their buying habits.

Concepts in Action Boxes

Found in every chapter, these boxes cover real-world cost accounting issues across a variety of industries including automobile racing, defense contracting, entertainment, manufacturing, and retailing. New examples include

- How Flexcar Helps Reduce Business Transportation Costs, p. 33
- Sky-High Fixed Costs Trouble XM Satellite Radio, p. 77
- Time-Driven Activity-Based Costing at Charles Schwab, p. 159
- The Growth vs. Profitability Choice at YouTube, p. 483

Streamlined Presentation

We continue to try to simplify and streamline our presentation of various topics to make it as easy as possible for a student to learn the concepts, tools, and frameworks introduced in different chapters. Examples of more streamlined presentations can be found in

- Chapter 2, p. 39 on the flow of revenues and costs for a manufacturing sector company
- Chapter 4, pp. 109–112 on the accounting entries for a normal job-costing system in manufacturing
- Chapter 9, which uses a single comprehensive example to integrate inventory costing and capacity concepts
- Chapters 17 and 18, which use a simpler sequence for the five-steps in process costing and so provides more structure for students to follow

Increased Excel Support

We continue to provide Professors and Students with Excel support inside and outside the classroom.

New Excel Manual: For those students who need more required or optional Excel support, we have added an Excel supplement specifically designed to support this book. It describes step-by-step how many of the Excel exhibits in the book were developed. The goal of the supplement is to introduce students to the varied Excel tools that management accountants use and to help them understand the relationships among different accounting numbers.

For Professors: Key Tables and Exhibits from the text are reproduced in Excel. Instructors can access the Excel worksheets to support in-class discussion, to demonstrate key concepts, to explain difficult points, or to perform what-if (sensitivity) analysis. The Excel Labs can be found on the Instructor's Resource Center (IRC) and instructor DVD.

For Students: Excel templates for selected end-of-chapter exercises and problems are available online at **www.prenhall.com/horngren/cost13e**. These templates allow students to complete selected exercises and problems using Excel. The focus is on having students use Excel to understand and apply chapter content. This Excel-based learning is completely optional; therefore, students may choose to solve these exercises and problems manually.

Selected Chapter-by-Chapter Content Changes

Thank you for your continued support of Cost Accounting. In every new edition, we strive to update this text thoroughly. To ease your transition from the twelfth edition, here are selected highlights of chapter changes for the thirteenth edition.

Chapter 1 focuses on decision making and introduces a new five-step decision-making framework that is featured in many chapters of the book. It introduces ideas of pre-decision information (for planning decisions) and post-decision information (for performance evaluation, control and learning).

Chapter 2 has been rewritten to emphasize managerial decisions. The chapter exhibits have been completely redone so students can follow all the concepts, steps, and numbers on the exhibits themselves.

Chapter 3 has been reorganized. It starts with an example that is then used to explain assumptions and terminology. The managerial aspects of the chapter have been strengthened and the sections on alternative fixed cost/variable cost structures, multiple product breakeven analysis, and contribution margin versus gross margin have been significantly revised and shortened.

Chapter 4 concepts are developed within the context of the five-step decision-making process introduced in Chapter 1. This allows for a richer managerial discussion of strategy, risk, and uncertainty. The section on normal job-costing system in manufacturing has been significantly shortened by adding a new exhibit.

Chapter 5 discusses the concepts of activity-based costing and activity-based management within a decision-making framework. The exhibits have been redone to provide a road map to the various steps in activity-based costing and to reduce chapter length. There is more discussion of how managers choose cost-allocation bases and implement activity-based costing.

Chapter 6 has been completely rewritten using a two-product example and two cost drivers in manufacturing and distribution. Chapter 6 integrates activity-based costing ideas from Chapter 5 into the budgeting discussion by describing how product quantities lead to activities, that, in turn, lead to costs in different areas to support these activities. The chapter frames the budgeting discussion within a decision-making framework. More material has been added on learning, budgetary slack, and participative budgeting. Exhibits have been redone to simplify the exposition.

Chapters 7 and 8 present a more streamlined discussion of different levels of variance analysis and tighten the links between production and sales volume variances.

Chapter 9 integrates the two parts of the chapter on inventory costing and denominator-level capacity concepts using a single comprehensive example.

Chapter 10 has greater discussion of managerial decision-making using quantitative analysis. The Chapter 10 Appendix includes more details on regression analysis.

Chapter 12 includes more discussion of product and customer life-cycles. Chapter 12 exhibits have also been streamlined.

Chapter 13 presents more discussion of strategy, including customer preference maps and strategy maps. The material on the balanced scorecard has been significantly rewritten to cover strategy maps, departmental scorecards, tests of anticipated cause-and-effect relationships, and performance evaluation uses of the scorecard.

Chapter 14 describes how the decision-making framework presented in Chapter 1 can be used to evaluate and manage customers.

Chapter 15 discusses alternative methods of cost and revenue allocations and simplifies the example to illustrate different methods for allocating costs of multiple support departments.

In Chapters 17 and 18, the sequence of the five-step procedure for process costing has been slightly revised. The new formats and exhibits are more structured and so should ease student learning.

Chapter 19 describes how theory of constraints can be implemented using a balanced scorecard. There is also greater discussion of the service sector.

Chapter 20 introduces lean accounting. Performance measures and control in JIT production is discussed in the context of the balanced scorecard.

Chapter 22 adds more material on market-based and negotiated transfer pricing.

Assignment Material

The thirteenth edition continues the widely applauded close connection between text and assignment material forged in previous editions.

- *Questions* require students to understand basic concepts and the meaning of key terms.
- *Exercises* are short structured assignments that test basic issues presented in the chapter.
- *Problems* are longer and more difficult assignments. Some problems span multiple chapters and test student comprehension of related issues.
- *Collaborative Learning Problems* require students to think critically about a particular problem or specific business situation.

Teaching and Learning Support

MyAccountingLab

MyAccountingLab is an online homework and assessment tool, designed to help students practice cost accounting problems and concepts, and give their instructors feedback on their performance. It lets cost accounting professors assign a homework deliverable that is automatically graded, but that also serves as a tutorial experience for students.

Based on a Pearson's MathXL platform that has graded over millions of assignments, MyAccountingLab provides a strong, reliable platform with a rock solid performance history. To learn more visit **www.myaccountinglab.com.**

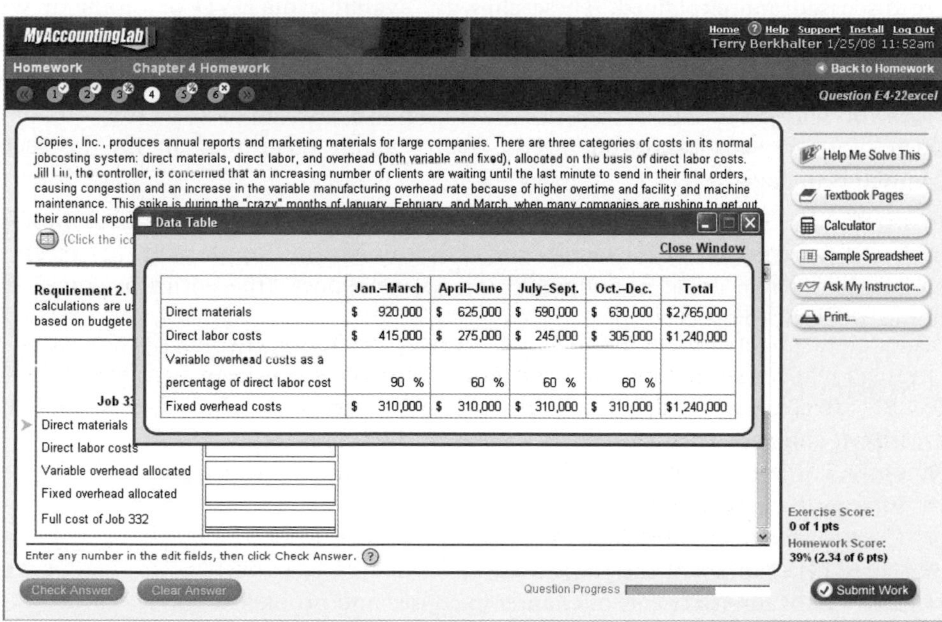

For Instructors

- *Instructor's Resource Center*

  These password-protected resources are accessible from **www.pearsonhighered.com** for *Cost Accounting*, 13th ed. Resources include:
  - Instructor's Manual
  - Test Item File

  - TestGen EQ—A computerized test item file.
  - Solutions Manual
  - Image Library—Access to most of the images and illustrations featured in the text.
  - Excel Labs and their solutions. Also included are the Excel files of the figures and tables in the text.
  - Complete PowerPoint Presentations
  - NEW PowerPoint slides of fully-worked-out solutions for selected problems.
  - Check Figures
  - Support for Blackboard and WebCT courses

- *Instructor's Resource Manual* by John Stancil of Florida Southern College offers helpful classroom suggestions and teaching tips.
- *Test Item File* with contributions from A.J. Cataldo II of West Chester University offers an array of questions ranging from easy to difficult. An electronic version of these questions is also available. The *Test Item File* now supports Association to Advance Collegiate Schools of Business (AACSB) International Accreditation. Each chapter of the *Test Item File* was prepared with the AACSB curricula standards in mind and the answer line of each question, where appropriate, indicates a category within which the question falls.
- *Solutions Manual* by Charles T. Horngren, Srikant M. Datar, George Foster, Madhav V. Rajan, and Christopher Ittner provides instructors with answers to all end-of-chapter material.
- *Cost Accounting Video Library* produced by Beverly Amer of Northern Arizona University and Aspenleaf Productions provide real-company scenarios. These brief videos take students "on location" to real companies where real accounting situations are discussed and explained. These clips are available on DVD or online at **www.prenhall.com/horngren/cost13e.**
- *PowerPoint Presentation* created by Michael Flores of Wichita State University provides you with a slide show ready for classroom use. Use the slides as they are, or edit them to meet your classroom needs. Each exhibit mentioned in the Instructor's Manual is included.
- *Instructor Resource Center on DVD* contains print and technology ancillaries. This makes it extremely easy for faculty to (1) customize any supplement, (2) access any supplement while using a computer, and (3) transport "the entire package" from home, to class, to office.

For Students

Prentice Hall Companion Website offers access to:

  - Online quizzes
  - Internet Exercises
  - *Cost Accounting* Video Library segments
  - Three (3) chapters of the *Student Guide*
  - Excel Labs for select end-of-chapter exercises and problems

- *Student Guide* by John K. Harris is a self study aid that helps reinforce key concepts with numerous review features for each chapter.
- *Student Solutions Manual* by Charles T. Horngren, Srikant M. Datar, George Foster, Madhav V. Rajan, and Christopher Ittner assists with solutions for all even-numbered end-of-chapter problems.
- NEW *Excel Manual for Cost Accounting* by Laurie Burney of Mississippi State University and Michele Matherly of Xavier University. This brief supplement is aligned to bring students up to speed with using Excel in this course.

- VangoNotes. Study on the go with VangoNotes—chapter reviews from your text in downloadable mp3 format. VangoNotes are flexible; download all the material directly to your player, or only the chapters you need. And they're efficient. Use them in your car, at the gym, walking to class, or wherever. So get yours today. And get studying. VangoNotes.com.

Acknowledgments

We are indebted to many people for their ideas and assistance. Our primary thanks go to the many academics and practitioners who have advanced our knowledge of cost accounting. The package of teaching materials we present is the work of skillful and valued team members developing some excellent end-of-chapter assignment material. Tommy Goodwin, Richard Saouma (UCLA), Jenny Shen (Berkeley), and Nandita Sommers (McKinsey) provided outstanding research assistance on technical issues and current developments. We would also like to thank the dedicated and hard working supplement author team of A.J. Cataldo II, Laurie Burney, Michele Matherly, Michael Flores, Ralph Greenberg, John R. McGowan, Diane Satin, Karen Schoenebeck, John Stancil, and GEX Publishing Services. The book is much better because of the efforts of these colleagues.

In shaping this edition, we in particular would like to thank a group of colleagues who worked closely with us and the editorial team. This group provided detailed feedback and participated in focus groups that guided the direction of this edition:

Jenny Dosch
Metropolitan State University

Joe Dowd
Eastern Washington University

Constance Hylton
George Mason University

Leslie Kren
University of Wisconsin-Milwaukee

Michele Matherly
Xavier University

Laurie Burney
Mississippi State University

Mike Morris
Notre Dame University

Cindy Nye
Bellevue University

Roy Regel
University of Montana

Margaret Shackell-Dowell
Notre Dame University

Marvin Bouillon
Iowa State University

Kreag Danvers
Clarion University

A.J. Cataldo II
West Chester University

Kenneth Danko
San Fransisco State University

T.S. Amer
Northern Arizona University

Robert Hartman
University of Iowa

We would also like to extend our thanks to those professors who provided detailed written reviews or comments on drafts. These professors include:

Robyn Alcock
Central Queensland University

David S. Baglia
Grove City College

Charles Bailey
University of Central Florida

Robert Bauman
Allan Hancock Joint Community College

David Bilker
University of Maryland, University College

Marvin Bouillon
Iowa State University

Dennis Caplan
Columbia University

Donald W. Gribbin
Southern Illinois University

Rosalie Hallbauer
Florida International University

John Haverty
St. Joseph's University

Jean Hawkins
William Jewell College

Jiunn C. Huang
San Francisco State University

Zafar U. Khan
Eastern Michigan University

Larry N. Killough
Virginia Polytechnic Institute & State University

Keith Kramer
Southern Oregon University

Jay Law
Central Washington University

Sandra Lazzarini
University of Queensland

Gary J. Mann
University of Texas at El Paso

Ronald Marshall
Michigan State University

Maureen Mascha
Marquette University

Pam Meyer
University of Louisiana at Lafayette

Marjorie Platt
Northeastern University

Roy W. Regel
University of Montana

Pradyot K. Sen
University of Cincinnati

Gim S. Seow
University of Connecticut

Rebekah A. Sheely
Northeastern University

Robert J. Shepherd
University of California, Santa Cruz

Kenneth Sinclair
Lehigh University

Vic Stanton
California State University, Hayward

Carolyn Streuly
Marquette University

Gerald Thalmann
North Central College

Peter D. Woodlock
Youngstown State University

James Williamson
San Diego State University

Sung-Soo Yoon
UCLA at Los Angeles

Jennifer Dosch
Metro State University

Joe Dowd
Eastern Washington University

Leslie Kren
University of Wisconsin-Madison

Michele Matherly
Xavier University

Laurie Burney
Mississippi State University

Mike Morris
Notre Dame University

Cinthia Nye
Bellevue University

Roy Regel
University of Montana

Margaret Shackell-Dowel
Notre Dame University

Marvin Bouillon
Iowa State University

Kreag Danvers
Clarion University of Pennsylvania

A.J. Cataldo II
West Chester University

Kenneth Danko
San Fransisco State University

T.S. Amer
Northern Arizona University

Robert Hartman
University of Iowa

Diane Satin
California State University East Bay

John Stancil
Florida Southern College

Michael Flores
Wichita University

Ralph Greenberg
Temple University

Paul Warrick
Westwood College

Karen Schoenebeck
Southwestern College

Thomas D. Fields
Washington University in St. Louis

Constance Hylton
George Mason University

Robert Alford
DePaul University

Michael Eames
Santa Clara University

We also would like to thank our colleagues who helped us greatly by accuracy checking the text and supplements including Constance Hylton, Michele Matherly, and Carolyn Streuly.

We thank the people at Prentice Hall for their hard work and dedication, including Steve Deitmer, Eric Svendsen, Kashey Sheehan Madara, Mauricio Escoto, Steve Sartori, Wendy Craven, Judy Leale, Kerri Tomasso, Kevin Holm, Arnold Vila, Michelle Klein, and Kelly Morrison at GEX Publishing Services. We must extend special thanks to Lori Ceretto, the development editor on this edition, who took charge of this project and directed it across the finish line. This book would not have been possible without her dedication and skill.

Alexandra Gural and others expertly managed the production aspects of all the manuscript preparation with superb skill and tremendous dedication. We are deeply appreciative of their good spirits, loyalty, and ability to stay calm in the most hectic of times. The constant support of Bianca Baggio is greatly appreciated.

Appreciation also goes to the American Institute of Certified Public Accountants, the Institute of Management Accountants, the Society of Management Accountants of Canada, the Certified General Accountants Association of Canada, the Financial

Executive Institute of America, and many other publishers and companies for their generous permission to quote from their publications. Problems from the Uniform CPA examinations are designated (CPA); problems from the Certified Management Accountant examination are designated (CMA); problems from the Canadian examinations administered by the Society of Management Accountants are designated (SMA); problems from the Certified General Accountants Association are designated (CGA). Many of these problems are adapted to highlight particular points.

We are grateful to the professors who contributed assignment material for this edition. Their names are indicated in parentheses at the start of their specific problems. Comments from users are welcome.

CHARLES T. HORNGREN
SRIKANT M. DATAR
GEORGE FOSTER
MADHAV V. RAJAN
CHRISTOPHER ITTNER

1 The Accountant's Role in the Organization

Learning Objectives

1. Describe how cost accounting supports management accounting and financial accounting
2. Understand how management accountants affect strategic decisions
3. Describe the set of business functions in the value chain and identify the dimensions of performance that customers are expecting of companies
4. Explain the five-step decision-making process and its role in management accounting
5. Describe three guidelines management accountants follow in supporting managers
6. Understand how management accounting fits into an organization's structure
7. Understand what professional ethics mean to management accountants

All businesses are concerned about costs. Whether their products are automobiles, fast food, or the latest designer fashions, managers must understand the cost behavior of their operations or risk losing control. Managers use cost accounting information to make decisions—including decisions related to strategy formulation, research and development, budgeting, production planning, and pricing, among others. Sometimes these decisions involve tradeoffs. The following article shows how companies like Xerox make those tradeoffs to increase their profits.

Xerox Keeps Its Eye on Key Success Factors: Copier Prices Are Down, but Profits Are Up[1]

Sometimes, low revenues portend good news.

Take the Xerox Corporation. For the fifth quarter in a row, its revenues from copiers and printers have gone down. But ask Anne M. Mulcahy, Xerox's chief executive, what she plans to do about that, and her answer is, absolutely nothing.

Dollars from equipment sales may be down because of lower copier and printer prices but Xerox is selling a lot of machines. And that, Ms. Mulcahy insists, is what counts.

In the document-processing world, that makes total sense. Printer and copier companies make the most money from sales of toners, inks and services. And those sales, of course, are directly proportional to the number of machines being used, leading to higher profits.

To increase profits, Xerox is also managing costs. Costs are down, and will soon go down more—Xerox is leaving its lush headquarters in Stamford, Connecticut, for sparser space in Norwalk.

Just like at Xerox, companies are concerned about both revenues and costs. Consider movies produced by the entertainment industry. *Lord of the Rings. Pirates of the Caribbean. Finding Nemo.* What do these movies have in common? Each was a major box office hit, generating hundreds of millions of dollars in revenue. Behind the

[1] *Source:* Claudia H. Deutsch, "Prices Are Lower, but Profits Are Up at Xerox," *The New York Times* (April 21, 2007).

scenes, studio accountants used modern cost accounting techniques to carefully track costs. At the end of each movie's run, the studios could tell just how successful the project had been.

The study of modern cost accounting yields insights into how managers and accountants can contribute to operations. It also prepares them for leadership roles. Many large companies, such as Teva Sport Sandals, Sony Pictures, and Nike, have senior executives with accounting backgrounds.

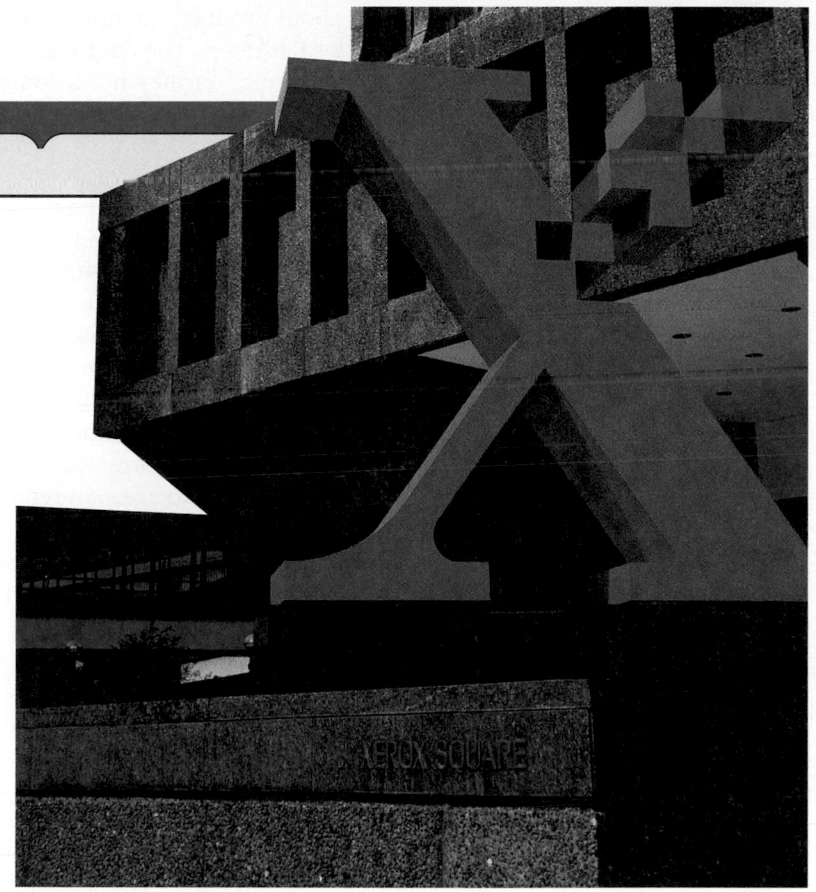

Management Accounting, Financial Accounting, and Cost Accounting

Accounting systems take economic events and transactions, such as sales and materials purchases, and process the data into information helpful to managers, sales representatives, production supervisors, and others. Processing any economic transaction means collecting, categorizing, summarizing, and analyzing. For example, costs are collected by category, such as materials, labor, and shipping. These costs are then summarized to determine total costs by month, quarter, or year. The results are analyzed to evaluate, say, how costs have changed relative to revenues from one period to the next. Accounting systems provide the information found in the income statement, the balance sheet, and the statement of cash flow and in performance reports, such as the cost of operating a plant or of providing a service. Managers use accounting information to administer the activities, businesses, or functional areas they oversee and to coordinate those activities, businesses, or functions within the framework of the organization. This book focuses on how accounting assists managers in these tasks.

Individual managers often require the information in an accounting system to be presented or reported differently. Consider, for example, sales order information. A sales manager may be interested in the total dollar amount of sales to determine the commissions to be paid. A distribution manager may be interested in the sales order quantities by geographic region and by customer-requested delivery dates to ensure timely deliveries. A manufacturing manager, to schedule production, may be interested in the quantities of various products and their desired delivery dates. An ideal database—sometimes called a data warehouse or infobarn—consists of small, detailed bits of information that can be used for multiple purposes. For instance, the sales order database will contain detailed information about product, quantity ordered, selling price, and delivery details (place and date) for each sales order. The database stores information in a way that allows managers to access the information they need. Many companies are building their own Enterprise Resource Planning (ERP) systems, single databases that collect data and feed it into applications that support the company's business activities, such as purchasing, production, distribution, and sales.

Learning Objective 1

Describe how cost accounting supports management accounting and financial accounting

. . . cost accounting measures costs of acquiring or using resources

Management accounting and financial accounting have different goals. **Management accounting** measures, analyzes, and reports financial and nonfinancial information that helps managers make decisions to fulfill the goals of an organization. Managers use management accounting information to choose, communicate, and implement strategy. They also use management accounting information to coordinate product design, production, and marketing decisions and to evaluate performance. Management accounting information and reports do not have to follow set principles or rules. The key questions are always (1) How will this information help managers do their jobs better, and (2) do the benefits of producing this information exceed the costs?

Financial accounting focuses on reporting to external parties such as investors, government agencies, banks, and suppliers. It measures and records business transactions and provides financial statements that are based on generally accepted accounting principles (GAAP). Managers' compensation is often directly affected by the numbers in these financial statements. Consequently, managers are interested in both management accounting and financial accounting.

Exhibit 1-1 summarizes the major differences between management accounting and financial accounting. Note, however, that reports such as balance sheets, income statements, and statements of cash flows are common to both management accounting and financial accounting.

Cost accounting provides information for management accounting and financial accounting. **Cost accounting** measures, analyzes, and reports financial and nonfinancial information relating to the costs of acquiring or using resources in an organization. For example, calculating the cost of a product is a cost accounting function that answers financial accounting's inventory-valuation needs and management accounting's decision-making needs (such as choosing which products to offer). Modern cost accounting takes

Exhibit 1-1

Major Differences Between Management Accounting and Financial Accounting

	Management Accounting	Financial Accounting
Purpose of information	Help managers make decisions to fulfill an organization's goals	Communicate organization's financial position to investors, banks, regulators, and other outside parties
Primary users	Managers of the organization	External users such as investors, banks, regulators, and suppliers
Focus and emphasis	Future-oriented (budget for 2008 prepared in 2007)	Past-oriented (reports on 2007 performance prepared in 2008)
Rules of measurement and reporting	Internal measures and reports do not have to follow GAAP but are based on cost-benefit analysis	Financial statements must be prepared in accordance with GAAP and be certified by external, independent auditors
Time span and type of reports	Varies from hourly information to 15 to 20 years, with financial and nonfinancial reports on products, departments, territories, and strategies	Annual and quarterly financial reports, primarily on the company as a whole
Behavioral implications	Designed to influence the behavior of managers and other employees	Primarily reports economic events but also influences behavior because manager's compensation is often based on reported financial results

the perspective that collecting cost information is a function of the management decisions being made. Thus, the distinction between management accounting and cost accounting is not so clear-cut, and we often use these terms interchangeably in the book.

We frequently hear business people use the term *cost management.* Unfortunately, that term has no uniform definition. We use **cost management** to describe the approaches and activities of managers to use resources to increase value to customers and to achieve organizational goals. Cost management decisions include decisions such as the amounts and kinds of materials used, changes in plant processes, and changes in product designs. Information from accounting systems helps managers to manage costs, but the information and the accounting systems themselves are not cost management.

Cost management has a broad focus and should not be interpreted to mean only continuous reduction in costs. Cost management is inextricably linked with revenue and profit planning. As part of cost management, managers often deliberately incur additional costs, for example in advertising and product modifications, to enhance revenues and profits.

Cost management is not practiced in isolation. It is an integral part of general management strategies and their implementation. Examples include programs that enhance customer satisfaction and quality, as well as research and development (R&D) and marketing programs to promote "blockbuster" new products.

Strategic Decisions and the Management Accountant

Learning Objective 2

Understand how management accountants affect strategic decisions

. . . they provide information about competitive advantages and resources

Strategy specifies how an organization matches its own capabilities with the opportunities in the marketplace to accomplish its objectives. In other words, strategy describes how an organization will compete and the opportunities its managers should seek and pursue. Businesses follow one of two broad strategies. Some companies, such as Southwest Airlines and Vanguard (the mutual fund company), have been profitable and have grown over the years on the basis of providing quality products or services at low prices. Other companies such as EMC Corporation, the manufacturer of data-storage equipment, and Pfizer, the pharmaceutical giant, generate their profits and growth on the basis of their ability to offer differentiated or unique products or services that are often priced higher than the products or services of their competitors.

Deciding between these strategies is a critical part of what managers do. Management accountants work closely with managers in formulating strategy by providing information about the sources of competitive advantage—for example, the cost, productivity, or efficiency advantage of their company relative to competitors or the premium prices a company can charge relative to the costs of adding features that make its products or services distinctive. **Strategic cost management** describes cost management that specifically focuses on strategic issues.

Management accountants help formulate strategy by helping managers answer questions such as:

- Who are our most important customers, and how do we deliver value to them? For example, after Amazon.com's success in selling books online, Barnes and Noble developed the capabilities to sell online by building its information and technology infrastructure. Toyota has built flexible computer-integrated manufacturing (CIM) plants that enable it to use the same equipment to produce a variety of cars in response to changing customer tastes.
- What substitute products exist in the marketplace, and how do they differ from our product in terms of price and quality? For example, Hewlett-Packard designs new printers after comparing the functionality, quality, and price of its printers to other printers available in the marketplace.
- What is our most critical capability? Is it technology, production, or marketing? How can we leverage it for new strategic initiatives? Kellogg Company, for example, uses the reputation of its brand to introduce new types of cereal.

- Will adequate cash be available to fund the strategy, or will additional funds need to be raised? Proctor & Gamble, for example, issued new debt and equity to fund its strategic acquisition of Gillette, a maker of shaving products.

The best-designed strategies and the best-developed capabilities are useless unless they are effectively executed. In the next section, we describe actions managers take to create value for their customers and how management accountants help them do it.

Value Chain and Supply Chain Analysis and Key Success Factors

Customers demand from companies much more than a fair price. They expect a quality product or service delivered in a timely way. These multiple factors drive how a customer experiences a product or service and the value or usefulness a customer derives from the product or service. How then does a company go about creating this value?

Value-Chain Analysis

Learning Objective 3

Describe the set of business functions in the value chain and identify the dimensions of performance that customers are expecting of companies

. . . R&D, design, production, marketing, distribution, and customer service to achieve cost and efficiency, quality, time, and innovation

Value chain is the sequence of business functions in which customer usefulness is added to products or services. Exhibit 1-2 shows six business functions: R&D, design, production, marketing, distribution, and customer service. We illustrate these business functions using SONY Corporation's television division.

1. **Research and development**—Generating and experimenting with ideas related to new products, services, or processes. At SONY, this function includes research on alternative television signal transmission (analog, digital, high-definition) and on the clarity of different shapes and thicknesses of television screens.
2. **Design of products, services, or processes**—Detailed planning and engineering of products, services, or processes. Design at Sony includes determining the number of component parts in a television set and the effect of alternative product designs on quality and manufacturing costs.
3. **Production**—Acquiring, coordinating, and assembling resources to produce a product or deliver a service. Production of a SONY television set includes the acquisition and assembly of the electronic parts, the cabinet, and the packaging used for shipping.
4. **Marketing**—Promoting and selling products or services to customers or prospective customers. SONY markets its televisions through trade shows, advertisements in newspapers and magazines, and on the Internet.
5. **Distribution**—Delivering products or services to customers. Distribution for SONY includes shipping to retail outlets, catalog vendors, direct sales via the Internet, and other channels through which customers purchase televisions.
6. **Customer service**—Providing after-sale support to customers. SONY provides customer service on its televisions in the form of customer-help telephone lines, support on the Internet, and warranty repair work.

Each of these business functions is essential to SONY satisfying its customers and keeping them satisfied (and loyal) over time. Companies use the term *customer relationship management (CRM)* to describe a strategy that integrates people and technology in all business functions to enhance relationships with customers, partners, and distributors. CRM initiatives use technology to coordinate all customer-facing activities (such as marketing, sales calls, distribution, and postsales support) and the design and production activities necessary to get products to customers.

Exhibit 1-2 depicts the usual order in which different business-function activities physically occur. Do not, however, interpret Exhibit 1-2 as implying that managers should proceed sequentially through the value chain when planning and managing their activities.

Exhibit 1-2 Managers in Different Parts of the Value Chain

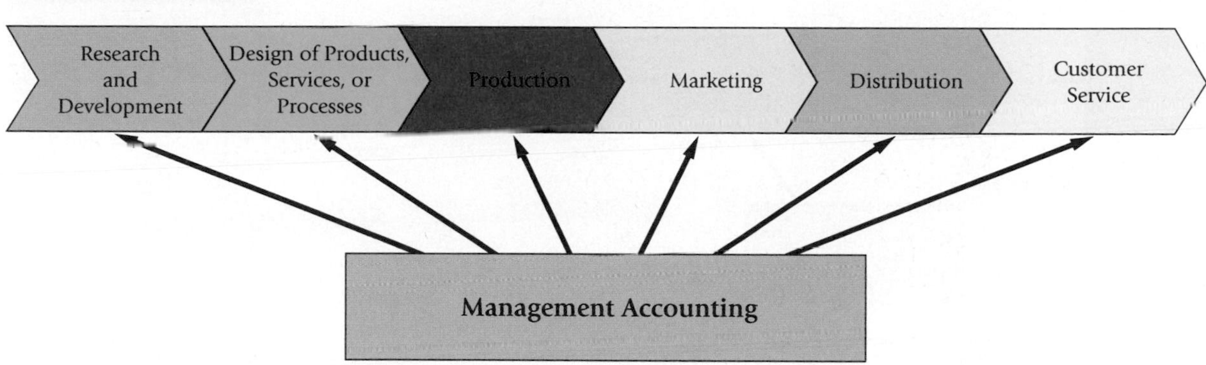

Companies gain (in terms of cost, quality, and the speed with which new products are developed) if two or more of the individual business functions of the value chain work concurrently as a team. For example, inputs into design decisions by production, marketing, distribution, and customer service managers often lead to design choices that reduce total costs of the company.

Management accountants track the costs incurred in each value-chain category. Their goal is to reduce costs in each category and to improve efficiency. Cost information also helps managers make cost-benefit tradeoffs. For example, is it cheaper to buy products from outside vendors or to do manufacturing in-house? Is it worthwhile to invest more resources in design and manufacturing if it reduces costs in marketing and customer service or increases revenues?

Supply-Chain Analysis

Companies can also implement strategy, cut costs, and create value by enhancing their supply chain. The term **supply chain** describes the flow of goods, services, and information from the initial sources of materials and services to the delivery of products to consumers, regardless of whether those activities occur in the same organization or in other organizations. Consider the soft drinks Coke and Pepsi. Many companies play a role in bringing these products to consumers. Exhibit 1-3 presents an overview of the supply chain. Cost management emphasizes integrating and coordinating activities across all companies in the supply chain, as well as across each business function in an individual company's value chain, to reduce costs. For example, both Coca-Cola Company and Pepsi Bottling Group contract with their suppliers (such as plastic and aluminum companies and sugar refiners) to frequently deliver small quantities of materials directly to the production floor to reduce materials-handling costs. Consider another example: To reduce inventory levels in the supply chain, Wal-Mart is asking its suppliers such as Coca-Cola to be responsible for and to manage inventory at both the Coca-Cola warehouse and Wal-Mart.

Key Success Factors

Customers want companies to use the value chain and supply chain to deliver ever improving levels of performance regarding several (or even all) of the following:

- **Cost and efficiency**—Companies face continuous pressure to reduce the cost of the products or services they sell. To calculate and manage the cost of products, the management accountant tries to understand the tasks or activities (such as setting up machines or distributing products) that cause costs to arise. Managers monitor the marketplace to determine prices that customers are willing to pay for products or services. Management accountants calculate a target cost for a product by subtracting

Exhibit 1-3 Supply Chain for a Cola Bottling Company

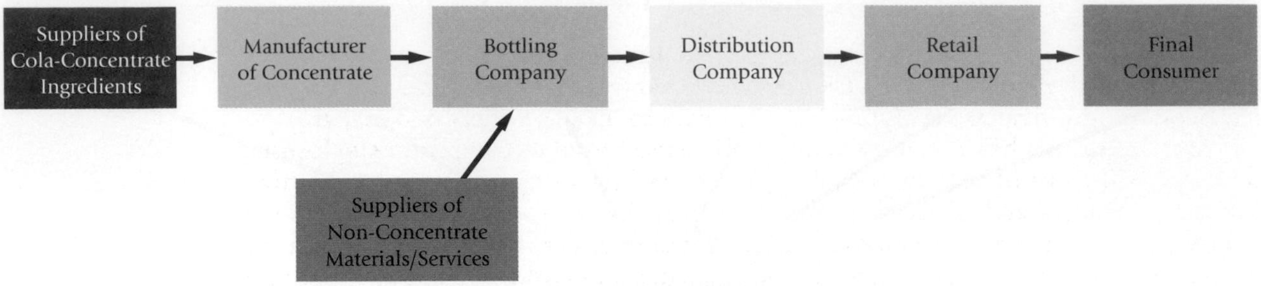

the operating income per unit of product that the company thinks it can earn from the "target price." Managers work with management accountants to achieve the target cost by eliminating some activities (such as rework) and by reducing the costs of performing activities in all value-chain functions—from initial R&D to customer service.

Increased global competition is placing even more pressure on companies to lower costs. U.S. companies are cutting costs by outsourcing some of their business functions. Nike, for example, has moved its manufacturing operations to China and Mexico. Citigroup and America Online are increasingly doing their software development in Spain, Eastern Europe, and India.

- **Quality**—Customers expect high levels of quality. Total quality management (TQM) is a philosophy in which management improves operations throughout the value chain to deliver products and services that exceed customer expectations. TQM encompasses designing the product or service to meet the needs and wants of customers, as well as making products with zero (or minimal) defects and waste and with low inventories. Management accountants evaluate the costs and revenue benefits of TQM initiatives.
- **Time**—Time has many components. New-product development time is the time it takes for new products to be created and brought to market. The increasing pace of technological innovation has led to shorter product life cycles and the need for companies to bring new products to market more rapidly. The management accountant measures the costs and benefits of a product over its life cycle.

  Customer-response time describes the speed at which an organization responds to customer requests. To increase customer satisfaction, organizations must complete activities faster and meet promised delivery dates reliably. Delays or bottlenecks occur when the work to be performed exceeds the available capacity. To increase output in these situations, managers need to increase the capacity of the bottleneck operation. The management accountant's role is to quantify the costs and benefits of relieving the bottleneck constraints.
- **Innovation**—A constant flow of innovative products or services is the basis for ongoing company success. The management accountant helps managers evaluate alternative investment decisions and R&D decisions.

Management accountants help managers track performance on the chosen key success factors relative to the performance of competitors on the same factors. Tracking what is happening in other companies serves as a *benchmark* and alerts managers to the changes their own customers are observing and evaluating. The goal is for a company to *continuously improve* its critical operations—for example, on-time arrival for Southwest Airlines, customer access for online auctions at eBay, and cost reduction at Sumitomo Electric. Sometimes more-fundamental changes in operations—such as redesigning a manufacturing process to reduce costs—may be necessary. However, successful strategy implementation requires more than value-chain and supply-chain analysis and execution of key success factors. It is the decisions that managers make that help them to develop, integrate, and implement their strategies.

Decision Making, Planning, and Control: The Five-Step Decision-Making Process

We illustrate the five-step decision-making process using the example of the *Daily News*, a newspaper in Denver, Colorado. In subsequent chapters of the book, we describe how managers use this five-step decision-making process to make a variety of decisions.

The *Daily News* has a strategy to differentiate itself from its competitors by focusing on in-depth analyses of news by its highly rated journalists, using color to enhance attractiveness to readers and advertisers, and developing its Web site to deliver up-to-the-minute news, interviews, and analyses. It has substantial capabilities to deliver on this strategy. It owns an automated, computer-integrated, state-of-the-art printing facility and has developed a Web-based information technology infrastructure. Its distribution network is one of the best in the newspaper industry.

A key challenge for Naomi Crawford, the manager of the *Daily News*, is to increase revenues. To decide what she should do, Naomi works through the five-step decision-making process.

Learning Objective 4

Explain the five-step decision making process

. . . identify the problem and uncertainties, obtain information, make predictions about the future, make decisions by choosing among alternatives, and implement the decision, evaluate performance, and learn

and its role in management accounting

. . . planning and control of operations and activities

1. **Identify the problem and uncertainties.** Naomi has two main choices:
   a. Increase the selling price per newspaper, or
   b. Increase the rate per page charged to advertisers.

   The key uncertainty is the effect on demand of any increase in price or rates. A decrease in demand could offset any increase in prices or rates and lead to lower overall revenues.
2. **Obtain information.** Gathering information before making a decision helps managers get a better handle on the uncertainties. Naomi asks her marketing manager to talk to some representative readers to gauge how they might react to an increase in the newspaper's selling price. She asks her advertising sales manager to talk to current and potential advertisers to get a better understanding of the advertising market. She also reviews the effect that past price increases had on readership. Ramon Sandoval, the management accountant at the *Daily News*, provides information about past increases or decreases in advertising rates and the subsequent changes in advertising revenues. He also collects and analyzes information on advertising rates charged by competing media outlets, including other newspapers.
3. **Make predictions about the future.** On the basis of information she has obtained, Naomi makes predictions about the future. She concludes that readers would be quite upset if she increased prices and is fairly certain that it would lead to a decrease in readership. She has a different view when it comes to advertising rates. She anticipates a marketwide increase in advertising rates and therefore believes that increasing these rates will have little effect on the number of pages of advertising sold.

   Naomi recognizes that making predictions requires considerable judgment. She carefully evaluates any biases that she might have. Has she correctly judged readers' sentiment or has her thinking been overly influenced by anticipation of all the negative publicity she would get rather than an actual decline in readership? How sure is she that her competitors will increase advertising rates? Is her thinking in this regard biased by their past actions? Have circumstances changed? How confident is she that her sales representatives can convince advertisers to pay higher rates? Naomi retests her assumptions and reviews her thinking. She feels confident about the predictions and judgments she has made.
4. **Make decisions by choosing among alternatives.** Naomi decides to increase advertising rates by 4% to $5,200 per page in March 2009. She communicates the new advertising rate schedule to the sales department. Ramon Sandoval estimates advertising revenues to be $4,160,000 ($5,200 per page × 800 pages predicted to be sold in March 2009).

Steps 1 through 4 are collectively referred to as *planning*. **Planning** comprises selecting organization goals, predicting results under various alternative ways of achieving those goals, deciding how to attain the desired goals, and communicating the goals and how to attain them to the entire organization. Management accountants serve as business partners in these planning activities because of their understanding of what creates value and the key success factors.

The most important planning tool is a budget. A **budget** is the quantitative expression of a proposed plan of action by management and is an aid to coordinating what needs to be done to implement that plan. For March 2009, budgeted advertising revenues equal $4,160,000. The full budget for March 2009 will include budgeted circulation revenue and the production, distribution, and customer-service costs that would be needed to achieve sales goals; the anticipated cash flows; and the potential financing needs. Because the process of preparing a budget crosses business functions, it forces coordination and communication throughout the company, as well as with the company's suppliers and customers.

5. **Implement the decision, evaluate performance, and learn.** Managers at the *Daily News* take actions to implement the March 2009 budget. Management accountants collect information to follow through on how actual performance compares to planned or budgeted performance (also referred to as scorekeeping). This information is very different from the *predecision* planning information Naomi collected in Step 2 to enable her to better understand uncertainties, to make predictions, and to make a decision. The comparison of actual performance to budgeted performance is the *control* or *postdecision* role of information. **Control** comprises taking actions that implement the planning decisions, deciding how to evaluate performance, and providing feedback and learning to help future decision making.

   Performance measures tell managers how well they and their subunits are doing. Linking rewards to performance helps motivate managers. These rewards are both intrinsic (self-satisfaction for a job well done) and extrinsic (salary, bonuses, and promotions linked to performance). A budget serves as much as a control tool as a planning tool. Why? Because a budget is a benchmark against which actual performance can be compared.

Consider performance evaluation at the *Daily News*. During March 2009, the newspaper sold advertising, issued invoices, and received payments. These invoices and receipts were recorded in the accounting system. Exhibit 1-4 shows the *Daily News*'s performance report of advertising revenues for March 2009. This report indicates that 760 pages of advertising (40 pages fewer than the budgeted 800 pages) were sold. The average rate per page was $5,080, compared with the budgeted $5,200 rate, yielding actual advertising revenues of $3,860,800. The actual advertising revenues were $299,200 less than the budgeted $4,160,000.

The performance report in Exhibit 1-4 spurs investigation and learning. **Learning** is examining past performance (the control function) and systematically exploring alternative ways to make better-informed decisions and plans in the future. Learning can lead to changes in goals, changes in the ways decision alternatives are identified, changes in the range of information collected when making predictions, and sometimes changes in managers.

The performance report in Exhibit 1-4 would prompt the management accountant to raise several questions directing the attention of managers to problems and opportunities. Did the marketing and sales department make sufficient efforts to convince advertisers that, even with the new higher rate of $5,200 per page, advertising in the *Daily News* was a good buy? Why was the actual average rate per page $5,080 instead of the budgeted

Exhibit 1-4

Performance Report of Advertising Revenues at the *Daily News* for March 2009

	Actual Result (1)	Budgeted Amount (2)	Difference: (Actual Result – Budgeted Amount) (3) = (1) – (2)	Difference as a Percentage of Budgeted Amount (4) = (3) ÷ (2)
Advertising pages sold	760 pages	800 pages	40 pages Unfavorable	5.0% Unfavorable
Average rate per page	$5,080	$5,200	$120 Unfavorable	2.3% Unfavorable
Advertising revenues	$3,860,800	$4,160,000	$299,200 Unfavorable	7.2% Unfavorable

rate of $5,200? Did some sales representatives offer discounted rates? Did economic conditions cause the decline in advertising revenues? Are revenues falling because editorial and production standards have declined? Answers to these questions could prompt the newspaper's publisher to take subsequent actions, including, for example, adding more sales personnel or making changes in editorial policy. Good implementation requires the marketing, editorial, and production departments to coordinate their actions.

The management accountant could go further by identifying the specific advertisers that cut back or stopped advertising after the rate increase went into effect. Managers could then decide when and how sales representatives should follow-up with these advertisers.

The left side of Exhibit 1-5 provides an overview of the decision-making processes at the *Daily News*. The right side of the exhibit highlights how the management accounting system aids in decision making.

Two final points: First, although budgets are primarily financial, managers use both financial and nonfinancial information to help implement their strategies. For example, action plans often include targets for market share, quality, new-product development, and employee satisfaction. When exercising control, managers compare actual and targeted nonfinancial measures as well as financial measures and take corrective actions.

Second, a plan must be flexible enough so that managers can seize sudden opportunities unforeseen at the time the plan is formulated. In no case should control mean that managers cling to a plan when unfolding events (such as a sensational news story) indicate that actions not encompassed by that plan (such as spending more money to cover the story) would offer better results for the company (from higher newspaper sales).

Key Management Accounting Guidelines

Three guidelines help management accountants provide the most value to their companies in strategic and operational decision making: Employ a cost-benefit approach, give

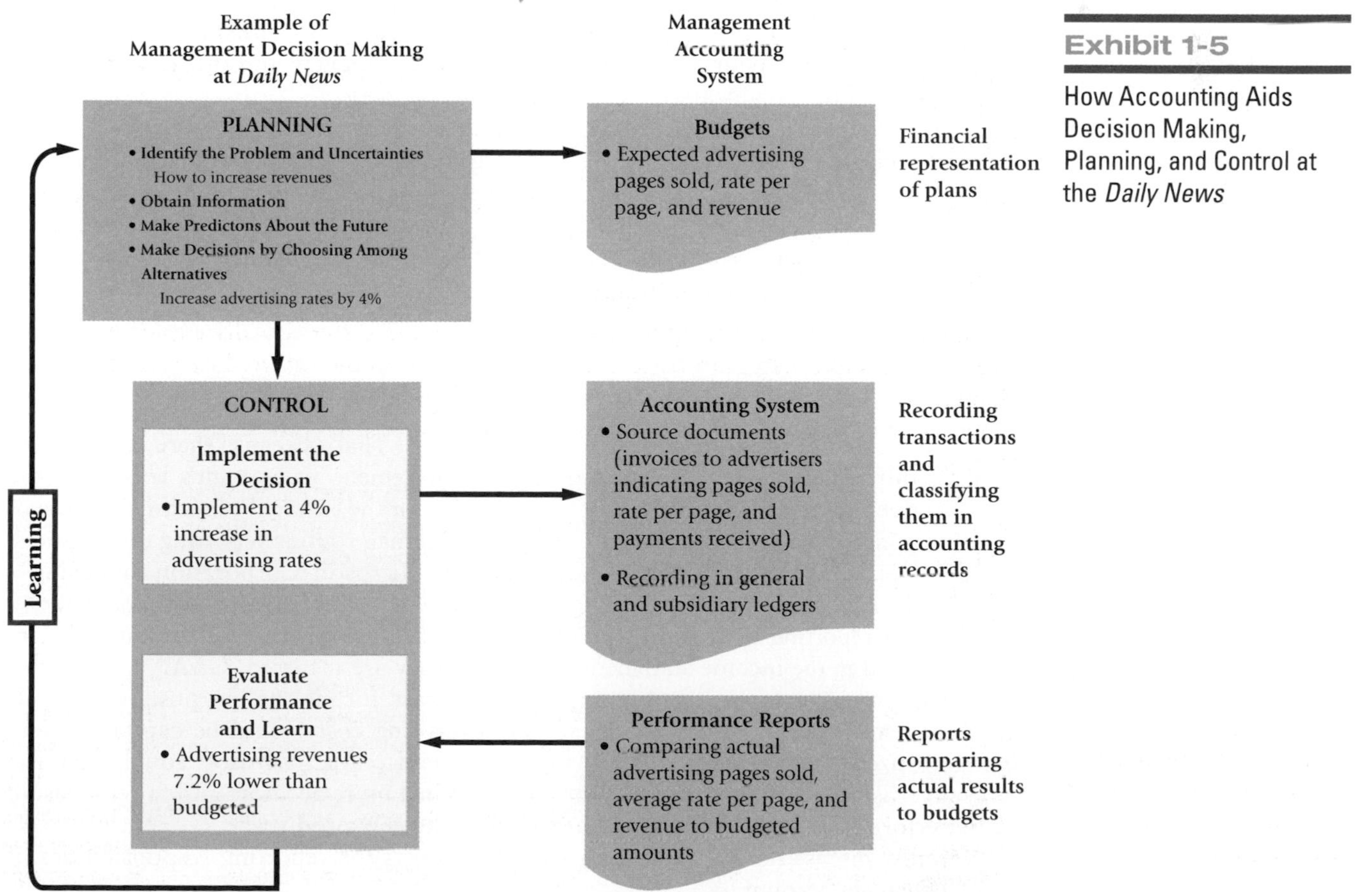

Exhibit 1-5

How Accounting Aids Decision Making, Planning, and Control at the *Daily News* full recognition to behavioral considerations as well as technical considerations, and use different costs for different purposes.

Cost-Benefit Approach

Learning Objective 5

Describe three guidelines management accountants follow in supporting managers

... employing a cost-benefit approach, recognizing behavioral as well as technical considerations, and calculating different costs for different purposes

Management accountants continually face resource-allocation decisions, such as whether to purchase a new software package or hire a new employee. The **cost-benefit approach** should be used in making these decisions: Resources should be spent if the expected benefits to the company exceed the expected costs. The expected benefits and costs may not be easy to quantify. Nevertheless, the cost-benefit approach is useful for making resource-allocation decisions.

Consider the installation of a company's first budgeting system. Previously, the company used historical recordkeeping and little formal planning. A major benefit of installing a budgeting system is that it compels managers to plan ahead, compare actual to budgeted information, and take corrective action. These actions lead to different decisions that create more profits than the decisions that would have been made using the historical system. The expected benefits exceed the expected costs of the new budgeting system. These costs include investments in physical assets, in training managers and others, and in ongoing operations.

Behavorial and Technical Considerations

The cost-benefit approach is the criterion that assists managers in deciding whether, say, to install a proposed budgeting system instead of continuing to use an existing historical system. Consider the human (the behavioral) side of why budgeting is used. Budgets induce a different set of decisions within an organization because of better collaboration, planning, and motivation. A management accounting system has two simultaneous missions, one technical and one behavioral. The technical considerations help managers make wise economic decisions by providing them with the desired information (for example, costs in various value-chain categories) in an appropriate format (for example, actual results versus budgeted amounts) and at the preferred frequency (for example, weekly versus monthly). The behavioral considerations motivate managers and other employees to aim for goals of the organization.

Both accountants and managers should always remember that management is not confined exclusively to technical matters. Management is primarily a human activity that should focus on how to help individuals do their jobs better—for example, by helping them to understand the activities that add value and those that do not. Moreover, when workers underperform, behavioral considerations suggest that managers should personally discuss with workers ways to improve performance and not just send them a report highlighting their underperformance.

Different Costs for Different Purposes

This book examines alternative ways to compute costs. That's because there are different costs for different purposes. This theme is the management accountant's version of the "one size does not fit all" notion. A cost concept used for the external-reporting purpose of accounting may not be an appropriate concept for internal, routine reporting to managers.

Consider the advertising costs associated with Microsoft Corporation launching a major new product. The product is expected to have a useful life of two years or more. For external reporting to shareholders, television advertising costs for this product are fully expensed in the income statement in the year they are incurred. GAAP requires this immediate expensing for external reporting. In contrast, for internal purposes of evaluating management performance, the television advertising costs could be capitalized and then amortized or written off as expenses over several years. Microsoft could capitalize these advertising costs if it believes doing so results in a more accurate and fairer measure of the performance of the managers that launched the new product.

We now discuss how organization structure affects the reporting responsibilities of the management accountant.

Organization Structure and the Management Accountant

We focus first on broad management functions and then look at the accounting and finance functions in more detail.

Line and Staff Relationships

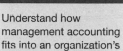

Learning Objective 6

Understand how management accounting fits into an organization's structure

. . . for example, the responsibilities of the controller

Most organizations distinguish between line management and staff management. **Line management**, such as production, marketing, and distribution management, is directly responsible for attaining the goals of the organization. For example, managers of manufacturing divisions may target particular levels of budgeted operating income, certain levels of product quality and safety, and compliance with environmental laws. Similarly, the pediatrics department in a hospital is responsible for patient billings, costs, and quality of service. **Staff management**, such as management accountants and information technology and human-resources management, exists to provide advice and assistance to line management. A plant manager (a line function) may be responsible for investing in new equipment. A management accountant (a staff function) works as a business partner of the plant manager by preparing detailed operating-cost comparisons of alternative pieces of equipment.

Increasingly, organizations such as Toyota and Dell are using teams to achieve their objectives. These teams include both line and staff management so that all inputs into a decision are available simultaneously. As a result, the traditional distinctions between line and staff have become less clear-cut than they were a decade ago.

The Chief Financial Officer and the Controller

The **chief financial officer** (CFO)—also called the **finance director** in many countries—is the executive responsible for overseeing the financial operations of an organization. The responsibilities of the CFO vary among organizations, but they usually include the following areas:

- **Controllership**—includes providing financial information for reports to managers and shareholders, and overseeing the overall operations of the accounting system
- **Treasury**—includes banking and short- and long-term financing, investments, and cash management
- **Risk management**—includes managing the financial risk of interest-rate and exchange-rate changes and derivatives management
- **Taxation**—includes income taxes, sales taxes, and international tax planning
- **Investor relations**—responding to and interacting with shareholders
- **Internal audit**—includes reviewing and analyzing financial and other records to attest to the integrity of the organization's financial reports and to adherence to its policies and procedures

The **controller** (also called the *chief accounting officer*) is the financial executive primarily responsible for management accounting and financial accounting. This book focuses on the controller as the chief management accounting executive. Modern controllers do not do any controlling in terms of line authority except over their own departments. Yet the modern concept of controllership maintains that the controller does control in a special sense. That is, by reporting and interpreting relevant data, the controller exerts a force or influence that impels line managers toward making better-informed decisions as they implement their strategies.

Exhibit 1-6 is an organization chart of the CFO and the corporate controller at Nike, the leading footwear and apparel company. The CFO is a staff manager who reports to the chief operating officer (COO), who reports to the chief executive officer (CEO). As in most organizations, the corporate controller at Nike reports to the CFO. Nike also has

Exhibit 1-6

Nike: Reporting Relationships for the CFO and the Corporate Controller

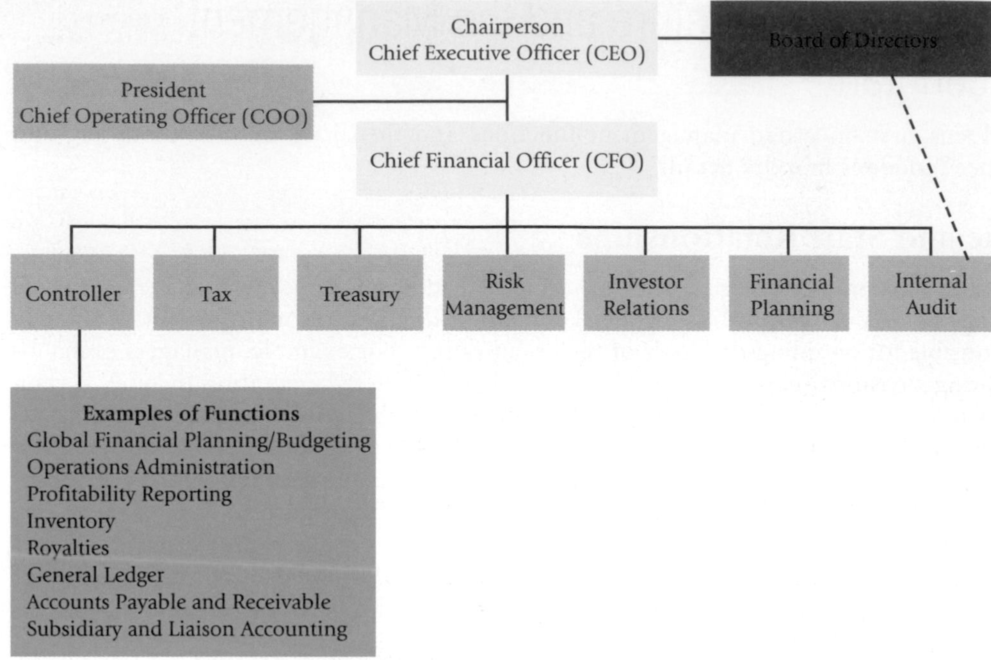

regional controllers for the major geographic regions in which it operates, such as the United States, Asia Pacific, Latin America, and Europe. Individual countries sometimes have a country controller. Organization charts such as the one in Exhibit 1-6 show formal reporting relationships. In most organizations, there also are informal relationships that must be understood when managers attempt to implement their decisions. Examples of informal relationships are friendships among managers (friendships of a professional or personal kind) and the personal preferences of top management about the managers they rely on in decision making.

Ponder what managers do to design and implement strategies and the organization structures within which they operate. Then think about the management accountants' and controllers' roles. It should be clear that the successful management accountant must have technical and analytical competence *as well as* behavioral and interpersonal skills. The Concepts in Action box on p. 15 describes some desirable values and behaviors and why they are so critical to the partnership between management accountants and managers. We will elaborate on these values and behaviors as we discuss different topics in subsequent chapters of this book.

At no time has the focus on ethical conduct been sharper than it is today. Corporate scandals at Enron, WorldCom, Arthur Andersen, Ahold, Health South, and Tyco have seriously eroded the public's confidence in corporations. All employees in a company, whether in line management or staff management, must comply with the organization's—and more broadly, society's—expectations of ethical standards.

Learning Objective 7

Understand what professional ethics mean to management accountants

. . . for example, management accountants must maintain integrity and credibility in every aspect of their jobs

Professional Ethics

Accountants have special obligations regarding ethics, given that they are responsible for the integrity of the financial information provided to internal and external parties. The Sarbanes–Oxley legislation in the United States, passed in 2002 in response to a series of corporate scandals, focuses on improving internal control, corporate governance, monitoring of managers, and disclosure practices of public corporations. These regulations legislate tough ethical standards on managers and accountants and provide a process for employees to report violations of illegal and unethical acts.

Concepts in Action

Management Accounting Beyond the Numbers

When you hear the job title "accountant," what comes to mind? The CPA who does your tax return each year? Individuals who prepare budgets at Dell or Unilever? To people outside the profession, it may seem like accountants are just "numbers people." It is true that most accountants are adept financial managers, yet their skills do not stop there. To be successful, management accountants must possess certain values and behaviors that reach well beyond basic analytical abilities.

Working in cross-functional teams and as a business partner of managers. It is not enough that management accountants simply be technically competent about management accounting. They need to be able to work in teams, to learn about business issues, to understand the motivations of different individuals, to respect the views of their colleagues, and to show empathy and trust.

Promoting fact-based analysis and making tough-minded, critical judgments without being adversarial. Management accountants must raise tough questions for managers to consider, especially when preparing budgets. They must do so thoughtfully and with the intent of improving plans and decisions. In the case of Enron, the once-thriving energy company that went bankrupt, management accountants should have raised questions about whether the company's complex business model would be profitable.

Leading and motivating people to change and be innovative. Implementing new ideas, however good they may be, is seldom easy. When Kanthal, the Swedish manufacturer of heating elements, introduced its innovative product-costing system, the controller and his team of management accountants made sure that the vision for the change was well understood and that all managers were educated and trained in the new methods. The managers who achieved early successes served as champions for the new system.

Communicating clearly, openly, and candidly. Communicating information is a large part of what management accountants do. A few years ago, Pitney Bowes, Inc. (PBI), a $4 billion global provider of integrated mail and document management solutions, implemented a reporting initiative to give managers feedback in key areas. The initiative succeeded because it was clearly designed and openly communicated by PBI's team of management accountants.

Having a strong sense of integrity and of doing the right things. Management accountants must never succumb to pressure from managers to manipulate financial information. They must always remember that their primary commitment is to the organization and its shareholders. At WorldCom, under pressure from senior managers, members of the accounting staff concealed billions of dollars in expenses. Because the accounting staff lacked the integrity and courage to do what was right, WorldCom landed in bankruptcy. Some members of the accounting staff served prison terms for their actions.

Source: Andy Serwer, "The Hole Story." *Fortune, July 7, 2003;* Mark Green, Jeannine Garrity, Andrea Gumbus and Bridget Lyons, "Pitney Bowes Calls for New Metrics," *Strategic Finance,* May 2002.

Ethical Guidelines

Professional accounting organizations promote high ethical standards, and such organizations representing management accountants exist in many countries. Appendix C at the end of the book discusses professional organizations in the United States, Canada, Australia, Japan, and the United Kingdom. Each of these organizations provides certification programs. For example, the **Institute of Management Accountants (IMA)**—the largest association of management accountants in the United States—provides programs leading to the **Certified Management Accountant (CMA)** certificate and the **Certified in Financial Management (CFM)** certificate. These certificates indicate that the holder has demonstrated the competency of technical knowledge required by the IMA in management accounting and financial management, respectively.

The IMA has issued a *Standards of Ethical Conduct for Practitioners of Management Accounting and Financial Management.* Exhibit 1-7 presents the IMA's guidance on issues

Exhibit 1-7

Standards of Ethical Conduct for Practitioners of Management Accounting and Financial Management

Practitioners of management accounting and financial management have an obligation to the public, their profession, the organizations they serve, and themselves to maintain the highest standards of ethical conduct. In recognition of this obligation, the Institute of Management Accountants has promulgated the following standards of ethical professional practice. Adherence to these standards, both domestically and internationally, is integral to achieving the Objectives of Management Accounting. Practitioners of management accounting and financial management shall not commit acts contrary to these standards nor shall they condone the commission of such acts by others within their organizations.

IMA STATEMENT OF ETHICAL PROFESSIONAL PRACTICE

Practitioners of management accounting and financial management shall behave ethically. A commitment to ethical professional practice includes overarching principles that express our values and standards that guide our conduct.

PRINCIPLES

IMA's overarching ethical principles include: Honesty, Fairness, Objectivity, and Responsibility. Practitioners shall act in accordance with these principles and shall encourage others within their organizations to adhere to them.

STANDARDS

A practitioner's failure to comply with the following standards may result in disciplinary action.

COMPETENCE

Each practitioner has a responsibility to:

1. Maintain an appropriate level of professional expertise by continually developing knowledge and skills.
2. Perform professional duties in accordance with relevant laws, regulations, and technical standards.
3. Provide decision support information and recommendations that are accurate, clear, concise, and timely.
4. Recognize and communicate professional limitations or other constraints that would preclude responsible judgment or successful performance of an activity.

CONFIDENTIALITY

Each practitioner has a responsibility to:

1. Keep information confidential except when disclosure is authorized or legally required.
2. Inform all relevant parties regarding appropriate use of confidential information. Monitor subordinates' activities to ensure compliance.
3. Refrain from using confidential information for unethical or illegal advantage.

INTEGRITY

Each practitioner has a responsibility to:

1. Mitigate actual conflicts of interest. Regularly communicate with business associates to avoid apparent conflicts of interest. Advise all parties of any potential conflicts.
2. Refrain from engaging in any conduct that would prejudice carrying out duties ethically.
3. Abstain from engaging in or supporting any activity that might discredit the profession.

CREDIBILITY

Each practitioner has a responsibility to:

1. Communicate information fairly and objectively.
2. Disclose all relevant information that could reasonably be expected to influence an intended user's understanding of the reports, analyses, or recommendations.
3. Disclose delays or deficiencies in information, timeliness, processing, or internal controls in conformance with organization policy and/or applicable law.

Source: Statement on Management Accounting Number 1-C, *Standards of Ethical Conduct for Practitioners of Management Accounting and Financial Management* (Montvale, NJ: Institute of Management Accountants, 2005). Reprinted with permission from the Institute of Management Accountants, Montvale, NJ, www.imanet.org.

relating to competence, confidentiality, integrity, and credibility. The IMA provides its members with an ethics hotline service. Members can call professional counselors at the IMA's Ethics Counseling Service to discuss their ethical dilemmas. The counselors help identify the key ethical issues and possible alternative ways of resolving them, and confidentiality is guaranteed.

Typical Ethical Challenges

Ethical issues can confront management accountants in many ways. Here are two examples:

- **Case A:** A management accountant, knowing that reporting a loss for a software division will result in yet another "rightsizing initiative" (a gentler term than "layoffs"), has concerns about the commercial potential of a software product for which development costs are currently being capitalized as an asset rather than being shown as an expense for internal reporting purposes. The division manager argues that showing development costs as an asset is justified because the new product will generate profits. However, the division manager presents little evidence to support his argument. The last two products from this division have been unsuccessful. The management accountant has many friends in the division and wants to avoid a personal confrontation with the division manager.
- **Case B:** A packaging supplier, bidding for a new contract, offers the management accountant of the purchasing company an all-expenses-paid weekend to the Super Bowl. The supplier does not mention the new contract when giving the invitation. The accountant is not a personal friend of the supplier. He knows cost issues are critical in approving the new contract and is concerned that the supplier will ask for details about bids by competing packaging companies.

In each case the management accountant is faced with an ethical dilemma. Case A involves competence, credibility, and integrity. The management accountant should request that the division manager provide credible evidence that the new product is commercially viable. If the manager does not provide such evidence, expensing development costs in the current period is appropriate. Case B involves confidentiality and integrity.

Ethical issues are not always clear-cut. The supplier in Case B may have no intention of raising issues associated with the bid. However, the appearance of a conflict of interest in Case B is sufficient for many companies to prohibit employees from accepting "favors" from suppliers. Exhibit 1-8 presents the IMA's guidance on "Resolution of Ethical Conflict." The accountant in Case B should discuss the invitation with his immediate supervisor. If the visit is approved, the supplier should be informed that the invitation has

Exhibit 1-8

Resolution of Ethical Conflict

In applying the Standards of Ethical Professional Practice, you may encounter problems identifying unethical behavior or resolving an ethical conflict. When faced with ethical issues, you should follow your organization's established policies on the resolution of such conflict. If these policies do not resolve the ethical conflict, you should consider the following courses of action:

1. Discuss the issue with your immediate supervisor except when it appears that the supervisor is involved. In that case, present the issue to the next level. If you cannot achieve a satisfactory resolution, submit the issue to the next management level. If your immediate superior is the chief executive officer or equivalent, the acceptable reviewing authority may be a group such as the audit committee, executive committee, board of directors, board of trustees, or owners. Contact with levels above the immediate superior should be initiated only with your superior's knowledge, assuming he or she is not involved. Communication of such problems to authorities or individuals not employed or engaged by the organization is not considered appropriate, unless you believe there is a clear violation of the law.
2. Clarify relevant ethical issues by initiating a confidential discussion with an IMA Ethics Counselor or other impartial advisor to obtain a better understanding of possible courses of action.
3. Consult your own attorney as to legal obligations and rights concerning the ethical conflict.

Source: Statement on Management Accounting Number 1-C, *Standards of Ethical Conduct for Practitioners of Management Accounting and Financial Management* (Montvale, NJ: Institute of Management Accountants, 2005). Reprinted with permission from the Institute of Management Accountants, Montvale, NJ, www.imanet.org.

been officially approved subject to his following corporate policy (which includes the confidentiality of information).

Most professional accounting organizations around the globe issue statements about professional ethics. These statements include many of the same issues discussed by the IMA in Exhibits 1-7 and 1-8. For example, the Chartered Institute of Management Accountants (CIMA) in the United Kingdom identifies the same four fundamental principles as in Exhibit 1-7: competency, confidentiality, integrity, and credibility.

Problem for Self-Study

Campbell Soup Company incurs the following costs:

a. Purchase of tomatoes by a canning plant for Campbell's tomato soup products
b. Materials purchased for redesigning Pepperidge Farm biscuit containers to make biscuits stay fresh longer
c. Payment to Backer, Spielvogel, Bates, the advertising agency, for advertising work on Healthy Request line of soup products
d. Salaries of food technologists researching feasibility of a Prego pizza sauce that has minimal calories
e. Payment to Safeway for redeeming coupons on Campbell's food products
f. Cost of a toll-free telephone line used for customer inquiries about using Campbell's soup products
g. Cost of gloves used by line operators on the Swanson Fiesta breakfast-food production line
h. Cost of handheld computers used by Pepperidge Farm delivery staff serving major supermarket accounts

Required Classify each cost item (**a–h**) as one of the business functions in the value chain in Exhibit 1-2 (p. 7)

Solution

a. Production
b Design of products, services, or processes
c. Marketing
d. Research and development
e. Marketing
f. Customer service
g. Production
h. Distribution

Decision Points

The following question-and-answer format summarizes the chapter's learning objectives. Each decision presents a key question related to a learning objective. The guidelines are the answer to that question.

Decision	Guidelines
1. What information does cost accounting provide?	Cost accounting measures, analyzes, and reports financial and nonfinancial information relating to the cost of acquiring or using resources in an organization. Cost accounting provides information to both management accounting and financial accounting.
2. How do management accountants support strategic decisions?	Management accountants contribute to strategic decisions by providing information about the sources of competitive advantage.

3. How do companies add value, and what are the dimensions of performance that customers are expecting of companies?	Companies add value through R&D; design of products, services, or processes; production; marketing; distribution; and customer service. Customers want companies to deliver performance through cost and efficiency, quality, timeliness, and innovation.
4. How do managers implement strategy?	Managers implement strategy by making decisions using a five-step decision-making process: (1) identify the problem and uncertainties, (2) obtain information, (3) make predictions about the future, (4) make decisions by choosing among alternatives, and (5) implement the decision, evaluate performance, and learn. The first four steps are the planning decisions, which include deciding on organization goals, predicting results under various alternative ways of achieving those goals, and then deciding how to attain the desired goals. Step 5 is the control decision, which includes taking actions to implement the planning decisions and deciding on performance evaluation and feedback that will help future decision making.
5. What guidelines do management accountants use?	Three guidelines that help management accountants increase their value to managers are (a) employ a cost-benefit approach, (b) recognize behavioral as well as technical considerations, and (c) identify different costs for different purposes.
6. Where does the management accounting function fit into an organization's structure?	Management accounting is an integral part of the controller's function in an organization. In most organizations, the controller reports to the chief financial officer, who is a key member of the top management team.
7. What are the ethical responsibilities of management accountants?	Management accountants have ethical responsibilities that are related to competence, confidentiality, integrity, and credibility.

TERMS TO LEARN

Each chapter will include this section. Like all technical terms, accounting terms have precise meanings. Learn the definitions of new terms when you initially encounter them. The meaning of each of the following terms is given in this chapter and in the Glossary at the end of this book.

budget (**p. 10**)
Certified in Financial Management (CFM) (**p. 15**)
Certified Management Accountant (CMA) (**p. 15**)
chief financial officer (CFO) (**p. 13**)
control (**p. 10**)
controller (**p. 13**)
cost accounting (**p. 4**)
cost-benefit approach (**p. 12**)
cost management (**p. 5**)
customer service (**p. 6**)
design of products, services, or processes (**p. 6**)
distribution (**p. 6**)
finance director (**p. 13**)
financial accounting (**p. 4**)
Institute of Management Accountants (IMA) (**p. 15**)
learning (**p. 10**)
line management (**p. 13**)
management accounting (**p. 4**)
marketing (**p. 6**)
planning (**p. 9**)
production (**p. 6**)
research and development (**p. 6**)
staff management (**p. 13**)
strategic cost management (**p. 5**)
strategy (**p. 5**)
supply chain (**p. 7**)
value chain (**p. 6**)

ASSIGNMENT MATERIAL

Questions

1-1 How does management accounting differ from financial accounting?

1-2 "Management accounting should not fit the straitjacket of financial accounting." Explain and give an example.

1-3 How can a management accountant help formulate a strategy?

1-4 Describe the business functions in the value chain.

1-5 Explain the term "supply chain" and its importance to cost management.

1-6 "Management accounting deals only with costs." Do you agree? Explain.

1-7 How can management accountants help improve quality and achieve timely product deliveries?

1-8 Describe the five-step decision-making process.

1-9 Distinguish planning decisions from control decisions.

1-10 What three guidelines help management accountants provide the most value to managers?

1-11 "Knowledge of technical issues such as computer technology is a necessary but not sufficient condition to becoming a successful management accountant." Do you agree? Why?

1-12 As a new controller, reply to this comment by a plant manager: "As I see it, our accountants may be needed to keep records for shareholders and Uncle Sam, but I don't want them sticking their noses in my day-to-day operations. I do the best I know how. No bean counter knows enough about my responsibilities to be of any use to me."

1-13 As used in accounting, what do IMA and CMA stand for?

1-14 Name the four areas in which standards of ethical conduct exist for management accountants in the United States. What organization sets forth these standards?

1-15 What steps should a management accountant take if established written policies provide insufficient guidance on how to handle an ethical conflict?

Exercises

1-16 Value chain and classification of costs, computer company. Compaq Computer incurs the following costs:

- **a.** Electricity costs for the plant assembling the Presario computer line of products
- **b.** Transportation costs for shipping the Presario line of products to a retail chain
- **c.** Payment to David Kelley Designs for design of the Armada Notebook
- **d.** Salary of computer scientist working on the next generation of minicomputers
- **e.** Cost of Compaq employees' visit to a major customer to demonstrate Compaq's ability to interconnect with other computers
- **f.** Purchase of competitors' products for testing against potential Compaq products
- **g.** Payment to television network for running Compaq advertisements
- **h.** Cost of cables purchased from outside supplier to be used with Compaq printers

Required Classify each of the cost items (**a–h**) into one of the business functions of the value chain shown in Exhibit 1-2 (p. 7).

1-17 Value chain and classification of costs, pharmaceutical company. Merck, a pharmaceutical company, incurs the following costs:

- **a.** Cost of redesigning blister packs to make drug containers more tamperproof
- **b.** Cost of videos sent to doctors to promote sales of a new drug
- **c.** Cost of a toll-free telephone line used for customer inquiries about drug usage, side effects of drugs, and so on
- **d.** Equipment purchased to conduct experiments on drugs yet to be approved by the government
- **e.** Payment to actors for a television infomercial promoting a new hair-growth product for balding men
- **f.** Labor costs of workers in the packaging area of a production facility
- **g.** Bonus paid to a salesperson for exceeding a monthly sales quota
- **h.** Cost of Federal Express courier service to deliver drugs to hospitals

Required Classify each of the cost items (**a–h**) as one of the business functions of the value chain shown in Exhibit 1-2 (p. 7).

1-18 Value chain and classification of costs, fast food restaurant. Burger King, a hamburger fast food restaurant, incurs the following costs:

- **a.** Cost of oil for the deep fryer
- **b.** Wages of the counter help who give customers the food they order
- **c.** Cost of the costume for the King on the Burger King television commercials
- **d.** Cost of children's toys given away free with kids' meals
- **e.** Cost of the posters indicating the special "two cheeseburgers for $2"
- **f.** Costs of frozen onion rings and French fries
- **g.** Salaries of the food specialists who create new sandwiches for the restaurant chain
- **h.** Cost of "to-go" bags requested by customers who could not finish their meals in the restaurant

Required Classify each of the cost items (**a–h**) as one of the business functions of the value chain shown in Exhibit 1-2 (p. 7).

1-19 Value chain, supply chain, and key success factors. A survey on the ways organizations are changing their management accounting systems reported the following:

a. Company A now prepares a value-chain income statement for each brand it sells.
b. Company B now presents in a single report all costs related to achieving high quality levels in its products.
c. Company C now presents in its performance reports estimates of the manufacturing costs of its two most important competitors, in addition to its own manufacturing costs.
d. Company D now contracts with its suppliers to frequently deliver small quantities of materials directly to the production floor.
e. Company E now reports the percentage of times it fails to meet delivery dates that it has promised to customers.

Required

Link each of these changes to value-chain or supply-chain analysis or to the key success factors that are important to managers.

1-20 Planning and control decisions. Conner Company makes and sells brooms and mops. It takes the following actions, not necessarily in the order given below. For each action (**a–e** below,) state whether it is a planning decision or a control decision.

a. Conner asks its marketing team to consider ways to get back market share from its newest competitor, Swiffer.
b. Conner calculates market share after introducing its newest product.
c. Conner compares costs it actually incurred with costs it expected to incur for the production of the new product.
d. Conner's design team proposes a new product to compete directly with the Swiffer.
e. Conner estimates the costs it will incur to sell 30,000 units of the new product in the first quarter of next fiscal year.

1-21 Five-step decision-making process, manufacturing. Garnicki Foods makes frozen dinners that it sells through grocery stores. Typical products include turkey dinners, pot roast, fried chicken, and meat loaf. The managers at Garnicki have recently introduced a line of frozen chicken pies. They take the following actions with regard to this decision.

Required

Classify each action (**a–g** below) as a step in the five-step decision-making process (identify the problem and uncertainties, obtain information, make predictions about the future, choose among alternatives, implement the decision, evaluate performance, and learn). The actions below are not listed in the order they are performed.

a. Garnicki performs a taste test at the local shopping mall to see if consumers like the taste of its proposed new chicken pie product.
b. Garnicki sales managers estimate they will sell more meat pies in their northern sales territory than in their southern sales territory.
c. Garnicki managers discuss the possibility of introducing a new product.
d. Garnicki managers compare actual costs of making chicken pies with their budgeted costs.
e. Costs for making chicken pies are budgeted.
f. Garnicki decides to make chicken pies.
g. The purchasing manager calls a supplier to check the prices of chicken.

1-22 Five-step decision-making process, service firm. Brite Exteriors is a firm that provides house painting services. Robert Brite, the owner, is trying to find new ways to increase revenues. Mr. Brite performs the following actions, not in the order listed.

Required

Classify each action below according to its step in the five-step decision-making process (identify the problem and uncertainties, obtain information, make predictions about the future, choose among alternatives, implement the decision, evaluate performance, and learn).

a. Mr. Brite calls Home Depot to ask the price of paint sprayers.
b. Mr. Brite discusses with his employees the possibility of growing revenues of the firm.
c. One of Mr. Brite's project managers suggests that using paint sprayers instead of hand painting will increase productivity and thus revenues.
d. The workers who are not familiar with paint sprayers take more time to finish a job than they did when painting by hand.
e. Mr. Brite compares the expected cost of buying sprayers to the expected cost of hiring more workers who paint by hand, and estimates profits from both alternatives.
f. The project scheduling manager confirms that demand for house painting services has increased.
g. Mr. Brite decides to buy the paint sprayers rather than hire additional painters.

1-23 Professional ethics and reporting division performance. Marcia Miller is division controller and Tom Maloney is division manager of the Ramses Shoe Company. Miller has line responsibility to Maloney, but she also has staff responsibility to the company controller.

Maloney is under severe pressure to achieve the budgeted division income for the year. He has asked Miller to book $200,000 of revenues on December 31. The customers' orders are firm, but the shoes are still in the production process. They will be shipped on or around January 4. Maloney says to Miller, "The key event is getting the sales order, not shipping the shoes. You should support me, not obstruct my reaching division goals."

Required

1. Describe Miller's ethical responsibilities.
2. What should Miller do if Maloney gives her a direct order to book the sales?

Problems

1-24 Planning and control decisions, Internet company. WebNews.com offers its subscribers several services, such as an annotated TV guide and local-area information on weather, restaurants, and movie theaters. Its main revenue sources are fees for banner advertisements and fees from subscribers. Recent data are:

Month/Year	Advertising Revenues	Actual Number of Subscribers	Monthly Fee Per Subscriber
June 2007	$ 400,988	28,642	$14.95
December 2007	833,158	54,813	19.95
June 2008	861,034	58,178	19.95
December 2008	1,478,072	86,437	19.95
June 2009	2,916,962	146,581	19.95

The following decisions were made from June through October 2009:

a. June 2009: Raised subscription fee to $24.95 per month from July 2009 onward. The budgeted number of subscribers for this monthly fee is shown in the following table.
b. June 2009: Informed existing subscribers that from July onward, monthly fee would be $24.95.
c. July 2009: Offered e-mail service to subscribers and upgraded other online services.
d. October 2009: Dismissed the vice president of marketing after significant slowdown in subscribers and subscription revenues, based on July through September 2009 data in table below.
e. October 2009: Reduced subscription fee to $21.95 per month from November 2009 onward.

Results for July–September 2009 are:

Month/Year	Budgeted Number of Subscribers	Actual Number of Subscribers	Monthly Fee per Subscriber
July 2009	140,000	128,933	$24.95
August 2009	150,000	139,419	24.95
September 2009	160,000	143,131	24.95

Required

1. Classify each of the decisions (**a**) to (**e**) as a planning or a control decision.
2. Give two examples of other planning decisions and two examples of other control decisions that may be made at WebNews.com.

1-25 Strategic decisions and management accounting. A series of independent situations in which a firm is about to make a strategic decision follow.

Decisions:

a. Roger Phones is about to decide whether to launch production and sale of a cell phone with standard features.
b. Computer Magic is trying to decide whether to produce and sell a new home computer software package that includes the ability to interface with a sewing machine and a vacuum cleaner. There is no such software currently on the market.
c. Christina Cosmetics has been asked to provide a "store brand" lip gloss that will be sold at discount retail stores.
d. Marcus Meats is entertaining the idea of developing a special line of gourmet bologna made with sun dried tomatoes, pine nuts, and artichoke hearts.

Required

1. For each decision, state whether the company is following a low price or a differentiated product strategy.
2. For each decision, discuss what information the management accountant can provide about the source of competitive advantage for these firms.

1-26 Management accounting guidelines. For each of the following items, identify which of the management accounting guidelines applies: cost-benefit approach, behavioral and technical considerations, or different costs for different purposes.

1. Analyzing whether to keep the billing function within an organization or outsource it
2. Deciding to give bonuses for superior performance to the employees in a Japanese subsidiary and extra vacation time to the employees in a Swedish subsidiary
3. Including costs of all the value-chain functions before deciding to launch a new product, but including only its manufacturing costs in determining its inventory valuation
4. Considering the desirability of hiring one more salesperson
5. Giving each salesperson the compensation option of choosing either a low salary and a high-percentage sales commission or a high salary and a low-percentage sales commission
6. Selecting the costlier computer system after considering two systems
7. Installing a participatory budgeting system in which managers set their own performance targets, instead of top management imposing performance targets on managers
8. Recording research costs as an expense for financial reporting purposes (as required by U.S. GAAP) but capitalizing and expensing them over a longer period for management performance-evaluation purposes
9. Introducing a profit-sharing plan for employees

1-27 Role of controller, role of chief financial officer. George Perez is the controller at Allied Electronics, a manufacturer of devices for the computer industry. He is being considered for a promotion to chief financial officer.

Required

1. In this table, indicate which executive is *primarily* responsible for each activity.

Activity	Controller	CFO
Managing accounts payable		
Communicating with investors		
Strategic review of different lines of businesses		
Budgeting funds for a plant upgrade		
Managing the company's short-term investments		
Negotiating fees with auditors		
Assessing profitability of various products		
Evaluating the costs and benefits of a new product design		

2. Based on this table and your understanding of the two roles, what types of training or experiences will George find most useful for the CFO position?

1-28 Software-procurement decision, ethics. Jorge Michaels is the Chicago-based controller of Fiesta Foods, a rapidly growing manufacturer and marketer of Mexican food products. Michaels is currently considering the purchase of a new cost-management package for use by each of the company's six manufacturing plants and its many marketing personnel. Four major, competing products are being considered by Michaels.

Horizon 1-2-3 is an aggressive software developer. It views Fiesta as a target of opportunity. Every six months, Horizon has a three-day users' conference in a Caribbean location. Each conference has substantial time allowed for "rest and recreation." Horizon offers Michaels an all-expenses-paid visit to the upcoming conference in Cancun, Mexico. Michaels accepts the offer, believing it will be very useful to talk to other users of Horizon software. He is especially looking forward to the visit because he has close relatives in the Cancun area.

Prior to leaving, Michaels receives a visit from the president of Fiesta. She shows him an anonymous letter sent to her. It argues that Horizon is receiving unfair favorable treatment in Fiesta's software decision-making process. The letter specifically mentions Michaels' upcoming "all-expenses-paid package to Cancun during Chicago's cold winter." Michaels is deeply offended. He says he has made no decision, and he believes he is very capable of making a software choice on the merits of each product. Fiesta currently does not have a formal, written code of ethics.

Required

1. Do you think Michaels faces an ethical problem in regard to his forthcoming visit to the Horizon users' group meeting? Refer to Exhibit 1-7 (p. 16). Explain.
2. Should Fiesta allow executives to attend user meetings while negotiating with other vendors about a purchase decision? Explain. If yes, what conditions on attending should apply?
3. Would you recommend that Fiesta develop its own code of ethics to handle situations such as this? What are the pros and cons of having such a written code?

1-29 Professional ethics and end-of-year actions. Janet Taylor is the new division controller of the snack-foods division of Gourmet Foods. Gourmet Foods has reported a minimum 15% growth in annual earnings for each of the past five years. The snack-foods division has reported annual earnings growth of more than 20% each year in this same period. During the current year, the economy went into a recession. The corporate controller estimates a 10% annual earnings growth rate for Gourmet Foods this year. One month before the December 31 fiscal year-end of the current year, Taylor estimates the snack-foods division will report an annual earnings growth of only 8%. Warren Ryan, the snack-foods division president, is not happy, but he notes that "the end-of-year actions" still need to be taken.

Taylor makes some inquiries and is able to compile the following list of end-of-year actions that were more or less accepted by the previous division controller:

a. Deferring December's routine monthly maintenance on packaging equipment by an independent contractor until January of next year
b. Extending the close of the current fiscal year beyond December 31 so that some sales of next year are included in the current year
c. Altering dates of shipping documents of next January's sales to record them as sales in December of the current year
d. Giving salespeople a double bonus to exceed December sales targets
e. Deferring the current period's advertising by reducing the number of television spots run in December and running more than planned in January of next year
f. Deferring the current period's reported advertising costs by having Gourmet Foods' outside advertising agency delay billing December advertisements until January of next year or by having the agency alter invoices to conceal the December date
g. Persuading carriers to accept merchandise for shipment in December of the current year although they normally would not have done so

Required

1. Why might the snack-foods division president want to take these end-of-year actions?
2. The division controller is deeply troubled and reads the "Standards of Ethical Conduct for Practitioners of Management Accounting and Financial Management" in Exhibit 1-7 (p. 16). Classify each of the end-of-year actions (**a–g**) as acceptable or unacceptable according to that document.
3. What should Taylor do if Ryan suggests that these end-of-year actions are taken in every division of Gourmet Foods and that she will greatly harm the snack-foods division if she does not cooperate and paint the rosiest picture possible of the division's results?

1-30 Professional ethics and earnings management. Harvest Day Corporation is a publishing company that produces trade magazines. The company's stockholders are awaiting the announcement of Harvest Day's earnings for the fiscal year, which ends on December 31. Market analysts have predicted earnings to be around $1.34 per share. The CEO of Harvest Day expects earnings to be only $1.20 per share, and knows this will cause the price of the stock to drop. The CEO suggests the following ideas to various managers to try to increase reported earnings by the end of the fiscal year:

a. Delaying recording of cancelled subscriptions for December until January.
b. Waiting until the new fiscal year to update the software on office computers.
c. Recognizing unearned subscription revenue (cash received in advance for magazines that will be sent in the future) as revenue when received in the current month (just before fiscal year end) instead of booking it as a liability.
d. Delay recording purchases of office supplies on account until after year end.
e. Booking advertising revenues that relate to January in December.
f. Waiting until after fiscal year end to do building repairs.
g. Switching from declining balance to straight line depreciation to reduce depreciation expense in the current year.

Required

1. Why would Harvest Day Corporation's CEO want to "manage" earnings?
2. From the point of view of the "Standards of Ethical Behavior for Practitioners of Management Accounting and Financial Management," which of the items in **a-g** above are acceptable to Harvest Day's Controller? Which are unacceptable?
3. What should the Controller do about the CEO's suggestions? What should the Controller do if the CEO refuses to change the suggestions?

Collaborative Learning Problem

1-31 Global company, ethical challenges. In June 2009, the government of Vartan invited bids for the construction of a cellular telephone network. ZenTel, an experienced communications company, was eager to enter the growing field of cellular telephone networks in countries with poor infrastructures for land lines. If ZenTel won a few of these early contracts, it would be sought after for its field experience and expertise. After careful analysis, it prepared a detailed bid for the Communications Ministry of Vartan, building in only half of its usual profit margin and providing a contractual guarantee that the project would be completed in two years or less. The multimillion-dollar bid was submitted before the deadline, and ZenTel received notification that it had reached the Vartan government. Then, despite repeated faxes, e-mails, and phone calls to the ministry, there was no news on the bids or the project from the Vartan government.

Steve Cheng, VP of Global Operations for ZenTel, contacted the U.S. commercial attaché in Vartan, who told him that his best chance was to go to Vartan and try to meet the deputy minister of communications in person. Cheng prepared thoroughly for the trip, rereading the proposal and making sure that he understood the details.

At the commercial attaché's office in Vartan's capital, Cheng waited nervously for the deputy minister and his assistant. Cheng had come to Vartan with a clear negotiating strategy to try to win the bid. Soon the deputy minister and his staff arrived, introductions were made, and pleasantries were exchanged. The deputy minister asked a few questions about ZenTel and the bid and then excused himself, leaving his assistant to talk to Cheng. After clearly indicating that many other compelling bids had been made by firms from around the world, the assistant said, "Mr. Cheng, I guarantee that ZenTel's bid will be accepted if you pay a $1 million commission. Of course, your excellent proposal doesn't have to be altered in any way." It was clear to Cheng that the "commission" was, in fact, a bribe. Tactfully, he pointed out that U.S. laws and ZenTel's corporate policy prohibited such a payment. The assistant wished him a good day and a pleasant flight home and left.

Required

1. As a shareholder in ZenTel, would you prefer that ZenTel executives agree to the payment of the "commission"?
2. When Cheng described his experience to his friend Hank Shorn, who managed international business development for another company, Hank said that his own "personal philosophy" was to make such payments if they were typical in the local culture. Do you agree with Hank's point of view? Explain.
3. Why would ZenTel have a corporate policy against such payments?
4. What should Steve Cheng do next?

2 An Introduction To Cost Terms and Purposes

Learning Objectives

1. Define and illustrate a cost object
2. Distinguish between direct costs and indirect costs
3. Explain variable costs and fixed costs
4. Interpret unit costs cautiously
5. Distinguish among manufacturing companies, merchandising companies, and service-sector companies
6. Describe the three categories of inventories commonly found in manufacturing companies
7. Distinguish inventoriable costs from period costs
8. Explain why product costs are computed in different ways for different purposes
9. Describe a framework for cost accounting and cost management

What does the word cost mean to you? Is it the price you pay for something of value? A cash outflow? Something that affects profitability? There are many different types of costs, and at different times organizations put more or less emphasis on them. When times are good companies often focus on selling as much as they can, with costs taking a backseat. But when times get tough, the emphasis usually shifts to costs and cutting them, as General Motors is doing.

GM Struggles Under the Weight of Its Fixed Costs[1]

It took more than 75 years, but after continually losing market share to Japan's Toyota Motor Company, General Motors (GM) finally lost its title as the world's largest automaker. The fact is that GM's competitiveness in the automobile market is drastically affected by its fixed costs—costs that do not change with the number of cars that GM makes.

After a decade of belt-tightening, GM's variable costs—costs such as material costs that vary with the number of cars that GM makes—finally began to fall in line with those of the Japanese. Unfortunately, a large percentage of GM's operating costs are fixed because union contracts make it difficult for the company to close its factories or reduce pensions and health benefits owed to retired workers.

To cover its high fixed costs, GM needed to sell a lot of cars. For a time, sales rebates did the trick. GM also expanded aggressively into China and Europe.

But in 2005-2006, when growth efforts did not succeed, GM began to steer in a different direction. It bought out tens of thousands of workers and closed more than a dozen plants, negotiated with the union for another $1 billion in annual savings, slashed retirement plan benefits for its 40,000-plus salaried employees, and froze its pension program.

---

[1] *Sources:* David Welch, "GM's U.S. Blues," *BusinessWeek Online* (March 14, 2007); Sholnn Freeman and Albert B. Crenshaw, "GM to Cut White-Collar Retirement Benefits," *The Washington Post* (March 8, 2006), p. D01; "GM Chief Says Results Will Improve," *Bloomberg News* (January 14, 2006); A. Gary Shilling, "What's Bad for GM," *Forbes* (April 25, 2005); Alex Taylor III, "GM Hits the Skids," *Fortune* (April 4, 2005); David Welch and Kathleen Kerwin, "For GM, Sweet Deals Are Smarter Than They Look," *BusinessWeek* Online (August 26, 2002).

The plan seems to be working—at least as a start. In 2006, GM reported a $2.2 billion operating profit.

Industry analysts, however, say more cuts are needed. Richard Wagoner, GM's CEO, has vowed to cut its fixed costs from 34 percent of revenue in 2006, to 25 percent by 2010.

As the General Motors story illustrates, managers must understand costs in order to interpret and act on accounting reports. Organizations such as the United Way, Stanford University Hospital, and Nokia generate reports containing a variety of cost concepts and terms that managers need to run their operations. If managers understand these concepts and terms, they can use the information provided. Moreover, they can avoid misusing it. This chapter discusses cost concepts and terms that are the basis of accounting information used for internal and external reporting.

Costs and Cost Terminology

Accountants define **cost** as a resource sacrificed or forgone to achieve a specific objective. A cost (such as direct materials or advertising) is usually measured as the monetary amount that must be paid to acquire goods or services. An **actual cost** is the cost incurred (a historical or past cost), as distinguished from a **budgeted cost**, which is a predicted or forecasted cost (a future cost).

When you think of cost, you invariably think of it in the context of finding the cost of a particular thing. We call this thing a **cost object**, which is anything for which a measurement of costs is desired. Suppose that you were a manager at BMW's Spartanburg, South Carolina, plant. BMW makes several different types of cars and sport activity vehicles (SAVs) at this plant. What cost objects can you think of? Now look at Exhibit 2-1.

> **Learning Objective 1**
>
> Define and illustrate a cost object
>
> . . . examples of cost objects are products, services, activities, processes, and customers

You will see that BMW managers want to know the cost of various products, such as the BMW X5, but that they also want to know the costs of things such as projects, services, and departments. Managers use their knowledge of these costs to guide decisions, for example, about product innovation, quality, and customer service.

Now think about whether a manager at BMW might want to know the *budgeted cost* of a cost object, or the *actual cost*. Managers almost always need to know both types of costs when making decisions. Comparing budgeted costs to actual costs helps managers evaluate how well they did and learn about how they can do better in the future.

How does a cost system determine the costs of various cost objects? Typically in two basic stages: accumulation, followed by assignment. **Cost accumulation** is the collection

Exhibit 2-1

Examples of Cost Objects at BMW

Cost Object	Illustration
Product	A BMW X5 sports activity vehicle
Service	Telephone hotline providing information and assistance to BMW dealers
Project	R&D project on enhancing the DVD system in BMW cars
Customer	Herb Chambers Motors, the BMW dealer that purchases a broad range of BMW vehicles
Activity	Setting up machines for production or maintaining production equipment
Department	Environmental, Health, and Safety Department

of cost data in some organized way by means of an accounting system. For example, at its Spartanburg plant, BMW collects (accumulates) costs in various categories such as different types of materials, different classifications of labor, and costs incurred for supervision. Managers and management accountants then *assign* these accumulated costs to designated cost objects, such as the different models of cars that BMW manufactures at that plant. How do BMW managers use this cost information? For two main purposes. To *make* decisions, for instance, how to price different models of cars or how much to invest in R&D and marketing. And to *implement* decisions by influencing and motivating employees to act and learn, for example, by rewarding employees for reducing costs.

Now that we know why it is useful to assign costs, we turn our attention to some concepts that will help us do it. Again, think of the different types of costs that we just discussed—materials, labor, and supervision. You are probably thinking that some costs, such as costs of materials, are easier to assign to a cost object than others, such as costs of supervision. As you will see, this is indeed the case.

Direct Costs and Indirect Costs

We now describe how costs are classified as direct and indirect costs and the methods used to assign these costs to cost objects.

Learning Objective 2

Distinguish between direct costs

. . . costs that are traced directly to the cost object

and indirect costs

. . . costs that are allocated to the cost object

- **Direct costs of a cost object** are related to the particular cost object and can be traced to it in an economically feasible (cost-effective) way. For example, the cost of steel or tires is a direct cost of BMW X5s. The cost of the steel or tires can be easily traced to or identified with the BMW X5. The workers on the BMW X5 line request materials from the warehouse and the material requisition document identifies the cost of the materials supplied to the X5. In a similar vein, individual workers record the time spent working on the X5 on time sheets. The cost of this labor can easily be traced to the X5 and is another example of a direct cost. The term **cost tracing** is used to describe the assignment of direct costs to a particular cost object.
- **Indirect costs of a cost object** are related to the particular cost object but cannot be traced to it in an economically feasible (cost-effective) way. For example, the salaries of plant administrators (including the plant manager) who oversee production of the many different types of cars produced at the Spartanburg plant are an indirect cost of the X5s. Plant administration costs are related to the cost object (X5s) because plant administration is necessary for managing the production of X5s. Plant administration costs are indirect costs because plant administrators also oversee the production of other products, such as the Z4 Roadster. Unlike the cost of steel or tires, there is no requisition of plant administration services and it is virtually impossible to trace plant administration costs to the X5 line. The term **cost allocation** is used to describe the assignment of indirect costs to a particular cost object. **Cost assignment** is a general term that encompasses both (1) tracing direct costs to a cost object and (2) allocating indirect costs to a cost object. Exhibit 2-2 depicts direct costs and indirect costs and both forms of cost assignment—cost tracing and cost allocation—using the example of the BMW X5.

An Example of Cost Assignment

Consider the cost to lease the Spartanburg plant. This cost is an indirect cost of the X5—there is no separate lease agreement for the space used to make the X5. But BMW *allocates* to the X5 a part of the lease cost of the building—for example, on the basis of an estimate of the percentage of the building's total floor space occupied for the production of the X5 relative to the total floor space used to produce all models of cars.

Managers want to assign costs accurately to cost objects. Inaccurate product costs will mislead managers about the profitability of different products. Consequently, managers might unknowingly promote unprofitable products while deemphasizing profitable products. Generally, managers are more confident about the accuracy of direct costs of cost objects, such as the cost of steel and tires of the X5.

Indirect costs pose more challenges. Consider the lease. Allocating the cost of the lease on the basis of the total floor space occupied by each car model makes sense. This approach measures the building resources used by each car model reasonably and accurately. The more floor space that a car model occupies, the greater the lease costs that should be assigned to it. Accurately allocating other indirect costs, such as plant administration to the X5, however, is more difficult. Should these costs be allocated on the basis of the number of workers working on each car model? The number of cars produced of each model? Some other measure? How to measure the share of plant administration used by each car model is not clearcut.

Factors Affecting Direct/Indirect Cost Classifications

Several factors affect the classification of a cost as direct or indirect:

- **The materiality of the cost in question.** The smaller the amount of a cost—that is, the more immaterial the cost is—the less likely that it is economically feasible to trace that cost to a particular cost object. Consider a mail-order catalog company such as Lands' End. It would be economically feasible to trace the courier charge for delivering a package to an individual customer as a direct cost. In contrast, the cost of the invoice paper included in the package would be classified as an indirect cost. Why? Because although the cost of the paper can be traced to each customer, it is not cost-effective to do so. The benefits of knowing that, say, exactly 0.5¢ worth of paper is included in each package do not exceed the data processing and administrative costs of tracing the cost to each package.
- **Available information-gathering technology.** Improvements in information-gathering technology make it possible to consider more and more costs as direct costs. Bar codes, for example, allow manufacturing plants to treat certain low-cost materials such as clips and screws, which were previously classified as indirect costs, as direct costs of products. At Dell, component parts such as the computer chip and the CD-ROM drive display a bar code that can be scanned at every point in the production process. Bar codes can be read into a manufacturing cost file by waving a "wand" in the same quick and efficient way supermarket checkout clerks enter the cost of each item purchased by a customer.
- **Design of operations.** Classifying a cost as direct is easier if a company's facility (or some part of it) is used exclusively for a specific cost object, such as a specific product or a particular customer. For example, the cost of the General Chemicals facility that is dedicated to manufacturing soda ash is a direct cost of soda ash.

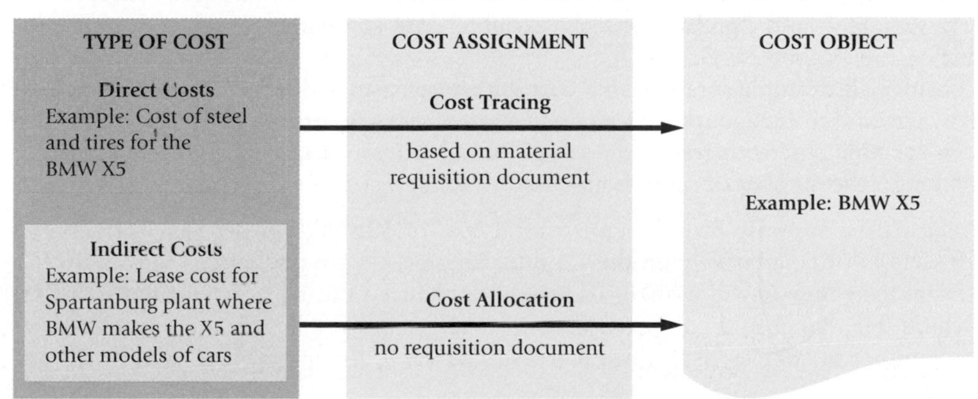

Exhibit 2-2

Cost Assignment to a Cost Object

Be aware that a specific cost may be both a direct cost of one cost object and an indirect cost of another cost object. *That is, the direct/indirect classification depends on the choice of the cost object.* For example, the salary of an Assembly Department supervisor at BMW is a direct cost if the cost object is the Assembly Department, but it is an indirect cost if the cost object is a product such as the BMW X5 SAV because the Assembly Department assembles many different models. A useful rule to remember is that the broader the definition of the cost object—the Assembly Department rather than the X5 SAV—the higher the proportion of total costs that are direct costs and the more confidence that a manager has in the accuracy of the resulting cost amounts.

Cost-Behavior Patterns: Variable Costs and Fixed Costs

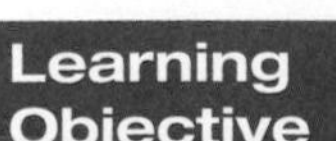

Learning Objective 3

Explain variable costs and fixed costs

. . . the two basic ways in which costs behave

Costing systems record the cost of resources acquired, such as materials, labor, and equipment, and track how those resources are used to produce and sell products or services. Recording the costs of resources acquired and used allows managers to see how costs behave. Consider two basic types of cost-behavior patterns found in many accounting systems. A **variable cost** changes *in total* in proportion to changes in the related level of total activity or volume. A **fixed cost** remains unchanged *in total* for a given time period, despite wide changes in the related level of total activity or volume. Costs are defined as variable or fixed with respect to *a specific activity* and for *a given time period.* Surveys of practice repeatedly show that identifying a cost as variable or fixed provides valuable information for making many management decisions and is an important input when evaluating performance. To illustrate these two basic types of costs, again consider costs at the Spartanburg, South Carolina, plant of BMW.

1. **Variable Costs:** If BMW buys a steering wheel at $60 for each of its BMW X5 vehicles, then the total cost of steering wheels should be $60 times the number of vehicles produced, as the following table illustrates.

Number of X5s Produced (1)	Variable Cost per Steering Wheel (2)	Total Variable Cost of Steering Wheels (3) = (1) × (2)
1	$60	$ 60
1,000	60	60,000
3,000	60	180,000

The steering wheel cost is an example of a variable cost because *total cost* changes in proportion to changes in the number of vehicles produced. The cost per unit of a variable cost is constant. It is precisely because the variable cost per steering wheel in column 2 is the same for each steering wheel that the total variable cost of steering wheels in column 3 changes proportionately with the number of X5s produced in column 1. When considering how variable costs behave, always focus on total costs.

Exhibit 2-3, Panel A, graphically illustrates the total variable cost of steering wheels. The cost is represented by a straight line that climbs from left to right. The phrases "strictly variable" and "proportionately variable" are sometimes used to describe the variable cost in Panel A.

Consider an example of a variable cost with respect to a different activity—the $20 hourly wage paid to each worker to set up machines at the Spartanburg plant. Setup labor cost is a variable cost with respect to setup hours because setup cost changes in total in proportion to the number of setup hours used.

2. **Fixed Costs:** Suppose BMW incurs a total cost of $2,000,000 per year for supervisors who work exclusively on the X5 line. These costs are unchanged in total over a designated range of the number of vehicles produced during a given time span (see Exhibit 2-3, Panel B). Fixed costs become smaller and smaller on a per unit basis as the number of vehicles assembled increases, as the following table shows.

Annual Total Fixed Supervision Costs for BMW X5 Assembly Line (1)	Number of X5s Produced (2)	Fixed Supervision Cost per X5 (3) = (1) ÷ (2)
$2,000,000	10,000	$200
$2,000,000	25,000	80
$2,000,000	50,000	40

It is precisely because *total* line supervision costs are fixed at $2,000,000 that fixed supervision cost per X5 decreases as the number of X5s produced increases; the same fixed cost is spread over a larger number of X5s. Do not be misled by the change in fixed cost per unit. Just as in the case of variable costs, when considering fixed costs, always focus on total costs. Costs are fixed when total costs remain unchanged despite significant changes in the level of total activity or volume.

Why are some costs variable and other costs fixed? Recall that a cost is usually measured as the amount of money that must be paid to acquire goods and services. Total cost of steering wheels is a variable cost because BMW buys the steering wheels only when they are needed. As more X5s are produced, proportionately more steering wheels are acquired and proportionately more costs are incurred.

Contrast the description of variable costs with the $2,000,000 of fixed costs per year incurred by BMW for supervision of the X5 assembly line. This level of supervision is acquired and put in place well before BMW uses it to produce X5s and before BMW even knows how many X5s it will produce. Suppose that BMW puts in place supervisors capable of supervising the production of 60,000 X5s each year. If the demand is for only 55,000 X5s, there will be idle capacity. Supervisors on the X5 line could have supervised the production of 60,000 X5s but will supervise only 55,000 X5s because of the lower demand. However, BMW must pay for the unused line supervision capacity because the cost of supervision cannot be reduced in the short run. If demand is even lower—say only 50,000 X5s—line supervision costs will not change; they will continue to be $2,000,000, and idle capacity will increase. Unlike variable costs, fixed costs of resources (such as for line supervision) cannot be quickly and easily changed to match the resources needed or used. Over time, however, managers can take actions to reduce fixed costs. For example, if the X5 line needs to be run for fewer hours because of low demand for X5s, BMW may lay off supervisors or move them to another production line.

Do not assume that individual cost items are inherently variable or fixed. Consider labor costs. Labor costs can be purely variable with respect to units produced when workers are paid on a piece-unit (piece-rate) basis. Some garment workers are paid on a per-shirt-sewed basis. In contrast, labor costs at a plant in the coming year are sometimes appropriately classified as fixed. For instance, a labor union agreement might set annual salaries and conditions, contain a no-layoff clause, and severely restrict a company's flexibility to assign workers to any other plant that has demand for labor. Japanese companies have for a long time had a policy of lifetime employment for their workers. Although such a policy entails higher labor costs, particularly in economic downturns, the benefits are increased loyalty and dedication to the company and higher productivity. The

Exhibit 2-3

Graphs of Variable and Fixed Costs

PANEL A: Variable Cost of Steering Wheels at $60 per BMW X5 Assembled

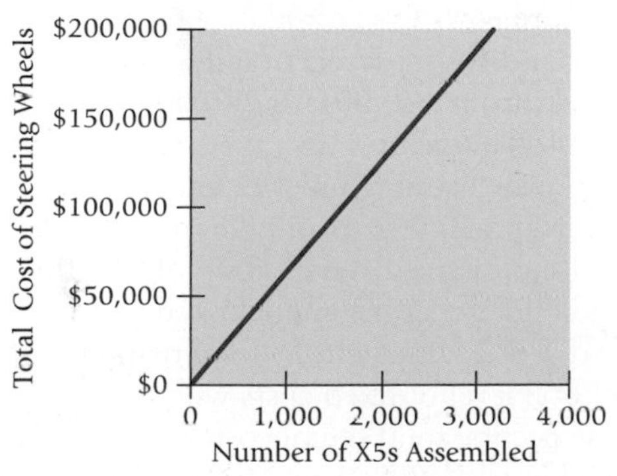

PANEL B: Supervision Costs for the BMW X5 assembly line (in millions)

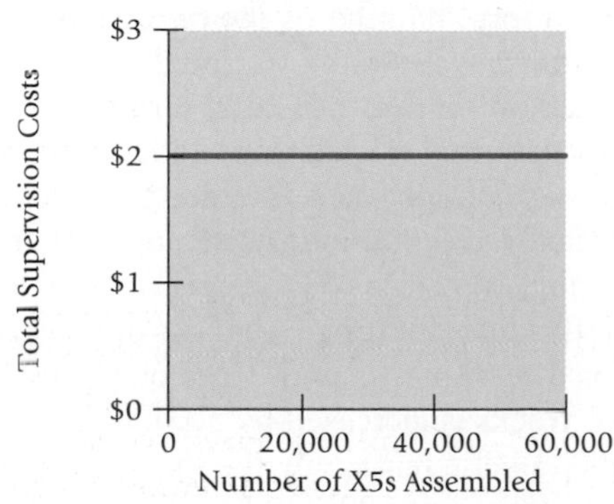

Concepts in Action on page 33 describes how a car-sharing service offers companies the opportunity to convert the fixed costs of owning corporate cars into variable costs by renting cars on an as-needed basis.

A particular cost item could be variable with respect to one level of activity and fixed with respect to another. Consider annual registration and license costs for a fleet of planes owned by an airline company. Registration and license costs would be a variable cost with respect to the number of planes owned. But registration and license costs for a particular plane are fixed with respect to the miles flown by that plane during a year.

To focus on key concepts, we have classified the behavior of costs as variable or fixed. Some costs have both fixed and variable elements and are called *mixed* or *semivariable* costs. For example, a company's telephone costs may have a fixed monthly payment and a charge per phone-minute used. We discuss mixed costs and techniques to separate out their fixed and variable components in Chapter 10.

Cost Drivers

A **cost driver** is a variable, such as the level of activity or volume, that causally affects costs over a given time span. That is, there is a cause-and-effect relationship between a change in the level of activity or volume and a change in the level of total costs. For example, if product-design costs change with the number of parts in a product, the number of parts is a cost driver of product-design costs. Similarly, miles driven is often a cost driver of distribution costs.

The cost driver of a variable cost is the level of activity or volume whose change causes proportionate changes in the variable cost. For example, the number of vehicles assembled is the cost driver of the total cost of steering wheels. If setup workers are paid an hourly wage, the number of setup hours is the cost driver of total (variable) setup costs.

Costs that are fixed in the short run have no cost driver in the short run but may have a cost driver in the long run. Consider the costs of testing color printers at Hewlett-Packard. These costs consist of Testing Department equipment and staff costs that are difficult to change and, hence, are fixed in the short run with respect to changes in the volume of production. In this case, volume of production is not a cost driver of testing costs in the short run. In the long run, however, Hewlett-Packard will increase or decrease the Testing Department's equipment and staff to the levels needed to support future production volumes. In the long run, volume of production is a cost driver of testing costs.

Relevant Range

Relevant range is the band of normal activity level or volume in which there is a specific relationship between the level of activity or volume and the cost in question. For example, a fixed cost is fixed only in relation to a given wide range of total activity or volume (at which the company is expected to operate) and only for a given time span (usually a particular budget period). Suppose that BMW contracts with Thomas Transport Company (TTC) to transport X5s to BMW dealers. Thomas Transport Company (TTC), rents two trucks. Each truck has annual fixed rental costs of $40,000. The maximum annual usage of each truck is 120,000 miles. In the current year (2009), the predicted combined total hauling of the two trucks is 170,000 miles.

Exhibit 2-4 shows how annual fixed costs behave at different levels of miles of hauling. Up to 120,000 miles, TTC can operate with one truck; from 120,001 to 240,000 miles, it operates with two trucks; from 240,001 to 360,000 miles, it operates with three trucks. This pattern will continue as TTC adds trucks to its fleet to provide more miles of hauling. Given the predicted 170,000-mile usage for 2009, the range from 120,001 to 240,000 miles hauled is the range in which TTC expects to operate, resulting in fixed rental costs of $80,000. Within this relevant range, changes in miles hauled will not affect the annual fixed costs.

Fixed costs may change from one year to the next. For example, if the total rental fee of the two trucks is increased by $2,000 for 2010, the total level of fixed costs will increase to $82,000 (all else remaining the same). If that increase occurs, total rental costs will be fixed at this new level of $82,000 for 2010 for miles hauled in the 120,001 to 240,000 range.

Concepts in Action

How Flexcar Helps Reduce Business Transportation Costs

Rising gas prices, high insurance costs, and hefty parking fees have forced many businesses to reexamine whether owning corporate cars is economical. In some cities, the Flexcar car-sharing service has emerged as an attractive alternative. Flexcar provides an "on demand" option for urban businesses and individuals to rent a car by the week, the day, or even the hour. Basically, members make a reservation by phone or Internet, go to the parking lot where the car is located (usually via walking or public transportation), swipe an electronic card over a sensor that unlocks the door, and then just climb in and drive away. Rental fees begin around $8 per hour and $63 per day and include gas, insurance, maintenance, 24-hour roadside assistance, and some mileage (usually 150 miles per day). Currently, business customers account for 30–40 percent of Flexcar's revenues.

Let's think about what the Flexcar option means for companies. Many small businesses own a company car or two for getting to meetings, making deliveries, and other errands. Similarly, several large companies own a fleet of cars to shuttle visiting executives and clients back and forth from appointments, business lunches, and the airport. Traditionally, owning these cars has involved very high fixed costs, including buying the asset (car), costs of the maintenance department, and insurance for multiple drivers. But businesses had no other options.

Now, companies can use Flexcar for on-demand transportation while reducing their transportation and overhead costs. In San Diego, most of the 20 employees at DCI Engineers, a consulting engineering firm, commute to work using mass transit and use Flexcars from a nearby lot to visit clients and attend business meetings, thus eliminating the need for corporate cars. In Seattle, Starbucks took it one step further by having Flexcar operate a pool of vehicles out of its corporate-headquarters parking lot exclusively for use by its employees.

From a business perspective, Flexcar allows companies to convert the fixed costs of owning a company car to variable costs. If business slows, or a car isn't required to visit a client, Flexcar customers are not saddled with the fixed costs of car ownership. Of course, if companies use Flexcars frequently, they can end up paying more overall than they would have paid if they had purchased and maintained the car themselves.

Flexcar believes that it is also contributing to society and the environment. The company estimates that for every car it operates, 20 private automobiles are kept off the road, thus reducing congestion on the roads. Conscious about the environment and global warming, Flexcar operates many hybrid and electric cars in its fleet. Is anyone really noticing car-sharing services like Flexcar? Here's one sign: *Flexcar One*, a Honda hybrid, was recently parked in a reserved spot directly outside the West Wing of the White House for business use by White House staff!

Sources: Mollie Neal, "Curb Auto Expenses with Car-Sharing Services," *Small Business Review*, April 25, 2006; Annys Shin, "Flexcar Receives Infusion of Cash," *The Washington Post*, June 20, 2006; Richard Blackwell, "When an Occasional Car Will Do the Trick," *Toronto Globe and Mail*, December 28, 2006.

The basic assumption of the relevant range also applies to variable costs. That is, outside the relevant range, variable costs, such as direct materials, may not change proportionately with changes in production volume. For example, above a certain volume, direct material costs may increase at a lower rate because of price discounts on purchases greater than a certain quantity.

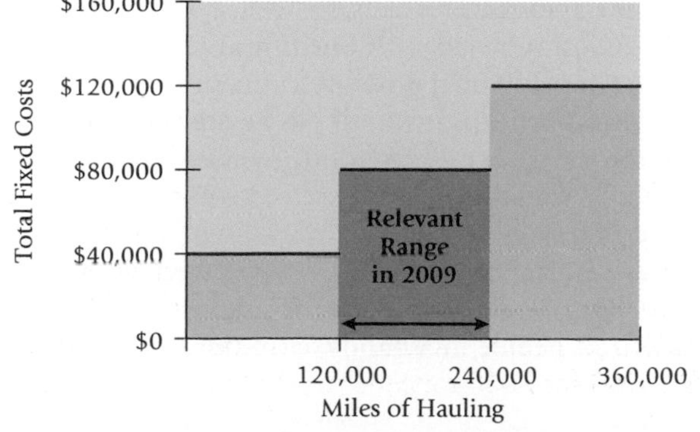

Exhibit 2-4

Fixed-Cost Behavior at Thomas Transport Company

Exhibit 2-5

Examples of Costs in Combinations of the Direct/Indirect and Variable/Fixed Cost Classifications for a Car Manufacturer

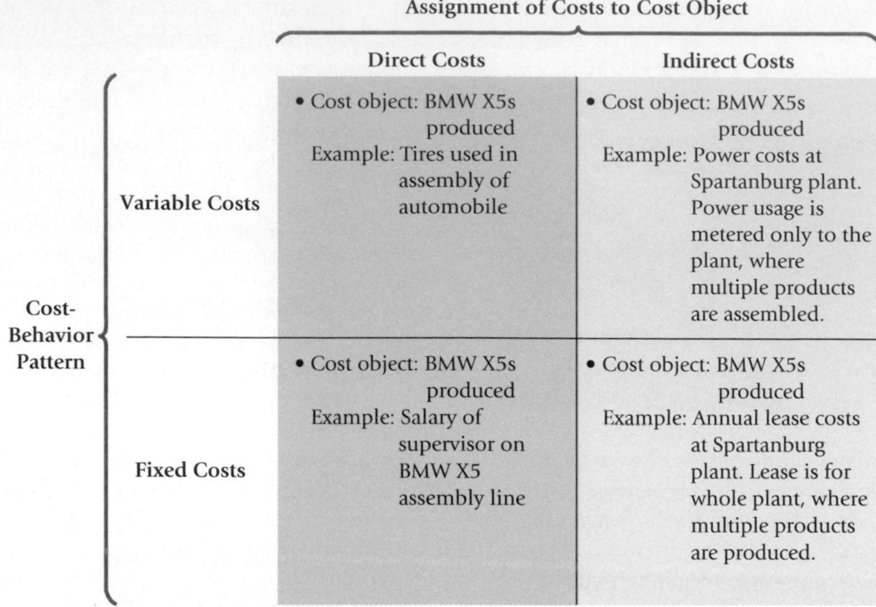

Relationships of Types of Costs

We have introduced two major classifications of costs: direct/indirect and variable/fixed. Costs may simultaneously be:

- Direct and variable
- Direct and fixed
- Indirect and variable
- Indirect and fixed

Exhibit 2-5 shows examples of costs in each of these four cost classifications for the BMW X5.

Total Costs and Unit Costs

The preceding section concentrated on the behavior patterns of total costs in relation to activity or volume levels. We now consider unit costs.

Unit Costs

Learning Objective 4

Interpret unit costs cautiously

. . . for many decisions, managers should use total costs, not unit costs

Generally, the decision maker should think in terms of total costs rather than unit costs. In many decision contexts, however, calculating a unit cost is essential. Consider the chairman of the social committee of a fraternity, who is trying to decide whether to hire a musical group for an upcoming party. He estimates the cost of hiring the group to be $1,000. This knowledge is helpful for the decision, but it is not enough.

Before a decision can be reached, the chairman also must predict the number of people who will attend. Without knowledge of both total cost and number of attendees, he cannot make an informed decision on a possible admission price to recover the cost of the party or even on whether to have a party at all. So he computes the unit cost of hiring the musical group by dividing the total cost ($1,000) by the expected number of people who will attend. If 1,000 people attend, the unit cost is $1 per person; if 100 attend, the unit cost soars to $10.

Unless the total cost is "unitized" (that is, averaged with respect to the level of activity or volume), the $1,000 cost is difficult to interpret. The unit cost combines the total cost and the number of people in a handy, communicative way.

Accounting systems typically report both total-cost amounts and average-cost-per-unit amounts. A **unit cost**, also called an **average cost**, is computed by dividing total cost by the number of units. The units might be expressed in various ways. Examples are automobiles assembled, packages delivered, or hours worked. Suppose that, in 2009, its first year of operations, $40,000,000 of manufacturing costs are incurred to produce 500,000 speaker systems at the Memphis plant of Tennessee Products. Then the unit cost is $80:

$$\frac{\text{Total manufacturing costs}}{\text{Number of units manufactured}} = \frac{\$40{,}000{,}000}{500{,}000 \text{ units}} = \$80 \text{ per unit}$$

If 480,000 units are sold and 20,000 units remain in ending inventory, the unit-cost concept helps in the determination of total costs in the income statement and balance sheet and, hence, the financial results reported by Tennessee Products to shareholders, banks, and the government.

Cost of goods sold in the income statement, 480,000 units × $80 per unit	$38,400,000
Ending inventory in the balance sheet, 20,000 units × $80 per unit	1,600,000
Total manufacturing costs of 500,000 units	$40,000,000

Unit costs are found in all areas of the value chain—for example, unit cost of product design, of sales visits, and of customer-service calls. By summing unit costs throughout the value chain, managers calculate the unit cost of the different products or services they deliver and determine the profitability of each product or service. Managers use this information, for example, to decide the products in which they should invest more resources, such as R&D and marketing, and the prices they should charge.

Use Unit Costs Cautiously

Although unit costs are regularly used in financial reports and for making product mix and pricing decisions, *managers should think in terms of total costs rather than unit costs for many decisions*. Consider the manager of the Memphis plant of Tennessee Products. Assume the $40,000,000 in costs in 2009 consist of $10,000,000 of fixed costs and $30,000,000 of variable costs (at $60 variable cost per speaker system produced). Suppose the total fixed cost and the variable cost per speaker system in 2010 are expected to be unchanged from 2009. The budgeted costs for 2010 at different production levels, calculated on the basis of total variable costs, total fixed costs, and total costs, are:

Units Produced (1)	Variable Cost per Unit (2)	Total Variable Costs (3)=(1)×(2)	Total Fixed Costs (4)	Total Costs (5)=(3)+(4)	Unit Cost (6)=(5)÷(1)
100,000	$60	$ 6,000,000	$10,000,000	$16,000,000	$160.00
200,000	$60	$12,000,000	$10,000,000	$22,000,000	$110.00
500,000	$60	$30,000,000	$10,000,000	$40,000,000	$ 80.00
800,000	$60	$48,000,000	$10,000,000	$58,000,000	$ 72.50
1,000,000	$60	$60,000,000	$10,000,000	$70,000,000	$ 70.00

A plant manager who uses the 2009 unit cost of $80 per unit will underestimate actual total costs if 2010 output is below the 2009 level of 500,000 units. If actual volume is 200,000 units due to, say, the presence of a new competitor, actual costs would be $22,000,000. The unit cost of $80 times 200,000 units equals $16,000,000, which underestimates the actual total costs by $6,000,000 ($22,000,000 – $16,000,000). *The unit cost of $80 applies only when 500,000 units are produced.* An overreliance on unit cost in this situation could lead to insufficient cash being available to pay costs if volume declines to 200,000 units. As the table indicates, for making this decision, managers should think in terms of total variable costs, total fixed costs, and total costs rather than unit cost. As a general rule, first calculate total costs, then compute a unit cost, if it is needed for a particular decision.

We now discuss cost concepts used in different sectors of the economy.

Manufacturing-, Merchandising-, and Service-Sector Companies

Learning Objective 5

Distinguish among manufacturing companies, merchandising companies, and service-sector companies

. . . different types of companies face different accounting issues

We define three sectors of the economy and provide examples of companies in each sector.

1. **Manufacturing-sector companies** purchase materials and components and convert them into various finished goods. Examples are automotive companies, cellular phone producers, food-processing companies, and textile companies.
2. **Merchandising-sector companies** purchase and then sell tangible products without changing their basic form. This sector includes companies engaged in retailing (such as bookstores or department stores), distribution, or wholesaling.
3. **Service-sector companies** provide services (intangible products)—for example, legal advice or audits—to their customers. Examples are law firms, accounting firms, banks, mutual fund companies, insurance companies, transportation companies, advertising agencies, radio and television stations, Internet-based companies such as Internet service providers, travel agencies, and brokerage firms.

Types of Inventory, Inventoriable Costs, and Period Costs

Learning Objective 6

Describe the three categories of inventories commonly found in manufacturing companies

. . . the categories are direct materials, work in process, and finished goods

In this section, we describe the different types of inventory that companies hold and some commonly used classifications of manufacturing costs.

Types of Inventory

Manufacturing-sector companies purchase materials and components and convert them into various finished goods. These companies typically have one or more of the following three types of inventory:

1. **Direct materials inventory.** Direct materials in stock and awaiting use in the manufacturing process (for example, computer chips and components needed to manufacture cellular phones).
2. **Work-in-process inventory.** Goods partially worked on but not yet completed (for example, cellular phones at various stages of completion in the manufacturing process). Also called **work in progress**.
3. **Finished goods inventory.** Goods (for example, cellular phones) completed but not yet sold.

Merchandising-sector companies purchase tangible products and then sell them without changing their basic form. They hold only one type of inventory, which is products in their original purchased form, called *merchandise inventory*. Service-sector companies provide only services or intangible products and so do not hold inventories of tangible products.

Commonly Used Classifications of Manufacturing Costs

Three terms commonly used when describing manufacturing costs are direct material costs, direct manufacturing labor costs, and indirect manufacturing costs.

1. **Direct material costs** are the acquisition costs of all materials that eventually become part of the cost object (work in process and then finished goods) and can be traced to the cost object in an economically feasible way. Acquisition costs of direct materials include freight-in (inward delivery) charges, sales taxes, and custom duties. Examples of direct material costs are the steel and tires used to make the BMW X5, and the computer chips used to make cellular phones.

2. **Direct manufacturing labor costs** include the compensation of all manufacturing labor that can be traced to the cost object (work in process and then finished goods) in an economically feasible way. Examples include wages and fringe benefits paid to machine operators and assembly-line workers who convert direct materials purchased to finished goods.
3. **Indirect manufacturing costs** are all manufacturing costs that are related to the cost object (work in process and then finished goods) but cannot be traced to that cost object in an economically feasible way. Examples include supplies, indirect materials such as lubricants, indirect manufacturing labor such as plant maintenance and cleaning labor, plant rent, plant insurance, property taxes on the plant, plant depreciation, and the compensation of plant managers. This cost category is also referred to as **manufacturing overhead costs** or **factory overhead costs.** We use *indirect manufacturing costs* and *manufacturing overhead costs* interchangeably in this book.

We now describe the distinction between inventoriable costs and period costs.

Inventoriable Costs

Learning Objective 7

Distinguish inventoriable costs

. . . assets when incurred, then cost of goods sold

from period costs

. . . expenses of the period when incurred

Inventoriable costs are all costs of a product that are considered as assets in the balance sheet when they are incurred and that become cost of goods sold only when the product is sold. For manufacturing-sector companies, all manufacturing costs are inventoriable costs. Consider Cellular Products, a manufacturer of cellular phones. Costs of direct materials, such as computer chips, issued to production (from direct material inventory), direct manufacturing labor costs, and manufacturing overhead costs create new assets, starting as work in process and becoming finished goods (the cellular phones). Hence, manufacturing costs are included in work-in-process inventory and in finished goods inventory (they are "inventoried") to accumulate the costs of creating these assets.

When the cellular phones are sold, the cost of manufacturing them is matched against **revenues,** which are inflows of assets (usually cash or accounts receivable) received for products or services provided to customers. The cost of goods sold includes all manufacturing costs (direct materials, direct manufacturing labor, and manufacturing overhead costs) incurred to produce them. The cellular phones may be sold during a different accounting period than the period in which they were manufactured. Thus, inventorying manufacturing costs in the balance sheet during the accounting period when goods are manufactured and expensing the manufacturing costs in a later income statement when the goods are sold matches revenues and expenses.

For merchandising-sector companies such as Wal-Mart, inventoriable costs are the costs of purchasing the goods that are resold in their same form. These costs comprise the costs of the goods themselves plus any incoming freight, insurance, and handling costs for those goods. Service-sector companies provide only services or intangible products. The absence of inventories of tangible products for sale means there are no inventoriable costs.

Period Costs

Period costs are all costs in the income statement other than cost of goods sold. Period costs are treated as expenses of the accounting period in which they are incurred because they are expected to benefit revenues in that period and are not expected to benefit revenues in future periods (because there is not sufficient evidence to conclude that such future benefit exists). Expensing these costs in the period they are incurred matches expenses to revenues.

For manufacturing-sector companies, period costs in the income statement are all nonmanufacturing costs (for example, design costs and distribution costs). For merchandising-sector companies, period costs in the income statement are all costs not related to the cost of goods purchased for resale. Examples of these period costs are labor costs of sales floor personnel and advertising costs. Because there are no inventoriable costs for service-sector companies, all costs in the income statement are period costs.

Exhibit 2-5 showed examples of inventoriable costs in direct/indirect and variable/fixed cost classifications for a car manufacturer. Exhibit 2-6 shows examples of period costs in direct/indirect and variable/fixed cost classifications at a bank.

Exhibit 2-6

Examples of Period Costs in Combinations of the Direct/Indirect and Variable/Fixed Cost Classifications at a Bank

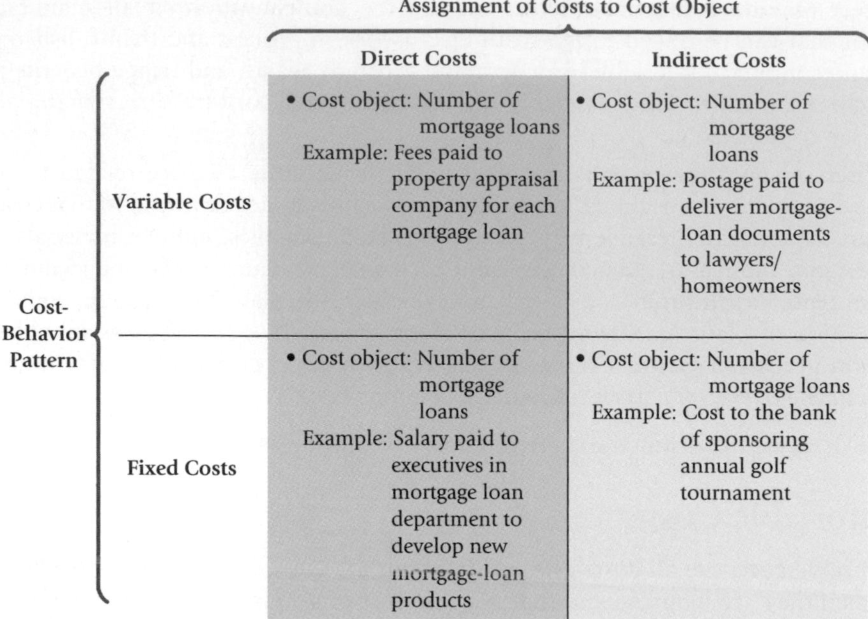

Illustrating the Flow of Inventoriable Costs and Period Costs

We illustrate the flow of inventoriable costs and period costs through the income statement of a manufacturing company, for which the distinction between inventoriable costs and period costs is most detailed.

Manufacturing-Sector Example

Follow the flow of costs for Cellular Products in Exhibit 2-7 and Exhibit 2-8. Exhibit 2-7 visually highlights the differences in the flow of inventoriable and period costs for a manufacturing-sector company. Note how, as described in the previous section, inventoriable costs go through the balance sheet accounts of work-in-process inventory and finished goods inventory before entering cost of goods sold in the income statement. Period costs are expensed directly in the income statement. Exhibit 2-8 takes the visual presentation in Exhibit 2-7 and shows how inventoriable costs and period expenses would appear in the income statement and schedule of cost of goods manufactured of a manufacturing company.

We start by tracking the flow of direct materials shown on the left of Exhibit 2-7 and in Panel B of Exhibit 2-8.

Step 1: Cost of direct materials used. Note how the arrows in Exhibit 2-7 for beginning inventory, \$11,000, and direct material purchases, \$73,000, "fill up" the direct material inventory box and how direct material used, \$76,000 "empties out" direct material inventory leaving an ending inventory of direct materials of \$8,000 that becomes the beginning inventory for the next year.

The cost of direct materials used is calculated in Exhibit 2-8, Panel B (light blue shaded area) as

Beginning inventory of direct materials, January 1, 2009	\$11,000
+ Purchases of direct materials in 2009	73,000
− Ending inventory of direct materials, December 31, 2009	8,000
= Direct materials used in 2009	\$76,000

Step 2: Total manufacturing costs incurred in 2009. Total manufacturing costs refers to all direct manufacturing costs and manufacturing overhead costs incurred during 2009 for all goods worked on during the year. Cellular Products classifies its manufacturing costs into the three categories described earlier.

(i) Direct materials used in 2009 (shaded light blue in Exhibit 2-8, Panel B)	$ 76,000
(ii) Direct manufacturing labor in 2009 (shaded blue in Exhibit 2-8, Panel B)	9,000
(iii) Manufacturing overhead costs (shaded dark blue in Exhibit 2-8, Panel B)	20,000
Total manufacturing costs incurred in 2009	$105,000

Note how in Exhibit 2-7, these costs increase work-in-process inventory.

Step 3: Cost of goods manufactured in 2009. Cost of goods manufactured refers to the cost of goods brought to completion, whether they were started before or during the current accounting period.

Note how the work-in-process inventory box in Exhibit 2-7 has a very similar structure to the direct material inventory box described in Step 1. Beginning work-in-process inventory of $6,000 and total manufacturing costs incurred in 2009 of $105,000 "fill-up" the work-in-process inventory box. Some of the manufacturing costs incurred during 2009 are held back as the cost of the ending work-in-process inventory. The ending work-in-process inventory of $7,000 becomes the beginning inventory for the next year, and the cost of goods manufactured during 2009 of $104,000 "empties out" the work-in-process inventory while "filling up" the finished goods inventory box.

The cost of goods manufactured in 2009 (shaded teal) is calculated in Exhibit 2-8, Panel B as:

Beginning work-in-process inventory, January 1, 2009	$ 6,000
+ Total manufacturing costs incurred in 2009	105,000
= Total manufacturing costs to account for	111,000
− Ending work-in-process inventory, December 31, 2009	7,000
= Cost of goods manufactured in 2009	$104,000

Step 4: Cost of goods sold in 2009. The cost of goods sold is the cost of finished goods inventory sold to customers during the current accounting period. Looking at the finished goods inventory box in Exhibit 2-7, we see that the beginning inventory of finished goods of $22,000 and cost of goods manufactured in 2009 of $104,000 "fill up" the finished goods inventory box. The ending inventory of finished goods of $18,000 becomes the beginning

Exhibit 2-7 Flow of Revenue and Costs for a Manufacturing-Sector Company, Cellular Products (in thousands)

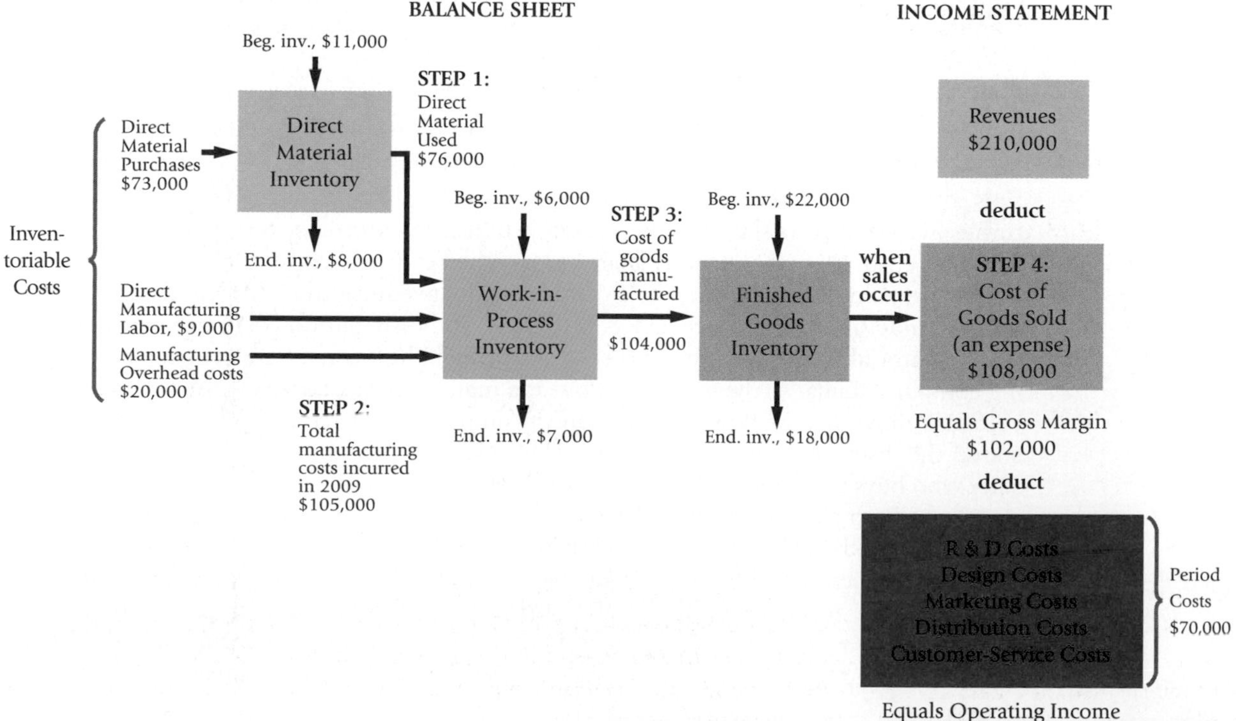

inventory for the next year, and the cost of goods sold during 2009 of $108,000 "empties out" the finished goods inventory.

This cost of goods sold is an expense that is matched against revenues. The cost of goods sold for Cellular Products (shaded brown) is computed in Exhibit 2-8, Panel A, as:

Beginning inventory of finished goods, January 1, 2009	$ 22,000
+ Cost of goods manufactured in 2009	104,000
− Ending inventory of finished goods, December 31, 2009	18,000
= Cost of goods sold in 2009	$108,000

Exhibit 2-9 shows related general-ledger T-accounts for Cellular Products' manufacturing cost flow. Note how the cost of goods manufactured ($104,000) is the cost of all goods completed during the accounting period. These costs are all inventoriable costs. Goods completed during the period are transferred to finished goods inventory. These costs become cost of goods sold in the accounting period when the goods are sold. Also note that the direct materials, direct manufacturing labor, and manufacturing overhead costs of the units in work-in-process inventory ($7,000) and finished goods inventory ($18,000) as of December 31, 2009, will appear as an asset in the balance sheet. These costs will become expenses next year, when these units are sold.

We are now in a position to prepare Cellular Products' income statement for 2009. The income statement of Cellular Products is shown on the right-hand side of Exhibit 2-7 and in Exhibit 2-8, Panel A. Revenues of Cellular Products are (in thousands) $210,000. Inventoriable costs expensed during 2009 equal cost of goods sold of $108,000. Gross margin = Revenues − Cost of goods sold = $210,000 − $108,000 = $102,000.

The $70,000 comprising R&D, design, marketing, distribution, and customer-service costs are period costs of Cellular Products. These period costs include, for example, salaries of salespersons, depreciation on computers and other equipment used in marketing, and the cost of leasing warehouse space for distribution. Period costs help to calculate **operating income**, which is total revenues from operations minus cost of goods sold and operating costs (excluding interest expense and income taxes). The operating income of Cellular Products is $32,000 (gross margin, $102,000 − period costs, $70,000).

Newcomers to cost accounting frequently assume that indirect costs such as rent, telephone, and depreciation are always costs of the period in which they are incurred and are not associated with inventories. When these costs are incurred in marketing or in corporate headquarters, they are period costs. However, when these costs are incurred in manufacturing, they are manufacturing overhead costs and are inventoriable.

Recap of Inventoriable Costs and Period Costs

Exhibit 2-7 highlights the differences between inventoriable costs and period costs for a manufacturing company. The manufacturing costs of finished goods include direct materials, other direct manufacturing costs such as direct manufacturing labor, and manufacturing overhead costs such as supervision, production control, and machine maintenance. All these costs are inventoriable: They are assigned to work-in-process inventory until the goods are completed and then to finished goods inventory until the goods are sold. All nonmanufacturing costs, such as R&D, design, and distribution costs, are period costs.

Inventoriable costs and period costs flow through the income statement at a merchandising company similar to the way costs flow at a manufacturing company. At a merchandising company, however, the flow of costs is much simpler to understand and track. Exhibit 2-10 shows the distribution between inventoriable costs and period costs for a retailer or wholesaler who buys goods for resale. The only inventoriable cost is the cost of merchandise. (This corresponds to the cost of finished goods manufactured for a manufacturing company.) Purchased goods are held as merchandise inventory, the cost of which is shown as an asset in the balance sheet. As the goods are sold, their costs are shown in the income statement as cost of goods sold. A retailer or wholesaler also has a variety of marketing, distribution, and customer-service costs, which are period costs. In the income statement, period costs are deducted from revenues without ever having been included as part of inventory.

Exhibit 2-8 Income Statement and Schedule of Cost of Goods Manufactured of a Manufacturing-Sector Company, Cellular Products

	A	B	C	D
1	**PANEL A: INCOME STATEMENT**			
2	**Cellular Products**			
3	**Income Statement**			
4	**For the Year Ended December 31, 2009 (in thousands)**			
5	Revenues		$210,000	
6	Cost of goods sold:			
7	Beginning finished goods inventory, January 1, 2009	$ 22,000		
8	Cost of goods manufactured (see Panel B)	104,000		
9	Cost of goods available for sale	126,000		
10	Ending finished goods inventory, December 31, 2009	18,000		
11	Cost of goods sold		108,000	
12	Gross margin (or gross profit)		102,000	
13	Operating costs:			
14	R&D, design, mktg., dist., & cust.-service cost	70,000		
15	Total operating costs		70,000	
16	Operating income		$ 32,000	
17				
18	**PANEL B: COST OF GOODS MANUFACTURED**			
19	**Cellular Products**			
20	**Schedule of Cost of Goods Manufactured[a]**			
21	**For the Year Ended December 31, 2009 (in thousands)**			
22	Direct materials:			
23	Beginning inventory, January 1, 2009	$11,000		
24	Purchases of direct materials	73,000		
25	Cost of direct materials available for use	84,000		
26	Ending inventory, December 31, 2009	8,000		
27	Direct materials used		$ 76,000	
28	Direct manufacturing labor		9,000	
29	Manufacturing overhead costs:			
30	Indirect manufacturing labor	$ 7,000		
31	Supplies	2,000		
32	Heat, light, and power	5,000		
33	Depreciation--plant building	2,000		
34	Depreciation--plant equipment	3,000		
35	Miscellaneous	1,000		
36	Total manufacturing overhead costs		20,000	
37	Manufacturing costs incurred during 2009		105,000	
38	Beginning work-in-process inventory, January 1, 2009		6,000	
39	Total manufacturing costs to account for		111,000	
40	Ending work-in-process inventory, December 31, 2009		7,000	
41	Cost of goods manufactured (to Income Statement)		$104,000	
42	[a]Note that this schedule can become a Schedule of Cost of Goods Manufactured and Sold simply by including the beginning and ending finished goods inventory figures in the supporting schedule rather than in the body of the income statement.			

STEP 4: rows 6–11. STEP 1: rows 22–27. STEP 2: rows 27–37. STEP 3: rows 37–41.

Exhibit 2-9 General-Ledger T-Accounts for Cellular Products' Manufacturing Cost Flow

Work-in-Process Inventory

Bal. Jan. 1, 2009	6,000	Cost of goods manufactured	104,000
Direct materials used	76,000		
Direct manuf. labor	9,000		
Indirect manuf. costs	20,000		
Bal. Dec. 31, 2009	7,000		

Finished Goods Inventory

Bal. Jan. 1, 2009	22,000	Cost of goods sold	108,000
	104,000		
Bal. Dec. 31, 2009	18,000		

Cost of Goods Sold

108,000	

Prime Costs and Conversion Costs

Two terms used to describe cost classifications in manufacturing costing systems are prime costs and conversion costs. **Prime costs** are all direct manufacturing costs. For Cellular Products,

$$\text{Prime costs} = \text{Direct material costs} + \text{Direct manufacturing labor costs} = \$76{,}000 + \$9{,}000 = \$85{,}000$$

As we have already discussed, the greater the proportion of prime costs in a company's cost structure, the more confident managers can be about the accuracy of the costs of products. As information-gathering technology improves, companies can add more and more direct-cost categories. For example, power costs might be metered in specific areas of a plant and identified with specific products. In this case, prime costs would include direct materials, direct manufacturing labor, and direct metered power. Furthermore, if a production line were dedicated to the manufacture of a specific product, the depreciation on the production equipment would be a direct manufacturing cost and would be included in prime costs. Computer software companies often have a "purchased technology" direct manufacturing cost item. This item, which represents payments to suppliers who develop software algorithms for a product, is also included in prime costs. **Conversion costs** are all manufacturing costs other than direct material costs. Conversion costs represent all manufacturing costs incurred to convert direct materials into finished goods. For Cellular Products,

$$\text{Conversion costs} = \frac{\text{Direct manufacturing}}{\text{labor costs}} + \frac{\text{Manufacturing}}{\text{overhead costs}} = \$9{,}000 + \$20{,}000 = \$29{,}000$$

Note that direct manufacturing labor costs are a part of both prime costs and conversion costs.

Some manufacturing operations, such as computer-integrated manufacturing (CIM) plants, have very few workers. The workers' roles are to monitor the manufacturing

Exhibit 2-10

Merchandising Company (Retailer or Wholesaler)

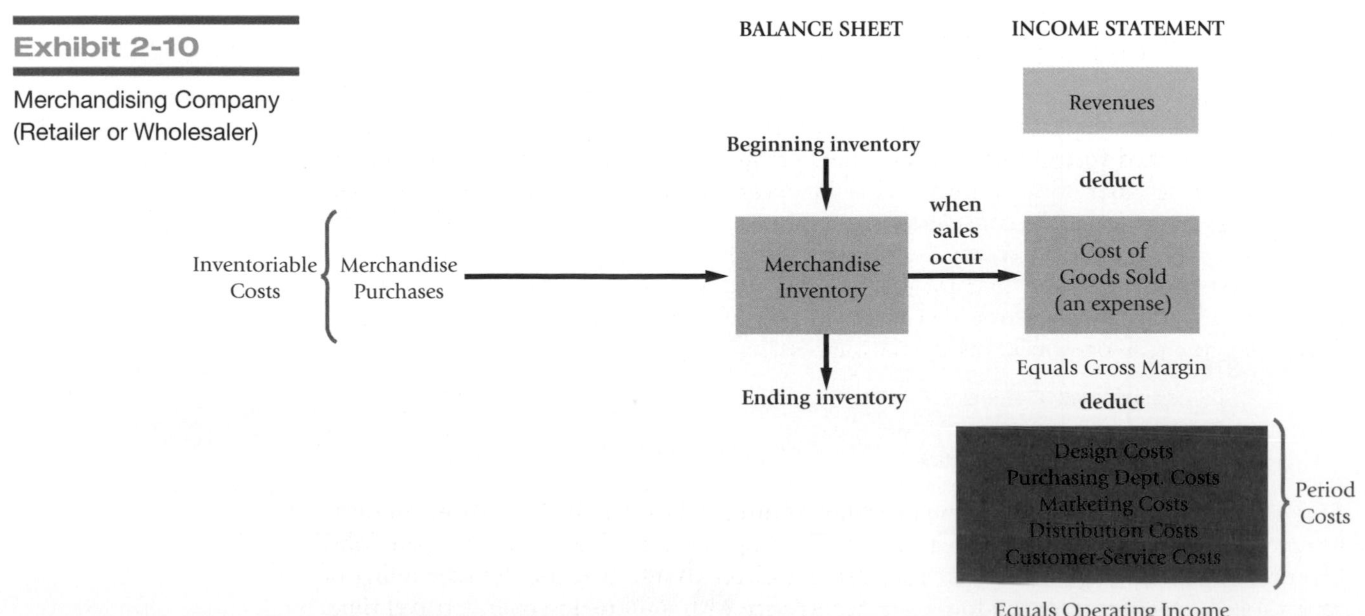

process and to maintain the equipment that produces multiple products. Costing systems in CIM plants do not have a direct manufacturing labor cost category because direct manufacturing labor cost is relatively small and because it is difficult to trace this cost to products. In CIM plants, the only prime cost is direct material costs, and conversion costs consist only of manufacturing overhead costs.

Measuring Costs Requires Judgment

Measuring costs requires judgment. That's because there are alternative ways in which costs can be defined and classified. Different companies or sometimes even different subunits within the same company may define and classify costs differently. Be careful to define and understand the ways costs are measured in a company or situation. We first illustrate this point with respect to labor cost measurement.

Measuring Labor Costs

Although manufacturing labor cost classifications vary among companies, most companies have the following categories:

- Direct manufacturing labor (labor that can be traced to individual products)
- Manufacturing overhead (examples of prominent labor components of manufacturing overhead follow):
  - Indirect labor (compensation)
    - Forklift truck operators (internal handling of materials)
    - Plant janitors
    - Plant guards
    - Rework labor (time spent by direct laborers redoing defective work)
    - Overtime premium paid to plant workers (explained next)
    - Idle time (explained next)
  - Managers', department heads', and supervisors' salaries
  - Payroll fringe costs, for example, health care premiums and pension costs (explained later)

Note how *indirect labor costs* are commonly divided into many subclassifications, for example, forklift operators and plant guards, to retain information on different categories of indirect labor. Note also that managers' salaries usually are not classified as indirect labor costs. Instead, the compensation of supervisors, department heads, and all others who are regarded as manufacturing management is placed in a separate classification of labor-related manufacturing overhead.

Overtime Premium and Idle Time

The purpose of classifying costs in detail is to associate an individual cost with a specific cause or reason for why it was incurred. Two classes of indirect labor—overtime premium and idle time—need special mention. **Overtime premium** is the wage rate paid to workers (for both direct labor and indirect labor) in *excess* of their straight-time wage rates. Overtime premium is usually considered to be a part of indirect costs or overhead. Consider an example from the service sector. George Flexner does home repairs for Sears Appliance Services. He is paid \$20 per hour for straight-time and \$30 per hour (time and a half) for overtime. His overtime premium is \$10 per overtime hour. If he works 44 hours, including 4 overtime hours, in one week, his gross compensation would be classified as follows:

Direct service labor: 44 hours × \$20 per hour	\$880
Overtime premium: 4 hours × \$10 per hour	40
Total compensation for 44 hours	\$920

In this example, why is the overtime premium of direct labor usually considered an overhead cost rather than a direct cost? After all, it can be traced to specific repair jobs. Overtime premium is generally not considered a direct charge because the scheduling of repair jobs is usually either random or in accordance with minimizing overall travel time.

For example, assume that jobs 1 through 5 are scheduled to be completed on a specific workday of 10 hours, including 2 overtime hours. Each job (service call) requires 2 hours. Should the job scheduled during hours 9 and 10 be assigned the overtime premium? Or should the premium be prorated over all five jobs? Prorating the overtime premium does not "penalize"—add to the cost of—a particular batch of work solely because it happened to be worked on during the overtime hours. *Instead, the overtime premium is considered to be attributable to the heavy overall volume of work. Its cost is regarded as part of service overhead, which is borne by all repair jobs.*

Sometimes overtime is not random. For example, a customer demanding a "rush job" may clearly be the sole source of overtime. In such instances, the overtime premium is regarded as a direct cost of that job.

Another subclassification of indirect labor is the idle time of both direct and indirect manufacturing or service labor. **Idle time** is wages paid for unproductive time caused by lack of orders, machine breakdowns, material shortages, poor scheduling, and the like. For example, if the Sears repair truck broke down for 3 hours, Flexner's earnings would be classified as follows:

Direct service labor: 41 hours × \$20/hour	\$820
Idle time (service overhead): 3 hours × \$20/hour	60
Overtime premium (service overhead): 4 hours × \$10/hour	40
Total earnings for 44 hours	\$920

Clearly, the idle time is not related to a particular job, nor, as we have already discussed, is the overtime premium. Both overtime premium and idle time are considered overhead costs.

Benefits of Defining Accounting Terms

Managers, accountants, suppliers, and others will avoid many problems if they thoroughly understand and agree on the classifications and meanings of the cost terms introduced in this chapter and later in this book.

Consider the classification of manufacturing labor *payroll fringe costs* (for example, employer payments for employee benefits such as Social Security, life insurance, health insurance, and pensions). Some companies classify these costs as manufacturing overhead costs. In other companies, the fringe benefits related to direct manufacturing labor are treated as an additional direct manufacturing labor cost. Consider, for example, a direct laborer, such as a lathe operator, whose gross wages are computed on the basis of a stated wage rate of \$20 an hour and fringe benefits totaling, say, \$5 per hour. Some companies classify the \$20 as direct manufacturing labor cost and the \$5 as manufacturing overhead cost. Other companies classify the entire \$25 as direct manufacturing labor cost. The latter approach is preferable because the stated wage and the fringe benefit costs together are a fundamental part of acquiring direct manufacturing labor services.

Caution: In every situation, pinpoint clearly what direct manufacturing labor includes and what direct manufacturing labor excludes. Achieving clarity may prevent disputes regarding cost-reimbursement contracts, income tax payments, and labor union matters. Consider that some countries such as Costa Rica and Mauritius offer substantial income tax savings to companies that locate plants within their borders. In some cases, to qualify for the tax benefits, the direct manufacturing labor costs of the plant must at least equal a specified percentage of the total manufacturing costs.

When direct manufacturing labor costs are not precisely defined, disputes have arisen as to whether payroll fringe costs should be included in direct manufacturing labor when calculating the direct manufacturing labor percentage for qualifying for such tax benefits. Companies have sought to classify payroll fringe costs as part of direct manufacturing labor costs to make direct manufacturing labor costs a higher percentage of total manufacturing costs. Tax authorities have argued that payroll fringe costs are part of manufacturing overhead. In addition to fringe benefits, other debated items are compensation for training time, idle time, vacations, sick leave, and overtime premium. To prevent disputes, contracts and laws should be as specific as possible regarding definitions and measurements.

Different Meanings of Product Costs

Learning Objective 8

Explain why product costs are computed in different ways for different purposes

. . . examples are pricing and product-mix decisions, government contracts, and financial statements

Many cost terms found in practice have ambiguous meanings. Consider the term *product cost*. A **product cost** is the sum of the costs assigned to a product for a specific purpose. Different purposes can result in different measures of product cost, as the brackets on the value chain in Exhibit 2-11 illustrate:

- **Pricing and product-mix decisions.** For the purposes of making decisions about pricing and which products provide the most profits, the manager is interested in the overall (total) profitability of different products and, consequently, assigns costs incurred in all business functions of the value chain to the different products.
- **Contracting with government agencies.** Government contracts often reimburse contractors on the basis of the "cost of a product" plus a prespecified margin of profit. Because of the cost-plus profit margin nature of the contract, government agencies provide detailed guidelines on the cost items they will allow and disallow when calculating the cost of a product. For example, some government agencies explicitly exclude marketing, distribution, and customer-service costs from the product costs that qualify for reimbursement, and they may only partially reimburse R&D costs. These agencies want to reimburse contractors for only those costs most closely related to delivering products under the contract. The second bracket in Exhibit 2-11 shows how the product-cost calculations for a specific contract may allow for all design and production costs but only part of R&D costs.
- **Preparing financial statements for external reporting under GAAP.** Under GAAP, only manufacturing costs can be assigned to inventories in the financial statements. For purposes of calculating inventory costs, product costs include only inventoriable (manufacturing) costs.

As Exhibit 2-11 illustrates, product-cost measures range from a narrow set of costs for financial statements—a set that includes only inventoriable costs—to a broader set of costs for reimbursement under a government contract to a still broader set of costs for pricing and product-mix decisions.

This section focused on how different purposes result in the inclusion of different cost items of the value chain of business functions when product costs are calculated. The same caution about the need to be clear and precise about cost concepts and their measurement applies to each cost classification introduced in this chapter. Exhibit 2-12 summarizes the key cost classifications.

Using the five-step process described in Chapter 1, think about how these different classifications of costs are helpful to managers when making decisions and evaluating performance.

1. *Identify the problem and uncertainties.* Consider a decision about how much to price a product. This decision often depends on how much it costs to make the product.

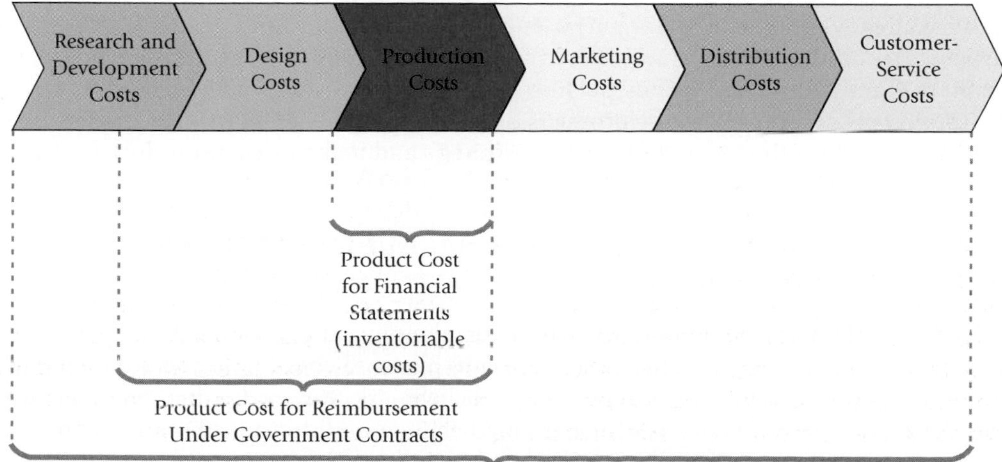

Exhibit 2-11

Different Product Costs for Different Purposes

Exhibit 2-12

Alternative Classifications of Costs

1. Business function
   a. Research and development
   b. Design of products, services, or processes
   c. Production
   d. Marketing
   e. Distribution
   f. Customer service
2. Assignment to a cost object
   a. Direct cost
   b. Indirect cost
3. Behavior pattern in relation to the level of activity or volume
   a. Variable cost
   b. Fixed cost
4. Aggregate or average
   a. Total cost
   b. Unit cost
5. Assets or expenses
   a. Inventoriable cost
   b Period cost

2. *Obtain information.* Managers identify direct and indirect costs of a product in each business function. Managers also gather other information about customers, competitors, and prices of substitute products.
3. *Make predictions about the future.* Managers estimate what it will cost to make the product in the future. This requires predictions about the quantity of product that managers expect to sell and an understanding of fixed and variable costs.
4. *Make decisions by choosing among alternatives.* Managers choose a price to charge based on a thorough understanding of costs and other information.
5. *Implement the decision, evaluate performance, and learn.* Managers control costs and learn by comparing actual total and unit costs against predicted amounts.

The next section describes how the basic concepts introduced in this chapter lead to a framework for understanding cost accounting and cost management that can then be applied to the study of many topics, such as strategy evaluation, quality, and investment decisions.

A Framework for Cost Accounting and Cost Management

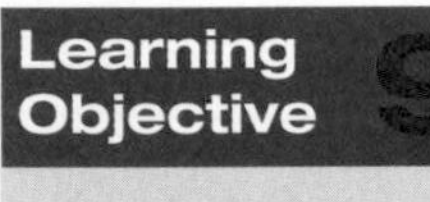

Describe a framework for cost accounting and cost management

. . . three features that help managers make decisions

Three features of cost accounting and cost management across a wide range of applications are:

1. Calculating the cost of products, services, and other cost objects
2. Obtaining information for planning and control and performance evaluation
3. Analyzing the relevant information for making decisions

We develop these ideas in Chapters 3 through 12. The ideas also form the foundation for the study of various topics later in the book.

Calculating the Cost of Products, Services, and Other Cost Objects

We have already seen the different purposes and measures of product costs. Whatever the purpose, the costing system traces direct costs and allocates indirect costs to products. Chapters 4 and 5 describe systems, such as activity-based costing systems, used to calculate total costs and unit costs of products and services. The chapters also discuss how managers use this information to formulate strategy and make pricing, product-mix, and cost-management decisions.

Obtaining Information for Planning and Control and Performance Evaluation

Budgeting is the most commonly used tool for planning and control. A budget forces managers to look ahead, to translate strategy into plans, to coordinate and communicate within the organization, and to provide a benchmark for evaluating performance. Budgeting often plays a major role in affecting behavior and decisions because managers strive to meet budget targets. Chapter 6 describes budgeting systems.

At the end of a reporting period, managers compare actual results to planned performance. The manager's tasks are to understand why differences (called variances) between actual and planned performances arise and to use the information provided by these variances as feedback to promote learning and future improvement. Managers also use variances as well as nonfinancial measures, such as defect rates and customer satisfaction ratings, to control and evaluate the performance of various departments, divisions, and managers. Chapters 7 and 8 discuss variance analysis. Chapter 9 describes planning, control, and inventory-costing issues relating to capacity. Chapters 6, 7, 8, and 9 focus on the management accountant's role in implementing strategy.

Analyzing the Relevant Information for Making Decisions

When making decisions about strategy design and strategy implementation, managers must understand which revenues and costs to consider and which ones to ignore. Management accountants help managers identify what information is relevant and what information is irrelevant. Consider a decision about whether to buy a product from an outside vendor or to make it in-house. The costing system indicates that it costs $25 per unit to make the product in-house. A vendor offers the product for $22 per unit. At first glance, it seems it will cost less for the company to buy the product rather than make it. Suppose, however, that of the $25 to make the product in-house, $5 consists of plant lease costs that the company will have to pay whether the product is made or bought. That is, if the product is bought, the plant will remain idle and the $5 in lease costs will still be incurred. Under this condition, it will cost less to make the product than to buy it. That's because making the product costs only an *additional* $20 per unit ($25 – $5), compared with an *additional* $22 per unit if it is bought. The $5 per unit of lease cost is irrelevant to the decision because it will be incurred whether the product is made or bought. Analyzing relevant information is a key aspect of making decisions.

When making strategic decisions about which products to produce, managers must know how revenues and costs vary with changes in output levels. For this purpose, managers need to distinguish fixed costs from variable costs. Chapter 3 analyzes how operating income changes with changes in units sold and how managers use this information to make decisions such as how much to spend on advertising. Chapter 10 describes methods to estimate the fixed and variable components of costs. Chapter 11 applies the concept of relevance to decision making in many different situations and describes methods managers use to maximize income given the resource constraints that they face. Chapter 12 describes how management accountants help managers determine prices and manage costs across the value chain and over a product's life cycle.

Later chapters in the book discuss topics such as strategy evaluation, customer profitability, quality, just-in-time systems, investment decisions, transfer pricing, and performance evaluation. Each of these topics invariably has product costing, planning and control, and decision-making perspectives. A command of the first 12 chapters will help you master these topics. For example, Chapter 13 on strategy describes the balanced scorecard, a set of financial and nonfinancial measures used to implement strategy that builds on the planning and control functions. The section on strategic analysis of operating income builds on ideas of product costing and variance analysis. The section on downsizing and managing capacity builds on ideas of relevant revenues and relevant costs.

Problem for Self-Study

Foxwood Company is a metal- and woodcutting manufacturer, selling products to the home construction market. Consider the following data for 2009:

Sandpaper	$ 2,000
Materials-handling costs	70,000
Lubricants and coolants	5,000
Miscellaneous indirect manufacturing labor	40,000
Direct manufacturing labor	300,000

Direct materials inventory Jan. 1, 2009	40,000
Direct materials inventory Dec. 31, 2009	50,000
Finished goods inventory Jan. 1, 2009	100,000
Finished goods inventory Dec. 31, 2009	150,000
Work-in-process inventory Jan. 1, 2009	10,000
Work-in-process inventory Dec. 31, 2009	14,000
Plant-leasing costs	54,000
Depreciation—plant equipment	36,000
Property taxes on plant equipment	4,000
Fire insurance on plant equipment	$ 3,000
Direct materials purchased	460,000
Revenues	1,360,000
Marketing promotions	60,000
Marketing salaries	100,000
Distribution costs	70,000
Customer-service costs	100,000

Required

1. Prepare an income statement with a separate supporting schedule of cost of goods manufactured. For all manufacturing items, classify costs as direct costs or indirect costs and indicate by V or F whether each is basically a variable cost or a fixed cost (when the cost object is a product unit). If in doubt, decide on the basis of whether the total cost will change substantially over a wide range of units produced.
2. Suppose that both the direct material costs and the plant-leasing costs are for the production of 900,000 units. What is the direct material cost of each unit produced? What is the plant-leasing cost per unit? Assume that the plant-leasing cost is a fixed cost.
3. Suppose Foxwood Company manufactures 1,000,000 units next year. Repeat the computation in requirement 2 for direct materials and plant-leasing costs. Assume the implied cost-behavior patterns persist.
4. As a management consultant, explain concisely to the company president why the unit cost for direct materials did not change in requirements 2 and 3 but the unit cost for plant-leasing costs did change.

Solution

1.

Foxwood Company
Income Statement
For the Year Ended December 31, 2009

Revenues		$1,360,000
Cost of goods sold		
Beginning finished goods inventory January 1, 2009	$ 100,000	
Cost of goods manufactured (see schedule below)	960,000	
Cost of goods available for sale	1,060,000	
Deduct ending finished goods inventory December 31, 2009	150,000	910,000
Gross margin (or gross profit)		450,000
Operating costs		
Marketing promotions	60,000	
Marketing salaries	100,000	
Distribution costs	70,000	
Customer-service costs	100,000	330,000
Operating income		$ 120,000

Foxwood Company
Schedule of Cost of Goods Manufactured
For the Year Ended December 31, 2009

Direct materials		
Beginning inventory, January 1, 2009		$ 40,000
Purchases of direct materials		460,000
Cost of direct materials available for use		500,000
Ending inventory, December 31, 2009		50,000
Direct materials used		450,000 (V)
Direct manufacturing labor		300,000 (V)
Indirect manufacturing costs		
Sandpaper	$ 2,000 (V)	
Materials-handling costs	70,000 (V)	
Lubricants and coolants	5,000 (V)	
Miscellaneous indirect manufacturing labor	40,000 (V)	
Plant-leasing costs	54,000 (F)	
Depreciation—plant equipment	36,000 (F)	
Property taxes on plant equipment	4,000 (F)	
Fire insurance on plant equipment	3,000 (F)	214,000
Manufacturing costs incurred during 2009		964,000
Beginning work-in-process inventory, January 1, 2009		10,000
Total manufacturing costs to account for		974,000
Ending work-in-process inventory, December 31, 2009		14,000
Cost of goods manufactured (to Income Statement)		$960,000

2. Direct material unit cost = Direct materials used ÷ Units produced
   = $450,000 ÷ 900,000 units = $0.50 per unit
   Plant-leasing unit cost = Plant-leasing costs ÷ Units produced
   = $54,000 ÷ 900,000 units = $0.06 per unit
3. The direct material costs are variable, so they would increase in total from $450,000 to $500,000 (1,000,000 units × $0.50 per unit). However, their unit cost would be unaffected: $500,000 ÷ 1,000,000 units = $0.50 per unit.

   In contrast, the plant-leasing costs of $54,000 are fixed, so they would not increase in total. However, the plant-leasing cost per unit would decline from $0.060 to $0.054: $54,000 ÷ 1,000,000 units = $0.054 per unit.
4. The explanation would begin with the answer to requirement 3. As a consultant, you should stress that the unitizing (averaging) of costs that have different behavior patterns can be misleading. A common error is to assume that a total unit cost, which is often a sum of variable unit cost and fixed unit cost, is an indicator that total costs change in proportion to changes in production levels. The next chapter demonstrates the necessity for distinguishing between cost-behavior patterns. You must be wary, especially about average fixed cost per unit. Too often, unit fixed cost is erroneously regarded as being indistinguishable from unit variable cost.

Decision Points

The following question-and-answer format summarizes the chapter's learning objectives. Each decision presents a key question related to a learning objective. The guidelines are the answer to that question.

Decision	Guidelines
1. How do managers choose a cost object?	A cost object is anything for which a separate measurement of cost is needed. Examples include a product, a service, a project, a customer, a brand category, an activity, and a department.
2. How do managers decide whether a cost is a direct or an indirect cost?	A direct cost is any cost that is related to a particular cost object and can be traced to that cost object in an economically feasible way. Indirect costs are related to the particular cost object but cannot be traced in an economically feasible way. The same cost can be direct for one cost object and indirect for other cost objects. This book uses *cost tracing* to describe the assignment of direct costs to a cost object and *cost allocation* to describe the assignment of indirect costs to a cost object.
3. How do managers decide whether a cost is a variable or a fixed cost?	A variable cost changes *in total* in proportion to changes in the related level of total activity or volume. A fixed cost remains unchanged *in total* for a given time period despite wide changes in the related level of total activity or volume.
4. How should costs be estimated?	In general, focus on total costs, not unit costs. When making total cost estimates, think of variable costs as an amount per unit and fixed costs as a total amount. The unit cost of a cost object should be interpreted cautiously when it includes a fixed-cost component.
5. How do you distinguish among manufacturing-, merchandising-, and service-sector companies?	Manufacturing-sector companies purchase materials and components and convert them into finished goods. Merchandising-sector companies purchase and then sell tangible products without changing their basic form. Service-sector companies provide services (intangible products) to their customers.
6. How do manufacturing companies categorize inventories?	The three categories of inventories found in many manufacturing companies depict stages in the conversion process: direct materials, work in process, and finished goods.
7. Which costs are initially treated as assets for external reporting, and which costs are expensed as they are incurred?	Inventoriable costs are all costs of a product that are regarded as an asset in the accounting period when they are incurred and then become cost of goods sold in the accounting period when the product is sold. Period costs are expensed in the accounting period in which they are incurred and are all of the costs in an income statement other than cost of goods sold.
8. How do managers assign costs to cost objects?	Managers can assign different costs to the same cost object depending on the purpose. For example, for the external reporting purpose in a manufacturing company, the inventoriable cost of a product includes only manufacturing costs. In contrast, costs from all business functions of the value chain often are assigned to a product for pricing and product-mix decisions.
9. What are the features of cost accounting and cost management?	Three features of cost accounting and cost management are (1) calculating the cost of products, services, and other cost objects; (2) obtaining information for planning and control and performance evaluation; and (3) analyzing the relevant information for making decisions.

TERMS TO LEARN

This chapter contains more basic terms than any other in this book. Do not proceed before you check your understanding of the following terms. Both the chapter and the Glossary at the end of the book contain definitions.

actual cost (**p. 27**)
average cost (**p. 35**)
budgeted cost (**p. 27**)
conversion costs (**p. 42**)
cost (**p. 27**)
cost accumulation (**p. 27**)
cost allocation (**p. 28**)
cost assignment (**p. 28**)
cost driver (**p. 32**)
cost object (**p. 27**)
cost of goods manufactured (**p. 39**)
cost tracing (**p. 28**)
direct costs of a cost object (**p. 28**)
direct manufacturing labor costs (**p. 37**)
direct material costs (**p. 36**)
direct materials inventory (**p. 36**)
factory overhead costs (**p. 37**)
finished goods inventory (**p. 36**)
fixed cost (**p. 30**)
idle time (**p. 44**)
indirect costs of a cost object (**p. 28**)
indirect manufacturing costs (**p. 37**)
inventoriable costs (**p. 37**)
manufacturing overhead costs (**p. 37**)
manufacturing-sector companies (**p. 36**)
merchandising-sector companies (**p. 36**)
operating income (**p. 40**)
overtime premium (**p. 43**)
period costs (**p. 37**)
prime costs (**p. 42**)
product cost (**p. 45**)
relevant range (**p. 32**)
revenues (**p. 37**)
service-sector companies (**p. 36**)
unit cost (**p. 35**)
variable cost (**p. 30**)
work-in-process inventory (**p. 36**)
work in progress (**p. 36**)

ASSIGNMENT MATERIAL

Questions

2-1 Define cost object and give three examples.

2-2 Define direct costs and indirect costs.

2-3 Why do managers consider direct costs to be more accurate than indirect costs?

2-4 Name three factors that will affect the classification of a cost as direct or indirect.

2-5 Define variable cost and fixed cost. Give an example of each.

2-6 What is a cost driver? Give one example.

2-7 What is the relevant range? What role does the relevant-range concept play in explaining how costs behave?

2-8 Explain why unit costs must often be interpreted with caution.

2-9 Describe how manufacturing-, merchandising-, and service-sector companies differ from each other.

2-10 What are three different types of inventory that manufacturing companies hold?

2-11 Distinguish between inventoriable costs and period costs.

2-12 Do service-sector companies have inventoriable costs? Explain.

2-13 Define the following: direct material costs, direct manufacturing-labor costs, manufacturing overhead costs, prime costs, and conversion costs.

2-14 Describe the overtime-premium and idle-time categories of indirect labor.

2-15 Define product cost. Describe three different purposes for computing product costs.

Exercises

2-16 Computing and interpreting manufacturing unit costs. Minnesota Office Products (MOP) produces three different paper products at its Vaasa lumber plant: Supreme, Deluxe, and Regular. Each product has its own dedicated production line at the plant. It currently uses the following three-part classification for its manufacturing costs: direct materials, direct manufacturing labor, and manufacturing overhead costs. Total manufacturing overhead costs of the plant in July 2008 are $150 million ($20 million of which are fixed). This total amount is allocated to each product line on the basis of the direct manufacturing labor costs of each line. Summary data (in millions) for July 2008 are as follows:

	Supreme	Deluxe	Regular
Direct material costs	$84	$54	$62
Direct manufacturing labor costs	$14	$28	$ 8
Manufacturing overhead costs	$42	$84	$24
Units produced	80	120	100

Required

1. Compute the manufacturing cost per unit for each product produced in July 2008.

2. Suppose that in August 2008, production was 120 million units of Supreme, 160 million units of Deluxe, and 180 million units of Regular. Why might the July 2008 information on manufacturing cost per unit be misleading when predicting total manufacturing costs in August 2008?

2-17 Direct, indirect, fixed and variable costs. Ceramica Company manufactures three kinds of hand-painted ceramic figurines in a two-step process. The first step is automated; in the Baking Department a machine presses the clay figurines into molds and bakes them. In the Painting Department the baked figurines are carefully removed from their molds and hand painted. After they dry, the figurines are packed and shipped to customers. Ceramica's two departments, Baking and Painting, are in a single factory building. Packaging takes place in the Painting Department.

Required

1. Costs involved in the process are listed below. For each cost below, indicate whether it is a direct variable, direct fixed, indirect variable or indirect fixed cost, assuming "units of production of each kind of figurine" is the cost object.

   Costs:
   Clay
   Paint
   Packaging materials
   Depreciation on machinery and molds
   Rent on factory
   Insurance on factory
   Factory utilities
   Painters
   Painting Department manager
   Baking Department manager
   Materials handlers
   Custodian in factory
   Night guard in factory
   Machinist (running the baking machine)
   Machine maintenance personnel
   Maintenance supplies for factory
   Cleaning supplies for factory
2. If the cost object were "Baking Department" rather than output, which costs above would now be direct instead of indirect costs?

2-18 Classification of costs, service sector. Consumer Focus is a marketing research firm that organizes focus groups for consumer-product companies. Each focus group has eight individuals who are paid $50 per session to provide comments on new products. These focus groups meet in hotels and are led by a trained, independent, marketing specialist hired by Consumer Focus. Each specialist is paid a fixed retainer to conduct a minimum number of sessions and a per session fee of $2,000. A Consumer Focus staff member attends each session to ensure that all the logistical aspects run smoothly.

Required

Classify each of the following cost items as:

a. Direct or indirect (D or I) costs with respect to each individual focus group.
b. Variable or fixed (V or F) costs with respect to how the total costs of Consumer Focus change as the number of focus groups conducted changes. (If in doubt, select on the basis of whether the total costs will change substantially if there is a large change in the number of groups conducted.)

You will have two answers (D or I; V or F) for each of the following items:

Cost Item	D or I	V or F
A. Payment to individuals in each focus group to provide comments on new products		
B. Annual subscription of Consumer Focus to *Consumer Reports* magazine		
C. Phone calls made by Consumer Focus staff member to confirm individuals will attend a focus group session (Records of individual calls are not kept.)		
D. Retainer paid to focus group leader to conduct 20 focus groups per year on new medical products		
E. Meals provided to participants in each focus group		
F. Lease payment by Consumer Focus for corporate office		
G. Cost of tapes used to record comments made by individuals in a focus group session (These tapes are sent to the company whose products are being tested.)		
H. Gasoline costs of Consumer Focus staff for company-owned vehicles (staff members submit monthly bills with no mileage breakdowns.)		

2-19 Classification of costs, merchandising sector. Home Entertainment Center (HEC) operates a large store in San Francisco. The store has both a video section and a music (compact disks and tapes) section. HEC reports revenues for the video section separately from the music section.

Required

Classify each of the following cost items as:

a. Direct or indirect (D or I) costs with respect to the total number of videos sold.

b. Variable or fixed (V or F) costs with respect to how the total costs of the video section change as the total number of videos sold changes. (If in doubt, select on the basis of whether the total costs will change substantially if there is a large change in the total number of videos sold.)

You will have two answers (D or I; V or F) for each of the following items:

Cost Item	D or I	V or F
A. Annual retainer paid to a video distributor		
B. Electricity costs of HEC store (single bill covers entire store)		
C. Costs of videos purchased for sale to customers		
D. Subscription to *Video Trends* magazine		
E. Leasing of computer software used for financial budgeting at HEC store		
F. Cost of popcorn provided free to all customers of HEC		
G. Earthquake insurance policy for HEC store		
H. Freight-in costs of videos purchased by HEC		

2-20 Classification of costs, manufacturing sector. The Fremont, California, plant of New United Motor Manufacturing, Inc. (NUMMI), a joint venture of General Motors and Toyota, assembles two types of cars (Corollas and Geo Prisms). Separate assembly lines are used for each type of car.

Required

Classify each of the following cost items as:

a. Direct or indirect (D or I) costs with respect to the total number of cars of each type assembled (Corolla or Geo Prism).

b. Variable or fixed (V or F) costs with respect to how the total costs of the plant change as the total number of cars of each type assembled changes. (If in doubt, select on the basis of whether the total costs will change substantially if there is a large change in the total number of cars of each type assembled.)

You will have two answers (D or I; V or F) for each of the following items:

Cost Item	D or I	V or F
A. Cost of tires used on Geo Prisms		
B. Salary of public relations manager for NUMMI plant		
C. Annual awards dinner for Corolla suppliers		
D. Salary of engineer who monitors design changes on Geo Prism		
E. Freight costs of Corolla engines shipped from Toyota City, Japan, to Fremont, California		
F. Electricity costs for NUMMI plant (single bill covers entire plant)		
G. Wages paid to temporary assembly-line workers hired in periods of high production (paid on hourly basis)		
H. Annual fire-insurance policy cost for NUMMI plant		

2-21 Variable costs, fixed costs, total costs. Ana Compo is getting ready to open a small restaurant. She is on a tight budget and must choose between the following long-distance phone plans:

Plan A: Pay 8 cents per minute of long-distance calling.

Plan B: Pay a fixed monthly fee of $16 for up to 300 long-distance minutes, and 5 cents per minute thereafter (if she uses fewer than 300 minutes in any month, she still pays $16 for the month).

Plan C: Pay a fixed monthly fee of $20 for up to 480 long-distance minutes and 4 cents per minute thereafter (if she uses fewer than 480 minutes, she still pays $20 for the month).

Required

1. Draw a graph of the total monthly costs of the three plans for different levels of monthly long-distance calling.
2. Which plan should Compo choose if she expects to make 100 minutes of long-distance calls? 300 minutes? 500 minutes?

2-22 Variable costs and fixed costs. Consolidated Minerals (CM) owns the rights to extract minerals from beach sands on Fraser Island. CM has costs in three areas:

a. Payment to a mining subcontractor who charges $80 per ton of beach sand mined and returned to the beach (after being processed on the mainland to extract three minerals: ilmenite, rutile, and zircon).

b. Payment of a government mining and environmental tax of $50 per ton of beach sand mined.

c. Payment to a barge operator. This operator charges $150,000 per month to transport each batch of beach sand—up to 100 tons per batch per day—to the mainland and then return to Fraser Island (that is, 0 to 100 tons per day = $150,000 per month; 101 to 200 tons per day = $300,000 per month, and so on).

Each barge operates 25 days per month. The $150,000 monthly charge must be paid even if fewer than 100 tons are transported on any day and even if CM requires fewer than 25 days of barge transportation in that month.

CM is currently mining 180 tons of beach sands per day for 25 days per month.

Required

1. What is the variable cost per ton of beach sand mined? What is the fixed cost to CM per month?
2. Plot a graph of the variable costs and another graph of the fixed costs of CM. Your graphs should be similar to Exhibit 2-3, Panel A (p. 31), and Exhibit 2-4 (p. 33). Is the concept of relevant range applicable to your graphs? Explain.
3. What is the unit cost per ton of beach sand mined (a) if 180 tons are mined each day and (b) if 220 tons are mined each day? Explain the difference in the unit-cost figures.

2-23 Variable costs, fixed costs, relevant range. Yumball Candies manufactures jaw-breaker candies in a fully automated process. The machine that produces candies was purchased recently and can make 4,000 per month. The machine costs $6,000 and is depreciated using straight line depreciation over ten years assuming zero residual value. Rent for the factory space and warehouse, and other fixed manufacturing overhead costs total $1,000 per month.

Yumball currently makes and sells 3,000 jaw-breakers per month. Yumball buys just enough materials each month to make the jaw-breakers it needs to sell. Materials cost 10 cents per jawbreaker.

Next year Yumball expects demand to increase by 100%. At this volume of materials purchased, it will get a 10% discount on price. Rent and other fixed manufacturing overhead costs will remain the same.

Required

1. What is Yumball's current annual relevant range of output?
2. What is Yumball's current annual fixed manufacturing cost within the relevant range? What is the variable manufacturing cost?
3. What will Yumball's relevant range of output be next year? How if at all, will total fixed and variable manufacturing costs change next year?

2-24 Cost drivers and value chain. Prentice-Hall Publishing is developing a new book for international accounting. For the development and publication of this book, the company has undertaken the following activities in its value chain:

Identify the customer need (what do faculty and students want in a book?)
Find an author
Market the book to faculty
Author writes book
Process orders from bookstores
Editor edits book
Receive unsold copies of book from bookstores
Author rewrites book
Provide on-line assistance to faculty and students (study guides, test banks, etc.)
Print and bind the books
Deliver the book to bookstores

During the process of product development, production, marketing, distribution and customer service, Prentice-Hall has kept track of the following cost drivers:

Number of books ordered by bookstores
Number of unsold books sent back from bookstores
Number of deliveries made to bookstores
Number of pages of text
Amount paid to the author
Machine hours for running the printing and binding equipment
Hours spent with prospective customers to sell the book
Number of potential authors interviewed
Number of changes editor makes
Number of times author must do rewrites
Number of schools the marketing representative visits to discuss book ideas
Number of schools the marketing representative visits to market the book
Marketing representative salary
Number of schools that adopt the new book
Number of faculty that adopt the new book

Required

1. Identify each value chain activity listed at the beginning of the exercise with one of the following value-chain categories.
   a) Product development, b) Production, c) Marketing, d) Distribution, and e) Customer Service
2. Use the list of cost drivers above to find one or more reasonable cost drivers for each of the activities in Prentice-Hall's value chain.

2-25 Cost drivers and functions. The list of representative cost drivers in the right column of this table are randomized with respect to the list of functions in the left column. That is, they do not match.

Function	Representative Cost Driver
1. Accounting	A. Number of invoices sent
2. Human resources	B. Number of purchase orders
3. Data processing	C. Number of research scientists
4. Research and development	D. Hours of computer processing unit (CPU)
5. Purchasing	E. Number of employees
6. Distribution	F. Number of transactions processed
7. Billing	G. Number of deliveries made

Required

1. Match each function with its representative cost driver.
2. Give a second example of a cost driver for each function.

2-26 Total costs and unit costs. A student association has hired a band and a caterer for a graduation party. The band will charge a fixed fee of $1,000 for an evening of music, and the caterer will charge a fixed fee of $600 for the party setup and an additional $9 per person who attends. Snacks and soft drinks will be provided by the caterer for the duration of the party. Students attending the party will pay $5 each at the door.

Required

1. Draw a graph depicting the fixed cost, the variable cost, and the total cost to the student association for different attendance levels.
2. Suppose 100 people attend the party. What will be the total cost to the student association? What will be the cost per person?
3. Suppose 500 people attend the party. What will be the total cost to the student association and the cost per attendee?
4. Draw a graph depicting the cost per attendee for different attendance levels. As president of the student association, you want to request a grant to cover some of the party costs. Will you use the per attendee cost numbers to make your case? Why or why not?

2-27 Total and unit cost, decision making. Graham's Glassworks makes glass flanges for scientific use. Materials cost $1 per flange, and the glass blowers are paid a wage rate of $20 per hour. A glass blower blows 10 flanges per hour. Fixed manufacturing costs for flanges are $20,000 per period. Period (non-manufacturing) costs associated with flanges are $10,000 per period, and are fixed.

Required

1. Graph the fixed, variable and total manufacturing cost for flanges, using units (number of flanges) on the *x*-axis.
2. Assume Graham's Glassworks manufactures and sells 5,000 flanges this period. Their competitor, Fred's Flasks, sells flanges for $8.25 each. Can Graham sell below Fred's price and still make a profit on the flanges?
3. How would your answer to requirement 2 differ if Graham's Glassworks made and sold 10,000 flanges this period? Why? What does this indicate about the use of unit cost in decision making?

2-28 Inventoriable costs versus period costs. Each of the following cost items pertains to one of these companies: General Electric (a manufacturing-sector company), Safeway (a merchandising-sector company), and Google (a service-sector company):

a. Perrier mineral water purchased by Safeway for sale to its customers
b. Electricity used to provide lighting for assembly-line workers at a General Electric refrigerator-assembly plant
c. Depreciation on Google's computer equipment used to update directories of Web sites
d. Electricity used to provide lighting for Safeway's store aisles
e. Depreciation on General Electric's computer equipment used for quality testing of refrigerator components during the assembly process
f. Salaries of Safeway's marketing personnel planning local-newspaper advertising campaigns
g. Perrier mineral water purchased by Google for consumption by its software engineers
h. Salaries of Google's marketing personnel selling banner advertising

Required

1. Distinguish between manufacturing-sector, merchandising-sector, and service-sector companies.
2. Distinguish between inventoriable costs and period costs.
3. Classify each of the cost items (**a–h**) as an inventoriable cost or a period cost. Explain your answers.

Problems

2-29 Flow of Inventoriable Costs. Hofstra Plastics' selected data for August 2008 are presented here (in millions):

Direct materials inventory 8/1/2008	$ 90
Direct materials purchased	360
Direct materials used	375
Total manufacturing overhead costs	480
Variable manufacturing overhead costs	250
Total manufacturing costs incurred during August 2008	1,600
Work-in-process inventory 8/1/2008	200
Cost of goods manufactured	1,650
Finished goods inventory 8/1/2008	125
Cost of goods sold	1,700

Required Calculate the following costs:

1. Direct materials inventory 8/31/2008
2. Fixed manufacturing overhead costs for August
3. Direct manufacturing labor costs for August
4. Work-in-process inventory 8/31/2008
5. Cost of goods available for sale in August
6. Finished goods inventory 8/31/2008

2-30 Computing cost of goods purchased and cost of goods sold. The following data are for Marvin Department Store. The account balances (in thousands) are for 2008.

Marketing, distribution, and customer-service costs	$ 37,000
Merchandise inventory, January 1, 2008	27,000
Utilities	17,000
General and administrative costs	43,000
Merchandise inventory, December 31, 2008	34,000
Purchases	155,000
Miscellaneous costs	4,000
Transportation-in	7,000
Purchase returns and allowances	4,000
Purchase discounts	6,000

Required Compute **(1)** the cost of goods purchased and **(2)** the cost of goods sold.

2-31 Cost of goods manufactured. Consider the following account balances (in thousands) for the Canseco Company:

File Edit View Insert Format Tools Data Window Help

	A	B	C
1	**Canseco Company**	**Beginning of**	**End of**
2		**2009**	**2009**
3	Direct materials inventory	$22,000	$26,000
4	Work-in-process inventory	21,000	20,000
5	Finished goods inventory	18,000	23,000
6	Purchases of direct materials		75,000
7	Direct manufacturing labor		25,000
8	Indirect manufacturing labor		15,000
9	Plant insurance		9,000
10	Depreciation -- plant, building, and equipment		11,000
11	Repairs and maintenance -- plant		4,000
12	Marketing, distribution, and customer-service costs		93,000
13	General and administrative costs		29,000

If you want to use Excel to solve this problem, go to the Excel Lab at **www.prenhall.com/horngren/cost13e** and download the template for Exhibit 2-8.

Required

1. Prepare a schedule for the cost of goods manufactured for 2009.
2. Revenues for 2009 were $300 million. Prepare the income statement for 2009.

2-32 Income statement and schedule of cost of goods manufactured. The Howell Corporation has the following account balances (in millions):

For Specific Date		For Year 2009	
Direct materials inventory, Jan. 1, 2009	$15	Purchases of direct materials	$325
Work-in-process inventory, Jan. 1, 2009	10	Direct manufacturing labor	100
Finished goods inventory, Jan. 1, 2009	70	Depreciation—plant and equipment	80
Direct materials inventory, Dec. 31, 2009	20	Plant supervisory salaries	5
Work-in-process inventory, Dec. 31, 2009	5	Miscellaneous plant overhead	35
Finished goods inventory, Dec. 31, 2009	55	Revenues	950
		Marketing, distribution, and customer-service costs	240
		Plant supplies used	10
		Plant utilities	30
		Indirect manufacturing labor	60

Required

Prepare an income statement and a supporting schedule of cost of goods manufactured for the year ended December 31, 2009. (For additional questions regarding these facts, see the next problem.)

2-33 Interpretation of statements (continuation of 2-32).

Required

1. How would the answer to Problem 2-32 be modified if you were asked for a schedule of cost of goods manufactured and sold instead of a schedule of cost of goods manufactured? Be specific.
2. Would the sales manager's salary (included in marketing, distribution, and customer-service costs) be accounted for any differently if the Howell Corporation were a merchandising-sector company instead of a manufacturing-sector company? Using the flow of manufacturing costs outlined in Exhibit 2-9 (p. 42), describe how the wages of an assembler in the plant would be accounted for in this manufacturing company.
3. Plant supervisory salaries are usually regarded as manufacturing overhead costs. When might some of these costs be regarded as direct manufacturing costs? Give an example.
4. Suppose that both the direct materials used and the plant and equipment depreciation are related to the manufacture of 1 million units of product. What is the unit cost for the direct materials assigned to those units? What is the unit cost for plant and equipment depreciation? Assume that yearly plant and equipment depreciation is computed on a straight-line basis.
5. Assume that the implied cost-behavior patterns in requirement 4 persist. That is, direct material costs behave as a variable cost, and plant and equipment depreciation behaves as a fixed cost. Repeat the computations in requirement 4, assuming that the costs are being predicted for the manufacture of 1.2 million units of product. How would the total costs be affected?
6. As a management accountant, explain concisely to the president why the unit costs differed in requirements 4 and 5.

2-34 Income statement and schedule of cost of goods manufactured. The following items (in millions) pertain to Chan Corporation:

For Specific Date		For Year 2009	
Work-in-process inventory, Jan. 1, 2009	$10	Plant utilities	$ 5
Direct materials inventory, Dec. 31, 2009	5	Indirect manufacturing labor	20
Finished goods inventory, Dec. 31, 2009	12	Depreciation—plant and equipment	
Accounts payable, Dec. 31, 2009	20		9
		Revenues	350
Accounts receivable, Jan. 1, 2009	50	Miscellaneous manufacturing overhead	
Work-in-process inventory, Dec. 31, 2009	2		10
Finished goods inventory, Jan 1, 2009	40	Marketing, distribution, and customer-service costs	
			90
Accounts receivable, Dec. 31, 2009	30	Direct materials purchased	80
Accounts payable, Jan. 1, 2009	40	Direct manufacturing labor	40
Direct materials inventory, Jan. 1, 2009	30	Plant supplies used	6
		Property taxes on plant	1

Chan's manufacturing costing system uses a three-part classification of direct materials, direct manufacturing labor, and manufacturing overhead costs.

Required

Prepare an income statement and a supporting schedule of cost of goods manufactured. (For additional questions regarding these facts, see the next problem.)

2-35 Terminology, interpretation of statements (continuation of 2-34).

1. Calculate total prime costs and total conversion costs.
2. Compute total inventoriable costs and period costs.
3. Design costs and R&D costs are not considered product costs for financial statement purposes. When might some of these costs be regarded as product costs? Give an example.

4. Suppose that both the direct materials used and the depreciation on plant and equipment are related to the manufacture of 1 million units of product. Determine the unit cost for the direct materials assigned to those units and the unit cost for depreciation on plant and equipment. Assume that yearly depreciation is computed on a straight-line basis.
5. Assume that the implied cost-behavior patterns in requirement 4 persist. That is, direct material costs behave as a variable cost and depreciation on plant and equipment behaves as a fixed cost. Repeat the computations in requirement 4, assuming that the costs are being predicted for the manufacture of 1.5 million units of product. Determine the effect on total costs.
6. Assume that depreciation on the equipment (but not the plant) is computed based on the number of units produced because the equipment deteriorates with units produced. The depreciation rate on equipment is $4 per unit. Calculate the depreciation on equipment assuming (a) 1 million units of product are produced and (b) 1.5 million units of product are produced.

2-36 Labor cost, overtime and idle time. Len Lippart is a line worker in the assembly department of Maxart Manufacturing. He normally earns $12 per hour, but gets time and a half ($18 per hour) for overtime, over 40 hours per week. He earns double time if he works holidays even if he has not worked 40 hours that week.

Sometimes the assembly line equipment goes down and Len has to wait for the mechanics to repair the equipment or there is a scheduling mix-up. Len is paid for this time and Maxart considers this idle time.

In May, Len worked two 42 hour weeks, one 43 hour week, and the last week he worked 40 hours, but one of those days was Memorial Day (holiday). During regular hours, the assembly line equipment was down 4.2 hours in May, and Len had one hour of idle time because of a scheduling mixup.

Required

1. Calculate (a) direct manufacturing labor, (b) idle time, (c) overtime holiday premium, and (d) total earnings for Len in May.
2. Is idle time and overtime premium a direct or indirect cost of the jobs that Len worked on in May? Explain.

2-37 Fire Loss, computing inventory costs. A distraught employee, Fang W. Arson, put a torch to a manufacturing plant on a blustery February 26. The resulting blaze destroyed the plant and its contents. Fortunately, certain accounting records were kept in another building. They reveal the following for the period from January 1, 2009, to February 26, 2009:

Direct materials purchased	$160,000
Work-in-process inventory, 1/1/2009	$34,000
Direct materials inventory, 1/1/2009	$16,000
Finished goods inventory, 1/1/2009	$30,000
Manufacturing overhead costs	40% of conversion costs
Revenues	$500,000
Direct manufacturing labor	$180,000
Prime costs	$294,000
Gross margin percentage based on revenues	20%
Cost of goods available for sale	$450,000

The loss is fully covered by insurance. The insurance company wants to know the historical cost of the inventories as a basis for negotiating a settlement, although the settlement is actually to be based on replacement cost, not historical cost.

Required

Calculate the cost of:

1. Finished goods inventory, 2/26/2009
2. Work-in-process inventory, 2/26/2009
3. Direct materials inventory, 2/26/2009

2-38 Comprehensive problem on unit costs, product costs. Tampa Office Equipment manufactures and sells metal shelving. It began operations on January 1, 2009. Costs incurred for 2009 are as follows (V stands for variable; F stands for fixed):

Direct materials used	$140,000 V
Direct manufacturing labor costs	30,000 V
Plant energy costs	5,000 V
Indirect manufacturing labor costs	10,000 V
Indirect manufacturing labor costs	16,000 F
Other indirect manufacturing costs	8,000 V
Other indirect manufacturing costs	24,000 F
Marketing, distribution, and customer-service costs	122,850 V
Marketing, distribution, and customer-service costs	40,000 F
Administrative costs	50,000 F

Variable manufacturing costs are variable with respect to units produced. Variable marketing, distribution, and customer-service costs are variable with respect to units sold.

Inventory data are:

	Beginning: January 1, 2009	Ending: December 31, 2009
Direct materials	0 lb.	2,000 lbs.
Work in process	0 units	0 units
Finished goods	0 units	? units

Production in 2009 was 100,000 units. Two pounds of direct materials are used to make one unit of finished product.

Revenues in 2009 were $436,800. The selling price per unit and the purchase price per pound of direct materials were stable throughout the year. The company's ending inventory of finished goods is carried at the average unit manufacturing cost for 2009. Finished-goods inventory at December 31, 2009, was $20,970.

Required

1. Calculate direct materials inventory, total cost, December 31, 2009
2. Calculate finished-goods inventory, total units, December 31, 2009.
3. Calculate selling price in 2009.
4. Calculate operating income for 2009.

2-39 Labor cost classification; ethics. Zix Manufacturing has recently opened a plant in Costa Melon in order to take advantage of certain tax benefits. In order to qualify for these tax benefits, the company's direct manufacturing labor costs must be at least 20% of total manufacturing costs for the period.

Zix Manufacturing normally classifies direct manufacturing labor wages as direct manufacturing labor, but classifies fringe benefits, overtime premiums, idle time, and vacation time and sick leave as indirect manufacturing labor.

During the first period of operations in Costa Melon, Zix incurs a total of $2,500,000 in manufacturing costs. Of that, $410,000 is direct manufacturing labor wages, $45,000 is overtime premium, $86,000 is fringe benefits, $20,500 is vacation time and sick leave, and $10,900 is idle time.

Required

1. Will Zix's direct manufacturing labor costs qualify them for the tax benefit?
2. Bob Zixson, the manager of the new Costa Melon plant, is concerned that he will not get a bonus this year because the plant will not get the tax benefit. What might he ask the plant controller to do to make sure Zix gets the tax benefit? How might these accounting changes be rationalized?
3. Should the plant controller do what the manager has asked in requirement 2? Why or why not?

Collaborative Learning Problem

2-40 Finding unknown amounts. An auditor for the Internal Revenue Service is trying to reconstruct some partially destroyed records of two taxpayers. For each of the cases in the accompanying list, find the unknowns designated by the letters A through D.

	Case 1	Case 2
	(in thousands)	
Accounts receivable, 12/31	$ 6,000	$ 2,100
Cost of goods sold	A	20,000
Accounts payable, 1/1	3,000	1,700
Accounts payable, 12/31	1,800	1,500
Finished goods inventory, 12/31	B	5,300
Gross margin	11,300	C
Work-in-process inventory, 1/1	0	800
Work-in-process inventory, 12/31	0	3,000
Finished goods inventory, 1/1	4,000	4,000
Direct materials used	8,000	12,000
Direct manufacturing labor	3,000	5,000
Manufacturing overhead costs	7,000	D
Purchases of direct materials	9,000	7,000
Revenues	32,000	31,800
Accounts receivable, 1/1	2,000	1,400

3 Cost-Volume-Profit Analysis

Learning Objectives

1. Explain the features of cost-volume-profit (CVP) analysis
2. Determine the breakeven point and output level needed to achieve a target operating income
3. Understand how income taxes affect CVP analysis
4. Explain CVP analysis in decision making and how sensitivity analysis helps managers cope with uncertainty
5. Use CVP analysis to plan variable and fixed costs
6. Apply CVP analysis to a company producing multiple products
7. Adapt CVP analysis to situations in which a product has more than one cost driver

All managers want to know how profits will change as the units sold of a product or service change. Home Depot managers, for example, might wonder how many units of a new product must be sold to break even or make a certain amount of profit. Procter & Gamble managers might ask: If we expand our business into a particular foreign market, how will that affect costs, selling price, and profits? These questions have a common "what-if" theme. Examining the results of these what-if possibilities and alternatives helps managers make better decisions.

Managers must also decide whether to produce more or less of a particular product, change the mix of products they sell, or change their sales prices. The following article explains the dilemma the high-end jeweler Tiffany & Co. recently faced—whether it should increase the prices on one of its best-selling jewelry lines recognizing that it will likely lower the quantity of jewelry sold. Does this sound like a wise strategy to you?

Tiffany Tinkers with Its Sales Mix—and Takes a Cost-Volume-Profit Gamble[1]

In the late 1990s, Tiffany's managers decided to create cheaper silver jewelry to address the then-emerging trend toward "affordable" luxury. Middle-class consumers were becoming increasingly brand-conscious. And silver had emerged as the "it" metal.

Tiffany's 1997 introduction of the silver "Return to Tiffany" collection, which offered jewelry inscribed with the Tiffany name for just over $100, was a huge hit. Teens jammed Tiffany's hushed stores, clamoring for the $110 must-have fashion accessory. Even Elle Woods, the ditzy law student in the 2001 hit movie ***Legally Blonde,*** accessorized her string bikini with a Tiffany charm bracelet and matching necklace. From 1997 to 2002, the company's profits more than doubled.

But Tiffany's managers were worried. On the one hand, they knew the cheaper, silver jewelry had become a fad that could eventually erode Tiffany's brand name and the sales of its higher-priced products, which were relatively more expensive to produce.

On the other hand, any effort to curb lower-end silver could dramatically slow sales and affect profitability. Nonetheless, in a dramatic gamble, Tiffany decided to slow down its "golden goose" by hiking prices on the fast-growing, highly profitable line while simultaneously introducing pricier jewelry collections.

---

[1] *Source:* Ellen Byron, "Fashion Victim: To Refurbish Its Image, Tiffany's Risks Profits," *The Wall Street Journal*, January 10, 2007, p. A1.

By 2005 the craze died down, sales of silver jewelry and other pieces under $500 declined, but with it the company's earnings and stock price. But by 2007, Tiffany could boast that its store sales were up in 2006, and that its biggest sales growth had come from jewelry items costing over $20,000 apiece. The jury is still out on whether the daring move has worked. The company's profit margins and stock price have yet to reach the highs of years past.

As you read this chapter, you will begin to understand Tiffany's challenges and the actions it would have had to take to sustain profitability as sales of lower-end jewelry declined. A key task in the face of declining sales is to reduce fixed costs. Many capital intensive companies, such as US Airways and United Airlines in the airlines industry and Global Crossing and WorldCom in the telecommunications industry, had to file for bankruptcy because, when sales declined at these companies during 2001 and 2002, fixed costs remained high. The methods of CVP analysis described in this chapter help management accountants alert managers to such risks.

Essentials of CVP Analysis

Learning Objective 1

Explain the features of cost-volume-profit (CVP) analysis

. . . how operating income changes with changes in output level, selling prices, variable costs, or fixed costs

Cost-volume-profit (CVP) analysis examines the behavior of total revenues, total costs, and operating income as changes occur in the units sold, the selling price, the variable cost per unit, or the fixed costs of a product. Let's consider an example to illustrate CVP analysis.

> Example: Mary Frost is considering selling Do-All Software, a home-office software package, at a computer convention in Chicago. Mary knows she can purchase this software from a computer software wholesaler at $120 per package, with the privilege of returning all unsold packages and receiving a full $120 refund per package. She also knows that she would pay $2,000 to Computer Conventions, Inc., for the booth rental at the convention. She will incur no other costs. She must decide whether she should rent a booth.

Mary, like most managers who face such a situation, works through a series of steps.

1. **Identify the problem and uncertainties.** The decision to rent the booth hinges critically on how Mary resolves two important uncertainties—the price she can charge and the number of packages she can sell at that price. Every decision deals with selecting a

course of action. The outcome of the chosen action is uncertain and will only be known in the future.

2. **Obtain information.** When faced with uncertainty, managers obtain information that might help them understand the uncertainties better. For example, Mary gathers information about the type of individuals likely to attend the convention and other software that might be sold at the convention. She also gathers data on her past experiences selling Do-All Software at conventions very much like the Chicago convention.
3. **Make predictions about the future.** Using all the information available to them, managers make predictions. Mary predicts that she can charge a price of $200 for Do-All Software. At that price she is reasonably confident that she will be able to sell 30 packages and possibly as many as 60. In making these predictions, Mary like most managers, must exercise considerable judgment. Her predictions rest on the belief that her experience at the Chicago convention will be similar to her experience at the San Francisco convention four months earlier. Yet, Mary ponders several questions. Is this comparison appropriate? Have conditions and circumstances changed over the last four months? Are there any biases creeping into her thinking? She is keen on selling at the Chicago convention because sales in the last couple of months have been lower than expected. Is this experience making her predictions overly optimistic? Has she ignored some of the competitive risks? Will the other software vendors at the convention reduce their prices?

   Mary reviews her thinking. She retests her assumptions. She also explores these questions with John Mills, a close friend, who has extensive experience selling software like Do-All. In the end, she feels quite confident that her predictions are reasonable and carefully thought through.
4. **Make decisions by choosing among alternatives.** Mary uses CVP analysis, described just below, and decides to rent the booth at the Chicago convention.
5. **Implement the decision, evaluate performance, and learn.** Thoughtful managers never stop learning. They compare their actual performance to predicted performance to understand why things worked out the way they did and what they might learn. At the end of the Chicago convention, for example, Mary would want to evaluate whether her predictions about price and the number of packages she could sell were correct. Such feedback would be very helpful to Mary as she makes decisions about renting booths at subsequent conventions.

How does Mary use CVP analysis in Step 4 to make her decision? Mary begins by identifying what costs are fixed and what costs are variable.

The booth-rental cost of $2,000 is a fixed cost because it will not change no matter how many packages Mary sells. The cost of the package itself is a variable cost because it increases in proportion to the number of packages sold. Mary will incur a cost of $120 for each package that she sells. To get an idea of how operating income will change as a result of selling different quantities of packages, Mary calculates operating income if sales are 5 packages and if sales are 40 packages.

	5 packages sold	40 packages sold
Revenues	$1,000 ($200 per package × 5 packages)	$8,000 ($200 per package × 40 packages)
Variable purchase costs	600 ($120 per package × 5 packages)	4,800 ($120 per package × 40 packages)
Fixed costs	2,000	2,000
Operating income	$(1,600)	$1,200

The only numbers that change from selling different quantities of packages are *total revenues* and *total variable costs*. The difference between total revenues and total variable costs is called **contribution margin**. Contribution margin indicates why operating income changes as the number of units sold changes. The contribution margin when Mary sells 5 packages is $400 ($1,000 in total revenues minus $600 in total variable costs); the contribution margin when Mary sells 40 packages is $3,200 ($8,000 in total revenues minus $4,800 in total variable costs). When calculating the contribution margin, be sure to subtract all variable costs. For example, if Mary had variable selling costs because she paid a commission to salespeople for each package they sold at the convention, variable costs would include the cost of each package plus the sales commission.

Contribution margin per unit is a useful tool for calculating contribution margin and operating income. **Contribution margin per unit** is the difference between selling price and variable cost per unit. In the Do-All Software example, contribution margin per package, or per unit, is $200 − $120 = $80. Contribution margin per unit recognizes the tight coupling of selling price and variable cost per unit. Unlike fixed costs, Mary will only incur the variable cost per unit of $120 when she sells a unit of Do-All Software for $200. Consequently, a second way to calculate contribution margin is:

$$\text{Contribution margin} = \text{Contribution margin per unit} \times \text{Number of units sold}$$

For example, when 40 packages are sold, contribution margin = $80 per unit × 40 units = $3,200.

Even before she gets to the convention, Mary incurs $2,000 in fixed costs. For each package that Mary sells at the convention, she recovers $80 of the $2,000. Mary hopes to sell enough packages to fully recover the $2,000 she spent for renting the booth and to then make a profit. Exhibit 3-1 presents contribution margins for different quantities of packages sold. The income statement in Exhibit 3-1 is called a **contribution income statement** because it groups costs into variable costs and fixed costs to highlight contribution margin. See how each additional package sold from 0 to 1 to 5 increases contribution margin by $80 per package, recovering more of the fixed costs and reducing the operating loss. If Mary sells 25 packages, contribution margin equals $2,000 ($80 per package × 25 packages), exactly recovering fixed costs and resulting in $0 operating income. If Mary sells 40 packages, contribution margin increases by another $1,200 ($3,200 − $2,000), all of which becomes operating income. As you look across Exhibit 3-1 from left to right, you see that the increase in contribution margin exactly equals the increase in operating income (or the decrease in operating loss).

Instead of expressing contribution margin as a dollar amount per unit, we can express it as a percentage. **Contribution margin percentage** (also called **contribution margin ratio**) equals contribution margin per unit divided by selling price.

In our example,

$$\text{Contribution margin percentage} = \frac{\$80}{\$200} = 0.40, \text{ or } 40\%$$

Contribution margin percentage is the contribution margin per dollar of revenue. In this example, contribution margin percentage is 40% of each dollar of revenue (equal to 40 cents).

Mary can calculate total contribution margin for different output levels by multiplying the contribution margin percentage by the total revenues shown in Exhibit 3-1. For example, if Mary sells 40 packages, revenues will be $8,000 and contribution margin will equal 40% of $8,000, or 0.40 × $8,000 = $3,200. Mary earns operating income of $1,200 ($3,200 − $2,000) by selling 40 packages for $8,000.

How was the Excel spreadsheet in Exhibit 3-1 constructed? Underlying the Exhibit are some equations that express the CVP relationships. To make good decisions using CVP analysis, we must understand these relationships and the structure of the

File Edit View Insert Format Tools Data Window Help

	A	B	C	D	E	F	G	H
1				Number of Packages Sold				
2				0	1	5	25	40
3	Revenues	$ 200	per package	$ 0	$ 200	$ 1,000	$5,000	$8,000
4	Variable costs	$ 120	per package	0	120	600	3,000	4,800
5	Contribution margin	$ 80	per package	0	80	400	2,000	3,200
6	Fixed costs	$2,000		2,000	2,000	2,000	2,000	2,000
7	Operating income			$(2,000)	$(1,920)	$(1,600)	$ 0	$1,200

Exhibit 3-1

Contribution Income Statement for Different Quantities of Do-All Software Packages Sold

contribution income statement in Exhibit 3-1. There are three related ways (we will call them methods) to think more deeply about and model CVP relationships: the equation method, the contribution margin method, and the graph method. The equation method and the contribution margin method are most useful when managers want to determine operating income at few specific levels of sales (for example 5, 15, 25, and 40 units sold). The graph method helps managers visualize the relationship between units sold and operating income over a wide range of quantities of units sold. As we shall see later in the chapter, different methods are useful for different decisions.

Equation Method

Each column in Exhibit 3-1 is expressed as an equation.

$$\text{Revenues} - \text{Variable costs} - \text{Fixed costs} = \text{Operating income}$$

How are revenues in each column calculated?

$$\text{Revenues} = \text{Selling price } (SP) \times \text{Quantity of units sold } (Q)$$

How are variable costs in each column calculated?

$$\text{Variable costs} = \text{Variable cost per unit } (VCU) \times \text{Quantity of units sold } (Q)$$

So,

$$\left[\begin{pmatrix}\text{Selling} \\ \text{price}\end{pmatrix} \times \begin{pmatrix}\text{Quantity of} \\ \text{units sold}\end{pmatrix} - \begin{pmatrix}\text{Variable cost} \\ \text{per unit}\end{pmatrix} \times \begin{pmatrix}\text{Quantity of} \\ \text{units sold}\end{pmatrix}\right] - \begin{matrix}\text{Fixed} \\ \text{costs}\end{matrix} = \begin{matrix}\text{Operating} \\ \text{income}\end{matrix} \qquad \textbf{(Equation 1)}$$

Equation 1 becomes the basis for calculating operating income for different quantities of units sold. For example, if you go to cell F7 in Exhibit 3-1, the calculation of operating income when Mary sells 5 packages is

$$(\$200 \times 5) - (\$120 \times 5) - \$2{,}000 = \$1{,}000 - \$600 - \$2{,}000 = -\$1{,}600$$

Contribution Margin Method

Rearranging equation 1,

$$\left[\begin{pmatrix}\text{Selling} \\ \text{price}\end{pmatrix} - \begin{pmatrix}\text{Variable cost} \\ \text{per unit}\end{pmatrix} \times \begin{pmatrix}\text{Quantity of} \\ \text{units sold}\end{pmatrix}\right] - \begin{matrix}\text{Fixed} \\ \text{costs}\end{matrix} = \begin{matrix}\text{Operating} \\ \text{income}\end{matrix}$$

$$\begin{pmatrix}\text{Contribution margin} \\ \text{per unit}\end{pmatrix} \times \begin{pmatrix}\text{Quantity of} \\ \text{units sold}\end{pmatrix} - \begin{matrix}\text{Fixed} \\ \text{costs}\end{matrix} = \begin{matrix}\text{Operating} \\ \text{income}\end{matrix} \qquad \textbf{(Equation 2)}$$

In our Do-All Software example, contribution margin per unit is $80 ($200 − $120), so when Mary sells 5 packages,

$$\text{Operating income} = (\$80 \times 5) - \$2{,}000 = -\$1{,}600$$

Equation 2 expresses the basic idea we described earlier—each unit sold helps Mary recover $80 (in contribution margin) of the $2,000 in fixed costs.

Graph Method

In the graph method, we represent total costs and total revenues graphically. Each is shown as a line on a graph. Exhibit 3-2 illustrates the graph method for Do-All Software. Because we have assumed that total costs and total revenues behave in a linear fashion, we need only two points to plot the line representing each of them.

1. **Total costs line.** The total costs line is the sum of fixed costs and variable costs. Fixed costs are $2,000 at all quantities of units sold within the relevant range. To plot the total costs line, use as one point the $2,000 fixed costs at zero units sold (point A), because variable costs are $0 when no units are sold. Select a second point by choosing any other convenient output level (say, 40 units sold) and determine the corresponding total costs. Total variable costs at this output level are $4,800 (40 units × $120 per unit).

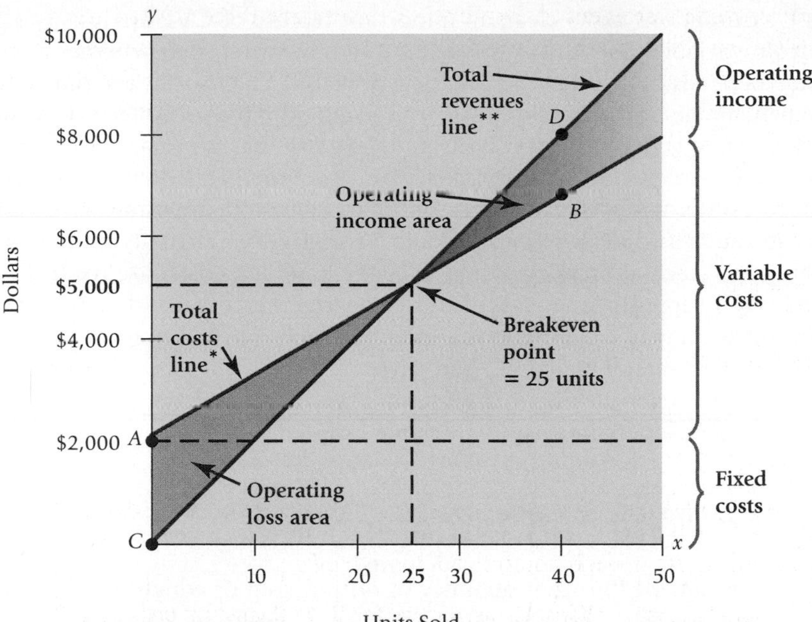

*Slope of the total costs line is the variable cost per unit = $120
**Slope of the total revenues line is the selling price = $200

Exhibit 3-2

Cost-Volume Graph for Do-All Software

Remember, fixed costs are $2,000 at all quantities of units sold within the relevant range, so total costs at 40 units sold equal $6,800 ($2,000 + $4,800), which is point B in Exhibit 3-2. The total costs line is the straight line from point A through point B.

2. **Total revenues line.** One convenient starting point is $0 revenues at 0 units sold, which is point C in Exhibit 3-2. Select a second point by choosing any other convenient output level and determining the corresponding total revenues. At 40 units sold, total revenues are $8,000 ($200 per unit × 40 units), which is point D in Exhibit 3-2. The total revenues line is the straight line from point C through point D.

   Profit or loss at any sales level can be determined by the vertical distance between the two lines at that level in Exhibit 3-2. For quantities fewer than 25 units sold, total costs exceed total revenues, and the purple area indicates operating losses. For quantities greater than 25 units sold, total revenues exceed total costs, and the blue-green area indicates operating incomes. At 25 units sold, total revenues equal total costs. Mary will break even by selling 25 packages.

Cost-Volume-Profit Assumptions

Now that you have seen how CVP analysis works, think about the following assumptions we made during the analysis:

1. Changes in the levels of revenues and costs arise only because of changes in the number of product (or service) units sold. The number of units sold is the only revenue driver and the only cost driver. Just as a cost driver is any factor that affects costs, a **revenue driver** is a variable, such as volume, that causally affects revenues.
2. Total costs can be separated into two components: a fixed component that does not vary with units sold and a variable component that changes with respect to units sold. Furthermore, you know from Chapter 2 (Exhibit 2-5, p. 34) that variable costs include both direct variable costs and indirect variable costs of a product. Similarly, fixed costs include both direct fixed costs and indirect fixed costs of a product.
3. When represented graphically, the behaviors of total revenues and total costs are linear (meaning they can be represented as a straight line) in relation to units sold within a relevant range (and time period).
4. Selling price, variable cost per unit, and total fixed costs (within a relevant range and time period) are known and constant.

As the CVP assumptions make clear, an important feature of CVP analysis is distinguishing fixed from variable costs. Always keep in mind, however, that whether a cost is variable or fixed depends on the time period for a decision. The shorter the time horizon, the higher the percentage of total costs considered fixed. Suppose an American Airlines plane will depart from its gate in the next hour and currently has 20 seats unsold. A potential passenger arrives with a transferable ticket from a competing airline. What are the variable costs to American of placing one more passenger in an otherwise empty seat? Variable costs (such as one more meal) would be negligible. Virtually all the costs in this decision situation (such as crew costs and baggage-handling costs) are fixed.

Alternatively, suppose American must decide whether to include another city in its routes. This decision may have a one-year planning horizon. Many more costs, including crew costs, baggage-handling costs, and airport fees, would be considered variable. Always consider the relevant range, the length of the time horizon, and the specific decision situation when classifying costs as variable or fixed.

Breakeven Point and Target Income

Learning Objective 2

Determine the breakeven point and output level needed to achieve a target operating income

. . . compare contribution margin and fixed costs

The **breakeven point (BEP)** is that quantity of output sold at which total revenues equal total costs—that is, the quantity of output sold that results in \$0 of operating income. Managers are interested in the breakeven point because they want to avoid operating losses. The breakeven point tells them how much output they must sell to avoid a loss. We have already seen how to use the graph method to calculate the breakeven point. Recall from Exhibit 3-1 that operating income was \$0 when Mary sold 25 units, the breakeven point. But by understanding the equations underlying the calculations in Exhibit 3-1, we can calculate the breakeven point directly for Do-All Software rather than trying out different quantities and checking when operating income equals \$0.

Recall the equation method (equation 1):

$$\left(\begin{array}{c}\text{Selling}\\\text{price}\end{array} \times \begin{array}{c}\text{Quantity of}\\\text{units sold}\end{array}\right) - \left(\begin{array}{c}\text{Variable cost}\\\text{per unit}\end{array} \times \begin{array}{c}\text{Quantity of}\\\text{units sold}\end{array}\right) - \begin{array}{c}\text{Fixed}\\\text{costs}\end{array} = \begin{array}{c}\text{Operating}\\\text{income}\end{array}$$

Setting operating income equal to \$0 and denoting quantity of output units that must be sold by Q,

$$\begin{aligned}(\$200 \times Q) - (\$120 \times Q) - \$2{,}000 &= \$0\\ \$80 \times Q &= \$2{,}000\\ Q &= \$2{,}000 \div \$80 \text{ per unit} = 25 \text{ units}\end{aligned}$$

If Mary sells fewer than 25 units, she will have a loss; if she sells 25 units, she will break even; and if she sells more than 25 units, she will make a profit. While this breakeven point is expressed in units, it can also be expressed in terms of revenues: 25 units × \$200 selling price = \$5,000.

Recall the contribution margin method (equation 2):

$$\left(\begin{array}{c}\text{Contribution}\\\text{margin per unit}\end{array} \times \begin{array}{c}\text{Quantity of}\\\text{units sold}\end{array}\right) - \text{Fixed costs} = \text{Operating income}$$

At the breakeven point, operating income is by definition \$0 and so:

$$\text{Contribution margin per unit} \times \text{Breakeven number of units} = \text{Fixed cost} \qquad \textbf{(Equation 3)}$$

Rearranging equation 3 and entering the data,

$$\begin{array}{c}\text{Breakeven}\\\text{number of units}\end{array} = \frac{\text{Fixed costs}}{\text{Contribution margin per unit}} = \frac{\$2{,}000}{\$80 \text{ per unit}} = 25 \text{ units}$$

To calculate the breakeven point in terms of revenues, recall that in the Do-All Software example,

$$\begin{array}{c}\text{Contribution margin}\\\text{percentage}\end{array} = \frac{\text{Contribution margin per unit}}{\text{Selling price}} = \frac{\$80}{\$200} = 0.40, \text{ or } 40\%$$

That is, 40% of each dollar of revenue, or 40 cents, is contribution margin. To break even, contribution margin must equal fixed costs of \$2,000. To earn \$2,000 of contribution margin, revenues must equal \$2,000 ÷ 0.40 = \$5,000.

$$\frac{\text{Breakeven}}{\text{revenues}} = \frac{\text{Fixed costs}}{\text{Contribution margin \%}} = \frac{\$2{,}000}{0.40} = \$5{,}000$$

The breakeven point tells managers how much they must sell to avoid a loss. But managers are equally interested in how they will achieve the operating income targets underlying their strategies and plans. For example, selling 25 units at a price of \$200 assures Mary that she will not lose money if she rents the booth. This news is comforting, but Mary is equally interested in learning how much she needs to sell to achieve a targeted amount of operating income.

Target Operating Income

We illustrate target operating income calculations by asking: How many units must Mary sell to earn an operating income of \$1,200? Exhibit 3-1 shows that operating income is \$1,200 when 40 packages are sold. Equation 1 helps us to find *Q* directly without plugging in different quantities into Exhibit 3-1 and checking when operating income equals \$1,200.

$$(\$200 \times Q) - (\$120 \times Q) - \$2{,}000 = \$1{,}200$$
$$\$80 \times Q = \$2{,}000 + \$1{,}200 = \$3{,}200$$
$$Q = \$3{,}200 \div \$80 \text{ per unit} = 40 \text{ units}$$

Alternatively, we could modify the contribution margin method and equation 2,

$$\frac{\text{Quantity of units}}{\text{required to be sold}} = \frac{\text{Fixed costs} + \text{Target operating income}}{\text{Contribution margin per unit}} \qquad \text{(Equation 4)}$$

$$\frac{\text{Quantity of units}}{\text{required to be sold}} = \frac{\$2{,}000 + \$1{,}200}{\$80 \text{ per unit}} = 40 \text{ units}$$

Proof:		
	Revenues, \$200 per unit × 40 units	\$8,000
	Variable costs, \$120 per unit × 40 units	4,800
	Contribution margin, \$80 per unit × 40 units	3,200
	Fixed costs	2,000
	Operating income	\$1,200

The revenues needed to earn an operating income of \$1,200 can also be calculated directly by recognizing (1) that \$3,200 of contribution margin must be earned (fixed costs of \$2,000 plus operating income of \$1,200) and (2) that each dollar of revenue earns 40 cents of contribution margin. To earn \$3,200 of contribution margin, revenues must equal \$3,200 ÷ 0.40 = \$8,000.

$$\text{Revenues needed to earn } \$1{,}200 = \frac{\$2{,}000 + \$1{,}200}{0.40} = \frac{\$3{,}200}{0.40} = \$8{,}000$$

The graph in Exhibit 3-2 is very difficult to use if the question is: How many units must Mary sell to earn an operating income of \$1,200. Why? Because it is not easy to determine from the graph the precise point at which the difference between the total revenues line and the total costs line equals \$1,200. However, recasting Exhibit 3-2 in the form of a profit-volume (PV) graph makes it easier to answer this question.

A **PV graph** shows how changes in the quantity of units sold affect operating income. Exhibit 3-3 is the PV graph for Do-All Software (fixed costs, \$2,000; selling price, \$200; and variable cost per unit, \$120). The PV line can be drawn using two points. One convenient point (M) is the operating loss at 0 units sold, which is equal to the fixed costs of \$2,000, shown at –\$2,000 on the vertical axis. A second convenient point (N) is the breakeven point, which is 25 units in our example (see p. 66). The PV line is the straight line from point M through point N. To find the number of units Mary must sell to earn an operating income of \$1,200, draw a horizontal line parallel to the *x*-axis corresponding to

$1,200 on the vertical axis (that's the y-axis). At the point where this line intersects the PV line, draw a vertical line down to the horizontal axis (that's the x-axis). The vertical line intersects the x-axis at 40 units, indicating that by selling 40 units Mary will earn an operating income of $1,200.

Target Net Income and Income Taxes

Learning Objective 3

Understand how income taxes affect CVP analysis

. . . focus on net income

Net income is operating income plus nonoperating revenues (such as interest revenue) minus nonoperating costs (such as interest cost) minus income taxes. For simplicity, throughout this chapter we assume nonoperating revenues and nonoperating costs are zero. Thus, net income is computed as operating income minus income taxes.

Thus far, we have ignored the effect of income taxes in our CVP analysis. In many companies, the income targets for managers in their strategic plans are expressed in terms of net income. That's because top management wants subordinate managers to take into account the effects their decisions have on operating income after income taxes are paid. Some decisions may not result in large operating incomes. But they may have favorable tax consequences and so may be attractive on a net income basis—the measure that drives shareholders' dividends and returns.

To make net income evaluations, CVP calculations for target income must be stated in terms of target net income instead of target operating income. For example, Mary may be interested in knowing the quantity of units she must sell to earn a net income of $960, assuming an income tax rate of 40%. Using the equation method,

$$\text{Revenues} - \text{Variable costs} - \text{Fixed costs} = \text{Target operating income}$$

And,

$$\text{Target net income} = \left(\begin{array}{c}\text{Target}\\ \text{operating income}\end{array}\right) - \left(\begin{array}{c}\text{Target}\\ \text{operating income}\end{array} \times \text{Tax rate}\right)$$

$$\text{Target net income} = (\text{Target operating income}) \times (1 - \text{Tax rate})$$

$$\text{Target operating income} = \frac{\text{Target net income}}{1 - \text{Tax rate}}$$

Substituting for target operating income:

$$\text{Revenues} - \text{Variable costs} - \text{Fixed costs} = \frac{\text{Target net income}}{1 - \text{Tax rate}}$$

Exhibit 3-3

Profit-Volume Graph for Do-All Software

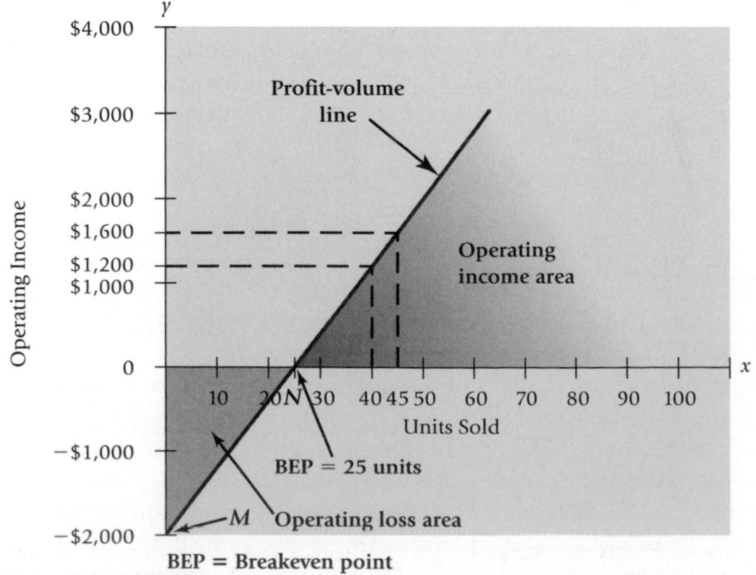

Substituting numbers from our Do-All Software example:

$$(\$200 \times Q) - (\$120 \times Q) - \$2{,}000 = \frac{\$960}{1 - 0.40}$$

$$(\$200 \times Q) - (\$120 \times Q) - \$2{,}000 = \$1{,}600$$

$$\$80 \times Q = \$3{,}600$$

$$Q = \$3{,}600 \div \$80 \text{ per unit} = 45 \text{ units}$$

Alternatively, we can use the contribution margin method and equation 4 and substitute:

$$\text{Target operating income} = \frac{\text{Target net income}}{1 - \text{Tax rate}}$$

$$\begin{array}{c}\text{Quantity of units}\\ \text{required to be sold}\end{array} = \frac{\text{Fixed costs} + \dfrac{\text{Target net income}}{1 - \text{Tax rate}}}{\text{Contribution margin per unit}}$$

$$\begin{array}{c}\text{Quantity of units}\\ \text{required to be sold}\end{array} = \frac{\$2{,}000 + \dfrac{\$960}{1 - 0.40}}{\$80} = \frac{\$2{,}000 + \$1{,}600}{\$80 \text{ per unit}} = 45 \text{ units}$$

Proof:

Revenues, $200 per unit × 45 units	$9,000
Variable costs, $120 per unit × 45 units	5,400
Contribution margin	3,600
Fixed costs	2,000
Operating income	1,600
Income taxes, $1,600 × 0.40	640
Net income	$ 960

Mary can also use the PV graph in Exhibit 3-3. For a target net income of $960,

$$\text{Target operating income} = \frac{\text{Target net income}}{1 - \text{Tax rate}} = \frac{\$960}{1 - 0.40} = \$1{,}600$$

From Exhibit 3-3, to earn target operating income of $1,600, Mary needs to sell 45 units.

Focusing the analysis on target net income instead of target operating income will not change the breakeven point. That's because, by definition, operating income at the breakeven point is $0, and no income taxes are paid when there is no operating income.

Using CVP Analysis for Decision Making

We have seen how CVP analysis is useful for calculating the units that need to be sold to break even, or to achieve a target operating income or target net income. Managers also use CVP analysis to guide other decisions, many of them strategic decisions. Consider a decision about choosing additional features for an existing product. Different choices can affect selling prices, variable cost per unit, fixed costs, units sold, and operating income. CVP analysis helps managers make product decisions by estimating the expected profitability of these choices.

Strategic decisions invariably entail risk. CVP analysis can be used to evaluate how operating income will be affected if the original predicted data are not achieved—say, if sales are 10% lower than estimated. Evaluating this risk affects other strategic decisions a company might make. For example, if the probability of a decline in sales seems high, a manager may take actions to change the cost structure to have more variable costs and fewer fixed costs. We return to our Do-All Software example to illustrate using CVP analysis for strategic decisions concerning advertising and selling price.

Learning Objective 4

Explain CVP analysis in decision making and how sensitivity analysis helps managers cope with uncertainty

. . . determine the effect on operating income of different assumptions

Decision to Advertise

Returning to Do-All Software, suppose Mary anticipates selling 40 units at the convention. Exhibit 3-3 indicates that Mary's operating income will be $1,200. Mary is considering placing an advertisement describing the product and its features in the convention brochure. The advertisement will cost $500. This cost is a fixed cost because it will not change regardless of the number of units Mary sells. She thinks that advertising will increase sales by 10% to 44 packages. Should Mary advertise? The following table presents the CVP analysis.

	40 Packages Sold with No Advertising (1)	44 Packages Sold with Advertising (2)	Difference (3) = (2) − (1)
Revenues ($200 × 40; $200 × 44)	$8,000	$8,800	$800
Variable costs ($120 × 40; $120 × 44)	4,800	5,280	480
Contribution margin ($80 × 40; $80 × 44)	3,200	3,520	320
Fixed costs	2,000	2,500	500
Operating income	$1,200	$1,020	$(180)

Operating income decreases from $1,200 to $1,020, so Mary should not advertise. Note that Mary could focus only on the difference column and come to the same conclusion: If Mary advertises, contribution margin will increase by $320 (revenues, $800−variable costs, $480), and fixed costs will increase by $500, resulting in a $180 decrease in operating income.

As you become more familiar with CVP analysis, try evaluating decisions based on differences rather than mechanically working through the contribution income statement. Analyzing differences gets to the heart of CVP analysis and sharpens intuition by focusing only on the revenues and costs that will change by implementing new decisions.

Decision to Reduce Selling Price

Having decided not to advertise, Mary is contemplating whether to reduce the selling price to $175. At this price, she thinks she will sell 50 units. At this quantity, the software wholesaler who supplies Do-All Software will sell the packages to Mary for $115 per unit instead of $120. Should Mary reduce the selling price? No, as the following CVP analysis shows.

Contribution margin from lowering price to $175: ($175 − $115) per unit × 50 units	$3,000
Contribution margin from maintaining price at $200: ($200 − $120) per unit × 40 units	3,200
Change in contribution margin from lowering price	$ (200)

Decreasing the price will reduce contribution margin by $200 and, because the fixed costs of $2,000 will not change, it will also reduce operating income by $200.

Mary could also ask "At what price can I sell 50 units (purchased at $115 per unit) and continue to earn an operating income of $1,200?" The answer is $179, as the following calculations show.

	Target operating income	$1,200
	Add fixed costs	2,000
	Target contribution margin	$3,200
	Divided by number of units sold	÷50 units
	Target contribution margin per unit	$ 64
	Add variable cost per unit	115
	Target selling price	$ 179
Proof:	Revenues, $179 per unit × 50 units	$8,950
	Variable costs, $115 per unit × 50 units	5,750
	Contribution margin	3,200
	Fixed costs	2,000
	Operating income	$1,200

Mary should also examine the effects of other decisions, such as simultaneously increasing advertising costs and lowering prices. In each case, Mary will compare the changes in contribution margin (through the effects on selling prices, variable costs, and quantities of units sold) to the changes in fixed costs, and she will choose the alternative that provides the highest operating income.

Sensitivity Analysis and Uncertainty

Before choosing strategies and plans about how to implement strategies, managers frequently analyze the sensitivity of their decisions to changes in underlying assumptions. **Sensitivity analysis** is a "what-if" technique that managers use to examine how an outcome will change if the original predicted data are not achieved or if an underlying assumption changes. In the context of CVP analysis, sensitivity analysis answers questions such as, What will operating income be if the quantity of units sold decreases by 5% from the original prediction? And, What will operating income be if variable cost per unit increases by 10%? The sensitivity of operating income to various possible outcomes broadens managers' perspectives about what might actually occur *before* they commit costs.

Electronic spreadsheets, such as Excel, enable managers to conduct CVP-based sensitivity analyses in a systematic and efficient way. Using spreadsheets, managers can conduct sensitivity analysis to examine the effect and interaction of changes in selling price, variable cost per unit, fixed costs, and target operating income. Exhibit 3-4 displays a spreadsheet for the Do-All Software example. Mary can immediately see how many units she needs to sell to achieve particular operating-income levels, given alternative levels of fixed costs and variable cost per unit that she may face. For example, 32 units must be sold to earn an operating income of $1,200 if fixed costs are $2,000 and variable cost per unit is $100. Mary can also use Exhibit 3-4 to determine that she needs to sell 56 units to break even (earn operating income of $0) if the booth rental at the Chicago convention is raised to $2,800 (increasing fixed costs to $2,800) and if the software supplier raises its price to $150 (increasing variable cost to $150 per unit). Mary can use information about costs and sensitivity analysis, together with realistic predictions about how much she can sell to decide if she should rent a booth at the convention.

Another aspect of sensitivity analysis is **margin of safety**, the amount by which budgeted (or actual) revenues exceed breakeven revenues. Expressed in units, *margin of safety* is the sales quantity minus the breakeven quantity. The margin of safety answers the "what-if" question: If budgeted revenues are above breakeven and drop, how far can they fall below budget before the breakeven point is reached? Such a fall could be a result of a competitor introducing a better product, or poorly executed marketing programs, and so on. Assume that Mary has fixed costs of $2,000, a selling price of $200, and variable cost per unit of $120. For 40 units sold, the budgeted revenues are $8,000 and the budgeted operating income is $1,200. The breakeven point for this set of assumptions is 25 units

Exhibit 3-4

Spreadsheet Analysis of CVP Relationships for Do-All Software

File Edit View Insert Format Tools Data Window Help

D5 ▼ fx =($A5+D$3)/(F1-$B5)

	A	B	C	D	E	F
1			Number of units required to be sold at $		200	
2			Selling Price to Earn Target Operating Income of			
3		Variable Costs	$0	$1,200	$1,600	$2,000
4	Fixed Costs	per Unit	(Breakeven point)			
5	$2,000	$100	20	32[a]	36	40
6	$2,000	$120	25	40	45	50
7	$2,000	$150	40	64	72	80
8	$2,400	$100	24	36	40	44
9	$2,400	$120	30	45	50	55
10	$2,400	$150	48	72	80	88
11	$2,800	$100	28	40	44	48
12	$2,800	$120	35	50	55	60
13	$2,800	$150	56	80	88	96
14						

[a]Number of units required to be sold $= \dfrac{\text{Fixed costs + Target operating income}}{\text{Contribution margin per unit}} = \dfrac{\$2,000 + \$1,200}{\$200 - \$100} = 32$

($2,000 ÷ $80 per unit), or $5,000 ($200 per unit × 25 units). Mary can determine the margin of safety by using the following equation:

$$\text{Margin of safety} = \frac{\text{Budgeted}}{\text{revenues}} - \frac{\text{Breakeven}}{\text{revenues}} = \$8{,}000 - \$5{,}000 = \$3{,}000$$

$$\frac{\text{Margin of}}{\text{safety (in units)}} = \frac{\text{Budgeted}}{\text{sales (units)}} - \frac{\text{Breakeven}}{\text{sales (units)}} = 40 - 25 = 15 \text{ units}$$

Sometimes margin of safety is expressed as a percentage:

$$\text{Margin of safety percentage} = \frac{\text{Margin of safety in dollars}}{\text{Budgeted (or actual) revenues}}$$

$$\text{In our example, margin of safety percentage} = \frac{\$3{,}000}{\$8{,}000} = 37.5\%$$

This result means that revenues would have to decrease substantially, by 37.5%, to reach breakeven revenues. The high margin of safety gives Mary confidence that she is unlikely to suffer a loss.

If, however, Mary expected to sell only 30 units, budgeted revenues would be $6,000 ($200 per unit × 30 units) and the margin of safety would equal:

$$\text{Budgeted revenues} - \text{Breakeven revenues} = \$6{,}000 - \$5{,}000 = \$1{,}000$$

$$\frac{\text{Margin of}}{\text{safety percentage}} = \frac{\text{Margin of safety in dollars}}{\text{Budgeted (or actual) revenues}} = \frac{\$1{,}000}{\$6{,}000} = 16.67\%$$

This result means that if revenues decrease by more than 16.67%, Mary would suffer a loss. A low margin of safety increases the risk of a loss. If Mary does not have the tolerance for this level of risk, she will prefer not to rent a booth at the convention.

Sensitivity analysis is a simple approach to recognizing **uncertainty**, which is the possibility that an actual amount will deviate from an expected amount. Sensitivity analysis gives managers a good feel for the risks involved. A more comprehensive approach to recognizing uncertainty is to compute expected values using probability distributions. This approach is illustrated in the appendix to this chapter.

Cost Planning and CVP

Use CVP analysis to plan variable and fixed costs

. . . compare risk of losses versus higher returns

Managers have the ability to choose the levels of fixed and variable costs in their cost structures. This is a strategic decision. In this section, we describe various factors that managers and management accountants consider as they make this decision.

Alternative Fixed-Cost/Variable-Cost Structures

CVP-based sensitivity analysis highlights the risks and returns as fixed costs are substituted for variable costs in a company's cost structure. In Exhibit 3-4, compare line 6 and line 11.

	Fixed Cost	Variable Cost	Number of units required to be sold at $200 selling price to earn target operating income of $0 (Breakeven point)	$2,000
Line 6	$2,000	$120	25	50
Line 11	$2,800	$100	28	48

Compared to Line 6, Line 11, with higher fixed costs, has more risk of loss (has a higher breakeven point) but requires fewer units to be sold (48 versus 50) to earn operating income of $2,000. CVP analysis can help managers evaluate various fixed-cost/variable-cost structures. We next consider the effects of these choices in more detail. Suppose Computer Conventions, Inc. offers Mary three rental alternatives:

Option 1: $2,000 fixed fee

Option 2: $800 fixed fee plus 15% of convention revenues

Option 3: 25% of convention revenues with no fixed fee

Mary's variable cost per unit is $120. Mary is interested in how her choice of a rental agreement will affect the income she earns and the risks she faces. Exhibit 3-5 graphically depicts the profit-volume relationship for each option. The line representing the relationship between units sold and operating income for Option 1 is the same as the line in the PV graph shown in Exhibit 3-3 (fixed costs of $2,000 and contribution margin per unit of $80). The line representing Option 2 shows fixed costs of $800 and a contribution margin per unit of $50 [selling price, $200, minus variable cost per unit, $120, minus variable rental fees per unit, $30, (0.15 × $200)]. The line representing Option 3 has fixed costs of $0 and a contribution margin per unit of $30 [$200 − $120 − $50 (0.25 × $200)].

Option 3 has the lowest breakeven point (0 units), and Option 1 has the highest breakeven point (25 units). Option 1 has the highest risk of loss if sales are low, but it also has the highest contribution margin per unit ($80) and hence the highest operating income when sales are high (greater than 40 units).

The choice among Options 1, 2, and 3 is a strategic decision that Mary faces. As in most strategic decisions, what she decides now will significantly affect her operating income (or loss), depending on the demand for Do-All Software. Faced with this uncertainty, Mary's choice will be influenced by her confidence in the level of demand for the software package and her willingness to risk losses if demand is low. For example, if Mary's tolerance for risk is high, she will choose Option 1 with its high potential rewards. If, however, Mary is averse to taking risk, she will prefer Option 3, where the rewards are smaller if sales are high but where she never suffers a loss if sales are low.

Operating Leverage

The risk-return trade-off across alternative cost structures can be measured as operating leverage. **Operating leverage** describes the effects that fixed costs have on changes in operating income as changes occur in units sold and contribution margin. Organizations with a high proportion of fixed costs in their cost structures, as is the case under Option 1, have high operating leverage. The line representing Option 1 in Exhibit 3-5 is the steepest of the three lines. Small increases in sales lead to large increases in operating income. Small decreases in sales result in relatively large decreases in operating income, leading to a greater risk of operating losses. *At any given level of sales,*

$$\text{Degree of operating leverage} = \frac{\text{Contribution margin}}{\text{Operating income}}$$

The following table shows the **degree of operating leverage** at sales of 40 units for the three rental options.

	Option 1	Option 2	Option 3
1. Contribution margin per unit (p. 73)	$ 80	$ 50	$ 30
2. Contribution margin (Row 1 × 40 units)	$3,200	$2,000	$1,200
3. Operating income (from Exhibit 3-5)	$1,200	$1,200	$1,200
4. Degree of operating leverage (Row 2 ÷ Row 3)	$\frac{\$3,200}{\$1,200} = 2.67$	$\frac{\$2,000}{\$1,200} = 1.67$	$\frac{\$1,200}{\$1,200} = 1.00$

These results indicate that, when sales are 40 units, a percentage change in sales and contribution margin will result in 2.67 times that percentage change in operating income for Option 1, but the same percentage change (1.00) in operating income for Option 3. Consider, for example, a sales increase of 50% from 40 to 60 units. Contribution margin will increase by 50% under each option. Operating income, however, will increase by 2.67 × 50% = 133% from $1,200 to $2,800 in Option 1, but it will increase by only 1.00 × 50% = 50% from $1,200 to $1,800 in Option 3 (see Exhibit 3-5). The degree of operating leverage at a given level of sales helps managers calculate the effect of fluctuations in sales on operating income.

Keep in mind that, in the presence of fixed costs, the degree of operating leverage is different at different levels of sales. For example, at sales of 60 units, the degree of operating leverage under each of the three options is as follows:

Exhibit 3-5

Profit-Volume Graph for Alternative Rental Options for Do-All Software

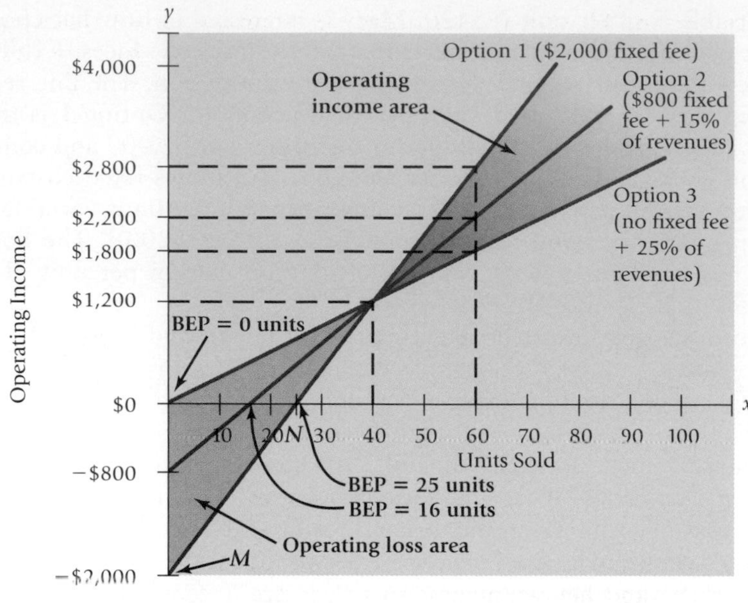

	Option 1	Option 2	Option 3
1. Contribution margin per unit (p. 73)	$ 80	$ 50	$ 30
2. Contribution margin (Row 1 × 60 units)	$4,800	$3,000	$1,800
3. Operating income (from Exhibit 3-5)	$2,800	$2,200	$1,800
4. Degree of operating leverage (Row 2 ÷ Row 3)	$\frac{\$4,800}{\$2,800} = 1.71$	$\frac{\$3,000}{\$2,200} = 1.36$	$\frac{\$1,800}{\$1,800} = 1.00$

The degree of operating leverage decreases from 2.67 (at sales of 40 units) to 1.71 (at sales of 60 units) under Option 1 and from 1.67 to 1.36 under Option 2. In general, whenever there are fixed costs, the degree of operating leverage decreases as the level of sales increases beyond the breakeven point. If fixed costs are $0 as in Option 3, contribution margin equals operating income, and the degree of operating leverage equals 1.00 at all sales levels.

But why must managers monitor operating leverage carefully? Again, consider companies such as US Airways, United Airlines, WorldCom, and Global Crossing. Their high operating leverage was a major reason for their financial problems. Anticipating high demand for their services, these companies borrowed money to acquire assets, resulting in high fixed costs. As sales declined in 2001 and 2002, these companies suffered losses and could not generate sufficient cash to service their interest and debt, causing them to seek bankruptcy protection.

Could these problems have been avoided? Perhaps, if managers had not built up assets and fixed costs too quickly to take advantage of the opportunities they saw in the marketplace. However, by doing so they simultaneously increased the risk of losses if demand for their products proved to be weak. Managers could also have reduced the magnitude of these problems by using equity rather than debt to finance the purchase of assets. Unlike debt, equity does not have a predetermined schedule of repayments. Equity financing would have given these companies more time to ride out the periods of weak demand for their services. So why didn't these companies use equity? Because relative to debt, equity financing is more costly. Managers and management accountants should always evaluate how the level of fixed costs and variable costs they choose will affect the risk-return trade-off. See Concepts in Action, p. 77, for another example of the risks of high fixed costs.

What actions are managers taking to reduce their fixed costs? Many companies are moving their manufacturing facilities from the United States to lower-cost countries, such as Mexico and China. To substitute high fixed costs with lower variable costs, companies are purchasing products from lower-cost suppliers instead of manufacturing products themselves. These actions reduce both costs and operating leverage. More recently,

General Electric and Hewlett-Packard began outsourcing service functions, such as post-sales customer service, by shifting their customer call centers to countries, such as India, where costs are lower. These decisions by companies are not without controversy. Some economists argue that outsourcing helps to keep costs, and therefore prices, low and enables U.S. companies to remain globally competitive. Others argue that outsourcing reduces job opportunities in the United States and hurts working-class families.

Effects of Sales Mix on Income

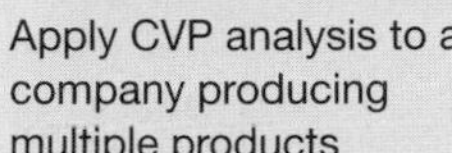

Learning Objective 6

Apply CVP analysis to a company producing multiple products

. . . assume sales mix of products remains constant as total units sold changes

Sales mix is the quantities (or proportion) of various products (or services) that constitute total unit sales of a company. Suppose Mary is now budgeting for a subsequent computer convention in Boston. She plans to sell two different software products—Do-All and Superword—and budgets the following:

	Do-All	Superword	Total
Expected sales	60	40	100
Revenues, $200 and $100 per unit	$12,000	$4,000	$16,000
Variable costs, $120 and $70 per unit	7,200	2,800	10,000
Contribution margin, $80 and $30 per unit	$4,800	$1,200	6,000
Fixed costs			4,500
Operating income			$1,500

What is the breakeven point? In contrast to the single-product (or service) situation, the number of total units that must be sold to break even in a multiproduct company depends on the sales mix—the combination of the number of units of Do-All sold and the number of units of Superword sold. We assume that the budgeted sales mix (60 units of Do-All sold for every 40 units of Superword sold, that is, 3 units of Do-All sold for every 2 units of Superword sold) will not change at different levels of total unit sales. That is, we think of Mary selling a bundle of 3 units of Do-All and 2 units of Superword. Note that this does not mean that Mary physically bundles the two products together into one big package. Instead, we think in terms of bundling to assist in budgeting.

Each bundle yields a contribution margin of $300 calculated as follows:

	Number of Units of Do-All and Superword in Each Bundle	Contribution Margin per Unit for Do-All and Superword	Contribution Margin of the Bundle
Do-All	3	$80	$240
Superword	2	30	60
Total			$300

To compute the breakeven point, we calculate the number of bundles Mary needs to sell.

$$\text{Breakeven point in bundles} = \frac{\text{Fixed costs}}{\text{Contribution margin per bundle}} = \frac{\$4{,}500}{\$300 \text{ per bundle}} = 15 \text{ bundles}$$

Breakeven point in units of Do-All and Superword is:

Do-All: 15 bundles × 3 units of Do-All per bundle	45 units
Superword: 15 bundles × 2 units of Superword per bundle	30 units
Total number of units to breakeven	75 units

Breakeven point in dollars for Do-All and Superword is:

Do-All: 45 units × $200 per unit	$9,000
Superword: 30 units × $100 per unit	3,000
Breakeven revenues	$12,000

We can also calculate the breakeven point in revenues for the multiple-products situation as follows:

	Number of Units of Do-All and Superword in Each Bundle	Selling Price for Do-All and Superword	Revenue of the Bundle
Do-All	3	$200	$600
Superword	2	100	200
Total			$800

$$\text{Contribution margin percentage for the bundle} = \frac{\text{Contribution margin of the bundle}}{\text{Revenue of the bundle}} = \frac{\$300}{\$800} = 0.375 \text{ or } 37.5\%$$

$$\text{Breakeven revenues} = \frac{\text{Fixed costs}}{\text{Contribution margin \% for the bundle}} = \frac{\$4{,}500}{0.375} = \$12{,}000$$

$$\text{Number of bundles required to be sold to break even} = \frac{\text{Breakeven revenues}}{\text{Revenue per bundle}} = \frac{\$12{,}000}{\$800 \text{ per bundle}} = 15 \text{ bundles}$$

That is, breakeven point in units and dollars for Do-All and Superword are:

Do-All: 15 bundles × 3 units of Do-All per bundle = 45 units × $200 per unit = $9,000
Superword: 15 bundles × 2 units of Superword per bundle = 30 units × $100 per unit = $3,000

Recall that in all our calculations, we have assumed that the budgeted sales mix (3 units of Do-All for every 2 units of Superword) will not change at different levels of total unit sales.

Of course, there are many different sales mixes (in units) that result in a contribution margin of $4,500 and cause Mary to break even, as the following table shows:

Sales Mix (Units)		Contribution Margin from		
Do-All (1)	Superword (2)	Do-All (3) = $80 × (1)	Superword (4) = $30 × (2)	Total Contribution Margin (5) = (3) + (4)
48	22	$3,840	$ 660	$4,500
36	54	2,880	1,620	4,500
30	70	2,400	2,100	4,500

If for example, the sales mix changes to 3 units of Do-All for every 7 units of Superword, you can see in the preceding table that the breakeven point increases from 75 units to 100 units, comprising 30 units of Do-All and 70 units of Superword. The breakeven quantity increases because the sales mix has shifted toward the lower-contribution-margin product, Superword ($30 per unit compared to Do-All's $80 per unit). In general, for any given total quantity of units sold, as the sales mix shifts toward units with lower contribution margins (more units of Superword compared to Do-All), operating income will be lower.

How do companies choose their sales mix? They adjust their mix to respond to demand changes. For example, as gasoline prices increase and customers want smaller cars, auto companies shift their production mix to produce additional smaller cars.

Learning Objective 7

Adapt CVP analysis to situations in which a product has more than one cost driver

. . . basic concepts apply but simple formulas do not

Multiple Cost Drivers

Throughout this chapter, we have assumed that the number of output units is the only revenue driver and the only cost driver. Now we describe how some aspects of CVP analysis can be adapted to the general case of multiple cost drivers.

Consider again the single-product Do-All Software example. Suppose Mary will incur a variable cost of $10 for preparing documents (including an invoice) for each customer who buys Do-All Software. That is, the cost driver of document-preparation costs is the number of customers who buy Do-All Software. Mary's operating income can then be expressed in terms of revenues and these costs:

Concepts in Action

Sky-High Fixed Costs Trouble XM Satellite Radio

Building up too much fixed costs can be hazardous to a company's health. Because fixed costs, unlike variable costs, do not automatically decrease as volume declines, companies with too much fixed costs can lose a considerable amount of money during lean times. XM Satellite Radio, once the market leader in satellite radio broadcasting, learned this lesson the hard way.

To begin broadcasting in 2001, XM had to spend over $1 billion on a broadcasting license, two space satellites, and other technology infrastructure. Once operational, the company also spent billions on other fixed items such as programming and content, satellite transmission, and R&D. In contrast, XM's variable costs were minimal, consisting mainly of artist-royalty fees and customer service and billing. In effect, this created a business model with a high operating leverage—that is, XM's cost structure had a very significant proportion of fixed costs. As such, the only way XM could be profitable was by amassing millions of paid subscribers and selling advertising.

The competitive disadvantage of this highly-leveraged business model became apparent almost immediately. In 2002, Sirius Satellite Radio entered the market with basically the same offering as its competitor, XM: 100+ channels of music and talk radio available nationwide for a monthly subscription fee. Using the same highly leveraged business model as XM, Sirius pursued a nearly identical growth strategy of selling radio advertisements while growing a huge subscriber base.

Other competitors lurked, as well. Traditional radio still held a huge share of the market, and around the same time as the launch of XM and Sirius, Apple released its first iPod portable digital-music player. Notably, Apple's iPod had a much lower operating leverage than satellite radio: R&D costs were much smaller, and its marginal costs were primarily tied to manufacturing and distribution. The iPod was profitable even at low sales volumes because of its low fixed costs.

In response to Sirius and other competitors, XM began spending extravagantly for exclusive programming content. XM spent $650 million on the exclusive satellite broadcasting rights for Major League Baseball and gave Oprah Winfrey $55 million to start her XM show. Sirius responded by inking an exclusive deal with the National Football League and paying "shock-jock" Howard Stern nearly $500 million to move to Sirius. This added to the highly leveraged operating position of both companies. By 2006, despite its nearly 8 million subscribers, XM never turned a profit and most analysts and observers felt that neither XM nor Sirius (with 6 million subscribers) would ever be able to recover its high fixed costs.

In 2007, XM bowed to cost and marketplace pressure and agreed to merge with Sirius. One observer called it the "stop us before we spend again" merger. Sirius CEO Mel Karmazin—who will head up the combined entity—noted that operating leverage drove the merger. He vowed to look for "synergies on every line of the income statement."

Sources: "XM Satellite Radio (A)," Harvard Business School Case No. 9-504-009; "Satellite Radio: An Industry Case Study," Kellogg School of Management (Northwestern University) Case No. 5-206-255; Testimony of Sean Buston, CFA, before the Copyright Royalty Board of the Library of Congress (October 2006); Justin Fox, "The 'stop us before we spend again' merger," Time.com, February 20, 2007. time-blog.com/curious_capitalist/2007/02/the_stop_us_before_we_spend_ag.html; Various analysts reports.

$$\text{Operating Income} = \text{Revenues} - \left(\begin{array}{c}\text{Cost of each}\\ \text{Do-All software}\\ \text{package}\end{array} \times \begin{array}{c}\text{Number of}\\ \text{packages}\\ \text{sold}\end{array}\right) - \left(\begin{array}{c}\text{Cost of preparing}\\ \text{documents for}\\ \text{each customer}\end{array} \times \begin{array}{c}\text{Number of}\\ \text{customers}\end{array}\right) - \text{Fixed costs}$$

If Mary sells 40 packages to 15 customers, then

$$\begin{aligned}\text{Operating income} &= (\$200 \text{ per package} \times 40 \text{ packages}) - (\$120 \text{ per package} \times 40 \text{ packages}) - \\ &\quad (\$10 \text{ per customer} \times 15 \text{ customers}) - \$2{,}000 \\ &= \$8{,}000 - \$4{,}800 - \$150 - \$2{,}000 = \$1{,}050\end{aligned}$$

If instead Mary sells 40 packages to 40 customers, then

$$\begin{aligned}\text{Operating income} &= (\$200 \times 40) - (\$120 \times 40) - (\$10 \times 40) - \$2{,}000 \\ &= \$8{,}000 - \$4{,}800 - \$400 - \$2{,}000 = \$800\end{aligned}$$

The number of packages sold is not the only determinant of Mary's operating income. For a given number of packages sold, Mary's operating income will be lower if she sells Do-All Software to more customers. Mary's costs depend on two cost drivers: the number of packages sold and the number of customers.

Just as in the case of multiple products, there is no unique breakeven point when there are multiple cost drivers. For example, Mary will break even if she sells 26 packages to 8 customers or 27 packages to 16 customers:

$$(\$200 \times 26) - (\$120 \times 26) - (\$10 \times 8) - \$2{,}000 = \$5{,}200 - \$3{,}120 - \$80 - \$2{,}000 = \$0$$
$$(\$200 \times 27) - (\$120 \times 27) - (\$10 \times 16) - \$2{,}000 = \$5{,}400 - \$3{,}240 - \$160 - \$2{,}000 = \$0$$

CVP Analysis in Service and Nonprofit Organizations

Thus far, our CVP analysis has focused on a merchandising company. CVP can also be applied to decisions by manufacturing, service, and nonprofit organizations. To apply CVP analysis in service and nonprofit organizations, we need to focus on measuring their output, which is different from the tangible units sold by manufacturing and merchandising companies. Examples of output measures in various service and nonprofit industries are:

Industry	Measure of Output
Airlines	Passenger miles
Hotels/motels	Room-nights occupied
Hospitals	Patient days
Universities	Student credit-hours

Consider an agency of the Massachusetts Department of Social Welfare with a \$900,000 budget appropriation (its revenues) for 2008. This nonprofit agency's purpose is to assist handicapped people seeking employment. On average, the agency supplements each person's income by \$5,000 annually. The agency's only other costs are fixed costs of rent and administrative salaries equal to \$270,000. The agency manager wants to know how many people could be assisted in 2008. We can use CVP analysis here by setting operating income to \$0. Let Q be the number of handicapped people to be assisted:

$$\text{Revenues} - \text{Variable costs} - \text{Fixed costs} = 0$$
$$\$900{,}000 - \$5{,}000\,Q - \$270{,}000 = 0$$
$$\$5{,}000\,Q = \$900{,}000 - \$270{,}000 = \$630{,}000$$
$$Q = \$630{,}000 \div \$5{,}000 \text{ per person} = 126 \text{ people}$$

Suppose the manager is concerned that the total budget appropriation for 2009 will be reduced by 15% to \$900,000 × (1 − 0.15) = \$765,000. The manager wants to know how many handicapped people could be assisted with this reduced budget. Assume the same amount of monetary assistance per person:

$$\$765{,}000 - \$5{,}000\,Q - \$270{,}000 = 0$$
$$\$5{,}000Q = \$765{,}000 - \$270{,}000 = \$495{,}000$$
$$Q = \$495{,}000 \div \$5{,}000 \text{ per person} = 99 \text{ people}$$

Note the following two characteristics of the CVP relationships in this nonprofit situation:

1. The percentage drop in the number of people assisted, (126 − 99) ÷ 126, or 21.4%, is greater than the 15% reduction in the budget appropriation. That's because the \$270,000 in fixed costs still must be paid, leaving a proportionately lower budget to assist people. The percentage drop in service exceeds the percentage drop in budget appropriation.
2. Given the reduced budget appropriation (revenues) of \$765,000, the manager can adjust operations to stay within this appropriation in one or more of three basic ways: (a) reduce the number of people assisted from the current 126, (b) reduce the

variable cost (the extent of assistance per person) from the current $5,000 per person, or (c) reduce the total fixed costs from the current $270,000.

Contribution Margin versus Gross Margin

Clearly distinguish contribution margin, which provides information for CVP analysis, from gross margin discussed in Chapter 2.

$$\text{Gross margin} = \text{Revenues} - \text{Cost of goods sold}$$
$$\text{Contribution margin} = \text{Revenues} - \text{All variable costs}$$

Gross margin is a measure of competitiveness—how much a company can charge for its products over and above the cost of acquiring or producing them. Companies, such as branded pharmaceuticals, have high gross margins because their products provide unique and distinctive benefits to consumers. Products such as televisions that operate in competitive markets, have low gross margins. Contribution margin indicates how much of a company's revenues are available to cover fixed costs. It helps in assessing risk of loss. Risk of loss is low (high) if, when sales are low, contribution margin exceeds (is less than) fixed costs. Gross margins and contribution margin are related but give different insights. For example, a company operating in a competitive market with a low gross margin will have a low risk of loss if its fixed costs are small.

Consider the distinction between gross margin and contribution margin in the context of manufacturing companies. In the manufacturing sector, contribution margin and gross margin differ in two respects: fixed manufacturing costs and variable nonmanufacturing costs. The following example (figures assumed) illustrates this difference:

Contribution Income Statement Emphasizing Contribution Margin (in 000s)		
Revenues		$1,000
Variable manufacturing costs	$250	
Variable nonmanufacturing costs	270	520
Contribution margin		480
Fixed manufacturing costs	160	
Fixed nonmanufacturing costs	138	298
Operating income		$ 182

Financial Accounting Income Statement Emphasizing Gross Margin (in 000s)	
Revenues	$1,000
Cost of goods sold ($250 + $160)	410
Gross margin	590
Nonmanufacturing costs ($270 + $138)	408
Operating income	$ 182

Fixed manufacturing costs of $160,000 are not deducted from revenues when computing contribution margin but are deducted when computing gross margin. Cost of goods sold in a manufacturing company includes all variable manufacturing costs and all fixed manufacturing costs ($250,000 + $160,000). Variable nonmanufacturing costs (such as commissions paid to salespersons) of $270,000 are deducted from revenues when computing contribution margin but are not deducted when computing gross margin.

Like contribution margin, gross margin can be expressed as a total, as an amount per unit, or as a percentage. For example, the **gross margin percentage** is the gross margin divided by revenues—59% ($590 ÷ $1,000) in our manufacturing-sector example.

Problem for Self-Study

Wembley Travel Agency specializes in flights between Los Angeles and London. It books passengers on United Airlines at $900 per round-trip ticket. Until last month, United paid Wembley a commission of 10% of the ticket price paid by each passenger. This commission was Wembley's only source of revenues. Wembley's fixed costs are $14,000 per month (for salaries, rent, and so on), and its variable costs are $20 per ticket purchased for a passenger. This $20 includes a $15 per ticket delivery fee paid to Federal Express. (To keep the analysis simple, we assume each round-trip ticket purchased is delivered in a separate package. Thus, the $15 delivery fee applies to each ticket.)

United Airlines has just announced a revised payment schedule for all travel agents. It will now pay travel agents a 10% commission per ticket up to a maximum of $50. Any ticket costing more than $500 generates only a $50 commission, regardless of the ticket price.

Required

1. Under the old 10% commission structure, how many round-trip tickets must Wembley sell each month (a) to break even and (b) to earn an operating income of $7,000?
2. How does United's revised payment schedule affect your answers to (a) and (b) in requirement 1?

Solution

1. Wembley receives a 10% commission on each ticket: 10% × $900 = $90. Thus,

$$\begin{aligned} \text{Selling price} &= \$90 \text{ per ticket} \\ \text{Variable cost per unit} &= \$20 \text{ per ticket} \\ \text{Contribution margin per unit} &= \$90 - \$20 = \$70 \text{ per ticket} \\ \text{Fixed costs} &= \$14{,}000 \text{ per month} \end{aligned}$$

a. $$\frac{\text{Breakeven number}}{\text{of tickets}} = \frac{\text{Fixed costs}}{\text{Contribution margin per unit}} = \frac{\$14{,}000}{\$70 \text{ per ticket}} = 200 \text{ tickets}$$

b. When target operating income = $7,000 per month:

$$\begin{aligned} \frac{\text{Quantity of tickets}}{\text{required to be sold}} &= \frac{\text{Fixed costs} + \text{Target operating income}}{\text{Contribution margin per unit}} \\ &= \frac{\$14{,}000 + \$7{,}000}{\$70 \text{ per ticket}} = \frac{\$21{,}000}{\$70 \text{ per ticket}} = 300 \text{ tickets} \end{aligned}$$

2. Under the new system, Wembley would receive only $50 on the $900 ticket. Thus,

$$\begin{aligned} \text{Selling price} &= \$50 \text{ per ticket} \\ \text{Variable cost per unit} &= \$20 \text{ per ticket} \\ \text{Contribution margin per unit} &= \$50 - \$20 = \$30 \text{ per ticket} \\ \text{Fixed costs} &= \$14{,}000 \text{ per month} \end{aligned}$$

a. $$\frac{\text{Breakeven number}}{\text{of tickets}} = \frac{\$14{,}000}{\$30 \text{ per ticket}} = 467 \text{ tickets (rounded up)}$$

b. $$\frac{\text{Quantity of tickets}}{\text{required to be sold}} = \frac{\$21{,}000}{\$30 \text{ per ticket}} = 700 \text{ tickets}$$

The $50 cap on the commission paid per ticket causes the breakeven point to more than double (from 200 to 467 tickets) and the tickets required to be sold to earn $7,000 per month to also more than double (from 300 to 700 tickets). As would be expected, travel agents reacted very negatively to the United Airlines announcement to change commission payments. Unfortunately for travel agents, other airlines also changed their commission structure in similar ways.

Decision Points

The following question-and-answer format summarizes the chapter's learning objectives. Each decision presents a key question related to a learning objective. The guidelines are the answer to that question.

Decision	Guidelines
1. How can CVP analysis assist managers?	CVP analysis assists managers in understanding the behavior of a product's or service's total costs, total revenues, and operating income as changes occur in the output level, selling price, variable costs, or fixed costs.

2. How do companies determine the breakeven point or the output needed to achieve a target operating income?	The breakeven point is the quantity of output at which total revenues equal total costs. The three methods for computing the breakeven point and the quantity of output to achieve target operating income are the equation method, the contribution margin method, and the graph method. Each method is merely a restatement of the others. Managers often select the method they find easiest to use in the specific decision situation.
3. How should companies incorporate income taxes into CVP analysis?	Income taxes can be incorporated into CVP analysis by using target net income rather than target operating income. The breakeven point is unaffected by income taxes because no income taxes are paid when operating income equals zero.
4. How should companies cope with uncertainty or changes in underlying assumptions?	Sensitivity analysis, a "what-if" technique, examines how an outcome will change if the original predicted data are not achieved or if an underlying assumption changes. When making decisions, managers use CVP analysis to compare contribution margins and fixed costs under different assumptions.
5. How should companies choose between different variable-cost/fixed-cost structures?	Choosing the variable-cost/fixed-cost structure is a strategic decision for companies. CVP analysis highlights the risk of losses when revenues are low and the upside profits when revenues are high for different proportions of variable and fixed costs in a company's cost structure.
6. Can CVP analysis be applied to a company producing multiple products?	CVP analysis can be applied to a company producing multiple products by assuming the sales mix of products sold remains constant as the total quantity of units sold changes.
7. Can CVP analysis be applied to a product that has multiple cost drivers?	The basic concepts of CVP analysis can be applied to multiple-cost-driver situations, but there is no unique breakeven point.

APPENDIX: DECISION MODELS AND UNCERTAINTY

This appendix explores the characteristics of uncertainty and describes an approach managers can use to make decisions in a world of uncertainty. We will also illustrate the insights gained when uncertainty is recognized in CVP analysis.

Coping with Uncertainty[2]

In the face of uncertainty, managers rely on decision models to help them make the right choices.

Role of a Decision Model

Uncertainty is the possibility that an actual amount will deviate from an expected amount. In the Do-All example, Mary might forecast sales at 40 units, but actual sales might turn out to be 30 units or 60 units. A decision model helps managers deal with such uncertainty. It is a formal method for making a choice, commonly involving both quantitative and qualitative analyses. The quantitative analysis usually includes the following steps:

Step 1: Identify a choice criterion. A **choice criterion** is an objective that can be quantified. This objective can take many forms. Most often the choice criterion is to maximize income or to minimize costs. The choice criterion provides a basis for choosing the best alternative action. Mary's choice criterion is to maximize expected operating income at the Chicago computer convention.

Step 2: Identify the set of alternative actions to be considered. We use the letter *a* with subscripts $_1$, $_2$, and $_3$ to distinguish each of Mary's three possible actions:

---

[2] The presentation here draws (in part) from teaching notes prepared by R. Williamson.

a_1 = Pay \$2,000 fixed fee

a_2 = Pay \$800 fixed fee plus 15% of convention revenues

a_3 = Pay 25% of convention revenues with no fixed fee

Step 3: Identify the set of events that can occur. An **event** is a possible relevant occurrence, such as the actual number of software packages Mary may sell at the convention. The set of events should be mutually exclusive and collectively exhaustive. Events are mutually exclusive if they cannot occur at the same time. Events are collectively exhaustive if, taken together, they make up the entire set of possible relevant occurrences (no other event can occur). Examples of mutually exclusive and collectively exhaustive events are growth, decline, or no change in industry demand, and increase, decrease, or no change in interest rates. Only one event out of the entire set of mutually exclusive and collectively exhaustive events will actually occur.

Suppose Mary's only uncertainty is the number of units of Do-All Software that she can sell. For simplicity, suppose Mary estimates that sales will be either 30 or 60 units. We use the letter x with subscripts $_1$ and $_2$ to distinguish the set of mutually exclusive and collectively exhaustive events:

$$x_1 = 30 \text{ units}$$
$$x_2 = 60 \text{ units}$$

Step 4: Assign a probability to each event that can occur. A **probability** is the likelihood or chance that an event will occur. The decision model approach to coping with uncertainty assigns probabilities to events. A **probability distribution** describes the likelihood, or the probability, that each of the mutually exclusive and collectively exhaustive set of events will occur. In some cases, there will be much evidence to guide the assignment of probabilities. For example, the probability of obtaining heads in the toss of a coin is 1/2 and that of drawing a particular playing card from a standard, well-shuffled deck is 1/52. In business, the probability of having a specified percentage of defective units may be assigned with great confidence on the basis of production experience with thousands of units. In other cases, there will be little evidence supporting estimated probabilities—for example, expected sales of a new pharmaceutical product next year.

Suppose that Mary, on the basis of past experience, assesses a 60% chance, or a 6/10 probability, that she will sell 30 units and a 40% chance, or a 4/10 probability, that she will sell 60 units. Using $P(x)$ as the notation for the probability of an event, the probabilities are:

$$P(x_1) = 6/10 = 0.60$$
$$P(x_2) = 4/10 = 0.40$$

The probabilities of these events add to 1.00 because they are mutually exclusive and collectively exhaustive.

Step 5: Identify the set of possible outcomes. Outcomes specify, in terms of the choice criterion, the predicted economic results of the various possible combinations of actions and events. The outcomes in the Do-All Software example take the form of six possible operating incomes that are displayed in a decision table in Exhibit 3-6. A **decision table** is a summary of the alternative actions, events, outcomes, and probabilities of events.

Distinguish actions from events. Actions are decision choices available to managers—for example, the particular rental alternatives that Mary can choose. Events are the set of all relevant occurrences that can happen—for example, the different quantities of software packages that may be sold at the convention. The outcome is operating income, which depends both on the action the manager selects (rental alternative chosen) and the event that occurs (the quantity of packages sold).

Exhibit 3-7 presents an overview of relationships among a decision model, the implementation of a chosen action, its outcome, and a subsequent performance evaluation. Thoughtful managers step back and evaluate what happened and learn from their experiences. This learning serves as feedback for adapting the decision model for future actions.

Exhibit 3-6 Decision Table for Do-All Software

	A	B	C	D	E	F	G	H	I
1	Selling price =	$200			Operating Income				
2	Package cost =	$120			Under Each Possible Event				
3			Percentage						
4		Fixed	of Convention	Event x_1 : Units Sold =		30	Event x_2 : Units Sold =		60
5	Actions	Fee	Revenues	Probability(x_1) =		0.60	Probability(x_2) =		0.40
6	a_1: Pay $2,000 fixed fee	$2,000	0%	$400[l]			$2,800[m]		
7	a_2: Pay $800 fixed fee plus 15% of convention revenues	$ 800	15%	$700[n]			$2,200[p]		
8	a_3: Pay 25% of convention revenues with no fixed fee	$ 0	25%	$900[q]			$1,000[r]		
9									
10	[l]Operating Income = ($200 - $120)(30) - $2,000	=	$ 400						
11	[m]Operating Income = ($200 - $120)(60) - $2,000	=	$2,800						
12	[n]Operating Income = ($200 - $120 - 15% x $200)(30) - $800	=	$ 700						
13	[p]Operating Income = ($200 - $120 - 15% x $200)(60) - $800	=	$2,200						
14	[q]Operating Income = ($200 - $120 - 25% x $200)(30)	=	$ 900						
15	[r]Operating Income = ($200 - $120 - 25% x $200)(60)	=	$1,800						

Expected Value

An **expected value** is the weighted average of the outcomes, with the probability of each outcome serving as the weight. When the outcomes are measured in monetary terms, expected value is often called **expected monetary value.** Using information in Exhibit 3-6, the expected monetary value of each booth-rental alternative denoted by $E(a_1)$, $E(a_2)$, and $E(a_3)$ is:

Pay $2,000 fixed fee:	$E(a_1) = 0.60(\$400) + 0.40(\$2{,}800) = \$1{,}360$
Pay $800 fixed fee plus 15% of revenues:	$E(a_2) = 0.60(\$700) + 0.40(\$2{,}200) = \$1{,}300$
Pay 25% of revenues with no fixed fee:	$E(a_3) = 0.60(\$900) + 0.40(\$1{,}800) = \$1{,}260$

To maximize expected operating income, Mary should select action a_1—pay Computer Conventions, Inc. a $2,000 fixed fee.

To interpret the expected value of selecting action a_1, imagine that Mary attends many conventions, each with the probability distribution of operating incomes given in Exhibit 3-6. For a specific convention, Mary will earn operating income of either $400, if she sells 30 units, or $2,800, if she sells 60 units. But if Mary attends 100 conventions, she will expect to earn $400 operating income 60% of the time (at 60 conventions), and $2,800 operating income 40% of the time (at 40 conventions), for a total operating income of $136,000 ($400 × 60 + $2,800 × 40). The expected value of $1,360 is the

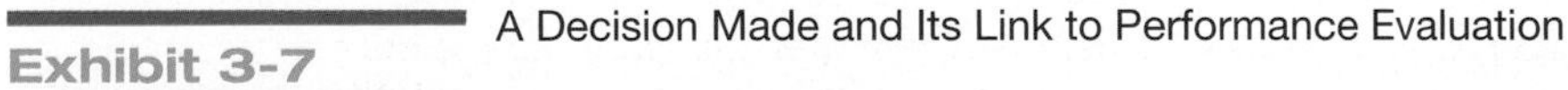
Exhibit 3-7 A Decision Made and Its Link to Performance Evaluation

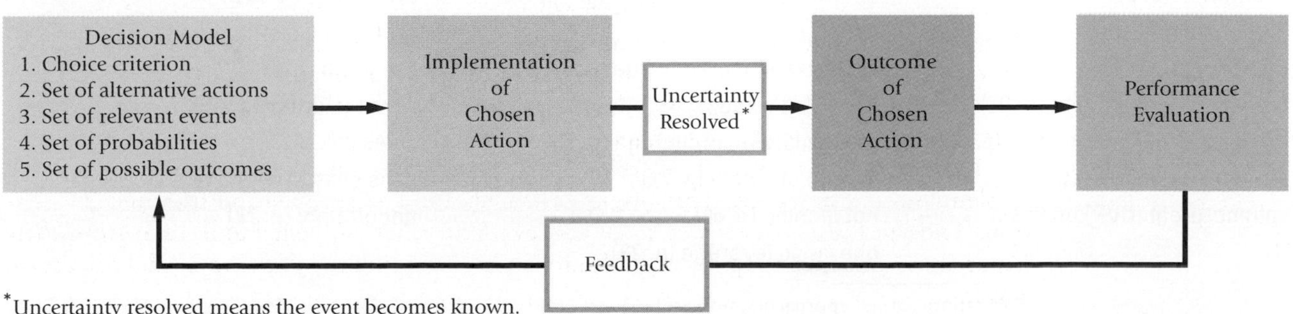

*Uncertainty resolved means the event becomes known.

operating income per convention that Mary will earn when averaged across all conventions ($136,000 ÷ 100). Of course, in many real-world situations, managers must make one-time decisions under uncertainty. Even in these cases, expected value is a useful tool for choosing among alternatives.

Consider the effect of uncertainty on the preferred action choice. If Mary were certain she would sell only 30 units (that is, $P(x_1) = 1$), she would prefer alternative a_3—pay 25% of convention revenues with no fixed fee. To follow this reasoning, examine Exhibit 3-6. When 30 units are sold, alternative a_3 yields the maximum operating income of $900. Because fixed costs are $0, booth-rental costs are lower, equal to $1,500 (25% of revenues = 0.25 × $200 per unit × 30 units), when sales are low.

However, if Mary were certain she would sell 60 software packages (that is, $P(x_2) = 1$), she would prefer alternative a_1—pay a $2,000 fixed fee. Exhibit 3-6 indicates that when 60 units are sold, alternative a_1 yields the maximum operating income of $2,800. Rental payments under a_2 and a_3 increase with units sold but are fixed under a_1.

Despite the high probability of selling only 30 units, Mary still prefers to take action a_1, which is to pay a fixed fee of $2,000. That's because the high risk of low operating income (the 60% probability of selling only 30 units) is more than offset by the high return from selling 60 units, which has a 40% probability. If Mary were more averse to risk (measured in our example by the difference between operating incomes when 30 versus 60 units are sold), she might have preferred action a_2 or a_3. For example, action a_2 ensures an operating income of at least $700, greater than the operating income of $400 that she would earn under action a_1 if only 30 units were sold. Of course, choosing a_2 limits the upside potential to $2,200 relative to $2,800 under a_1, if 60 units are sold. If Mary is very concerned about downside risk, however, she may be willing to forgo some upside benefits to protect against a $400 outcome by choosing a_2.[3]

Good Decisions and Good Outcomes

Always distinguish between a good decision and a good outcome. One can exist without the other. Suppose you are offered a one-time-only gamble tossing a coin. You will win $20 if the event is heads, but you will lose $1 if the event is tails. As a decision maker, you proceed through the logical phases: gathering information, assessing outcomes, and making a choice. You accept the bet. Why? Because the expected value is $9.50 [0.5($20) + 0.5(− $1)]. The coin is tossed and the event is tails. You lose. From your viewpoint, this was a good decision but a bad outcome.

A decision can be made only on the basis of information that is available at the time of evaluating and making the decision. By definition, uncertainty rules out guaranteeing that the best outcome will always be obtained. As in our example, it is possible that bad luck will produce bad outcomes even when good decisions have been made. A bad outcome does not mean a bad decision was made. The best protection against a bad outcome is a good decision.

TERMS TO LEARN

This chapter and the Glossary at the end of the book contain definitions of the following important terms:

breakeven point (BEP) (**p. 66**)
choice criterion (**p. 81**)
contribution income statement (**p. 63**)
contribution margin (**p. 62**)
contribution margin per unit (**p. 63**)
contribution margin percentage (**p. 63**)
contribution margin ratio (**p. 63**)
cost-volume-profit (CVP) analysis (**p. 61**)
decision table (**p. 82**)
degree of operating leverage (**p. 73**)
event (**p. 82**)
expected monetary value (**p. 83**)
expected value (**p. 83**)
gross margin percentage (**p. 79**)
margin of safety (**p. 71**)
net income (**p. 68**)
operating leverage (**p. 73**)
outcomes (**p. 82**)
probability (**p. 82**)
probability distribution (**p. 82**)
PV graph (**p. 67**)
revenue driver (**p. 65**)
sales mix (**p. 75**)
sensitivity analysis (**p. 71**)
uncertainty (**p. 72**)

[3] For more formal approaches, refer to J. Moore and L. Weatherford, *Decision Modeling with Microsoft Excel*, 6th ed. (Upper Saddle River, NJ: Prentice Hall, 2001).

ASSIGNMENT MATERIAL

Note: To underscore the basic CVP relationships, the assignment material ignores income taxes unless stated otherwise.

Questions

3-1 Define cost-volume-profit analysis.

3-2 Describe the assumptions underlying CVP analysis.

3-3 Distinguish between operating income and net income.

3-4 Define contribution margin, contribution margin per unit, and contribution margin percentage.

3-5 Describe three methods that can be used to express CVP relationships.

3-6 Why is it more accurate to describe the subject matter of this chapter as CVP analysis rather than as breakeven analysis?

3-7 "CVP analysis is both simple and simplistic. If you want realistic analysis to underpin your decisions, look beyond CVP analysis." Do you agree? Explain.

3-8 How does an increase in the income tax rate affect the breakeven point?

3-9 Describe sensitivity analysis. How has the advent of the electronic spreadsheet affected the use of sensitivity analysis?

3-10 Give an example of how a manager can decrease variable costs while increasing fixed costs.

3-11 Give an example of how a manager can increase variable costs while decreasing fixed costs.

3-12 What is operating leverage? How is knowing the degree of operating leverage helpful to managers?

3-13 "There is no such thing as a fixed cost. All costs can be 'unfixed' given sufficient time." Do you agree? What is the implication of your answer for CVP analysis?

3-14 How can a company with multiple products compute its breakeven point?

3-15 "In CVP analysis, gross margin is a less-useful concept than contribution margin." Do you agree? Explain briefly.

Exercises

3-16 CVP computations. Fill in the blanks for each of the following independent cases.

Case	Revenues	Variable Costs	Fixed Costs	Total Costs	Operating Income	Contribution Margin Percentage
a.		$500		$ 800	$1,200	
b.	$2,000		$300		$ 200	
c.	$1,000	$700		$1,000		
d.	$1,500		$300			40%

3-17 CVP computations. Patel Manufacturing sold 200,000 units of its product for $30 per unit in 2008. Variable cost per unit is $25 and total fixed costs are $800,000.

Required

1. Calculate (a) contribution margin and (b) operating income.
2. Patel's current manufacturing process is labor intensive. Kate Schoenen, Patel's production manager, has proposed investing in state-of-the-art manufacturing equipment, which will increase the annual fixed costs to $2,400,000. The variable costs are expected to decrease to $16 per unit. Patel expects to maintain the same sales volume and selling price next year. How would acceptance of Schoenen's proposal affect your answers to (a) and (b) in requirement 1?
3. Should Patel accept Schoenen's proposal? Explain.

3-18 CVP analysis, changing revenues and costs. Sunshine Travel Agency specializes in flights between Toronto and Jamaica. It books passengers on Canadian Air. Sunshine's fixed costs are $22,000 per month. Canadian Air charges passengers $1,000 per round-trip ticket.

Required

Calculate the number of tickets Sunshine must sell each month to (a) break even and (b) make a target operating income of $10,000 per month in each of the following independent cases.

1. Sunshine's variable costs are $35 per ticket. Canadian Air pays Sunshine 8% commission on ticket price.
2. Sunshine's variable costs are $29 per ticket. Canadian Air pays Sunshine 8% commission on ticket price.
3. Sunshine's variable costs are $29 per ticket. Canadian Air pays $48 fixed commission per ticket to Sunshine. Comment on the results.
4. Sunshine's variable costs are $29 per ticket. It receives $48 commission per ticket from Canadian Air. It charges its customers a delivery fee of $5 per ticket. Comment on the results.

3-19 CVP exercises. The Super Donut owns and operates six doughnut outlets in and around Kansas City. You are given the following corporate budget data for next year:

Revenues	$10,000,000
Fixed costs	$ 1,800,000
Variable costs	$ 8,000,000

Variable costs change with respect to the number of doughnuts sold.

Required Compute the budgeted operating income for each of the following deviations from the original budget data. (Consider each case independently.)

1. A 10% increase in contribution margin, holding revenues constant
2. A 10% decrease in contribution margin, holding revenues constant
3. A 5% increase in fixed costs
4. A 5% decrease in fixed costs
5. An 8% increase in units sold
6. An 8% decrease in units sold
7. A 10% increase in fixed costs and a 10% increase in units sold
8. A 5% increase in fixed costs and a 5% decrease in variable costs

3-20 CVP exercises. The Doral Company manufactures and sells pens. Currently, 5,000,000 units are sold per year at $0.50 per unit. Fixed costs are $900,000 per year. Variable costs are $0.30 per unit.

Required Consider each case separately:

1. **a.** What is the current annual operating income?
   b. What is the present breakeven point in revenues?

Compute the new operating income for each of the following changes:

2. A $0.04 per unit increase in variable costs
3. A 10% increase in fixed costs and a 10% increase in units sold
4. A 20% decrease in fixed costs, a 20% decrease in selling price, a 10% decrease in variable cost per unit, and a 40% increase in units sold

Compute the new breakeven point in units for each of the following changes:

5. A 10% increase in fixed costs
6. A 10% increase in selling price and a $20,000 increase in fixed costs

3-21 CVP analysis, income taxes. Diego Motors is a small car dealership. On average, it sells a car for $26,000, which it purchases from the manufacturer for $22,000. Each month, Diego Motors pays $60,000 in rent and utilities and $70,000 for salespeople's salaries. In addition to their salaries, salespeople are paid a commission of $500 for each car they sell. Diego Motors also spends $10,000 each month for local advertisements. Its tax rate is 40%.

Required

1. How many cars must Diego Motors sell each month to break even?
2. Diego Motors has a target monthly net income of $63,000. What is its target monthly operating income? How many cars must be sold each month to reach the target monthly net income of $63,000?

3-22 CVP analysis, income taxes. The Rapid Meal has two restaurants that are open 24 hours a day. Fixed costs for the two restaurants together total $450,000 per year. Service varies from a cup of coffee to full meals. The average sales check per customer is $8.00. The average cost of food and other variable costs for each customer is $3.20. The income tax rate is 30%. Target net income is $105,000.

Required

1. Compute the revenues needed to earn the target net income.
2. How many customers are needed to break even? To earn net income of $105,000?
3. Compute net income if the number of customers is 150,000.

3-23 CVP analysis, sensitivity analysis. Hoot Washington is the newly elected leader of the Republican Party. Media Publishers is negotiating to publish Hoot's Manifesto, a new book that promises to be an instant best-seller. The fixed costs of producing and marketing the book will be $500,000. The variable costs of producing and marketing will be $4.00 per copy sold. These costs are before any payments to Hoot. Hoot negotiates an up-front payment of $3 million, plus a 15% royalty rate on the net sales price of each book. The net sales price is the listed bookstore price of $30, minus the margin paid to the bookstore to sell the book. The normal bookstore margin of 30% of the listed bookstore price is expected to apply.

Required

1. Prepare a PV graph for Media Publishers.
2. How many copies must Media Publishers sell to (a) break even and (b) earn a target operating income of $2 million?
3. Examine the sensitivity of the breakeven point to the following changes:
   a. Decreasing the normal bookstore margin to 20% of the listed bookstore price of $30.

b. Increasing the listed bookstore price to $40 while keeping the bookstore margin at 30%.
c. Comment on the results.

3-24 CVP analysis, margin of safety. Suppose Lattin Corp.'s breakeven point is revenues of $1,500,000. Fixed costs are $600,000.

Required

1. Compute the contribution margin percentage.
2. Compute the selling price if variable costs are $15 per unit.
3. Suppose 80,000 units are sold. Compute the margin of safety in units and dollars.

3-25 Operating leverage. Color Rugs is holding a two-week carpet sale at Jerry's Club, a local warehouse store. Color Rugs plans to sell carpets for $500 each. The company will purchase the carpets from a local distributor for $350 each, with the privilege of returning any unsold units for a full refund. Jerry's Club has offered Color Rugs two payment alternatives for the use of space.

- Option 1: A fixed payment of $5,000 for the sale period
- Option 2: 10% of total revenues earned during the sale period

Assume Color Rugs will incur no other costs.

Required

1. Calculate the breakeven point in units for (a) option 1 and (b) option 2.
2. At what level of revenues will Color Rugs earn the same operating income under either option?
   a. For what range of unit sales will Color Rugs prefer option 1?
   b. For what range of unit sales will Color Rugs prefer option 2?
3. Calculate the degree of operating leverage at sales of 100 units for the two rental options.
4. Briefly explain and interpret your answer to requirement 3.

3-26 CVP analysis, international cost structure differences. Knitwear, Inc., is considering three countries for the sole manufacturing site of its new sweater: Singapore, Thailand, or the United States. All sweaters are to be sold to retail outlets in the United States at $32 per unit. These retail outlets add their own markup when selling to final customers. Fixed costs and variable cost per unit (sweater) differ in the three countries.

File Edit View Insert Format Tools Data Window Help

	A	B	C	D
1		Annual	Variable	Variable
2		Fixed	Manufacturing	Marketing &
3		Costs	Cost	Distribution Cost
4	Country	(Millions)	per Sweater	per Sweater
5	Singapore	$ 6.5	$ 8.00	$11.00
6	Thailand	$ 4.5	$ 5.50	$11.50
7	United States	$12.0	$13.00	$ 9.00

If you want to use Excel to solve this exercise, go to the Excel Lab at **www.prenhall.com/horngren/cost13e** and download the template for Exercise 3-26.

Required

1. Compute the breakeven point for Knitwear, Inc., in each country in (a) units sold (b) revenues.
2. If Knitwear, Inc., plans to produce and sell 800,000 sweaters in 2009, what is the budgeted operating income for each of the three manufacturing locations? Comment on the results.

3-27 Sales mix, new and upgrade customers. Zapo 1-2-3 is a top-selling electronic spreadsheet product. Zapo is about to release version 5.0. It divides its customers into two groups: new customers and upgrade customers (those who previously purchased Zapo 1-2-3, 4.0 or earlier versions). Although the same physical product is provided to each customer group, sizable differences exist in selling prices and variable marketing costs:

	New Customers		Upgrade Customers	
Selling price		$210		$120
Variable costs				
Manufacturing	$25		$25	
Marketing	65	90	15	40
Contribution margin		$120		$80

The fixed costs of Zapo 1-2-3 5.0 are $14,000,000. The planned sales mix in units is 60% new customers and 40% upgrade customers.

Required

1. What is the Zapo 1-2-3 5.0 breakeven point in units, assuming that the planned 60%/40% sales mix is attained?
2. If the sales mix is attained, what is the operating income when 200,000 units are sold?
3. Show how the breakeven point in units changes with the following customer mixes:
   a. New 50%/Upgrade 50%
   b. New 90%/Upgrade 10%
   c. Comment on the results.

3-28 CVP analysis, multiple cost drivers. Susan Wong is a distributor of brass picture frames. For 2008, she plans to purchase frames for $30 each and sell them for $45 each. Susan's fixed costs are expected to be $240,000. Susan's only other costs will be variable costs of $60 per shipment for preparing the invoice and delivery documents, organizing the delivery, and following up for collecting accounts receivable. The $60 cost will be incurred each time Susan ships an order of picture frames, regardless of the number of frames in the order.

Required

1. a. Suppose Susan sells 40,000 picture frames in 1,000 shipments in 2008. Calculate Susan's 2008 operating income.
   b. Suppose Susan sells 40,000 picture frames in 800 shipments in 2008. Calculate Susan's 2008 operating income.
2. Suppose Susan anticipates making 500 shipments in 2008. How many picture frames must Susan sell to break even in 2008?
3. Calculate another breakeven point for 2008, different from the one described in requirement 2. Explain briefly why Susan has multiple breakeven points.

3-29 CVP, Not for profit. The Sunrise Group (SG) is an environmentally conscious organization that buys land with the objective of preserving the natural environment. SG receives private contributions and takes no assistance from the government.

Fixed costs of operating the organization are $1,000,000 per year. Variable costs (including purchase of land, environmental impact reports and title search) average $3,000 per acre. In 2009, SG expects to receive contributions of $19,000,000. All contributions in excess of operating costs will be used to purchase land.

Required

1. How many acres will SG be able to purchase in 2009?
2. SG is considering participating in a new government program that will provide $1,000 per acre to subsidize the purchase of environmentally sensitive land. If SG participates in this program they estimate they will lose $5,000,000 in contributions from supporters who believe that accepting money from the government is not consistent with SG's mission. If SG participates in the program, how many acres of land will SG be able to buy in 2009? On financial considerations alone, should SG take the $1,000 per acre of subsidy?
3. SG is worried that contributions may drop by more than $5,000,000 if it takes the government subsidy. By how much can contributions decrease for SG to be able to buy the same amount of land if it takes the government subsidy or rejects it?

3-30 Contribution margin, decision making. Schmidt Men's Clothing's revenues and cost data for 2009 are:

Revenues		$500,000
Cost of goods sold (40% of sales)		200,000
Gross margin		300,000
Operating costs:		
Salaries fixed	$150,000	
Sales commissions (10% of sales)	50,000	
Depreciation of equipment and fixtures	12,000	
Store rent ($4,000 per month)	48,000	
Other operating costs	50,000	310,000
Operating income (loss)		$(10,000)

Mr. Schmidt, the owner of the store, is unhappy with the operating results. An analysis of other operating costs reveals that it includes $40,000 variable costs, which vary with sales volume, and $10,000 (fixed) costs.

Required

1. Compute the contribution margin of Schmidt Men's Clothing.
2. Compute the contribution margin percentage.
3. Mr. Schmidt estimates that he can increase revenues by 20% by incurring additional advertising costs of $10,000. Calculate the impact of the additional advertising costs on operating income.

3-31 Contribution margin, gross margin, and margin of safety. Mirabella Cosmetics manufactures and sells a face cream to small ethnic stores in the greater New York area. It presents the monthly operating income statement shown here to George Lopez, a potential investor in the business. Help Mr. Lopez understand Mirabella's cost structure.

File Edit View Insert Format Tools Data Window Help

	A	B	C	D
1		Mirabella Cosmetics		
2		Operating Income Statement, June 2008		
3	Units sold			10,000
4	Revenues			$100,000
5	Cost of goods sold			
6	Variable manufacturing costs		$55,000	
7	Fixed manufacturing costs		20,000	
8	Total			75,000
9	Gross margin			25,000
10	Operating costs			
11	Variable marketing costs		$ 5,000	
12	Fixed marketing & administration costs		10,000	
13	Total operating costs			15,000
14	Operating income			$ 10,000

If you want to use Excel to solve this exercise, go to the Excel Lab at **www.prenhall.com/horngren/cost13e** and download the template for Exercise 3-31.

Required

1. Recast the income statement to emphasize contribution margin.
2. Calculate the contribution margin percentage and breakeven point in units and revenues for June 2008.
3. What is the margin of safety (in units) for June 2008?
4. If sales in June were only 8,000 units and Mirabella's tax rate is 30%, calculate its net income.

3-32 Uncertainty and expected costs. Dawmart Corp, an international retail giant, is considering implementing a new business to business (B2B) information system for processing purchase orders. The current system costs Dawmart $1,000,000 per month and $40 per order. Dawmart has two options, a partially automated B2B and a fully automated B2B system. The partially automated B2B system will have a fixed cost of $5,000,000 per month and a variable cost of $30 per order. The fully automated B2B system has a fixed cost of $10,000,000 per month and $20 per order.

Based on data from the last two years, Dawmart has determined the following distribution on monthly orders:

Monthly Number of Orders	Probability
300,000	. 1
400,000	.25
500,000	. 4
600,000	.15
700,000	. 1

Required

1. Prepare a table showing the cost of each plan for each quantity of monthly orders.
2. What is the expected cost of each plan?
3. In addition to the information systems costs, what other factors should Dawmart consider before deciding to implement a new B2B system?

Problems

3-33 CVP analysis, service firm. Wildlife Escapes generates average revenue of $4,000 per person on its five-day package tours to wildlife parks in Kenya. The variable costs per person are:

Airfare	$1,500
Hotel accommodations	1,000
Meals	300
Ground transportation	600
Park tickets and other costs	200
Total	$3,600

Annual fixed costs total $480,000.

Required

1. Calculate the number of package tours that must be sold to break even.
2. Calculate the revenue needed to earn a target operating income of $100,000.
3. If fixed costs increase by $24,000, what decrease in variable cost per person must be achieved to maintain the breakeven point calculated in requirement 1?

3-34 CVP, target operating income, service firm. Teddy Bear Daycare provides daycare for children Mondays through Fridays. Its monthly variable costs per child are:

Lunch and snacks	$100
Educational supplies	75
Other supplies (paper products, toiletries, etc.)	25
Total	$200

Monthly fixed costs consist of:

Rent	$2,000
Utilities	300
Insurance	300
Salaries	2,500
Miscellaneous	500
Total	$5,600

Teddy Bear charges each parent $600 per child.

Required

1. Calculate the breakeven point.
2. Teddy Bear's target operating income is $10,400 per month. Compute the number of children who must be enrolled to achieve the target operating income.
3. Teddy Bear lost its lease and had to move to another building. Monthly rent for the new building is $3,000. At the suggestion of parents, Teddy Bear plans to take children on field trips. Monthly costs of the field trips are $1,000. By how much should Teddy Bear increase fees per child to meet the target operating income of $10,400 per month, assuming the same number of children as in requirement 2?

3-35 CVP analysis. (CMA, adapted) Galaxy Disk's projected operating income for 2008 is $200,000, based on a sales volume of 200,000 units. Galaxy sells disks for $16 each. Variable costs consist of the $10 purchase price and a $2 shipping and handling cost. Galaxy's annual fixed costs are $600,000.

Required

1. Calculate Galaxy's breakeven point and margin of safety in units.
2. Calculate the company's operating income for 2008 if there is a 10% increase in projected unit sales.
3. For 2009, management expects that the unit purchase price of the disks will increase by 30%. Calculate the sales revenue Galaxy must generate for 2009 to maintain the current year's operating income if the selling price remains unchanged.

3-36 CVP analysis, income taxes. (CMA, adapted) R. A. Ro and Company, a manufacturer of quality handmade walnut bowls, has had a steady growth in sales for the past five years. However, increased competition has led Mr. Ro, the president, to believe that an aggressive marketing campaign will be necessary next year to maintain the company's present growth. To prepare for next year's marketing campaign, the company's controller has prepared and presented Mr. Ro with the following data for the current year, 2008:

Variable cost (per bowl)	
Direct materials	$ 3.25
Direct manufacturing labor	8.00
Variable overhead (manufacturing, marketing, distribution and customer service)	2.50
Total variable cost per bowl	$ 13.75
Fixed costs	
Manufacturing	$25,000s
Marketing, distribution, and customer service	110,000
Total fixed costs	$135,000
Selling price	25.00
Expected sales, 20,000 units	$500,000
Income tax rate	40%

Required

1. What is the projected net income for 2008?
2. What is the breakeven point in units for 2008?

3. Mr. Ro has set the revenue target for 2009 at a level of $550,000 (or 22,000 bowls). He believes an additional marketing cost of $11,250 for advertising in 2009, with all other costs remaining constant, will be necessary to attain the revenue target. What is the net income for 2009 if the additional $11,250 is spent and the revenue target is met?
4. What is the breakeven point in revenues for 2009 if the additional $11,250 is spent for advertising?
5. If the additional $11,250 is spent, what are the required 2009 revenues for 2009 net income to equal 2008 net income?
6. At a sales level of 22,000 units, what maximum amount can be spent on advertising if a 2009 net income of $60,000 is desired?

3-37 CVP, sensitivity analysis. Technology of the Past (TOP) produces old-fashioned simple corkscrews. Last year was not a good year for sales but TOP expects the market to pick up this year. Last year's income statement was:

Sales revenue ($4 per corkscrew)	$40,000
Variable cost ($3 per corkscrew)	30,000
Contribution margin	10,000
Fixed cost	6,000
Operating income	$ 4,000

To take advantage of the anticipated growth in the market, TOP is considering the following courses of action.

Required

1. Do nothing. If TOP does nothing, it expects sales to increase by 10%.
2. Spend $2,000 on a new advertising campaign that is expected to increase sales by 50%.
3. Raise the price of the corkscrew to $5. This is expected to decrease sales quantities by 20%.
4. Redesign the classic corkscrew and increase the selling price to $6 while increasing the variable cost by $1 per corkscrew. The sales level is not expected to change from last year.

Evaluate each of the alternatives considered by TOP. What should TOP do?

3-38 CVP analysis, shoe stores. The WalkRite Shoe Company operates a chain of shoe stores that sell 10 different styles of inexpensive men's shoes with identical unit costs and selling prices. A unit is defined as a pair of shoes. Each store has a store manager who is paid a fixed salary. Individual salespeople receive a fixed salary and a sales commission. WalkRite is considering opening another store that is expected to have the revenue and cost relationships shown here:

File Edit View Insert Format Tools Data Window Help

	A	B	C	D	E
1	Unit Variable Data (per pair of shoes)			Annual Fixed Costs	
2	Selling price	$30.00		Rent	$ 60,000
3	Cost of shoes	$19.50		Salaries	200,000
4	Sales commission	1.50		Advertising	80,000
5	Variable cost per unit	$21.00		Other fixed costs	20,000
6				Total fixed costs	$360,000

If you want to use Excel to solve this problem, go to the Excel Lab at **www.prenhall.com/horngren/cost13e** and download the template for Problem 3-38. Consider each question independently:

Required

1. What is the annual breakeven point in (a) units sold and (b) revenues?
2. If 35,000 units are sold, what will be the store's operating income (loss)?
3. If sales commissions are discontinued and fixed salaries are raised by a total of $81,000, what would be the annual breakeven point in (a) units sold and (b) revenues?
4. Refer to the original data. If, in addition to his fixed salary, the store manager is paid a commission of $0.30 per unit sold, what would be the annual breakeven point in (a) units sold and (b) revenues?
5. Refer to the original data. If, in addition to his fixed salary, the store manager is paid a commission of $0.30 *per unit in excess of the breakeven point,* what would be the store's operating income if 50,000 units were sold?

3-39 CVP analysis, shoe stores (continuation of 3-38). Refer to requirement 3 of Problem 3-38. In this problem, assume the role of the owner of WalkRite. If you want to use Excel to solve this problem, go to the Excel Lab at **www.prenhall.com/horngren/cost13e** and download the template for Problem 3-38.

Required

1. Calculate the number of units sold at which the owner of WalkRite would be indifferent between the original salary-plus-commissions plan for salespeople and the higher fixed-salaries-only plan.
2. As owner, which sales compensation plan would you choose if forecasted annual sales of the new store were at least 55,000 units? What do you think of the motivational aspect of your chosen compensation plan?
3. Suppose the target operating income is $168,000. How many units must be sold to reach the target operating income under (a) the original salary-plus-commissions plan and (b) the higher-fixed-salaries-only plan?
4. You open the new store on January 1, 2008, with the original salary-plus-commission compensation plan in place. Because you expect the cost of the shoes to rise due to inflation, you place a firm bulk order for 50,000 shoes and lock in the $19.50 price per unit. But, toward the end of the year, only 48,000 shoes are sold, and you authorize a markdown of the remaining inventory to $18 per unit. Finally, all units are sold. Salespeople, as usual, get paid a commission of 5% of revenues. What is the annual operating income for the store?

3-40 Alternate cost structures, uncertainty, and sensitivity analysis. Edible Bouquets (EB) makes and sells flower bouquets. EB is considering opening a new store in the local mall. The mall has several empty shops and EB is unsure of the demand for its product. The mall has offered EB two alternative rental agreements. The first is a standard fixed rent agreement where EB will pay the mall $5,000 per month. The second is a royalty agreement where the mall receives $10 for each bouquet sold.

EB estimates that a bouquet will sell for $50 and have a variable cost of $30 to make (including the cost of flowers, and commission for the salesperson).

Required

1. What is the breakeven point in units under each rental agreement?
2. For what range of sales levels will EB prefer (a) the fixed rent agreement (b) the royalty agreement?
3. If EB signs a sales agreement with a local flower stand, it will save $5 in variable costs per bouquet. How would this affect your answer in requirement 2?
4. Do this question only if you have covered the chapter appendix in your class. EB estimates that the store is equally likely to sell 200, 400, 600, 800 or 1,000 arrangements. Using information from the original problem, prepare a table that shows the expected profit at each sales level under each rental agreement. What is the expected value of each rental agreement? Which rental agreement should EB choose?

3-41 CVP, alternative cost structures. Kids Lemonade Stand (KLS) is run by Sarah, who sells lemonade for $0.50 per glass. Lemons, sugar and water cost $0.15 per glass. Sarah's friend, Jessica, helps out by squeezing the lemons for $0.10 each. (Each lemon will provide enough juice for 2 glasses of lemonade.) Sarah uses tables, chairs and pitchers that belong to David who gathered the furniture when he had the stand last summer. David charges $6 per day for use of the furniture.

Required

1. How many glasses of lemonade does Sarah have to sell each day to breakeven?
2. Sarah wants to earn $3 per day after expenses. How many glasses does she have to sell to earn $3.
3. David wants more money, so he has offered to squeeze all the lemons Sarah needs for $1.70 per day. If Sarah hires David instead of Jessica, how many glasses will Sarah have to sell each day to breakeven?
4. At what sales level will Sarah be indifferent between hiring Jessica or David to squeeze the lemons? At what sales levels would she prefer to (a) hire Jessica (b) hire David?

3-42 CVP analysis, income taxes, sensitivity. (CMA, adapted) Almo Company manufactures and sells adjustable canopies that attach to motor homes and trailers. For its 2009 budget, Almo estimates the following:

Selling price	$ 400
Variable cost per canopy	$ 200
Annual fixed costs	$100,000
Net income	$240,000
Income tax rate	40%

The May income statement reported that sales were not meeting expectations. For the first five months of the year, only 350 units had been sold at the established price, with variable costs as planned, and it was clear that the net income projection for 2009 would not be reached unless some actions were taken. A management committee presented the following mutually exclusive alternatives to the president:

a. Reduce the selling price by $40. The sales organization forecasts that at this significantly reduced price, 2,700 units can be sold during the remainder of the year. Total fixed costs and variable cost per unit will stay as budgeted.
b. Lower variable cost per unit by $10 through the use of less-expensive direct materials and slightly modified manufacturing techniques. The selling price will also be reduced by $30, and sales of 2,200 units are expected for the remainder of the year.
c. Reduce fixed costs by $10,000 and lower the selling price by 5%. Variable cost per unit will be unchanged. Sales of 2,000 units are expected for the remainder of the year.

Required

1. If no changes are made to the selling price or cost structure, determine the number of units that Almo Company must sell (a) to break even and (b) to achieve its net income objective.
2. Determine which alternative Almo should select to achieve its net income objective. Show your calculations.

3-43 Choosing between compensation plans, operating leverage. (CMA, adapted) Marston Corporation manufactures pharmaceutical products that are sold through a network of external sales agents. The agents are paid a commission of 10% of revenues. Marston is considering replacing the sales agents with its own salespeople, who would be paid a commission of 10% of revenues and total salaries of $2,080,000. The income statement for the year ending December 31, 2008, under the two scenarios is shown here.

	A	B	C	D	E
1	Marston Corporation				
2	Income Statement				
3	For the Year Ended December 31, 2008				
4		Using Sales Agents		Using Own Sales Force	
5	Revenues		$26,000,000		$26,000,000
6	Cost of goods sold				
7	Variable	$11,700,000		$11,700,000	
8	Fixed	2,870,000	14,570,000	2,870,000	14,570,000
9	Gross margin		11,430,000		11,430,000
10	Marketing costs				
11	Commissions	$ 4,680,000		$ 2,600,000	
12	Fixed costs	3,420,000	8,100,000	5,500,000	8,100,000
13	Operating income		$ 3,330,000		$ 3,330,000

If you want to use Excel to solve this problem, go to the Excel Lab at **www.prenhall.com/horngren/cost13e** and download the template for Problem 3-43.

Required

1. Calculate Marston's 2008 contribution margin percentage, breakeven revenues, and degree of operating leverage under the two scenarios.
2. Describe the advantages and disadvantages of each type of sales alternative.
3. In 2009, Marston uses its own salespeople, who demand a 15% commission. If all other cost behavior patterns are unchanged, how much revenue must the salespeople generate in order to earn the same operating income as in 2008?

3-44 Sales mix, three products. The Ronowski Company has three product lines of belts—A, B, and C—with contribution margins of $3, $2, and $1, respectively. The president foresees sales of 200,000 units in the coming period, consisting of 20,000 units of A, 100,000 units of B, and 80,000 units of C. The company's fixed costs for the period are $255,000.

Required

1. What is the company's breakeven point in units, assuming that the given sales mix is maintained?
2. If the sales mix is maintained, what is the total contribution margin when 200,000 units are sold? What is the operating income?
3. What would operating income be if 20,000 units of A, 80,000 units of B, and 100,000 units of C were sold? What is the new breakeven point in units if these relationships persist in the next period?

3-45 Multi-product CVP and decision making. Pure Water Products produces 2 types of water filters. One attaches to the faucet and cleans all water that passes through the faucet. The other is a pitcher-cum-filter that only purifies water meant for drinking.

The unit that attaches to the faucet is sold for $80 and has variable costs of $20.

The pitcher-cum-filter sells for $90 and has variable costs of $25.

Pure Water sells 2 faucet models for every 3 pitchers sold. Fixed costs equal $945,000.

Required

1. What is the breakeven point in unit sales and dollars for each type of filter at the current sales mix?
2. Pure Water is considering buying new production equipment. The new equipment will increase fixed cost by $181,400 per year and will decrease the variable cost of the faucet and the pitcher units by $5 and $9 respectively. Assuming the same sales mix, how many of each type of filter does Pure Water need to sell to breakeven?
3. Assuming the same sales mix, at what total sales level would Pure Water be indifferent between using the old equipment and buying the new production equipment? If total sales are expected to be 30,000 units, should Pure Water buy the new production equipment?

3-46 Sales mix, two products. The Goldman Company retails two products: a standard and a deluxe version of a luggage carrier. The budgeted income statement for next period is as follows:

	Standard Carrier	Deluxe Carrier	Total
Units sold	150,000	50,000	200,000
Revenues at $20 and $30 per unit	$3,000,000	$1,500,000	$4,500,000
Variable costs at $14 and $18 per unit	2,100,000	900,000	3,000,000
Contribution margins at $6 and $12 per unit	$ 900,000	$ 600,000	1,500,000
Fixed costs			1,200,000
Operating income			$ 300,000

Required

1. Compute the breakeven point in units, assuming that the planned sales mix is attained.
2. Compute the breakeven point in units (a) if only standard carriers are sold and (b) if only deluxe carriers are sold.
3. Suppose 200,000 units are sold but only 20,000 of them are deluxe. Compute the operating income. Compute the breakeven point in units. Compare your answer with the answer to requirement 1. What is the major lesson of this problem?

3-47 Gross margin and contribution margin. The Museum of Art is preparing for its annual appreciation dinner for contributing members. Last year, 500 members attended the dinner. Tickets for the dinner were $20 per attendee. The profit report for last year's dinner follows.

Ticket sales	$10,000
Cost of dinner	11,000
Gross margin	(1,000)
Invitations and paperwork	3,000
Profit (loss)	$(4,000)

This year the dinner committee does not want to lose money on the dinner. To help achieve its goal, the committee analyzed last year's costs. Of the $11,000 cost of the dinner, $6,000 were fixed costs and $5,000 were variable costs. Of the $3,000 cost of invitation and paperwork, $2,500 were fixed and $500 were variable.

Required

1. Prepare last year's profit report using the contribution margin format.
2. The committee is considering expanding this year's dinner invitation list to include volunteer members (in addition to contributing members). If they expand the dinner invitation list, they expect attendance to double. Calculate the effect this will have on the profitability of the dinner.

3-48 Ethics, CVP analysis. Allen Corporation produces a molded plastic casing, LX201, for desktop computers. Summary data from its 2008 income statement are as follows:

Revenues	$5,000,000
Variable costs	3,000,000
Fixed costs	2,160,000
Operating income	$ (160,000)

Jane Woodall, Allen's president, is very concerned about Allen Corporation's poor profitability. She asks Max Lemond, production manager, and Lester Bush, controller, to see if there are ways to reduce costs.

After two weeks, Max returns with a proposal to reduce variable costs to 52% of revenues by reducing the costs Allen currently incurs for safe disposal of wasted plastic. Lester is concerned that this would expose the company to potential environmental liabilities. He tells Max, "We would need to estimate some of these potential environmental costs and include them in our analysis." "You can't do that," Max replies. "We are not violating any laws. There is some possibility that we may have to incur environmental costs in the future, but if we bring it up now, this proposal will not go through because our senior management always assumes these costs to be larger than they turn out to be. The market is very tough, and we are in danger of shutting down the company. We don't want all our colleagues to lose their jobs. The only reason our competitors are making money is because they are doing exactly what I am proposing."

Required

1. Calculate Allen Corporation's breakeven revenues for 2008.
2. Calculate Allen Corporation's breakeven revenues if variable costs are 52% of revenues.
3. Calculate Allen Corporation's operating income for 2008 if variable costs had been 52% of revenues.
4. Given Max Lemond's comments, what should Lester Bush do?

Collaborative Learning Problem

3-49 Deciding where to produce. (CMA, adapted) The Domestic Engines Co. produces the same power generators in two Illinois plants, a new plant in Peoria and an older plant in Moline. The following data are available for the two plants:

	A	B	C	D	E
1		Peoria		Moline	
2	Selling price		$150.00		$150.00
3	Variable manufacturing cost per unit	$72.00		$88.00	
4	Fixed manufacturing cost per unit	30.00		15.00	
5	Variable marketing and distribution cost per unit	14.00		14.00	
6	Fixed marketing and distribution cost per unit	19.00		14.50	
7	Total cost per unit		135.00		131.50
8	Operating income per unit		$ 15.00		$ 18.50
9	Production rate per day	400	units	320	units
10	Normal annual capacity usage	240	days	240	days
11	Maximum annual capacity	300	days	300	days

All fixed costs per unit are calculated based on a normal capacity usage consisting of 240 working days. When the number of working days exceeds 240, overtime charges raise the variable manufacturing costs of additional units by $3.00 per unit in Peoria and $8.00 per unit in Moline.

Domestic Engines Co. is expected to produce and sell 192,000 power generators during the coming year. Wanting to take advantage of the higher operating income per unit at Moline, the company's production manager has decided to manufacture 96,000 units at each plant, resulting in a plan in which Moline operates at capacity (320 units per day × 300 days) and Peoria operates at its normal volume (400 units per day × 240 days).

If you want to use Excel to solve this problem, go to the Excel Lab at **www.prenhall.com/horngren/cost13e** and download the template for Problem 3-49.

Required

1. Calculate the breakeven point in units for the Peoria plant and for the Moline plant.
2. Calculate the operating income that would result from the production manager's plan to produce 96,000 units at each plant.
3. Determine how the production of 192,000 units should be allocated between the Peoria and Moline plants to maximize operating income for Domestic Engines. Show your calculations.

4 Job Costing

Learning Objectives

1. Describe the building-block concepts of costing systems
2. Distinguish job costing from process costing
3. Outline the seven-step approach to job costing
4. Distinguish actual costing from normal costing
5. Track the flow of costs in a job-costing system
6. Dispose of under or over-allocated manufacturing overhead costs at the end of the fiscal year using alternative methods
7. Apply variations from normal costing

It's fair to say that no one likes to lose money. Whether a company is a new startup venture providing marketing consulting services or an established manufacturer of custom-built motorcycles, knowing how to job cost—how much it costs to produce an individual product—is critical if a profit is to be generated. As the following article shows, no one knows this better than Mike Sutton, the owner of Sutton Siding and Remodeling, a Springfield, Illinois, company.

Job Costing Is Job 1 at Sutton Siding[1]

Making a profit on a project depends on pricing it right. To do so, building remodelers, for example, calculate how much it will cost to complete a job and add a markup to the cost. At Sutton Siding and Remodeling, Mike Sutton, vice president of construction, is responsible for job costing. Mike carefully examines each job and verifies job costs as part of the contract-approval process.

Contract coordinator Ed Green double-checks all the numbers, watching especially for any unusual costs that could wreak havoc with the net profit on the job. Adds Sutton, "If the costs are too high on a particular job, the contract is not approved."

Each Thursday, sales, production, and administrative staff go through each job scheduled for start-up. Once a project is under way, the crews working on it detail every phase of construction in a written report. Sutton uses a checklist with 60 job-phase categories, such as finish carpentry and roofing, to track each one accurately. Every day, workers at each site log the percentage of each phase completed, giving the homeowner, workers, and Sutton management, a clear picture of what was accomplished.

Everyone working on jobs attends weekly Friday meetings. At these meetings, lead carpenters provide, and superintendents check, job-labor summaries of all the activities on every project. Sutton posts them for all to see.

Labor is a key element of job costing. The company includes a comprehensive list of labor costs besides the actual wages paid to employees: federal taxes, workers' compensation insurance, health insurance, life and disability insurance, retirement, profit sharing, vacations and holidays, sick days, and paid days off.

[1] *Source: Professional Remodeler,* June 1, 2001, pp. 77–78. © 2007, Reed Business Information, a division of Reed Elsevier Inc. All Rights Reserved.

Sutton is just as exacting about materials used in a job. All materials must be bought through a purchase order, with copies going to the lead carpenter, the superintendent for the project, the vendor, and accounts payable. Keeping track of materials has helped Sutton rein in how much the company spends on materials.

All of the information for every job is kept in a master notebook, which Sutton calls his bible. Every job has a number, and everything associated with that job—from purchase orders to daily logs—must have that number on it.

Just like at Sutton Siding, DaimlerChrysler managers need to know how much it costs to manufacture the Mercedes S-Class and PriceWaterhouseCoopers needs to know what it costs to audit Novartis AG, the Swiss pharmaceutical company. Knowing the costs and profitability of jobs helps managers pursue their business strategies, develop pricing plans, and meet external reporting requirements. Of course, when making decisions, managers combine cost information with noncost information, such as personal observations of operations, and nonfinancial performance measures, such as quality and customer satisfaction.

Building-Block Concepts of Costing Systems

Let's review some terms discussed in Chapter 2 that we'll use to introduce costing systems:

- *Cost object*—anything for which a measurement of costs is desired—for example, a product, such as an iMac computer, or a service, such as the cost of repairing an iMac computer.
- *Direct costs of a cost object*—costs related to a particular cost object that can be traced to that cost object in an economically feasible (cost-effective) way—for example the cost of purchasing the main computer board or the cost of parts used to make an iMac computer. Costs can be traced because making more computers directly causes more computer board costs to be incurred.
- *Indirect costs of a cost object*—costs related to a particular cost object that cannot be traced to that cost object in an economically feasible (cost-effective) way—for example, the costs of supervisors who oversee multiple products, one of which is the iMac, or the rent paid for the repair facility that repairs many different Apple computer products besides the iMac. Indirect costs are allocated to the cost object using a cost-allocation method.

Learning Objective 1

Describe the building-block concepts of costing systems

. . . the building blocks are cost object, direct costs, indirect costs, cost pools, and cost-allocation bases

Recall that *cost assignment* is a general term for assigning costs, whether direct or indirect, to a cost object. *Cost tracing* is a specific term for assigning direct costs; *cost allocation* refers to assigning indirect costs. The relationship among these three concepts can be graphically represented as

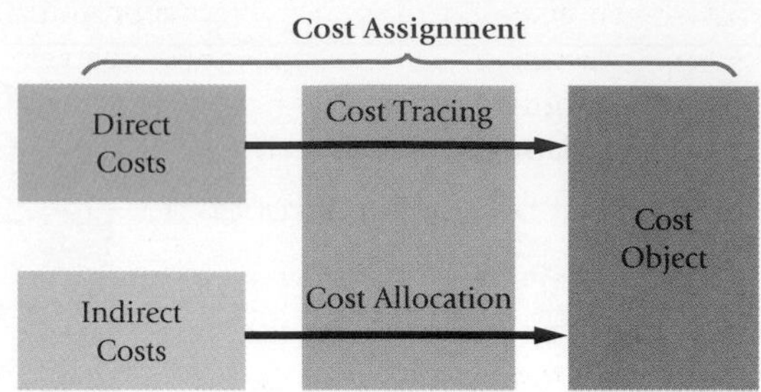

Throughout this chapter, the costs assigned to a cost object, for example, a product such as a Mini Cooper or a service such as an audit of MTV, include both variable and fixed costs. Managers use costs of products and services to guide long-run strategic decisions (for example, what mix of products and services to produce and sell and what prices to charge for them). In making these decisions, managers include all costs for two reasons. First, in the long run more costs can be managed and fewer costs are regarded as fixed. Second, also in the long run, a business cannot survive unless the prices of the products and services it chooses to sell cover both variable and fixed costs.

We need to introduce and explain two more terms to discuss costing systems:

1. **Cost pool.** A **cost pool** is a grouping of individual indirect cost items. Cost pools can range from broad, such as all manufacturing-plant costs, to narrow, such as the costs of operating metal-cutting machines. Cost pools are often organized in conjunction with cost-allocation bases.
2. **Cost-allocation base.** How should a company allocate costs to operate metal-cutting machines among different products? One way would be to allocate the costs based on the number of machine-hours used to produce the different products. The **cost-allocation base** (in our example, the number of machine-hours) is a systematic way to link an indirect cost or group of indirect costs (in our example, operating costs of all metal-cutting machines) to a cost object (in our example, different products). For example, if overhead costs of operating metal-cutting machines is $500,000 based on running these machines for 10,000 hours, the cost allocation rate is $500,000 ÷ 10,000 hours = $50 per machine-hour, where machine-hours is the cost allocation base. If a product uses 800 machine-hours, it will be allocated $40,000, $50 per machine-hour × 800 machine hours. Companies often use the cost driver of indirect costs as the cost-allocation base because of the cause-and-effect relationship between changes in the level of the cost driver and changes in indirect costs over the long run. A cost-allocation base can be either financial (such as direct labor costs) or nonfinancial (such as the number of machine-hours). When the cost object is a job, product, or customer, the cost-allocation base is also called a **cost-application base.**

The concepts represented by these five terms constitute the building blocks that we will use to design the costing systems described in this chapter.

Managers and management accountants choose cost objects to help them make decisions. As we described earlier, one major type of cost object of an accounting system is a *product* or *service*. Another major type of cost object is a *responsibility center*, which is a part, segment, or subunit of an organization whose manager is accountable for specified activities. Examples of responsibility centers are departments or groups of departments (such as operations and sales at eBay), divisions (such as Cadillac and Buick at General Motors), and geographic territories (such as North America, Europe, and Asia Pacific at Nike).

The most common responsibility center is a department. Identifying department costs helps managers control the costs for which they are responsible. This process also enables senior managers to evaluate the performance of their subordinates and the performance of subunits as economic investments. In manufacturing companies, the costs of the Manufacturing Department include direct costs, such as materials and manufacturing labor, and indirect costs, such as supervision, engineering, production, and quality control.

Be aware that supervision, engineering, and quality control costs, which are considered indirect or overhead costs when costing individual jobs or products, are considered direct costs of the Manufacturing Department. The reason is these costs are difficult to trace in an economically feasible way to individual jobs or products within the Manufacturing Department, but they are easily identified with and traced to the department itself.

Job-Costing and Process-Costing Systems

Learning Objective 2

Distinguish job costing

. . . job costing is used to cost a distinct product

from process costing

. . . process costing is used to cost masses of identical or similar units

Management accountants use two basic types of costing systems to assign costs to products or services:

1. **Job-costing system.** In this system, the cost object is a unit or multiple units of a distinct product or service called a **job**. Each job generally uses different amounts of resources. The product or service is often a single unit, such as a specialized machine made at Hitachi, a construction project managed by Bechtel Corporation, a repair job done at an Audi Service Center, or an advertising campaign produced by Saatchi & Saatchi. Each special machine made by Hitachi is unique and distinct. An advertising campaign for one client at Saatchi and Saatchi is unique and distinct from advertising campaigns for other clients. Job costing is also used to cost multiple identical units of a distinct product, such as the costs incurred by Raytheon Corporation to manufacture multiple units of the Patriot missile for the U.S. Department of Defense. Because the products and services are distinct, job-costing systems accumulate costs separately for each product or service.
2. **Process-costing system.** In this system, the cost object is masses of identical or similar units of a product or service. For example, Citibank provides the same service to all its customers when processing customer deposits. Intel provides the same product (say, a Pentium 4 chip) to each of its customers. Customers of Minute Maid all receive the same frozen orange juice product. In each period, process-costing systems divide the total costs of producing an identical or similar product or service by the total number of units produced to obtain a per-unit cost. This per-unit cost is the average unit cost that applies to each of the identical or similar units produced in that period.

Exhibit 4-1 presents examples of job costing and process costing in the service, merchandising, and manufacturing sectors. These two types of costing systems are best considered as opposite ends of a continuum; in between, one type of system can blur into the other to some degree.

Many companies have costing systems that are neither pure job costing nor pure process costing but have elements of both. Costing systems, therefore, need to be tailored to the underlying operations. For example, Kellogg Corporation uses job costing to calculate the total cost to manufacture each of its different and distinct types of products—such as Corn Flakes, Crispix, and Froot Loops—but process costing to calculate the per-unit cost of producing each identical box of Corn Flakes. In this chapter, we focus on job-costing systems. Chapters 17 and 18 discuss process-costing systems.

Exhibit 4-1

Examples of Job Costing and Process Costing in the Service, Merchandising, and Manufacturing Sectors

	Service Sector	Merchandising Sector	Manufacturing Sector
Job Costing Used	• Audit engagements done by Price Waterhouse Coopers • Consulting engagements done by McKinsey & Co. • Advertising-agency campaigns run by Ogilvy and Mather • Individual legal cases argued by Hale & Dorr • Computer-repair jobs done by CompUSA • Movies produced by Universal Studios	• L. L. Bean sending individual items by mail order • Special promotion of new products by Wal-Mart	• Assembly of individual aircrafts at Boeing • Construction of ships at Litton Industries
Process Costing Used	• Bank-check clearing at Bank of America • Postal delivery (standard items) by U.S. Postal Service	• Grain dealing by Arthur Daniel Midlands • Lumber dealing by Weyerhauser	• Oil refining by Shell Oil • Beverage production by PepsiCo

Job Costing: An Example

We illustrate job costing using the example of Robinson Company, a company that manufactures and installs specialized machinery for the paper-making industry. In early 2008, Robinson receives a request to bid for the manufacturing and installation of a new paper-making machine for the Western Pulp and Paper Company (WPP). Robinson has never made a machine quite like this one, and its managers wonder what to bid for the job. Robinson's management works through the five-step decision-making process.

1. **Identify the problems and uncertainties.** The decision of whether and how much to bid for the WPP job depends on how management resolves two critical uncertainties—what it will cost to complete the job and the prices that its competitors are likely to bid.
2. **Obtain information.** Robinson's managers first evaluate whether doing the WPP job is consistent with the company's strategy. Are these the kinds of jobs they want to be doing more of? Is this an attractive segment of the market? Will Robinson be able to develop a competitive advantage over its competitors? Strategy is as much about what to do as it is about what not to do. Robinson's managers conclude that the WPP job fits well with the company's strategic ambitions.

   Robinson's managers study the drawings and engineering specifications provided by WPP and decide on technical details of the machine. They compare the specifications of this machine to similar machines they have made in the past. They identify competitors who might bid on the job and speculate on what these bids might be.
3. **Make predictions about the future.** Robinson's managers estimate the cost of direct materials, direct manufacturing labor, and overhead for the WPP job. They also consider qualitative factors and risk factors and think through any biases they might have. For example, do engineers and employees working on the WPP job have the necessary skills and technical competence? Would they find the experience valuable and challenging. If the project runs into trouble, what effect might it have on employee morale and on other jobs? How accurate are the cost estimates, and what is the likelihood of cost overruns? What biases do Robinson's managers have to be careful about? Remember, Robinson has not made a machine quite like this one. The predictions about costs are based on other similar machines. Robinson's managers need to be careful not to draw inappropriate analogies and to seek the most relevant information when making their judgments.

4. **Make decisions by choosing among alternatives.** Robinson bids $15,000 for the WPP job. This bid is based on a manufacturing cost estimate of $10,000 and a markup of 50% over manufacturing cost. The $15,000 price takes into account likely bids by competitors, the technical and business risks, and qualitative factors. Robinson's managers are very confident that they have obtained the best possible information in reaching their decision.
5. **Implement the decision, evaluate performance, and learn.** Robinson wins the bid for the WPP job. As Robinson works on the WPP job, it keeps careful track of all the costs it has incurred (which are detailed later in this chapter). Ultimately, Robinson's managers compare the predicted amounts against actual costs to evaluate how well they did on the WPP job.

Actual Costing

Actual costing is a costing system that traces direct costs to a cost object by using the actual direct-cost rates times the actual quantities of the direct-cost inputs. It allocates indirect costs based on the actual indirect-cost rates times the actual quantities of the cost-allocation bases.

In its job-costing system, Robinson accumulates costs incurred on a job in different parts of the value chain—for example, manufacturing, marketing, and customer service. We focus on Robinson's manufacturing function (which also includes product installation). To make a machine, Robinson purchases some components from outside suppliers and makes others itself. Each of Robinson's jobs also has a service element: installing a machine at a customer's site, integrating it with the customer's other machines and processes, and ensuring the machine meets customer expectations.

General Approach to Job Costing

Robinson uses the following seven steps to assign costs to an individual job. This approach is commonly used by companies in the manufacturing, merchandising, and service sectors.

Learning Objective 3

Outline the seven-step approach to job costing

. . . the seven-step approach is used to compute direct and indirect costs of a job

Step 1: Identify the Job That Is the Chosen Cost Object. The cost object in the Robinson Company example is Job WPP 298, manufacturing a paper-making machine for the Western Pulp and Paper Company in 2008. Robinson's managers and management accountants gather information to cost jobs through source documents. A **source document** is an original record (such as a labor time card on which an employee's work hours are recorded) that supports journal entries in an accounting system. The main source document for Job WPP 298 is a job-cost record. A **job-cost record,** also called a **job-cost sheet,** records and accumulates all the costs assigned to a specific job, starting when work begins. Exhibit 4-2 shows the job-cost record for the paper-making machine ordered by Western Pulp and Paper Company. Follow the various steps in costing Job WPP 298 on the job-cost record in Exhibit 4-2.

Step 2: Identify the Direct Costs of the Job. Robinson identifies two direct-manufacturing cost categories: direct materials and direct manufacturing labor.

- **Direct materials:** On the basis of the engineering specifications and drawings provided by WPP, a manufacturing engineer orders materials from the storeroom. The order is placed using a basic source document called a **materials-requisition record,** which contains information about the cost of direct materials used on a specific job and in a specific department. Exhibit 4-3, Panel A, shows a materials-requisition record for the Robinson Company. See how the record specifies the job for which the material is requested (WPP 298), the description of the material (Part Number MB 468-A, metal brackets), the actual quantity (8), the actual unit cost ($14), and the actual total cost ($112). The $112 actual total cost also appears on the job-cost record in Exhibit 4-2. If we add the cost of all material requisitions, the total actual direct material cost is $4,606, which is shown in the Direct Materials panel of the job-cost record in Exhibit 4-2.

Exhibit 4-2 Source Documents at Robinson Company: Job-Cost Record

File Edit View Insert Format Tools Data Window Help

	A	B	C	D	E	
1			**JOB-COST RECORD**			
2	JOB NO:	WPP 298		CUSTOMER:	Western Pulp and Paper	
3	Date Started:	Feb. 4, 2008		Date Completed	Feb. 28, 2008	
4						
5						
6	**DIRECT MATERIALS**					
7	Date	Materials		Quantity	Unit	Total
8	Received	Requisition No.	Part No.	Used	Cost	Costs
9	Feb. 4, 2008	2008: 198	MB 468-A	8	$14	$ 112
10	Feb. 4, 2008	2008: 199	TB 267-F	12	63	756
11						•
12						•
13	Total					$ 4,606
14						
15	**DIRECT MANUFACTURING LABOR**					
16	Period	Labor Time	Employee	Hours	Hourly	Total
17	Covered	Record No.	No.	Used	Rate	Costs
18	Feb. 4-10, 2008	LT 232	551-87-3076	25	$18	$ 450
19	Feb. 4-10, 2008	LT 247	287-31-4671	5	19	95
20						•
21						•
22	Total					$ 1,579
23						
24	**MANUFACTURING OVERHEAD***					
25		Cost Pool		Allocation-Base	Allocation-	Total
26	Date	Category	Allocation-Base	Quantity Used	Base Rate	Costs
27	Dec. 31, 2008	Manufacturing	Direct Manufacturing	88 hours	$45	$ 3,960
28			Labor-Hours			
29						
30	Total					$ 3,960
31	**TOTAL MANUFACTURING COST OF JOB**					$10,145
32						
33						
34	*The Robinson Company uses a single manufacturing-overhead cost pool. The use of multiple overhead cost pools					
35	would mean multiple entries in the "Manufacturing Overhead" section of the job-cost record.					
36						

- **Direct manufacturing labor:** The accounting for direct manufacturing labor is similar to the accounting described for direct materials. The source document for direct manufacturing labor is a **labor-time record**, which contains information about the amount of labor time used for a specific job in a specific department. Exhibit 4-3, Panel B, shows a typical weekly labor-time record for a particular employee (G. L. Cook). Each day Cook records the time spent on individual jobs (in this case WPP 298 and JL 256), as well as the time spent on other tasks, such as maintenance of machines or cleaning, that are not related to a specific job.

  The 25 hours that Cook spent on Job WPP 298 appears on the job-cost record in Exhibit 4-2 at a cost of $450 (25 hours × $18 per hour). Similarly, the job-cost record for Job JL 256 will carry a cost of $216 (12 hours × $18 per hour). The three hours of time spent on maintenance and cleaning at $18 per hour equals $54.

Exhibit 4-3 Source Documents at Robinson Company: Materials Requisition Record and Labor-Time Record.

PANEL A:

MATERIALS-REQUISITION RECORD

Materials-Requisition Record No. 2008: 198

Job No. WPP 298 Date: FEB. 4, 2008

Part No.	Part Description	Quantity	Unit Cost	Total Cost
MB 468-A	Metal Brackets	8	$14	$112

Issued By: B. Clyde Date: Feb. 4, 2008

Received By: L. Daley Date: Feb. 4, 2008

PANEL B:

LABOR-TIME RECORD

Labor-Time Record No: LT 232

Employee Name: O. L. Cook Employee No. 551-07-3070

Employee Classification Code: Grade 3 Machinist

Hourly Rate: $18

Week Start: Feb. 4, 2008 Week End: Feb. 10, 2008

Job. No.	M	T	W	Th	F	S	Su	Total
WPP 298	4	8	3	6	4	0	0	25
JL 256	3	0	4	2	3	0	0	12
Maintenance	1	0	1	0	1	0	0	3
Total	8	8	8	8	8	0	0	40

Supervisor: R. Stuart Date: Feb. 10, 2008

This cost is part of indirect manufacturing costs because it is not traceable to any particular job. This indirect cost is included as part of the manufacturing-overhead cost pool allocated to jobs. The total direct manufacturing labor costs of $1,579 for the paper-making machine that appears in the Direct Manufacturing Labor panel of the job-cost record in Exhibit 4-2 is the sum of all the direct manufacturing labor costs charged to this job by different employees.

All costs other than direct materials and direct manufacturing labor are classified as indirect costs.

Step 3: Select the Cost-Allocation Bases to Use for Allocating Indirect Costs to the Job. Indirect manufacturing costs are costs that are necessary to do a job but that cannot be traced to a specific job. It would be impossible to complete a job without incurring indirect costs such as supervision, manufacturing engineering, utilities, and repairs. Because these costs cannot be traced to a specific job, they must be allocated to all jobs in a systematic way. Different jobs require different quantities of indirect resources. The objective is to allocate the costs of indirect resources in a systematic way to their related jobs.

Companies often use multiple cost-allocation bases to allocate indirect costs because different indirect costs have different cost drivers. For example, some indirect costs such as depreciation and repairs of machines are more closely related to machine-hours. Other indirect costs such as supervision and production support are more closely related to direct manufacturing labor-hours. Robinson, however, chooses direct manufacturing labor-hours as the sole allocation base for linking all indirect manufacturing costs to jobs. That's because, in its labor-intensive environment, Robinson believes that the number of direct manufacturing labor-hours is a good measure of how individual jobs use all the manufacturing overhead resources, such as salaries paid to supervisors, engineers, production support staff, and quality management staff. There is a cause-and-effect relationship between the direct manufacturing labor-hours required by an individual job—the cause—and the indirect manufacturing resources demanded by that job—the effect. (We will see in Chapter 5 that, in many manufacturing environments, we need to broaden the set of cost drivers.) In 2008, Robinson records 27,000 actual direct manufacturing labor-hours.

Step 4: Identify the Indirect Costs Associated with Each Cost-Allocation Base. Because Robinson believes that a single cost-allocation base—direct manufacturing labor-hours—can be used to allocate indirect manufacturing costs to jobs, Robinson creates a single cost pool called manufacturing overhead costs. This pool represents all indirect costs of the Manufacturing Department that are difficult to trace directly to individual jobs. In 2008, actual manufacturing overhead costs total $1,215,000.

As we saw in Steps 3 and 4, managers first identify cost-allocation bases and then identify the costs related to each cost-allocation base, not the other way around. That's because managers must first understand the cost driver, the reasons why costs are being incurred (for example, setting up machines, moving materials, or designing jobs), before they can determine the costs associated with each cost driver. The reason for not doing

Step 4 before Step 3 is that there is nothing to guide the creation of the cost pools. As a result, the cost pools created may not have cost-allocation bases that are cost drivers of the costs in the cost pool. Of course, Steps 3 and 4 can be done almost simultaneously.

Step 5: Compute the Rate per Unit of Each Cost-Allocation Base Used to Allocate Indirect Costs to the Job. For each cost pool, the **actual indirect-cost rate** is calculated by dividing actual total indirect costs in the pool (determined in Step 4) by the actual total quantity of the cost-allocation base (determined in Step 3). Robinson calculates the allocation rate for its single manufacturing overhead cost pool as follows:

$$\text{Actual manufacturing overhead rate} = \frac{\text{Actual manufacturing overhead costs}}{\text{Actual total quantity of cost-allocation base}}$$

$$= \frac{\$1{,}215{,}000}{27{,}000 \text{ direct manufacturing labor-hours}}$$

$$= \$45 \text{ per direct manufacturing labor-hour}$$

Step 6: Compute the Indirect Costs Allocated to the Job. The indirect costs of a job are computed by multiplying the actual quantity of each different allocation base (one allocation base for each cost pool) associated with the job by the indirect cost rate of each allocation base (computed in Step 5). Recall that Robinson's managers selected direct manufacturing labor-hours as the only cost-allocation base. Out of the 27,000 total direct manufacturing labor-hours for 2008, Robinson uses 88 direct manufacturing labor-hours on the WPP 298 job. Manufacturing overhead costs allocated to WPP 298 equal \$3,960 (\$45 per direct manufacturing labor-hour × 88 hours) and appear in the Manufacturing Overhead panel of the WPP 298 job-cost record in Exhibit 4-2.

Step 7: Compute the Total Cost of the Job by Adding All Direct and Indirect Costs Assigned to the Job. Exhibit 4-2 shows that the total manufacturing costs of the WPP job are \$10,145.

Direct manufacturing costs		
Direct materials	\$4,606	
Direct manufacturing labor	1,579	\$ 6,185
Manufacturing overhead costs		
(\$45 per direct manuf. labor-hour × 88 hours)		3,960
Total manufacturing costs of job WPP 298		\$10,145

Recall that Robinson bid a price of \$15,000 for the job. At that revenue, the actual-costing system shows a gross margin of \$4,855 (\$15,000 − \$10,145) and a gross-margin percentage of 32.4% (\$4,855 ÷ \$15,000 = 0.324).

Robinson's manufacturing managers and sales managers can use the gross-margin and gross-margin percentage calculations to compare the profitability of different jobs (see Concepts in Action on p. 106) to try to understand the reasons why some jobs show low profitability. Have direct materials been wasted? Was direct manufacturing labor too high? Were there ways to improve the efficiency of these jobs? Were these jobs simply underpriced? Job-cost analysis provides the information needed for judging the performance of manufacturing and sales managers and for making future improvements.

Exhibit 4-4 is an overview of Robinson Company's job-costing system. This exhibit represents the concepts comprising the five building blocks—cost object, direct costs of a cost object, indirect costs of a cost object, indirect-cost pool, and cost-allocation base—of job-costing systems that were first introduced at the beginning of this chapter. Costing-system overviews such as Exhibit 4-4 are important learning tools. We urge you to sketch one when you need to understand a costing system in manufacturing, merchandising, or service companies. (The symbols in Exhibit 4-4 are used consistently in the costing-system overviews presented in this book. A triangle always identifies a direct cost; a rectangle represents the indirect-cost pool; and an octagon describes the cost-allocation base.) Note the parallel between the overview diagram and the cost of the WPP 298 job described in Step 7. Exhibit 4-4 shows two direct-cost categories (direct materials and direct manufacturing labor) and one indirect-cost category (manufacturing overhead) used to allocate

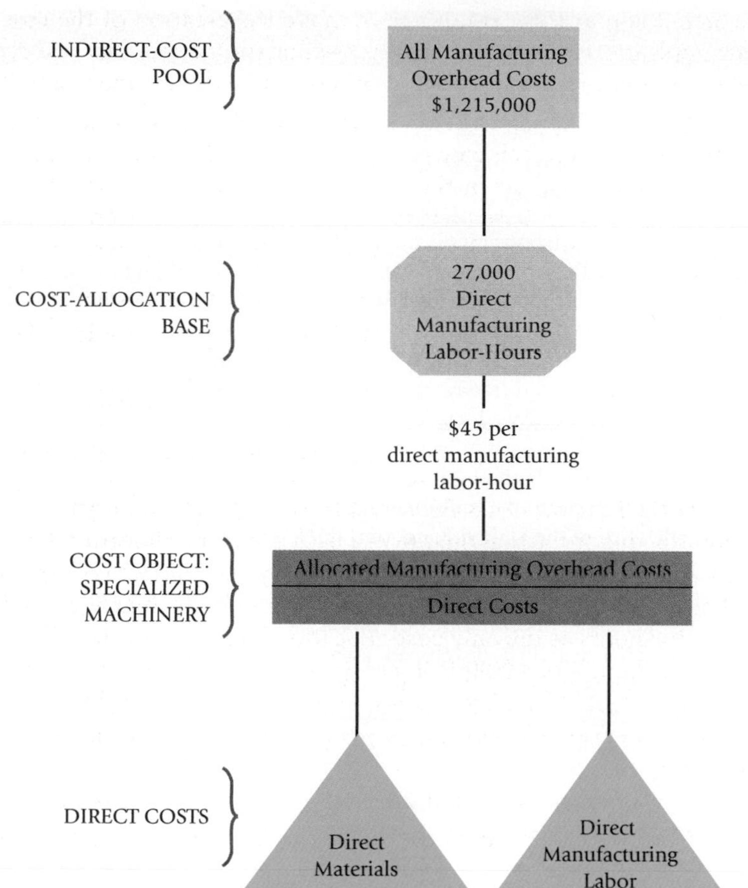

Exhibit 4-4

Job-Costing Overview for Determining Manufacturing Costs of Jobs at Robinson Company

indirect costs. The costs in Step 7 also have three dollar amounts, each corresponding respectively to the two direct-cost and one indirect-cost categories.

The Role of Technology

To improve the efficiency of their operations, managers use costing information about products and jobs to control materials, labor, and overhead costs. Modern information technology provides managers with quick and accurate product-cost information, making it easier to manage and control jobs. For example, in many costing systems, source documents exist only in the form of computer records. We next describe bar coding and other forms of online information recording that reduce human intervention and improve the accuracy of the records of materials and labor time for individual jobs.

Consider, for example, direct materials charged to jobs for product-costing purposes. Managers control these costs as materials are purchased and used. Using Electronic Data Interchange (EDI) technology, companies like Robinson order materials from their suppliers by clicking a few keys on a computer keyboard. EDI, an electronic computer link between a company and its suppliers, ensures that the order is transmitted quickly and accurately with minimum paperwork and costs. A bar code scanner records the receipt of incoming materials. The computer matches the receipt with the order, prints out a check to the supplier, and records the material received. When an operator on the production floor transmits a request for materials via a computer terminal, the computer prepares a materials-requisition record, instantly recording the issue of materials in the materials and job-cost records. Each day, the computer sums the materials-requisition records charged to a particular job or manufacturing department. A performance report is then prepared comparing budgeted costs and actual costs of direct materials. Direct material usage can be reported hourly—if the benefits exceed the cost of such frequent reporting.

Similarly, information about direct manufacturing labor is obtained as employees log into computer terminals and key in the job numbers, their employee numbers, and start

Concepts in Action

Job Costing on the Next-Generation Military Fighter Plane

Northrop Grumman, Inc. is a leading provider of systems and technologies for the U.S. Department of Defense. Competitive bidding processes and increased public and congressional oversight make understanding costs critical in pricing decisions, as well as in winning and retaining government contracts. Each job must be estimated individually because the unique end-products demand different amounts of Northrop Grumman's resources.

The team of Northrop Grumman, Lockheed Martin, and BAE Systems was awarded the System Design and Demonstration contract to build the F-35 Lightning II aircraft—also known as the Joint Strike Fighter—in late 2001. This project, worth over $200 billion over at least seven years, will create a family of supersonic, multi-role fighter airplanes designed for the U.S. Air Force, Navy, and Marine Corps, as well as militaries of the United Kingdom, Italy, The Netherlands, Turkey, Canada, Australia, Denmark, and Norway.

The F-35 Lightning II project has five primary stages: (1) conceptualization, (2) design and review, (3) manufacturing, (4) assembly, and (5) testing and delivery. In the conceptualization phase, detailed plans for each aircraft model are created. Technologies for these plans are researched, developed, and approved during the design and review phase. Subsequently, thousands of components, created by the primary contractors and various subcontractors, are manufactured, assembled in multiple locations, and tested prior to delivery to the purchasing organizations. Finally, the aircraft is assembled and tested prior to delivery. In December 2006, the F-35 Lightning II production model successfully completed its first test flight.

To ensure proper allocation and accounting of resources, F-35 Lightning II project managers use a job-costing system. The system first calculates the budgeted cost of direct materials and direct-labor hours for the project. It then allocates all overhead costs (supervisor salaries, rent, depreciation, materials handling, and so on) to jobs using budgeted direct material costs and direct-labor hours as allocation bases. Northrop Grumman's job-costing system allows managers to assign costs to processes and projects. Northrop Grumman continually estimates the profitability of these projects based on the percentage of work completed and the related revenue earned. Managers use the job-costing system to actively manage costs, while program representatives from the Department of Defense and members of Congress have access to clear, concise, and transparent costing data.

Sources: Conversations with Northrop Grumman, Inc. management, www.jsf.mil, and various program announcements and press releases.

and end times of their work on different jobs. The computer automatically prints the labor time record and, using hourly rates stored for each employee, calculates the direct manufacturing labor costs of individual jobs. Information technology also provides managers with instantaneous feedback to help control manufacturing overhead costs, jobs in process, jobs completed, and jobs shipped and installed at customer sites.

Time Period Used to Compute Indirect-Cost Rates

Robinson Company computes indirect-cost rates in Step 5 of the job-costing system (p. 104) on an annual basis. Why doesn't Robinson calculate indirect-cost rates each week? or each month? If Robinson could calculate actual indirect cost rates each week or each month, Robinson would be able to calculate actual costs of jobs much earlier and not have to wait until the end of the fiscal year. There are two reasons for using longer periods, such as a year, to calculate indirect-cost rates. One reason is related to the dollar amount in the numerator. The other reason is related to the quantity of the cost-allocation base in the denominator of the calculation.

1. **The numerator reason (indirect-cost pool).** The shorter the period, the greater the influence of seasonal patterns on the amount of costs. For example, if indirect-cost

rates were calculated each month, costs of heating (included in the numerator) would be charged to production only during the winter months. But an annual period incorporates the effects of all four seasons into a single, annual indirect-cost rate.

Levels of total indirect costs are also affected by nonseasonal erratic costs. Examples of nonseasonal erratic costs include costs incurred in a particular month that benefit operations during future months, such as costs of repairs and maintenance of equipment, and costs of vacation and holiday pay. If monthly indirect-cost rates were calculated, jobs done in a month with high, nonseasonal erratic costs would be charged with these costs. Pooling all indirect costs together over the course of a full year and calculating a single annual indirect-cost rate helps to smooth some of the erratic bumps in costs associated with shorter periods.

2. **The denominator reason (quantity of the cost-allocation base).** Another reason for longer periods is the need to spread monthly fixed indirect costs over fluctuating levels of monthly output and hence fluctuating quantities of the cost-allocation base. Consider the following example.

Suppose a company deliberately schedules its production to correspond with a highly seasonal sales pattern. Assume the following mix of variable indirect costs (such as supplies, repairs, and indirect manufacturing labor) that vary with the quantity of the cost-allocation base and fixed indirect costs (plant depreciation and engineering support) that do not vary with the quantity of the cost-allocation base:

	Indirect Costs			Direct Manufacturing Labor-Hours	Allocation Rate per Direct Manufacturing Labor-Hour
	Variable (1)	Fixed (2)	Total (3)	(4)	(5) = (3) ÷ (4)
High-output month	$40,000	$60,000	$100,000	3,200	$31.25
Low-output month	10,000	60,000	70,000	800	87.50

You can see that variable indirect costs change in proportion to changes in direct manufacturing labor-hours. Therefore, the variable indirect-cost rate is the same in both the high-output months and the low-output months ($40,000 ÷ 3,200 labor-hours = $12.50 per labor-hour; $10,000 ÷ 800 labor-hours = $12.50 per labor-hour). Sometimes overtime payments or excessive machine maintenance can cause the variable indirect-cost rate to be higher in high-output months. In such cases, variable indirect costs should be allocated at a higher rate to production in high-output months relative to production in low-output months.

Consider now the fixed costs of $60,000. The fixed costs cause monthly total indirect-cost rates to vary considerably—from $31.25 per hour to $87.50 per hour. Few managers believe that identical jobs done in different months should be allocated indirect-cost charges per hour that differ so significantly ($87.50 ÷ $31.25 = 2.80, or 280%) because of fixed costs. Furthermore, if bids are based on costs, bids would be high in low-output months leading to lost bids, when in fact management wants to accept more bids to utilize idle capacity. In our example, management chose a specific level of capacity based on a time horizon far beyond a mere month. An average, annualized rate based on the relationship of total annual indirect costs to the total annual level of output will smooth the effect of monthly variations in output levels.

There are a couple more reasons for using annual overhead rates. One is that the calculation of monthly indirect-cost rates is affected by the number of Monday-to-Friday workdays in a month. The number of workdays per month varies from 20 to 23 during a year. If separate rates are computed each month, jobs in February would bear a greater share of indirect costs (such as depreciation and property taxes) than jobs in other months because February has the fewest workdays in a month. Many managers believe such results to be an unrepresentative and unreasonable way to assign indirect costs to jobs. An annual period reduces the effect that the number of working days per month has on unit costs. Another reason is that setting annual overhead rates once a year saves management time that would be needed 12 times per year if overhead rates were set monthly.

Normal Costing

Learning Objective 4

Distinguish actual costing

. . . actual costing uses actual indirect-cost rates

from normal costing

. . . normal costing uses budgeted indirect-cost rates

The difficulty of calculating actual indirect-cost rates on a weekly or monthly basis means managers cannot calculate the actual costs of jobs as they are completed. However, managers, including those at Robinson, want a close approximation of the costs of various jobs regularly during the year, not just at the end of the fiscal year. Managers want manufacturing costs (and other costs, such as marketing costs) for ongoing uses, including pricing jobs, monitoring and managing costs, evaluating the success of the job, learning about what worked and what didn't, bidding on new jobs, and preparing interim financial statements. Because of the need for immediate access to job costs, few companies wait to allocate overhead costs until year-end when the actual manufacturing overhead is finally known. Instead, a *predetermined* or *budgeted* indirect-cost rate is calculated for each cost pool at the beginning of a fiscal year, and overhead costs are allocated to jobs as work progresses. For the numerator and denominator reasons already described, the **budgeted indirect-cost rate** for each cost pool is computed as follows:

$$\text{Budgeted indirect cost rate} = \frac{\text{Budgeted annual indirect costs}}{\text{Budgeted annual quantity of the cost-allocation base}}$$

Using budgeted indirect-cost rates gives rise to normal costing.

Normal costing is a costing system that (1) traces direct costs to a cost object by using the actual direct-cost rates times the actual quantities of the direct-cost inputs and (2) allocates indirect costs based on the *budgeted* indirect-cost rates times the actual quantities of the cost-allocation bases. Both actual costing and normal costing trace direct costs to jobs in the same way. Source documents identify the actual quantities and actual rates of direct materials and direct manufacturing labor for a job as the work is being done. The only difference between costing a job with actual costing and normal costing is that actual costing uses *actual* indirect-cost rates, whereas normal costing uses *budgeted* indirect-cost rates. Exhibit 4-5 distinguishes between actual costing and normal costing.

We illustrate normal costing for the Robinson Company example using the seven-step procedure presented earlier. The following budgeted data for 2008 are for its manufacturing operations:

	Budget
Total manufacturing overhead costs	$1,120,000
Total direct manufacturing labor-hours	28,000

Steps 1 and 2 are exactly as before: Step 1 identifies WPP 298 as the cost object; Step 2 calculates actual direct material costs of $4,606, and actual direct manufacturing labor costs of $1,579. Recall from Step 3 that Robinson uses a single cost-allocation base, direct manufacturing labor-hours, to allocate all manufacturing overhead costs to jobs. The budgeted quantity of direct manufacturing labor-hours for 2008 is 28,000 hours. In Step 4, Robinson groups all the indirect manufacturing costs into a single manufacturing overhead cost pool. In Step 5, the budgeted manufacturing overhead rate for 2008 is calculated as:

$$\begin{aligned}\text{Budgeted manufacturing overhead rate} &= \frac{\text{Budgeted annual manufacturing indirect costs}}{\text{Budgeted annual quantity of the cost-allocation base}}\\ &= \frac{\$1{,}120{,}000}{28{,}000 \text{ direct manufacturing labor-hours}}\\ &= \$40 \text{ per direct manufacturing labor-hour}\end{aligned}$$

Exhibit 4-5

Actual Costing and Normal Costing Methods

	Actual Costing	**Normal Costing**
Direct Costs	*Actual direct-cost rates* × actual quantities of direct-cost inputs	*Actual direct-cost rates* × actual quantities of direct-cost inputs
Indirect Costs	*Actual indirect-cost rates* × actual quantities of cost-allocation bases	*Budgeted indirect-cost rates* × actual quantities of cost-allocation bases

In Step 6, under a normal-costing system,

$$\text{Manufacturing overhead costs allocated to WPP 298} = \text{Budgeted manufacturing overhead rate} \times \text{Actual quantity of direct manufacturing labor-hours}$$

$$= \$40 \text{ per direct manuf. labor-hour} \times 88 \text{ direct manufacturing labor-hours}$$

$$= \$3{,}520$$

In Step 7, the cost of the job under normal costing is $9,705, calculated as

Direct manufacturing costs		
Direct materials	$4,606	
Direct manufacturing labor	1,579	$6,185
Manufacturing overhead costs		
($40 per direct manufacturing labor-hour × 88 actual direct manufacturing labor-hours)		3,520
Total manufacturing costs of job		$9,705

The manufacturing cost of the WPP 298 job is lower by $440 under normal costing ($9,705) than it is under actual costing ($10,145) because the budgeted indirect-cost rate is $40 per hour, whereas the actual indirect-cost rate is $45 per hour. That is, ($45 − $40) × 88 actual direct manufacturing labor-hours = $440.

As we discussed previously, manufacturing costs of a job are available much earlier under a normal-costing system. Consequently, Robinson's manufacturing and sales managers can evaluate the profitability of different jobs, the efficiency with which the jobs are done, and the pricing of different jobs as soon as the jobs are completed, while the experience is still fresh in everyone's mind. Another advantage of normal costing is that corrective actions can be implemented much sooner. At the end of the year, though, costs allocated using normal costing will not, in general, equal actual costs incurred. If material, adjustments will need to be made so that the cost of jobs and the costs in various inventory accounts are based on actual rather that normal costing. We describe these adjustments later in the chapter.

A Normal Job-Costing System in Manufacturing

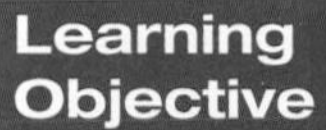

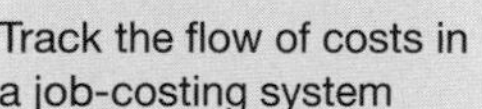

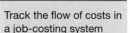

Learning Objective 5

Track the flow of costs in a job-costing system

. . . from purchase of materials to sale of finished goods

We now explain how a normal job-costing system operates in manufacturing. Continuing with the Robinson Company example, the following illustration considers events that occurred in February 2008. Before getting into details, study Exhibit 4-6, which provides a broad framework for understanding the flow of costs in job costing.

The upper part of Exhibit 4-6 shows the flow of inventoriable costs from the purchase of materials and other manufacturing inputs, to their conversion into work-in-process and finished goods, to the sale of finished goods.

Direct materials used and direct manufacturing labor can be easily traced to jobs. They become part of work-in-process inventory on the balance sheet because direct manufacturing labor transforms direct materials into another asset, work-in-process inventory. Robinson also incurs manufacturing overhead costs (including indirect materials and indirect manufacturing labor) to convert direct materials into work-in-process inventory. These overhead (indirect) costs, however, cannot be easily traced to individual jobs. Manufacturing overhead costs, therefore, are first accumulated in a manufacturing overhead account and then allocated to individual jobs. As manufacturing overhead costs are allocated, they become part of work-in-process inventory.

As individual jobs are completed, work-in-process inventory becomes another balance sheet asset, finished goods inventory. Only when finished goods are sold is an expense, cost of goods sold, recognized in the income statement and matched against revenues earned.

The lower part of Exhibit 4-6 shows the period costs—marketing and customer-service costs. These costs do not create any assets on the balance sheet because they are

Exhibit 4-6 Flow of Costs in Job Costing

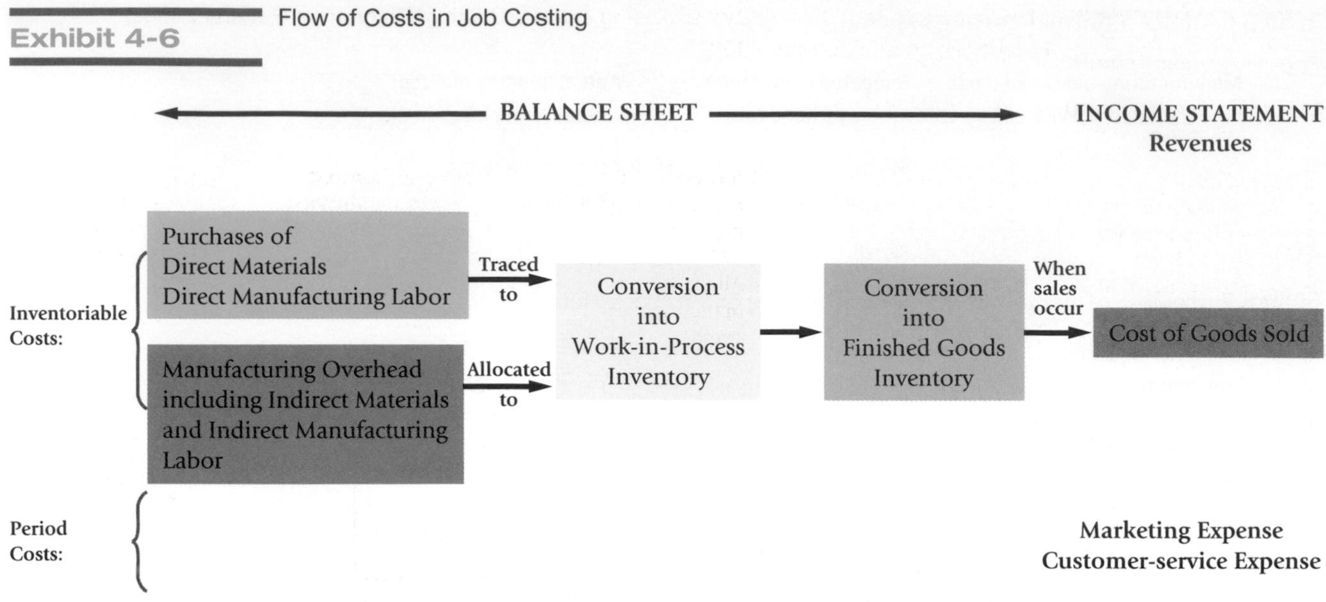

not incurred to transform materials into a finished product. Instead, they are expensed in the income statement as they are incurred to best match revenues.

We next describe the entries made in the general ledger.

General Ledger

You know by this point that a job-costing system has a separate job-cost record for each job. A summary of the job-cost record is typically found in a subsidiary ledger. The general ledger account Work-in-Process Control presents the total of these separate job-cost records pertaining to all unfinished jobs. The job-cost records and Work-in-Process Control account track job costs from when jobs start until they are complete.

Exhibit 4-7 shows T-account relationships for Robinson Company's general ledger. The general ledger gives a "bird's-eye view" of the costing system. The amounts shown in Exhibit 4-7 are based on the transactions and journal entries that follow. As you go through each journal entry, use Exhibit 4-7 to see how the various entries being made come together. General ledger accounts with "Control" in the titles (for example, Materials Control and Accounts Payable Control) have underlying subsidiary ledgers that contain additional details, such as each type of material in inventory and individual suppliers that Robinson must pay.

Software programs process the transactions in most accounting systems. Some programs make general ledger entries simultaneously with entries in the subsidiary ledger accounts. Other software programs make general ledger entries at, say, weekly or monthly intervals, with entries in the subsidiary ledger accounts made more frequently. The Robinson Company makes entries in its subsidiary ledger when transactions occur and then makes entries in its general ledger on a monthly basis.

A general ledger should be viewed as only one of many tools that assist management in planning and control. To control operations, managers rely on not only the source documents used to record amounts in the subsidiary ledgers, but also nonfinancial information such as the percentage of jobs requiring rework.

Explanations of Transactions

We next look at a summary of Robinson Company's transactions for February 2008 and the corresponding journal entries for those transactions.

1. Purchases of materials (direct and indirect) on credit, $89,000

Materials Control	89,000	
Accounts Payable Control		89,000

Exhibit 4-7 Manufacturing Job-Costing System Using Normal Costing: Diagram of General Ledger Relationships for February 2008

GENERAL LEDGER

① Purchase of direct and indirect materials, $89,000
② Usage of direct materials, $81,000, and indirect materials, $4,000

③ Cash paid for direct manufacturing labor, $39,000, and indirect manufacturing labor, $15,000

④ Incurrence of other manufacturing dept. overhead, $75,000
⑤ Allocation of manufacturing overhead, $80,000

⑥ Completion and transfer to finished goods, $188,800
⑦ Cost of goods sold, $180,000

⑧ Incurrence of marketing and customer-service costs, $60,000
⑨ Sales, $270,000

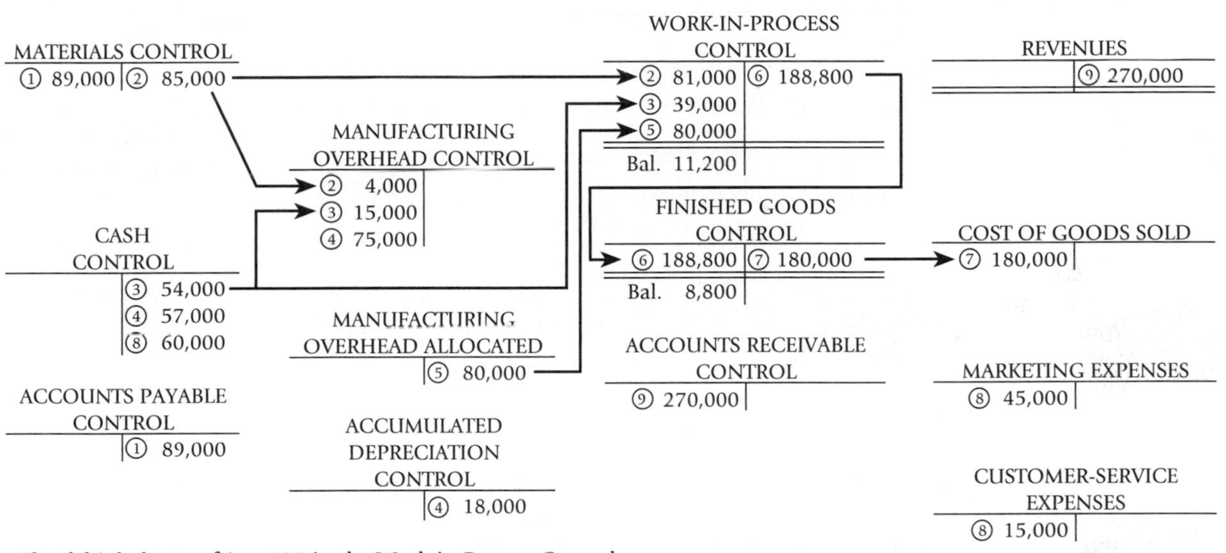

The debit balance of $11,200 in the Work-in-Process Control account represents the total cost of all jobs that have not been completed as of the end of February 2008.

The debit balance of $8,800 in the Finished Goods Control account represents the cost of all jobs that have been completed but not sold as of the end of February 2008.

2. Usage of direct materials, $81,000 and indirect materials, $4,000

Work-in-Process Control	81,000	
Manufacturing Overhead Control	4,000	
Materials Control		85,000

3. Manufacturing payroll for February: direct labor, $39,000 and indirect labor, $15,000 paid in cash

Work-in- Process Control	39,000	
Manufacturing Overhead Control	15,000	
Cash Control		54,000

4. Other manufacturing overhead costs incurred during February, $75,000, consisting of supervision and engineering salaries, $44,000 (paid in cash); plant utilities, repairs, and insurance, $13,000 (paid in cash); and plant depreciation, $18,000

Manufacturing Overhead Control	75,000	
Cash Control		57,000
Accumulated Depreciation Control		18,000

5. Allocation of manufacturing overhead to jobs, $80,000

Work-in-Process Control	80,000	
Manufacturing Overhead Allocated		80,000

Under normal costing, **manufacturing overhead allocated**—also called **manufacturing overhead applied**—is the amount of manufacturing overhead costs allocated to individual jobs based on the budgeted rate multiplied by actual quantity used of the allocation base. Manufacturing overhead allocated contains all manufacturing overhead costs. They are assigned to jobs using a cost-allocation base because these costs cannot be traced specifically to jobs in an economically feasible way.

Keep in mind the distinct difference between transactions 4 and 5. In transaction 4, actual overhead costs incurred throughout the month are added (debited) to the Manufacturing Overhead Control account. These costs are not debited to Work-in-Process Control. Manufacturing overhead costs are added (debited) to Work-in-Process Control *only when* manufacturing overhead costs are allocated in transaction 5. At the time these costs are allocated, Manufacturing Overhead Control is, *in effect,* decreased (credited) via its contra account, Manufacturing Overhead Allocated. Under the normal-costing system described in our illustration, the budgeted manufacturing overhead rate of $40 per direct manufacturing labor-hour is calculated at the beginning of the year on the basis of predictions of annual manufacturing overhead costs and the annual quantity of the cost-allocation base. Almost certainly, the actual amounts allocated will differ from the predictions. In a later section, we discuss what to do with this difference.

6. Completion and transfer of individual jobs to finished goods, $188,800

Finished Goods Control	188,800	
Work-in- Process Control		188,800

7. Cost of goods sold, $180,000

Cost of Goods Sold	180,000	
Finished Goods Control		180,000

8. Marketing costs for February, $45,000 and customer service costs for February $15,000, paid in cash

Marketing Expenses	45,000	
Customer Service Expenses	15,000	
Cash Control		60,000

9. Sales revenues, all on credit, $270,000

Accounts Receivable Control	270,000	
Revenues		270,000

Subsidiary Ledgers

Exhibits 4-8 and 4-9 present subsidiary ledgers that contain the underlying details—the "worm's-eye view" as opposed to the "bird's-eye view" of the general ledger—such as each type of materials in inventory and costs accumulated in individual jobs. The sum of all entries in underlying subsidiary ledgers equals the total amount in the corresponding general ledger control accounts.

Material Records by Type of Materials The subsidiary ledger for materials at Robinson Company—called *Materials Records*— keeps a continuous record of quantity received, quantity issued to jobs, and inventory balances for each type of material. Panel A of Exhibit 4-8 shows the Materials Record for Metal Brackets (Part No. MB 468-A). In many companies, the source documents supporting the receipt and issue of materials are scanned into a computer. Software programs then automatically update the Materials Records and make all the necessary accounting entries in the subsidiary and general ledgers.

As direct materials are used, they are recorded as issued in the Materials Records (see Exhibit 4-8, Panel A, for a record of the Metal Brackets issued for the Western Pulp and Paper [WPP] machine job). Direct materials are also charged to individual job records, which are the subsidiary ledger accounts for the Work-in-Process Control account in the general ledger. For example, the metal brackets used in the WPP machine job appear as direct material costs of $112 in the subsidiary ledger under the job-cost record for WPP 298 (Exhibit 4-9, Panel A). The cost of direct materials used across all job-cost records for February 2008 is $81,000 (Exhibit 4-9, Panel A).

Exhibit 4-8 Subsidiary Ledger for Materials, Labor, and Manufacturing Department Overhead[1]

PANEL A: Materials Records by Type of Materials

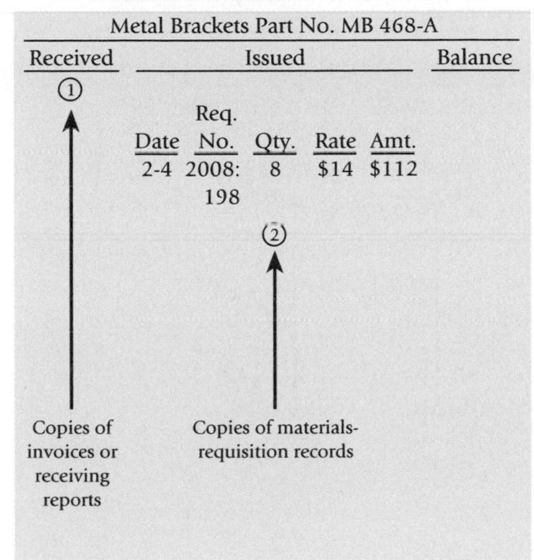

Metal Brackets Part No. MB 468-A

Received	Issued					Balance
	Date	Req. No.	Qty.	Rate	Amt.	
①	2-4	2008: 198	8	$14	$112	
		②				

PANEL B: Labor Records by Employee

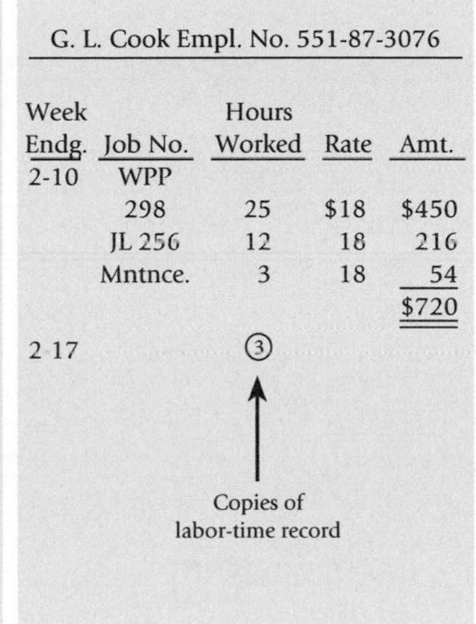

G. L. Cook Empl. No. 551-87-3076

Week Endg.	Job No.	Hours Worked	Rate	Amt.
2-10	WPP 298	25	$18	$450
	JL 256	12	18	216
	Mntnce.	3	18	54
				$720
2-17		③		

PANEL C: Manufacturing Department Overhead Records by Month

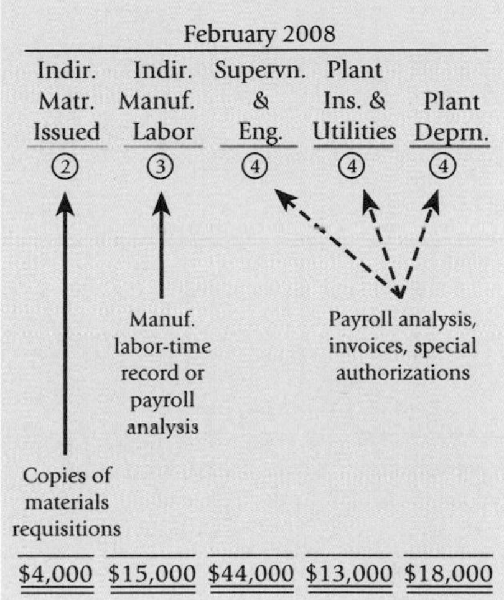

February 2008

Indir. Matr. Issued	Indir. Manuf. Labor	Supervn. & Eng.	Plant Ins. & Utilities	Plant Deprn.
②	③	④	④	④
$4,000	$15,000	$44,000	$13,000	$18,000

Total cost of all types of materials received in February, $89,000

Total cost of all types of materials issued in February, $85,000

Total cost of all direct and indirect manufacturing labor incurred in February, $54,000 ($39,000 + $15,000)

Other manufacturing overhead costs incurred in February, $75,000

[1]The arrows show how the supporting documentation (for example, copies of materials requisition records) results in the journal entry number shown in circles (for example, journal entry number 2) that corresponds to the entries in Exhibit 4-7.

As indirect materials (for example, lubricants) are used, they are charged to the Manufacturing Department overhead records (Exhibit 4-8, Panel C), which comprise the subsidiary ledger for Manufacturing Overhead Control. The Manufacturing Department overhead records accumulate actual costs in individual overhead categories by each indirect-cost-pool account in the general ledger. Recall that Robinson has only one indirect-cost pool: Manufacturing Overhead. The cost of indirect materials used is not added directly to individual job records. Instead, the cost of these indirect materials is allocated to individual job records as a part of manufacturing overhead.

Labor Records by Employee Labor-time records (see Exhibit 4-8, Panel B) are used to trace direct manufacturing labor to individual jobs and to accumulate the indirect manufacturing labor in Manufacturing Department overhead records (Exhibit 4-8, Panel C). The subsidiary ledger for employee labor records shows the different jobs that G. L. Cook, Employee No. 551-87-3076 worked on and the $720 of wages owed to Cook, for the week ending February 10. The sum of total wages owed to all employees for February 2008 is $54,000. The job-cost record for WPP 298 shows direct manufacturing labor costs of $450 for the time Cook spent on the WPP machine job (Exhibit 4-9, Panel A). Total direct manufacturing labor costs recorded in all job-cost records (the subsidiary ledger for Work-in-Process Control) for February 2008 is $39,000.

G. L. Cook's employee record shows $54 for maintenance, which is an indirect manufacturing labor cost. The total indirect manufacturing labor costs of $15,000 for February 2008 appear in the Manufacturing Department overhead records in the subsidiary ledger (Exhibit 4-8, Panel C). These costs, by definition, are not traced to an individual job. Instead, they are allocated to individual jobs as a part of manufacturing overhead.

Manufacturing Department Overhead Records by Month The Manufacturing Department overhead records (see Exhibit 4-8, Panel C) that make up the subsidiary

Exhibit 4-9 Subsidiary Ledger for Individual Jobs[1]

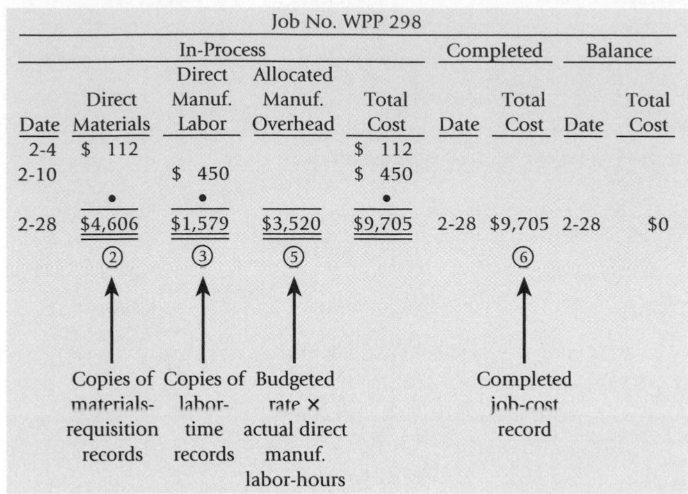

PANEL A: Work-in-Process Inventory Records by Jobs

Job No. WPP 298								
In-Process					Completed		Balance	
Date	Direct Materials	Direct Manuf. Labor	Allocated Manuf. Overhead	Total Cost	Date	Total Cost	Date	Total Cost
2-4	$ 112			$ 112				
2-10		$ 450		$ 450				
	•	•		•				
2-28	$4,606	$1,579	$3,520	$9,705	2-28	$9,705	2-28	$0
	②	③	⑤			⑥		

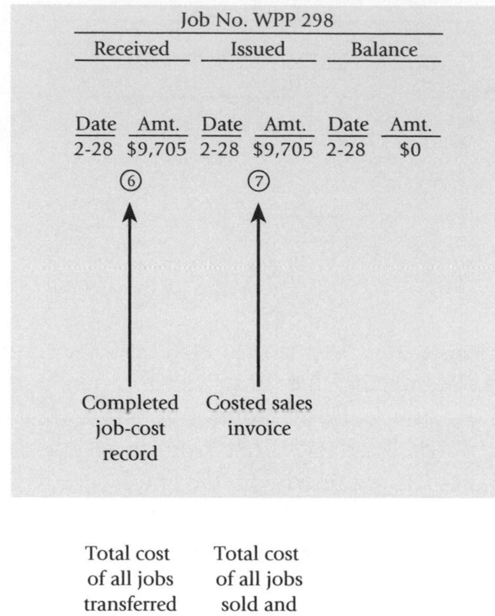

PANEL B: Finished Goods Inventory Records by Job

Job No. WPP 298					
Received		Issued		Balance	
Date	Amt.	Date	Amt.	Date	Amt.
2-28	$9,705	2-28	$9,705	2-28	$0
	⑥		⑦		

Total cost of direct materials issued to all jobs in Feb., $81,000

Total cost of direct manuf. labor used on all jobs in Feb., $39,000

Total manuf. overhead allocated to all jobs in Feb., $80,000

Total cost of all jobs completed and transferred to finished goods in Feb., $188,800

Total cost of all jobs transferred to finished goods in Feb., $188,800

Total cost of all jobs sold and invoiced in Feb., $180,000

[1]The arrows show how the supporting documentation (for example, copies of materials requisition records) results in the journal entry number shown in circles (for example, journal entry number 2) that corresponds to the entries in Exhibit 4-7.

ledger for Manufacturing Overhead Control show details of different categories of overhead costs such as indirect materials, indirect manufacturing labor, supervision and engineering, plant insurance and utilities, and plant depreciation. The source documents for these entries include invoices (for example, a utility bill) and special schedules (for example, a depreciation schedule) from the responsible accounting officer.

Work-in-Process Inventory Records by Jobs As we have already discussed, the job-cost record for each individual job in the subsidiary ledger will be debited by the cost of direct materials and direct manufacturing labor used by individual jobs. The job-cost record for each individual job in the subsidiary ledger will also be debited for manufacturing overhead allocated for the actual direct manufacturing labor-hours used in that job. For example, the job-cost record for Job WPP 298 (Exhibit 4-9, Panel A) shows Manufacturing Overhead Allocated of \$3,520 (budgeted rate of \$40 per labor-hour × 88 actual direct manufacturing labor-hours used). We assume 2,000 actual direct manufacturing labor-hours were used for all jobs in February 2008, resulting in a total manufacturing overhead allocation of \$40 per labor-hour × 2,000 direct manufacturing labor-hours = \$80,000.

Finished Goods Inventory Records by Jobs Exhibit 4-9, Panel A, shows that Job WPP 298 was completed at a cost of \$9,705. Job WPP 298 also simultaneously appears in the finished goods records of the subsidiary ledger. Given Robinson's use of normal costing, cost of goods completed consists of actual direct materials, actual direct manufacturing labor, and manufacturing overhead allocated to each job based on the budgeted manufacturing overhead rate times actual direct manufacturing labor-hours.

Exhibit 4-9, Panel B, indicates that Job WPP 298 was sold and delivered to the customer on February 28, 2008.

Other Subsidiary Records Just as in the case of the manufacturing payroll, Robinson maintains employee labor records in subsidiary ledgers for marketing and customer service payroll as well as records for different types of advertising costs (print, television, and radio). An accounts receivable subsidiary ledger is also used to record the February 2008 amounts due from each customer, including the $15,000 due from the sale of Job WPP 298.

At this point, pause and review the nine entries in this illustration. Exhibit 4-7 is a handy summary of all nine general-ledger entries presented in T-account form. Be sure to trace each journal entry, step-by-step, to T-accounts in the general ledger presented in Exhibit 4-7.

Exhibit 4-10 provides Robinson's income statement for February 2008 using information from entries 7, 8, and 9. If desired, the cost of goods sold calculations can be further subdivided and presented in the format of Exhibit 2-8, page 41.

Nonmanufacturing Costs and Job Costing Chapter 2 (pp. 26–59) pointed out that companies use product costs for different purposes. The product costs reported as inventoriable costs to shareholders may differ from product costs reported for government contracting and may also differ from product costs reported to managers for guiding pricing and product-mix decisions. We emphasize that even though, as described previously, marketing and customer-service costs are expensed when incurred for financial accounting purposes, companies often trace or allocate these costs to individual jobs for pricing, product-mix, and cost-management decisions.

To identify marketing and customer-service costs of individual jobs, Robinson can use the same approach to job costing described earlier in this chapter in the context of manufacturing. Robinson can trace the direct marketing costs and customer-service costs to jobs. Assume marketing and customer-service costs have the same cost-allocation base, revenues, and are included in a single cost pool. Robinson can then calculate a budgeted indirect-cost rate by dividing budgeted indirect marketing costs plus budgeted indirect customer-service costs by budgeted revenues. Robinson can use this rate to allocate these indirect costs to jobs. For example, if this rate were 15% of revenues, Robinson would allocate $2,250 to Job WPP 298 (0.15 × $15,000, the revenue from the job). By assigning both manufacturing costs and nonmanufacturing costs to jobs, Robinson can compare all costs against the revenues that different jobs generate.

Budgeted Indirect Costs and End-of-Accounting-Year Adjustments

Using budgeted indirect-cost rates and normal costing instead of actual costing has the advantage that indirect costs can be assigned to individual jobs on an ongoing and timely

Exhibit 4-10

Robinson Company Income Statement for the Month Ending February 2008

Revenues		$270,000
Cost of goods sold ($180,000 + $14,000[1])		194,000
Gross margin		76,000
Operating costs		
Marketing costs	$45,000	
Customer-service costs	15,000	
Total operating costs		60,000
Operating income		$ 16,000

[1]Cost of goods sold has been increased by $14,000, the difference between the Manufacturing overhead control account ($94,000) and the Manufacturing overhead allocated ($80,000). In a later section of this chapter, we discuss this adjustment, which represents the amount by which actual manufacturing overhead cost exceeds the manufacturing overhead allocated to jobs during February 2008.

basis, rather than only at the end of the fiscal year when actual costs are known. However, budgeted rates are unlikely to equal actual rates because they are based on estimates made up to 12 months before actual costs are incurred. We now consider adjustments that are needed when, at the end of the fiscal year, indirect costs allocated differ from actual indirect costs incurred. Recall that for the numerator and denominator reasons discussed earlier (pp. 106–107), we do *not* expect actual overhead costs incurred each month to equal overhead costs allocated each month.

Learning Objective 6

Dispose of under- or overallocated manufacturing overhead costs at the end of the fiscal year using alternative methods

. . . for example, writing off this amount to the Cost of Goods Sold account

Underallocated indirect costs occur when the allocated amount of indirect costs in an accounting period is less than the actual (incurred) amount. **Overallocated indirect costs** occur when the allocated amount of indirect costs in an accounting period is greater than the actual (incurred) amount.

Underallocated (overallocated) indirect costs = Actual indirect costs incurred − Indirect costs allocated

Underallocated (overallocated) indirect costs are also called **underapplied (overapplied) indirect costs** and **underabsorbed (overabsorbed) indirect costs.**

Consider the manufacturing overhead indirect-cost pool at Robinson Company. There are two indirect-cost accounts in the general ledger that have to do with manufacturing overhead:

1. Manufacturing Overhead Control, the record of the actual costs in all the individual overhead categories (such as indirect materials, indirect manufacturing labor, supervision, engineering, utilities, and plant depreciation)
2. Manufacturing Overhead Allocated, the record of the manufacturing overhead allocated to individual jobs on the basis of the budgeted rate multiplied by actual direct manufacturing labor-hours

Assume the following annual data for the Robinson Company:

Manufacturing Overhead Control			Manufacturing Overhead Allocated	
Bal. Dec 31, 2008	1,215,000		Bal. Dec 31, 2008	1,080,000

The $1,080,000 credit balance in Manufacturing Overhead Allocated results from multiplying the 27,000 actual direct manufacturing labor-hours worked on all jobs in 2008 by the budgeted rate of $40 per direct manufacturing labor-hour.

The $135,000 difference (a net debit) is an underallocated amount because actual manufacturing overhead costs are greater than the allocated amount. This difference arises from two reasons related to the computation of the $40 budgeted hourly rate:

1. **Numerator reason (indirect-cost pool).** Actual manufacturing overhead costs of $1,215,000 are greater than the budgeted amount of $1,120,000.
2. **Denominator reason (quantity of allocation base).** Actual direct manufacturing labor-hours of 27,000 are fewer than the budgeted 28,000 hours.

There are three main approaches to accounting for the $135,000 underallocated manufacturing overhead caused by Robinson underestimating manufacturing overhead costs and overestimating the quantity of the cost-allocation base: (1) adjusted allocation-rate approach, (2) proration approach, and (3) write-off to cost of goods sold approach.

Adjusted Allocation-Rate Approach

The **adjusted allocation-rate approach** restates all overhead entries in the general ledger and subsidiary ledgers using actual cost rates rather than budgeted cost rates. First, the actual manufacturing overhead rate is computed at the end of the fiscal year. Then, the manufacturing overhead costs allocated to every job during the year are recomputed using the actual manufacturing overhead rate (rather than the budgeted manufacturing overhead rate). Finally, end-of-year closing entries are made. The result is that at year-end, every job-cost record and finished goods record—as well as the ending Work-in-Process Control, Finished Goods Control, and Cost of Goods Sold accounts—represent actual manufacturing overhead costs incurred.

The widespread adoption of computerized accounting systems has greatly reduced the cost of using the adjusted allocation-rate approach. Consider the Robinson example. The actual manufacturing overhead ($1,215,000) exceeds the manufacturing overhead allocated ($1,080,000) by 12.5% [($1,215,000 − $1,080,000) ÷ $1,080,000]. At year-end, Robinson could increase the manufacturing overhead allocated to each job in 2008 by 12.5% using a single software command. The command would adjust both the subsidiary ledgers and the general ledger.

Consider the Western Pulp and Paper machine job, WPP 298. Under normal costing, the manufacturing overhead allocated to the job is $3,520 (the budgeted rate of $40 per direct manufacturing labor-hour × 88 hours). Increasing the manufacturing overhead allocated by 12.5%, or $440 ($3,520 × 0.125), means the adjusted amount of manufacturing overhead allocated to Job WPP 298 equals $3,960 ($3,520 + $440). Note from page 104 that using actual costing, manufacturing overhead allocated to this job is also $3,960 (the actual rate of $45 per direct manufacturing labor-hour × 88 hours). Making this adjustment under normal costing for each job in the subsidiary ledgers ensures that all $1,215,000 of manufacturing overhead is allocated to jobs.

The adjusted allocation-rate approach yields the benefits of both the *timeliness and convenience of normal costing during the year and the allocation of actual manufacturing overhead costs at year-end*. Each individual job-cost record and the end-of-year account balances for inventories and cost of goods sold are adjusted to actual costs. After-the-fact analysis of actual profitability of individual jobs provides managers with accurate and useful insights for future decisions about job pricing, which jobs to emphasize, and ways to manage job costs.

Proration Approach

Proration spreads underallocated overhead or overallocated overhead among ending work in process inventory, finished goods inventory, and cost of goods sold. Materials inventory is not included in this proration because no manufacturing overhead costs have been allocated to it. In our Robinson example, end-of-year proration is made to the ending balances in Work-in-Process Control, Finished Goods Control, and Cost of Goods Sold. Assume the following actual results for Robinson Company in 2008:

	A	B	C
1	Account	Account Balance (Before Proration)	Allocated Manufacturing Overhead Included in Each Account Balance (Before Proration)
2	Work in process control	$ 50,000	$ 16,200
3	Finished goods control	75,000	31,320
4	Cost of goods sold	2,375,000	1,032,480
5		$2,500,000	$1,080,000

How should Robinson prorate the underallocated $135,000 of manufacturing overhead at the end of 2008?

Robinson prorates underallocated or overallocated amounts on the basis of the total amount of manufacturing overhead allocated in 2008 (before proration) in the ending balances of Work-in-Process Control, Finished Goods Control, and Cost of Goods Sold. The $135,000 underallocated overhead is prorated over the three affected accounts in proportion to their total amount of manufacturing overhead allocated (before proration) in column 2 of the following table, resulting in the ending balances (after proration) in column 5 at actual costs.

	A	B	C	D	E	F	G
10		Account Balance (Before Proration)	Allocated Manufacturing Overhead Included in Each Account Balance (Before Proration)	Allocated Manufacturing Overhead Included in Each Account Balance as a Percent of Total	Proration of $135,000 of Underallocated Manufacturing Overhead		Account Balance (After Proration)
11	Account	(1)	(2)	(3) = (2) / $1,080,000	(4) = (3) x $135,000		(5) = (1) + (4)
12	Work in process control	$ 50,000	$ 16,200	1.5%	0.015 x $135,000 =	$ 2,025	$ 52,025
13	Finished goods control	75,000	31,320	2.9%	0.029 x 135,000 =	3,915	78,915
14	Cost of goods sold	2,375,000	1,032,480	95.6%	0.956 x 135,000 =	129,060	2,504,060
15	Total	$2,500,000	$1,080,000	100.0%		$135,000	$2,635,000

Prorating on the basis of the manufacturing overhead allocated (before proration) results in allocating manufacturing overhead based on actual manufacturing overhead costs. Recall that the actual manufacturing overhead ($1,215,000) in 2008 exceeds the manufacturing overhead allocated ($1,080,000) in 2008 by 12.5%. The proration amounts in column 4 can also be derived by multiplying the balances in column 2 by 0.125. For example, the $3,915 proration to Finished Goods is 0.125 × $31,320. Adding these amounts effectively means allocating manufacturing overhead at 112.5% of what had been allocated before. The journal entry to record this proration is:

Work-in-Process Control	2,025	
Finished Goods Control	3,915	
Cost of Goods Sold	129,060	
Manufacturing Overhead Allocated	1,080,000	
Manufacturing Overhead Control		1,215,000

If manufacturing overhead had been overallocated, the Work-in-Process Control, Finished Goods Control, and Cost of Goods Sold accounts would be decreased (credited) instead of increased (debited).

This journal entry closes (brings to zero) the manufacturing overhead-related accounts and restates the 2008 ending balances for Work-in-Process Control, Finished Goods Control, and Cost of Goods Sold to what they would have been if actual manufacturing overhead rates had been used rather than budgeted manufacturing overhead rates. This method reports the same 2008 ending balances in the general ledger as the adjusted allocation-rate approach.

Some companies use the proration approach but base it on the column 1 amounts of the preceding table—that is, the ending balances of Work-in-Process Control, Finished Goods Control, and Cost of Goods Sold before proration. The following table shows that prorations based on ending account balances are not the same as the more-accurate prorations calculated earlier based on the amount of manufacturing overhead allocated to the accounts because the proportions of manufacturing overhead costs to total costs in these accounts are not the same.

	A	B	C	D	E	F
1		Account Balance (Before Proration)	Account Balance as a Percent of Total	Proration of $135,000 of Underallocated Manufacturing Overhead		Account Balance (After Proration)
2	Account	(1)	(2) = (1) / $2,500,000	(3) = (2) x $135,000		(4) = (1) + (3)
3	Work in process control	$ 50,000	2.0%	0.02 x $135,000 =	$ 2,700	$ 52,700
4	Finished goods control	75,000	3.0%	0.03 x 135,000 =	4,050	79,050
5	Cost of goods sold	2,375,000	95.0%	0.95 x 135,000 =	128,250	2,503,250
6	Total	$2,500,000	100.0%		$135,000	$2,635,000

However, proration based on ending balances is frequently justified as being an expedient way of approximating the more-accurate results from using indirect costs allocated.

Write-Off to Cost of Goods Sold Approach

Under this approach, the total under- or overallocated manufacturing overhead is included in this year's Cost of Goods Sold. For Robinson, the journal entry would be:

Cost of Goods Sold	135,000	
Manufacturing Overhead Allocated	1,080,000	
Manufacturing Overhead Control		1,215,000

Robinson's two Manufacturing Overhead accounts are closed with the difference between them included in cost of goods sold. The Cost of Goods Sold account after the write-off equals $2,510,000, the balance before the write-off of $2,375,000 *plus the underallocated* manufacturing overhead amount of $135,000.

Choice Among Approaches

Which of these three approaches is the best one to use? In making this decision, managers should be guided by the causes for underallocation or overallocation and how the information will be used. Many management accountants, industrial engineers, and managers argue that to the extent that the under- or overallocated overhead cost measures inefficiency during the period, it should be written off to Cost of Goods Sold instead of being prorated. This line of reasoning argues for applying a combination of the write-off and proration methods. For example, the portion of the underallocated overhead cost that is due to inefficiency (say, because of excessive spending) and that could have been avoided should be written off to Cost of Goods Sold, whereas the portion that is unavoidable should be prorated. Unlike full proration, this approach avoids carrying the costs of inefficiency as part of inventory assets.

Proration should be based on the manufacturing overhead allocated component in the ending balances of Work-in-Process Control, Finished Goods Control, and Cost of Goods Sold. Prorating to each individual job (as in the adjusted allocation-rate approach) is useful if the goal is to develop the most accurate record of individual job costs for profitability analysis purposes.

The write-off to Cost of Goods Sold is the simplest approach for dealing with under- or overallocated overhead. If the amount of under- or overallocated overhead is small—in comparison with total operating income or some other measure of materiality—the write-off to Cost of Goods Sold approach yields a good approximation to more-accurate, but more-complex, approaches. Companies are also becoming increasingly conscious of inventory control, and quantities of inventories are lower than they were in earlier years. As a result, cost of goods sold tends to be higher in relation to the dollar amount of work-in-process and finished goods inventories. Also, the inventory balances of job-costing companies are usually small because goods are often made in response to customer orders. Consequently, as is true in our Robinson example, writing off, instead of prorating, under- or overallocated overhead is unlikely to result in significant distortions in financial statements.

Note that regardless of which of the three approaches is used, the underallocated overhead is not carried in the overhead accounts beyond the end of the fiscal year. Why? Because the ending balances in Manufacturing Overhead Control and Manufacturing Overhead Allocated are closed to Work-in-Process Control, Finished Goods Control, and Cost of Goods Sold, and therefore become zero at the end of each year.

Multiple Overhead Cost Pools

The Robinson Company illustration assumed that a single manufacturing overhead cost pool with direct manufacturing labor-hours as the cost-allocation base was appropriate for allocating all manufacturing overhead costs to jobs. Robinson could have used multiple cost-allocation bases, say, direct manufacturing labor-hours and machine-hours, to allocate manufacturing overhead costs to jobs. But Robinson would use multiple cost-allocation bases only if its managers believed that the benefits of the information generated by adding one or more pools (more-accurate costing and pricing of jobs and better ability to manage costs) exceeded the additional costs of that costing system. (We discuss these issues in Chapter 5.)

To implement a normal-costing system with two overhead cost pools, Robinson would determine, say, the budgeted total direct manufacturing labor-hours and the budgeted total machine-hours for 2008, and identify the associated total budgeted overhead costs for each cost pool. It would then calculate two budgeted overhead rates, one based on direct manufacturing labor-hours and the other on machine-hours. Manufacturing overhead costs would be allocated to jobs using these two budgeted overhead rates and the actual direct manufacturing labor-hours and actual machine hours used by various jobs. The general ledger would contain Manufacturing Overhead Control and Manufacturing Overhead Allocated amounts for each cost pool. End-of-year adjustments for under- or overallocated overhead costs would then be made separately for each cost pool.

Variations from Normal Costing: A Service-Sector Example

Apply variations from normal costing

. . . variations from normal costing use budgeted direct-cost rates

Job costing is also very useful in service industries such as accounting and consulting firms, advertising agencies, auto repair shops, and hospitals. In an accounting firm, each audit is a job. The costs of each audit are accumulated in a job-cost record, much like the document used by Robinson Company, based on the seven-step approach described earlier. On the basis of labor-time records, direct labor costs of the professional staff—audit partners, audit managers, and audit staff—are traced to individual jobs. Other direct costs such as travel, out-of-town meals and lodging, phone, fax, and copying are also traced to jobs. The costs of secretarial support, office staff, rent, and depreciation of furniture and equipment are indirect costs because these costs cannot be traced to jobs in an economically feasible way. Indirect costs are allocated to jobs, for example, using a cost-allocation base such as number of professional labor-hours.

In some service organizations, a variation from normal costing is helpful because actual direct-labor costs—the largest component of total costs—can be difficult to trace to jobs as they are completed. For example, in our audit illustration, the actual direct-labor costs may include bonuses that become known only at the end of the year (a numerator reason). Also, the hours worked each period might vary significantly depending on the number of working days each month and the demand from clients (a denominator reason). In situations like these, a company needing timely information during the progress of an audit (and not wanting to wait until the end of the fiscal year) will use budgeted rates for some direct costs and budgeted rates for indirect costs. All budgeted rates are calculated at the start of the fiscal year. In contrast, normal costing uses actual cost rates for all direct costs and budgeted cost rates only for indirect costs.

The mechanics of using budgeted rates for direct costs are similar to the methods employed when using budgeted rates for indirect costs in normal costing. We illustrate this for Lindsay and Associates, a public accounting firm. For 2008, Lindsay budgets total direct-labor costs of \$14,400,000, total indirect costs of \$12,960,000, and total direct (professional) labor-hours of 288,000. In this case,

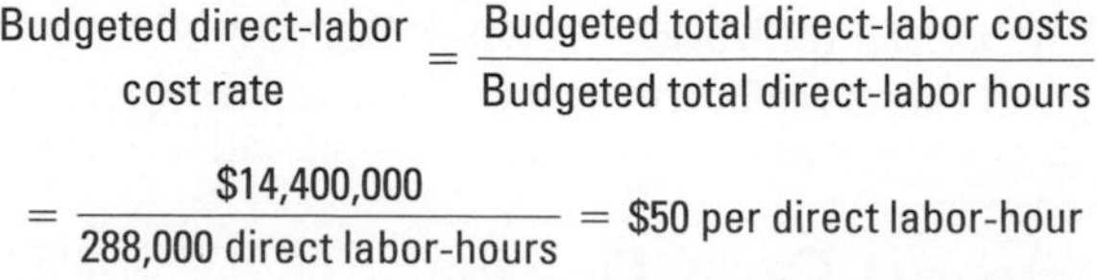

$$\text{Budgeted direct-labor cost rate} = \frac{\text{Budgeted total direct-labor costs}}{\text{Budgeted total direct-labor hours}}$$

$$= \frac{\$14{,}400{,}000}{288{,}000 \text{ direct labor-hours}} = \$50 \text{ per direct labor-hour}$$

Assuming only one indirect-cost pool and total direct-labor costs as the cost-allocation base,

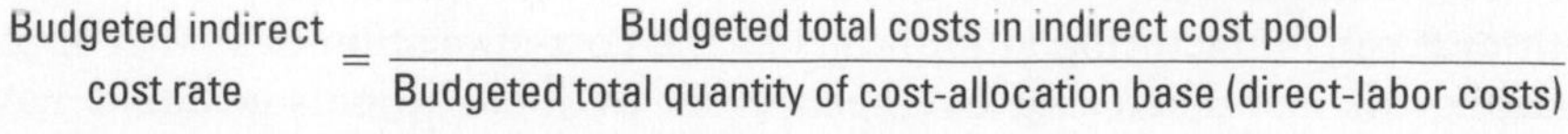

$$\text{Budgeted indirect cost rate} = \frac{\text{Budgeted total costs in indirect cost pool}}{\text{Budgeted total quantity of cost-allocation base (direct-labor costs)}}$$

$$= \frac{\$12{,}960{,}000}{\$14{,}400{,}000} = 0.90\text{, or } 90\% \text{ of direct-labor costs}$$

Suppose that in March 2008, an audit of Tracy Transport, a client of Lindsay, uses 800 direct labor-hours. Lindsay calculates the direct-labor costs of the Tracy Transport audit by multiplying the budgeted direct-labor cost rate, $50 per direct labor-hour, by 800, the actual quantity of direct labor-hours. The indirect costs allocated to the Tracy Transport audit are determined by multiplying the budgeted indirect-cost rate (90%) by the direct-labor costs assigned to the job ($40,000). Assuming no other direct costs for travel and the like, the cost of the Tracy Transport audit is:

Direct-labor costs, $50 × 800	$40,000
Indirect costs allocated, 90% × $40,000	36,000
Total	$76,000

At the end of the fiscal year, the direct costs traced to jobs using budgeted rates will generally not equal actual direct costs because the actual rate and the budgeted rate are developed at different times using different information. End-of-year adjustments for under- or overallocated direct costs would need to be made in the same way that adjustments are made for under- or overallocated indirect costs.

The Lindsay and Associates example illustrates that all costing systems do not exactly match either the actual-costing system or the normal-costing system described earlier in the chapter. As another example, engineering consulting firms often have some actual direct costs (cost of making blueprints or fees paid to outside experts), other direct costs (professional labor costs) assigned to jobs using a budgeted rate, and indirect costs (engineering and office-support costs) allocated to jobs using a budgeted rate. Therefore, users of costing systems should be aware of the different systems that they may encounter.

Problem for Self-Study

You are asked to bring the following incomplete accounts of Endeavor Printing, Inc., up-to-date through January 31, 2009. Consider the data that appear in the T-accounts as well as the following information in items (a) through (j).

Endeavor's normal-costing system has two direct-cost categories (direct material costs and direct manufacturing labor costs) and one indirect-cost pool (manufacturing overhead costs, which are allocated using direct manufacturing labor costs).

Materials Control

12-31-2008 Bal. 15,000	

Wages Payable Control

	1-31-2009 Bal. 3,000

Work-in-Process Control

Manufacturing Overhead Control

1-31-2009 Bal. 57,000	

Finished Goods Control

12-31-2008 Bal. 20,000	

Costs of Goods Sold

Additional Information:

a. Manufacturing overhead is allocated using a budgeted rate that is set every December. Management forecasts next year's manufacturing overhead costs and next year's direct manufacturing labor costs. The budget for 2009 is $600,000 for manufacturing overhead costs and $400,000 for direct manufacturing labor costs.

b. The only job unfinished on January 31, 2009, is No. 419, on which direct manufacturing labor costs are $2,000 (125 direct manufacturing labor-hours) and direct material costs are $8,000.

c. Total direct materials issued to production during January 2009 are $90,000.

d. Cost of goods completed during January is $180,000.

e. Materials inventory as of January 31, 2009, is $20,000.

f. Finished goods inventory as of January 31, 2009, is $15,000.

g. All plant workers earn the same wage rate. Direct manufacturing labor-hours used for January total 2,500 hours. Other labor costs total $10,000.
h. The gross plant payroll paid in January equals $52,000. Ignore withholdings.
i. All "actual" manufacturing overhead incurred during January has already been posted.
j. All materials are direct materials.

Required **Calculate:**

1. Materials purchased during January
2. Cost of Goods Sold during January
3. Direct manufacturing labor costs incurred during January
4. Manufacturing Overhead Allocated during January
5. Balance, Wages Payable Control, December 31, 2008
6. Balance, Work-in-Process Control, January 31, 2009
7. Balance, Work-in-Process Control, December 31, 2008
8. Manufacturing Overhead Underallocated or Overallocated for January 2009

Solution

Amounts from the T-accounts are labeled "(T)"

1. From Materials Control T-account, Materials purchased: $90,000 (c) + $20,000 (e) − $15,000 (T) = $95,000
2. From Finished Goods Control T-account, Cost of Goods Sold: $20,000 (T) + $180,000 (d) − $15,000 (f) = $185,000
3. Direct manufacturing wage rate: $2,000 (b) ÷ 125 direct manufacturing labor-hours (b) = $16 per direct manufacturing labor-hour
   Direct manufacturing labor costs: 2,500 direct manufacturing labor-hours (g) × $16 per hour = $40,000
4. Manufacturing overhead rate: $600,000 (a) ÷ $400,000 (a) = 150%

Manufacturing Overhead Allocated: 150% of $40,000 = 1.50 × $40,000 (see 3) = $60,000

5. From Wages Payable Control T-account, Wages Payable Control, December 31, 2008: $52,000 (h) + $3,000 (T) − $40,000 (see 3) − $10,000 (g) = $5,000
6. Work-in-Process Control, January 31, 2009: $8,000 (b) + $2,000 (b) + 150% of $2,000 (b) = $13,000 (This answer is used in item 7.)
7. From Work-in-Process Control T-account, Work-in-Process Control, December 31, 2008: $180,000 (d) + $13,000 (see 6) − $90,000 (c) − $40,000 (see 3) − $60,000 (see 4) = $3,000
8. Manufacturing overhead overallocated: $60,000 (see 4) − $57,000 (T) = $3,000.

Letters alongside entries in T-accounts correspond to letters in the preceding additional information. Numbers alongside entries in T-accounts correspond to numbers in the requirements above.

Materials Control

December 31,2008 Bal.	(given)	15,000		
	(1)	95,000[1]	(c)	90,000
January 31, 2009 Bal.	(e)	20,000		

[1] Can be computed only after all other postings in the account have been found.

Work-in-Process Control

December 31,2008 Bal.	(7) 3,000		(d) 180,000
Direct materials	(c) 90,000		
Direct manufacturing labor	(b) (g) (3) 40,000		
Manufacturing overhead allocated	(3) (a) (4) 60,000		
January 31, 2009 Bal.	(b) (6) 13,000		

Finished Goods Control

December 31, 2008 Bal.	(given) 20,000		(2) 185,000
	(d) 180,000		
January 31, 2009 Bal.	(f) 15,000		

Wages Payable Control

	(h) 52,000	December 31,2008 Bal.	(5) 5,000
			(g) (3) 40,000
			(g) 10,000
		January 31, 2009	(given) 3,000

Manufacturing Overhead Control

Total January charges	(given) 57,000		

Manufacturing Overhead Allocated

			(3) (a) (4) 60,000

Cost of Goods Sold

	(d) (f) (2) 185,000		

Decision Points

The following question-and-answer format summarizes the chapter's learning objectives. Each decision presents a key question related to a learning objective. The guidelines are the answer to that question.

Decision	Guidelines
1. What are the building-block concepts of a costing system?	The building-block concepts of a costing system are cost object, direct costs of a cost object, indirect costs of a cost object, cost pool, and cost-allocation base. Costing-system overview diagrams represent these concepts in a systematic way. Costing systems aim to report cost numbers that reflect the way chosen cost objects (such as products or services) use the resources of an organization.
2. How do you distinguish job costing from process costing?	Job-costing systems assign costs to distinct units of a product or service. Process-costing systems assign costs to masses of identical or similar units and compute unit costs on an average basis. These two costing systems represent opposite ends of a continuum. The costing systems of many companies combine some elements of both job costing and process costing.
3. How do you implement a job-costing system?	A general seven-step approach to job costing requires identifying (1) the job, (2) the direct-cost categories, (3) the cost-allocation bases, (4) the indirect-cost categories, (5) the cost-allocation rates, (6) the allocated indirect costs of a job, and (7) the total direct and indirect costs of a job.

4. How do you distinguish actual costing from normal costing?	Actual costing and normal costing differ in the type of indirect-cost rates used:

	Actual Costing	Normal Costing
Direct-cost rates	Actual rates	Actual rates
Indirect-cost rates	Actual rates	Budgeted rates

Both systems use actual quantities of inputs for tracing direct costs and actual quantities of the allocation bases for allocating indirect costs.

5. When are transactions recorded in a manufacturing job-costing system?	A job-costing system in manufacturing records the flow of inventoriable costs: (a) acquisition of materials and other manufacturing inputs; (b) their conversion into work in process; (c) their conversion into finished goods; and (d) the sale of finished goods. The job costing system also expenses period costs such as marketing costs as these costs are incurred.
6. How should you dispose of under- or overallocated manufacturing overhead costs at the end of the fiscal year?	The two theoretically correct approaches to disposing of under- or overallocated manufacturing overhead costs at the end of the fiscal year are (1) to adjust the allocation rate and (2) to prorate on the basis of the total amount of the allocated manufacturing overhead cost in the ending balances of Work-in-Process Control, Finished Goods Control, and Cost of Goods Sold. Many companies, however, simply write off amounts of under- or overallocated manufacturing overhead to Cost of Goods Sold when amounts are immaterial.
7. What variations from normal costing can be used?	In some variations from normal costing, organizations use budgeted rates to assign direct costs, as well as indirect costs, to jobs.

TERMS TO LEARN

This chapter and the Glossary at the end of the book contain definitions of:

actual costing (**p. 101**)
actual indirect-cost rate (**p. 104**)
adjusted allocation-rate approach (**p. 116**)
budgeted indirect-cost rate (**p. 108**)
cost-allocation base (**p. 98**)
cost-application base (**p. 98**)
cost pool (**p. 98**)
job (**p. 99**)
job-cost record (**p. 101**)
job-cost sheet (**p. 101**)
job-costing system (**p. 99**)
labor-time record (**p. 102**)
manufacturing overhead allocated (**p. 111**)
manufacturing overhead applied (**p. 111**)
materials-requisition record (**p. 101**)
normal costing (**p. 108**)
overabsorbed indirect costs (**p. 116**)
overallocated indirect costs (**p. 116**)
overapplied indirect costs (**p. 116**)
process-costing system (**p. 99**)
proration (**p. 117**)
source document (**p. 101**)
underabsorbed indirect costs (**p. 116**)
underallocated indirect costs (**p. 116**)
underapplied indirect costs (**p. 116**)

ASSIGNMENT MATERIAL

Questions

4-1 Define cost pool, cost tracing, cost allocation, and cost-allocation base.

4-2 How does a job-costing system differ from a process-costing system?

4-3 Why might an advertising agency use job costing for an advertising campaign by Pepsi, whereas a bank might use process costing to determine the cost of checking account deposits?

4-4 Describe the seven steps in job costing.

4-5 What are the two major cost objects that managers focus on in companies using job costing?

4-6 Describe three major source documents used in job-costing systems.

4-7 What is the main concern about source documents used to prepare job-cost records?

4-8 Give two reasons why most organizations use an annual period rather than a weekly or monthly period to compute budgeted indirect-cost rates.

4-9 Distinguish between actual costing and normal costing.

4-10 Describe two ways in which a house construction company may use job-cost information.

4-11 Comment on the following statement: "In a normal-costing system, the amounts in the Manufacturing Overhead Control account will always equal the amounts in the Manufacturing Overhead Allocated account."

4-12 Describe three different debit entries to the Work-in-Process Control T-account under normal costing.

4-13 Describe three alternative ways to dispose of under- or overallocated overhead costs.

4-14 When might a company use budgeted costs rather than actual costs to compute direct-labor rates?

4-15 Describe briefly why modern technology such as Electronic Data Interchange (EDI) is helpful to managers.

Exercises

4-16 Job costing, process costing. In each of the following situations, determine whether job costing or process costing would be more appropriate.

a. A CPA firm
b. An oil refinery
c. A custom furniture manufacturer
d. A tire manufacturer
e. A textbook publisher
f. A pharmaceutical company
g. An advertising agency
h. An apparel manufacturing plant
i. A flour mill
j. A paint manufacturer
k. A medical care facility
l. A landscaping company
m. A cola-drink-concentrate producer
n. A movie studio
o. A law firm
p. A commercial aircraft manufacturer
q. A management consulting firm
r. A breakfast-cereal company
s. A catering service
t. A paper mill
u. An auto repair shop

4-17 Actual costing, normal costing, accounting for manufacturing overhead. Destin Products uses a job-costing system with two direct-cost categories (direct materials and direct manufacturing labor) and one manufacturing overhead cost pool. Destin allocates manufacturing overhead costs using direct manufacturing labor costs. Destin provides the following information:

	Budget for 2009	Actual Results for 2009
Direct material costs	$2,000,000	$1,900,000
Direct manufacturing labor costs	1,500,000	1,450,000
Manufacturing overhead costs	2,700,000	2,755,000

Required

1. Compute the actual and budgeted manufacturing overhead rates for 2009.
2. During March, the job-cost record for Job 626 contained the following information:

Direct materials used	$40,000
Direct manufacturing labor costs	$30,000

   Compute the cost of Job 626 using (a) actual costing and (b) normal costing.
3. At the end of 2009, compute the under- or overallocated manufacturing overhead under normal costing. Why is there no under- or overallocated overhead under actual costing?

4-18 Job costing, normal and actual costing. Anderson Construction assembles residential houses. It uses a job-costing system with two direct-cost categories (direct materials and direct labor) and one indirect-cost pool (assembly support). Direct labor-hours is the allocation base for assembly support costs. In December 2007, Anderson budgets 2008 assembly-support costs to be $8,000,000 and 2008 direct labor-hours to be 160,000.

At the end of 2008, Anderson is comparing the costs of several jobs that were started and completed in 2008.

	Laguna Model	Mission Model
Construction period	Feb-June 2008	May-Oct 2008
Direct material costs	$106,450	$127,604
Direct labor costs	$ 36,276	$ 41,410
Direct labor-hours	900	1,010

Direct materials and direct labor are paid for on a contract basis. The costs of each are known when direct materials are used or when direct labor-hours are worked. The 2008 actual assembly-support costs were $6,888,000, and the actual direct labor-hours were 164,000.

Required

1. Compute the (a) budgeted indirect-cost rate and (b) actual indirect-cost rate. Why do they differ?
2. What are the job costs of the Laguna Model and the Mission Model using (a) normal costing and (b) actual costing?
3. Why might Anderson Construction prefer normal costing over actual costing?

4-19 Budgeted manufacturing overhead rate, allocated manufacturing overhead. Waheed Company uses normal costing. It allocates manufacturing overhead costs using a budgeted rate per machine-hour. The following data are available for 2008:

Budgeted manufacturing overhead costs	$4,000,000
Budgeted machine-hours	200,000
Actual manufacturing overhead costs	$3,860,000
Actual machine-hours	195,000

Required

1. Calculate the budgeted manufacturing overhead rate.
2. Calculate the manufacturing overhead allocated during 2008.
3. Calculate the amount of under- or overallocated manufacturing overhead.

4-20 Job costing, accounting for manufacturing overhead, budgeted rates. The Lynn Company uses a job-costing system at its Minneapolis plant. The plant has a Machining Department and an Assembly Department. Its job-costing system has two direct-cost categories (direct materials and direct manufacturing labor) and two manufacturing overhead cost pools (the Machining Department overhead, allocated to jobs based on actual machine-hours, and the Assembly Department overhead, allocated to jobs based on actual direct manufacturing labor costs). The 2009 budget for the plant is:

	Machining Department	Assembly Department
Manufacturing overhead	$1,800,000	$3,600,000
Direct manufacturing labor costs	$1,400,000	$2,000,000
Direct manufacturing labor-hours	100,000	200,000
Machine-hours	50,000	200,000

Required

1. Present an overview diagram of Lynn's job-costing system. Compute the budgeted manufacturing overhead rate for each department.
2. During February, the job-cost record for Job 494 contained the following:

	Machining Department	Assembly Department
Direct materials used	$45,000	$70,000
Direct manufacturing labor costs	$14,000	$15,000
Direct manufacturing labor-hours	1,000	1,500
Machine-hours	2,000	1,000

Compute the total manufacturing overhead costs allocated to Job 494.

3. At the end of 2009, the actual manufacturing overhead costs were $2,100,000 in Machining and $3,700,000 in Assembly. Assume that 55,000 actual machine-hours were used in Machining and that actual direct manufacturing labor costs in Assembly were $2,200,000. Compute the over- or underallocated manufacturing overhead for each department.

4-21 Job costing, consulting firm. Taylor & Associates, a consulting firm, has the following condensed budget for 2009:

Revenues		$20,000,000
Total costs:		
Direct costs		
Professional Labor	$ 5,000,000	
Indirect costs		
Client support	13,000,000	18,000,000
Operating income		$ 2,000,000

Taylor has a single direct-cost category (professional labor) and a single indirect-cost pool (client support). Indirect costs are allocated to jobs on the basis of professional labor costs.

Required

1. Prepare an overview diagram of the job-costing system. Compute the 2009 budgeted indirect-cost rate for Taylor & Associates.

2. The markup rate for pricing jobs is intended to produce operating income equal to 10% of revenues. Compute the markup rate as a percentage of professional labor costs.
3. Taylor is bidding on a consulting job for Red Rooster, a fast-food chain specializing in poultry meats. The budgeted breakdown of professional labor on the job is as follows:

Professional Labor Category	Budgeted Rate per Hour	Budgeted Hours
Director	$200	3
Partner	100	16
Associate	50	40
Assistant	30	160

Compute the budgeted cost of the Red Rooster job. How much will Taylor bid for the job if it is to earn its target operating income of 10% of revenues?

4-22 Service industry, time period used to compute indirect cost rates. Printers, Inc. produces annual reports and marketing materials for large companies. There are three categories of costs in its normal job-costing system: direct materials, direct labor, and overhead (both variable and fixed), allocated on the basis of direct labor costs. Jill Liu, the controller, is concerned that an increasing number of clients are waiting until the last minute to send in their final orders, causing congestion and an increase in the variable manufacturing overhead rate because of higher overtime and facility and machine maintenance. This spike is during the "crazy" months of January, February, and March, when many companies are rushing to get out their annual reports and marketing materials. Liu obtains the following budgeted data for 2008:

File Edit View Insert Format Tools Data Window Help

	A	B	C	D	E	F
1		Jan.-March	April-June	July-Sept.	Oct.-Dec.	Total
2	Direct materials	$900,000	$620,000	$595,000	$605,000	$2,720,000
3	Direct labor costs	$400,000	$280,000	$250,000	$270,000	$1,200,000
4	Variable overhead costs as a percentage of direct labor cost	90%	60%	60%	60%	
5	Fixed overhead costs	$300,000	$300,000	$300,000	$300,000	$1,200,000

If you want to use Excel to solve this exercise, go to the Excel Lab at **www.prenhall.com/horngren/cost13e** and download the template for Exercise 4-22.

Required

1. Consider Job 332, an order for 100,000 sales catalogs for the local mall. Actual direct material costs for this job are $10,000 and actual labor costs are $6,000. Calculate the cost of Job 332 (a) if it is completed in January–March 2008 and if the budgeted overhead rate for that quarter is used to allocate overhead costs, (b) if it is done in July–September 2008 and if the budgeted overhead rate for that quarter is used to allocate overhead costs, and (c) if the average budgeted overhead rate for the year 2008 is used to allocate overhead costs.
2. To cost each job, Printers, Inc. currently uses the budgeted variable overhead rate for the quarter in which the job is completed and a budgeted fixed overhead rate based on budgeted annual fixed overhead costs and budgeted annual direct labor costs. Calculate the cost of Job 332 using this method if it is done in (a) January–March 2008 and (b) July–September 2008.
3. Printers, Inc., prices each job at 125% of costs. Which method of costing jobs for pricing purposes would you recommend? Why? Explain briefly.

4-23 Accounting for manufacturing overhead. Consider the following selected cost data for the Pittsburgh Forging Company for 2008.

Budgeted manufacturing overhead costs	$7,500,000
Budgeted machine-hours	250,000
Actual manufacturing overhead costs	$7,300,000
Actual machine-hours	245,000

The company uses normal costing. Its job-costing system has a single manufacturing overhead cost pool. Costs are allocated to jobs using a budgeted machine-hour rate. Any amount of under- or overallocation is written off to Cost of Goods Sold.

Required

1. Compute the budgeted manufacturing overhead rate.
2. Prepare the journal entries to record the allocation of manufacturing overhead.
3. Compute the amount of under- or overallocation of manufacturing overhead. Is the amount material? Prepare a journal entry to dispose of this amount.

4-24 Job costing, journal entries. The University of Chicago Press is wholly owned by the university. It performs the bulk of its work for other university departments, which pay as though the press were an outside business enterprise. The press also publishes and maintains a stock of books for general sale. The Press uses normal costing to cost each job. Its job-costing system has two direct-cost categories (direct materials and direct manufacturing labor) and one indirect-cost pool (manufacturing overhead, allocated on the basis of direct manufacturing labor costs).

The following data (in thousands) pertain to 2009:

Direct materials and supplies purchased on credit	$ 800
Direct materials used	710
Indirect materials issued to various production departments	100
Direct manufacturing labor	1,300
Indirect manufacturing labor incurred by various production departments	900
Depreciation on building and manufacturing equipment	400
Miscellaneous manufacturing overhead* incurred by various production departments (ordinarily would be detailed as repairs, photocopying, utilities, etc.)	550
Manufacturing overhead allocated at 160% of direct manufacturing labor costs	?
Cost of goods manufactured	4,120
Revenues	8,000
Cost of goods sold	4,020
Inventories, December 31, 2008 (not 2009):	
Materials Control	100
Work-in-Process Control	60
Finished Goods Control	500

*The term manufacturing overhead is not used uniformly. Other terms that are often encountered in printing companies include job overhead and shop overhead.

Required

1. Prepare an overview diagram of the job-costing system at the University of Chicago Press.
2. Prepare journal entries to summarize the 2009 transactions. As your final entry, dispose of the year-end under- or overallocated manufacturing overhead as a write-off to Cost of Goods Sold. Number your entries. Explanations for each entry may be omitted.
3. Show posted T-accounts for all inventories, Cost of Goods Sold, Manufacturing Overhead Control, and Manufacturing Overhead Allocated.

4-25 Journal entries, T-accounts and source documents. Production Company produces gadgets for the coveted small appliance market. The following data reflects activity for the year 2008.

Costs incurred:	
Purchases of direct materials (net) on credit	$124,000
Direct manufacturing labor cost	80,000
Indirect labor	54,500
Depreciation, factory equipment	30,000
Depreciation, office equipment	7,000
Maintenance, factory equipment	20,000
Miscellaneous factory overhead	9,500
Rent, factory building	70,000
Advertising expense	90,000
Sales commissions	30,000

Inventories:

	January 1, 2008	December 31, 2008
Direct materials	$ 9,000	$11,000
Work in process	6,000	21,000
Finished goods	69,000	24,000

Production Co. uses a normal cost system and allocates overhead to work in process at a rate of $2.50 per direct manufacturing labor dollar. Indirect materials are insignificant so there is no inventory account for indirect materials.

Required

1. Prepare journal entries to record the transactions for 2008 including an entry to close out over- or underallocated overhead to cost of goods sold. For each journal entry indicate the source document that would be used to authorize each entry. Also note which subsidiary ledger, if any, should be referenced as backup for the entry.
2. Post the journal entries to T-accounts for all of the inventories, Cost of Goods Sold, the Manufacturing Overhead Control Account, and the Manufacturing Overhead Allocated Account.

4-26 Job costing, journal entries. Donnell Transport assembles prestige manufactured homes. Its job costing system has two direct-cost categories (direct materials and direct manufacturing labor) and one indirect-cost pool (manufacturing overhead allocated at a budgeted $30 per machine-hour in 2009). The following data (in millions) pertain to operations for 2009:

Materials Control, beginning balance, January 1, 2009	$ 12
Work-in-Process Control, beginning balance, January 1, 2009	2
Finished Goods Control, beginning balance, January 1, 2009	6
Materials and supplies purchased on credit	150
Direct materials used	145
Indirect materials (supplies) issued to various production departments	10
Direct manufacturing labor	90
Indirect manufacturing labor incurred by various production departments	30
Depreciation on plant and manufacturing equipment	19
Miscellaneous manufacturing overhead incurred (ordinarily would be detailed as repairs, utilities, etc., with a corresponding credit to various liability accounts)	9
Manufacturing overhead allocated, 2,100,000 actual machine-hours	?
Cost of goods manufactured	294
Revenues	400
Cost of goods sold	292

Required

1. Prepare an overview diagram of Donnell Transport's job-costing system.
2. Prepare journal entries. Number your entries. Post to T-accounts. What is the ending balance of Work-in-Process Control?
3. Show the journal entry for disposing of under- or overallocated manufacturing overhead directly as a year-end write-off to Cost of Goods Sold. Post the entry to T-accounts.

4-27 Job costing, unit cost, ending work in process. Raymond Company produces pipes for concert-quality organs. Each job is unique. In April 2009, it completed all outstanding orders, and then, in May 2009, it worked on only two jobs, M1 and M2:

	A	B	C
1	**Raymond Company, May 2009**	**Job M1**	**Job M2**
2	Direct materials	$ 75,000	$ 50,000
3	Direct manufacturing labor	275,000	200,000

Direct manufacturing labor is paid at the rate of $25 per hour. Manufacturing overhead costs are allocated at a budgeted rate of $20 per direct manufacturing labor-hour. Only Job M1 was completed in May.

If you want to use Excel to solve this exercise, go to the Excel Lab at **www.prenhall.com/horngren/cost13e** and download the template for Exercise 4-27.

Required

1. Compute the total cost for Job M1.
2. 1,500 pipes were produced for Job M1. Calculate the cost per pipe.
3. Prepare the journal entry transferring Job M1 to finished goods.
4. What is the ending balance in the Work-in-Process Control account?

4-28 Job costing; actual, normal, and variation from normal costing. Chirac & Partners, a Quebec-based public accounting partnership, specializes in audit services. Its job-costing system has a single direct-cost category (professional labor) and a single indirect-cost pool (audit support, which contains all costs of the Audit Support Department). Audit support costs are allocated to individual jobs using actual professional labor-hours. Chirac & Partners employs 10 professionals to perform audit services.

Budgeted and actual amounts for 2009 are as follows:

	A	B	C
1	**Chirac & Partners**		
2	**Budget for 2009**		
3	Professional labor compensation	$960,000	
4	Audit support department costs	$720,000	
5	Professional labor-hours billed to clients	16,000	hours
6			
7	**Actual results for 2009**		
8	Audit support department costs	$744,000	
9	Professional labor-hours billed to clients	15,500	hours
10	Actual professional labor cost rate	$58	per hour

If you want to use Excel to solve this exercise, go to the Excel Lab at **www.prenhall.com/horngren/cost13e** and download the template for Exercise 4-28.

Required

1. Compute the direct-cost rate and the indirect-cost rate per professional labor-hour for 2009 under (a) actual costing, (b) normal costing, and (c) the variation from normal costing that uses budgeted rates for direct costs.
2. Chirac's 2009 audit of Pierre & Co. was budgeted to take 110 hours of professional labor time. The actual professional labor time spent on the audit was 120 hours. Compute the cost of the Pierre & Co. audit using (a) actual costing, (b) normal costing, and (c) the variation from normal costing that uses budgeted rates for direct costs. Explain any differences in the job cost.

4-29 Job order costing: actual, normal, and variation from normal costing. Thanatos & Hades (T&H) is a law firm that specializes in writing wills. Its job-costing system has one direct cost pool, professional labor, and a single indirect cost pool that includes all supporting costs of running the law office. The support costs are allocated to clients on the basis of professional labor hours. In addition to the two senior partners, T&H have six associates who work directly with clients. Each of the eight lawyers is expected to work for approximately 2,500 hours a year.

Budgeted and actual costs for 2008 were:

Budgeted professional labor costs	$1,100,000
Budgeted support costs	$2,000,000
Actual professional labor costs	$1,320,000
Actual support costs	$2,400,000
Actual total professional hours	22,000 hours

Required

1. Compute the direct cost rate and the indirect cost rate per professional labor hour under
   a. actual costing
   b. normal costing
   c. variation from normal costing that uses budgeted rates for direct costs.
2. The will for a rich tycoon, Ari Apostolus, was very complex and took four lawyers at the firm, 1,000 hours each to prepare. What would the cost of writing this will be under each of the costing methods in requirement 1?

4-30 Proration of overhead. The Ride-On-Water Company (ROW) produces a line of non-motorized boats. ROW uses a normal costing system and allocates manufacturing overhead using direct manufacturing labor cost. The following data is for 2009:

Budgeted manufacturing overhead cost	$100,000
Budgeted direct manufacturing labor cost	$200,000
Actual manufacturing overhead cost	$106,000
Actual direct manufacturing labor cost	$220,000

Inventory balances on December 31, 2009 were:

Account	Ending balance	2009 direct manufacturing labor cost in ending balance
Work in process	$ 50,000	$ 20,000
Finished goods	240,000	60,000
Cost of goods sold	560,000	140,000

Required

1. Calculate the overhead allocation rate.
2. Compute the amount of under- or overallocated overhead
3. Calculate the ending balances in work in process, finished goods and cost of goods sold if under-overallocated overhead is:
   a. Written off to cost of goods sold
   b. Prorated based on ending balances (before proration) in each of the three accounts.
   c. Prorated based on the overhead allocated in 2009 in the ending balances (before proration) in each of the three accounts.
4. Which method makes the most sense? Justify your answer.

Problems

4-31 Job costing, accounting for manufacturing overhead, budgeted rates. The Solomon Company uses a job-costing system at its Dover, Delaware, plant. The plant has a Machining Department and a Finishing Department. Solomon uses normal costing with two direct-cost categories (direct materials and direct manufacturing labor) and two manufacturing overhead cost pools (the Machining Department, with machine hours as the allocation base, and the Finishing Department, with direct manufacturing labor costs as the allocation base). The 2009 budget for the plant is as follows:

	Machining Department	Finishing Department
Manufacturing overhead costs	$10,000,000	$8,000,000
Direct manufacturing labor costs	$ 900,000	$4,000,000
Direct manufacturing labor-hours	30,000	160,000
Machine-hours	200,000	33,000

Required

1. Prepare an overview diagram of Solomon's job-costing system.
2. What is the budgeted overhead rate in the Machining Department? In the Finishing Department?
3. During the month of January, the job-cost record for Job 431 shows the following:

	Machining Department	Finishing Department
Direct materials used	$14,000	$3,000
Direct manufacturing labor costs	$ 600	$1,250
Direct manufacturing labor-hours	30	50
Machine-hours	130	10

   Compute the total manufacturing overhead allocated to Job 431.
4. Assuming that Job 431 consisted of 200 units of product, what is the cost per unit?
5. Amounts at the end of 2009 are as follows:

	Machining Department	Finishing Department
Manufacturing overhead incurred	$11,200,000	$7,900,000
Direct manufacturing labor costs	$ 950,000	$4,100,000
Machine-hours	220,000	32,000

   Compute the under- or overallocated manufacturing overhead for each department and for the Dover plant as a whole.
6. Why might Solomon use two different manufacturing overhead cost pools in its job-costing system?

4-32 Service industry, job costing, law firm. Keating & Associates is a law firm specializing in labor relations and employee-related work. It employs 25 professionals (5 partners and 20 associates) who work directly with its clients. The average budgeted total compensation per professional for 2008 is $104,000. Each professional is budgeted to have 1,600 billable hours to clients in 2008. All professionals work for clients to their maximum 1,600 billable hours available. All professional labor costs are included in a single direct-cost category and are traced to jobs on a per-hour basis. All costs of Keating & Associates other than professional labor costs are included in a single indirect-cost pool (legal support) and are allocated to jobs using professional labor-hours as the allocation base. The budgeted level of indirect costs in 2008 is $2,200,000.

Required

1. Prepare an overview diagram of Keating's job-costing system.
2. Compute the 2008 budgeted direct-cost rate per hour of professional labor.
3. Compute the 2008 budgeted indirect-cost rate per hour of professional labor.
4. Keating & Associates is considering bidding on two jobs:
   a. Litigation work for Richardson, Inc., which requires 100 budgeted hours of professional labor
   b. Labor contract work for Punch, Inc., which requires 150 budgeted hours of professional labor

   Prepare a cost estimate for each job.

4-33 Service industry, job costing, two direct- and two indirect-cost categories, law firm (continuation of 4-32). Keating has just completed a review of its job-costing system. This review included a detailed analysis of how past jobs used the firm's resources and interviews with personnel about what factors drive the level of indirect costs. Management concluded that a system with two direct-cost categories (professional partner labor and professional associate labor) and two indirect-cost categories (general support and secretarial support) would yield more-accurate job costs. Budgeted information for 2008 related to the two direct-cost categories is as follows:

	Professional Partner Labor	Professional Associate Labor
Number of professionals	5	20
Hours of billable time per professional	1,600 per year	1,600 per year
Total compensation (average per professional)	$200,000	$80,000

Budgeted information for 2008 relating to the two indirect-cost categories is

	General Support	Secretarial Support
Total costs	$1,800,000	$400,000
Cost-allocation base	Professional labor-hours	Partner labor-hours

Required

1. Compute the 2008 budgeted direct-cost rates for (a) professional partners and (b) professional associates.
2. Compute the 2008 budgeted indirect-cost rates for (a) general support and (b) secretarial support.
3. Compute the budgeted costs for the Richardson and Punch jobs, given the following information:

	Richardson, Inc.	Punch, Inc.
Professional partners	60 hours	30 hours
Professional associates	40 hours	120 hours

4. Comment on the results in requirement 3. Why are the job costs different from those computed in Problem 4-32?

4-34 Proration of overhead. (Z. Iqbal, adapted) The Zaf Radiator Company uses a normal-costing system with a single manufacturing overhead cost pool and machine-hours as the cost-allocation base. The following data are for 2009:

Budgeted manufacturing overhead costs	$4,800,000
Overhead allocation base	Machine-hours
Budgeted machine-hours	80,000
Manufacturing overhead costs incurred	$4,900,000
Actual machine-hours	75,000

Machine-hours data and the ending balances (before proration of under- or overallocated overhead) are as follows:

	Actual Machine-Hours	2009 End-of-Year Balance
Cost of Goods Sold	60,000	$8,000,000
Finished Goods Control	11,000	1,250,000
Work-in-Process Control	4,000	750,000

Required

1. Compute the budgeted manufacturing overhead rate for 2009.
2. Compute the under- or overallocated manufacturing overhead of Zaf Radiator in 2009. Dispose of this amount using
   - **a.** Write-off to Cost of Goods Sold
   - **b.** Proration based on ending balances (before proration) in Work-in-Process Control, Finished Goods Control, and Cost of Goods Sold
   - **c.** Proration based on the overhead allocated in 2009 (before proration) in the ending balances of Work-in-Process Control, Finished Goods Control, and Cost of Goods Sold
3. Which method do you prefer in requirement 2? Explain.

4-35 Normal costing, overhead allocation, working backward. (M. Rajan, adapted) Gibson Manufacturing uses normal costing for its job-costing system, which has two direct-cost categories (direct materials and direct manufacturing labor) and one indirect-cost category (manufacturing overhead). The following information is obtained for 2009:

- Total manufacturing costs, $8,000,000
- Manufacturing overhead allocated, $3,600,000 (allocated at a rate of 200% of direct manufacturing labor costs)

- Work-in-process inventory on January 1, 2009, $320,000
- Cost of finished goods manufactured, $7,920,000

Required

1. Use information in the first two bullet points to calculate (a) direct manufacturing labor costs in 2009 and (b) cost of direct materials used in 2009.
2. Calculate the ending work-in-process inventory on December 31, 2009.

4-36 Proration of overhead with two indirect cost pools. The Finer Furniture Company produces expensive desks for executives. The wood for the desks are cut into standard sizes and the desks are assembled in the Construction and Assembly (C&A) department. The assembled desks are then sent to the Finishing Department to be stained. Overhead costs in the C&A department are allocated to production using machine-hours, and overhead costs in the Finishing Department are allocated using direct labor-hours.

Finer Furniture uses a normal costing system and has the following data for 2008

	C&A	Finishing
Budgeted overhead rate	$40 per machine-hour	$50 per direct labor-hour
Actual overhead cost	$163,000	$87,000
Actual hours	4,000 machine-hours	2,000 labor-hours

Ending balances, machine-hours and direct labor-hours data are as follows:

Account	Balance Before Proration December 31, 2008	Actual Machine-Hours	Actual Direct Labor-Hours
Work in process	$ 150,000	200	100
Finished goods	250,000	600	400
Cost of goods sold	1,600,000	3,200	1,500

Required

1. Calculate the over- or underallocated overhead for each of the C&A and Finishing departments in 2008.
2. Calculate the ending balances in work in process, finished goods and cost of goods sold if the under- or overallocated overhead amounts in *each* department are:
   a. Written off to cost of goods sold
   b. Prorated based on the ending balance (before proration) in each of the three accounts
   c. Prorated based on the overhead allocated in 2008 (before proration) in the ending balances in each of the three accounts.
3. Which method would you choose? Explain.

4-37 General ledger relationships, under- and overallocation. (S. Sridhar, adapted) Needham Company uses normal costing in its job-costing system. Partially completed T-accounts and additional information for Needham for 2008 are as follows:

Direct Materials Control

	Debit	Credit
1-1-2008	30,000	380,000
	400,000	

Work-in-Process Control

	Debit	Credit
1-1-2008	20,000	
Dir. manuf. labor	360,000	

Finished Goods Control

	Debit	Credit
1-1-2008	10,000	900,000
	940,000	

Manufacturing Overhead Control

Debit	Credit
540,000	

Manufacturing Overhead Allocated

Debit	Credit

Cost of Goods Sold

Debit	Credit

Additional Information:

a. Direct manufacturing labor wage rate was $15 per hour.
b. Manufacturing overhead was allocated at $20 per direct manufacturing labor-hour.
c. During the year, sales revenues were $1,090,000, and marketing and distribution costs were $140,000.

Required

1. What was the amount of direct materials issued to production during 2008?
2. What was the amount of manufacturing overhead allocated to jobs during 2008?
3. What was the total cost of jobs completed during 2008?
4. What was the balance of work-in-process inventory on December 31, 2008?
5. What was the cost of goods sold before proration of under- or overallocated overhead?
6. What was the under- or overallocated manufacturing overhead in 2008?
7. Dispose of the under- or overallocated manufacturing overhead using
   a. Write-off to Cost of Goods Sold
   b. Proration based on ending balances (before proration) in Work-in-Process Control, Finished Goods Control, and Cost of Goods Sold

8. Using each of the approaches in requirement 7, calculate Needham's operating income for 2008.
9. Which approach in requirement 7 do you recommend Needham use? Explain your answer briefly.

4-38 Overview of general ledger relationships. The Blakely Company is a small machine shop that uses normal costing in its job-costing system. The total debits and credits in certain accounts *one day before year-end* are as follows:

	December 30, 2008	
	Total Debits	**Total Credits**
Materials Control	$100,000	$ 70,000
Work-in-Process Control	320,000	305,000
Manufacturing Department Overhead Control	85,000	—
Finished Goods Control	325,000	300,000
Cost of Goods Sold	300,000	—
Manufacturing Overhead Allocated	—	90,000

All materials purchased are direct materials. Note that "total debits" in the inventory accounts would include beginning inventory balances on January 1, 2008, if any.

The total debits and total credits above *do not include* the following:

a. The manufacturing labor costs for the December 31 working day: direct manufacturing labor, $5,000, and indirect manufacturing labor, $1,000.
b. Miscellaneous manufacturing overhead incurred on December 31: $1,000.

Additional Information:

a. Manufacturing overhead has been allocated as a percentage of direct manufacturing labor costs through December 30.
b. Direct materials purchased during 2008 were $85,000.
c. No direct materials were returned to suppliers.
d. Direct manufacturing labor costs during 2008 totaled $150,000, not including the December 31 working day described previously.

Required

1. Use T-accounts to compute the January 1, 2008 beginning balances for the Materials Control, Work-in-Process Control, and Finished Goods Control accounts.
2. Prepare all adjusting and closing journal entries for the preceding accounts. Assume that all under- or overallocated manufacturing overhead is closed directly to Cost of Goods Sold.
3. Compute the ending inventory balances on December 31, 2008, after adjustments and closing, for Materials Control, Work-in-Process Control, and Finished Goods Control accounts.

4-39 Allocation and proration of overhead. Franklin & Son Printing designed and printed sales brochures, catalogues, and pamphlets. The business was dissolved in early 1763.

Franklin & Son Printing used a normal costing system. It has two direct cost pools, materials and labor and one indirect cost pool, overhead. Overhead was charged to printing jobs on the basis of direct labor cost. The following information was known about the firm for 1762.

Budgeted material costs	£1000
Budgeted labor costs	£2000
Budgeted overhead costs	£1500
Actual material costs	£ 900
Actual labor costs	£1800
Actual overhead costs	£1250

There was no work in process on Jan. 1, 1762 and there were two jobs in process on Dec. 31, 1762. The first job had used £25 of materials so far and £20 of labor. The second job had used £15 worth of material and £32 of labor. Franklin & Son Printing had no finished goods inventories because all printing jobs were based on orders that, when completed, were transferred to cost of goods sold.

Required

1. Compute the overhead allocation rate.
2. Calculate the balance in ending work in process and in cost of goods sold.
3. Calculate under- or overallocated overhead.
4. Calculate the ending balances in work in process and cost of goods sold if the under- or overallocated overhead amount is:
   a. Written off to cost of goods sold
   b. Prorated using the ending balance (before proration) in cost of goods sold and work-in-process control accounts.
5. Which of the methods in requirement 4 would you choose? Explain.

4-40 Job costing, contracting, ethics. Jack Halpern is the owner and CEO of Aerospace Comfort, a firm specializing in the manufacture of seats for airplanes. He has just received a copy of a letter written to the General Audit Section of the U.S. Navy. He believes it is from an ex-employee of Aerospace.

Dear Sir,

Aerospace Comfort manufactured 100 X7 seats for the Navy in 2009. The following may be of interest.

1. *Direct material costs billed for the 100 X7 seats were $25,000.*
2. *Direct manufacturing labor costs billed for 100 X7 seats were $6,000. These costs include 16 hours of setup labor at $25 per hour, an amount included in the manufacturing overhead cost pool as well. The $6,000 also includes 12 hours of design time at $50 an hour. Design time was explicitly identified as a cost the Navy would not reimburse.*
3. *Manufacturing overhead costs billed for 100 X7 seats were $9,000 (150% of direct manufacturing labor costs). This amount includes the 16 hours of setup labor at $25 per hour that is incorrectly included as part of direct manufacturing labor costs.*

You may also want to know that over 40% of the direct materials is purchased from Frontier Tech, a company that is 51% owned by Jack Halpern's brother. For obvious reasons, this letter will not be signed.

cc: The Wall Street Journal, Jack Halpern, CEO of Aerospace Comfort

Aerospace Comfort's contract states that the Navy reimburses Aerospace at 130% of total manufacturing costs. Assume that the facts in the letter are correct as you answer the following questions.

Required

1. What is the cost amount per X7 seat that Aerospace Comfort billed the Navy? Assume that the actual direct material costs were $25,000.
2. What is the amount per X7 seat that Aerospace Comfort should have billed the Navy? Assume that the actual direct material costs were $25,000.
3. What should the Navy do to tighten its procurement procedures to reduce the likelihood of such situations recurring in the future?

Collaborative Learning Problem

4-41 Job costing—service industry. Michael Scott books tours for new bands and arranges to print T-shirts and produce demo CDs to sell on the tour. Scott's agency uses a normal costing system with two direct cost pools, labor and materials, and one indirect cost pool, general overhead. General overhead is allocated to each tour at 150% of labor cost. The following information relates to the agency for June 2009.

1. As of June 1, there were tours for two bands, *Grunge Express* and *Different Strokes* in progress.
2. During June both *Grunge Express* and *Different Strokes* finished their tours.
3. New tours were started for three bands: *As I Lay Dieing, Ask Me Later* and *Maybe Tomorrow.* Of these bands, only *Maybe Tomorrow* finished its tour by the end of June.
4. All costs incurred during the planning stage for a tour and during the tour are gathered in a balance sheet account called "Tours in Progress (TIP)." When a tour is completed, the costs are transferred to an income statement account called "Cost of Completed Tours (CCT)."

Following is cost information for June 2009:

	From Beginning TIP		Incurred in June	
Band	**Materials**	**Labor**	**Materials**	**Labor**
Grunge Express	$400	$600	$ 0	$100
Different Strokes	300	400	175	300
As I Lay Dieing	---	---	250	400
Ask Me Later	---	---	350	200
Maybe Tomorrow	---	---	275	400

Actual overhead in June was $2,500.

Required

1. Calculate TIP for the end of June.
2. Calculate CCT for June.
3. Calculate under/over allocated overhead at the end of June.
4. Calculate the ending balances in TIP and CCT if the under/over allocated overhead amount is:
   a. Written off to CCT
   b. Prorated based on the ending balances (before proration) in TIP and CCT
   c. Prorated based on the overhead allocated in June in the ending balances of TIP and CCT (before proration).
5. Which of the methods in requirement 4 would you choose?

5 Activity-Based Costing and Activity-Based Management

Learning Objectives

1. Explain how broad averaging undercosts and overcosts products or services
2. Present three guidelines for refining a costing system
3. Distinguish between simple and activity-based costing systems
4. Describe a four-part cost hierarchy
5. Cost products or services using activity-based costing
6. Explain how activity-based costing systems are used in activity-based management
7. Compare activity-based costing systems and department costing systems
8. Evaluate the costs and benefits of implementing activity-based costing systems

A good mystery never fails to capture the imagination. Money is stolen or lost; property disappears or someone meets with foul play. On the surface, what appears unremarkable to the untrained eye can turn out to be quite a revelation once the facts and details are uncovered. Getting to the bottom of the case, understanding what happened and why, and taking action can make the difference between a solved case and an unsolved one. Business and organizations are much the same. Their costing systems are often mysteries, with unresolved questions: Why are we bleeding red ink? Are we pricing our products accurately? Activity-based costing can help unravel the mystery and result in improved operations, as Scotland Yard discovers in the following article.

Mystery Solved: London Police Spend $1 Billion-Plus a Year on Paperwork versus Fighting Crime, ABC Analysis Uncovers[1]

London police spend more than £120 million a year [more than $250 million] on paperwork—a sum greater than that spent fighting robberies and house burglaries. The findings emerged from an "activity based costing" (ABC) review of policing, which produced the most detailed picture of where the money goes. It covered time spent by officers and staff on filling out forms, writing letters, sending memos, and checking paperwork, and the figure would be higher if paperwork linked to particular crimes, such as interview notes or arrest warrants, were included.

Since 2003, every force in England and Wales has been required to carry out an annual ABC review. Each pound spent must be allocated to one of 60 categories, from counterterrorism and solving crimes to training and sick leave to general correspondence not related to any specific incident.

The London Police accounts for almost a quarter of Britain's £12.8 billion total annual bill for policing. On the basis that other forces do a similar amount of paper-pushing, the nationwide annual cost of police paperwork is around £500 million.

Alan Gordon, the vice-chairman of the Police Federation, said: "These figures illustrate what we have been saying for years—that

[1] *Source:* Ben Leapman, "Police Spend £500m Filling in Forms," *Telegraph.co.uk* (January 22, 2006).

officers are overburdened with paperwork at the expense of response-based policing."

In response, the Home Office scrapped 7,700 unnecessary police forms and saved time for frontline officers by expanding the role of civilian staff. Scotland Yard said it would use the findings to redirect cash to frontline activities.

Most companies—such as Oracle, JP Morgan Chase, and Honda—offer more than one product (or service). Dell Computer, for example, produces desktops, laptops, and servers. The three basic activities for manufacturing computers are (a) designing computers, (b) ordering component parts, and (c) assembly. The different products require different quantities of the three activities. For example, a server has a more complex design, many more parts, and more complex assembly than a desktop.

To measure the cost of producing each product, Dell separately tracks activity costs for each product. In this chapter, we describe activity-based costing systems and how they help companies make better decisions about pricing and product mix. And, just as in the case of Scotland Yard, we show how ABC systems assist in cost management decisions by improving product designs, processes, and efficiency.

Broad Averaging and Its Consequences

Historically, companies (for example, television and automobile manufacturers) produced a limited variety of products. Indirect (or overhead) costs were a relatively small percentage of total costs. So, using simple costing systems to allocate costs broadly was easy, inexpensive, and reasonably accurate. However, as product diversity and indirect costs have increased, broad averaging has resulted in greater inaccuracy of product costs. For example, the use of a single, plant-wide manufacturing overhead rate to allocate costs to products often produces unreliable cost data. The term *peanut-butter costing* (yes, that's what it's called) describes a particular costing approach that uses broad averages for assigning (or spreading, as in spreading peanut butter) the cost of resources uniformly to cost objects (such as products or services) when the individual products or services, may in fact, use those resources in nonuniform ways.

Learning Objective 1

Explain how broad averaging undercosts and overcosts products or services

. . . this problem arises when reported costs of products do not equal their actual costs

Undercosting and Overcosting

The following example illustrates how averaging can provide inaccurate and misleading cost data. Consider the cost of a restaurant bill for four colleagues who meet monthly to discuss business developments. Each diner orders separate entrees, desserts, and drinks. The restaurant bill for the most recent meeting is:

	Emma	James	Jessica	Matthew	Total	Average
Entree	$11	$20	$15	$14	$ 60	$15
Dessert	0	8	4	4	16	4
Drinks	4	14	8	6	32	8
Total	$15	$42	$27	$24	$108	$27

If the $108 total restaurant bill is divided evenly, $27 is the average cost per diner. This cost-averaging approach treats each diner the same. Emma would probably object to paying $27 because her actual cost is only $15; she ordered the lowest-cost entree, had no dessert, and had the lowest-cost drink. When costs are averaged across all four diners, both Emma and Matthew are overcosted, James is undercosted, and Jessica is (by coincidence) accurately costed.

Broad averaging can lead to undercosting or overcosting of products or services:

- **Product undercosting**—a product consumes a high level of resources but is reported to have a low cost per unit (James's dinner).
- **Product overcosting**—a product consumes a low level of resources but is reported to have a high cost per unit (Emma's dinner).

What are the strategic consequences of product undercosting and overcosting? Think of a company that uses cost information about its products to guide pricing decisions. Undercosted products will be underpriced, increasing demand for these products but lowering profits. In fact, undercosted products may lead to sales that actually result in losses—the sales bring in less revenue than the cost of resources they use—although the company has the erroneous impression that these sales are profitable. Overcosted products lead to overpricing, causing these products to lose market share to competitors producing similar products. Worse still, product undercosting and overcosting draws managerial attention to the wrong products. A manager will try to reduce costs of overcosted products because the reported costs of these products are high, yet, instead, the manager needs to focus on planning and managing activities for products that are undercosted because these products consume high levels of resources even though their reported costs are low.

Product-Cost Cross-Subsidization

Product-cost cross-subsidization means that if a company undercosts one of its products, then it will overcost at least one of its other products. Similarly, if a company overcosts one of its products, it will undercost at least one of its other products. Product-cost cross-subsidization is very common in situations in which a cost is uniformly spread—meaning it is broadly averaged—across multiple products without recognizing the amount of resources consumed by each product.

In the restaurant-bill example, the amount of cost cross-subsidization of each diner can be readily computed *because all cost items can be traced as direct costs to each diner*. If all diners pay $27, Emma is paying $12 more than her actual cost of $15. She is cross-subsidizing James who is paying $15 less than his actual cost of $42. Calculating the amount of cost cross-subsidization takes more work when there are indirect costs to be considered. Why? Because the resources represented by the indirect costs are used by two or more diners, and we need to find a way to allocate costs to each diner. Consider, for example, a $40 bottle of wine whose cost is shared equally. Each diner would pay $10 ($40 ÷ 4). Suppose Matthew drinks 2 glasses of wine while Emma, James, and Jessica drink one glass each for a total of 5 glasses. Allocating the cost of the bottle of wine on the basis of the glasses of wine that each diner drinks would result in Matthew paying $16 ($40 × 2/5) and each of the others $8 ($40 × 1/5). In this case, sharing the cost equally, Emma, James, and Jessica are each paying $2 ($10 − $8) more and are cross-subsidizing Matthew who is paying $6 ($16 − $10) less for the wine he consumes.

To see the effects of broad averaging on direct and indirect costs, we consider Plastim Corporation's costing system.

Simple Costing System at Plastim Corporation

Plastim Corporation manufactures lenses for the rear taillights of automobiles. A lens, made from black, red, orange, or white plastic, is the part of the lamp visible on the automobile's exterior. Lenses are made by injecting molten plastic into a mold to give the lamp its desired shape. The mold is cooled to allow the molten plastic to solidify, and the lens is removed.

Under its contract with Giovanni Motors, a major automobile manufacturer, Plastim makes two types of lenses: a complex lens, CL5, and a simple lens, S3. The complex lens is a large lens with special features, such as multicolor molding (when more than one color is injected into the mold) and a complex shape that wraps around the corner of the car. Manufacturing CL5 lenses is more complex because various parts in the mold must align and fit precisely. The S3 lens is simpler to make because it has a single color and few special features.

Design, Manufacturing, and Distribution Processes

The sequence of steps to design, produce, and distribute lenses, whether simple or complex, is:

- **Design products and processes.** Each year Giovanni Motors specifies some modifications to the simple and complex lenses. Plastim's Design Department designs the molds from which the lenses will be made and specifies the processes needed (that is, details of the manufacturing operations).
- **Manufacture lenses.** The lenses are molded, finished, cleaned, and inspected.
- **Distribute lenses.** Finished lenses are packed and sent to Giovanni Motors.

Plastim is operating at capacity and incurs very low marketing costs. Because of its high-quality products, Plastim has minimal customer-service costs. Plastim's business environment is very competitive with respect to simple lenses. At a recent meeting, Giovanni's purchasing manager indicates that a new supplier, Bandix, which makes only simple lenses, is offering to supply the S3 lens to Giovanni at a price of $53, well below Plastim's $63 price. Unless Plastim can lower its selling price, it will lose the Giovanni business for the simple lens for the upcoming model year. Fortunately, the same competitive pressures do not exist for the complex lens, which Plastim currently sells to Giovanni at $137 per lens.

Plastim's management has various options available to it.

- Plastim can give up the Giovanni business in simple lenses if it is unprofitable. Bandix makes only simple lenses and perhaps, therefore, uses simpler technology and processes than Plastim, which makes both simple and complex lenses. The simpler operations may give Bandix a cost advantage that Plastim cannot match. If so, it is better for Plastim to not supply the S3 lens to Giovanni.
- Plastim can reduce the price of the simple lens and either accept a lower margin or aggressively seek to reduce costs.

To make these long-run strategic decisions, management needs to first understand the costs to design, make, and distribute the S3 and CL5 lenses.

Bandix makes essentially one product, simple lenses. It therefore has a very simple costing environment where the cost of a lens can be calculated fairly accurately by dividing total costs incurred by units produced. Plastim's costing environment is more challenging. The processes to make simple and complex lenses are quite different and Plastim needs to determine what it costs to make each type of lens.

In computing these costs, Plastim assigns both variable costs and costs that are fixed in the short run to the S3 and CL5 lenses. Why? For two reasons. First because, in the long run, almost all costs can be changed and managed including those that are fixed in the short run. Second because, to survive and prosper in the long run, the prices charged for S3 and CL5 must exceed total costs (variable and fixed) to design, make and distribute the lenses.

Consequently, to guide their pricing and cost-management decisions, Plastim's managers assign all costs, both manufacturing and nonmanufacturing, to the S3 and CL5 lenses. Had the purpose been inventory costing to comply with generally accepted accounting principles, Plastim's management accountants would have assigned only manufacturing costs to the lenses. Surveys of company practice across the globe overwhelmingly indicate that the vast majority of companies use costing systems not just for inventory costing but also for strategic purposes such as pricing and product-mix decisions and decisions about cost reduction, process improvement, design, and planning and budgeting. As a result, even merchandising-sector companies (for whom inventory costing is straightforward) and service-sector companies (who have no inventory) expend considerable resources in designing and operating their costing systems. In this chapter, we take this more strategic focus and describe cost system design across the value chain.

Simple Costing System Using a Single Indirect-Cost Pool

Plastim has historically had a simple costing system that allocates indirect costs using a single indirect-cost rate, the type of system described in Chapter 4. To budget costs for 2010, we first describe Plastim's simple costing system and later contrast it with a different costing system: activity-based costing. (Note that instead of jobs, as in Chapter 4, we now have products as the cost objects.) Exhibit 5-1 shows an overview of Plastim's simple costing system. Use this exhibit as a guide as you study the following steps, each of which is marked in Exhibit 5-1.

Step 1: Identify the Products That Are the Chosen Cost Objects. The cost objects are the 60,000 simple S3 lenses and the 15,000 complex CL5 lenses that Plastim will produce in 2010. Plastim's goal is to first calculate the total costs and then the unit cost of designing, manufacturing, and distributing these lenses.

Step 2: Identify the Direct Costs of the Products. Plastim identifies the direct costs—direct materials and direct manufacturing labor—of the lenses. Exhibit 5-2 shows the direct and indirect costs for the S3 and the CL5 lenses using the simple costing system. The direct cost calculations appear on lines 5, 6, and 7 of Exhibit 5-2. Plastim classifies all other costs as indirect costs.

Step 3: Select the Cost-Allocation Bases to Use for Allocating Indirect (or Overhead) Costs to the Products. A majority of the indirect costs consist of salaries paid to supervisors, engineers, manufacturing support, and maintenance staff, all supporting direct manufacturing labor. Plastim uses direct manufacturing labor-hours as the only allocation base to allocate all manufacturing and nonmanufacturing indirect costs to S3 and CL5. In 2010, Plastim plans to use 39,750 direct manufacturing labor-hours.

Step 4: Identify the Indirect Costs Associated with Each Cost-Allocation Base. Because Plastim uses only a single cost-allocation base, Plastim groups all budgeted indirect costs of \$2,385,000 for 2010 into a single overhead cost pool.

Step 5: Compute the Rate per Unit of Each Cost-Allocation Base.

$$\text{Budgeted indirect-cost rate} = \frac{\text{Budgeted total costs in indirect-cost pool}}{\text{Budgeted total quantity of cost-allocation base}}$$

$$= \frac{\$2{,}385{,}000}{39{,}750 \text{ direct manufacturing labor-hours}}$$

$$= \$60 \text{ per direct manufacturing labor-hour}$$

Step 6: Compute the Indirect Costs Allocated to the Products. Plastim expects to use 30,000 total direct manufacturing labor-hours to make the 60,000 S3 lenses and 9,750 total direct manufacturing labor-hours to make the 15,000 CL5 lenses. Exhibit 5-2 shows indirect costs of \$1,800,000 (\$60 per direct manufacturing labor-hour × 30,000 direct manufacturing labor-hours) allocated to the simple lens and \$585,000 (\$60 per direct manufacturing labor-hour × 9,750 direct manufacturing labor-hours) allocated to the complex lens.

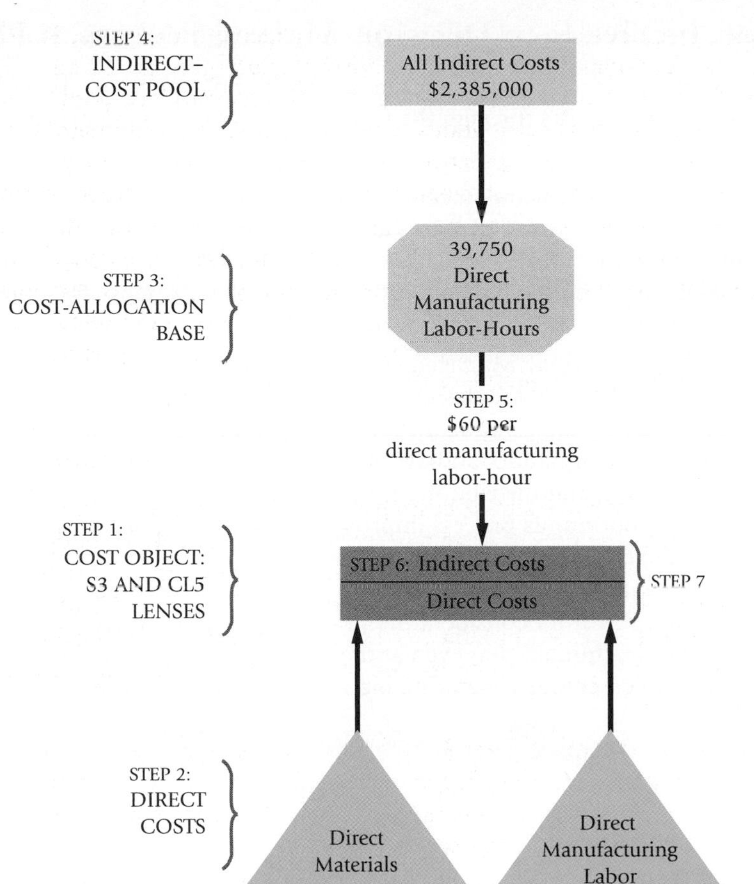

Exhibit 5-1

Overview of Plastim's Simple Costing System

Step 7: Compute the Total Cost of the Products by Adding All Direct and Indirect Costs Assigned to the Products. Exhibit 5-2 presents the product costs for the simple and complex lenses. The direct costs are calculated in step 2 and the indirect costs in step 6. Be sure you see the parallel between the simple costing system overview diagram (Exhibit 5-1) and the costs calculated in step 7. Exhibit 5-1 shows two direct-cost categories and one indirect-cost category. Hence, the budgeted cost of each type of lens in step 7 (Exhibit 5-2) has three line items: two for direct costs and one for allocated indirect costs. The unit cost of the S3 lens will be $58.75, well above the $53 selling price quoted by Bandix. The cost per CL5 lens is $97.

Exhibit 5-2

Plastim's Product Costs Using the Simple Costing System

File Edit View Insert Format Tools Data Window Help

	A	B	C	D	E	F	G
1		60,000			15,000		
2		Simple Lenses (S3)			Complex Lenses (CL5)		
3		Total	per Unit		Total	per Unit	Total
4		(1)	(2) = (1) ÷ 60,000		(3)	(4) = (3) ÷ 15,000	(5) = (1) + (3)
5	Direct materials	$1,125,000	$18.75		$ 675,000	$45.00	$1,800,000
6	Direct manufacturing labor	600,000	10.00		195,000	13.00	795,000
7	Total direct costs (Step 2)	1,725,000	28.75		870,000	58.00	2,595,000
8	Indirect costs allocated (Step 6)	1,800,000	30.00		585,000	39.00	2,385,000
9	Total costs (Step 7)	$3,525,000	$58.75		$1,455,000	$97.00	$4,980,000
10							

Applying the Five-Step Decision-Making Process at Plastim

To decide how it should respond to the threat that Bandix poses to its S3 lens business, Plastim's management works through the five-step decision-making process introduced in Chapter 1.

Step 1: Identify the problem and uncertainties. The problem is clear—if Plastim wants to retain the Giovanni business for S3 lenses and make a profit, it must find a way to reduce the price and costs of the S3 lens. The two major uncertainties Plastim faces are (1) whether Plastim's technology and processes for the S3 lens are competitive with Bandix's and (2) whether the S3 lens is overcosted by the simple costing system.

Step 2: Obtain information. Management asks a team of its design and process engineers to analyze and evaluate the design, manufacturing, and distribution operations for the S3 lens. The team is very confident that the technology and processes for the S3 lens are not inferior to those of Bandix and other competitors. Plastim has many years of experience in manufacturing and distributing simple lenses like the S3. Plastim also has a history and culture of continuous process improvements. If anything, the team is less certain about Plastim's capabilities in manufacturing and distributing complex lenses because it has only recently started making this type of lens. Given these doubts, management is happy that Giovanni Motors considers the price of the CL5 lens to be competitive. It is somewhat of a puzzle, though, that even at these prices Plastim is budgeted to earn a very large profit margin percentage (operating income ÷ revenues) on the CL5 lenses:

	60,000 Simple Lenses (S3)		15,000 Complex Lenses (CL5)		
	Total (1)	per Unit (2) = (1) ÷ 60,000	Total (3)	per Unit (4) = (3) ÷ 15,000	Total (5) = (1) + (3)
Revenues	$3,780,000	$63.00	$2,055,000	$137.00	$5,835,000
Total costs	3,525,000	58.75	1,455,000	97.00	4,980,000
Operating income	$ 255,000	$ 4.25	$ 600,000	$ 40.00	$ 855,000
Profit margin percentage		6.75%		29.20%	

As it continues to gather information, Plastim's management begins to ponder why the profit margin percentage is low for the S3 lens, where the company has strong capabilities, but high on the newer, less-established CL5 lens. Plastim is not deliberately charging a low price for S3, so management starts to believe that perhaps the problem lies with its costing system. Plastim's simple costing system may be overcosting the simple S3 lens (assigning too much cost to it) and undercosting the complex CL5 lens (assigning too little cost to it).

Step 3: Make predictions about the future. Plastim's key challenge is to get a better estimate of what it will cost to design, make, and distribute the S3 and CL5 lenses. Management is fairly confident about the direct material and direct manufacturing labor costs of each lens because these costs are easily traced to the lenses. But management is quite concerned about how accurately the simple costing system measures the indirect resources used by each type of lens. It believes it can do much better.

At the same time, management wants to ensure that no biases enter its thinking. In particular, it wants to be careful that the desire to be competitive on the S3 lens should not lead to assumptions that bias in favor of lowering costs of the S3 lens.

Step 4: Make decisions by choosing among alternatives. On the basis of predicted costs, and taking into account how Bandix might respond, Plastim must decide whether to bid for the Giovanni Motors' S3 lens business and if it does bid, what price it should offer.

Step 5: Implement the decision, evaluate performance, and learn. If Plastim wins Giovanni's S3 lens business, it must compare actual costs, as it makes and ships S3 lenses, to predicted costs and learn why actual costs deviate from predicted costs. Such evaluation and learning form the basis for future improvements.

The next few sections focus on Steps 3, 4 and 5—how Plastim improves the allocation of indirect costs to the S3 and CL5 lenses, how it uses these predictions to bid for the S3 lens business, and how it makes product design and process improvements.

Refining a Costing System

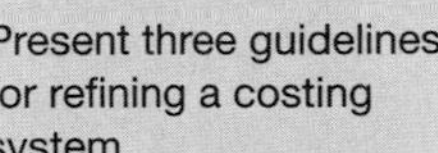

Learning Objective 2

Present three guidelines for refining a costing system

. . . classify more costs as direct costs, expand the number of indirect-cost pools, and identify cost drivers

A **refined costing system** reduces the use of broad averages for assigning the cost of resources to cost objects (such as jobs, products, and services) and provides better measurement of the costs of indirect resources used by different cost objects—no matter how differently various cost objects use indirect resources. There are three principal reasons that have accelerated the demand for such refinements.

1. **Increase in product diversity.** The growing demand for customized products has led companies to increase the variety of products and services they offer. Kanthal, the Swedish manufacturer of heating elements, for example, produces more than 10,000 different types of electrical heating wires and thermostats. Banks, such as the Cooperative Bank in the United Kingdom, offer many different types of accounts and services: special passbook accounts, ATMs, credit cards, and electronic banking. These products differ in the demands they place on the resources needed to produce them because of differences in volume, process, and complexity. The use of broad averages is likely to lead to distorted and inaccurate cost information.
2. **Increase in indirect costs.** The use of product and process technology such as computer-integrated manufacturing (CIM) and flexible manufacturing systems (FMS), has led to an increase in indirect costs and a decrease in direct costs, particularly direct manufacturing labor costs. In CIM and FMS, computers on the manufacturing floor give instructions to set up and run equipment quickly and automatically. The computers accurately measure hundreds of production parameters and directly control the manufacturing processes to achieve high-quality output. Managing more complex technology and producing very diverse products also requires committing an increasing amount of resources for various support functions, such as production scheduling and product and process design and engineering. Because direct manufacturing labor is not a cost driver of these costs, allocating indirect costs on the basis of direct manufacturing labor (which was the common practice) often does not accurately measure how resources are being used by different products.
3. **Competition in product markets.** As markets have become more competitive, managers have felt the need to obtain more accurate cost information to help them make important strategic decisions, such as how to price products and which products to sell. Making correct pricing and product mix decisions is critical in competitive markets because competitors quickly capitalize on a company's mistakes.

   Whereas the above factors point to reasons for the increase in *demand* for refined cost systems, *advances in information technology* have enabled companies to implement these refinements. Costing system refinements require more data gathering and more analysis, and improvements in information technology have drastically reduced the costs to gather, validate, store, and analyze vast quantities of data.

This chapter describes three guidelines for refining a costing system:

1. **Direct-cost tracing.** Identify as many direct costs as is economically feasible. This guideline aims to reduce the amount of costs classified as indirect, thereby minimizing the extent to which costs have to be allocated, rather than traced.
2. **Indirect-cost pools.** Expand the number of indirect-cost pools until each of these pools is more homogeneous. In a *homogeneous cost pool,* all of the costs have the same or a similar cause-and-effect (or benefits-received) relationship with a single cost driver that is used as the cost-allocation base. Consider, for example, a single indirect-cost pool containing both indirect machining costs and indirect distribution costs that are allocated to products using machine-hours. This pool is not homogeneous because machining costs and distribution costs do not have the same cause-and-effect relationship with machine-hours. Increases in machine-hours—the cause—have the effect of increasing machining costs but not distribution costs. Now suppose that machining costs and distribution costs are separated into two indirect-cost pools with machine-hours as the cost-allocation base for the machining cost pool and the number of shipments as the cost-allocation base for the distribution cost pool. Each

indirect-cost pool would now be homogeneous, which means that within each cost pool, all costs have the same cause-and-effect relationship with their respective cost-allocation base.

3. **Cost-allocation bases.** As we describe later in the chapter, whenever possible, use the cost driver (the cause of indirect costs) as the cost-allocation base for each homogenous indirect-cost pool (the effect).

Activity-Based Costing Systems

Learning Objective 3

Distinguish between simple and activity-based costing systems

. . . unlike simple systems, ABC systems calculate costs of individual activities to cost products

One of the best tools for refining a costing system is activity-based costing. **Activity-based costing (ABC)** refines a costing system by identifying individual activities as the fundamental cost objects. An **activity** is an event, task, or unit of work with a specified purpose—for example, designing products, setting up machines, operating machines, and distributing products. More informally, activities are verbs; they are things that a firm does. Consistent with their more strategic focus, ABC systems identify activities in all functions of the value chain. ABC systems first calculate the costs of individual activities and then assign costs to cost objects such as products and services on the basis of the mix of activities needed to produce each product or service:[2]

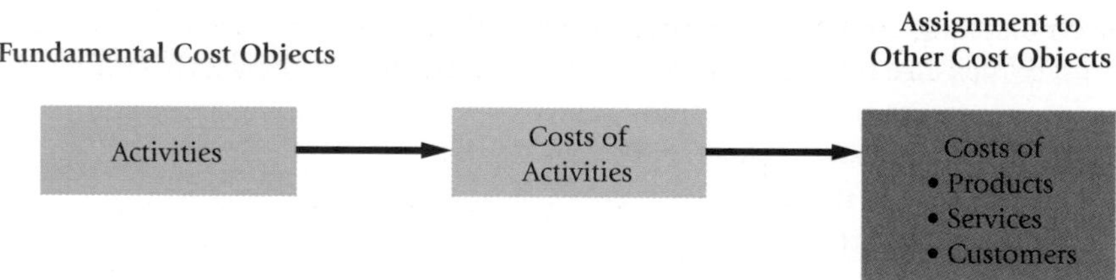

Plastim's ABC System

After reviewing its simple costing system and the potential miscosting of product costs, Plastim decides to implement an ABC system. Direct costs can be traced to products easily, so the ABC system focuses on refining the assignment of indirect costs to departments, processes, products, or other cost objects. Plastim's ABC system identifies various activities that help explain why Plastim incurs the costs it currently classifies as indirect. In other words, it breaks up the current indirect cost pool into finer pools of costs related to various activities. To identify these activities, Plastim organizes a team comprised of managers from design, manufacturing, distribution, accounting, and administration.

Defining activities is not a simple matter. The team evaluates hundreds of tasks performed at Plastim before choosing the activities that form the basis of its ABC system. For example, it decides if maintenance of molding machines, operations of molding machines, process control, and product inspection should each be regarded as a separate activity or should be combined into a single activity. An activity-based costing system with many activities becomes overly detailed and unwieldy to operate. An activity-based costing system with too few activities may not be refined enough to measure cause-and-effect relationships between cost drivers and various indirect costs. In choosing activities, Plastim's team identifies those that account for a sizable fraction of indirect costs and combines activities that have the same cost driver into a single activity. For example, the team decides to combine maintenance of molding machines, operations of molding machines, process control, and product inspection into a single activity—molding machine operations—because all these activities have the same cost driver: molding machine-hours.

[2] For more details on ABC systems, see R. Cooper and R. S. Kaplan, *The Design of Cost Management Systems* (Upper Saddle River, NJ: Prentice Hall, 1999); G. Cokins, *Activity-Based Cost Management: An Executive's Guide* (Hoboken, NJ: John Wiley & Sons, 2001); and R. S. Kaplan and S. Anderson, *Time-Driven Activity-Based Costing: A Simpler and More Powerful Path to Higher Profits* (Boston: Harvard Business School Press, 2007).

The team identifies the following seven activities by developing a flowchart of all the steps and processes needed to design, manufacture, and distribute S3 and CL5 lenses.

a. Design products and processes
b. Set up molding machines to ensure that the molds are properly held in place and parts are properly aligned before manufacturing starts
c. Operate molding machines to manufacture lenses
d. Clean and maintain the molds after lenses are manufactured
e. Prepare batches of finished lenses for shipment
f. Distribute lenses to customers
g. Administer and manage all processes at Plastim

These activity descriptions form the basis of the activity-based costing system—sometimes called an *activity list* or an *activity dictionary*. The list of tasks, however, is only the first step in implementing activity-based costing systems. Plastim must also identify the cost of each activity and the related cost driver. To do so, Plastim uses the three guidelines for refining a costing system described on pages 143–144.

1. **Direct-cost tracing.** Plastim's ABC system subdivides the single indirect cost pool into seven smaller cost pools related to the different activities. Plastim determines that the costs in the cleaning and maintenance activity cost pool (item d) is a direct cost. The costs of cleaning and maintenance consist of salaries and wages paid to workers responsible for cleaning the mold. These costs can be economically traced to the specific mold used to produce the lens.
2. **Indirect-cost pools.** Plastim considers the remaining six activity cost pools as indirect cost pools. Unlike the single indirect cost pool of Plastim's simple costing system, each of the activity-related cost pools is homogeneous. That is, each activity cost pool includes only those narrow and focused set of costs that have the same cost driver. For example, the distribution cost pool includes only those costs (such as wages of truck drivers) that, over time, increase as the cost driver of distribution costs, cubic feet of packages delivered, increases. In the simple costing system, all costs were lumped together and changes in the cost-allocation base, direct manufacturing labor-hours, had no effect on the costs in the single cost pool.

   Determining costs of activity pools requires assigning and reassigning costs accumulated in support departments, such as human resources and information systems, to each of the activity cost pools on the basis of how various activities use support department resources. In the 2-stage allocation model, this is the *first-stage allocation*—the allocation of costs accumulated in support departments to each activity cost pool. We focus here on the *second-stage allocation*—the allocation of costs of activity cost pools to products. We defer a detailed discussion of how costs of activity pools are determined until Chapters 14 and 15.
3. **Cost-allocation bases.** For each activity cost pool, the cost driver is used (whenever possible) as the cost-allocation base. For example, in the long run, setup-hours is the cost driver for the setup activity so setup hours is used as the cost-allocation base for setup costs. How do Plastim's managers know that setup hours is the cost driver? They consider various alternatives and use their knowledge of operations to choose among them. For example, Plastim's managers must decide whether setup hours or the number of setups is the cost driver of setup costs. On the basis of their knowledge of operations, Plastim's managers believe that setup time, not just the number of setups, drive setup costs because more complex setups take more time and are more costly. Plastim's managers can also test their beliefs with data. Over time, a plot of the data should show a proportionate change in setup costs as setup hours change. The relation between setup costs and number of setups would be much weaker. (Chapter 10 discusses several methods to estimate the relationship between a cost driver and costs.)

The logic of ABC systems is twofold. First, structuring activity cost pools more finely with cost drivers for each activity cost pool as the cost-allocation base leads to more accurate costing of activities. Second, allocating these costs to products by measuring the cost-allocation bases of different activities used by different products leads to more accurate product costs. We illustrate this logic by focusing on the setup activity at Plastim.

Setting up molding machines frequently entails trial runs, fine-tuning, and adjustments. Improper setups cause quality problems such as scratches on the surface of the lens. The resources needed for each setup depend on the complexity of the manufacturing operation. Complex lenses require more setup resources per setup than simple lenses. Furthermore, complex lenses can be produced only in small batches because the molds for complex lenses need to be cleaned more often than molds for simple lenses. Thus, relative to simple lenses, complex lenses not only use more resources per setup, but they also require more frequent setups.

Setup data for the simple S3 lens and the complex CL5 lens are:

		Simple S3 Lens	Complex CL5 Lens	Total
1	Quantity of lenses produced	60,000	15,000	
2	Number of lenses produced per batch	240	50	
3 = (1) ÷ (2)	Number of batches	250	300	
4	Setup time per batch	2 hours	5 hours	
5 = (3) × (4)	Total setup-hours	500 hours	1,500 hours	2,000 hours

Setup hours represents the demand that each product places on setup resources.

Of the $2,385,000 in the total indirect-cost pool, Plastim identifies the total costs of setups (consisting mainly of allocated costs of process engineers, quality engineers, supervisors, and depreciation on setup equipment) to be $300,000. The following table illustrates the effect of using direct manufacturing labor-hours—the cost-allocation base for all indirect costs in Plastim's pre-ABC costing system—versus setup-hours—the cost-allocation base for setup costs in the ABC system—to allocate setup costs to the simple and complex lenses. Of the $60 total rate per direct manufacturing labor-hour (p. 140), the setup cost per direct manufacturing labor-hour amounts to $7.54717 ($300,000 ÷ 39,750 total direct manufacturing labor-hours). The setup cost per setup-hour equals $150 ($300,000 ÷ 2,000 total setup-hours).

	Simple S3 Lens	Complex CL5 Lens	Total
Setup cost allocated using direct manufacturing labor-hours: $7.54717 × 30,000; $7.54717 × 9,750	$226,415	$ 73,585	$300,000
Setup cost allocated using setup-hours: $150 × 500; $150 × 1,500	$ 75,000	$225,000	$300,000

As we have already discussed when presenting guidelines 2 and 3, setup hours, not direct manufacturing labor hours, are the cost driver of set-up costs. Setup costs depend on the number of batches and the difficulty of the setups, both of which result in more setup-hours. The CL5 lens uses substantially more setup-hours than the S3 lens (1,500 hours ÷ 2,000 hours = 75% of the total setup hours) because the CL5 requires a greater number of setups (batches) and each setup is more challenging. The ABC system therefore allocates substantially more setup costs to CL5 than to S3 because of the greater demand that CL5 places on setup resources. When direct manufacturing labor-hours rather than setup-hours are used to allocate setup costs in the simple costing system, it is the S3 lens that is allocated a very large share of the setup costs because the S3 lens uses a larger proportion of direct manufacturing labor-hours (30,000 ÷ 39,750 = 75.47%). As a result, the simple costing system overcosts the S3 lens with regard to setup costs.

Note that setup-hours are related to batches (or groups) of lenses made, not the number of individual lenses. Activity-based costing attempts to identify the most relevant cause-and-effect relationship for each activity pool, without restricting the cost driver to only units of output or variables related to units of output (such as direct manufacturing labor-hours). As our discussion of setups illustrates, limiting cost-allocation bases in this manner weakens the cause-and-effect relationship between the cost allocation base and the costs in a cost pool. Under an ABC system, when the cost in a cost pool relates to batches of output (such as set-up costs), the cost-allocation bases chosen are cost drivers based on batches of output (such as setup hours). ABC systems classify costs in a *cost hierarchy*, distinguishing costs by whether the cost driver is a unit of output (or variables such as machine-hours or direct manufacturing labor-hours that are related to units of output); or a group of units of a product, such as a batch in the case of setup costs; or the complexity of the product itself as in the case of design costs.

Cost Hierarchies

Learning Objective 4

Describe a four-part cost hierarchy

. . . a four-part cost hierarchy is used to categorize costs based on different types of cost drivers—for example, costs that vary with each unit of a product versus costs that vary with each batch of products

A **cost hierarchy** categorizes various activity cost pools on the basis of the different types of cost drivers, or cost-allocation bases, or different degrees of difficulty in determining cause-and-effect (or benefits-received) relationships. ABC systems commonly use a cost hierarchy having four levels—output unit-level costs, batch-level costs, product-sustaining costs, and facility-sustaining costs—to identify cost-allocation bases that are, whenever possible, drivers of costs in activity cost pools.

Output unit-level costs are the costs of activities performed on each individual unit of a product or service. Machine operations costs (such as the cost of energy, machine depreciation, and repair) related to the activity of running the automated molding machines are output unit-level costs. They are output unit-level costs because, over time, the cost of this activity increases with additional units of output produced (or machine-hours used).

Suppose that in our Plastim example, each S3 lens requires 0.15 molding machine-hours. Then S3 lenses require a total of 9,000 molding machine-hours (0.15 molding machine-hours per lens × 60,000 lenses). Similarly, suppose each CL5 lens requires 0.25 molding machine-hours. Then the CL5 lenses require 3,750 molding machine-hours (0.25 molding machine-hours per lens × 15,000 lenses). The *total* machine operations costs allocated to S3 and CL5 depend on the quantity of each type of lens produced, regardless of the number of batches in which the lenses are made. Plastim's ABC system uses machine-hours—an output unit-level cost-allocation base—to allocate machine operations costs to products.

Batch-level costs are the costs of activities related to a group of units of products or services rather than to each individual unit of product or service. In the Plastim example, setup costs are batch-level costs because, over time, the cost of this setup activity increases with setup-hours needed to produce batches of lenses. As described in the table on page 146, the S3 lens requires 500 setup-hours (2 setup-hours per batch × 250 batches). The CL5 lens requires 1,500 setup-hours (5 setup-hours per batch × 300 batches). The total setup costs allocated to S3 and CL5 depend on the total setup-hours required by each type of lens, not on the number of units of S3 and CL5 produced. (Setup costs being a batch-level cost cannot be avoided by producing one less unit of S3 or CL5.) Plastim's ABC system uses setup-hours—a batch-level cost-allocation base—to allocate setup costs to products.

Consider another example. In companies that purchase many different types of direct materials (Plastim purchases mainly plastic pellets), procurement costs can be significant. Procurement costs include the costs of placing purchase orders, receiving materials, and paying invoices. These costs are batch-level costs because they are related to the number of purchase orders placed rather than to the quantity or value of materials purchased. Other examples of batch-level costs are materials-handling and quality-inspection costs associated with batches of products produced.

Product-sustaining costs (service-sustaining costs) are the costs of activities undertaken to support individual products or services regardless of the number of units or batches in which the units are produced. In the Plastim example, design costs are product-sustaining costs. Over time, design costs depend largely on the time designers spend on designing and modifying the product, the mold, and the process. These design costs are a function of the complexity of the mold, measured by the number of parts in the mold multiplied by the area (in square feet) over which the molten plastic must flow (12 parts × 2.5 square feet, or 30 parts-square feet for the S3 lens, and 14 parts × 5 square feet, or 70 parts-square feet for the CL5 lens). The total design costs allocated to S3 and CL5 depend on the complexity of the mold, regardless of the number of units or batches of production. Design costs cannot be avoided by producing fewer units or running fewer batches. Plastim's ABC system uses parts-square feet—a product-sustaining cost-allocation base—to allocate design costs to products. Other examples of product-sustaining costs are product research and development costs, costs of making engineering changes, and marketing costs to launch new products.

Facility-sustaining costs are the costs of activities that cannot be traced to individual products or services but that support the organization as a whole. In the Plastim example, the general administration costs (including top management compensation, rent, and building security) are facility-sustaining costs. It is usually difficult to find a good cause-and-effect relationship between these costs and the cost-allocation base. This lack of a cause-and-effect relationship causes some companies not to allocate these costs to products and instead to deduct them separately from operating income. Other companies, such as Plastim, allocate facility-sustaining costs to products on some basis—for example, direct manufacturing labor-hours—because management believes all costs should be allocated to products. Allocating all costs to products or services becomes important when management wants to set selling prices on the basis of an amount of cost that includes all costs.

Implementing Activity-Based Costing at Plastim

Learning Objective 5

Cost products or services using activity-based costing

. . . use cost rates for different activities to compute indirect costs of a product

Now that you understand the basic concepts of ABC, let's use them to refine Plastim's simple costing system. We again follow the seven-step approach to costing and the three guidelines for refining costing systems (the guidelines are increasing direct-cost tracing, creating homogeneous indirect-cost pools, and identifying cost-allocation bases that have cause-and-effect relationships with costs in the cost pool). Exhibit 5-3 shows an overview of Plastim's ABC system. Use this exhibit as a guide as you study the following steps, each of which is marked in Exhibit 5-3.

Step 1: Identify the Products That Are the Chosen Cost Objects. The cost objects are the 60,000 S3 and the 15,000 CL5 lenses that Plastim will produce in 2010. Plastim's goal is to first calculate the total costs and then the per-unit cost of designing, manufacturing, and distributing these lenses.

Step 2: Identify the Direct Costs of the Products. Plastim identifies as direct costs of the lenses: direct material costs, direct manufacturing labor costs, and mold cleaning and maintenance costs. Plastim has been classifying mold cleaning and maintenance costs as indirect costs and has allocated them to products using direct manufacturing labor-hours. However, following guideline 1 for refining a costing system, these costs, consisting of workers' wages for cleaning molds after each batch of lenses is produced, can be traced directly as a batch-level cost because each type of lens can only be produced from a specific mold. Complex lenses incur more mold cleaning and maintenance costs than simple lenses because Plastim produces more batches of complex lenses than simple lenses and because the molds of complex lenses are more difficult to clean. Direct manufacturing labor-hours is not a good cost driver of the demand that simple and complex lenses place on mold cleaning and maintenance resources.

Exhibit 5-5 shows the direct and indirect costs for the S3 and CL5 lenses using the ABC system. The direct costs calculations appear on lines 6, 7, 8 and 9 of Exhibit 5-5. Plastim classifies all other costs as indirect costs, as we will see in Exhibit 5-4.

Step 3: Select the Activities and Cost-Allocation Bases to Use for Allocating Indirect Costs to the Products. Following guidelines 2 and 3 for refining a costing system, Plastim identifies six activities—(a) design, (b) molding machine setups, (c) machine operations, (d) shipment setup, (e) distribution, and (f) administration—for allocating indirect costs to products. Exhibit 5-4, column 2, shows the cost hierarchy category, and column 4 shows the cost-allocation base and the budgeted quantity of the cost-allocation base for each activity described in column 1.

Identifying the cost-allocation bases defines the number of activity pools into which costs must be grouped in an ABC system. For example, rather than define the design activities of product design, process design, and prototyping as separate activities, Plastim defines these three activities together as a combined "design" activity and forms a homogeneous design cost pool. Why? Because the complexity of the mold is an appropriate cost driver for costs incurred in each of the three separate design activities.

A second consideration before choosing a cost-allocation base is the availability of reliable data and measures. Consider the problem of determining a cost-allocation base for the design activity. The driver of design cost, which is a product-sustaining cost, is the complexity of the mold; more-complex molds take more time to design. In its ABC system, Plastim measures mold complexity in terms of the number of parts in the mold and the surface area of the mold (parts-square feet). If these data are difficult to obtain or measure, Plastim may be forced to use some other measure of complexity, such as the amount of material flowing through the mold. A potential problem with this measure is that the quantity of material flow may not adequately represent the cost of the design activity.

Step 4: Identify the Indirect Costs Associated with Each Cost-Allocation Base. In this step, Plastim assigns budgeted indirect costs for 2010 to activities (see Exhibit 5-4, column 3), to the extent possible, on the basis of a cause-and-effect relationship between the cost-allocation base for an activity and the costs of the activity. For example, all costs that have a cause-and-effect relationship to cubic feet of packages moved are assigned to the distribution cost pool. Of course, the strength of the cause-and-effect relationship between the cost-allocation base and the respective cost of the activity varies across cost pools. For example, the cause-and-effect relationship between direct manufacturing labor-hours and administration activity costs is not as strong as the relationship between setup-hours and setup activity costs.

Some costs can be directly identified with a particular activity. For example, cost of materials used when designing products, salaries paid to design engineers, and depreciation of equipment used in the design department are directly identified with the design activity. Other costs need to be allocated across activities. For example, on the basis of interviews or time records, manufacturing engineers and supervisors estimate the time they will spend on design, molding machine setup, and machine operations. The time to be spent on these activities serves as a basis for allocating each manufacturing engineer's and supervisor's salary costs to various activities.

Plastim allocates support costs to activity-cost pools using allocation bases that best describe how support costs are used by the different activities. For example, rent costs are allocated to activity cost pools on the basis of square-feet area used by different activities.

The point here is that all costs do not fit neatly into activity categories. Often, costs may first need to be allocated to activities (Stage 1 of the 2-stage cost-allocation model) before the costs of the activities can be allocated to products (Stage 2). Chapters 14 and 15 describe Stage 1 allocations in greater detail.

Step 5: Compute the Rate per Unit of Each Cost-Allocation Base. Exhibit 5-4, column 5, summarizes the calculation of the budgeted indirect cost rates using the budgeted quantity of the cost-allocation base from step 3 and the total budgeted indirect costs of each activity from step 4.

Step 6: Compute the Indirect Costs Allocated to the Products. Exhibit 5-5 shows total budgeted indirect costs of $1,153,953 allocated to the simple lens and $961,047 allocated to the complex lens. Follow the budgeted indirect cost calculations for each lens in Exhibit 5-5. For each activity, Plastim's operations personnel indicate the total quantity of the cost-allocation base that will be used for each lens (recall that Plastim operates at capacity). For example, lines 15 and 16 of Exhibit 5-5 show that of the 2,000 total setups hours, the S3 lens is budgeted to use 500 hours and the CL5 lens 1,500 hours. The budgeted indirect cost rate is $150 per setup hour (Exhibit 5-4, column 5, line 5).

Therefore, total budgeted cost of setup activity allocated to the S3 lens is $75,000 (500 setup-hours × $150 per setup-hour) and to the CL5 lens is $225,000 (1,500 setup-hours × $150 per setup-hour). Budgeted setup cost per unit equals $1.25 ($75,000 ÷ 60,000 units) for the S3 lens and $15 ($225,000 ÷ 15,000 units) for the CL5 lens.

Step 7: Compute the Total Cost of the Products by Adding All Direct and Indirect Costs Assigned to the Products. Exhibit 5-5 presents the product costs for the simple and complex

Exhibit 5-3 Overview of Plastim's Activity-Based Costing System

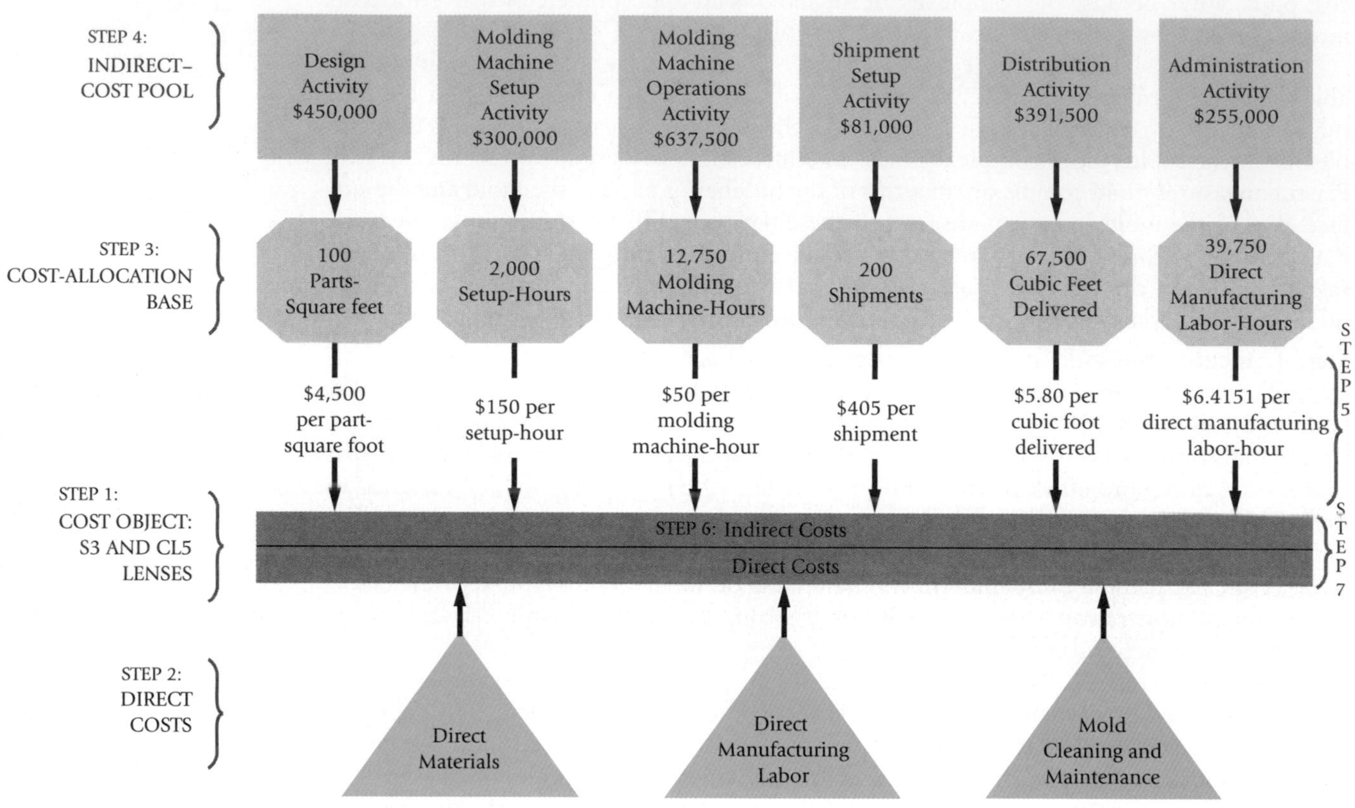

Exhibit 5-4 Activity-Cost Rates for Indirect-Cost Pools

	A	B	C	D	E	F	G	H
1			(Step 4)	(Step 3)		(Step 5)		
2	Activity	Cost Hierarchy Category	Total Budgeted Indirect Costs	Budgeted Quantity of Cost-Allocation Base		Budgeted Indirect Cost Rate		Cause-and-Effect Relationship Between Allocation Base and Activity Cost
3	(1)	(2)	(3)	(4)		(5) = (3) ÷ (4)		(6)
4	Design	Product-sustaining	$450,000	100	parts-square feet	$ 4,500	per part-square foot	Design Department indirect costs increase with more complex molds (more parts, larger surface area).
5	Setup molding machines	Batch-level	$300,000	2,000	setup-hours	$ 150	per setup-hour	Indirect setup costs increase with setup-hours.
6	Machine operations	Output unit-level	$637,500	12,750	molding machine-hours	$ 50	per molding machine-hour	Indirect costs of operating molding machines increases with molding machine-hours.
7	Shipment setup	Batch-level	$ 81,000	200	shipments	$ 405	per shipment	Shipping costs incurred to prepare batches for shipment increase with the number of shipments.
8	Distribution	Output-unit-level	$391,500	67,500	cubic feet delivered	$ 5.80	per cubic foot delivered	Distribution costs increase with the cubic feet of packages delivered.
9	Administration	Facility sustaining	$255,000	39,750	direct manuf. labor-hours	$6.4151	per direct manuf. labor-hour	The demand for Administrative resources increases with direct manufacturing labor-hours.

Exhibit 5-5 Plastim's Product Costs Using Activity-Based Costing System

	A	B	C	D	E	F	G
1		60,000			15,000		
2		Simple Lenses (S3)			Complex Lenses (CL5)		
3		Total	per Unit		Total	per Unit	Total
4	Cost Description	(1)	(2) = (1) ÷ 60,000		(3)	(4) = (3) ÷ 15,000	(5) = (1) + (3)
5	Direct costs						
6	Direct materials	$1,125,000	$18.75		$ 675,000	$ 45.00	$1,800,000
7	Direct manufacturing labor	600,000	10.00		195,000	13.00	795,000
8	Direct mold cleaning and maintenance costs	120,000	2.00		150,000	10.00	270,000
9	Total direct costs (Step 2)	1,845,000	30.75		1,020,000	68.00	2,865,000
10	Indirect Costs of Activities						
11	Design						
12	S3, 30 parts-sq.ft. x $4,500	135,000	2.25				} 450,000
13	CL5, 70 parts-sq.ft. x $4,500				315,000	21.00	
14	Setup of molding machines						
15	S3, 500 setup-hours x $150	75,000	1.25				} 300,000
16	CL5, 1,500 setup-hours x $150				225,000	15.00	
17	Machine operations						
18	S3, 9,000 molding machine-hours x $50	450,000	7.50				} 637,500
19	CL5, 3,750 molding machine-hours x $50				187,500	12.50	
20	Shipment setup						
21	S3, 100 shipments x $405	40,500	0.67				} 81,000
22	CL5, 100 shipments x $405				40,500	2.70	
23	Distribution						
24	S3, 45,000 cubic feet delivered x $5.80	261,000	4.35				} 391,500
25	CL5, 22,500 cubic feet delivered x $5.80				130,500	8.70	
26	Administration						
27	S3, 30,000 dir. manuf. labor-hours x $6.4151	192,453	3.21				} 255,000
28	CL5, 9,750 dir. manuf. labor-hours x $6.4151				62,547	4.17	
29	Total indirect costs allocated (Step 6)	1,153,953	19.23		961,047	64.07	2,115,000
30	Total Costs (Step 7)	$2,998,953	$49.98		$1,981,047	$132.07	$4,980,000
31							

lenses. The direct costs are calculated in step 2, and the indirect costs are calculated in step 6. The ABC system overview in Exhibit 5-3 shows three direct-cost categories and six indirect-cost categories. The budgeted cost of each lens type in Exhibit 5-5 has nine line items, three for direct costs and six for indirect costs. The differences between the ABC product costs of S3 and CL5 calculated in Exhibit 5-5 highlight how each of these products uses different amounts of direct and indirect costs in each activity area.

We emphasize two features of ABC systems. First, these systems identify all costs used by products, whether the costs are variable or fixed in the short run. That's because the focus of ABC systems is on long-run decisions when more of the costs can be managed and fewer costs are regarded as fixed. As we saw in Chapter 3, if Plastim's managers were interested in short-run decisions, they would need to focus on only the variable costs of activities used by products and not all costs. Second, recognizing the hierarchy of costs is critical when allocating costs to products. It is easiest to use the cost hierarchy to first calculate the total costs of each product. The per-unit costs can then be derived by dividing total costs by the number of units produced.

Comparing Alternative Costing Systems

Exhibit 5-6 compares the simple costing system using a single indirect-cost pool (Exhibit 5-1 and Exhibit 5-2) Plastim had been using and the ABC system (Exhibit 5-3 and Exhibit 5-5). Note three points in Exhibit 5-6, consistent with the guidelines for refining a costing system: (1) ABC systems trace more costs as direct costs; (2) ABC systems create homogeneous cost pools linked to different activities; and (3) for each activity-cost pool, ABC systems seek a cost-allocation base that has a cause-and-effect relationship with costs in the cost pool.

The homogeneous cost pools and the choice of cost-allocation bases, tied to the cost hierarchy, give Plastim's managers greater confidence in the activity and product cost numbers from the ABC system. The bottom part of Exhibit 5-6 shows that allocating costs to lenses using only an output unit-level allocation base—direct manufacturing labor-hours, as in the single indirect-cost pool system used prior to ABC—overcosts the simple S3 lens by $8.77 per unit and undercosts the complex CL5 lens by $35.07 per unit. The CL5 lens uses a disproportionately larger amount of output unit-level, batch-level, and product-sustaining costs than is represented by the direct manufacturing labor-hour cost-allocation base. The S3 lens uses a disproportionately smaller amount of these costs. The ABC system, by its use of multiple indirect cost pools and activity-specific drivers at various levels of the cost hierarchy, is able to better recognize the resources used by the S3 and CL5 lenses.

The benefit of an ABC system is that it provides information to make better decisions. But this benefit must be weighed against the measurement and implementation costs of an ABC system. We elaborate on these costs later in this chapter.

Using ABC Systems for Improving Cost Management and Profitability

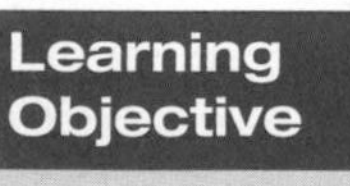

Explain how activity-based costing systems are used in activity-based management

. . . such as pricing decisions, product-mix decisions, and cost reduction

The emphasis of this chapter so far has been on the role of ABC systems in obtaining better product costs. But Plastim's managers must now use this information to make decisions (step 4 of the 5-step decision process, p. 142) and to implement the decision, evaluate performance, and learn (step 5, p. 142). **Activity-based management (ABM)** is a method of management decision-making that uses activity-based costing information to improve customer satisfaction and profitability. We define ABM broadly to include decisions about pricing and product mix, how to reduce costs, how to improve processes, and decisions relating to product design.

Pricing and Product-Mix Decisions

An ABC system gives managers information about the costs of making and selling diverse products. With this information, managers can make pricing and product-mix decisions. For example, the ABC system indicates that Plastim can match its competitor's price of $53 for the S3 lens and still make a profit because the ABC cost of S3 is $49.98 (see Exhibit 5-5).

Plastim's managers offer Giovanni Motors a price of $52 for the S3 lens. Plastim's managers are confident that they can use the deeper understanding of costs that the ABC system provides to improve efficiency and further reduce the cost of the S3 lens. Without information from the ABC system, Plastim managers might have erroneously concluded that they would incur an operating loss on the S3 lens at a price of $53. This incorrect conclusion would have probably caused Plastim to reduce its business in simple lenses and focus instead on complex lenses, where its single indirect-cost-pool system indicated it is very profitable.

Focusing on complex lenses would have been a mistake. The ABC system indicates that the cost of making the complex lens is much higher—$132.07 versus $97 under the direct manufacturing labor-hour-based costing system Plastim had been using. As Plastim's operations staff had thought all along, Plastim has no competitive advantage in making CL5 lenses. At a price of $137 per lens for CL5, the profit margin is very small

Exhibit 5-6

Comparing Alternative Costing Systems

	Simple Costing System Using a Single Indirect-Cost Pool (1)	ABC System (2)	Difference (3) = (2) – (1)
Direct-cost categories	2	3	1
	Direct materials Direct manufacturing labor	Direct materials Direct manufacturing labor Direct mold cleaning and maintenance labor	
Total direct costs	$2,595,000	$2,865,000	$270,000
Indirect-cost pools	1	6	5
	Single indirect-cost pool allocated using direct manufacturing labor-hours	Design (parts-square feet)[1] Molding machine setup (setup-hours) Machine operations (molding machine-hours) Shipment setup (number of shipments) Distribution (cubic feet delivered) Administration (direct manufacturing labor-hours)	
Total indirect costs	$2,385,000	$2,115,000	($270,000)
Total costs assigned to simple (S3) lens	$3,525,000	$2,998,953	($526,047)
Cost per unit of simple (S3) lens	$58.75	$49.98	($8.77)
Total costs assigned to complex (CL5) lens	$1,455,000	$1,981,047	$526,047
Cost per unit of complex (CL5) lens	$97.00	$132.07	$35.07

[1]Cost drivers for the various indirect-cost pools are shown in parentheses.

($137.00– $132.07 = $4.93). As Plastim reduces its prices on simple lenses, it would need to negotiate a higher price for complex lenses.

Cost Reduction and Process Improvement Decisions

Manufacturing and distribution personnel use ABC systems to focus on how and where to reduce costs. Managers set cost reduction targets in terms of reducing the cost per unit of the cost-allocation base in different activity areas. For example, the supervisor of the distribution activity area at Plastim could have a performance target of decreasing distribution cost per cubic foot of products delivered from $5.80 to $5.40 by reducing distribution labor and warehouse rental costs. The goal is to reduce these costs without compromising customer service or the actual or perceived value (usefulness) customers obtain from the product or service. That is, Plastim will attempt to take out only those costs that are *nonvalue added.*

Doing an analysis of the factors that cause costs to be incurred (cost drivers) reveals many opportunities for improving the way work is done. Management can evaluate whether particular nonvalue-added activities can be reduced or eliminated. Each of the cost-allocation bases in Plastim's ABC system is a nonfinancial variable (number of setup-hours, cubic feet delivered, and so on). Controlling physical items such as setup-hours or cubic feet delivered is often the most fundamental way that operating personnel manage costs. For example, Plastim can decrease distribution costs by packing the lenses in a way that reduces the bulkiness of the packages delivered.

The following table shows the reduction in distribution costs of the S3 and CL5 lenses as a result of actions that lower cost per cubic foot delivered (from $5.80 to $5.40) and total cubic feet of deliveries (from 45,000 to 40,000 for S3 and 22,500 to 20,000 for CL5).

	60,000 (S3) Lenses		15,000 (CL5) Lenses	
	Total (1)	per Unit (2) = (1) ÷ 60,000	Total (3)	per Unit (4) = (3) ÷ 15,000
Distribution costs (from Exhibit 5-5)				
S3, 45,000 cubic feet × $5.80/cubic foot	$261,000	$4.35		
CL5, 22,500 cubic feet × $5.80/cubic foot			$130,500	$8.70
Distribution costs as a result of process improvements				
S3, 40,000 cubic feet × $5.40/cubic foot	216,000	3.60		
CL5, 20,000 cubic feet × $5.40/cubic foot			108,000	7.20
Savings in distribution costs from process improvements	$ 45,000	$0.75	$ 22,500	$1.50

Taking the long-term strategic view of ABC systems, we assume in the preceding example that total distribution costs will decrease from $391,500 ($261,000 + $130,500) to $324,000 ($216,000 + $108,000) as Plastim reduces distribution cost per cubic foot and cubic feet of packages delivered. In the short run, however, distribution costs may be fixed and may not decrease. Suppose all $391,500 of distribution costs are fixed costs in the short run. In this case, how should costs be allocated to the S3 and CL5 lenses? Note that this situation did not arise in our example so far. That's because Plastim is expected to operate at capacity, and all $391,500 of distribution costs support the distribution of S3 and CL5 lenses.

Many ABC systems distinguish *costs incurred* from *resources used* to design, manufacture, and deliver products and services. For the distribution activity, after process improvements,

Costs incurred = $391,500

Resources used = $216,000 (for S3 lens) + $108 000 (for CL5 lens) = $324,000

ABC systems focus on the resources used by each product and hence would allocate $216,000 to S3 and $108,000 to CL5 for a total of $324,000, which is less than the costs incurred of $391,500. The difference of $67,500 ($391,500−$324,000) represents costs of unused but available distribution capacity—that is,

Costs incurred = Resources used + Costs of unused capacity

= $324,000 + $67,500 = $391,500

This unused capacity arises from efficiency improvements (using less distribution labor and space) that result in a decrease in the distribution cost per cubic foot from $5.80 to $5.40, as the following calculations show:

Number of cubic feet of lenses that Plastim can deliver as a result of efficiency improvements	= $391,500 / $5.40 per cubic feet	= 72,500 cubic feet
Number of cubic feet that Plastim needs to deliver (S3 lens, 40, 000; CL5 lens, 20,000	= 40,000 + 20,000	= 60,000 cubic feet
Unused distribution capacity		= 12,500 cubic feet

Costs of unused distribution capacity = 12,500 cubic feet × $5.40 per cubic foot = $67,500

An advantage of ABC systems is that they do not allocate the costs of unused capacity to products. Instead, these systems highlight the amount of unused capacity as a separate line item. Highlighting unused capacity signals to managers an opportunity for reducing costs. Managers will seek to reduce unused capacity—for example, by redeploying labor to other uses or by laying off workers. At the same time, product costs for S3 and CL5 are not burdened by the cost of resources not supporting these products. Chapter 9 discusses issues related to unused capacity in more detail.

Design Decisions

Management can evaluate how its current product and process designs affect activities and costs as a way of identifying new designs to reduce costs. For example, design decisions that decrease complexity of the mold reduce costs of design, materials, labor, machine setups, machine operations, and mold cleaning and maintenance. Plastim's customers may be willing to give up some features of the lens in exchange for a lower price.

Had Plastim continued to use its direct manufacturing labor-hour-based system to choose among alternative designs, which design choices would Plastim have favored? Answer: Those designs that reduced direct manufacturing labor-hours the most. That's because the costing system would signal that reducing direct manufacturing labor-hours reduces indirect costs. However, this is a false signal. As our discussion of Plastim's ABC system reveals, the cause-and-effect relationship between direct manufacturing labor-hours and Plastim's indirect costs is weak, so reducing direct manufacturing labor-hours would have only a minimal effect on reducing indirect costs.

Planning and Managing Activities

Many companies implementing ABC systems for the first time analyze actual costs to identify activity-cost pools and activity-cost rates. To be useful for planning, making decisions, and managing activities, companies specify budgeted costs for activities and use budgeted cost rates to cost products as we saw in the Plastim example. At year-end, budgeted costs and actual costs are compared to provide feedback on how well activities were managed. As activities and processes are changed, new activity-cost rates are calculated. At the end of the year, adjustments must also be made for underallocated or overallocated indirect costs for each activity area using methods described in Chapter 4.

We will return to activity-based management in later chapters. Management decisions that use activity-based costing information are described in Chapter 6, in which we discuss activity-based budgeting; Chapter 11, in which we discuss outsourcing and adding or dropping business segments; in Chapter 12, in which we evaluate alternative design choices to improve efficiency and reduce nonvalue-added costs; in Chapter 13, in which we cover reengineering and downsizing; in Chapter 14, in which we explore managing customer profitability; in Chapter 19, in which we explain quality improvements; and in Chapter 20, in which we describe how to evaluate suppliers.

Activity-Based Costing and Department Costing Systems

Learning Objective 7

Compare activity-based costing systems and department costing systems

. . . activity-based costing systems are a refinement of department costing systems into more-focused and homogenous cost pools

Companies often use costing systems that have features of ABC systems—such as multiple cost pools and multiple cost-allocation bases—but that do not emphasize individual activities. Many companies have evolved their costing systems from using a single indirect cost rate system to using separate indirect cost rates for each department (for example, design, manufacturing, distribution, and so on) or each subdepartment (for example, machining and assembly departments within manufacturing) that can be thought of as representing broad tasks. ABC systems, with its focus on specific activities, are a further refinement of department costing systems. In this section, we compare ABC systems and department costing systems.

Plastim uses the Design Department indirect cost rate to cost its design activity. Plastim calculates the design activity rate by dividing total Design Department costs by total parts-square feet, a measure of the complexity of the mold and the driver of Design Department costs. Plastim does not find it worthwhile to calculate separate activity rates within the Design Department for the different design activities, such as designing products, making temporary molds, and designing processes. Why? Because complexity of a mold is an appropriate cost-allocation base for costs incurred for all those design activities: The Design Department costs are homogeneous with respect to this cost-allocation base.

In contrast, using ABC, Plastim identifies in the Manufacturing Department, two activity cost pools—a setup cost pool and a machine operations cost pool—instead of using a single Manufacturing Department overhead cost pool. It identifies these activity cost pools for two reasons. First, each of these activities within manufacturing incurs significant costs and has a different cost driver. Second, the S3 and CL5 lenses do not use resources from these two activity areas in the same proportion. For example, CL5 uses 75% (1,500 ÷ 2,000) of the setup-hours but only 29.4% (3,750 ÷ 12,750) of the machine-hours. Using only machine-hours, say, to allocate all Manufacturing Department costs at Plastim would result in CL5 being undercosted because it would not be charged for the significant amounts of setup resources it actually uses.

Based on what we just explained, using department indirect cost rates to allocate costs to products results in similar information as activity cost rates if: (1) a single activity accounts for a sizable proportion of the department's costs; or (2) significant costs are incurred on different activities within a department but each activity has the same cost driver and hence cost-allocation base (as was the case in Plastim's Design Department). From a purely product costing standpoint, department and activity indirect cost rates will also give the same product costs if significant costs are incurred for different activities with different cost-allocation bases within a department but different products use resources from the different activity areas in the same proportions (for example, if CL5 had used 65%, say, of the setup-hours and 65% of the machine-hours). In this case, though, not identifying activities and cost drivers within departments conceals activity cost information that would be valuable for cost management and design and process improvements.

We close this section with a note of caution. Do not assume that because department costing systems require the creation of multiple indirect cost pools that they properly recognize the drivers of costs within departments as well as how resources are used by products. As we have indicated, in many situations, department costing systems can be refined using ABC. Emphasizing activities leads to more-focused and homogeneous cost pools, aids in identifying cost-allocation bases for activities that have a better cause-and-effect relationship with the costs in activity cost pools, and leads to better design and process decisions. But the benefits of an ABC system must be balanced against its costs and limitations.

Implementing ABC Systems

Learning Objective 8

Evaluate the costs and benefits of implementing activity-based costing systems

. . . measurement difficulties versus more accurate costs that aid in decision making

Managers choose the level of detail to use in a costing system by evaluating the expected costs of the system against the expected benefits that will come from using it to make better decisions. There are telltale signs of when an ABC system is likely to provide the most benefits. Here are some of these signs:

- Significant amounts of indirect costs are allocated using only one or two cost pools.
- All or most indirect costs are identified as output unit-level costs (few indirect costs are described as batch-level costs, product-sustaining costs, or facility-sustaining costs).
- Products make diverse demands on resources because of differences in volume, process steps, batch size, or complexity.
- Products that a company is well suited to make and sell show small profits; whereas products that a company is less suited to produce and sell show large profits.
- Operations staff have substantial disagreement with the reported costs of manufacturing and marketing products and services.

When a company decides to implement ABC, it must make important choices about the level of detail to use. Should it choose many finely specified activities, cost drivers, and cost pools, or would a few suffice? For example, Plastim could identify a different molding machine-hour rate for each different type of molding machine. In making such choices, managers weigh the benefits against the costs and limitations of implementing a more detailed costing system.

The main costs and limitations of an ABC system are the measurements necessary to implement it. ABC systems require management to estimate costs of activity pools and to identify and measure cost drivers for these pools to serve as cost-allocation bases. Even basic ABC systems require many calculations to determine costs of products and services. These measurements are costly. Activity cost rates also need to be updated regularly.

As ABC systems get very detailed and more cost pools are created, more allocations are necessary to calculate activity costs for each cost pool. This increases the chances of misidentifying the costs of different activity cost pools. For example, supervisors are more prone to incorrectly identify the time they spent on different activities if they have to allocate their time over five activities rather than only two activities.

At times, companies are also forced to use allocation bases for which data are readily available rather than allocation bases they would have liked to use. For example, a company might be forced to use the number of loads moved, instead of the degree of difficulty and distance of different loads moved, as the allocation base for material-handling costs, because data on degree of difficulty and distance of moves are difficult to obtain. When erroneous cost-allocation bases are used, activity-cost information can be misleading. For example, if the cost per load moved decreases, a company may conclude that it has become more efficient in its materials-handling operations. In fact, the lower cost per load moved may have resulted solely from moving many lighter loads over shorter distances.

Many companies, such as Kanthal, a Swedish manufacturer of heating elements, have found the strategic and operational benefits of a less-detailed ABC system to be good enough to not warrant incurring the costs and challenges of operating a more-detailed system. Other organizations, such as Hewlett-Packard, implement ABC in chosen divisions or functions. As improvements in information technology and accompanying declines in measurement costs continue, more-detailed ABC systems have become a practical alternative in many companies, such as The Cooperative Bank in the United Kingdom. As such trends persist, more detailed ABC systems should be better able to pass the cost–benefit test.

Global surveys of company practice suggest that ABC implementation varies among companies. Nevertheless, its framework and ideas provide a standard for judging whether any simple costing system is good enough for a particular management's purposes. Any contemplated changes in a simple costing system will inevitably be improved by ABC thinking. The Concepts in Action box on p. 158 describes some of the behavioral issues that management accountants must be sensitive to as they seek to immerse an organization in ABC thinking.

ABC in Service and Merchandising Companies

Although many of the early examples of ABC originated in manufacturing, ABC has many applications in service and merchandising companies. In addition to manufacturing activities, the Plastim example includes the application of ABC to a service activity—design—and to a merchandising activity—distribution. Companies such as The Cooperative Bank, Braintree Hospital, BCTel in the telecommunications industry, and Union Pacific in the railroad industry have implemented some form of ABC system to identify profitable product mixes, improve efficiency, and satisfy customers. Similarly, many retail and wholesale companies—for example, Supervalu, a retailer and distributor of grocery store products, and Owens and Minor, a medical supplies distributor—have used ABC systems. The Problem for Self-Study describes an application of ABC in a supermarket. Finally, as we describe in Chapter 14, a large number of financial services companies (as well as other companies) employ variations of ABC systems to analyze and improve the profitability of their customer interactions.

The widespread use of ABC systems in service and merchandising companies reinforces the idea that ABC systems are used by managers for strategic decisions rather than for inventory valuation. (Inventory valuation is fairly straightforward in merchandising companies and not needed in service companies.) Service companies, in particular, find great value from ABC because a vast majority of their cost structure comprises indirect costs. After all, there are few direct costs when a bank makes a loan, or when a representative answers a phone call at a call center. As we have seen, a major benefit of ABC is its ability to assign indirect costs to cost objects by identifying activities and cost drivers. As

Concepts in Action

Successfully Championing ABC

Successfully implementing ABC systems requires more than an understanding of the technical details. ABC implementation often represents a significant change in the costing system and, as the chapter indicates, it requires a manager to make major choices with respect to the definition of activities and the level of detail. What then are some of the behavioral issues that the management accountant must be sensitive to?

1. **Gaining support of top management and creating a sense of urgency for the ABC effort.** This requires management accountants to lay out the vision for the ABC project and to clearly communicate its strategic benefits (for example, the resulting improvements in product and process design). It also requires selling the idea to end users, working with members of other departments and as business partners of the managers in the various areas affected by the ABC project. For example, at USAA Federal Savings Bank, project managers demonstrated how the information gained from ABC would provide insights into the efficiency of bank operations, which was previously unavailable. Now the finance area communicates regularly with operations about new reports and proposed changes to the financial reporting package that managers receive.
2. **Creating a guiding coalition of managers throughout the value chain for the ABC effort.** ABC systems measure how the resources of an organization are used. Managers responsible for these resources have the best knowledge about activities and cost drivers. Getting managers to cooperate and take the initiative for implementing ABC is essential for gaining the required expertise, the proper credibility, and the necessary leadership.

   There are several other benefits to gaining wide participation among managers. First, implementing ABC requires a significant time commitment. If managers feel more involved in the process, they are more likely to be willing to commit their time to the ABC effort. Second, there inevitably will be some managers who may be, or may perceive themselves to be, negatively affected by the ABC information. In our Plastim example, the manager of the complex CL5 lens may feel that ABC disadvantages him because it assigns more costs to the CL5 lens. Involving managers who are skeptical of the ABC process and giving them an opportunity to express their concerns reduces the likelihood of these managers negatively affecting the process. Finally, engaging managers throughout the value chain creates greater opportunities for coordination and cooperation across the different functions. For example, an ABC analysis might reveal that a company is incurring high manufacturing costs because of quality problems in its plant. The best way to reduce costs may be to redesign the product. This requires that the design department and the manufacturing department work closely together.
3. **Educating and training employees in ABC as a basis for employee empowerment.** Disseminating information about ABC throughout an organization allows workers in all areas of a business to use their knowledge of ABC to make improvements. For example, WS Industries, an Indian manufacturer of insulators, not only shared ABC information with its workers but also established an incentive plan that gave employees a percentage of the cost savings. The results were dramatic because employees were empowered and motivated to implement numerous cost-saving projects.
4. **Seeking small short-run successes as proof that the ABC implementation is yielding results.** Too often, managers and management accountants seek big results and major changes far too quickly. In many situations, achieving a significant change overnight is difficult. However, showing how ABC information has helped improve a process and save costs, even if only in small ways, motivates the team to stay on course and build momentum. The credibility gained from small victories leads to additional and bigger improvements involving larger numbers of people and different parts of the organization. Eventually ABC and ABM will be rooted in the culture of the organization. Sharing short-term successes may also help motivate employees to be innovative. At USAA Federal Savings Bank, managers created a "process improvement" mailbox in Microsoft Outlook to facilitate the sharing of process improvement ideas.
5. **Recognizing that ABC information is not perfect because it balances the need for better information against the costs of creating a complex system that few managers and employees can understand.** The management accountant must help managers recognize both the value and the limitations of ABC and not oversell it. Open and honest communication about ABC ensures that managers use ABC thoughtfully to make good decisions. Critical judgments can then be made without being adversarial, and tough questions can be asked to help drive better decisions about the system.

a result, ABC systems provide greater insight than traditional systems into the management of these indirect costs. The general approach to ABC in service and merchandising companies is similar to the ABC approach in manufacturing.

Concepts in Action

Time-Driven Activity-Based Costing at Charles Schwab

Time-driven activity-based costing ("TDABC") helps Charles Schwab—the leading stock brokerage—with strategic-analysis, measurement, and management of its service delivery. This support is critical because Charles Schwab offers its core service—stock trading—through multiple channels including branches, call centers, and the Internet. Because the costs for each channel are different, TDABC can help answer questions such as: What are the total costs associated with branch transactions versus online transactions? Which channels help reduce overall costs? How can Charles Schwab price its services to drive customer behavior change? To answer these questions, TDABC identifies and measures the costs of activities aimed at servicing Charles Schwab's more than seven million clients.

TDABC assigns all of the company's resource costs to cost objects using a framework that requires two sets of estimates. TDABC first calculates the cost of supplying resource capacity, such as broker time. The total cost of resources including personnel, management, occupancy, technology, and supplies is divided by the available capacity—the time available for brokers to do the work—to obtain the capacity cost rate. Next, TDABC uses the capacity cost rate to drive resource costs to cost objects, such as stock trades executed through brokers at a branch, by estimating the demand for resource capacity (time) that the cost object requires.

Realizing that trades executed online cost much less than trades completed through brokers, Charles Schwab took action to reduce costs. One executive noted, "The system revealed that we had lots of no-fee trades of mutual funds in the broker-assisted channel, which was very expensive relative to the online channel. We turned many customers profitable by developing a fee structure to stimulate the use of cheaper channels."

In addition to the mutual-fund trading change, Charles Schwab has used TDABC information to lower process costs by several hundred million dollars annually and to better align product pricing and account management to the company's diverse client segments. The company is working on other opportunities, including priority-call routing and email marketing, to further reduce costs while maintaining or enhancing Charles Schwab's already top-rated customer service.

Sources: Kaplan, R. S. and Anderson, S. R., "The Innovation of Time-Driven Activity-Based Costing," *Cost Management,* March-April 2007, pp. 5–15; R.S. Kaplan and S.R. Anderson, *Time-Driven Activity-Based Costing* (Boston, MA: Harvard Business School Press, 2007); Martinez-Jerez, F. Asis, "Understanding Customer Profitability at Charles Schwab," Harvard Business School Case Study No. 9-106-102, January 2007.

The Cooperative Bank followed the approach described in this chapter when it implemented ABC in its retail banking operations. It calculated the costs of various activities, such as performing ATM transactions, opening and closing accounts, administering mortgages, and processing Visa transactions. It then used the activity cost rates to calculate costs of various products, such as checking accounts, mortgages, and Visa cards and the costs of supporting different customers. ABC information helped The Cooperative Bank to improve its processes and to identify profitable products and customer segments. The Concepts in Action feature above describes how Charles Schwab has similarly benefited from using ABC analysis.

Activity-based costing raises some interesting issues when it is applied to a public service institution such as the U.S. Postal Service. The costs of delivering mail to remote locations are far greater than the costs of delivering mail within urban areas. However, for fairness and community-building reasons, the Postal Service cannot charge customers in remote areas higher prices. In this case, activity-based costing is valuable for understanding, managing, and reducing costs but not for pricing decisions.

Problem for Self-Study

Family Supermarkets (FS) has decided to increase the size of its Memphis store. It wants information about the profitability of individual product lines: soft drinks, fresh produce, and packaged food. FS provides the following data for 2010 for each product line:

	Soft Drinks	Fresh Produce	Packaged Food
Revenues	$317,400	$840,240	$483,960
Cost of goods sold	$240,000	$600,000	$360,000
Cost of bottles returned	$ 4,800	$ 0	$ 0
Number of purchase orders placed	144	336	144
Number of deliveries received	120	876	264
Hours of shelf-stocking time	216	2,160	1,080
Items sold	50,400	441,600	122,400

FS also provides the following information for 2010:

Activity (1)	Description of Activity (2)	Total Support Costs (3)	Cost-Allocation Base (4)
1. Bottle returns	Returning of empty bottles to store	$ 4,800	Direct tracing to soft-drink line
2. Ordering	Placing of orders for purchases	$ 62,400	624 purchase orders
3. Delivery	Physical delivery and receipt of merchandise	$100,800	1,260 deliveries
4. Shelf-stocking	Stocking of merchandise on store shelves and ongoing restocking	$ 69,120	3,456 hours of shelf-stocking time
5. Customer support	Assistance provided to customers, including checkout and bagging	$122,880	614,400 items sold
Total		$360,000	

Required

1. Family Supermarkets currently allocates store support costs (all costs other than cost of goods sold) to product lines on the basis of cost of goods sold of each product line. Calculate the operating income and operating income as a percentage of revenues for each product line.
2. If Family Supermarkets allocates store support costs (all costs other than cost of goods sold) to product lines using an ABC system, calculate the operating income and operating income as a percentage of revenues for each product line.
3. Comment on your answers in requirements 1 and 2.

Solution

1. The following table shows the operating income and operating income as a percentage of revenues for each product line. All store support costs (all costs other than cost of goods sold) are allocated to product lines using cost of goods sold of each product line as the cost-allocation base. Total store support costs equal $360,000 (cost of bottles returned, $4,800 + cost of purchase orders, $62,400 + cost of deliveries, $100,800 + cost of shelf-stocking, $69,120 + cost of customer support, $122,880). The allocation rate for store support costs = $360,000 ÷ $1,200,000 (soft drinks $240,000 + fresh produce $600,000 + packaged food, $360,000) = 30% of cost of goods sold. To allocate support costs to each product line, FS multiplies the cost of goods sold of each product line by 0.30.

	Soft Drinks	Fresh Produce	Packaged Food	Total
Revenues	$317,400	$840,240	$483,960	$1,641,600
Cost of goods sold	240,000	600,000	360,000	1,200,000
Store support cost ($240,000; $600,000; $360,000) × 0.30	72,000	180,000	108,000	360,000
Total costs	312,000	780,000	468,000	1,560,000
Operating income	$ 5,400	$ 60,240	$ 15,960	$ 81,600
Operating income ÷ Revenues	1.70%	7.17%	3.30%	4.97%

2. Under an ABC system, FS identifies bottle-return costs as a direct cost because these costs can be traced to the soft drink product line. FS then calculates cost-allocation rates for each activity area (as in step 5 of the seven-step costing system, described in the chapter, p. 149). The activity rates are as follows:

Activity (1)	Cost Hierarchy (2)	Total Costs (3)	Quantity of Cost-Allocation Base (4)	Overhead Allocation Rate (5) = (3) ÷ (4)
Ordering	Batch-level	$ 62,400	624 purchase orders	$100 per purchase order
Delivery	Batch-level	$100,800	1,260 deliveries	$80 per delivery
Shelf-stocking	Output unit-level	$ 69,120	3,456 shelf-stocking-hours	$20 per stocking-hour
Customer support	Output unit-level	$122,880	614,400 items sold	$0.20 per item sold

Store support costs for each product line by activity are obtained by multiplying the total quantity of the cost-allocation base for each product line by the activity cost rate. Operating income and operating income as a percentage of revenues for each product line are as follows:

	Soft Drinks	Fresh Produce	Packaged Food	Total
Revenues	$317,400	$840,240	$483,960	$1,641,600
Cost of goods sold	240,000	600,000	360,000	1,200,000
Bottle-return costs	4,800	0	0	4,800
Ordering costs				
(144; 336; 144) purchase orders × $100	14,400	33,600	14,400	62,400
Delivery costs				
(120; 876; 264) deliveries × $80	9,600	70,080	21,120	100,800
Shelf-stocking costs				
(216; 2,160; 1,080) stocking-hours × $20	4,320	43,200	21,600	69,120
Customer-support costs				
(50,400; 441,600; 122,400) items sold × $0.20	10,080	88,320	24,480	122,880
Total costs	283,200	835,200	441,600	1,560,000
Operating income	$ 34,200	$ 5,040	$ 42,360	$ 81,600
Operating income ÷ Revenues	10.78%	0.60%	8.75%	4.97%

3. Managers believe the ABC system is more credible than the simple costing system. The ABC system distinguishes the different types of activities at FS more precisely. It also tracks more accurately how individual product lines use resources. Rankings of relative profitability—operating income as a percentage of revenues—of the three product lines under the simple costing system and under the ABC system are:

Simple Costing System		ABC System	
1. Fresh produce	7.17%	1. Soft drinks	10.78%
2. Packaged food	3.30%	2. Packaged food	8.75%
3. Soft drinks	1.70%	3. Fresh produce	0.60%

The percentage of revenues, cost of goods sold, and activity costs for each product line are as follows:

	Soft Drinks	Fresh Produce	Packaged Food
Revenues	19.34%	51.18%	29.48%
Cost of goods sold	20.00	50.00	30.00
Bottle returns	100.00	0	0
Activity areas:			
Ordering	23.08	53.84	23.08
Delivery	9.53	69.52	20.95
Shelf-stocking	6.25	62.50	31.25
Customer-support	8.20	71.88	19.92

Soft drinks consume fewer resources than either fresh produce or packaged food. Soft drinks have fewer deliveries and require less shelf-stocking time than required for either fresh produce or packaged food. Most major soft-drink suppliers deliver merchandise to the store shelves and stock the shelves themselves. In contrast, the fresh produce area has the most deliveries and consumes a large percentage of shelf-stocking time. It also has the highest number of individual sales items. The simple costing system assumed that each product line used the resources in each activity area in the same ratio as their respective individual cost of goods sold to total cost of goods sold. Clearly, this assumption is incorrect. The simple costing system is an example of averaging that is too broad.

FS managers can use the ABC information to guide decisions such as how to allocate a planned increase in floor space. An increase in the percentage of space allocated to soft drinks is warranted. Note, however, that ABC information should be but one input into decisions about shelf-space allocation. FS may have minimum limits on the shelf space allocated to fresh produce because of shoppers' expectations that supermarkets will carry products from this product line. In many situations, companies cannot make product decisions in isolation but must consider the effect that dropping a product might have on customer demand for other products.

Pricing decisions can also be made in a more informed way with ABC information. For example, suppose a competitor announces a 5% reduction in soft-drink prices. Given the 10.77% margin FS currently earns on its soft-drink product line, it has flexibility to reduce prices and still make a profit on this product line. In contrast, the simple costing system erroneously implied that soft drinks only had a 1.70% margin, leaving little room to counter a competitor's pricing initiatives.

Decision Points

The following question-and-answer format summarizes the chapter's learning objectives. Each decision presents a key question related to a learning objective. The guidelines are the answer to that question.

Decision	Guidelines
1. When does product undercosting or overcosting occur?	Product undercosting (overcosting) occurs when a product or service consumes a high (low) level of resources but is reported to have a low (high) cost. Broad averaging, or peanut-butter costing, a common cause of undercosting or overcosting, is the result of using broad averages that uniformly assign, or spread, the cost of resources to products when the individual products use those resources in a nonuniform way. Product-cost cross-subsidization exists when one undercosted (overcosted) product results in at least one other product being overcosted (undercosted).
2. How do managers refine a costing system?	Refining a costing system means making changes that result in cost numbers that better measure the way different cost objects, such as products, use different amounts of resources of the company. These changes can require additional direct-cost tracing, the choice of more-homogeneous indirect cost pools, or the use of different cost-allocation bases.
3. What is the difference between the design of a simple costing system and an activity-based costing (ABC) system?	The ABC system differs from the simple system by its fundamental focus on activities. The ABC system typically has more-homogeneous indirect-cost pools than the simple system, and more cost drivers are used as cost-allocation bases.
4. What is a cost hierarchy?	A cost hierarchy categorizes costs into different cost pools on the basis of the different types of cost-allocation bases or different degrees of difficulty in determining cause-and-effect (or benefits-received) relationships. A four-part cost hierarchy consists of output unit-level costs, batch-level costs, product-sustaining or service-sustaining costs, and facility-sustaining costs.

5. How do managers cost products or services using ABC systems?	In ABC, costs of activities are used to assign costs to other cost objects such as products or services based on the activities the products or services consume.
6. How can ABC systems be used to manage better?	Activity-based management (ABM) is a management method of decision-making that uses ABC information to satisfy customers and improve profits. ABC systems are used for such management decisions as pricing, product-mix, cost reduction, process improvement, product and process redesign, and planning and managing activities.
7. When can department costing systems be used instead of ABC systems?	Cost information in department costing systems approximates cost information in ABC systems only when each department has a single activity, or a single cost driver for different activities, or when different products use the different activities of the department in the same proportions.
8. When should managers use ABC systems?	ABC systems are likely to yield the most benefits when indirect costs are a high percentage of total costs or when products and services make diverse demands on indirect resources. The main costs of ABC systems are the difficulties of the measurements necessary to implement and update the systems.

TERMS TO LEARN

This chapter and the Glossary at the end of this book contain definitions of:

activity (**p. 144**)
activity-based costing (ABC) (**p. 144**)
activity-based management (ABM) (**p. 152**)
batch-level costs (**p. 147**)
cost hierarchy (**p. 147**)
facility-sustaining costs (**p. 148**)
output unit-level costs (**p. 147**)
product-cost cross-subsidization (**p. 138**)
product overcosting (**p. 138**)
product-sustaining costs (**p. 147**)
product undercosting (**p. 138**)
refined costing system (**p. 143**)
service-sustaining costs (**p. 147**)

ASSIGNMENT MATERIAL

Questions

5-1 What is broad averaging and what consequences can it have on costs?

5-2 Why should managers worry about product overcosting or undercosting?

5-3 What is costing system refinement? Describe three guidelines for refinement.

5-4 What is an activity-based approach to designing a costing system?

5-5 Describe four levels of a cost hierarchy.

5-6 Why is it important to classify costs into a cost hierarchy?

5-7 What are the key reasons for product cost differences between simple costing systems and ABC systems?

5-8 Describe four decisions for which ABC information is useful.

5-9 "Department indirect-cost rates are never activity-cost rates." Do you agree? Explain.

5-10 Describe four signs that help indicate when ABC systems are likely to provide the most benefits.

5-11 What are the main costs and limitations of implementing ABC systems?

5-12 "ABC systems only apply to manufacturing companies." Do you agree? Explain.

5-13 "Activity-based costing is the wave of the present and the future. All companies should adopt it." Do you agree? Explain.

5-14 "Increasing the number of indirect-cost pools is guaranteed to sizably increase the accuracy of product or service costs." Do you agree? Why?

5-15 The controller of a retail company has just had a $50,000 request to implement an ABC system quickly turned down. A senior vice president, in rejecting the request, noted, "Given a choice, I will always prefer a $50,000 investment in improving things a customer sees or experiences, such as our shelves or our store layout. How does a customer benefit by our spending $50,000 on a supposedly better accounting system?" How should the controller respond?

Exercises

5-16 Cost hierarchy. Teledor, Inc., manufactures boom boxes (music systems with radio, cassette, and compact disc players) for several well-known companies. The boom boxes differ significantly in their complexity and their manufacturing batch sizes. The following costs were incurred in 2009.

- **a.** Indirect manufacturing labor costs such as supervision that supports direct manufacturing labor, $1,200,000
- **b.** Procurement costs of placing purchase orders, receiving materials, and paying suppliers related to the number of purchase orders placed, $600,000
- **c.** Cost of indirect materials, $350,000
- **d.** Costs incurred to set up machines each time a different product needs to be manufactured, $700,000
- **e.** Designing processes, drawing process charts, making engineering process changes for products, $900,000
- **f.** Machine-related overhead costs such as depreciation, maintenance, production engineering, $1,200,000 (These resources relate to the activity of running the machines.)
- **g.** Plant management, plant rent, and plant insurance, $950,000

Required

1. Classify each of the preceding costs as output unit-level, batch-level, product-sustaining, or facility-sustaining. Explain each answer.
2. Consider two types of boom boxes made by Teledor, Inc. One boom box is complex to make and is produced in many batches. The other boom box is simple to make and is produced in few batches. Suppose that Teledor needs the same number of machine-hours to make each type of boom box and that Teledor allocates all overhead costs using machine-hours as the only allocation base. How, if at all, would the boom boxes be miscosted? Briefly explain why.
3. How is the cost hierarchy helpful to Teledor in managing its business?

5-17 ABC, cost hierarchy, service. (CMA, adapted) Plymouth Test Laboratories does heat testing (HT) and stress testing (ST) on materials and operates at capacity. Under its current simple costing system, Plymouth aggregates all operating costs of $1,280,000 into a single overhead cost pool. Plymouth calculates a rate per test-hour of $16 ($1,280,000 ÷ 80,000 total test-hours). HT uses 50,000 test-hours, and ST uses 30,000 test-hours. Gary Celeste, Plymouth's controller, believes that there is enough variation in test procedures and cost structures to establish separate costing and billing rates for HT and ST. The market for test services is becoming competitive. Without this information, any miscosting and mispricing of its services could cause Plymouth to lose business. Celeste divides Plymouth's costs into four activity-cost categories.

- **a.** Direct-labor costs, $243,000. These costs can be directly traced to HT, $183,000, and ST, $60,000.
- **b.** Equipment-related costs (rent, maintenance, energy, and so on), $400,000. These costs are allocated to HT and ST on the basis of test-hours.
- **c.** Setup costs, $385,000. These costs are allocated to HT and ST on the basis of the number of setup-hours required. HT requires 13,500 setup-hours, and ST requires 4,000 setup-hours.
- **d.** Costs of designing tests, $252,000. These costs are allocated to HT and ST on the basis of the time required to design the tests. HT requires 2,800 hours, and ST requires 1,400 hours.

Required

1. Classify each activity cost as output unit-level, batch-level, product- or service-sustaining, or facility-sustaining. Explain each answer.
2. Calculate the cost per test-hour for HT and ST. Explain briefly the reasons why these numbers differ from the $16 per test-hour that Plymouth calculated using its simple costing system.
3. Explain the accuracy of the product costs calculated using the simple costing system and the ABC system. How might Plymouth's management use the cost hierarchy and ABC information to better manage its business?

5-18 Alternative allocation bases for a professional services firm. The Wolfson Group (WG) provides tax advice to multinational firms. WG charges clients for (a) direct professional time (at an hourly rate) and (b) support services (at 30% of the direct professional costs billed). The three professionals in WG and their rates per professional hour are:

Professional	Billing Rate per Hour
Myron Wolfson	$500
Ann Brown	120
John Anderson	80

WG has just prepared the May 2009 bills for two clients. The hours of professional time spent on each client are as follows:

	Hours per Client	
Professional	Seattle Dominion	Tokyo Enterprises
Wolfson	15	2
Brown	3	8
Anderson	22	30
Total	40	40

Required

1. What amounts did WG bill to Seattle Dominion and Tokyo Enterprises for May 2009?
2. Suppose support services were billed at $50 per professional labor-hour (instead of 30% of professional labor costs). How would this change affect the amounts WG billed to the two clients for May 2009? Comment on the differences between the amounts billed in requirements 1 and 2.
3. How would you determine whether professional labor costs or professional labor-hours is the more appropriate allocation base for WG's support services?

5-19 Plantwide, department, and ABC indirect cost rates. Automotive Products (AP) designs and produces automotive parts. In 2009, actual variable manufacturing overhead is $308,600. AP's simple costing system allocates variable manufacturing overhead to its three customers based on machine-hours and prices its contracts based on full costs. One of its customers has regularly complained of being charged noncompetitive prices, so AP's controller Devon Smith realizes that it is time to examine the consumption of overhead resources more closely. He knows that there are three main departments that consume overhead resources: design, production, and engineering. Interviews with the department personnel and examination of time records yield the following detailed information:

	A	B	C	D	E	F
1				Usage of Cost Drivers by Customer Contract		
2	Department	Cost Driver	Variable Manufacturing Overhead in 2009	United Motors	Holden Motors	Leland Vehicle
3	Design	CAD-design hours	$ 39,000	110	200	80
4	Production	Engineering hours	29,600	70	60	240
5	Engineering	Machine hours	240,000	120	2,800	1,080
6	Total		$308,600			

If you want to use Excel to solve this exercise, go to the Excel Lab at **www.prenhall.com/horngren/cost13e** and download the template for Exercise 5-19.

Required

1. Compute the variable manufacturing overhead allocated to each customer in 2009 using the simple costing system that has machine-hours as the allocation base.
2. Compute the variable manufacturing overhead allocated to each customer in 2009 using department-based variable manufacturing overhead rates.
3. Comment on your answers in requirements 1 and 2. Which customer do you think was complaining about being overcharged in the simple system? If the new department-based rates are used to price contracts, which customer(s) will be unhappy? How would you respond to these concerns?
4. How else might AP use the information available from its department-by-department analysis of variable manufacturing overhead costs?
5. AP's managers are wondering if they should further refine the department-by-department costing system into an ABC system by identifying different activities within each department. Under what conditions would it not be worthwhile to further refine the department costing system into an ABC system?

5-20 ABC, process costing. Parker Company produces mathematical and financial calculators and operates at capacity. Data related to the two products are presented here.

	Mathematical	Financial
Annual production in units	50,000	100,000
Direct material costs	$150,000	$300,000
Direct manufacturing labor costs	$ 50,000	$100,000
Direct manufacturing labor-hours	2,500	5,000
Machine-hours	25,000	50,000
Number of production runs	50	50
Inspection hours	1,000	500

Total manufacturing overhead costs are:

	Total
Machining costs	$375,000
Setup costs	120,000
Inspection costs	105,000

Required

1. Compute the manufacturing overhead cost per unit for each product.
2. Compute the manufacturing cost per unit for each product.

5-21 Activity-based costing, service company. Quikprint Corporation owns a small printing press that prints leaflets, brochures, and advertising materials. Quikprint classifies its various printing jobs as standard jobs or special jobs. Quikprint's simple job-costing system has two direct-cost categories (direct materials and direct labor) and a single indirect-cost pool. Quikprint operates at capacity and allocates all indirect costs using printing machine-hours as the allocation base.

Quikprint is concerned about the accuracy of the costs assigned to standard and special jobs and therefore is planning to implement an activity-based costing system. Quickprint's ABC system would have the same direct-cost categories as its simple costing system. However, instead of a single indirect-cost pool there would now be six categories for assigning indirect costs: design, purchasing, setup, printing machine operations, marketing, and administration. To see how activity-based costing would affect the costs of standard and special jobs, Quikprint collects the following information for the fiscal year 2009 that just ended.

	A	B	C	D	E–H
1		Standard Job	Special Job	Total	Cause-and-Effect Relationship between Allocation Base and Activity Cost
2	Number of printing jobs	400	200		
3	Price per job	$1,200	$ 1,500		
4	Cost of supplies per job	$ 200	$ 250		
5	Direct labor costs per job	$ 180	$ 200		
6	Printing machine hours per job	10	10		
7	Cost of printing machine operations			$150,000	Indirect costs of operating printing machines
8					increase with printing machine hours
9	Setup hours per job	4	7		
10	Setup costs			$ 90,000	Indirect setup costs increase with setup hours
11	Number of purchase orders	400	500		
12	Purchase order costs			$ 36,000	Indirect purchase order costs increase with
13					number of purchase orders
14	Design costs	$8,000	$32,000	$ 40,000	Design costs are allocated to standard and special
15					jobs based on a special study of the design department
16	Marketing costs as a percentage of sales price	5%	5%	$ 39,000	
17	Administration costs			$ 48,000	Demand for administrative resources increases with direct labor hours

If you want to use Excel to solve this exercise, go to the Excel Lab at **www.prenhall.com/horngren/cost13e** and download the template for Exercise 5-21.

Required

1. Calculate the cost of a standard job and a special job under the simple costing system.
2. Calculate the cost of a standard job and a special job under the activity-based costing system.
3. Compare the costs of a standard job and a special job in requirements 1 and 2. Why do the simple and activity-based costing systems differ in the cost of a standard job and a special job?
4. How might Quikprint use the new cost information from its activity-based costing system to better manage its business?

5-22 Allocation of costs to activities, unused capacity. Harmon Academy, a private school for boys, serves 500 students: 200 in the middle school (grades 6–8) and 300 in the high school (grades 9–12). Each school has its own assistant principal, and there is one principal, Brian Smith, for all of Harmon Academy. For any single student, almost all of Harmon's costs are indirect. Harmon currently has five indirect cost categories, which are listed in column A of the following table. Smith wants to develop an activity-based costing system for the school. He identifies four activities—academic instruction, administration, sports training, and community relationships—related to the educational enterprise, which are shown in columns B, C, D, and E of the following table.

Smith and his team identify number of students as the cost driver of academic instruction and administration costs, and the number of team sports offered by the school as the cost driver of sports training costs. The cost of maintaining community relationships—dealing with the town board and participating in local activities—is a facility-sustaining cost that the school has to incur each year. This table shows the percentage of costs in each line item used by each activity.

	A	B	C	D	E	F
1		Percentage of Costs Used by Each Activity				
2	Indirect Cost Categories	Academic Instruction	Administration	Sports Training	Community Relationships	2009 Expenditures
3	Teachers' salaries and benefits	60%	20%	8%	12%	$4,000,000
4	Principals' salaries and benefits	10%	60%	5%	25%	400,000
5	Facilities cost	35%	15%	45%	5%	2,600,000
6	Office staff salaries and benefits	5%	60%	10%	25%	300,000
7	Sports program staff salaries and benefits	35%	10%	45%	10%	500,000
8						$7,800,000

If you want to use Excel to solve this exercise, go to the Excel Lab at **www.prenhall.com/horngren/cost13e** and download the template for Exercise 5-22.

Required

1. What is the overall cost of educating each student? Of this cost, what percentage is the cost of academic instruction? Of administration?
2. Smith is dismayed at the high cost of sports training. Further examination reveals that $300,000 of those costs are for ice hockey, a sport pursued by a total of 40 students. What would the overall cost of educating each student be if the ice hockey program is eliminated and its cost saved?
3. For the 2010 school year, Harmon charges an annual fee of $1,000 for any student who wants to play ice hockey. As a result, 10 of the less-motivated students drop the sport. Assuming the costs of the school in 2010 are the same as in 2009, what is the overall cost of educating each student in 2010?
4. Consider the costs of the academic instruction activity and assume they are fixed in the short run. At these costs, Harmon could serve 600 students. What is the cost of the academic instruction resources used by Harmon's current 500 students? What is the cost of unused academic instruction capacity? What actions can Smith take to reduce the cost of academic instruction per student in the short run? In the long run?

5-23 ABC, retail product-line profitability. Family Supermarkets (FS) operates at capacity and decides to apply ABC analysis to three product lines: baked goods, milk and fruit juice, and frozen foods. It identifies four activities and their activity cost rates as:

Ordering	$100 per purchase order
Delivery and receipt of merchandise	$80 per delivery
Shelf-stocking	$20 per hour
Customer support and assistance	$0.20 per item sold

The revenues, cost of goods sold, store support costs, and activity-area usage of the three product lines are:

	Baked Goods	Milk and Fruit Juice	Frozen Products
Financial data			
Revenues	$57,000	$63,000	$52,000
Cost of goods sold	$38,000	$47,000	$35,000
Store support	$11,400	$14,100	$10,500
Activity-area usage (cost-allocation base)			
Ordering (purchase orders)	30	25	13
Delivery (deliveries)	98	36	28
Shelf-stocking (hours)	183	166	24
Customer support (items sold)	15,500	20,500	7,900

Under its simple costing system, FS allocated support costs to products at the rate of 30% of cost of goods sold.

Required

1. Use the simple costing system to prepare a product-line profitability report for FS.
2. Use the ABC system to prepare a product-line profitability report for FS.
3. What new insights does the ABC system in requirement 2 provide to FS managers?

5-24 ABC, wholesale, customer profitability. Villeagas Wholesalers operates at capacity and sells furniture items to four department-store chains (customers). Mr. Villeagas commented, "We apply ABC to determine product-line profitability. The same ideas apply to customer profitability, and we should find out our customer profitability as well." Villeagas Wholesalers sends catalogs to corporate purchasing departments on a monthly basis. The customers are entitled to return unsold merchandise within a six-month period from the purchase date and receive a full purchase price refund. The following data were collected from last year's operations:

	Chain			
	1	2	3	4
Gross sales	$50,000	$30,000	$100,000	$70,000
Sales returns:				
Number of items	100	26	60	40
Amount	$10,000	$ 5,000	$ 7,000	$ 6,000
Number of orders:				
Regular	40	150	50	70
Rush	10	50	10	30

Villeagas has calculated the following activity rates.

Activity	Cost-Driver Rate
Regular order processing	$20 per regular order
Rush order processing	$100 per rush order
Returned items processing	$10 per item
Catalogs and customer support	$1,000 per customer

Customers pay the transportation costs. The cost of goods sold averages 80% of sales.

Required Determine the contribution to profit from each chain last year. Comment on your solution.

5-25 ABC, activity area cost-driver rates, product cross-subsidization. Idaho Potatoes (IP) operates at capacity and processes potatoes into potato cuts at its highly automated Pocatello plant. It sells potatoes to the retail consumer market and to the institutional market, which includes hospitals, cafeterias, and university dormitories.

IP's simple costing system has a single direct-cost category (direct materials, which are the raw potatoes) and a single indirect-cost pool (production support). Support costs are allocated on the basis of pounds of potato cuts processed. Support costs include packaging materials. The 2009 total actual costs for producing 1,000,000 pounds of potato cuts (900,000 for the retail market and 100,000 for the institutional market) are:

Direct materials used	$150,000
Production support	$983,000

The simple costing system does not distinguish between potato cuts produced for the retail and the institutional markets.

At the end of 2009, IP unsuccessfully bid for a large institutional contract. Its bid was reported to be 30% above the winning bid. This feedback came as a shock because IP included only a minimum profit margin on its bid. Moreover, the Pocatello plant was acknowledged as the most efficient in the industry.

As a result of its review process of the lost contract bid, IP decided to explore ways to refine its costing system. First, it identified that $188,000 of the $983,000 pertaining to packaging materials could be traced to individual jobs ($180,000 for retail and $8,000 for institutional). These costs will now be classified as direct materials. The $150,000 of direct materials used were classified as $135,000 for retail and $15,000 for institutional. Second, it used ABC to examine how the two products (retail potato cuts and institutional potato cuts) used indirect support resources. The finding was that three activity areas could be distinguished.

- **Cleaning Activity Area**—IP uses 1,200,000 pounds of raw potatoes to yield 1,000,000 pounds of potato cuts. The cost-allocation base is pounds of raw potatoes cleaned. Costs in the cleaning activity area are $120,000.
- **Cutting Activity Area**—IP processes raw potatoes for the retail market independently of those processed for the institutional market. The production line produces (a) 250 pounds of retail potato cuts per cutting-hour and (b) 400 pounds of institutional potato cuts per cutting-hour. The cost-allocation base is cutting-hours on the production line. Costs in the cutting activity area are $231,000.
- **Packaging Activity Area**—IP packages potato cuts for the retail market independently of those packaged for the institutional market. The packaging line packages (a) 25 pounds of retail potato

cuts per packaging-hour and (b) 100 pounds of institutional potato cuts per packaging-hour. The cost-allocation base is packaging-hours on the production line. Costs in the packaging activity area are $444,000.

Required

1. Using the simple costing system, what is the cost per pound of potato cuts produced by IP?
2. Calculate the cost rate per unit of the cost driver in the (a) cleaning, (b) cutting, and (c) packaging activity areas.
3. Suppose IP uses information from its activity cost rates to calculate costs incurred on retail potato cuts and institutional potato cuts. Using the ABC system, what is the cost per pound of (a) retail potato cuts and (b) institutional potato cuts?
4. Comment on the cost differences between the two costing systems in 1 and 3. How might IP use the information in 3 to make better decisions?

5-26 Activity-based costing, job-costing system. The Hewlett-Packard (HP) plant in Roseville, California, operates at capacity and assembles and tests printed-circuit (PC) boards. The job-costing system at this plant has two direct-cost categories (direct materials and direct manufacturing labor) and seven indirect-cost pools. These indirect-cost pools represent the seven activity areas that operating personnel at the plant determined are sufficiently different (in terms of cost-behavior patterns or individual products being assembled) to warrant separate cost pools. The cost-allocation base chosen for each activity area is the cost driver at that activity area.

Debbie Berlant, a newly appointed marketing manager at HP, is attending a training session that describes how an activity-based costing approach was used to design the Roseville plant's job-costing system. Berlant is provided with the following incomplete information for a specific job (an order for a single PC board, No. A82):

Direct materials	$75.00	
Direct manufacturing labor	15.00	$90.00
Manufacturing overhead (see below)		?
Total manufacturing cost		$?

Manufacturing Overhead Cost Pool	Cost-Allocation Base	Cost-Allocation Rate	Units of Cost-Allocation Base Used on Job No. A82	Manufacturing Overhead Allocated to Job
1. Axial insertion	Axial insertions	0.08	45	?
2. Dip insertion	Dip insertions	0.25	?	6.00
3. Manual insertion	Manual insertions	?	11	5.50
4. Wave solder	Boards soldered	3.50	?	3.50
5. Backload	Backload insertions	?	6	4.20
6. Test	Budgeted time that board is in test activity	90.00	0.25	?
7. Defect analysis	Budgeted time for defect analysis and repair	?	0.10	8.00

Required

1. Prepare an overview diagram of the activity-based job-costing system at the Roseville plant.
2. Fill in the blanks (noted by question marks) in the cost information provided to Berlant for Job No. A82.
3. Why might manufacturing managers and marketing managers favor this ABC job-costing system over the simple costing system, which had the same two direct-cost categories but only a single indirect-cost pool (manufacturing overhead allocated using direct manufacturing labor costs)?

5-27 ABC, product costing at banks, cross-subsidization. First International Bank (FIB) is examining the profitability of its Premier Account, a combined savings and checking account. Depositors receive a 7% annual interest rate on their average deposit. FIB earns an interest rate spread of 3% (the difference between the rate at which it lends money and the rate it pays depositors) by lending money for home loan purposes at 10%. Thus, FIB would gain $60 on the interest spread if a depositor had an average Premier Account balance of $2,000 in 2008 ($2,000 × 3% = $60).

The Premier Account allows depositors unlimited use of services such as deposits, withdrawals, checking accounts, and foreign currency drafts. Depositors with Premier Account balances of $1,000 or more receive unlimited free use of services. Depositors with minimum balances of less than $1,000 pay a $20-a-month service fee for their Premier Account.

FIB recently conducted an activity-based costing study of its services. It assessed the following costs for six individual services. The use of these services in 2008 by three customers is as follows:

	Activity-Based Cost per "Transaction"	Account Usage		
		Robinson	Skerrett	Farrel
Deposit/withdrawal with teller	$ 2.50	40	50	5
Deposit/withdrawal with automatic teller machine (ATM)	0.80	10	20	16
Deposit/withdrawal on prearranged monthly basis	0.50	0	12	60
Bank checks written	8.00	9	3	2
Foreign currency drafts	12.00	4	1	6
Inquiries about account balance	1.50	10	18	9
Average Premier Account balance for 2008		$1,100	$800	$25,000

Assume Robinson and Farrel always maintain a balance above $1,000, whereas Skerrett always has a balance below $1,000.

Required

1. Compute the 2008 profitability of the Robinson, Skerrett, and Farrel Premier Accounts at FIB.
2. What evidence is there of cross-subsidization among the three Premier Accounts? Why might FIB worry about this cross-subsidization if the Premier Account product offering is profitable as a whole?
3. What changes would you recommend for FIB's Premier Account?

Problems

5-28 Job costing with single direct-cost category, single indirect-cost pool, law firm. Wigan Associates is a recently formed law partnership. Ellery Hanley, the managing partner of Wigan Associates, has just finished a tense phone call with Martin Offiah, president of Widnes Coal. Offiah strongly complained about the price Wigan charged for some legal work done for Widnes Coal.

Hanley also received a phone call from its only other client (St. Helen's Glass), which was very pleased with both the quality of the work and the price charged on its most recent job.

Wigan Associates operates at capacity and uses a cost-based approach to pricing (billing) each job. Currently it uses a simple costing system with a single direct-cost category (professional labor-hours) and a single indirect-cost pool (general support). Indirect costs are allocated to cases on the basis of professional labor-hours per case. The job files show the following:

	Widnes Coal	St. Helen's Glass
Professional labor	104 hours	96 hours

Professional labor costs at Wigan Associates are $70 an hour. Indirect costs are allocated to cases at $105 an hour. Total indirect costs in the most recent period were $21,000.

Required

1. Why is it important for Wigan Associates to understand the costs associated with individual jobs?
2. Compute the costs of the Widnes Coal and St. Helen's Glass jobs using Wigan's simple costing system.

5-29 Job costing with multiple direct-cost categories, single indirect-cost pool, law firm (continuation of 5-28). Hanley asks his assistant to collect details on those costs included in the $21,000 indirect-cost pool that can be traced to each individual job. After analysis, Wigan is able to reclassify $14,000 of the $21,000 as direct costs:

Other Direct Costs	Widnes Coal	St. Helen's Glass
Research support labor	$1,600	$ 3,400
Computer time	500	1,300
Travel and allowances	600	4,400
Telephones/faxes	200	1,000
Photocopying	250	750
Total	$3,150	$10,850

Hanley decides to calculate the costs of each job as if Wigan had used six direct cost-pools and a single indirect-cost pool. The single indirect-cost pool would have $7,000 of costs and would be allocated to each case using the professional labor-hours base.

Required

1. What is the revised indirect-cost allocation rate per professional labor-hour for Wigan Associates when total indirect costs are $7,000?

2. Compute the costs of the Widnes and St. Helen's jobs if Wigan Associates had used its refined costing system with multiple direct-cost categories and one indirect-cost pool.
3. Compare the costs of Widnes and St. Helen's jobs in requirement 2 with those in requirement 2 of Problem 5-28. Comment on the results.

5-30 Job costing with multiple direct-cost categories, multiple indirect-cost pools, law firm (continuation of 5-28 and 5-29). Wigan has two classifications of professional staff: partners and associates. Hanley asks his assistant to examine the relative use of partners and associates on the recent Widnes Coal and St. Helen's jobs. The Widnes job used 24 partner-hours and 80 associate-hours. The St. Helen's job used 56 partner-hours and 40 associate-hours. Therefore, totals of the two jobs together were 80 partner-hours and 120 associate-hours. Hanley decides to examine how using separate direct-cost rates for partners and associates and using separate indirect-cost pools for partners and associates would have affected the costs of the Widnes and St. Helen's jobs. Indirect costs in each indirect-cost pool would be allocated on the basis of total hours of that category of professional labor. From the total indirect cost-pool of $7,000, $4,600 is attributable to the activities of partners, and $2,400 is attributable to the activities of associates.

The rates per category of professional labor are as follows:

Category of Professional Labor	Direct Cost per Hour	Indirect Cost per Hour
Partner	$100.00	$4,600 ÷ 80 hours = $57.50
Associate	50.00	$2,400 ÷ 120 hours = $20.00

Required

1. Compute the costs of the Widnes and St. Helen's cases using Wigan's further refined system, with multiple direct-cost categories and multiple indirect-cost pools.
2. For what decisions might Wigan Associates find it more useful to use this job-costing approach rather than the approaches in Problem 5-28 or 5-29?

5-31 Plantwide, department, and activity-cost rates. Tarquin's Trophies makes trophies, plaques, and medallions and operates at capacity. Tarquin does large custom orders, for example the participant trophies for the Mishawaka Little League. The Controller has asked you to compare plantwide, department, and activity-based cost allocation.

Tarquin's Trophies
Budgeted Information per unit
For the year ended 30 November 2009

Forming Department	**Trophies**	**Plaques**	**Medallions**
Direct materials	$2.50	$1.50	$0.50
Direct labor	3.00	1.20	0.60
	$5.50	$2.70	$1.10
Assembly Department	**Trophies**	**Plaques**	**Medallions**
Direct materials	$0.50	$1.25	$0.25
Direct labor	1.50	1.50	0.50
	$2.00	$2.75	$0.75
Packaging Department	**Trophies**	**Plaques**	**Medallions**
Direct materials	$0.75	$0.50	$0.10
Direct labor	0.75	0.25	0.10
	$1.50	$0.75	$0.20
Number of units produced	5,200	7,500	16,700

The overhead cost for each department is:

Forming Department	
Materials handling	$ 5,700
Quality inspection	6,300
Utilities	10,386
	$22,386

Assembly Department	
Materials handling	$ 9,200
Quality inspection	13,800
Utilities	10,960
	$33,960

Packaging Department	
Materials handling	$18,315
Quality inspection	14,985
Utilities	8,934
	$42,234

Other information:

Materials handling and quality inspection costs vary with the number of batches processed in each department. The number of batches for each product line in each department is as follows:

	Trophies	Plaques	Medallions
Forming department	116	40	44
Assembly department	63	83	84
Packaging department	80	100	190

Utilities costs vary with direct labor costs in each department.

Required

1. Calculate the cost per unit of Trophies, Plaques and Medallions based on a single plantwide overhead rate, if total overhead is allocated based on total direct costs.
2. Calculate the cost per unit of Trophies, Plaques and Medallions based on departmental overhead rates, where forming department overhead costs are allocated based on direct labor costs of the forming department, assembly department overhead costs are allocated based on total direct costs of the assembly department and packaging department overhead costs are allocated based on direct materials costs of the packaging department.
3. Calculate the cost per unit of Trophies, Plaques and Medallions if Tarquin allocates overhead costs in each department using activity-based costing.
4. Explain how the disaggregation of information could improve or reduce decision quality.

5-32 Department and activity-cost rates, service sector. Radhika's Radiology Center (RRC) performs x-rays, ultrasounds, CT scans, and MRIs. RRC has developed a reputation as a top Radiology Center in the state. RRC has achieved this status because it constantly re-examines its processes and procedures. RRC has been using a single, facility-wide overhead allocation rate. The VP of Finance believes that RRC can make better process improvements if it uses more disaggegated cost information. She says, "We have state of the art medical imaging technology. Can't we have state of the art accounting technology?"

Radhika's Radiology Center
Budgeted Information
For the year ended May 30, 2011

	X-rays	Ultrasound	CT scan	MRI	Total
Technician labor	$ 61,440	$105,600	$ 96,000	$105,000	$ 368,040
Depreciation	32,240	268,000	439,000	897,500	1,636,740
Materials	22,080	16,500	24,000	31,250	93,830
Administration					20,610
Maintenance					247,320
Sanitation					196,180
Utilities					134,350
	$115,760	$390,100	$559,000	$1,033,750	$2,697,070
Number of procedures	3,840	4,400	3,000	2,500	
Minutes to clean after each procedure	5	5	15	35	
Minutes for each procedure	5	15	20	45	

RRC operates at capacity. The proposed allocation bases for overhead are as follows:

Administration	Number of procedures
Maintenance (including parts)	Capital Cost of the Equipment (use Depreciation)
Sanitation	Total cleaning minutes
Utilities	Total procedure minutes

Required

1. Calculate the budgeted cost per service for X-rays, Ultrasounds, CT scans, and MRIs using direct technician labor costs as the allocation basis.
2. Calculate the budgeted cost per service of X-rays, Ultrasounds, CT scans, and MRIs if RRC allocated overhead costs using activity-based costing.
3. Explain how the disaggregation of information could be helpful to RRC's intention to continuously improve their services.

5-33 Choosing cost drivers, activity-based costing, activity-based management. Annie Warbucks runs a dance studio with childcare and adult fitness classes. Annie's budget for the upcoming year is as follows:

Annie Warbuck's Dance Studio
Budgeted Costs and Activities
For the Year Ended June 30, 2010

Dance teacher salaries—school year	$48,600	
Dance teacher salaries—summer programme	13,500	
Child care teacher salaries	24,300	
Fitness instructor salaries	39,060	
Total salaries		$125,460
Supplies (art, dance accessories, fitness)		21,984
Rent, maintenance and utilities		97,511
Administration salaries		50,075
Marketing expenses		21,000
Total		$316,030

Other information:

Dance classes	3 per hour
Hours of operation (Dance, Childcare and Fitness)—school year (36 weeks)	2 p.m. to 8 p.m. M–F
Hours of operation (Dance, Childcare and Fitness)—summer programme (10 weeks)	9 a.m. to noon; 1 p.m. to 4 p.m. M–F

Other information:

	Dance	Childcare	Fitness	Total
Square footage	6,000	3,150	2,500	11,650
Number of participants	1,485	450	270	2,205
Teachers per hour	3	3	1	7
Number of advertisements	26	24	20	70

Required

1. Determine which costs are direct costs and which costs are indirect costs of different programs.
2. Choose a cost driver for the indirect costs and calculate the cost per unit of the cost driver. Explain briefly your choice of cost driver.
3. Calculate the budgeted costs of each program.
4. How can Annie use this information for pricing? What other factors should she consider?

5-34 Activity-based costing, merchandising. Pharmacare, Inc., a distributor of special pharmaceutical products, operates at capacity and has three main market segments:

a. General supermarket chains
b. Drugstore chains
c. Mom-and-Pop single-store pharmacies

Rick Flair, the new controller of Pharmacare, reported the following data for 2008:

	A	B	C	D	E
1					
2	**Pharmacare, 2008**	**General**			
3		**Supermarket**	**Drugstore**	**Mom-and-Pop**	
4		**Chains**	**Chains**	**Single Stores**	**Pharmacare**
5	Revenues	$3,708,000	$3,150,000	$1,980,000	$8,838,000
6	Cost of goods sold	3,600,000	3,000,000	1,800,000	8,400,000
7	Gross Margin	$ 108,000	$ 150,000	$ 180,000	438,000
8	Other operating costs				301,080
9	Operating income				$ 136,920

For many years, Pharmacare has used gross margin percentage [(Revenue − Cost of goods sold) ÷ Revenue] to evaluate the relative profitability of its market segments. But, Flair recently attended a seminar on activity-based costing and is considering using it at Pharmacare to analyze and allocate "other operating costs." He meets with all the key managers and several of his operations and sales staff and they agree that there are five key activities that drive other operating costs at Pharmacare:

Activity Area	Cost Driver
Order processing	Number of customer purchase orders
Line-item processing	Number of line items ordered by customers
Delivering to stores	Number of store deliveries
Cartons shipped to store	Number of cartons shipped
Stocking of customer store shelves	Hours of shelf-stocking

Each customer order consists of one or more line items. A line item represents a single product (such as Extra-Strength Tylenol Tablets). Each product line item is delivered in one or more separate cartons. Each store delivery entails the delivery of one or more cartons of products to a customer. Pharmacare's staff stacks cartons directly onto display shelves in customers' stores. Currently, there is no additional charge to the customer for shelf-stocking, and not all customers use Pharmacare for this activity. The level of each activity in the three market segments and the total cost incurred for each activity in 2008 is shown below:

	A	B	C	D	E
13					
14	**Activity-based Cost Data**		**Activity Level**		
15	**Pharmacare 2008**	**General**			**Total Cost**
16		**Supermarket**	**Drugstore**	**Mom-and-Pop**	**of Activity**
17	**Activity**	**Chains**	**Chains**	**Single Stores**	**in 2008**
18	Orders processed (number)	140	360	1,500	$ 80,000
19	Line-items ordered (number)	1,960	4,320	15,000	63,840
20	Store deliveries made (number)	120	360	1,000	71,000
21	Cartons shipped to stores (number)	36,000	24,000	16,000	76,000
22	Shelf stocking (hours)	360	180	100	10,240
23					$301,080

If you want to use Excel to solve this problem, go to the Excel Lab at **www.prenhall.com/horngren/cost13e** and download the template for Problem 5-34.

Required

1. Compute the 2008 gross-margin percentage for each of Pharmacare's three market segments.
2. Compute the cost driver rates for each of the five activity areas.
3. Use the activity-based costing information to allocate the $301,080 of "other operating costs" to each of the market segments. Compute the operating income for each market segment.
4. Comment on the results. What new insights are available with the activity-based costing information?

5-35 Choosing cost drivers, activity-based costing, activity-based management. Pumpkin Bags (PB) is a designer of high quality backpacks and purses. Each design is made in small batches. Each spring, PB comes out with new designs for the backpack and for the purse. They use these designs for a year, and then move on to the next trend. The bags are all made on the same fabrication equipment that is expected to operate at capacity. The equipment must be switched over to a new design and set up to prepare for the production of each new batch of products. When completed, each batch of products is immediately shipped to a wholesaler. Shipping costs vary with the number of shipments. Budgeted information for the year is as follows:

Pumpkin Bags Budget for costs and Activities For the year ended February 28, 2009	
Direct materials—purses	$ 362,000
Direct materials—backpacks	427,000
Direct manufacturing labor—purses	98,000
Direct manufacturing labor—backpacks	115,597
Setup	64,960
Shipping	72,065
Design	167,000
Plant utilities and administration	225,000
Total	$1,531,622

Other information:

	Backpacks	Purses	Total
Number of bags	6,000	3,150	9,150
Hours of production	1,560	2,600	4,160
Number of batches	133	70	203
Number of designs	3	2	5

Required

1. Identify the cost hierarchy level for each cost category.
2. Identify the most appropriate cost driver for each cost category. Explain briefly your choice of cost driver.
3. Calculate the cost per unit of cost driver for each cost category.
4. Calculate the total costs and cost per unit for each product line.
5. Explain how you could use the information in requirement 4 to reduce costs.

5-36 ABC, health care. Uppervale Health Center runs three programs: (1) alcoholic rehabilitation, (2) drug addict rehabilitation, and (3) aftercare (counseling and support of patients after release from a mental hospital). The center's budget for 2009 follows:

Professional salaries:		
4 physicians × $150,000	$ 600,000	
18 psychologists × $75,000	1,350,000	
20 nurses × $30,000	600,000	$2,550,000
Medical supplies		300,000
General overhead (administrative salaries, rent, utilities, etc.)		880,000
Total		$3,730,000

Muriel Clayton, the director of the center, is keen on determining the cost of each program. Clayton compiled the following data describing employee allocations to individual programs:

	Alcohol	Drug	Aftercare	Total Employees
Physicians		4		4
Psychologists	6	4	8	18
Nurses	4	6	10	20

Eighty patients are in residence in the alcohol program, each staying about six months. Thus, the clinic provides 40 patient-years of service in the alcohol program. Similarly, 100 patients are involved in the drug program for about six months each. Thus, the clinic provides 50 patient-years of service in the drug program.

Clayton has recently become aware of activity-based costing as a method to refine costing systems. She asks her accountant, Huey Deluth, how she should apply this technique. Deluth obtains the following information:

1. Consumption of medical supplies depends on the number of patient-years.
2. General overhead costs consists of:

Rent and clinic maintenance	$180,000
Administrative costs to manage patient charts, food, laundry	600,000
Laboratory services	100,000
Total	$880,000

3. Other information about individual departments are:

	Alcohol	Drug	Aftercare	Total Employees
Square feet of space occupied by each program	9,000	9,000	12,000	30,000
Patient-years of service	40	50	60	150
Number of laboratory tests	400	1,400	700	2,500

Required

1. a. Selecting cost-allocation bases that you believe are the most appropriate for allocating indirect costs to programs, calculate the indirect cost rates for medical supplies; rent and clinic maintenance; administrative costs for patient charts, food, and laundry; and laboratory services.
   b. Using an activity-based costing approach to cost analysis, calculate the cost of each program and the cost per patient-year of the alcohol and drug programs.
   c. What benefits can Uppervale Health Center obtain by implementing the ABC system?
2. What factors, other than cost, do you think Uppervale Health Center should consider in allocating resources to its programs?

5-37 Unused capacity, activity-based costing, activity-based management. Nivag's Netballs is a manufacturer of high quality basketballs and volleyballs. Setup costs are driven by the number of batches. Equipment and maintenance costs increase with the number of machine hours, and lease rent is paid per square foot. Capacity of the facility is 12,000 square feet and Nivag is using only 70% of this capacity. Nivag records the cost of unused capacity as a separate line item, and not as a product cost. Below is the budgeted information for Nivag:

Nivag's Netballs
Budgeted Costs and Activities
For the Year Ended August 31, 2010

Direct materials—basketballs	$ 209,750
Direct materials—volleyballs	358,290
Direct manufacturing labor—basketballs	107,333
Direct manufacturing labor—volleyballs	102,969
Setup	143,500
Equipment and maintenance costs	109,900
Lease rent	216,000
Total	$1,247,742

Other information:

	Basketballs	Volleyballs
Number of balls	66,000	100,000
Machine hours	11,000	12,500
Number of batches	300	400
Square footage of production space used	3,360	5,040

Required

1. Calculate the cost per unit of cost driver for each indirect cost pool.
2. What is the cost of unused capacity?
3. What is the total cost and the cost per unit of resources used to produce (a) basketballs and (b) volleyballs?
4. What factors should Nivag consider if it has the opportunity to manufacture a new line of footballs?

5-38 Activity-based job costing, unit-cost comparisons. The Tracy Corporation has a machining facility specializing in jobs for the aircraft-components market. Tracy's previous simple job-costing system had two direct-cost categories (direct materials and direct manufacturing labor) and a single indirect-cost pool (manufacturing overhead, allocated using direct manufacturing labor-hours). The indirect cost-allocation rate of the simple system for 2010 would have been $115 per direct manufacturing labor-hour.

Recently a team with members from product design, manufacturing, and accounting used an ABC approach to refine its job-costing system. The two direct-cost categories were retained. The team decided to replace the single indirect-cost pool with five indirect-cost pools. The cost pools represent five activity areas at the plant, each with its own supervisor and budget responsibility. Pertinent data are as follows:

Activity Area	Cost-Allocation Base	Cost-Allocation Rate
Materials handling	Parts	$ 0.40
Lathe work	Lathe turns	0.20
Milling	Machine-hours	20.00
Grinding	Parts	0.80
Testing	Units tested	15.00

Information-gathering technology has advanced to the point at which the data necessary for budgeting in these five activity areas are collected automatically.

Two representative jobs processed under the ABC system at the plant in the most recent period had the following characteristics:

	Job 410	Job 411
Direct material cost per job	$ 9,700	$59,900
Direct manufacturing labor cost per job	$750	$11,250
Number of direct manufacturing labor-hours per job	25	375
Parts per job	500	2,000
Lathe turns per job	20,000	60,000
Machine-hours per job	150	1,050
Units per job (all units are tested)	10	200

Required

1. Compute the manufacturing cost per unit for each job under the previous simple job-costing system.
2. Compute the manufacturing cost per unit for each job under the activity-based costing system.
3. Compare the per-unit cost figures for Jobs 410 and 411 computed in requirements 1 and 2. Why do the simple and the activity-based costing systems differ in the manufacturing cost per unit for each job? Why might these differences be important to Tracy Corporation?
4. How might Tracy Corporation use information from its ABC system to better manage its business?

5-39 ABC, implementation, ethics. (CMA, adapted) Applewood Electronics, a division of Elgin Corporation, manufactures two large-screen television models: the Monarch, which has been produced since 2004 and sells for $900, and the Regal, a newer model introduced in early 2007 that sells for $1,140. Based on the following income statement for the year ended November 30, 2008, senior management at Elgin have decided to concentrate Applewood's marketing resources on the Regal model and to begin to phase out the Monarch model.

Applewood Electronics Income Statement For the Fiscal Year Ended November 30, 2008

	Monarch	Regal	Total
Revenues	$19,800,000	$4,560,000	$24,360,000
Cost of goods sold	12,540,000	3,192,000	15,732,000
Gross margin	7,260,000	1,368,000	8,628,000
Selling and administrative expense	5,830,000	978,000	6,808,000
Operating income	$ 1,430,000	$ 390,000	$ 1,820,000
Units produced and sold	22,000	4,000	
Net income per unit sold	$65.00	$97.50	

Unit costs for Monarch and Regal are as follows:

	Monarch	Regal
Direct materials	$208	$584
Direct manufacturing labor		
Monarch (1.5 hours × $12)	18	
Regal (3.5 hours × $12)		42
Machine costs [a]		
Monarch (8 hours × $18)	144	
Regal (4 hours × $18)		72
Manufacturing overhead other than machine costs [b]	200	100
Total cost	$570	$798

[a] Machine costs include lease costs of the machine, repairs, and maintenance.
[b] Manufacturing overhead was allocated to products based on machine-hours at the rate of $25 per hour.

Applewood's controller, Susan Benzo, is advocating the use of activity-based costing and activity-based management and has gathered the following information about the company's manufacturing overhead costs for the year ended November 30, 2008.

Activity Center (Cost Allocation Base)	Total Activity Costs	Units of the Cost-Allocation Base Monarch	Regal	Total
Soldering (number of solder points)	$ 942,000	1,185,000	385,000	1,570,000
Shipments (number of shipments)	860,000	16,200	3,800	20,000
Quality control (number of inspections)	1,240,000	56,200	21,300	77,500
Purchase orders (number of orders)	950,400	80,100	109,980	190,080
Machine power (machine-hours)	57,600	176,000	16,000	192,000
Machine setups (number of setups)	750,000	16,000	14,000	30,000
Total manufacturing overhead	$4,800,000			

After completing her analysis, Benzo shows the results to Fred Duval, the Applewood division president. Duval does not like what he sees. "If you show headquarters this analysis, they are going to ask us to phase out the Regal line, which we have just introduced. This whole costing stuff has been a major problem for us. First Monarch was not profitable and now Regal."

"Looking at the ABC analysis, I see two problems. First, we do many more activities than the ones you have listed. If you had included all activities, maybe your conclusions would be different. Second, you used number of setups and number of inspections as allocation bases. The numbers would be different had you used setup-hours and inspection-hours instead. I know that measurement problems precluded you from using these other cost-allocation bases, but I believe you ought to make some adjustments to our current numbers to compensate for these issues. I know you can do better. We can't afford to phase out either product."

Benzo knows that her numbers are fairly accurate. As a quick check, she calculates the profitability of Regal and Monarch using more and different allocation bases. The set of activities and activity rates she had used resulted in numbers that closely approximate those based on more detailed analyses. She is confident that headquarters, knowing that Regal was introduced only recently, will not ask Applewood to phase it out. She is also aware that a sizable portion of Duval's bonus is based on division revenues. Phasing out either product would adversely affect his bonus. Still, she feels some pressure from Duval to do something.

Required

1. Using activity-based costing, calculate the profitability of the Regal and Monarch models.
2. Explain briefly why these numbers differ from the profitability of the Regal and Monarch models calculated using Applewood's existing simple costing system.
3. Comment on Duval's concerns about the accuracy and limitations of ABC.
4. How might Applewood find the ABC information helpful in managing its business?
5. What should Susan Benzo do in response to Duval's comments?

Collaborative Learning Problem

5-40 Activity-based costing, activity-based management, merchandising. Super Bookstore (SB) is a large city bookstore that sells books and music CDs, and has a café. SB operates at capacity and allocates selling, general and administration (S, G & A) costs to each product line using the cost of merchandise of each product line. SB wants to optimize the pricing and cost management of each product line. SB is wondering if its accounting system is providing it with the best information for making such decisions.

Super Bookstore
Product Line Information
For the Year Ended December 31, 2010

	Books	CDs	Café
Revenues	$3,720,480	$2,315,360	$736,216
Cost of Merchandise	$2,656,727	$1,722,311	$556,685
Cost of Café Cleaning	–	–	$ 18,250
Number of Purchase orders Placed	2,800	2,500	2,000
Number of Deliveries Received	1,400	1,700	1,600
Hours of Shelf Stocking Time	15,000	14,000	10,000
Items sold	124,016	115,768	368,108

Super Bookstore incurs the following Selling, General & Administration costs:

Super Bookstore
Selling, General & Administration (S, G & A) costs
For the Year Ended December 31, 2010

Purchasing department expenses	$ 474,500
Receiving department expenses	432,400
Shelf stocking labor expense	487,500
Customer support expense (cashiers and floor employees)	91,184
	$1,485,584

Required

1. Suppose Super bookstore uses cost of merchandise to allocate all S, G & A costs. Prepare product line and total company income statements.
2. Identify an improved method for allocating costs to the three product lines. Explain. Use the method for allocating S, G & A costs that you propose to prepare new product line and total company income statements. Compare your results to the results in requirement 1.
3. Write a memo to Super Bookstore's management describing the state of its accounting system, any improvements that you would recommend, and how the information may be useful for product line decisions.

6 Master Budget and Responsibility Accounting

Learning Objectives

1. Describe the master budget and explain its benefits
2. Describe the advantages of budgets
3. Prepare the operating budget and its supporting schedules
4. Use computer-based financial planning models in sensitivity analysis
5. Explain kaizen budgeting and how it is used for cost management
6. Describe responsibility centers and responsibility accounting
7. Explain how controllability relates to responsibility accounting
8. Recognize the human aspects of budgeting

Budgets are make or break in businesses. You might think a budget is only for companies whose profit margins are slim—Wal-Mart, for example. As the following article shows, even companies that sell high-dollar value goods and services adhere to budgets. Without budgets, it's difficult for managers and their employees to know whether they're on target for their growth and spending goals.

"Scrimping" at the Ritz: Master Budgets

"Ladies and gentlemen serving ladies and gentlemen." That's the motto of the Ritz-Carlton. With locations ranging from Bahrain to China, the grand hotel chain is known for its indulgent luxury and sumptuous surroundings. However, the aura of the chain's old-world elegance stands in contrast to its rather heavy emphasis—behind the scenes, of course—on cost control and budgets. Yet, it is this very approach that makes it possible for the Ritz to offer the legendary grandeur its guests expect during their stay.

A Ritz hotel's performance is the responsibility of its general manager and controller at each location worldwide. Local forecasts and budgets are prepared annually and are the basis of subsequent performance evaluations for the hotel and people who work there.

The preparation of a hotel's budget begins with the hotel's sales director, who is responsible for all hotel revenues. Sources of revenue include hotel rooms, conventions, weddings, meeting facilities, merchandise, and food and beverage. The controller then seeks input about costs. Standard costs, based on cost per occupied room, are used to build the budget for guest room stays. Other standard costs are used to calculate costs for meeting rooms and food and beverages. The completed sales budget and annual operating budget are sent to corporate headquarters. From there, the hotel's actual monthly performance is monitored against the approved budget.

The managers of each hotel meet daily to review the hotel's performance to date. They have the ability to adjust prices in the reservation system if they so choose. Adjusting prices can be particularly important if a hotel anticipates low occupancy rates.

Each month, the controller of each hotel receives a report from corporate headquarters that shows how the hotel performed against budget, as well as against the actual performance of other Ritz hotels. Any ideas for boosting revenues and reducing costs are regularly shared among hotel controllers.

As the Ritz-Carlton example illustrates, budgeting is widespread in organizations. Southwest Airlines, for example, uses budgets to monitor and manage fuel costs. Costco depends on its budget to maintain razor-thin margins as a result of strong competition from Wal-Mart. Gillette uses budgets to plan marketing campaigns for its razors and blades.

Budgeting is a common accounting tool companies use for implementing strategy. Management uses budgets to communicate directions and goals throughout a company. Budgets turn managers' perspectives forward and aid in planning and controlling the actions managers must undertake to satisfy their customers and succeed in the marketplace. Budgets provide measures of the financial results a company expects from its planned activities. By planning, managers learn to anticipate and avoid potential problems. Instead of dealing with unexpected problems, managers can focus their energies on exploiting opportunities. Remember: "Few businesses plan to fail, but many of those that flop failed to plan."

Budgets and the Budgeting Cycle

A *budget* is (a) the quantitative expression of a proposed plan of action by management for a specified period and (b) an aid to coordinate what needs to be done to implement that plan. A budget generally includes both financial and non-financial aspects of the plan, and it serves as a blueprint for the company to follow in an upcoming period. A financial budget quantifies management's expectations regarding income, cash flows, and financial position. Just as financial statements are prepared for past periods, financial statements can be prepared for future periods—for example, a budgeted income statement, a budgeted statement of cash flows, and a budgeted balance sheet. Underlying these financial budgets are nonfinancial budgets for, say, units manufactured or sold, number of employees, and number of new products being introduced to the marketplace.

Strategic Plans and Operating Plans

Budgeting is most useful when it is integrated with a company's strategy. *Strategy* specifies how an organization matches its own capabilities with the opportunities in the marketplace to accomplish its objectives. In developing successful strategies, managers consider questions such as:

- What are our objectives?
- How do we create value for our customers while distinguishing ourselves from our competitors?
- Are the markets for our products local, regional, national, or global? What trends affect our markets? How are we affected by the economy, our industry, and our competitors?
- What organizational and financial structures serve us best?
- What are the risks and opportunities of alternative strategies, and what are our contingency plans if our preferred plan fails?

A company, such as Home Depot, can have a strategy of providing quality products or services at a low price. Another company, such as Pfizer or Porsche, can have a strategy of providing a unique product or service that is priced higher than the products or services of competitors. Exhibit 6-1 shows that strategic plans are expressed through long-run budgets and operating plans are expressed via short-run budgets. But there is more to the story! The exhibit shows arrows pointing backward as well as forward. The backward arrows are a way of graphically indicating that budgets can lead to changes in plans and strategies. Budgets help managers assess strategic risks and opportunities by providing them with feedback about the likely effects of their strategies and plans. And sometimes the feedback signals to managers that they need to revise their plans and possibly their strategies.

DaimlerChrysler's decision about the pricing of its Dodge Durango illustrates how budgets helped its managers rework their operating plans. The Durango competes in the sport activity vehicle (SAV) market with the lower-priced Subaru Forrester and Isuzu Rodeo, as well as the comparably priced Chevrolet Blazer. DaimlerChrysler was considering reducing the Durango's price, to stimulate demand and increase profits. The budget, however, indicated that the anticipated increase in sales would not compensate for the lower prices and would, in fact, decrease Durango's profits. For its strategy of reducing price to succeed, DaimlerChrysler also would need to reduce Durango's manufacturing and marketing costs. This feedback led management to refocus attention on developing new product and pricing strategies for the Durango.

Budgeting Cycle and Master Budget

Well-managed companies usually cycle through the following budgeting steps during the course of the fiscal year:

1. Working together, managers and management accountants plan the performance of the company as a whole and the performance of its subunits (such as departments or divisions). Taking into account past performance and anticipated changes in the future, managers at all levels reach a common understanding on what is expected.
2. Senior managers give subordinate managers a frame of reference, a set of specific financial or nonfinancial expectations against which actual results will be compared.
3. Management accountants help managers investigate variations from plans, such as an unexpected decline in sales. If necessary, corrective action follows, such as a reduction in price to boost sales or cutting of costs to maintain profitability.
4. Managers and management accountants take into account market feedback, changed conditions, and their own experiences as they begin to make plans for the next period. For example, a decline in sales may cause managers to make changes in product features for the next period.

Exhibit 6-1

Strategy, Planning, and Budgets

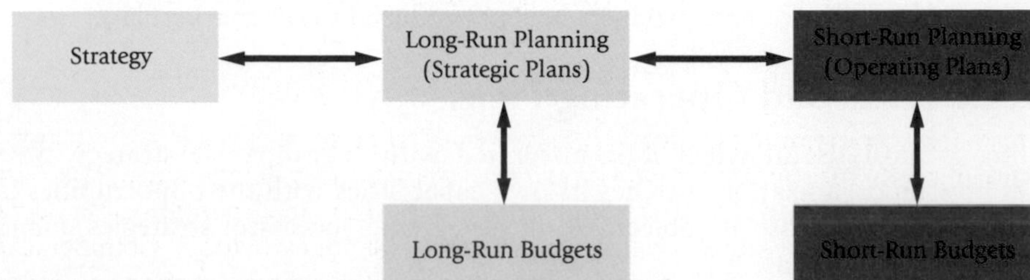

The preceding four steps describe the ongoing budget process. The working document at the core of this process is called the master budget. The **master budget** expresses management's operating and financial plans for a specified period (usually a fiscal year), and it includes a set of budgeted financial statements. The master budget is the initial plan of what the company intends to accomplish in the budget period. The master budget evolves from both operating and financing decisions made by managers.

- Operating decisions deal with how to best use the limited resources of an organization.
- Financing decisions deal with how to obtain the funds to acquire those resources.

The terminology used to describe budgets varies among companies. For example, budgeted financial statements are sometimes called **pro forma statements**. Some companies, such as Hewlett-Packard, refer to budgeting as *targeting*. And many companies, such as Nissan Motor Company and Owens Corning, refer to the budget as a *profit plan*.

The focus of this book is how management accounting helps managers make operating decisions. That's why this chapter emphasizes operating budgets. Managers spend a significant part of their time preparing and analyzing budgets. The many advantages of budgeting make spending time on budgeting a worthwhile investment of managers' energies.

Learning Objective 1

Describe the master budget

. . . The master budget is the initial budget prepared before the start of a period

and explain its benefits

. . . benefits include planning, coordination, and control

Advantages of Budgets

Budgets are an integral part of management control systems. When administered thoughtfully by managers, budgets:

- Promote coordination and communication among subunits within the company
- Provide a framework for judging performance and facilitating learning
- Motivate managers and other employees

Learning Objective 2

Describe the advantages of budgets

. . . advantages include coordination, communication, performance evaluation, and managerial motivation

Coordination and Communication

Coordination is meshing and balancing all aspects of production or service and all departments in a company in the best way for the company to meet its goals. *Communication* is making sure those goals are understood by all employees.

Coordination forces executives to think of relationships among individual departments and the company as a whole, and across companies. Consider budgeting at Pace, a United Kingdom–based manufacturer of electronic products. A key product is Pace's decoder boxes for cable television. The production manager can achieve more timely production by coordinating and communicating with the company's marketing team to understand when decoder boxes will be needed. In turn, the marketing team can make better predictions of future demand for decoder boxes by coordinating and communicating with Pace's customers.

Suppose BSKYB, one of Pace's largest customers, is planning to launch a new digital satellite service nine months from now. If Pace's marketing group is able to obtain information about the launch date for the satellite service, it can share this information with Pace's manufacturing group. The manufacturing group must then coordinate and communicate with Pace's materials-procurement group, and so on. The point to understand is that Pace is more likely to have satisfied customers (by having decoder boxes in the demanded quantities at the times demanded) if Pace coordinates and communicates both within its business functions and with its suppliers and customers during the budgeting process as well as during the production process.

Framework for Judging Performance and Facilitating Learning

Budgets enable a company's managers to measure actual performance against predicted performance. Budgets can overcome two limitations of using past performance as a basis for judging actual results. One limitation is that past results often incorporate past miscues and substandard performance. Consider a cellular telephone company (Mobile Communications) examining the current-year (2010) performance of its sales force. Suppose the performance for

2009 incorporated the efforts of many salespeople who have since left Mobile because they did not have a good understanding of the marketplace. (The president of Mobile said, "They could not sell ice cream in a heat wave.") Using the sales record of those departed employees would set the performance bar for 2010 much too low.

The other limitation of using past performance is that future conditions can be expected to differ from the past. Consider again Mobile Communications. Suppose, in 2010, Mobile had a 20% revenue increase, compared with a 10% revenue increase in 2009. Does this increase indicate outstanding sales performance? Before you say yes, consider the following facts. In November 2009, an industry trade association forecast that the 2010 growth rate in industry revenues would be 40%, which also turned out to be the actual growth rate. As a result, Mobile's 20% actual revenue gain in 2010 takes on a negative connotation, even though it exceeded the 2009 actual growth rate of 10%. Using the 40% budgeted sales growth rate provides a better measure of the 2010 sales performance than using the 2009 actual growth rate of 10%.

However, it is important to remember that a company's budget should not be the only benchmark used to evaluate performance. Many companies also consider performance relative to peers as well as improvement over prior years. The problem with evaluating performance relative only to a budget is it creates an incentive for subordinates to set a target that is relatively easy to achieve.[1] Of course, managers at all levels recognize this incentive, and therefore they work to make the budget more challenging to achieve for the individuals who report to them. Negotiations occur among managers at each of these levels to understand what is possible and what is not. The budget is the end product of these negotiations.

One of the most valuable benefits of budgeting is that it helps managers learn. When actual performance falls short of budgeted or planned performance, it prompts thoughtful senior managers to ask questions about what happened and why, and how performance can be improved in the future. This probing and learning is one of the most important reasons why budgeting helps improve performance.

Motivating Managers and Other Employees[2]

Research shows that challenging budgets improve employee performance. That's because employees view falling short of budgeted numbers as a failure. Most employees are motivated to work more intensely to avoid failure than to achieve success. As employees get closer to a goal, they work harder to achieve it. Therefore, many executives like to set demanding but achievable goals for their subordinate managers and employees. Creating a little anxiety improves performance, but overly ambitious and unachievable budgets increase anxiety without motivation—that's because employees see little chance of avoiding failure. General Electric's former CEO, Jack Welch, describes challenging budgets that subordinates buy into as energizing, motivating, and satisfying for managers and other employees, and capable of unleashing out-of-the-box and creative thinking.

Challenges in Administering Budgets

Budgeting is a time-consuming process that involves all levels of management. Top managers want lower-level managers to participate in the budgeting process because lower-level managers have more specialized knowledge and first-hand experience with day-to-day aspects of running the business. Participation creates greater commitment and accountability toward the budget among lower-level managers. This is the bottom-up aspect of the budgeting process.

The widespread prevalence of budgets in companies ranging from major corporations with international presence to smaller local businesses indicates that the advantages of budgeting systems outweigh the costs. To gain the benefits of budgeting, management at all levels of a company should understand and support the budget and all aspects of the management control system. Top management support is critical for obtaining lower-level

---

[1] See J. Hope and R. Fraser, *Beyond Budgeting* (Boston, MA: Harvard Business School Press, 2003) for several examples.

[2] For a more-detailed discussion, see R. Larnick, G. Wu, and C. Heath, "Raising the Bar on Goals," Graduate School of Business Publication, University of Chicago, Spring 1999.

management's participation in the formulation of budgets and for successful administration of budgets. Lower-level managers who feel that top management does not "believe" in a budget are unlikely to be active participants in a budget process.

Budgets should not be administered rigidly. Changing conditions usually call for changes in plans. A manager may commit to a budget, but a situation might develop in which some unplanned repairs or an unplanned advertising program would better serve the interests of the company. The manager should not defer the repairs or the advertising as a way of meeting the budget if doing so will hurt the company in the long run. Attaining the budget should not be an end in itself. In fact, critics of budgeting cite the temptation on the part of managers to administer budgets rigidly as one of the most negative aspects of budgeting.[3]

Time Coverage of Budgets

Budgets typically have a set period, such as a month, quarter, year, and so on. The set period can itself be broken into subperiods. For example, a 12-month cash budget may be broken into 12 monthly periods so that cash inflows and outflows can be better coordinated.

The motive for creating a budget should guide a manager in choosing the period for the budget. For example, consider budgeting for a new Harley-Davidson 500-cc motorcycle. If the purpose is to budget for the total profitability of this new model, a five-year period (or more) may be suitable and long enough to cover the product from design through to manufacture, sales, and after-sales support. In contrast, consider budgeting for a school play. If the purpose is to estimate all cash outlays, a six-month period from the planning stage to the final performance may be adequate.

The most frequently used budget period is one year, which is often subdivided into months and quarters. The budgeted data for a year are frequently revised as the year goes on. For example, at the end of the first quarter, management may change the budget for the next three quarters in light of new information obtained during the first quarter.

Businesses are increasingly using rolling budgets. A **rolling budget**, also called a **continuous budget**, is a budget that is always available for a specified future period. It is created by continually adding a month, quarter, or year to the period that just ended. Consider Electrolux, the global appliance company, which has a three- to five-year strategic plan and a four-quarter rolling budget. A four-quarter rolling budget for the April 2009 to March 2010 period is superseded in the next quarter—that is in June 2009—by a four-quarter rolling budget for July 2009 to June 2010, and so on. There is always a 12-month budget (for the next year) in place. Rolling budgets constantly force Electrolux's management to think about the forthcoming 12 months, regardless of the quarter at hand.

Steps in Developing an Operating Budget

The best way to explain how to prepare an operating budget is with an example. Consider Stylistic Furniture, a company that makes two types of granite-top coffee tables —Casual and Deluxe. It is late 2009 and Stylistic's CEO, Rex Jordan, is very concerned about how he is going to respond to the Board of Directors' mandate to increase profits by 10% in the coming year. Jordan goes through the five-step decision-making process introduced in Chapter 1.

1. **Identify the problem and uncertainties.** The problem is to identify a strategy and to build a budget to achieve a 10% profit growth. There are several uncertainties. Can Stylistic dramatically increase sales for its more profitable Deluxe tables? What price pressures is Stylistic likely to face? Will the cost of materials increase? Can costs be reduced through efficiency improvements?
2. **Obtain information.** Stylistic's managers gather information about sales of Deluxe tables in the current year. They are delighted to learn that sales have been stronger than

[3] J. Hope and R. Fraser, *Beyond Budgeting* (Boston, MA: Harvard Business School Press, 2003), pp. 3–17.

expected. Moreover, one of Stylistic's key competitors in its line of Casual tables has had quality problems that are unlikely to be resolved until early 2010. Unfortunately, they also discover that the prices of direct materials have increased slightly during 2009.

3. **Make predictions about the future.** Stylistic's managers feel confident that with a little more marketing, they will be able to grow the Deluxe tables business and even increase prices slightly relative to 2009. They also do not expect significant price pressures on Casual tables in the early part of the year because of the quality problems faced by a key competitor. They are concerned, however, that when the competitor does start selling again, pressure on prices could increase. The purchasing manager anticipates that prices of direct materials will be about the same as in 2009. The manufacturing manager believes that efficiency improvements would allow costs of manufacturing tables to be maintained at 2009 costs despite an increase in the prices of other inputs. Achieving these efficiency improvements is important if Stylistic is to maintain its 12% operating margin (that is, operating income ÷ sales = 12%) and to grow sales and operating income.
4. **Make decisions by choosing among alternatives.** Jordan and his managers feel confident in their strategy of pushing sales of Deluxe tables. This decision has some risks but is easily the best option available for Stylistic to increase profits by 10%.
5. **Implement the decision, evaluate performance, and learn.** As we will discuss in Chapters 7 and 8, managers compare actual to predicted performance to learn about why things turned out the way they did and how to do things better. Stylistic's managers would want to know whether their predictions about prices of Casual and Deluxe tables were correct. Did prices of direct materials increase more or less than anticipated? Did efficiency improvements occur? Such learning would be very helpful as Stylistic plans its budgets in subsequent years.

Learning Objective 3

Prepare the operating budget

. . . the budgeted income statement

and its supporting schedules

. . . such as cost of goods sold and nonmanufacturing costs

Stylistic's managers begin their work toward the 2010 budget. Exhibit 6-2 shows a diagram of the various parts of the *master budget*. The master budget comprises the financial projections of all the individual budgets for a company for a specified period, usually a fiscal year. The light, medium and dark purple boxes in Exhibit 6-2 represent the budgeted income statement and its supporting budget schedules—together called the **operating budget.**

We show the revenues budget box in a light purple color to indicate that it is often the starting point of the operating budget. The supporting schedules—shown in medium purple—quantify the budgets for various business functions of the value chain, from research and development to distribution costs. These schedules build up to the budgeted income statement—the key summary statement in the operating budget—shown in dark purple.

The light and dark blue boxes in the exhibit are the **financial budget**, which is that part of the master budget made up of the capital expenditures budget, the cash budget, the budgeted balance sheet, and the budgeted statement of cash flows. A financial budget focuses on how operations and planned capital outlays affect cash—shown in light blue.

The cash budget and the budgeted income statement can then be used to prepare two other summary financial statements—the budgeted balance sheet and the budgeted statement of cash flows—shown in dark blue. The master budget is finalized only after several rounds of discussions between top management and managers responsible for various business functions in the value chain.

We next present the steps in preparing an operating budget for Stylistic Furniture for 2010. Use Exhibit 6-2 as a guide for the steps that follow. The appendix to this chapter presents Stylistic's cash budget, which is another key component of the master budget. Details needed to prepare the budget follow:

- Stylistic sells two models of granite-top coffee tables—Casual and Deluxe. Nonsales-related revenue, such as interest income, is zero.
- Work-in-process inventory is negligible and is ignored.
- Direct materials inventory and finished goods inventory are costed using the first-in, first-out (FIFO) method. Unit costs of direct materials purchased and unit costs of finished goods sold remain unchanged throughout each budget year but can change from year to year.

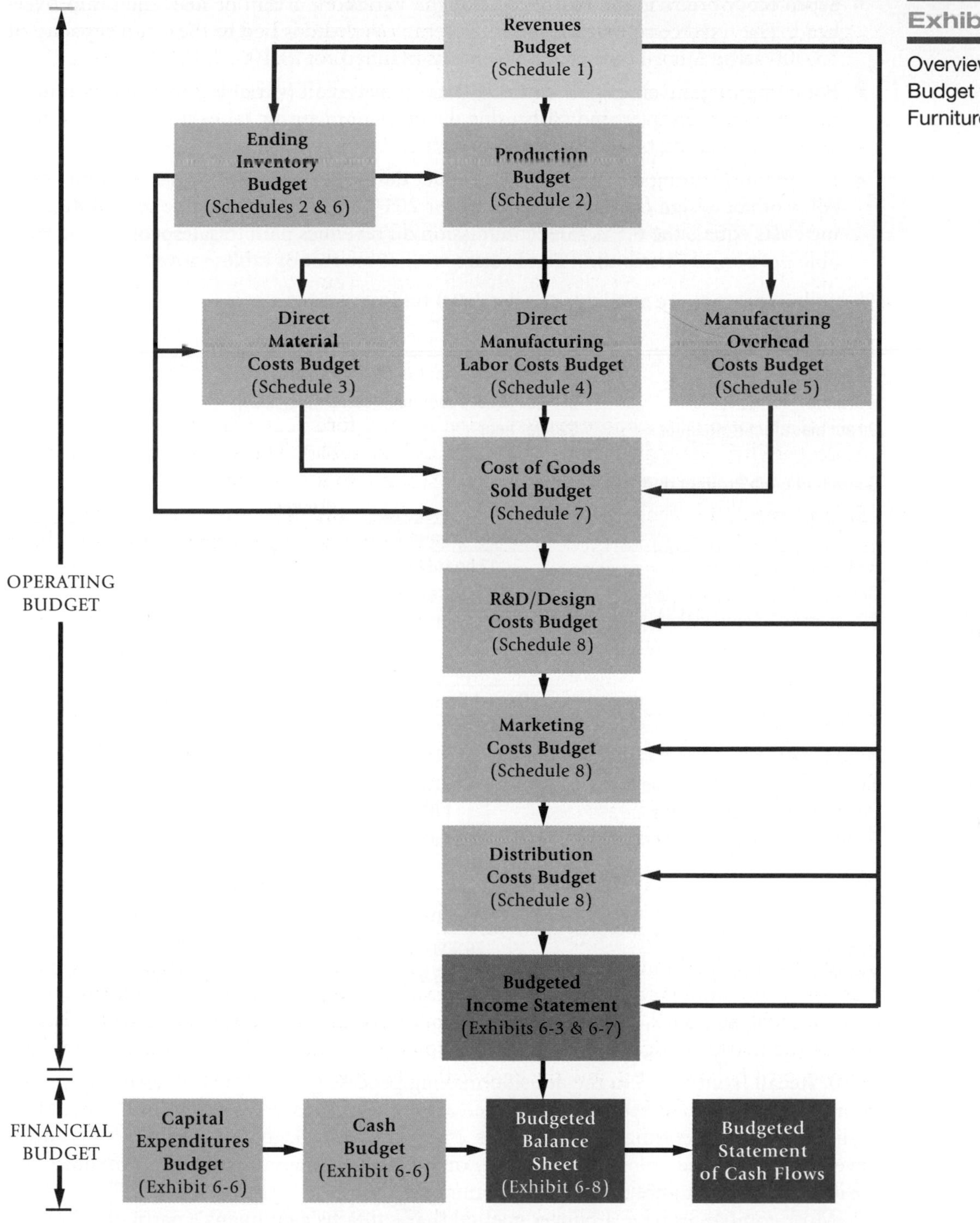

Exhibit 6-2

Overview of the Master Budget for Stylistic Furniture

- There are two types of direct materials: red oak (RO) and granite slabs (GS). Direct material costs are variable with respect to units of output—coffee tables.
- Direct manufacturing labor workers are hired on an hourly basis; no overtime is worked.
- There are two cost drivers for manufacturing overhead costs—direct manufacturing labor-hours and setup labor-hours.
- Direct manufacturing labor hours is the cost driver for the variable portion of manufacturing operations overhead. The fixed component of manufacturing operations overhead is tied to the manufacturing capacity of 300,000 direct manufacturing labor-hours that Stylistic has planned for 2010.

- Setup labor-hours is the cost driver for the variable portion of machine setup overhead. The fixed component of machine setup overhead is tied to the setup capacity of 15,000 setup labor-hours that Stylistic has planned for 2010.
- For computing inventoriable costs, Stylistic allocates all (variable and fixed) manufacturing operations overhead costs using direct manufacturing labor-hours and machine setup overhead costs using setup labor-hours.
- Nonmanufacturing costs consist of product design, marketing and distribution costs. All product design costs are fixed costs for 2010. The variable component of marketing costs equals the 6.5% sales commission on revenues paid to salespeople. The variable portion of distribution costs varies with cubic feet of tables moved.

The following data are available for the 2010 budget:

Direct materials	
Red Oak	$ 7 per board foot (b.f.) (same as in 2009)
Granite	$10 per square foot (s.f.) (same as in 2009)
Direct manufacturing labor	$20 per hour

Content of Each Product Unit

	Product	
	Casual Granite Table	Deluxe Granite Table
Red Oak	12 board feet	12 board feet
Granite	6 square feet	8 square feet
Direct manufacturing labor	4 hours	6 hours

	Product	
	Casual Granite Table	Deluxe Granite Table
Expected sales in units	50,000	10,000
Selling price	$ 600	$ 800
Target ending inventory in units	11,000	500
Beginning inventory in units	1,000	500
Beginning inventory in dollars	$384,000	$262,000

	Direct Materials	
	Red Oak	Granite
Beginning inventory	70,000 b.f.	60,000 s.f.
Target ending inventory	80,000 b.f.	20,000 s.f.

Stylistic bases its budgeted cost information on the costs it predicts it will incur to support its revenue budget, taking into account the efficiency improvements it expects to make in 2010. Recall from step 3 in the decision-making process (p. 186) that efficiency improvements are critical to offset anticipated increases in direct materials prices and to maintain Stylistic's 12% operating margin. Some companies rely heavily on past results when developing budgeted amounts; others rely on detailed engineering studies. Companies differ in how they compute their budgeted amounts.

Most companies have a budget manual that contains a company's particular instructions and relevant information for preparing its budgets. Although the details differ among companies, the following basic steps are common for developing the operating budget for a manufacturing company. Beginning with the revenues budget, each of the other budgets follows step-by-step in logical fashion.

Step 1: Prepare the Revenues Budget. A revenues budget, calculated in Schedule 1, is the usual starting point for the operating budget. That's because the production level and the inventory level—and therefore manufacturing costs—as well as nonmanufacturing costs, generally depend on the forecasted level of unit sales or revenues. Many factors influence the sales forecast, including the sales volume in recent periods, general economic and industry conditions, market research studies, pricing policies, advertising and sales promotions, competition, and regulatory policies. In Stylistic's case, the revenues budget for

2010 reflects Stylistic's strategy to grow revenues by increasing sales of Deluxe tables from 8,000 tables in 2009 to 10,000 tables in 2010.

Schedule 1: Revenues Budget
For the Year Ending December 31, 2010

	Units	Selling Price	Total Revenues
Casual	50,000	$600	$30,000,000
Deluxe	10,000	800	8,000,000
Total			$38,000,000

The $38,000,000 is the amount of revenues in the budgeted income statement. The revenues budget is often the result of elaborate information gathering and discussions among sales managers and sales representatives who have a detailed understanding of customer needs, market potential, and competitors' products. This information is often gathered through a customer response management (CRM) or sales management system. Statistical approaches such as regression and trend analysis can also help in sales forecasting. These techniques use indicators of economic activity and past sales data to forecast future sales. Managers should use statistical analysis only as one input to forecast sales. In the final analysis, the sales forecast should represent the collective experience and judgment of managers.

The usual starting point for step 1 is to base revenues on expected demand. Occasionally, a factor other than demand limits budgeted revenues. For example, when demand is greater than available production capacity or a manufacturing input is in short supply, the revenues budget would be based on the maximum units that could be produced. Why? Because sales would be limited by the amount produced.

Step 2: Prepare the Production Budget (in Units). After revenues are budgeted, the manufacturing manager prepares the production budget, which is calculated in Schedule 2. The total finished goods units to be produced depends on budgeted unit sales and expected changes in units of inventory levels:

$$\begin{array}{c}\text{Budget}\\\text{production}\\\text{(units)}\end{array} = \begin{array}{c}\text{Budget}\\\text{sales}\\\text{(units)}\end{array} + \begin{array}{c}\text{Target ending}\\\text{finished goods}\\\text{inventory}\\\text{(units)}\end{array} - \begin{array}{c}\text{Beginning}\\\text{finished goods}\\\text{inventory}\\\text{(units)}\end{array}$$

Schedule 2: Production Budget (in Units)
For the Year Ending December 31, 2010

	Product	
	Casual	Deluxe
Budgeted unit sales (Schedule 1)	50,000	10,000
Add target ending finished goods inventory	11,000	500
Total required units	61,000	10,500
Deduct beginning finished goods inventory	1,000	500
Units of finished goods to be produced	60,000	10,000

Step 3: Prepare the Direct Material Usage Budget and Direct Material Purchases Budget. The number of units to be produced, calculated in Schedule 2, is the key to computing the usage of direct materials in quantities and in dollars. The direct material quantities used depend on the efficiency with which materials are consumed to produce a table. In determining budgets, managers are constantly anticipating ways to make process improvements that increase quality and reduce waste, thereby reducing direct material usage and costs.

Like many companies, Stylistic has a *bill of materials,* stored and updated in its computer systems. This document identifies how each product is manufactured, specifying all materials (and components), the sequence in which the materials are used, the quantity of materials in each finished unit, and the work centers where the operations are performed. For example, the bill of materials would indicate that 12 board feet of red oak and 6 square feet of granite are needed to produce each Casual coffee table, and 12 board feet of red oak and 8 square feet of granite to produce each Deluxe coffee table. This information is then used to calculate the amounts in Schedule 3A.

Schedule 3A: Direct Material Usage Budget in Quantity and Dollars
For the Year Ending December 31, 2010

	Material		
	Red Oak	Granite	Total
Physical Units Budget			
Direct materials required for			
Casual tables (60,000 units × 12 b.f. and 6 s.f.)	720,000 b.f.	360,000 s.f.	
Direct materials required for			
Deluxe tables (10,000 units × 12 b.f. and 8 s.f.)	120,000 b.f.	80,000 s.f.	
Total quantity of direct materials to be used	840,000 b.f.	440,000 s.f.	
Cost Budget			
Available from beginning direct materials inventory			
(under a FIFO cost-flow assumption)			
Red Oak: 70,000 b.f. × $7 per b.f.	$ 490,000		
Granite: 60,000 s.f. × $10 per s.f.		$ 600,000	
To be purchased this period			
Red Oak: (840,000 − 70,000) b.f. × $7 per b.f.	5,390,000		
Granite: (440,000 − 60,000) s.f. × $10 per s.f.		3,800,000	
Direct materials to be used this period	$5,880,000	$4,400,000	$10,280,000

The purchasing manager prepares the budget for direct material purchases, calculated in Schedule 3B, based on the budgeted direct materials to be used, the beginning inventory of direct materials, and the target ending inventory of direct materials:

$$\text{Purchases of direct materials} = \text{Direct materials used in production} + \text{Target ending inventory of direct materials} - \text{Beginning inventory of direct material}$$

Schedule 3B: Direct Material Purchases Budget
For the Year Ending December 31, 2010

	Material		
	Red Oak	Granite	Total
Physical Units Budget			
To be used in production (from Schedule 3A)	840,000 b.f.	440,000 s.f.	
Add target ending inventory	80,000 b.f.	20,000 s.f.	
Total requirements	920,000 b.f.	460,000 s.f.	
Deduct beginning inventory	70,000 b.f.	60,000 s.f.	
Purchases to be made	850,000 b.f.	400,000 s.f.	
Cost Budget			
Red Oak: 850,000 b.f. × $7 per b.f.	$5,950,000		
Granite: 400,000 s.f. × $10 per s.f.		$4,000,000	
Purchases	$5,950,000	$4,000,000	$9,950,000

Step 4: Prepare the Direct Manufacturing Labor Costs Budget. In this step, manufacturing managers use *labor standards*, the time allowed per unit of output, to calculate the direct manufacturing labor costs budget in Schedule 4. These costs depend on wage rates, production methods, process and efficiency improvements and hiring plans.

Schedule 4: Direct Manufacturing Labor Costs Budget
For the Year Ending December 31, 2010

	Output Units Produced (Schedule 2)	Direct Manufacturing Labor-Hours per Unit	Total Hours	Hourly Wage Rate	Total
Casual	60,000	4	240,000	$20	$4,800,000
Deluxe	10,000	6	60,000	20	1,200,000
Total			300,000		$6,000,000

Step 5: Prepare the Manufacturing Overhead Costs Budget. As we described earlier, direct manufacturing labor-hours is the cost driver for the variable portion of manufacturing operations overhead and setup labor-hours is the cost driver for the variable portion of machine setup overhead costs. The use of activity-based cost drivers such as these gives rise to *activity-based budgeting*. **Activity-based budgeting (ABB)** focuses on the budgeted cost of the activities necessary to produce and sell products and services.

For the 300,000 direct manufacturing labor-hours, Stylistic's manufacturing managers estimate various line items of overhead costs that constitute manufacturing operations overhead (that is, all costs for which direct manufacturing labor-hours is the cost driver). Managers identify opportunities for process improvements and determine budgeted manufacturing operations overhead costs in the operating department. They also determine the resources that they will need from the two support departments—kilowatt hours of energy from the power department and hours of maintenance service from the maintenance department. The support department managers, in turn, plan the costs of personnel and supplies that they will need to provide the operating department with the support services it requires. The costs of the support departments are then allocated (first-stage cost allocation) as part of manufacturing operations overhead. Chapter 15 describes how the allocation of support department costs to operating departments is done when support departments provide services to each other and to operating departments. The upper half of Schedule 5 shows the various line items of costs that constitute manufacturing operations overhead costs—that is, all overhead costs that are caused by the 300,000 direct manufacturing labor-hours (the cost driver).

Stylistic's managers determine how setups should be done for the Casual and Deluxe line of tables, taking into account past experiences and potential improvements in setup efficiency.

For example, managers consider:

- Increasing the length of the production run per batch so that fewer batches (and therefore fewer setups) are needed for the budgeted production of tables.
- Decreasing the setup time per batch.
- Reducing the supervisory time needed, for instance by increasing the skill base of workers.

Stylistic's managers forecast the following setup information for the Casual and Deluxe tables:

	Casual Tables	Deluxe Tables	Total
1. Quantity of tables to be produced	60,000 tables	10,000 tables	
2. Number of tables to be produced per batch	50 tables/batch	40 tables/batch	
3. Number of batches (1) ÷ (2)	1,200 batches	250 batches	
4. Setup time per batch	10 hours/batch	12 hours/batch	
5. Total setup-hours (3) × (4)	12,000 hours	3,000 hours	15,000 hours
6. Setup-hour per table (5) ÷ (1)	0.2 hour	0.3 hour	

Using an approach similar to the one described for manufacturing operations overhead costs, Stylistic's managers estimate various line items of costs that comprise machine setup overhead costs—that is, all costs that are caused by the 15,000 setup labor-hours (the cost driver). Note how using activity-based cost drivers provides more-detailed information that improves decision making compared with budgeting based solely on output-based cost drivers. Of course, managers must always evaluate whether the expected benefit of adding more cost drivers exceeds the expected cost.[4] The bottom half of Schedule 5 summarizes these costs.

[4] The Stylistic example illustrates ABB using setup costs included in Stylistic's manufacturing overhead costs budget. ABB implementations in practice include costs in many parts of the value chain. For an example, see S. Borjesson, "A Case Study on Activity-Based Budgeting," *Journal of Cost Management,* Vol. 10, No. 4, pp. 7–18.

Schedule 5: Manufacturing Overhead Costs Budget
For the Year Ending December 31, 2010
Manufacturing Operations Overhead Costs

Variable costs		
Supplies	$1,500,000	
Indirect manufacturing labor	1,680,000	
Power (support department costs)	2,100,000	
Maintenance (support department costs)	1,200,000	$6,480,000
Fixed costs (to support capacity of 300,000 direct manufacturing labor-hours)		
Depreciation	1,020,000	
Supervision	390,000	
Power (support department costs)	630,000	
Maintenance (support department costs)	480,000	2,520,000
Total manufacturing operations overhead costs		$9,000,000

Machine Setup Overhead Costs

Variable costs		
Supplies	$ 390,000	
Indirect manufacturing labor	840,000	
Power (support department costs)	90,000	$ 1,320,000
Fixed costs (to support capacity of 15,000 setup labor-hours)		
Depreciation	603,000	
Supervision	1,050,000	
Power (support department costs)	27,000	1,680,000
Total machine setup overhead costs		$ 3,000,000
Total manufacturing operations overhead costs		$12,000,000

Step 6: Prepare the Ending Inventories Budget. The management accountant prepares the ending inventories budget, calculated in Schedules 6A and 6B. In accordance with generally accepted accounting principles, Stylistic treats both variable and fixed manufacturing overhead as inventoriable (product) costs. Stylistic is budgeted to operate at capacity. Manufacturing operations overhead costs are allocated to finished goods inventory at the budgeted rate of $30 per direct manufacturing labor-hour (total budgeted manufacturing operations overhead, $9,000,000 ÷ 300,000 budgeted direct manufacturing labor-hours). Machine setup overhead costs are allocated to finished goods inventory at the budgeted rate of $200 per setup-hour (total budgeted machine setup overhead, $3,000,000 ÷ 15,000 budgeted setup labor-hours). Schedule 6A shows the computation of the unit cost of coffee tables started and completed in 2010.

Schedule 6A: Unit Costs of Ending Finished Goods Inventory
December 31, 2010

		Product			
		Casual Tables		Deluxe Tables	
	Cost per Unit of Input	Input per Unit of Output	Total	Input per Unit of Output	Total
Red Oak	$ 7	12 b.f.	$ 84	12 b.f.	$ 84
Granite	10	6 s.f.	60	8 s.f.	80
Direct manufacturing labor	20	4 hrs.	80	6 hrs.	120
Manufacturing overhead	30	4 hrs.	120	6 hrs.	180
Machine setup overhead	200	0.2 hrs.	40	0.3 hrs	60
Total			$384		$524

Under the FIFO method, this unit cost is used to calculate the cost of target ending inventories of finished goods in Schedule 6B.

Schedule 6B: Ending Inventories Budget
December 31, 2010

	Quantity	Cost per Unit	Total	
Direct Materials				
Red Oak	80,000*	$ 7	$ 560,000	
Granite	20,000*	10	200,000	$ 760,000
Finished Goods				
Casual	11,000**	$384***	$4,224,000	
Deluxe	500**	524***	262,000	4,486,000
Total ending inventory				$5,246,000

*Data are from p. 188. **Data are from p. 188. ***From Schedule 6A, this is based on 2010 costs of manufacturing finished goods because under the FIFO costing method, the units in finished goods ending inventory consists of units that are produced during 2010.

Step 7: Prepare the Cost of Goods Sold Budget. The manufacturing and purchase managers, together with the management accountant, use information from Schedules 3 through 6 to prepare Schedule 7.

Schedule 7: Cost of Goods Sold Budget
For the Year Ending December 31, 2010

	From Schedule	Total	
Beginning finished goods inventory, January 1, 2010	Given*		$ 646,000
Direct materials used	3A	$10,280,000	
Direct manufacturing labor	4	6,000,000	
Manufacturing overhead	5	12,000,000	
Cost of goods manufactured			28,280,000
Cost of goods available for sale			28,926,000
Deduct ending finished goods inventory, December 31, 2010	6B		4,486,000
Cost of Goods Sold			$24,440,000

*Given in the description of basic data and requirements (Casual, $384,000, Deluxe $262,000).

Step 8: Prepare the Nonmanufacturing Costs Budget. Schedules 2 through 7 cover budgeting for Stylistic's production function of the value chain. For brevity, other parts of the value chain—product design, marketing and distribution—are combined into a single schedule. Just as in the case of manufacturing costs, managers in other functions of the value chain build in process and efficiency improvements and prepare nonmanufacturing cost budgets on the basis of the quantities of cost drivers planned for 2010.

Product design costs are fixed costs, determined on the basis of the product design work anticipated for 2010. The variable component of budgeted marketing costs is the commissions paid to sales people equal to 6.5% of revenues. The fixed component of budgeted marketing costs equal to $1,330,000 is tied to the marketing capacity for 2010. The cost driver of the variable component of budgeted distribution costs is cubic feet of tables moved (Casual: 18 cubic feet × 50,000 tables + Deluxe: 24 cubic feet × 10,000 tables = 1,140,000 cubic feet). Variable distribution costs equal $2 per cubic foot. The fixed component of budgeted distribution costs equals $1,596,000 and is tied to the distribution capacity for 2010. Schedule 8 shows the product design, marketing, and distribution costs budget for 2010.

Schedule 8: Nonmanufacturing Costs Budget
For the Year Ending December 31, 2010

Business Function	Variable Costs	Fixed Costs	Total Costs
Product Design	—	$1,024,000	$1,024,000
Marketing			
(Variable cost: $38,000,000 × 0.065)	$2,470,000	1,330,000	3,800,000
Distribution			
(Variable cost: $2 × 1,140,000 cu. ft.)	2,280,000	1,596,000	3,876,000
	$4,750,000	$3,950,000	$8,700,000

Exhibit 6-3

Budgeted Income Statement for Stylistic Furniture

	A	B	C	D
1	**Budgeted Income Statement for Stylistic Furniture**			
2	**For the Year Ending December 31, 2010**			
3	Revenues	Schedule 1		$38,000,000
4	Cost of goods sold	Schedule 7		24,440,000
5	Gross margin			13,560,000
6	Operating costs			
7	Product design costs	Schedule 8	$1,024,000	
8	Marketing costs	Schedule 8	3,800,000	
9	Distribution costs	Schedule 8	3,876,000	8,700,000
10	Operating income			$ 4,860,000

Step 9: Prepare the Budgeted Income Statement. The CEO and managers of various business functions, with help from the management accountant, use information in Schedules 1, 7, and 8 to finalize the budgeted income statement, shown in Exhibit 6-3. The style used in Exhibit 6-3 is typical, but more details could be included in the income statement; the more details that are put in the income statement, the fewer supporting schedules that are needed for the income statement.

Budgeting is a cross-functional activity. Top management's strategies for achieving revenue and operating income goals influence the costs planned for the different business functions of the value chain. For example, a budgeted increase in sales based on spending more for marketing must be matched with higher production costs to ensure that there is an adequate supply of tables and with higher distribution costs to ensure timely delivery of tables to customers.

Rex Jordan, the CEO of Stylistic Furniture, is very pleased with the 2010 budget. It calls for a 10% increase in operating income compared with 2009. The keys to achieving a higher operating income are a significant increase in sales of Deluxe tables, and process improvements and efficiency gains throughout the value chain. As Rex studies the budget more carefully, however, he is struck by two comments appended to the budget: First, to achieve the budgeted number of tables sold, Stylistic may need to reduce its selling prices by 3% to $582 for Casual tables and to $776 for Deluxe tables. Second, a supply shortage in direct materials may result in a 5% increase in the prices of direct materials (red oak and granite) above the material prices anticipated in the 2010 budget. If direct materials prices increase, however, no reduction in selling prices is anticipated. He asks Tina Larsen, the management accountant, to use Stylistic's financial planning model to evaluate how these outcomes will affect budgeted operating income.

Learning Objective 4

Use computer-based financial planning models in sensitivity analysis

. . . for example, understand the effects of changes in selling prices and direct material prices on budgeted income

Computer-Based Financial Planning Models

Financial planning models are mathematical representations of the relationships among operating activities, financing activities, and other factors that affect the master budget. Companies can use computer-based systems, such as Enterprise Resource Planning (ERP) systems, to perform calculations for these planning models. Companies that use ERP systems, and other such budgeting tools, find that these systems simplify budgeting and reduce the computational burden and time required to prepare budgets. The Concepts in Action box on p. 196 provides an example of one such company. ERP systems store vast quantities of information about the materials, machines and equipment, labor, power, maintenance, and setups needed to manufacture different products. Once sales quantities for different products have been identified, the software can quickly compute the budgeted costs for manufacturing these products. The software packages have a module on sensitivity analysis to assist managers in their planning and budgeting activities.

Exhibit 6-4 Effect of Changes in Budget Assumptions on Budgeted Operating Income for Stylistic Furniture

File Edit View Insert Format Tools Data Window Help

	A	B	C	D	E	F	G	H	I
1	Key Assumptions								
2		Units Sold		Selling Price		Direct Material Cost		Budgeted Operating Income	
3	What-If Scenario	Casual	Deluxe	Casual	Deluxe	Red Oak	Granite	Dollars	Change from Master Budget
4	Master budget	50,000	10,000	$600	$800	$7.00	$10.00	$4,860,000	
5	Scenario 1	50,000	10,000	582	776	$7.00	$10.00	3,794,100	22% decrease
6	Scenario 2	50,000	10,000	600	800	$7.35	$10.50	4,483,800	8% decrease

Sensitivity analysis is a "what-if" technique that examines how a result will change if the original predicted data are not achieved or if an underlying assumption changes.

To see how sensitivity analysis works, we consider two scenarios identified as possibly affecting Stylistic Furniture's budget model for 2010.

Scenario 1: A 3% decrease in the selling price of the Casual table and a 3% decrease in the selling price of the Deluxe table.

Scenario 2: A 5% increase in the price per board foot of red oak and a 5% increase in the price per square foot of granite.

Exhibit 6-4 presents the budgeted operating income for the two scenarios.

Note that under Scenario 1, a change in selling prices per table affects revenues (Schedule 1) as well as variable marketing costs (sales commissions, Schedule 8). The Problem for Self-Study at the end of the chapter shows the revised schedules for Scenario 1. Similarly, a change in the price of direct materials affects the direct material usage budget (Schedule 3A), the unit cost of ending finished goods inventory (Schedule 6A), the ending finished goods inventories budget (in Schedule 6B) and the cost of goods sold budget (Schedule 7). Sensitivity analysis is especially useful in incorporating such interrelationships into budgeting decisions by managers.

Exhibit 6-4 shows a substantial decrease in operating income as a result of decreases in selling prices but a smaller decline in operating income if direct material prices increase by 5%. The sensitivity analysis prompts Stylistic's managers to put in place contingency plans. For example, should selling prices decline in 2010, Stylistic may choose to postpone some product development programs that it had included in its 2010 budget but that could be deferred to a later year. More generally, when the success or viability of a venture is highly dependent on attaining one or more targets, managers should frequently update their budgets as uncertainty is resolved. These updated budgets can help managers to adjust expenditure levels as circumstances change.

Instructors and students who, at this point, want to explore the cash budget and the budgeted balance sheet for the Stylistic Furniture example can skip ahead to the appendix on page 203.

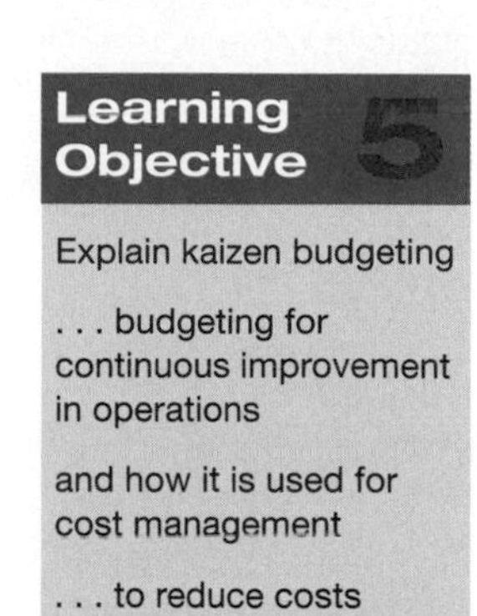

Learning Objective 5
Explain kaizen budgeting
. . . budgeting for continuous improvement in operations
and how it is used for cost management
. . . to reduce costs

Kaizen Budgeting

Chapter 1 noted the importance of continuous improvement, or *kaizen* in Japanese. **Kaizen budgeting** explicitly incorporates continuous improvement anticipated during the budget period into the budget numbers. Many companies that have cost reduction as a strategic focus, including General Electric in the United States and Citizens Watch and Toyota in Japan, use kaizen budgeting to continuously reduce costs. Much of the cost reduction associated with kaizen budgeting arises from many small improvements rather than "quantum leaps." A significant aspect of kaizen budgeting is employee suggestions.

Concepts in Action

Web-Enabled Budgeting and Hendrick Motorsports

In recent years, an increasing number of companies have implemented comprehensive software packages that manage budgeting and forecasting functions across the organization. One such option is Microsoft Corporation's Forecaster package, which is designed for businesses looking to gain control over their budgeting and forecasting process within a fully integrated Web-based environment.

Among the more unique companies implementing Web-enabled budgeting is Hendrick Motorsports. Featuring champion drivers Jeff Gordon and Jimmie Johnson, Hendrick is the premier NASCAR Sprint Cup (formerly NEXTEL Cup) stock car racing organization. Headquartered on a 12 building, 600,000-square-foot campus near Charlotte, North Carolina, Hendrick operates four full-time teams in the Sprint Cup series, which runs annually from February through November and features 36 races at 23 speedways across the United States. The Hendrick organization has annual operating costs of $100 million and 550 employees, with tasks ranging from accounting and marketing to engine building and racecar driving. Such an environment features multiple functional areas and units, varied worksites, and ever-changing circumstances. Patrick Perkins, director of marketing, noted, "Racing is a fast business. It's just as fast off the track as it is on it. With the work that we put into development of our teams and technologies, and having to respond to change as well as anticipate change, I like to think of us in this business as change experts."

Microsoft Forecaster, Hendrick's Web-enabled budgeting package, has allowed Hendrick's financial managers to seamlessly manage the planning and budgeting process. Authorized users from each functional area or team sign on to the application through the corporate intranet. Security on the system is tight: Access is limited to only the accounts that a manager is authorized to budget. That way, for example, Jeff Gordon's crew chief can't see what Jimmie Johnson's team members are doing. Forecaster also allows users at the racetrack to access the application remotely, which allows mangers to receive or update real-time "actuals" from the system. This way, team managers know their allotted expenses for each race. Forecaster also provides users with additional features, including seamless links with general ledger accounts and the option to perform what-if (sensitivity) analyses. Scott Lampe, chief financial officer, said, "Forecaster allows us to change our forecasts to respond to changes, either rule changes [such as changes in the series' points system] or technology changes [such as pilot testing NASCAR's new, safer "Car of Tomorrow"] throughout the racing season."

Hendrick's Web-enabled budgeting system frees the finance department so it can work on strategy, analysis, and decision-making. It also allows Hendrick to complete its annual budgeting process in only six weeks, a 50 percent reduction in the time spent budgeting and planning, which is critical given NASCAR's extremely short off-season. Patrick Pearson from Hendrick Motorsports believes the system gives the organization a competitive advantage, "In racing, the team that wins is not only the team with the fastest car, but the team that is the most disciplined and prepared week in and week out. Forecaster allows us to respond to that changing landscape."

Source: Ryan, Nate, "Hendrick Empire Strikes Back with Three Contenders in Chase for Nextel Cup," *USA Today*, September 17, 2006; Hendrick Motorsports, "About Hendrick Motorsports," Hendrick Motorsports Web site www.hendrickmotorsports.com (April 12, 2007); Microsoft Corporation, "Microsoft Forecaster: Hendrick Motorsports Customer Video," Microsoft Corporation Web site www.microsoft.com (April 12, 2007); Goff, John, "In the Fast Lane," *CFO Magazine*, December 1, 2004; Lampe, Scott, "NASCAR Racing Team Stays on Track with FRx Software's Comprehensive Budget Planning Solution," *DM Review*, July 1, 2003.

Companies implementing kaizen budgeting believe that employees who actually do the job, whether in manufacturing, sales, or distribution, have the best information and knowledge of how the job can be done better. These companies create a culture in which employee suggestions are valued, recognized, and rewarded.

Throughout our nine budgeting steps for Stylistic Furniture, we assumed four hours of direct labor time to manufacture each Casual coffee table. A kaizen budgeting approach would incorporate continuous improvement resulting from, for example, employee suggestions for doing the work faster or reducing idle time. The kaizen budget for direct manufacturing labor-hours for 2010 would then be as follows:

	Budgeted Direct Manufacturing Labor-Hours per Table
January–March 2010	4.00
April–June 2010	3.95
July–September 2010	3.90
October–December 2010	3.85

The implications of these direct manufacturing labor-hour reductions would be lower direct manufacturing labor costs, as well as lower variable manufacturing operations overhead costs, because direct manufacturing labor is the driver of these costs. Unless Stylistic meets these continuous improvement goals, actual hours used will exceed budgeted hours in the latter quarters of the year. Should that happen, Stylistic's managers will explore reasons for the goals not being met and either adjust the targets or implement process changes that will accelerate continuous improvement.

Kaizen budgeting can also be applied to activities such as setups with the goal of reducing setup time and setup costs, or distribution with the goal of reducing the cost of moving each cubic foot of table. Kaizen budgeting and budgeting for specific activities are key building blocks of the master budget.

Budgeting and Responsibility Accounting

To attain the goals described in the master budget, a company must coordinate the efforts of all its employees—from the top executive through all levels of management to every supervised worker. Coordinating the company's efforts means assigning responsibility to managers who are accountable for their actions in planning and controlling human and other resources. How each company structures its own organization significantly shapes how the company's efforts will be coordinated.

Learning Objective 6

Describe responsibility centers

. . . a part of an organization that a manager is accountable for

and responsibility accounting

. . . measurement of plans and actual results that a manager is accountable for

Organization Structure and Responsibility

Organization structure is an arrangement of lines of responsibility within the organization. A company such as British Petroleum may be organized primarily by business function—exploration, refining, and marketing—with each manager having decision-making authority over her function. Another company, such as Procter & Gamble, the household-products giant, may be organized by product line or brand. The managers of the individual divisions (toothpaste, soap, and so on) would each have decision-making authority concerning all the business functions (manufacturing, marketing, and so on) within that division.

Each manager, regardless of level, is in charge of a responsibility center. A **responsibility center** is a part, segment, or subunit of an organization whose manager is accountable for a specified set of activities. The higher the manager's level, the broader the responsibility center and, generally, the larger the number of his or her subordinates. **Responsibility accounting** is a system that measures the plans, budgets, actions, and actual results of each responsibility center. Four types of responsibility centers are:

1. **Cost center**—the manager is accountable for costs only.
2. **Revenue center**—the manager is accountable for revenues only.
3. **Profit center**—the manager is accountable for revenues and costs.
4. **Investment center**—the manager is accountable for investments, revenues, and costs.

The Maintenance Department of a Marriott hotel is a cost center because the maintenance manager is responsible only for costs, so this budget is based on costs. The Sales Department is a revenue center because the sales manager is responsible primarily for revenues, so this budget is based on revenues. The hotel manager is in charge of a profit center because the manager is accountable for both revenues and costs, so this budget is based on revenues and costs. The regional manager responsible for determining the amount to be invested in new hotel projects and for revenues and costs generated from these investments is in charge of an investment center, so this budget is based on revenues, costs, and the investment base.

A responsibility center can be structured to promote better alignment of individual and company goals. For example, until recently, OPD, an office products distributor, operated its Sales Department as a revenue center. Each salesperson received a commission of 3% of the revenues per order, regardless of its size, the cost of processing it, or the cost of delivering the office products. An analysis of customer profitability at OPD found that many customers were unprofitable. The main reason was the high ordering and delivery costs of small orders. OPD's managers decided to make the Sales Department a profit center, accountable for revenues and costs, and to change the incentive system for salespeople to 15% of the monthly profits per customer. The costs for each customer included the ordering and delivery costs. The effect of this change was immediate. The Sales Department began charging customers for ordering and delivery, and salespeople at OPD actively encouraged customers to consolidate their purchases into fewer orders. As a result, each order began producing larger revenues. Customer profitability increased because of a 40% reduction in ordering and delivery costs in one year.

Feedback

Budgets coupled with responsibility accounting provide feedback to top management about the performance relative to the budget of different responsibility center managers.

Differences between actual results and budgeted amounts—called *variances*—if properly used, can help managers implement and evaluate strategies in three ways:

1. ***Early warning.*** Variances alert managers early to events not easily nor immediately evident. Managers can then take corrective actions or exploit the available opportunities. For example, after observing a small decline in sales this period, managers may want to investigate if this is an indication of an even steeper decline to follow later in the year.
2. ***Performance evaluation.*** Variances prompt managers to probe how well the company has performed in implementing its strategies. Were materials and labor used efficiently? Was R&D spending increased as planned? Did product warranty costs decrease as planned?
3. ***Evaluating strategy.*** Variances sometimes signal to managers that their strategies are ineffective. For example, a company seeking to compete by reducing costs and improving quality may find that it is achieving these goals but that it is having little effect on sales and profits. Top management may then want to re-evaluate the strategy.

Responsibility and Controllability

Learning Objective 7

Explain how controllability relates to responsibility accounting

. . . managers cannot control all of the costs that they are accountable for; responsibility accounting focuses on obtaining information, not fixing blame

Controllability is the degree of influence that a specific manager has over costs, revenues, or related items for which he or she is responsible. A **controllable cost** is any cost that is primarily subject to the influence of a given *responsibility center manager* for a given *period*. A responsibility accounting system could either exclude all uncontrollable costs from a manager's performance report or segregate such costs from the controllable costs. For example, a machining supervisor's performance report might be confined to direct materials, direct manufacturing labor, power, and machine maintenance costs and might exclude costs such as rent and taxes paid on the plant.

In practice, controllability is difficult to pinpoint for at least two reasons:

1. Few costs are clearly under the sole influence of one manager. For example, prices of direct materials may be influenced by a purchasing manager, but these prices also depend on market conditions beyond the manager's control. Quantities used may be influenced by a production manager, but quantities used also depend on the quality of materials purchased. Moreover, managers often work in teams. Think about how difficult it is to evaluate individual responsibility in a team situation.
2. With a long enough time span, all costs will come under somebody's control. However, most performance reports focus on periods of a year or less. A current manager may

benefit from a predecessor's accomplishments or may inherit a predecessor's problems and inefficiencies. For example, present managers may have to work under undesirable contracts with suppliers or labor unions that were negotiated by their predecessors. How can we separate what the current manager actually controls from the results of decisions made by others? Exactly what is the current manager accountable for? Answers may not be clear-cut.

Executives differ in how they embrace the controllability notion when evaluating those reporting to them. Some CEOs regard the budget as a firm commitment that subordinates must meet. Failure to meet the budget is viewed unfavorably. Other CEOs believe a more risk-sharing approach with managers is preferable, in which noncontrollable factors and performance relative to competitors are taken into account when judging the performance of managers who fail to meet their budgets.

Managers should avoid overemphasizing controllability. Responsibility accounting is more far-reaching. It focuses on gaining *information and knowledge*, not only on control. *Responsibility accounting helps managers to first focus on whom they should ask to obtain information and not on whom they should blame.* For example, if actual revenues at a Marriott hotel are less than budgeted revenues, the managers of the hotel may be tempted to blame the sales manager for the poor performance. The fundamental purpose of responsibility accounting, however, is not to fix blame but to gather information to enable future improvement.

The question is, Who can tell us the most about the specific item in question, regardless of that person's ability to exert personal control over that item? For instance, purchasing managers may be held accountable for total purchase costs, not because of their ability to control market prices, but because of their ability to predict uncontrollable prices and to explain uncontrollable price changes. Similarly, managers at a Pizza Hut unit may be held responsible for operating income of their units, even though they (a) do not fully control selling prices nor the costs of many food items and (b) have minimal flexibility about what items to sell or the ingredients in the items they sell. They are, however, in the best position to explain differences between their actual operating incomes and their budgeted operating incomes.

Performance reports for responsibility centers are sometimes designed to change managers' behavior in the direction top management desires. For example, some companies have changed the accountability of a cost center to a profit center. That's because the manager will probably behave differently. A cost-center manager may emphasize production efficiency and deemphasize the pleas of sales personnel for faster service and rush orders. In a profit center, the manager is responsible for costs and revenues. Even though the manager still has no control over sales personnel, the manager can influence activities that affect sales and will more likely weigh the impact of decisions on costs and revenues rather than on costs alone.

Human Aspects of Budgeting

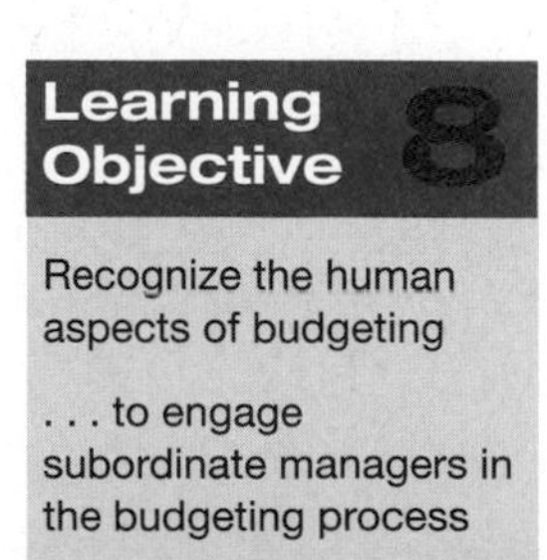

Learning Objective 8
Recognize the human aspects of budgeting
. . . to engage subordinate managers in the budgeting process

Why did we discuss the two major topics, the master budget and responsibility accounting, in the same chapter? Primarily to emphasize that human factors are crucial in budgeting. Too often, budgeting is thought of as a mechanical tool. The budgeting techniques themselves are free of emotion. However, the administration of budgeting requires education, persuasion, and intelligent interpretation.

As we discussed earlier in this chapter, budgeting is most effective when lower-level managers actively participate and meaningfully engage in the budgeting process. Participation adds credibility to the budgeting process and creates greater commitment and accountability toward the budget. But participation requires "honest" communication about the business from subordinates and lower-level managers to their bosses.

At times, subordinates may try to "play games" and build in *budgetary slack*. **Budgetary slack** describes the practice of underestimating budgeted revenues, or overestimating budgeted costs, to make budgeted targets more easily achievable. It frequently occurs when budget variances (the differences between actual results and budgeted amounts) are used to evaluate performance. Line managers are also unlikely to be fully honest in their budget communications if top management mechanically institutes across-the-board cost reductions (say, a 10% reduction in all areas) in the face of projected revenue reductions.

Budgetary slack provides managers with a hedge against unexpected adverse circumstances. But budgetary slack also misleads top management about the true profit potential of the company, which leads to inefficient resource planning and allocation and poor coordination of activities across different parts of the company.

To avoid problems of budgetary slack, some companies use budgets primarily for planning purposes. They evaluate managerial performance using multiple indicators that take into account various factors such as the prevailing business environment and performance relative to competitors. But evaluating performance in this way takes time and requires careful exercise of judgment. Other companies use budgets for both planning and performance evaluation and use different approaches to obtain accurate information.

To explain one approach, let's consider the plant manager of a beverage bottler who is suspected by top management of understating the productivity potential of the bottling lines in his forecasts for the coming year. His presumed motivation is to increase the likelihood of meeting next year's production bonus targets. Suppose top management could purchase a consulting firm's study that reports productivity levels—such as the number of bottles filled per hour—at a number of comparable plants owned by other bottling companies. This report shows that its own plant manager's productivity forecasts are well below actual productivity levels being achieved at other comparable plants.

Top management could share this independent information source with the plant manager and ask him to explain why his productivity differs from that at other similar plants. They could also base part of the plant manager's compensation on his plant's productivity in comparison with other "benchmark" plants rather than on the forecasts he provided. Using external benchmark performance measures reduces a manager's ability to set budget levels that are easy to achieve.[5]

Another approach to reducing budgetary slack is for managers to involve themselves regularly in understanding what their subordinates are doing. Such involvement should not result in managers dictating the decisions and actions of subordinates. Rather, a manager's involvement should take the form of providing support, challenging in a motivational way the assumptions subordinates make, and enhancing mutual learning about the operations. Regular interaction with subordinates allows managers to become knowledgeable about the operations and diminishes the ability of subordinates to create slack in their budgets.

Part of top management's responsibility is to promote commitment among the employees to a set of core values and norms. These values and norms describe what constitutes acceptable and unacceptable behavior. For example, Johnson & Johnson (J&J) has a credo that describes its responsibilities to doctors, patients, employees, communities, and shareholders. Employees are trained in the credo to help them understand the behavior that is expected of them. Managers are often promoted from within and are therefore very familiar with the work of the employees reporting to them. Managers also have the responsibility to interact with and mentor their subordinates. These values and practices create a culture at J&J that discourages budgetary slack.

Some companies, such as IBM and Kodak, have designed innovative performance evaluation measures that reward managers based on the subsequent accuracy of the forecasts used in preparing budgets. For example, the *higher and more accurate* the budgeted profit forecasts of division managers, the higher their incentive bonuses.

Many of the best performing companies, such as General Electric, Microsoft, and Novartis, set "stretch" targets. Stretch targets are challenging but achievable levels of expected performance, intended to create a little discomfort and to motivate employees to exert extra effort and attain better performance.

Many managers regard budgets negatively. To them, the word budget is about as popular as, say, *downsizing*, *layoff*, or *strike*. Top managers must convince their subordinates

---

[5] For an excellent discussion of these issues, see Chapter 14 ("Formal Models in Budgeting and Incentive Contracts") of R. S. Kaplan and A. A. Atkinson, *Advanced Management Accounting*, 3rd ed. (Upper Saddle River, NJ: Prentice Hall, 1998).

that the budget is a tool designed to help them set and reach goals. But whatever the manager's perspective on budgets—pro or con—budgets are not remedies for weak management talent, faulty organization, or a poor accounting system.

The management style of executives is a factor in how budgets are perceived in companies. Some CEOs argue that "numbers always tell the story." An executive once noted, "You can miss your plan once, but you wouldn't want to miss it twice." Other CEOs believe "too much focus on making the numbers in a budget" can lead to poor decision-making and unethical practices.

Budgeting in Multinational Companies

Multinational companies, such as Federal Express, Kraft, and Pfizer, have operations in many countries. An international presence carries with it positives—access to new markets and resources—and negatives—operating in less-familiar business environments and exposure to currency fluctuations. For example, multinational companies earn revenues and incur expenses in many different currencies, and they must translate their operating performance into a single currency (say, U.S. dollars) for reporting results to their shareholders each quarter. This translation is based on the average exchange rates that prevail during the quarter. That is, in addition to budgeting in different currencies, management accountants in multinational companies also need to budget for foreign exchange rates. This is difficult because management accountants need to anticipate potential changes that might take place during the year. Exchange rates are constantly fluctuating, so to reduce the possible negative impact on performance caused by unfavorable exchange rate movements, finance managers will frequently use sophisticated techniques such as forward, future, and option contracts to minimize exposure to foreign currency fluctuations. Besides currency issues, multinational companies need to understand the political, legal, and, in particular, economic environments of the different countries in which they operate. For example, in Turkey and some Latin American countries, annual inflation rates can be 100%, resulting in sharp declines in the value of the local currency.

Multinational companies find budgeting to be a valuable tool when operating in very uncertain environments. As circumstances and conditions change, companies revise their budgets. The purpose of budgeting in such environments is not to evaluate performance relative to budgets—a meaningless comparison when conditions are so volatile. Instead, the goal of budgeting is to help managers throughout the organization to learn and to adapt their plans to the changing conditions and to communicate and coordinate the actions that need to be taken throughout the company. Senior managers evaluate performance more subjectively, based on how well subordinate managers have managed in these uncertain environments.

Problem for Self-Study

Consider the Stylistic Furniture example described earlier. Suppose that to maintain its sales quantities, Stylistic needs to decrease selling prices to $582 per Casual table and $776 per Deluxe table, a 3% decrease in the selling prices used in the chapter illustration. All other data are unchanged.

Required

Prepare a budgeted income statement, including all necessary detailed supporting budget schedules that are different from the schedules presented in the chapter. Indicate those schedules that will remain unchanged.

Solution

Schedules 1 and 8 will change. Schedule 1 changes because a change in selling price affects revenues. Schedule 8 changes because revenues are a cost driver of marketing costs (sales commissions). The remaining schedules will not change because a change in selling price has no effect on manufacturing costs. The revised schedules and the new budgeted income statement follow.

Schedule 1: Revenue Budget
For the Year Ending December 31, 2010

	Selling Price	Units	Total Revenues
Casual tables	$582	50,000	$29,100,000
Deluxe tables	776	10,000	7,760,000
Total			$36,860,000

Schedule 8: Nonmanufacturing Costs Budget
For the Year Ending December 31, 2010

Business Function	Variable Costs	Fixed Costs (as in Schedule 8, p. 193)	Total Costs
Product Design		$1,024,000	$1,024,000
Marketing			
(Variable cost: $36,860,000 × 0.065)	$2,395,900	1,330,000	3,725,900
Distribution			
(Variable cost: $2 × 1,140,000 cu. ft.)	2,280,000	1,596,000	3,876,000
	$4,675,900	$3,950,000	$8,625,900

Stylistic Furniture
Budgeted Income Statement
For the Year Ending December 31, 2010

Revenues	Schedule 1		$36,860,000
Cost of goods sold	Schedule 7		24,440,000
Gross margin			12,420,000
Operating costs			
Product design	Schedule 8	$1,024,000	
Marketing costs	Schedule 8	3,725,900	
Distribution costs	Schedule 8	3,876,000	8,625,900
Operating income			$ 3,794,100

Decision Points

The following question-and-answer format summarizes the chapter's learning objectives. Each decision presents a key question related to a learning objective. The guidelines are the answer to that question.

Decision	Guidelines
1. What is the master budget and why is it useful?	The master budget summarizes the financial projections of all the company's budgets. It expresses management's operating and financing plans—the formalized outline of the company's financial objectives and how they will be attained. Budgets are tools that, by themselves, are neither good nor bad. Budgets are useful when administered skillfully.
2. When should a company prepare budgets? What are the advantages of preparing budgets?	Budgets should be prepared when their expected benefits exceed their expected costs. The advantages of budgets include: (a) they compel strategic analysis and planning, (b) they promote coordination and communication among subunits of the company, (c) they provide a framework for judging performance and facilitating learning, and (d) they motivate managers and other employees.

3. What is the operating budget and why is it useful?	The operating budget is the budgeted income statement and its supporting budget schedules. The starting point for the operating budget is generally the revenues budget. The following supporting schedules are derived from the revenues budget and the activities needed to support the revenues budget: production budget, direct material usage budget, direct material purchases budget, direct manufacturing labor cost budget, manufacturing overhead costs budget, ending inventories budget, cost of goods sold budget, R&D/product design cost budget, marketing cost budget, distribution cost budget, and customer-service cost budget.
4. How can managers plan for changes in the underlying budget assumptions?	Managers can use financial planning models—mathematical statements of the relationships among operating activities, financing activities, and other factors that affect the budget. These models make it possible for management to conduct what-if (sensitivity) analysis of the effects that changes in the original predicted data or changes in underlying assumptions would have on the master budget and to develop plans to respond to changed conditions.
5. How can budgets include the effects of future improvements?	Kaizen budgeting is based on the idea that it is possible to continuously reduce costs over time. Costs in kaizen budgeting are based on improvements that are yet to be implemented rather than on current practices or methods.
6. How do companies use responsibility centers and responsibility accounting?	A responsibility center is a part, segment, or subunit of an organization whose manager is accountable for a specified set of activities. Four types of responsibility centers are cost centers, revenue centers, profit centers, and investment centers. Responsibility accounting systems are useful because they measure the plans, budgets, actions, and actual results of each responsibility center.
7. Should performance reports of responsibility center managers include only costs the manager can control?	No. Controllable costs are costs primarily subject to the influence of a given responsibility center manager for a given time period. Performance reports of responsibility center managers often include costs, revenues, and investments that the managers cannot control. Responsibility accounting associates financial items with managers on the basis of which manager has the most knowledge and information about the specific items, regardless of the manager's ability to exercise full control.
8. Why are human factors crucial in budgeting?	The administration of budgets requires education, participation, persuasion, and intelligent interpretation. When wisely administered, budgets create commitment, accountability and honest communication. When badly managed, budgeting can lead to game-playing and budgetary slack—the practice of making budget targets more easily achievable.

APPENDIX: THE CASH BUDGET

The chapter illustrated the operating budget, which is one part of the master budget. The other part is the financial budget, which comprises the capital expenditures budget, the cash budget, the budgeted balance sheet, and the budgeted statement of cash flows. This appendix focuses on the cash budget and the budgeted balance sheet. Capital budgeting is discussed in Chapter 21. The budgeted statement of cash flows is beyond the scope of this book, and generally is covered in financial accounting and corporate finance courses.

Suppose Stylistic Furniture had the balance sheet for the year ended December 31, 2009, shown in Exhibit 6-5. The budgeted cash flows for 2010 are:

	Quarters			
	1	2	3	4
Collections from customers	$9,136,600	$10,122,000	$10,263,200	$8,561,200
Disbursements				
Direct materials	2,947,605	2,714,612	2,157,963	2,155,356
Payroll	3,604,512	2,671,742	2,320,946	2,562,800
Manufacturing overhead costs	2,109,018	1,530,964	1,313,568	1,463,450
Nonmanufacturing costs	1,847,750	1,979,000	1,968,250	1,705,000
Machinery purchase	—	—	758,000	—
Income taxes	725,000	400,000	400,000	400,000

The quarterly data are based on the budgeted cash effects of the operations formulated in Schedules 1 through 8 in the chapter, but the details of that formulation are not shown here to keep this illustration as brief and as focused as possible.

The company wants to maintain a $350,000 minimum cash balance at the end of each quarter. The company can borrow or repay money at an interest rate of 12% per year. Management does not want to borrow any more short-term cash than is necessary. By special arrangement, interest is computed and paid when the principal is repaid. Assume, for simplicity, that borrowing takes place at the beginning and repayment at the end of the quarter under consideration (in multiples of $1,000). Interest is computed to the nearest dollar.

Suppose the management accountant at Stylistic is given the preceding data and the other data contained in the budgets in the chapter (pp. 186–194). She is instructed as follows:

1. Prepare a cash budget for 2010 by quarter. That is, prepare a statement of cash receipts and disbursements by quarter, including details of borrowing, repayment, and interest.
2. Prepare a budgeted income statement for the year ending December 31, 2010. This statement should include interest expense and income taxes (at a rate of 40% of operating income).
3. Prepare a budgeted balance sheet on December 31, 2010.

Exhibit 6-5

Balance Sheet for Stylistic Furniture, December 31, 2009

File Edit View Insert Format Tools Data Window Help

	A	B	C	D
1		Stylistic Furniture Balance Sheet		
2		December 31, 2009		
3		Assets		
4	Current Assets			
5	Cash		$ 300,000	
6	Accounts receivable		1,711,000	
7	Direct materials inventory		1,090,000	
8	Finished goods inventory		646,000	$ 3,747,000
9	Property, plant, and equipment:			
10	Land		2,000,000	
11	Building and equipment	$22,000,000		
12	Accumulated depreciation	(6,900,000)	15,100,000	17,100,000
13	Total			$20,847,000
14		Liabilities and Stockholders' Equity		
15	Current Liabilities			
16	Accounts payable		$ 904,000	
17	Income taxes payable		325,000	$ 1,229,000
18	Stockholders' equity			
19	Common stock, no-par,			
20	25,000 shares outstanding		3,500,000	
21	Retained earnings		16,118,000	19,618,000
22	Total			$20,847,000

Preparation of Budgets

1. The **cash budget** (Exhibit 6-6) is a schedule of expected cash receipts and disbursements. It predicts the effects on the cash position at the given level of operations. Exhibit 6-6 presents the cash budget by quarters to show the impact of cash flow timing on bank loans and their repayment. In practice, monthly—and sometimes weekly or even daily—cash budgets are critical for cash planning and control. Cash budgets help avoid unnecessary idle cash and unexpected cash deficiencies. They thus keep cash balances in line with needs. Ordinarily, the cash budget has these main sections:

   a. **Cash available for needs (before any financing).** The beginning cash balance plus cash receipts equals the total cash available for needs before any financing. Cash receipts depend on collections of accounts receivable, cash sales, and miscellaneous recurring sources, such as rental or royalty receipts. Information on the expected collectibility of accounts receivable is needed for accurate predictions. Key factors include bad-debt (uncollectible accounts) experience (not an issue in the Stylistic case because Stylistic sells to only a few large wholesalers) and average time lag between sales and collections.

Exhibit 6-6 Cash Budget for Stylistic Furniture for the Year Ending December 31, 2010

File Edit View Insert Format Tools Data Window Help

	A	B	C	D	E	F
1		**Stylistic Furniture**				
2		**Cash Budget**				
3		**For Year Ending December 31, 2010**				
4				**Quarters**		**Year as a**
5		**1**	**2**	**3**	**4**	**Whole**
6	Cash balance, beginning	$ 300,000	$ 350,715	$ 350,657	$ 350,070	$ 300,000
7	Add receipts					
8	Collections from customers	9,136,600	10,122,000	10,263,200	8,561,200	38,083,000
9	Total cash available for needs (x)	9,436,600	10,472,715	10,613,857	8,911,270	38,383,000
10	Deduct disbursements					
11	Direct materials	2,947,605	2,714,612	2,157,963	2,155,356	9,975,536
12	Payroll	3,604,512	2,671,742	2,320,946	2,562,800	11,160,000
13	Manufacturing overhead costs	2,109,018	1,530,964	1,313,568	1,463,450	6,417,000
14	Nonmanufacturing costs	1,847,750	1,979,000	1,968,250	1,705,000	7,500,000
15	Machinery purchase			758,000		758,000
16	Income taxes	725,000	400,000	400,000	400,000	1,925,000
17	Total disbursements (y)	11,233,885	9,296,318	8,918,727	8,286,606	37,735,536
18	Minimum cash balance desired	350,000	350,000	350,000	350,000	350,000
19	Total cash needed	11,583,885	9,646,318	9,268,727	8,636,606	38,085,536
20	Cash excess (deficiency)*	$(2,147,285)	$ 826,397	$ 1,345,130	$ 274,664	$ 297,464
21	Financing					
22	Borrowing (at beginning)	$ 2,148,000	$ 0	$ 0	$ 0	$ 2,148,000
23	Repayment (at end)	0	(779,000)	(1,234,000)	(135,000)	(2,148,000)
24	Interest (at 12% per year)**	0	(46,740)	(111,060)	(16,200)	(174,000)
25	Total effects of financing (z)	$ 2,148,000	$ (825,740)	$ (1,345,060)	$ (151,200)	$ (174,000)
26	Cash balance, ending***	$ 350,715	$ 350,657	$ 350,070	$ 473,464	$ 473,464
27	*Excess of total cash available for needs − Total cash needed before financing.					
28	**Note that the short-term interest payments pertain only to the amount of principal being repaid at the end of a quarter. The specific computations regarding interest are $779,000 x 0.12 x 0.5 = $46,740; $1,234,000 x 0.12 x 0.75 = $111,060; $135,000 x 0.12 = $16,200. Also note that *depreciation does not require a cash outlay.*					
29	***Ending cash balance = Total cash available for needs (x) − Total disbursements (y) + Total effects of financing (z)					

b. **Cash disbursements.** Cash disbursements by Stylistic Furniture include:
   i. *Direct material purchases.* Suppliers are paid in full three weeks after the goods are delivered.
   ii. *Direct labor and other wage and salary outlays.* All payroll-related costs are paid in the month in which the labor effort occurs.
   iii. *Other costs.* These depend on timing and credit terms. (In the Stylistic case, all other costs are paid in the month in which the cost is incurred.) *Note, depreciation does not require a cash outlay.*
   iv. *Other disbursements.* These include outlays for property, plant, equipment, and other long-term investments.
   v. Income tax payments.

c. **Financing effects.** Short-term financing requirements depend on how the total cash available for needs (keyed as (x) in Exhibit 6-6) compares with the total cash disbursements (keyed as (y)), plus the minimum ending cash balance desired. The financing plans will depend on the relationship between total cash available for needs and total cash needed. If there is a deficiency of cash, loans will be obtained. If there is excess cash, any outstanding loans will be repaid.

d. **Ending cash balance.**

The cash budget in Exhibit 6-6 shows the pattern of short-term "self-liquidating" cash loans. In quarter 1, Stylistic budgets a $2,147,285 cash deficiency. Hence, it undertakes short-term borrowing of $2,148,000 that it pays off over the course of the year. Seasonal peaks of production or sales often result in heavy cash disbursements for purchases, payroll, and other operating outlays as the products are produced and sold. Cash receipts from customers typically lag behind sales. The loan is *self-liquidating* in the sense that the borrowed money is used to acquire resources that are used to produce and sell finished goods, and the proceeds from sales are used to repay the loan. This self-liquidating cycle is the movement from cash to inventories to receivables and back to cash.

2. The budgeted income statement is presented in Exhibit 6-7. It is merely the budgeted operating income statement in Exhibit 6-3 (p. 194) expanded to include interest expense and income taxes.

3. The budgeted balance sheet is presented in Exhibit 6-8. Each item is projected in light of the details of the business plan as expressed in all the previous budget schedules. For example, the ending balance of accounts receivable of $1,628,000 is

Exhibit 6-7

Budgeted Income Statement for Stylistic Furniture for the Year Ending December 31, 2010

File Edit View Insert Format Tools Data Window Help

	A	B	C	D
1	**Stylistic Furniture**			
2	**Budgeted Income Statement**			
3	**For the Year Ending December 31, 2010**			
4	Revenues	Schedule 1		$38,000,000
5	Cost of goods sold	Schedule 7		24,440,000
6	Gross margin			13,560,000
7	Operating costs			
8	Product design costs	Schedule 8	$1,024,000	
9	Marketing costs	Schedule 8	3,800,000	
10	Distribution costs	Schedule 8	3,876,000	8,700,000
11	Operating income			4,860,000
12	Interest expense	Exhibit 6-6		174,000
13	Income before income taxes			4,686,000
14	Income taxes (at 40%)			1,874,400
15	Net income			$ 2,811,600

computed by adding the budgeted revenues of $38,000,000 (from Schedule 1) to the beginning balance of accounts receivable of $1,711,000 (from Exhibit 6-5) and subtracting cash receipts of $38,083,000 (from Exhibit 6-6).

For simplicity, the cash receipts and disbursements were given explicitly in this illustration. Usually, the receipts and disbursements are calculated based on the lags between the items reported on the accrual basis of accounting in an income statement and balance sheet and their related cash receipts and disbursements. Consider accounts receivable. In the first three quarters, Stylistic estimates that 80% of all sales made in a quarter are collected in the same quarter and 20% are collected in the following quarter. Estimated collections from customers each quarter are calculated in the following table (assuming sales by quarter of $9,282,000, $10,332,000, $10,246,000, and $8,140,000 that equal 2010 budgeted sales of $38,000,000).

Schedule of Cash Collections

	Quarters			
	1	2	3	4
Accounts receivable balance on 1-1-2010 (p. 204) (Fourth quarter sales from prior year collected in first quarter of 2010)	$1,711,000			
From first-quarter 2010 sales (9,282,000 × 0.80; 9,282,000 × 0.20)	7,425,600	$ 1,856,400		
From second-quarter 2010 sales (10,332,000 × 0.80; 10,332,000 × 0.20)		8,265,600	$ 2,066,400	
From third-quarter 2010 sales (10,246,000 × 0.80; 10,246,000 × 0.20)			8,196,800	$2,049,200
From fourth-quarter 2010 sales (8,140,000 × 0.80)				6,512,000
Total collections	$9,136,600	$10,122,000	$10,263,200	$8,561,200

Note that the quarterly cash collections from customers calculated in this schedule equal the cash collections by quarter shown on page 204. Furthermore, the difference between fourth-quarter sales and the cash collected from fourth-quarter sales, $8,140,000 − $6,512,000 = $1,628,000 appears as accounts receivable in the budgeted balance sheet as of December 31, 2010 (see Exhibit 6-8).

Sensitivity Analysis and Cash Flows

Exhibit 6-4 (p. 195) shows how differing assumptions about selling prices of coffee tables and direct material prices led to differing amounts for budgeted operating income for Stylistic Furniture. A key use of sensitivity analysis is to budget cash flow. Exhibit 6-9 outlines the short-term borrowing implications of the two combinations examined in Exhibit 6-4. Scenario 1, with the lower selling prices per table ($582 for the Casual table and $776 for the Deluxe table), requires $2,352,000 of short-term borrowing in quarter 1 that cannot be fully repaid as of December 31, 2010. Scenario 2, with the 5% higher direct material costs, requires $2,250,000 borrowing by Stylistic Furniture, that also cannot be repaid by December 31, 2010. Sensitivity analysis helps managers anticipate such outcomes and take steps to minimize the effects of expected reductions in cash flows from operations.

Exhibit 6-8 Budgeted Balance Sheet for Stylistic Furniture, December 31, 2010

File Edit View Insert Format Tools Data Window Help

	A	B	C	D
1	**Stylistic Furniture**			
2	**Budgeted Balance Sheet**			
3	**December 31, 2010**			
4	**Assets**			
5	Current Assets			
6	Cash (from Exhibit 6-6)		$ 473,464	
7	Accounts receivable (1)		1,628,000	
8	Direct materials inventory (2)		760,000	
9	Finished goods inventory (2)		4,486,000	$ 7,347,464
10	Property, plant, and equipment			
11	Land (3)		2,000,000	
12	Building and equipment (4)	$22,758,000		
13	Accumulated depreciation (5)	(8,523,000)	14,235,000	16,235,000
14	Total			$23,582,464
15	**Liabilities and Stockholders' Equity**			
16	Current Liabilities			
17	Accounts payable (6)		$ 878,464	
18	Income taxes payable (7)		274,400	$ 1,152,864
19	Stockholders' equity			
20	Common stock, no-par, 25,000 shares outstanding (8)		3,500,000	
21	Retained earnings (9)		18,929,600	22,429,600
22	Total			$23,582,464
23				
24	Notes:			
25	Beginning balances are used as the starting point for most of the following computations:			
26	(1) $1,711,000 + $38,000,000 revenues − $38,083,000 receipts (Exhibit 6-6) = $1,628,000			
27	(2) From Schedule 6B, p. 193			
28	(3) From beginning balance sheet, p. 204			
29	(4) $22,000,000 + $758,000 purchases = $22,758,0000			
30	(5) $6,900,000 + $1,020,000 + $603,000 depreciation from Schedule 5, p. 192			
31	(6) $904,000 + $9,950,000 (Schedule 3B) − $9,975,536 (Exhibit 6-6) = $878,464			
32	There are no other current liabilities. Cash flows for payroll, manufacturing overhead and nonmanufacturing costs totaling $25,077,000 on the cash budget (Exhibit 6-6) consists of direct manufacturing labor costs of $6,000,000 from Schedule 4 + cash manufacturing overhead costs of $10,377,000 ($12,000,000 − depreciation of $1,623,000) from Schedule 5 + cash nonmanufacturing costs of $8,700,000 from Schedule 8.			
33	(7) $325,000 + $1,874,400 current year − $1,925,0000 payment = $274,4000.			
34	(8) From beginning balance sheet.			
35	(9) $16,118,000 + $2,811,600 net income per Exhibit 6-7 = $18,929,600			

Exhibit 6-9 Sensitivity Analysis: Effects of Key Budget Assumptions in Exhibit 6-4 on 2010 Short-Term Borrowing for Stylistic Furniture

File Edit View Insert Format Tools Data Window Help

	A	B	C	D	E	F	G	H	I	J
1				Direct Material			Short-Term Borrowing and Repayment by Quarter			
2		Selling Price		Purchase Costs		Budgeted	Quarters			
3	Scenario	Casual	Deluxe	Red Oak	Granite	Operating Income	1	2	3	4
4	1	$582	$776	$7.00	$10.00	$3,794,100	$2,352,000	($511,000)	($ 969,000)	($ 30,000)
5	2	$600	$800	7.35	10.50	4,483,800	2,250,000	(651,000)	(1,134,000)	(149,000)

TERMS TO LEARN

The chapter and the Glossary at the end of the book contain definitions of:

activity-based budgeting (ABB) (**p. 191**)
budgetary slack (**p. 199**)
cash budget (**p. 205**)
continuous budget (**p. 185**)
controllability (**p. 198**)
controllable cost (**p. 198**)
cost center (**p. 197**)
financial budget (**p. 186**)
financial planning models (**p. 194**)
investment center (**p. 197**)
kaizen budgeting (**p. 195**)
master budget (**p. 183**)
operating budget (**p. 186**)
organization structure (**p. 197**)
pro forma statements (**p. 183**)
profit center (**p. 197**)
responsibility accounting (**p. 197**)
responsibility center (**p. 197**)
revenue center (**p. 197**)
rolling budget (**p. 185**)

ASSIGNMENT MATERIAL

Questions

6-1 What are the four elements of the budgeting cycle?

6-2 Define master budget.

6-3 "Strategy, plans, and budgets are unrelated to one another." Do you agree? Explain.

6-4 "Budgeted performance is a better criterion than past performance for judging managers." Do you agree? Explain.

6-5 "Production managers and marketing managers are like oil and water. They just don't mix." How can a budget assist in reducing battles between these two areas?

6-6 "Budgets meet the cost-benefit test. They force managers to act differently." Do you agree? Explain.

6-7 Define rolling budget. Give an example.

6-8 Outline the steps in preparing an operating budget.

6-9 "The sales forecast is the cornerstone for budgeting." Why?

6-10 How can sensitivity analysis be used to increase the benefits of budgeting?

6-11 Define kaizen budgeting.

6-12 Describe how nonoutput-based cost drivers can be incorporated into budgeting.

6-13 Explain how the choice of the type of responsibility center (cost, revenue, profit, or investment) affects behavior.

6-14 What are some additional considerations that arise when budgeting in multinational companies?

6-15 "Cash budgets must be prepared before the operating income budget." Do you agree? Explain.

Exercises

6-16 Sales budget, service setting. In 2009, McGrath & Sons, a small environmental-testing firm, performed 11,000 radon tests for $250 each and 15,200 lead tests for $200 each. Because newer homes are being built with lead-free pipes, lead-testing volume is expected to decrease by 10% next year. However, awareness of radon-related health hazards is expected to result in a 5% increase in radon-test volume each year in the near future. Jim McGrath feels that if he lowers his price for lead testing to $190 per test, he will have to face only a 5% decline in lead-test sales in 2010.

Required

1. Prepare a 2010 sales budget for McGrath & Sons assuming that McGrath holds prices at 2009 levels.
2. Prepare a 2010 sales budget for McGrath & Sons assuming that McGrath lowers the price of a lead test to $190. Should McGrath lower the price of a lead test in 2010 if its goal is to maximize sales revenue?

6-17 Sales and production budget. The Mendez Company expects sales in 2010 of 200,000 units of serving trays. Mendez's beginning inventory for 2010 is 15,000 trays; target ending inventory, 25,000 trays. Compute the number of trays budgeted for production in 2010.

6-18 Direct material budget. Inglenook Co. produces wine. The company expects to produce 2,500,000 two-liter bottles of Chablis in 2010. Inglenook purchases empty glass bottles from an outside vendor. Its target ending inventory of such bottles is 80,000; its beginning inventory is 50,000. For simplicity, ignore breakage. Compute the number of bottles to be purchased in 2010.

6-19 Budgeting material purchases. The Mahoney Company has prepared a sales budget of 45,000 finished units for a three-month period. The company has an inventory of 16,000 units of finished goods on hand at December 31 and has a target finished goods inventory of 18,000 units at the end of the succeeding quarter.

It takes three gallons of direct materials to make one unit of finished product. The company has an inventory of 60,000 gallons of direct materials at December 31 and has a target ending inventory of 50,000 gallons at the end of the succeeding quarter. How many gallons of direct materials should be purchased during the three months ending March 31?

6-20 Revenues and production budget. Purity, Inc., bottles and distributes mineral water from the company's natural springs in northern Oregon. Purity markets two products: twelve-ounce disposable plastic bottles and four-gallon reusable plastic containers.

Required

1. For 2010, Purity marketing managers project monthly sales of 400,000 twelve-ounce bottles and 100,000 four-gallon containers. Average selling prices are estimated at $0.25 per twelve-ounce bottle and $1.50 per four-gallon container. Prepare a revenues budget for Purity, Inc., for the year ending December 31, 2010.
2. Purity begins 2010 with 900,000 twelve-ounce bottles in inventory. The vice president of operations requests that twelve-ounce bottles ending inventory on December 31, 2010, be no less than 600,000 bottles. Based on sales projections as budgeted above, what is the minimum number of twelve-ounce bottles Purity must produce during 2010?
3. The VP of operations requests that ending inventory of four-gallon containers on December 31, 2010, be 200,000 units. If the production budget calls for Purity to produce 1,300,000 four-gallon containers during 2010, what is the beginning inventory of four-gallon containers on January 1, 2010?

6-21 Budgeting; direct material usage, manufacturing cost and gross margin. Xerxes Manufacturing Company manufactures blue rugs, using wool and dye as direct materials. All other materials are indirect. At the beginning of the year Xerxes has an inventory of 349,000 skeins of wool at a cost of $715,450 and 5,000 gallons of dye at a cost of $24,850. Target ending inventory of wool and dye is zero. Xerxes uses the FIFO inventory cost flow method.

One blue rug is budgeted to use 30 skeins of wool at a cost of $2 per skein and 1/2 gallon of dye at a cost of $5 per gallon.

Xerxes blue rugs are very popular and demand is high, but because of capacity constraints the firm will produce only 100,000 blue rugs per year. The budgeted selling price is $2,000 each. There are no rugs in beginning inventory. Target ending inventory of rugs is also zero.

Xerxes makes rugs by hand, but uses a machine to dye the wool. Thus, overhead costs are accumulated in two cost pools—one for weaving and the other for dyeing. Weaving overhead is allocated to product based on direct manufacturing labor-hours (DMLH). Dyeing overhead is allocated to product based on machine-hours (MH).

There is no direct manufacturing labor cost for dyeing. Xerxes budgets 56 direct manufacturing labor-hours to weave a rug at a budgeted rate of $15 per hour. It budgets 0.15 machine-hours to dye each skein in the dyeing process.

The following table presents the budgeted overhead costs for the dyeing and weaving cost pools:

	Dyeing (based on 450,000 MH)	Weaving (based on 5,600,000 DMLH)
Variable costs		
Indirect materials	$ 0	$11,200,000
Maintenance	4,950,000	2,240,000
Utilities	5,400,000	1,680,000
Fixed costs		
Indirect labor	239,000	1,300,000
Depreciation	1,900,000	52,000
Other	320,000	2,380,000
Total budgeted costs	$12,809,000	$18,852,000

Required

1. Prepare a direct material usage budget in both units and dollars.
2. Calculate the budgeted overhead allocation rates for weaving and dyeing.
3. Calculate the budgeted unit cost of a blue rug for the year.
4. Prepare a revenue budget for blue rugs for the year, assuming Xerxes sells (a) 100,000 or (b) 95,000 blue rugs (that is at two different sales levels).
5. Calculate the budgeted cost of goods sold for blue rugs under each sales assumption.
6. Find the budgeted gross margin for blue rugs under each sales assumption.

6-22 Revenues, production, and purchases budgets. The Suzuki Co. in Japan has a division that manufactures two-wheel motorcycles. Its budgeted sales for Model G in 2010 is 900,000 units. Suzuki's target ending inventory is 80,000 units, and its beginning inventory is 100,000 units. The company's budgeted selling price to its distributors and dealers is 400,000 yen (¥) per motorcycle.

Suzuki buys all its wheels from an outside supplier. No defective wheels are accepted. (Suzuki's needs for extra wheels for replacement parts are ordered by a separate division of the company.) The company's target ending inventory is 60,000 wheels, and its beginning inventory is 50,000 wheels. The budgeted purchase price is 16,000 yen (¥) per wheel.

Required

1. Compute the budgeted revenues in yen.
2. Compute the number of motorcycles to be produced.
3. Compute the budgeted purchases of wheels in units and in yen.

6-23 Budgets for production and direct manufacturing labor. (CMA, adapted) Roletter Company makes and sells artistic frames for pictures of weddings, graduations, and other special events. Bob Anderson, the controller, is responsible for preparing Roletter's master budget and has accumulated the following information for 2010:

	2010				
	January	February	March	April	May
Estimated sales in units	10,000	12,000	8,000	9,000	9,000
Selling price	$54.00	$51.50	$51.50	$51.50	$51.50
Direct manufacturing labor-hours per unit	2.0	2.0	1.5	1.5	1.5
Wage per direct manufacturing labor-hour	$10.00	$10.00	$10.00	$11.00	$11.00

In addition to wages, direct manufacturing labor-related costs include pension contributions of $0.50 per hour, worker's compensation insurance of $0.15 per hour, employee medical insurance of $0.40 per hour, and social security taxes. Assume that as of January 1, 2010, the social security tax rates are 7.5% for employers and 7.5% for employees. The cost of employee benefits paid by Roletter on its employees is treated as a direct manufacturing labor cost.

Roletter has a labor contract that calls for a wage increase to $11 per hour on April 1, 2010. New labor-saving machinery has been installed and will be fully operational by March 1, 2010. Roletter expects to have 16,000 frames on hand at December 31, 2009, and it has a policy of carrying an end-of-month inventory of 100% of the following month's sales plus 50% of the second following month's sales.

Required

Prepare a production budget and a direct manufacturing labor budget for Roletter Company by month and for the first quarter of 2010. Both budgets may be combined in one schedule. The direct manufacturing labor budget should include labor-hours, and show the details for each labor cost category.

6-24 Activity-based budgeting. The Chelsea store of Family Supermarket (FS), a chain of small neighborhood grocery stores, is preparing its activity-based budget for January 2008. FS has three product categories: soft drinks, fresh produce, and packaged food. The following table shows the four activities that consume indirect resources at the Chelsea store, the cost drivers and their rates, and the cost-driver amount budgeted to be consumed by each activity in January 2008.

	A	B	C	D	E	F
1			January 2008	January 2008 Budgeted		
2			Budgeted	Amount of Cost Driver Used		
3	Activity	Cost Driver	Cost-Driver Rate	Soft Drinks	Fresh Produce	Packaged Food
4	Ordering	Number of purchase orders	$90	14	24	14
5	Delivery	Number of deliveries	$82	12	62	19
6	Shelf-stocking	Hours of stocking time	$21	16	172	94
7	Customer support	Number of items sold	$ 0.18	4,600	34,200	10,750

If you want to use Excel to solve this exercise, go to the Excel Lab at **www.prenhall.com/horngren/cost13e** and download the template for Exercise 6-24.

Required

1. What is the total budgeted indirect cost at the Chelsea store in January 2008? What is the total budgeted cost of each activity at the Chelsea store for January 2008? What is the budgeted indirect cost of each product category for January 2008?
2. Which product category has the largest fraction of total budgeted indirect costs?
3. Given your answer in requirement 2, what advantage does FS gain by using an activity-based approach to budgeting over, say, allocating indirect costs to products based on cost of goods sold?

6-25 Kaizen approach to activity-based budgeting (continuation of 6-24). Family Supermarkets (FS) has a kaizen (continuous improvement) approach to budgeting monthly activity costs for each month of 2008.

Each successive month, the budgeted cost-driver rate decreases by 0.2% relative to the preceding month (so, for example, February's budgeted cost-driver rate is 0.998 times January's budgeted cost-driver rate, and March's budgeted cost-driver rate is 0.998 times the budgeted February 2008 rate). FS assumes that the budgeted amount of cost-driver usage remains the same each month.

If you want to use Excel to solve this exercise, go to the Excel Lab at **www.prenhall.com/horngren/cost13e** and download the template for Exercise 6-24.

Required

1. What is the total budgeted cost for each activity and the total budgeted indirect cost for March 2008?
2. What are the benefits of using a kaizen approach to budgeting? What are the limitations of this approach, and how might FS management overcome them?

6-26 Responsibility and controllability. Consider each of the following independent situations:

1. A very successful salesman at Amcorp Computers regularly ignores the published sales catalog and offers lowered prices to his customers in order to close sales. The VP of sales notices that revenues are substantially lower than budgeted.
2. Every "special deal" offered to a customer by any salesperson at Amcorp Computers has to be cleared by the VP of sales. Revenues for the second quarter have been lower than budgeted.
3. The shipping department of Amcorp has limited capacity, and sales orders are being cancelled by customers because of delays in delivery. Revenues for the past month have been lower than budgeted.
4. At Planetel Corp., a manufacturer of telecommunications equipment, the production supervisor notices that a significantly larger number of direct manufacturing labor-hours were used than had been budgeted. Investigation revealed that it was due to a decline in educational standards required by the Human Resources department when it interviewed applicants for hourly production jobs six months earlier.
5. At Planetel Corp., a relatively new production supervisor finds that more direct manufacturing labor-hours were used than had been budgeted. Interviews revealed that workers were unhappy with the supervisor's management style and were intentionally working slowly and inefficiently.
6. At Planetel Corp., the production supervisor traces the excessive consumption of direct materials (relative to the budget) to the fact that waste was high on machines that had not been properly maintained.

Required

For each situation described, determine where (that is, with whom) (a) responsibility and (b) controllability lie. Suggest what might be done to solve the problem or to improve the situation.

6-27 Cash flow analysis, chapter appendix. (CMA, adapted) TabComp, Inc., is a retail distributor for MZB-33 computer hardware and related software and support services. TabComp prepares annual sales forecasts of which the first six months for 2009 are presented here.

Cash sales account for 25% of TabComp's total sales, 30% of the total sales are paid by bank credit card, and the remaining 45% are on open account (TabComp's own charge accounts). The cash sales and cash from bank credit-card sales are received in the month of the sale. Bank credit-card sales are subject to a 4% discount deducted at the time of the daily deposit. The cash receipts for sales on open account are 70% in the month following the sale and 28% in the second month after the sale. The remaining accounts receivable are estimated to be uncollectible.

TabComp's month-end inventory requirements for computer hardware units are 30% of the next month's sales. A one-month lead time is required for delivery from the manufacturer. Thus, orders for computer hardware units are placed on the 25th of each month to assure that they will be in the store by the first day of the month needed. The computer hardware units are purchased under terms of n/45 (payment in full within 45 days of invoice), measured from the time the units are delivered to TabComp. TabComp's purchase price for the computer units is 60% of the selling price.

TabComp Inc.
Sales Forecast for First Six Months of 2009

	Hardware Sales		Software Sales	
	Units	Dollars	and Support	Total Revenues
January	130	$ 390,000	$160,000	$ 550,000
February	120	360,000	140,000	500,000
March	110	330,000	150,000	480,000
April	90	270,000	130,000	400,000
May	100	300,000	125,000	425,000
June	125	375,000	225,000	600,000
Total	675	$2,025,000	$930,000	$2,955,000

Required

1. Calculate the cash that TabComp, Inc., can expect to collect during April 2009. Be sure to show all of your calculations.

2. TabComp, Inc., is determining how many MZB-33 computer hardware units to order on January 25, 2009.
   a. Determine the projected number of computer hardware units that will be ordered.
   b. Calculate the dollar amount of the order that TabComp will place for these computer hardware units.
3. As part of the annual budget process, TabComp prepares a cash budget by month for the entire year. Explain why a company such as TabComp prepares a cash budget by month for the entire year.

Problems

6-28 Budget schedules for a manufacturer. Sierra Furniture is an elite desk manufacturer. It makes two products:

- Executive desks—3' × 5' oak desks
- Chairman desks—6' × 4' red oak desks

The budgeted direct-cost inputs for each product in 2009 are:

	Executive Line	Chairman Line
Oak top	16 square feet	0
Red oak top	0	25 square feet
Oak legs	4	0
Red oak legs	0	4
Direct manufacturing labor	3 hours	5 hours

Unit data pertaining to the direct materials for March 2009 are:

Actual Beginning Direct Materials Inventory (3/1/2009)

	Executive Line	Chairman Line
Oak top (square feet)	320	0
Red oak top (square feet)	0	150
Oak legs	100	0
Red oak legs	0	40

Target Ending Direct Materials Inventory (3/31/2009)

	Executive Line	Chairman Line
Oak top (square feet)	192	0
Red oak top (square feet)	0	200
Oak legs	80	0
Red oak legs	0	44

Unit cost data for direct-cost inputs pertaining to February 2009 and March 2009 are:

	February 2009 (actual)	March 2009 (budgeted)
Oak top (per square foot)	$18	$20
Red oak top (per square foot)	23	25
Oak legs (per leg)	11	12
Red oak legs (per leg)	17	18
Manufacturing labor cost per hour	30	30

Manufacturing overhead (both variable and fixed) is allocated to each desk on the basis of budgeted direct manufacturing labor-hours per desk. The budgeted variable manufacturing overhead rate for March 2009 is $35 per direct manufacturing labor-hour. The budgeted fixed manufacturing overhead for March 2009 is $42,500. Both variable and fixed manufacturing overhead costs are allocated to each unit of finished goods.

Data relating to finished goods inventory for March 2009 are:

	Executive Line	Chairman Line
Beginning inventory in units	20	5
Beginning inventory in dollars (cost)	$10,480	$4,850
Target ending inventory in units	30	15

Budgeted sales for March 2009 are 740 units of the executive line and 390 units of the chairman line. The budgeted selling prices per unit in March 2009 are $1,020 for the executive-line desk and $1,600 for the chairman-line desk. Assume the following in your answer:

- Work-in-process inventories are negligible and ignored.
- Direct materials inventory and finished goods inventory are costed using the FIFO method.
- Unit costs of direct materials purchased and finished goods are constant in March 2009.

Required

1. Prepare the following budgets for March 2009:
   a. Revenues budget
   b. Production budget in units
   c. Direct material usage budget and direct material purchases budget
   d. Direct manufacturing labor budget
   e. Manufacturing overhead budget
   f. Ending inventories budget (direct materials and finished goods)
   g. Cost of goods sold budget
2. Suppose Sierra Furniture decides to incorporate continuous improvement into its budgeting process. Describe two areas where Sierra could incorporate continuous improvement into the budget schedules in requirement 1.

6-29 Activity based budget; kaizen improvements. Korna Company manufactures a product, gizmo, that uses the following direct inputs:

	Price	Quantity	Cost per unit of output
Direct materials	$4 per ounce	10 ounces per unit	$40 per unit
Direct manufacturing labor-hours (DMLH)	$15 per DMLH	2 DMLH per unit	$30 per unit

Korna has no direct materials inventory. All manufacturing overhead costs are variable costs. The manufacturing overhead cost is comprised of two activities: Setup and Operations. The cost driver for setup is setup hours, and the cost driver for operations is direct manufacturing labor-hours. Korna allocates setup cost at a rate of $80 per setup-hour, and each setup takes two hours. Korna Company makes gizmos in batches of 100 units. Operations costs are allocated at a rate of $1.60 per direct manufacturing labor-hour.

Required

1. Korna plans to make and sell 20,000 gizmos in the first quarter of next year. The selling price for the product is $120. Prepare the revenues budget for the first quarter.
2. Prepare the direct material usage budget for the first quarter of next year.
3. Prepare the direct manufacturing labor usage budget for the first quarter of next year.
4. Prepare the manufacturing overhead cost budget for each activity for the first quarter of next year.
5. Compute the budgeted unit cost of a gizmo for the first quarter of next year.
6. Prepare the cost of goods sold budget for the first quarter of next year. Assume Korna budgets 1,000 units of beginning finished goods inventory at a cost of $72 per unit. Korna uses the LIFO cost flow assumption for finished goods inventory. Korna expects to sell all 20,000 gizmos made in the first quarter.
7. Calculate the budgeted gross margin for the first quarter of next year.
8. Korna Company managers want to implement kaizen costing. They budget a 1% decrease in materials quantity and direct manufacturing labor-hours and a 3% decrease in setup time per unit for each subsequent quarter. Calculate the budgeted unit cost and gross margin for quarters two and three. Assume no change in budgeted output.
9. Refer to requirement 8 above. How could the reduction in materials and time be accomplished? Are there any problems with this plan?

6-30 Revenue and production budgets. (CPA, adapted) The Scarborough Corporation manufactures and sells two products: Thingone and Thingtwo. In July 2009, Scarborough's budget department gathered the following data to prepare budgets for 2010:

2010 Projected Sales

Product	Units	Price
Thingone	60,000	$165
Thingtwo	40,000	$250

2010 Inventories in Units

	Expected	Target
Product	January 1, 2010	December 31, 2010
Thingone	20,000	25,000
Thingtwo	8,000	9,000

The following direct materials are used in the two products:

	Amount Used per Unit		
Direct Material	**Unit**	**Thingone**	**Thingtwo**
A	pound	4	5
B	pound	2	3
C	each	0	1

Projected data for 2010 with respect to direct materials are as follows:

Direct Material	Anticipated Purchase Price	Expected Inventories January 1, 2010	Target Inventories December 31, 2010
A	$12	32,000 lb.	36,000 lb.
B	5	29,000 lb.	32,000 lb.
C	3	6,000 units	7,000 units

Projected direct manufacturing labor requirements and rates for 2010 are as follows:

Product	Hours per Unit	Rate per Hour
Thingone	2	$12
Thingtwo	3	16

Manufacturing overhead is allocated at the rate of $20 per direct manufacturing labor-hour.

Based on the preceding projections and budget requirements for Thingone and Thingtwo, prepare the following budgets for 2010:

Required

1. Revenues budget (in dollars)
2. Production budget (in units)
3. Direct material purchases budget (in quantities)
4. Direct material purchases budget (in dollars)
5. Direct manufacturing labor budget (in dollars)
6. Budgeted finished goods inventory at December 31, 2010 (in dollars)

6-31 Budgeted income statement. (CMA, adapted) Easecom Company is a manufacturer of video-conferencing products. Regular units are manufactured to meet marketing projections, and specialized units are made after an order is received. Maintaining the video-conferencing equipment is an important area of customer satisfaction. With the recent downturn in the computer industry, the video-conferencing equipment segment has suffered, leading to a decline in Easecom's financial performance. The following income statement shows results for 2010.

Easecom Company
Income Statement
For the Year Ended December 31, 2010 (in thousands)

Revenues:		
Equipment	$6,000	
Maintenance contracts	1,800	
Total revenues		$7,800
Cost of goods sold		4,600
Gross margin		3,200
Operating costs		
Marketing	600	
Distribution	150	
Customer maintenance	1,000	
Administration	900	
Total operating costs		2,650
Operating income		$ 550

Easecom's management team is in the process of preparing the 2011 budget and is studying the following information:

1. Selling prices of equipment are expected to increase by 10% as the economic recovery begins. The selling price of each maintenance contract is expected to remain unchanged from 2010.
2. Equipment sales in units are expected to increase by 6%, with a corresponding 6% growth in units of maintenance contracts.
3. Cost of each unit sold is expected to increase by 3% to pay for the necessary technology and quality improvements.
4. Marketing costs are expected to increase by $250,000, but administration costs are expected to remain at 2010 levels.
5. Distribution costs vary in proportion to the number of units of equipment sold.
6. Two maintenance technicians are to be hired at a total cost of $130,000, which covers wages and related travel costs. The objective is to improve customer service and shorten response time.
7. There is no beginning or ending inventory of equipment.

Required Prepare a budgeted income statement for the year ending December 31, 2011.

6-32 Responsibility of purchasing agent. (Adapted from a description by R. Villers) Mark Richards is the purchasing agent for the Hart Manufacturing Company. Kent Sampson is head of the Production Planning and Control Department. Every six months, Sampson gives Richards a general purchasing program. Richards gets specifications from the Engineering Department. He then selects suppliers and negotiates prices. When he took this job, Richards was informed very clearly that he bore responsibility for meeting the general purchasing program once he accepted it from Sampson.

During week 24, Richards is advised that Part No. 1234—a critical part—would be needed for assembly on Tuesday morning of week 32. He found that the regular supplier could not deliver. He called everywhere and finally found a supplier in the Midwest who accepted the commitment.

He followed up by e-mail. Yes, the supplier assured him, the part would be ready. The matter was so important that on Thursday of week 31, Richards checked by phone. Yes, the shipment had left in time. Richards was reassured and did not check further. But on Tuesday of week 32, the part had not arrived. Inquiry revealed that the shipment had been misdirected by the railroad and was still in Chicago.

Required What department should bear the costs of time lost in the plant due to the delayed shipment? Why? As purchasing agent, do you think it is fair that such costs be charged to your department?

6-33 Comprehensive problem with ABC costing. Pet Transport Company makes two pet carriers, the Cat-allac and the Dog-eriffic. They are both made of plastic with metal doors, but the Cat-allac is smaller. Information for the two products for the month of April is given in the following tables:

Input prices	
Direct materials	
Plastic	$4 per pound
Metal	$3 per pound
Direct manufacturing labor	$10 per direct manufacturing labor hour

Input quantities per unit of output	**Cat-allac**	**Dog-eriffic**
Direct materials		
Plastic	4 pounds	6 pounds
Metal	0.5 pounds	1 pound
Direct manufacturing labor-hours (DMLH)	3 hours	5 hours
Machine-hours (MH)	10 MH	18 MH

Inventory information, direct materials	**Plastic**	**Metal**
Beginning inventory	250 pounds	60 pounds
Target ending inventory	380 pounds	55 pounds
Cost of beginning inventory	$950	$180

Pet Transport accounts for direct materials using a FIFO cost flow assumption.

Sales and inventory information, finished goods	**Cat-allac**	**Dog-eriffic**
Expected sales in units	500	300
Selling price	$160	$250
Target ending inventory in units	35	15
Beginning inventory in units	15	30
Beginning inventory in dollars	$1,500	$5,580

Pet Transport uses a FIFO cost flow assumption for finished good inventory.

Pet Transport uses an activity-based costing system and classifies overhead into three activity pools: Setup, Processing and Inspection. Activity rates for these activities are $100 per setup hour, $5 per machine hour, and $16 per inspection hour, respectively. Other information follows:

Cost driver information

	Cat-allac	Dog-eriffic
Number of units per batch	20	15
Setup time per batch	1.5 hours	1.75 hours
Inspection time per batch	0.5 hour	0.6 hour

Nonmanufacturing fixed costs for March equal $36,000, of which half are salaries. Salaries are expected to increase 5% in April. The only variable nonmanufacturing cost is sales commission, equal to 1% of sales revenue.

Required

Prepare the following for April:

1. Revenues budget
2. Production budget in units
3. Direct material usage budget and direct material purchases budget
4. Direct manufacturing labor cost budget
5. Manufacturing overhead cost budgets for each of the three activities
6. Budgeted unit cost of ending finished goods inventory and ending inventories budget
7. Cost of goods sold budget
8. Nonmanufacturing costs budget
9. Budgeted income statement (ignore income taxes)

6-34 (Continuation of 6-33) Cash budget (appendix.) Refer to the information in problem 6-33.

Assume the following: Pet Transport (PT) does not make any sales on credit. PT sells only to the public, and accepts cash and credit cards. 90% of its sales are to customers using credit cards, for which PT gets the cash right away less a 3% transaction fee.

Purchases of materials are on account. PT pays for half the purchases in the period of the purchase, and the other half in the following period. At the end of March, PT owes suppliers $8,500.

PT plans to replace a machine in April at a net cash cost of $13,700.

Labor, other manufacturing costs and nonmanufacturing costs are paid in cash in the month incurred except of course, depreciation, which is not a cash flow. $20,000 of the manufacturing cost and $10,000 of the nonmanufacturing cost for April is depreciation.

PT currently has a $2,000 loan at an annual interest rate of 12%. The interest is paid at the end of each month. If PT has more than $10,000 cash at the end of April it will pay back the loan. PT owes $5,000 in income taxes that need to be remitted in April. PT has cash of $5,360 on hand at the end of March.

Required

Prepare a cash budget for April for Pet Transport.

6-35 Comprehensive operating budget, budgeted balance sheet. Slopes, Inc., manufactures and sells snowboards. Slopes manufactures a single model, the Pipex. In the summer of 2009, Slopes's management accountant gathered the following data to prepare budgets for 2010:

Materials and labor requirements

Direct materials	
Wood	5 board feet (b.f.) per snowboard
Fiberglass	6 yards per snowboard
Direct manufacturing labor	5 hours per snowboard

Slopes's CEO expects to sell 1,000 snowboards during 2010 at an estimated retail price of $450 per board. Further, the CEO expects 2010 beginning inventory of 100 snowboards and would like to end 2010 with 200 snowboards in stock.

Direct materials Inventories

	Beginning Inventory 1/1/2010	Ending Inventory 12/31/2010
Wood	2,000 b.f.	1,500 b.f.
Fiberglass	1,000 yards	2,000 yards

Variable manufacturing overhead is $7 per direct manufacturing labor-hour. There are also $66,000 in fixed manufacturing overhead costs budgeted for 2010. Slopes combines both variable and fixed manufacturing overhead into a single rate based on direct manufacturing labor-hours. Variable marketing costs are allocated at the rate of $250 per sales visit. The marketing plan calls for 30 sales visits during 2010. Finally, there are $30,000 in fixed nonmanufacturing costs budgeted for 2010.

Other data includes:

	2009 Unit Price	2010 Unit Price
Wood	$28.00 per b.f.	$30.00 per b.f.
Fiberglass	$ 4.80 per yard	$ 5.00 per yard
Direct manufacturing labor	$24.00 per hour	$25.00 per hour

The inventoriable unit cost for ending finished goods inventory on December 31, 2009, is $374.80. Assume Slopes uses a FIFO inventory method for both direct materials and finished goods. Ignore work in process in your calculations.

Budgeted balances at December 31, 2010, in the selected accounts are:

Cash	$ 10,000
Property, plant, and equipment (net)	850,000
Current liabilities	17,000
Long-term liabilities	178,000
Stockholders' equity	800,000

Required

1. Prepare the 2010 revenues budget (in dollars).
2. Prepare the 2010 production budget (in units).
3. Prepare the direct material usage and purchases budgets for 2010.
4. Prepare a direct manufacturing labor budget for 2010.
5. Prepare a manufacturing overhead budget for 2010.
6. What is the budgeted manufacturing overhead rate for 2010?
7. What is the budgeted manufacturing overhead cost per output unit in 2010?
8. Calculate the cost of a snowboard manufactured in 2010.
9. Prepare an ending inventory budget for both direct materials and finished goods for 2010.
10. Prepare a cost of goods sold budget for 2010.
11. Prepare the budgeted income statement for Slopes, Inc., for the year ending December 31, 2010.
12. Prepare the budgeted balance sheet for Slopes, Inc., as of December 31, 2010.

6-36 Cash budgeting, chapter appendix. Retail outlets purchase snowboards from Slopes, Inc., throughout the year. However, in anticipation of late summer and early fall purchases, outlets ramp up inventories from May through August. Outlets are billed when boards are ordered. Invoices are payable within 60 days. From past experience, Slopes's accountant projects 20% of invoices are paid in the month invoiced, 50% are paid in the following month, and 30% of invoices are paid two months after the month of invoice. The average selling price per snowboard is $450.

To meet demand, Slopes increases production from April through July, because the snowboards are produced a month prior to their projected sale. Direct materials are purchased in the month of production and are paid for during the following month (terms are payment in full within 30 days of the invoice date). During this period there is no production for inventory, and no materials are purchased for inventory.

Direct manufacturing labor and manufacturing overhead are paid monthly. Variable manufacturing overhead is incurred at the rate of $7 per direct manufacturing labor-hour. Variable marketing costs are driven by the number of sales visits. However, there are no sales visits during the months studied. Slopes, Inc., also incurs fixed manufacturing overhead costs of $5,500 per month and fixed nonmanufacturing overhead costs of $2,500 per month.

Projected Sales

May 80 units	August 100 units
June 120 units	September 60 units
July 200 units	October 40 units

Direct Materials and Direct Manufacturing Labor Utilization and Cost

	Units per Board	Price per Unit	Unit
Wood	5	$30	Board feet
Fiberglass	6	5	Yard
Direct manufacturing labor	5	25	Hour

The beginning cash balance for July 1, 2010, is $10,000. On October 1, 2009, Slopes had a cash crunch and borrowed $30,000 on a 6% one-year note with interest payable monthly. The note is due October 1, 2010. Using the information provided, you will need to determine whether Slopes will be in a position to pay off this short-term debt on October 1, 2010.

Required

1. Prepare a cash budget for the months of July through September 2010. Show supporting schedules for the calculation of receivables and payables.
2. Will Slopes be in a position to pay off the $30,000 one-year note that is due on October 1, 2010? If not, what actions would you recommend to Slopes's management?
3. Suppose Slopes is interested in maintaining a minimum cash balance of $10,000. Will the company be able to maintain such a balance during all three months analyzed? If not, suggest a suitable cash management strategy.

6-37 Cash budgeting, chapter appendix. On December 1, 2009, the Itami Wholesale Co. is attempting to project cash receipts and disbursements through January 31, 2010. On this latter date, a note will be payable in the amount of $100,000. This amount was borrowed in September to carry the company through the seasonal peak in November and December.

Selected general ledger balances on December 1 are:

Cash	$ 10,000	
Accounts receivable	280,000	
Allowance for bad debts		$15,800
Inventory	87,500	
Accounts payable		92,000

Sales terms call for a 2% discount if payment is made within the first 10 days of the month after sale, with the balance due by the end of the month after sale. Experience has shown that 70% of the billings will be collected within the discount period, 20% by the end of the month after purchase, and 8% in the following month. The remaining 2% will be uncollectible. There are no cash sales.

The average selling price of the company's products is $100 per unit. Actual and projected sales are:

October actual	$ 180,000
November actual	250,000
December estimated	300,000
January estimated	150,000
February estimated	120,000
Total estimated for year ending June 30, 2010	$1,500,000

All purchases are payable within 15 days. Thus, approximately 50% of the purchases in a month are due and payable in the next month. The average unit purchase cost is $70. Target ending inventories are 500 units plus 25% of the next month's unit sales.

Total budgeted marketing, distribution, and customer-service costs for the year are $400,000. Of this amount, $150,000 are considered fixed (and include depreciation of $30,000). The remainder vary with sales. Both fixed and variable marketing, distribution, and customer-service costs are paid as incurred.

Required

Prepare a cash budget for December 2009 and January 2010. Supply supporting schedules for collections of receivables; payments for merchandise; and marketing, distribution, and customer-service costs.

6-38 Comprehensive problem; ABC manufacturing, two products. Dinettes Inc. operates at capacity and makes glass topped dining tables and wooden chairs, which are then typically sold as sets of four chairs with one table. However, some customers purchase replacement or extra chairs, and others buy some chairs or a table only, so the sales mix is not exactly 4:1. Dinettes Inc. is planning its annual budget for fiscal year 2009. Information for 2009 follows:

Input prices

Direct materials	
Wood	$ 1.60 per board foot
Glass	$12 per sheet
Direct manufacturing labor	$15 per direct manufacturing labor-hour

Input quantities per unit of output

	Chairs	Tables
Direct materials		
Wood	5 board feet	7 board feet
Glass	—	2 sheets
Direct manufacturing labor	4 hours	8 hours
Machine-hours (MH)	3 MH	5 MH

Inventory information, direct materials

	Wood	Glass
Beginning inventory	109,200 board feet	8,750 sheets
Target ending inventory	117,500 board feet	9,000 sheets
Cost of beginning inventory	$170,352	$109,375

Dinettes Inc. accounts for direct materials using a FIFO cost flow.

Sales and inventory information, finished goods

	Chairs	Tables
Expected sales in units	172,000	45,000
Selling price	$80	$900
Target ending inventory in units	8,500	2,250
Beginning inventory in units	8,000	2,100
Beginning inventory in dollars	$760,000	$477,000

Dinette Inc. uses a FIFO cost flow assumption for finished goods inventory.

Chairs are manufactured in batches of 500, and tables are manufactured in batches of 50. It takes three hours to set up for a batch of chairs, and two hours to set up for a batch of tables.

Dinette Inc. uses activity-based costing and has classified all overhead costs as shown in the table below:

Cost type	Budgeted variable	Budgeted fixed	Cost driver/Allocation base
Manufacturing:			
Materials handling	$342,840	$ 600,000	Number of board feet used
Setup	97,000	300,740	Setup hours
Processing	789,250	5,900,000	Machine hours
Nonmanufacturing:			
Marketing	2,011,200	4,500,000	Sales revenue
Distribution	54,000	380,000	Number of deliveries

Delivery trucks transport units sold in delivery sizes of 500 chairs or 500 tables.

Required Do the following for the year 2009:

1. Prepare the revenues budget.
2. Use the revenue budget to:
   a. Find the budgeted allocation rate for marketing costs.
   b. Find the budgeted number of deliveries and allocation rate for distribution costs.
3. Prepare the production budget in units.

4. Use the production budget to:
   a. Find the budgeted number of setups, setup hours, and the allocation rate for setup costs.
   b. Find the budgeted total machine hours and the allocation rate for processing costs.
5. Prepare the direct material usage budget and the direct material purchases budgets.
6. Use the direct material usage budget to find the budgeted allocation rate for materials handling costs.
7. Prepare the direct manufacturing labor cost budget.
8. Prepare the manufacturing overhead cost budget for materials handling, setup, and processing
9. Prepare the budgeted unit cost of ending finished goods inventory and ending inventories budget.
10. Prepare cost of goods sold budget.
11. Prepare the nonmanufacturing overhead costs budget for marketing and distribution.
12. Prepare a budgeted income statement (ignore income taxes).
13. Compare the budgeted unit cost of a chair to its budgeted selling price. Why might Dinette Inc. continue to sell the chairs for only $80?

6-39 Budgeting and ethics. Delma Company manufactures a variety of products in a variety of departments, and evaluates departments and departmental managers by comparing actual cost and output relative to the budget. Departmental managers help create the budgets, and usually provide information about input quantities for materials, labor and overhead costs.

Wert Mimble is the manager of the department that produces Product Z. Wert has estimated these inputs for Product Z:

Input	Budget Quantity per Unit of Output
Direct material	3 pounds
Direct manufacturing labor	20 minutes
Machine time	10 minutes

The department produces about 100 units of Product Z each day. Wert's department always gets excellent evaluations, sometimes exceeding budgeted production quantities. Each 100 units of product Z uses, on average, about 32 hours of direct manufacturing labor (four people working eight hours each,) 295 pounds of material, and 16.5 machine hours.

Top management of Delma Company has decided to implement budget standards that will challenge the workers in each department, and it has asked Wert to design more challenging input standards for Product Z. Wert provides top management with the following input quantities:

Input	Budget Quantity per Unit of Output
Direct material	2.95 pounds
Direct manufacturing labor	19.2 minutes
Machine time	9.9 minutes

Required

Discuss the following:

1. Are these standards, challenging standards for Department Z?
2. Why do you suppose Wert picked these particular standards?
3. What steps can Delma Company top management take to make sure Wert's standards really meet the goals of the firm?

Collaborative Learning Problem

6-40 Comprehensive budgeting problem; activity based costing, operating and financial budgets. (Chapter Appendix) Yummi-Lik makes really big lollipops in two sizes, large and giant. Yummi-Lik sells these lollipops to convenience stores, fairs, schools for fundraisers, and in bulk on the internet. Summer is approaching, and Yummi-Lik is preparing its budget for the month of June. The lollipops are hand made, mostly out of sugar, and attached to wooden sticks. Expected sales are based on past experience.

Other information for the month of June follows:

Input prices

Direct materials	
Sugar	$0.50 per pound (lb)
Sticks	$0.30 each
Direct manufacturing labor	$8 per direct manufacturing labor-hour

Input quantities per unit of output

	Large	Giant
Direct materials		
Sugar	0.25 lb	0.5 lb
Sticks	1	1
Direct manufacturing labor-hours (DMLH)	0.2 hour	0.25 hour
Setup hours per batch	0.08 hour	0.09 hour

Inventory information, direct materials

	Sugar	Sticks
Beginning inventory	125 lb	350
Target ending inventory	240 lb	480
Cost of beginning inventory	$64	$105

Yummi-Lik accounts for direct materials using a FIFO cost flow assumption.

Sales and inventory information, finished goods

	Large	Giant
Expected sales in units	3,000	1,800
Selling price	$ 3	$ 4
Target ending inventory in units	300	180
Beginning inventory in units	200	150
Beginning inventory in dollars	$ 500	$ 474

Yummi-Lik uses a FIFO cost flow assumption for finished goods inventory.

All the lollipops are made in batches of 10. Yummi-Lik incurs manufacturing overhead costs, and marketing and general administration costs, but customers pay for shipping. Other than manufacturing labor costs, monthly processing costs are very small. Yummy-Lik uses activity-based costing and has classified all overhead costs for the month of June as shown in the following chart:

Cost type	Denominator Activity	Rate
Manufacturing:		
Setup	Setup hours	$20 per setup hr
Processing	Direct manufacturing labor-hours (DMLH)	$1.70 per DMLH
Nonmanufacturing:		
Marketing and general administration	Sales revenue	10%

Required

1. Prepare each of the following for June:
   - **a.** Revenues budget
   - **b.** Production budget in units
   - **c.** Direct material usage budget and direct material purchases budget
   - **d.** Direct manufacturing labor cost budget
   - **e.** Manufacturing overhead cost budgets for processing and setup activities
   - **f.** Budgeted unit cost of ending finished goods inventory and ending inventories budget
   - **g.** Cost of goods sold budget
   - **h.** Marketing and general administration costs budget
2. Yummi-Lik's Balance Sheet for May 31 follows. Use it and the following information to prepare a Cash Budget for Yummi-Lik for June.
   - 80% of sales are on account of which half are collected in the month of the sale, 49% are collected the following month, and 1% are never collected and written off as bad debts.
   - All purchases of materials are on account. Yummi-Lik pays for 70% of purchases in the month of purchase and 30% in the following month.
   - All other costs are paid in the month incurred.
   - Yummi-Lik is making monthly interest payments of 1% (12% per year) on a $20,000 long term loan.
   - Yummi-Lik plans to pay the $500 of taxes owed as of May 31 in the month of June. Income tax expense for June is zero.
   - 40% of processing and setup costs, and 30% of marketing and general administration costs are depreciation.

Yummi-Lik
Balance Sheet
as of May 31

Assets		
Cash		$ 587
Accounts receivable	$ 4,800	
Less: Allowance for bad debts	96	4,704
Inventories		
Direct materials		169
Finished goods		974
Fixed assets	$190,000	
Less: Accumulated depreciation	55,759	134,241
Total assets		$140,675

Liabilities and Equity	
Accounts payable	$ 696
Taxes payable	500
Interest payable	200
Long term debt	20,000
Common stock	10,000
Retained earnings	109,279
Total liabilities and equity	$140,675

3. Prepare a budgeted income statement for June and a budgeted balance sheet for Yummi-Lik as of June 30.

7 Flexible Budgets, Direct-Cost Variances, and Mangement Control

Learning Objectives

1. Distinguish a static budget from a flexible budget
2. Develop flexible budgets and compute flexible-budget variances and sales-volume variances
3. Explain why standard costs are often used in variance analysis
4. Compute price variances and efficiency variances for direct-cost categories
5. Understand how managers use variances
6. Perform variance analysis in activity-based costing systems
7. Describe benchmarking and explain its role in cost management

What goes into your favorite Starbucks drink? Espresso and steamed milk? Sure, but the price of your latte includes costs beyond just coffee and milk. At Starbucks, and across the service industry, employee labor also makes up a large share of each store's direct costs. Starbucks has an extensive budgeting system that incorporates sales, food costs, and labor expenses for each store. Each day, managers check their store's actual activity against budgeted performance to prevent negative variances. This variance analysis is especially critical at Starbucks, where the tension between rising direct costs and increasing prices is weighing on customer satisfaction, profitability, and the company's aggressive expansion plan.

Starbucks Tries to Keep a Lid on Costs Amid Expansion[1]

In October 2006, Starbucks set a new long-term goal to have 40,000 coffee stores worldwide, more than triple its current number. Welcome to the Starbucks store on 49th Street and Seventh Avenue in Manhattan. At 9:45 a.m. in August 2006, as four baristas scrambled to take orders, about 20 people were in two lines that snaked around the inside of the Starbucks store. But not everyone was happy. That morning, the company raised prices on its drinks for the seventh time since 1997. Coupled with the long lines, some people question whether Starbucks can pull off such a rapid expansion strategy.

In the year that followed Starbucks' announcement of its expansion plans, store-level operating margins decreased from 10.9% to 10.4%. And while sales at stores open for more than one year increased by 4%, 3% of that came from an increase in the value per customer transaction, which included price hikes. With margins under pressure, and increasing competition from Dunkin' Donuts, Caribou Coffee, and McDonald's, Starbucks has begun emphasizing cost control and operating-variance reduction to keep from having to raises its prices more than necessary.

[1] *Sources:* Helm, B. and J. Goudreau, "Is Starbucks Pushing Prices Too High?" *BusinessWeek* (July 31, 2007); Harris, C., "Starbucks Slips; Lattes Rise," *The Seattle Post Intelligencer* (July 23, 2007); Saporito, B., "Starbucks: Wake Up, Smell the Coffee," *Time* (February 26, 2007); Linn, A., "Starbucks Wants 40,000 Stores Worldwide, Up From 30,000 Goal," *International Herald Tribune* (October 6, 2006); Internal company information (as posted at starbucksgossip.typepad.com on November 3, 2006).

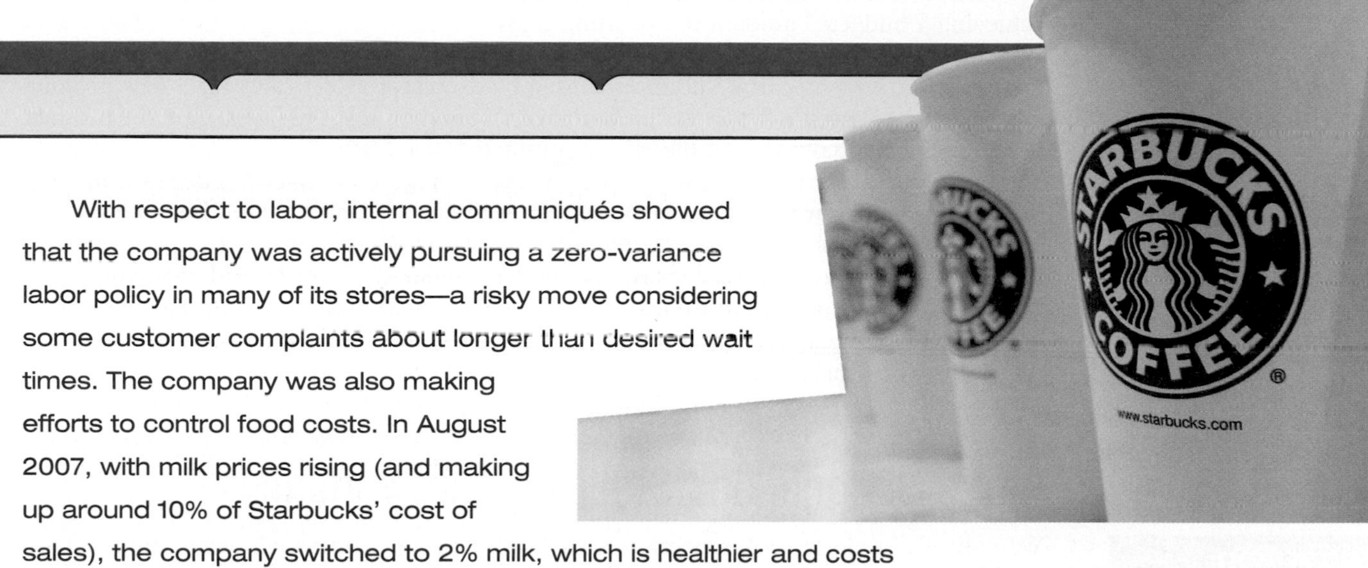

With respect to labor, internal communiqués showed that the company was actively pursuing a zero-variance labor policy in many of its stores—a risky move considering some customer complaints about longer than desired wait times. The company was also making efforts to control food costs. In August 2007, with milk prices rising (and making up around 10% of Starbucks' cost of sales), the company switched to 2% milk, which is healthier and costs less, and redoubled efforts to reduce milk-related spoilage.

In Chapter 6, you saw how budgets help managers with their planning function. We now explain how budgets, specifically flexible budgets, are used to compute variances, which assist managers in their control function. Flexible budgets and variances enable managers to make meaningful comparisons of actual results with planned performance, and to obtain insights into why actual results differ from planned performance. They form the critical final function in the five-step decision-making process, by making it possible for managers to *evaluate performance and learn* after decisions are implemented. In this chapter and the next, we explain how.

The Use of Variances

A **variance** is the difference between actual results and expected performance. The expected performance is also called **budgeted performance**, which is a point of reference for making comparisons.

Variances lie at the point where the planning and control functions of management come together. They assist managers in implementing their strategies by enabling **management by exception.** This is the practice of focusing management attention on areas that are not operating as expected (such as a large shortfall in sales of a product) and devoting less time to areas operating as expected. In other words, by highlighting the areas that have deviated most from expectations, variances enable managers to focus their efforts on the most critical areas. Consider scrap and rework costs at a Maytag appliances plant. If actual costs are much higher than budgeted, the variances will guide managers to seek explanations and to take early corrective action, ensuring that future operations result in less scrap and rework. Sometimes a large positive variance may occur, such as a significant decrease in manufacturing costs of a product. Managers will try to understand the reasons for this decrease, for example, better operator training or changes in manufacturing methods, so these practices can be appropriately continued and transferred to other divisions within the organization.

Variances are also used in performance evaluation and to motivate managers. Production-line managers at Maytag may have quarterly efficiency incentives linked to achieving a budgeted amount of operating costs.

Sometimes variances suggest that the company should consider a change in strategy. For example, large negative variances caused by excessive defect rates for a new product may suggest a flawed product design. Managers may then want to investigate the product design and potentially change the mix of products being offered.

Variance analysis contributes in many ways to making the five-step decision-making process more effective. It allows managers to evaluate performance and learn by providing a framework for correctly assessing current performance. In turn, managers take corrective actions to ensure that decisions are implemented correctly and that previously budgeted results are in fact attained. Variances also enable managers to generate more informed predictions about the future, and thereby improve the quality of the five-step decision-making process.

Static Budgets and Static-Budget Variances

Learning Objective 1

Distinguish a static budget

. . . the master budget based on output planned at start of period

from a flexible budget

. . . the budget that is adjusted (flexed) to recognize the actual output level

We will take a closer look at variances by examining one company's accounting system. Note as you study the exhibits in this chapter that "level" followed by a number denotes the amount of detail shown by a variance analysis. Level 1 reports the least detail, level 2 offers more information, and so on.

Consider Webb Company, a firm that manufactures and sells jackets. The jackets require tailoring and many hand operations. Webb sells exclusively to distributors, who in turn sell to independent clothing stores and retail chains. For simplicity, we assume that Webb's only costs are in the manufacturing function; Webb incurs no costs in other value-chain functions, such as marketing and distribution. We also assume that all units manufactured in April 2008 are sold in April 2008. Therefore, all direct materials are purchased and used in the same budget period, and there is no direct materials inventory at either the beginning or the end of the period. No work-in-process or finished goods inventories exist at either the beginning or the end of the period. The Problem for Self-Study (pp. 246–247) relaxes some of these assumptions. Webb has three variable-cost categories. The budgeted variable cost per jacket for each category is:

Cost Category	Variable Cost per Jacket
Direct material costs	$60
Direct manufacturing labor costs	16
Variable manufacturing overhead costs	12
Total variable costs	$88

The *number of units manufactured* is the cost driver for direct materials, direct manufacturing labor, and variable manufacturing overhead. The relevant range for the cost driver is from 0 to 12,000 jackets. Budgeted and actual data for April 2008 follow:

Budgeted fixed costs for production between 0 and 12,000 jackets	$276,000
Budgeted selling price	$120 per jacket
Budgeted production and sales	12,000 jackets
Actual production and sales	10,000 jackets

The **static budget**, or master budget, is based on the level of output planned at the start of the budget period. The master budget is called a static budget because the budget for the period is developed around a single (static) planned output level. Exhibit 7-1, column 3, presents the static budget for Webb Company for April 2008 that was prepared at the end of 2007. For each line item in the income statement, Exhibit 7-1, column 1, displays data for the actual April results. For example, actual revenues are $1,250,000, and the actual selling price is $1,250,000 ÷ 10,000 jackets = $125 per jacket—compared with the budgeted selling price of $120 per jacket. Similarly, actual direct material costs are $621,600, and the direct material cost per jacket is $621,600 ÷ 10,000 = $62.16 per jacket—compared with the budgeted

Exhibit 7-1

Static-Budget-Based Variance Analysis for Webb Company for April 2008[a]

Level 1 Analysis

	Actual Results (1)	Static-Budget Variances (2) = (1) – (3)	Static Budget (3)
Units sold	10,000	2,000 U	12,000
Revenues	$1,250,000	$190,000 U	$1,440,000
Variable costs			
Direct materials	621,600	98,400 F	720,000
Direct manufacturing labor	198,000	6,000 U	192,000
Variable manufacturing overhead	130,500	13,500 F	144,000
Total variable costs	950,100	105,900 F	1,056,000
Contribution margin	299,900[b]	84,100 U	384,000[c]
Fixed costs	285,000	9,000 U	276,000
Operating income	$ 14,900	$ 93,100 U	$ 108,000

$ 93,100 U
Static-budget variance

[a]F = favorable effect on operating income; U = unfavorable effect on operating income.
[b]Contribution margin percentage = $299,900 ÷ $1,250,000 = 24.0%.
[c]Contribution margin percentage = $384,000 ÷ $1,440,000 = 26.7%.

direct material cost per jacket of $60. We describe potential reasons and explanations for these differences as we discuss different variances throughout the chapter.

The **static-budget variance** (see Exhibit 7-1, column 2) is the difference between the actual result and the corresponding budgeted amount in the static budget.

A **favorable variance**—denoted F in this book—has the effect, when considered in isolation, of increasing operating income relative to the budgeted amount. For revenue items, F means actual revenues exceed budgeted revenues. For cost items, F means actual costs are less than budgeted costs. An **unfavorable variance**—denoted U in this book—has the effect, when viewed in isolation, of decreasing operating income relative to the budgeted amount. Unfavorable variances are also called *adverse variances* in some countries, for example, the United Kingdom.

The unfavorable static-budget variance for operating income of $93,100 in Exhibit 7-1 is calculated by subtracting static-budget operating income of $108,000 from actual operating income of $14,900:

$$\begin{aligned}\text{Static-budget variance for operating income} &= \text{Actual result} - \text{Static-budget amount}\\ &= \$14{,}900 - \$108{,}000\\ &= \$93{,}100\ \text{U}.\end{aligned}$$

The analysis in Exhibit 7-1 provides managers with additional information on the static-budget variance for operating income of $93,100 U. The more detailed breakdown indicates how the line items that comprise operating income—revenues, individual variable costs, and fixed costs—add up to the static-budget variance of $93,100.

Remember, Webb produced and sold only 10,000 jackets, although managers anticipated an output of 12,000 jackets in the static budget. *Managers want to know how much of the static-budget variance is because of inaccurate forecasting of output units sold and how much is due to Webb's performance in manufacturing and selling 10,000 jackets.* Managers, therefore, create a flexible budget, which enables a more in-depth understanding of deviations from the static budget.

Flexible Budgets

Learning Objective 2

Develop flexible budgets

. . . proportionately increase variable costs; keep fixed costs the same

and compute flexible-budget variances

. . . each flexible-budget variance is the difference between an actual result and a flexible-budget amount

and sales-volume variances

. . . each sales-volume variance is the difference between a flexible-budget amount and a static-budget amount

A **flexible budget** calculates budgeted revenues and budgeted costs based on *the actual output in the budget period.* The flexible budget is prepared at the end of the period (April 2008), after the actual output of 10,000 jackets is known. The flexible budget is the *hypothetical* budget that Webb would have prepared at the start of the budget period if it had correctly forecast the actual output of 10,000 jackets. In preparing the flexible budget:

- The budgeted selling price is the same \$120 per jacket used in preparing the static budget.
- The budgeted variable costs are the same \$88 per jacket used in the static budget.
- The budgeted fixed costs are the same static-budget amount of \$276,000. Why? Because the 10,000 jackets produced falls within the relevant range of 0 to 12,000 jackets. Therefore, Webb would have budgeted the same amount of fixed costs, \$276,000, whether it anticipated making 10,000 or 12,000 jackets.

The *only* difference between the static budget and the flexible budget is that the static budget is prepared for the planned output of 12,000 jackets, whereas the flexible budget is based on the actual output of 10,000 jackets. The static budget is being "flexed," or adjusted, from 12,000 jackets to 10,000 jackets. The flexible budget for 10,000 jackets assumes that all costs are either completely variable or completely fixed with respect to the number of jackets produced.

Webb develops its flexible budget in three steps.

Step 1: Identify the Actual Quantity of Output. In April 2008, Webb produced and sold 10,000 jackets.

Step 2: Calculate the Flexible Budget for Revenues Based on Budgeted Selling Price and Actual Quantity of Output.

$$\text{Flexible-budget revenues} = \$120 \text{ per jacket} \times 10{,}000 \text{ jackets} = \$1{,}200{,}000$$

Step 3: Calculate the Flexible Budget for Costs Based on Budgeted Variable Cost per Output Unit, Actual Quantity of Output, and Budgeted Fixed Costs.

Flexible-budget variable costs	
Direct materials, \$60 per jacket × 10,000 jackets	\$ 600,000
Direct manufacturing labor, \$16 per jacket × 10,000 jackets	160,000
Variable manufacturing overhead, \$12 per jacket × 10,000 jackets	120,000
Total flexible-budget variable costs	880,000
Flexible-budget fixed costs	276,000
Flexible-budget total costs	\$1,156,000

These three steps enable Webb to prepare a flexible budget, as shown in Exhibit 7-2, column 3. The flexible budget allows for a more detailed analysis of the \$93,100 unfavorable static-budget variance for operating income.

Flexible-Budget Variances and Sales-Volume Variances

Exhibit 7-2 shows the flexible-budget-based variance analysis for Webb, which subdivides the \$93,100 unfavorable static-budget variance for operating income into two parts: a flexible-budget variance of \$29,100 U and a sales-volume variance of \$64,000 U. The **sales-volume variance** is the difference between a flexible-budget amount and the corresponding static-budget amount. The **flexible-budget variance** is the difference between an actual result and the corresponding flexible-budget amount.

Exhibit 7-2 Level 2 Flexible-Budget-Based Variance Analysis for Webb Company for April 2008[a]

Level 2 Analysis

	Actual Results (1)	Flexible-Budget Variances (2) = (1) – (3)	Flexible Budget (3)	Sales-Volume Variances (4) = (3) – (5)	Static Budget (5)
Units sold	10,000	0	10,000	2,000 U	12,000
Revenues	$1,250,000	$50,000 F	$1,200,000	$240,000 U	$1,440,000
Variable costs					
Direct materials	621,600	21,600 U	600,000	120,000 F	720,000
Direct manufacturing labor	198,000	38,000 U	160,000	32,000 F	192,000
Variable manufacturing overhead	130,500	10,500 U	120,000	24,000 F	144,000
Total variable costs	950,100	70,100 U	880,000	176,000 F	1,056,000
Contribution margin	299,900	20,100 U	320,000	64,000 U	384,000
Fixed manufacturing costs	285,000	9,000 U	276,000	0	276,000
Operating income	$ 14,900	$29,100 U	$ 44,000	$ 64,000 U	$ 108,000

Level 2: $29,100 U Flexible-budget variance; $ 64,000 U Sales-volume variance

Level 1: $93,100 U Static-budget variance

[a]F = favorable effect on operating income; U = unfavorable effect on operating income.

Sales-Volume Variances

Keep in mind that the flexible-budget amounts in column 3 of Exhibit 7-2 and the static-budget amounts in column 5 are both computed using budgeted selling prices, budgeted variable cost per jacket, and budgeted fixed costs. The difference between the static-budget and the flexible-budget amounts is called the sales-volume variance because it arises *solely* from the difference between the 10,000 actual quantity (or volume) of jackets sold and the 12,000 quantity of jackets expected to be sold in the static budget.

$$\text{Sales-volume variance for operating income} = \text{Flexible-budget amount} - \text{Static-budget amount}$$
$$= \$44{,}000 - \$108{,}000$$
$$= \$64{,}000\ \text{U}$$

The sales-volume variance in operating income for Webb measures the change in budgeted contribution margin because Webb sold only 10,000 jackets rather than the budgeted 12,000.

$$\text{Sales-volume variance for operating income} = \left(\text{Budgeted contribution margin per unit}\right) \times \left(\text{Actual units sold} - \text{Static-budget units sold}\right)$$
$$= \left(\text{Budgeted selling price} - \text{Budgeted variable cost per unit}\right) \times \left(\text{Actual units sold} - \text{Static-budget units sold}\right)$$
$$= (\$120 \text{ per jacket} - \$88 \text{ per jacket}) \times (10{,}000 \text{ jackets} - 12{,}000 \text{ jackets})$$
$$= \$32 \text{ per jacket} \times (-2{,}000 \text{ jackets})$$
$$= \$64{,}000\ \text{U}$$

Exhibit 7-2, column 4, shows the components of this overall variance by identifying the sales-volume variance for each of the line items in the income statement. Webb's managers determine that the unfavorable sales-volume variance in operating income could be because of one or more of the following reasons:

1. The overall demand for jackets is not growing at the rate that was anticipated.
2. Competitors are taking away market share from Webb.
3. Webb did not adapt quickly to changes in customer preferences and tastes.
4. Budgeted sales targets were set without careful analysis of market conditions.
5. Quality problems developed that led to customer dissatisfaction with Webb's jackets.

How Webb responds to the unfavorable sales-volume variance will be influenced by what management believes to be the cause of the variance. For example, if Webb's managers believe the unfavorable sales-volume variance was caused by market-related reasons (reasons 1, 2, 3, or 4), the sales manager would be in the best position to explain what happened and to suggest corrective actions, such as sales promotions, that may be needed. If, however, managers believe the unfavorable sales-volume variance was caused by quality problems (reason 5), the production manager would be in the best position to analyze the causes and to suggest strategies for improvement, such as changes in the manufacturing process or investments in new machines.

The static-budget variances compared actual revenues and costs for 10,000 jackets against budgeted revenues and costs for 12,000 jackets. Separating the sales-volume variance—which reflects the effects of inaccurate forecasting of output units sold—from the static-budget variance enables managers to compare actual revenues earned and costs incurred for April 2008 against the revenues and costs Webb would have budgeted for the 10,000 jackets actually produced and sold—the flexible budget. *These flexible-budget variances are a better measure of operating performance than static-budget variances because they compare actual revenues to budgeted revenues and actual costs to budgeted costs for the same 10,000 jackets of output.*

Flexible-Budget Variances

The first three columns of Exhibit 7-2 compare actual results with flexible-budget amounts. Flexible-budget variances are in column 2 for each line item in the income statement:

$$\text{Flexible-budget variance} = \text{Actual result} - \text{Flexible-budget amount}$$

The operating income line in Exhibit 7-2 shows the flexible-budget variance is $29,100 U ($14,900 − $44,000). The $29,100 U arises because actual selling price, actual variable cost per unit, and actual fixed costs differ from their budgeted amounts. The actual results and budgeted amounts for the selling price and variable cost per unit are:

	Actual Result	Budgeted Amount
Selling price	$125.00 ($1,250,000 ÷ 10,000 jackets)	$120.00 ($1,200,000 ÷ 10,000 jackets)
Variable cost per jacket	$ 95.01 ($ 950,100 ÷ 10,000 jackets)	$ 88.00 ($ 880,000 ÷ 10,000 jackets)

The flexible-budget variance for revenues is called the **selling-price variance** because it arises solely from the difference between the actual selling price and the budgeted selling price:

$$\begin{aligned}\text{Selling-price variance} &= \left(\text{Actual selling price} - \text{Budgeted selling price}\right) \times \text{Actual units sold} \\ &= (\$125 \text{ per jacket} - \$120 \text{ per jacket}) \times 10{,}000 \text{ jackets} \\ &= \$50{,}000 \text{ F}\end{aligned}$$

Webb has a favorable selling-price variance because the $125 actual selling price exceeds the $120 budgeted amount, which increases operating income. Marketing managers are generally in the best position to understand and explain the reason for this selling price difference. For example, was the difference due to better quality? Or was it due to an overall increase in market prices? Webb's managers concluded it was due to a general increase in prices.

The flexible-budget variance for total variable costs is unfavorable ($70,100 U) for the actual output of 10,000 jackets. It's unfavorable because of one or both of the following:

- Webb used greater quantities of inputs (such as direct manufacturing labor-hours) compared to the budgeted quantities of inputs.
- Webb incurred higher prices per unit for the inputs (such as the wage rate per direct manufacturing labor-hour) compared to the budgeted prices per unit of the inputs.

Higher input quantities and/or higher input prices relative to the budgeted amounts could be the result of Webb deciding to produce a better product than what was planned or the result of inefficiencies in Webb's manufacturing and purchasing, or both. *You should always think of variance analysis as providing suggestions for further investigation rather than as establishing conclusive evidence of good or bad performance.*

The actual fixed costs of $285,000 are $9,000 more than the budgeted amount of $276,000. This unfavorable flexible-budget variance reflects unexpected increases in the cost of fixed indirect resources, such as factory rent or supervisory salaries.

In the rest of this chapter, we will focus on variable direct-cost input variances. Chapter 8 emphasizes indirect (overhead) cost variances.

Price Variances and Efficiency Variances for Direct-Cost Inputs

To gain further insight, almost all companies subdivide the flexible-budget variance for direct-cost inputs into two more-detailed variances:

1. A price variance that reflects the difference between an actual input price and a budgeted input price
2. An efficiency variance that reflects the difference between an actual input quantity and a budgeted input quantity

The information available from these variances (which we call level 3 variances) helps managers to better understand past performance and take corrective actions to implement superior strategies in the future. Managers generally have more control over efficiency variances than price variances. That's because the quantity of inputs used is primarily affected by factors inside the company, but price changes are primarily due to market forces outside the company.

Obtaining Budgeted Input Prices and Budgeted Input Quantities

To calculate price and efficiency variances, Webb needs to obtain budgeted input prices and budgeted input quantities. Webb's three main sources for this information are:

1. **Actual input data from past periods.** Most companies have past data on actual input prices and actual input quantities. These past prices and quantities could be used as the budgeted prices and quantities in a flexible budget. The advantage of past data is that they represent quantities and prices that are "real" rather than hypothetical and can serve as benchmarks for continuous improvement. Another advantage is that past data are typically available at low cost. However, there are limitations to using past data. Past data can include inefficiencies such as wastage of direct materials. Past data also do not incorporate any changes expected for the budget period.
2. **Data from other companies that have similar processes.** The benefit of using this data is that the budget numbers represent competitive benchmarks from other companies.

Learning Objective 3

Explain why standard costs are often used in variance analysis

. . . standard costs exclude past inefficiencies and take into account future changes

The main difficulty of using this source is that comparable input-price and input quantity data from other companies are often not available.

3. **Standards developed by Webb.** A **standard** is a carefully determined price, cost, or quantity that is used as a benchmark for judging performance. A standard is usually expressed on a per-unit basis. Consider how Webb determines its direct manufacturing labor standards. Webb conducts engineering studies to obtain a detailed breakdown of the steps required to make a jacket. Each step is assigned a standard time based on work performed by a *skilled* worker using equipment operating in an *efficient* manner. There are two advantages of using standard times: (i) they aim to exclude past inefficiencies and (ii) they aim to take into account changes expected to occur in the budget period. An example of (ii) is the decision by Webb, for strategic reasons, to lease new sewing machines that operate at a faster speed and enable output to be produced with lower defect rates. Similarly, Webb determines the standard quantity of square yards of cloth required by a skilled operator to make each jacket.

When developing standards for indirect costs, using detailed engineering studies to determine the standard times spent by support staff on different products is quite difficult. Instead, management accountants develop standard times based on interviews that identify the time spent by support staff on various activities (such as setups, supervision, and quality control) and the amount of time of each activity required by different products. However, this process requires care by management accountants because support staff may bias their estimates of the amount of time they spend on activities. The staff may want to seem busy or have lenient standards for the future.

The term "standard" refers to many different things. Always clarify its meaning and how it is being used. A **standard input** is a carefully determined quantity of input—such as square yards of cloth or direct manufacturing labor-hours—required for one unit of output, such as a jacket. A **standard price** is a carefully determined price that a company expects to pay for a unit of input. In the Webb example, the standard wage rate that Webb expects to pay its operators is an example of a standard price of a direct manufacturing labor-hour. A **standard cost** is a carefully determined cost of a unit of output—for example, the standard direct manufacturing labor cost of a jacket at Webb.

$$\frac{\text{Standard cost per output unit for}}{\text{each variable direct-cost input}} \quad \text{Standard cost per output unit for each variable direct-cost input} = \text{Standard input allowed for one output unit} \times \text{Standard price per input unit}$$

Standard direct material cost per jacket: 2 square yards of cloth input allowed per output unit (jacket) manufactured, at $30 standard price per square yard

$$\text{Standard direct material cost per jacket} = 2 \text{ square yards} \times \$30 \text{ per square yard} = \$60$$

Standard direct manufacturing labor cost per jacket: 0.8 manufacturing labor-hour of input allowed per output unit manufactured, at $20 standard price per hour

$$\text{Standard direct manufacturing labor cost per jacket} = 0.8 \text{ labor-hour} \times \$20 \text{ per labor-hour} = \$16$$

How are the words "budget" and "standard" related? Budget is the broader term. To clarify: Budgeted input prices, budgeted input quantities, and budgeted costs need *not* be based on standards. However, when standards *are* used to obtain budgeted input quantities and budgeted input prices, the terms "standard" and "budget" are used interchangeably. The standard cost of each input required for one unit of output is determined by the standard quantity of each input required for one unit of output and the standard price per input unit. See how the standard-cost computations for direct materials and direct manufacturing labor equal the budgeted direct material cost per jacket of $60 and the budgeted direct manufacturing labor cost of $16 referred to earlier (p. 226).

In its standard costing system, Webb uses standards that are attainable through efficient operations but that allow for normal disruptions. An alternative is to set more-challenging standards that are more difficult to attain. As we discussed in Chapter 6, setting challenging standards can increase motivation and performance. If, however, standards are regarded by workers as essentially unachievable, it can increase frustration and hurt performance.

Data for Calculating Webb's Price Variances and Efficiency Variances

Learning Objective 4

Compute price variances

. . . each price variance is the difference between an actual input price and a budgeted input price

and efficiency variances

. . . each efficiency variance is the difference between an actual input quantity and a budgeted input quantity for actual output

for direct-cost categories

Consider Webb's two direct-cost categories. The actual cost for each of these categories for the 10,000 jackets manufactured and sold in April 2008 is:

Direct materials purchased and used	
1. Square yards of cloth input purchased and used	22,200
2. Actual price incurred per square yard	$28
3. Direct material costs (22,200 × $28) [shown in Exhibit 7-2, column 1]	$621,600
Direct manufacturing labor	
1. Direct manufacturing labor-hours	9,000
2. Actual price incurred per direct manufacturing labor-hour	$22
3. Direct manufacturing labor costs (9,000 × $22) [shown in Exhibit 7-2, column 1]	$198,000

For simplicity, we assume the quantity of direct materials used equals the quantity of direct materials purchased. The Problem for Self-Study (pp. 246–247) relaxes this assumption. Let's use the Webb Company data to illustrate the price variance and the efficiency variance for direct-cost inputs.

A **price variance** is the difference between actual price and budgeted price multiplied by actual input quantity, such as direct materials purchased or used. A price variance is sometimes called an **input-price variance** or **rate variance,** especially when referring to a price variance for direct manufacturing labor. An **efficiency variance** is the difference between actual input quantity used—such as square yards of cloth of direct materials—and budgeted input quantity allowed for actual output, multiplied by budgeted price. An efficiency variance is sometimes called a **usage variance.**

Exhibit 7-3 shows how the price variance and the efficiency variance subdivide the flexible-budget variance. Consider direct materials. The direct materials flexible-budget variance of $21,600 U is the difference between actual costs incurred (actual input quantity × actual price) of $621,600 shown in column 1 and the flexible budget (budgeted input quantity allowed for actual output × budgeted price) of $600,000 shown in column 3. Column 2 (actual input quantity × budgeted price) is inserted between column 1 and column 3. The difference between columns 1 and 2 is the price variance of $44,400 F. This price variance occurs because the same actual input quantity (22,200 sq. yds.) is multiplied by *actual price* ($28) in column 1 and *budgeted price* ($30) in column 2. The difference between columns 2 and 3 is the efficiency variance of $66,000 U, because the same budgeted price ($30) is multiplied by *actual input quantity* (22,200 sq. yds) in column 2 and *budgeted input quantity allowed for actual output* (20,000 sq. yds.) in column 3. See how the direct materials price variance, $44,400 F, plus the direct materials efficiency variance, $66,000 U, equals the direct materials flexible budget variance, $21,600 U. Let's explore price variances and efficiency variances in greater detail so we can see how managers use these variances to improve their future performance.

Price Variances

The formula for computing the price variance is:

$$\text{Price variance} = \left(\begin{array}{c}\text{Actual price}\\ \text{of input}\end{array} - \begin{array}{c}\text{Budgeted price}\\ \text{of input}\end{array}\right) \times \begin{array}{c}\text{Actual quanity}\\ \text{of input}\end{array}$$

Exhibit 7-3 Columnar Presentation of Variance Analysis: Direct Costs for Webb Company for April 2008[a]

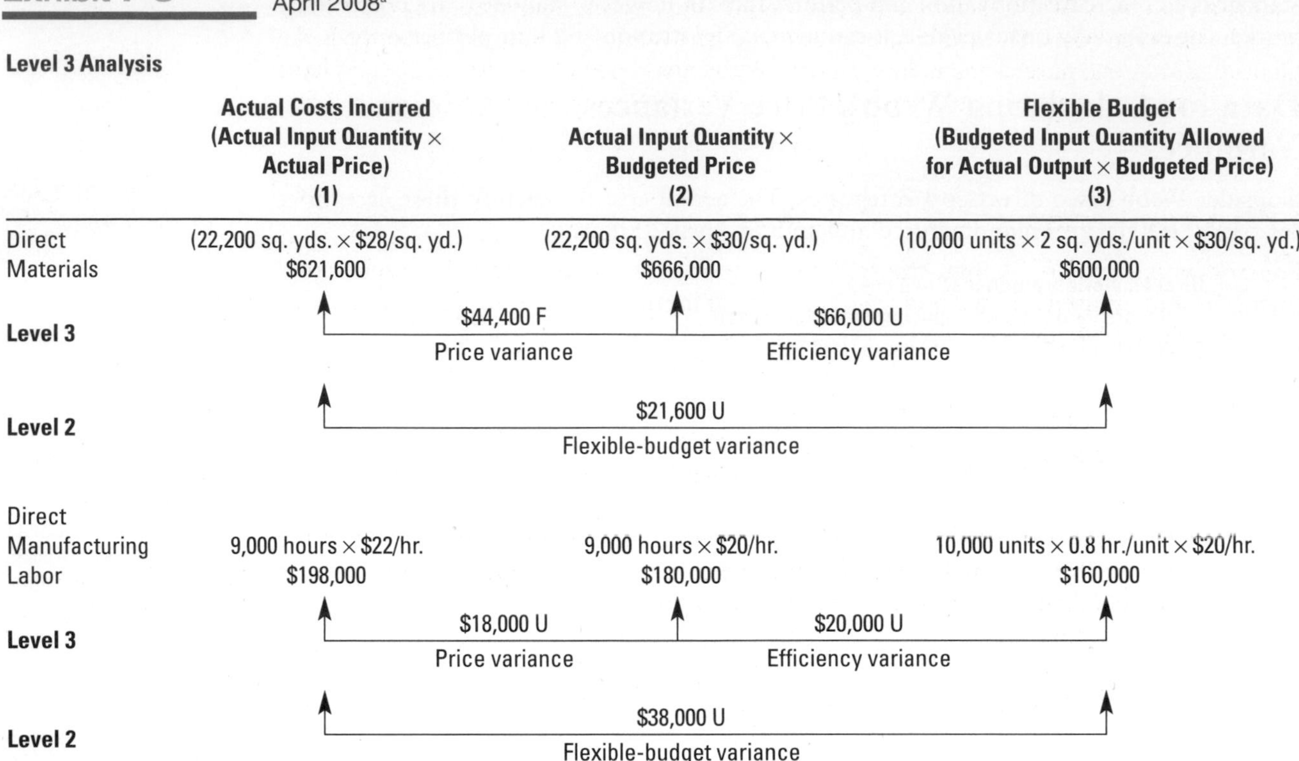

[a]F = favorable effect on operating income; U = unfavorable effect on operating income.

Price variances for Webb's two direct-cost categories are:

Direct-Cost Category	(Actual price of input − Budgeted price of input)	×	Actual quantity of input	=	Price Variance
Direct materials	($28 per sq. yard − $30 per sq. yard)	×	22,200 square yards	=	$44,400 F
Direct manufacturing labor	($22 per hour − $20 per hour)	×	9,000 hours	=	$18,000 U

The direct materials price variance is favorable because actual price of cloth is less than budgeted price, resulting in an increase in operating income. The direct manufacturing labor price variance is unfavorable because actual wage rate paid to labor is more than the budgeted rate, resulting in a decrease in operating income.

Always consider a broad range of possible causes for a price variance. For example, Webb's favorable direct materials price variance could be due to one or more of the following:

- Webb's purchasing manager negotiated the direct materials prices more skillfully than was planned for in the budget.
- The purchasing manager changed to a lower-price supplier.
- Webb's purchasing manager ordered larger quantities than the quantities budgeted, thereby obtaining quantity discounts.
- Direct material prices decreased unexpectedly because of, say, industry oversupply.
- Budgeted purchase prices of direct materials were set too high without careful analysis of market conditions.
- The purchasing manager received favorable prices because he was willing to accept unfavorable terms on factors other than prices (such as lower-quality material).

Webb's response to a direct materials price variance depends on what is believed to be the cause of the variance. Assume Webb's managers attribute the favorable price variance to the purchasing manager ordering in larger quantities than budgeted, thereby receiving quantity discounts. Webb could examine if purchasing in these larger quantities resulted in higher storage costs. If the increase in storage and inventory holding costs exceeds the quantity discounts, purchasing in larger quantities is not beneficial. Some companies have reduced their materials storage areas to prevent their purchasing managers from ordering in larger quantities.

Efficiency Variance

For any actual level of output, the efficiency variance is the difference between actual quantity of input used and the budgeted quantity of input allowed to produce actual output, multiplied by budgeted price:

$$\text{Efficiency Variance} = \left(\begin{array}{c}\text{Actual} \\ \text{quantity of} \\ \text{input used}\end{array} - \begin{array}{c}\text{Budgeted quantity} \\ \text{of unput allowed} \\ \text{for actual output}\end{array}\right) \times \begin{array}{c}\text{Budgeted price} \\ \text{of input}\end{array}$$

The idea here is that a company is inefficient if it uses a larger quantity of input than the budgeted quantity for its actual level of output; the company is efficient if it uses a smaller quantity of inputs than was budgeted for that output level.

The efficiency variances for each of Webb's direct-cost categories are:

Direct-Cost Category	(Actual quantity of input used − Budgeted quantity of input allowed for actual output)	× Budgeted price of input	=	Efficiency Variance
Direct materials	[22,200 sq. yds. − (10,000 units × 2 sq. yds./unit)]	× $30 per sq. yard		
	= (22,200 sq. yds. − 20,000 sq. yds.)	× $30 per sq. yard	=	$66,000 U
Direct manufacturing	[9,000 hours − (10,000 units × 0.8 hour/unit)]	× $20 per hour		
labor	= (9,000 hours − 8,000 hours)	× $20 per hour	=	20,000 U

The two manufacturing efficiency variances—direct materials efficiency variance and direct manufacturing labor efficiency variance—are each unfavorable because more input was used than was budgeted for the actual output, resulting in a decrease in operating income.

As with price variances, there is a broad range of possible causes for these efficiency variances (see also the Concepts in Action feature on p. 237). For example, Webb's unfavorable efficiency variance for direct manufacturing labor could be because of one or more of the following:

- Webb's personnel manager hired underskilled workers.
- Webb's production scheduler inefficiently scheduled work, resulting in more manufacturing labor time than budgeted being used per jacket.
- Webb's maintenance department did not properly maintain machines, resulting in more manufacturing labor time than budgeted being used per jacket.
- Budgeted time standards were set too tight without careful analysis of the operating conditions and the employees' skills.

Suppose Webb's managers determine that the unfavorable variance is due to poor machine maintenance. Webb may then establish a team consisting of plant engineers and machine operators to develop a maintenance schedule that will reduce future breakdowns and thereby prevent adverse effects on labor time and product quality.

Summary of Variances

Exhibit 7-4 provides a summary of the different variances. Note how the variances at each higher level provide disaggregated and more detailed information for evaluating performance.

Exhibit 7-4 Summary of Levels 1, 2, and 3 Variance Analysis

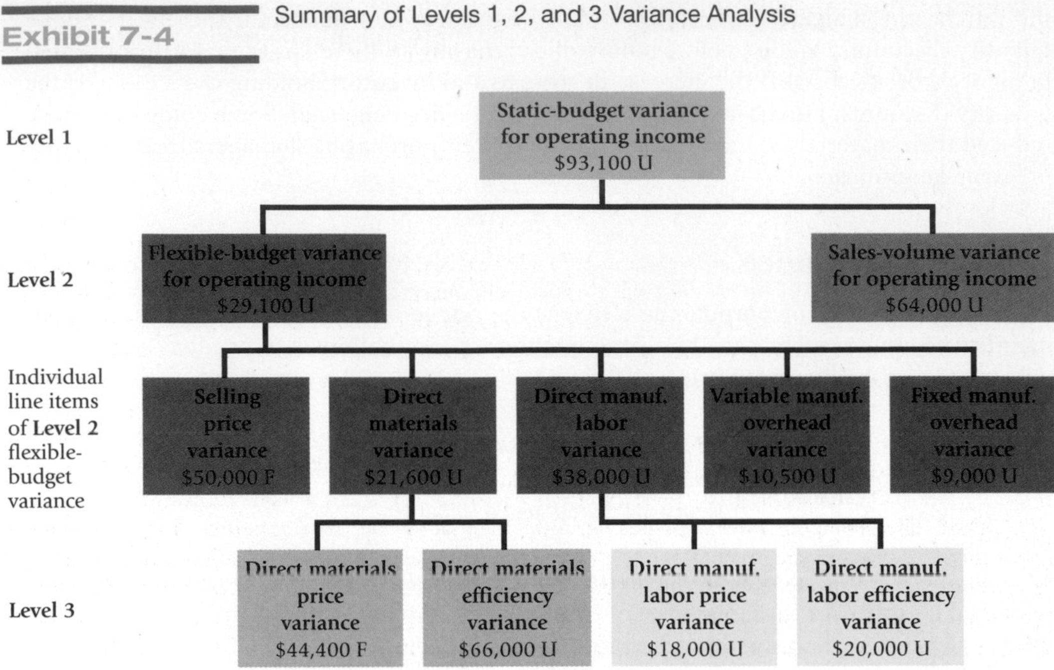

The following computations show why actual operating income is $14,900 when the static budget operating income is $108,000. The numbers in the computations can be found in Exhibits 7-2 and 7-3.

Static budget operating income			$108,000
Unfavorable sales-volume variance for operating income			(64,000)
Flexible-budget operating income			44,000
Flexible-budget variances for operating income:			
Favorable selling-price variance		$ 50,000	
Direct materials variances:			
Favorable direct materials price variance	$ 44,400		
Unfavorable direct materials efficiency variance	(66,000)		
Unfavorable direct materials variance		(21,600)	
Direct manufacturing labor variances:			
Unfavorable direct manufacturing labor price variance	(18,000)		
Unfavorable direct manufacturing labor efficiency variance	(20,000)		
Unfavorable direct manufacturing labor variance		(38,000)	
Unfavorable variable manufacturing overhead variance		(10,500)	
Unfavorable fixed manufacturing overhead variance		(9,000)	
Unfavorable flexible-budget variance for operating income			(29,100)
Actual operating income			$ 14,900

The summary of variances highlights three main effects.

1. Webb sold 2,000 fewer units than budgeted, resulting in an unfavorable sales volume variance of $64,000. Sales declined because of quality problems and new styles of jackets introduced by Webb's competitors.
2. Webb sold units at a higher price than budgeted, resulting in a favorable selling-price variance of $50,000. Webb's prices, however, were lower than the prices charged by Webb's competitors.
3. Manufacturing costs for the actual output produced were higher than budgeted—direct materials by $21,600; direct manufacturing labor by $38,000; variable manufacturing overhead by $10,500; and fixed overhead by $9,000—because of poor quality of cloth, poor maintenance of machines, and underskilled workers.

Concepts in Action

Weapons Against Waste: Sandoz Uses Variance Analysis to Cut Its Product Costs and Improve Profits

Sandoz US, the $1.5 billion subsidiary of Swiss-based Novartis AG, develops generic pharmaceutical substitutes for market-leading therapeutic drugs. To ensure success, the 1,500 employees of Sandoz must develop and deliver its products to wholesalers and retailers at the lowest possible cost. Because the generic drug industry is so competitive, an intricate understanding of product costs is critical. Variance analysis helps managers assess and maintain product profitability.

At its Broomfield, Colorado manufacturing facility, Sandoz uses standard costs, based on the recipes for each product, to predict the costs associated with producing batches of each generic drug. To monitor and control costs, the plant controller regularly reviews detailed costing information received from the managers on the production floor. The plant controller then uses variance analysis to improve operations. Variance analysis helps support improvements in the manufacturing process, forecast financial results, and set manufacturing standards. Most important, it also helps managers find the root cause of process deficiencies. Let's take a closer look at how Sandoz's managers use variance analysis.

Materials cost variances are reviewed on a weekly basis and are analyzed in terms of yield loss. Yield loss is a measure of direct materials efficiency—that is, the difference between the actual quantity of materials used and the expected quantity of materials that should have been used.

Each week, management accountants at Sandoz analyze which products have the top dollar value and the highest volume of yield losses. They forward their findings to production for review. Year-to-date trends are examined by engineers and scientists to determine if changes in processes, materials, and equipment are necessary or if the standards that have been set require modification. Maintaining accurate standards is important because managers use standards to plan direct materials purchases. Inaccuracies about direct material requirements could lead to direct material stock-outs, cycle time increases, and customer back orders.

But direct material costs are not the only costs getting attention. Consider direct manufacturing labor costs. Management accountants calculate a standard direct manufacturing labor rate for each manufacturing area (for example, mixing, blending, tableting, and packaging). Managers then review direct manufacturing labor efficiency variances, and management accountants report and track products and work centers with consistently high unfavorable variances. Teams of workers analyze root causes and recommend process and equipment enhancements to improve direct manufacturing labor efficiency and to make standard labor-time adjustments. Accurate labor-time standards are critical because they drive direct manufacturing labor staffing levels.

With intense margin pressures, these practices are employed throughout the generic pharmaceutical business. With the average price for US generic drug prescription at $30.56 (versus $84.20 for branded prescription drugs), generic manufacturers must aggressively contain costs in such a high volume, low margin environment. But how has variance analysis and standard costing helped Sandoz specifically? Over the years, the plant has decreased yield and destruction losses enhancing the company's ability to deliver products that meet customers' expectations and contributing significantly to overall profitability. This will be critical in the years ahead, as analysts believe Sandoz will be responsible for 30% of Novartis' overall growth by 2012.

Sources: Conversations with, and documents prepared by, Eric Evans and Erich Erchr (of Sandoz US) on March 20, 2004 and May 28, 2004; Dumrese, T., et al., *Novartis AG - Reinitiating Coverage* (Oppenheim Research, August 15, 2007); conversations with, and documents prepared by, John Niedermayer (pharmaceutical consultant), August 31, 2007.

We now present Webb's journal entries under its standard costing system.

Journal Entries Using Standard Costs

Chapter 4 illustrated journal entries when normal costing is used. We will now illustrate journal entries for Webb Company using standard costs. Our focus is on direct materials and direct manufacturing labor. All the numbers included in the following journal entries are found in Exhibit 7-3.

Note: In each of the following entries, unfavorable variances are always debits (they decrease operating income), and favorable variances are always credits (they increase operating income).

JOURNAL ENTRY 1A: Isolate the direct materials price variance at the time of purchase by increasing (debiting) Direct Materials Control at standard prices. This is the earliest time possible to isolate this variance.

1a. Direct Materials Control		
(22,200 square yards × $30 per square yard)	666,000	
Direct Materials Price Variance		
(22,200 square yards × $2 per square yard)		44,400
Accounts Payable Control		
(22,200 square yards × $28 per square yard)		621,600
To record direct materials purchased.		

JOURNAL ENTRY 1B: Isolate the direct materials efficiency variance at the time the direct materials are used by increasing (debiting) Work-in-Process Control at standard quantities allowed for actual output units manufactured times standard prices.

1b. Work-in-Process Control		
(10,000 jackets × 2 yards per jacket × $30 per square yard)	600,000	
Direct Materials Efficiency Variance		
(2,200 square yards × $30 per square yard)	66,000	
Direct Materials Control		
(22,200 square yards × $30 per square yard)		666,000
To record direct materials used.		

JOURNAL ENTRY 2: Isolate the direct manufacturing labor price variance and efficiency variance at the time this labor is used by increasing (debiting) Work-in-Process Control at standard quantities allowed for actual output units manufactured at standard prices. Note that Wages Payable Control measures the actual amounts payable to workers based on actual hours worked and actual wage rates.

2. Work-in-Process Control		
(10,000 jackets × 0.80 hour per jacket × $20 per hour)	160,000	
Direct Manufacturing Labor Price Variance		
(9,000 hours × $2 per hour)	18,000	
Direct Manufacturing Labor Efficiency Variance		
(1,000 hours × $20 per hour)	20,000	
Wages Payable Control		
(9,000 hours × $22 per hour)		198,000
To record liability for direct manufacturing labor costs.		

We have seen how standard costing and variance analysis help to focus management attention on areas not operating as expected. The journal entries here point to another advantage of standard costing systems—that is, standard costs simplify product costing. As each unit is manufactured, costs are assigned to it using the standard cost of direct materials, the standard cost of direct manufacturing labor and, as you will see in Chapter 8, standard manufacturing overhead cost.

From the perspective of control, all variances are isolated at the earliest possible time. For example, by isolating the direct materials price variance at the time of purchase, corrective actions—such as seeking cost reductions from the current supplier or obtaining price quotes from other potential suppliers—can be taken immediately when a large unfavorable variance is first known rather than waiting until after the materials are used in production.

At the end of the fiscal year, the variance accounts are written off to cost of goods sold if they are immaterial in amount. For simplicity, we assume that the balances in the different direct cost variance accounts as of April 2008 are also the balances at the end of 2008 and therefore immaterial in total. Webb would record the following journal entry to write off the direct cost variance accounts to Cost of Goods Sold.

Cost of Goods Sold	59,600	
Direct Materials Price Variance	44,400	
Direct Materials Efficiency Variance		66,000
Direct Manufacturing Labor Price Variance		18,000
Direct Manufacturing Labor Efficiency Variance		20,000

Alternatively, assuming Webb has inventories at the end of the fiscal year, and the variances are material in their amounts, the variance accounts are prorated between cost of goods sold and various inventory accounts using the methods described in Chapter 4 (pp. 115–119). For example, Direct Materials Price Variance is prorated among Materials Control, Work-in-Process Control, Finished Goods Control and Cost of Goods Sold on the basis of the standard costs of direct materials in each account's ending balance. Direct Materials Efficiency Variance is prorated among Work-in-Process Control, Finished Goods Control and Cost of Goods Sold on the basis of the direct material costs in each account's ending balance (after proration of the direct materials price variance).

Many accountants, industrial engineers, and managers maintain that to the extent that variances measure inefficiency or abnormal efficiency during the year, they should be written off instead of being prorated among inventories and cost of goods sold. This reasoning argues for applying a combination of the write-off and proration methods for each individual variance. Consider the efficiency variance. The portion of the efficiency variance that is due to inefficiency and could have been avoided should be written off to cost of goods sold while the portion that is unavoidable should be prorated. If another variance, such as the direct materials price variance, is considered unavoidable because it is entirely caused by general market conditions, it should be prorated. Unlike full proration, this approach avoids carrying the costs of inefficiency as part of inventoriable costs.

Implementing Standard Costing

Standard costing provides valuable information for the management and control of materials, labor, and other activities related to production.

Standard Costing and Information Technology

Modern information technology promotes the increased use of standard costing systems for product costing and control. Companies such as Dell and Sandoz (the manufacturer of generic pharmaceuticals) store standard prices and standard quantities in their computer systems. A bar code scanner records the receipt of materials, immediately costing each material using its stored standard price. The receipt of materials is then matched with the purchase order to record accounts payable and to isolate the direct materials price variance.

The direct materials efficiency variance is calculated as output is completed by comparing the standard quantity of direct materials that should have been used with the computerized request for direct materials submitted by an operator on the production floor. Labor variances are calculated as employees log into production-floor terminals and punch in their employee numbers, start and end times, and the quantity of product they helped produce. Managers use this instantaneous feedback from variances to initiate immediate corrective action, as needed.

Wide Applicability of Standard Costing

Companies that have implemented total quality management and computer-integrated manufacturing (CIM) systems, as well as companies in the service sector, find standard costing to be a useful tool. Companies implementing total quality management programs use standard costing to control materials costs. Service-sector companies such as McDonald's are labor intensive and use standard costs to control labor costs. Companies that have implemented CIM, such as Toyota, use flexible budgeting and standard costing to manage activities such as materials handling and setups. The growing use of Enterprise Resource Planning (ERP) systems, as described in Chapter 6, has made it easy for firms to keep track of standard, average, and actual costs for inventory items and to make real-time assessments of variances. Managers use variance information to identify areas of the firm's manufacturing or purchasing process that most need attention.

Management Uses of Variances

Managers and management accountants use variances to evaluate performance after decisions are implemented, to trigger organization learning, and to make continuous improvements. Variances serve as an early warning system to alert managers to existing problems or to prospective opportunities. Variance analysis enables managers to evaluate the effectiveness of the actions and performance of personnel in the current period, as well as to fine-tune strategies for achieving improved performance in the future. To make sure that managers interpret variances correctly and make appropriate decisions based on them, managers need to recognize that variances can have multiple causes.

Multiple Causes of Variances

Managers must not interpret variances in isolation of each other. The causes of variances in one part of the value chain can be the result of decisions made in another part of the value chain. Consider an unfavorable direct materials efficiency variance on Webb's production line. Possible operational causes of this variance across the value chain of the company are:

1. Poor design of products or processes
2. Poor work on the production line because of underskilled workers or faulty machines
3. Inappropriate assignment of labor or machines to specific jobs
4. Congestion due to scheduling a large number of rush orders from Webb's sales representatives
5. Webb's suppliers not manufacturing cloth materials of uniformly high quality

Item 5 offers an even broader reason for the cause of the unfavorable direct materials efficiency variance by considering inefficiencies in the supply chain of companies—in this case, by the cloth suppliers for Webb's jackets. Whenever possible, managers must attempt to understand the root causes of the variances.

When to Investigate Variances

Managers realize that a standard is not a single measure but rather a range of possible acceptable input quantities, costs, output quantities, or prices. Consequently, they expect small variances to arise. A variance within an acceptable range is considered to be an "in control occurrence" and calls for no investigation or action by managers. So when would managers need to investigate variances?

Frequently, managers investigate variances based on subjective judgments or rules of thumb. For critical items, such as product defects, even a small variance may prompt investigations and actions. For other items, such as direct material costs, labor costs, and repair costs, companies generally have rules such as "investigate all variances exceeding $5,000 or 25% of budgeted cost, whichever is lower." The idea is that a 4% variance in direct material costs of $1 million—a $40,000 variance—deserves more attention than a 20% variance in repair costs of $10,000—a $2,000 variance. Variance analysis is subject to the same cost-benefit test as all other phases of a management control system.

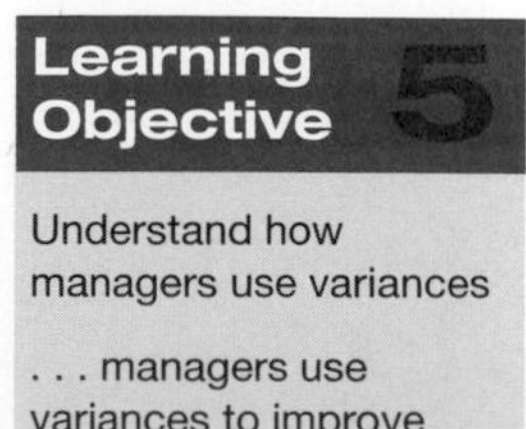

Performance Measurement Using Variances

Managers often use variance analysis when evaluating the performance of their subordinates. Two attributes of performance are commonly evaluated:

1. **Effectiveness:** the degree to which a predetermined objective or target is met—for example, sales, customer satisfaction, and quality of Motorola's new line of cell phones.
2. **Efficiency:** the relative amount of inputs used to achieve a given output level—the smaller the quantity of inputs used to make a given number of cell phones or the greater the number of cell phones made from a given quantity of input, the greater the efficiency.

As we discussed earlier, managers must be sure they understand the causes of a variance before using it for performance evaluation. Suppose a Webb purchasing manager has just negotiated a deal that results in a favorable price variance for direct materials. The deal could have achieved a favorable variance for any or all of the following reasons:

1. The purchasing manager bargained effectively with suppliers.
2. The purchasing manager secured a discount for buying in bulk with fewer purchase orders. However, buying larger quantities than necessary for the short run resulted in excessive inventory.
3. The purchasing manager accepted a bid from the lowest-priced supplier after only minimal effort to check quality amid concerns about the supplier's materials.

If the purchasing manager's performance is evaluated solely on price variances, then the evaluation will be positive. Reason 1 would support this favorable conclusion: The purchasing manager bargained effectively. Reasons 2 and 3 have short-run gains, buying in bulk or making only minimal effort to check the supplier's quality-monitoring procedures. However, these short-run gains could be offset by higher inventory storage costs or higher inspection costs and defect rates on Webb's production line, leading to unfavorable direct manufacturing labor and direct materials efficiency variances. Webb may ultimately lose more money because of reasons 2 and 3 than it gains from the favorable price variance.

Bottom line: Managers should not automatically interpret a favorable variance as "good news."

Managers benefit from variance analysis because it highlights individual aspects of performance. However, if any single performance measure (for example, a labor efficiency variance or a consumer rating report) receives excessive emphasis, managers will tend to make decisions that will cause the particular performance measure to look good. These actions may conflict with the company's overall goals, inhibiting the goals from being achieved. This faulty perspective on performance usually arises when top management designs a performance evaluation and reward system that does not emphasize total company objectives.

Organization Learning

The goal of variance analysis is for managers to understand why variances arise, to learn, and to improve future performance. For instance, to reduce the unfavorable direct materials efficiency variance, Webb's managers may seek improvements in product design, in the commitment of workers to do the job right the first time, and in the quality of supplied materials, among other improvements. Sometimes an unfavorable direct materials efficiency variance may signal a need to change product strategy, perhaps because the product cannot be made at a low enough cost. Variance analysis should not be a tool to "play the blame game" (that is, seeking a person to blame for every unfavorable variance). Rather, it should help the company learn about what happened and how to perform better in the future.

Managers need to strike a delicate balance between the two uses of variances we have discussed: performance evaluation and organization learning. Variance analysis is helpful for performance evaluation, but an overemphasis on performance evaluation and meeting individual variance targets can undermine learning and continuous improvement. Why? Because achieving the standard becomes an end in and of itself. As a result, managers will seek targets that are easy to attain rather than targets that are challenging and that require creativity and resourcefulness. For example, if performance evaluation is overemphasized, Webb's manufacturing manager will prefer an easy standard that allows workers ample time to manufacture a jacket; he will then have little incentive to improve processes and methods to reduce manufacturing time and cost.

An overemphasis on performance evaluation may also cause managers to take actions to achieve the budget and avoid an unfavorable variance, even if such actions could hurt the company in the long run. For example, the manufacturing manager may push workers to produce jackets within the time allowed, even if this action could lead to poorer quality jackets being produced, which could later hurt revenues. Such negative impacts are less likely to occur if variance analysis is seen as a way of promoting organization learning.

Continuous Improvement

Managers can also use variance analysis to create a virtuous cycle of continuous improvement. How? By repeatedly identifying causes of variances, initiating corrective actions, and evaluating results of actions. Improvement opportunities are often easier to identify when products are first produced. Once the easy opportunities have been identified ("the low-hanging fruit picked"), much more ingenuity may be required to identify successive improvement opportunities. Some companies use kaizen budgeting (Chapter 6, p. 195) to specifically target reductions in budgeted costs over successive periods. The advantage of kaizen budgeting is that it makes continuous improvement goals explicit.

Financial and Nonfinancial Performance Measures

Almost all companies use a combination of financial and nonfinancial performance measures for planning and control rather than relying exclusively on either type of measure. To control a production process, supervisors cannot wait for an accounting report with variances reported in dollars. Instead, timely nonfinancial performance measures are frequently used for control purposes in such situations. For example, a Nissan plant compiles data such as defect rates and production-schedule attainment and broadcasts them in ticker-tape fashion on screens throughout the plant.

In Webb's cutting room, cloth is laid out and cut into pieces, which are then matched and assembled. Managers exercise control in the cutting room by observing workers and by focusing on *nonfinancial measures*, such as number of square yards of cloth used to produce 1,000 jackets or percentage of jackets started and completed without requiring any rework. Webb production workers find these nonfinancial measures easy to understand. At the same time, Webb production managers will also use *financial measures* to evaluate the overall cost efficiency with which operations are being run and to help guide decisions about, say, changing the mix of inputs used in manufacturing jackets. Financial measures are often critical in a company because they indicate the economic impact of diverse physical activities. This knowledge allows managers to make trade-offs—increase the costs of one physical activity (say, cutting) to reduce the costs of another physical measure (say, defects).

We next describe how the management insights gained from standard costing and variance analysis help companies that use activity-based costing systems.

Variance Analysis and Activity-Based Costing

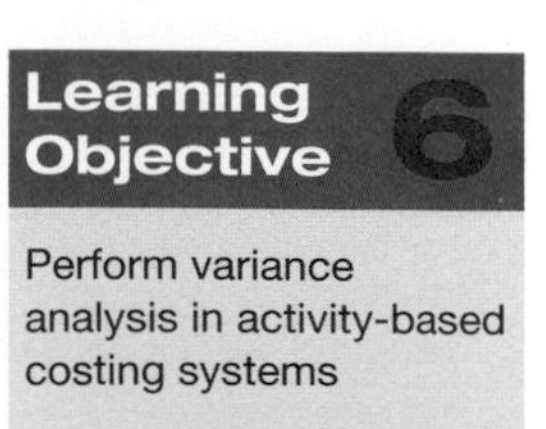

Learning Objective 6
Perform variance analysis in activity-based costing systems
. . . by comparing budgeted costs and actual costs of activities

Activity-based costing (ABC) systems focus on individual activities as the fundamental cost objects. ABC systems classify the costs of various activities into a cost hierarchy—output unit-level costs, batch-level costs, product-sustaining costs, and facility-sustaining costs (see pp. 147–148). In this section, we show how a company that has an ABC system and batch-level direct costs can benefit from variance analysis. Batch-level costs are the costs of activities related to a group of units of products or services rather than to each individual unit of product or service.

Relating Batch Costs to Product Output

Consider Lyco Brass Works, which manufactures many different types of faucets and brass fittings. Because of the wide range of products it produces, Lyco uses an activity-based costing system. In contrast, Webb uses a simple costing system because it makes only one type of jacket. One of Lyco's products is Elegance, a decorative brass faucet for home spas. Lyco produces Elegance in batches. For each product Lyco makes, it uses dedicated materials-handling labor to bring materials to the production floor, transport work in process from one work center to the next, and take the finished goods to the shipping area. Therefore, materials-handling labor costs for Elegance are direct costs of Elegance. Because the materials for a batch are moved together, materials-handling labor costs vary with number of batches rather than with number of units in a batch. Materials-handling labor costs are variable direct batch-level costs.

Information regarding Elegance for 2009 follows:

	Static-Budget Amount	Actual Result
1. Units of Elegance produced and sold	180,000	151,200
2. Batch size (units per batch)	150	140
3. Number of batches (Line 1 ÷ Line 2)	1,200	1,080
4. Materials-handling labor-hours per batch	5	5.25
5. Total materials-handling labor-hours (Line 3 × Line 4)	6,000	5,670
6. Cost per materials-handling labor-hour	$ 14	$ 14.50
7. Total materials-handling labor costs (Line 5 × Line 6)	$84,000	$82,215

To prepare the flexible budget for materials-handling labor costs, Lyco starts with the actual units of output produced, 151,200 units, and proceeds with the following steps.

Step 1: Using Budgeted Batch Size, Calculate the Number of Batches that Should Have Been Used to Produce Actual Output. At the budgeted batch size of 150 units per batch, Lyco should have produced the 151,200 units of output in 1,008 batches (151,200 units ÷ 150 units per batch).

Step 2: Using Budgeted Materials-Handling Labor-Hours per Batch, Calculate the Number of Materials-Handling Labor-Hours that Should Have Been Used. At the budgeted quantity of 5 hours per batch, 1,008 batches should have required 5,040 materials-handling labor-hours (1,008 batches × 5 hours per batch).

Step 3: Using Budgeted Cost per Materials-Handling Labor-Hour, Calculate the Flexible-Budget Amount for Materials-Handling Labor-Hours. The flexible-budget amount is 5,040 materials-handling labor-hours × $14 budgeted cost per materials-handling labor-hour = $70,560.

Note how the flexible-budget calculations for materials-handling labor costs focus on batch-level quantities (materials-handling labor-hours per batch rather than per unit). The flexible-budget variance for materials-handling labor costs can then be calculated as:

$$
\begin{aligned}
\text{Flexible-budget variance} &= \text{Actual costs} - \text{Flexible-budget costs} \\
&= (5{,}670 \text{ hours} \times \$14.50 \text{ per hour}) - (5{,}040 \text{ hours} \times \$14 \text{ per hour}) \\
&= \$82{,}215 - \$70{,}560 \\
&= \$11{,}655 \text{ U}
\end{aligned}
$$

The unfavorable variance indicates that materials-handling labor costs were $11,655 higher than the flexible-budget target.

Price and Efficiency Variances

We can get some insight into the possible reasons for this $11,655 unfavorable variance by examining the price and efficiency components of the flexible-budget variance.

$$
\begin{aligned}
\text{Price variance} &= \left(\begin{array}{c}\text{Actual price}\\ \text{of input}\end{array} - \begin{array}{c}\text{Budgeted price}\\ \text{of input}\end{array}\right) \times \begin{array}{c}\text{Actual quantity}\\ \text{of input}\end{array} \\
&= (\$14.50 \text{ per hour} - \$14 \text{ per hour}) \times 5{,}670 \text{ hours} \\
&= \$0.50 \text{ per hour} \times 5{,}670 \text{ hours} \\
&= \$2{,}835 \text{ U}
\end{aligned}
$$

The unfavorable price variance for materials-handling labor indicates that the \$14.50 actual cost per materials-handling labor-hour exceeds the \$14.00 budgeted cost per materials-handling labor-hour. This variance could be the result of Lyco's human resources manager negotiating wage rates less skillfully or of wage rates increasing unexpectedly due to scarcity of labor.

$$\text{Efficiency variance} = \left(\begin{array}{c}\text{Actual}\\ \text{quantity of}\\ \text{input used}\end{array} - \begin{array}{c}\text{Budgeted quantity}\\ \text{of input allowed}\\ \text{for actual output}\end{array}\right) \times \begin{array}{c}\text{Budgeted price}\\ \text{of input}\end{array}$$

$$= (5{,}670 \text{ hours} - 5{,}040 \text{ hours}) \times \$14 \text{ per hour}$$

$$= 630 \text{ hours} \times \$14 \text{ per hour}$$

$$= \$8{,}820 \text{ U}$$

The unfavorable efficiency variance indicates that the 5,670 actual materials-handling labor-hours exceeded the 5,040 budgeted materials-handling labor-hours for actual output. Possible reasons for the unfavorable efficiency variance are:

- Smaller actual batch sizes of 140 units, instead of the budgeted batch sizes of 150 units, resulting in Lyco producing the 151,200 units in 1,080 batches instead of 1,008 (151,200 ÷ 150) batches
- Higher actual materials-handling labor-hours per batch of 5.25 hours instead of budgeted materials-handling labor-hours of 5 hours

Reasons for smaller-than-budgeted batch sizes could include quality problems when batch sizes exceed 140 faucets and high costs of carrying inventory.

Possible reasons for larger actual materials-handling labor-hours per batch are:

- Inefficient layout of the Elegance production line
- Materials-handling labor having to wait at work centers before picking up or delivering materials
- Unmotivated, inexperienced, and underskilled employees
- Very tight standards for materials-handling time

Identifying the reasons for the efficiency variance helps Lyco's managers develop a plan for improving materials-handling labor efficiency.

Focus on Hierarchy

Flexible-budget quantity computations focus at the appropriate level of the cost hierarchy. For example, because materials handling is a batch-level cost, the flexible-budget quantity calculations are made at the batch level—the quantity of materials-handling labor-hours that Lyco should have used based on the number of batches it should have used to produce the actual quantity of 151,200 units. If a cost had been a product-sustaining cost—such as product design cost—the flexible-budget quantity computations would focus at the product-sustaining level, for example, by evaluating the actual complexity of product design relative to the budget.

Learning Objective 7

Describe benchmarking and explain its role in cost management

. . . benchmarking compares actual performance against the best levels of performance

Benchmarking and Variance Analysis

The budgeted amounts in the Webb Company and Lyco Brass Works illustrations are based on analysis of operations within their own respective companies. We now turn to the situation in which companies develop standards based on an analysis of operations at other companies. **Benchmarking** is the continuous process of comparing the levels of performance in producing products and services and executing activities against the best levels of performance in competing companies or in companies having similar processes. When benchmarks are used as standards, managers and management accountants know that the company will be competitive in the marketplace if it can attain the standards.

Companies develop benchmarks and calculate variances on items that are the most important to their businesses. Consider the cost per available seat mile (ASM) for United Airlines; ASMs equal the total seats in a plane multiplied by the distance traveled, and are a measure of airline size. Assume United uses data from each of eight competing U.S. airlines in its benchmark cost comparisons. Summary data are in Exhibit 7-5. The benchmark companies are ranked from lowest to highest operating cost per ASM in column 1. Also reported in Exhibit 7-5 are operating revenue per ASM, operating income per ASM, labor cost per ASM, fuel cost per ASM, and total available seat miles.

How well did United manage its costs? The answer depends on which specific benchmark is being used for comparison. United's actual operating cost of $0.1320 per ASM is above the average operating cost of $0.1151 per ASM of the eight other airlines. Moreover, United's operating cost per ASM is 68.8% higher than JetBlue Airways, the lowest-cost competitor at $0.0782 per ASM [($0.1320 − $0.0782) ÷ $0.0782 = 68.8%)]. So why is United's operating cost per ASM so high? Column 5 suggests that labor cost is one reason ($0.0298 for United compared with $0.0193 for JetBlue). These benchmarking data alert management at United that they need to cut labor costs to become more cost competitive.

Using benchmarks such as those in Exhibit 7-5 is not without problems. Finding appropriate benchmarks is a major issue in implementing benchmarking. Many companies purchase benchmark data from consulting firms. Another problem is ensuring the benchmark numbers are comparable. In other words, there needs to be an "apples to apples" comparison. Differences can exist across companies in their strategies, inventory costing methods, depreciation methods, and so on. For example, JetBlue serves fewer cities and has mostly long-haul flights compared with United, which serves almost all major U.S. cities and several international cities and has both long-haul and short-haul flights. Southwest Airlines differs from United because it specializes in short-haul direct flights and offers fewer services on board its planes. Because United's strategy is different from the strategies of JetBlue and Southwest, one might expect its cost per ASM to be different too. United's strategy is more comparable to the strategies of American, Continental, Delta, Northwest, and U.S. Airways. Note that its costs per ASM are more competitive with these airlines. But United competes head-to-head with JetBlue and Southwest in several cities and markets, so it still needs to benchmark against these carriers as well.

United's management accountants can use benchmarking data to address several questions. How do factors such as plane size and type, or the duration of flights, affect the cost per ASM? Do airlines differ in their fixed cost/variable cost structures? Can performance

Exhibit 7-5 Available Seat Mile (ASM) Benchmark Comparison of United Airlines with Eight Other Airlines

File Edit View Insert Format Tools Data Window Help

	A	B	C	D	E	F	G
1		Operating Cost	Operating Revenue	Operating Income	Fuel Cost	Labor Cost	Total ASMs
2		per ASM	per ASM	per ASM	per ASM	per ASM	(Millions)
3	Airline	(1)	(2)	(3) = (2) - (1)	(4)	(5)	(6)
4							
5	United Airlines	$0.1320	$0.1352	$0.0031	$0.0337	$0.0298	143,095
6	Airlines used as benchmarkers:						
7	JetBlue Airways	$0.0782	$0.0826	$0.0044	$0.0263	$0.0193	28,594
8	Southwest Airlines	$0.0880	$0.0981	$0.0101	$0.0231	$0.0329	92,663
9	Continental Airlines	$0.1141	$0.1184	$0.0042	$0.0274	$0.0259	110,918
10	Delta Airlines	$0.1156	$0.1160	$0.0004	$0.0292	$0.0279	147,995
11	Alaska Airlines	$0.1198	$0.1157	- $0.0041	$0.0325	$0.0319	23,278
12	American Airlines	$1.1246	$0.1293	$0.0047	$0.0332	$0.0356	174,000
13	Northwest Airlines	$0.1380	$0.1466	$0.0086	$0.0395	$0.0310	85,738
14	U.S. Airways/American West	$0.1429	$0.1501	$0.0072	$0.0327	$0.0271	76,983
15	Average of airlines						
16	used as benchmarks	$0.1151	$0.1196	$0.0044	$0.0305	$0.0290	92,521
17							
18							
19	*Source:* Individual companines' 10-K reports for the year ending December 31,2006						

be improved by rerouting flights, using different types of aircraft on different routes, or changing the frequency or timing of specific flights? What explains revenue differences per ASM across airlines? Is it differences in perceived quality of service or differences in competitive power at specific airports? Management accountants are more valuable to managers when they use benchmarking data to provide insight into *why* costs or revenues differ across companies, or within plants of the same company, as distinguished from simply reporting the magnitude of such differences.

Problem for Self-Study

O'Shea Company manufactures ceramic vases. It uses its standard costing system when developing its flexible-budget amounts. In April 2009, 2,000 finished units were produced. The following information relates to its two direct manufacturing cost categories: direct materials and direct manufacturing labor.

Direct materials used were 4,400 kilograms (kg). The standard direct materials input allowed for one output unit is 2 kilograms at $15 per kilogram. O'Shea purchased 5,000 kilograms of materials at $16.50 per kilogram, a total of $82,500. (This Problem for Self-Study illustrates how to calculate direct materials variances when the quantity of materials *purchased* in a period differs from the quantity of materials *used* in that period.)

Actual direct manufacturing labor-hours were 3,250, at a total cost of $66,300. Standard manufacturing labor time allowed is 1.5 hours per output unit, and the standard direct manufacturing labor cost is $20 per hour.

Required

1. Calculate the direct materials price variance and efficiency variance, and the direct manufacturing labor price variance and efficiency variance. Base the direct materials price variance on a flexible budget for *actual quantity purchased*, but base the direct materials efficiency variance on a flexible budget for *actual quantity used*.
2. Prepare journal entries for a standard costing system that isolates variances at the earliest possible time.

Solution

1. Exhibit 7-6 shows how the columnar presentation of variances introduced in Exhibit 7-3 can be adjusted for the difference in timing between purchase and use of materials. Note, in particular, the two sets of computations in column 2 for direct materials—the $75,000 for direct materials purchased and the $66,000 for direct materials used. The direct materials price variance is calculated on purchases so that managers responsible for the purchase can immediately identify and isolate reasons for the variance and initiate any desired corrective action. The efficiency variance is the responsibility of the production manager, so this variance is identified only at the time materials are used.
2. Journal entries:

Account	Debit	Credit
Materials Control (5,000 kg × $15 per kg)	75,000	
Direct Materials Price Variance (5,000 kg × $1.50 per kg)	7,500	
Accounts Payable Control (5,000 kg × $16.50 per kg)		82,500
Work in Process Control (2,000 units × 2 kg per unit × $15 per kg)	60,000	
Direct Materials Efficiency Variance (400 kg × $15 per kg)	6,000	
Materials Control (4,400 kg × $15 per kg)		66,000
Work in Process Control (2,000 units × 1.5 hours per unit × $20 per hour)	60,000	
Direct Manufacturing Labor Price Variance (3,250 hours × $0.40 per hour)	1,300	
Direct Manufacturing Labor Efficiency Variance (250 hours × $20 per hour)	5,000	
Wages Payable Control (3,250 hours × $20.40 per hour)		66,300

Note: All the variances are debits because they are unfavorable and therefore reduce operating income.

Exhibit 7-6 Columnar Presentation of Variance Analysis for O'Shea Company: Direct Materials and Direct Manufacturing Labor for April 2009[a]

Level 3 Analysis

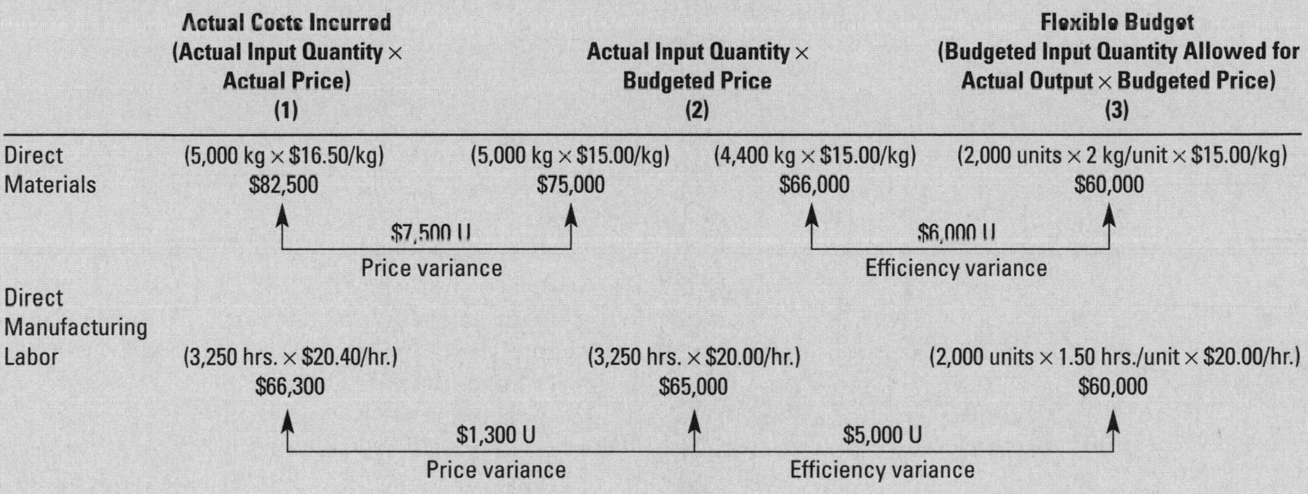

	Actual Costs Incurred (Actual Input Quantity × Actual Price) (1)		Actual Input Quantity × Budgeted Price (2)		Flexible Budget (Budgeted Input Quantity Allowed for Actual Output × Budgeted Price) (3)
Direct Materials	(5,000 kg × $16.50/kg) $82,500		(5,000 kg × $15.00/kg) $75,000 / (4,400 kg × $15.00/kg) $66,000		(2,000 units × 2 kg/unit × $15.00/kg) $60,000
		$7,500 U Price variance		$6,000 U Efficiency variance	
Direct Manufacturing Labor	(3,250 hrs. × $20.40/hr.) $66,300		(3,250 hrs. × $20.00/hr.) $65,000		(2,000 units × 1.50 hrs./unit × $20.00/hr.) $60,000
		$1,300 U Price variance		$5,000 U Efficiency variance	

[a]F = favorable effect on operating income; U = unfavorable effect on operating income.

Decision Points

The following question-and-answer format summarizes the chapter's learning objectives. Each decision presents a key question related to a learning objective. The guidelines are the answer to that question.

Decision	Guidelines
1. How does a flexible budget differ from a static budget, and why should companies use flexible budgets?	A static budget is based on the level of output planned at the start of the budget period. A flexible budget is adjusted (flexed) to recognize the actual output level of the budget period. Flexible budgets help managers gain more insight into the causes of variances than is available from static budgets.
2. How can managers develop a flexible budget and compute the flexible-budget variance and the sales-volume variance?	Managers use a three-step procedure to develop a flexible budget. When all costs are either variable with respect to output units or fixed, these three steps require only information about budgeted selling price, budgeted variable cost per output unit, budgeted fixed costs, and actual quantity of output units. The static-budget variance can be subdivided into a flexible-budget variance (the difference between an actual result and the corresponding flexible-budget amount) and a sales-volume variance (the difference between the flexible-budget amount and the corresponding static-budget amount).
3. What is a standard cost and what are its purposes?	A standard cost is a carefully determined cost used as a benchmark for judging performance. The purposes of a standard cost are to exclude past inefficiencies and to take into account changes expected to occur in the budget period.
4. Why should a company calculate price and efficiency variables?	The computation of price and efficiency variances helps managers gain insight into two different—but not independent—aspects of performance. The price variance focuses on the difference between actual input price and budgeted input price. The efficiency variance focuses on the difference between actual quantity of input and budgeted quantity of input allowed for actual output.

5. How do managers use variances?

Managers use variances for control, decision implementation, performance evaluation, organization learning, and continuous improvement. When using variances for these purposes, managers consider several variances together rather than focusing only on an individual variance.

6. Can variance analysis be used with an activity-based costing system?

Variance analysis can be applied to activity costs (such as setup costs) to gain insight into why actual activity costs differ from activity costs in the static budget or in the flexible budget. Interpreting cost variances for different activities requires understanding whether the costs are output unit-level, batch-level, product-sustaining, or facility-sustaining costs.

7. What is benchmarking and why is it useful?

Benchmarking is the process of comparing the level of performance in producing products and services and executing activities against the best levels of performance in competing companies or companies with similar processes. Benchmarking measures how well a company and its managers are doing in comparison to other organizations.

TERMS TO LEARN

This chapter and the Glossary at the end of the book contain definitions of:

benchmarking **(p. 244)**
budgeted performance **(p. 225)**
effectiveness **(p. 241)**
efficiency **(p. 241)**
efficiency variance **(p. 233)**
favorable variance **(p. 227)**
flexible budget **(p. 228)**
flexible-budget variance **(p. 228)**
input-price variance **(p. 233)**
management by exception **(p. 225)**
price variance **(p. 233)**
rate variance **(p. 233)**
sales-volume variance **(p. 228)**
selling-price variance **(p. 230)**
standard **(p. 232)**
standard cost **(p. 232)**
standard input **(p. 232)**
standard price **(p. 232)**
static budget **(p. 227)**
static-budget variance **(p. 227)**
unfavorable variance **(p. 227)**
usage variance **(p. 233)**
variance **(p. 225)**

ASSIGNMENT MATERIAL

Questions

7-1 What is the relationship between management by exception and variance analysis?

7-2 What are two possible sources of information a company might use to compute the budgeted amount in variance analysis?

7-3 Distinguish between a favorable variance and an unfavorable variance.

7-4 What is the key difference between a static budget and a flexible budget?

7-5 Why might managers find a flexible-budget analysis more informative than a static-budget analysis?

7-6 Describe the steps in developing a flexible budget.

7-7 List four reasons for using standard costs.

7-8 How might a manager gain insight into the causes of a flexible-budget variance for direct materials?

7-9 List three causes of a favorable direct materials price variance.

7-10 Describe three reasons for an unfavorable direct manufacturing labor efficiency variance.

7-11 How does variance analysis help in continuous improvement?

7-12 Why might an analyst examining variances in the production area look beyond that business function for explanations of those variances?

7-13 Comment on the following statement made by a plant manager: "Meetings with my plant accountant are frustrating. All he wants to do is pin the blame on someone for the many variances he reports."

7-14 How can variances be used to analyze costs in individual activity areas?

7-15 "Benchmarking against other companies enables a company to identify the lowest-cost producer. This amount should become the performance measure for next year." Do you agree?

Exercises

7-16 Flexible budget. Brabham Enterprises manufactures tires for the Formula I motor racing circuit. For August 2009, it budgeted to manufacture and sell 3,000 tires at a variable cost of $74 per tire and total fixed costs of $54,000. The budgeted selling price was $110 per tire. Actual results in August 2009 were 2,800 tires manufactured and sold at a selling price of $112 per tire. The actual total variable costs were $229,600, and the actual total fixed costs were $50,000.

Required

1. Prepare a performance report (akin to Exhibit 7-2, p. 229) that uses a flexible budget and a static budget.
2. Comment on the results in requirement 1.

7-17 Flexible budget. Connor Company's budgeted prices for direct materials, direct manufacturing labor, and direct marketing (distribution) labor per attaché case are $40, $8, and $12, respectively. The president is pleased with the following performance report:

	Actual Costs	Static Budget	Variance
Direct materials	$364,000	$400,000	$36,000 F
Direct manufacturing labor	78,000	80,000	2,000 F
Direct marketing (distribution) labor	110,000	120,000	10,000 F

Actual output was 8,800 attaché cases. Assume all three direct-cost items above are variable costs.

Required

Is the president's pleasure justified? Prepare a revised performance report that uses a flexible budget and a static budget.

7-18 Flexible-budget preparation and analysis. Bank Management Printers, Inc., produces luxury checkbooks with three checks and stubs per page. Each checkbook is designed for an individual customer and is ordered through the customer's bank. The company's operating budget for September 2009 included these data:

Number of checkbooks	15,000
Selling price per book	$ 20
Variable cost per book	$ 8
Fixed costs for the month	$145,000

The actual results for September 2009 were:

Number of checkbooks produced and sold	12,000
Average selling price per book	$ 21
Variable cost per book	$ 7
Fixed costs for the month	$150,000

The executive vice president of the company observed that the operating income for September was much lower than anticipated, despite a higher-than-budgeted selling price and a lower-than-budgeted variable cost per unit. As the company's management accountant, you have been asked to provide explanations for the disappointing September results.

Bank Management develops its flexible budget on the basis of budgeted per-output-unit revenue and per-output-unit variable costs without detailed analysis of budgeted inputs.

Required

1. Prepare a static-budget-based variance analysis of the September performance.
2. Prepare a flexible-budget-based variance analysis of the September performance.
3. Why might Bank Management find the flexible-budget-based variance analysis more informative than the static-budget-based variance analysis? Explain your answer.

7-19 Flexible budget, working backward. The Clarkson Company produces engine parts for car manufacturers. A new accountant intern at Clarkson has accidentally deleted the calculations on the company's variance analysis calculations for the year ended December 31, 2009. The following table is what remains of the data.

File Edit View Insert Format Tools Data Window Help

	A	B	C	D	E	F
1	Performance Report, Year Ended December 31, 2009					
2						
3		Actual Results	Flexible-Budget Variances	Flexible Budget	Sales-Volume Variances	Static Budget
4	Units sold	130,000				120,000
5	Revenues (sales)	$715,000				$420,000
6	Variable costs	515,000				240,000
7	Contribution margin	200,000				180,000
8	Fixed costs	140,000				120,000
9	Operating income	$ 60,000				$ 60,000

If you want to use Excel to solve this exercise, go to the Excel Lab at **www.prenhall.com/horngren/cost13e** and download the template for Exercise 7-19.

Required

1. Calculate all the required variances. (If your work is accurate, you will find that the total static-budget variance is $0.)
2. What are the actual and budgeted selling prices? What are the actual and budgeted variable costs per unit?
3. Review the variances you have calculated and discuss possible causes and potential problems. What is the important lesson learned here?

7-20 Flexible-budget and sales volume variances. Marron, Inc. produces the basic fillings used in many popular frozen desserts and treats—vanilla and chocolate ice creams, puddings, meringues, and fudge. Marron uses standard costing and carries over no inventory from one month to the next. The ice-cream product group's results for June 2009 were:

	A	B	C
1	**Performance Report, June 2009**		
2		**Actual Results**	**Static Budget**
3	Units (pounds)	525,000	500,000
4	Revenues	$3,360,000	$3,250,000
5	Variable manufacturing costs	1,890,000	1,750,000
6	Contribution margin	$1,470,000	$1,500,000

Ted Levine, the business manager for ice-cream products, is pleased that more pounds of ice cream were sold than budgeted and that revenues were up. Unfortunately, variable manufacturing costs went up too. The bottom line is that contribution margin declined by $30,000, which is less than 1% of the budgeted revenues of $3,250,000. Overall, Levine feels that the business is running fine.

If you want to use Excel to solve this exercise, go to the Excel Lab at **www.prenhall.com/horngren/cost13e** and download the template for Exercise 7-20.

Required

1. Calculate the static-budget variance in units, revenues, variable manufacturing costs, and contribution margin? What percentage is each static-budget variance relative to its static-budget amount?
2. Break down each static-budget variance into a flexible-budget variance and a sales-volume variance.
3. Calculate the selling-price variance.
4. Assume the role of management accountant at Marron. How would you present the results to Ted Levine? Should he be more concerned? If so, why?

7-21 Price and efficiency variances. Peterson Foods manufactures pumpkin scones. For January 2009, it budgeted to purchase and use 15,000 pounds of pumpkin at $0.89 a pound. Actual purchases and usage for January 2009 were 16,000 pounds at $0.82 a pound. It budgets for 60,000 pumpkin scones. Actual output was 60,800 pumpkin scones.

Required

1. Compute the flexible-budget variance.
2. Compute the price and efficiency variances.
3. Comment on the above results and provide a possible explanation for them.

7-22 Materials and manufacturing labor variances. Consider the following data collected for Great Homes, Inc.:

	Direct Materials	Direct Manufacturing Labor
Cost incurred: actual inputs × actual prices	$200,000	$90,000
Actual inputs × standard prices	214,000	86,000
Standard inputs allowed for actual output × standard prices	225,000	80,000

Required Compute the price, efficiency, and flexible-budget variances for direct materials and direct manufacturing labor.

7-23 Direct materials and direct manufacturing labor variances. GloriaDee, Inc., designs and manufactures T-shirts. It sells its T-shirts to brand-name clothes retailers in lots of one dozen. GloriaDee's May 2009 static budget and actual results for direct inputs are:

Static Budget	
Number of T-shirt lots (1 lot = 1 dozen)	500
Per lot of T-shirts:	
Direct materials	12 meters at $1.50 per meter = $18.00
Direct manufacturing labor	2 hours at $8.00 per hour = $16.00
Actual Results	
Number of T-shirt lots sold	550
Total direct inputs:	
Direct materials	7,260 meters at $1.75 per meter = $12,705.00
Direct manufacturing labor	1,045 hours at $8.10 per hour = $8,464.50

GloriaDee has a policy of analyzing all input variances when they add up to more than 10% of the total cost of materials and labor in the flexible budget, and this is true in May 2009. The production manager discusses the sources of the variances: "A new type of material was purchased in May. This led to faster cutting and sewing, but the workers used more material than usual as they learned to work with it. For now, the standards are fine."

Required

1. Calculate the direct materials and direct manufacturing labor price and efficiency variances in May 2009. What is the total flexible-budget variance for both inputs (direct materials and direct manufacturing labor) combined? What percentage is this variance of the total cost of direct materials and direct manufacturing labor in the flexible budget?
2. Gloria Denham, the CEO, is concerned about the input variances. But, she likes the quality and feel of the new material and agrees to use it for one more year. In May 2010, GloriaDee again produces 550 lots of T-shirts. Relative to May 2009, 2% less direct material is used, direct material price is down 5%, and 2% less direct manufacturing labor is used. Labor price has remained the same as in May 2009. Calculate the direct materials and direct manufacturing labor price and efficiency variances in May 2010. What is the total flexible-budget variance for both inputs (direct materials and direct manufacturing labor) combined? What percentage is this variance of the total cost of direct materials and direct manufacturing labor in the flexible budget?
3. Comment on the May 2010 results. Would you continue the "experiment" of using the new material?

7-24 Price and efficiency variances, journal entries. The Monroe Corporation manufactures lamps. It has set up the following standards per finished unit for direct materials and direct manufacturing labor:

Direct materials: 10 lbs. at $4.50 per lb.	$45.00
Direct manufacturing labor: 0.5 hour at $30 per hour	15.00

The number of finished units budgeted for January 2009 was 10,000; 9,850 units were actually produced.

Actual results in January 2009 were:

Direct materials: 98,055 lbs. used	
Direct manufacturing labor: 4,900 hours	$154,350

Assume that there was no beginning inventory of either direct materials or finished units.

During the month, materials purchases amounted to 100,000 lbs., at a total cost of $465,000. Input price variances are isolated upon purchase. Input-efficiency variances are isolated at the time of usage.

Required

1. Compute the January 2009 price and efficiency variances of direct materials and direct manufacturing labor.
2. Prepare journal entries to record the variances in requirement 1.
3. Comment on the January 2009 price and efficiency variances of Monroe Corporation.
4. Why might Monroe calculate direct materials price variances and direct materials efficiency variances with reference to different points in time?

7-25 Continuous improvement (continuation of 7-24). The Monroe Corporation sets monthly standard costs using a continuous-improvement approach. In January 2009, the standard direct material cost is $45 per unit and the standard direct manufacturing labor cost is $15 per unit. Due to more efficient operations, the standard quantities for February 2009 are set at 0.988 of the standard quantities for January. In March 2009, the standard quantities are set at 0.988 of the standard quantities for February 2009. Assume the same information for March 2009 as in Exercise 7-24, except for these revised standard quantities.

Required

1. Compute the March 2009 standard quantities for direct materials and direct manufacturing labor.
2. Compute the March 2009 price and efficiency variances for direct materials and direct manufacturing labor.

7-26 Materials and manufacturing labor variances, standard costs. Dunn, Inc. is a privately held furniture manufacturer. For August 2009, Dunn had the following standards for one of its products, a wicker chair:

	Standards per Chair
Direct materials	2 square yards of input at $5 per square yard
Direct manufacturing labor	0.5 hour of input at $10 per hour

The following data were compiled regarding *actual performance*: actual output units (chairs) produced, 2,000; square yards of input purchased and used, 3,700; price per square yard, $5.10; direct manufacturing labor costs, $8,820; actual hours of input, 900; labor price per hour, $9.80.

1. Show computations of price and efficiency variances for direct materials and direct manufacturing labor. Give a plausible explanation of why each variance occurred.
2. Suppose 6,000 square yards of materials were purchased (at $5.10 per square yard), even though only 3,700 square yards were used. Suppose further that variances are identified at their most timely control point; accordingly, direct materials price variances are isolated and traced at the time of purchase to the Purchasing Department rather than to the Production Department. Compute the price and efficiency variances under this approach.

7-27 Journal entries and T-accounts (continuation of 7-26). Prepare journal entries and post them to T-accounts for all transactions in Exercise 7-26, including requirement 2. Summarize how these journal entries differ from the normal-costing entries described in Chapter 4, pages 110–112.

7-28 Flexible budget. (Refer to data in Exercise 7-26). Suppose the static budget was for 2,500 units of output. Actual output was 2,000 units. The variances are shown in the following report:

	Actual Results	Static Budget	Variance
Direct materials	$18,870	$25,000	$6,130 F
Direct manufacturing labor	$ 8,820	$12,500	$3,680 F

Required What are the price, efficiency, and sales-volume variances for direct materials and direct manufacturing labor? Based on your results, explain why the static budget was not achieved.

7-29 Activity-based costing, flexible-budget variances for finance-function activities. FastGrocery.com, an online company that delivers groceries to its customers, has the following information for its three finance activities in 2008:

			Rate per Unit of Cost Driver	
Activity	Level Activity	Driver Cost	Static Budget	Actual
Receivables	Output unit	Remittances	$0.639	$0.80
Payables	Batch	Invoices	2.900	2.85
Travel expenses	Batch	Travel claims	7.600	7.45

The output measure is the number of deliveries, which is the same as the number of remittances. The following is additional information.

	Static-Budget Amounts	Actual Amount
Number of deliveries	1,000,000	945,000
Batch size in terms of deliveries:		
Payables	5	4.468
Travel expenses	500	501.587

Required

1. Calculate the flexible-budget variance for each activity in 2008.
2. Calculate the price and efficiency variances for each activity in 2008.

Problems

7-30 Flexible budget, direct materials and direct manufacturing labor variances. Tuscany Statuary manufactures bust statues of famous historical figures. All statues are the same size. Each unit requires the same amount of resources. The following information is from the static budget for 2009:

Expected production and sales	5,000 units
Direct materials	50,000 pounds
Direct manufacturing labor	20,000 hours
Total fixed costs	$1,000,000

Standard quantities, standard prices, and standard unit costs follow for direct materials and direct manufacturing labor.

	Standard Quantity	Standard Price	Standard Unit Cost
Direct materials	10 pounds	$10 per pound	$100
Direct manufacturing labor	4 hours	$40 per hour	$160

During 2009, actual number of units produced and sold was 6,000. Actual cost of direct materials used was $594,000, based on 54,000 pounds purchased at $11 per pound. Direct manufacturing labor-hours actually used were 25,000, at the rate of $38 per hour. As a result, actual direct manufacturing labor costs were $950,000. Actual fixed costs were $1,005,000. There were no beginning or ending inventories.

Required

1. Calculate the sales-volume variance and flexible-budget variance for each cost category.
2. Compute price and efficiency variances for direct materials and direct manufacturing labor.

7-31 Variance analysis, nonmanufacturing setting

Stevie McQueen has run Lightning Car Detailing for the past 10 years. His static budget and actual results for June 2011 are provided below. Stevie has one employee who has been with him for all ten years that he has been in business. He has not been as lucky with his second and third employees. Stevie is hiring new employees in those positions almost every second month. It usually takes 2 hours to detail a vehicle. It takes as long for the seasoned employee as for the new ones, as the former tends to put more into the job. Stevie pays his long-term employee $20 per hour and the other two employees $10 per hour. Stevie pays all employees for 2 hours of work on each car, regardless of how long the work actually takes them. There were no wage increases in June.

Lightning Car Detailing
Actual and Budgeted Income Statements
For the month ended June 30, 2011

	Budget	Actual
Cars detailed	200	225
Revenue	$30,000	$39,375
Variable costs		
Costs of supplies	1,500	2,250
Labor	5,600	6,000
Total variable costs	7,100	8,250
Contribution margin	22,900	31,125
Fixed costs	9,500	9,500
Operating income	$13,400	$21,625

Required

1. Prepare a statement of the static budget variances that Stevie would be interested in.
2. Compute any flexible budget variances that you believe would be appropriate.
3. What information, in addition to that provided in the income statements, would you want Stevie to gather, if you wanted to improve operational efficiency?
4. How many cars, on average, did Stevie budget for each employee? How many cars did they actually detail?
5. What advice would you give Stevie about motivating his employees?

7-32 Comprehensive variance analysis, responsibility issues. (CMA, adapted) Styles, Inc. manufactures a full line of well-known sunglasses frames and lenses. Styles uses a standard costing system to set attainable standards for direct materials, labor, and overhead costs. Styles reviews and revises standards annually, as necessary. Department managers, whose evaluations and bonuses are affected by their department's performance, are held responsible to explain variances in their department performance reports.

Recently, the manufacturing variances in the Image prestige line of sunglasses have caused some concern. For no apparent reason, unfavorable materials and labor variances have occurred. At the monthly staff meeting, Jack Barton, manager of the Image line, will be expected to explain his variances and suggest ways of improving performance. Barton will be asked to explain the following performance report for 2008:

	Actual Results	Static-Budget Amounts
Units sold	7,275	7,500
Revenues	$596,550	$600,000
Variable manufacturing costs	351,965	324,000
Fixed manufacturing costs	108,398	112,500
Gross margin	136,187	163,500

Barton collected the following information:

Three items comprised the standard variable manufacturing costs in 2008:

- Direct materials: Frames. Static budget cost of $49,500. The standard input for 2008 is 3.00 ounces per unit.
- Direct materials: Lenses. Static budget costs of $139,500. The standard input for 2008 is 6.00 ounces per unit.
- Direct manufacturing labor: Static budget costs of $135,000. The standard input for 2008 is 1.20 hours per unit.

Assume there are no variable manufacturing overhead costs.

The actual variable manufacturing costs in 2008 were:

- Direct materials: Frames. Actual costs of $55,872. Actual ounces used were 3.20 ounces per unit.
- Direct materials: Lenses. Actual costs of $150,738. Actual ounces used were 7.00 ounces per unit.
- Direct manufacturing labor: Actual costs of $145,355. The actual labor rate was $14.80 per hour.

Required

1. Prepare a report that includes:
   a. Selling-price variance
   b. Sales-volume variance and flexible-budget variance for operating income in the format of the analysis in Exhibit 7-2
   c. Price and efficiency variances for:
      - Direct materials: frames
      - Direct materials: lenses
      - Direct manufacturing labor
2. Give three possible explanations for each of the three price and efficiency variances at Styles in requirement 1c.

7-33 Possible causes for price and efficiency variances

You are a student preparing for a job interview with a Fortune 100 consumer products manufacturer. You are applying for a job in the Finance Department. This company is known for its rigorous case-based interview process. One of the students who successfully obtained a job with them upon graduation last year advised you to "know your variances cold!" When you inquired further, she told you that she had been asked to pretend that she was investigating wage and materials variances. Per her advice, you have been studying the causes and consequences of variances. You are excited when you walk in and find that the first case deals with variance analysis. You are given the following data for May for a detergent bottling plant located in Mexico:

Actual	
Bottles filled	360,000
Direct materials used in production	6,000,000 ozs
Actual direct material cost	2,125,000 pesos
Actual direct manufacturing labor-hours	22,040 hours
Actual direct labor cost	664,940 pesos
Standards	
Purchase price of direct materials	0.35 pesos/oz
Bottle size	15 oz
Wage rate	29.30 pesos/hour
Bottles per minute	0.50

Required

Please respond to the following questions as if you were in an interview situation:

1. Calculate the materials efficiency and price variance, and the wage and labor efficiency variances for the month of May.
2. You are given the following context: "Union organizers are targeting our detergent bottling plant in Puebla, Mexico for a union." Can you provide a better explanation for the variances that you have calculated on the basis of this information?

7-34 Material cost variances, use of variances for performance evaluation

Katharine Stanley is the owner of Better Bikes, a company that produces high quality cross-country bicycles. Better Bikes participates in a supply chain that consists of suppliers, manufacturers, distributors, and elite bicycle shops. For several years Better Bikes has purchased titanium from suppliers in the supply chain. Better Bikes uses titanium for the bicycle frames because it is stronger and lighter than other metals and therefore increases the quality of the bicycle. Earlier this year, Better Bikes hired Michael Scott, a recent graduate from State University, as purchasing manager. Michael believed that he could reduce costs if he purchased titanium from an on-line marketplace at a lower price.

Better Bikes established the following standards based upon their experience with their previous suppliers. The standards are:

Cost of titanium	$20 per pound
Titanium used per bicycle	8 lbs

Actual results for the first month using the online supplier of titanium are:

Bicycles produced	500
Titanium purchased	6000 lbs for $108,000
Titanium used in production	5000 lbs.

Required

1. Compute the direct materials price and efficiency variances.
2. What factors can explain the variances identified in requirement 1? Could any other variances be affected?
3. Was switching suppliers a good idea for Better Bikes? Explain why or why not.
4. Should Michael Scott's performance evaluation be based solely on price variances? Should the production manager's evaluation be based solely on efficiency variances? Why it is important for Katharine Stanley to understand the causes of a variance before she evaluates performance?
5. Other than performance evaluation, what reasons are there for calculating variances?
6. What future problems could result from Better Bikes' decision to buy a lower quality of titanium from the on-line marketplace?

7-35 Direct manufacturing labor and direct materials variances, missing data. (CMA, heavily adapted). Morro Bay Surfboards manufactures fiberglass surfboards. The standard cost of direct materials and direct manufacturing labor is $100 per board. This includes 20 pounds of direct materials, at the budgeted price of $2 per pound, and five hours of direct manufacturing labor, at the budgeted rate of $12 per hour. Following are additional data for the month of July:

Units completed	6,000 units
Direct material purchases	150,000 pounds
Cost of direct material purchases	$292,500
Actual direct manufacturing labor-hours	32,000 hours
Actual direct-labor cost	$368,000
Direct materials efficiency variance	$ 12,500 U

There were no beginning inventories.

Required

1. Compute direct manufacturing labor variances for July.
2. Compute the actual pounds of direct materials used in production in July.
3. Calculate the actual price per pound of direct materials purchased.
4. Calculate the direct materials price variance.

7-36 Direct materials and manufacturing labor variances, solving unknowns. (CPA, adapted) On May 1, 2009, Bovar Company began the manufacture of a new paging machine known as Dandy. The company installed a standard costing system to account for manufacturing costs. The standard costs for a unit of Dandy follow:

Direct materials (3 lbs. at $5 per lb.)	$15.00
Direct manufacturing labor (1/2 hour at $20 per hour)	10.00
Manufacturing overhead (75% of direct manufacturing labor costs)	7.50
	$32.50

The following data were obtained from Bovar's records for the month of May:

	Debit	Credit
Revenues		$125,000
Accounts payable control (for May's purchases of direct materials)		68,250
Direct materials price variance	$3,250	
Direct materials efficiency variance	2,500	
Direct manufacturing labor price variance	1,900	
Direct manufacturing labor efficiency variance		2,000

Actual production in May was 4,000 units of Dandy, and actual sales in May were 2,500 units.

The amount shown for direct materials price variance applies to materials purchased during May. There was no beginning inventory of materials on May 1, 2009.

Compute each of the following items for Bovar for the month of May. Show your computations.

Required

1. Standard direct manufacturing labor-hours allowed for actual output produced
2. Actual direct manufacturing labor-hours worked
3. Actual direct manufacturing labor wage rate

4. Standard quantity of direct materials allowed (in pounds)
5. Actual quantity of direct materials used (in pounds)
6. Actual quantity of direct materials purchased (in pounds)
7. Actual direct materials price per pound

7-37 Direct materials and manufacturing labor variances, journal entries. Shayna's Smart Shawls Inc. is a small business that Shayna developed while in college. She began hand-knitting shawls for her dorm friends to wear while studying. As demand grew, she hired some workers and began to manage the operation. Shayna's shawls require wool and labor. She experiments with the type of wool that she uses, and she has great variety in the shawls she produces. Shayna has bi-modal turnover in her labor. She has some employees who have been with her for a very long time and others who are new and inexperienced.

Shayna uses standard costing for her shawls. She expects that a typical shawl should take 3.5 hours to produce, and the standard wage rate is $10.50 per hour. An average shawl uses 12 skeins of wool. Shayna shops around for good deals, and expects to pay $3.00 per skein.

Shayna uses a just-in-time inventory system, as she has clients tell her what type and color of wool they would like her to use.

For the month of April, Shayna's workers produced 230 shawls using 836 hours and 2,633.50 skeins of wool. Shayna bought wool for $8,295.50 (and used the entire quantity), and incurred labor costs of $7,814.50.

Required

1. Calculate the price and efficiency variances for the wool, and the price and efficiency variances for direct manufacturing labor.
2. Record the journal entries for the variances incurred.
3. Discuss logical explanations for the combination of variances that Shayna experienced.

7-38 Use of materials and manufacturing labor variances for benchmarking

You are a new junior accountant at Clearview Corporation, maker of lenses for eyeglasses. Your company sells generic-quality lenses for a moderate price. Your boss, the Controller, has given you the latest month's report for the lens trade association. You do not know which firm is which, except that you know that you are firm A.

Unit Variable Costs - Member Firms
For the month ended September 30, 2010

	Firm A	Firm B	Firm C	Firm D	
Materials input	2.00	1.95	2.15	2.50	oz. of glass
Materials price	$ 5.00	$ 5.50	$ 5.00	$ 4.50	per oz.
Labor hours used	0.75	1.10	0.80	0.85	hours
Wage rate	$15.00	$15.50	$16.00	$16.50	per DLH
Variable overhead rate	$ 9.00	$13.50	$ 7.50	$11.25	per DLH

Required

1. Calculate the total variable cost per unit for each firm in the trade association. Compute the percent of total for the material, labor, and variable overhead components.
2. Using Firm A as the benchmark, calculate direct materials and direct manufacturing labor price and efficiency variances for the other three firms. Calculate the percent over standard for each firm and each variance.
3. Write a brief memo to your boss outlining the advantages and disadvantages of belonging to this trade association for benchmarking purposes. Include a few ideas to improve productivity that you want your boss to take to the department heads' meeting.

7-39 Comprehensive variance analysis review. Sonnet, Inc. has the following budgeted standards for the month of March 2010:

Average selling price per diskette	$ 5.00
Total direct material cost per diskette	$ 0.85
Direct manufacturing labor	
Direct manufacturing labor cost per hour	$ 15.00
Average labor productivity rate (diskettes per hour)	300
Direct marketing cost per unit	$ 0.30
Fixed overhead	$850,000

Sales of 2,000,000 units are budgeted for March. Actual March results are:

- Unit sales and production totaled 90% of plan.
- Actual average selling price declined to $4.80.
- Productivity dropped to 250 diskettes per hour.
- Actual direct manufacturing labor cost is $15 per hour.
- Actual total direct material cost per unit dropped to $0.80.
- Actual direct marketing costs were $0.30 per unit.
- Fixed overhead costs were $30,000 below plan.

Calculate the following:

Required

1. Static-budget and actual operating income
2. Static-budget variance for operating income
3. Flexible-budget operating income
4. Flexible-budget variance for operating income
5. Sales-volume variance for operating income
6. Price and efficiency variances for direct manufacturing labor
7. Flexible-budget variance for direct manufacturing labor

7-40 Comprehensive variance analysis. Sol Electronics, a fast-growing electronic device producer, uses a standard costing system, with standards set at the beginning of each year.

In the second quarter of 2009, Sol faced two challenges: it had to negotiate and sign a new short-term labor agreement with its workers' union, and it also had to pay a higher rate to its suppliers for direct materials. The new labor contract raised the cost of direct manufacturing labor relative to the company's 2009 standards. Similarly, the new rate for direct materials exceeded the company's 2009 standards. However, the materials were of better quality than expected, so Sol's management was confident that there would be less waste and less rework in the manufacturing process. They also speculated that the per-unit direct manufacturing labor cost might decline as a result of the materials' improved quality.

At the end of the second quarter, Sol's CFO, Terence Shaw, reviewed the following results:

	A	B	C	D	E	F	G	H	I	J	K	L	M	N	O	P	Q	R	S
1		Variable Costs Per Unit																	
2	Per Unit Variable Costs	Standard						First-Quarter 2009 Actual Results						Second-Quarter 2009 Actual Results					
3	Direct materials	2.2	lbs	at	$5.70	per lb	$12.54	2.3	lbs	at	$ 5.80	per lb	$13.34	2.0	lbs	at	$ 6.00	per lb	$12.00
4	Direct manufacturing labor	0.5	hrs	at	$ 12	per hr	$ 6.00	0.52	hrs	at	$ 12	per hr	$ 6.24	0.45	hrs	at	$ 14	per hr	$ 6.30
5	Other variable costs						$10.00						$10.00						$ 9.85
6							$28.54						$29.58						$28.15

	U	V	W	X
1				
2		Static Budget for Each Quarter Based on 2009	First-Quarter 2009 Results	Second-Quarter 2009 Results
3	Units	4,000	4,400	4,800
4	Selling price	$ 70	$ 72	$ 71.50
5	Sales	$280,000	$316,800	$343,200
6	Variable costs			
7	Direct materials	50,160	58,696	57,600
8	Direct manufacturing labor	24,000	27,456	30,240
9	Other variable costs	40,000	44,000	47,280
10	Total variable costs	114,160	130,152	135,120
11	Contribution margin	165,840	186,648	208,080
12	Fixed costs	68,000	66,000	68,400
13	Operating income	$ 97,840	$120,640	$139,680

Shaw was relieved to see that the anticipated savings in material waste and rework seemed to have materialized. But, he was concerned that the union would press hard for higher wages given that actual unit costs came in below standard unit costs and operating income continued to climb.

If you want to use Excel to solve this problem, go to the Excel Lab at **www.prenhall.com/horngren/cost13e** and download the template for Problem 7-40.

Required

1. Prepare a detailed variance analysis of the second-quarter results relative to the static budget. Show how much of the improvement in operating income arose due to changes in sales volume and how much arose for other reasons. Calculate variances that isolate the effects of price and usage changes in direct materials and direct manufacturing labor.

2. Use the results of requirement 1 to prepare a rebuttal to the union's anticipated demands in light of the second-quarter results.
3. Terence Shaw thinks that the company can negotiate better if it changes the standards. Without performing any calculations, discuss the pros and cons of immediately changing the standards.

7-41 Comprehensive variance analysis. (CMA) Iceland, Inc. is a fast-growing ice-cream maker. The company's new ice-cream flavor, Cherry Star, sells for $8 per pound. The standard monthly production level is 200,000 pounds, and the standard inputs and costs per pound are:

	A	B	C	D	E
1		Quantity per		Standard	
2	Cost Item	Pound of Ice Cream		Unit Costs	
3	Direct materials				
4	Cream	10	oz.	$ 0.02	/oz.
5	Vanilla Extract	5	oz.	0.15	/oz.
6	Cherry	1	oz.	0.50	/oz.
7					
8	Direct manufacturing labor [a]				
9	Preparing	1	min.	14.40	/hr.
10	Stirring	2	min.	18.00	/hr.
11					
12	Variable overhead [b]	3	min.	32.40	/hr.
13					
14	[a] Direct manufacturing labor rates include employee benefits.				
15	[b] Allocated on the basis of direct manufacturing labor-hours.				

Molly Cates, the CFO, is disappointed with the results for May 2009, prepared based on these standard costs:

	A	B	C	D	E	F	G
17		Performance Report, May 2009					
18		Actual		Budget		Variance	
19	Units (pounds)	225,000		200,000		25,000	F
20	Revenues	$1,777,500		$1,600,000		$177,500	F
21	Direct materials	432,500		290,000		142,500	U
22	Direct manufacturing labor	174,000		168,000		6,000	U

Cates notes that despite a sizable increase in the pounds of ice cream sold in May, Cherry Star's contribution to the company's overall profitability has been lower than expected. Cates gathers the following information to help analyze the situation:

	A	B	C	D
25		Usage Report, May 2009		
26	Cost Item	Quantity		Actual Cost
27	Direct materials			
28	Cream	2,325,000	oz.	$ 46,500
29	Vanilla Extract	1,330,000	oz.	266,000
30	Cherry	240,000	oz.	120,000
31				
32	Direct manufacturing labor			
33	Preparing	225,000	min.	54,000
34	Stirring	400,000	min.	120,000

If you want to use Excel to solve this problem, go to the Excel Lab at **www.prenhall.com/horngren/cost13e** and download the template for Problem 7-41.

Compute the following variances. Comment on the variances, with particular attention to the variances that may be related to each other and the controllability of each variance: **Required**

1. Selling-price variance
2. Direct materials price variance
3. Direct materials efficiency variance
4. Direct manufacturing labor efficiency variance

7-42 Variance analysis with activity-based costing and batch-level direct costs

Electric Eels Company produces high quality electric eels for Museums and Aquaria to sell in their gift shops. It accounts for the production of these eels with an ABC system. For 2009, Electric Eels expected to produce and sell 16,000 units, but actual output was only 15,000 units.

You are a new management accountant at the company. You have been asked to calculate the variances for the batch-level costs. The two main batch-level costs are setup and quality inspection. Quality inspection is driven by inspection hours, and setup is driven by the number of setup hours.

		Setup	Quality Inspection
Static-Budget:	Batch size (units per batch)	100	120
	Cost driver (hours) per batch	8	10
	Cost per hour	$10.75	$17.50
Actual Result:	Batch size (units per batch)	75	100
	Cost driver (hours) per batch	7	9
	Cost per hour	$12.00	$15.50

Required

1. Calculate the flexible-budget, price, and efficiency variances for both batch activities.
2. Write a short memo to your boss, the Controller, explaining the variances that you calculated.

Collaborative Learning Problem

7-43 Price and efficiency variances, problems in standard-setting, benchmarking.

New Fashions manufactures shirts for retail chains. Andy Jorgenson, the controller, is becoming increasingly disenchanted with New Fashion's standard costing system. The budgeted and actual amounts for direct materials and direct manufacturing labor for June 2009 were:

	Budgeted Amounts	Actual Amounts
Shirts manufactured	6,000	6,732
Direct material costs	$30,000	$30,294
Direct material units (rolls of cloth)	600	612
Direct manufacturing labor costs	$27,000	$27,693
Direct manufacturing labor-hours	1,500	1,530

There were no beginning or ending inventories of materials.

Standard costs are based on a study of the operations conducted by an independent consultant six months earlier. Jorgenson observes that since that study he has rarely seen an unfavorable variance of any magnitude. He notes that even at their current output levels, the workers seem to have a lot of time for sitting around and gossiping. Jorgenson is concerned that the production manager, Charlie Fenton, is aware of this but does not want to tighten up the standards because the lax standards make his performance look good.

Required

1. Compute the price and efficiency variances of New Fashions for direct materials and direct manufacturing labor in June 2009.
2. Describe the types of actions the employees at New Fashions may have taken to reduce the accuracy of the standards set by the independent consultant. Why would employees take those actions? Is this behavior ethical?
3. If Jorgenson does nothing about the standard costs, will his behavior violate any of the Standards of Ethical Conduct for Management Accountants described in Exhibit 1-7 on p. 16?
4. What actions should Jorgenson take?
5. Jorgenson can obtain benchmarking information about the estimated costs of New Fashion's major competitors from Benchmarking Clearing House (BCH). Discuss the pros and cons of using the BCH information to compute the variances in requirement 1.

8 Flexible Budgets, Overhead Cost Variances, and Management Control

Learning Objectives

1. Explain the similarities and differences in planning variable overhead costs and fixed overhead costs
2. Develop budgeted variable overhead cost rates
3. Compute the variable overhead flexible-budget variance, the variable overhead efficiency variance, and the variable overhead spending variance
4. Develop budgeted fixed overhead cost rates
5. Compute the fixed overhead flexible-budget variance, the fixed overhead spending variance, and the fixed overhead production-volume variance
6. Show how the 4-variance analysis approach reconciles the actual overhead incurred with the overhead amounts allocated during the period
7. Calculate overhead variances in activity-based costing

What do this week's weather forecast, courtroom witness testimony, and organization performance have in common? Most of the time, reality doesn't match expectations: It doesn't rain when forecast, and the witness swears the defendant was at the scene of the crime even though a solid alibi exists. The organization discovers at the end of the month that its skyrocketing costs have significantly reduced its profits, or perhaps that dramatically lower costs have improved its profits tremendously. Differences, or variances, are all around us.

For organizations, variances can have unpleasant consequences. This is especially true when executives and employees don't tell the truth about why and how the variances occurred, as the following article shows.

CEO Claims He Didn't See Variances, but Jurors Did[1]

In the Bernard Ebbers trial, the decisive evidence may not have been the star witnesses on either side. It may have been the hundreds of papers the jurors pored through during their deliberations.

Several jurors said in interviews after the guilty verdict that they didn't entirely believe either Mr. Ebbers, the former head of WorldCom, or Scott Sullivan, the former chief financial officer who testified against his ex-boss. Because of that, they resorted to picking through dense financial documents presented by the defense and prosecution to figure out the truth about how much the former CEO knew.

The jury convicted Mr. Ebbers of participating in the $11 billion accounting fraud at WorldCom, which was driven into bankruptcy and has since reemerged as MCI Inc. A pivotal concept was the judge's instruction to the jury about willful ignorance. The prosecution did not have to prove accounting fraud, but rather that Mr. Ebbers knew about it—or made an effort not to. Two jurors said that reports, called "management budget variance reports," were crucial.

Betty Vinson, a former WorldCom accountant testified that her group distributed those reports to Mr. Ebbers. Not only was Mr. Ebbers one of just four other executives who received the reports, but his version was prepared on special, extra-large "green bar paper" with lines that made it easier for him to read.

[1] *Source:* Jesse Drucker and Li Yuan, "Executives on Trial: 'How Could He Not See?': Documents Swayed Ebbers Jury," *The Wall Street Journal,* March 17, 2005, p.c1.

Jurors Ms. Strong and Ms. Nulty said looking at those reports was critical, since the "line costs"—the main focus of the accounting fraud—were very high. Then there was a drop-off. "Something clearly happened to make them cut the costs in half," said Ms. Nulty. "We found it impossible that he didn't ask questions or wasn't aware."

Companies such as DuPont, International Paper and U.S. Steel that invest heavily in capital equipment or Amazon.com and Yahoo! that invest large amounts in software have high overhead costs. As the WorldCom example suggests, understanding the behavior of overhead costs, planning for them, performing variance analysis, and acting appropriately on the results are critical for a company.

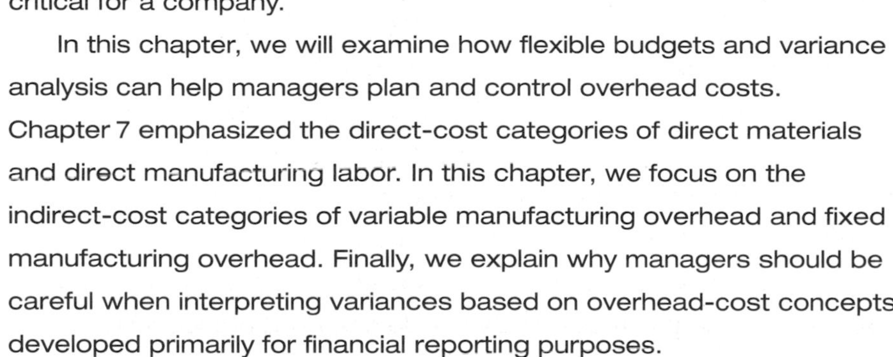

In this chapter, we will examine how flexible budgets and variance analysis can help managers plan and control overhead costs. Chapter 7 emphasized the direct-cost categories of direct materials and direct manufacturing labor. In this chapter, we focus on the indirect-cost categories of variable manufacturing overhead and fixed manufacturing overhead. Finally, we explain why managers should be careful when interpreting variances based on overhead-cost concepts developed primarily for financial reporting purposes.

Planning of Variable and Fixed Overhead Costs

We'll use the Webb Company example again to illustrate the planning and control of variable and fixed overhead costs. Recall that Webb manufactures jackets that are sold to distributors, who in turn sell to independent clothing stores and retail chains. For simplicity, we assume Webb's only costs are *manufacturing* costs. For ease of exposition, we use the term overhead costs instead of manufacturing overhead costs. Variable (manufacturing) overhead costs for Webb include energy, machine maintenance, engineering support, and indirect materials. Fixed (manufacturing) overhead costs include plant leasing costs, depreciation on plant equipment, and the salaries of the plant managers.

Learning Objective 1

Explain the similarities and differences in planning variable overhead costs and fixed overhead costs

. . . for both, plan only essential activities and be efficient; fixed overhead costs are usually determined well before the budget period begins

Planning Variable Overhead Costs

To effectively plan variable overhead costs for a product or service, managers must eliminate the activities that do not add value to the product or service. By doing this, managers can focus their attention on the activities that create a superior product or service for their customers. Webb's managers examine how each of their variable overhead costs relates to delivering a superior product or service to customers. For example, customers expect Webb's jackets to last. So managers at Webb consider sewing to be an essential activity.

Therefore, maintenance activities for sewing machines—included in Webb's variable overhead costs—are also essential activities for which management must plan. In addition, such maintenance should be done in a cost-effective way. This means, for example, scheduling periodic equipment maintenance rather than waiting for sewing machines to break down.

Planning Fixed Overhead Costs

Effective planning of fixed overhead costs is similar to effective planning for variable overhead costs—planning to undertake only essential activities and then planning to be efficient in that undertaking. But in planning fixed overhead costs, there is one more strategic issue that managers must take into consideration: choosing the appropriate level of capacity or investment that will benefit the company in the long run. Consider Webb's leasing of sewing machines, each having a fixed cost per year. Leasing insufficient machine capacity—say, because Webb underestimates demand or because of limited space in the plant—will result in an inability to meet demand and lost sales of jackets. Leasing more machines than necessary—if Webb overestimates demand—will result in additional fixed leasing costs on machines not fully used during the year.

The planning of fixed overhead costs differs from the planning of variable overhead costs in one important respect: timing. At the start of a budget period, management will have made most of the decisions that determine the level of fixed overhead costs to be incurred. But, it's the day-to-day, ongoing operating decisions that mainly determine the level of variable overhead costs incurred in that period.

Standard Costing at Webb Company

Webb uses standard costing. The development of standards for Webb's direct manufacturing costs was described in Chapter 7. This chapter discusses the development of standards for Webb's manufacturing overhead costs. **Standard costing** is a costing system that (a) traces direct costs to output produced by multiplying the standard prices or rates by the standard quantities of inputs allowed for actual outputs produced and (b) allocates overhead costs on the basis of the standard overhead-cost rates times the standard quantities of the allocation bases allowed for the actual outputs produced.

The standard cost of Webb's jackets can be computed at the start of the budget period. This feature of standard costing simplifies record keeping. That is because no record is needed of the actual overhead costs or of the actual quantities of the cost-allocation bases used for making the jackets. What is needed are the standard overhead cost rates for variable and fixed overhead. Webb's management accountants calculate these cost rates based on the planned amounts of variable and fixed overhead and the standard quantities of the allocation bases. We describe these computations in the following sections. Note that once standards have been set, the costs of using standard costing are low relative to the costs of using actual costing or normal costing.

Developing Budgeted Variable Overhead Cost Rates

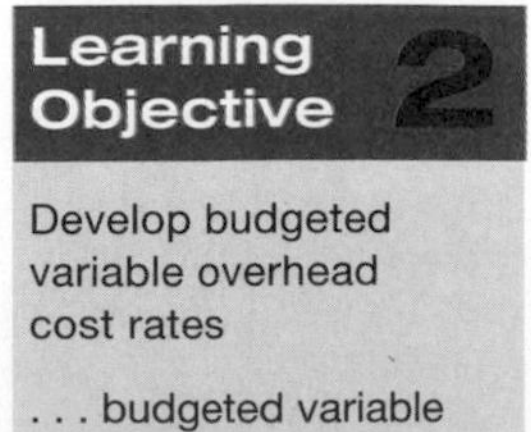
Learning Objective 2

Develop budgeted variable overhead cost rates

. . . budgeted variable costs divided by quantity of cost-allocation base

Budgeted variable overhead cost-allocation rates can be developed in four steps. We use the Webb example to illustrate these steps. Throughout the chapter, we use the broader term "budgeted rate" rather than "standard rate" to be consistent with the term used in describing normal costing in earlier chapters. In standard costing, the budgeted rates are standard rates.

Step 1: Choose the Period to Be Used for the Budget. Webb uses a 12-month budget period to help smooth out seasonal effects.

Step 2: Select the Cost-Allocation Bases to Use in Allocating Variable Overhead Costs to Output Produced. Webb's operating managers select machine-hours as the cost-allocation base because they believe that machine-hours is the only cost driver of variable overhead. Based on an engineering study, Webb estimates it will take 0.40 of a machine-hour per actual output unit. For its budgeted output of 144,000 jackets in 2008, Webb budgets 57,600 (0.40 × 144,000) machine-hours.

Step 3: Identify the Variable Overhead Costs Associated with Each Cost-Allocation Base. Webb groups all of its variable overhead costs, including costs of energy, machine maintenance, engineering support, indirect materials, and indirect manufacturing labor in a single cost pool. Webb's total budgeted variable overhead costs for 2008 are $1,728,000.

Step 4: Compute the Rate per Unit of Each Cost-Allocation Base Used to Allocate Variable Overhead Costs to Output Produced. Dividing the amount in step 3 ($1,728,000) by the amount in step 2 (57,600 machine-hours), Webb estimates a rate of $30 per standard machine-hour for allocating its variable overhead costs.

In standard costing, the variable overhead rate per unit of the cost-allocation base ($30 per machine-hour for Webb) is generally expressed as a standard rate per output unit. Webb calculates the budgeted variable overhead cost rate per output unit as:

$$\begin{array}{c} \text{Budgeted variable} \\ \text{overhead cost rate} \\ \text{per output unit} \end{array} = \begin{array}{c} \text{Budgeted input} \\ \text{allowed per} \\ \text{output unit} \end{array} \times \begin{array}{c} \text{Budgeted variable} \\ \text{overhead cost rate} \\ \text{per input unit} \end{array}$$

$$= 0.40 \text{ hour per jacket} \times \$30 \text{ per hour}$$

$$= \$12 \text{ per jacket}$$

Webb uses $12 per jacket as the budgeted variable overhead cost rate in both its static budget for 2008 and in the monthly performance reports it prepares during 2008.

The $12 per jacket represents the amount by which Webb's variable overhead costs are expected to change with respect to output units (jackets) for the planning and control (budgeting) purpose and also for the inventory costing purpose. As the number of jackets manufactured increases, budgeted variable overhead costs (for the planning and control purpose of cost accounting) and variable overhead costs allocated to output units (for the inventory costing purpose) both increase at the rate of $12 per jacket. Of course, this presents an overall picture of total variable overhead costs, which in reality consist of many items, including energy, repairs, indirect labor, and so on. Managers help control variable overhead costs by budgeting each line item and then investigating possible causes for any significant variances.

Variable Overhead Cost Variances

We now illustrate how the budgeted variable overhead rate is used in computing Webb's variable overhead cost variances. The following data are for April 2008, when Webb produced and sold 10,000 jackets:

	Actual Result	Flexible-Budget Amount
1. Output units (jackets)	10,000	10,000
2. Machine-hours per output unit	0.45	0.40
3. Machine-hours (1 × 2)	4,500	4,000
4. Variable overhead costs	$130,500	$120,000
5. Variable overhead costs per machine-hour (4 ÷ 3)	$ 29.00	$ 30.00
6. Variable overhead costs per output unit (4 ÷ 1)	$ 13.05	$ 12.00

As we saw in Chapter 7, the flexible budget enables Webb to highlight the differences between actual costs and actual quantities versus budgeted costs and budgeted quantities for the actual output level of 10,000 jackets.

Learning Objective 3

Compute the variable overhead flexible-budget variance,

. . . difference between actual variable overhead costs and flexible-budget variable overhead amounts

the variable overhead efficiency variance,

. . . difference between actual quantity of cost-allocation base and budgeted quantity of cost-allocation base

and the variable overhead spending variance

. . . difference between actual variable overhead cost rate and budgeted variable overhead cost rate

Flexible-Budget Analysis

The **variable overhead flexible-budget variance** measures the difference between actual variable overhead costs incurred and flexible-budget variable overhead amounts.

$$\begin{aligned}\text{Variable overhead flexible-budget variance} &= \text{Actual costs incurred} - \text{Flexible-budget amount}\\ &= \$130{,}500 - \$120{,}000\\ &= \$10{,}500\text{ U}\end{aligned}$$

This $10,500 unfavorable flexible-budget variance means Webb's actual variable overhead exceeded the flexible-budget amount by $10,500 for the 10,000 jackets actually produced and sold. Webb's managers would want to know the reasons why actual costs exceeded the flexible-budget amount. Did Webb use more machine-hours than planned to produce the 10,000 jackets? If so, was it because workers were less skilled than expected in using machines? Or did Webb spend more on variable overhead costs, such as maintenance?

Just as we illustrated in Chapter 7 with the flexible-budget variance for direct-cost items, Webb's managers can get further insight into the reason for the $10,500 unfavorable variance by subdividing it into the efficiency variance and spending variance.

Variable Overhead Efficiency Variance

The **variable overhead efficiency variance** is the difference between actual quantity of the cost-allocation base used and budgeted quantity of the cost-allocation base that should have been used to produce actual output, multiplied by budgeted variable overhead cost per unit of the cost-allocation base.

$$\begin{aligned}\text{Variable overhead efficiency variance} &= \left(\begin{array}{c}\text{Actual quantity of variable overhead}\\ \text{cost-allocation base used for actual output}\end{array} - \begin{array}{c}\text{Budgeted quantity of variable overhead}\\ \text{cost-allocation base allowed for actual output}\end{array}\right) \times \begin{array}{c}\text{Budgeted variable overhead cost per unit}\\ \text{of cost-allocation base}\end{array}\\ &= (4{,}500\text{ hours} - 0.40\text{ hr./unit} \times 10{,}000\text{ units}) \times \$30\text{ per hour}\\ &= (4{,}500\text{ hours} - 4{,}000\text{ hours}) \times \$30\text{ per hour}\\ &= \$15{,}000\text{ U}\end{aligned}$$

Columns 2 and 3 of Exhibit 8-1 depict the variable overhead efficiency variance. Note the variance arises solely because of the difference between actual quantity (4,500 hours) and

Exhibit 8-1

Columnar Presentation of Variable Overhead Variance Analysis: Webb Company for April 2008[a]

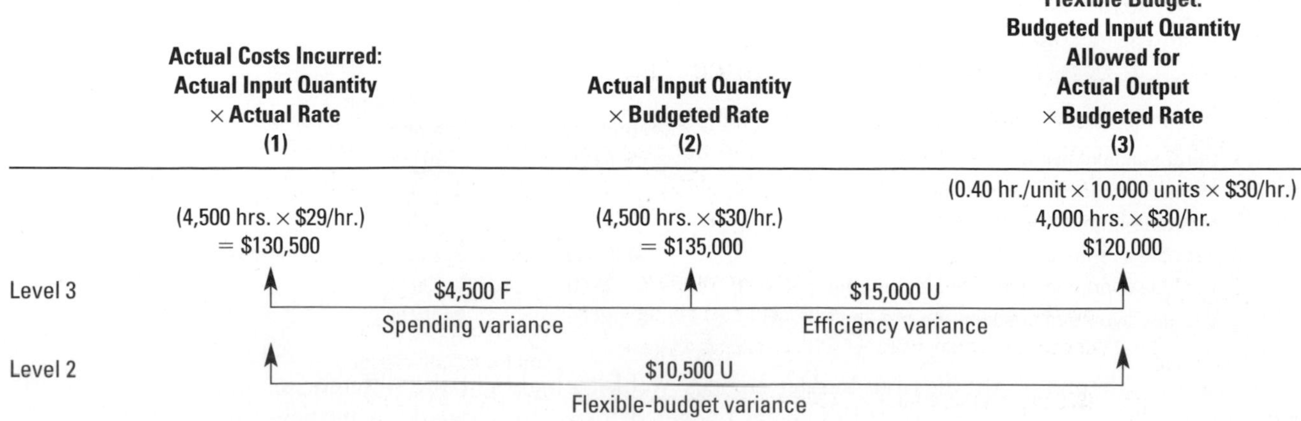

[a]F = favorable effect on operating income; U = unfavorable effect on operating income.

budgeted quantity (4,000 hours) of the cost-allocation base. The variable overhead efficiency variance is computed the same way as the efficiency variance for direct-cost items (Chapter 7, p. 235). But the interpretation of the variable overhead efficiency variance differs from the interpretation of direct-cost efficiency variances. In Chapter 7, efficiency variances for direct-cost items are based on differences between actual inputs used and budgeted inputs allowed for actual output produced. For example, an efficiency variance for direct manufacturing labor for Webb will indicate whether more or fewer direct labor-hours are used per jacket than were budgeted for actual output produced. In contrast, the efficiency variance for variable overhead cost is based on the efficiency with which *the cost-allocation base* is used. Webb's unfavorable variable overhead efficiency variance of $15,000 means that the actual machine-hours (the cost-allocation base) of 4,500 hours turned out to be higher than the budgeted machine-hours of 4,000 hours allowed to manufacture 10,000 jackets.

The following table shows possible causes for Webb's actual machine-hours exceeding budgeted machine-hours and management's potential responses to each of these causes.

Possible Causes for Exceeding Budget	Potential Management Responses
1. Workers were less skilled than expected in using machines.	**1.** Encourage the human resources department to implement better employee-hiring practices and training procedures.
2. Production scheduler inefficiently scheduled jobs, resulting in more machine-hours used than budgeted.	**2.** Improve plant operations by installing production scheduling software.
3. Machines were not maintained in good operating condition.	**3.** Ensure preventive maintenance is done on all machines.
4. Webb's sales staff promised a distributor a rush delivery, which resulted in more machine-hours used than budgeted.	**4.** Coordinate production schedules with sales staff and distributors and share information with them.
5. Budgeted machine time standards were set too tight.	**5.** Commit more resources to develop appropriate standards.

Management's response to this $15,000 U variance would be guided by which cause(s) best describes the April 2008 results. Note how, depending on the cause(s) of the variance, corrective actions may need to be taken not just in manufacturing but also in other business functions of the value chain, such as sales and distribution.

Webb's managers discovered that one reason the machines operated below budgeted efficiency levels in April 2008 was insufficient maintenance performed in the prior two months. A former plant manager delayed maintenance in a presumed attempt to meet monthly budget cost targets. As we discussed in Chapter 6, managers should not be focused on meeting short-run budget targets if it is likely to result in harmful long-run consequences. Webb is now strengthening its internal maintenance procedures so that failure to do monthly maintenance as needed will raise a "red flag" that must be immediately explained to management. Another reason for actual machine-hours exceeding budgeted machine-hours was the use of underskilled workers. As a result, Webb is initiating steps to improve hiring and training practices.

Variable Overhead Spending Variance

The **variable overhead spending variance** is the difference between actual variable overhead cost per unit of the cost-allocation base and budgeted variable overhead cost per unit of the cost-allocation base, multiplied by the actual quantity of variable overhead cost-allocation base used for actual output.

$$\begin{aligned}\text{Variable overhead spending variance} &= \left(\begin{array}{c}\text{Actual variable}\\\text{overhead cost per unit}\\\text{of cost-allocation base}\end{array} - \begin{array}{c}\text{Budgeted variable}\\\text{overhead cost per unit}\\\text{of cost-allocation base}\end{array}\right) \times \begin{array}{c}\text{Actual quantity of}\\\text{variable overhead}\\\text{cost-allocation base}\\\text{used for actual output}\end{array}\\ &= (\$29 \text{ per machine-hour} - \$30 \text{ per machine-hour}) \times 4{,}500 \text{ machine-hours}\\ &= (-\$1 \text{ per machine-hour}) \times 4{,}500 \text{ machine-hours}\\ &= \$4{,}500 \text{ F}\end{aligned}$$

Webb operated in April 2008 with a lower-than-budgeted variable overhead cost per machine-hour. Hence, there is a favorable variable overhead spending variance. Columns 1 and 2 in Exhibit 8-1 depict this variance.

To understand the favorable variable overhead spending variance and its implications, Webb's managers need to recognize why *actual* variable overhead cost per unit of the cost-allocation base ($29 per machine-hour) is *lower* than *budgeted* variable overhead cost per unit of the cost-allocation base ($30 per machine-hour). The 4,500 actual machine-hours are 12.5% greater than the flexible-budget amount of 4,000 machine hours [(4,500 − 4,000) ÷ 4,000 = 0.125, or 12.5%]. Actual variable overhead costs of $130,500 are only 8.75% greater than the flexible-budget amount of $120,000 [($130,500 − $120,000) ÷ $120,000 = 0.0875, or 8.75%]. Relative to the flexible budget, the percentage increase in actual variable overhead costs is *less* than the percentage increase in machine-hours. Consequently, actual variable overhead cost per machine-hour is lower than the budgeted amount.

Recall that variable overhead costs include costs of energy, machine maintenance, indirect materials, and indirect labor. Two reasons why the percentage increase in actual variable overhead costs is less than the percentage increase in machine-hours are:

1. Actual prices of individual inputs included in variable overhead costs, such as the price of energy, indirect materials, or indirect labor, are lower than budgeted prices of these inputs. For example, the actual price of electricity may only be $0.09 per kilowatt-hour, compared with a price of $0.10 per kilowatt-hour in the flexible budget.
2. Relative to the flexible budget, the percentage increase in the actual quantity usage of individual items in the variable overhead-cost pool is less than the percentage increase in machine-hours. Suppose actual energy used is 32,400 kilowatt-hours, compared with the flexible-budget amount of 30,000 kilowatt-hours. The 8% [(32,400 − 30,000) ÷ 30,000] increase in energy usage compared with the 12.5% [(4,500 − 4,000) ÷ 4,000] increase in machine-hours will lead to a favorable variable overhead spending variance. The favorable spending variance can be partially or completely traced to the efficient use of energy and other variable overhead items.

As part of the last stage of the five-step decision-making process, Webb's managers will need to examine the signals provided by the variable overhead variances to *evaluate performance and learn*. By understanding the reasons for these variances, Webb can take appropriate actions and make more precise predictions in order to achieve improved results in future periods.

For example, Webb's managers must examine why actual prices of variable overhead cost items are different from budgeted prices. The price effects could be the result of skillful negotiation on the part of the purchasing manager, oversupply in the market, or lower quality of inputs such as indirect materials. Webb's response depends on what is believed to be the cause of the variance. If the concerns are about quality, for instance, Webb may want to put in place new quality management systems.

Similarly, Webb's managers should understand the possible causes for the efficiency with which variable overhead resources are used. These causes include skill levels of workers, maintenance of machines and the efficiency of the manufacturing process. Webb's managers discovered that Webb used fewer supervision resources per machine hour because of manufacturing process improvements. As a result, they began organizing cross-functional teams to see if more process improvements could be achieved.

We emphasize that a favorable variable overhead spending variance is not always desirable. For example, the variable overhead spending variance is not would be favorable if Webb's managers purchased lower-priced, poor-quality indirect materials, hired less-talented supervisors, or performed less machine maintenance. These decisions, however, are likely to hurt product quality and harm the long-run prospects of the business.

To clarify the concepts of variable overhead efficiency variance and variable overhead spending variance, consider the following example, assuming that (a) energy is the only item of variable overhead cost and machine-hours is the cost-allocation base, (b) actual machine-hours used to produce actual output equals budgeted machine-hours, and (c) actual price of energy equals budgeted price. Under those assumptions, there would be no efficiency variance, but there could be a spending variance. The company has been efficient with respect to the number of machine-hours used to produce the actual output. But it could be using too much energy—not because of excessive machine-hours but because of waste (using more energy per machine-hour). The cost of this higher energy usage is reflected in the spending variance. Managers would try to find ways to reduce energy consumption per machine-hour via better machine maintenance or by making modifications to the manufacturing process.

Journal Entries for Variable Overhead Costs and Variances

We now prepare journal entries for Variable Overhead Control and the contra account Variable Overhead Allocated.

Entries for variable overhead for April 2008 (data from Exhibit 8-1) are:

1.	Variable Overhead Control	130,500	
	Accounts Payable and various other accounts		130,500
	To record actual variable overhead costs incurred.		
2.	Work-in-Process Control	120,000	
	Variable Overhead Allocated		120,000
	To record variable overhead cost allocated (0.40 machine-hour/unit × 10,000 units × $30/machine-hour). (The costs accumulated in Work-in-Process Control are transferred to Finished Goods Control when production is completed and to Cost of Goods Sold when the products are sold.)		
3.	Variable Overhead Allocated	120,000	
	Variable Overhead Efficiency Variance	15,000	
	Variable Overhead Control		130,500
	Variable Overhead Spending Variance		4,500
	To record variances for the accounting period.		

These variances are the underallocated or overallocated variable overhead costs. At the end of the fiscal year, the variance accounts are written off to cost of goods sold if immaterial in amount. If the variances are material in amount, they are prorated among Work-in-Process Control, Finished Goods Control, and Cost of Goods Sold on the basis of the variable overhead allocated to these accounts, as described in Chapter 4, pp. 115–119. As we discussed in Chapter 7, only unavoidable costs are prorated. Any part of the variances attributable to avoidable inefficiency are written off in the period. Assume that the balances in the variable overhead variance accounts as of April 2008 are also the balances at the end of the 2008 fiscal year and are immaterial in amount. The following journal entry records the write-off of the variance accounts to cost of goods sold.

Cost of Goods Sold	10,500	
Variable Overhead Spending Variance	4,500	
Variable Overhead Efficiency Variance		15,000

We next consider fixed overhead costs.

Developing Budgeted Fixed Overhead Rates

Learning Objective 4

Develop budgeted fixed overhead cost rates

. . . budgeted fixed costs divided by quantity of cost-allocation base

Fixed overhead costs are, by definition, a lump sum of costs that remains unchanged in total for a given period despite wide changes in the level of total activity or volume related to those overhead costs. Fixed costs are usually included in flexible budgets, but they remain the same total amount within the relevant range of activity regardless of the output level chosen to "flex" the variable costs and revenues. Recall from Exhibit 7-2, p. 229, and the steps in developing a flexible budget that the fixed-cost amount is the same $276,000 in the static budget and in the flexible budget. Do not assume, however, that fixed overhead costs can never be changed. Managers can reduce fixed overhead costs by selling equipment or by laying off employees. But they are fixed in the sense that, unlike variable costs such as direct material costs, fixed costs do not *automatically* increase or decrease with the level of activity within the relevant range. The steps in developing the budgeted fixed overhead rate are:

Step 1: Choose the Period to Use for the Budget. As with variable overhead costs, the budget period for fixed overhead costs is typically 12 months. Chapter 4 (pp. 106–107) provides two reasons for using annual overhead rates rather than, say, monthly rates: the numerator reason—such as reducing the influence of seasonality—and the denominator reason—such as reducing the effect of varying output and number of days in a month. In addition, setting annual overhead rates once a year saves management the time they would need 12 times during the year if budget rates had to be set monthly.

Step 2: Select the Cost-Allocation Bases to Use in Allocating Fixed Overhead Costs to Output Produced. Webb uses machine-hours as the only cost-allocation base for fixed overhead costs. Why? Because Webb's managers believe that, in the long run, fixed overhead costs will increase or decrease to the levels needed to support the amount of machine-hours. Therefore, in the long run, the amount of machine-hours used is the only cost driver of fixed overhead costs. The number of machine-hours is the denominator in the budgeted fixed overhead rate computation and is called the **denominator level** or, in manufacturing settings, the **production-denominator level.** For simplicity, we assume Webb expects to operate at capacity in fiscal year 2008—with a budgeted usage of 57,600 machine-hours for a budgeted output of 144,000 jackets.[2]

Step 3: Identify the Fixed Overhead Costs Associated with Each Cost-Allocation Base. Because Webb identifies only a single cost-allocation base—machine-hours—to allocate fixed overhead costs, it groups all such costs into a single cost pool. Costs in this pool include depreciation on plant and equipment, plant and equipment leasing costs, and the plant manager's salary. Webb's fixed overhead budget for 2008 is $3,312,000.

Step 4: Compute the Rate per Unit of Each Cost-Allocation Base Used to Allocate Fixed Overhead Costs to Output Produced. Dividing the $3,312,000 from step 3 by the 57,600 machine-hours from step 2, Webb estimates a fixed overhead cost rate of $57.50 per machine-hour:

$$\text{Budgeted fixed overhead cost per unit of cost-allocation base} = \frac{\text{Budgeted total costs in fixed overhead cost pool}}{\text{Budgeted total quantity of cost-allocation base}} = \frac{\$3{,}312{,}000}{57{,}600} = \$57.50 \text{ per machine-hour}$$

In standard costing, the $57.50 fixed overhead cost per machine-hour is usually expressed as a standard cost per output unit. Recall that Webb's engineering study estimates that it will take 0.40 machine-hour per output unit. Webb can now calculate the budgeted fixed overhead cost per output unit as:

$$\begin{aligned}\text{Budgeted fixed overhead cost per output unit} &= \text{Budgeted quantity of cost-allocation base allowed per output unit} \times \text{Budgeted fixed overhead cost per unit of cost-allocation base}\\ &= 0.40 \text{ of a machine-hour per jacket} \times \$57.50 \text{ per machine-hour}\\ &= \$23.00 \text{ per jacket}\end{aligned}$$

When preparing monthly budgets for 2008, Webb divides the $3,312,000 annual total fixed costs into 12 equal monthly amounts of $276,000.

---

[2] Because Webb plans its capacity over multiple periods, anticipated demand in 2008 could be such that budgeted output for 2008 is less than capacity. Companies vary in the denominator levels they choose; some may choose budgeted output and others may choose capacity. In either case, the basic approach and analysis presented in this chapter is unchanged. Chapter 9 discusses choosing a denominator level and its implications in more detail.

Fixed Overhead Cost Variances

The flexible-budget amount for a fixed-cost item is also the amount included in the static budget prepared at the start of the period. No adjustment is required for differences between actual output and budgeted output for fixed costs. That's because fixed costs are unaffected by changes in the output level within the relevant range. At the start of 2008, Webb budgeted fixed overhead costs to be $276,000 per month. The actual amount for April 2008 turned out to be $285,000. The **fixed overhead flexible-budget variance** is the difference between actual fixed overhead costs and fixed overhead costs in the flexible budget:

Learning Objective 5

Compute the fixed overhead flexible-budget variance,

. . . difference between actual fixed overhead costs and flexible-budget fixed overhead amounts

the fixed overhead spending variance,

. . . same as above

and the fixed overhead production-volume variance

. . . difference between budgeted fixed overhead and fixed overhead allocated on the basis of actual output produced

$$\begin{aligned}\text{Fixed overhead flexible-budget variance} &= \text{Actual costs incurred} - \text{Flexible budget amount}\\ &= \$285{,}000 - \$276{,}000\\ &= \$9{,}000\text{ U}\end{aligned}$$

The variance is unfavorable because $285,000 actual fixed overhead costs exceed the $276,000 budgeted for April 2008, which decreases that month's operating income by $9,000.

The variable overhead flexible-budget variance described earlier in this chapter was subdivided into a spending variance and an efficiency variance. There is not an efficiency variance for fixed overhead costs. That's because a given lump sum of fixed overhead costs will be unaffected by how efficiently machine-hours are used to produce output in a given budget period. As we will see later on, this does not mean that a company cannot be efficient or inefficient in its use of fixed-overhead-cost resources. As Exhibit 8-2 shows, because there is no efficiency variance, the **fixed overhead spending variance** is the same amount as the fixed overhead flexible-budget variance:

$$\begin{aligned}\text{Fixed overhead spending variance} &= \text{Actual costs incurred} - \text{Flexible-budget amount}\\ &= \$285{,}000 - \$276{,}000\\ &= \$9{,}000\text{ U}\end{aligned}$$

Reasons for the unfavorable spending variance could be higher plant-leasing costs, higher depreciation on plant and equipment, and higher administrative costs such as a higher-than-budgeted salary paid to the plant manager. Webb investigated this variance and found that there was a $9,000 per month unexpected increase in its equipment-leasing costs. However, management concluded that the new lease rates were competitive with

Exhibit 8-2

Columnar Presentation of Fixed Overhead Variance Analysis: Webb Company for April 2008[a]

	Actual Costs Incurred (1)		**Flexible Budget: Same Budgeted Lump Sum (as in Static Budget) Regardless of Output Level (2)**		**Allocated: Budgeted Input Quantity Allowed for Actual Output × Budgeted Rate (3)**
					(0.40 hr./unit × 10,000 units × $57.50/hr.)
					(4,000 hrs. × $57.50/hr.)
	$285,000		$276,000		$230,000
Level 3		9,000 U Spending variance		$46,000 U Production-volume variance	
Level 2		$9,000 U Flexible-budget variance			

[a]F = favorable effect on operating income; U = unfavorable effect on operating income.

lease rates available elsewhere. If this were not the case, management would look to lease equipment from other suppliers.

Production-Volume Variance

We now consider a variance—the production-volume variance—that arises only for fixed costs.

Computing the Production-Volume Variance

Using standard costing, Webb's budgeted fixed overhead costs are allocated to actual output produced during the period at the budgeted rate of \$57.50 per standard machine-hour or \$23 per jacket (0.40 machine-hour per jacket × \$57.50 per machine-hour). So, if Webb produces 1,000 jackets, \$23,000 (\$23 per jacket × 1,000 jackets) out of April's budgeted fixed overhead costs of \$276,000 will be allocated to the jackets. If Webb produces 10,000 jackets, \$230,000 (\$23 per jacket × 10,000 jackets) will be allocated. Only if Webb produces 12,000 jackets (that is, operates at capacity), will all \$276,000 (\$23 per jacket × 12,000 jackets) of the budgeted fixed overhead cost be allocated to the jacket output. The key point here is that even though Webb budgets fixed overhead costs to be \$276,000 it does not necessarily allocate all these costs to output. The reason is that Webb budgets \$276,000 of fixed costs to support its planned production of 12,000 jackets. If Webb produces fewer than 12,000 jackets, it only allocates the budgeted cost of capacity actually needed and used to produce the jackets.

The **production-volume variance**, also referred to as the **denominator-level variance**, is the difference between budgeted fixed overhead and fixed overhead allocated on the basis of actual output produced. The allocated fixed overhead can be expressed in terms of allocation-base units (machine-hours for Webb) or in terms of the budgeted fixed cost per unit:

$$
\begin{aligned}
\text{Production volume variance} &= \text{Budgeted fixed overhead} - \text{Fixed overhead allocated for actual output units produced} \\
&= \$276{,}000 - (0.40 \text{ hour per jacket} \times \$57.50 \text{ per hour} \times 10{,}000 \text{ jackets}) \\
&= \$276{,}000 - (\$23 \text{ per jacket} \times 10{,}000 \text{ jackets}) \\
&= \$276{,}000 - \$230{,}000 \\
&= \$46{,}000 \text{ U}
\end{aligned}
$$

As shown in Exhibit 8-2, the budgeted fixed overhead (\$276,000) will be the lump sum shown in the static budget and also in any flexible budget within the relevant range. Fixed overhead allocated (\$230,000) is the amount of fixed overhead costs allocated; it is calculated by multiplying the number of output units produced during the budget period (10,000 units) by the budgeted cost per output unit (\$23). The \$46,000 U production-volume variance can also be thought of as \$23 per jacket × 2,000 jackets that were *not* produced (12,000 jackets planned − 10,000 jackets produced). We will explore possible causes for the unfavorable production-volume variance and its management implications in the following section.

Exhibit 8-3 is a graphic presentation of the production-volume variance. Exhibit 8-3 shows that for planning and control purposes, fixed (manufacturing) overhead costs do not change in the 0- to 12,000-unit relevant range. Contrast this behavior of fixed costs with how these costs are depicted for the inventory costing purpose in Exhibit 8-3. Under generally accepted accounting principles, fixed (manufacturing) overhead costs are allocated as an inventoriable cost to the output units produced. Every output unit that Webb manufactures will increase the fixed overhead allocated to products by \$23. That is, for purposes of allocating fixed overhead costs to jackets, these costs are viewed *as if* they had a variable-cost behavior pattern. As the graph in Exhibit 8-3 shows, the difference between the fixed overhead costs budgeted of \$276,000 and the \$230,000 of costs allocated is the \$46,000 unfavorable production-volume variance.

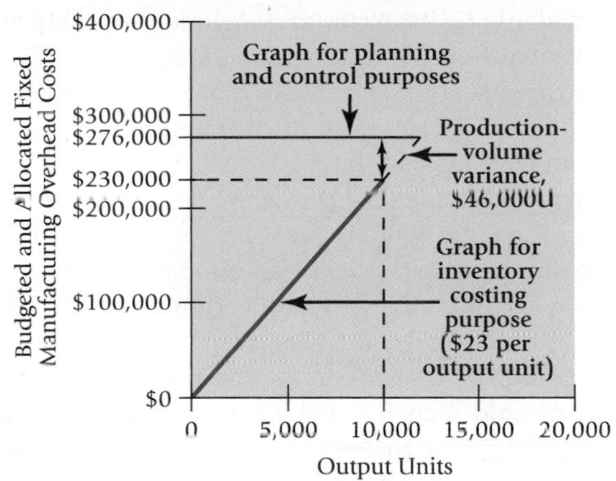

Exhibit 8-3

Behavior of Fixed Manufacturing Overhead Costs; Budgeted for Planning and Control Purposes and Allocated for Inventory Costing Purposes for Webb Company for April 2008

Managers should always be careful to distinguish the behavior of fixed costs from how fixed costs are allocated to products. In particular, managers should not use the unitization of fixed overhead costs for planning and control decisions, where it is important to understand how fixed costs behave. When forecasting fixed costs, managers should concentrate on total lump-sum costs.

Interpreting the Production-Volume Variance

Lump-sum fixed costs represent costs of acquiring capacity, such as plant and equipment leases, that do not decrease automatically if the resources needed turn out to be less than the resources acquired. Sometimes costs are fixed for contractual reasons such as a lease contract; at other times, costs are fixed because of lumpiness in acquiring and disposing of capacity—for example, Webb may be able to add capacity to produce jackets only in increments of say 1,000 jackets. If this is the case, Webb may choose capacity levels of 10,000, 11,000, or 12,000 jackets but nothing in between.

Webb's management would want to analyze why this overcapacity occurred. Is demand weak? Should Webb reevaluate its product and marketing strategies? Is there a quality problem? Or did Webb make a strategic mistake by acquiring too much capacity? The causes of the $46,000 unfavorable production-volume variance will drive the actions Webb's managers will take in response to this variance.

In contrast, a favorable production-volume variance indicates an overallocation of fixed overhead costs. That is, the overhead costs allocated to the actual output produced exceed the budgeted fixed overhead costs of $276,000. The favorable production-volume variance comprises the fixed costs recorded in excess of $276,000.

Be careful when drawing conclusions regarding a company's decisions about capacity planning and usage from the type (that is, favorable, F, or unfavorable, U) or the magnitude associated with a production-volume variance. To interpret the $46,000 unfavorable variance, Webb should consider why it sold only 10,000 jackets in April. Suppose a new competitor had gained market share by pricing below Webb's selling price. To sell the budgeted 12,000 jackets, Webb might have had to reduce its own selling price on all 12,000 jackets. Suppose it decided that selling 10,000 jackets at a higher price yielded higher operating income than selling 12,000 jackets at a lower price. The production-volume variance does not take into account such information. That's why Webb should not interpret the $46,000 U amount as the total economic cost of selling 2,000 jackets fewer than the 12,000 jackets budgeted. If, however, Webb's managers anticipate they will not need capacity beyond 10,000 jackets, they may reduce the excess capacity, say, by canceling the lease on some of the machines.

Companies plan their plant capacity strategically on the basis of market information about how much capacity will be needed over some future time horizon. For 2008, Webb's budgeted quantity of output is equal to the maximum capacity of the plant for that budget period. Actual demand (and quantity produced) turned out to be below the budgeted quantity of output, so Webb reports an unfavorable production-volume variance for

April 2008. However, it would be incorrect to conclude that Webb's management made a poor planning decision regarding plant capacity. Demand for Webb's jackets might be highly uncertain. Given this uncertainty and the cost of not having sufficient capacity to meet sudden demand surges (for example, lost contribution margins and reduced follow-on business), Webb's management may have made a wise choice in planning 2008 plant capacity. Of course, if demand is unlikely to pick up again, Webb's managers may look to cancel the lease on some of the machines or to sublease the machines to other parties with the goal of reducing the unfavorable production-volume variance.

Managers must always explore the why of a variance before concluding that the label unfavorable or favorable necessarily indicates, respectively, poor or good management performance. Understanding the reasons for a variance also helps managers decide on future courses of action. Should Webb's managers try to reduce capacity, increase sales, or do nothing? Based on their analysis of the situation, Webb's managers decided to reduce some capacity but continued to maintain some excess capacity to accommodate unexpected surges in demand. Chapter 9 and Chapter 13 examine these issues in more detail. The Concepts in Action feature on p. 273 highlights another example of managers using variances, and the reasons behind them, to help guide their decisions.

Next we describe the journal entries Webb would make to record fixed overhead costs using standard costing.

Journal Entries for Fixed Overhead Costs and Variances

We illustrate journal entries for fixed overhead costs for April 2008 using Fixed Overhead Control and the contra account Fixed Overhead Allocated (data from Exhibit 8-2).

1.	Fixed Overhead Control	285,000	
	Salaries Payable, Accumulated Depreciation, and various other accounts		285,000
	To record actual fixed overhead costs incurred.		
2.	Work-in-Process Control	230,000	
	Fixed Overhead Allocated		230,000
	To record fixed overhead costs allocated, (0.40 machine-hour/unit × 10,000 units × $57.50/machine-hour). (The costs accumulated in Work-in-Process Control are transferred to Finished Goods Control when production is completed and to Cost of Goods Sold when the products are sold.)		
3.	Fixed Overhead Allocated	230,000	
	Fixed Overhead Spending Variance	9,000	
	Fixed Overhead Production-Volume Variance	46,000	
	Fixed Overhead Control		285,000
	To record variances for the accounting period.		

Note how the fixed overhead spending variance and the fixed overhead production-volume variance record the $55,000 ($285,000 − $230,000) of fixed overhead costs that have been incurred but not allocated to jackets. These variances are the underallocated fixed overhead costs that we introduced when studying normal costing in Chapter 4.

At the end of the fiscal year, the fixed overhead spending variance is written off to cost of goods sold if it is immaterial in amount, or prorated among Work-in-Process Control, Finished Goods Control and Cost of Goods Sold on the basis of the fixed overhead allocated to these accounts as described in Chapter 4, pages 115–119. Some companies combine the write-off and proration methods—that is, they write off the portion of the variance that is due to inefficiency and could have been avoided and prorate the portion of the variance that is unavoidable. Assume that the balance in the Fixed Overhead Spending

Concepts in Action

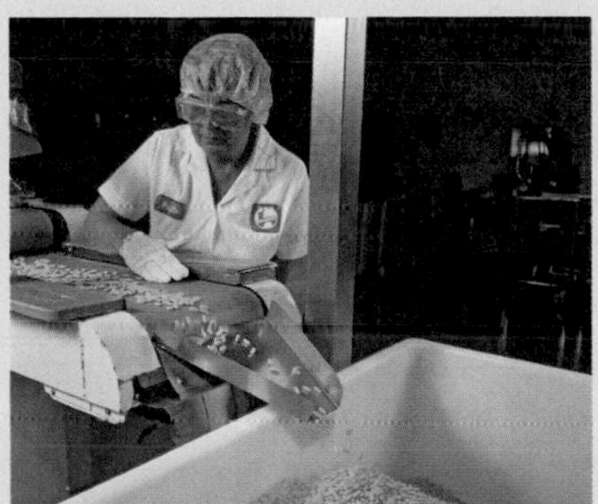

Variance Analysis and Standard Costing Help Sandoz Manage Its Overhead Costs

How does a major manufacturing company, such as Sandoz US, maintain its competitive advantage? In addition to its intricate analysis of direct cost variances, Sandoz must also tackle the challenge of accounting for overhead cost variances. With generic pharmaceutical companies operating on very thin profit margins, it is important to examine how Sandoz uses variance analysis and standard costing to manage its overhead costs.

Each year, Sandoz prepares an overhead budget based on a detailed product production plan, planned overhead spending, and other factors, including inflation, efficiency initiatives, and anticipated capital expenditures and depreciation. Sandoz then uses activity-based costing techniques to assign budgeted overhead costs to different work centers (for example, mixing, blending, tableting, testing, and packaging). Finally, overhead costs are assigned to products based on the activity levels required by each product at each work center. The resulting standard product cost is used in product profitability analysis and as a basis for making pricing decisions. The two main focal points in Sandoz's performance analyses are overhead absorption analysis and manufacturing overhead variance analysis.

Each month, Sandoz uses absorption analysis to compare actual production and actual costs to the standard costs of processed inventory. The monthly analysis evaluates two key trends:

1. Are costs in line with the budget? If not, the reasons are examined and the accountable managers notified.
2. Are production volume and product mix conforming to plan? If not, Sandoz reviews and adjusts machine capacities and the absorption trend is deemed to be permanent. Plant management uses absorption analysis as a compass to determine if they are on budget and have an appropriate capacity level to efficiently satisfy the needs of their customers.

Manufacturing overhead variances are examined at the work center level. These variances help determine when equipment is not running as expected, which leads to repair or replacement. Variances also help in identifying inefficiencies in processing and setup and cleaning times, which leads to more efficient ways to use equipment. Sometimes, manufacturing overhead variance analysis leads to the review and improvement of the standards themselves—a critical element in planning the level of plant capacity. Management reviews current and future capacity use on a monthly basis, using standard hours entered into the plan's Enterprise Resource Planning system. The standards are a useful tool in identifying capacity constraints and future capital needs.

As the plant controller remarked, "Standard costing at Sandoz produces costs that are not only understood by management accountants and industrial engineers, but by decision makers in marketing and on the production floor. Management accountants at Sandoz achieve this by having a high degree of process understanding and involvement. The result is better pricing and product mix decisions, lower waste, process improvements, and efficient capacity choices—all contributing to overall profitability." With continued price pressures on generic pharmaceuticals, like Wal-Mart's recent decision to sell many popular generic drugs for $4 per prescription, Sandoz's focus on overhead cost variances will be critical to maintain profitability and growth.

Source: Conversations with, and documents prepared by, Eric Evans and Erich Erchr (of Sandoz US) on March 20, 2004 and May 28, 2004; "Wal-Mart Cuts Generic Prescription Medicines to $4," Wal-Mart Stores, Inc. press release, Bentonville, Arkansas, September 21, 2006; conversations with, and documents prepared by, John Niedermayer (pharmaceutical consultant) August 31, 2007.

Variance account as of April 2008 is also the balance at the end of 2008 and is immaterial in amount. The following journal entry records the write-off to Cost of Goods Sold.

Cost of Goods Sold	9,000	
Fixed Overhead Spending Variance		9,000

We now consider the production-volume variance. Assume that the balance in Fixed Overhead Production-Volume Variance as of April 2008 is also the balance at the end of 2008. Also assume that some of the jackets manufactured during 2008 are in work-in-process and finished goods inventory at the end of the year. Many management accountants make a strong argument for writing off to Cost of Goods Sold and not prorating an unfavorable production-volume variance. Proponents of this argument contend that the unfavorable production-volume variance of $46,000 measures the cost of resources expended for 2,000 jackets that were not produced ($23 per jacket × 2,000 jackets = $46,000). Prorating these costs would inappropriately allocate fixed overhead costs incurred for the 2,000 jackets that were not produced to the jackets that were produced. The jackets produced already bear their representative share of fixed overhead costs of $23 per jacket. Therefore, this argument favors charging the unfavorable production-volume variance against the year's revenues so that fixed costs of unused capacity are not carried in work-in-process inventory and finished goods inventory.

There is, however, an alternative view. This view regards the denominator level chosen as a "soft" rather than a "hard" measure of the fixed resources required and needed to produce each jacket. Suppose that either because of the design of the jacket or the functioning of the machines, it took more machine-hours than previously thought to manufacture each jacket. Consequently, Webb could make only 10,000 jackets rather than the planned 12,000 in April. In this case, the $276,000 of budgeted fixed overhead costs support the production of the 10,000 jackets manufactured. Under this reasoning, prorating the fixed overhead production-volume variance would appropriately spread fixed overhead costs among Work-in-Process Control, Finished Goods Control, and Cost of Goods Sold.

What about a favorable production-volume variance? Suppose Webb manufactured 13,800 jackets in April 2008.

Production-volume variance	=	Budgeted fixed overhead	−	Fixed overhead allocated using budgeted cost per output unit overhead allowed for actual output produced
	=	$276,000	−	($23 per jacket × 13,800 jackets)
	=	$276,000	−	$317,400 = $41,400 F

Because actual production exceeded the planned capacity level, clearly the fixed overhead costs of $276,000 supported production of, and so should be allocated to, all 13,800 jackets. Prorating the favorable production-volume variance achieves this outcome and reduces the amounts in Work-in-Process Control, Finished Goods Control, and Cost of Goods Sold. Proration is also the more conservative approach in the sense that it results in a lower operating income than if the entire favorable production-volume variance were credited to Cost of Goods Sold.

One more point is relevant to the discussion of whether to prorate the production-volume variance or to write it off to cost of goods sold. If variances are always written off to cost of goods sold, a company could set its standards to either increase (for financial reporting purposes) or decrease (for tax purposes) operating income. In other words, always writing off variances invites gaming behavior. For example, Webb could generate a favorable (unfavorable) production-volume variance by setting the denominator level used to allocate fixed overhead costs low (high) and thereby increase (decrease) operating income. The proration method has the effect of approximating the allocation of fixed costs based on actual costs and actual output so it is not susceptible to the manipulation of operating income via the choice of the denominator level.

There is no clear-cut or preferred approach for closing out the production-volume variance. The appropriate accounting procedure is a matter of judgment and depends on the circumstances of each case. Variations of the proration method may be desirable. For example, a company may choose to write off a portion of the production-volume variance and prorate the rest. The goal is to write off that part of the production-volume variance that represents the cost of capacity not used to support the production of output during the period. The rest of the production-volume variance is prorated to Work-in-Process Control, Finished Goods Control, and Cost of Goods Sold.

If Webb were to write off the production-volume variance to cost of goods sold, it would make the following journal entry.

Cost of Goods Sold	46,000	
Fixed Overhead Production-Volume Variance		46,000

Integrated Analysis of Overhead Cost Variances

Learning Objective 6

Show how the 4-variance analysis approach reconciles the actual overhead incurred with the overhead amounts allocated during the period

. . . the 4-variance analysis approach identifies spending and efficiency variances for variable overhead costs and spending and production-volume variances for fixed overhead costs

As our discussion indicates, the variance calculations for variable overhead and fixed overhead differ.

- Variable overhead has no production-volume variance.
- Fixed overhead has no efficiency variance.

Exhibit 8-4 presents an integrated summary of the variable overhead variances and the fixed overhead variances computed using standard costs for April 2008. Panel A shows the variances for variable overhead, while Panel B contains the fixed overhead variances. As you study Exhibit 8-4, note how the columns in Panels A and B are aligned to measure the different variances. In both Panels A and B,

- The difference between columns 1 and 2 measures the spending variance.
- The difference between columns 2 and 3 measures the efficiency variance (if applicable).
- The difference between columns 3 and 4 measures the production-volume variance (if applicable).

Panel A contains an efficiency variance; Panel B has no efficiency variance for fixed overhead. As discussed earlier, a lump-sum amount of fixed costs will be unaffected by the degree of operating efficiency in a given budget period.

Panel A does not have a production-volume variance. That's because the amount of variable overhead allocated is always the same as the flexible-budget amount. Variable costs never have any unused capacity. When production and sales decline from 12,000 jackets to 10,000 jackets, budgeted variable overhead costs proportionately decline. Fixed costs are different. Panel B has a production-volume variance (see Exhibit 8-3) because Webb had to acquire the fixed manufacturing overhead resources it had committed to when it planned production of 12,000 jackets, even though it produced only 10,000 jackets and did not use some of its capacity.

4-Variance Analysis

When all of the overhead variances are presented together as in Exhibit 8-4, we refer to it as a 4-variance analysis:

4-Variance Analysis

	Spending Variance	Efficiency Variance	Production-Volume Variance
Variable overhead	$4,500 F	$15,000 U	Never a variance
Fixed overhead	$9,000 U	Never a variance	$46,000 U

Note that the 4-variance analysis provides the same level of information as the variance analysis carried out earlier for variable overhead and fixed overhead separately (in Exhibits 8-1 and 8-2, respectively), but it does so in a unified presentation that also indicates those variances that are never present.

As you have seen in the case of other variances, the variances in Webb's 4-variance analysis are not necessarily independent of each other. For example, Webb may purchase lower-quality machine fluids (leading to a favorable variable overhead spending variance), which results in the machines taking longer to operate than budgeted (causing an unfavorable variable overhead efficiency variance), and producing less than budgeted output (causing an unfavorable production-volume variance).

Combined Variance Analysis

Detailed 4-variance analyses are most common in large, complex businesses. That's because it is impossible for managers at a company such as General Electric to keep track of all that is happening within their areas of responsibility. The detailed analyses help

Exhibit 8-4 Columnar Presentation of Integrated Variance Analysis: Webb Company for April 2008[a]

PANEL A: Variable (Manufacturing) Overhead

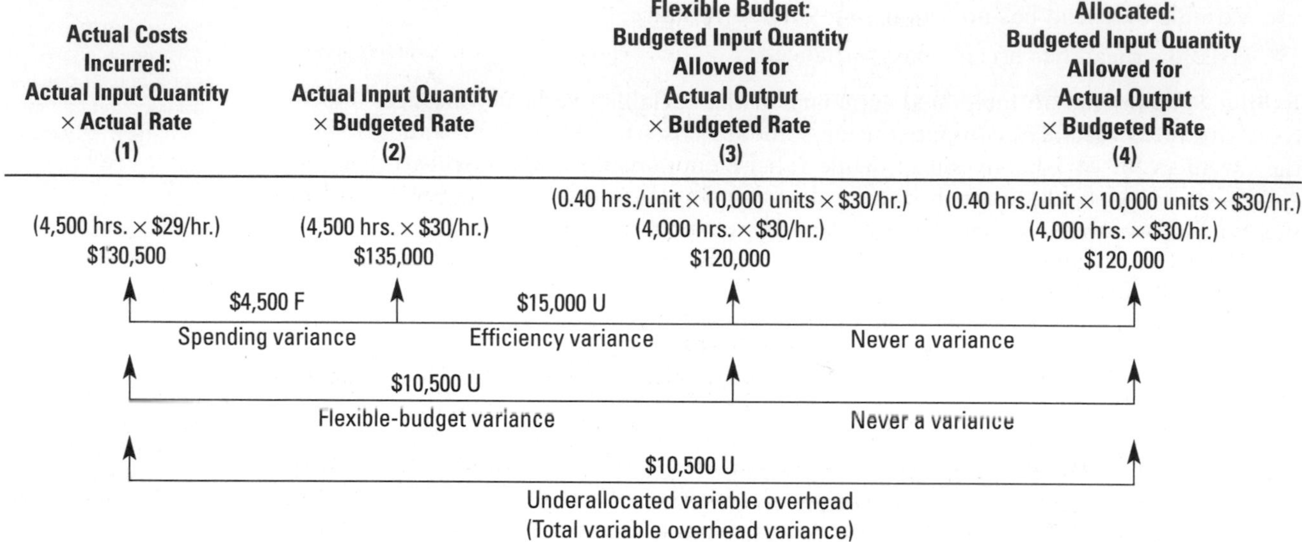

PANEL B: Fixed (Manufacturing) Overhead

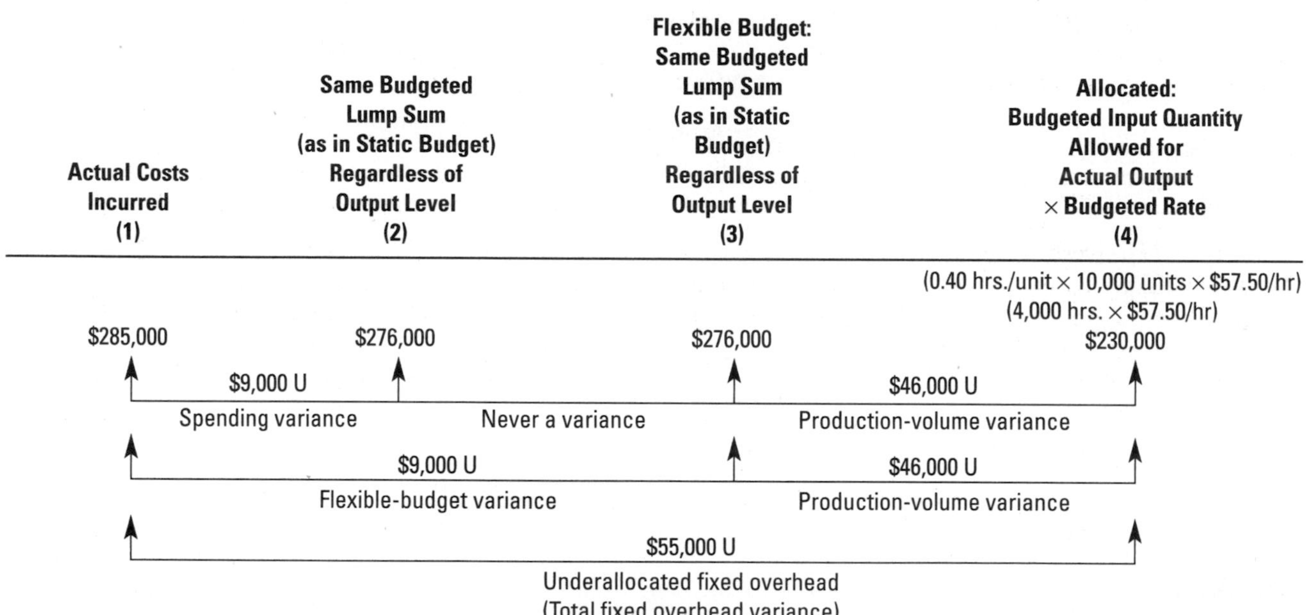

[a]F = favorable effect on operating income; U = unfavorable effect on operating income.

managers identify and focus attention on the areas not operating as expected. Managers of small businesses understand their operations better based on personal observations and nonfinancial measures. They find less value in doing the additional measurements required for 4-variance analyses. For example, to simplify their costing systems, small companies may not distinguish variable overhead incurred from fixed overhead incurred because making this distinction is often not clear-cut. As we saw in Chapter 2 and will see in Chapter 10, many costs such as supervision, quality control, and materials handling have both variable- and fixed-cost components that may not be easy to separate. Managers may therefore use a less detailed analysis that *combines* the variable overhead and fixed overhead into a single total overhead.

When a single total overhead cost category is used, it can still be analyzed at varying levels of detail. For each level of detail, the variances are the sums of the variable overhead and fixed overhead variances for that level, as computed in Exhibit 8-4. At its most detailed level of analysis, the combined variance analysis looks as follows.

Combined 3-Variance Analysis

	Spending Variance	Efficiency Variance	Production-Volume Variance
Total overhead	$4,500 U	$15,000 U	$46,000 U

The accounting for 3-variance analysis is simpler than for 4-variance analysis, but some information is lost. In particular, the 3-variance analysis combines the variable and fixed overhead spending variances into a single total overhead spending variance.

A 2-variance analysis aggregates the spending and efficiency variances from the 3-variance analysis.

Combined 2-Variance Analysis

	Flexible-Budget Variance	Production-Volume Variance
Total overhead	$19,500 U	$46,000 U

The combined 2-variance analysis compares actual costs to the flexible budget to compute the flexible-budget variance and the budgeted and allocated fixed costs to compute the production-volume variance. Unlike 3-variance analysis, 2-variance analysis does not use information about the actual inputs (machine-hours) used in April (the information required in Exhibit 8-4, Panel A, column 2, to subdivide the variable overhead flexible-budget variance into the spending variance and the efficiency variance).

Finally, a combined 1-variance analysis combines the flexible-budget variance and the production-volume variance into a single overhead variance figure:

Combined 1-Variance Analysis

	Total Overhead Variance
Total overhead	$65,500 U

The single **total-overhead variance** equals the total amount of underallocated (or underapplied) overhead costs. (Recall our discussion of underallocated overhead costs in normal costing from Chapter 4, page 116.) Using figures from Exhibit 8-4, the $65,500 U total-overhead variance is the difference between (a) the total actual overhead incurred ($130,500 + $285,000 = $415,500) and (b) the overhead allocated ($120,000 + $230,000 = $350,000) to the actual output produced.

Production-Volume Variance and Sales-Volume Variance

As we complete our study of variance analysis for Webb Company, it is helpful to step back to see the "big picture" and to link the accounting and performance evaluation functions of standard costing. Exhibit 7-2, page 229, subdivided the static-budget variance of $93,100 U into a flexible budget variance of $29,100 U and a sales-volume variance of $64,000 U. In both Chapter 7 and this chapter, we presented more detailed variances that subdivided, whenever possible, individual flexible-budget variances for selling price, direct materials, direct manufacturing labor, variable overhead, and fixed overhead. Here is a summary:

Selling price	$50,000 F
Direct materials (Price, $44,400 F + Efficiency, $66,000 U)	21,600 U
Direct labor (Price, $18,000 U + Efficiency, $20,000 U)	38,000 U
Variable overhead (Spending, $4,500 F + Efficiency, $15,000 U)	10,500 U
Fixed overhead (Spending, $9,000 U)	9,000 U
Total flexible budget variance	$29,100 U

We also calculated one other variance in this chapter, the production-volume variance, which is not part of the flexible-budget variance. The natural question that arises is: where does the production-volume variance fit into the "big picture?" As we shall see, the production-volume variance is a component of the sales-volume variance.

Under our assumption of actual production and sales of 10,000 jackets, Webb's costing system debits to Work-in-Process Control the standard costs of the 10,000 jackets produced, which are then transferred to Finished Goods and finally to Cost of Goods Sold:

Direct materials (Chapter 7, p. 238, Entry 1b)	
($60 per jacket × 10,000 jackets)	$ 600,000
Direct manufacturing labor (Chapter 7, p. 238, Entry 2)	
($16 per jacket × 10,000 jackets)	160,000
Variable overhead (Chapter 8, p. 267, Entry 2)	
($12 per jacket × 10,000 jackets)	120,000
Fixed overhead (Chapter 8, p. 272, Entry 2)	
($23 per jacket × 10,000 jackets)	230,000
Cost of goods sold at standard cost	
($111 per jacket × 10,000 jackets)	$1,110,000

Webb's costing system also records the revenues from the 10,000 jackets sold at the budgeted selling price of $120 per jacket. The net effect of these entries on Webb's budgeted operating income is as follows:

Revenues at budgeted selling price	
($120 per jacket × 10,000 jackets)	$1,200,000
Cost of goods sold at standard cost	
($111 per jacket × 10,000 jackets)	1,110,000
Operating income based on budgeted profit per jacket	
($9 per jacket × 10,000 jackets)	$ 90,000

A crucial point to keep in mind is that in standard costing, fixed overhead cost is treated as if it is a variable cost. That is, in determining the budgeted operating income of $90,000, only $230,000 ($23 per jacket × 10,000 jackets) of fixed overhead is considered, whereas the budgeted fixed overhead costs are $276,000. Webb's accountants then record the $46,000 unfavorable production-volume variance (the difference between budgeted fixed overhead costs, $276,000, and allocated fixed overhead costs, $230,000, p. 272, Entry 2), as well as the various flexible-budget variances (including the fixed overhead spending variance) that total $29,100 unfavorable (see Exhibit 7-2, p. 229). This results in actual operating income of $14,900 as follows:

Operating income based on budgeted profit per jacket	
($9 per jacket × 10,000 jackets)	$90,000
Unfavorable production-volume variance	(46,000)
Flexible-budget operating income (Exhibit 7-2)	44,000
Unfavorable flexible-budget variance for operating income (Exhibit 7-2)	(29,100)
Actual operating income (Exhibit 7-2)	$14,900

In contrast, the static-budget operating income of $108,000 (p. 227) is not entered in Webb's costing system. The reason is that standard costing records budgeted revenues, standard costs, and variances only for the 10,000 jackets actually produced and sold, not for the 12,000 jackets that were *planned* to be produced and sold. It follows that the sales-volume variance of $64,000 U, which is the difference between static-budget operating income, $108,000, and flexible-budget operating income, $44,000 (Exhibit 7-2, p. 229), is never actually recorded in standard costing. Nevertheless, the sales-volume variance is useful because it helps managers understand the lost contribution margin from selling 2,000 fewer jackets (the sales-volume variance assumes fixed costs remain at the budgeted level of $276,000).

What are the components of the sales-volume variance? First, consider the difference between the static-budget operating income of $108,000 for 12,000 jackets and budgeted operating income of $90,000 for 10,000 jackets. This is the *operating-income volume variance* of $18,000 U ($108,000 − $90,000), and reflects the fact that Webb produced and sold 2,000 fewer units than budgeted. The second component of the sales-volume variance is the difference between the budgeted operating income of $90,000 and the flexible budget operating income of $44,000 (Exhibit 7-2, p. 229) for the 10,000 actual units. This difference arises because Webb's costing system treats fixed costs as if they behave in a variable manner and so assumes fixed costs equal the allocated amount of $230,000 rather than the budgeted fixed costs of $276,000. Of course, the difference between the allocated and budgeted fixed costs is precisely the production-volume variance of $46,000 U. Therefore,

	Operating-income volume variance	$18,000 U
(+)	Production-volume variance	46,000 U
Equals	Sales-volume variance	$64,000 U

That is, the sales-volume variance is comprised of production volume and operating income volume variances.

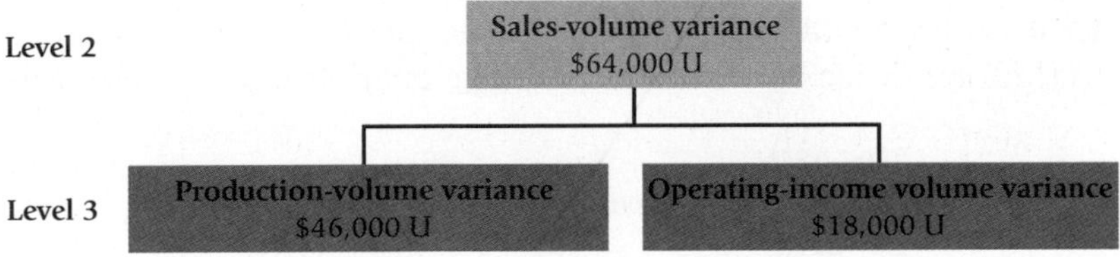

Financial and Nonfinancial Performance Measures

The overhead variances discussed in this chapter are examples of financial performance measures. Managers also find that nonfinancial measures provide useful information. Nonfinancial measures that Webb would likely find helpful in planning and controlling its overhead costs are:

1. Quantity of actual indirect materials used per machine-hour, relative to quantity of budgeted indirect materials used per machine-hour
2. Actual energy used per machine-hour, relative to budgeted energy used per machine-hour
3. Actual machine-hours per jacket, relative to budgeted machine-hours per jacket

These performance measures, like the financial variances discussed in this chapter and Chapter 7, can be described as signals to direct managers' attention to problems. These nonfinancial performance measures probably would be reported daily or hourly on the production floor. The overhead variances we discussed in this chapter capture the financial effects of items such as the three factors listed above, which in many cases first appear as nonfinancial performance measures.

Both financial and nonfinancial performance measures are used to evaluate the performance of managers. Exclusive reliance on either is always too simplistic because each gives a different perspective on performance. Nonfinancial measures (such as those described above) provide feedback on individual aspects of a manager's performance, whereas financial measures evaluate the overall effect of and the tradeoffs among different nonfinancial performance measures.

Overhead Cost Variances in Nonmanufacturing and Service Settings

Our Webb Company example examines variable manufacturing overhead costs and fixed manufacturing overhead costs. Should the overhead costs of the nonmanufacturing areas of the company be examined using the variance analysis framework discussed in this chapter? Companies often use variable-cost information pertaining to nonmanufacturing, as well as manufacturing, costs in pricing and product mix decisions. Managers consider variance analysis of all variable overhead costs when making such decisions and when managing costs. For example, managers in industries in which distribution costs are high, such as automobiles, consumer durables, and cement and steel, may use standard costing to give reliable and timely information on variable distribution overhead spending variances and efficiency variances.

Consider service-sector companies such as airlines, hospitals, hotels, and railroads. The measures of output commonly used in these companies are passenger-miles flown, patient days provided, room-days occupied, and ton-miles of freight hauled, respectively. Few costs can be traced to these outputs in a cost-effective way. The majority of costs are fixed overhead costs (for example, costs of equipment, buildings, and staff). Using capacity effectively is the key to profitability, and fixed overhead variances can help managers in this task. Retail businesses, such as Kmart, also have high capacity-related fixed costs (lease and occupancy costs). In the case of Kmart, sales declines resulted in unused capacity and unfavorable fixed-cost variances. Kmart reduced fixed costs by closing some of its stores, but it also had to file for Chapter 11 bankruptcy.

Consider the following data for United Airlines for 2000, 2003 and 2006. Available seat miles (ASMs) are the actual seats in an airplane multiplied by the distance traveled.

Year	Total ASMs (Millions) (1)	Revenue per ASM (2)	Cost per ASM (3)	Operating Income per ASM (4)=(2) − (3)
2000	175,485	$0.1103	$0.1066	$0.0037
2003	136,630	$0.1006	$0.1104	− $0.0098
2006	143,095	$0.1352	$0.1320	$0.0031

After September 11, 2001, as air travel declined, United's revenues decreased but a majority of its costs comprising fixed costs of airport facilities, equipment, and personnel did not. United had a large unfavorable production-volume variance as its capacity was underutilized. As column 1 of the table indicates, United responded by reducing its capacity from 175,485 million ASMs to 136,630 million, but it was unable to fill even the planes it had retained, so revenue per ASM declined (column 2) and cost per ASM increased (column 3). United filed for Chapter 11 bankruptcy and began seeking government guarantees to obtain the loans it needed. Since then, strong demand for airline travel, as well as yield improvements gained by more efficient use of resources and networks, have led to increased traffic and higher average ticket prices. By maintaining a disciplined approach to capacity and tight control over growth, United saw a 34.4% jump in its revenue per ASM between 2003 and 2006. Despite the 19.6% increase in cost per ASM over this period, due in part to soaring aircraft fuel expenses, the overall improvement in performance allowed United to come out of bankruptcy on February 1, 2006.

Activity-Based Costing and Variance Analysis

Learning Objective 7

Calculate overhead variance in activity-based costing

. . . compare budgeted and actual overhead costs of activities

ABC systems classify costs of various activities into a cost hierarchy: output unit-level, batch-level, product-sustaining, and facility-sustaining (see pp. 147–148). The basic principles and concepts for variable overhead costs and fixed overhead costs presented earlier in the chapter can be applied to ABC systems. In this section, we illustrate variance analysis for variable batch-level setup overhead costs and fixed batch-level setup overhead costs. Batch-level costs are costs of activities that are related to a group of units of products or services rather than to each individual unit.

We continue the Chapter 7 example of Lyco Brass Works, which manufactures Elegance, a line of decorative brass faucets for home spas. Lyco produces Elegance in batches. To manufacture a batch of Elegance, Lyco must set up the machines and molds. Setting up the machines and molds requires highly trained skills. Hence, a separate Setup Department is responsible for setting up machines and molds for different batches of products. Setup costs are overhead costs of products.

Setup costs consist of some costs that are variable and some that are fixed with respect to the number of setup-hours. Variable setup costs consist of wages paid to direct setup labor and indirect support labor, costs of maintenance of setup equipment, and costs of indirect materials and energy used during setups. Fixed setup costs consist of salaries paid to engineers and supervisors and costs of leasing setup equipment.

Information regarding Elegance for 2009 follows:

	Static-Budget Amount	Actual Amount
1. Units of Elegance produced and sold	180,000	151,200
2. Batch size (units per batch)	150	140
3. Number of batches (Line 1 ÷ Line 2)	1,200	1,080
4. Setup hours per batch	6	6.25
5. Total setup-hours (Line 3 × Line 4)	7,200	6,750
6. Variable overhead cost per setup-hour	$20	$21
7. Variable setup overhead costs (Line 5 × Line 6)	$144,000	$141,750
8. Total fixed setup overhead costs	$216,000	$220,000

Flexible Budget and Variance Analysis for Variable Setup Overhead Costs

To prepare the flexible budget for variable setup overhead costs, Lyco starts with the actual units of output produced, 151,200 units, and proceeds using the following steps.

Step 1: Using Budgeted Batch Size, Calculate the Number of Batches That Should Have Been Used to Produce Actual Output. Lyco should have manufactured the 151,200 units of output in 1,008 batches (151,200 units ÷ 150 units per batch).

Step 2: Using Budgeted Setup-Hours per Batch, Calculate the Number of Setup-Hours That Should Have Been Used. At the budgeted quantity of 6 setup-hours per batch, 1,008 batches should have required 6,048 setup-hours (1,008 batches × 6 setup-hours per batch).

Step 3: Using Budgeted Variable Cost per Setup-Hour, Calculate the Flexible Budget for Variable Setup Overhead Costs. The flexible-budget amount is 6,048 setup-hours × $20 per setup-hour = $120,960.

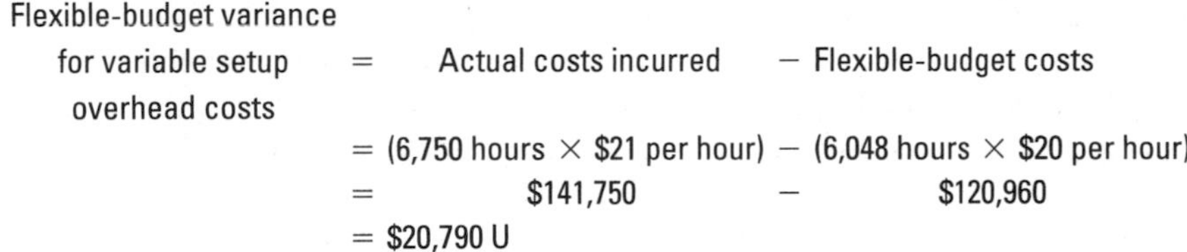
Flexible-budget variance for variable setup overhead costs = Actual costs incurred − Flexible-budget costs
= (6,750 hours × $21 per hour) − (6,048 hours × $20 per hour)
= $141,750 − $120,960
= $20,790 U

Exhibit 8-5 presents the variances for variable setup overhead costs in columnar form.

Exhibit 8-5

Columnar Presentation of Variable Setup Overhead Variance Analysis for Lyco Brass Works for 2009[a]

	Actual Costs Incurred: Actual Input Quantity × Actual Rate (1)		Actual Input Quantity × Budgeted Rate (2)		Flexible Budget: Budgeted Input Quantity Allowed for Actual Output × Budgeted Rate (3)
	(6,750 hours × $21 per hour) $141,750		(6,750 hours × $20 per hour) $135,000		(6,048 hours × $20 per hour) $120,960
Level 3		$6,750 U Spending variance		$14,040 U Efficiency variance	
Level 2			$20,790 U Flexible-budget variance		

[a]F = favorable effect on operating income; U = unfavorable effect on operating income.

The flexible-budget variance for variable setup overhead costs can be subdivided into efficiency and spending variances.

$$\begin{aligned}\text{Variable setup overhead efficiency variance} &= \left(\begin{array}{c}\text{Actual quantity of variable overhead cost-allocation base used for actual output}\end{array} - \begin{array}{c}\text{Budgeted quantity of variable overhead cost-allocation base allowed for actual output}\end{array}\right) \times \begin{array}{c}\text{Budgeted variable overhead cost per unit of cost-allocation base}\end{array}\\ &= (6{,}750 \text{ hours} - 6{,}048 \text{ hours}) \times \$20 \text{ per hour}\\ &= 702 \text{ hours} \times \$20 \text{ per hour}\\ &= \$14{,}040\ \text{U}\end{aligned}$$

The unfavorable variable setup overhead efficiency variance of $14,040 arises because the 6,750 actual setup-hours exceed the 6,048 setup-hours Lyco planned to use for the number of units it produced. Two reasons for the unfavorable efficiency variance are (1) smaller actual batch sizes of 140 units per batch, instead of budgeted batch sizes of 150 units, which resulted in Lyco producing the 151,200 units in 1,080 batches instead of 1,008 batches; and (2) higher actual setup-hours per batch of 6.25 hours instead of the budgeted 6 hours.

Explanations for smaller-than-budgeted batch sizes could include (1) quality problems if batch sizes exceed 140 units (faucets) and (2) high costs of carrying inventory. Explanations for higher actual setup-hours per batch include (1) problems with equipment; (2) undermotivated, inexperienced, or underskilled employees; and (3) inappropriate setup-time standards.

Lyco's variable setup overhead spending variance is calculated as follows:

$$\begin{aligned}\text{Variable setup overhead spending variance} &= \left(\begin{array}{c}\text{Actual variable overhead cost per unit of cost-allocation base}\end{array} - \begin{array}{c}\text{Budgeted variable overhead cost per unit of cost-allocation base}\end{array}\right) \times \begin{array}{c}\text{Actual quantity of variable overhead cost-allocation base used for actual output}\end{array}\\ &= (\$21 \text{ per hour} - \$20 \text{ per hour}) \times 6{,}750 \text{ hours}\\ &= \$1 \text{ per hour} \times 6{,}750 \text{ hours}\\ &= \$6{,}750\ \text{U}\end{aligned}$$

The unfavorable spending variance indicates that in 2009 Lyco operated with a higher-than-budgeted variable overhead cost per setup-hour. Two main reasons that could account for the unfavorable spending variance are (1) actual prices of individual items included in variable overhead, such as setup labor, indirect support labor, or energy, are higher than budgeted prices; and (2) actual quantity usage of individual items, such as indirect support labor and energy, increased more than the increase in setup-hours, due perhaps to setups becoming more complex because of equipment problems. Thus, equipment problems could lead to an unfavorable efficiency variance because setup-hours increase, but they could also lead to an unfavorable spending variance, because each setup-hour requires more resources from the setup cost pool than was budgeted.

Identifying the reasons for these variances is important because it helps managers take corrective action that will be incorporated in future budgets. We now consider fixed setup overhead costs.

Flexible Budget and Variance Analysis for Fixed Setup Overhead Costs

Lyco's fixed setup overhead flexible-budget variance is calculated as follows:

$$\begin{aligned}\text{Fixed-setup overhead flexible-budget variance} &= \text{Actual costs incurred} - \text{Flexible-budget costs}\\ &= \$220{,}000 - \$216{,}000\\ &= \$4{,}000\ \text{U}\end{aligned}$$

Note that the flexible-budget amount for fixed setup overhead costs equals the static-budget amount of $216,000. That's because there is no "flexing" of fixed costs. Moreover, because fixed overhead costs have no efficiency variance, the fixed setup overhead spending variance is the same as the fixed overhead flexible-budget variance. The spending variance could be unfavorable because of higher leasing costs of new setup equipment or higher salaries paid to engineers and supervisors. Lyco may have incurred these costs to alleviate some of the difficulties it was having in setting up machines.

To calculate the production-volume variance, Lyco first computes the budgeted cost-allocation rate for fixed setup overhead costs using the same four-step approach described on page 268.

Step 1: Choose the Period to Use for the Budget. Lyco uses a period of 12 months (the year 2009).

Step 2: Select the Cost-Allocation Base to Use in Allocating Fixed Overhead Costs to Output Produced. Lyco uses budgeted setup-hours as the cost-allocation base for fixed setup overhead costs. Budgeted setup-hours in the static budget for 2009 are 7,200 hours.

Step 3: Identify the Fixed Overhead Costs Associated with the Cost-Allocation Base. Lyco's fixed setup overhead cost budget for 2009 is $216,000.

Step 4: Compute the Rate per Unit of the Cost-Allocation Base Used to Allocate Fixed Overhead Costs to Output Produced. Dividing the $216,000 from step 3 by the 7,200 setup-hours from step 2, Lyco estimates a fixed setup overhead cost rate of $30 per setup-hour:

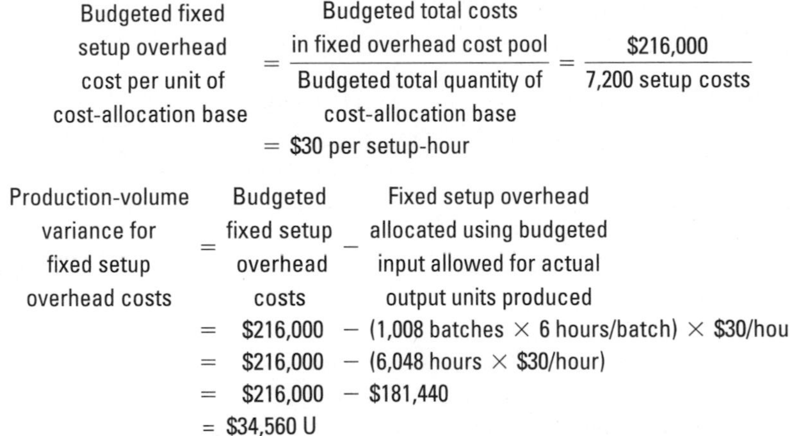

$$\begin{array}{c}\text{Budgeted fixed}\\\text{setup overhead}\\\text{cost per unit of}\\\text{cost-allocation base}\end{array} = \frac{\begin{array}{c}\text{Budgeted total costs}\\\text{in fixed overhead cost pool}\end{array}}{\begin{array}{c}\text{Budgeted total quantity of}\\\text{cost-allocation base}\end{array}} = \frac{\$216{,}000}{7{,}200 \text{ setup costs}}$$

$$= \$30 \text{ per setup-hour}$$

$$\begin{array}{c}\text{Production-volume}\\\text{variance for}\\\text{fixed setup}\\\text{overhead costs}\end{array} = \begin{array}{c}\text{Budgeted}\\\text{fixed setup}\\\text{overhead}\\\text{costs}\end{array} - \begin{array}{c}\text{Fixed setup overhead}\\\text{allocated using budgeted}\\\text{input allowed for actual}\\\text{output units produced}\end{array}$$

$$= \$216{,}000 - (1{,}008 \text{ batches} \times 6 \text{ hours/batch}) \times \$30\text{/hour}$$

$$= \$216{,}000 - (6{,}048 \text{ hours} \times \$30\text{/hour})$$

$$= \$216{,}000 - \$181{,}440$$

$$= \$34{,}560 \text{ U}$$

Exhibit 8-6 presents the variances for fixed setup overhead costs in columnar form.

During 2009, Lyco planned to produce 180,000 units of Elegance but actually produced 151,200 units. The unfavorable production-volume variance measures the amount

Exhibit 8-6

Columnar Presentation of Fixed Setup Overhead Variance Analysis: Lyco Brass Works for 2009[a]

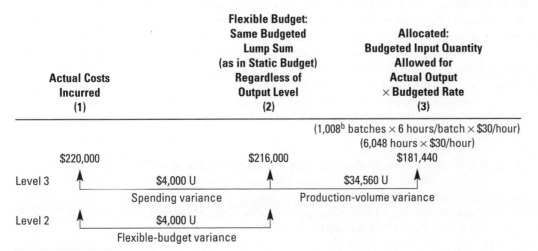

	Actual Costs Incurred (1)		Flexible Budget: Same Budgeted Lump Sum (as in Static Budget) Regardless of Output Level (2)		Allocated: Budgeted Input Quantity Allowed for Actual Output × Budgeted Rate (3)
					(1,008[b] batches × 6 hours/batch × $30/hour)
					(6,048 hours × $30/hour)
	$220,000		$216,000		$181,440
Level 3		$4,000 U Spending variance		$34,560 U Production-volume variance	
Level 2		$4,000 U Flexible-budget variance			

[a]F = favorable effect on operating income; U = unfavorable effect on operating income.

[b]1,008 batches = 151,200 units ÷ 150 units per batch.

of extra fixed setup costs that Lyco incurred for setup capacity it had but did not use. One interpretation is that the unfavorable $34,560 production-volume variance represents inefficient use of setup capacity. However, Lyco may have earned higher operating income by selling 151,200 units at a higher price than 180,000 units at a lower price. As a result, Lyco's managers should interpret the production-volume variance cautiously because it does not consider effects on selling prices and operating income.

Problem for Self-Study

Nina Garcia is the newly appointed president of Laser Products. She is examining the May 2009 results for the Aerospace Products Division. This division manufactures wing parts for satellites. Lopez's current concern is with manufacturing overhead costs at the Aerospace Products Division. Both variable and fixed overhead costs are allocated to the wing parts on the basis of laser-cutting-hours. The following budget information is available:

Budgeted variable overhead rate	$200 per hour
Budgeted fixed overhead rate	$240 per hour
Budgeted laser-cutting time per wing part	1.5 hours
Budgeted production and sales for May 2009	5,000 wing parts
Budgeted fixed overhead costs for May 2009	$1,800,000

Actual results for May 2009 are:

Wing parts produced and sold	4,800 units
Laser-cutting-hours used	8,400 hours
Variable overhead costs	$1,478,400
Fixed overhead costs	$1,832,200

Required

1. Compute the spending variance and the efficiency variance for variable overhead.
2. Compute the spending variance and the production-volume variance for fixed overhead.
3. Give two explanations for each of the variances calculated in requirements 1 and 2.

Solution

1. and 2. See Exhibit 8-7.

3. *a.* Variable overhead spending variance, $201,600 F. One possible reason for this variance is that the actual prices of individual items included in variable overhead (such as cutting fluids) are lower than budgeted prices. A second possible reason is that the percentage increase in the actual quantity usage of individual items in the variable overhead cost pool is less than the percentage increase in laser-cutting-hours compared to the flexible budget.

   b. Variable overhead efficiency variance, $240,000 U. One possible reason for this variance is inadequate maintenance of laser machines, causing them to take more laser-cutting time per wing part. A second possible reason is use of undermotivated, inexperienced, or underskilled workers with the laser-cutting machines, resulting in more laser-cutting time per wing part.

   c. Fixed overhead spending variance, $32,200 U. One possible reason for this variance is that the actual prices of individual items in the fixed-cost pool unexpectedly increased from the prices budgeted (such as an unexpected increase in machine leasing costs). A second possible reason is misclassification of items as fixed that are in fact variable.

d. Production-volume variance, $72,000 U. Actual production of wing parts is 4,800 units, compared with 5,000 units budgeted. One possible reason for this variance is demand factors, such as a decline in an aerospace program that led to a decline in demand for aircraft parts. A second possible reason is supply factors, such as a production stoppage due to labor problems or machine breakdowns.

Exhibit 8-7 Columnar Presentation of Integrated Variance Analysis: Laser Products for May 2009[a]

PANEL A: Variable (Manufacturing) Overhead

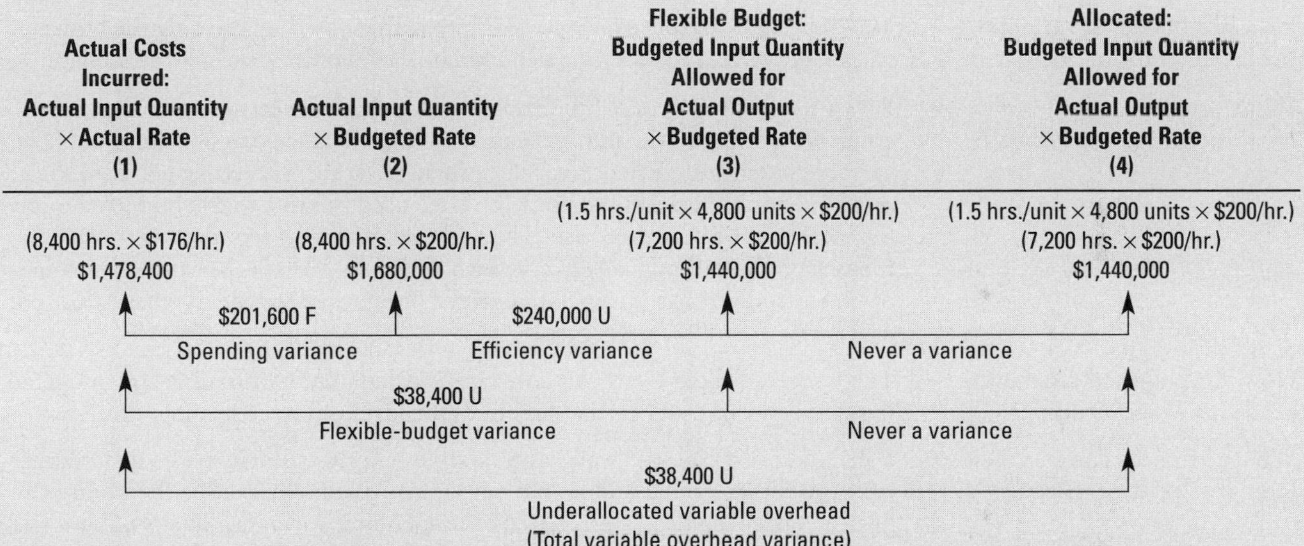

PANEL B: Fixed (Manufacturing) Overhead

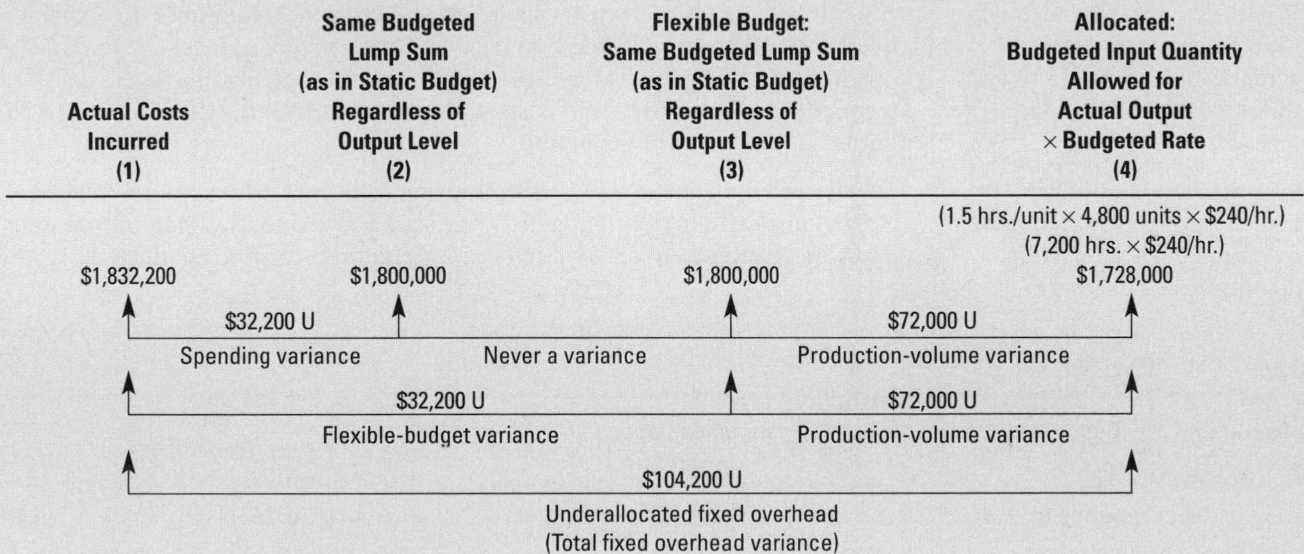

[a]F = favorable effect on operating income; U = unfavorable effect on operating income.

Source: From "The Case for Management Accounting" by Paul Sherman. Used with permission from STRATEGIC FINANCE, October 2003, published by the Institute of Management Accountants, Montvale, NJ, www.imanet.org.

Decision Points

The following question-and-answer format summarizes the chapter's learning objectives. Each decision presents a key question related to a learning objective. The guidelines are the answer to that question.

Decision	Guidelines
1. How do managers plan variable overhead costs and fixed overhead costs?	Planning of both variable and fixed overhead costs involves undertaking only activities that add value and then being efficient in that undertaking. The key difference is that for variable-cost planning, ongoing decisions during the budget period play a much larger role; whereas for fixed-cost planning, most key decisions are made before the start of the period.
2. How is a budgeted variable overhead cost rate calculated?	The budgeted variable overhead cost rate is calculated by dividing the budgeted variable overhead costs by the denominator level of the cost-allocation base.
3. What variances can be calculated for variable overhead?	When the flexible budget for variable overhead is developed, an overhead efficiency variance and an overhead spending variance can be computed. The variable overhead efficiency variance focuses on the difference between the actual quantity of the cost-allocation base used relative to the budgeted quantity of the cost-allocation base. The variable overhead spending variance focuses on the difference between the actual variable overhead cost per unit of the cost-allocation base relative to the budgeted variable overhead cost per unit of the cost-allocation base.
4. How is a budgeted fixed overhead cost rate calculated?	The budgeted fixed overhead cost rate is calculated by dividing the budgeted fixed ovzerhead costs by the denominator level of the cost-allocation base.
5. What variances can be calculated for fixed overhead?	For fixed overhead, the static and flexible budgets coincide. The difference between the budgeted and actual amount of fixed overhead is the flexible-budget variance, also referred to as the spending variance. The production-volume variance measures the difference between budgeted fixed overhead and fixed overhead allocated on the basis of actual output produced.
6. What is the most detailed way for a company to reconcile actual overhead incurred with the amount allocated during a period?	A 4-variance analysis presents spending and efficiency variances for variable overhead costs and spending and production-volume variances for fixed overhead costs. By analyzing these four variances together, managers can reconcile the actual overhead costs with the amount of overhead allocated to output produced during a period.
7. Can the flexible-budget variance approach for analyzing overhead costs be used in activity-based costing?	Yes, flexible budgets in ABC systems give insight into why actual overhead activity costs differ from budgeted overhead activity costs. Using output and input measures for an activity, a 4-variance analysis can be conducted.

TERMS TO LEARN

The chapter and the Glossary at the end of the book contain definitions of:

denominator level (**p. 268**)
denominator-level variance (**p. 270**)
fixed overhead flexible-budget variance (**p. 269**)
fixed overhead spending variance (**p. 269**)
production-denominator level (**p. 268**)
production-volume variance (**p. 270**)
standard costing (**p. 262**)
total-overhead variance (**p. 277**)
variable overhead efficiency variance (**p. 264**)
variable overhead flexible-budget variance (**p. 264**)
variable overhead spending variance (**p. 265**)

ASSIGNMENT MATERIAL

Questions

8-1 How do managers plan for variable overhead costs?

8-2 How does the planning of fixed overhead costs differ from the planning of variable overhead costs?

8-3 How does standard costing differ from actual costing?

8-4 What are the steps in developing a budgeted variable overhead cost-allocation rate?

8-5 What are the factors that affect the spending variance for variable manufacturing overhead?

8-6 Assume variable manufacturing overhead is allocated using machine-hours. Give three possible reasons for a favorable variable overhead efficiency variance.

8-7 Describe the difference between a direct materials efficiency variance and a variable manufacturing overhead efficiency variance.

8-8 What are the steps in developing a budgeted fixed overhead rate?

8-9 Why is the flexible-budget variance the same amount as the spending variance for fixed manufacturing overhead?

8-10 Explain how the analysis of fixed manufacturing overhead costs differs for (a) planning and control on the one hand and (b) inventory costing for financial reporting on the other hand.

8-11 Provide one caveat that will affect whether a production-volume variance is a good measure of the economic cost of unused capacity.

8-12 "The production-volume variance should always be written off to Cost of Goods Sold." Do you agree? Explain.

8-13 What are the variances in a 4-variance analysis?

8-14 "Overhead variances should be viewed as interdependent rather than independent." Give an example.

8-15 Describe how flexible-budget variance analysis can be used in the control of costs of activity areas.

Exercises

8-16 Variable manufacturing overhead, variance analysis. Esquire Clothing is a manufacturer of designer suits. The cost of each suit is the sum of three variable costs (direct material costs, direct manufacturing labor costs, and manufacturing overhead costs) and one fixed-cost category (manufacturing overhead costs). Variable manufacturing overhead cost is allocated to each suit on the basis of budgeted direct manufacturing labor-hours per suit. For June 2009, each suit is budgeted to take four labor-hours. Budgeted variable manufacturing overhead cost per labor-hour is \$12. The budgeted number of suits to be manufactured in June 2009 is 1,040.

Actual variable manufacturing costs in June 2009 were \$52,164 for 1,080 suits started and completed. There were no beginning or ending inventories of suits. Actual direct manufacturing labor-hours for June were 4,536.

Required

1. Compute the flexible-budget variance, the spending variance, and the efficiency variance for variable manufacturing overhead.
2. Comment on the results.

8-17 Fixed manufacturing overhead, variance analysis (continuation of 8-16). Esquire Clothing allocates fixed manufacturing overhead to each suit using budgeted direct manufacturing labor-hours per suit. Data pertaining to fixed manufacturing overhead costs for June 2009 are budgeted, \$62,400, and actual, \$63,916.

Required

1. Compute the spending variance for fixed manufacturing overhead. Comment on the results.
2. Compute the production-volume variance for June 2009. What inferences can Esquire Clothing draw from this variance?

8-18 Variable manufacturing overhead variance analysis. The French Bread Company bakes baguettes for distribution to upscale grocery stores. The company has two direct-cost categories: direct materials and direct manufacturing labor. Variable manufacturing overhead is allocated to products on the basis of standard direct manufacturing labor-hours. Following is some budget data for the French Bread Company:

Direct manufacturing labor use	0.02 hours per baguette
Variable manufacturing overhead	\$10.00 per direct manufacturing labor-hour

The French Bread Company provides the following additional data for the year ended December 31, 2009:

Planned (budgeted) output	3,200,000 baguettes
Actual production	2,800,000 baguettes
Direct manufacturing labor	50,400 hours
Actual variable manufacturing overhead	$680,400

Required

1. What is the denominator level used for allocating variable manufacturing overhead? (That is, for how many direct manufacturing labor-hours is French Bread budgeting?)
2. Prepare a variance analysis of variable manufacturing overhead. Use Exhibit 8-4 (p. 276) for reference.
3. Discuss the variances you have calculated and give possible explanations for them.

8-19 Fixed manufacturing overhead variance analysis (continuation of 8-18). The French Bread Company also allocates fixed manufacturing overhead to products on the basis of standard direct manufacturing labor-hours. For 2009, fixed manufacturing overhead was budgeted at $4.00 per direct manufacturing labor-hour. Actual fixed manufacturing overhead incurred during the year was $272,000.

Required

1. Prepare a variance analysis of fixed manufacturing overhead cost. Use Exhibit 8-4 (p. 276) as a guide.
2. Is fixed overhead underallocated or overallocated? By what amount?
3. Comment on your results. Discuss the variances and explain what may be driving them.

8-20 Manufacturing overhead, variance analysis. The Solutions Corporation is a manufacturer of centrifuges. Fixed and variable manufacturing overheads are allocated to each centrifuge using budgeted assembly-hours. Budgeted assembly time is two hours per unit. The following table shows the budgeted amounts and actual results related to overhead for June 2009.

	A–E	F	G
1	**The Solutions Corporation (June 2009)**	**Actual Results**	**Static Budget**
2	Number of centrifuges assembled and sold	216	200
3	Hours of assembly time	411	
4	Variable manufacturing overhead cost per hour of assembly time		$30.00
5	Variable manufacturing overhead costs	$12,420	
6	Fixed manufacturing overhead costs	$20,560	$19,200

If you want to use Excel to solve this exercise, go to the Excel Lab at **www.prenhall.com/horngren/cost13e** and download the template for Exercise 8-20.

Required

1. Prepare an analysis of all variable manufacturing overhead and fixed manufacturing overhead variances using the columnar approach in Exhibit 8-4 (p. 276).
2. Prepare journal entries for Solutions' June 2009 variable and fixed manufacturing overhead costs and variances; write off these variances to cost of goods sold for the quarter ending June 30, 2009.
3. How does the planning and control of variable manufacturing overhead costs differ from the planning and control of fixed manufacturing overhead costs?

8-21 4-variance analysis, fill in the blanks. Pandom, Inc. produces chemicals for large biotech companies. It has the following data for manufacturing overhead costs during August 2010:

	Variable	**Fixed**
Actual costs incurred	$35,700	$18,000
Costs allocated to products	27,000	14,400
Flexible budget: Budgeted input allowed for actual output produced × budgeted rate	27,000	15,000
Actual input × budgeted rate	31,500	15,000

Use F for favorable and U for unfavorable:

	Variable	Fixed
(1) Spending variance	$____	$____
(2) Efficiency variance	____	____
(3) Production-volume variance	____	____
(4) Flexible-budget variance	____	____
(5) Underallocated (overallocated) manufacturing overhead	____	____

8-22 Straightforward 4-variance overhead analysis. The Lopez Company uses standard costing in its manufacturing plant for auto parts. The standard cost of a particular auto part, based on a denominator level of 4,000 output units per year, included 6 machine-hours of variable manufacturing overhead at $8 per hour and 6 machine-hours of fixed manufacturing overhead at $15 per hour. Actual output produced was 4,400 units. Variable manufacturing overhead incurred was $245,000. Fixed manufacturing overhead incurred was $373,000. Actual machine-hours were 28,400.

Required

1. Prepare an analysis of all variable manufacturing overhead and fixed manufacturing overhead variances, using the 4-variance analysis in Exhibit 8-4 (p. 276).
2. Prepare journal entries using the 4-variance analysis.
3. Describe how individual fixed manufacturing overhead items are controlled from day to day.
4. Discuss possible causes of the fixed manufacturing overhead variances.

8-23 Straightforward coverage of manufacturing overhead, standard-costing system. The Singapore division of a Canadian telecommunications company uses standard costing for its machine-paced production of telephone equipment. Data regarding production during June are as follows:

Variable manufacturing overhead costs incurred	$155,100
Variable manufacturing overhead cost rate	$12 per standard machine-hour
Fixed manufacturing overhead costs incurred	$401,000
Fixed manufacturing overhead costs budgeted	$390,000
Denominator level in machine-hours	13,000
Standard machine-hour allowed per unit of output	0.30
Units of output	41,000
Actual machine-hours used	13,300
Ending work-in-process inventory	0

Required

1. Prepare an analysis of all manufacturing overhead variances. Use the 4-variance analysis framework illustrated in Exhibit 8-4 (p. 276).
2. Prepare journal entries for manufacturing overhead costs and their variances.
3. Describe how individual variable manufacturing overhead items are controlled from day to day.
4. Discuss possible causes of the variable manufacturing overhead variances.

8-24 Overhead variances, service sector. Meals on Wheels (MOW) operates a meal home-delivery service. It has agreements with 20 restaurants to pick up and deliver meals to customers who phone or fax orders to MOW. MOW allocates variable and fixed overhead costs on the basis of delivery time. MOW's owner, Josh Carter, obtains the following information for May 2009 overhead costs:

File Edit View Insert Format Tools Data Window Help

	A	B	C
1	**Meals on Wheels (May 2009)**	**Actual Results**	**Static Budget**
2	Output units (number of deliveries)	8,800	10,000
3	Hours per delivery		0.70
4	Hours of delivery time	5,720	
5	Variable overhead cost per hour of delivery time		$ 1.50
6	Variable overhead costs	$10,296	
7	Fixed overhead costs	$38,600	$35,000

If you want to use Excel to solve this exercise, go to the Excel Lab at **www.prenhall.com/horngren/cost13e** and download the template for Exercise 8-24.

Required

1. Compute spending and efficiency variances for MOW's variable overhead in May 2009.
2. Compute the spending variance and production-volume variance for MOW's fixed overhead in May 2009.
3. Comment on MOW's overhead variances and suggest how Josh Carter might manage MOW's variable overhead differently from its fixed overhead costs.

8-25 Total overhead, 3-variance analysis. Furniture, Inc. specializes in the production of futons. It uses standard costing and flexible budgets to account for the production of a new line of futons. For 2010, budgeted variable overhead at a level of 3,200 standard monthly direct labor-hours was $25,600; budgeted total overhead at 4,000 standard monthly direct labor-hours was $79,040. The standard cost allocated to each output included a total overhead rate of 120% of standard direct labor costs. For October, Furniture, Inc. incurred total overhead of $99,600 and direct labor costs of $80,976. The direct labor price variance was $3,856 unfavorable. The direct labor flexible-budget variance was $5,776 unfavorable. The standard labor price was $16 per hour. The production-volume variance was $5,600, favorable.

Required

1. Compute the direct labor efficiency variance and the spending and efficiency variances for overhead. Also, compute the denominator level.
2. Describe how individual variable overhead items are controlled from day to day. Also, describe how individual fixed overhead items are controlled.

8-26 Overhead variances, missing information. Dvent budgets 18,000 machine-hours for the production of computer chips in August 2009. The budgeted variable overhead rate is $6 per machine-hour. At the end of August, there is a $375 favorable spending variance for variable overhead and a $1,575 unfavorable spending variance for fixed overhead. For the computer chips produced, 14,850 machine-hours are budgeted and 15,000 machine-hours are actually used. Total actual overhead costs are $120,000.

Required

1. Compute efficiency and flexible-budget variances for Dvent's variable overhead in August 2009. Will variable overhead be over- or underallocated? By how much?
2. Compute production-volume and flexible-budget variances for Dvent's fixed overhead in August 2009. Will fixed overhead be over- or underallocated? By how much?

8-27 Identifying favorable and unfavorable variances. Purdue Inc., manufactures tires for large auto companies. It uses standard costing and allocates variable and fixed manufacturing overhead based on machine-hours. For each independent scenario given, indicate whether each of the manufacturing variances will be favorable or unfavorable or, in case of insufficient information, indicate "cannot be determined."

Scenario	Variable Overhead Spending Variance	Variable Overhead Efficiency Variance	Fixed Overhead Spending Variance	Fixed Overhead Production-Volume Variance
Production output is 5% more than budgeted, and actual fixed manufacturing overhead costs are 6% more than budgeted				
Production output is 10% more than budgeted; actual machine-hours are 5% less than budgeted				
Production output is 8% less than budgeted				
Actual machine-hours are 15% greater than flexible-budget machine-hours				
Relative to the flexible budget, actual machine-hours are 10% greater, and actual variable manufacturing overhead costs are 15% greater				

8-28 Flexible-budget variances, review of Chapters 7 and 8. David James is a cost accountant and business analyst for Doorknob Design Company (DDC), which manufactures expensive brass doorknobs. DDC uses two direct cost categories: direct materials and direct manufacturing labor. James feels that manufacturing overhead is most closely related to material usage. Therefore, DDC allocates manufacturing overhead to production based upon pounds of materials used.

At the beginning of 2009, DDC budgeted production of 100,000 doorknobs and adopted the following standards for each doorknob:

Required

	Input	Cost/Doorknob
Direct materials (brass)	0.5 lbs @ $20/lb	$10.00
Direct manufacturing labor	0.25 hours @ $30/hour	7.50
Manufacturing overhead:		
Variable	$10/lb × 0.5 lbs	5.00
Fixed	$ 5/lb × 0.5 lbs	2.50
Standard cost per doorknob		$25.00

Actual results for April 2009 were:

Production	95,000 doorknobs
Direct materials purchased	50,000 lbs at $22/lb
Direct materials used	45,000 lbs
Direct manufacturing labor	20,000 hours for $650,000
Variable manufacturing overhead	$400,000
Fixed manufacturing overhead	$350,000

Required

1. For the month of April, compute the following variances, indicating whether each is favorable (F) or unfavorable (U).
   a. Direct materials price variance (based on purchases).
   b. Direct materials efficiency variance.
   c. Direct manufacturing labor price variance
   d. Direct manufacturing labor efficiency variance
   e. Variable manufacturing overhead spending variance
   f. Variable manufacturing overhead efficiency variance
   g. Production-volume variance
   h. Fixed manufacturing overhead spending variance
2. Can James use any of the variances to help explain any of the other variances? Give examples.

Problems

8-29 Comprehensive variance analysis. Kitchen Whiz manufactures premium food processors. The following is some manufacturing overhead data for Kitchen Whiz for the year ended December 31, 2010:

Manufacturing Overhead	Actual Results	Flexible Budget	Allocated Amount
Variable	$ 76,608	$ 76,800	$ 76,800
Fixed	350,208	348,096	376,320

Budgeted number of output units: 888
Planned allocation rate: 2 machine-hours per unit
Actual number of machine-hours used: 1,824
Static-budget variable manufacturing overhead costs: $71,040
Compute the following quantities (you should be able to do so in the prescribed order):

Required

1. Budgeted number of machine-hours planned
2. Budgeted fixed manufacturing overhead costs per machine-hour
3. Budgeted variable manufacturing overhead costs per machine-hour
4. Budgeted number of machine-hours allowed for actual output produced
5. Actual number of output units
6. Actual number of machine-hours used per output unit

8-30 Journal entries (continuation of 8-29).

Required

1. Prepare journal entries for variable and fixed manufacturing overhead (you will need to calculate the various variances to accomplish this).
2. Overhead variances are written off to the Cost of Goods Sold (COGS) account at the end of the fiscal year. Show how COGS is adjusted through journal entries.

8-31 Graphs and overhead variances. Fresh, Inc. is a manufacturer of vacuums and uses standard costing. Manufacturing overhead (both variable and fixed) is allocated to products on the basis of budgeted machine-hours. In 2009, budgeted fixed manufacturing overhead cost was $18,000,000. Budgeted variable manufacturing overhead was $9 per machine-hour. The denominator level was 1,000,000 machine-hours.

Required

1. Prepare a graph for fixed manufacturing overhead. The graph should display how Fresh, Inc.'s fixed manufacturing overhead costs will be depicted for the purposes of (a) planning and control and (b) inventory costing.
2. Suppose that 875,000 machine-hours were allowed for actual output produced in 2009, but 950,000 actual machine-hours were used. Actual manufacturing overhead was $9,025,000, variable, and $18,050,000, fixed. Compute (a) the variable manufacturing overhead spending and efficiency variances and (b) the fixed manufacturing overhead spending and production-volume variances. Use the columnar presentation illustrated in Exhibit 8-4 (p. 276).
3. What is the amount of the under- or overallocated variable manufacturing overhead and the under- or overallocated fixed manufacturing overhead? Why are the flexible-budget variance and the under- or overallocated overhead amount always the same for variable manufacturing overhead but rarely the same for fixed manufacturing overhead?
4. Suppose the denominator level was 750,000 rather than 1,000,000 machine-hours. What variances in requirement 2 would be affected? Recompute them.

8-32 4-variance analysis, find the unknowns. Consider each of the following situations—cases A, B, and C—independently. Data refer to operations for April 2009. For each situation, assume standard costing. Also assume the use of a flexible budget for control of variable and fixed manufacturing overhead based on machine-hours.

	Cases		
	A	**B**	**C**
(1) Fixed manufacturing overhead incurred	$26,500	—	$30,000
(2) Variable manufacturing overhead incurred	$15,000	—	—
(3) Denominator level in machine-hours	1,250	—	2,750
(4) Standard machine-hours allowed for actual output achieved	—	1,625	—
(5) Fixed manufacturing overhead (per standard machine-hour)	—	—	—
Flexible-budget data:			
(6) Variable manufacturing overhead (per standard machine-hour)	—	$ 8.50	$ 5.00
(7) Budgeted fixed manufacturing overhead	$25,000	—	$27,500
(8) Budgeted variable manufacturing overhead[a]	—	—	—
(9) Total budgeted manufacturing overhead[a]	—	$31,313	—
Additional data:			
(10) Standard variable manufacturing overhead allocated	$18,750	—	—
(11) Standard fixed manufacturing overhead allocated	$25,000	—	—
(12) Production-volume variance	—	$ 1,250 U	$ 1,250 F
(13) Variable manufacturing overhead spending variance	$ 4,875 F	$ 0	$ 875 U
(14) Variable manufacturing overhead efficiency variance	—	$ 0	$ 250 U
(15) Fixed manufacturing overhead spending variance	—	$ 750 F	—
(16) Actual machine-hours used	—	—	—

[a]For standard machine-hours allowed for actual output produced.

Required

Fill in the blanks under each case. [*Hint:* Prepare a worksheet similar to that in Exhibit 8-4 (p. 276). Fill in the knowns and then solve for the unknowns.]

8-33 Flexible budgets, 4-variance analysis. (CMA, adapted) Nolton Products uses standard costing. It allocates manufacturing overhead (both variable and fixed) to products on the basis of standard direct manufacturing labor-hours (DLH). Nolton develops its manufacturing overhead rate from the current annual budget. The manufacturing overhead budget for 2009 is based on budgeted output of 720,000 units, requiring 3,600,000 DLH. The company is able to schedule production uniformly throughout the year.

A total of 66,000 output units requiring 315,000 DLH was produced during May 2009. Manufacturing overhead (MOH) costs incurred for May amounted to $375,000. The actual costs, compared with the annual budget and 1/12 of the annual budget, are as follows:

Annual Manufacturing Overhead Budget 2009

	Total Amount	Per Output Unit	Per DLH Input Unit	Monthly MOH Budget May 2009	Actual MOH Costs for May 2009
Variable MOH					
Indirect manufacturing labor	$ 900,000	$1.25	$0.25	$ 75,000	$ 75,000
Supplies	1,224,000	1.70	0.34	102,000	111,000
Fixed MOH					
Supervision	648,000	0.90	0.18	54,000	51,000
Utilities	540,000	0.75	0.15	45,000	54,000
Depreciation	1,008,000	1.40	0.28	84,000	84,000
Total	$4,320,000	$6.00	$1.20	$360,000	$375,000

Required

Calculate the following amounts for Nolton Products for May 2009:

1. Total manufacturing overhead costs allocated
2. Variable manufacturing overhead spending variance
3. Fixed manufacturing overhead spending variance
4. Variable manufacturing overhead efficiency variance
5. Production-volume variance

Be sure to identify each variance as favorable (F) or unfavorable (U).

8-34 Direct Manufacturing Labor and Variable Manufacturing Overhead Variances. Sarah Beth's Art Supply Company produces various types of paints. Actual direct manufacturing labor hours in the factory that produces paint have been higher than budgeted hours for the last few months and the owner, Sarah B. Jones, is concerned about the effect this has had on the company's cost overruns. Because variable manufacturing overhead is allocated to units produced using direct manufacturing labor hours, Sarah feels that the mismanagement of labor will have a twofold effect on company profitability. Following are the relevant budgeted and actual results for the second quarter of 2008.

	Budget Information	Actual Results
Paint set production	10,000	13,000
Direct manuf. labor hours per paint set	0.5 hour	0.75 hour
Direct manufacturing labor rate	$20/hour	$20.20/hour
Variable manufacturing overhead rate	$10/hour	$ 9.75/hour

Required

1. Calculate the direct manufacturing labor price and efficiency variances and indicate whether each is favorable (F) or unfavorable (U).
2. Calculate the variable manufacturing overhead spending and efficiency variances and indicate whether each is favorable (F) or unfavorable (U).
3. For both direct manufacturing labor and variable manufacturing overhead, do the price/spending variances help Sarah explain the efficiency variances?
4. Is Sarah correct in her assertion that the mismanagement of labor has a twofold effect on cost overruns? Why might the variable manufacturing overhead efficiency variance not be an accurate representation of the effect of labor overruns on variable manufacturing overhead costs?

8-35 Causes of Indirect Variances. Heather's Horse Spa (HHS) is an establishment that boards, trains, and pampers horses while their owners are on vacation. Heather sells her service as an "enchanting vacation experience for your horse while you vacation elsewhere." Horse feed, shampoos, ribbons, and other supplies are treated as variable indirect costs. Consequently, there are no direct materials involved in the vacation service. Other overhead costs including indirect labor, depreciation on the barn, and advertising are fixed. Both variable and fixed overhead are allocated to each horse guest-week using the weight of the horse as the basis of allocation.

HHS budgeted amounts for August 2009 were:

Horse guest-weeks	40
Average weight per horse	900 lbs.
Variable overhead cost per pound of horse	$0.20/lb
Fixed overhead rate	$1.50/lb

Actual results for August 2009 were:

Horse guest-weeks	38
Average weight per horse	950 lbs
Actual variable overhead	$7,500
Actual fixed overhead	$50,000

Required

1. Calculate the variable overhead spending and efficiency variances and indicate whether each is favorable (F) or unfavorable (U).
2. Calculate the fixed overhead spending and production-volume variances and indicate whether each is favorable (F) or unfavorable (U).
3. Explain what the variable overhead spending variance means. What factors could have caused it?
4. What factors could have caused the variable overhead efficiency variance?
5. If fixed overhead is, in fact, fixed, how could a fixed overhead spending variance occur?
6. What caused the fixed overhead production-volume variance? What does it mean? What are the negative implications, if any, of the production-volume variance?

8-36 Activity-based costing, batch-level variance analysis. Rica's Fleet Feet, Inc., produces dance shoes for stores all over the world. While the pairs of shoes are boxed individually, they are crated and shipped in batches. The shipping department records both variable and fixed overhead costs. The following information pertains to shipping costs for 2008.

	Static-Budget Amounts	Actual Results
Pairs of shoes shipped	240,000	180,000
Average number of pairs of shoes per crate	12	10
Packing hours per crate	1.2 hours	1.1 hours
Variable overhead cost per hour	$20	$21
Fixed overhead cost	$60,000	$55,000

Required

1. What is the static budget number of crates for 2008?
2. What is the flexible budget number of crates for 2008?
3. What is the actual number of crates shipped in 2008?
4. Assuming fixed overhead is allocated using crate-packing hours, what is the predetermined fixed overhead allocation rate?
5. For variable overhead costs, compute the spending and efficiency variances.
6. For fixed overhead costs, compute the spending and the production-volume variances.

8-37 Activity-based costing, batch-level variance analysis. Jo Nathan Publishing Company specializes in printing specialty textbooks for a small but profitable college market. Due to the high setup costs for each batch printed, Jo Nathan holds the book requests until demand for a book is approximately 500. At that point Jo Nathan will schedule the setup and production of the book. For rush orders, Jo Nathan will produce smaller batches for an additional charge of $700 per setup.

Budgeted and actual costs for the printing process for 2009 were:

	Static-Budget Amounts	Actual Results
Number of books produced	200,000	216,000
Average number of books per setup	500	480
Hours to set up printers	6 hours	6.5 hours
Variable overhead cost per setup-hour	$100	$90
Total fixed setup overhead costs	$72,000	$79,000

Required

1. What is the static budget number of setups for 2009?
2. What is the flexible budget number of setups for 2009?
3. What is the actual number of setups in 2009?
4. Assuming fixed setup overhead costs are allocated using setup-hours, what is the predetermined fixed setup overhead allocation rate?

5. Does Jo Nathan's charge of $700 cover the budgeted variable overhead cost of an order? The budgeted total overhead cost?
6. For variable setup overhead costs, compute the spending and efficiency variances.
7. For fixed setup overhead costs, compute the spending and the production-volume variances.
8. What qualitative factors should Jo Nathan consider before accepting or rejecting a special order?

8-38 Production-Volume Variance Analysis and Sales Volume Variance. Dawn Floral Creations, Inc., makes jewelry in the shape of flowers. Each piece is hand-made and takes an average of 1.5 hours to produce because of the intricate design and scrollwork. Dawn uses direct labor hours to allocate the overhead cost to production. Fixed overhead costs, including rent, depreciation, supervisory salaries and other production expenses, are budgeted at $9,000 per month. These costs are incurred for a facility large enough to produce 1,000 pieces of jewelry a month.

During the month of February, Dawn produced 600 pieces of jewelry and actual fixed costs were $9,200.

Required

1. Calculate the fixed overhead spending variance and indicate whether it is favorable (F) or unfavorable (U).
2. If Dawn uses direct labor hours available at capacity to calculate the budgeted fixed overhead rate, what is the production-volume variance? Indicate whether it is favorable (F) or unfavorable (U).
3. An unfavorable production-volume variance is a measure of the under-allocation of fixed overhead cost caused by production levels at less than capacity. It therefore could be interpreted as the economic cost of unused capacity. Why would Dawn be willing to incur this cost? Your answer should separately consider the following two unrelated factors:
   a. Demand could vary from month to month while available capacity remains constant.
   b. Dawn would not want to produce at capacity unless it could sell all the units produced. What does Dawn need to do to raise demand and what effect would this have on profit?
4. Dawn's budgeted variable cost per unit is $25 and she expects to sell her jewelry for $55 apiece. Compute the sales-volume variance and reconcile it with the production-volume variance calculated in requirement 2. What does each concept measure?

8-39 Comprehensive review of Chapters 7 and 8, working backward from given variances. The Mancusco Company uses a flexible budget and standard costs to aid planning and control of its machining manufacturing operations. Its costing system for manufacturing has two direct-cost categories (direct materials and direct manufacturing labor—both variable) and two overhead-cost categories (variable manufacturing overhead and fixed manufacturing overhead, both allocated using direct manufacturing labor-hours).

At the 40,000 budgeted direct manufacturing labor-hour level for August, budgeted direct manufacturing labor is $800,000, budgeted variable manufacturing overhead is $480,000, and budgeted fixed manufacturing overhead is $640,000.

The following actual results are for August:

Direct materials price variance (based on purchases)	$176,000 F
Direct materials efficiency variance	69,000 U
Direct manufacturing labor costs incurred	522,750
Variable manufacturing overhead flexible-budget variance	10,350 U
Variable manufacturing overhead efficiency variance	18,000 U
Fixed manufacturing overhead incurred	597,460
Fixed manufacturing overhead spending variance	42,540 F

The standard cost per pound of direct materials is $11.50. The standard allowance is three pounds of direct materials for each unit of product. During August, 30,000 units of product were produced. There was no beginning inventory of direct materials. There was no beginning or ending work in process. In August, the direct materials price variance was $1.10 per pound.

In July, labor unrest caused a major slowdown in the pace of production, resulting in an unfavorable direct manufacturing labor efficiency variance of $45,000. There was no direct manufacturing labor price variance. Labor unrest persisted into August. Some workers quit. Their replacements had to be hired at higher wage rates, which had to be extended to all workers. The actual average wage rate in August exceeded the standard average wage rate by $0.50 per hour.

Required

1. Compute the following for August:
   a. Total pounds of direct materials purchased
   b. Total number of pounds of excess direct materials used
   c. Variable manufacturing overhead spending variance
   d. Total number of actual direct manufacturing labor-hours used
   e. Total number of standard direct manufacturing labor-hours allowed for the units produced
   f. Production-volume variance
2. Describe how Mancusco's control of variable manufacturing overhead items differs from its control of fixed manufacturing overhead items.

8-40 Review of Chapters 7 and 8, 3-variance analysis. (CPA, adapted) The Beal Manufacturing Company's costing system has two direct-cost categories: direct materials and direct manufacturing labor. Manufacturing overhead (both variable and fixed) is allocated to products on the basis of standard direct manufacturing labor-hours (DLH). At the beginning of 2009, Beal adopted the following standards for its manufacturing costs:

	Input	Cost per Output Unit
Direct materials	3 lbs. at $5 per lb.	$ 15.00
Direct manufacturing labor	5 hrs. at $15 per hr.	75.00
Manufacturing overhead:		
Variable	$6 per DLH	30.00
Fixed	$8 per DLH	40.00
Standard manufacturing cost per output unit		$160.00

The denominator level for total manufacturing overhead per month in 2009 is 40,000 direct manufacturing labor-hours. Beal's flexible budget for January 2009 was based on this denominator level. The records for January indicated the following:

Direct materials purchased	25,000 lbs. at $5.20 per lb.
Direct materials used	23,100 lbs.
Direct manufacturing labor	40,100 hrs. at $14.60 per hr.
Total actual manufacturing overhead (variable and fixed)	$600,000
Actual production	7,800 output units

Required

1. Prepare a schedule of total standard manufacturing costs for the 7,800 output units in January 2009.
2. For the month of January 2009, compute the following variances, indicating whether each is favorable (F) or unfavorable (U):
   a. Direct materials price variance, based on purchases
   b. Direct materials efficiency variance
   c. Direct manufacturing labor price variance
   d. Direct manufacturing labor efficiency variance
   e. Total manufacturing overhead spending variance
   f. Variable manufacturing overhead efficiency variance
   g. Production-volume variance

8-41 Non-financial variances. Daisy Canine Products produces high quality dog food distributed only through veterinary offices. To ensure that the food is of the highest quality and has taste appeal, Daisy has a rigorous inspection process. For quality control purposes, Daisy has a standard based on the pounds of food inspected per hour and the number of pounds that pass or fail the inspection.

Daisy expects that for every 10,000 pounds of food produced, 1,000 pounds of food will be inspected. Inspection of 1,000 pounds of dog food should take 1 hour. Daisy also expects that 2% of the food inspected will fail the inspection. During the month of May, Daisy produced 2,250,000 pounds of food and inspected 200,000 pounds of food in 210 hours. Of the 200,000 pounds of food inspected, 3,500 pounds of food failed to pass the inspection.

Required

1. Compute two variances that help determine whether the time spent on inspections was more or less than expected. (Follow a format similar to the one used for the variable overhead spending and efficiency variances, but without prices.)
2. Compute two variances that can be used to evaluate the percentage of the food that fails the inspection.

8-42 Non-financial performance measures. Rollie Manufacturing makes, among other things, wheels for roller skates. Manufacturing Department B receives plastic wheel casings from Manufacturing Department A and puts them on axles along with some ball bearings. The wheel casings have been inspected in Department A and should be free from major defects.

Most of the work in Department B is done by machine, but before the wheels are sent to the Packaging Department they are inspected for defects. Poorly made wheels are disassembled by hand and sent back to the beginning of the Department B line for rework. Thus any wheel that was made incorrectly and fixed takes more than twice as long to finish as a wheel that was made correctly the first time. Any wheels still not useable after rework are thrown away.

The same amount of ball bearings is requisitioned from the materials storeroom daily. Any leftover ball bearings at the end of the day are discarded. Ball bearings are measured by weight.

The machines in Department B are serviced only at night after the manufacturing run is over to save on intentional downtime. There are three machines in Department B, so if one does go down during processing there are still two workable machines until the next day. Rollie's goal in Department B is to produce 400 usable wheels per day.

Required

1. Under what circumstance would you consider ball bearings indirect rather than direct materials? Would you consider them direct materials or overhead in this problem?
2. What non-financial measures can Rollie use in Department B to control overhead costs?
3. Suggest some ways Rollie can better plan for and reduce overhead costs, given your answer to requirement 2.

Collaborative Learning Problem

8-43 Overhead variances, ethics. Zeller Company uses standard costing. The company prepared its static budget for 2008 at 2,500,000 machine-hours for the year. Total budgeted overhead cost is $31,250,000. The variable overhead rate is $10 per machine-hour ($20 per unit). Actual results for 2008 follow:

Machine-hours	2,400,000 hours
Output	1,245,000 units
Variable overhead	$25,200,000
Fixed overhead spending variance	$1,500,000 U

Required

1. Compute for the fixed overhead:
   a. Budgeted amount
   b. Budgeted cost per machine-hour
   c. Actual cost
   d. Production-volume variance
2. Compute the variable overhead spending variance and the variable overhead efficiency variance.
3. Jack Remich, the controller, prepares the variance analysis. It is common knowledge in the company that he and Ronald Monroe, the production manager, are not on the best of terms. In a recent executive committee meeting, Monroe had complained about the lack of usefulness of the accounting reports he receives. To get back at him, Remich manipulated the actual fixed overhead amount by assigning a greater-than-normal share of allocated costs to the production area. And, he decided to depreciate all of the newly acquired production equipment using the double-declining-balance method rather than the straight-line method, contrary to company practice. As a result, there was a sizable unfavorable fixed overhead spending variance. He boasted to one of his confidants, "I am just returning the favor." Discuss Remich's actions and their ramifications.

9 Inventory Costing and Capacity Analysis

Learning Objectives

1. Identify what distinguishes variable costing from absorption costing
2. Compute income under absorption costing and variable costing, and explain the difference in income
3. Understand how absorption costing can provide undesirable incentives for managers to build up inventory
4. Differentiate throughput costing from variable costing and absorption costing
5. Describe the various capacity concepts that can be used in absorption costing
6. Examine the key factors in choosing a capacity level to compute the budgeted fixed manufacturing cost rate
7. Describe how attempts to recover fixed costs of capacity may lead to price increases and lower demand

Few numbers capture the attention of managers and shareholders more than operating profits. Moreover, different costing-method decisions can have a big impact on profit margins. This is especially true when it comes to inventory-costing methods: Not only does the inventory-costing method managers choose affect the bottom line, so does the amount of inventory they decide to produce in conjunction with it. This can magnify the effect of the costing method on the firm's profits. That's the situation the computer chipmaker Intel ended up in, as the following article shows.

Intel's Inventory Strategy Backfires[1]

When Intel dropped the bomb. . . ratcheting down its forecast for both sales and profit margins in the second quarter of 2002, Wall Street analysts were caught again like deer in the headlights. As Intel's stock plummeted on the news in after-hours trading, Joseph A. Osha, Merrill Lynch's semiconductor analyst, said, "Nobody saw this coming."

In truth, somebody did see it coming—Fred Hickey, publisher of *The High-Tech Strategist* in Nashua, N.H. . . . Mr. Hickey. . . repeatedly warned his subscribers that shares of Intel, the largest producer of computer chips, were headed for a fall. For instance, back in March 2002, Intel management predicted that gross margins in the second quarter would be 53 percent. But Mr. Hickey speculated that Intel's impressive margins were mostly a result of a buildup in inventory, not sales to end users, and that the margins were therefore unsustainable unless demand picked up. It obviously did not.

Mr. Hickey said Intel "tried to be a hero in the first quarter." "They continued to produce at high levels, which improved their gross margins, and then talked about efficiencies and productivity when it was only an inventory buildup," he added. "Now they have to pay the piper."

Hickey noted that Intel's costs were mostly fixed from quarter-to-quarter. Intel's gross margin goes up when it builds more units and down when it builds fewer units. Running close to capacity amortizes

[1] *Source:* Gretchen Morgenson, "Far From Wall Street, Intel's Bad News Was No Surprise," *The New York Times,* June 9, 2002, p. 1; Melanie Hollands, "IT Investor's Journal: Did Intel 'accidentally' make too many CPUs this quarter?" *www.itmanagersjournal.com/feature/747*, September 02, 2004; and "Intel Profit Rises, But Shares Fall on Gross Margin Concerns," *today.msnbc.msn.com/id/19812891*, July 17, 2007.

Intel's nearly-fixed costs across more parts, improving gross margins. Unsold inventory nominally enjoys the same gross-margin improvement—assuming its value does not decline by the time it's sold!

Managers in companies with high fixed costs must manage capacity levels and make decisions about the use of available capacity. Managers must also decide on a production and inventory policy (as Intel did). These decisions and the accounting choices managers make affect the operating incomes of manufacturing companies. This chapter focuses on two types of cost accounting choices:

1. *The inventory-costing choice* determines which manufacturing costs are treated as inventoriable costs. Recall from Chapter 2 (p. 37), *inventoriable costs* are all costs of a product that are regarded as assets when they are incurred and expensed as cost of goods sold when the product is sold. There are three types of inventory costing methods: absorption costing, variable costing, and throughput costing. We discuss each in Part One of this chapter.
2. *The denominator-level capacity choice* focuses on the preselected level of the cost allocation base used to set budgeted fixed manufacturing cost rates. There are four possible choices of capacity levels: theoretical capacity, practical capacity, normal capacity utilization, and master-budget capacity utilization. We discuss each in Part Two of this chapter.

PART ONE: INVENTORY COSTING FOR MANUFACTURING COMPANIES

The two most common methods of costing inventories in manufacturing companies are variable costing and absorption costing. We discuss them first and then explain throughput costing, a more recent and less common method.

Variable Costing and Absorption Costing

The easiest way to understand the difference between variable costing and absorption costing is with an example. We will study Stassen Company, an optical consumer-products manufacturer. We focus in particular on its product line of high-end telescopes for aspiring astronomers.

Data for Stassen Company for 2009

Stassen uses standard costing:

- Direct costs are traced to products using standard prices and standard inputs allowed for actual outputs produced.
- Indirect (overhead) manufacturing costs are allocated using standard indirect rates times standard inputs allowed for actual outputs produced.

Stassen's management wants to prepare an income statement for 2009 (the fiscal year just ended) to evaluate the performance of the telescope product line. The operating information for the year is:

	A	B
1		**Units**
2	Beginning Inventory	0
3	Production	8,000
4	Sales	6,000
5	Ending Inventory	2,000

Actual price and cost data for 2009 are:

	A	B
10	Selling price	$ 1,000
11	Variable manufacturing cost per unit	
12	Direct material cost per unit	$ 110
13	Direct manufacturing labor cost per unit	40
14	Manufacturing overhead cost per unit	50
15	Total variable manufacturing cost per unit	$ 200
16	Variable marketing cost per unit sold	$ 185
17	Fixed manufacturing costs (all indirect)	$1,080,000
18	Fixed marketing costs (all indirect)	$1,380,000

For simplicity and to focus on the main ideas, we assume the following about Stassen:

- Stassen incurs manufacturing and marketing costs only. The cost driver for all variable manufacturing costs is units produced; the cost driver for variable marketing costs is units sold. There are no batch-level costs and no product-sustaining costs.
- There are no price variances, efficiency variances, or spending variances. Therefore, the *budgeted* (standard) price and cost data for 2009 are the same as the *actual* price and cost data.
- Work-in-process inventory is zero.
- Stassen budgeted production of 8,000 units for 2009. This was used to calculate the budgeted fixed manufacturing cost per unit of $135 ($1,080,000/8,000 units).
- Stassen budgeted sales of 6,000 units for 2009, which is the same as the actual sales for 2009.
- The actual production for 2009 is 8,000 units. As a result, there is no production-volume variance for manufacturing costs in 2009. Later examples, based on data for 2010 and 2011, do include production-volume variances. However, even in those cases, the income statements contain no variances other than the production-volume variance.
- All variances are written off to cost of goods sold in the period (year) in which they occur.

Learning Objective 1

Identify what distinguishes variable costing

. . . fixed manufacturing costs excluded from inventoriable costs

from absorption costing

. . . fixed manufacturing costs included in inventoriable costs

Variable costing is a method of inventory costing in which all variable manufacturing costs (direct and indirect) are included as inventoriable costs. All fixed manufacturing costs are excluded from inventoriable costs and are instead treated as costs of the period in which they are incurred. Note that *variable costing* is a less-than-perfect term to describe this inventory-costing method because not all variable costs are inventoriable costs. Only variable manufacturing costs are inventoriable. Another common term used to describe this method is **direct costing**, which is even more of a misnomer because variable costing considers variable manufacturing overhead (an indirect cost) as inventoriable, while excluding direct nonmanufacturing costs.

Absorption costing is a method of inventory costing in which all variable manufacturing costs and all fixed manufacturing costs are included as inventoriable costs. That is, inventory "absorbs" all manufacturing costs.

Under both variable costing and absorption costing, all variable manufacturing costs are inventoriable costs and all nonmanufacturing costs in the value chain (such as research and development and marketing), whether variable or fixed, are period costs and are recorded as expenses when incurred.

To summarize: The main difference between variable costing and absorption costing is the way in which fixed manufacturing costs are accounted for.

- Under variable costing, fixed manufacturing costs are treated as an expense of the period.
- Under absorption costing, fixed manufacturing costs are inventoriable costs. In our example, the standard fixed manufacturing cost is \$135 per unit (\$1,080,000 ÷ 8,000 units) produced.

For Stassen, inventoriable costs per unit produced in 2009 under the two methods are:

	Variable Costing		Absorption Costing	
Variable manufacturing cost per unit produced:				
Direct materials	\$110		\$110	
Direct manufacturing labor	40		40	
Manufacturing overhead	50	\$200	50	\$200
Fixed manufacturing cost per unit produced		—		135
Total inventoriable cost per unit produced		\$200		\$335

Comparing Income Statements for One Year

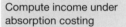

Learning Objective 2

Compute income under absorption costing

. . . using the gross-margin format

and variable costing,

. . . using the contribution-margin format

and explain the difference in income

. . . affected by the unit level of production and sales under absorption costing, but only the unit level of sales under variable costing

What will Stassen's operating income be if it uses variable costing or absorption costing? The differences between these methods are apparent in Exhibit 9-1. Panel A shows the variable costing income statement and Panel B the absorption-costing income statement for Stassen's telescope product line for 2009. The variable-costing income statement uses the contribution-margin format introduced in Chapter 3. The absorption-costing income statement uses the gross-margin format introduced in Chapter 2. Why these differences in format? The distinction between variable costs and fixed costs is central to variable costing, and it is highlighted by the contribution-margin format. Similarly, the distinction between manufacturing and nonmanufacturing costs is central to absorption costing, and it is highlighted by the gross-margin format.

Absorption-costing income statements need not differentiate between variable and fixed costs. However, we will make this distinction between variable and fixed costs in the Stassen example to show how individual line items are classified differently under variable costing and absorption costing. In Exhibit 9-1, Panel B, note that inventoriable cost is \$335 per unit under absorption costing: allocated fixed manufacturing costs of \$135 per unit plus variable manufacturing costs of \$200 per unit.

Notice how the fixed manufacturing costs of \$1,080,000 are accounted for under variable costing and absorption costing in Exhibit 9-1. The income statement under variable costing deducts the \$1,080,000 lump sum as an expense for 2009. In contrast, the income statement under absorption costing regards each finished unit as absorbing \$135 of fixed manufacturing cost. Under absorption costing, the \$1,080,000 (\$135 per unit × 8,000 units) is initially treated as an inventoriable cost in 2009. Of this, \$810,000 (\$135 per unit × 6,000 units sold) subsequently becomes a part of cost of goods sold in 2009, and \$270,000 (\$135 per unit × 2,000 units) remains an asset—part of ending finished goods inventory on December 31, 2009.

Operating income is \$270,000 higher under absorption costing compared with variable costing, because only \$810,000 of fixed manufacturing costs are expensed under absorption costing, whereas all \$1,080,000 of fixed manufacturing costs are expensed

Exhibit 9-1 Comparison of Variable Costing and Absorption Costing for Stassen Company: Telescope Product-Line Income Statements for 2009

	A	B	C	D	E	F	G
1	Panel A: VARIABLE COSTING				Panel B: ABSORPTION COSTING		
2	Revenues: $1,000 x 6,000 units		$6,000,000		Revenues: $1,000 x 6,000 units		$6,000,000
3	Variable cost of goods sold:				Cost of goods sold:		
4	Beginning inventory	$ 0			Beginning inventory	$ 0	
5	Variable manufacturing costs: $200 x 8,000 units	1,600,000			Variable manufacturing costs: $200 x 8,000 units	1,600,000	
6					Allocated fixed manufacturing costs: $135 x 8,000 units	1,080,000	
7	Cost of goods available for sale	1,600,000			Cost of goods available for sale	2,680,000	
8	Deduct ending inventory: $200 x 2,000 units	(400,000)			Deduct ending inventory: $335 x 2,000 units	(670,000)	
9	Variable cost of goods sold		1,200,000		Cost of goods sold		2,010,000
10	Variable marketing costs: $185 x 6,000 units sold		1,110,000				
11	Contribution margin		3,690,000		Gross Margin		3,990,000
12	Fixed manufacturing costs		1,080,000		Variable marketing costs: $185 x 6,000 units sold		1,110,000
13	Fixed marketing cost		1,380,000		Fixed marketing costs		1,380,000
14	Operating income		$1,230,000		Operating Income		$1,500,000
15							
16	Manufacturing costs expensed in Panel A:				Manufacturing costs expensed in Panel B:		
17	Variable cost of goods sold		$1,200,000				
18	Fixed manufacturing costs		1,080,000				
19	Total		$2,280,000		Cost of goods sold		$2,010,000

under variable costing. Note that the variable manufacturing cost of $200 per unit is accounted for the same way in both income statements in Exhibit 9-1.

These points can be summarized as follows:

	Variable Costing	Absorption Costing
Variable manufacturing costs: $200 per telescope produced	Inventoriable	Inventoriable
Fixed manufacturing costs: $1,080,000 per year	Deducted as an expense of the period	Inventoriable at $135 per telescope produced using budgeted denominator level of 8,000 units produced per year ($1,080,000 ÷ 8,000 units = $135 per unit)

The basis of the difference between variable costing and absorption costing is how fixed manufacturing costs are accounted for. If inventory levels change, operating income will differ between the two methods because of the difference in accounting for fixed manufacturing costs. To see this, let's compare telescope sales of 6,000, 7,000, and 8,000 units by Stassen in 2009, when 8,000 units were produced. Of the $1,080,000 total fixed manufacturing costs, the amount expensed in the 2009 income statement under each of these scenarios would be:

	A	B	C	D	E	G	H
1			Variable Costing			Absorption Costing	
2						Fixed Manufacturing Costs	
3	Units	Ending	Fixed Manufacturing Costs			Included in Inventory	Amount Expensed
4	Sold	Inventory	Included in Inventory	Amount Expensed		=$135 x Ending Inv.	=$135 x Units Sold
5	6,000	2,000	$0	$1,080,000		$270,000	$ 810,000
6	7,000	1,000	$0	$1,080,000		$135,000	$ 945,000
7	8,000	0	$0	$1,080,000		$ 0	$1,080,000

In the last scenario, where 8,000 units are produced and sold, both variable and absorption costing report the same net income because inventory levels are unchanged. This chapter's appendix describes how the choice of variable costing or absorption costing affects the breakeven quantity of sales when inventory levels are allowed to vary.

Explaining Differences in Operating Income

To get a more-comprehensive view of the effects of variable costing and absorption costing, Stassen's management accountants prepare income statements for three years of operations.

Data for Stassen Company for 2009, 2010, and 2011

In both 2010 and 2011, Stassen has a production-volume variance because actual telescope production differs from the budgeted level of production of 8,000 units per year used to calculate budgeted fixed manufacturing cost per unit. The actual quantities sold for 2010 and 2011 are the same as the sales quantities budgeted for these respective years, which are given in units in the following table:

	E	F	G	H
1		**2009**	**2010**	**2011**
2	Beginning inventory	0	2,000	500
3	Production	8,000	5,000	10,000
4	Sales	6,000	6,500	7,500
5	Ending inventory	2,000	500	3,000

All other 2009 data given earlier for Stassen also apply for 2010 and 2011.

Comparing Income Statements for Three Years

Exhibit 9-2 presents the income statement under variable costing in Panel A and the income statement under absorption costing in Panel B for 2009, 2010, and 2011. As you study Exhibit 9-2, note that the 2009 columns in both Panels A and B show the same figures as Exhibit 9-1. The 2010 and 2011 columns are similar to 2009 *except for the production-volume variance line item under absorption costing in Panel B*. Keep in mind the following points about absorption costing as you study Panel B of Exhibit 9-2:

1. The $135 fixed manufacturing cost rate is based on the budgeted denominator capacity level of 8,000 units in 2009, 2010, and 2011 ($1,080,000 ÷ 8,000 units = $135 per unit). Whenever production—that's the quantity produced, not the quantity sold—deviates from the denominator level, there will be a production-volume variance. The amount of Stassen's production-volume variance is determined by multiplying $135 per unit by the difference between the actual level of production and the denominator level.

   In 2010, production was 5,000 units, 3,000 lower than the denominator level of 8,000 units. The result is an unfavorable production-volume variance of $405,000 ($135 per unit × 3,000 units). The year 2011 has a favorable production-volume variance of $270,000 ($135 per unit × 2,000 units), due to production of 10,000 units, which exceeds the denominator level of 8,000 units.

   Recall how standard costing works under absorption costing. Each time a unit is manufactured, $135 of fixed manufacturing costs is included in the cost of goods manufactured and available for sale. In 2010, when 5,000 units are manufactured, $675,000 ($135 per unit × 5,000 units) of fixed manufacturing costs is included in the cost of goods available for sale (see Exhibit 9-2, Panel B, line 22). Total fixed manufacturing costs for 2010 are $1,080,000. The production-volume variance of $405,000 U equals the difference between $1,080,000 and $675,000. In Panel B, note how, for each year, the fixed manufacturing costs included in the cost of goods available for sale plus the production-volume variance always equals $1,080,000.

2. The production-volume variance, which relates only to fixed manufacturing overhead, exists under absorption costing but not under variable costing. That's because under variable costing, fixed manufacturing costs of $1,080,000 are always treated as an expense of the period, regardless of the level of production (and sales).

Exhibit 9-2 Comparison of Variable Costing and Absorption Costing for Stassen Company: Telescope Product-Line Income Statements for 2009, 2010, and 2011

	A	B	C	D	E	F	G
1	**Panel A: VARIABLE COSTING**						
2		2009		2010		2011	
3	Revenues: \$1,000 x 6,000; 6,500; 7,500 units		\$6,000,000		\$6,500,000		\$7,500,000
4	Variable cost of goods sold:						
5	Beginning inventory: \$200 x 0; 2,000; 500 units	\$ 0		\$ 400,000		\$ 100,000	
6	Variable manufacturing costs: \$200 x 8,000; 5,000; 10,000 units	1,600,000		1,000,000		2,000,000	
7	Cost of goods available for sale	1,600,000		1,400,000		2,100,000	
8	Deduct ending inventory: \$200 x 2,000; 500; 3,000 units	(400,000)		(100,000)		(600,000)	
9	Variable cost of goods sold		1,200,000		1,300,000		1,500,000
10	Variable marketing costs: \$185 x 6,000; 6,500; 7,500 units		1,110,000		1,202,500		1,387,500
11	Contribution margin		3,690,000		3,997,500		4,612,500
12	Fixed manufacturing costs		1,080,000		1,080,000		1,080,000
13	Fixed marketing costs		1,380,000		1,380,000		1,380,000
14	Operating income		\$1,230,000		\$1,537,500		\$2,152,500
15							
16	**Panel B: ABSORPTION COSTING**						
17		2009		2010		2011	
18	Revenues: \$1,000 x 6,000; 6,500; 7,500 units		\$6,000,000		\$6,500,000		\$7,500,000
19	Cost of goods sold:						
20	Beginning inventory: \$335 x 0; 2,000; 500 units	\$ 0		\$ 670,000		\$ 167,500	
21	Variable manufacturing costs: \$200 x 8,000; 5,000; 10,000 units	1,600,000		1,000,000		2,000,000	
22	Allocated fixed manufacturing costs: \$135 x 8,000; 5,000; 10,000 units	1,080,000		675,000		1,350,000	
23	Cost of goods available for sale	2,680,000		2,345,000		3,517,500	
24	Deduct ending inventory: \$335 x 2,000; 500; 3,000 units	(670,000)		(167,500)		(1,005,000)	
25	Adjustment for production-volume variance[a]	0		405,000	U	(270,000)	F
26	Cost of goods sold		2,010,000		2,582,500		2,242,500
27	Gross Margin		3,990,000		3,917,500		5,257,500
28	Variable marketing costs: \$185 x 6,000; 6,500; 7,500 units		1,110,000		1,202,500		1,387,500
29	Fixed marketing costs		1,380,000		1,380,000		1,380,000
30	Operating Income		\$1,500,000		\$1,335,000		\$2,490,000
31							
32	[a]Production-volume variance = Budgeted fixed manufacturing costs - Fixed manufacturing overhead allocated using budgeted cost per output unit allowed for actual output produced (Panel B, line 22)						
33	2009: \$1,080,000 - (\$135 x 8,000) = \$1,080,000 - \$1,080,000 = \$0						
34	2010: \$1,080,000 - (\$135 x 5,000) = \$1,080,000 - \$675,000 = \$405,000 U						
35	2009: \$1,080,000 - (\$135 x 10,000) = \$1,080,000 - \$1,350,000 = (\$270,000) F						
36							
37	Production volume variance can also be calculated as:						
38	Fixed manufacturing cost per unit x (Denominator level - Actual output units produced)						
39	2009: \$135 x (8,000 - 8,000) units = \$135 x 0 = \$0						
40	2010: \$135 x (8,000 - 5,000) units = \$135 x 3,000 = \$405,000 U						
41	2011: \$135 x (8,000 - 10,000) units = \$135 x (2,000) = (\$270,000) F						

Here's a summary (using information from Exhibit 9-2) of the operating-income differences for Stassen Company during the 2009 to 2011 period:

	2009	2010	2011
1. Absorption-costing operating income	\$1,500,000	\$1,335,000	\$2,490,000
2. Variable-costing operating income	\$1,230,000	\$1,537,500	\$2,152,500
3. Difference: (1) − (2)	\$ 270,000	\$ (202,500)	\$ 337,500
4. Difference as a % of absorption-costing operating income	18.0%	(15.2%)	13.6%

The percentage differences in the preceding table illustrate why managers whose performance is measured by reported income are concerned about the choice between variable costing and absorption costing.

Why do variable costing and absorption costing usually report different operating income numbers? In general, if inventory increases during an accounting period, less operating income will be reported under variable costing than absorption costing. Conversely, if inventory decreases, more operating income will be reported under variable costing than absorption costing. The difference in reported operating income is due solely to (a) moving fixed manufacturing costs into inventories as inventories increase and (b) moving fixed manufacturing costs out of inventories as inventories decrease.

The difference between operating income under absorption costing and variable costing can be computed by formula 1, which focuses on fixed manufacturing costs in beginning inventory and ending inventory:

	A	B	C	D	E	F	G	H
1	Formula 1							
2						Fixed manufacturing		Fixed manufacturing
3		Absorption-costing	-	Variable-costing	=	costs in ending inventory	-	costs in beginning inventory
4		operating income		operation income		under absorption costing		under absorption costing
5	2009	$1,500,000	-	$1,230,000	=	($135 x 2,000 units)	-	($135 x 0 units)
6				$ 270,000	=	$270,000		
7								
8	2010	$1,335,000	-	$1,537,500	=	($135 x 500 units)	-	($135 x 2,000 units)
9				($ 202,500)	=	($202,500)		
10								
11	2011	$2,490,000	-	$2,152,500	=	($135 x 3,000 units)	-	($135 x 500 units)
12				$ 337,500	=	$337,500		

Fixed manufacturing costs in ending inventory are deferred to a future period under absorption costing. For example, $270,000 of fixed manufacturing overhead is deferred to 2010 at December 31, 2009. Under variable costing, all $1,080,000 of fixed manufacturing costs are treated as an expense of 2009.

Recall that,

$$\text{Beginning inventory} + \text{Cost of goods manufactured} = \text{Cost of goods sold} + \text{Ending Inventory}$$

Therefore, instead of focusing on fixed manufacturing costs in ending and beginning inventory, we could alternatively focus on fixed manufacturing costs in units produced and units sold. This approach highlights how fixed manufacturing costs move between units produced and units sold during the fiscal year.

	A	B	C	D	E	F	G	H
16	Formula 2							
17						Fixed manufacturing costs		Fixed manufacturing costs
18		Absorption-costing	-	Variable-costing	=	inventoried in units produced	-	in cost of goods sold
19		operating income		operation income		under absorption costing		under absorption costing
20	2009	$1,500,000	-	$1,230,000	=	($135 x 8,000 units)	-	($135 x 6,000 units)
21				$ 270,000	=	$270,000		
22								
23	2010	$1,335,000	-	$1,537,500	=	($135 x 5,000 units)	-	($135 x 6,500 units)
24				($ 202,500)	=	($202,500)		
25								
26	2011	$2,490,000	-	$2,152,500	=	($135 x 10,000 units)	-	($135 x 7,500 units)
27				$ 337,500	=	$337,500		

Managers face increasing pressure to reduce inventory levels. Some companies are achieving steep reductions in inventory levels using policies such as just-in-time production—a production system under which products are manufactured only when needed. Formula 1 illustrates that, as Stassen reduces its inventory levels, operating income differences between absorption costing and variable costing become immaterial. Consider, for example, the formula for 2009. If instead of 2,000 units in ending inventory, Stassen had only 2 units in ending inventory, the difference between absorption-costing operating income and variable-costing operating income would drop from \$270,000 to \$270 [(\$135 per unit × 2) − (\$135 per unit × 0)].

Effect of Sales and Production on Operating Income under Variable Costing

Given a constant contribution margin per unit and constant fixed costs, the period-to-period change in operating income under variable costing is *driven solely by changes in the quantity of units actually sold*. Consider the variable-costing operating income of Stassen in (a) 2010 versus 2009 and (b) 2011 versus 2010. Recall that:

$$\text{Contribution margin per unit} = \text{Selling price} - \text{Variable manufacturing cost per unit} - \text{Variable marketing cost per unit}$$

$$= \$1{,}000 \text{ per unit} - \$200 \text{ per unit} - \$185 \text{ per unit}$$

$$= \$615 \text{ per unit.}$$

$$\text{Change in variable-costing operating income} = \text{Contribution margin per unit} \times \text{Change in quantity of units sold}$$

(a) 2010 vs. 2009: \$1,537,500 − \$1,230,000 = \$615 per unit × (6,500 units − 6,000 units)
\$307,500 = \$307,500

(b) 2011 vs. 2010: \$2,152,500 − \$1,537,500 = \$615 per unit × (7,500 units − 6,500 units)
\$615,000 = \$615,000

Under variable costing, Stassen managers cannot increase operating income by "producing for inventory." Why not? Because, as you can see from the preceding computations, when using variable costing, only the quantity of units sold drives operating income. We'll explain later in this chapter that absorption costing enables managers to increase operating income by increasing the unit level of sales, as well as by producing more units. Before you proceed to the next section, make sure that you examine Exhibit 9-3 for a detailed comparison of the differences between variable costing and absorption costing.

Performance Measures and Absorption Costing

Absorption costing is the required inventory method for external reporting in most countries. Many companies use absorption costing for internal accounting as well. Why? Because it is cost-effective and less confusing to managers to use one common method of inventory costing for both external and internal reporting and performance evaluation. A common method of inventory costing can also help prevent managers from taking actions that make their performance measure look good but that hurt the income they report to shareholders. Another advantage of absorption costing is that it measures the cost of all manufacturing resources, whether variable or fixed, necessary to produce inventory. Many companies use inventory costing information for long-run decisions such as pricing and choosing a product mix. For these long-run decisions, inventory costs should include both variable *and* fixed costs.

One problem with absorption costing is that it enables a manager to increase operating income in a specific period by increasing production—even if there is no customer demand for the additional production! The chapter opener illustrated this effect—Intel's margins and income were higher because the firm produced more ending inventory. Stassen's managers may be tempted to do this to get higher bonuses based on absorption-costing operating income. Generally, higher operating income also has a positive effect on stock price, which increases managers' stock-based compensation.

To reduce the undesirable incentives to build up inventories that absorption costing can create, a number of companies use variable costing for internal reporting. Variable costing focuses attention on distinguishing variable manufacturing costs from fixed manufacturing costs. This distinction is important for short-run decision making (as in cost-volume-profit analysis in Chapter 3 and in planning and control in Chapters 6, 7, and 8).

Companies that use both methods for internal reporting—variable costing for short-run decisions and performance evaluation and absorption costing for long-run

Exhibit 9-3 Comparative Income Effects of Variable Costing and Absorption Costing

Question	Variable Costing	Absorption Costing	Comment
Are fixed manufacturing costs inventoried?	No	Yes	Basic theoretical question of when these costs should be expensed
Is there a production-volume variance?	No	Yes	Choice of denominator level affects measurement of operating income under absorption costing only
Are classifications between variable and fixed costs routinely made?	Yes	Infrequently	Absorption costing can be easily modified to obtain subclassifications for variable and fixed costs, if desired (for example, see Exhibit 9-1, Panel B)
How do changes in unit inventory levels affect operating income?[a]			Differences are attributable to the timing of when fixed manufacturing costs are expensed
Production = sales	Equal	Equal	
Production > sales	Lower[b]	Higher[c]	
Production < sales	Higher	Lower	
What are the effects on cost-volume-profit relationship (for a given level of fixed costs and a given contribution margin per unit)?	Driven by unit level of sales	Driven by (a) unit level of sales, (b) unit level of production, and (c) chosen denominator level	Management control benefit: Effects of changes in production level on operating income are easier to understand under variable costing

[a]Assuming that all manufacturing variances are written off as period costs, that no change occurs in work-in-process inventory, and no change occurs in the budgeted fixed manufacturing cost rate between accounting periods.

[b]That is, lower operating income than under absorption costing.

[c]That is, higher operating income than under variable costing.

decisions—benefit from the different advantages of both. In the next section, we explore in more detail the challenges that arise from absorption costing.

Undesirable Buildup of Inventories

Learning Objective 3

Understand how absorption costing can provide undesirable incentives for managers to build up inventory

. . . producing more units for inventory absorbs fixed manufacturing costs and increases operating income

Recall that one motivation for an undesirable buildup of inventories could be because a manager's bonus is based on reported absorption-costing operating income. Assume that Stassen's managers have such a bonus plan. Exhibit 9-4 shows how Stassen's absorption-costing operating income for 2010 changes as the production level changes. This exhibit assumes that the production-volume variance is written off to cost of goods sold at the end of each year. Beginning inventory of 2,000 units and sales of 6,500 units for 2010 are unchanged from the case shown in Exhibit 9-2. *As you review Exhibit 9-4, keep in mind that the computations are basically the same as those in Exhibit 9-2.*

Exhibit 9-4 shows that production of 4,500 units meets the 2010 sales budget of 6,500 units (2,000 units from beginning inventory + 4,500 units produced). Operating income at this production level is $1,267,500. By producing more than 4,500 units, commonly referred to as *producing for inventory*, Stassen increases absorption-costing operating income. Each additional unit in 2010 ending inventory will increase operating income by $135. For example, if 8,000 units are produced, ending inventory will be 3,500 units and operating income increases to $1,740,000. This amount is $472,500 more than the operating income with zero ending inventory ($1,740,000 − $1,267,500, or 3,500 units × $135 per unit = $472,500). Under absorption costing, the company, by producing 3,500 units for inventory, includes $472,500 of fixed manufacturing costs in finished goods inventory, so they are not expensed in 2010.

Can top management implement checks and balances that limit managers from producing for inventory under absorption costing? The answer is yes, as we will see in the next section, but producing for inventory cannot be completely prevented. There are many subtle ways a manager can produce for inventory that, if done to a limited extent, may not be easy to detect. For example,

Exhibit 9-4 Effect on Absorption-Costing Operating Income of Different Production Levels for Stassen Company: Telescope Product-Line Income Statement for 2010 at Sales of 6,500 Units

File Edit View Insert Format Tools Data Window Help

	A	B	C	D	E	F	G	H	I	J	K
1	**Unit Data**										
2	Beginning inventory	2,000		2,000		2,000		2,000		2,000	
3	Production	4,500		5,000		6,500		8,000		9,000	
4	Goods available for sale	6,500		7,000		8,500		10,000		11,000	
5	Sales	6,500		6,500		6,500		6,500		6,500	
6	Ending inventory	0		500		2,000		3,500		4,500	
7											
8	**Income Statement**										
9	Revenues	$6,500,000		$6,500,000		$6,500,000		$6,500,000		$6,500,000	
10	Cost of goods sold:										
11	Beginning inventory ($335 x 2,000)	670,000		670,000		670,000		670,000		670,000	
12	Variable manufacturing costs: $200 x production	900,000		1,000,000		1,300,000		1,600,000		1,800,000	
13	Allocated fixed manufacturing costs: $135 x production	607,500		675,000		877,500		1,080,000		1,215,000	
14	Cost of goods available for sale	2,177,500		2,345,000		2,847,500		3,350,000		3,685,000	
15	Deduct ending inventory: $335 x ending inventory	0		(167,500)		(670,000)		(1,172,500)		(1,507,500)	
16	Adjustment for production-volume variance[a]	472,500	U	405,000	U	202,500	U	0		(135,000)	F
17	Cost of goods sold	2,650,000		2,582,500		2,380,000		2,177,500		2,042,500	
18	Gross Margin	3,850,000		3,917,500		4,120,000		4,322,500		4,457,500	
19	Marketing costs: ($1,380,000 + $185 per unit x 6,500 units sold)	2,582,500		2,582,500		2,582,500		2,582,500		2,582,500	
20	Operating Income	$1,267,500		$1,335,000		$1,537,500		$1,740,000		$1,875,000	
21											
22	[a]Production-volume variance = Budgeted fixed manufacturing costs - Allocated fixed manufacturing costs (Income Statement, line 13)										
23	At production of 4,500 units: $1,080,000 - $607,500 = $472,500 U										
24	At production of 5,000 units: $1,080,000 - $675,000 = $405,000 U										
25	At production of 6,500 units: $1,080,000 - $877,500 = $202,500 U										
26	At production of 8,000 units: $1,080,000 - $1,080,000 = $0										
27	At production of 9,000 units: $1,080,000 - $1,215,000 = ($135,000) F										

- A plant manager may switch to manufacturing products that absorb the highest amount of fixed manufacturing costs, regardless of the customer demand for these products (called "cherry picking" the production line). Production of items that absorb the least or lower fixed manufacturing costs may be delayed, resulting in failure to meet promised customer delivery dates (which, over time, can result in unhappy customers).
- A plant manager may accept a particular order to increase production, even though another plant in the same company is better suited to handle that order.
- To increase production, a manager may defer maintenance beyond the current period. Although operating income in this period may increase as a result, future operating income could decrease by a larger amount if repair costs increase and equipment becomes less efficient.

The example in Exhibit 9-4 focuses on only one year (2010). A Stassen manager who built up ending inventories of telescopes to 4,500 units in 2010 would have to further increase ending inventories in 2011 to increase that year's operating income by producing for inventory. There are limits to how much inventory levels can be increased over time (because of physical constraints on storage space and management supervision and controls). Such limits reduce the likelihood of incurring some of absorption costing's undesirable effects.

Proposals for Revising Performance Evaluation

Top management, with help from the controller and management accountants, can take several steps to reduce the undesirable effects of absorption costing.

- Focus on careful budgeting and inventory planning to reduce management's freedom to build up excess inventory. For example, the budgeted monthly balance sheets have estimates of the dollar amount of inventories. If actual inventories exceed these dollar amounts, top management can investigate the inventory buildups.
- Incorporate a carrying charge for inventory in the internal accounting system. For example, the company could assess an inventory carrying charge of 1% per month on the investment tied up in inventory and for spoilage and obsolescence when it

evaluates a manager's performance. An increasing number of companies are beginning to adopt this inventory carrying charge.

- Change the period used to evaluate performance. Critics of absorption costing give examples in which managers take actions that maximize quarterly or annual income at the potential expense of long-run income. When their performance is evaluated over a three- to five-year period, managers will be less tempted to produce for inventory.
- Include nonfinancial as well as financial variables in the measures used to evaluate performance (see the Concepts in Action feature, p. 310). Examples of nonfinancial measures that can be used to monitor the performance of Stassen's managers in 2011 (see data on p. 303) are:

$$\textbf{(a)}\ \frac{\text{Ending inventory in units in 2011}}{\text{Beginning inventory in units in 2011}} = \frac{3{,}000}{500} = 6$$

$$\textbf{(b)}\ \frac{\text{Units produced in 2011}}{\text{Units sold in 2011}} = \frac{10{,}000}{7{,}500} = 1.33$$

Top management would want to see production equal to sales and relatively stable levels of inventory. Companies that manufacture or sell several products could report these two measures for each of the products they manufacture and sell.

Throughput Costing

Learning Objective 4

Differentiate throughput costing

. . . direct material costs inventoried

from variable costing

. . . variable manufacturing costs inventoried

and absorption costing

. . . variable and fixed manufacturing costs inventoried

Some managers maintain that even variable costing promotes an excessive amount of costs being inventoried. They argue that only direct materials are "truly variable." **Throughput costing,** which also is called **super-variable costing** because it is an extreme form of variable costing, is a method of inventory costing in which only direct material costs are included as inventoriable costs. All other costs are costs of the period in which they are incurred. In particular, variable direct manufacturing labor costs and variable manufacturing overhead costs are regarded as period costs and are deducted as expenses of the period.

Exhibit 9-5 is the throughput-costing income statement for Stassen Company for 2009, 2010, and 2011. *Throughput contribution* equals revenues minus all direct material cost of the goods sold. Compare the operating income amounts reported in Exhibit 9-5 with those for absorption costing and variable costing:

	2009	2010	2011
Absorption-costing operating income	$1,500,000	$1,335,000	$2,490,000
Variable-costing operating income	$1,230,000	$1,537,500	$2,152,500
Throughput-costing operating income	$1,050,000	$1,672,500	$1,927,500

Only the $110 direct material cost per unit is inventoriable under throughput costing, compared with $335 per unit for absorption costing and $200 per unit for variable costing. When the production quantity exceeds sales as in 2009 and 2011, throughput costing results in the largest amount of expenses in the current period's income statement. Advocates of throughput costing say it provides less incentive to produce for inventory than either variable costing or, especially, absorption costing. Throughput costing is a more recent phenomenon in comparison with variable costing and absorption costing and has avid supporters, but so far it has not been widely adopted.[2]

Comparison of Alternative Inventory-Costing Methods

Variable costing and absorption costing (as well as throughput costing) may be combined with actual, normal, or standard costing. Exhibit 9-6 compares product costing under six alternative inventory-costing systems.

---

[2] See E. Goldratt, *The Theory of Constraints* (New York: North River Press, 1990); E. Noreen, D. Smith, and J. Mackey, *The Theory of Constraints and Its Implications for Management Accounting* (New York: North River Press, 1995).

Concepts in Action

Yield Improvements and the Production-Volume Variance at Analog Devices

Analog Devices, Inc. (ADI) produces integrated circuits and systems used in computers, broadband modems, medical instruments, and consumer electronics. Improving yield— the quantity of good die produced on a silicon wafer divided by the total number of die that could be printed and produced on the wafer—is critical to delivering high-quality products at low cost. For internal-reporting purposes, ADI uses variable costing. Fixed costs—comprising fixed overhead costs—are allocated to products only for the purposes of external reporting. The denominator level used to allocate standard fixed overhead costs to products is machine capacity assuming efficient operations—for example, machines working six hours per day. However, suppose running the machines only four hours a day is adequate to meet actual demand. The result is an unfavorable production-volume variance because budgeted fixed overhead costs exceed the overhead costs allocated to production.

How do improvements in yield affect ADI's production-volume variance? As yields improve, machines need to be run for fewer hours to produce the actual output. That's because fewer silicon wafers need to be started to get the desired quantity of good product. Consequently, even fewer of the budgeted fixed overhead costs get allocated to production, the costs in inventory decline, and the unfavorable production-volume variance gets bigger. As the production-volume variance is written off to cost of goods sold at year-end, profit margins decline. Thus, quality improvements can have negative operating-income effects!

ADI weighted the performance evaluation of its production planners more toward satisfying customer orders than reducing inventory levels. Thus, even as yields improved, planners were reluctant to reduce the number of wafer starts until they were sure that the higher yields would continue. They did not want to be in a position in which ADI lacked inventory to meet customer requests. Building up inventory also improved short-run operating income.

Commenting on the tensions and trade-offs, ADI's chairman and president warned, "Unless quality improvement and other more-fundamental performance measures are elevated to the same level of importance as financial measures, when conflicts arise, financial considerations win out." However, believing in the long-run benefits of higher quality, ADI continued to improve yield, and it developed a scorecard of financial and nonfinancial performance measures that gave incentives to production planners and operations managers to not produce more product simply to absorb fixed overhead costs into inventory. This strategy has proven very successful. ADI has been one of the longest-standing, highest-growth companies in the technology sector. It had 2006 revenues of almost $2.6 billion, serving over 60,000 customers worldwide.

Source: Analog Devices: The Half-Life System, Harvard Business School case number 9-190-061, Analog Devices 2006 Annual Report; and discussions with company management.

Variable Costing	Absorption Costing
Actual costing	Actual costing
Standard costing	Standard costing
Normal costing	Normal costing

Variable costing has been controversial among accountants—not because of disagreement about the need to delineate between variable and fixed costs for internal planning and control, but as it pertains to *external reporting*. Accountants who favor variable costing for external reporting maintain that the fixed portion of manufacturing costs is more closely related to the capacity to produce than to the actual production of specific units. Hence, fixed costs should be expensed, not inventoried.

Accountants who support absorption costing for *external reporting* maintain that inventories should carry a fixed-manufacturing-cost component. Why? Because both variable manufacturing costs and fixed manufacturing costs are necessary to produce goods. Therefore, both types of costs should be inventoried in order to match all manufacturing costs to revenues, regardless of their different behavior patterns.

For external reporting to shareholders, companies around the globe tend to follow the generally accepted accounting principle that all manufacturing costs are inventoriable. For tax reporting in the United States, all manufacturing costs plus some product design

	A	B	C	D
1		2009	2010	2011
2	Revenues: $1,000 x 6,000; 6,500; 7,500 units	$6,000,000	$6,500,000	$7,500,000
3	Direct material cost of goods sold			
4	Beginning inventory: $110 x 0; 2,000; 500 units	0	220,000	55,000
5	Direct materials: $110 x 8,000; 5,000; 10,000 units	880,000	550,000	1,100,000
6	Cost of goods available for sale	880,000	770,000	1,155,000
7	Deduct ending inventory: $110 x 2,000; 500; 3,000 units	(220,000)	(55,000)	(330,000)
8	Direct material cost of goods sold	660,000	715,000	825,000
9	Throughput contribution[a]	5,340,000	5,785,000	6,675,000
10	Manufacturing costs (other than direct materials)[b]	1,800,000	1,530,000	1,980,000
11	Marketing costs[c]	2,490,000	2,582,500	2,767,500
12	Operating income	$1,050,000	$1,672,500	$1,927,500
13				
14	[a]Throughput contribution equals revenues minus all direct material cost of goods sold			
15	[b]Fixed manuf. costs + [(variable manuf. labor cost per unit + variable manuf. overhead cost per unit)			
16	x units produced]; $1,080,000 + [($40 + $50) x 8,000; 5,000; 10,000 units]			
17	[c]Fixed marketing costs + (variable marketing cost per unit x units sold);			
18	$1,380,000 + ($185 x 6,000; 6,500; 7,500 units)			

Exhibit 9-5

Throughput Costing for Stassen Company: Telescope Product-Line Income Statements for 2009, 2010, and 2011

and administrative costs (such as legal costs) must be included as inventoriable costs.[3] Administrative costs must be allocated between those costs related to manufacturing activities (inventoriable costs) and those not related to manufacturing.

A key issue in absorption costing is the choice of the capacity level used to compute fixed manufacturing cost per unit produced. Part Two of this chapter discusses this issue.

Exhibit 9-6 Comparison of Alternative Inventory-Costing Systems

			Actual Costing	Normal Costing	Standard Costing
Absorption Costing	Variable Costing	**Variable Direct Manufacturing Cost**	Actual prices × Actual quantity of inputs used	Actual prices × Actual quantity of inputs used	Standard prices × Standard quantity of inputs allowed for actual output achieved
Absorption Costing	Variable Costing	**Variable Manufacturing Overhead Costs**	Actual variable overhead rates × Actual quantity of cost-allocation bases used	Budgeted variable overhead rates × Actual quantity of cost-allocation bases used	Standard variable overhead rates × Standard quantity of cost-allocation bases allowed for actual output achieved
Absorption Costing		**Fixed Direct Manufacturing Costs**	Actual prices × Actual quantity of inputs used	Actual prices × Actual quantity of inputs used	Standard prices × Standard quantity of inputs allowed for actual output achieved
Absorption Costing		**Fixed Manufacturing Overhead Costs**	Actual fixed overhead rates × Actual quantity of cost-allocation bases used	Budgeted fixed overhead rates × Actual quantity of cost-allocation bases used	Standard fixed overhead rates × Standard quantity of cost-allocation bases allowed for actual output achieved

[3] Section 1.471-11 of the U.S. Internal Revenue Code (Inventories of Manufacturers) states that "both direct and indirect production costs must be taken into account in the computation of inventoriable costs in accordance with the 'full absorption' method of inventory costing . . . Costs are considered to be production costs to the extent that they are incident to and necessary for production or manufacturing operations or processes. Production costs include direct production costs and fixed and variable indirect production costs." Case law is useful to examine when determining the precise boundaries between inventoriable and noninventoriable costs.

Problem for Self-Study

Assume Stassen Company on January 1, 2009, decides to contract with another company to preassemble a large percentage of the components of its telescopes. The revised manufacturing cost structure during the 2009-to-2011 period is:

Variable manufacturing cost per unit produced	
Direct materials	$ 295
Direct manufacturing labor	20
Manufacturing overhead	5
Total variable manufacturing cost per unit produced	$ 320
Fixed manufacturing costs	$120,000

Under the revised cost structure, a larger percentage of Stassen's manufacturing costs are variable with respect to units produced. The denominator level of production used to calculate budgeted fixed manufacturing cost per unit in 2009, 2010, and 2011 is 8,000 units. Assume no other change from the data underlying Exhibits 9-1 and 9-2. Summary information pertaining to absorption-costing operating income and variable costing operating income with this revised cost structure is:

	2009	2010	2011
Absorption-costing operating income	$1,500,000	$1,695,000	$2,250,000
Variable-costing operating income	1,470,000	1,717,500	2,212,500
Difference	$ 30,000	$ (22,500)	$ 37,500

Required

1. Compute the budgeted fixed manufacturing cost per unit in 2009, 2010, and 2011.
2. Explain the difference between absorption-costing operating income and variable-costing operating income in 2009, 2010, and 2011, focusing on fixed manufacturing costs in beginning and ending inventory.
3. Why are these differences smaller than the differences in Exhibit 9-2?

Solution

1. $$\text{Budgeted fixed manufacturing cost per unit} = \frac{\text{Budgeted fixed manufacturing costs}}{\text{Budgeted production units}}$$

$$= \frac{\$120{,}000}{8{,}000 \text{ units}}$$

$$= \$15 \text{ per unit}$$

2.

	Absorption-costing operating income	−	Variable-costing operating income	=	Fixed manufacturing costs in ending inventory under absorption costing	−	Fixed manufacturing costs in beginning inventory under absorption costing
2009:	$1,500,000	−	$1,470,000	=	($15 per unit × 2,000 units)	−	($15 per unit × 0 units)
			$30,000	=	$30,000		
2010:	$1,695,000	−	$1,717,500	=	($15 per unit × 500 units)	−	($15 per unit × 2,000 units)
			−$22,500	=	−$22,500		
2011:	$2,250,000	−	$2,212,500	=	($15 per unit × 3,000 units)	−	($15 per unit × 500 units)
			$37,500		$37,500		

3. Subcontracting a large part of manufacturing has greatly reduced the magnitude of fixed manufacturing costs. This reduction, in turn, means differences between absorption costing and variable costing are much smaller than in Exhibit 9-2.

PART TWO: DENOMINATOR-LEVEL CAPACITY CONCEPTS AND FIXED-COST CAPACITY ANALYSIS

Determining the "right" level of capacity is one of the most strategic and most difficult decisions managers face. Having too much capacity to produce relative to that needed to meet market demand means incurring some costs of unused capacity. Having too little capacity to produce means that demand from some customers may be unfilled. These customers may go to other sources of supply and never return. Therefore, both managers and accountants should have a clear understanding of the issues that arise with capacity costs.

Alternative Denominator-Level Capacity Concepts for Absorption Costing

Learning Objective 5

Describe the various capacity concepts that can be used in absorption costing

. . . theoretical capacity, practical capacity, normal capacity utilization, and master-budget capacity utilization

Earlier chapters, especially Chapters 4, 5, and 8, have highlighted how normal costing and standard costing report costs in an ongoing timely manner throughout a fiscal year. The choice of the capacity level used to allocate budgeted fixed manufacturing costs to products can greatly affect the operating income reported under normal costing or standard costing and the product-cost information available to managers.

Consider the Stassen Company example again. Recall that the annual fixed manufacturing costs of the production facility are $1,080,000. Stassen currently uses absorption costing with standard costs for external reporting purposes, and it calculates its budgeted fixed manufacturing rate on a per unit basis. We will now examine four different capacity levels used as the denominator to compute the budgeted fixed manufacturing cost rate: theoretical capacity, practical capacity, normal capacity utilization, and master-budget capacity utilization.

Theoretical Capacity and Practical Capacity

In business and accounting, *capacity* ordinarily means a "constraint," an "upper limit." **Theoretical capacity** is the level of capacity based on producing at full efficiency all the time. Stassen can produce 25 units per shift when the production lines are operating at maximum speed. If we assume 360 days per year, the theoretical annual capacity for two shifts per day is:

$$25 \text{ units per shift} \times 2 \text{ shifts per day} \times 360 \text{ days} = 18{,}000 \text{ units}$$

Theoretical capacity is theoretical in the sense that it does not allow for any plant maintenance, shutdown periods, interruptions because of downtime on the assembly lines, or any other factors. Theoretical capacity represents an ideal goal of capacity utilization. Theoretical capacity levels are unattainable in the real world but they provide a target for a company to aspire to.

Practical capacity is the level of capacity that reduces theoretical capacity by considering unavoidable operating interruptions, such as scheduled maintenance time, shutdowns for holidays, and so on. Assume that practical capacity is the practical production rate of 20 units per shift (as opposed to 25 units per shift under theoretical capacity) for two shifts per day for 300 days a year (as distinguished from 360 days a year under theoretical capacity). The practical annual capacity is:

$$20 \text{ units per shift} \times 2 \text{ shifts per day} \times 300 \text{ days} = 12{,}000 \text{ units}$$

Engineering and human resource factors are both important when estimating theoretical or practical capacity. Engineers at the Stassen facility can provide input on the technical capabilities of machines for cutting and polishing lenses. Human-safety factors, such as increased injury risk when the line operates at faster speeds, are also necessary considerations in estimating practical capacity. With difficulty, practical capacity is attainable.

Normal Capacity Utilization and Master-Budget Capacity Utilization

Both theoretical capacity and practical capacity measure capacity levels in terms of what a plant can *supply*—available capacity. In contrast, normal capacity utilization and master-budget capacity utilization measure capacity levels in terms of *demand* for the output of the plant—the amount of available capacity that the plant expects to use based on the demand for its products. In many cases, budgeted demand is well below production capacity available.

Normal capacity utilization is the level of capacity utilization that satisfies average customer demand over a period (say, two to three years) that includes seasonal, cyclical, and trend factors. **Master-budget capacity utilization** is the level of capacity utilization that managers expect for the current budget period, which is typically one year. These two capacity-utilization levels can differ—for example, when an industry, such as automobiles or semiconductors, has cyclical periods of high and low demand or when management believes that budgeted production for the coming period is not representative of long-run demand.

Consider Stassen's master budget for 2009, based on production of 8,000 telescopes per year. Despite using this master-budget capacity-utilization level of 8,000 telescopes for 2009, top management believes that over the next three years the normal (average) annual production level will be 10,000 telescopes. They view 2009's budgeted production level of 8,000 telescopes to be "abnormally" low. That's because a major competitor has been sharply reducing its selling price and spending large amounts on advertising. Stassen expects that the competitor's lower price and advertising blitz will not be a long-run phenomenon and that, by 2011 and beyond, Stassen's production and sales will be higher.

Effect on Budgeted Fixed Manufacturing Cost Rate

We now illustrate how each of these four denominator levels affects the budgeted fixed manufacturing cost rate. Stassen has budgeted (standard) fixed manufacturing overhead costs of $1,080,000 for 2009. This lump-sum is incurred to provide the capacity to produce telescopes. The amount includes, among other costs, leasing costs for the facility and the compensation of the facility managers. The budgeted fixed manufacturing cost rates for 2009 for each of the four capacity-level concepts are:

	A	B	C	D
1		Budgeted Fixed	Budget	Budgeted Fixed
2	Denominator-Level	Manufacturing	Capacity Level	Manufacturing
3	Capacity Concept	Costs per Year	(in units)	Cost per Unit
4	(1)	(2)	(3)	(4) = (2) / (3)
5	Theoretical capacity	$1,080,000	18,000	$ 60
6	Practical capacity	$1,080,000	12,000	$ 90
7	Normal capacity utilization	$1,080,000	10,000	$108
8	Master-budget capacity utilization	$1,080,000	8,000	$135

The significant difference in cost rates (from $60 to $135) arises because of large differences in budgeted capacity levels under the different capacity concepts.

Budgeted (standard) variable manufacturing cost is $200 per unit. The total budgeted (standard) manufacturing cost per unit for alternative capacity-level concepts is:

	A	B	C	D
1		Budgeted Variable	Budgeted Fixed	Budgeted Total
2	Denominator-Level	Manufacturing	Manufacturing	Manufacturing
3	Capacity Concept	Cost per Unit	Cost per Unit	Cost per Unit
4	(1)	(2)	(3)	(4) = (2) + (3)
5	Theoretical capacity	$200	$ 60	$260
6	Practical capacity	$200	$ 90	$290
7	Normal capacity utilization	$200	$108	$308
8	Master-budget capacity utilization	$200	$135	$335

Because different denominator-level capacity concepts yield different budgeted fixed manufacturing costs per unit, Stassen must decide which capacity level to use. Stassen is not required to use the same capacity-level concept, say, for management planning and control, external reporting to shareholders, and income tax purposes.

Choosing a Capacity Level

Learning Objective 6

Examine the key factors in choosing a capacity level to compute the budgeted fixed manufacturing cost rate

. . . managers must consider the effect a capacity level has on product costing, capacity management, pricing decisions, and financial statements

As we just saw, at the start of each fiscal year, managers determine different denominator levels for the different capacity concepts and calculate different budgeted fixed manufacturing costs per unit. We now discuss the problems with and effects of different denominator-level choices for different purposes, including (a) product costing and capacity management, (b) pricing, (c) performance evaluation, (d) external reporting, (e) regulatory requirements, and (f) difficulties in forecasting capacity levels.

Product Costing and Capacity Management

Data from normal costing or standard costing are often used in pricing or product-mix decisions. As the Stassen example illustrates, use of theoretical capacity results in an unrealistically small fixed manufacturing cost per unit because it is based on an idealistic and unattainable level of capacity. Theoretical capacity is rarely used to calculate budgeted fixed manufacturing cost per unit because it departs significantly from the real capacity available to a company.

Many companies favor practical capacity as the denominator to calculate budgeted fixed manufacturing cost per unit. Practical capacity in the Stassen example represents the maximum number of units (12,000) that Stassen can reasonably expect to produce per year for the $1,080,000 it will spend annually on capacity. If Stassen had consistently planned to produce fewer units, say 6,000 telescopes each year, it would have built a smaller plant and incurred lower costs.

Stassen budgets $90 in fixed manufacturing cost per unit based on the $1,080,000 it costs to acquire the capacity to produce 12,000 units. This level of plant capacity is an important strategic decision that managers make well before Stassen uses the capacity and even before Stassen knows how much of the capacity it will actually use. That is, budgeted fixed manufacturing cost of $90 per unit measures the *cost per unit of supplying the capacity*.

Demand for Stassen's telescopes in 2009 is expected to be 8,000 units, which is 4,000 units lower than the practical capacity of 12,000 units. However, the cost of *supplying* the capacity needed to make 12,000 units is still $90 per unit. That's because it costs Stassen $1,080,000 per year to acquire the capacity to make 12,000 units. The capacity and its cost are fixed *in the short run*; unlike variable costs, the capacity supplied does not automatically reduce to match the capacity needed in 2010. As a result, not all of the capacity supplied at $90 per unit will be needed or used in 2010. Using practical capacity as the denominator level, managers can subdivide the cost of resources supplied into used and unused components. At the supply cost of $90 per unit, the manufacturing resources that Stassen will use equal $720,000 ($90 per unit × 8,000 units). Manufacturing resources that Stassen will not use are $360,000 [$90 per unit × (12,000 − 8,000) units].

Using practical capacity as the denominator level sets the cost of capacity at the cost of supplying the capacity, regardless of the demand for the capacity. Highlighting the cost of capacity acquired but not used directs managers' attention toward managing unused capacity, perhaps by designing new products to fill unused capacity, by leasing unused capacity to others, or by eliminating unused capacity. In contrast, using either of the capacity levels based on the demand for Stassen's telescopes—master-budget capacity utilization or normal capacity utilization—hides the amount of unused capacity. If Stassen had used master-budget capacity utilization as the capacity level, it would have calculated budgeted fixed manufacturing cost per unit as $135 ($1,080,000 ÷ 8,000 units). This calculation does not use data about practical capacity, so it does not separately identify the cost of unused capacity. Note, however, that the cost of $135 per unit includes a charge for unused capacity: it comprises the $90 fixed manufacturing resource that would be used to produce each unit at practical capacity plus the cost of unused capacity allocated to each unit, $45 per unit ($360,000 ÷ 8,000 units).

From the perspective of long-run product costing, which cost of capacity should Stassen use for pricing purposes or for benchmarking its product cost structure against competitors: $90 per unit based on practical capacity or $135 per unit based on master-budget capacity utilization? Probably the $90 per unit based on practical capacity. Why? Because $90 per unit represents the budgeted cost per unit of only the capacity used to produce the product, and it explicitly excludes the cost of any unused capacity. Stassen's customers will be willing to pay a price that covers the cost of the capacity actually used but will not want to pay for unused capacity that provides no other benefits to them. Customers expect Stassen to manage its unused capacity or to bear the cost of unused capacity, not pass it along to them. Moreover, if Stassen's competitors manage unused capacity more effectively, the cost of capacity in the competitors' cost structures (which guides competitors' pricing decisions) is likely to approach $90. In the next section we show how the use of normal capacity utilization or master-budget capacity utilization can result in setting selling prices that are not competitive.

Pricing Decisions and the Downward Demand Spiral

Learning Objective 7

Describe how attempts to recover fixed costs of capacity may lead to price increases and lower demand

. . . this situation is the downward demand spiral, which explains why customers are unwilling to pay for a company's unused capacity

The **downward demand spiral** for a company is the continuing reduction in the demand for its products that occurs when competitor prices are not met; as demand drops further, higher and higher unit costs result in greater reluctance to meet competitors' prices.

The easiest way to understand the downward demand spiral is via an example. Assume Stassen uses master-budget capacity utilization of 8,000 units for product costing in 2009. The resulting manufacturing cost is $335 per unit ($200 variable manufacturing cost per unit + $135 fixed manufacturing cost per unit). Assume that in December 2008, a competitor offers to supply a major customer of Stassen (a customer who was expected to purchase 2,000 units in 2009) telescopes at $300 per unit. The Stassen manager, not wanting to show a loss on the account and wanting to recoup all costs in the long run, declines to match the competitor's price. The account is lost. The loss means budgeted fixed manufacturing costs of $1,080,000 will be spread over the remaining master-budget volume of 6,000 units at a rate of $180 per unit ($1,080,000 ÷ 6,000 units).

Suppose yet another Stassen customer—who also accounts for 2,000 units of budgeted volume—receives a bid from a competitor at a price of $350 per unit. The Stassen manager compares this bid with his revised unit cost of $380 ($200 + $180), declines to match the competition, and the account is lost. Planned output would shrink further to 4,000 units. Budgeted fixed manufacturing cost per unit for the remaining 4,000 telescopes would now be $270 ($1,080,000 ÷ 4,000 units). The following table shows the effect of spreading fixed manufacturing costs over a shrinking amount of master-budget capacity utilization:

	A	B	C	D
1	**Master-Budget**		**Budgeted Fixed**	
2	**Capacity Utilization**	**Budgeted Variable**	**Manufacturing**	**Budgeted Total**
3	**Denominator Level**	**Manufacturing Cost**	**Cost per Unit**	**Manufacturing**
4	**(Units)**	**per Unit**	**[$1,080,000 ÷ (1)]**	**Cost per Unit**
5	(1)	(2)	(3)	(4) = (2) + (3)
6	8,000	$200	$135	$335
7	6,000	$200	$180	$380
8	4,000	$200	$270	$470
9	3,000	$200	$360	$560

Practical capacity, by contrast, is a stable measure. The use of practical capacity as the denominator to calculate budgeted fixed manufacturing cost per unit avoids the recalculation of unit costs when expected demand levels change. That's because the fixed cost rate would be calculated based on *capacity available* rather than *capacity used to meet demand*. Managers who use reported unit costs in a mechanical way to set prices are less likely to promote a downward demand spiral when they use practical capacity than when they use normal capacity utilization or master-budget capacity utilization.

Using practical capacity as the denominator level also gives the manager a more accurate idea of the resources needed and used to produce a unit by excluding the cost of unused capacity. As discussed earlier, the cost of manufacturing resources supplied to produce a telescope is $290 ($200 variable manufacturing cost per unit plus $90 fixed manufacturing cost per unit). This cost is lower than the prices offered by Stassen's competitors and would have correctly led the manager to match the prices and retain the accounts (assuming for purposes of this discussion that Stassen has no other costs). If, however, the prices offered by competitors were lower than $290 per unit, the Stassen manager would not recover the cost of resources used to supply telescopes. This would signal to the manager that Stassen was noncompetitive even if it had no unused capacity. The only way then for Stassen to be profitable and retain customers in the long run would be to reduce its manufacturing cost per unit.

Performance Evaluation

Consider how the choice among normal capacity utilization, master-budget capacity utilization, and practical capacity affects the evaluation of a marketing manager. Normal capacity utilization is often used as a basis for long-run plans. Normal capacity utilization depends on the time span selected and the forecasts made for each year. *However, normal capacity utilization is an average that provides no meaningful feedback to the marketing manager for a particular year.* Using normal capacity utilization as a reference for judging current performance of a marketing manager is an example of misusing a long-run measure for a short-run purpose. Master-budget capacity utilization, rather than normal capacity utilization or practical capacity, should be used to evaluate a marketing manager's performance in the current year. That's because the master budget is the principal short-run planning and control tool. Managers feel more obligated to reach the levels specified in the master budget, which should have been carefully set in relation to the maximum opportunities for sales in the current year.

When large differences exist between practical capacity and master-budget capacity utilization, several companies (such as Texas Instruments, Polysar, and Sandoz) classify the difference as *planned unused capacity*. One reason for this approach is performance evaluation. Consider our Stassen telescope example. The managers in charge of capacity planning usually do not make pricing decisions. Top management decided to build a production facility with 12,000 units of practical capacity, focusing on demand over the next five years. But Stassen's marketing managers, who are mid-level managers, make the pricing decisions. These marketing managers believe they should be held accountable only for the manufacturing overhead costs related to their potential customer base in 2009. The master-budget capacity utilization suggests a customer base in 2009 of 8,000 units (2/3 of the 12,000 practical capacity). Using responsibility accounting principles (see Chapter 6, pp. 197–199), only 2/3 of the budgeted total fixed manufacturing costs ($1,080,000 × 2/3 = $720,000) would be attributed to the fixed capacity costs of meeting 2009 demand. The remaining 1/3 of the numerator ($1,080,000 × 1/3 = $360,000) would be separately shown as the capacity cost of meeting increases in long-run demand expected to occur beyond 2009.[4]

External Reporting

The magnitude of the favorable/unfavorable production-volume variance under absorption costing is affected by the choice of the denominator level used to calculate the budgeted fixed manufacturing cost per unit. Assume the following actual operating information for Stassen in 2009:

	A	B	C
1	Beginning inventory	0	
2	Production	8,000	units
3	Sales	6,000	units
4	Ending inventory	2,000	units
5	Selling price	$ 1,000	per unit
6	Variable manufacturing cost	$ 200	per unit
7	Fixed manufacturing costs	$ 1,080,000	
8	Variable marketing cost	$ 185	per unit sold
9	Fixed marketing costs	$ 1,380,000	

Note that this is the same data used to calculate the income under variable and absorption costing for Stassen in Exhibit 9-1. As before, we assume that there are no price, spending, or efficiency variances in manufacturing costs.

Recall from Chapter 8 the equation used to calculate the production-volume variance:

$$\text{Production-volume variance} = \left(\begin{array}{c}\text{Budgeted}\\ \text{fixed}\\ \text{manufacturing}\\ \text{overhead}\end{array}\right) - \left(\begin{array}{c}\text{Fixed manufacturing overhead allocated using}\\ \text{budgeted cost per output unit}\\ \text{allowed for acutal output produced}\end{array}\right)$$

The four different capacity-level concepts result in four different budgeted fixed manufacturing overhead cost rates per unit. The different rates will result in different amounts of fixed manufacturing overhead costs allocated to the 8,000 units actually produced and different amounts of production-volume variance. Using the budgeted fixed manufacturing costs of $1,080,000 (equal to actual fixed manufacturing costs) and the rates calculated on page 314 for different denominator levels, the production-volume variance computations are as follows:

$$\begin{aligned}\text{Production-volume variance (theoretical capacity)} &= \$1{,}080{,}000 - (8{,}000 \text{ units} \times \$60 \text{ per unit})\\ &= \$1{,}080{,}000 - 480{,}000\\ &= 600{,}000 \text{ U}\end{aligned}$$

[4] For further discussion, see T. Klammer, *Capacity Measurement and Improvement* (Chicago: Irwin, 1996). This research was facilitated by CAM-I, an organization promoting innovative cost management practices. CAM-I's research on capacity costs explores ways in which companies can identify types of capacity costs that can be reduced (or eliminated) without affecting the required output to meet customer demand. An example is improving processes to successfully eliminate the costs of capacity held in anticipation of handling difficulties due to imperfect coordination with suppliers and customers.

Production-volume variance (practical capacity) = \$1,080,000 – (8,000 units × \$90 per unit)
= \$1,080,000 – 720,000
= 360,000 U

Production-volume variance (normal capacity utilization) = \$1,080,000 – (8,000 units × \$108 per unit)
= \$1,080,000 – 864,000
= 216,000 U

Production-volume variance (master-budget capacity utilization) = \$1,080,000 – (8,000 units × \$135 per unit)
= \$1,080,000 – 1,080,000
= 0

How Stassen disposes of its production-volume variance at the end of the fiscal year will determine the effect this variance has on the company's operating income. We now discuss the three alternative approaches Stassen can use to dispose of the production-volume variance. These approaches were first discussed in Chapter 4 (pp. 115–119).

1. **Adjusted allocation-rate approach.** This approach restates all amounts in the general and subsidiary ledgers by using actual rather than budgeted cost rates. Given that actual fixed manufacturing costs are \$1,080,000 and actual production is 8,000 units, the recalculated fixed manufacturing cost is \$135 per unit (\$1,080,000 ÷ 8,000 actual units). Under the adjusted allocation-rate approach, the choice of the capacity level used to calculate the budgeted fixed manufacturing cost per unit has no effect on year-end financial statements. In effect, actual costing is adopted at the end of the fiscal year.
2. **Proration approach.** The underallocated or overallocated overhead is spread among ending balances in Work-in-Process Control, Finished Goods Control, and Cost of Goods Sold. The proration restates the ending balances in these accounts to what they would have been if actual cost rates had been used rather than budgeted cost rates. The proration approach also results in the choice of the capacity level used to calculate the budgeted fixed manufacturing cost per unit having no effect on year-end financial statements.
3. **Write-off variances to cost of goods sold approach.** Exhibit 9-7 shows how use of this approach affects Stassen's operating income for 2009. Recall that Stassen had no beginning inventory, and it had production of 8,000 units and sales of 6,000 units. Therefore, the ending inventory on December 31, 2009, is 2,000 units. Using master-budget capacity utilization as the denominator level results in assigning the highest amount of fixed manufacturing cost per unit to the 2,000 units in ending inventory (see the line item "deduct ending inventory" in Exhibit 9-7). Accordingly, operating income is highest using master-budget capacity utilization. The differences in operating income for the four denominator-level concepts in Exhibit 9-7 are due to different amounts of fixed manufacturing overhead being inventoried at the end of 2009:

	Fixed Manufacturing Overhead in Dec. 31, 2009 Inventory		
Theoretical capacity	2,000 units × \$60 per unit	=	\$120,000
Practical capacity	2,000 units × \$90 per unit	=	\$180,000
Normal capacity utilization	2,000 units × \$108 per unit	=	\$216,000
Master-budget capacity utilization	2,000 units × \$135 per unit	=	\$270,000

In Exhibit 9-7, for example, the \$54,000 difference (\$1,500,000 – \$1,446,000) in operating income between master-budget capacity utilization and normal capacity utilization is due to the difference in fixed manufacturing overhead inventoried (\$270,000 \$216,000).

What is the common reason and explanation for the increasing operating-income numbers in Exhibit 9-4 (p. 308) and Exhibit 9-7? It is the amount of fixed manufacturing costs incurred that is included in ending inventory at the end of the year. As this amount increases, so does operating income. The amount of fixed manufacturing costs inventoried depends on two factors: the number of units in ending inventory and the rate at which fixed manufacturing costs are allocated to each unit. Exhibit 9-4 shows the effect on operating income of increasing the number of units in ending inventory (by increasing production). Exhibit 9-7 shows the effect on operating income of increasing the fixed manufacturing cost allocated per unit (by decreasing the denominator level used to calculate the rate).

Chapter 8 (pp. 273–274) discusses the various issues managers and management accountants must consider when deciding whether to prorate the production-volume variance among inventories and cost of goods sold or to simply write off the variance to cost of goods sold. The objective is to write off the portion of the production-volume variance that represents the cost of capacity not used to support the production of output during the period. Determining this amount is almost always a matter of judgment.

Tax Requirements

For tax reporting purposes in the United States, the Internal Revenue Service (IRS) requires companies to use practical capacity to calculate budgeted fixed manufacturing cost per unit. At year-end, proration of any variances between inventories and cost of

Exhibit 9-7 Income-Statement Effects of Using Alternative Capacity-Level Concepts: Stassen Company for 2009

	A	B	C	D	E	F	G	H
1		Theoretical Capacity		Practical Capacity		Normal Capacity Utilization		Master-Budget Capacity Utilization
2	Denominator level in cases	18,000		12,000		10,000		8,000
3	Revenues[a]	$6,000,000		$6,000,000		$6,000,000		$6,000,000
4	Cost of goods sold							
5	Beginning inventory	0		0		0		0
6	Variable manufacturing costs[b]	1,600,000		1,600,000		1,600,000		1,600,000
7	Fixed manufacturing costs[c]	480,000		720,000		864,000		1,080,000
8	Cost of goods available for sale	2,080,000		2,320,000		2,464,000		2,680,000
9	Deduct ending inventory[d]	(520,000)		(580,000)		(616,000)		(670,000)
10	Cost of goods sold (at standard cost)	1,560,000		1,740,000		1,848,000		2,010,000
11	Adjustment for production-volume variance	600,000	U	360,000	U	216,000	U	0
12	Cost of goods sold	2,160,000		2,100,000		2,064,000		2,010,000
13	Gross margin	3,840,000		3,900,000		3,936,000		3,990,000
14	Marketing costs[e]	2,490,000		2,490,000		2,490,000		2,490,000
15	Operating income	$1,350,000		$1,410,000		$1,446,000		$1,500,000
16								
17	[a]$1,000 x 6,000 units = $6,000,000			[d]Ending inventory costs:				
18	[b]$200 x 8,000 units = $1,600,000			($200 + $60) x 2,000 units = $520,000				
19	[c]Fixed manufacturing overhead costs:			($200 + $90) x 2,000 units = $580,000				
20	$60 x 8,000 units = $ 480,000			($200 + $108) x 2,000 units = $616,000				
21	$90 x 8,000 units = $ 720,000			($200 + $135) x 2,000 units = $670,000				
22	$108 x 8,000 units = $ 864,000			[e]Marketing costs:				
23	$135 x 8,000 units = $1,080,000			$1,380,000 + $185 x 6,000 units = $2,490,000				

goods sold is required (unless the variance is immaterial in amount) to calculate the company's operating income.[5]

Difficulties in Forecasting Chosen Denominator-Level Concept

Practical capacity measures the available supply of capacity. Managers can usually use engineering studies and human-resource considerations (such as worker safety) to obtain a reliable estimate of this denominator level for the budget period. However, it is more difficult to estimate normal capacity utilization reliably. For example, many U.S. steel companies in the 1980s believed they were in the downturn of a demand cycle that would have an upturn within two or three years. After all, steel had been a cyclical business in which upturns followed downturns, making the notion of normal capacity utilization appear reasonable. Unfortunately, the steel cycle in the 1980s did not turn up; some companies and numerous plants closed. Another example is that marketing managers are often prone to overestimate their ability to regain lost sales and market share. Their estimate of "normal" demand for their product may consequently be based on an overly optimistic outlook. Master-budget capacity utilization typically focuses only on the expected capacity utilization for the next year. Therefore, master-budget capacity utilization can be more reliably estimated than normal capacity utilization.

Capacity Costs and Denominator-Level Issues

We now present more factors that affect the planning and control of capacity costs.

1. Costing systems, such as normal costing or standard costing, do not recognize uncertainty the way managers recognize it. Managers use a *single* amount rather than a range of possible amounts as the denominator level when calculating budgeted fixed manufacturing cost per unit in absorption costing. Yet, managers face uncertainty about demand: they even face uncertainty about their capability to supply. Stassen's facility has an estimated practical capacity of 12,000 units. The estimated master-budget capacity utilization for 2009 is 8,000 units. These estimates are uncertain. Managers recognize uncertainty in their capacity-planning decisions. Stassen built its current plant with a 12,000 unit practical capacity in part to provide the capability to meet possible demand surges. Even if such surges do not occur in a given period, do not conclude that capacity unused in a given period is wasted resources. *The gains from meeting sudden demand surges may well require having unused capacity in some periods.*
2. The fixed manufacturing cost rate is based on a numerator—budgeted fixed manufacturing costs—and a denominator—some measure of capacity or capacity utilization. Our discussion so far has emphasized issues concerning the choice of the denominator. Challenging issues also arise in measuring the numerator. For example, deregulation of the U.S. electric utility industry has resulted in many electric utilities becoming unprofitable. This situation has led to write-downs in the values of the utilities' plants and equipment. The write-downs reduce the numerator because there is less depreciation expense included in the calculation of fixed capacity cost per kilowatt-hour of electricity produced. The difficulty that managers face in this situation is that the amount of write-downs is not clear-cut but, rather, a matter of judgment.
3. Capacity costs also arise in nonmanufacturing parts of the value chain. Stassen may acquire a fleet of vehicles capable of distributing the practical capacity of its production facility. When actual production is below practical capacity, there will be unused-capacity cost issues with the distribution function, as well as with the manufacturing function.

[5] U.S. tax reporting requires the use of either the adjusted allocation-rate approach or the proration approach. Section 1.471-11 of the U.S. Internal Revenue Code states: "The proper use of the standard cost method requires that a taxpayer must reallocate to the goods in ending inventory a pro rata portion of any net negative or net positive overhead variances."

As you saw in Chapter 8, capacity cost issues are prominent in many service-sector companies, such as airlines, hospitals, and railroads, even though these companies carry no inventory and so have no inventory costing problems. For example, in calculating the fixed overhead cost per patient-day in its obstetrics and gynecology department, a hospital must decide which denominator level to use: practical capacity, normal capacity utilization, or master-budget capacity utilization. Its decision may have implications for capacity management, as well as pricing and performance evaluation.

4. For simplicity and to focus on the main ideas about choosing a denominator to calculate a budgeted fixed manufacturing cost rate, our Stassen example assumed that all fixed manufacturing costs had a single cost driver: telescope units produced. As you saw in Chapter 5, activity-based costing systems have multiple overhead cost pools at the output-unit, batch, product-sustaining, and facility-sustaining levels, each with its own cost driver. In calculating activity cost rates (for fixed costs of setups and material handling, say), management must choose a capacity level for the quantity of the cost driver (setup-hours or loads moved). Should management use practical capacity, normal capacity utilization, or master-budget capacity utilization? For all the reasons described in this chapter (such as pricing and capacity management), most proponents of activity-based costing argue that practical capacity should be used as the denominator level to calculate activity cost rates.

Problem for Self-Study

Suppose Stassen Company is computing its operating income for 2013. That year's results are identical to the results for 2009, shown in Exhibit 9-7, except that master-budget capacity utilization for 2013 is 9,000 units instead of 8,000. Production in 2013 is 8,000 units and sales are 6,000 units. There is no beginning inventory on January 1, 2013, and there are no variances other than the production-volume variance. Stassen writes off this variance to cost of goods sold.

Required How would the results for Stassen Company in Exhibit 9-7 differ if the year were 2013 rather than 2009? Show your computations.

Solution

The only change in Exhibit 9-7 results would be for the master-budget capacity utilization level. The budgeted fixed manufacturing cost rate for 2013 is:

$$\frac{\$1{,}080{,}000}{9{,}000 \text{ units}} = \$120 \text{ per unit}$$

The manufacturing cost per unit is \$320 (\$200 + \$120). So, the production-volume variance for 2013 is:

$$(9{,}000 \text{ units} - 8{,}000 \text{ units}) \times \$120 \text{ per unit} = \$120{,}000 \text{ U}$$

The income statement for 2013 is as follows:

Revenues: \$1,000 per unit × 6,000 units	\$6,000,000
Cost of goods sold:	
Beginning inventory	0
Variable manufacturing costs: \$200 per unit × 8,000 units	1,600,000
Fixed manufacturing costs: \$120 per unit × 8,000 units	960,000
Cost of goods available for sale	2,560,000
Deduct ending inventory: \$320 per unit × 2,000 units	(640,000)
Cost of goods sold (at standard costs)	1,920,000
Adjustment for production-volume variance	120,000 U
Cost of goods sold	2,040,000
Gross margin	3,960,000
Marketing costs: \$1,380,000 fixed + (\$185 per unit) × (6,000 units sold)	2,490,000
Operating income	\$1,470,000

The higher denominator level used to calculate budgeted fixed manufacturing cost per unit in the 2013 master budget means that fewer fixed manufacturing costs are inventoried in 2013 ($120 per unit × 2,000 units = $240,000) than in 2009 ($135 per unit × 2,000 units = $270,000). This difference of $30,000 ($270,000 − $240,000) results in operating income being lower by $30,000 in 2013 relative to 2009 ($1,500,000 − $1,470,000).

Decision Points

The following question-and-answer format summarizes the chapter's learning objectives. Each decision presents a key question related to a learning objective. The guidelines are the answer to that question.

Decision	Guidelines
1. How does variable costing differ from absorption costing?	Variable costing and absorption costing differ in only one respect: how to account for fixed manufacturing costs. Under variable costing, fixed manufacturing costs are excluded from inventoriable costs and are a cost of the period in which they are incurred. Under absorption costing, fixed manufacturing costs are inventoriable and become a part of cost of goods sold in the period when sales occur.
2. How does income differ under variable and absorption costing?	The variable-costing income statement is based on the contribution-margin format. Under it, operating income is driven by the unit level of sales. Under absorption costing, the income statement follows the gross-margin format. Operating income is driven by the unit level of production, the unit level of sales, and the denominator level used for assigning fixed costs.
3. Why might managers build up finished goods inventory if they use absorption costing?	When absorption costing is used, managers can increase current operating income by producing more units for inventory. Producing for inventory absorbs more fixed manufacturing costs into inventory and reduces costs expensed in the period. Critics of absorption costing label this manipulation of income as the major negative consequence of treating fixed manufacturing costs as inventoriable costs.
4. How does throughput costing differ from variable costing and absorption costing?	Throughput costing treats all costs except direct materials as costs of the period in which they are incurred. Throughput costing results in a lower amount of manufacturing costs being inventoried than either variable or absorption costing.
5. What are the various capacity levels a company can use to compute the budgeted fixed manufacturing cost rate?	Capacity levels can be measured in terms of capacity supplied—theoretical capacity or practical capacity. Capacity can also be measured in terms of output demanded—normal capacity utilization or master-budget capacity utilization.
6. What are the major factors managers consider in choosing the capacity level to compute the budgeted fixed manufacturing cost rate?	The major factors managers consider in choosing the capacity level to compute the budgeted fixed manufacturing cost rate are (a) effect on product costing and capacity management, (b) effect on pricing decisions, (c) effect on performance evaluation, (d) effect on financial statements, (e) regulatory requirements, and (f) difficulties in forecasting chosen capacity-level concepts.
7. Should a company with high fixed costs and unused capacity raise selling prices to try to fully recoup its costs?	No, companies with high fixed costs and unused capacity may encounter ongoing and increasingly greater reductions in demand if they continue to raise selling prices to try to fully recoup variable and fixed costs from a declining sales base. This phenomenon is called the downward demand spiral.

APPENDIX: BREAKEVEN POINTS IN VARIABLE COSTING AND ABSORPTION COSTING

Chapter 3 introduced cost-volume-profit analysis. If variable costing is used, the breakeven point (that's where operating income is \$0) is computed in the usual manner. There is only one breakeven point in this case, and it depends on (1) fixed (manufacturing and operating) costs and (2) contribution margin per unit.

The formula for computing breakeven point under variable costing is a special case of the more-general target operating income formula from Chapter 3 (p. 67):

$$\text{Let } Q = \text{Number of units sold to earn the target operating income}$$

$$\text{Then } Q = \frac{\text{Total fixed costs} + \text{Target operating income}}{\text{Contribution margin per unit}}$$

Breakeven occurs when the target operating income is \$0. In our Stassen illustration for 2009 (see Exhibit 9-1, p. 302):

$$Q = \frac{(\$1{,}080{,}000 + \$1{,}380{,}000) + \$0}{(\$1{,}000 - (\$200 + \$185))} = \frac{\$2{,}460{,}000}{\$615}$$
$$= 4{,}000 \text{ units.}$$

Proof of breakeven point:

Revenues, \$1,000 × 4,000 units	\$4,000,000
Variable costs, \$385 × 4,000 units	1,540,000
Contribution margin, \$615 × 4,000 units	2,460,000
Fixed costs	2,460,000
Operating income	\$ 0

If absorption costing is used, the required number of units to be sold to earn a specific target operating income is not unique because of the number of variables involved. The following formula shows the factors that will affect the target operating income under absorption costing:

$$Q = \frac{\begin{matrix}\text{Total}\\\text{fixed}\\\text{costs}\end{matrix} + \begin{matrix}\text{Target}\\\text{operating}\\\text{income}\end{matrix} + \left[\begin{matrix}\text{Fixed}\\\text{manufacturing}\\\text{cost rate}\end{matrix} \times \left(\begin{matrix}\text{Breakeven}\\\text{sales}\\\text{in units}\end{matrix} - \begin{matrix}\text{Units}\\\text{produced}\end{matrix}\right)\right]}{\text{Contribution margin per unit}}$$

In this formula, the numerator is the sum of three terms (from the perspective of the two "+" signs), compared with two terms in the numerator of the variable-costing formula stated earlier. The additional term in the numerator under absorption costing is:

$$\left[\begin{matrix}\text{Fixed manufacturing}\\\text{cost rate}\end{matrix} \times \left(\begin{matrix}\text{Breakeven sales}\\\text{in units}\end{matrix} - \begin{matrix}\text{Units}\\\text{produced}\end{matrix}\right)\right]$$

This term reduces the fixed costs that need to be recovered when units produced exceed the breakeven sales quantity. When production exceeds the breakeven sales quantity, some of the fixed manufacturing costs that are expensed under variable costing are not expensed under absorption costing; they are instead included in finished goods inventory.

For Stassen Company in 2009, suppose that actual production is 5,280 units. Then, one breakeven point, Q, under absorption costing is:

$$Q = \frac{(\$1{,}080{,}000 + \$1{,}380{,}000) + \$0 + [\$135 \times (Q - 5{,}280)]}{(\$1{,}000 - (\$200 + \$185))}$$
$$= \frac{(\$2{,}460{,}000 + \$135Q - \$712{,}800)}{\$615}$$
$$\$615Q = \$1{,}747{,}200 + \$135Q$$
$$\$480Q = \$1{,}747{,}200$$
$$Q = 3{,}640$$

Proof of breakeven point:

Revenues, $1,000 × 3,640 units		$3,640,000
Cost of goods sold:		
Cost of goods sold at standard cost, $335 × 3,640 units	$1,219,400	
Production-volume variance, $135 × (8,000 − 5,280) units	367,200 U	1,586,600
Gross margin		2,053,400
Marketing costs:		
Variable marketing costs, $185 × 3,640 units	673,400	
Fixed marketing costs	1,380,000	2,053,400
Operating income		$ 0

The breakeven point under absorption costing depends on (1) fixed manufacturing costs, (2) fixed operating (marketing) costs, (3) contribution margin per unit, (4) unit level of production, and (5) the capacity level chosen as the denominator to set the fixed manufacturing cost rate. For Stassen in 2009, a combination of 3,640 units sold, fixed manufacturing costs of $1,080,000, fixed marketing costs of $1,380,000, contribution margin per unit of $615, an 8,000-unit denominator level, and production of 5,280 units would result in an operating income of $0. *Note, however, that there are many combinations of these five factors that would give an operating income of $0.* For example, holding all other factors constant, a combination of 6,240 units produced and 3,370 units sold also results in an operating income of $0 under absorption costing.

Proof of breakeven point:

Revenues, $1,000 × 3,370 units		$3,370,000
Cost of goods sold:		
Cost of goods sold at standard cost, $335 × 3,370 units	$1,128,950	
Production-volume variance, $135 × (8,000 − 6,240) units	237,600 U	1,366,550
Gross margin		2,003,450
Marketing costs:		
Variable marketing costs, $185 × 3,370 units	623,450	
Fixed marketing costs	1,380,000	2,003,450
Operating income		$ 0

Suppose actual production in 2009 was equal to the denominator level, 8,000 units, and there were no units sold and no fixed marketing costs. All the units produced would be placed in inventory, so all the fixed manufacturing costs would be included in inventory. There would be no production-volume variance. Under these conditions, the company could break even with no sales whatsoever! In contrast, under variable costing, the operating loss would be equal to the fixed manufacturing costs of $1,080,000.

TERMS TO LEARN

This chapter and the Glossary at the end of the book contain definitions of:

absorption costing (**p. 301**)
direct costing (**p. 301**)
downward demand spiral (**p. 316**)
master-budget capacity utilization (**p. 314**)
normal capacity utilization (**p. 314**)
practical capacity (**p. 313**)
super-variable costing (**p. 309**)
theoretical capacity (**p. 313**)
throughput costing (**p. 309**)
variable costing (**p. 300**)

ASSIGNMENT MATERIAL

Questions

9-1 Differences in operating income between variable costing and absorption costing are due solely to accounting for fixed costs. Do you agree? Explain.

9-2 Why is the term *direct costing* a misnomer?

9-3 Do companies in either the service sector or the merchandising sector make choices about absorption costing versus variable costing?

9-4 Explain the main conceptual issue under variable costing and absorption costing regarding the timing for the release of fixed manufacturing overhead as expense.

9-5 "Companies that make no variable-cost/fixed-cost distinctions must use absorption costing, and those that do make variable-cost/fixed-cost distinctions must use variable costing." Do you agree? Explain.

9-6 The main trouble with variable costing is that it ignores the increasing importance of fixed costs in manufacturing companies. Do you agree? Why?

9-7 Give an example of how, under absorption costing, operating income could fall even though the unit sales level rises.

9-8 What are the factors that affect the breakeven point under (a) variable costing and (b) absorption costing?

9-9 Critics of absorption costing have increasingly emphasized its potential for leading to undesirable incentives for managers. Give an example.

9-10 What are two ways of reducing the negative aspects associated with using absorption costing to evaluate the performance of a plant manager?

9-11 What denominator-level capacity concepts emphasize the output a plant can supply? What denominator-level capacity concepts emphasize the output customers demand for products produced by a plant?

9-12 Describe the downward demand spiral and its implications for pricing decisions.

9-13 Will the financial statements of a company always differ when different choices at the start of the accounting period are made regarding the denominator-level capacity concept?

9-14 What is the IRS's requirement for tax reporting regarding the choice of a denominator-level capacity concept?

9-15 "The difference between practical capacity and master-budget capacity utilization is the best measure of management's ability to balance the costs of having too much capacity and having too little capacity." Do you agree? Explain.

Exercises

9-16 Variable and absorption costing, explaining operating-income differences. Nascar Motors assembles and sells motor vehicles and uses standard costing. Actual data relating to April and May 2008 are:

File Edit View Insert Format Tools Data Window Help

	A	B	C	D
1		**April**		**May**
2	Unit data			
3	Beginning inventory	0		150
4	Production	500		400
5	Sales	350		520
6	Variable costs			
7	Manufacturing cost per unit produced	$ 10,000		$ 10,000
8	Operating (marketing) cost per unit sold	3,000		3,000
9	Fixed costs			
10	Manufacturing costs	$2,000,000		$2,000,000
11	Operating (marketing) costs	600,000		600,000

The selling price per vehicle is $24,000. The budgeted level of production used to calculate the budgeted fixed manufacturing cost per unit is 500 units. There are no price, efficiency, or spending variances. Any production-volume variance is written off to cost of goods sold in the month in which it occurs.

If you want to use Excel to solve this exercise, go to the Excel Lab at **www.prenhall.com/horngren/cost13e** and download the template for Exercise 9-16.

Required

1. Prepare April and May 2008 income statements for Nascar Motors under (a) variable costing and (b) absorption costing.
2. Prepare a numerical reconciliation and explanation of the difference between operating income for each month under variable costing and absorption costing.

9-17 Throughput costing (continuation of 9-16). The variable manufacturing costs per unit of Nascar Motors are:

	A	B	C
1		April	May
7	Direct material cost per unit	$6,700	$6,700
8	Direct manufacturing labor cost per unit	1,500	1,500
9	Manufacturing overhead cost per unit	1,800	1,800

If you want to use Excel to solve this exercise, go to the Excel Lab at **www.prenhall.com/horngren/cost13e** and download the template for Exercise 9-17.

Required

1. Prepare income statements for Nascar Motors in April and May of 2008 under throughput costing.
2. Contrast the results in requirement 1 with those in requirement 1 of Exercise 9-16.
3. Give one motivation for Nascar Motors to adopt throughput costing.

9-18 Variable and absorption costing, explaining operating-income differences. BigScreen Corporation manufactures and sells 50-inch television sets and uses standard costing. Actual data relating to January, February, and March of 2009 are:

	January	February	March
Unit data			
Beginning inventory	0	300	300
Production	1,000	800	1,250
Sales	700	800	1,500
Variable costs			
Manufacturing cost per unit produced	$900	$900	$900
Operating (marketing) cost per unit sold	$600	$600	$600
Fixed costs			
Manufacturing costs	$400,000	$400,000	$400,000
Operating (marketing) costs	$140,000	$140,000	$140,000

The selling price per unit is $2,500. The budgeted level of production used to calculate the budgeted fixed manufacturing cost per unit is 1,000 units. There are no price, efficiency, or spending variances. Any production-volume variance is written off to cost of goods sold in the month in which it occurs.

Required

1. Prepare income statements for BigScreen in January, February, and March of 2009 under (a) variable costing and (b) absorption costing.
2. Explain the difference in operating income for January, February, and March under variable costing and absorption costing.

9-19 Throughput costing (continuation of 9-18). The variable manufacturing costs per unit of BigScreen Corporation are:

	January	February	March
Direct material cost per unit	$500	$500	$500
Direct manufacturing labor cost per unit	100	100	100
Manufacturing overhead cost per unit	300	300	300
	$900	$900	$900

Required

1. Prepare income statements for BigScreen in January, February, and March of 2009 under throughput costing.
2. Contrast the results in requirement 1 with those in requirement 1 of Exercise 9-18.
3. Give one motivation for BigScreen to adopt throughput costing.

9-20 Variable versus absorption costing. The Zwatch Company manufactures trendy, high-quality moderately priced watches. As Zwatch's senior financial analyst, you are asked to recommend a method of inventory costing. The CFO will use your recommendation to prepare Zwatch's 2009 income statement. The following data are for the year ended December 31, 2009:

Beginning inventory, January 1, 2009	85,000 units
Ending inventory, December 31, 2009	34,500 units
2009 sales	345,400 units
Selling price (to distributor)	$22.00 per unit
Variable manufacturing cost per unit, including direct materials	$5.10 per unit
Variable operating (marketing) cost per unit sold	$1.10 per unit sold
Fixed manufacturing costs	$1,440,000
Denominator-level machine-hours	6,000
Standard production rate	50 units per machine-hour
Fixed operating (marketing) costs	$1,080,000

Assume standard costs per unit are the same for units in beginning inventory and units produced during the year. Also, assume no price, spending, or efficiency variances. Any production-volume variance is written off to cost of goods sold in the month in which it occurs.

Required

1. Prepare income statements under variable and absorption costing for the year ended December 31, 2009.
2. What is Zwatch's operating income as percentage of revenues under each costing method?
3. Explain the difference in operating income between the two methods.
4. Which costing method would you recommend to the CFO? Why?

9-21 Absorption and variable costing. (CMA) Osawa, Inc., planned and actually manufactured 200,000 units of its single product in 2009, its first year of operation. Variable manufacturing cost was $20 per unit produced. Variable operating (non-manufacturing) cost was $10 per unit sold. Planned and actual fixed manufacturing costs were $600,000. Planned and actual fixed operating (non-manufacturing) costs totaled $400,000. Osawa sold 120,000 units of product at $40 per unit.

Required

1. Osawa's 2009 operating income using absorption costing is (a) $440,000, (b) $200,000, (c) $600,000, (d) $840,000, or (e) none of these. Show supporting calculations.
2. Osawa's 2009 operating income using variable costing is (a) $800,000, (b) $440,000, (c) $200,000, (d) $600,000, or (e) none of these. Show supporting calculations.

9-22 Absorption versus variable costing. Electron, Inc. is a semiconductor company based in San Jose. In 2009, it produced a new router system for its corporate clients. The average wholesale selling price of the system is $1,200 each. For 2009, Electron estimates that it will sell 10,000 router systems and so produces 10,000 units. Actual 2009 sales are 8,960 units. Electron's actual 2009 costs are:

	A	B
1	Variable cost per unit:	
2	Manufacturing cost per unit produced	
3	Direct materials	$ 55
4	Direct manufacturing labor	45
5	Manufacturing overhead	120
6	Marketing cost per unit sold	75
7	Fixed costs:	
8	Manufacturing costs	$1,471,680
9	R&D	981,120
10	Marketing	3,124,480

If you want to use Excel to solve this exercise, go to the Excel Lab at **www.prenhall.com/horngren/cost13e** and download the template for Exercise 9-22.

Required

1. Calculate the operating income under variable costing.
2. Each router unit produced is allocated $165 in fixed manufacturing costs. If the production-volume variance is written off to cost of goods sold, and there are no price, spending, or efficiency variances, calculate the operating income under absorption costing.
3. Explain the differences in operating incomes obtained in requirement 1 and requirement 2.
4. Electron's management is considering implementing a bonus for the supervisors based on gross margin under absorption costing. What incentives will this create for the supervisors? Do you think this new bonus plan is a good idea? Explain briefly.

9-23 Comparison of actual-costing methods. The Rehe Company sells its razors at $3 per unit. The company uses a first-in, first-out actual costing system. A fixed manufacturing cost rate is computed at the end of each year by dividing the actual fixed manufacturing costs by the actual production units. The following data are related to its first two years of operation:

	2008	2009
Sales	1,000 units	1,200 units
Production	1,400 units	1,000 units
Costs:		
Variable manufacturing	$ 700	$ 500
Fixed manufacturing	700	700
Variable operating (marketing)	1,000	1,200
Fixed operating (marketing)	400	400

Required

1. Prepare income statements based on variable costing for each of the two years.
2. Prepare income statements based on absorption costing for each of the two years.
3. Prepare a numerical reconciliation and explanation of the difference between operating income for each year under absorption costing and variable costing.
4. Critics have claimed that a widely used accounting system has led to undesirable buildups of inventory levels. (a) Is variable costing or absorption costing more likely to lead to such buildups? Why? (b) What can be done to counteract undesirable inventory buildups?

9-24 Variable and absorption costing, sales, and operating-income changes. Headsmart, a three-year-old company, has been producing and selling a single type of bicycle helmet. Headsmart uses standard costing. After reviewing the income statements for the first three years, Stuart Weil, president of Headsmart, commented, "I was told by our accountants—and in fact, I have memorized—that our breakeven volume is 50,000 units. I was happy that we reached that sales goal in each of our first two years. But, here's the strange thing: in our first year, we sold 50,000 units and indeed we broke even. Then, in our second year we sold the same volume and had a positive operating income. I didn't complain, of course. . . but here's the bad part. In our third year, we *sold 20% more* helmets, but our *operating income fell by more than 80%* relative to the second year! We didn't change our selling price or cost structure over the past three years and have no price, efficiency, or spending variances . . . so what's going on?!"

File Edit View Insert Format Tools Data Window Help

	A	B	C	D
1	**Absorption Costing**			
2		**2008**	**2009**	**2010**
3	Sales (units)	50,000	50,000	60,000
4	Revenues	$2,100,000	$2,100,000	$2,520,000
5	Cost of goods sold			
6	Beginning inventory	0	0	380,000
7	Production	1,900,000	2,280,000	1,900,000
8	Available for sale	1,900,000	2,280,000	2,280,000
9	Deduct ending inventory	0	(380,000)	0
10	Adjustment for production-volume variance	0	(240,000)	0
11	Cost of goods sold	1,900,000	1,660,000	2,280,000
12	Gross margin	200,000	440,000	240,000
13	Selling and administrative expenses (all fixed)	200,000	200,000	200,000
14	Operating income	$ 0	$ 240,000	$ 40,000
15				
16	Beginning inventory	0	0	10,000
17	Production (units)	50,000	60,000	50,000
18	Sales (units)	50,000	50,000	60,000
19	Ending inventory	0	10,000	0
20	Variable manufacturing cost per unit	$ 14	$ 14	$ 14
21	Fixed manufacturing overhead costs	$1,200,000	$1,200,000	$1,200,000
22	Fixed manuf. costs allocated per unit produced	$ 24	$ 24	$ 24

If you want to use Excel to solve this exercise, go to the Excel Lab at **www.prenhall.com/horngren/cost13e** and download the template for Exercise 9-24.

Required

1. What denominator level is Headsmart using to allocate fixed manufacturing costs to the bicycle helmets? How is Headsmart disposing of any favorable or unfavorable production-volume variance at the end of the year? Explain your answer briefly.
2. How did Headsmart's accountants arrive at the breakeven volume of 50,000 units?
3. Prepare a variable costing–based income statement for each year. Explain the variation in variable costing operating income for each year based on contribution margin per unit and sales volume.
4. Reconcile the operating incomes under variable costing and absorption costing for each year, and use this information to explain to Stuart Weil the positive operating income in 2009 and the drop in operating income in 2010.

9-25 Capacity management, denominator-level capacity concepts. Match each of the following items with one or more of the denominator-level capacity concepts by putting the appropriate letter(s) by each item:

a. Theoretical capacity
b. Practical capacity
c. Normal capacity utilization
d. Master-budget capacity utilization

1. Measures the denominator level in terms of what a plant can supply
2. Is based on producing at full efficiency all the time
3. Represents the expected level of capacity utilization for the next budget period
4. Measures the denominator level in terms of demand for the output of the plant
5. Takes into account seasonal, cyclical, and trend factors
6. Should be used for performance evaluation
7. Represents an ideal benchmark
8. Highlights the cost of capacity acquired but not used
9. Should be used for long-term pricing purposes
10. Hides the cost of capacity acquired but not used
11. If used as the denominator-level concept, would avoid the restatement of unit costs when expected demand levels change

9-26 Denominator-level problem. Speedy, Inc. is a manufacturer of the very popular G36 motorcycles. The management at Speedy has recently adopted absorption costing and is debating which denominator-level concept to use. The G36 motorcycles sell for an average price of $8,500. Budgeted fixed manufacturing overhead costs for 2009 are estimated at $4,000,000. Speedy, Inc. uses subassembly operators that provide component parts. The following are the denominator-level options that management has been considering:

a. Theoretical capacity—based on two shifts, completion of four motorcycles per shift, and a 360-day year—$2 \times 4 \times 360 = 2{,}880$.
b. Practical capacity—theoretical capacity adjusted for unavoidable interruptions, breakdowns, and so forth—$2 \times 3 \times 320 = 1{,}920$.
c. Normal capacity utilization—estimated at 1,200 units.
d. Master-budget capacity utilization—the strengthening stock market and the growing popularity of motorcycles have prompted the Marketing Department to issue an estimate for 2009 of 1,500 units.

Required

1. Calculate the budgeted fixed manufacturing overhead cost rates under the four denominator-level concepts.
2. What are the benefits to Speedy, Inc. of using either theoretical capacity or practical capacity?
3. Under a cost-based pricing system, what are the negative aspects of a master-budget denominator level? What are the positive aspects?

9-27 Variable and absorption costing and breakeven points (chapter appendix). Tammy Cat Tree Co (TCTC) builds luxury cat trees and sells them through the Internet to cat owners who want to provide their cats with a more natural environment. At the start of 2008, TCTC carried no inventory. During the year, they produced 1,000 cat trees and sold 800 cat trees for $300 each. Fixed production costs were $100,000 and variable production costs were $75 per cat tree. Fixed advertising, Web page and other general and administrative expenses were $50,000 and variable shipping costs were $25 per tree.

Required

1. Prepare an income statement assuming TCTC uses:
   a. Variable costing
   b. Absorption costing.
2. Compute the breakeven point in units assuming TCTC uses:
   a. Variable costing
   b. Absorption costing.
3. Due to recent changes in local conservation laws, the price of the wood used in the cat trees is expected to increase by $25 for each tree. What effect would this have on the breakeven points calculated above?
4. Using the original data in the problem and the breakeven/target income formulas, show that it would be necessary to sell 800 cat trees to earn the income calculated in requirements 1a and 1b above.

Problems

9-28 Variable costing versus absorption costing. The Mavis Company uses an absorption-costing system based on standard costs. Total variable manufacturing cost, including direct material cost, is $3 per unit; the standard production rate is 10 units per machine-hour. Total budgeted and actual fixed manufacturing overhead costs are $420,000. Fixed manufacturing overhead is allocated at $7 per machine-hour ($420,000 ÷ 60,000 machine-hours of denominator level). Selling price is $5 per unit. Variable operating (non-manufacturing) cost, which is driven by units sold, is $1 per unit. Fixed operating (non-manufacturing) costs are $120,000. Beginning inventory in 2009 is 30,000 units; ending inventory is 40,000 units. Sales in 2009 are 540,000 units. The same standard unit costs persisted throughout 2008 and 2009. For simplicity, assume that there are no price, spending, or efficiency variances.

Required

1. Prepare an income statement for 2009 assuming that the production-volume variance is written off at year-end as an adjustment to cost of goods sold.
2. The president has heard about variable costing. She asks you to recast the 2009 statement as it would appear under variable costing.
3. Explain the difference in operating income as calculated in requirements 1 and 2.
4. Graph how fixed manufacturing overhead is accounted for under absorption costing. That is, there will be two lines: one for the budgeted fixed manufacturing overhead (which is equal to the actual fixed manufacturing overhead in this case) and one for the fixed manufacturing overhead allocated. Show how the production-volume variance might be indicated in the graph.
5. Critics have claimed that a widely used accounting system has led to undesirable buildups of inventory levels. (a) Is variable costing or absorption costing more likely to lead to such buildups? Why? (b) What can be done to counteract undesirable inventory buildups?

9-29 Variable costing and absorption costing, the All-Fixed Company. (R. Marple, adapted) It is the end of 2009. The All-Fixed Company began operations in January 2008. The company is so named because it has no variable costs. All its costs are fixed; they do not vary with output.

The All-Fixed Company is located on the bank of a river and has its own hydroelectric plant to supply power, light, and heat. The company manufactures a synthetic fertilizer from air and river water and sells its product at a price that is not expected to change. It has a small staff of employees, all paid fixed annual salaries. The output of the plant can be increased or decreased by adjusting a few dials on a control panel.

The following budgeted and actual data are for the operations of the All-Fixed Company. All-Fixed uses budgeted production as the denominator level and writes off any production-volume variance to cost of goods sold.

	2008	2009[a]
Sales	10,000 tons	10,000 tons
Production	20,000 tons	0 tons
Selling price	$ 30 per ton	$ 30 per ton
Costs (all fixed):		
Manufacturing	$280,000	$280,000
Operating (non-manufacturing)	$ 40,000	$ 40,000

[a]Management adopted the policy, effective January 1, 2009, of producing only as much product as needed to fill sales orders. During 2009, sales were the same as for 2008 and were filled entirely from inventory at the start of 2009.

Required

1. Prepare income statements with one column for 2008, one column for 2009, and one column for the two years together, using (a) variable costing and (b) absorption costing.
2. What is the breakeven point under (a) variable costing and (b) absorption costing?
3. What inventory costs would be carried in the balance sheet on December 31, 2008 and 2009, under each method?
4. Assume that the performance of the top manager of the company is evaluated and rewarded largely on the basis of reported operating income. Which costing method would the manager prefer? Why?

9-30 Comparison of variable costing and absorption costing. Hinkle Company uses standard costing. Tim Bartina, the new president of Hinkle Company, is presented with the following data for 2009:

	A	B	C
1	Hinkle Company		
2	Income Statements for the Year Ended December 31, 2009		
3		Variable	Absorption
4		Costing	Costing
5	Revenues	$9,000,000	$9,000,000
6	Cost of goods sold (at standard costs)	4,680,000	5,860,000
7	Fixed manufacturing overhead (budgeted)	1,200,000	-
8	Fixed manufacturing overhead variances (all unfavorable):		
9	Spending	100,000	100,000
10	Production volume	-	400,000
11	Total marketing and administrative costs (all fixed)	1,500,000	1,500,000
12	Total costs	7,480,000	7,860,000
13	Operating income	$1,520,000	$1,140,000
14			
15	Inventories (at standard costs)		
16	December 31, 2008	$1,200,000	$1,720,000
17	December 31, 2009	66,000	206,000

If you want to use Excel to solve this problem, go to the Excel Lab at **www.prenhall.com/horngren/cost13e** and download the template for Problem 9-30.

Required

1. At what percentage of denominator level was the plant operating during 2009?
2. How much fixed manufacturing overhead was included in the 2008 and the 2009 ending inventory under absorption costing?
3. Reconcile and explain the difference in 2009 operating incomes under variable and absorption costing.
4. Tim Bartina is concerned: He notes that despite an increase in sales over 2008, 2009 operating income has actually declined under absorption costing. Explain how this occurred.

9-31 Effects of differing production levels on absorption costing income: Metrics to minimize inventory buildups. University Press produces textbooks for college courses. They recently hired a new editor, Leslie White, to handle production and sales of books for an introduction to accounting course. Leslie's compensation depends on the gross margin associated with sales of this book. Leslie needs to decide how many copies of the book to produce. The following information is available for the fall semester 2010:

Estimated sales	10,000 books
Beginning inventory	0 books
Average selling price	$100 per book
Variable production costs	$60 per book
Fixed production costs	$120,000 per semester

The fixed cost allocation rate is based on expected sales and is therefore equal to
$120,000/10,000 books = $12 per book

Leslie has decided to produce either 10,000, 12,000, or 16,000 books.

Required

1. Calculate expected gross margin if Leslie produces 10,000, 12,000, or 16,000 books. (Make sure you include the production-volume variance as part of cost of goods sold)
2. Calculate ending inventory in units and in dollars for each production level.
3. Managers who are paid a bonus that is a function of gross margin may be inspired to produce product in excess of demand to maximize their own bonus. The chapter suggested metrics to discourage managers from producing products in excess of demand. Do you think the following metrics will accomplish this objective? Show your work.
   a. Incorporate a charge of 10% of the cost of the ending inventory as an expense for evaluating the manager.
   b. Include non-financial measures (such as the ones recommended on pp. 308–309) when evaluating management and rewarding performance.

9-32 Alternative denominator-level capacity concepts, effect on operating income. Lucky Lager has just purchased the Austin Brewery. The brewery is two years old and uses absorption costing. It will "sell" its product to Lucky Lager at $45 per barrel. Paul Brandon, Lucky Lager's controller, obtains the following information about Austin Brewery's capacity and budgeted fixed manufacturing costs for 2009:

	A	B	C	D	E
1		Budgeted Fixed	Days of	Hours of	
2	Denominator-Level	Manufacturing	Production	Production	Barrels
3	Capacity Concept	Overhead per Period	per Period	per Day	per Hour
4	Theoretical capacity	$28,000,000	360	24	540
5	Practical capacity	$28,000,000	350	20	500
6	Normal capacity utilization	$28,000,000	350	20	400
7	Master-budget capacity for each half year				
8	(a) January-June 2009	$14,000,000	175	20	320
9	(b) July-December 2009	$14,000,000	175	20	480

If you want to use Excel to solve this problem, go to the Excel Lab at **www.prenhall.com/horngren/cost13e** and download the template for Problem 9-32.

Required

1. Compute the budgeted fixed manufacturing overhead rate per barrel for each of the denominator-level capacity concepts. Explain why they are different.
2. In 2009, the Austin Brewery reported these production results:

	A	B
12	Beginning inventory in barrels, 1-1-2009	0
13	Production in barrels	2,600,000
14	Ending inventory in barrels, 12-31-2009	200,000
15	Actual variable manufacturing costs	$78,520,000
16	Actual fixed manufacturing overhead costs	$27,088,000

There are no variable cost variances. Fixed manufacturing overhead cost variances are written off to cost of goods sold in the period in which they occur. Compute the Austin Brewery's operating income when the denominator-level capacity is (a) theoretical capacity, (b) practical capacity, and (c) normal capacity utilization.

9-33 Motivational considerations in denominator-level capacity selection (continuation of 9-32). If you want to use Excel to solve this problem, go to the Excel Lab at **www.prenhall.com/horngren/cost13e** and download the template for Problem 9-32.

Required

1. If the plant manager of the Austin Brewery gets a bonus based on operating income, which denominator-level capacity concept would he prefer to use? Explain.
2. What denominator-level capacity concept would Lucky Lager prefer to use for U.S. income-tax reporting? Explain.
3. How might the IRS limit the flexibility of an absorption-costing company like Lucky Lager attempting to minimize its taxable income?

9-34 Denominator-level choices, changes in inventory levels, effect on operating income. Koshu Corporation is a manufacturer of computer accessories. It uses absorption costing based on standard costs and reports the following data for 2009:

	A	B	C
1	Theoretical capacity	144,000	units
2	Practical capacity	120,000	units
3	Normal capacity utilization	96,000	units
4	Selling price	$ 30	per unit
5	Beginning inventory	10,000	units
6	Production	104,000	units
7	Sales volume	112,000	units
8	Variable budgeted manufacturing cost	$ 3	per unit
9	Total budgeted fixed manufacturing costs	$1,440,000	
10	Total budgeted operating (non-manuf.) costs (all fixed)	$ 400,000	

There are no price, spending, or efficiency variances. Actual operating costs equal budgeted operating costs. The production-volume variance is written off to cost of goods sold. For each choice of denominator level, the budgeted production cost per unit is also the cost per unit of beginning inventory.

If you want to use Excel to solve this problem, go to the Excel Lab at **www.prenhall.com/horngren/cost13e** and download the template for Problem 9-34.

Required

1. What is the production-volume variance in 2009 when the denominator level is (a) theoretical capacity, (b) practical capacity, and (c) normal capacity utilization?
2. Prepare absorption costing–based income statements for Koshu Corporation using theoretical capacity, practical capacity, and normal capacity utilization as the denominator levels.
3. Why is the operating income under normal capacity utilization lower than the other two scenarios?
4. Reconcile the difference in operating income based on theoretical capacity and practical capacity with the difference in fixed manufacturing overhead included in inventory.

9-35 Effects of denominator-level choice. The Shen Company is a manufacturer of MP3 players. It installed standard costs and a flexible budget on January 1, 2009. The president has been pondering how fixed manufacturing overhead should be allocated to products. Machine-hours have been chosen as the allocation base. Her remaining uncertainty is the denominator level for machine-hours. She decides to wait for the first month's results before making a final choice of what denominator level should be used from that day forward.

In January 2009, the actual units of output had a standard of 28,000 machine-hours allowed. If the company used practical capacity as the denominator level, the fixed manufacturing overhead spending variance would be $4,000, unfavorable, and the production-volume variance would be $14,400, unfavorable. If the company used normal capacity utilization as the denominator level, the production-volume variance would be $8,000, favorable. Budgeted fixed manufacturing overhead was $48,000 for the month.

Required

1. Compute the denominator level, assuming that the normal-capacity-utilization concept is chosen.
2. Compute the denominator level, assuming that the practical-capacity concept is chosen.
3. Suppose you are the executive vice president. You want to maximize your 2009 bonus, which depends on 2009 operating income. Assume that the production-volume variance is written off to cost of goods sold at year-end. Which denominator level would you favor? Why?

9-36 Downward demand spiral. Network Company is a large manufacturer of optical storage systems based in Arizona. Its practical annual capacity is 7,500 units, and, for the past few years, its budgeted and actual sales and production volume have been 7,500 units per year. Network's budgeted and actual variable manufacturing costs are $100 per unit, and budgeted and actual total fixed manufacturing costs are $2,250,000 per year. Network calculates full manufacturing cost per unit as the sum of the variable manufacturing cost per unit and the fixed manufacturing costs allocated to the budgeted units produced. Selling price is set at a 100% markup to full manufacturing cost per unit.

Required

1. Compute Network's selling price.
2. Recent competition from abroad has caused a drop in budgeted production and sales volume to 6,000 units per year, and analysts are predicting further declines. If Network continues to use budgeted production as the denominator level, calculate its new selling price.
3. Comment on the effect that changes in budgeted production have on selling price. Suggest another denominator level that Network might use for its pricing decision. Justify your choice.
4. Network has received an offer to buy identical storage units for $400 each instead of manufacturing the units in-house. Shutting down the manufacturing plant would reduce fixed costs to $450,000 per year. At what level of expected annual sales (in units) should Network accept this offer? Explain your answer.

9-37 Absorption costing and production-volume variance—alternative capacity bases. Earth Light First (ELF), a producer of energy-efficient light bulbs, expects that demand will increase markedly over the next decade. Due to the high fixed costs involved in the business, ELF has decided to evaluate its financial performance using absorption costing income. The production-volume variance is written off to cost of goods sold. The variable cost of production is $2.50 per bulb. Fixed manufacturing costs are $1,000,000 per year. Variable and fixed selling and administrative expenses are $0.25 per bulb sold and $250,000, respectively. Because its light bulbs are currently popular with environmentally-conscious customers, ELF can sell the bulbs for $9.00 each.

ELF is deciding whether to use, when calculating the cost of each unit produced:

Theoretical capacity	800,000 bulbs
Practical capacity	500,000 bulbs
Normal capacity	250,000 bulbs (average production for the next three years)
Master budget capacity	200,000 bulbs produced this year

Required

1. Calculate the inventoriable cost per unit using each level of capacity to compute fixed manufacturing cost per unit.

2. Calculate the production-volume variance using each level of capacity to compute the fixed manufacturing overhead allocation rate and this year's production of 220,000 bulbs.
3. Assuming ELF has no beginning inventory, calculate operating income for ELF using each type of capacity to compute fixed manufacturing cost per unit and this year's sales of 200,000 bulbs.

9-38 Operating income effects of denominator-level choice and disposal of production-volume variance (continuation of 9-37)

Required

1. If ELF sells all 220,000 bulbs produced, what would be the effect on operating income of using each type of capacity as a basis for calculating manufacturing cost per unit?
2. Compare the results of operating income at different capacity levels when 200,000 bulbs are sold and when 220,000 bulbs are sold. What conclusion can you draw from the comparison?
3. Using the original data (that is, 220,000 units produced and 200,000 units sold) if ELF had used the proration approach to allocate the production-volume variance, what would operating income have been under each level of capacity? (Assume that there is no ending work in process.)

9-39 Cost allocation, downward demand spiral. Deli One operates a chain of 10 hospitals in the Los Angeles area. Its central food-catering facility, Deliman, prepares and delivers meals to the hospitals. It has the capacity to deliver up to 1,460,000 meals a year. In 2009, based on estimates from each hospital controller, Deliman budgeted for 1,022,000 meals a year. Budgeted fixed costs in 2009 were $1,533,000. Each hospital was charged $6.00 per meal—$4.50 variable costs plus $1.50 allocated budgeted fixed cost.

Recently, the hospitals have been complaining about the quality of Deliman's meals and their rising costs. In mid-2009, Deli One's president announces that all Deli One hospitals and support facilities will be run as profit centers. Hospitals will be free to purchase quality-certified services from outside the system. Ron Smith, Deliman's controller, is preparing the 2010 budget. He hears that three hospitals have decided to use outside suppliers for their meals; this will reduce the 2010 estimated demand to 876,000 meals. No change in variable cost per meal or total fixed costs is expected in 2010.

Required

1. How did Smith calculate the budgeted fixed cost per meal of $1.50 in 2009?
2. Using the same approach to calculating budgeted fixed cost per meal and pricing as in 2009, how much would hospitals be charged for each Deliman meal in 2010? What would their reaction be?
3. Suggest an alternative cost-based price per meal that Smith might propose and that might be more acceptable to the hospitals. What can Deliman and Smith do to make this price profitable in the long run?

9-40 Cost allocation, responsibility accounting, ethics (continuation of 9-39). In 2010, only 806,840 Deliman meals were produced and sold to the hospitals. Smith suspects that hospital controllers had systematically inflated their 2010 meal estimates.

Required

1. Recall that Deliman uses the master-budget capacity utilization to allocate fixed costs and to price meals. What was the effect of production-volume variance on Deliman's operating income in 2010?
2. Why might hospital controllers deliberately overestimate their future meal counts?
3. What other evidence should Deli One's controller seek to investigate Smith's concerns?
4. Suggest two specific steps that Deli One's controller might take to reduce hospital controllers' incentives to inflate their estimated meal counts.

Collaborative Learning Problem

9-41 Absorption, variable, and throughput costing. EnRG, Inc. produces trail mix packaged for sale in convenience stores in the Northeast section of the United States. At the beginning of April 2008, EnRG has no inventory of trail mix. Demand for the next three months is expected to remain constant at 50,000 bags per month. EnRG plans to produce to demand, 50,000 bags in April. However, many of the employees take vacation in June, so EnRG plans to produce 70,000 bags in May and only 30,000 bags in June.

Costs for the three months are expected to remain unchanged. The costs and revenues for April, May and June are expected to be:

Sales revenue	$6.00 per bag	Variable selling cost	$0.15 per bag
Direct material cost	$0.80 per bag	Fixed manufacturing overhead costs	$105,000 per month
Direct manufacturing labor cost	$0.45 per bag	Fixed administrative costs	$ 35,000 per month
Variable manufacturing overhead cost	$0.30 per bag		

Suppose the actual costs, market demand, and levels of production for April, May, and June are as expected.

Required

1. Compute operating income for April, May, and June under variable costing.
2. Compute operating income for April, May, and June under absorption costing. Assume that the denominator level for each month is that month's expected level of output.
3. Compute operating income for April, May, and June under throughput costing.
4. Discuss the benefits and problems associated with using throughput costing.

10 Determining How Costs Behave

Learning Objectives

1. Explain the two assumptions frequently used in cost-behavior estimation.
2. Describe linear cost functions and three common ways in which they behave
3. Understand various methods of cost estimation
4. Outline six steps in estimating a cost function using quantitative analysis
5. Describe three criteria used to evaluate and choose cost drivers
6. Explain and give examples of nonlinear cost functions
7. Distinguish the cumulative average-time learning model from the incremental unit-time learning model
8. Be aware of data problems encountered in estimating cost functions

What is the value of looking at the past? Perhaps it is to recall fond memories you've had or help you understand historical events. Or, maybe your return to the past enables you to better understand and predict the future. When an organization looks at the past, it typically does so to analyze its results, so that the best decisions can be made for the company's future. This activity requires gathering information about costs and how they behave so that managers can predict what they will be "down the road." But sometimes looking at the past isn't enough—especially when the firm is undertaking new opportunities, as the following article shows.

Management Accountants at Boeing Embrace Opportunities, Tackle Challenges[1]

Understanding how costs behave is a valuable technical skill. Managers look to management accountants to help them identify cost drivers, estimate cost relationships, and determine the fixed and variable components of costs. To be effective, management accountants must have a clear understanding of the business's strategy and operations. They must also be able to communicate their findings in a way that helps managers make better decisions.

Let's consider an example. In 2004, Chicago-based Boeing landed the job as lead systems integrator (LSI) for a multiyear, $14.8 billion defense missile-shield contract with the U.S. government. This deal could further lead to 20 years and more than $100 billion worth of work for Boeing. The contract shifts Boeing into a more software-based managerial role instead of its traditional role as a pure military hardware manufacturer.

The deal is a great opportunity for Boeing, of course. But new opportunities such as this also create many challenges. As the lead systems integrator on the project, Boeing is responsible for hiring contractors and overseeing projects related to the contract. As the company's strategy shifts, Boeing's management accountants help the firm's managers understand new cost relationships and estimate new fixed and variable costs.

[1] *Source:* Julie Creswell, "Boeing Plays Defense Beset by Airbus and Rocked by Scandal the Aircraft Maker Turns to a New CEO—and the Pentagon—for Help," *Fortune,* April 19, 2004 and Government Accountability Office, *Missile Defense Acquisition Strategy Generates Results but Delivers Less at a Higher Cost*, Washington, DC: Government Accountability Office, March 2007.

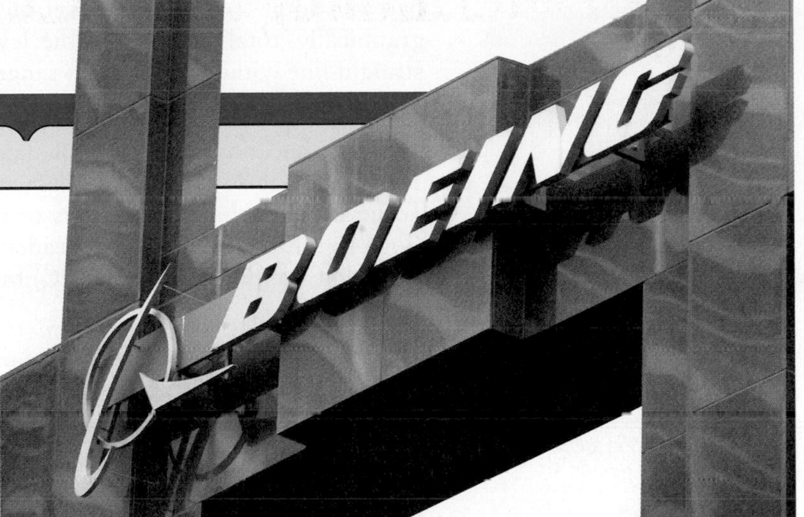

But when it comes to new, cutting-edge technology, determining cost drivers and estimating costs are not easy tasks. As of 2007, Boeing has overrun its contract budget by $600 million. So how have Boeing's management accountants responded? They have identified testing delays as the reason for the cost overruns, and Boeing has begun making process changes to address this problem.

As the Boeing example illustrates, managers must understand how costs behave to make strategic and operating decisions. Consider several examples. Managers at Sony must decide which alternative product design to choose for a new line of Plasma televisions. At Bank of America, managers might want to explore whether it should seek a 5% increase in customers. Managers at Owens and Minor might want to know which cost drivers to choose in its activity-based costing system.

In each situation, knowledge of cost behavior is needed to answer these questions. This chapter will focus on how managers determine cost-behavior patterns—that is, how costs change in relation to changes in activity levels, in the quantity of products produced, and so on.

General Issues in Estimating Cost Functions

Managers are able to understand cost behavior through cost functions. A **cost function** is a mathematical description of how a cost changes with changes in the level of an activity relating to that cost. Examples of activities are preparing setups for production runs and operating machines. Cost functions can be plotted on a graph by measuring the level of an activity, such as number of batches produced or number of machine-hours used, on the horizontal axis (called the x-axis) and the amount of total costs corresponding to—or, preferably, dependent on—the levels of that activity on the vertical axis (called the y-axis).

Learning Objective 1

Explain the two assumptions frequently used in cost-behavior estimation

. . . cost functions are linear and have a single cost driver

Basic Assumptions and Examples of Cost Functions

Managers often estimate cost functions based on two assumptions:

1. Variations in the level of a single activity (the cost driver) explain the variations in the related total costs.
2. Cost behavior is approximated by a linear cost function within the relevant range. Recall that a relevant range is the range of the activity in which there is a relationship

between total cost and the level of activity. For a **linear cost function** represented graphically, total cost versus the level of a single activity related to that cost is a straight line within the relevant range.

We use these two assumptions throughout most, but not all, of this chapter. Not all cost functions are linear and can be explained by a single activity. Later sections will discuss cost functions that do not rely on these assumptions.

Learning Objective 2

Describe linear cost functions

. . . graph of cost function is a straight line

and three common ways in which they behave

. . . variable, fixed, and mixed

To understand three basic types of linear cost functions and to see the role of cost functions in business decisions, consider the negotiations between Cannon Services and World Wide Communications (WWC) for exclusive use of a telephone line between New York and Paris.

- **Alternative 1:** $5 per phone-minute used. Total cost to Cannon changes in proportion to the number of phone-minutes used. The number of phone-minutes used is the only factor whose change causes a change in total cost.

  Panel A in Exhibit 10-1 presents this *variable cost* for Cannon Services. Under alternative 1, there is no fixed cost. We write the cost function in Panel A of Exhibit 10-1 as

  $$y = \$5X$$

  where X measures the actual number of phone-minutes used (on the x-axis), and y measures the total cost of the phone-minutes used (on the y-axis) calculated using the cost function. Panel A illustrates the $5 **slope coefficient,** the amount by which total cost changes when a one-unit change occurs in the level of activity (one phone-minute in the Cannon example). *Throughout the chapter, uppercase letters, such as X, refer to the actual observations, and lowercase letters, such as y, represent estimates or calculations made using a cost function.*

- **Alternative 2:** Total cost will be fixed at $10,000 per month, regardless of the number of phone-minutes used. (We use the same activity measure, number of phone-minutes used, to compare cost-behavior patterns under the three alternatives.)

  Panel B in Exhibit 10-1 presents this *fixed cost* for Cannon Services. We write the cost function in Panel B as

  $$y = \$10{,}000$$

  The fixed cost of $10,000 is called a **constant;** it is the component of total cost that does not vary with changes in the level of the activity. Under alternative 2, the constant accounts for all the cost because there is no variable cost. Graphically, the slope coefficient of the cost function is zero; this cost function intersects the y-axis at the constant value, and therefore the *constant* is also called the **intercept.**

- **Alternative 3:** $3,000 per month plus $2 per phone-minute used. This is an example of a mixed cost. A **mixed cost**—also called a **semivariable cost**—is a cost that has both fixed and variable elements.

Exhibit 10-1 Examples of Linear Cost Functions

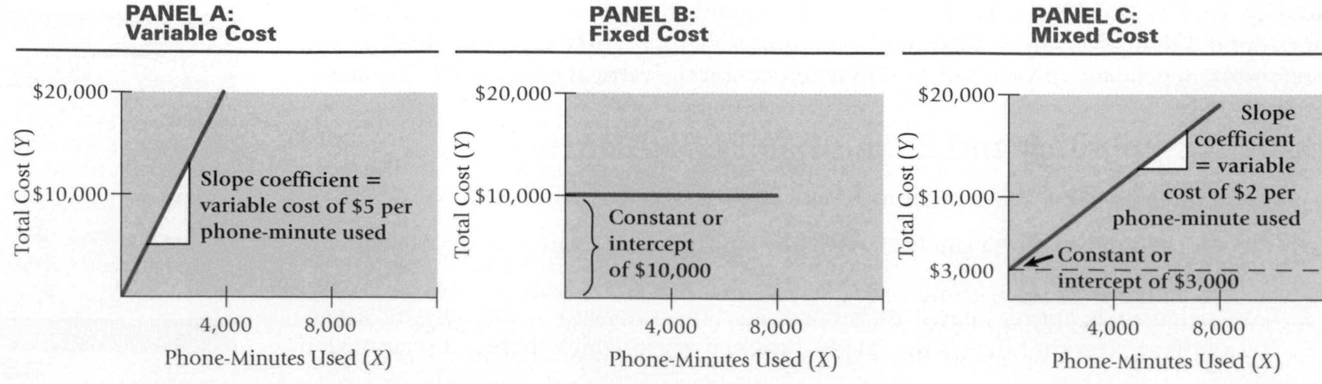

Panel C in Exhibit 10-1 presents this *mixed cost* for Cannon Services. We write the cost function in Panel C of Exhibit 10-1 as

$$y = \$3{,}000 + \$2X$$

Unlike the graphs for alternatives 1 and 2, Panel C has both a constant, or intercept, value of \$3,000 and a slope coefficient of \$2. In the case of a mixed cost, total cost in the relevant range increases as the number of phone-minutes used increases. Note, total cost does not vary strictly in proportion to the number of phone-minutes used within the relevant range. For example, when 4,000 phone-minutes are used, the total cost equals \$11,000 [\$3,000 + (\$2 per phone-minute × 4,000 phone-minutes)], but when 8,000 phone-minutes are used, total cost equals \$19,000 [\$3,000 + (\$2 per phone-minute × 8,000 phone-minutes)]. Although the number of phone-minutes used has doubled, total cost has increased by only about 73% [(\$19,000 − \$11,000) ÷ \$11,000].

Cannon's managers must understand the cost-behavior patterns in the three alternatives to choose the best deal with WWC. Suppose Cannon expects to use at least 4,000 phone-minutes per month. Its cost for 4,000 phone-minutes under the three alternatives would be as follows:

- **Alternative 1:** \$20,000 (\$5 per phone-minute × 4,000 phone-minutes)
- **Alternative 2:** \$10,000
- **Alternative 3:** \$11,000 [\$3,000 + (\$2 per phone-minute × 4,000 phone-minutes)]

Alternative 2 is the least costly. Moreover, if Cannon were to use more than 4,000 phone-minutes, as is likely to be the case, alternatives 1 and 3 would be even more costly. Cannon's managers, therefore, should choose alternative 2.

Note that the graphs in Exhibit 10-1 are linear. That is, they appear as straight lines. We simply need to know the constant, or intercept, amount (commonly designated a) and the slope coefficient (commonly designated b). For any linear cost function based on a single activity (recall our two assumptions discussed at the start of the chapter), knowing a and b is sufficient to describe and graphically plot all the values within the relevant range of number of phone-minutes used. We write a general form of this linear cost function as

$$y = a + bX$$

Under alternative 1, a = \$0 and b = \$5 per phone-minute used; under alternative 2, a = \$10,000 and b = \$0 per phone-minute used; and under alternative 3, a = \$3,000 and b = \$2 per phone-minute used. To plot the mixed-cost function in Panel C, we draw a line starting from the point marked \$3,000 on the y-axis and increasing at a rate of \$2 per phone-minute used, so that at 1,000 phone-minutes, total costs increase by \$2,000 (\$2 per phone-minute × 1,000 phone-minutes) to \$5,000 (\$3,000 + \$2,000) and at 2,000 phone-minutes, total costs increase by \$4,000 (\$2 per phone-minute × 2,000 phone-minutes) to \$7,000 (\$3,000 + \$4,000) and so on.

Brief Review of Cost Classification

Let's review briefly Chapter 2's three criteria for classifying a cost into its variable and fixed components.

Choice of Cost Object A particular cost item could be variable with respect to one cost object and fixed with respect to another cost object. Consider Super Shuttle, an airport transportation company. If the fleet of vans it owns is the cost object, then the annual van registration and license costs would be variable costs with respect to the number of vans owned. But if a particular van is the cost object, then the registration and license costs for that van are fixed costs with respect to the miles driven during a year.

Time Horizon Whether a cost is variable or fixed with respect to a particular activity depends on the time horizon being considered in the decision situation. The longer the time horizon, all other things being equal, the more likely that the cost will be variable. For example, inspection costs at Boeing Company are typically fixed in the short run with respect to inspection-hours used because inspectors earn a fixed salary in a given year regardless of the number of inspection-hours of work done. But, in the long run, Boeing's total inspection costs will vary with the inspection-hours required: More inspectors will be hired if more inspection-hours are needed, and some inspectors will be reassigned to other tasks or laid off if fewer inspection-hours are needed.

Relevant Range Managers should never forget that variable and fixed cost-behavior patterns are valid for linear cost functions only within the given relevant range. Outside the relevant range, variable and fixed cost-behavior patterns change, causing costs to become nonlinear (nonlinear means the plot of the relationship on a graph is not a straight line). For example, Exhibit 10-2 plots the relationship (over several years) between total direct manufacturing labor costs and the number of snowboards produced each year by Ski Authority at its Vermont plant. In this case, the nonlinearities outside the relevant range occur because of labor and other inefficiencies (first because workers are learning to produce snowboards and later because capacity limits are being stretched). Knowing the relevant range is essential to properly classify costs.

Cost Estimation

The Cannon Services/WWC example illustrates variable-, fixed-, and mixed-cost functions using information about *future* cost structures proposed to Cannon by WWC. Often, however, cost functions are estimated from *past* cost data. Managers use **cost estimation** to measure a relationship based on data from past costs and the related level of an activity. For example, marketing managers at Volkswagen could use cost estimation to understand what causes their marketing costs to change from year to year (for example, the number of cars sold or the number of new car models introduced) and the fixed and variable components of these costs. Managers are interested in estimating past cost-behavior functions primarily because these estimates can help them make more-accurate **cost predictions**, or forecasts, about future costs. Better cost predictions help managers make more-informed planning and control decisions, such as preparing next year's marketing budget. But better management decisions, cost predictions, and estimation of cost functions can be achieved only if managers correctly identify the factors that affect costs.

The Cause-and-Effect Criterion in Choosing Cost Drivers

The most important issue in estimating a cost function is determining whether a cause-and-effect relationship exists between the level of an activity and the costs related to that level of activity. Without a cause-and-effect relationship, managers will be less confident about their ability to estimate or predict costs. Recall from Chapter 2 that when a cause-and-effect relationship exists between a change in the level of an activity and a change in the level of total costs, we refer to the activity measure as a *cost driver*. We use the terms *level of activity* and *level of cost driver* interchangeably when estimating cost functions.

Exhibit 10-2

Linearity Within Relevant Range for Ski Authority, Inc.

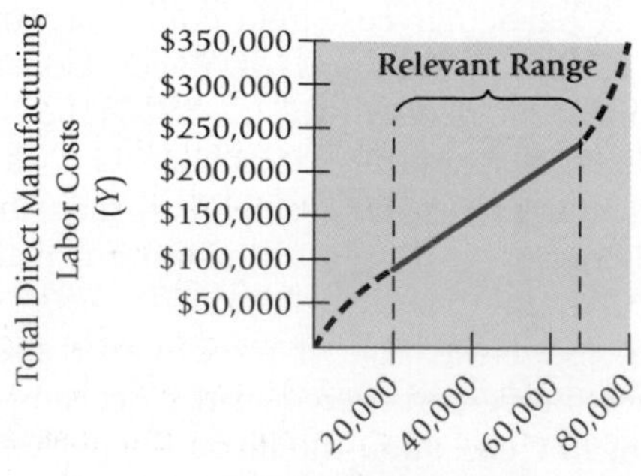

Understanding the drivers of costs is crucially important for managing costs. The cause-and-effect relationship might arise as a result of:

- **A physical relationship between the level of activity and costs.** An example is when units of production is used as the activity that affects direct material costs. Producing more units requires more direct materials, which results in higher total direct material costs.
- **A contractual arrangement.** In alternative 1 of the Cannon Services example described earlier, number of phone-minutes used is specified in the contract as the level of activity that affects the telephone line costs.
- **Knowledge of operations.** An example is when number of parts is used as the activity measure of ordering costs. A product with many parts will incur higher ordering costs than a product with few parts.

Managers must be careful not to interpret a high correlation, or connection, in the relationship between two variables to mean that either variable causes the other. Consider direct material costs and labor costs. For a given product mix, producing more units generally results in higher material costs and higher labor costs. Material costs and labor costs are highly correlated, but neither causes the other. Using labor costs to predict material costs is problematic. Some products require more labor costs relative to material costs, while other products require more material costs relative to labor costs. If the product mix changes toward more labor-intensive products, say, labor costs will increase while material costs will decrease. Labor costs are a poor predictor of material costs. By contrast, factors that drive material costs such as product mix, product designs, and manufacturing processes, would have more accurately predicted the changes in material costs.

Only a cause-and-effect relationship—not merely correlation—establishes an economically plausible relationship between the level of an activity and its costs. Economic plausibility is critical because it gives analysts and managers confidence that the estimated relationship will appear again and again in other sets of data from the same situation. Identifying cost drivers also gives managers insights into ways to reduce costs and the confidence that reducing the quantity of the cost drivers will lead to a decrease in costs.

To identify cost drivers on the basis of data gathered over time, always use a long time horizon. Why? Because, as our example of inspection costs at Boeing Company illustrates (pp. 336–337), costs may be fixed in the short run (during which time they have no cost driver), but they are usually variable and have a cost driver in the long run.

Consider Elegant Rugs, which uses state-of-the-art automated weaving machines to produce carpets for homes and offices. Management has made many changes in manufacturing processes and wants to introduce new styles of carpets. It would like to evaluate how these changes have affected costs and what styles of carpets it should introduce. It follows the five-step decision-making process outlined in Chapter 1.

Step 1: Identify the problem and uncertainties. The changes in the manufacturing process were specifically targeted at reducing indirect manufacturing labor costs, and management wants to know whether costs such as supervision, maintenance, and quality control did, in fact, decrease. One option is to simply compare indirect manufacturing labor costs before and after the process change. The problem with this approach is that the volume of activity before and after the process change was very different so costs need to be compared after taking into account the change in activity volume.

Managers were fairly confident about the direct material and direct manufacturing labor costs of the new styles of carpets. They were less certain about the impact that the choice of different styles would have on indirect manufacturing costs.

Step 2: Obtain information. Managers gathered information about potential cost drivers—factors such as machine-hours or direct manufacturing labor-hours that cause indirect manufacturing labor costs to be incurred. They also began considering different techniques (discussed in the next section) such as the industrial engineering method, the conference method, the account analysis method, the high-low method, and the regression method for estimating the magnitude of the effect of the cost driver on indirect manufacturing labor costs. Their goal was to identify the best possible single cost driver.

Step 3: Make predictions about the future. Managers used past data to estimate the relationship between cost drivers and costs and used this relationship to predict future costs.

Step 4: Make decisions by choosing among alternatives. As we will describe later (pp. 349–351), Elegant Rugs chose machine-hours as the cost driver of indirect manufacturing labor costs. Using the regression analysis estimate of indirect manufacturing labor cost per machine-hour, managers estimated the costs of alternative styles of carpets and chose to introduce the most profitable styles.

Step 5: Implement the decision, evaluate performance, and learn. After the managers at Elegant Rugs introduced the new carpet styles, they focused on evaluating the results of their decision. Comparing predicted to actual costs helped managers to learn how accurate the estimates were, to set targets for continuous improvement, and to constantly seek ways to improve efficiency and effectiveness.

Cost Estimation Methods

Learning Objective 3

Understand various methods of cost estimation

. . . for example, the regression analysis method determines the line that best fits past data

As we mentioned in Step 2, four methods of cost estimation are the industrial engineering method, the conference method, the account analysis method, and the quantitative analysis method (which takes different forms). These methods differ with respect to how expensive they are to implement, the assumptions they make, and the information they provide about the accuracy of the estimated cost function. They are not mutually exclusive, and many organizations use a combination of these methods.

Industrial Engineering Method

The **industrial engineering method**, also called the **work-measurement method**, estimates cost functions by analyzing the relationship between inputs and outputs in physical terms. Consider Elegant Rugs. It uses inputs of cotton, wool, dyes, direct manufacturing labor, machine time, and power. Production output is square yards of carpet. Time-and-motion studies analyze the time required to perform the various operations to produce the carpet. For example, a time-and-motion study may conclude that to produce 10 square yards of carpet requires one hour of direct manufacturing labor. Standards and budgets transform these physical input measures into costs. The result is an estimated cost function relating direct manufacturing labor costs to the cost driver, square yards of carpet produced.

The industrial engineering method is a very thorough and detailed way to estimate a cost function when there is a physical relationship between inputs and outputs, but it can be very time-consuming. Some government contracts mandate its use. Many organizations, such as Bose and Nokia, use it to estimate direct manufacturing costs but find it too costly or impractical for analyzing their entire cost structure. For example, physical relationships between inputs and outputs are difficult to specify for some items, such as indirect manufacturing costs, R&D costs and advertising costs.

Conference Method

The **conference method** estimates cost functions on the basis of analysis and opinions about costs and their drivers gathered from various departments of a company (purchasing, process engineering, manufacturing, employee relations, and so on). The Cooperative Bank in the United Kingdom has a Cost-Estimating Department that develops cost functions for its retail banking products (checking accounts, VISA cards, mortgages, and so on) based on the consensus of estimates from personnel of the particular departments. Elegant Rugs gathers opinions from supervisors and production engineers about how indirect manufacturing labor costs vary with machine-hours and direct manufacturing labor-hours.

The conference method encourages interdepartmental cooperation. The pooling of expert knowledge from different business functions of the value chain gives the conference method credibility. Because the conference method does not require detailed analysis of data, cost functions and cost estimates can be developed quickly. However, the emphasis on opinions rather than systematic estimation means that the accuracy of the cost estimates depends largely on the care and skill of the people providing the inputs.

Account Analysis Method

The **account analysis method** estimates cost functions by classifying various cost accounts as variable, fixed, or mixed with respect to the identified level of activity. Typically, managers use qualitative rather than quantitative analysis when making these cost-classification decisions. The account analysis approach is widely used because it is reasonably accurate, cost-effective, and easy to use.

Consider indirect manufacturing labor costs for a small production area (or cell) at Elegant Rugs. Indirect manufacturing labor costs include wages paid for supervision, maintenance, quality control, and setups. During the most recent 12-week period, Elegant Rugs ran the machines in the cell for a total of 862 hours and incurred total indirect manufacturing labor costs of $12,501. Using qualitative analysis, the manager and the cost analyst determine that over this 12-week period indirect manufacturing labor costs are mixed costs with only one cost driver—machine hours. As machine-hours vary, one component of the cost (such as supervision cost) is fixed, whereas another component (such as maintenance cost) is variable. The goal is to use account analysis to estimate a linear cost function for indirect manufacturing labor costs with number of machine-hours as the cost driver. The cost analyst uses experience and judgment to separate total indirect manufacturing labor costs ($12,501) into costs that are fixed ($2,157, based on 950 hours of machine capacity for the cell over a 12-week period) and costs that are variable ($10,344) with respect to the number of machine-hours used. Variable cost per machine-hour is $10,344 ÷ 862 machine-hours = $12 per machine-hour. The linear cost equation, $y = a + bX$, in this example is:

Indirect manufacturing labor costs = $2,157 + ($12 per machine-hour × Number of machine-hours)

The indirect manufacturing labor cost per machine-hour is $12,501 ÷ 862 machine-hours = $14.50 per machine-hour. Management at Elegant Rugs can use the cost function to estimate the indirect manufacturing labor costs of using, say, 950 machine-hours to produce carpet in the next 12-week period. Estimated costs equal $2,157 + (950 machine-hours × $12 per machine-hour) = $13,557. The indirect manufacturing labor cost per machine-hour decreases to $13,557 ÷ 950 machine-hours = $14.27 per machine-hour, as fixed costs of $2,157 are spread over a greater number of machine-hours.

To obtain reliable estimates of the fixed and variable components of cost, organizations such as Target take care to ensure that individuals thoroughly knowledgeable about the operations make the cost-classification decisions. Supplementing the account analysis method with the conference method improves credibility.

Quantitative Analysis Method

Quantitative analysis uses a formal mathematical method to fit cost functions to past data observations. Excel is a useful tool for performing quantitative analysis. Columns B and C of Exhibit 10-3 show the breakdown of Elegant Rugs's total machine-hours (862) and total indirect manufacturing labor costs ($12,501) into weekly data for the most recent 12-week period. Note that the data are paired—for each week there is data for the number of machine-hours and corresponding indirect manufacturing labor costs. For example, week 12 shows 48 machine-hours and indirect manufacturing labor costs of $963. The next section uses the data in Exhibit 10-3 to illustrate how to estimate a cost function using quantitative analysis.

Exhibit 10-3

Weekly Indirect Manufacturing Labor Costs and Machine-Hours for Elegant Rugs

	A	B	C
1	**Week**	**Cost Driver: Machine-Hours**	**Indirect Manufacturing Labor Costs**
2		**(*X*)**	**(*Y*)**
3	1	68	$ 1,190
4	2	88	1,211
5	3	62	1,004
6	4	72	917
7	5	60	770
8	6	96	1,456
9	7	78	1,180
10	8	46	710
11	9	82	1,316
12	10	94	1,032
13	11	68	752
14	12	48	963
15	Total	862	$12,501
16			

Steps in Estimating a Cost Function Using Quantitative Analysis

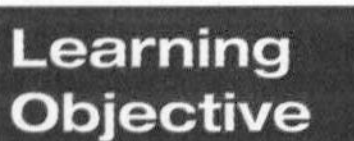

Learning Objective 4

Outline six steps in estimating a cost function using quantitative analysis

. . . the end result (step 6) is to evaluate the cost driver of the estimated cost function

There are six steps in estimating a cost function using a quantitative analysis of a past cost relationship.

Step 1: Choose the dependent variable

Step 2: Identify the independent variable, or cost driver

Step 3: Collect data on the dependent variable and the cost driver

Step 4: Plot the data

Step 5: Estimate the cost function

Step 6: Evaluate the cost driver of the estimated cost function

Let's take a closer look at quantitative analysis using the Elegant Rugs example.

Step 1: Choose the dependent variable. Choice of the **dependent variable** (the cost to be predicted and managed) will depend on the cost function being estimated. In the Elegant Rugs example, the dependent variable is indirect manufacturing labor costs.

Step 2: Identify the independent variable, or cost driver. The **independent variable** (level of activity or cost driver) is the factor used to predict the dependent variable (costs). When the cost is an indirect cost, as with Elegant Rugs, the independent variable is also called a cost-allocation base. Although these terms are sometimes used interchangeably, we use the term *cost driver* to describe the independent variable. Frequently, the cost analyst, working with the management team, will cycle through the six steps several times, trying alternative economically plausible cost drivers to identify a cost driver that best fits the data.

A cost driver should have an *economically plausible* relationship with the dependent variable and be measurable. Economic plausibility means that the relationship (describing how changes in the cost driver lead to changes in the costs being considered) is based on a physical relationship, a contract, or knowledge of operations and makes economic sense to the operating manager and the management accountant. As we saw in Chapter 5, all the individual items of costs included in the dependent variable should have the same cost driver, that is, the cost pool should be homogenous. When all items of costs in the dependent variable do not have the same cost driver, the cost analyst should investigate the possibility of creating homogenous cost pools and estimating more than one cost function, one for each cost item/cost driver pair.

As an example, consider several types of fringe benefits paid to employees and the cost drivers of the benefits:

Fringe Benefit	Cost Driver
Health benefits	Number of employees
Cafeteria meals	Number of employees
Pension benefits	Salaries of employees
Life insurance	Salaries of employees

The costs of health benefits and cafeteria meals can be combined into one homogenous cost pool because they have the same cost driver—the number of employees. Pension benefits and life insurance costs have a different cost driver—the salaries of employees—and, therefore, should not be combined with health benefits and cafeteria meals. Instead, pension benefits and life insurance costs should be combined into a separate homogenous cost pool. The cost pool comprising pension benefits and life insurance costs can be estimated using salaries of employees receiving these benefits as the cost driver.

Step 3: Collect data on the dependent variable and the cost driver. This is usually the most difficult step in cost analysis. Cost analysts obtain data from company documents, from interviews with managers, and through special studies. These data may be time-series data or cross-sectional data.

Time-series data pertain to the same entity (organization, plant, activity, and so on) over successive past periods. Weekly observations of indirect manufacturing labor costs and number of machine-hours at Elegant Rugs are examples of time-series data. The ideal time-series database would contain numerous observations for a company whose operations have not been affected by economic or technological change. A stable economy and technology ensure that data collected during the estimation period represent the same underlying relationship between the cost driver and the dependent variable. Moreover, the periods (for example, daily, weekly, or monthly) used to measure the dependent variable and the cost driver should be consistent throughout the observations.

Cross-sectional data pertain to different entities during the same period. For example, studies of loans processed and the related personnel costs at 50 individual, yet similar branches of a bank during March 2009 would produce cross-sectional data for that month. The cross-sectional data should be drawn from entities that, within each entity, have a similar relationship between the cost driver and costs. Later in this chapter, we describe the problems that arise in data collection.

Step 4: Plot the data. The general relationship between the cost driver and costs can be readily observed in a graphical representation of the data, which is commonly called a plot of the data. Moreover, the plot highlights extreme observations (observations outside the general pattern) that analysts should check. Was there an error in recording the data or an unusual event, such as a work stoppage, that makes these observations unrepresentative of the normal relationship between the cost driver and the costs? Plotting the data

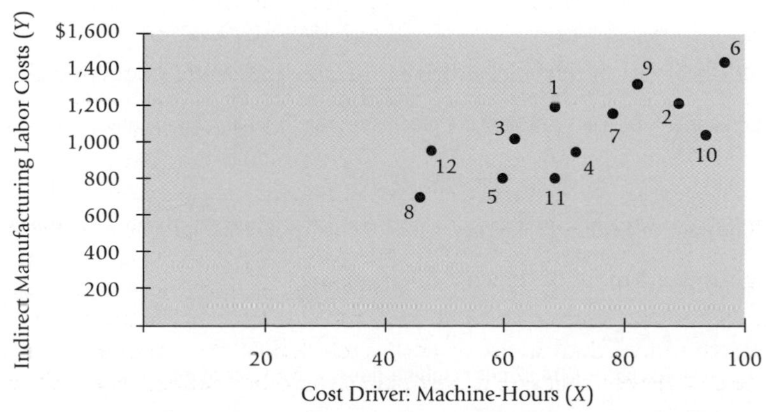

Exhibit 10-4

Plot of Weekly Indirect Manufacturing Labor Costs and Machine-Hours for Elegant Rugs

also provides insight into whether the relationship is approximately linear and what the relevant range of the cost function is.

Exhibit 10-4 is a plot of the weekly data from columns B and C of the Excel spreadsheet in Exhibit 10-3. This graph provides strong visual evidence of a positive linear relationship between number of machine-hours and indirect manufacturing labor costs (that is, when machine-hours go up, so do indirect manufacturing labor costs). There do not appear to be any extreme observations in Exhibit 10-4. The relevant range is from 46 to 96 machine-hours per week (weeks 8 and 6, respectively).

Step 5: Estimate the cost function. We will show two ways to estimate the cost function for our Elegant Rugs data. One uses the high-low method, and the other uses regression analysis, the two most frequently described forms of quantitative analysis. The widespread availability of computer packages such as Excel makes regression analysis much more easy to use. Still, we describe the high-low method to provide some basic intuition for the idea of drawing a line to "fit" a number of data points. We present these methods after Step 6.

Step 6: Evaluate the cost driver of the estimated cost function. In this step, we describe criteria for evaluating the cost driver of the estimated cost function. We do this after illustrating the high-low method and regression analysis.

High-Low Method

The simplest form of quantitative analysis to "fit" a line to data points is the **high-low method**. It uses only the highest and lowest observed values of the cost driver within the relevant range and their respective costs to estimate the slope coefficient and the constant of the cost function. It provides a first cut at understanding the relationship between a cost driver and costs. We illustrate the high-low method using data from Exhibit 10-3.

	Cost Driver: Machine-Hours (X)	Indirect Manufacturing Labor Costs (Y)
Highest observation of cost driver (week 6)	96	$1,456
Lowest observation of cost driver (week 8)	46	710
Difference	50	$ 746

The slope coefficient, *b*, is calculated as:

$$\text{Slope coefficient} = \frac{\text{Difference between costs associated with highest and lowest observations of the cost driver}}{\text{Difference between highest and lowest observations of the cost driver}}$$

$$= \$746 \div 50 \text{ machine-hours} = \$14.92 \text{ per machine-hour}$$

To compute the constant, we can use either the highest or the lowest observation of the cost driver. Both calculations yield the same answer because the solution technique solves two linear equations with two unknowns, the slope coefficient and the constant. Because

$$y = a + bX$$
$$a = y - bX$$

At the highest observation of the cost driver, the constant, *a*, is calculated as:

$$\text{Constant} = \$1{,}456 - (\$14.92 \text{ per machine-hour} \times 96 \text{ machine-hours}) = \$23.68$$

And at the lowest observation of the cost driver,

$$\text{Constant} = \$710 - (\$14.92 \text{ per machine-hour} \times 46 \text{ machine-hours}) = \$23.68$$

Thus, the high-low estimate of the cost function is:

$$y = a + bX$$
$$y = \$23.68 + (\$14.92 \text{ per machine-hour} \times \text{Number of machine-hours})$$

The maroon line in Exhibit 10-5 shows the estimated cost function using the high-low method (based on the data in Exhibit 10-3). The estimated cost function is a straight line joining the observations with the highest and lowest values of the cost driver (number of machine-hours). Note how this simple high-low line falls "in-between" the data points with three observations on the line, four above it and five below it. The intercept (a = \$23.68), the point where the dashed extension of the maroon line meets the y-axis, is the constant component of the equation that provides the best linear approximation of how a cost behaves *within the relevant range* of 46 to 96 machine-hours. The intercept should *not* be interpreted as an estimate of the fixed costs of Elegant Rugs if no machines were run. That's because running no machines and shutting down the plant—that is, using zero machine-hours—is *outside the relevant range.*

Suppose indirect manufacturing labor costs in week 6 were \$1,280, instead of \$1,456, while 96 machine-hours were used. In this case, the highest observation of the cost driver (96 machine-hours in week 6) will not coincide with the newer highest observation of the costs (\$1,316 in week 9). How would this change affect our high-low calculation? Given that the cause-and-effect relationship runs *from* the cost driver *to* the costs in a cost function, we choose the highest and lowest observations of the cost driver (the factor that causes the costs to change). The high-low method would still estimate the new cost function using data from weeks 6 (high) and 8 (low).

There is a danger of relying on only two observations to estimate a cost function. Suppose that because a labor contract guarantees certain minimum payments in week 8, indirect manufacturing labor costs in week 8 were \$1,000, instead of \$710, when only 46 machine-hours were used. The blue-green line in Exhibit 10-5 shows the cost function that would be estimated by the high-low method using this revised cost. Other than the two points used to draw the line, all other data lie on or below the line! In this case, choosing the highest and lowest observations for machine-hours would result in an estimated cost function that poorly describes the underlying linear cost relationship between number of machine-hours and indirect manufacturing labor costs. In this case, the high-low method can be modified so that the two observations chosen are a *representative high* and a *representative low*. Managers use this modification to avoid having extreme observations, which arise from abnormal events, affect the cost function. The modification allows managers to estimate a cost function that is representative of the relationship between the cost driver and costs and, therefore, is more useful for making decisions (such as pricing and performance evaluation).

The advantage of the high-low method is that it is simple to compute and easy to understand; it gives a quick, initial insight into how the cost driver—number of machine hours—affects indirect manufacturing labor costs. The disadvantage is that it ignores information from all but two observations when estimating the cost function. We next describe the regression analysis method of quantitative analysis that uses all available data to estimate the cost function.

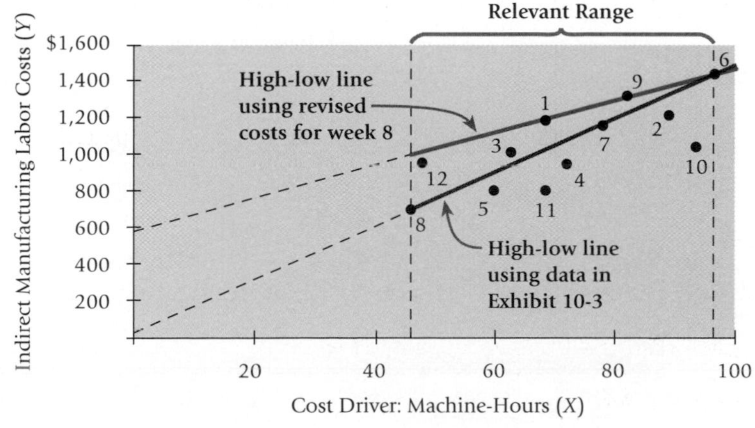

Exhibit 10-5

High-Low Method for Weekly Indirect Manufacturing Labor Costs and Machine-Hours for Elegant Rugs

Regression Analysis Method

Regression analysis is a statistical method that measures the average amount of change in the dependent variable associated with a unit change in one or more independent variables. In the Elegant Rugs example, the dependent variable is total indirect manufacturing labor costs. The independent variable, or cost driver, is number of machine-hours. **Simple regression** analysis estimates the relationship between the dependent variable and *one* independent variable. **Multiple regression** analysis estimates the relationship between the dependent variable and *two or more* independent variables. Multiple regression analysis for Elegant Rugs might use as the independent variables, or cost drivers, number of machine-hours and number of batches. The appendix to this chapter will explore simple regression and multiple regression in more detail.

In later sections, we will illustrate how Excel performs the calculations associated with regression analysis. The following discussion emphasizes how managers interpret and use the output from Excel to make critical strategic decisions. Exhibit 10-6 shows the line developed using regression analysis that best fits the data in columns B and C of Exhibit 10-3. Excel estimates the cost function to be

$$y = \$300.98 + \$10.31X$$

The regression line in Exhibit 10-6 is derived using the least-squares technique. The least-squares technique determines the regression line by minimizing the sum of the squared vertical differences from the data points (the various points in the graph) to the regression line. The vertical difference, called **residual term**, measures the distance between actual cost and estimated cost for each observation. Exhibit 10-6 shows the residual term for the week 1 data. The line from the observation to the regression line is drawn perpendicular to the horizontal axis, or x-axis. The smaller the residual terms, the better the fit between actual cost observations and estimated costs. *Goodness of fit* indicates the strength of the relationship between the cost driver and costs. The regression line in Exhibit 10-6 rises from left to right. The positive slope of this line and small residual terms indicate that, on average, indirect manufacturing labor costs increase as the number of machine-hours increases. The vertical dashed lines in Exhibit 10-6 indicate the relevant range, the range within which the cost function applies.

Instructors and students who want to explore the technical details of estimating the least-squares regression line, can go to the Appendix, pp. 363–367 and return to this point without any loss of continuity.

The estimate of the slope coefficient, b, indicates that indirect manufacturing labor costs vary at the average amount of \$10.31 for every machine-hour used within the relevant range. Management can use the regression equation when budgeting for future indirect manufacturing labor costs. For instance, if 90 machine-hours are budgeted for the upcoming week, the predicted indirect manufacturing labor costs would be

$$y = \$300.98 + (\$10.31 \text{ per machine-hour} \times 90 \text{ machine-hours}) = \$1{,}228.88$$

Exhibit 10-6

Regression Model for Weekly Indirect Manufacturing Labor Costs and Machine-Hours for Elegant Rugs

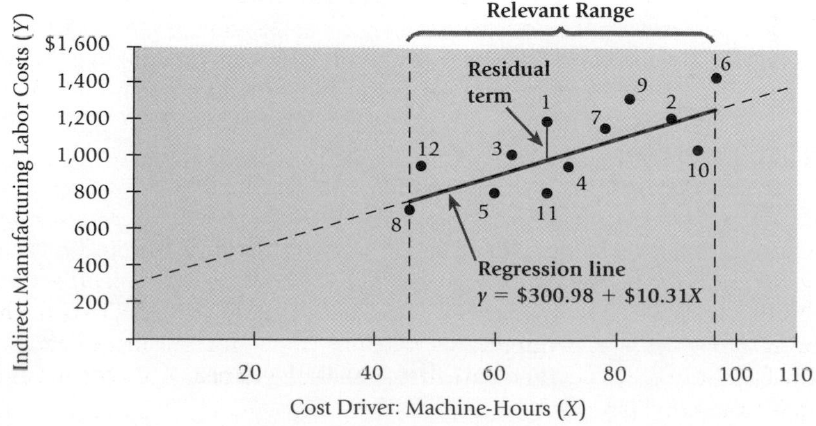

As we have already mentioned, the regression method is more accurate than the high-low method because the regression equation estimates costs using information from all observations, whereas the high-low equation uses information from only two observations. The inaccuracies of the high-low method can mislead managers. Consider the high-low method equation in the preceding section, y = \$23.68 + \$14.92 per machine-hour × Number of machine-hours. For 90 machine-hours, the predicted weekly cost based on the high-low method equation is \$23.68 + (\$14.92 per machine-hour × 90 machine-hours) = \$1,366.48. Suppose that for 7 weeks over the next 12-week period, Elegant Rugs runs its machines for 90 hours each week. Assume average indirect manufacturing labor costs for those 7 weeks are \$1,300. Based on the high-low method prediction of \$1,366.48, Elegant Rugs would conclude it has performed well because actual costs are less than predicted costs. But comparing the \$1,300 performance with the more-accurate \$1,228.88 prediction of the regression model tells a much different story and would probably prompt Elegant Rugs to search for ways to improve its cost performance.

Accurate cost estimation helps managers predict future costs and evaluate the success of cost-reduction initiatives. Suppose the manager at Elegant Rugs is interested in evaluating whether recent strategic decisions that led to changes in the production process and resulted in the data in Exhibit 10-3 have reduced indirect manufacturing labor costs, such as supervision, maintenance, and quality control. Using data on number of machine-hours used and indirect manufacturing labor costs of the previous process (not shown here), the manager estimates the regression equation,

y = \$545.26 + (\$15.86 per machine-hour × Number of machine-hours)

The constant (\$300.98 versus \$545.26) and the slope coefficient (\$10.31 versus \$15.86) are both smaller for the new process relative to the old process. It appears that the new process has decreased indirect manufacturing labor costs.

Evaluating Cost Drivers of the Estimated Cost Function

How does a company determine the best cost driver when estimating a cost function? In many cases, the choice of a cost driver is aided substantially by understanding both operations and cost accounting.

To see why understanding operations is needed, consider the costs to maintain and repair metal-cutting machines at Helix Corporation, a manufacturer of treadmills. Helix schedules repairs and maintenance at a time when production is at a low level to avoid having to take machines out of service when they are needed most. An analysis of the monthly data will then show high repair costs in months of low production and low repair costs in months of high production. Someone unfamiliar with operations might conclude that there is an inverse relationship between production and repair costs. The engineering link between units produced and repair costs, however, is usually clear-cut. Over time, there is a cause-and-effect relationship: the higher the level of production, the higher the repair costs. To estimate the relationship correctly, operating managers and analysts will recognize that repair costs will tend to lag behind periods of high production, and hence, they will use production of prior periods as the cost driver.

In other cases, choosing a cost driver is more subtle and difficult. Consider again indirect manufacturing labor costs at Elegant Rugs. Management believes that both the number of machine-hours and the number of direct manufacturing labor-hours are plausible cost drivers of indirect manufacturing labor costs. However, management is not sure which is the better cost driver. Exhibit 10-7 presents weekly data (in Excel) on indirect manufacturing labor costs and number of machine-hours for the most recent 12-week period from Exhibit 10-3, together with data on the number of direct manufacturing labor-hours for the same period.

Exhibit 10-7

Weekly Indirect Manufacturing Labor Costs, Machine-Hours, and Direct Manufacturing Labor-Hours for Elegant Rugs

	A	B	C	D
1	Week	Original Cost Driver: Machine-Hours	Alternate Cost Driver: Direct Manufacturing Labor-Hours (*X*)	Indirect Manufacturing Labor Costs (*Y*)
2	1	68	30	$ 1,190
3	2	88	35	1,211
4	3	62	36	1,004
5	4	72	20	917
6	5	60	47	770
7	6	96	45	1,456
8	7	78	44	1,180
9	8	46	38	710
10	9	82	70	1,316
11	10	94	30	1,032
12	11	68	29	752
13	12	48	38	963
14	Total	862	462	$12,501
15				

What guidance do the different cost-estimation methods provide for choosing among cost drivers? The industrial engineering method relies on analyzing physical relationships between cost drivers and costs, relationships that are difficult to specify in this case. The conference method and the account analysis method use subjective assessments to choose a cost driver and to estimate the fixed and variable components of the cost function. In these cases, managers must rely on their best judgment. Managers cannot use these methods to test and try alternative cost drivers. The major advantages of quantitative methods are that they are objective—a given data set and estimation method result in a unique estimated cost function—and managers can use them to evaluate different cost drivers. We use the regression analysis approach to illustrate how to evaluate different cost drivers.

First, the cost analyst at Elegant Rugs enters data in columns C and D of Exhibit 10-7 in Excel and estimates the following regression equation of indirect manufacturing labor costs based on number of direct manufacturing labor-hours:

$$y = \$744.67 + \$7.72X$$

Exhibit 10-8 shows the plot of the data points for number of direct manufacturing labor-hours and indirect manufacturing labor costs, and the regression line that best fits the data. Exhibit 10-6 shows the corresponding graph when number of machine-hours is the cost driver. To decide which of the two cost drivers Elegant Rugs should choose, the analyst compares the machine-hour regression equation and the direct manufacturing labor-hour regression equation. There are three criteria used to make this evaluation.

Learning Objective 5

Describe three criteria used to evaluate and choose cost drivers

. . . economically plausible relationships, goodness of fit, and significant effect of the cost driver on costs

1. **Economic plausibility.** Both cost drivers are economically plausible. However, in the state-of-the-art, highly automated production environment at Elegant Rugs, managers familiar with the operations believe that costs such as machine maintenance are likely to be more closely related to number of machine-hours used than to number of direct manufacturing labor-hours used.
2. **Goodness of fit.** Compare Exhibits 10-6 and 10-8. The vertical differences between actual costs and predicted costs are much smaller for the machine-hours regression than for the direct manufacturing labor-hours regression. Number of machine-hours used, therefore, has a stronger relationship—or goodness of fit—with indirect manufacturing labor costs.

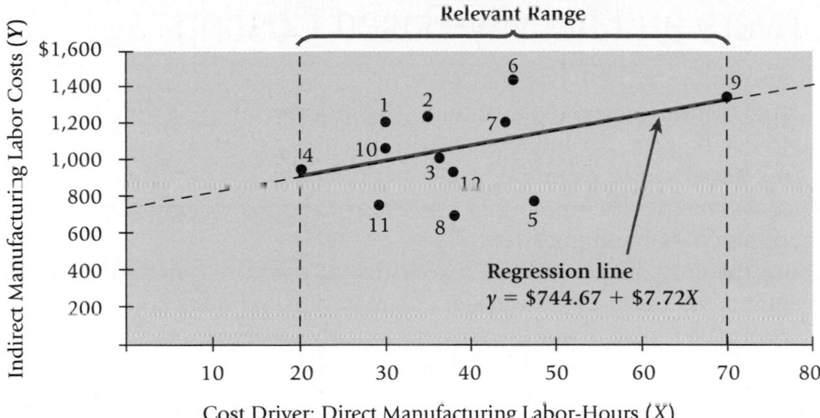

Exhibit 10-8

Regression Model for Weekly Indirect Manufacturing Labor Costs and Direct Manufacturing Labor-Hours for Elegant Rugs

3. **Significance of independent variable.** Again compare Exhibits 10-6 and 10-8 (both of which have been drawn to roughly the same scale). The machine-hours regression line has a steep slope relative to the slope of the direct manufacturing labor-hours regression line. *For the same (or more) scatter of observations about the line (goodness of fit)*, a flat, or slightly sloped regression line indicates a weak relationship between the cost driver and costs. In our example, changes in direct manufacturing labor-hours appear to have a small influence or effect on indirect manufacturing labor costs.

Based on this evaluation, managers at Elegant Rugs select number of machine-hours as the cost driver and use the cost function y = $300.98 + ($10.31 per machine-hour × Number of machine-hours) to predict future indirect manufacturing labor costs.

Instructors and students who want to explore how regression analysis techniques can be used to choose among different cost drivers can go to the Appendix, pp. 367–369 and return to this point without any loss of continuity.

Why is choosing the correct cost driver to estimate indirect manufacturing labor costs important? Consider the following strategic decision that management at Elegant Rugs must make. The company is thinking of introducing a new style of carpet that, from a manufacturing standpoint, is similar to the carpets it has manufactured in the past. Prices are set by the market and sales of 650 square yards of this carpet are expected each week. Management estimates 72 machine-hours and 21 direct manufacturing labor-hours would be required per week to produce the 650 square yards of carpet needed. Using the machine-hour regression equation, Elegant Rugs would predict indirect manufacturing labor costs of y = $300.98 + ($10.31 per machine-hour × 72 machine-hours) = $1,043.30. If it used direct manufacturing labor-hours as the cost driver, it would incorrectly predict costs of $744.67 + ($7.72 per labor-hour × 21 labor-hours) = $906.79. If Elegant Rugs chose similarly incorrect cost drivers for other indirect costs as well and systematically underestimated costs, it would conclude that the costs of manufacturing the new style of carpet would be low and basically fixed (fixed because the regression line is nearly flat). But the actual costs driven by number of machine-hours used and other correct cost drivers would be higher. By failing to identify the proper cost drivers, management would be misled into believing the new style of carpet would be more profitable than it actually is. It might decide to introduce the new style of carpet, whereas if Elegant identifies the correct cost driver it might decide not to introduce the new carpet.

Incorrectly estimating the cost function would also have repercussions for cost management and cost control. Suppose number of direct manufacturing labor-hours were used as the cost driver, and actual indirect manufacturing labor costs for the new carpet were $970. Actual costs would then be higher than the predicted costs of $906.79. Management would feel compelled to find ways to cut costs. In fact, on the basis of the preferred machine-hour cost driver, the plant would have actual costs lower than the $1,043.30 predicted costs—a performance that management should seek to replicate, not change!

Cost Drivers and Activity-Based Costing

Activity-based costing (ABC) systems focus on individual activities—such as product design, machine setup, materials handling, distribution, and customer service—as the fundamental cost objects. To implement ABC systems, managers must identify a cost driver for each activity. For example, using methods described in this chapter, the manager must decide whether the number of loads moved or the weight of loads moved is the cost driver of materials-handling costs.

To choose the cost driver and use it to estimate the cost function in our materials-handling example, the manager collects data on materials-handling costs and the quantities of the two competing cost drivers over a reasonably long period. Why a long period? Because in the short run, materials-handling costs may be fixed and, therefore, will not vary with changes in the level of the cost driver. In the long run, however, there is a clear cause-and-effect relationship between materials-handling costs and the cost driver. Suppose number of loads moved is the cost driver of materials-handling costs. Increases in the number of loads moved will require more materials-handling labor and equipment; decreases will result in equipment being sold and labor being reassigned to other tasks.

ABC systems have a great number and variety of cost drivers and cost pools. That means ABC systems require many cost relationships to be estimated. In estimating the cost function for each cost pool, the manager must pay careful attention to the cost hierarchy. For example, if a cost is a batch-level cost such as setup cost, the manager must only consider batch-level cost drivers like number of setup-hours. In some cases, the costs in a cost pool may have more than one cost driver from different levels of the cost hierarchy. In the Elegant Rugs example, the cost drivers for indirect manufacturing labor costs could be machine-hours and number of production batches of carpet manufactured. Furthermore, it may be difficult to subdivide the indirect manufacturing labor costs into two cost pools and to measure the costs associated with each cost driver. In these cases, companies use multiple regression to estimate costs based on more than one independent variable. The appendix to this chapter discusses multiple regression in more detail.

As the Concepts in Action feature (p. 354) illustrates, managers implementing ABC systems use a variety of methods—industrial engineering, conference, and regression analysis—to estimate slope coefficients. In making these choices, managers trade off level of detail, accuracy, feasibility, and costs of estimating cost functions.

Nonlinearity and Cost Functions

Explain and give examples of nonlinear cost functions

... graph of cost function is not a straight line, for example, because of quantity discounts or costs changing in steps

In practice, cost functions are not always linear. A **nonlinear cost function** is a cost function for which the graph of total costs (based on the level of a single activity) is not a straight line within the relevant range. To see what a nonlinear cost function looks like, return to Exhibit 10-2 (p. 340), but now let's expand the relevant range from 0 to 80,000 snowboards produced from the original relevant range of 20,000 to 65,000. You can see that the cost function over this expanded range is graphically represented by a line that is not a straight line.

Consider another example. Economies of scale in advertising may enable an advertising agency to produce double the number of advertisements for less than double the costs. Even direct material costs are not always linear variable costs because of quantity discounts on direct material purchases. As shown in Exhibit 10-9 (p. 353), Panel A, total direct material costs rise as the units of direct materials purchased increase. But, because of quantity discounts, these costs rise more slowly (as indicated by the slope coefficient) as the units of direct materials purchased increase. This cost function has $b = \$25$ per unit for 1 to 1,000 units purchased, $b = \$15$ per unit for 1,001 to 2,000 units purchased, and $b = \$10$ per unit for 2,001 to 3,000 units purchased. The direct material cost per unit falls at each price break—that is, the cost per unit decreases with larger purchase orders. If managers are interested in understanding cost behavior over the relevant range from 1 to 3,000 units, the cost function is nonlinear—not a straight line. If, however, managers are only interested in understanding cost behavior over a more narrow relevant range (for example, from 1 to 1,000 units), the cost function is linear.

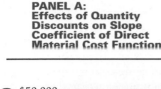

Exhibit 10-9 Examples of Nonlinear Cost Functions

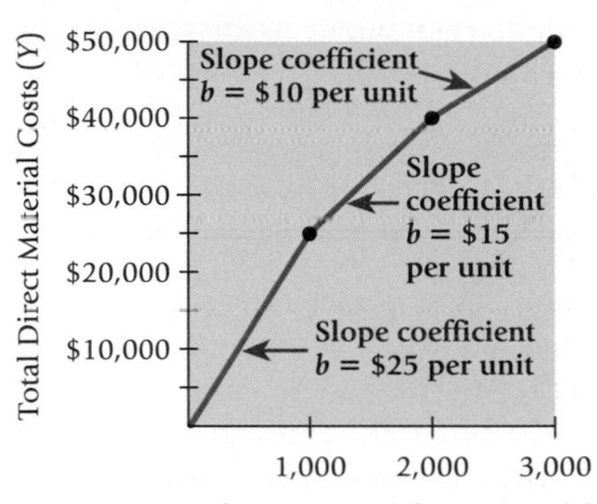

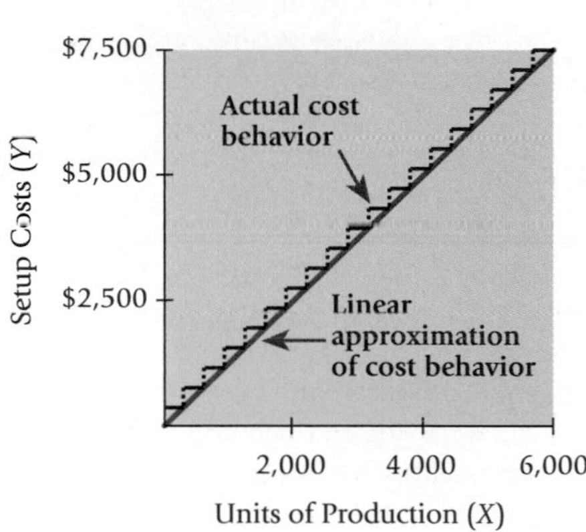

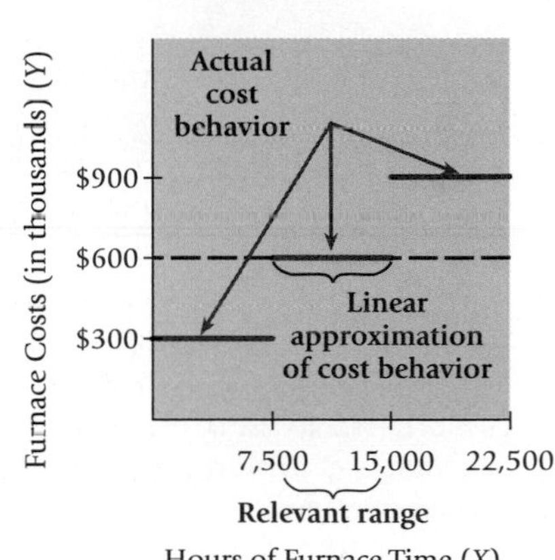

Step cost functions are also examples of nonlinear cost functions. A **step cost function** is a cost function in which the cost remains the same over various ranges of the level of activity, but the cost increases by discrete amounts—that is, increases in steps—as the level of activity increases from one range to the next. Panel B in Exhibit 10-9 shows a *step variable-cost function*, a step cost function in which cost remains the same over *narrow* ranges of the level of activity in each relevant range. Panel B presents the relationship between units of production and setup costs. The pattern is a step cost function because, as we described in Chapter 5 on activity-based costing, setup costs are related to each production batch started. If the relevant range is considered to be from 0 to 6,000 production units, the cost function is nonlinear. However, as shown by the blue-green line in Panel B, managers often approximate step variable costs with a continuously-variable cost function. This type of step cost pattern also occurs when production inputs such as materials-handling labor, supervision, and process engineering labor are acquired in discrete quantities but used in fractional quantities.

Panel C in Exhibit 10-9 shows a *step fixed-cost function* for Crofton Steel, a company that operates large heat-treatment furnaces to harden steel parts. Looking at Panel C and Panel B, you can see that the main difference between a step variable-cost function and a step fixed-cost function is that the cost in a step fixed-cost function remains the same over *wide* ranges of the activity in each relevant range. The ranges indicate the number of furnaces being used (each furnace costs $300,000). The cost increases from one range to the next higher range when the hours of furnace time needed require the use of another furnace. The relevant range of 7,500 to 15,000 hours of furnace time indicates that the company expects to operate with two furnaces at a cost of $600,000. Management considers the cost of operating furnaces as a fixed cost within this relevant range of operation. However, if the relevant range is considered to be from 0 to 22,500 hours, the cost function is nonlinear: The graph in Panel C is not a single straight line; it is three broken lines.

Learning Curves and Nonlinear Cost Functions

Nonlinear cost functions also result from learning curves. A **learning curve** is a function that measures how labor-hours per unit decline as units of production increase because workers are learning and becoming better at their jobs. Managers use learning curves to predict how labor-hours, or labor costs, will increase as more units are produced.

Concepts in Action

Activity-Based Costing: Identifying Cost and Revenue Drivers

Many cost estimation methods presented in this chapter are essential to service-, manufacturing-, and retail-sector implementations of activity-based costing across the globe. To determine the cost of an activity in the banking industry, ABC systems often rely on expert analyses and opinions gathered from operating personnel (the conference method). For example, the Loan Department staff at the Cooperative Bank in the United Kingdom subjectively estimate the costs of the loan processing activity and the quantity of the related cost driver—the number of loans processed, a batch-level cost driver, as distinguished from the amount of the loans, an output unit-level cost driver—to derive the cost of processing a loan.

Other global banks, in contrast, use input-output relationships (the industrial engineering method) to identify cost drivers and the cost of an activity. Bankinter—the Spanish joint venture of Bank of America and Banco Santander—uses work and time measurement methods to determine the total costs associated with routine activities, such as opening an account and making a transfer payment. In the United States, the Boeing Commercial Airplane Group's Wichita Division uses detailed analyses of its commercial airplane-manufacturing methods to support make/buy decisions for complex parts required in airplane assembly. The Industrial engineering method is also used by federal government agencies such as the U.S. Postal Service to determine the cost of each post office transaction and the Patent and Trademark Office to identify the costs of each patent examination.

Regression analysis is another helpful tool for determining the cost drivers of activities. Consider how fuel service retailers (that is, gas stations with convenience stores) identify the principal cost driver for labor within their operations. Two possible cost drivers are gasoline sales and convenience store sales. Gasoline sales are batch-level activities because payment transactions occur only once for each gasoline purchase, regardless of the volume of gasoline purchased; whereas convenience store sales are output unit-level activities that vary based on the amount of food, drink, and other products sold. Fuel service retailers generally use convenience store sales as the basis for assigning labor costs because multiple regression analyses confirm that convenience store sales, not gasoline sales, are the major cost driver of labor within their operations.

First Tennessee Banking Corporation used insights from cost estimation to restructure its certificate of deposit (CD) offerings. First Tennessee recognized that the cost of processing a CD was fixed regardless of the amount of the certificate, but that the revenue was a function of the dollar amount of the certificate. Therefore, a 90-day $500 CD that was reopened four times a year generated only $5 per year on a 1% interest spread, which was considerably less revenue than the cost of processing the transactions. By applying ABC concepts and using the conference method, First Tennessee found that 30% of its CD offerings were providing 88% of CD profits, while another 30% of CDs were serviced at a loss of 7%. As a result, of these findings, management worked to enhance revenues through a combination of higher minimum balances, new products and process redesign. Using a similar analysis, Bankinter restructured its enrollment incentives and outreach strategy to attract more profitable customers to its Internet banking service.

Sources: "The Cooperative Bank," Harvard Business School Case No. N9-195-196; "Internet Customer Acquisition Strategy at Bankinter," Harvard Business School Case No. 9-103-021 (2007); "Boeing Commercial Airplane Group Wichita Division (Boeing Co.)," Massachusetts Institute of Technology Labor Aerospace Research Agenda (2001); Barton, T., and J. MacArthur, "Activity-Based Costing and Predatory Pricing: The Case of the Retail Industry," *Management Accounting Quarterly* (Spring 2003); Carter, T., A. Sedaghat, and T. Williams, "How ABC Changed the Post Office," *Management Accounting* (February 1998); Peckenpaugh, J., "Teaching the ABCs," *Government Executive* (April 1, 2002); Sweeney, R., and J. Mays, "ABM," *Management Accounting* (March 1997).

The aircraft-assembly industry first documented the effect that learning has on efficiency. In general, as workers become more familiar with their tasks, their efficiency improves. Managers learn how to improve the scheduling of work shifts and how to operate the plant better. As a result of improved efficiency, unit costs decrease as productivity increases, and the unit-cost function behaves nonlinearly. These nonlinearities must be considered when estimating and predicting unit costs.

Managers have extended the learning-curve notion to other business functions in the value chain, such as marketing, distribution, and customer service, and to costs other than labor costs. The term *experience curve* describes this broader application of the learning curve. An **experience curve** is a function that measures the decline in cost per unit in various business functions of the value chain—marketing, distribution, and so on—as the amount of these activities increases. For companies such as Dell Computer, Wal-Mart, and McDonald's, learning curves and experience curves are key elements of their strategies. These companies use learning curves and experience curves to reduce costs and increase customer satisfaction, market share, and profitability.

We now describe two learning-curve models: the cumulative average-time learning model and the incremental unit-time learning model.

Cumulative Average-Time Learning Model

Learning Objective 7

Distinguish the cumulative average-time learning model

. . . average time per unit declines by constant percentage, as units produced double from the incremental unit-time learning model

. . . incremental time to produce last unit declines by constant percentage, as units produced double

In the **cumulative average-time learning model**, cumulative average time per unit declines by a constant percentage each time the cumulative quantity of units produced doubles. Consider Rayburn Corporation, a radar systems manufacturer. Rayburn has an 80% learning curve. The 80% means that when the quantity of units produced is doubled from *X* to 2*X*, cumulative average time *per unit* for 2*X* units is 80% of cumulative average time *per unit* for *X* units. Average time per unit has dropped by 20% (100% − 80%). Exhibit 10-10 is an Excel spreadsheet showing the calculations for the cumulative average-time learning model for Rayburn Corporation. Note that as the number of units produced doubles from 1 to 2 in column A, cumulative average time per unit declines from 100 hours to 80% of 100 hours (0.80 × 100 hours = 80 hours) in column B. As the number of units doubles from 2 to 4, cumulative average time per unit declines to 80% of 80 hours = 64 hours, and so on. To obtain the cumulative total time in column D, multiply cumulative average time per unit by the cumulative number of units produced. For example, to produce 4 cumulative units would require 256 labor-hours (4 units × 64 cumulative average labor-hours per unit).

Incremental Unit-Time Learning Model

In the **incremental unit-time learning model**, incremental time needed to produce the last unit declines by a constant percentage each time the cumulative quantity of units produced doubles. Again, consider Rayburn Corporation and an 80% learning curve. The 80% here means that when the quantity of units produced is doubled from *X* to 2*X*, the time needed to produce the last unit when 2*X* total units are produced is 80% of the time needed to produce the last unit when *X* total units are produced. Exhibit 10-11 is an Excel spreadsheet showing the calculations for the incremental unit-time learning model for Rayburn Corporation based on an 80% learning curve. Note how when units produced double from 2 to 4 in column A, the time to produce unit 4 (the last unit when 4 units are produced) is 64 hours in column B, which is 80% of the 80 hours needed to produce unit 2 (the last unit when 2 units are produced). We obtain the cumulative total time in column D by summing individual unit times in column B. For example, to produce 4 cumulative units would require 314.21 labor-hours (100.00 + 80.00 + 70.21 + 64.00).

Exhibit 10-12 presents graphs using Excel for the cumulative average-time learning model (using data from Exhibit 10-10) and the incremental unit-time learning model (using data from Exhibit 10-11). Panel A graphically illustrates cumulative average time per unit as a function of cumulative units produced for each model. The curve for the cumulative average-time learning model is plotted using the data from Exhibit 10-10, column B, versus column A. The curve for the incremental unit-time learning model is plotted using the data from Exhibit 10-11, column E, versus column A. Panel B graphically illustrates cumulative total labor-hours as a function of cumulative units produced for each model. The curve for the cumulative average-time learning model is plotted using the data from Exhibit 10-10, column D, versus column A. The curve for the incremental unit-time learning model is plotted using the data from Exhibit 10-11, column D, versus column A.

The incremental unit-time learning model predicts a higher cumulative total time to produce two or more units than the cumulative average-time learning model, assuming the same learning rate for both models. That is, in Exhibit 10-12, Panel B, the graph for the 80% incremental unit-time learning model lies above the graph for the 80% cumulative average-time learning model. If we compare the results in Exhibit 10-10 (column D)

Exhibit 10-10 Cumulative Average-Time Learning Model for Rayburn Corporation

	A	B	C	D	E
1	Cumulative Average-Time Learning Model for Rayburn Corporation				
2					
3		80% Learning Curve			
4					
5	Cumulative	Cumulative		Cumulative	Individual Unit
6	Number	Average Time		Total Time:	Time for *X* th
7	of Units (*X*)	per Unit (*y*)*: Labor Hours		Labor-Hours	Unit: Labor Hours
8					
9				D = Col A x Col B	
10					
11	1	100.00		100.00	100.00
12	2	80.00	=(100x0.8)	160.00	60.00
13	3	70.21		210.63	50.63
14	4	64.00	=(80x0.8)	256.00	45.37
15	5	59.56		297.82	41.82
16	6	56.17		337.01	39.19
17	7	53.45		374.14	37.13
18	8	51.20	=(64x0.8)	409.60	35.46
19	9	49.29		443.65	34.05
20	10	47.65		476.51	32.86
21	11	46.21		508.32	31.81
22	12	44.93		539.22	30.89
23	13	43.79		569.29	30.07
24	14	42.76		598.63	29.34
25	15	41.82		627.30	28.67
26	16	40.96	=(51.2x0.8)	655.36	28.06
27					

E13 = D13 - D12
= 210.63 - 160.00

*The mathematical relationship underlying the cumulative average-time learning model is:

$$y = aX^b$$

where y = Cumulative average time (labor-hours) per unit
X = Cumulative number of units produced
a = Time (labor-hours) required to produce the first unit
b = Factor used to calculate cumulative average time to produce units

The value of b is calculated as

$$\frac{\ln\,(\text{learning-curve \% in decimal form})}{\ln 2}$$

For an 80% learning curve, $b = \ln 0.8/\ln 2 = -0.2231/0.6931 = -0.3219$
when $X = 3$, $a = 100$, $b = -0.3219$,

$$y = 100 \times 3^{-0.3219} = 70.21 \text{ labor hours}$$

Numbers in table may not be exact because of rounding.

with the results in Exhibit 10-11 (column D), to produce 4 cumulative units, the 80% incremental unit-time learning model predicts 314.21 labor-hours versus 256.00 labor-hours predicted by the 80% cumulative average-time learning model. That's because under the cumulative average-time learning model *average labor-hours needed to produce all 4 units* is 64 hours; the labor-hour amount needed to produce unit 4 is much less than 64 hours—it is 45.37 hours (see Exhibit 10-10). Under the incremental unit-time learning model, the labor-hour amount needed to produce unit 4 is 64 hours, and the labor-hours needed to produce the first 3 units are more than 64 hours, so average time needed to produce all 4 units is more than 64 hours.

How do managers choose which model and what percent learning curve to use? They make their choices on a case-by-case basis. For example, if the behavior of manufacturing labor-hour usage as production levels increase follows a pattern like the one predicted by the 80% learning curve cumulative average-time learning model, then the 80% learning curve cumulative average-time learning model should be used. Engineers, plant managers, and workers are good sources of information on the amount and type of learning actually occurring as production increases. Plotting this information and estimating the model that best fits the data is helpful in selecting the appropriate model.[2]

Setting Prices, Budgets, and Standards

How do companies use learning curves? Consider the data in Exhibit 10-10 for the cumulative average-time learning model at Rayburn Corporation. Suppose variable costs

[2] For details, see C. Bailey, "Learning Curve Estimation of Production Costs and Labor-Hours Using a Free Excel Add-In," *Management Accounting Quarterly*, Summer 2000: 25–31. Free software for estimating learning curves is available at Dr. Bailey's Web site (www.profbailey.com).

Exhibit 10-11 Incremental Unit-Time Learning Model for Rayburn Corporation

File Edit View Insert Format Tools Data Window Help

	A	B	C	D	E
1	Incremental Unit-Time Learning Model for Rayburn Corporation				
2					
3		80% Learning Curve			
4					
5	Cumulative	Individual Unit Time		Cumulative	Cumulative
6	Number	for Xth Unit (y)*:		Total Time:	Average Time
7	of Units (X)	Labor Hours		Labor-Hours	per Unit:
8					Labor-Hours
9					
10					E = Col D ÷ Col A
11					
12	1	100.00		100.00	100.00
13	2	80.00	=(100x0.8)	180.00	90.00
14	3	70.21		250.21	83.40
15	4	64.00	=(80x0.8)	314.21	78.55
16	5	59.56		373.77	74.75
17	6	56.17		429.94	71.66
18	7	53.45		483.39	69.06
19	8	51.20	=(64x0.8)	534.59	66.82
20	9	49.29		583.89	64.88
21	10	47.65		631.54	63.15
22	11	46.21		677.75	61.61
23	12	44.93		722.68	60.22
24	13	43.79		766.47	58.96
25	14	42.76		809.23	57.80
26	15	41.82		851.05	56.74
27	16	40.96	=(51.2x0.8)	892.01	55.75
28					

D14 = D13 + B14
= 180.00 + 70.21

*The mathematical relationship underlying the incremental unit-time learning model is:

$$y = aX^b$$

where y = Time (labor-hours) taken to produce the last single unit
X = Cumulative number of units produced
a = Time (labor-hours) required to produce the first unit
b = Factor used to calculate incremental unit time to produce units
$= \frac{\ln\text{(learning-curve \% in decimal form)}}{\ln 2}$

For an 80% learning curve, $b = \ln 0.8 \div \ln 2 = -0.2231 \div 0.6931 = -0.3219$
Where $X = 3$, $a = 100$, $b = -0.3219$,
$y = 100 \times 3^{-0.3219} = 70.21$ labor hours
The cumulative total time when $X = 3$ is 100+80+70.21=250.21 labor-hours.
Numbers in the table may not be exact because of rounding.

subject to learning effects consist of direct manufacturing labor, at \$20 per hour, and related overhead, at \$30 per direct manufacturing labor-hour. Managers should predict the costs shown in Exhibit 10-13.

These data show that the effects of the learning curve could have a major influence on decisions. For example, managers at Rayburn Corporation might set an extremely low

Exhibit 10-12 Plots for Cumulative Average-Time Learning Model and Incremental Unit-Time Learning Model for Rayburn Corporation

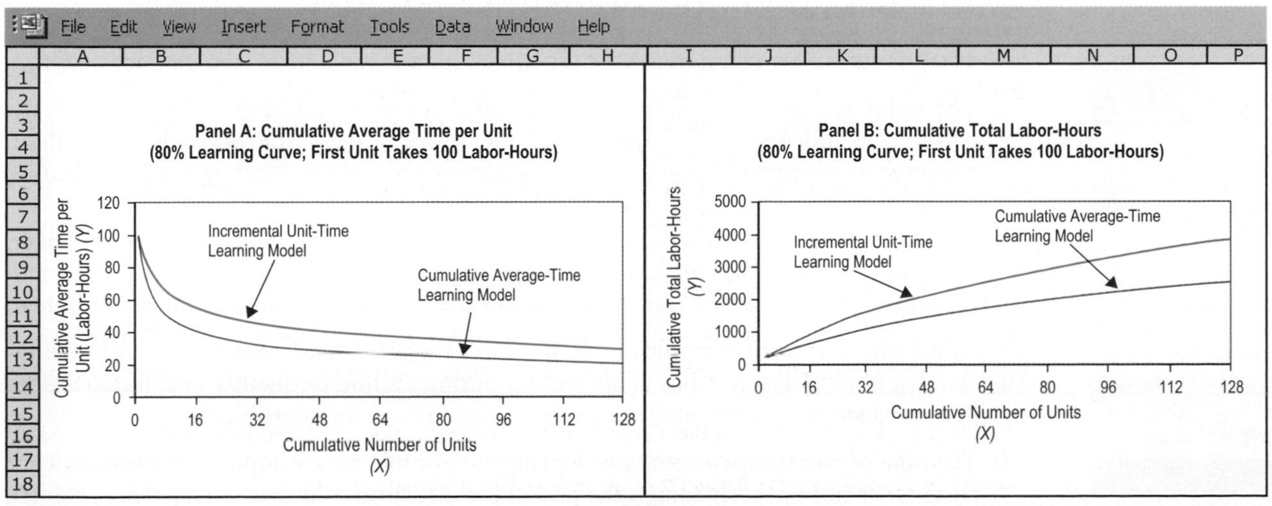

Exhibit 10-13

Predicting Costs Using Learning Curves at Rayburn Corporation

	A	B	C	D	E	F
1		Cumulative				
2	Cumulative	Average Time	Cumulative	Cumulative Costs		Additions to
3	Number of	per Unit:	Total Time:	at $50 per		Cumulative
4	Units	Labor-Hours[a]	Labor-Hours[a]	Labor-Hour		Costs
5	1	100.00	100.00	$ 5,000	(100.00 x $50)	$ 5,000
6	2	80.00	160.00	8,000	(160.00 x $50)	3,000
7	4	64.00	256.00	12,800	(256.00 x $50)	4,800
8	8	51.20	409.60	20,480	(409.60 x $50)	7,680
9	16	40.96	655.36	32,768	(655.36 x $50)	12,288
10						
11	[a]Based on the cumulative average-time learning model. See Exhibit 10-10 for the computations					
12	of these amounts.					

selling price on its radar systems to generate high demand. As its production increases to meet this growing demand, cost per unit drops. Rayburn "rides the product down the learning curve" as it establishes a larger market share. Although it may have earned little operating income on its first unit sold—it may actually have lost money on that unit—Rayburn earns more operating income per unit as output increases.

Alternatively, subject to legal and other considerations, Rayburn's managers might set a low price on just the final 8 units. After all, the total labor and related overhead costs per unit for these final 8 units are predicted to be only $12,288 ($32,768 − $20,480). On these final 8 units, the $1,536 cost per unit ($12,288 ÷ 8 units) is much lower than the $5,000 cost per unit of the first unit produced.

Many companies, such as Pizza Hut and Home Depot, incorporate learning-curve effects when evaluating performance. The Nissan Motor Company expects its workers to learn and improve on the job and evaluates performance accordingly. It sets assembly-labor efficiency standards for new models of cars after taking into account the learning that will occur as more units are produced.

The learning-curve models examined in Exhibits 10-10 to 10-13 assume that learning is driven by a single variable (production output). Other models of learning have been developed (by companies such as Analog Devices and Yokogawa Hewlett-Packard) that focus on how quality—rather than manufacturing labor-hours—will change over time, regardless of whether more units are produced. Studies indicate that factors other than production output, such as job rotation and organizing workers into teams, contribute to learning that improves quality.

Data Collection and Adjustment Issues

Learning Objective 8

Be aware of data problems encountered in estimating cost functions

. . . for example, unreliable data and poor recordkeeping, extreme observations, treating fixed costs as if they are variable, and a changing relationship between a cost driver and cost

The ideal database for estimating cost functions quantitatively has two characteristics:

1. **The database should contain numerous reliably measured observations of the cost driver (the independent variable) and the related costs (the dependent variable).** Errors in measuring the costs and the cost driver are serious. They result in inaccurate estimates of the effect of the cost driver on costs.
2. **The database should consider many values spanning a wide range for the cost driver.** Using only a few values of the cost driver that are grouped closely considers too small a segment of the relevant range and reduces the confidence in the estimates obtained.

Unfortunately, cost analysts typically do not have the advantage of working with a database having both characteristics. This section outlines some frequently encountered data problems and steps the cost analyst can take to overcome these problems.

1. The time period for measuring the dependent variable (for example, machine-lubricant costs) does not properly match the period for measuring the cost driver. This problem

often arises when accounting records are not kept on the accrual basis. Consider a cost function with machine-lubricant costs as the dependent variable and number of machine-hours as the cost driver. Assume that the lubricant is purchased sporadically and stored for later use. Records maintained on the basis of lubricants purchased will indicate little lubricant costs in many months and large lubricant costs in other months. These records present an obviously inaccurate picture of what is actually taking place. The analyst should use accrual accounting to measure cost of lubricants consumed to better match costs with the machine-hours cost driver in this example.

2. Fixed costs are allocated as if they are variable. For example, costs such as depreciation, insurance, or rent may be allocated to products to calculate cost per unit of output. *The danger is to regard these costs as variable rather than as fixed. They seem to be variable because of the allocation methods used.* To avoid this problem, the analyst should distinguish carefully fixed costs from variable costs and not treat allocated fixed cost per unit as a variable cost.
3. Data are either not available for all observations or are not uniformly reliable. Missing cost observations often arise from a failure to record a cost or from classifying a cost incorrectly. For example, marketing costs may be understated because costs of sales visits to customers may be incorrectly recorded as customer-service costs. Recording data manually rather than electronically tends to result in a higher percentage of missing observations and erroneously entered observations. Errors also arise when data on cost drivers originate outside the internal accounting system. For example, the Accounting Department may obtain data on testing-hours for medical instruments from the company's Manufacturing Department and data on number of items shipped to customers from the Distribution Department. One or both of these departments might not keep accurate records. To minimize these problems, the cost analyst should design data collection reports that regularly and routinely obtain the required data and should follow up immediately whenever data are missing.
4. Extreme values of observations occur from errors in recording costs (for example, a misplaced decimal point), from nonrepresentative periods (for example, from a period in which a major machine breakdown occurred or from a period in which a delay in delivery of materials from an international supplier curtailed production), or from observations outside the relevant range. Analysts should adjust or eliminate unusual observations before estimating a cost relationship.
5. There is no homogeneous relationship between the cost driver and the individual cost items in the dependent variable-cost pool. A homogeneous relationship exists when each activity whose costs are included in the dependent variable has the same cost driver. In this case, a single cost function can be estimated. As discussed in step 2 for estimating a cost function using quantitative analysis (p. 344), when the cost driver for each activity is different, separate cost functions, each with its own cost driver, should be estimated for each activity. Alternatively, as discussed on pp. 368–371, the cost function should be estimated with more than one independent variable using multiple regression.
6. The relationship between the cost driver and the cost is not stationary. That is, the underlying process that generated the observations has not remained stable over time. For example, the relationship between number of machine-hours and manufacturing overhead costs is unlikely to be stationary when the data cover a period in which new technology was introduced. One way to see if the relationship is stationary is to split the sample into two parts and estimate separate cost relationships—one for the period before the technology was introduced and one for the period after the technology was introduced. Then, if the estimated coefficients for the two periods are similar, the analyst can pool the data to estimate a single cost relationship. When feasible, pooling data provides a larger data set for the estimation, which increases confidence in the cost predictions being made.
7. Inflation has affected costs, the cost driver, or both. For example, inflation may cause costs to change even when there is no change in the level of the cost driver. To study the underlying cause-and-effect relationship between the level of the cost driver and costs, the analyst should remove purely inflationary price effects from the data by dividing each cost by the price index on the date the cost was incurred.

In many cases, a cost analyst must expend considerable effort to reduce the effect of these problems before estimating a cost function on the basis of past data.

Problem for Self-Study

The Helicopter Division of GLD, Inc. is examining helicopter assembly costs at its Indiana plant. It has received an initial order for eight of its new land-surveying helicopters. GLD can adopt one of two methods of assembling the helicopters:

	A	B	C	D	E
1		Labor-Intensive Assembly Method		Machine-Intensive Assembly Method	
2	Direct material cost per helicopter	$ 40,000		$36,000	
3	Direct-assembly labor time for first helicopter	2,000	labor-hours	800	labor-hours
4	Learning curve for assembly labor time per helicopter	85%	cumulative average time*	90%	incremental unit time**
5	Direct-assembly labor cost	$ 30	per hour	$ 30	per hour
6	Equipment-related indirect manufacturing cost	$ 12	per direct-assembly labor-hour	$ 45	per direct-assembly labor-hour
7	Material-handling-related indirect manufacturing cost	50%	of direct material cost	50%	of direct material cost
8					
9					
10	*Using the formula (p. 356), for an 85% learning curve, $b = \frac{\ln 0.85}{\ln 2} = \frac{-0.162519}{0.693147} = -0.234465$				
11					
12					
13					
14					
15	**Using the formula (p. 357), for a 90% learning curve, $b = \frac{\ln 0.90}{\ln 2} = \frac{-0.105361}{0.693147} = -0.152004$				
16					
17					

Required

1. How many direct-assembly labor-hours are required to assemble the first eight helicopters under (a) the labor-intensive method and (b) the machine-intensive method?
2. What is the total cost of assembling the first eight helicopters under (a) the labor-intensive method and (b) the machine-intensive method?

Solution

1. a. The following calculations show the labor-intensive assembly method based on an 85% cumulative average-time learning model (using Excel):

	G	H	I	J	K
1	Cumulative	Cumulative		Cumulative	Individual
2	Number	Average Time		Total Time:	time for
3	of Units	per Unit (*y*):		Labor-Hours	*X*th unit:
4		Labor Hours			Labor-Hours
5				Col J = Col G x Col H	
6	1	2,000		2,000	2,000
7	2	1,700	(2,000 x 0.85)	3,400	1,400
8	3	1,546		4,637	1,237
9	4	1,445	(1,700 x 0.85)	5,780	1,143
10	5	1,371		6,857	1,077
11	6	1,314		7,884	1,027
12	7	1,267		8,871	987
13	8	1,228.25	(1,445 x 0.85)	9,826	955
14					

Cumulative average-time per unit for the Xth unit in column H is calculated as $y = aX^b$; see Exhibit 10-10 (p. 356). For example, when $X = 3$, $y = 2{,}000 \times 3^{-0.234465} = 1{,}546$ labor-hours.

b. The following calculations show the machine-intensive assembly method based on a 90% incremental unit-time learning model:

	G	H	I	J	K
1	Cumulative	Individual		Cumulative	Cumulative
2	Number	Unit Time		Total Time:	Average Time
3	of Units	for *X*th Unit (*y*):		Labor-Hours	Per Unit:
4		Labor Hours			Labor-Hours
5					Col K = Col J ÷ Col G
6	1	800		800	800
7	2	720	(800 x 0.9)	1,520	760
8	3	677		2,197	732
9	4	648	(720 x 0.9)	2,845	711
10	5	626		3,471	694
11	6	609		4,081	680
12	7	595		4,676	668
13	8	583	(648 x 0.9)	5,258	657

Individual unit time for the Xth unit in column H is calculated as $y = aX^b$; see Exhibit 10-11 (p. 357). For example, when $X = 3$, $y = 800 \times 3^{-0.152004} = 677$ labor-hours.

2. Total costs of assembling the first eight helicopters are:

	O	P	Q
1		Labor-Intensive	Machine-Intensive
2		Assembly Method	Assembly Method
3		(using data from part 1a)	(using data from part 1b)
4	Direct materials:		
5	8 helicopters x $40,000; $36,000 per helicopter	$320,000	$288,000
6	Direct-assembly labor:		
7	9,826 hrs.; 5,258 hrs. x $30/hr.	294,780	157,740
8	Indirect manufacturing costs		
9	Equipment related		
10	9,826 hrs. x $12/hr.; 5,258 hrs. x $45/hr.	117,912	236,610
11	Materials-handling related		
12	0.50 x $320,000; $288,000	160,000	144,000
13	Total assembly costs	$892,692	$826,350

The machine-intensive method's assembly costs are $66,342 lower than the labor-intensive method ($892,692 − $826,350).

Decision Points

The following question-and-answer format summarizes the chapter's learning objectives. Each decision presents a key question related to a learning objective. The guidelines are the answer to that question.

Decision	Guidelines
1. What assumptions are usually made when estimating a cost function?	The two assumptions frequently made in cost-behavior estimation are (a) changes in the level of a single activity explain changes in total costs and (b) cost behavior can adequately be approximated by a linear function of the activity level within the relevant range.
2. What is a linear cost function and what types of cost behavior can it represent?	A linear cost function is a cost function in which, within the relevant range, the graph of total costs based on the level of a single activity is a straight line. Linear cost functions can be described by a constant, *a*, which represents the estimate of the total cost component that, within the relevant range, does not vary with changes in the level of the activity; and a slope coefficient, *b*, which represents the estimate of the amount by which total costs change for each unit change in the level of the activity within the relevant range. Three types of linear cost functions are variable, fixed, and mixed (or semivariable).
3. What are the different methods that can be used to estimate a cost function?	Four methods for estimating cost functions are the industrial engineering method, the conference method, the account analysis method, and the quantitative analysis method (which includes the high-low method and the regression analysis method). If possible, the cost analyst should apply more than one method. Each method is a check on the others.
4. What are the steps to estimate a cost function using quantitative analysis?	There are six steps to estimate a cost function using quantitative analysis: (a) Choose the dependent variable; (b) identify the cost driver; (c) collect data on the dependent variable and the cost driver; (d) plot the data; (e) estimate the cost function; and (f) evaluate the cost driver of the estimated cost function. In most situations, working closely with operations managers, the cost analyst will cycle through these steps several times before identifying an acceptable cost function.
5. How should a company evaluate and choose cost drivers?	Three criteria for evaluating and choosing cost drivers are (a) economic plausibility, (b) goodness of fit, and (c) significance of independent variable.
6. What is a nonlinear cost function and how does it arise?	A nonlinear cost function is a cost function in which the graph of total costs based on the level of a single activity is not a straight line within the relevant range. Nonlinear costs can arise because of quantity discounts, step cost functions, and learning-curve effects.
7. What are two types of learning curve models that a company can use?	The learning curve is an example of a nonlinear cost function. Labor-hours per unit decline as units of production increase. In the cumulative average-time learning model, cumulative average-time per unit declines by a constant percentage each time the cumulative quantity of units produced doubles. In the incremental unit-time learning model, incremental unit time (the time needed to produce the last unit) declines by a constant percentage each time the cumulative quantity of units produced doubles. A company should use the model that better fits its observed labor-hour usage.
8. What are the common data problems a company must watch for when estimating costs?	The most difficult task in cost estimation is collecting high-quality, reliably measured data on the costs and the cost driver. Common problems include missing data, extreme values of observations, changes in technology, and distortions resulting from inflation.

APPENDIX: REGRESSION ANALYSIS

This appendix describes estimation of the regression equation, several commonly used regression statistics, and how to choose among cost functions that have been estimated by regression analysis. We use the data for Elegant Rugs presented in Exhibit 10-3 (p. 344) and displayed here again for easy reference.

Week	Cost Driver: Machine-Hours (*X*)	Indirect Manufacturing Labor Costs (*Y*)
1	68	$ 1,190
2	88	1,211
3	62	1,004
4	72	917
5	60	770
6	96	1,456
7	78	1,180
8	46	710
9	82	1,316
10	94	1,032
11	68	752
12	48	963
Total	862	$12,501

Estimating the Regression Line

The least-squares technique for estimating the regression line minimizes the sum of the squares of the vertical deviations from the data points to the estimated regression line (also called *residual term* in Exhibit 10-6, p. 348). The objective is to find the values of a and b in the linear cost function $y = a + bX$, where y is the *predicted* cost value as distinguished from the *observed* cost value, which we denote by Y. We wish to find the numerical values of a and b that minimize $\Sigma(Y - y)^2$, the sum of the squares of the vertical deviations between Y and y. Generally, these computations are done using software packages such as Excel. For the data in our example,[3] $a = \$300.98$ and $b = \$10.31$, so that the equation of the regression line is $y = \$300.98 + \$10.31X$.

[3] The formulae for a and b are:

$$a = \frac{(\Sigma Y)(\Sigma X^2) - (\Sigma X)(\Sigma XY)}{n(\Sigma X^2) - (\Sigma X)(\Sigma X)} \text{ and } b = \frac{n(\Sigma XY) - (\Sigma X)(\Sigma Y)}{n(\Sigma X^2) - (\Sigma X)(\Sigma X)}$$

where for the Elegant Rugs data in Exhibit 10-3,

n = number of data points = 12

ΣX = sum of the given X values = 68 + 88 + ... + 48 = 862

ΣX^2 = sum of squares of the X values = $(68)^2 + (88)^2 + \ldots + (48)^2$ = 4,624 + 7,744 + ... + 2,304 = 64,900

ΣY = sum of given Y values = 1,190 + 1,211 + ... + 963 = 12,501

ΣXY = sum of the amounts obtained by multiplying each of the given X values by the associated observed Y value = (68) (1,190) + (88)(1,211) + ... + (48) (963) = 80,920 + 106,568 + ... + 46,224 = 928,716

$$a = \frac{(12{,}501)(64{,}900) - (862)(928{,}716)}{12(64{,}900) - (862)(862)} = \$300.98$$

$$b = \frac{12(928{,}716) - (862)(12{,}501)}{12(64{,}900) - (862)(862)} = \$10.31$$

Goodness of Fit

Goodness of fit measures how well the predicted values, y, based on the cost driver, X, match actual cost observations, Y. The regression analysis method computes a measure of goodness of fit, called the coefficient of determination. The **coefficient of determination, r^2,** measures the percentage of variation in Y explained by X (the independent variable). That is, the coefficient of determination indicates the proportion of the variance of Y that is explained by the independent variable X. It is more convenient to express the coefficient of determination as 1 minus the proportion of total variance that is *not* explained by the independent variable—that is, 1 minus the ratio of unexplained variation to total variation. The unexplained variance arises because of differences between the actual values, Y, and the predicted values, y, which in the Elegant Rugs example is given by[4]

$$r^2 = 1 - \frac{\text{Unexplained variation}}{\text{Total variation}} = 1 - \frac{\Sigma(Y - y)^2}{\Sigma(Y - \overline{Y})^2} = 1 - \frac{290{,}824}{607{,}699} = 0.52$$

The calculations indicate that r^2 increases as the predicted values, y, more closely approximate the actual observations, Y. The range of r^2 is from 0 (implying no explanatory power) to 1 (implying perfect explanatory power). Generally, an r^2 of 0.30 or higher passes the goodness-of-fit test. However, do not rely exclusively on goodness of fit. It can lead to the indiscriminate inclusion of independent variables that increase r^2 but have no economic plausibility as cost drivers. *Goodness of fit has meaning only if the relationship between the cost drivers and costs is economically plausible.*

An alternative and related way to evaluate goodness of fit is to calculate the *standard error of the regression.* The **standard error of the regression** is the variance of the residuals. It is equal to

$$S = \sqrt{\frac{\Sigma(Y - y)^2}{\text{Degrees of freedom}}} = \sqrt{\frac{\Sigma(Y - y)^2}{n - 2}} = \sqrt{\frac{290{,}824}{12 - 2}} = \$170.54$$

Degrees of freedom equal the number of observations, 12, *minus* the number of coefficients estimated in the regression (in this case two, a and b). On average, actual Y and the predicted value, y, differ by \$170.54. For comparison, the average value of $Y = \overline{Y}$ is \$1,041.75. The smaller the standard error of the regression, the better the fit and the better the predictions for different values of X.

Significance of Independent Variables

Do changes in the economically plausible independent variable result in significant changes in the dependent variable? Or alternatively stated, is the slope coefficient, b = \$10.31, of the regression line statistically significant (that is, different from \$0)? Recall, for example, that in the regression of number of machine-hours and indirect manufacturing labor costs in the Elegant Rugs illustration, b is estimated from a sample of 12 weekly observations. The estimate, b, is subject to random factors, as are all sample statistics. That is, a different sample of 12 data points would undoubtedly give a different estimate of b. The **standard error of the estimated coefficient** indicates how much the estimated value, b, is likely to be affected by random factors. The t-value of the b coefficient measures how large the value of the estimated coefficient is relative to its standard error.

The cutoff t-value for making inferences about the b coefficient is a function of the number of degrees of freedom, the significance level and whether it is a one-sided or two-sided test. A 5% level of significance indicates that there is less than a 5% probability that

[4] From footnote 3, $\Sigma Y = 12{,}501$ and $\overline{Y} = 12{,}501 \div 12 = 1{,}041.75$

$$\Sigma(Y - \overline{Y})^2 = (1{,}190 - 1{,}041.75)^2 + (1{,}211 - 1{,}041.75)^2 + \ldots + (963 - 1{,}041.75)^2 = 607{,}699$$

Each value of X generates a predicted value of y. For example, in week 1, y = \$300.98 + (\$10.31 × 68) = \$1002.06; in week 2, y = \$300.98 + (\$10.31 × 88) = \$1,208.26; and in week 12, y = \$300.98 + (\$10.31 × 48) = \$795.86.

$$\Sigma(Y - y)^2 = (1{,}190 - 1{,}002.06)^2 + (1{,}211 - 1208.26)^2 + \ldots + (963 - 795.86)^2 = 290{,}824$$

random factors could have affected the coefficient *b*. A two-sided test assumes that random factors could have caused the coefficient to be either greater than \$10.31 or less than \$10.31 with equal probability. At a 5% level of significance, this means that there is less than a 2.5% (5% ÷ 2) probability that random factors could have caused the coefficient to be greater than \$10.31 and less than 2.5% probability that random factors could have caused the coefficient to be less than \$10.31. Under the expectation that the coefficient of *b* is positive, a one-sided test at the 5% level of significance assumes that there is less than 5% probability that random factors would have caused the coefficient to be less than \$10.31. The cutoff *t*-value at the 5% significance level and 10 degrees of freedom for a two-sided test is 2.228. If there were more observations and 60 degrees of freedom, the cutoff *t*-value would be 2.00 at a 5% significance level for a two-sided test.

The *t*-value (called *t* Stat in the Excel output) for the slope coefficient *b* is the value of the estimated coefficient, \$10.31 ÷ the standard error of the estimated coefficient \$3.12 = 3.30, which exceeds the cutoff *t*-value of 2.228. In other words, a relationship exists between the independent variable, machine-hours, and the dependent variable that cannot be attributed to random chance alone. Exhibit 10-14 shows a convenient format (in Excel) for summarizing the regression results for number of machine-hours and indirect manufacturing labor costs.

An alternative way to test that the coefficient *b* is significantly different from zero is in terms of a *confidence interval*: There is less than a 5% chance that the true value of the machine-hours coefficient lies outside the range \$10.31 ± (2.228 × \$3.12), or \$10.31 ± \$6.95, or from \$3.36 to \$17.26. Because 0 does not appear in the confidence interval, we can conclude that changes in the number of machine-hours do affect indirect manufacturing labor costs. Similarly, using data from Exhibit 10-14, the *t*-value for the constant term *a* is \$300.98 ÷ \$229.75 = 1.31, which is less than 2.228. This *t*-value indicates that, within the relevant range, the constant term is *not* significantly different from zero. The Durbin-Watson statistic in Exhibit 10-14 will be discussed in the following section.

Specification Analysis of Estimation Assumptions

Specification analysis is the testing of the assumptions of regression analysis. If the assumptions of (1) linearity within the relevant range, (2) constant variance of residuals, (3) independence of residuals, and (4) normality of residuals all hold, then the simple regression procedures give reliable estimates of coefficient values. This section provides a brief overview of specification analysis. When these assumptions are not satisfied, more-complex regression procedures are necessary to obtain the best estimates.[5]

1. **Linearity within the relevant range.** A common assumption—and one that appears to be reasonable in many business applications—is that a linear relationship exists

Exhibit 10-14 Simple Regression Results with Indirect Manufacturing Labor Costs as Dependent Variable and Machine-Hours as Independent Variable (Cost Driver) for Elegant Rugs

File Edit View Insert Format Tools Data Window Help

	A	B	C	D	E	F
1		**Coefficients**	**Standard Error**	***t* Stat**		= Coefficient/Standard Error
2		**(1)**	**(2)**	**(3) = (1) ÷ (2)**		= B3/C3
3	Intercept	\$300.98	\$229.75	1.31 →		= 300.98/229.75
4	Independent Variable: Machine-Hours (*X*)	\$ 10.31	\$ 3.12	3.30		
5						
6	**Regression Statistics**					
7	R Square	0.52				
8	Durbin-Watson Statistic	2.05				

[5] For details see, for example, W. H. Greene, *Econometric Analysis*, 4th ed. (Upper Saddle River, NJ: Prentice Hall, 2000).

between the independent variable X and the dependent variable Y within the relevant range. If a linear regression model is used to estimate a nonlinear relationship, however, the coefficient estimates obtained will be inaccurate.

When there is only one independent variable, the easiest way to check for linearity is to study the data plotted in a scatter diagram, a step that often is unwisely skipped. Exhibit 10-6 (p. 348) presents a scatter diagram for the indirect manufacturing labor costs and machine-hours variables of Elegant Rugs shown in Exhibit 10-3 (p. 344). The scatter diagram reveals that linearity appears to be a reasonable assumption for these data.

The learning-curve models discussed in this chapter (pp. 353–358) are examples of nonlinear cost functions. Costs increase when the level of production increases, but by lesser amounts than would occur with a linear cost function. In this case, the analyst should estimate a nonlinear cost function that incorporates learning effects.

2. **Constant variance of residuals.** The vertical deviation of the observed value Y from the regression line estimate y is called the *residual term, disturbance term*, or *error term*, $u = Y - y$. The assumption of constant variance implies that the residual terms are unaffected by the level of the cost driver. The assumption also implies that there is a uniform scatter, or dispersion, of the data points about the regression line as in Exhibit 10-15, Panel A. This assumption is likely to be violated, for example, in cross-sectional estimation of costs in operations of different sizes. For example, suppose Elegant Rugs has production areas of varying sizes. The company collects data from these different production areas to estimate the relationship between machine-hours and indirect manufacturing labor costs. It is very possible that the residual terms in this regression will be larger for the larger production areas that have higher machine-hours and higher indirect manufacturing labor costs. There would not be a uniform scatter of data points about the regression line (see Exhibit 10-15, Panel B). Constant variance is also known as *homoscedasticity.* Violation of this assumption is called *heteroscedasticity*.

   Heteroscedasticity does not affect the accuracy of the regression estimates a and b. It does, however, reduce the reliability of the estimates of the standard errors and thus affects the precision with which inferences about the population parameters can be drawn from the regression estimates.

3. **Independence of residuals.** The assumption of independence of residuals is that the residual term for any one observation is not related to the residual term for any other observation. The problem of *serial correlation* (also called *autocorrelation*) in the residuals arises when there is a systematic pattern in the sequence of residuals such that the residual in observation n conveys information about the residuals in observations $n + 1$, $n + 2$, and so on. Consider another production cell at Elegant Rugs that has, over a 20-week period, seen an increase in production and hence machine-hours. Exhibit 10-16 Panel B is a scatter diagram of machine-hours and indirect manufacturing labor costs. Observe the systematic pattern of the residuals in Panel B—positive residuals for extreme (high and low) quantities of machine-hours and negative residuals for moderate quantities of machine-hours. One reason for this observed pattern at low values of the cost driver is the "stickiness" of costs. When machine hours are below 50 hours, indirect manufacturing labor costs do not decline. When machine-hours increase over time as production is ramped up, indirect manufacturing labor costs increase more as managers at Elegant Rugs struggle to manage the higher volume. How would the plot of residuals look if there were no auto-correlation? Like the plot in Exhibit 10-16, Panel A that shows no pattern in the residuals.

   Like nonconstant variance of residuals, serial correlation does not affect the accuracy of the regression estimates a and b. It does, however, affect the standard errors of the coefficients, which in turn affect the precision with which inferences about the population parameters can be drawn from the regression estimates.

   The Durbin-Watson statistic is one measure of serial correlation in the estimated residuals. For samples of 10 to 20 observations, a Durbin-Watson statistic in the 1.10-to-2.90 range indicates that the residuals are independent. The Durbin-Watson statistic for the regression results of Elegant Rugs in Exhibit 10-14 is 2.05. Therefore,

Exhibit 10-15 Constant Variance of Residuals Assumption

PANEL A: Constant Variance (Uniform Scatter of Data Points Around Regression Line)

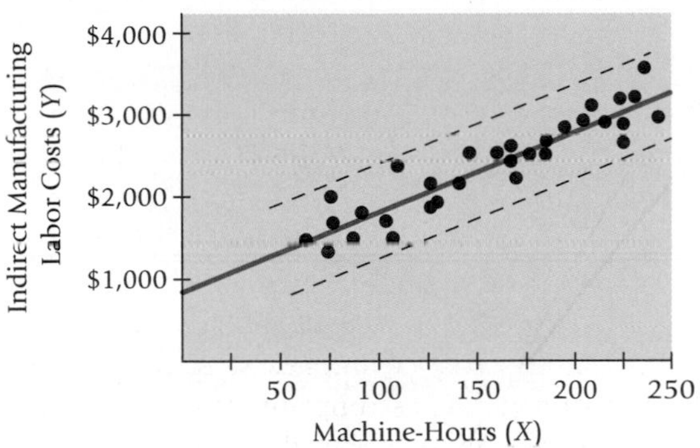

PANEL B: Nonconstant Variance (Higher Outputs Have Larger Residuals)

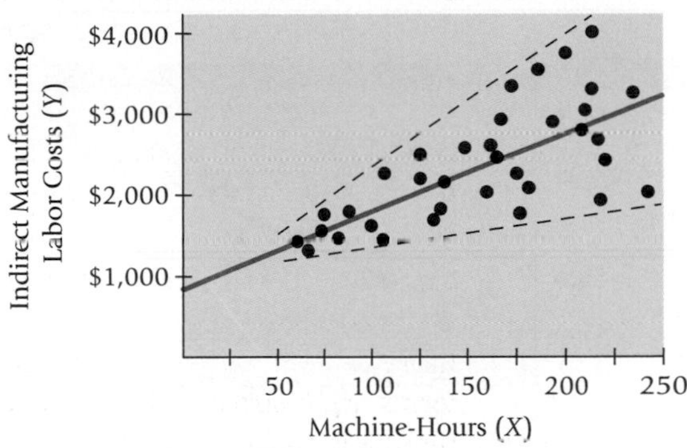

an assumption of independence in the estimated residuals is reasonable for this regression model.

4. **Normality of residuals.** The normality of residuals assumption means that the residuals are distributed normally around the regression line. The normality of residuals assumption is frequently satisfied when using regression analysis on real cost data. Even when the assumption does not hold, accountants can still generate accurate estimates based on the regression equation, but the resulting confidence interval around these estimates is likely to be inaccurate.

Using Regression Output to Choose Cost Drivers of Cost Functions

Consider the two choices of cost drivers we described earlier in this chapter for indirect manufacturing labor costs (y):

$$y = a + (b \times \text{Number of machine-hours})$$

$$y = a + (b \times \text{Number of direct manufacturing labor-hours})$$

Exhibits 10-6 and 10-8 show plots of the data for the two regressions. Exhibit 10-14 reports regression results for the cost function using number of machine-hours as the independent variable. Exhibit 10-17 presents comparable regression results (in Excel) for the cost function using number of direct manufacturing labor-hours as the independent variable.

On the basis of the material presented in this appendix, which regression is better? Exhibit 10-18 compares these two cost functions in a systematic way. For several criteria, the cost function based on machine-hours is preferable to the cost function based on direct manufacturing labor-hours. The economic plausibility criterion is especially important.

Do not always assume that any one cost function will perfectly satisfy all the criteria in Exhibit 10-18. A cost analyst must often make a choice among "imperfect" cost functions, in the sense that the data of any particular cost function will not perfectly meet one or more of the assumptions underlying regression analysis. For example, both of the cost functions in Exhibit 10-18 are imperfect because, as stated in the section on specification analysis of estimation assumptions, inferences drawn from only 12 observations are not reliable.

Exhibit 10-16 Independence of Residuals Assumption

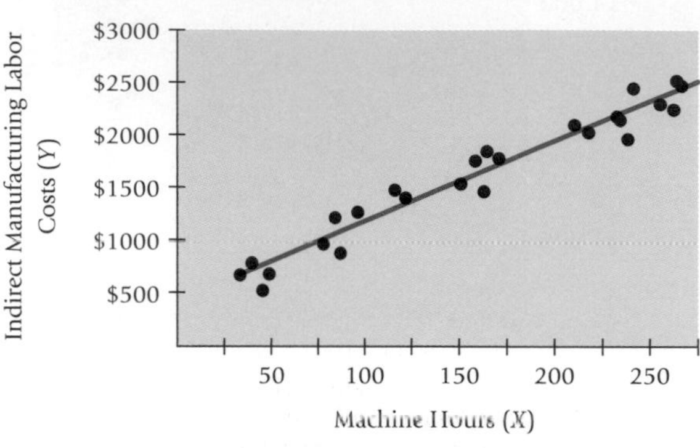

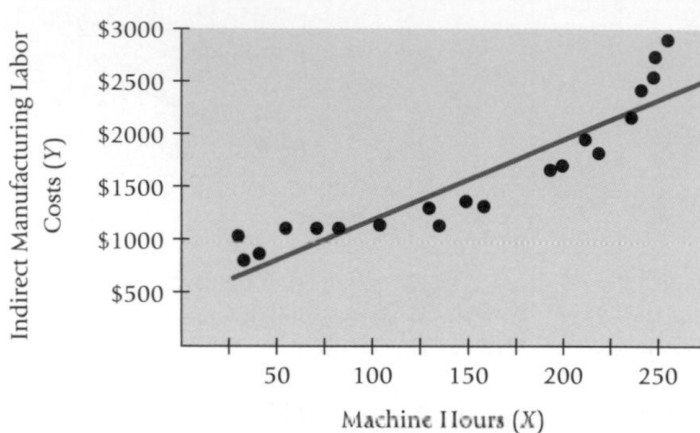

Exhibit 10-17 Simple Regression Results with Indirect Manufacturing Labor Costs as Dependent Variable and Direct Manufacturing Labor-Hours as Independent Variable (Cost Driver) for Elegant Rugs

File Edit View Insert Format Tools Data Window Help

	A	B	C	D	E	F	G	H
1		**Coefficients**	**Standard Error**	***t* Stat**				
2		**(1)**	**(2)**	**(3) = (1) ÷ (2)**				
3	Intercept	$744.67	$217.61	3.42				
4	Independent Variable: Direct Manufacturing Labor-Hours (*X*)	$ 7.72	$ 5.40	1.43 →		= Coefficient/Standard Error = B4/C4 = 7.72/5.40		
5								
6	**Regression Statistics**							
7	R Square	0.17						
8	Durbin-Watson Statistic	2.26						

Multiple Regression and Cost Hierarchies

In some cases, a satisfactory estimation of a cost function may be based on only one independent variable, such as number of machine-hours. In many cases, however, basing the estimation on more than one independent variable (that is, *multiple regression*) is more economically plausible and improves accuracy. The most widely used equations to express relationships between two or more independent variables and a dependent variable are linear in the form

$$y = a + b_1X_1 + b_2X_2 + \ldots + u$$

where,

y = Cost to be predicted
$X_1, X_2, \ldots$ = Independent variables on which the prediction is to be based
$a, b_1, b_2, \ldots$ = Estimated coefficients of the regression model
u = Residual term that includes the net effect of other factors not in the model as well as measurement errors in the dependent and independent variables

Criterion	Cost Function 1: Machine-Hours as Independent Variable	Cost Function 2: Direct Manufacturing Labor-Hours as Independent Variable
Economic plausibility	A positive relationship between indirect manufacturing labor costs (technical support labor) and machine-hours is economically plausible in Elegant Rugs's highly automated plant	A positive relationship between indirect manufacturing labor costs and direct manufacturing labor-hours is economically plausible, but less so than machine-hours in Elegant Rugs's highly automated plant on a week-to-week basis.
Goodness of fit[a]	$r^2 = 0.52$; standard error of regression = \$170.50. Excellent goodness of fit.	$r^2 = 0.17$; standard error of regression = \$224.60. Poor goodness of fit.
Significance of independent variable(s)	The *t*-value of 3.30 is significant at the 0.05 level.	The *t*-value of 1.43 is not significant at the 0.05 level.
Specification analysis of estimation assumptions	Plot of the data indicates that assumptions of linearity, constant variance, independence of residuals, (Durbin-Watson statistic = 2.05), and normality of residuals hold, but inferences drawn from only 12 observations are not reliable.	Plot of the data indicates that assumptions of linearity, constant variance, independence of residuals (Durbin-Watson statistic = 2.26) and normality of residuals hold, but inferences drawn from only 12 observations are not reliable.

[a]If the number of observations available to estimate the machine-hours regression differs from the number of observations available to estimate the direct manufacturing labor-hours regression, an *adjusted* r^2 can be calculated to take this difference (in degrees of freedom) into account. Programs such as Excel calculate and present *adjusted* r^2.

Exhibit 10-18

Comparison of Alternative Cost Functions for Indirect Manufacturing Labor Costs Estimated with Simple Regression for Elegant Rugs

Example Consider the Elegant Rugs data in Exhibit 10-19. The company's ABC analysis indicates that indirect manufacturing labor costs include large amounts incurred for setup and changeover costs when a new batch of carpets is started. Management believes that in addition to number of machine-hours (an output unit-level cost driver), indirect manufacturing labor costs are also affected by the number of batches of carpet produced during each week (a batch-level driver). Elegant Rugs estimates the relationship between two independent variables, number of machine-hours and number of production batches of carpet manufactured during the week, and indirect manufacturing labor costs.

Exhibit 10-20 presents results (in Excel) for the following multiple regression model, using data in columns B, C, and E of Exhibit 10-19:

$$y = \$42.58 + \$7.60X_1 + \$37.77X_2$$

where X_1 is the number of machine-hours and X_2 is the number of production batches. It is economically plausible that both number of machine-hours and number of production batches would help explain variations in indirect manufacturing labor costs at Elegant Rugs. The r^2 of 0.52 for the simple regression using number of machine-hours (Exhibit 10-14) increases to 0.72 with the multiple regression in Exhibit 10-20. The *t*-values suggest that the independent variable coefficients of both number of machine-hours (\$7.60) and number of production batches (\$37.77) are significantly different from zero ($t = 2.74$ is the *t*-value for number of machine-hours, and $t = 2.48$ is the *t*-value for number of production batches compared to the cut-off *t*-value of 2.26). The multiple regression model in Exhibit 10-20 satisfies both economic plausibility and statistical criteria, and it explains much greater variation (that is, r^2 of 0.72 versus r^2 of 0.52) in indirect manufacturing labor costs than the simple

Exhibit 10-19

Weekly Indirect Manufacturing Labor Costs, Machine-Hours, Direct Manufacturing Labor-Hours, and Number of Production Batches for Elegant Rugs

	A	B	C	D	E
1	Week	Machine-Hours (X_1)	Number of Production Batches (X_2)	Direct Manufacturing Labor-Hours	Indirect Manufacturing Labor Costs (Y)
2	1	68	12	30	$ 1,190
3	2	88	15	35	1,211
4	3	62	13	36	1,004
5	4	72	11	20	917
6	5	60	10	47	770
7	6	96	12	45	1,456
8	7	78	17	44	1,180
9	8	46	7	38	710
10	9	82	14	70	1,316
11	10	94	12	30	1,032
12	11	68	7	29	752
13	12	48	14	38	963
14	Total	862	144	462	$12,501
15					

regression model using only number of machine-hours as the independent variable.[6] The standard error of the regression equation that includes number of batches as an independent variable is

$$\sqrt{\frac{\Sigma(Y - y)^2}{n - 3}} = \sqrt{\frac{170{,}156}{9}} = \$137.50$$

which is lower than the standard error of the regression with only machine-hours as the independent variable, $170.50. That is, even though adding a variable reduces the degrees of freedom in the denominator, it substantially improves fit so that the numerator, $\Sigma(Y - y)^2$, decreases even more. Number of machine-hours and number of production batches are both important cost drivers of indirect manufacturing labor costs at Elegant Rugs.

In Exhibit 10-20, the slope coefficients—$7.60 for number of machine-hours and $37.77 for number of production batches—measure the change in indirect manufacturing labor costs associated with a unit change in an independent variable (assuming that the other independent variable is held constant). For example, indirect manufacturing labor costs increase by $37.77 when one more production batch is added, assuming that the number of machine-hours is held constant.

---

[6] Adding another variable always increases r^2. The question is whether adding another variable increases r^2 sufficiently. One way to get insight into this question is to calculate an adjusted r^2 as follows:

Adjusted $r^2 = 1 - (1 - r^2)\frac{n-1}{n-p-1}$, where n is the number of observations and p is the number of coefficients estimated. In the model with only machine-hours as the independent variable, Adjusted $r^2 = 1 - (1 - 0.52)\frac{12-1}{12-2-1} = 0.41$. In the model with both machine-hours and number of batches as independent variables, Adjusted $r^2 = 1-(1-0.72)\frac{12-1}{12-3-1} = 0.62$. Adjusted r^2 does not have the same interpretation as r^2 but the increase in adjusted r^2 when number of batches is added as an independent variable suggests that adding this variable significantly improves the fit of the model in a way that more than compensates for the degree of freedom lost by estimating another coefficient.

Exhibit 10-20 Multiple Regression Results with Indirect Manufacturing Labor Costs and Two Independent Variables of Cost Drivers (Machine-Hours and Production Batches) for Elegant Rugs

File Edit View Insert Format Tools Data Window Help

	A	B	C	D	E	F
1		**Coefficients**	**Standard Error**	**t Stat**		
2		**(1)**	**(2)**	**(3) = (1) ÷ (2)**		
3	Intercept	$42.58	$213.91	0.20		
4	Independent variable 1: Machine-Hours (*X1*)	$ 7.60	$ 2.77	2.74 →		= Coefficient/Standard Error = B4/C4 = 7.60/2.77
5	Independent variable 2: Number of production batches (*X2*)	$37.77	$ 15.25	2.48		
6						
7	**Regression Statistics**					
8	R Square	0.72				
9	Durbin-Watson Statistic	2.49				

An alternative approach would create two separate cost pools for indirect manufacturing labor costs: one for costs related to number of machine-hours and another for costs related to number of production batches. Elegant Rugs would then estimate the relationship between the cost driver and the costs in each cost pool. The difficult task under this approach is to properly subdivide the indirect manufacturing labor costs into the two cost pools.

Multicollinearity

A major concern that arises with multiple regression is multicollinearity. **Multicollinearity** exists when two or more independent variables are highly correlated with each other. Generally, users of regression analysis believe that a *coefficient of correlation* between independent variables greater than 0.70 indicates multicollinearity. Multicollinearity increases the standard errors of the coefficients of the individual variables. That is, variables that are economically and statistically significant will appear not to be significantly different from zero.

The matrix of correlation coefficients of the different variables described in Exhibit 10-19 are:

	Indirect manufacturing labor costs	**Machine-hours**	**Number of production batches**	**Direct manufacturing labor-hours**
Indirect manufacturing labor costs	1			
Machine-hours	0.72	1		
Number of production batches	0.69	0.4	1	
Direct manufacturing labor-hours	0.41	0.12	0.31	1

These results indicate that multiple regressions using any pair of the independent variables in Exhibit 10-19 are not likely to encounter multicollinearity problems.

When multicollinearity exists, try to obtain new data that do not suffer from multicollinearity problems. Do not drop an independent variable (cost driver) that should be included in a model because it is correlated with another independent variable. Omitting such a variable will cause the estimated coefficient of the independent variable included in the model to be biased away from its true value.

TERMS TO LEARN

This chapter and the Glossary at the end of this book contain definitions of:

account analysis method (**p. 343**)
coefficient of determination (r^2) (**p. 364**)
conference method (**p. 342**)
constant (**p. 338**)
cost estimation (**p. 340**)
cost function (**p. 337**)
cost predictions (**p. 340**)
cumulative average-time learning model (**p. 355**)
dependent variable (**p. 344**)
experience curve (**p. 354**)
high-low method (**p. 346**)
incremental unit-time learning model (**p. 355**)
independent variable (**p. 344**)
industrial engineering method (**p. 342**)
intercept (**p. 338**)
learning curve (**p. 353**)
linear cost function (**p. 338**)
mixed cost (**p. 338**)
multicollinearity (**p. 371**)
multiple regression (**p. 348**)
nonlinear cost function (**p. 352**)
regression analysis (**p. 348**)
residual term (**p. 348**)
semivariable cost (**p. 338**)
simple regression (**p. 348**)
slope coefficient (**p. 338**)
specification analysis (**p. 365**)
standard error of the estimated coefficient (**p. 364**)
standard error of the regression (**p. 364**)
step cost function (**p. 353**)
work-measurement method (**p. 342**)

ASSIGNMENT MATERIAL

Questions

10-1 What two assumptions are frequently made when estimating a cost function?

10-2 Describe three alternative linear cost functions.

10-3 What is the difference between a linear and a nonlinear cost function? Give an example of each type of cost function.

10-4 "High correlation between two variables means that one is the cause and the other is the effect." Do you agree? Explain.

10-5 Name four approaches to estimating a cost function.

10-6 Describe the conference method for estimating a cost function. What are two advantages of this method?

10-7 Describe the account analysis method for estimating a cost function.

10-8 List the six steps in estimating a cost function on the basis of an analysis of a past cost relationship. Which step is typically the most difficult for the cost analyst?

10-9 When using the high-low method, should you base the high and low observations on the dependent variable or on the cost driver?

10-10 Describe three criteria for evaluating cost functions and choosing cost drivers.

10-11 Define learning curve. Outline two models that can be used when incorporating learning into the estimation of cost functions.

10-12 Discuss four frequently encountered problems when collecting cost data on variables included in a cost function.

10-13 What are the four key assumptions examined in specification analysis in the case of simple regression?

10-14 "All the independent variables in a cost function estimated with regression analysis are cost drivers." Do you agree? Explain.

10-15 "Multicollinearity exists when the dependent variable and the independent variable are highly correlated." Do you agree? Explain.

Exercises

10-16 Estimating a cost function. The controller of the Ijiri Company wants you to estimate a cost function from the following two observations in a general ledger account called Maintenance:

Month	Machine-Hours	Maintenance Costs Incurred
January	6,000	$4,000
February	10,000	5,400

Required

1. Estimate the cost function for maintenance.
2. Can the constant in the cost function be used as an estimate of fixed maintenance cost per month? Explain.

10-17 Identifying variable-, fixed-, and mixed-cost functions. The Pacific Corporation operates car rental agencies at more than 20 airports. Customers can choose from one of three contracts for car rentals of one day or less:

- Contract 1: $50 for the day
- Contract 2: $30 for the day plus $0.20 per mile traveled
- Contract 3: $1 per mile traveled

Required

1. Plot separate graphs for each of the three contracts, with costs on the vertical axis and miles traveled on the horizontal axis.
2. Express each contract as a linear cost function of the form $y = a + bX$.
3. Identify each contract as a variable-, fixed-, or mixed-cost function.

10-18 Various cost-behavior patterns. (CPA, adapted) Select the graph that matches the numbered manufacturing cost data. Indicate by letter which graph best fits the situation or item described.

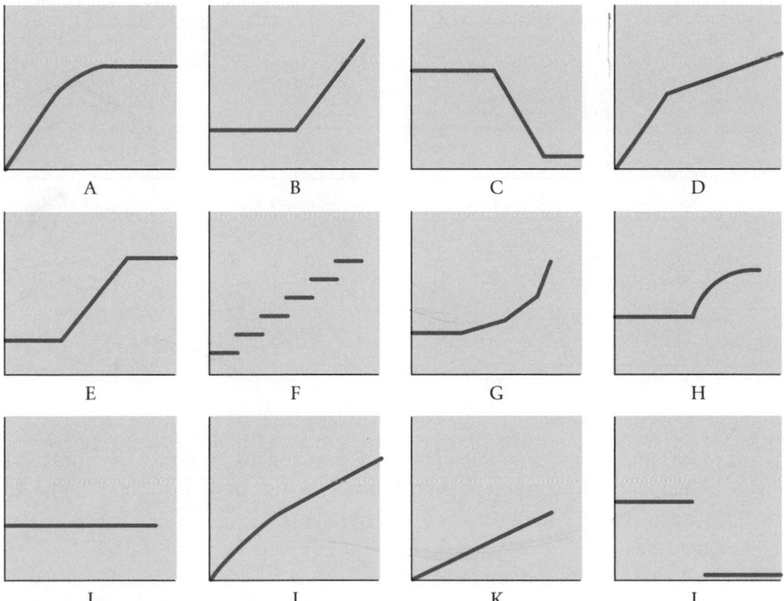

The vertical axes of the graphs represent total cost, and the horizontal axes represent units produced during a calendar year. In each case, the zero point of dollars and production is at the intersection of the two axes. The graphs may be used more than once.

Required

1. Annual depreciation of equipment, where the amount of depreciation charged is computed by the machine-hours method.
2. Electricity bill—a flat fixed charge, plus a variable cost after a certain number of kilowatt-hours are used, in which the quantity of kilowatt-hours used varies proportionately with quantity of units produced.
3. City water bill, which is computed as follows:

First 1,000,000 gallons or less	$1,000 flat fee
Next 10,000 gallons	$0.003 per gallon used
Next 10,000 gallons	$0.006 per gallon used
Next 10,000 gallons	$0.009 per gallon used
and so on	and so on

   The gallons of water used vary proportionately with the quantity of production output.
4. Cost of direct materials, where direct material cost per unit produced decreases with each pound of material used (for example, if 1 pound is used, the cost is $10; if 2 pounds are used, the cost is $19.98; if 3 pounds are used, the cost is $29.94), with a minimum cost per unit of $9.20.
5. Annual depreciation of equipment, where the amount is computed by the straight-line method. When the depreciation schedule was prepared, it was anticipated that the obsolescence factor would be greater than the wear-and-tear factor.

6. Rent on a manufacturing plant donated by the city, where the agreement calls for a fixed-fee payment unless 200,000 labor-hours are worked, in which case no rent is paid.
7. Salaries of repair personnel, where one person is needed for every 1,000 machine-hours or less (that is, 0 to 1,000 hours requires one person, 1,001 to 2,000 hours requires two people, and so on).
8. Cost of direct materials used (assume no quantity discounts).
9. Rent on a manufacturing plant donated by the county, where the agreement calls for rent of $100,000 to be reduced by $1 for each direct manufacturing labor-hour worked in excess of 200,000 hours, but a minimum rental fee of $20,000 must be paid.

10-19 Matching graphs with descriptions of cost and revenue behavior. (D. Green, adapted) Given here are a number of graphs.

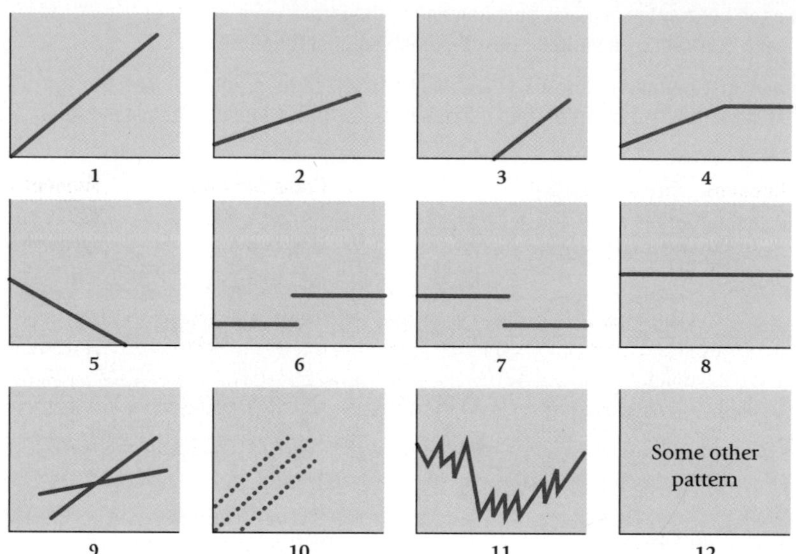

The horizontal axis represents the units produced over the year and the vertical axis represents total cost or revenues. Indicate by number which graph best fits the situation or item described. Some graphs may be used more than once; some may not apply to any of the situations.

a. Direct material costs
b. Supervisors' salaries for one shift and two shifts
c. A cost-volume-profit graph
d. Mixed costs—for example, car rental fixed charge plus a rate per mile driven
e. Depreciation of plant, computed on a straight-line basis
f. Data supporting the use of a variable-cost rate, such as manufacturing labor cost of $14 per unit produced
g. Incentive bonus plan that pays managers $0.10 for every unit produced above some level of production
h. Interest expense on $2 million borrowed at a fixed rate of interest

10-20 Account analysis method. Lorenzo operates a car wash. Incoming cars are put on an automatic conveyor belt. Cars are washed as the conveyor belt carries them from the start station to the finish station. After a car moves off the conveyor belt, it is dried manually. Workers then clean and vacuum the inside of the car. Lorenzo serviced 80,000 cars in 2009. Lorenzo reports the following costs for 2009.

Account Description	Costs
Car wash labor	$260,000
Soap, cloth, and supplies	42,000
Water	38,000
Electric power to move conveyor belt	72,000
Depreciation	64,000
Salaries	46,000

Required

1. Classify each account as variable or fixed with respect to the number of cars washed. Explain.
2. Suppose Lorenzo washed 90,000 cars in 2009. Use the cost classification you developed in requirement 1 to estimate Lorenzo's total costs in 2009. Depreciation is computed on a straight-line basis.

10-21 Account analysis. Raymondo's Restaurant wants to find an equation to estimate monthly utility costs. Raymondo's has only been in business for one month, January 2008, and has the following information for utilities:

a. Electricity is billed by kilowatt hour. According to its first bill, Raymondo's paid $573 for 3,000 kilowatt hours in January.

b. Raymondo's contract with Waste Management for garbage pickup has Raymondo's paying $270 once a quarter.

c. Raymondo's phone contract includes a flat monthly fee of $20 and an additional charge of $0.03 per call. Raymondo's made 1,200 calls in January.

Required

1. Which of the above costs is variable? Fixed? Mixed? Explain.
2. Combine the information above to get a utility cost function for January.
3. If Raymondo's expects to use 4,000 kilowatt hours of electricity in February, and makes the same number of calls as in January, estimate total utilities costs for February.

10-22 Account analysis method. Gower, Inc., a manufacturer of plastic products, reports the following manufacturing costs and account analysis classification for the year ended December 31, 2009.

Account	Classification	Amount
Direct materials	All variable	$300,000
Direct manufacturing labor	All variable	225,000
Power	All variable	37,500
Supervision labor	20% variable	56,250
Materials-handling labor	50% variable	60,000
Maintenance labor	40% variable	75,000
Depreciation	0% variable	95,000
Rent, property taxes, and administration	0% variable	100,000

Gower, Inc., produced 75,000 units of product in 2009. Gower's management is estimating costs for 2010 on the basis of 2009 numbers. The following additional information is available for 2010.

a. Direct materials prices in 2010 are expected to increase by 5% compared with 2009.

b. Under the terms of the labor contract, direct manufacturing labor wage rates are expected to increase by 10% in 2010 compared with 2009.

c. Power rates and wage rates for supervision, materials handling, and maintenance are not expected to change from 2009 to 2010.

d. Depreciation costs are expected to increase by 5%, and rent, property taxes, and administration costs are expected to increase by 7%.

e. Gower expects to manufacture and sell 80,000 units in 2010.

Required

1. Prepare a schedule of variable, fixed, and total manufacturing costs for each account category in 2010. Estimate total manufacturing costs for 2010.
2. Calculate Gower's total manufacturing cost per unit in 2009, and estimate total manufacturing cost per unit in 2010.
3. How can you obtain better estimates of fixed and variable costs? Why would these better estimates be useful to Gower?

10-23 Estimating a cost function, high-low method. Reisen Travel offers helicopter service from suburban towns to John F. Kennedy International Airport in New York City. Each of its 10 helicopters makes between 1,000 and 2,000 round-trips per year. The records indicate that a helicopter that has made 1,000 round-trips in the year incurs an average operating cost of $350 per round-trip, and one that has made 2,000 round-trips in the year incurs an average operating cost of $300 per round-trip.

Required

1. Using the high-low method, estimate the linear relationship $y = a + bX$, where y is the total annual operating cost of a helicopter and X is the number of round-trips it makes to JFK airport during the year.
2. Give examples of costs that would be included in *a* and in *b*.
3. If Reisen Travel expects each helicopter to make, on average, 1,200 round-trips in the coming year, what should its estimated operating budget for the helicopter fleet be?

10-24 Estimating a cost function, high-low method. Laurie Daley is examining customer-service costs in the southern region of Capitol Products. Capitol Products has more than 200 separate electrical products that are sold with a 6-month guarantee of full repair or replacement with a new product. When a product is returned by a customer, a service report is prepared. This service report includes details of the problem and the time and cost of resolving the problem. Weekly data for the most recent 10-week period are:

Week	Customer-Service Department Costs	Number of Service Reports
1	$13,845	201
2	20,624	276
3	12,941	122
4	18,452	386
5	14,843	274
6	21,890	436
7	16,831	321
8	21,429	328
9	18,267	243
10	16,832	161

Required

1. Plot the relationship between customer-service costs and number of service reports. Is the relationship economically plausible?
2. Use the high-low method to compute the cost function, relating customer-service costs to the number of service reports.
3. What variables, in addition to number of service reports, might be cost drivers of weekly customer-service costs of Capitol Products?

10-25 Linear cost approximation. Terry Lawler, managing director of the Memphis Consulting Group, is examining how overhead costs behave with changes in monthly professional labor-hours billed to clients. Assume the following historical data:

Total Overhead Costs	Professional Labor-Hours Billed to Clients
$340,000	3,000
400,000	4,000
435,000	5,000
477,000	6,000
529,000	7,000
587,000	8,000

Required

1. Compute the linear cost function, relating total overhead costs to professional labor-hours, using the representative observations of 4,000 and 7,000 hours. Plot the linear cost function. Does the constant component of the cost function represent the fixed overhead costs of the Memphis Consulting Group? Why?
2. What would be the predicted total overhead costs for (a) 5,000 hours and (b) 8,000 hours using the cost function estimated in requirement 1? Plot the predicted costs and actual costs for 5,000 and 8,000 hours.
3. Lawler had a chance to accept a special job that would have boosted professional labor-hours from 4,000 to 5,000 hours. Suppose Lawler, guided by the linear cost function, rejected this job because it would have brought a total increase in contribution margin of $38,000, before deducting the predicted increase in total overhead cost, $43,000. What is the total contribution margin actually forgone?

10-26 Cost-volume-profit and regression analysis. Garvin Corporation manufactures a children's bicycle, model CT8. Garvin currently manufactures the bicycle frame. During 2009, Garvin made 30,000 frames at a total cost of $900,000. Ryan Corporation has offered to supply as many frames as Garvin wants at a cost of $28.50 per frame. Garvin anticipates needing 36,000 frames each year for the next few years.

Required

1. **a.** What is the average cost of manufacturing a bicycle frame in 2009? How does it compare to Ryan's offer?
   b. Can Garvin use the answer in requirement 1a to determine the cost of manufacturing 36,000 bicycle frames? Explain.
2. Garvin's cost analyst uses annual data from past years to estimate the following regression equation with total manufacturing costs of the bicycle frame as the dependent variable and bicycle frames produced as the independent variable:

$$y = \$432{,}000 + \$15X$$

   During the years used to estimate the regression equation, the production of bicycle frames varied from 28,000 to 36,000. Using this equation, estimate how much it would cost Garvin to manufacture 36,000 bicycle frames. How much more or less costly is it to manufacture the frames rather than to acquire them from Ryan?
3. What other information would you need to be confident that the equation in requirement 2 accurately predicts the cost of manufacturing bicycle frames?

10-27 Regression analysis, service company. (CMA, adapted) Bob Jones owns a catering company that prepares food and beverages for banquets and parties. For a standard party the cost on a per-person basis is:

Food and beverages	$15
Labor (0.5 hour × $10 per hour)	5
Overhead (0.5 hour × $14 per hour)	7
Total cost per person	$27

Jones is quite certain about his estimates of the food, beverages, and labor costs but is not as comfortable with the overhead estimate. The overhead estimate was based on the actual data for the past 12 months, which are presented here. These data indicate that overhead costs vary with the direct labor-hours used. The $14 estimate was determined by dividing total overhead costs for the 12 months by total labor-hours.

Month	Labor-Hours	Overhead Costs
January	2,500	$ 55,000
February	2,700	59,000
March	3,000	60,000
April	4,200	64,000
May	7,500	77,000
June	5,500	71,000
July	6,500	74,000
August	4,500	67,000
September	7,000	75,000
October	4,500	68,000
November	3,100	62,000
December	6,500	73,000
Total	57,500	$805,000

Jones has recently become aware of regression analysis. He estimated the following regression equation with overhead costs as the dependent variable and labor-hours as the independent variable:

$$y = \$48,271 + \$3.93X$$

Required

1. Plot the relationship between overhead costs and labor-hours. Draw the regression line and evaluate it using the criteria of economic plausibility, goodness of fit, and slope of the regression line.
2. Using data from the regression analysis, what is the variable cost per person for a standard party?
3. Bob Jones has been asked to prepare a bid for a 200-person standard party to be given next month. Determine the minimum bid price that Jones would be willing to submit to recoup variable costs.

10-28 High-low, regression. Pat Flip is the new manager of the materials storeroom for Serth Manufacturing. Pat has been asked to estimate future monthly purchase costs for part #4599, used in two of Serth's products. Pat has purchase cost and quantity data for the past nine months as follows:

Month	Cost of purchase	Quantity purchased
January	$13,900	2,350 parts
February	14,650	2,450
March	11,560	1,910
April	20,420	3,220
May	16,640	2,590
June	16,880	2,780
July	16,810	3,130
August	20,500	3,400
September	18,460	3,060

Estimated monthly purchases for this part based on expected demand of the two products for the rest of the year are:

Month	Purchase quantity expected
October	3,000 parts
November	3,200
December	2,500

Required

1. The computer in Pat's office is down and Pat has been asked to immediately provide an equation to estimate the future purchase cost for part # 4599. Pat grabs a calculator and uses the high-low method to estimate a cost equation. What equation does Pat get?

2. Using the equation from requirement 1, calculate the future expected purchase costs for each of the last three months of the year.
3. After a few hours Pat's computer is fixed. Pat uses the first nine months of data and regression analysis to estimate the relationship between the quantity purchased and purchase costs of part #4599. The regression line Pat obtains is:

$$y = \$501.54 + \$5.84X$$

Evaluate the regression line using the criteria of economic plausibility, goodness of fit, and significance of the independent variable. Compare the regression equation to the equation based on the high-low method. Which is a better fit? Why?
4. Use the regression results to calculate the expected purchase costs for October, November, and December. Compare the expected purchase costs to the expected purchase costs calculated using the high-low method in requirement 2. Comment on your results.

10-29 Learning curve, cumulative average-time learning model. Global Defense manufactures radar systems. It has just completed the manufacture of its first newly designed system, RS-32. Manufacturing data for the RS-32 follow:

File Edit View Insert Format Tools Data Window Help

	A	B	C
1	Direct material cost	$80,000	per unit of RS-32
2	Direct manufacturing labor time for first unit	3,000	direct manufacturing labor-hours
3	Learning curve for manufacturing labor time per radar system	90%	cumulative average time[a]
4	Direct manufacturing labor cost	$ 25	per direct manufacturing labor-hour
5	Variable manufacturing overhead cost	$ 15	per direct manufacturing labor-hour
6			
7	[a]Using the formula (p. 356), for a 90% learning curve, $b = \frac{\ln 0.90}{\ln 2} =$	$\frac{-0.105361}{0.693147}$	= -0.152004
8			

If you want to use Excel to solve this exercise, go to the Excel Lab at **www.prenhall.com/horngren/cost13e** and download the template for Exercise 10-29.

Required Calculate the total variable costs of producing 2, 4, and 8 units.

10-30 Learning curve, incremental unit-time learning model. Assume the same information for Global Defense as in Exercise 10-29, except that Global Defense uses a 90% incremental unit-time learning model as a basis for predicting direct manufacturing labor-hours. (A 90% learning curve means $b = -0.152004$.)

If you want to use Excel to solve this exercise, go to the Excel Lab at **www.prenhall.com/horngren/cost13e** and download the template for Exercise 10-29.

Required

1. Calculate the total variable costs of producing 2, 3, and 4 units.
2. If you solved Exercise 10-29, compare your cost predictions in the two exercises for 2 and 4 units. Why are the predictions different? How should Global Defense decide which model it should use?

Problems

10-31 High-low method. Ken Howard, financial analyst at JVR Corporation, is examining the behavior of quarterly maintenance costs for budgeting purposes. Howard collects the following data on machine-hours worked and maintenance costs for the past 12 quarters:

Quarter	Machine-Hours	Maintenance Costs
1	90,000	$185,000
2	110,000	220,000
3	100,000	200,000
4	120,000	240,000
5	85,000	170,000
6	105,000	215,000
7	95,000	195,000
8	115,000	235,000
9	95,000	190,000
10	115,000	225,000
11	105,000	180,000
12	125,000	250,000

Required

1. Estimate the cost function for the quarterly data using the high low method.
2. Plot and comment on the estimated cost function.
3. Howard anticipates that JVR will operate machines for 90,000 hours in quarter 13. Calculate the predicted maintenance costs in quarter 13 using the cost function estimated in requirement 1.

10-32 High-low method and regression analysis. Happy Business College has recently opened a restaurant as part of its hospitality major. For the first 10 weeks the manager did not estimate any costs, but instead hoped revenues would cover costs. One of the new waiters, who happens to be taking a cost accounting class, suggests that the manager take the past known weekly costs and try to determine a cost equation by relating the cost to the number of customers served. The cost and customer data are as follows:

Week	Number of Customers per Week	Weekly Total Costs of Restaurant
1	751	$16,800
2	745	16,597
3	810	17,800
4	833	18,600
5	825	17,900
6	876	19,600
7	855	18,900
8	897	18,500
9	925	20,305
10	910	20,000

The manager gives this information to the waiter, who runs a regression and gets the following equation:

Weekly total restaurant costs = \$2,453 + (\$19.04 × Number of customers per week)

Required

1. Plot the relationship between number of customers per week and weekly total restaurant costs.
2. Estimate the cost equation using the high-low method, and draw this line on your graph.
3. Draw the regression line on your graph. Use your graph to evaluate the regression line using the criteria of economic plausibility, goodness of fit, and significance of the independent variable. Is the cost function estimated using the high-low method a close approximation to the cost function estimated using the regression method. Explain briefly.
4. At what point (number of customers) will the expected total cost based on the high-low equation equal the expected total cost based on the regression equation?

10-33 High-low method; regression analysis. (CIMA, adapted) Anna Martinez, the financial manager at the Casa Real restaurant, is checking to see if there is any relationship between newspaper advertising and sales revenues at the restaurant. She obtains the following data for the past 10 months:

Month	Revenues	Advertising Costs
March	$50,000	$2,000
April	70,000	3,000
May	55,000	1,500
June	65,000	3,500
July	55,000	1,000
August	65,000	2,000
September	45,000	1,500
October	80,000	4,000
November	55,000	2,500
December	60,000	2,500

She estimates the following regression equation:

Monthly revenues = \$39,502 + (\$8.723 × Advertising costs)

Required

1. Plot the relationship between advertising costs and revenues.
2. Draw the regression line and evaluate it using the criteria of economic plausibility, goodness of fit, and slope of the regression line.
3. Use the high-low method to compute the function, relating advertising costs and revenues.
4. Using (a) the regression equation and (b) the high-low equation, what is the increase in revenues for each $1,000 spent on advertising within the relevant range? Which method should Martinez use to predict the effect of advertising costs on revenues? Explain briefly.

10-34 Regression, activity-based costing, choosing cost drivers. Newroute Manufacturing has been using activity-based costing to determine the cost of product X-678. One of the activities, "Inspection," occurs just before the product is finished. Newroute inspects every 10th unit, and has been using "number of units inspected" as the cost driver for inspection costs. A significant component of inspection costs is the cost of the test-kit used in each inspection.

Neela McFeen, the line manager, is wondering if inspection labor-hours might be a better cost driver for inspection costs. Neela gathers information for weekly inspection costs, units inspected, and inspection labor-hours as shown below:

Week	Units Inspected	Inspection Labor-Hours	Inspection Costs
1	1,500	200	$3,900
2	500	80	2,000
3	1,800	240	4,700
4	2,500	250	6,000
5	2,200	220	5,500
6	800	90	2,600
7	1,000	120	3,100

Neela runs regressions on each of the possible cost drivers and estimates these cost functions:

Inspection Costs = $1,004 + ($2.02 × Number of units inspected)
Inspection Costs = $626 + ($19.51 × Inspection labor-hours)

Required

1. Explain why number of units inspected and inspection labor-hours are plausible cost drivers of inspection costs.
2. Plot the data and regression line for units inspected and inspection costs. Plot the data and regression line for inspection labor-hours and inspection costs. Which cost driver of inspection costs would you choose? Explain.
3. Neela expects inspectors to work 150 hours next period and to inspect 1,200 units. Using the cost driver you chose in requirement 2, what amount of inspection costs should Neela budget? Explain any implications of Neela choosing the cost driver you did not choose in requirement 2 to budget inspection costs.

10-35 Interpreting regression results, matching time periods. Brickman Apparel produces equipment for the extreme-sports market. It has four peak periods, each lasting two months, for manufacturing the merchandise suited for spring, summer, fall, and winter. In the off-peak periods, Brickman schedules equipment maintenance and runs advertising to generate demand for its upcoming seasonal merchandise. Brickman's controller, Sascha Green, wants to understand the drivers of equipment maintenance costs and the effect of advertising expenditures on sales. A regression analysis of two years of monthly data yields the following relationships:

Maintenance costs = $21,000 − ($2.20 per machine-hour × Number of machine-hours)
Sales revenue = $310,000 − ($1.80 × advertising expenditure)

Upon examining the results, Green comments, "So, all I have to do to reduce maintenance costs is run my machines longer?! And, clearly our advertising function is broken: The more we spend on advertising, the lower our sales revenue."

Required

1. Explain why Green made this comment.
2. Suggest a more economically plausible relationship between monthly maintenance costs and monthly machine-hours. Justify your choice.
3. Suggest a more economically plausible relationship between monthly sales and advertising expenditures. Justify your choice.

10-36 Cost estimation, cumulative average-time learning curve. The Nautilus Company, which is under contract to the U.S. Navy, assembles troop deployment boats. As part of its research program, it completes the assembly of the first of a new model (PT109) of deployment boats. The Navy is impressed with the PT109. It requests that Nautilus submit a proposal on the cost of producing another seven PT109s.

Nautilus reports the following cost information for the first PT109 assembled and uses an 85% cumulative average-time learning model as a basis for forecasting direct manufacturing labor-hours for the next seven PT109s. (An 85% learning curve means $b = -0.234465$.):

	A	B	C
1	Direct material	$100,000	
2	Direct manufacturing labor time for first boat	10,000	labor-hours
3	Direct manufacturing labor rate	$ 30	per direct manufacturing labor-hour
4	Variable manufacturing overhead cost	$ 20	per direct manufacturing labor-hour
5	Other manufacturing overhead	25%	of direct manufacturing labor costs
6	Tooling costs[a]	$500,000	
7	Learning curve for manufacturing labor time per boat	85%	cumulative average time[b]
8			
9	[a]Tooling can be reused at no extra cost because all of its cost has been assigned to the first deployment boat.		
10			
11	[b]Using the formula (p. 356), for an 85% learning curve, $b = \frac{\ln 0.85}{\ln 2} = \frac{-0.162519}{0.693147} = -0.234465$		
12			

If you want to use Excel to solve this problem, go to the Excel Lab at **www.prenhall.com/horngren/cost13e** and download the template for Problem 10-36.

Required

1. Calculate predicted total costs of producing the seven PT109s for the Navy. (Nautilus will keep the first deployment boat assembled, costed at $725,000, as a demonstration model for potential customers.)
2. What is the dollar amount of the difference between (a) the predicted total costs for producing the seven PT109s in requirement 1, and (b) the predicted total costs for producing the seven PT109s, assuming that there is no learning curve for direct manufacturing labor? That is, for (b) assume a linear function for units produced and direct manufacturing labor-hours.

10-37 Cost estimation, incremental unit-time learning model. Assume the same information for the Nautilus Company as in Problem 10-36 with one exception. This exception is that Nautilus uses an 85% incremental unit-time learning model as a basis for predicting direct manufacturing labor-hours in its assembling operations. (An 85% learning curve means $b = -0.234465$.)

If you want to use Excel to solve this problem, go to the Excel Lab at **www.prenhall.com/horngren/cost13e** and download the template for Problem 10-36.

Required

1. Prepare a prediction of the total costs for producing the seven PT109s for the Navy.
2. If you solved requirement 1 of Problem 10-36, compare your cost prediction there with the one you made here. Why are the predictions different? How should Nautilus decide which model it should use?

10-38 Regression; choosing among models (chapter appendix). Tilbert Toys (TT) makes the popular Floppin' Freddy Frog and Jumpin' Jill Junebug dolls in batches. TT has recently adopted activity-based costing. TT incurs setup costs for each batch of dolls that it produces. TT uses "number of setups" as the cost driver for setup costs.

TT has just hired Bebe Williams, an accountant. Bebe thinks that "number of setup hours" might be a better cost driver because the setup time for each product is different. Bebe collects the following data.

Month	Number of setups	Number of setup hours	Setup costs
1	195	920	$52,300
2	240	1,340	63,850
3	100	580	28,740
4	220	1,900	118,420
5	140	1,840	89,440
6	230	1,950	106,880
7	210	1,490	104,810
8	150	600	45,040
9	185	1,640	110,520

If you want to use Excel to solve this problem, go to the Excel Lab at **www.prenhall.com/horngren/cost13e** and download the template for Problem 10-38.

Required

1. Estimate the regression equation for (a) setup costs and number of setups and (b) setup costs and number of setup hours. You should obtain the following results:

Regression 1: Setup costs = $a + (b \times$ Number of setups)

Variable	Coefficient	Standard Error	*t*-Value
Constant	\$3,905	\$41,439	0.09
Independent variable 1: No. of setups	\$410	\$217	1.89
$r^2 = 0.34$; Durbin-Watson statistic = 1.12			

Regression 2: Setup costs = $a + (b \times$ Number of setup-hours)

Variable	Coefficient	Standard Error	*t*-Value
Constant	\$3,349	\$12,879	0.26
Independent variable 1: No. of setup-hours	\$56.27	\$8.85	6.36
$r^2 = 0.85$; Durbin-Watson statistic = 1.50			

2. On two different graphs plot the data and the regression lines for each of the following cost functions.
   a. Setup costs = $a + (b \times$ Number of setups)
   b. Setup costs = $a + (b \times$ Number of setup hours)
3. Evaluate the regression models for "Number of setups" and "Number of setup-hours" as the cost driver according to the format of Exhibit 10-18 (p. 369).
4. Based on your analysis, which cost driver should Tilbert Toys use for setup costs, and why?

10-39 Multiple regression (continuation of 10-38) (chapter appendix). Bebe Williams wonders if she should run a multiple regression with both number of setups and number of setup hours, as cost drivers.

If you want to use Excel to solve this problem, go to the Excel Lab at **www.prenhall.com/horngren/cost13e** and download the template for Problem 10-38.

Required

1. Run a multiple regression to estimate the regression equation for setup costs using both number of setups and number of setup hours as independent variables. You should obtain the following result:

Regression 3: Setup costs = $a + (b_1 \times$ No. of setups) + $(b_2 \times$ No. of setup-hours)

Variable	Coefficient	Standard Error	*t*-Value
Constant	–\$3,895	\$20,831	–0.19
Independent variable 1: No. of setups	\$60.84	\$132.02	0.46
Independent variable 2: No. of setup-hours	\$53.30	\$11.39	4.68
$r^2 = 0.86$; Durbin-Watson statistic = 1.36			

2. Evaluate the multiple regression output using the criteria of economic plausibility goodness of fit, significance of independent variables, and specification of estimation assumptions. (Assume linearity, constant variance, and normality of residuals.)
3. What difficulties do not arise in simple regression analysis that may arise in multiple regression analysis? Is there evidence of such difficulties in the multiple regression presented in this problem? Explain.
4. Which of the regression models from problems 10-38 and 10-39 would you recommend Bebe Williams use? Explain.

10-40 Purchasing Department cost drivers, activity-based costing, simple regression analysis (chapter appendix). Fashion Flair operates a chain of 10 retail department stores. Each department store makes its own purchasing decisions. Barry Lee, assistant to the president of Fashion Flair, is interested in better understanding the drivers of Purchasing Department costs. For many years, Fashion Flair has allocated Purchasing Department costs to products on the basis of the dollar value of merchandise purchased. A \$100 item is allocated 10 times as many overhead costs associated with the Purchasing Department as a \$10 item.

Lee recently attended a seminar titled "Cost Drivers in the Retail Industry." In a presentation at the seminar, Couture Fabrics, a leading competitor that has implemented activity-based costing, reported number of purchase orders and number of suppliers to be the two most important cost drivers of Purchasing Department costs. The dollar value of merchandise purchased in each purchase order was not found to be a significant cost driver. Lee interviewed several members of the Purchasing Department at the Fashion Flair store in Miami. They believed that Couture Fabrics's conclusions also applied to their Purchasing Department.

Lee collects the following data for the most recent year for Fashion Flair's 10 retail department stores:

Department Store	Purchasing Department Costs (PDC)	Dollar Value of Merchandise Purchased (MP$)	Number of Purchase Orders (No. of PO's)	Number of Suppliers (No. of S's)
Baltimore	$1,523,000	$ 68,315,000	4,357	132
Chicago	1,100,000	33,456,000	2,550	222
Los Angeles	547,000	121,160,000	1,433	11
Miami	2,049,000	119,500,000	5,944	190
New York	1,056,000	33,505,000	2,793	23
Phoenix	529,000	29,854,000	1,327	33
Seattle	1,538,000	102,875,000	7,586	104
St. Louis	1,754,000	38,674,000	3,617	119
Toronto	1,612,000	139,312,000	1,707	208
Vancouver	1,257,000	130,944,000	4,731	201

Lee decides to use simple regression analysis to examine whether one or more of three variables (the last three columns in the table) are cost drivers of Purchasing Department costs. Summary results for these regressions are as follows:

Regression 1: PDC $= a + (b \times \text{MP\$})$

Variable	Coefficient	Standard Error	*t*-Value
Constant	$1,039,061	$343,439	3.03
Independent variable 1: MP$	0.0031	0.0037	0.84

$r^2 = 0.08$; Durbin-Watson statistic $= 2.41$

Regression 2: PDC $= a + (b \times \text{No. of PO's})$

Variable	Coefficient	Standard Error	*t*-Value
Constant	$730,716	$265,419	2.75
Independent variable 1: No. of PO's	$ 156.97	$ 64.69	2.43

$r^2 = 0.42$; Durbin-Watson statistic $= 1.98$

Regression 3: PDC $= a + (b \times \text{No. of S's})$

Variable	Coefficient	Standard Error	*t*-Value
Constant	$814,862	$247,821	3.29
Independent variable 1: No. of S's	$ 3,875	$ 1,697	2.28

$r^2 = 0.39$; Durbin-Watson statistic $= 1.97$

Required

1. Compare and evaluate the three simple regression models estimated by Lee. Graph each one. Also, use the format employed in Exhibit 10-18 (p. 369) to evaluate the information.
2. Do the regression results support the Couture Fabrics's presentation about the Purchasing Department's cost drivers? Which of these cost drivers would you recommend in designing an ABC system?
3. How might Lee gain additional evidence on drivers of Purchasing Department costs at each of Fashion Flair's stores?

10-41 Purchasing Department cost drivers, multiple regression analysis (continuation of 10-40) (chapter appendix). Barry Lee decides that the simple regression analysis used in Problem 10-40 could be extended to a multiple regression analysis. He finds the following results for two multiple regression analyses:

Regression 4: PDC $= a + (b_1 \times \text{No. of PO's}) + (b_2 \times \text{No. of S's})$

Variable	Coefficient	Standard Error	*t*-Value
Constant	$485,384	$257,477	1.89
Independent variable 1: No. of PO's	$ 123.22	$ 57.69	2.14
Independent variable 2: No. of S's	$ 2,952	$ 1,476	2.00

$r^2 = 0.63$; Durbin-Watson statistic $= 1.90$

Regression 5: PDC $= a + (b_1 \times$ No. of PO's$) + (b_2 \times$ No. of S's$) + (b_3 \times$ MP$)

Variable	Coefficient	Standard Error	*t*-Value
Constant	$494,684	$310,205	1.59
Independent variable 1: No. of PO's	$ 124.05	$ 63.49	1.95
Independent variable 2: No. of S's	$ 2,984	$ 1,622	1.84
Independent variable 3: MP$	–0.0002	0.0030	–0.07

$r^2 = 0.63$; Durbin-Watson statistic = 1.90

The coefficients of correlation between combinations of pairs of the variables are:

	PDC	MP$	No. of PO's
MP$	0.29		
No. of PO's	0.65	0.27	
No. of S's	0.63	0.34	0.29

Required

1. Evaluate regression 4 using the criteria of economic plausibility, goodness of fit, significance of independent variables and specification analysis. Compare regression 4 with regressions 2 and 3 in Problem 10-40. Which one of these models would you recommend that Lee use? Why?
2. Compare regression 5 with regression 4. Which one of these models would you recommend that Lee use? Why?
3. Lee estimates the following data for the Baltimore store for next year: dollar value of merchandise purchased, $75,000,000; number of purchase orders, 3,900; number of suppliers, 110. How much should Lee budget for Purchasing Department costs for the Baltimore store for next year?
4. What difficulties do not arise in simple regression analysis that may arise in multiple regression analysis? Is there evidence of such difficulties in either of the multiple regressions presented in this problem? Explain.
5. Give two examples of decisions in which the regression results reported here (and in Problem 10-40) could be informative.

Collaborative Learning Problem

10-42 High-low method, alternative regression functions, accrual accounting adjustments, ethics. Trevor Kennedy, the cost analyst at a can manufacturing plant of United Packaging, is examining the relationship between total engineering support costs reported in the plant records and machine-hours. These costs have two components: (1) labor, which is paid monthly, and (2) materials and parts, which are purchased from an outside vendor every three months. After further discussion with the operating manager, Kennedy discovers that the materials and parts numbers reported in the monthly records are on an "as purchased" or cash accounting basis and not on an "as used" or accrual accounting basis. By examining materials and parts usage records, Kennedy is able to restate the materials and parts costs to an "as used" basis. (No restatement of the labor costs was necessary.) The reported and restated costs are as follows:

Month	Labor: Reported Costs (1)	Materials and Parts: Reported Costs (2)	Materials and Parts: Restated Costs (3)	Total Engineering Support: Reported Costs (4) = (1) + (2)	Total Engineering Support: Restated Costs (5) = (1) + (3)	Machine-Hours (6)
March	$347	$847	$182	$1,194	$529	30
April	521	0	411	521	932	63
May	398	0	268	398	666	49
June	355	961	228	1,316	583	38
July	473	0	348	473	821	57
August	617	0	349	617	966	73
September	245	821	125	1,066	370	19
October	487	0	364	487	851	53
November	431	0	290	431	721	42

The regression results for total engineering support reported costs as the dependent variable, are:

Regression 1: Engineering support reported costs = $a + (b \times$ Machine-hours)

Variable	Coefficient	Standard Error	*t*-Value
Constant	$1,393.20	$305.68	4.56
Independent variable 1: Machine-hours	–$ 14.23	$ 6.15	–2.31

$r^2 = 0.43$; Durbin-Watson statistic = 2.26

The regression results for total engineering support restated costs as the dependent variable, are:

Regression 2: Engineering support restated costs = $a + (b \times$ Machine-hours)

Variable	Coefficient	Standard Error	*t*-Value
Constant	$176.38	$53.99	3.27
Independent variable 1: Machine-hours	$ 11.44	$ 1.08	10.59

$r^2 = 0.94$; Durbin-Watson statistic = 1.31

Required

1. Plot the cost functions relating (i) the *reported costs* for total engineering support to machine-hours and (ii) the *restated costs* for total engineering support to machine-hours. Comment on the plots.
2. Use the high-low method to compute estimates of the cost functions $y = a + bX$ for (a) reported engineering support costs and machine-hours and (b) restated engineering support costs and machine-hours.
3. Contrast and evaluate the cost function estimated with regression analysis using restated data for materials and parts with the cost function estimated with regression analysis using the data reported in the plant records. Use the comparison format employed in Exhibit 10-18 (p. 369).
4. Of all the cost functions estimated in requirements 2 and 3, which one would you choose to best represent the relationship between engineering support costs and machine-hours? Explain briefly.
5. What problems might Kennedy encounter when restating the materials and parts costs recorded to an "as used" or accrual accounting basis?
6. Why is it important for Kennedy to choose the correct cost function? That is, illustrate two potential problems Kennedy could encounter by choosing a cost function other than the one you chose in requirement 4.
7. John Mason, the plant manager, is not pleased when he sees the restated numbers. He tells Kennedy, "I think the restated engineering support costs are too high. Please recheck your numbers. They ought to be lower." Kennedy is aware that lower costs will result in a higher bonus for Mason. He is also certain that his numbers are correct. What should Kennedy do?

11 Decision Making and Relevant Information

Learning Objectives

1. Use the five-step decision-making process to make decisions
2. Distinguish relevant from irrelevant information in decision situations
3. Explain the opportunity-cost concept and why it is used in decision making
4. Know how to choose which products to produce when there are capacity constraints
5. Discuss factors managers must consider when adding or dropping customers or segments
6. Explain why book value of equipment is irrelevant in equipment-replacement decisions
7. Explain how conflicts can arise between the decision model used by a manager and the performance-evaluation model used to evaluate the manager

How many decisions have you made today? Maybe you made a big one, such as accepting a job offer. Or maybe your decision was as simple as settling on your plans for the weekend or choosing a restaurant for dinner. Regardless of whether decisions are big or routine, most people follow a simple, logical process of making them. This process involves gathering information, making predictions, making a choice, acting on the choice, and evaluating results. It also includes deciding what costs and benefits each choice affords. Some costs are irrelevant. They are what they are. For example, they were incurred in the past, and the money is spent and can't be recouped. This chapter will explain which costs and benefits are relevant and which are not—and how you should think of them when choosing among alternatives.

Relevant Costs, the Internet, and Delta Airlines

What does it cost Delta Airlines to fly a customer on a round-trip flight from Orlando to San Francisco, leaving on Saturday, August 11, 2007, and returning on Tuesday, August 14, 2007? The incremental costs are very small—mainly food costs of, say, $15—because the other costs are fixed—the plane, pilots, ticket agents, fuel, airport landing fees, and baggage handlers. So would it be worthwhile for Delta to fill a seat provided it earns at least $15 for that seat? After all, it will incur all the other costs regardless of whether the seat is filled. The answer depends on whether the flight is full. Suppose Delta normally charges $440 for this round-trip ticket. If the flight is full, Delta would not sell the ticket for anything less than $440 because there are other customers willing to pay this fare for the flight. But what if there are empty seats? Selling a ticket for something more than $15 is better than leaving the seat empty and earning nothing.

If a customer calls or uses the Internet to purchase the ticket in early July 2007, Delta may quote $440 because it expects the flight to be full. But what if on Wednesday, August 8, 2007, Delta finds that the plane will not be full? At the last minute, Delta may be willing to lower its prices drastically in hopes of attracting more customers while still earning a profit on each additional passenger.

The Internet makes it possible for Delta to tell potential customers cheaply and quickly about lowered fares. Using what is called "push" technology, Delta broadcasts information about all flights on which seats are available often at fares ranging from $80 to $200. In addition, Delta offers seats to various Web sites specializing in last-minute travel packages, including lastminute.com, (**www.lastminute.com**), LastMinuteTravel (**www.lastminutetravel.com**), and Priceline (**www.priceline.com**). Using this sophisticated pricing strategy requires a deep understanding of how to think about costs in different decision situations.

Just like at Delta Airlines, managers in corporations around the world use a decision process to help them make decisions. Managers at Citibank gather information about financial markets, consumer preferences, and economic trends before determining whether to offer new services to customers. Macy's managers examine the relevant information related to domestic and international clothing manufacturing before selecting vendors. And managers at Porsche gather cost information to decide whether to manufacture a component part or purchase it from a supplier. The decision process may not always be an easy one, but as Napoleon Bonaparte said, "Nothing is more difficult, and therefore more precious, than to be able to decide."

Information and the Decision Process

Managers usually follow a *decision model* for choosing among different courses of action. A **decision model** is a formal method of making a choice, and it often involves both quantitative and qualitative analyses. Management accountants work with managers by analyzing and presenting relevant data to guide decisions.

Consider a strategic decision facing management at Precision Sporting Goods, a manufacturer of golf clubs: Should it reorganize its manufacturing operations to reduce manufacturing labor costs? Assume that there are only two alternatives: do not reorganize or reorganize.

The reorganization will eliminate all manual handling of materials. The current manufacturing labor consists of 20 workers—15 workers operate machines, and 5 workers handle materials. The 5 materials-handling workers have been hired on contracts that permit layoffs without additional payments. Each worker works 2,000 hours annually. The cost of reorganization (consisting mostly of new equipment leases) is predicted to be $90,000 each year. The predicted production output of 25,000 units will be unaffected by the decision. Also unaffected will be the predicted selling price of $250, the direct material cost per unit of $50, manufacturing overhead of $750,000, and marketing costs of $2,000,000.

Managers use the five-step decision-making process presented in Exhibit 11-1 and first introduced in Chapter 1 to make decisions such as whether to reorganize. In this exhibit, study the sequence of the steps and note how step 5 evaluates performance to provide feedback about actions taken in the previous steps. This feedback might affect future predictions, the prediction methods used, the way choices are made, or the implementation of the decision.

Learning Objective 1

Use the five-step decision-making process to make decisions

. . . the five steps are identify the problem and uncertainties, obtain information, make predictions about the future, make decisions by choosing among alternatives, and implement the decision, evaluate performance, and learn

Exhibit 11-1

Five-Step Decision-Making Process for Precision Sporting Goods

Step 1: Identify the Problem and Uncertainties

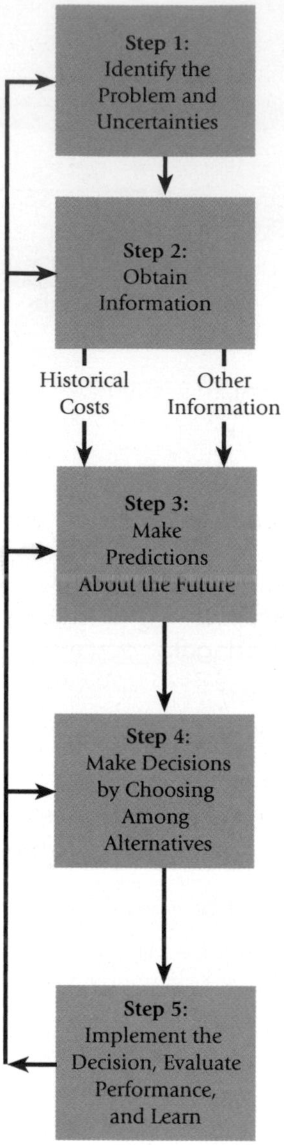

Should Precision Sporting Goods reorganize its manufacturing operations to reduce manufacturing labor costs? An important uncertainty is how the reorganization will affect employee morale.

Step 2: Obtain Information

Historical hourly wage rates are \$14 per hour. However, a recently negotiated increase in employee benefits of \$2 per hour will increase wages to \$16 per hour. The reorganization of manufacturing operations is expected to reduce the number of workers from 20 to 15 by eliminating all 5 workers who handle materials. The reorganization is likely to have negative effects on employee morale.

Historical Costs → Step 3; Other Information → Step 3

Step 3: Make Predictions About the Future

Managers use information from step 2 together with an assessment of probability as a basis for predicting future manufacturing labor costs. Under the existing do-not-reorganize alternative, costs are predicted to be \$640,000 (20 workers × 2,000 hours per worker per year × \$16 per hour), and under the reorganize alternative, costs are predicted to be \$480,000 (15 workers × 2,000 hours per worker per year ×\$16 per hour). Recall, the reorganization is predicted to cost \$90,000 per year.

Step 4: Make Decisions by Choosing Among Alternatives

Managers compare the predicted benefits calculated in step 3 (\$640,000 − \$480,000 = \$160,000—that is, savings from eliminating materials-handling labor costs, 5 workers × 2,000 hours per worker per year × \$16 per hour = \$160,000) against the cost of the reorganization (\$90,000) along with other considerations (such as likely negative effects on employee morale). Management chooses the reorganize alternative because the financial benefits are significant and the effects on employee morale are expected to be temporary and relatively small.

Step 5: Implement the Decision, Evaluate Performance, and Learn

Evaluating performance after the decision is implemented provides critical feedback for managers, and the five-step sequence is then repeated in whole or in part. Managers learn from actual results that the new manufacturing labor costs are \$540,000, rather than the predicted \$480,000, because of lower-than-expected manufacturing labor productivity. This (now) historical information can help managers make better subsequent predictions that allow for more learning time. Alternatively, managers may improve implementation via employee training and better supervision.

The Concept of Relevance

Learning Objective 2

Distinguish relevant from irrelevant information in decision situations

. . . only costs and revenues that are expected to occur in the future and differ among alternative courses of action are relevant

Much of this chapter focuses on step 4 in Exhibit 11-1 and on the concepts of relevant costs and relevant revenues when choosing among alternatives.

Relevant Costs and Relevant Revenues

Relevant costs are *expected future costs* and **relevant revenues** are *expected future revenues* that differ among the alternative courses of action being considered. Revenues and costs that are *not relevant* are said to be *irrelevant*. Be sure you understand that to be relevant costs and relevant revenues they *must*

- **Occur in the future**—every decision deals with selecting a course of action based on its expected future results—and
- **Differ among the alternative courses of action**—costs and revenues that do not differ will not matter and, hence, will have no bearing on the decision being made.

The question is always, "What difference will an action make?"

Exhibit 11-2 presents the financial data underlying the choice between the do-not-reorganize and reorganize alternatives for Precision Sporting Goods. There are two ways to do the analysis. The first considers "All revenues and costs," whereas the second considers only "Relevant revenues and costs."

The first two columns describe the first way and present *all data*. The last two columns describe the second way and present *only relevant costs*—the $640,000 and $480,000 expected future manufacturing labor costs and the $90,000 expected future reorganization costs that differ between the two alternatives. The revenues, direct materials, manufacturing overhead, and marketing items can be ignored because they will remain the same whether or not Precision Sporting Goods reorganizes. They do not differ between the alternatives and, therefore, are irrelevant.

Note, the past (historical) manufacturing hourly wage rate of $14 and total past (historical) manufacturing labor costs of $560,000 (20 workers × 2,000 hours per worker per year × $14 per hour) do not appear in Exhibit 11-2. *Although they may be a useful basis for making informed predictions of the expected future manufacturing labor costs of $640,000 and $480,000, historical costs themselves are past costs that, therefore, are irrelevant to decision making.* Past costs are also called **sunk costs** because they are unavoidable and cannot be changed no matter what action is taken.

The analysis in Exhibit 11-2 indicates that reorganizing the manufacturing operations will increase predicted operating income by $70,000 each year. Note that the managers at Precision Sporting Goods reach the same conclusion whether they use all data or include only relevant data in the analysis. By confining the analysis to only the relevant data, managers can clear away the clutter of potentially confusing irrelevant data. Focusing on the relevant data is especially helpful when all the information needed to prepare a detailed income statement is unavailable. Understanding which costs are relevant and which are irrelevant helps the decision maker concentrate on obtaining only the pertinent data and saves time.

Qualitative and Quantitative Relevant Information

Managers divide the outcomes of decisions into two broad categories: *quantitative* and *qualitative*. **Quantitative factors** are outcomes that are measured in numerical terms. Some quantitative factors are financial; they can be expressed in monetary terms. Examples include the cost of direct materials, direct manufacturing labor, and marketing. Other quantitative factors are nonfinancial; they can be measured numerically, but they are not expressed in monetary terms. Reduction in new product-development time for a manufacturing company and the percentage of on-time flight arrivals for an airline company are examples of quantitative nonfinancial factors. **Qualitative factors** are outcomes that are difficult to measure accurately in numerical terms. Employee morale is an example.

Exhibit 11-2

Determining Relevant Revenues and Relevant Costs for Precision Sporting Goods

	All Revenues and Costs		Relevant Revenues and Costs	
	Alternative 1: Do Not Reorganize	Alternative 2: Reorganize	Alternative 1: Do Not Reorganize	Alternative 2: Reorganize
Revenues[a]	$6,250,000	$6,250,000	—	—
Costs:				
Direct materials[b]	1,250,000	1,250,000	—	—
Manufacturing labor	640,000[c]	480,000[d]	$ 640,000[c]	$ 480,000[d]
Manufacturing overhead	750,000	750,000	—	—
Marketing	2,000,000	2,000,000	—	—
Reorganization costs	—	90,000	—	90,000
Total costs	4,640,000	4,570,000	640,000	570,000
Operating income	$1,610,000	$1,680,000	$(640,000)	$(570,000)
	$70,000 Difference		$70,000 Difference	

[a]25,000 units × $250 per unit = $6,250,000
[b]25,000 units × $50 per unit = $1,250,000
[c]20 workers × 2,000 hours per worker × $16 per hour = $640,000
[d]15 workers × 2,000 hours per worker × $16 per hour = $480,000

Relevant-cost analysis generally emphasizes quantitative factors that can be expressed in financial terms. *But just because qualitative factors and quantitative nonfinancial factors cannot be measured easily in financial terms does not make them unimportant.* In fact, managers must at times give more weight to these factors. For example, managers at Precision Sporting Goods carefully considered the negative effect on employee morale of laying off materials-handling workers, a qualitative factor, before choosing the reorganize alternative. Comparing and trading off nonfinancial and financial considerations is seldom easy.

Exhibit 11-3 summarizes the key features of relevant information.

An Illustration of Relevance: Choosing Output Levels

The concept of relevance applies to all decision situations. In this and the following several sections of this chapter, we present some of these decision situations. Later chapters describe other decision situations that require application of the relevance concept, such as Chapter 12 on pricing, Chapter 16 on joint costs, Chapter 19 on quality and timeliness, Chapter 20 on inventory management and supplier evaluation, Chapter 21 on capital investment, and Chapter 22 on transfer pricing. We start by considering decisions that affect output levels such as whether to introduce a new product or to try to sell more units of an existing product.

One-Time-Only Special Orders

One type of decision that affects output levels is accepting or rejecting special orders when there is idle production capacity and the special orders have no long-run implications. We use the term **one-time-only special order** to describe these conditions.

Example 1: Surf Gear manufactures quality beach towels at its highly automated Burlington, North Carolina, plant. The plant has a production capacity of 48,000 towels each month. Current monthly production is 30,000 towels. Retail department stores account for all existing sales. Expected results for the coming month (August) are shown in Exhibit 11-4. (These amounts are predictions based on past costs.) We assume all costs can be classified as either fixed or variable with respect to a single cost driver (units of output).

As a result of a strike at its existing towel supplier, a luxury hotel chain has offered to buy 5,000 towels from Surf Gear in August at $11 per towel. No subsequent sales to this hotel chain are anticipated. Fixed manufacturing costs are tied to the 48,000-towel production capacity. That is, fixed manufacturing costs relate to the production capacity available, regardless of the capacity used. If Surf Gear accepts the special order, it will use existing idle capacity to produce the 5,000 towels, and fixed manufacturing costs will not change. No marketing costs will be necessary for the 5,000-unit one-time-only special order. Accepting this special order is not expected to affect the selling price or the quantity of towels sold to regular customers. Should Surf Gear accept the hotel chain's offer?

Exhibit 11-4 presents data for this example on an absorption-costing basis (that is, both variable and fixed manufacturing costs are included in inventoriable costs and cost of goods sold). In this exhibit, the manufacturing cost of $12 per unit and the marketing cost of $7 per unit include both variable and fixed costs. The sum of all costs (variable and

Exhibit 11-3

Key Features of Relevant Information

- Past (historical) costs may be helpful as a basis for making *predictions*. However, past costs themselves are always irrelevant when making *decisions*.
- Different alternatives can be compared by examining differences in expected total future revenues and expected total future costs.
- Not all expected future revenues and expected future costs are relevant. Expected future revenues and expected future costs that do not differ among alternatives are irrelevant and, hence, can be eliminated from the analysis. The key question is always, What difference will an action make?
- Appropriate weight must be given to qualitative factors and quantitative nonfinancial factors.

Exhibit 11-4

Budgeted Income Statement for August, Absorption-Costing Format for Surf Gear[a]

	A	B	C	D
1		**Total**	**Per Unit**	
2	Units sold	30,000		
3				
4	Revenues	$600,000	$20.00	
5	Cost of goods sold (manufacturing costs)			
6	Variable manufacturing costs	225,000	7.50[b]	
7	Fixed manufacturing costs	135,000	4.50[c]	
8	Total cost of goods sold	360,000	12.00	
9	Marketing costs			
10	Variable marketing costs	150,000	5.00	
11	Fixed marketing costs	60,000	2.00	
12	Total marketing costs	210,000	7.00	
13	Full costs of the product	570,000	19.00	
14	Operating income	$ 30,000	$ 1.00	
15				
16	[a]Surf Gear incurs no R&D, product-design, distribution or customer-service costs			
17	[b]Variable manufacturing cost per unit = Direct material cost per unit + Direct manufacturing labor cost per unit + Variable manufacturing overhead cost per unit			
19	= $6.00 + $0.50 + $1.00 = $7.50			
20	[c]Fixed manufacturing cost per unit = Fixed direct manufacturing labor cost per unit + Fixed manufacturing overhead cost per unit			
22	= $1.50 + $3.00 = $4.50			

fixed) in a particular business function of the value chain, such as manufacturing costs or marketing costs, are called **business function costs. Full costs of the product**, in this case $19 per unit, are the sum of all variable and fixed costs in all business functions of the value chain (R&D, design, production, marketing, distribution, and customer service). For Surf Gear, full costs of the product consist of costs in manufacturing and marketing because these are the only business functions. No marketing costs are necessary for the special order, so the manager of Surf Gear will focus only on manufacturing costs. Based on the manufacturing cost per unit of $12—which is greater than the $11-per-unit price offered by the hotel chain—the manager might decide to reject the offer.

Exhibit 11-5 separates manufacturing and marketing costs into their variable- and fixed-cost components and presents data in the format of a contribution income statement. The relevant revenues and costs are the expected future revenues and costs that differ as a result of accepting the special offer—revenues of $55,000 ($11 per unit × 5,000 units) and variable manufacturing costs of $37,500 ($7.50 per unit × 5,000 units). The fixed manufacturing costs and all marketing costs (*including variable marketing costs*) are irrelevant in this case. That's because these costs will not change in total whether the special order is accepted or rejected. Surf Gear would gain an additional $17,500 (relevant revenues, $55,000—relevant costs, $37,500) in operating income by accepting the special order. In this example, comparing total amounts for 30,000 units versus 35,000 units or focusing only on the relevant amounts in the difference column in Exhibit 11-5 avoids a misleading implication—the implication that would result from comparing the $11-per-unit selling price against the manufacturing cost per unit of $12 (Exhibit 11-4), which includes both variable and fixed manufacturing costs.

The assumption of no long-run or strategic implications is crucial to management's analysis of the one-time-only special-order decision. Suppose Surf Gear concludes that the retail department stores (its regular customers) will demand a lower price if it sells towels at $11 apiece to the luxury hotel chain. In this case, revenues from regular customers will be relevant. Why? Because the future revenues from regular customers will differ depending on whether the special order is accepted or rejected. The relevant-revenue and relevant-cost analysis of the hotel-chain order would have to be modified to consider both the short-run benefits from accepting the order and the long-run consequences on profitability if prices were lowered to all regular customers.

Exhibit 11-5

One-Time-Only Special-Order Decision for Surf Gear: Comparative Contribution Income Statements

File Edit View Insert Format Tools Data Window Help

	A	B	C	D	E	F	G	H
1		Without the Special Order				With the Special Order		Difference: Relevant Amounts
2		30,000				35,000		for the
3		Units to be Sold				Units to be Sold		5,000
4		Per Unit		Total		Total		Units Special Order
5		(1)		(2) = (1) x 30,000		(3)		(4) = (3) – (2)
6	Revenues	$20.00		$600,000		$655,000		$55,000[a]
7	Variable costs:							
8	Manufacturing	7.50		225,000		262,500		37,500[b]
9	Marketing	5.00		150,000		150,000		0[c]
10	Total variable costs	12.50		375,000		412,500		37,500
11	Contribution margin	7.50		225,000		242,500		17,500
12	Fixed costs:							
13	Manufacturing	4.50		135,000		135,000		0[d]
14	Marketing	2.00		60,000		60,000		0[d]
15	Total fixed costs	6.50		195,000		195,000		0
16	Operating income	$ 1.00		$ 30,000		$ 47,500		$17,500
17								
18	[a]5,000 units x $11.00 per unit = $55,000.							
19	[b]5,000 units x $7.50 per unit = $37,500.							
20	[c]No variable marketing costs would be incurred for the 5,000-unit one-time-only special order.							
21	[d]Fixed manufacturing costs and fixed marketing costs would be unaffected by the special order.							

Potential Problems in Relevant-Cost Analysis

Managers should avoid two potential problems in relevant-cost analysis. First, they must watch for incorrect general assumptions, such as all variable costs are relevant and all fixed costs are irrelevant. In the Surf Gear example, the variable marketing cost of $5 per unit is irrelevant because Surf Gear will incur no extra marketing costs by accepting the special order. But fixed manufacturing costs could be relevant. The extra production of 5,000 towels per month does not affect fixed manufacturing costs because we assumed that the relevant range is from 30,000 to 48,000 towels per month. In some cases, however, producing the extra 5,000 towels might increase fixed manufacturing costs. Suppose Surf Gear would need to run three shifts of 16,000 towels per shift to achieve full capacity of 48,000 towels per month. Increasing the monthly production from 30,000 to 35,000 would require a partial third shift because two shifts could produce only 32,000 towels. The extra shift would increase fixed manufacturing costs, thereby making these additional fixed manufacturing costs relevant for this decision.

Second, unit-cost data can potentially mislead decision makers in two ways:

1. **When irrelevant costs are included.** Consider the $4.50 of fixed manufacturing cost per unit (direct manufacturing labor, $1.50 per unit, plus manufacturing overhead, $3.00 per unit) included in the $12-per-unit manufacturing cost in the one-time-only special-order decision (see Exhibits 11-4 and 11-5). This $4.50-per-unit cost is irrelevant, given the assumptions in our example, so it should be excluded.
2. **When the same unit costs are used at different output levels.** Generally, managers use total costs rather than unit costs because total costs are easier to work with and reduce the chance for erroneous conclusions. Then, if desired, the total costs can be unitized. In the Surf Gear example, total fixed manufacturing costs remain at $135,000 even if Surf Gear accepts the special order and produces 35,000 towels.

Including the fixed manufacturing cost per unit of $4.50 as a cost of the special order would lead to the erroneous conclusion that total fixed manufacturing costs would increase to $157,500 ($4.50 per towel × 35,000 towels).

The best way for managers to avoid these two potential problems is to keep focusing on (1) total revenues and total costs (rather than unit revenue and unit cost) and (2) the relevance concept. Managers should always require all items included in an analysis to be expected total future revenues and expected total future costs that differ among the alternatives.

Insourcing-versus-Outsourcing and Make-versus-Buy Decisions

We now apply the concept of relevance to another strategic decision: whether a company should make a component part or buy it from a supplier. We again assume idle capacity.

Outsourcing and Idle Facilities

Outsourcing is purchasing goods and services from outside vendors rather than **insourcing**, which is producing the same goods or providing the same services within the organization. For example, Kodak prefers to manufacture its own film (insourcing), but it has IBM do its data processing (outsourcing). Toyota relies on outside vendors to supply some component parts but chooses to manufacture other parts internally.

Decisions about whether a producer of goods or services will insource or outsource are also called **make-or-buy decisions**. Surveys of companies indicate that managers consider quality, dependability of suppliers, and costs as the most important factors in the make-or-buy decision. Sometimes, however, qualitative factors dominate management's make-or-buy decision. For example, Dell Computer buys the Pentium chip for its personal computers from Intel because Dell does not have the know-how and technology to make the chip itself. To maintain the secrecy of its formula, Coca-Cola does not outsource the manufacture of its concentrate.

Example 2: The Soho Company manufactures a three-in-one stereo consisting of a CD player, a cassette deck, and a digital radio. Columns 1 and 2 of the following table show the current costs for manufacturing the CD-player unit of the stereo system based on an analysis of various manufacturing activities:

	Total Current Costs of Producing 1,000,000 Units in 2,500 Batches (1)	**Current Cost per Unit (2) = (1) ÷ 1,000,000**	**Expected Total Costs of Producing 1,000,000 Units in 5,000 Batches Next Year (3)**	**Expected Cost per Unit (4) = (3) ÷ 1,000,000**
Direct materials	$ 9,000,000	$ 9.00	$ 9,000,000	$ 9.00
Direct manufacturing labor	2,400,000	2.40	2,400,000	2.40
Variable manufacturing overhead costs of power and utilities	1,600,000	1.60	1,600,000	1.60
Mixed (variable and fixed) manufacturing overhead costs of materials handling and setup	1,750,000	1.75	2,000,000	2.00
Fixed manufacturing overhead costs of plant lease, insurance, and administration	3,000,000	3.00	3,000,000	3.00
Total manufacturing cost	$17,750,000	$17.75	$18,000,000	$18.00

Currently, materials-handling and setup activities occur each time a batch of CD players is made. Soho produces 1,000,000 CD players in 2,500 batches, with 400 units in each batch. The number of batches is the cost driver for these costs. Total materials-handling costs and setup costs equal fixed costs of $500,000 plus variable costs of $500 per batch [$500,000 + (2,500 batches × $500 per batch) = $1,750,000]. Soho is considering producing CD players in smaller batch sizes. Soho anticipates producing the same 1,000,000 CD players next year in 5,000 batches of 200 units per batch. Through continuous improvement, the company expects to reduce variable costs for materials handling and setup to $300 per batch. Expected materials-handling and setup costs equal $500,000 + (5,000 batches × the cost per batch of $300) = $2,000,000. That is, batch-level costs increase even though the total production quantity of CD players is expected to be the same. No other changes in variable cost per unit or fixed costs are anticipated for next year, so expected costs of direct materials, direct manufacturing labor, variable manufacturing overhead, and fixed manufacturing overhead for next year are the same as for this year.

Another manufacturer offers to sell Soho 1,000,000 CD players next year for $16 per unit on whatever delivery schedule Soho wants. Assume that financial factors will be the basis of this make-or-buy decision. Should Soho make or buy the CD player?

Columns 3 and 4 of the preceding table indicate the expected total costs and expected cost per unit of producing 1,000,000 CD players next year. The expected manufacturing cost per unit for next year is $18. At first glance, it appears that the company should buy CD players because the expected $18-per-unit cost of making the CD player is more than the $16 per unit to buy it. But a make-or-buy decision is rarely obvious. To make a decision, management needs to answer the question: What is the difference in relevant costs between the alternatives?

For the moment, suppose (a) the capacity now used to make the CD players will become idle next year if the CD players are purchased and (b) the $3,000,000 of fixed manufacturing overhead will continue to be incurred next year regardless of the decision made. Assume the $500,000 in fixed salaries to support materials handling and setup will not be incurred if the manufacture of CD players is completely shut down.

Exhibit 11-6 presents the relevant-cost computations. Note that Soho will *save* $1,000,000 by making CD players rather than buying them from the outside supplier. Making CD players is the preferred alternative.

Exhibit 11-6

Relevant (Incremental) Items for Make-or-Buy Decision for CD Players at Soho Company

	Total Relevant Costs		Relevant Cost Per Unit	
Relevant Items	**Make**	**Buy**	**Make**	**Buy**
Outside purchase of parts		$16,000,000		$16.00
Direct materials	$ 9,000,000		$ 9.00	
Direct manufacturing labor	2,400,000		2.40	
Variable manufacturing overhead	1,600,000		1.60	
Mixed (variable and fixed) materials-handling and setup overhead	2,000,000		2.00	
Total relevant costs[a]	$15,000,000	$16,000,000	$15.00	$16.00
Difference in favor of making CD players	$1,000,000		$1.00	

[a]The $3,000,000 of plant-lease, plant-insurance, and plant-administration costs could be included under both alternatives. Conceptually, they do not belong in a listing of relevant costs because these costs are irrelevant to the decision. Practically, some managers may want to include them in order to list all costs that will be incurred under each alternative.

Note how the key concepts of relevance presented in Exhibit 11-3 apply here:

- Current-cost data in Example 2, columns 1 and 2 (pp. 393–394), play no role in the analysis in Exhibit 11-6 because for next year's make-or-buy decision these costs are past costs and, hence, irrelevant. They only help in predicting future costs.
- Exhibit 11-6 shows $2,000,000 of future materials-handling and setup costs under the make alternative but not under the buy alternative. Why? Because buying CD players and not manufacturing them will save $2,000,000 in future variable costs per batch and avoidable fixed costs. The $2,000,000 represents future costs that differ between the alternatives and so is relevant to the make-or-buy decision.
- Exhibit 11-6 excludes the $3,000,000 of plant-lease, insurance, and administration costs under both alternatives. Why? Because these future costs will not differ between the alternatives, so they are irrelevant.

A common term in decision making is *incremental cost.* An **incremental cost** is the additional total cost incurred for an activity. In Exhibit 11-6, the incremental cost of making CD players is the additional total cost of $15,000,000 that Soho will incur if it decides to make CD players. The $3,000,000 of fixed manufacturing overhead is not an incremental cost because Soho will incur these costs whether or not it makes CD players. Similarly, the incremental cost of buying CD players from an outside supplier is the additional total cost of $16,000,000 that Soho will incur if it decides to buy CD players. A **differential cost** is the difference in total cost between two alternatives. In Exhibit 11-6, the differential cost between the make-CD-players and buy-CD-players alternatives is $1,000,000 ($16,000,000 − $15,000,000). Note that *incremental cost* and *differential cost* are sometimes used interchangeably in practice. When faced with these terms, always be sure what they mean.

We define *incremental revenue* and *differential revenue* similarly to incremental cost and differential cost. **Incremental revenue** is the additional total revenue from an activity. **Differential revenue** is the difference in total revenue between two alternatives.

Strategic and Qualitative Factors

Strategic and qualitative factors affect outsourcing decisions. For example, Soho may prefer to manufacture CD players in-house to retain control over the design, quality, reliability, and delivery schedules of the CD players it uses in its stereos. Conversely, despite the cost advantages documented in Exhibit 11-6, Soho may prefer to outsource, become a leaner organization, and focus on areas of its core competencies—the manufacture and sale of stereos. As an example of focus, advertising companies, such as J. Walter Thompson, only do the creative and planning aspects of advertising (their core competencies), and they outsource production activities, such as film, photographs, and illustrations.

Outsourcing is not without risks. As a company's dependence on its suppliers increases, suppliers could increase prices and let quality and delivery performance slip. To minimize these risks, companies generally enter into long-run contracts specifying costs, quality, and delivery schedules with their suppliers. Intelligent managers build close partnerships or alliances with a few key suppliers. Toyota goes so far as to send its own engineers to improve suppliers' processes. Suppliers of companies such as Ford, Hyundai, Panasonic, and Sony have researched and developed innovative products, met demands for increased quantities, maintained quality and on-time delivery, and lowered costs—actions that the companies themselves would not have had the competencies to achieve. The Concepts in Action feature (p. 398) describes how companies are outsourcing services to lower-cost countries, which is also called *offshoring*.

Outsourcing decisions invariably have a long-run horizon in which the financial costs and benefits of outsourcing become more uncertain. Almost always, strategic and qualitative factors such as those described here become important determinants of the outsourcing decision. Weighing all these factors requires the exercise of considerable management judgment and care.

Opportunity Costs and Outsourcing

Learning Objective 3

Explain the opportunity-cost concept and why it is used in decision making

. . . in all decisions, it is important to consider the contribution to income forgone by choosing a particular alternative and rejecting others

In the simple make-or-buy decision in Exhibit 11-6, we assumed that the capacity currently used to make CD players will remain idle if Soho purchases the parts from the outside manufacturer. Often, however, the released capacity can be used for other, more-profitable purposes. Then, the choice Soho's managers are faced with is not whether to make or buy. It is how best to use available production capacity.

Example 3: Suppose that if Soho decides to buy CD players for its stereos from the outside supplier, then Soho's best use of the capacity that becomes available is to produce 500,000 Discmans, a portable, stand-alone CD player. From a manufacturing standpoint, Discmans are similar to stereo CD players. With help from operating managers, John Marquez, Soho's management accountant, estimates the following future revenues and costs if Soho decides to manufacture and sell Discmans:

Incremental future revenues		$8,000,000
Incremental future costs		
Direct materials	$3,400,000	
Direct manufacturing labor	1,000,000	
Variable overhead (such as power, utilities)	600,000	
Materials-handling and setup overheads	500,000	
Total incremental future costs		5,500,000
Incremental future operating income		$2,500,000

Because of capacity constraints, Soho can make either CD players for its stereo unit or Discmans, but not both. Which of the following three alternatives should Soho choose?

1. Make stereo CD players and do not make Discmans
2. Buy stereo CD players and do not make Discmans
3. Buy stereo CD players and make Discmans

Exhibit 11-7, Panel A, summarizes the "total-alternatives" approach—the future costs and revenues for *all* alternatives. Alternative 3, buying stereo CD players and using the available capacity to make and sell Discmans, is the preferred alternative. The future incremental costs of buying stereo CD players from an outside supplier ($16,000,000) are more than the future incremental costs of making stereo CD players in-house ($15,000,000). But Soho can use the capacity freed up by buying stereo CD players to gain $2,500,000 in operating income (incremental future revenues of $8,000,000 minus total incremental future costs of $5,500,000) by making and selling Discmans. The *net relevant* costs of buying stereo CD players and making and selling Discmans are $16,000,000 − $2,500,000 = $13,500,000.

The Opportunity-Cost Approach

Deciding to use a resource in a particular way causes a manager to forgo the opportunity to use the resource in alternative ways. This lost opportunity is a cost that the manager must consider when making a decision. **Opportunity cost** is the contribution to operating income that is forgone by not using a limited resource in its next-best alternative use. For example, the (relevant) cost of going to school for an MBA degree is not only the cost of tuition, books, lodging, and food, but also the income sacrificed (opportunity cost) by not working. Presumably the estimated future benefits of obtaining an MBA (for example, a higher-paying career) will exceed these costs.

Exhibit 11-7, Panel B, displays the opportunity-cost approach for analyzing the alternatives faced by Soho. *When using the opportunity-cost approach, Soho's managers should focus on the costs of making or buying stereo CD players.*

Exhibit 11-7

Total-Alternatives Approach and Opportunity-Cost Approach to Make-or-Buy Decisions for Soho Company

Relevant Items	Alternatives for Soho: 1. Make Stereo CD Players and Do Not Make Discmans	2. Buy Stereo CD Players and Do Not Make Discmans	3. Buy Stereo CD Players and Make Discmans
PANEL A Total-Alternatives Approach to Make-or-Buy Decisions			
Total incremental future costs of making/buying stereo CD players (from Exhibit 11-6)	$15,000,000	$16,000,000	$16,000,000
Deduct excess of future revenues over future costs from Discmans	0	0	(2,500,000)
Total relevant costs under total-alternatives approach	$15,000,000	$16,000,000	$13,500,000
PANEL B Opportunity-Cost Approach to Make-or-Buy Decisions			
Total incremental future costs of making/buying stereo CD players (from Exhibit 11-6)	$15,000,000	$16,000,000	$16,000,000
Opportunity cost: Profit contribution forgone because capacity will not be used to make Discmans, the next-best alternative	2,500,000	2,500,000	0
Total relevant costs under opportunity-cost approach	$17,500,000	$18,500,000	$16,000,000

Note that the differences in costs across the columns in Panels A and B are the same: The cost of alternative 3 is $1,500,000 less than the cost of alternative 1, and $2,500,000 less than the cost of alternative 2.

Consider alternative 1, make stereo CD players and do not make Discmans. Ask, what are all the costs of making stereo CD players under this alternative? Certainly Soho will incur $15,000,000 of incremental costs to make stereo CD players. But is this the entire cost? No, because by deciding to use limited manufacturing resources to make stereo CD players, Soho will give up the opportunity to earn $2,500,000 by not using these resources to make Discmans. Therefore, the relevant costs of making stereo CD players are the incremental costs of $15,000,000 plus the opportunity cost of $2,500,000.

Next consider alternative 2, buy stereo CD players and do not make Discmans. The incremental cost of buying stereo CD players will be $16,000,000. Similar to alternative 1, there is also an opportunity cost of $2,500,000 as a result of deciding not to make Discmans.

Finally, consider alternative 3, buy stereo CD players and make Discmans. The incremental cost of buying stereo CD players will be $16,000,000. The opportunity cost is zero. Why? Because by choosing this alternative, Soho will not forgo the profit it can earn from making and selling Discmans.

Panel B leads management to the same conclusion as Panel A: buying stereo CD players and making Discmans is the preferred alternative.

Panels A and B of Exhibit 11-7 describe two consistent approaches to decision making with capacity constraints. The total-alternatives approach in Panel A includes all future incremental costs and revenues. For example, under alternative 3, the additional future operating income from *using capacity to make and sell Discmans* ($2,500,000) is subtracted from the future incremental cost of buying stereo CD players ($16,000,000). The opportunity-cost analysis in Panel B takes the opposite approach. It focuses on stereo CD players. *Whenever capacity is not going to be used to make and sell Discmans*, the future forgone operating income is added as an opportunity cost of making or buying stereo CD players, as in alternatives 1 and 2. (Note that when Discmans are made, as in alternative 3, there is no "opportunity cost of not making Discmans.") Therefore, whereas Panel A *subtracts* $2,500,000 under alternative 3, Panel B *adds* $2,500,000 under alternative 1 and also under alternative 2. *Panel B highlights the idea that when capacity is constrained, the relevant revenues and costs of any alternative equal the incremental future revenues and costs plus the opportunity cost.*

Concepts in Action

The Changing Benefits and Costs of "Offshoring"

In recent years, many companies in the United States have engaged in the rapidly-evolving practice of "offshoring," which is the outsourcing of business processes and jobs to other countries. Offshoring was initially popular with companies because it yielded significant cost savings. Within the high-tech sector, for example, in 2004 the average computer programmer in the United States made $65,000 per year plus benefits, whereas one in India earned only $7,500 annually. Along with India, companies headquartered in the United States also outsourced jobs to China, the Philippines, and Latin America. Similar opportunities for cost savings also arose in the customer-service, technical-support, manufacturing, and supply-chain functions. Savings resulting from offshoring either increased profits or were passed on to consumers via lower prices. McKinsey & Company, a consulting firm, initially estimated that in the long run outsourcing could result in as much as a 50% increase in profits for some American businesses.

Despite the benefits, offshoring came with costs. A study by Hewitt Associates found that many companies failed to account for many of costs associated with offshoring, including the costs of international taxation, of coordinating the global supply chain, and of shuttering domestic facilities. Additionally, offshoring generated great controversy among public-policy experts, laid-off workers, and labor leaders who criticized the practice as "unfair."

But the offshoring environment is changing. First, the cost savings from offshoring are not what they used to be as labor costs for the right talent in China, India, Eastern Europe, and Latin America continue to increase. Second, companies are recognizing that for more complex, higher-end work, individuals providing the service need to have deep knowledge of the business and organizational needs of the customer. That is, they need to be located close to the customer and the business.

A case in point is IBM's work with Center Point Energy, a Texas utility, to install computerized electric meters, sensors and software in a "smart" grid to improve service and reduce cost. The business expertise needed to design the software to work with the production of electric power and to attach sensors to power lines to collect data on electricity flows cannot be outsourced. To do this well requires a team on the ground observing, coordinating, and negotiating. Of course, some of the software for the project continues to be written in India. Nevertheless, the shifting of work away from math-based rules to custom work that requires deep local knowledge creates natural limits to offshoring.

Sources: M. Baily, *Exploding the Myths About Offshoring* (April 2004), Available from McKinsey & Company. www.mckinsey.com; "Study Notes Offshoring Downside," *CNN/Money*, March 5, 2004; *Research Summary: Total Cost of Offshoring (TCO): Understanding the True Offshore Financial Rewards and Costs* (May 2004), Available from neoIT. www.neoit.com; D. Farrell, et al., *U.S. Offshoring: Rethinking the Response* (December 2005), Available from McKinsey & Company. www.mckinsey.com; M. Mandel, "The Real Cost of Offshoring," *BusinessWeek*, June 18, 2007; S. Lohr, "At IBM, A Smarter Way to Outsource," *The New York Times*, July 5, 2007.

However, when more than two alternatives are being considered simultaneously, it is generally easier to use the total-alternatives approach.

Opportunity costs are not incorporated into formal financial accounting records. Why? Because historical record keeping is limited to transactions involving alternatives that were *actually selected*, rather than alternatives that were rejected. Rejected alternatives do not produce transactions and so they are not recorded. If Soho makes stereo CD players, it will not make Discmans, and it will not record any accounting entries for Discmans. Yet the opportunity cost of making stereo CD players, which equals the operating income that Soho forgoes by not making Discmans, is a crucial input into the make-or-buy decision. Consider again Exhibit 11-7, Panel B. On the basis of only the incremental costs systematically recorded in the accounting system, it is less costly for Soho to make rather than buy stereo CD players. Recognizing the opportunity cost of $2,500,000 leads to the different conclusion: buying stereo CD players is preferable.

Suppose Soho has sufficient capacity to make Discmans even if it makes stereo CD players. In this case, Soho has a fourth alternative: make stereo CD players and make Discmans. For this alternative, the opportunity cost of making stereo CD players is $0 because Soho does not give up the $2,500,000 operating income from making

Discmans even if it chooses to make stereo CD players. The relevant costs are \$15,000,000 (incremental costs of \$15,000,000 plus opportunity cost of \$0). Under these conditions, Soho would prefer to make stereo CD players, rather than buy them, and also make Discmans.

Besides quantitative considerations, the make-or-buy decision should also consider strategic and qualitative factors. If Soho decides to buy stereo CD players from an outside supplier, it should consider factors such as the supplier's reputation for quality and timely delivery. Soho would also want to consider the strategic consequences of selling Discmans. For example, will selling Discmans take Soho's focus away from its stereo business?

Carrying Costs of Inventory

To see another example of an opportunity cost, consider the following data for Soho:

Annual estimated stereo CD player requirements for next year	1,000,000 units
Cost per unit when each purchase is equal to 10,000 units	\$16.00
Cost per unit when each purchase is equal to or greater than 500,000 units; \$16 minus 1% discount	\$15.84
Cost of a purchase order	\$500
Alternatives under consideration:	
A. Make 100 purchases of 10,000 units each during next year	
B. Make 2 purchases of 500,000 units during the year	
Average investment in inventory:	
A. (10,000 units × \$16.00 per unit) ÷ 2[a]	\$80,000
B. (500,000 units × \$15.84 per unit) ÷ 2[a]	\$3,960,000
Annual rate of return if cash is invested elsewhere (for example, bonds or stocks) at the same level of risk as investment in inventory)	9%

[a] The example assumes that stereo-CD-player purchases will be used uniformly throughout the year. The average investment in inventory during the year is the cost of the inventory when a purchase is received plus the cost of inventory just before the next purchase is delivered (in our example, zero) divided by 2.

Soho will pay cash for the stereo CD players it buys. Which purchasing alternative is more economical for Soho? The following table presents the two alternatives.

	Alternative A: Make 100 Purchases of 10,000 Units Each During the Year (1)	Alternative B: Make 2 Purchases of 500,000 Units Each During the Year (2)	Difference (3) = (1) − (2)
Annual purchase-order costs (100 purch. orders × \$500/purch. order; 2 purch. orders × \$500/purch. order)	\$ 50,000	\$ 1,000	\$ 49,000
Annual purchase costs (1,000,000 units × \$16.00/unit; 1,000,000 units × \$15.84/unit)	16,000,000	15,840,000	160,000
Opportunity cost: Annual rate of return that could be earned if investment in inventory were invested elsewhere at the same level of risk (0.09 × \$80,000; 0.09 × \$3,960,000)	7,200	356,400	(349,200)
Relevant costs	\$16,057,200	\$16,197,400	\$(140,200)

The opportunity cost of holding inventory is the income forgone by tying up money in inventory and not investing it elsewhere. The opportunity cost would not be recorded in the accounting system because, once the alternative of investing money elsewhere is rejected, there are no transactions related to this alternative to record. On the basis of the costs recorded in the accounting system (purchase-order costs and purchase costs), Soho would erroneously conclude that making two purchases of 500,000 units each is the less costly alternative. Column 3, however, indicates that, consistent with the trends toward holding smaller inventories, purchasing smaller quantities of 10,000 units 100 times a year is preferred to purchasing 500,000 units twice during the year. Why? Because the lower opportunity cost of holding smaller inventory exceeds the higher purchase and ordering costs. If the opportunity cost of money tied up in inventory were greater than 9% per year, or if other incremental benefits of holding lower inventory were considered—such as lower insurance, materials-handling, storage, obsolescence, and breakage costs—making 100 purchases would be even more economical.

Product-Mix Decisions with Capacity Constraints

Learning Objective 4

Know how to choose which products to produce when there are capacity constraints

. . . select the product with the highest contribution margin per unit of the limiting resource

We now examine how the concept of relevance applies to **product-mix decisions**—the decisions made by a company about which products to sell and in what quantities. These decisions usually have only a short-run focus because the level of capacity can be expanded in the long run. For example, BMW, the German car manufacturer, must continually adapt the mix of its different models of cars (for example, 325i, 525i, and 740i) to short-run fluctuations in selling prices and demand. To determine product mix, a company maximizes operating income, given constraints such as capacity and demand. Throughout this section, we assume that as short-run changes in product mix occur, the only costs that change are costs that are variable with respect to the number of units produced (and sold). Under this assumption, the analysis of individual product contribution margins provides insight into the product mix that maximizes operating income.

Example 4: Power Recreation assembles two engines—a snowmobile engine and a boat engine—at its Lexington, Kentucky, plant.

	Snowmobile Engine	Boat Engine
Selling price	$800	$1,000
Variable cost per unit	560	625
Contribution margin per unit	$240	$ 375
Contribution margin percentage		
($240 ÷ $800; $375 ÷ $1,000)	30%	37.5%

Assume that only 600 machine-hours are available daily for assembling engines. Additional capacity cannot be obtained in the short run. Power Recreation can sell as many engines as it produces. The constraining resource, then, is machine-hours. It takes two machine-hours to produce one snowmobile engine and five machine-hours to produce one boat engine. What product mix should Power Recreation's managers choose to maximize its operating income?

In terms of contribution margin per unit and contribution margin percentage, boat engines are more profitable than snowmobile engines. The product that Power Recreation should produce and sell, however, is not necessarily the product with the higher individual contribution margin per unit or contribution margin percentage. Managers should choose the product with *the highest contribution margin per unit of the constraining resource (factor)*. That's the resource that restricts or limits the production or sale of products.

	Snowmobile Engine	Boat Engine
Contribution margin per unit	$240	$375
Machine-hours required to produce one unit	2 machine-hours	5 machine-hours
Contribution margin per machine-hour		
$240 per unit ÷ 2 machine-hours/unit	$120/machine-hour	
$375 per unit ÷ 5 machine-hours/unit		$75/machine-hour
Total contribution margin for 600 machine-hours		
$120/machine-hour × 600 machine-hours	$72,000	
$75/machine-hour × 600 machine-hours		$45,000

Producing snowmobile engines earns more contribution margin per machine-hour, which is the constraining resource in this example. Therefore, choosing to produce and sell snowmobile engines maximizes *total* contribution margin and operating income. Other constraints in manufacturing settings can be the availability of direct materials, components, or skilled labor, as well as financial and sales factors. In a retail department store, the constraining resource may be linear feet of display space. Regardless of the specific constraining resource, managers should always focus on maximizing *total* contribution margin by choosing products that give the highest contribution margin per unit of the constraining resource.

In many cases, a manufacturer or retailer has the challenge of trying to maximize total operating income for a variety of products, each with more than one constraining resource. Some constraints may require a manufacturer or retailer to stock minimum quantities of products even if these products are not very profitable. For example, supermarkets must stock less-profitable products because customers will be willing to shop at a supermarket only if it carries a wide range of products that customers desire. To determine the most profitable production schedule and the most profitable product mix, the manufacturer or retailer needs to determine the maximum total contribution margin in the face of many constraints. Optimization techniques, such as linear programming discussed in the appendix to this chapter, help solve these more-complex problems.

Finally, there is the question of managing the bottleneck constraint to increase output and, therefore, contribution margin. Can the available machine-hours for assembling engines be increased beyond 600, for example, by reducing idle time? Can the time needed to assemble each snowmobile engine (two machine-hours) and each boat engine (five machine-hours) be reduced, for example, by reducing setup time and processing time of assembly? Can quality be improved so that constrained capacity is used to produce only good units rather than some good and some defective units? Can some of the assembly operations be outsourced to allow more engines to be built? Implementing any of these options will likely require Power Recreation to incur incremental costs. Power Recreation will implement only those options where the increase in contribution margins exceeds the increase in costs. *Instructors and students who, at this point, want to explore these issues in more detail can go to the section in Chapter 19, pages 680–684, titled "Theory of Constraints and Throughput Contribution Analysis" and then return to this chapter without any loss of continuity.*

Customer Profitability, Activity-Based Costing, and Relevant Costs

Learning Objective 5

Discuss factors managers must consider when adding or dropping customers or segments

. . . managers should focus on how total costs differ among alternatives and ignore allocated overhead costs

Not only must companies make choices regarding which products and how much of each product to produce, they must often make decisions about adding or dropping a product line or a business segment. Similarly, if the cost object is a customer, companies must make decisions about adding or dropping customers (analogous to a product line) or a branch office (analogous to a business segment). We illustrate relevant-revenue and relevant-cost analysis for these kinds of decisions using customers rather than products as the cost object.

Example 5: Allied West, the West Coast sales office of Allied Furniture, a wholesaler of specialized furniture, supplies furniture to three local retailers: Vogel, Brenner, and Wisk. Exhibit 11-8 presents expected revenues and costs of Allied West by customer for the upcoming year using its activity-based costing system. Allied West assigns costs to customers based on the activities needed to support each customer. Information on Allied West's costs for different activities at various levels of the cost hierarchy follows:

- Furniture-handling labor costs vary with the number of units of furniture shipped to customers.

Exhibit 11-8

Customer Profitability Analysis for Allied West

	Customer			
	Vogel	Brenner	Wisk	Total
Revenues	$500,000	$300,000	$400,000	$1,200,000
Cost of goods sold	370,000	220,000	330,000	920,000
Furniture-handling labor	41,000	18,000	33,000	92,000
Furniture-handling equipment cost written off as depreciation	12,000	4,000	9,000	25,000
Rent	14,000	8,000	14,000	36,000
Marketing support	11,000	9,000	10,000	30,000
Sales-order and delivery processing	13,000	7,000	12,000	32,000
General administration	20,000	12,000	16,000	48,000
Allocated corporate-office costs	10,000	6,000	8,000	24,000
Total costs	491,000	284,000	432,000	1,207,000
Operating income	$ 9,000	$ 16,000	$ (32,000)	$ (7,000)

- Allied West reserves different areas of the warehouse to stock furniture for different customers. For simplicity, assume that furniture-handling equipment in an area and depreciation costs on the equipment are identified with individual customers (customer-level costs). Any unused equipment remains idle. The equipment has a one-year useful life and zero disposal value.
- Allied West allocates rent to each customer on the basis of the amount of warehouse space reserved for that customer.
- Marketing costs vary with the number of sales visits made to customers.
- Sales-order costs are batch-level costs that vary with the number of sales orders received from customers; delivery-processing costs are batch-level costs that vary with the number of shipments made.
- Allied West allocates fixed general-administration costs (facility-level costs) to customers on the basis of customer revenues.
- Allied Furniture allocates its fixed corporate-office costs to sales offices on the basis of the square feet area of each sales office. Allied West then allocates these costs to customers on the basis of customer revenues.

In the following sections, we consider several decisions that Allied West's managers face: Should Allied West drop the Wisk account? Should it add a fourth customer, Loral? Should Allied Furniture close down Allied West? Should it open another sales office, Allied South, whose revenues and costs are identical to those of Allied West?

Relevant-Revenue and Relevant-Cost Analysis of Dropping a Customer

Exhibit 11-8 indicates a loss of $32,000 on the Wisk account. Allied West's managers believe the reason for the loss is that Wisk places low-margin orders with Allied, and has relatively high sales-order, delivery-processing, furniture-handling, and marketing costs. Allied West is considering several possible actions with respect to the Wisk account: reducing its own costs of supporting Wisk by becoming more efficient, cutting back on some of the services it offers Wisk, asking Wisk to place larger, less frequent orders, charging Wisk higher prices, or dropping the Wisk account. The following analysis focuses on the operating-income effect of dropping the Wisk account.

To determine what to do, Allied West's managers must answer the question, What are the relevant revenues and relevant costs? Information about the effect of dropping the Wisk account follows.

Exhibit 11-9

Relevant-Revenue and Relevant-Cost Analysis for Dropping the Wisk Account and Adding the Loral Account

	(Loss in Revenues) and Savings in Costs from Dropping Wisk Account (1)	Incremental Revenues and (Incremental Costs) from Adding Loral Account (2)
Revenues	$(400,000)	$400,000
Cost of goods sold	330,000	(330,000)
Furniture-handling labor	33,000	(33,000)
Furniture-handling equipment cost written off as depreciation	0	(9,000)
Rent	0	0
Marketing support	10,000	(10,000)
Sales-order and delivery processing	12,000	(12,000)
General administration	0	0
Corporate-office costs	0	0
Total costs	385,000	(394,000)
Effect on operating income (loss)	$ (15,000)	$ 6,000

- Dropping the Wisk account will save cost of goods sold, furniture-handling labor, marketing support, sales-order, and delivery-processing costs incurred on the account.
- Dropping the Wisk account will leave idle the warehouse space and furniture-handling equipment currently used to supply products to Wisk.
- Dropping the Wisk account will have no effect on fixed general-administration costs or corporate-office costs.

Exhibit 11-9, column 1, presents the relevant-revenue and relevant-cost analysis using data from the Wisk column in Exhibit 11-8. Allied West's operating income will be $15,000 lower if it drops the Wisk account—the cost savings from dropping the Wisk account, $385,000, will not be enough to offset the loss of $400,000 in revenues—so Allied West's managers decide to keep the account. Note that there is no opportunity cost of using warehouse space for Wisk because without Wisk, the space and equipment will remain idle.

Depreciation is a past cost, therefore it is irrelevant; rent, general-administration, and corporate-office costs are irrelevant because they are future costs that will not change if Allied West drops the Wisk account. For purposes of this decision, Allied West's managers should be particularly mindful of allocated overhead costs such as corporate-office costs. They should ignore amounts allocated to the sales office and individual customers. The question Allied West's managers must ask when deciding whether corporate-office costs are relevant is, will expected total corporate-office costs decrease as a result of dropping the Wisk account? In our example, they will not, so these costs are irrelevant. *If expected total corporate-office costs* decreased by dropping the Wisk account, those savings would be relevant even if *the amount allocated to Allied West did not change.*

Now suppose that if Allied West drops the Wisk account, it could lease the extra warehouse space to Sanchez Corporation for $20,000 per year. Then $20,000 would be Allied's opportunity cost of continuing to use the warehouse to service Wisk. Allied West would gain $5,000 by dropping the Wisk account ($20,000 from lease revenue minus lost operating income of $15,000). Before reaching a decision, Allied West's managers must examine whether Wisk can be made more profitable so that supplying products to Wisk earns more than the $20,000 from leasing to Sanchez. The managers must also consider strategic factors such as the effect of the decision on Allied West's reputation for developing stable, long-run business relationships with its customers.

Relevant-Revenue and Relevant-Cost Analysis of Adding a Customer

Suppose that in addition to Vogel, Brenner, and Wisk, Allied West's managers are evaluating the profitability of adding a customer, Loral. Allied West is already incurring annual costs of $36,000 for warehouse rent and $48,000 for general-administration costs. These costs together with *actual total* corporate-office costs will not change if Loral is added as a customer. Loral has a customer profile much like Wisk's. Suppose Allied West's managers predict revenues and costs of doing business with Loral to be the same as the revenues and costs described under the Wisk column of Exhibit 11-8. In particular, Allied West would have to acquire furniture-handling equipment for the Loral account costing $9,000, with a one-year useful life and zero disposal value. Should Allied West add Loral as a customer?

Exhibit 11-9, column 2, shows incremental revenues exceed incremental costs by $6,000. On the basis of this analysis, Allied West's managers would recommend adding Loral as a customer. Rent, general-administration, and corporate-office costs are irrelevant because these costs will not change if Loral is added as a customer. However, the cost of new equipment to support the Loral order (written off as depreciation of $9,000 in Exhibit 11-9, column 2) is relevant. That's because this cost can be avoided if Allied West decides not to add Loral as a customer. Note the critical distinction here: *Depreciation cost is irrelevant in deciding whether to drop Wisk as a customer because depreciation is a past cost, but the cost of purchasing new equipment that will then be written off as depreciation in the future is relevant in deciding whether to add Loral as a customer.*

Relevant-Revenue and Relevant-Cost Analysis of Closing or Adding Branch Offices or Segments

Companies periodically confront decisions about closing or adding branch offices or business segments. For example, given Allied West's expected loss of $7,000 (see Exhibit 11-8), should it be closed? Assume that closing Allied West will have no effect on total corporate-office costs.

Exhibit 11-10, column 1, presents the relevant-revenue and relevant-cost analysis using data from the Total column in Exhibit 11-8. The revenue losses of $1,200,000 will exceed the cost savings of $1,158,000, leading to a decrease in operating income of $42,000. Allied West should not be closed. The key reasons are that closing Allied West will not save depreciation cost of $25,000, which is a past or sunk cost, or actual total corporate-office costs. Corporate-office costs allocated to various sales offices will change *but the total amount of these costs will not decline*. The $24,000 no longer allocated to Allied West will be allocated to other sales offices. Therefore, the $24,000 of allocated corporate-office costs should not be included as expected cost savings from closing Allied West.

Now suppose Allied Furniture has the opportunity to open another sales office, Allied South, whose revenues and costs would be identical to Allied West's costs, including a cost of $25,000 to acquire furniture-handling equipment with a one-year useful life and zero disposal value. Opening this office will have no effect on total corporate-office costs. Should Allied Furniture open Allied South? Exhibit 11-10, column 2, indicates that it should do so because opening Allied South will increase operating income by $17,000. As

Exhibit 11-10

Relevant-Revenue and Relevant-Cost Analysis for Closing Allied West and Opening Allied South

	(Loss in Revenues) and Savings in Costs from Closing Allied West (1)	Incremental Revenues and (Incremental Costs) from Opening Allied South (2)
Revenues	$(1,200,000)	$1,200,000
Cost of goods sold	920,000	(920,000)
Furniture-handling labor	92,000	(92,000)
Furniture-handling equipment cost written off as depreciation	0	(25,000)
Rent	36,000	(36,000)
Marketing support	30,000	(30,000)
Sales-order and delivery processing	32,000	(32,000)
General administration	48,000	(48,000)
Corporate-office costs	0	0
Total costs	1,158,000	(1,183,000)
Effect on operating income (loss)	$ (42,000)	$ 17,000

before, the cost of new equipment (written off as depreciation) is relevant. But the point here is to ignore *allocated* corporate-office costs and focus on *total* corporate-office costs. Total corporate-office costs will not change if Allied South is opened, therefore these costs are irrelevant.

Irrelevance of Past Costs and Equipment-Replacement Decisions

Learning Objective 6

Explain why book value of equipment is irrelevant in equipment-replacement decisions

. . . it is a past cost

At several points in this chapter, when discussing the concept of relevance, we reasoned that past (historical or sunk) costs are irrelevant to decision making. That's because a decision cannot change something that has already happened. We now apply this concept to decisions about replacing equipment. We stress the idea that **book value**—original cost minus accumulated depreciation—of existing equipment is a past cost that is irrelevant.

Example 6: Toledo Company is considering replacing a metal-cutting machine with a newer model. The new machine is more efficient than the old machine, but it has a shorter life. Revenues from aircraft parts ($1.1 million per year) will be unaffected by the replacement decision. Here are the data the management accountant prepares for the existing (old) machine and the replacement (new) machine:

	Old Machine	New Machine
Original cost	$1,000,000	$600,000
Useful life	5 years	2 years
Current age	3 years	0 years
Remaining useful life	2 years	2 years
Accumulated depreciation	$600,000	Not acquired yet
Book value	$400,000	Not acquired yet
Current disposal value (in cash)	$40,000	Not acquired yet
Terminal disposal value (in cash 2 years from now)	$0	$0
Annual operating costs (maintenance, energy, repairs, coolants, and so on)	$800,000	$460,000

Toledo Corporation uses straight-line depreciation. To focus on relevance, we ignore the time value of money and income taxes.[1] Should Toledo replace its old machine?

Exhibit 11-11 presents a cost comparison of the two machines. Consider why each of the four items in Toledo's equipment-replacement decision is relevant or irrelevant:

1. **Book value of old machine, $400,000.** Irrelevant, because it is a past or sunk cost. All past costs are "down the drain." Nothing can change what has already been spent or what has already happened.
2. **Current disposal value of old machine, $40,000.** Relevant, because it is an expected future benefit that will only occur if the machine is replaced.
3. **Loss on disposal, $360,000.** This is the difference between amounts in items 1 and 2. It is a meaningless combination blurring the distinction between the irrelevant book value and the relevant disposal value. Each should be considered separately, as was done in items 1 and 2.
4. **Cost of new machine, $600,000.** Relevant, because it is an expected future cost that will only occur if the machine is purchased.

[1] See Chapter 21 for a discussion of time-value-of-money and income-tax considerations in capital investment decisions.

Exhibit 11-11

Operating Income Comparison: Replacement of Machine, Relevant and Irrelevant Items for Toledo Company

	Two Years Together		
	Keep (1)	Replace (2)	Difference (3) = (1) – (2)
Revenues	$2,200,000	$2,200,000	—
Operating costs			
Cash operating costs ($800,000/yr. × 2 years; $460,000/yr. × 2 years)	1,600,000	920,000	$ 680,000
Book value of old machine			
Periodic write-off as depreciation or	400,000	—	—
Lump-sum write-off	—	400,000[a]	
Current disposal value of old machine	—	(40,000)[a]	40,000
New machine cost, written off periodically as depreciation	—	600,000	(600,000)
Total operating costs	2,000,000	1,880,000	120,000
Operating income	$ 200,000	$ 320,000	$(120,000)

[a]In a formal income statement, these two items would be combined as "loss on disposal of machine" of $360,000.

Exhibit 11-11 should clarify these four assertions. Column 3 in Exhibit 11-11 shows that the book value of the old machine does not differ between the alternatives and could be ignored for decision-making purposes. No matter what the timing of the write-off—whether a lump-sum charge in the current year or depreciation charges over the next two years—the total amount is still $400,000 because it is a past (historical) cost. In contrast, the $600,000 cost of the new machine and the current disposal value of $40,000 for the old machine are relevant because they would not arise if Toledo's managers decided not to replace the machine. Note that the operating income from replacing is $120,000 higher for the two years together.

To provide focus, Exhibit 11-12 concentrates only on relevant items. Note that the same answer—higher operating income as a result of lower costs of $120,000 by replacing the machine—is obtained even though the book value is omitted from the calculations. The only relevant items are the cash operating costs, the disposal value of the old machine, and the cost of the new machine, which is represented as depreciation in Exhibit 11-12.

Learning Objective 7

Explain how conflicts can arise between the decision model used by a manager and the performance-evaluation model used to evaluate the manager

. . . tell managers to take a multiple-year view in decision making but judge their performance only on the basis of the current year's operating income

Decisions and Performance Evaluation

Consider our equipment-replacement example in light of the five-step sequence in Exhibit 11-1 (p. 388).

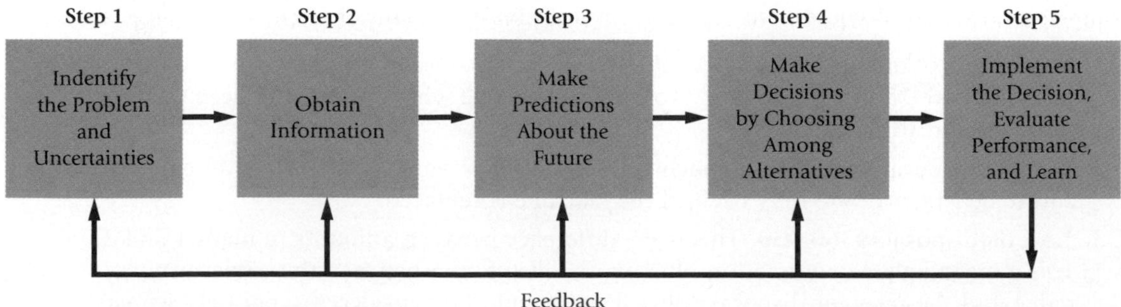

The decision model analysis (step 4), which is presented in Exhibits 11-11 and 11-12, dictates replacing the machine rather than keeping it. In the real world, however, would the manager replace? An important factor in replacement decisions is the manager's perception of whether the decision model is consistent with how the manager's performance will be judged after the decision is implemented (the performance-evaluation model in step 5).

Exhibit 11-12

Cost Comparison: Replacement of Machine, Relevant Items Only, for Toledo Company

	Two Years Together		
	Keep (1)	**Replace (2)**	**Difference (3) = (1) – (2)**
Cash operating costs	$1,600,000	$ 920,000	$680,000
Current disposal value of old machine	—	(40,000)	40,000
New machine, written off periodically as depreciation	—	600,000	(600,000)
Total relevant costs	$1,600,000	$1,480,000	$120,000

From the perspective of their own careers, it is no surprise that managers tend to favor the alternative that makes their performance look better. If the performance-evaluation model conflicts with the decision model, the performance-evaluation model often prevails in influencing managers' decisions. For example, if the promotion or bonus of the manager at Toledo hinges on his or her first year's operating income performance under accrual accounting, the manager's temptation *not* to replace will be overwhelming. Why? Because the accrual accounting model for measuring performance will show a higher first-year operating income if the old machine is kept rather than replaced (as the following table shows):

First-Year Results: Accrual Accounting

	Keep		Replace	
Revenues		$1,100,000		$1,100,000
Operating costs				
Cash-operating costs	$800,000		$460,000	
Depreciation	200,000		300,000	
Loss on disposal	—		360,000	
Total operating costs		1,000,000		1,120,000
Operating income (loss)		$ 100,000		$ (20,000)

Even though top management's goals encompass the two-year period (consistent with the decision model), the manager will focus on first-year results if his or her evaluation is based on short-run measures such as the first-year's operating income.

Resolving the conflict between the decision model and the performance-evaluation model is frequently a baffling problem in practice. In theory, resolving the difficulty seems obvious: Design models that are consistent. Consider our replacement example. Year-by-year effects on operating income of replacement can be budgeted for the two-year planning horizon. The manager then would be evaluated on the expectation that the first year would be poor and the next year would be much better. Doing this for every decision, however, makes the performance evaluation model very cumbersome. As a result of these practical difficulties, accounting systems rarely track each decision separately. Performance evaluation focuses on responsibility centers for a specific period, not on projects or individual items of equipment over their useful lives. Thus, the impacts of many different decisions are combined in a single performance report and evaluation measure, say operating income. Lower-level managers make decisions to maximize operating income, and top management—through the reporting system—is rarely aware of particular desirable alternatives that were *not* chosen by lower-level managers because of conflicts between the decision and performance-evaluation models.

Consider another conflict between the decision model and the performance-evaluation model. Suppose a manager buys a particular machine only to discover shortly thereafter that a better machine could have been purchased instead. The decision model may suggest replacing the machine that was just bought with the better machine, but will the manager do so? Probably not. Why? Because replacing the machine so soon after its purchase will reflect badly on the manager's capabilities and performance. If the manager's bosses have no knowledge of the better machine, the manager may prefer to keep the recently purchased machine rather than alert them to the better machine.

Chapter 23 discusses performance evaluation models in more detail.

Problem for Self-Study

Wally Lewis is manager of the engineering development division of Goldcoast Products. Lewis has just received a proposal signed by all 15 of his engineers to replace the workstations with networked personal computers (networked PCs). Lewis is not enthusiastic about the proposal.

Data on workstations and networked PCs are:

	Workstations	Networked PCs
Original cost	$300,000	$135,000
Useful life	5 years	3 years
Current age	2 years	0 years
Remaining useful life	3 years	3 years
Accumulated depreciation	$120,000	Not acquired yet
Current book value	$180,000	Not acquired yet
Current disposal value (in cash)	$95,000	Not acquired yet
Terminal disposal value (in cash 3 years from now)	$0	$0
Annual computer-related cash operating costs	$40,000	$10,000
Annual revenues	$1,000,000	$1,000,000
Annual noncomputer-related operating costs	$880,000	$880,000

Lewis's annual bonus includes a component based on division operating income. He has a promotion possibility next year that would make him a group vice president of Goldcoast Products.

Required

1. Compare the costs of workstations and networked PCs. Consider the cumulative results for the three years together, ignoring the time value of money and income taxes.
2. Why might Lewis be reluctant to purchase the networked PCs?

Solution

1. The following table considers all cost items when comparing future costs of workstations and networked PCs:

	Three Years Together		
All Items	**Workstations (1)**	**Networked PCs (2)**	**Difference (3) = (1) − (2)**
Revenues	$3,000,000	$3,000,000	—
Operating costs			
Noncomputer-related operating costs	2,640,000	2,640,000	—
Computer-related cash operating costs	120,000	30,000	$ 90,000
Workstations' book value			
Periodic write-off as depreciation or	180,000	— }	—
Lump-sum write-off	—	180,000 }	
Current disposal value of workstations	—	(95,000)	95,000
Networked PCs, written off periodically as depreciation	—	135,000	(135,000)
Total operating costs	2,940,000	2,890,000	50,000
Operating income	$ 60,000	$ 110,000	$ (50,000)

Alternatively, the analysis could focus on only those items in the preceding table that differ between the alternatives.

	Three Years Together		
Relevant Items	**Workstations**	**Networked PCs**	**Difference**
Computer-related cash operating costs	$120,000	$ 30,000	$ 90,000
Current disposal value of workstations	—	(95,000)	95,000
Networked PCs, written off periodically as depreciation	—	135,000	(135,000)
Total relevant costs	$120,000	$ 70,000	$ 50,000

The analysis suggests that it is cost-effective to replace the workstations with the networked PCs.

2. The accrual-accounting operating incomes *for the first year* under the keep-workstations versus the buy-networked-PCs alternatives are:

	Keep Workstations		Buy Networked PCs	
Revenues		$1,000,000		$1,000,000
Operating costs				
Noncomputer-related operating costs	$880,000		$880,000	
Computer-related cash operating costs	40,000		10,000	
Depreciation	60,000		45,000	
Loss on disposal of workstations	—		85,000[a]	
Total operating costs		980,000		1,020,000
Operating income (loss)		$ 20,000		$ (20,000)

[a] $85,000 = Book value of workstations, $180,000 – Current disposal value, $95,000.

Lewis would be less happy with the expected operating loss of $20,000 if the networked PCs are purchased than he would be with the expected operating income of $20,000 if the workstations are kept. Buying the networked PCs would eliminate the component of his bonus based on operating income. He might also perceive the $20,000 operating loss as reducing his chances of being promoted to a group vice president.

Decision Points

The following question-and-answer format summarizes the chapter's learning objectives. Each decision presents a key question related to a learning objective. The guidelines are the answer to that question.

Decision	Guidelines
1. What is the five-step process that can be used to make decisions?	The five-step decision-making process is (a) identify the problem and uncertainties, (b) obtain information, (c) make predictions about the future, (d) make decisions by choosing among alternatives, and (e) implement the decision, evaluate performance, and learn.
2. When is a revenue or cost item relevant for a particular decision and what potential problems should be avoided in relevant-cost analysis?	To be relevant for a particular decision, a revenue or cost item must meet two criteria: (a) it must be an expected future revenue or expected future cost, and (b) it must differ among alternative courses of action. The outcomes of alternative actions can be quantitative and qualitative. Quantitative outcomes are measured in numerical terms. Some quantitative outcomes can be expressed in financial terms, others cannot. Qualitative factors, such as employee morale, are difficult to measure accurately in numerical terms. Consideration must be given to relevant quantitative and qualitative factors in making decisions. Two potential problems to avoid in relevant-cost analysis are (a) making incorrect general assumptions—such as all variable costs are relevant and all fixed costs are irrelevant—and (b) losing sight of total amounts, focusing instead on unit amounts.
3. What is an opportunity cost and why should it be included when making decisions?	Opportunity cost is the contribution to income that is forgone by not using a limited resource in its next-best alternative use. Opportunity cost is included in decision making because it represents the best alternative way in which an organization may have used its resources had it not made the decision it did.

4. When resources are constrained, how should managers choose which of multiple products to produce and sell?	Under these conditions, managers should select the product that yields the highest contribution margin per unit of the constraining or limiting resource (factor). In this way, total contribution margin will be maximized.
5. In deciding to add or drop customers or to add or discontinue branch offices or segments, what should managers focus on and how should they take into account allocated overhead costs?	Managers should focus on what costs will change when making decisions about adding or dropping customers or adding or discontinuing branch offices and segments. Managers should ignore allocated overhead costs.
6. Is book value of existing equipment relevant in equipment-replacement decisions?	Book value of existing equipment is a past (historical or sunk) cost and, therefore, is irrelevant in equipment-replacement decisions.
7. How can conflicts arise between the decision model used by a manager and the performance-evaluation model used to evaluate that manager?	Top management faces a persistent challenge: making sure that the performance-evaluation model of lower-level managers is consistent with the decision model. A common inconsistency is to tell these managers to take a multiple-year view in their decision making but then to judge their performance only on the basis of the current year's operating income.

APPENDIX: LINEAR PROGRAMMING

In this chapter's Power Recreation example (pp. 400–401), suppose both the snowmobile and boat engines must be tested on a very expensive machine before they are shipped to customers. The available machine-hours for testing are limited. Production data are:

Department	Available Daily Capacity in Hours	Use of Capacity in Hours per Unit of Product		Daily Maximum Production in Units	
		Snowmobile Engine	Boat Engine	Snowmobile Engine	Boat Engine
Assembly	600 machine-hours	2.0 machine-hours	5.0 machine-hours	300[a] snow engines	120 boat engines
Testing	120 testing-hours	1.0 machine-hour	0.5 machine-hour	120 snow engines	240 boat engines

[a] For example, 600 machine-hours ÷ 2.0 machine-hours per snowmobile engine = 300, the maximum number of snowmobile engines that the Assembly Department can make if it works exclusively on snowmobile engines.

Exhibit 11-13 summarizes these and other relevant data. In addition, as a result of material shortages for boat engines, Power Recreation cannot produce more than 110 boat engines per day. How many engines of each type should Power Recreation produce and sell daily to maximize operating income?

Exhibit 11-13

Operating Data for Power Recreation

	Department Capacity (per Day) In Product Units				
	Assembly	Testing	Selling Price	Variable Cost per Unit	Contribution Margin per Unit
Only snowmobile engines	300	120	$ 800	$560	$240
Only boat engines	120	240	$1,000	$625	$375

Because there are multiple constraints, a technique called *linear programming* or *LP* can be used to determine the number of each type of engine Power Recreation should produce. LP models typically assume that all costs are either variable or fixed with respect to a single cost driver (units of output). As we shall see, LP models also require certain other linear assumptions to hold. When these assumptions fail, other decision models should be considered.[2]

Steps in Solving an LP Problem

We use the data in Exhibit 11-13 to illustrate the three steps in solving an LP problem. Throughout this discussion, *S* equals the number of units of snowmobile engines produced and sold, and *B* equals the number of units of boat engines produced and sold.

Step 1: Determine the objective function. The **objective function** of a linear program expresses the objective or goal to be maximized (say, operating income) or minimized (say, operating costs). In our example, the objective is to find the combination of snowmobile engines and boat engines that maximizes total contribution margin. Fixed costs remain the same regardless of the product-mix decision and are irrelevant. The linear function expressing the objective for the total contribution margin (*TCM*) is:

$$TCM = \$240S + \$375B$$

Step 2: Specify the constraints. A **constraint** is a mathematical inequality or equality that must be satisfied by the variables in a mathematical model. The following linear inequalities express the relationships in our example:

Assembly Department constraint	$2S + 5B \leq 600$
Testing Department constraint	$1S + 0.5B \leq 120$
Materials-shortage constraint for boat engines	$B \leq 110$
Negative production is impossible	$S \geq 0$ and $B \geq 0$

The three solid lines on the graph in Exhibit 11-14 show the existing constraints for Assembly and Testing and the materials-shortage constraint.[3] The feasible or technically possible alternatives are those combinations of quantities of snowmobile engines and boat engines that satisfy all the constraining resources or factors. The shaded "area of feasible solutions" in Exhibit 11-14 shows the boundaries of those product combinations that are feasible.

Step 3: Compute the optimal solution. Linear programming (LP) is an optimization technique used to maximize the *objective function* when there are multiple *constraints*. We present two approaches for finding the optimal solution using LP: trial-and-error approach and graphic approach. These approaches are easy to use in our example because there are only two variables in the objective function and a small number of constraints. Understanding these approaches provides insight into LP. In most real-world LP applications, managers use computer software packages to calculate the optimal solution.[4]

---

[2] Other decision models are described in J. Moore and L. Weatherford, *Decision Modeling with Microsoft Excel*, 7th ed. (Upper Saddle River, NJ: Prentice Hall, 2005); and S. Nahmias, *Production and Operations Analysis*, 5th ed. (New York: McGraw-Hill/Irwin, 2006).

[3] As an example of how the lines are plotted in Exhibit 11-14, use equal signs instead of inequality signs and assume for the Assembly Department that $B = 0$; then $S = 300$ (600 machine-hours ÷ 2 machine-hours per snowmobile engine). Assume that $S = 0$; then $B = 120$ (600 machine-hours ÷ 5 machine-hours per boat engine). Connect those two points with a straight line.

[4] Standard computer software packages rely on the simplex method. The *simplex method* is an iterative step-by-step procedure for determining the optimal solution to an LP problem. It starts with a specific feasible solution and then tests it by substitution to see whether the result can be improved. These substitutions continue until no further improvement is possible and the optimal solution is obtained.

Exhibit 11-14

Linear Programming: Graphic Solution for Power Recreation

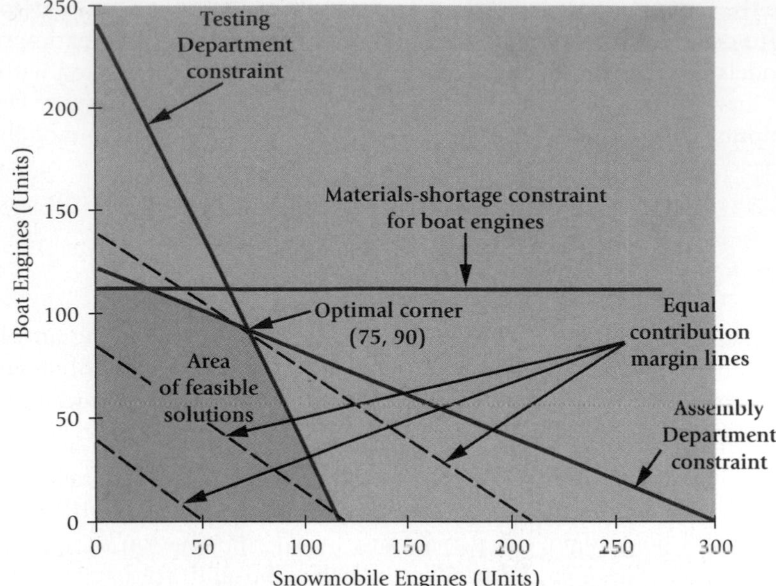

Trial-and-error approach The optimal solution can be found by trial and error, by working with coordinates of the corners of the area of feasible solutions.

First, select any set of corner points and compute the total contribution margin. Five corner points appear in Exhibit 11-14. It is helpful to use simultaneous equations to obtain the exact coordinates in the graph. To illustrate, the corner point ($S = 75$, $B = 90$) can be derived by solving the two pertinent constraint inequalities as simultaneous equations:

	$2S + 5B = 600$	(1)
	$1S + 0.5B = 120$	(2)
Multiplying (2) by 2:	$2S + B = 240$	(3)
Subtracting (3) from (1):	$4B = 360$	
Therefore,	$B = 360 \div 4 = 90$	
Substituting for B in (2):	$1S + 0.5(90) = 120$	
	$S = 120 - 45 = 75$	

Given $S = 75$ snowmobile engines and $B = 90$ boat engines, TCM = ($240 per snowmobile engine × 75 snowmobile engines) + ($375 per boat engine × 90 boat engines) = $51,750.

Second, move from corner point to corner point and compute the total contribution margin at each corner point.

Trial	Corner Point (S, B)	Snowmobile Engines (S)	Boat Engines (B)	Total Contribution Margin
1	(0, 0)	0	0	$240(0) + $375(0) = $0
2	(0, 110)	0	110	$240(0) + $375(110) = $41,250
3	(25,110)	25	110	$240(25) + $375(110) = $47,250
4	(75, 90)	75	90	$240(75) + $375(90) = $51,750[a]
5	(120, 0)	120	0	$240(120) + $375(0) = $28,800

[a]The optimal solution.

The optimal product mix is the mix that yields the highest total contribution: 75 snowmobile engines and 90 boat engines. To understand the solution, consider what happens when moving from the point (25,110) to (75,90). Power Recreation gives up $7,500 [$375 × (110 – 90)] in contribution margin from boat engines while gaining $12,000 [$240 × (75 – 25)] in contribution margin from snowmobile engines. This results in a net increase in contribution margin of $4,500 ($12,000 – $7,500), from $47,250 to $51,750.

Graphic approach Consider all possible combinations that will produce the same total contribution margin of, say, \$12,000. That is,

$$\$240S + \$375B = \$12,000$$

This set of \$12,000 contribution margins is a straight dashed line through [$S = 50$ (\$12,000 ÷ \$240); $B = 0$)] and [$S = 0$, $B = 32$ (\$12,000 ÷ \$375)] in Exhibit 11-14. Other equal total contribution margins can be represented by lines parallel to this one. In Exhibit 11-14, we show three dashed lines. Lines drawn farther from the origin represent more sales of both products and higher amounts of equal contribution margins.

The optimal line is the one farthest from the origin but still passing through a point in the area of feasible solutions. This line represents the highest total contribution margin. The optimal solution—the number of snowmobile engines and boat engines that will maximize the objective function, total contribution margin—is the corner point ($S = 75$, $B = 90$). This solution will become apparent if you put a straight-edge ruler on the graph and move it outward from the origin and parallel with the \$12,000 line. Move the ruler as far away from the origin as possible—that is, increase the total contribution margin—without leaving the area of feasible solutions. In general, the optimal solution in a maximization problem lies at the corner where the dashed line intersects an extreme point of the area of feasible solutions. Moving the ruler out any farther puts it outside the area of feasible solutions.

Sensitivity Analysis

What are the implications of uncertainty about the accounting or technical coefficients used in the objective function (such as the contribution margin per unit of snowmobile engines or boat engines) or the constraints (such as the number of machine-hours it takes to make a snowmobile engine or a boat engine)? Consider how a change in the contribution margin of snowmobile engines from \$240 to \$300 per unit would affect the optimal solution. Assume the contribution margin for boat engines remains unchanged at \$375 per unit. The revised objective function will be:

$$TCM = \$300S + \$375B$$

Using the trial-and-error approach to calculate the total contribution margin for each of the five corner points described in the previous table, the optimal solution is still ($S = 75$, $B = 90$). What if the contribution margin of snowmobile engines falls to \$160 per unit? The optimal solution remains the same ($S = 75$, $B = 90$). Thus, big changes in the contribution margin per unit of snowmobile engines have no effect on the optimal solution in this case. That's because, although the slopes of the equal contribution margin lines in Exhibit 11-14 change as the contribution margin of snowmobile engines changes from \$240 to \$300 to \$160 per unit, the farthest point at which the equal contribution margin lines intersect the area of feasible solutions is still ($S = 75$, $B = 90$).

TERMS TO LEARN

This chapter and the Glossary at the end of the book contain definitions of:

book value (**p. 405**)
business function costs (**p. 391**)
constraint (**p. 411**)
decision model (**p. 387**)
differential cost (**p. 395**)
differential revenue (**p. 395**)
full costs of the product (**p. 391**)
incremental cost (**p. 395**)
incremental revenue (**p. 395**)
insourcing (**p. 393**)
linear programming (LP) (**p. 411**)
make-or-buy decisions (**p. 393**)
objective function (**p. 411**)
one-time-only special order (**p. 390**)
opportunity cost (**p. 396**)
outsourcing (**p. 393**)
product-mix decisions (**p. 400**)
qualitative factors (**p. 389**)
quantitative factors (**p. 389**)
relevant costs (**p. 388**)
relevant revenues (**p. 388**)
sunk costs (**p. 389**)

ASSIGNMENT MATERIAL

Questions

11-1 Outline the five-step sequence in a decision process.

11-2 Define relevant costs. Why are historical costs irrelevant?

11-3 "All future costs are relevant." Do you agree? Why?

11-4 Distinguish between quantitative and qualitative factors in decision making.

11-5 Describe two potential problems that should be avoided in relevant-cost analysis.

11-6 "Variable costs are always relevant, and fixed costs are always irrelevant." Do you agree? Why?

11-7 "A component part should be purchased whenever the purchase price is less than its total manufacturing cost per unit." Do you agree? Why?

11-8 Define opportunity cost.

11-9 "Managers should always buy inventory in quantities that result in the lowest purchase cost per unit." Do you agree? Why?

11-10 "Management should always maximize sales of the product with the highest contribution margin per unit." Do you agree? Why?

11-11 "A branch office or business segment that shows negative operating income should be shut down." Do you agree? Explain briefly.

11-12 "Cost written off as depreciation on equipment already purchased is always irrelevant." Do you agree? Why?

11-13 "Managers will always choose the alternative that maximizes operating income or minimizes costs in the decision model." Do you agree? Why?

11-14 Describe the three steps in solving a linear programming problem.

11-15 How might the optimal solution of a linear programming problem be determined?

Exercises

11-16 Disposal of assets. Answer the following questions.

1. A company has an inventory of 1,000 assorted parts for a line of missiles that has been discontinued. The inventory cost is $75,000. The parts can be either (a) re-machined at total additional costs of $25,000 and then sold for $30,000 or (b) sold as scrap for $3,000. Which action is more profitable? Show your calculations.
2. A truck, costing $100,000 and uninsured, is wrecked its first day in use. It can be either (a) disposed of for $15,000 cash and replaced with a similar truck costing $105,000 or (b) rebuilt for $85,000, and thus be brand-new as far as operating characteristics and looks are concerned. Which action is less costly? Show your calculations.

11-17 Relevant and irrelevant costs. Answer the following questions.

1. Dalton computers makes 5,000 units of a circuit board, CB76 at a cost of $230 each. Variable cost per unit is $180 and fixed cost per unit is $50. Peach Electronics offers to supply 5,000 units of CB76 for $210. If Dalton buys from Peach it will be able to save $20 per unit in fixed costs but continue to incur the remaining $30 per unit. Should Dalton accept Peach's offer? Explain.
2. AP Manufacturing is deciding whether to keep or replace an old machine. It obtains the following information:

	Old Machine	New Machine
Original cost	$10,000	$8,000
Useful life	10 years	4 years
Current age	6 years	0 years
Remaining useful life	4 years	4 years
Accumulated depreciation	$6,000	Not acquired yet
Book value	$4,000	Not acquired yet
Current disposal value (in cash)	$2,500	Not acquired yet
Terminal disposal value (4 years from now)	$0	$0
Annual cash operating costs	$20,000	$12,000

AP Manufacturing uses straight-line depreciation. Ignore the time value of money and income taxes. Should AP Manufacturing replace the old machine? Explain.

11-18 Multiple choice. (CPA) Choose the best answer.

1. The Woody Company manufactures slippers and sells them at $10 a pair. Variable manufacturing cost is $4.50 a pair, and allocated fixed manufacturing cost is $1.50 a pair. It has enough idle capacity available to accept a one-time-only special order of 20,000 pairs of slippers at $6 a pair. Woody will not incur any marketing costs as a result of the special order. What would the effect on operating income be if the special order could be accepted without affecting normal sales? (a) $0, (b) $30,000 increase, (c) $90,000 increase, or (d) $120,000 increase. Show your calculations.
2. The Reno Company manufactures Part No. 498 for use in its production line. The manufacturing cost per unit for 20,000 units of Part No. 498 is as follows:

Direct materials	$ 6
Direct manufacturing labor	30
Variable manufacturing overhead	12
Fixed manufacturing overhead allocated	16
Total manufacturing cost per unit	$64

The Tray Company has offered to sell 20,000 units of Part No. 498 to Reno for $60 per unit. Reno will make the decision to buy the part from Tray if there is an overall savings of at least $25,000 for Reno. If Reno accepts Tray's offer, $9 per unit of the fixed overhead allocated would be eliminated. Furthermore, Reno has determined that the released facilities could be used to save relevant costs in the manufacture of Part No. 575. For Reno to achieve an overall savings of $25,000, the amount of relevant costs that would have to be saved by using the released facilities in the manufacture of Part No. 575 would be (a) $80,000, (b) $85,000, (c) $125,000, or (d) $140,000. Show your calculations.

11-19 Special order, activity-based costing. (CMA, adapted) The Award Plus Company manufactures medals for winners of athletic events and other contests. Its manufacturing plant has the capacity to produce 10,000 medals each month. Current production and sales are 7,500 medals per month. The company normally charges $150 per medal. Cost information for the current activity level is as follows:

Variable costs that vary with number of units produced	
Direct materials	$ 262,500
Direct manufacturing labor	300,000
Variable costs (for setups, materials handling, quality control, and so on) that vary with number of batches, 150 batches × $500 per batch	75,000
Fixed manufacturing costs	275,000
Fixed marketing costs	175,000
Total costs	$1,087,500

Award Plus has just received a special one-time-only order for 2,500 medals at $100 per medal. Accepting the special order would not affect the company's regular business. Award Plus makes medals for its existing customers in batch sizes of 50 medals (150 batches × 50 medals per batch = 7,500 medals). The special order requires Award Plus to make the medals in 25 batches of 100 each.

Required

1. Should Award Plus accept this special order? Show your calculations.
2. Suppose plant capacity were only 9,000 medals instead of 10,000 medals each month. The special order must either be taken in full or be rejected completely. Should Award Plus accept the special order? Show your calculations.
3. As in requirement 1, assume that monthly capacity is 10,000 medals. Award Plus is concerned that if it accepts the special order, its existing customers will immediately demand a price discount of $10 in the month in which the special order is being filled. They would argue that Award Plus's capacity costs are now being spread over more units and that existing customers should get the benefit of these lower costs. Should Award Plus accept the special order under these conditions? Show your calculations.

11-20 Make versus buy, activity-based costing. The Svenson Corporation manufactures cellular modems. It manufactures its own cellular modem circuit boards (CMCB), an important part of the cellular modem. It reports the following cost information about the costs of making CMCBs in 2008 and the expected costs in 2009:

	Current Costs in 2008	Expected Costs in 2009
Variable manufacturing costs		
Direct material cost per CMCB	$ 180	$ 170
Direct manufacturing labor cost per CMCB	50	45
Variable manufacturing cost per batch for setups, materials handling, and quality control	1,600	1,500
Fixed manufacturing cost		
Fixed manufacturing overhead costs that can be avoided if CMCBs are not made	320,000	320,000
Fixed manufacturing overhead costs of plant depreciation, insurance, and administration that cannot be avoided even if CMCBs are not made	800,000	800,000

Svenson manufactured 8,000 CMCBs in 2008 in 40 batches of 200 each. In 2009, Svenson anticipates needing 10,000 CMCBs. The CMCBs would be produced in 80 batches of 125 each.

The Minton Corporation has approached Svenson about supplying CMCBs to Svenson in 2009 at $300 per CMCB on whatever delivery schedule Svenson wants.

Required

1. Calculate the total expected manufacturing cost per unit of making CMCBs in 2009.
2. Suppose the capacity currently used to make CMCBs will become idle if Svenson purchases CMCBs from Minton. On the basis of financial considerations alone, should Svenson make CMCBs or buy them from Minton? Show your calculations.
3. Now suppose that if Svenson purchases CMCBs from Minton, its best alternative use of the capacity currently used for CMCBs is to make and sell special circuit boards (CB3s) to the Essex Corporation. Svenson estimates the following incremental revenues and costs from CB3s:

Total expected incremental future revenues	$2,000,000
Total expected incremental future costs	$2,150,000

On the basis of financial considerations alone, should Svenson make CMCBs or buy them from Minton? Show your calculations.

11-21 Inventory decision, opportunity costs. Lawnox, a manufacturer of lawn mowers, predicts that it will purchase 240,000 spark plugs next year. Lawnox estimates that 20,000 spark plugs will be required each month. A supplier quotes a price of $9 per spark plug. The supplier also offers a special discount option: If all 240,000 spark plugs are purchased at the start of the year, a discount of 4% off the $9 price will be given. Lawnox can invest its cash at 10% per year. It costs Lawnox $200 to place each purchase order.

Required

1. What is the opportunity cost of interest forgone from purchasing all 240,000 units at the start of the year instead of in 12 monthly purchases of 20,000 units per order?
2. Would this opportunity cost be recorded in the accounting system? Why?
3. Should Lawnox purchase 240,000 units at the start of the year or 20,000 units each month? Show your calculations.

11-22 Relevant costs, contribution margin, product emphasis. The Beach Comber is a take-out food store at a popular beach resort. Susan Sexton, owner of the Beach Comber, is deciding how much refrigerator space to devote to four different drinks. Pertinent data on these four drinks are as follows:

	Cola	Lemonade	Punch	Natural Orange Juice
Selling price per case	$18.80	$20.00	$27.10	$39.20
Variable cost per case	$14.20	$16.10	$20.70	$30.20
Cases sold per foot of shelf space per day	25	24	4	5

Sexton has a maximum front shelf space of 12 feet to devote to the four drinks. She wants a minimum of 1 foot and a maximum of 6 feet of front shelf space for each drink.

Required

1. Compute the contribution margin per case of each type of drink.
2. A co-worker of Sexton's recommends that she maximize the shelf space devoted to those drinks with the highest contribution margin per case. Evaluate this recommendation.
3. What shelf-space allocation for the four drinks would you recommend for the Beach Comber? Show your calculations.

11-23 Selection of most profitable product. Body-Builders, Inc., produces two basic types of weight-lifting equipment, Model 9 and Model 14. Pertinent data are as follows:

	A	B	C
1		Per Unit	
2		Model 19	Model 14
3	Selling Price	$100.00	$70.00
4	Costs		
5	Direct material	28.00	13.00
6	Direct manufacturing labor	15.00	25.00
7	Variable manufacturing overhead*	25.00	12.50
8	Fixed manufacturing overhead*	10.00	5.00
9	Marketing (all variable)	14.00	10.00
10	Total cost	92.00	65.50
11	Operating income	$ 8.00	$ 4.50
12			
13	*Allocated on the basis of machine-hours		

The weight-lifting craze is such that enough of either Model 9 or Model 14 can be sold to keep the plant operating at full capacity. Both products are processed through the same production departments.

If you want to use Excel to solve this exercise, go to the Excel Lab at **www.prenhall.com/horngren/cost13e** and download the template for Exercise 11-23.

Required

Which products should be produced? Briefly explain your answer.

11-24 Which base to close, relevant-cost analysis, opportunity costs. The U.S. Defense Department has the difficult decision of deciding which military bases to shut down. Military and political factors obviously matter, but cost savings are also an important factor. Consider two naval bases located on the West Coast—one in Alameda, California, and the other in Everett, Washington. The Navy has decided that it needs only one of those two bases permanently, so one must be shut down. The decision regarding which base to shut down will be made on cost considerations alone. The following information is available:

a. The Alameda base was built at a cost of $100 million. The operating costs of the base are $400 million per year. The base is built on land owned by the Navy, so the Navy pays nothing for the use of the property. If the base is closed, the land will be sold to developers for $500 million.
b. The Everett base was built at a cost of $150 million on land leased by the Navy from private citizens. The Navy can choose to lease the land permanently for a lease payment of $3 million per year. If it decides to keep the Everett base open, the Navy plans to invest $60 million in a fixed income note, which at 5% interest will earn the $3 million the government needs for the lease payments. The land and buildings will immediately revert back to the owner if the base is closed. The operating costs of the base, excluding lease payments, are $300 million per year.
c. If the Alameda base is shut down, the Navy will have to transfer some personnel to the Everett facility. As a result, the yearly operating costs at Everett will increase by $100 million per year. If the Everett facility is closed down, no extra costs will be incurred to operate the Alameda facility.

Required

The California delegation in Congress argues that it is cheaper to shut down the Everett base for two reasons: (1) it would save $100 million per year in additional costs required to operate the Everett base, and (2) it would save the lease payment of $3 million per year. (Recall that the Alameda base requires no cash payments for use of the land because the land is owned by the Navy.) Do you agree with the California delegation's arguments and conclusions? In your answer, identify and explain all costs that you consider relevant and all costs that you consider irrelevant for the base-closing decision.

11-25 Closing and opening stores. Sanchez Corporation runs two convenience stores, one in Connecticut and one in Rhode Island. Operating income for each store in 2009 is as follows:

	Connecticut Store	Rhode Island Store
Revenues	$1,070,000	$860,000
Operating costs		
Cost of goods sold	750,000	660,000
Lease rent (renewable each year)	90,000	75,000
Labor costs (paid on an hourly basis)	42,000	42,000
Depreciation of equipment	25,000	22,000
Utilities (electricity, heating)	43,000	46,000
Allocated corporate overhead	50,000	40,000
Total operating costs	1,000,000	885,000
Operating income (loss)	$ 70,000	$(25,000)

The equipment has a zero disposal value. In a senior management meeting, Maria Lopez, the management accountant at Sanchez Corporation, makes the following comment, "Sanchez can increase its profitability by closing down the Rhode Island store or by adding another store like it."

Required

1. By closing down the Rhode Island store, Sanchez can reduce overall corporate overhead costs by $44,000. Calculate Sanchez's operating income if it closes the Rhode Island store. Is Maria Lopez's statement about the effect of closing the Rhode Island store correct? Explain.
2. Calculate Sanchez's operating income if it keeps the Rhode Island store open and opens another store with revenues and costs identical to the Rhode Island store (including a cost of $22,000 to acquire equipment with a one-year useful life and zero disposal value). Opening this store will increase corporate overhead costs by $4,000. Is Maria Lopez's statement about the effect of adding another store like the Rhode Island store correct? Explain.

11-26 Choosing customers. Broadway Printers operates a printing press with a monthly capacity of 2,000 machine-hours. Broadway has two main customers: Taylor Corporation and Kelly Corporation. Data on each customer for January follows:

	Taylor Corporation	Kelly Corporation	Total
Revenues	$120,000	$80,000	$200,000
Variable costs	42,000	48,000	90,000
Contribution margin	78,000	32,000	110,000
Fixed costs (allocated)	60,000	40,000	100,000
Operating income	$ 18,000	$(8,000)	$ 10,000
Machine-hours required	1,500 hours	500 hours	2,000 hours

Kelly Corporation indicates that it wants Broadway to do an *additional* $80,000 worth of printing jobs during February. These jobs are identical to the existing business Broadway did for Kelly in January in terms of variable costs and machine-hours required. Broadway anticipates that the business from Taylor Corporation in February will be the same as that in January. Broadway can choose to accept as much of the Taylor and Kelly business for February as its capacity allows. Assume that total machine-hours and fixed costs for February will be the same as in January.

Required

What action should Broadway take to maximize its operating income? Show your calculations.

11-27 Relevance of equipment costs. The Auto Wash Company has just today paid for and installed a special machine for polishing cars at one of its several outlets. It is the first day of the company's fiscal year. The machine costs $20,000. Its annual cash operating costs total $15,000. The machine will have a four-year useful life and a zero terminal disposal value.

After the machine has been used for only one day, a salesperson offers a different machine that promises to do the same job at annual cash operating costs of $9,000. The new machine will cost $24,000 cash, installed. The "old" machine is unique and can be sold outright for only $10,000, minus $2,000 removal cost. The new machine, like the old one, will have a four-year useful life and zero terminal disposal value.

Revenues, all in cash, will be $150,000 annually, and other cash costs will be $110,000 annually, regardless of this decision.

For simplicity, ignore income taxes and the time value of money.

Required

1. **a.** Prepare a statement of cash receipts and disbursements for each of the four years under each alternative. What is the cumulative difference in cash flow for the four years taken together?
   b. Prepare income statements for each of the four years under each alternative. Assume straight-line depreciation. What is the cumulative difference in operating income for the four years taken together?
   c. What are the irrelevant items in your presentations in requirements a and b? Why are they irrelevant?
2. Suppose the cost of the "old" machine was $1 million rather than $20,000. Nevertheless, the old machine can be sold outright for only $10,000, minus $2,000 removal cost. Would the net differences in requirements 1a and 1b change? Explain.
3. Is there any conflict between the decision model and the incentives of the manager who has just purchased the "old" machine and is considering replacing it a day later?

11-28 Equipment upgrade versus replacement. (A. Spero, adapted) The TechMech Company produces and sells 6,000 modular computer desks per year at a selling price of $500 each. Its current production equipment, purchased for $1,500,000 and with a five-year useful life, is only two years old. It has a terminal disposal value of $0 and is depreciated on a straight-line basis. The equipment has a current disposal price of $600,000. However, the emergence of a new molding technology has led TechMech to consider either upgrading or replacing the production equipment. The following table presents data for the two alternatives:

	A	B	C
1		**Upgrade**	**Replace**
2	One-time equipment costs	$2,700,000	$4,200,000
3	Variable manufacturing cost per desk	$ 140	$ 80
4	Remaining useful life of equipment (years)	3	3
5	Terminal disposal value of equipment	$ 0	$ 0

All equipment costs will continue to be depreciated on a straight-line basis. For simplicity, ignore income taxes and the time value of money.

If you want to use Excel to solve this exercise, go to the Excel Lab at **www.prenhall.com/horngren/cost13e** and download the template for Exercise 11-28.

Required

1. Should TechMech upgrade its production line or replace it? Show your calculations.
2. Now suppose the one-time equipment cost to replace the production equipment is somewhat negotiable. All other data are as given previously. What is the maximum one-time equipment cost that TechMech would be willing to pay to replace the old equipment rather than upgrade it?
3. Assume that the capital expenditures to replace and upgrade the production equipment are as given in the original exercise, but that the production and sales quantity is not known. For what production and sales quantity would TechMech (i) upgrade the equipment or (ii) replace the equipment?
4. Assume that all data are as given in the original exercise. Dan Doria is TechMech's manager, and his bonus is based on operating income. Because he is likely to relocate after about a year, his current bonus is his primary concern. Which alternative would Doria choose? Explain.

Problems

11-29 Special Order. Louisville Corporation produces baseball bats for kids that it sells for $32 each. At capacity, the company can produce 50,000 bats a year. The costs of producing and selling 50,000 bats are as follows:

	Cost per Bat	Total Costs
Direct materials	$12	$ 600,000
Direct manufacturing labor	3	150,000
Variable manufacturing overhead	1	50,000
Fixed manufacturing overhead	5	250,000
Variable selling expenses	2	100,000
Fixed selling expenses	4	200,000
Total costs	$27	$1,350,000

Required

1. Suppose Louisville is currently producing and selling 40,000 bats. At this level of production and sales, its fixed costs are the same as given in the table above. Ripkin Corporation wants to place a one-time special order for 10,000 bats at $25 each. Louisville will incur no variable selling costs for this special order. Should Louisville accept this one-time special order? Show your calculations.
2. Now suppose Louisville is currently producing and selling 50,000 bats. If Louisville accepts Ripkin's offer it will have to sell 10,000 fewer bats to its regular customers. (a) On financial considerations alone, should Louisville accept this one-time special order? Show your calculations. (b) On financial considerations alone, at what price would Louisville be indifferent between accepting the special order and continuing to sell to its regular customers at $32 per bat. (c) What other factors should Louisville consider in deciding whether to accept the one-time special order?

11-30 Contribution approach, relevant costs. Air Frisco has leased a single jet aircraft that it operates between San Francisco and the Fijian Islands. Only tourist-class seats are available on its planes. An analyst has collected the following information:

Seating capacity per plane	360 passengers
Average number of passengers per flight	200 passengers
Average one-way fare	$500
Variable fuel costs	$14,000 per flight
Food and beverage service costs (no charge to passenger)	$20 per passenger
Commission to travel agents paid by Air Frisco (all tickets are booked by travel agents)	8% of fare
Fixed annual lease costs allocated to each flight	$53,000 per flight
Fixed ground-services (maintenance, check in, baggage handling) costs allocated to each flight	$7,000 per flight
Fixed flight-crew salaries allocated to each flight	$4,000 per flight

Assume that fuel costs are unaffected by the actual number of passengers on a flight.

Required

1. Calculate the total contribution margin from passengers that Air Frisco earns on each one-way flight between San Francisco and Fiji.
2. The Market Research Department of Air Frisco indicates that lowering the average one-way fare to $480 will increase the average number of passengers per flight to 212. On the basis of financial considerations alone, should Air Frisco lower its fare? Show your calculations.
3. Travel International, a tour operator, approaches Air Frisco with the possibility of chartering its aircraft. The terms of charter are as follows: (a) For each one-way flight, Travel International will pay Air Frisco $74,500 to charter the plane and to use its flight crew and ground-service staff; (b) Travel International will pay for fuel costs; and (c) Travel International will pay for all food costs. On the basis of financial considerations alone, should Air Frisco accept Travel International's offer? Show your calculations. What other factors should Air Frisco consider in deciding whether to charter its plane to Travel International?

11-31 Relevant costs, opportunity costs. Larry Miller, the general manager of Basil Software, must decide when to release the new version of Basil's spreadsheet package, Easyspread 2.0. Development of Easyspread 2.0 is complete; however, the diskettes, compact discs, and user manuals have not yet been produced. The product can be shipped starting July 1, 2009.

The major problem is that Basil has overstocked the previous version of its spreadsheet package, Easyspread 1.0. Miller knows that once Easyspread 2.0 is introduced, Basil will not be able to sell any more units of Easyspread 1.0. Rather than just throwing away the inventory of Easyspread 1.0, Miller is wondering if it might be better to continue to sell Easyspread 1.0 for the next three months and introduce Easyspread 2.0 on October 1, 2009, when the inventory of Easyspread 1.0 will be sold out.

The following information is available:

	Easyspread 1.0	Easyspread 2.0
Selling price	$160	$195
Variable cost per unit of diskettes, compact discs, user manuals	25	30
Development cost per unit	70	100
Marketing and administrative cost per unit	35	40
Total cost per unit	130	170
Operating income per unit	$ 30	$ 25

Development cost per unit for each product equals the total costs of developing the software product divided by the anticipated unit sales over the life of the product. Marketing and administrative costs are fixed costs in 2009, incurred to support all marketing and administrative activities of Basil Software. Marketing and administrative costs are allocated to products on the basis of the budgeted revenues of each product. The preceding unit costs assume Easyspread 2.0 will be introduced on October 1, 2009.

Required

1. On the basis of financial considerations alone, should Miller introduce Easyspread 2.0 on July 1, 2009, or wait until October 1, 2009? Show your calculations, clearly identifying relevant and irrelevant revenues and costs.
2. What other factors might Larry Miller consider in making a decision?

11-32 Opportunity costs. (H. Schaefer) The Wolverine Corporation is working at full production capacity producing 10,000 units of a unique product, Rosebo. Manufacturing cost per unit for Rosebo is as follows:

Direct materials	$ 2
Direct manufacturing labor	3
Manufacturing overhead	5
Total manufacturing cost	$10

Manufacturing overhead cost per unit is based on variable cost per unit of $2 and fixed costs of $30,000 (at full capacity of 10,000 units). Marketing cost per unit, all variable, is $4, and the selling price is $20.

A customer, the Miami Company, has asked Wolverine to produce 2,000 units of Orangebo, a modification of Rosebo. Orangebo would require the same manufacturing processes as Rosebo. Miami has offered to pay Wolverine $15 for a unit of Orangebo plus half of the marketing cost per unit.

Required

1. What is the opportunity cost to Wolverine of producing the 2,000 units of Orangebo? (Assume that no overtime is worked.)
2. The Buckeye Corporation has offered to produce 2,000 units of Rosebo for Wolverine so that Wolverine may accept the Miami offer. That is, if Wolverine accepts the Buckeye offer, Wolverine would manufacture 8,000 units of Rosebo and 2,000 units of Orangebo and purchase 2,000 units of Rosebo from Buckeye. Buckeye would charge Wolverine $14 per unit to manufacture Rosebo. On the basis of financial considerations alone, should Wolverine accept the Buckeye offer? Show your calculations.
3. Suppose Wolverine had been working at less than full capacity, producing 8,000 units of Rosebo at the time the Miami offer was made. Calculate the minimum price Wolverine should accept for Orangebo under these conditions. (Ignore the previous $15 selling price.)

11-33 Product mix, special order. (N. Melumad, adapted) Pendleton Engineering makes cutting tools for metalworking operations. It makes two types of tools: R3, a regular cutting tool, and HP6, a high-precision cutting tool. R3 is manufactured on a regular machine, but HP6 must be manufactured on both the regular machine and a high-precision machine. The following information is available.

	R3	HP6
Selling price	$ 100	$ 150
Variable manufacturing cost per unit	$ 60	$ 100
Variable marketing cost per unit	$ 15	$ 35
Budgeted total fixed overhead costs	$350,000	$550,000
Hours required to produce one unit on the regular machine	1.0	0.5

Additional information includes:

a. Pendleton faces a capacity constraint on the regular machine of 50,000 hours per year.
b. The capacity of the high-precision machine is not a constraint.
c. Of the $550,000 budgeted fixed overhead costs of HP6, $300,000 are lease payments for the high-precision machine. This cost is charged entirely to HP6 because Pendleton uses the machine exclusively to produce HP6. The lease agreement for the high-precision machine can be canceled at any time without penalties.
d. All other overhead costs are fixed and cannot be changed.

Required

1. What product mix—that is, how many units of R3 and HP6—will maximize Pendleton's operating income? Show your calculations.
2. Suppose Pendleton can increase the annual capacity of its regular machines by 15,000 machine-hours at a cost of $150,000. Should Pendleton increase the capacity of the regular machines by 15,000 machine-hours? By how much will Pendleton's operating income increase? Show your calculations.

3. Suppose that the capacity of the regular machines has been increased to 65,000 hours. Pendleton has been approached by Carter Corporation to supply 20,000 units of another cutting tool, S3, for $120 per unit. Pendleton must either accept the order for all 20,000 units or reject it totally. S3 is exactly like R3 except that its variable manufacturing cost is $70 per unit. (It takes one hour to produce one unit of S3 on the regular machine, and variable marketing cost equals $15 per unit.) What product mix should Pendleton choose to maximize operating income? Show your calculations.

11-34 Dropping a product line, selling more units. The Northern Division of Grossman Corporation makes and sells tables and beds. The following estimated revenue and cost information from the division's activity-based costing system is available for 2008.

	4,000 Tables	5,000 Beds	Total
Revenues ($125 × 4,000; $200 × 5,000)	$500,000	$1,000,000	$1,500,000
Variable direct materials and direct manufacturing labor costs ($75 × 4,000; $105 × 5,000)	300,000	525,000	825,000
Depreciation on equipment used exclusively by each product line	42,000	58,000	100,000
Marketing and distribution costs			
$40,000 (fixed) + ($750 per shipment × 40 shipments)	70,000		205,000
$60,000 (fixed) + ($750 per shipment × 100 shipments)		135,000	
Fixed general-administration costs of the division allocated to product lines on the basis of revenue	110,000	220,000	330,000
Corporate-office costs allocated to product lines on the basis of revenues	50,000	100,000	150,000
Total costs	572,000	1,038,000	1,610,000
Operating income (loss)	$(72,000)	$ (38,000)	$ (110,000)

Additional information includes:

a. On January 1, 2008, the equipment has a book value of $100,000 and zero disposal value. Any equipment not used will remain idle.
b. Fixed marketing and distribution costs of a product line can be avoided if the line is discontinued.
c. Fixed general-administration costs of the division and corporate-office costs will not change if sales of individual product lines are increased or decreased or if product lines are added or dropped.

Required

1. On the basis of financial considerations alone, should the Northern Division discontinue the tables product line, assuming the released facilities remain idle? Show your calculations.
2. What would be the effect on Northern Division's operating income if it were to sell 4,000 more tables? Assume that to do so the division would have to acquire additional equipment costing $42,000 with a one-year useful life and zero terminal disposal value. Assume further that the fixed marketing and distribution costs would not change but that the number of shipments would double. Show your calculations.
3. Given the Northern Division's expected operating loss of $110,000, should Grossman Corporation shut it down? Assume that shutting down the Northern Division will have no effect on corporate-office costs but will lead to savings of all general-administration costs of the division. Show your calculations.
4. Suppose Grossman Corporation has the opportunity to open another division, the Southern Division, whose revenues and costs are expected to be identical to the Northern Division's revenues and costs (including a cost of $100,000 to acquire equipment with a one-year useful life and zero terminal disposal value). Opening the new division will have no effect on corporate-office costs. Should Grossman open the Southern Division? Show your calculations.

11-35 Make or buy, unknown level of volume. (A. Atkinson) Oxford Engineering manufactures small engines. The engines are sold to manufacturers who install them in such products as lawn mowers. The company currently manufactures all the parts used in these engines but is considering a proposal from an external supplier who wishes to supply the starter assemblies used in these engines.

The starter assemblies are currently manufactured in Division 3 of Oxford Engineering. The costs relating to the starter assemblies for the past 12 months were as follows:

Direct materials	$200,000
Direct manufacturing labor	150,000
Manufacturing overhead	400,000
Total	$750,000

Over the past year, Division 3 manufactured 150,000 starter assemblies. The average cost for each starter assembly is $5 ($750,000 ÷ 150,000).

Further analysis of manufacturing overhead revealed the following information. Of the total manufacturing overhead, only 25% is considered variable. Of the fixed portion, $150,000 is an allocation of general overhead that will remain unchanged for the company as a whole if production of the starter assemblies is discontinued. A further $100,000 of the fixed overhead is avoidable if production of the starter assemblies is discontinued. The balance of the current fixed overhead, $50,000, is the division manager's salary. If production of the starter assemblies is discontinued, the manager of Division 3 will be transferred to Division 2 at the same salary. This move will allow the company to save the $40,000 salary that would otherwise be paid to attract an outsider to this position.

Required

1. Tidnish Electronics, a reliable supplier, has offered to supply starter-assembly units at $4 per unit. Because this price is less than the current average cost of $5 per unit, the vice president of manufacturing is eager to accept this offer. On the basis of financial considerations alone, should the outside offer be accepted? Show your calculations. (*Hint:* Production output in the coming year may be different from production output in the past year.)
2. How, if at all, would your response to requirement 1 change if the company could use the vacated plant space for storage and, in so doing, avoid $50,000 of outside storage charges currently incurred? Why is this information relevant or irrelevant?

11-36 Make versus buy, activity-based costing, opportunity costs. (N. Melumad and S. Reichelstein, adapted) The Ace Company produces bicycles. This year's expected production is 10,000 units. Currently, Ace makes the chains for its bicycles. Ace's management accountant reports the following costs for making the 10,000 bicycle chains:

	Cost per Unit	Costs for 10,000 Units
Direct materials	$4.00	$ 40,000
Direct manufacturing labor	2.00	20,000
Variable manufacturing overhead (power and utilities)	1.50	15,000
Inspection, setup, materials handling		2,000
Machine rent		3,000
Allocated fixed costs of plant administration, taxes, and insurance		30,000
Total costs		$110,000

Ace has received an offer from an outside vendor to supply any number of chains Ace requires at $8.20 per chain. The following additional information is available:

a. Inspection, setup, and materials-handling costs vary with the number of batches in which the chains are produced. Ace produces chains in batch sizes of 1,000 units. Ace will produce the 10,000 units in 10 batches.

b. Ace rents the machine used to make the chains. If Ace buys all of its chains from the outside vendor, it does not need to pay rent on this machine.

Required

1. Assume that if Ace purchases the chains from the outside vendor, the facility where the chains are currently made will remain idle. On the basis of financial considerations alone, should Ace accept the outside vendor's offer at the anticipated production (and sales) volume of 10,000 units? Show your calculations.
2. For this question, assume that if the chains are purchased outside, the facilities where the chains are currently made will be used to upgrade the bicycles by adding mud flaps and reflectors. As a consequence, the selling price of bicycles will be raised by $20. The variable cost per unit of the upgrade would be $18, and additional tooling costs of $16,000 would be incurred. On the basis of financial considerations alone, should Ace make or buy the chains, assuming that 10,000 units are produced (and sold)? Show your calculations.
3. The sales manager at Ace is concerned that the estimate of 10,000 units may be high and believes that only 6,200 units will be sold. Production will be cut back, freeing up work space. This space can be used to add the mud flaps and reflectors whether Ace buys the chains or makes them in-house. At this lower output, Ace will produce the chains in 8 batches of 775 units each. On the basis of financial considerations alone, should Ace purchase the chains from the outside vendor? Show your calculations.

11-37 Multiple choice, comprehensive problem on relevant costs. The following are the Class Company's unit costs of manufacturing and marketing a high-style pen at an output level of 20,000 units per month:

Manufacturing cost	
Direct materials	$1.00
Direct manufacturing labor	1.20
Variable manufacturing overhead cost	0.80
Fixed manufacturing overhead cost	0.50
Marketing cost	
Variable	1.50
Fixed	0.90

Required The following situations refer only to the preceding data; there is *no connection* between the situations. Unless stated otherwise, assume a regular selling price of $6 per unit. Choose the best answer to each question. Show your calculations.

1. For an inventory of 10,000 units of the high-style pen presented in the balance sheet, the appropriate unit cost to use is (a) $3.00, (b) $3.50, (c) $5.00, (d) $2.20, or (e) $5.90.
2. The pen is usually produced and sold at the rate of 240,000 units per year (an average of 20,000 per month). The selling price is $6 per unit, which yields total annual revenues of $1,440,000. Total costs are $1,416,000, and operating income is $24,000, or $0.10 per unit. Market research estimates that unit sales could be increased by 10% if prices were cut to $5.80. Assuming the implied cost-behavior patterns continue, this action, if taken, would
   a. Decrease operating income by $7,200
   b. Decrease operating income by $0.20 per unit ($48,000) but increase operating income by 10% of revenues ($144,000), for a net increase of $96,000
   c. Decrease fixed cost per unit by 10%, or $0.14, per unit, and thus decrease operating income by $0.06 ($0.20 − $0.14) per unit
   d. Increase unit sales to 264,000 units, which at the $5.80 price would give total revenues of $1,531,200 and lead to costs of $5.90 per unit for 264,000 units, which would equal $1,557,600, and result in an operating loss of $26,400
   e. None of these
3. A contract with the government for 5,000 units of the pens calls for the reimbursement of all manufacturing costs plus a fixed fee of $1,000. No variable marketing costs are incurred on the government contract. You are asked to compare the following two alternatives:

Sales Each Month to	Alternative A	Alternative B
Regular customers	15,000 units	15,000 units
Government	0 units	5,000 units

Operating income under alternative B is greater than that under alternative A by (a) $1,000, (b) $2,500, (c) $3,500, (d) $300, or (e) none of these.

4. Assume the same data with respect to the government contract as in requirement 3 except that the two alternatives to be compared are:

Sales Each Month to	Alternative A	Alternative B
Regular customers	20,000 units	15,000 units
Government	0 units	5,000 units

Operating income under alternative B relative to that under alternative A is (a) $4,000 less, (b) $3,000 greater, (c) $6,500 less, (d) $500 greater, or (e) none of these.

5. The company wants to enter a foreign market in which price competition is keen. The company seeks a one-time-only special order for 10,000 units on a minimum-unit-price basis. It expects that shipping costs for this order will amount to only $0.75 per unit, but the fixed costs of obtaining the contract will be $4,000. The company incurs no variable marketing costs other than shipping costs. Domestic business will be unaffected. The selling price to break even is (a) $3.50, (b) $4.15, (c) $4.25, (d) $3.00, or (e) $5.00.
6. The company has an inventory of 1,000 units of pens that must be sold immediately at reduced prices. Otherwise, the inventory will become worthless. The unit cost that is relevant for establishing the minimum selling price is (a) $4.50, (b) $4.00, (c) $3.00, (d) $5.90, or (e) $1.50.
7. A proposal is received from an outside supplier who will make and ship the high-style pens directly to the Class Company's customers as sales orders are forwarded from Class's sales staff. Class's fixed marketing costs will be unaffected, but its variable marketing costs will be slashed by 20%. Class's

plant will be idle, but its fixed manufacturing overhead will continue at 50% of present levels. How much per unit would the company be able to pay the supplier without decreasing operating income? (a) $4.75, (b) $3.95, (c) $2.95, (d) $5.35, or (e) none of these.

11-38 Closing down divisions. Aristide corporation has four operating divisions. During the first quarter of 2009, the company reported total income from operations of $61,000 and the following results for each division:

	Division			
	A	B	C	D
Sales	$530,000	$730,000	$920,000	$450,000
Cost of goods sold	450,000	480,000	576,000	390,000
Selling, general, and administrative expenses	100,000	207,000	246,000	120,000
Operating income/loss	$(20,000)	$ 43,000	$ 98,000	$(60,000)

Further analysis of costs reveals the following percentages of variable costs in each division

	A	B	C	D
Cost of goods sold	90%	80%	90%	95%
Selling, general, and administrative expenses	60%	60%	70%	80%

Closing down any division would result in savings of 60% of the fixed costs of that division.

Top management is very concerned about the unprofitable divisions (A and D) and is considering shutting them down.

Required

1. Calculate the contribution margin for the two unprofitable divisions (A and D).
2. On the basis of financial considerations alone, should the top management of Aristide shut down Division A? Division D?
3. What other factors should the top management of Aristide consider before making a decision?

11-39 Product mix, constrained resource. Westford Company produces three products, A110, B382 and C657. Unit data for the three products follows:

	Product		
	A110	B382	C657
Selling price	$84	$56	70
Variable costs			
Direct materials	24	15	9
Labor and other costs	28	27	40

All three products use the same direct material, Bistide. The demand for the products far exceeds the direct materials available to produce the products. Bistide costs $3 per pound and a maximum of 5,000 pounds is available each month. Westford must produce a minimum of 200 units of each product.

Required

1. How many units of product A110, B382, and C657 should Westford produce?
2. What is the maximum amount Westford would be willing to pay for another 1,000 pounds of Bistide?

11-40 Optimal product mix (chapter appendix). (CMA adapted) Della Simpson, Inc., sells two popular brands of cookies: Della's Delight and Bonny's Bourbon. Della's Delight goes through the Mixing and Baking departments, and Bonny's Bourbon, a filled cookie, goes through the Mixing, Filling, and Baking departments.

Michael Shirra, vice president for sales, believes that at the current price, Della Simpson can sell all of its daily production of Della's Delight and Bonny's Bourbon. Both cookies are made in batches of 3,000. In each department, the time required per batch and the total time available each day are as follows:

File Edit View Insert Format Tools Data Window Help

	A	B	C	D
1		Department Minutes		
2		Mixing	Filling	Baking
3	Della's Delight	30	0	10
4	Bonny's Bourbon	15	15	15
5	Total available per day	660	270	300

Revenue and cost data for each type of cookie are:

	A	B	C
7		Della's	Bonny's
8		Delight	Bourbon
9	Revenue per batch	$ 475	$ 375
10	Variable cost per batch	175	125
11	Contribution margin per batch	$ 300	$ 250
12	Monthly fixed costs		
13	(allocated to each product)	$18,650	$22,350

If you want to use Excel to solve this problem, go to the Excel Lab at **www.prenhall.com/horngren/cost13e** and download the template for Problem 11-40.

Required

1. Using *D* to represent the batches of Della's Delight and *B* to represent the batches of Bonny's Bourbon made and sold each day, formulate Shirra's decision as an LP model.
2. Compute the optimal number of batches of each type of cookie that Della Simpson, Inc., should make and sell each day to maximize operating income.

11-41 Make versus buy, ethics. (CMA, adapted) Lynn Hart is a management accountant at Paibec Corporation. Paibec is under intense cost competition. Hart has been asked to evaluate whether Paibec should continue to manufacture MTR-2000 or purchase it from Marley Company. Marley has submitted a bid to supply the 32,000 MTR-2000 units that Paibec will need for 2009 at a price of $17.30 each. Paibec has capacity available to produce 32,000 units.

From plant records and interviews with John Porter, the plant manager, Hart gathered the following information regarding Paibec's costs to manufacture 30,000 units of MTR-2000 in 2008:

	A	B
1		Costs for
2		30,000
3		units in 2008
4	Direct materials	$195,000
5	Direct manufacturing labor	120,000
6	Plant space rental	84,000
7	Equipment leasing	36,000
8	Other manufacturing overhead	225,000
9	Total manufacturing costs	$660,000
10		

Additionally, Porter tells her that:

- Variable costs per unit in 2009 will be the same as variable costs per unit in 2008.
- Plant rental and equipment lease are annual contracts that are going to be expensive to wiggle out of. Porter estimates it will cost $10,000 to terminate the plant rental contract and $5,000 to terminate the equipment-lease contract.
- 40% of the other manufacturing overhead is variable, proportionate to the direct manufacturing labor costs. The fixed component of other manufacturing overhead is expected to remain the same whether MTR-2000 is manufactured by Paibec or outsourced to Marley.
- Paibec's just-in-time policy means that inventory is negligible.

Hart is aware that cost studies can be threatening to current employees because the findings may lead to reorganizations and layoffs. She knows that Porter is concerned that outsourcing MTR-2000 will result in some of his close friends being laid off. Therefore, she performs her own independent analysis of competitive and other economic data, which reveals that:

- Prices of direct materials are likely to be higher by 8% in 2009 compared to 2008.
- Direct manufacturing labor rates are likely to be higher by 5% in 2009 compared to 2008.

- The plant-rental contract can, in fact, be terminated by paying $10,000. Paibec will not have any need for this space if MTR-2000 is outsourced.
- The equipment lease can be terminated by paying $3,000.

Hart shows Porter her analysis. Porter argues that Hart is ignoring the amazing continuous improvement that is occurring at the plant and that increases in direct material prices and direct manufacturing labor rates assumed by Hart will not occur. But Hart is very confident about the accuracy of the information she has collected.

If you want to use Excel to solve this problem, go to the Excel Lab at **www.prenhall.com/horngren/cost13e** and download the template for Problem 11-41.

Required

1. On the basis of the material and labor cost estimates originally compiled with Porter's help, should Hart recommend that MTR-2000 be produced at Paibec or purchased from Marley? Show your calculations.
2. On the basis of Hart's own independent estimates, should she recommend that MTR-2000 be produced or purchased? Show your calculations.
3. What other factors should Hart examine before recommending whether Paibec should manufacture or buy MTR-2000?
4. What should Hart do in response to Porter's inputs and comments?

Collaborative Learning Problem

11-42 Product mix, constrained resource. Taylor Furniture produces and sells specialty mattresses. Production is a machine-intensive process. Taylor's variable costs are direct material costs, variable machining costs, and sales commissions. Marion Taylor, the owner, is planning production for the coming year and collects the following data:

	Estimated Demand (units)	Selling Price	Direct Material Cost Per Unit	Variable Machining Cost Per Unit
Nealy	1,800	$3,000	$750	$600
Tersa	4,500	2,100	500	500
Pelta	39,000	800	100	200

- Salespeople are paid a 5% commission on each Nealy or Tersa sold, and a 10% commission on each Pelta sold. All other marketing and administrative costs are fixed and, along with the fixed manufacturing costs, total $8,750,000.
- Annual capacity is 50,000 machine-hours, which is limited by the availability of machines. Variable machining costs are $200 per hour.
- Taylor Furniture holds negligible inventories to minimize business risk.

Required

1. Calculate the machine-hours required to satisfy the estimated demand for each type of mattress.
2. What is the contribution margin per unit earned from each type of mattress?
3. Advise Marion Taylor about the most profitable production levels of the three products.
4. Suppose Taylor Furniture can lease additional machining capacity on an as-needed basis. What is the maximum amount that Marion Taylor would be willing to pay for each hour of additional machining capacity in the coming year?

12 Pricing Decisions and Cost Management

Learning Objectives

1. Discuss the three major influences on pricing decisions
2. Distinguish short-run from long-run pricing decisions
3. Price products using the target-costing approach
4. Apply the concepts of cost incurrence and locked-in costs
5. Price products using the cost-plus approach
6. Use life-cycle budgeting and costing when making pricing decisions
7. Describe two pricing practices in which noncost factors are important when setting prices
8. Explain the effects of antitrust laws on pricing

Most companies make a tremendous effort to analyze their costs and prices. They know if the price is too high, the sale will be lost to a competitor. Too low, and the firm's earnings targets won't be met. But some companies fall into a rut, continuing to price their products the way they always have in the past, even if it doesn't make sense. Parker Hannifin Corp., was one such company until its CEO, Donald Washkewicz, decided to change all of that.

Seeking Perfect Prices, CEO Tears Up the Rules[1]

For years, Parker Hannifin, the big industrial-parts maker, had used the same simple formula to determine prices of its 800,000 parts—from heat-resistant seals for jet engines to steel valves that hoist buckets on cherry pickers. Managers would calculate how much it cost to make and deliver each product and add a flat percentage on top, usually aiming for about 35%. They liked the method because it was straightforward and gave them broad authority to negotiate deals.

But Mr. Washkewicz, who took over as CEO in 2001, thought that Parker, which had revenues of $9.4 billion in 2006, had stuck itself in a profit-margin rut. No matter how much a product improved, the company charged the same premium for it that it did for a more standard item. And if it found a way to make a product less expensively, it cut the product's price as well.

While touring the company's 225 facilities in 2001, Mr. Washkewicz had an epiphany: Parker had to stop thinking like a widget maker and start thinking like a retailer, determining prices by what a customer is willing to pay rather than what a product costs to make. Such "strategic" pricing schemes are used in many different industries. Airlines charge more for a seat to Florida in January than in August. Sports teams raise ticket prices if they're playing a well-known opponent. Why shouldn't Parker do the same, Mr. Washkewicz reasoned. Today, the company says its new pricing approach boosted operating income by $200 million from 2002 through 2006.

Mr. Washkewicz hired consultants to analyze each of Parker's products and divide them into categories. "A" items were the high-volume commodities where there was at least one big competitor

[1] *Source:* Timothy Aeppel, "Changing the Formula: Seeking Perfect Prices, CEO Tears Up the Rules," *The Wall Street Journal,* March 27, 2007.

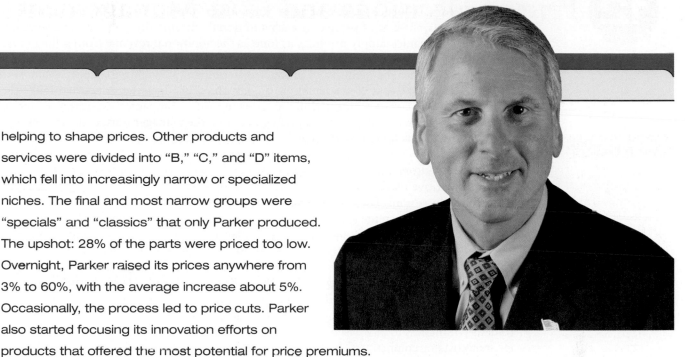

helping to shape prices. Other products and services were divided into "B," "C," and "D" items, which fell into increasingly narrow or specialized niches. The final and most narrow groups were "specials" and "classics" that only Parker produced. The upshot: 28% of the parts were priced too low. Overnight, Parker raised its prices anywhere from 3% to 60%, with the average increase about 5%. Occasionally, the process led to price cuts. Parker also started focusing its innovation efforts on products that offered the most potential for price premiums.

Just like at Parker, managers at many other companies often need to make strategic pricing decisions. This chapter describes how managers evaluate demand at different prices and manage costs across the value chain and over a product's life cycle to increase profitability.

Major Influences on Pricing Decisions

Learning Objective 1

Discuss the three major influences on pricing decisions

. . . customers, competitors, and costs

Consider for a moment how managers at Adidas might price their newest line of sneakers, or how decision makers at Microsoft would determine how much to charge for a monthly subscription of MSN Internet service. How companies price a product or a service ultimately depends on the demand and supply for it. Three influences on demand and supply are customers, competitors, and costs.

Customers, Competitors, and Costs

Customers Customers influence price through their effect on the demand for a product or service, based on factors such as the features of a product and its quality. As the Parker-Hannifin example illustrates, companies must always examine pricing decisions through the eyes of their customers. Too high a price relative to the value customers place on a product may cause customers to choose a competing or substitute product. Too low a price means lost profit opportunities.

Competitors No business operates in a vacuum. Companies must always be aware of the actions of their competitors. At one extreme, alternative or substitute products of competitors can affect demand and force a company to lower its prices. At the other extreme, a company without a competitor can set higher prices. When there are competitors, knowledge of rivals' technology, plant capacity, and operating strategies enables a company to estimate its competitors' costs—valuable information in setting its own prices.

Because competition spans international borders, costs and pricing decisions are also affected by fluctuations in the exchange rates between different countries' currencies. For example, if the yen weakens against the U.S. dollar, Japanese products become cheaper for American consumers and, consequently, more competitive in U.S. markets.

Costs Costs influence prices because they affect supply. Generally, as companies increase supply, the cost of producing each additional unit initially declines but eventually increases. Companies supply products as long as the additional revenue from selling more units exceeds the additional cost of producing them. The lower the cost of producing a product, the greater the quantity of product the company is willing to supply. Managers who understand the cost of producing their companies' products set prices that make the products attractive to customers while maximizing their companies' operating incomes. In computing the relevant costs for a pricing decision, the manager must consider relevant costs in all business functions of the value chain, from R&D to customer service.

Surveys of how managers make pricing decisions reveal that companies weigh customers, competitors, and costs differently. At one extreme, companies operating in a perfectly competitive market sell very similar commodity-type products, such as wheat, rice, steel, and aluminum. These companies have no control over setting prices and must accept the price determined by a market consisting of many participants. Cost information helps a company decide only on the output level that maximizes its operating income.

In less-competitive markets, such as those for cameras, televisions, and cellular phones, products are differentiated, and all three factors affect prices: The value customers place on a product and the prices charged for competing products affect demand, and the costs of producing and delivering the product influence supply.

As competition lessens even more, the key factor affecting pricing decisions is the customer's willingness to pay based on the value that customers place on the product or service, not costs or competitors. In the extreme, there are monopolies. A monopolist has no competitors and has much more leeway to set high prices. Nevertheless, there are limits. The higher the price a monopolist sets, the lower the demand for the monopolist's product as customers seek substitute products.

Time Horizon of Pricing Decisions

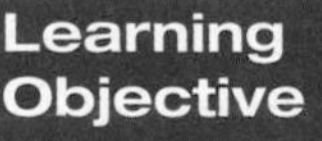

Learning Objective 2

Distinguish short-run

. . . less-than-one-year time horizon with mostly incremental costs being relevant

from long-run pricing decisions

. . . more-than-one-year time horizon with all product costs being relevant

Short-run pricing decisions typically have a time horizon of less than a year and include decisions such as (a) pricing a *one-time-only special order* with no long-run implications and (b) adjusting product mix and output volume in a competitive market. Long-run pricing decisions have a time horizon of a year or longer and include pricing a product in a major market in which there is some leeway in setting price. Two key differences affect pricing for the long run versus the short run.

1. Costs that are often irrelevant for short-run pricing decisions, such as fixed costs that cannot be changed, are generally relevant in the long run because fixed costs can be altered in the long run.
2. Profit margins in long-run pricing decisions are often set to earn a reasonable return on investment. Short-run pricing is more opportunistic: Prices are decreased when demand is weak and increased when demand is strong.

Costing and Pricing for the Short Run

Consider a short-run pricing decision facing the management team at Astel Computers. Astel manufactures two brands of personal computers (PCs)—Deskpoint, Astel's top-of-the-line product, and Provalue, a less-powerful Pentium chip-based machine. Datatech Corporation has asked Astel to bid on supplying 5,000 Provalue computers over the last three months of 2008. After this three-month period, Datatech is unlikely to place any future sales orders with Astel. Datatech will sell Provalue computers under its own brand name in regions and markets where Astel does not sell Provalue. Whether Astel accepts or rejects this order will not affect Astel's revenues—neither the units sold nor the selling price—from existing sales channels.

Relevant Costs for Short-Run Pricing Decisions

Before Astel can bid on Datatech's offer, Astel's managers must estimate how much it will cost to supply the 5,000 computers. Similar to the Surf Gear example in Chapter 11, the relevant costs Astel's managers must focus on include all direct and indirect costs throughout the value chain that will change in total by accepting the one-time-only special order from Datatech. Astel's managers outline the relevant costs in the following table:

Direct materials ($460 per computer × 5,000 computers)	$2,300,000
Direct manufacturing labor ($64 per computer × 5,000 computers)	320,000
Fixed costs of additional capacity to manufacture Provalue	250,000
Total costs	$2,870,000*

*No additional costs will be required for R&D, design, marketing, distribution, or customer service.

The relevant cost per computer is $574 ($2,870,000 ÷ 5,000). Therefore, any selling price above $574 will improve Astel's profitability in the short run. What price should Astel's managers bid for the 5,000-computer order?

Strategic and Other Factors in Short-Run Pricing

If Astel were the only supplier, Astel's managers would have to consider other effects of their pricing decision, such as whether Datatech would undercut Astel's selling price in Astel's current markets. If Astel's managers believed this to be a significant risk, the relevant costs of the bidding decision would include the contribution margin lost on sales to existing customers. In the current situation, Astel's managers know that many parties are eager to win the Datatech contract so its existing business can be undercut by Datatech regardless of whether Astel wins the contract. Hence the effect on the existing business is irrelevant to the decision. Moreover, after carefully evaluating the situation, Astel's managers conclude that Datatech will not undercut prices to Astel's customers.

Based on its market intelligence, Astel believes that competing bids will be between $596 and $610 per computer, Astel makes a bid of $595 per computer. If it wins this bid, operating income will increase by $105,000 (relevant revenues, $595 × 5,000 = $2,975,000 minus relevant costs, $2,870,000). Management's strategy is to bid as high above $574 as possible while remaining lower than competitors' bids.

In Astel's short-run pricing decision it had extra capacity and faced competition, so its focus was on identifying a sufficiently low price at which Astel would still make a profit. In other short-run situations, companies experience strong demand for their products or have limited capacity. In these cases, companies strategically increase prices in the short run to as much as the market will bear. We observe high short-run prices in the case of new products or new models of older products, such as microprocessors, computer chips, cellular telephones, and software.

Costing and Pricing for the Long Run

Short-run pricing decisions are responses to short-run demand and supply conditions. The relevant costs are only those costs that change in the short run. Long-run pricing is a strategic decision designed to build long-run relationships with customers based on stable and predictable prices. A stable price reduces the need for continuous monitoring of prices, improves planning, and builds long-run buyer–seller relationships. But to charge a stable price and earn the target long-run return, a company must, over the long run, know and manage its costs of supplying product to customers. As we will see, relevant costs for long-run pricing decisions include *all* future fixed and variable costs.

Calculating Product Costs for Long-Run Pricing Decisions

Let's return to the Astel example. However, this time we consider the long-run pricing decision for Provalue.

Astel has no beginning or ending inventory of Provalue in 2009 and manufactures and sells 150,000 units during the year. The manufacturing cost of Provalue is calculated using activity-based costing (ABC). Astel has three direct manufacturing costs—direct materials, direct manufacturing labor, and direct machining costs—and three manufacturing overhead cost pools—ordering and receiving components, testing and inspection of final products, and rework (correcting and fixing errors and defects)—in its accounting system. Astel treats machining costs as a direct cost of Provalue because Provalue is manufactured on machines that are dedicated to its production.[2]

Astel uses a long-run time horizon to price Provalue. Over this horizon, Astel's management observes the following:

- Direct material costs vary with number of units of Provalue produced.
- Direct manufacturing labor costs vary with number of direct manufacturing labor-hours used.
- Direct machining costs, such as rental and lease charges, do not vary with number of machine-hours used over this time horizon. They are fixed in the long run based on Astel's capacity of 300,000 machine-hours. Each unit of Provalue requires 2 machine-hours. Therefore, the entire machining capacity is used to manufacture Provalue (2 machine-hours per unit × 150,000 units = 300,000 machine-hours).
- Ordering and receiving, testing and inspection, and rework costs vary with the quantity of their respective cost driver. For example, ordering and receiving costs vary with the number of orders. Staff members responsible for placing orders can be reassigned or laid off in the long run if fewer orders need to be placed, or the number of staff members can be increased in the long run to process more orders.

The following Excel spreadsheet summarizes manufacturing cost information to produce 150,000 units of Provalue.

File Edit View Insert Format Tools Data Window Help

	A	B	C	D	E	F	G	H
1		**Manufacturing cost information**						
2		**to produce 150,000 units of Provalue**						
3	**Cost Category**	**Cost Driver**	**Details of Cost Driver Quantities**				**Total Quantity of Cost Driver**	**Cost per Unit of Cost Driver**
4	**(1)**	**(2)**		**(3)**		**(4)**	**(5)=(3)x(4)**	**(6)**
5	**Direct Manufacturing Costs**							
6	Direct materials	No. of kits	1	kit per unit	150,000	units	150,000	$460
7	Direct manufacturing labor (DML)	DML hours	3.2	DML hours per unit	150,000	units	480,000	$ 20
8	Direct machining (fixed)	Machine-hours					300,000	$ 38
9	**Manufacturing Overhead Costs**							
10	Ordering and receiving	No. of orders	50	orders per component	450	components	22,500	$ 80
11	Testing and inspection	Testing-hours	30	testing-hours per unit	150,000	units	4,500,000	$ 2
12	Rework				8%	defect rate		
13		Rework-hours	2.5	rework-hours per defective unit	12,000[a]	defective units	30,000	$ 40
14								
15	[a]8% defect rate x 150,000 units = 12,000 defective units							

[2] Recall that Astel makes two types of PCs: Deskpoint and Provalue. If Deskpoint and Provalue had shared the same machines, Astel would have allocated machining costs on the basis of the budgeted machine-hours used to manufacture the two products and would have treated these costs as fixed overhead costs. The basic analysis of Provalue would be exactly as described in the chapter except that machining costs would appear as overhead rather than direct fixed costs.

Exhibit 12-1 indicates that the total cost of manufacturing Provalue is $102 million, and the manufacturing cost per unit is $680. Manufacturing, however, is just one business function in the value chain. To set long-run prices, Astel's managers must calculate the *full cost* of producing and selling Provalue.

For its nonmanufacturing business functions in the value chain, Astel's managers identify direct costs and choose cost drivers and cost pools for indirect costs that measure cause-and-effect relationships. Astel's managers allocate costs to Provalue based on the quantity of cost-driver units that Provalue uses. Exhibit 12-2 summarizes the operating income for Provalue for 2009 based on an activity-based analysis of costs in all business functions. (For brevity, supporting calculations for nonmanufacturing business functions are not given.) Astel earns $15 million from Provalue, or $100 per unit sold in 2009.

Alternative Long-Run Pricing Approaches

How do companies use product cost information to make long-run pricing decisions? Two different approaches for pricing decisions are:

1. Market-based
2. Cost-based, which is also called cost-plus

The market-based approach to pricing starts by management asking, "Given what our customers want and how our competitors will react to what we do, what price should we charge?" The cost-based approach to pricing starts by management asking, "Given what it costs us to make this product, what price should we charge that will recoup our costs and achieve a target return on investment?"

Companies operating in *competitive* markets (for example, commodities such as steel, oil, and natural gas) use the market-based approach. The items produced or services provided by one company are very similar to items produced or services provided by others. Companies in these markets must accept the prices set by the market.

Companies operating in *less competitive* markets offering products or services that differ from each other (for example, automobiles, computers, management consulting, and

Exhibit 12-1

Manufacturing Costs of Provalue for 2009 Using Activity-Based Costing

File Edit View Insert Format Tools Data Window Help

	A	B	C
1		Total Manufacturing	
2		Costs for	Manufacturing
3		150,000 Units	Cost per Unit
4		(1)	(2) = (1) ÷ 150,000
5	Direct manufacturing costs		
6	Direct material costs		
7	(150,000 kits x $460 per kit)	$ 69,000,000	$460
8	Direct manufacturing labor costs		
9	(480,000 DML-hours x $20 per hour)	9,600,000	64
10	Direct machining costs		
11	(300,000 machine-hours x $38 per machine-hour)	11,400,000	76
12	Direct manufacturing costs	90,000,000	600
13			
14	Manufacturing overhead costs		
15	Ordering and receiving costs		
16	(22,500 orders x $80 per order)	1,800,000	12
17	Testing and inspection costs		
18	(4,500,000 testing-hours x $2 per hour)	9,000,000	60
19	Rework costs		
20	(30,000 rework-hours x $40 per hour)	1,200,000	8
21	Manufacturing overhead cost	12,000,000	80
22	Total manufacturing costs	$102,000,000	$680

Exhibit 12-2

Product Profitability of Provalue for 2009 Using Value-Chain Activity-Based Costing

File Edit View Insert Format Tools Data Window Help

	A	B	C
1		Total Amounts	
2		for 150,000 Units	Per Unit
3		(1)	(2) = (1) ÷ 150,000
4	Revenues	$150,000,000	$1,000
5	Costs of goods sold[a] (from Exhibit 12-1)	102,000,000	680
6	Operating costs[b]		
7	R&D costs	5,400,000	36
8	Design cost of product and process	6,000,000	40
9	Marketing costs	15,000,000	100
10	Distribution costs	3,600,000	24
11	Customer-service costs	3,000,000	20
12	Operating costs	33,000,000	220
13	Full cost of the product	135,000,000	900
14	Operating income	$ 15,000,000	$ 100
15			
16	[a]Cost of goods sold = Total manufacturing costs because there is no beginning or ending inventory		
17	of Provalue in 2009		
18	[b]Numbers for operating cost line-items are assumed without supporting calculations		

legal services), can use either the market-based or cost-based approach as the starting point for pricing decisions. Some companies first look at costs because cost information is more easily available and then consider customers or competitors—the cost-based approach. Others start by considering customers and competitors and then look at costs—the market-based approach. Both approaches consider customers, competitors, and costs. Only their starting points differ. Management must always keep in mind market forces, regardless of which pricing approach is used. For instance, a price set via cost-plus thinking may simply be unacceptable to customers, perhaps because a competitor has introduced a new, lower-priced product. So the "plus" in cost-plus is reduced to a price acceptable to the market.

Companies operating in markets that are *not competitive* favor cost-based approaches. That's because these companies do not need to respond or react to competitors' prices. The margin they add to costs to determine price depends on the value customers place on the product or service.

We consider first the market-based approach.

Target Costing for Target Pricing

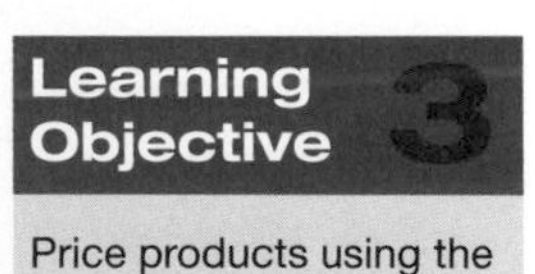

Price products using the target-costing approach

. . . target costing identifies an estimated price customers are willing to pay and then computes a target cost to earn the desired profit

Market-based pricing starts with a target price. A **target price** is the estimated price for a product or service that potential customers will pay. This estimate is based on an understanding of customers' perceived value for a product or service and how competitors will price competing products or services. Having this understanding of customers and competitors has become important for three reasons:

1. Competition from lower-cost producers has meant that prices cannot be increased.
2. Products are on the market for shorter periods of time, leaving less time and opportunity to recover from pricing mistakes, loss of market share, and loss of profitability.
3. Customers have become more knowledgeable and demand quality products at reasonable prices.

Understanding Customers' Perceived Value

A company's sales and marketing organization, through close contact and interaction with customers, is usually in the best position to identify customers' needs and their perceptions of the value of a product or service. Companies also conduct market research studies about product features that customers want and the prices they are willing to pay for those features.

Doing Competitor Analysis

To gauge how competitors might react to a prospective price, a company must understand competitors' technologies, products or services, costs, and financial conditions. For example, knowing competitors' technologies and products helps a company (a) to evaluate how distinctive its own products or services will be in the market and (b) to determine the prices it might be able to charge as a result of being distinctive. Where does a company obtain information about its competitors? Usually from former customers, suppliers, and employees of competitors. Another source of information is *reverse engineering*—that's disassembling and analyzing competitors' products to determine product designs and materials and to become acquainted with the technologies competitors use. Many companies, including Ford, General Motors, and PPG Industries, have departments whose sole purpose is to analyze competitors with respect to these considerations. At no time should a company resort to illegal or unethical means to obtain information from competitors. For example, a company should never pay off current employees or pose as a supplier or customer in order to obtain competitor information.

Implementing Target Pricing and Target Costing

There are five steps in developing target prices and target costs. We illustrate these steps using our Provalue example.

Step 1: Develop a product that satisfies the needs of potential customers. Based on an understanding of customer requirements and an analysis of competitors' products, Astel plans the product features and design modifications for Provalue for 2010. Astel's market research indicates that customers do not value Provalue's extra features, such as special audio features and designs that accommodate upgrades that can make the PC run faster. They want Astel to redesign Provalue into a no-frills but reliable PC and to sell it at a much lower price.

Step 2: Choose a target price. Based on Astel's research of its competitors' products and technologies, Astel expects its competitors to lower the prices of PCs that compete with Provalue to $850. Astel's management wants to respond aggressively by reducing Provalue's price by 20%, from $1,000 to $800 per unit. At this lower price, Astel's marketing manager forecasts an increase in annual sales from 150,000 to 200,000 units.

Step 3: Derive a target cost per unit by subtracting target operating income per unit from the target price. The target price is the basis for calculating target cost per unit. *Target cost per unit* is the target price minus *target operating income per unit.* **Target operating income per unit** is the operating income that a company aims to earn per unit of a product or service sold. **Target cost per unit** is the estimated long-run cost per unit of a product or service that enables the company to achieve its target operating income per unit when selling at the target price.[3] Target cost per unit is often lower than the existing *full cost per unit of the product.* Target cost per unit is really just that—a target—something the company must commit to achieve.

To earn the target return on the capital invested in the business, Astel's management needs a 10% target operating income on target revenues.

Total target revenues	= $800 per unit × 200,000 units = $160,000,000
Total target operating income	= 10% × $160,000,000 = $16,000,000
Target operating income per unit	= $16,000,000 ÷ 200,000 units = $80 per unit
Target cost per unit	= Target price − Target operating income per unit
	= $800 per unit − $80 per unit = $720 per unit
Total current full costs of Provalue	= $135,000,000 (from Exhibit 12-2)
Current full cost per unit of Provalue	= $135,000,000 ÷ 150,000 units = $900 per unit Exhibit 12-2

[3] For a more-detailed discussion of target costing, see S. Ansari, J. Bell and The CAM-I Target Cost Core Group, *Target Costing: The Next Frontier in Strategic Cost Management* (Homewood, IL: Irwin McGraw-Hill, 1997). For implementation information, see S. Ansari, L. D. Swenson, and J. Bell, "A Template for Implementing Target Costing," *Cost Management* (September–October 2006): 20–27.

Provalue's $720 target cost per unit is well below its existing $900 unit cost. Astel must reduce its unit cost by $180 to reach its goal. Cost-reduction efforts need to extend to all parts of the value chain—from R&D to customer service—including seeking lower prices from suppliers for materials and components, while maintaining quality.

What costs do Astel's managers include in the target-cost calculations? The relevant costs are *all* future costs, both variable and fixed, because in the long run, a company's prices and revenues must recover all its costs. If all these costs cannot be recovered, the company's best alternative is to shut down—an action that results in forgoing all future revenues and saving all future costs, whether fixed or variable. Contrast relevant costs for long-run pricing decisions (all variable and fixed costs) with relevant costs for short-run pricing decisions (costs that change in the short run, mostly but not exclusively variable costs).

Step 4: Perform cost analysis. This step analyzes which aspects of a product or service to target for cost reduction. For Provalue, Astel's managers consider the following:

- The functions performed by different component parts such as the motherboard, disc drives, and the graphics and video cards.
- The current costs of the different component parts.
- The importance that customers place on different product features. For example, Astel's targeted customers place greater emphasis on the reliability of the computer than on video quality.
- How different features relate to the functions performed by different component parts. For example, the reliability of the computer can be enhanced by using a simpler motherboard. By choosing a simpler motherboard, the newly designed computer will be unable to support the top-of-the-line video card. This is, however, of little concern to Astel because video quality is not as important to Astel's target customers.

Step 5: Perform value engineering to achieve target cost. Value engineering is a systematic evaluation of all aspects of the value chain; its objective is to reduce costs and achieve a quality level that satisfies customers. As we describe next, value engineering encompasses improvements in product designs, changes in materials specifications, and modifications in process methods. (See the Concepts in Action feature on p. 437 to learn about IKEA's approach to target pricing and target costing.)

Value Engineering, Cost Incurrence, and Locked-In Costs

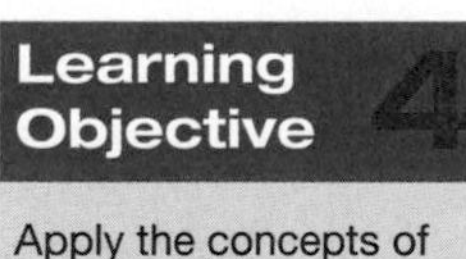

Apply the concepts of cost incurrence

. . . when resources are consumed

and locked-in costs

. . . when resources are committed to be incurred in the future

To implement value engineering, managers distinguish value-added activities and costs from nonvalue-added activities and costs. A **value-added cost** is a cost that, if eliminated, would reduce the actual or perceived value or utility (usefulness) customers obtain from using the product or service. Examples are costs of specific product features and attributes desired by customers. For Provalue, these features and attributes are a reliable PC, adequate memory, desired preloaded software, clear images on the monitor, and prompt customer service. A **nonvalue-added cost** is a cost that, if eliminated, would not reduce the actual or perceived value or utility (usefulness) customers obtain from using the product or service. It is a cost that the customer is unwilling to pay for. Examples of nonvalue-added costs are costs of producing defective products and machine breakdowns. Successful companies keep nonvalue-added costs to a minimum.

Activities and their costs do not always fall neatly into value-added or nonvalue-added categories. Some costs, such as supervision and production control, fall in a gray area because they include mostly value-added but also some nonvalue-added aspects. Despite these troublesome gray areas, attempts to distinguish value-added from nonvalue-added costs provide a useful overall framework for value engineering.

In the Provalue example, direct materials, direct manufacturing labor, and direct machining costs are value-added costs. Ordering, receiving, testing, and inspection costs fall in the gray area. Customers perceive some portion, but not all, of these costs as necessary for adding value. Rework costs, including costs of delivering reworked products, are nonvalue-added costs because these costs could have been avoided if a defective product had not been produced in the first place.

Concepts in Action

Extreme Target Pricing and Cost Management at IKEA

For millions of loyal customers throughout the world, Swedish furniture giant IKEA has achieved an almost cult-like status. Known for products with unpronounceable names, utilitarian design, flat packaging, and do-it-yourself instructions, IKEA has grown from humble beginnings to become the world's largest furniture retailer with 252 stores in 35 countries. How did this happen? Through aggressive target pricing, coupled with relentless cost management. IKEA's prices typically run 30% to 50% below their competitors' prices.

To achieve such low prices, the process of driving down costs begins with product conceptualization. First, product developers identify gaps in IKEA's current product portfolio. For example, product developers might identify the need to create a new low-price, modern-style couch designed for smaller apartments. Second, product developers and their team survey competitors to determine how much they charge for similar items, if offered, and then select a target price that is 30% to 50% less than the competitor's price. With a product and price established, product developers then determine what materials will be used and what manufacturer will do the assembly work—all before the new item is fully designed. A brief describing the new couch's target cost and basic specifications is submitted for bidding among IKEA's 1,800 suppliers in 55 countries. Suppliers vie to offer the most attractive bid based on price, function, and materials to be used. This value-engineering process promotes volume-based cost efficiencies throughout the design and production process.

But aggressive cost management does not stop there! All IKEA products are designed to be shipped unassembled in flat packages. The company estimates that shipping costs would be at least six times greater if all products were shipped assembled. In addition, IKEA stores *do not* offer many of the amenities their competitors offer, including salespeople, conspicuous price reductions, and product delivery.

But where does IKEA go from here? IKEA recently introduced a three-tier pricing system in its stores, so upscale customers can find fancier products in the same store in which cash-strapped shoppers pick up bargains. And those bargains are becoming less expensive. The company now works to decrease prices on its most popular items each year. Pernille Lopez, President of IKEA North America, stated, "The more popular our products are, the bigger the orders we can place. In return, our suppliers reduce their prices, and we pass the savings on." This relentless focus on lean design, cost containment, and customer focus remains a hallmark at IKEA. As founder Ingvar Kamprad once noted, "Waste of resources is a mortal sin at IKEA. Expensive solutions are often a sign of mediocrity, and an idea without a price tag is never acceptable."

Sources: L. Margonelli, "How IKEA Designs Its Sexy Price Tags," *Business 2.0* (October 2002); *Ingvar Kamprad and IKEA*, Harvard Business School case number 9-390-132; O. Burkeman, "The Miracle of Älmhult," *The Guardian* (June 17, 2004); T. Howard, "IKEA Builds on Furnishings Success," *Detroit News* (January 9, 2005); IKEA Group corporate site (www.ikea-group.ikea.com/corporate); IKEA Group US site (www.ikea.com/ms/en_US/campaigns/new_lower_price.html).

Astel's goal in value engineering is to reduce, and possibly eliminate, nonvalue-added costs and increase the efficiency of value-added activities. To do value engineering, Astel's managers must distinguish when costs are incurred from when costs are locked in. **Cost incurrence** describes when a resource is consumed (or benefit forgone) to meet a specific objective. Costing systems emphasize cost incurrence. For example, Astel's costing system recognizes direct material costs of Provalue as each unit of Provalue is assembled and sold. But Provalue's direct material cost per unit is *locked in*, or *designed in*, much earlier, when product designers choose the components that will go into Provalue. **Locked-in costs—designed-in costs**—are costs that have not yet been incurred but, based on decisions that have already been made, will be incurred in the future.

To manage costs well, a company must identify how design choices lock in costs, *before* the costs are incurred. For example, scrap and rework costs incurred during manufacturing are often locked in much earlier by faulty design. Similarly, in the software industry, software development costs are often locked in at the design-and-analysis stage. Costly and difficult-to-fix errors that appear during coding and testing are frequently locked in by bad software designs.

Exhibit 12-3

Pattern of Cost Incurrence and Locked-In Costs for Provalue

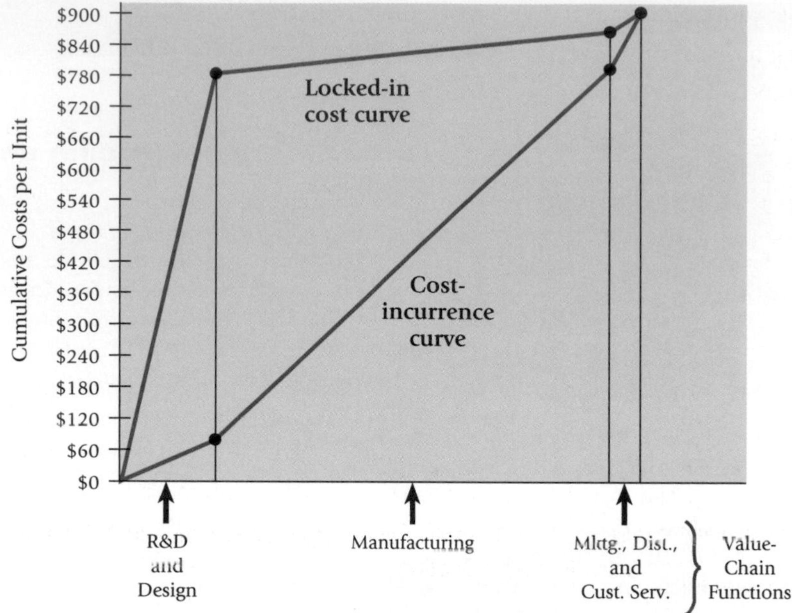

Exhibit 12-3 illustrates the locked-in cost curve and the cost-incurrence curve for Provalue. The bottom curve, graphically representing cost incurrence, uses information from Exhibit 12-2 to plot the cumulative cost per unit incurred in different business functions of the value chain. The top curve plots how cumulative costs are locked in. (The specific numbers underlying this curve are not presented.) Total cumulative cost per unit for both curves is $900. *However, the graph emphasizes the wide divergence between the time when costs are locked in and when they are incurred.* For example, once the product is designed and the operations to manufacture, market, distribute, and support the product are determined, more than 86% ($780 ÷ $900) of the unit cost of Provalue (for example, direct materials, ordering, testing and rework) is locked in, when only about 8% ($76 ÷ $900) of the unit cost is actually incurred!

Value-Chain Analysis and Cross-Functional Teams

To help reduce costs and achieve a quality level their customers want, Astel's managers focus on the design stage. The company organizes a cross-functional value-engineering team consisting of marketing managers, product designers, manufacturing engineers, purchasing managers, suppliers, dealers, and management accountants. The team modifies Provalue's design to reduce costs while retaining features that customers value. Here are some of the team's ideas:

- Use a simpler, more-reliable motherboard without complex features.
- Design Provalue so that various parts snap-fit together, rather than solder together, to decrease direct manufacturing labor-hours and related costs.
- Simplify the Provalue design and use fewer components to decrease ordering and receiving costs and also decrease testing and inspection costs.
- Design Provalue to be lighter and smaller to reduce distribution and packaging costs.
- Design Provalue to reduce repairs at customer sites.

Management accountants use their understanding of the technical and business aspects of the entire value chain to estimate cost savings.

Not all costs are locked in at the design stage. Managers always have opportunities to reduce costs by improving operating efficiency and productivity. Many companies combine value engineering with *kaizen*, or *continuous improvement* methods that seek to reduce the time it takes to do a task and to eliminate waste during production and delivery of products.

In summary, the target-pricing, target-costing, and value-engineering process has five key aspects:

1. Understanding customer requirements and competitor actions
2. Selecting a target price and determining a target cost
3. Anticipating how costs are locked in before they are incurred
4. Improving product and process designs and efficiency to achieve target costs and better quality
5. Using cross-functional teams to coordinate actions that need to be taken throughout the value chain

Achieving the Target Cost per Unit for Provalue

Exhibit 12-4 uses an activity-based approach to compare cost-driver quantities and rates for the 150,000 units of Provalue manufactured and sold in 2009 and the 200,000 units of Provalue II budgeted for 2010. Value engineering reduces both value-added costs (by

Exhibit 12-4 Cost-Driver Quantities and Rates for Provalue in 2009 and Provalue II for 2010 Using Activity-Based Costing

	A	B	C	D	E	F	G	H	I	J	K	L	M	N
1–2			Manufacturing cost information for 150,000 units of Provalue in 2009						Manufacturing cost information for 200,000 units of Provalue II for 2010					
3	Cost Category	Cost Driver	Details of Actual Cost Driver Quantities				Actual Total Quantity of Cost Driver	Actual Cost per Unit of Cost Driver (p.432)	Details of Budgeted Cost Driver Quantities				Budgeted Total Quantity of Cost Driver	Budgeted Cost per Unit of Cost Driver (Given)
4	(1)	(2)	(3)		(4)		(5)=(3)x(4)	(6)	(7)		(8)		(9)=(7)x(8)	(10)
5	**Direct Manufacturing Costs**													
6	Direct materials	No. of kits	1	kit per unit	150,000	units	150,000	$460	1	kit per unit	200,000	units	200,000	$385
7	Direct manuf. labor (DML)	DML hours	3.2	DML hours per unit	150,000	units	480,000	$ 20	2.65	DML hours per unit	200,000	units	530,000	$ 20
8	Direct machining (fixed)	Machine-hours					300,000	$ 38					300,000	$ 38
9	**Manufacturing Overhead Costs**													
10	Ordering and receiving	No. of orders	50	orders per component	450	components	22,500	$ 80	50	orders per component	425	components	21,250	$ 80
11	Testing and inspection	Testing-hours	30	testing-hours per unit	150,000	units	4,500,000	$ 2	15	testing hours per unit	200,000	units	3,000,000	$ 2
12	Rework				8%	defect rate					6.5%	defect rate		
13		Rework-hours	2.5	rework-hours per defective unit	12,000[a]	defective units	30,000	$ 40	2.5	rework-hours per defective unit	13,000[b]	defective units	32,500	$ 40
14														
15	[a]8% defect rate x 150,000 units = 12,000 defective units													
16	[b]6.5% defect rate x 200,000 units = 13,000 defective units													

Exhibit 12-5 Target Manufacturing Costs of Provalue II for 2010

	A	B	C	D	E	F
1		PROVALUE II				PROVALUE
2		Budgeted		Budgeted		Actual Manufacturing
3		Manufacturing Costs		Manufacturing		Cost per Unit
4		for 200,000 Units		Cost per Unit		(Exhibit 12-1)
5		(1)		(2) = (1) ÷ 200,000		(3)
6	Direct manufacturing costs					
7	Direct material costs					
8	(200,000 kits x $385 per kit)	$ 77,000,000		$385.00		$460.00
9	Direct manufacturing labor costs					
10	(530,000 DML-hours x $20 per hour)	10,600,000		53.00		64.00
11	Direct machining costs					
12	(300,000 machine-hours x $38 per machine-hour)	11,400,000		57.00		76.00
13	Direct manufacturing costs	99,000,000		495.00		600.00
14	Manufacturing overhead costs					
15	Ordering and receiving costs					
16	(21,250 orders x $80 per order)	1,700,000		8.50		12.00
17	Testing and inspection costs					
18	(3,000,000 testing-hours x $2 per hour)	6,000,000		30.00		60.00
19	Rework costs					
20	(32,500 rework-hours x $40 per hour)	1,300,000		6.50		8.00
21	Manufacturing overhead costs	9,000,000		45.00		80.00
22	Total manufaturing costs	$108,000,000		$540.00		$ 680.00

designing Provalue II to need fewer and less costly direct materials and components in each kit, and fewer direct manufacturing labor-hours and testing-hours per unit) and nonvalue-added costs (by simplifying Provalue II's design to reduce the percentage of units that require rework). Astel maintains 300,000 machine-hours of capacity but through value engineering reduces the machine-hours required to make Provalue II to 1.5 hours per unit. This reduction allows Astel to use the 300,000 machine-hours of capacity to make and sell more units of Provalue II (200,000 units versus 150,000 units for Provalue), thereby reducing machining cost per unit. For simplicity, we assume that value engineering will not reduce the $20 cost per direct manufacturing labor-hour, the $80 cost per order, the $2 cost per testing-hour, or the $40 cost per rework-hour. By making these activities more efficient, value engineering can also reduce costs by reducing these cost-driver rates (see the Problem for Self-Study, p. 448).

Exhibit 12-5 presents the target manufacturing costs of Provalue II, using data for the quantity of the cost driver and the cost-driver rate from the Provalue II columns in Exhibit 12-4. For comparison, Exhibit 12-5 also shows the actual 2009 manufacturing cost per unit of Provalue from Exhibit 12-1. The new design is budgeted to reduce total manufacturing cost per unit by $140 (from $680 to $540) at the budgeted sales quantity of 200,000 units. Astel's managers also expect the new design to reduce costs in other business functions from $220 (Exhibit 12-2) to $180 (calculations not shown). The budgeted full unit cost of Provalue II is $720—the target cost per unit. At the end of 2010, Astel's managers will compare actual costs and target costs to gain insight about improvements that can be made in subsequent target-costing efforts.

Unless managed properly, value engineering and target costing can have undesirable effects:

- Employees may feel frustrated if they fail to attain targets.
- The cross-functional team may add too many features just to accommodate the different wishes of team members.
- A product may be in development for a long time as alternative designs are evaluated repeatedly.

- Organizational conflicts may develop as the burden of cutting costs falls unequally on different business functions in the company's value chain, for example, more on manufacturing than on marketing.

To avoid these pitfalls, target-costing efforts should always (a) encourage employee participation and celebrate small improvements toward achieving the target, (b) focus on the customer, (c) pay attention to schedules, and (d) set cost-cutting targets for all value-chain functions to encourage a culture of teamwork and cooperation.

Cost-Based (Cost-Plus) Pricing

Learning Objective 5

Price products using the cost-plus approach

. . . cost-plus pricing is based on some measure of cost plus a markup

Instead of using the market-based approach for their long-run pricing decisions, managers sometimes use a cost-based approach. The general formula for setting a cost-based price adds a markup component to the cost base to determine a prospective selling price. Because a markup is added, cost-based pricing is often called cost-plus pricing, with the plus referring to the markup component. Managers use the cost-plus pricing formula only as a starting point for pricing decisions. Therefore, the markup component is rarely a rigid number. Instead, it is flexible, depending on the behavior of customers and competitors. The markup component is ultimately determined by the market.[4]

Cost-Plus Target Rate of Return on Investment

We illustrate a cost-plus pricing formula for our Astel example. Assume Astel's engineers have redesigned Provalue into Provalue II and that Astel uses a 12% markup on the full unit cost of the product in developing the prospective selling price.

Cost base (full unit cost of Provalue II)	$720.00
Markup component of 12% (0.12 × $720)	86.40
Prospective selling price	$806.40

How is the markup percentage of 12% determined? One way is to choose a markup to earn a *target rate of return on investment*. The **target rate of return on investment** is the target annual operating income that an organization aims to achieve divided by invested capital. Invested capital can be defined in many ways. In this chapter, we define invested capital as total assets—that is, long-term assets plus current assets. Suppose Astel's (pretax) target rate of return on investment is 18% and Provalue II's capital investment is $96 million. The target annual operating income for Provalue II is:

Invested capital	$96,000,000
Target rate of return on investment	18%
Target annual operating income (0.18 × $96,000,000)	$17,280,000
Target operating income per unit of Provalue II ($17,280,000 ÷ 200,000 units)	$86.40

This calculation indicates that Astel needs to earn a target operating income of $86.40 on each unit of Provalue II. The markup of $86.40 expressed as a percentage of the full product cost per unit of $720 equals 12% ($86.40 ÷ $720).

Do not confuse the 18% target rate of return on investment with the 12% markup percentage.

- The 18% target rate of return on investment expresses Astel's expected annual operating income as a percentage of investment.
- The 12% markup expresses operating income per unit as a percentage of the full product cost per unit.

[4] Exceptions are pricing of electricity and natural gas in many countries, where prices are set by the government on the basis of costs plus a return on invested capital. Chapter 15 discusses the use of costs to set prices in the defense-contracting industry. In these situations, products are not subject to competitive forces and cost accounting techniques substitute for markets as the basis for setting prices.

Astel first calculates target rate of return on investment and then determines markup percentage.

Alternative Cost-Plus Methods

Companies sometimes find it difficult to determine the specific amount of capital they invested to support a specific product. That's because computing the specific amount of invested capital requires knowing, for example, the allocations of investments in equipment and buildings to produce individual products—a difficult and somewhat arbitrary task. Some companies prefer to use alternative cost bases and markup percentages that still earn a return on invested capital but do not require explicit calculations of invested capital to set prices.

The following table presents some alternative cost bases for Provalue II without providing details of the calculations and using assumed markup percentages.

Cost Base	Estimated Cost per Unit (1)	Markup Percentage (2)	Markup Component (3) = (1) × (2)	Prospective Selling Price (4) = (1) + (3)
Variable manufacturing cost	$475.00	65%	$308.75	$783.75
Variable cost of the product	547.00	45	246.15	793.15
Manufacturing cost	540.00	50	270.00	810.00
Full cost of the product	720.00	12	86.40	806.40

The different cost bases and markup percentages give four prospective selling prices that are close to each other. In practice, a company will choose a cost base that it regards as reliable and a markup percentage that is based on its experience in pricing products to recover its costs and earn a target return on investment. For example, a company may choose the full cost of the product as a base if it is unsure about distinguishing variable costs from fixed costs.

The markup percentages in the preceding table vary a great deal, from a high of 65% on variable manufacturing cost to a low of 12% on full cost of the product. Why the wide variation? Because cost bases that include fewer costs have a higher markup percentage to compensate for the costs excluded from the base. The markup percentage also depends on the extent of competition in the marketplace. Markups and profit margins tend to be lower in more-competitive markets.

Surveys indicate that most managers use the full cost of the product for their cost-based pricing decisions—that is, they include both fixed and variable costs when calculating the cost per unit. Managers cite the following advantages for including fixed cost per unit in the cost base for pricing decisions:

1. **Full recovery of all costs of the product.** For long-run pricing decisions, full cost of the product informs managers of the minimum cost they need to recover to continue in business. Using just the variable cost as a base does not give managers this information. There is then a temptation, as has happened in the airline industry, to engage in excessive long-run price cutting as long as prices provide a positive contribution margin. Long-run price cutting, however, will result in losses if long-run revenues are less than the long-run full cost of the product.
2. **Price stability.** Managers believe that basing prices on the full cost of the product promotes price stability, because it limits the ability and temptations of salespersons to cut prices. Managers prefer price stability because it facilitates more-accurate forecasting and planning.
3. **Simplicity.** A full-cost formula for pricing does not require a detailed analysis of cost-behavior patterns to separate costs into fixed and variable components for each product. Many costs—for example, testing, inspection, and setups—have both variable- and fixed-cost components. Determining the variable cost of each activity and product is not straightforward.

Including fixed cost per unit in the cost base for pricing is not without problems. Allocating fixed costs to products can be arbitrary. Also, calculating fixed cost per unit requires a denominator level that is likely only an estimate of capacity or expected units of future sales. Errors in these estimates will cause actual full cost per unit of the product to differ from the estimated amount.

Cost-Plus Pricing and Target Pricing

The selling prices computed under cost-plus pricing are *prospective* prices. Suppose Astel's initial product design results in a $750 full cost for Provalue II. Assuming a 12% markup, Astel sets a prospective price of $840 [$750 + (0.12 × $750)]. In the competitive personal computer market, customer and competitor reactions to this price may force Astel to reduce the markup percentage and lower the price to, say, $800. Astel may then want to redesign Provalue II to reduce the full cost to $720 per unit, as in our example, and achieve a markup close to 12% while keeping the price at $800. The eventual design and cost-plus price chosen must balance the trade-offs among costs, markup, and customer reactions.

The target-pricing approach reduces the need to go back and forth among prospective cost-plus prices, customer reactions, and design modifications. Relative to cost-plus pricing, target pricing first determines product characteristics and target price on the basis of customer preferences and expected competitor responses, and then a target cost. Target pricing is not without its own challenges. Determining a target price can be difficult in markets where products are differentiated from one another. In these situations, managers go back and forth between target price and cost-plus approaches.

Suppliers who provide unique products and services—accountants and management consultants, for example—usually use cost-plus pricing. Professional service firms set prices based on hourly cost-plus billing rates of partners, managers, and associates. These prices are, however, reduced in competitive situations. Professional service firms also take a multiple-year client perspective when deciding prices. Certified public accountants, for example, sometimes charge a client a low price initially and a higher price later.

Service companies such as home repair services, automobile repair services, and architectural firms use a cost-plus pricing method called the *time-and-materials method*. Individual jobs are priced based on materials and labor time. The price charged for materials equals the cost of materials plus a markup. The price charged for labor represents the cost of labor plus a markup. That is, the price charged for each direct cost item includes its own markup. The markups are chosen to recover overhead costs and earn a profit.

Life-Cycle Product Budgeting and Costing

Learning Objective 6

Use life-cycle budgeting and costing when making pricing decisions

. . . accumulate all costs of a product from initial R&D to final customer service for each year of its life

Companies sometimes need to consider target prices and target costs for a product over a multiple-year product life cycle. The **product life cycle** spans the time from initial R&D on a product to when customer service and support is no longer offered for that product. For automobile companies such as DaimlerChrysler, Ford, and Nissan, the product life cycle for different car models ranges from 12 to 15 years. For pharmaceutical products, the life cycle at companies such as Pfizer, Merck, and Glaxo Smith Kline may be 15 to 20 years. For banks such as Wachovia and Chase Manhattan Bank, a product such as a newly designed savings account with specific privileges can have a life cycle of 10 to 20 years. Personal computers have a shorter life-cycle of 3 to 5 years, because rapid innovations in the computing power and speed of microprocessors that run the computers makes older models obsolete. The sales part of the product life cycle has four stages: when a product is introduced to the market, when sales grow, when sales stabilize as the product matures, and when sales decline as the product loses market acceptance.

In **life-cycle budgeting**, managers estimate the revenues and business function costs of the value chain attributable to each product from its initial R&D to its final customer service and support. **Life-cycle costing** tracks and accumulates business function costs of the value chain attributable to each product from initial R&D to final customer service and support. Life-cycle budgeting and life-cycle costing span several years.

Life-Cycle Budgeting and Pricing Decisions

Budgeted life-cycle costs can provide useful information for strategically evaluating pricing decisions. Consider Insight, Inc., a computer software company, which is developing a new accounting package, "General Ledger." Assume the following budgeted amounts for General Ledger over a six-year product life cycle:

Years 1 and 2

	Total Fixed Costs
R&D costs	$240,000
Design costs	160,000

Years 3 to 6

	Total Fixed Costs	Variable Cost per Package
Production costs	$100,000	$25
Marketing costs	70,000	24
Distribution costs	50,000	16
Customer-service costs	80,000	30

To be profitable, Insight must generate enough revenue to recover the costs in all six business functions of the value chain and, in particular, its high fixed nonproduction costs, which total $600,000. Exhibit 12-6 presents the life-cycle budget for General Ledger for three alternative selling-price/sales-quantity combinations.

Several features make life-cycle budgeting particularly important:

1. **The development period for R&D and design is long and costly.** In the General Ledger example, R&D and design span two years and constitute more than 30% of total costs for each of the three combinations of selling price and predicted sales quantity. When a high percentage of total life-cycle costs are incurred before any production begins and before any revenues are received, the company especially needs to consider revenues and costs over the life-cycle of the product. It uses this information to decide whether to begin the costly R&D and design activities.
2. **Many costs are locked in at R&D and design stages—even if R&D and design costs themselves are small.** In our General Ledger example, a poorly designed accounting software package that is difficult to install and use would result in higher marketing, distribution, and customer-service costs in several subsequent years. These costs would be even higher if the product failed to meet promised quality-performance levels. A life-cycle revenue-and-cost budget prevents these relationships among business-function costs across years from being overlooked in decision making. Life-cycle budgeting highlights costs throughout the product's life cycle and so facilitates target pricing, target costing, and value engineering at the design stage before costs are locked in. The amounts presented in Exhibit 12-6 are the outcome of value engineering.

Insight decides to sell the General Ledger package for $480 per package because this price maximizes life-cycle operating income. Insight's managers will eventually compare actual costs incurred to life-cycle budgets to obtain feedback and learn about how to estimate costs for subsequent products. Exhibit 12-6 assumes that the selling price per package is the same over the entire life cycle. For strategic reasons, however, Insight may decide to skim the market—charging higher prices to customers eager to try General Ledger when it is first introduced and lowering prices later as the product matures. In these later stages, Insight may even add new features to differentiate the product to maintain prices and sales. The life-cycle budget must then incorporate this strategy.

Management of environmental costs provides another example of life-cycle costing and value engineering. Environmental laws—for example, the U.S. Clean Air Act and the U.S. Superfund Amendment and Reauthorization Act—have introduced tougher environmental standards, imposed stringent cleanup requirements, and introduced severe penalties for polluting the air and contaminating subsurface soil and groundwater. Environmental costs that are incurred over several years of the product's life-cycle are often locked in at the product- and process-design stage. To avoid environmental liabilities, companies in industries such as oil refining, chemical processing, and automobiles do value engineering; they design products and processes to prevent and reduce pollution over the product's life cycle. Laptop computer manufacturers—for example, Hewlett Packard and Apple—have

Exhibit 12-6

Budgeting Life-Cycle Revenues and Costs for "General Ledger" Software Package of Insight, Inc.[a]

	Alternative Selling-Price/ Sales-Quantity Combinations		
	A	B	C
Selling price per package	$400	$480	$600
Sales quantity in units	5,000	4,000	2,500
Life-cycle revenues			
($400 × 5,000; $480 × 4,000; $600 × 2,500)	$2,000,000	$1,920,000	$1,500,000
Life-cycle costs			
R&D costs	240,000	240,000	240,000
Design costs of product/process	160,000	160,000	160,000
Production costs			
$100,000 + ($25 × 5,000); $100,000 + ($25 × 4,000); $100,000 + ($25 × 2,500)	225,000	200,000	162,500
Marketing costs			
$70,000 + ($24 × 5,000); $70,000 + ($24 × 4,000); $70,000 + ($24 × 2,500)	190,000	166,000	130,000
Distribution costs			
$50,000 + ($16 × 5,000); $50,000 + ($16 × 4,000); $50,000 + ($16 × 2,500)	130,000	114,000	90,000
Customer-service costs			
$80,000 + ($30 × 5,000); $80,000 + ($30 × 4,000); $80,000 + ($30 × 2,500)	230,000	200,000	155,000
Total life-cycle costs	1,175,000	1,080,000	937,500
Life-cycle operating income	$ 825,000	$ 840,000	$ 562,500

[a]This exhibit does not take into consideration the time value of money when computing life-cycle revenues or life-cycle costs. Chapter 21 outlines how this important factor can be incorporated into such calculations.

introduced costly recycling programs to ensure that nickel-cadmium batteries that can leak hazardous chemicals into the soil are disposed of in an environmentally safe way at the end of the batteries' lives.

Customer Life-Cycle Costing

A different notion of life-cycle costs is *customer life-cycle costs*. **Customer life-cycle costs** focus on the total costs incurred by a customer to acquire, use, maintain, and dispose of a product or service. Customer life-cycle costs for a car include the cost of the car itself plus the costs of operating and maintaining the car minus the disposal value of the car. Customer life-cycle costs can be an important consideration in the pricing decision.

For example, Ford's goal is to design cars that require minimal maintenance for 100,000 miles. Ford expects to charge a higher price and/or to gain greater market share by selling cars designed to meet this goal. Similarly, Maytag, the home-appliance manufacturer, charges higher prices for models that save electricity and have low maintenance costs. Boeing Corporation paid special attention to customer life-cycle costs when it designed the Boeing 777. The plane's design allows mechanics easier access to different areas of the plane to perform routine maintenance. The goal was to reduce the time and cost of plane maintenance and significantly decrease the life-cycle cost of owning a plane, allowing Boeing to justify a higher price for the 777.

Learning Objective 7

Describe two pricing practices in which noncost factors are important when setting prices

. . . price discrimination—charging different customers different prices for the same product; and peak-load pricing—charging higher prices when demand approaches capacity

Considerations Other than Costs in Pricing Decisions

In some cases, cost is *not* a major factor in setting prices. Consider the prices airlines charge for a round-trip flight from San Francisco to Cleveland. A coach-class ticket for a flight with 21-day advance purchase is $400 if the passenger stays in Cleveland over a Saturday night. It is $1,800 if the passenger returns without staying over a Saturday night. Can this price difference be explained by the difference in the cost to the airline of these round-trip flights? No; it costs the same amount to transport the passenger from San Francisco to Cleveland and back, regardless of whether the passenger stays in

Cleveland over a Saturday night. To explain this difference in price, we must recognize the potential for *price discrimination*.

Price discrimination is the practice of charging different customers different prices for the same product or service. How does price discrimination work in our airline example? The demand for airline tickets comes from two main sources: business travelers and pleasure travelers. Business travelers must travel to conduct business for their organizations, so their demand for air travel is relatively insensitive to price and airlines can earn higher operating incomes by charging business travelers higher prices. Insensitivity of demand to price changes is called *demand inelasticity*. Also, business travelers generally go to their destinations, complete their work, and return home without staying over a Saturday night. Pleasure travelers, however, usually don't need to return home during the week, and they prefer to spend weekends at their destinations. Because they pay for their tickets themselves, pleasure travelers' demand is more price-elastic—that is, they are much more sensitive to price than business travelers. Therefore, it is profitable for the airlines to charge low fares to stimulate demand among pleasure travelers.

How can airlines keep fares high for business travelers while, at the same time, keeping fares low for pleasure travelers? Requiring a Saturday night stay discriminates between the two customer segments. The airlines price-discriminate to take advantage of different sensitivities to prices exhibited by business travelers and pleasure travelers. Price differences exist even though there is no cost difference in serving the two segments of customers.

What if economic conditions weaken such that business travelers become more sensitive to price? The airlines may then need to lower the prices charged to business travelers. Following the events of September 11, 2001, airlines started offering discounted fares on certain routes without requiring a Saturday night stay to stimulate business travel. Business travel picked up and airlines started filling more seats than they otherwise would have. Unfortunately, travel did not pick up enough, and the airline industry as a whole suffered severe losses over the next few years.

In addition to price discrimination, pricing decisions also consider other noncost factors such as capacity constraints. **Peak-load pricing** is the practice of charging a higher price for the same product or service when the demand for it approaches the physical limit of the capacity to produce that product or service. Prices charged during periods when demand on the production capacity is high represent what customers are willing to pay for the product or service. These prices are greater than the prices charged when slack or excess capacity is available when the goal is to utilize capacity by lowering prices to stimulate demand. Peak-load pricing occurs in the telephone, telecommunications, hotel, car rental, and electric-utility industries. For the 2004 Summer Olympics in Athens, hotels charged very high rates and required multiple-night stays. Airlines charged high fares for flights into and out of many cities in the region for roughly a month around the time of the games. Given that demand far exceeded capacity, the hospitality industry and airlines employed peak-load pricing to increase their profits.

Consider the daily rental rates charged by Avis Corporation in January 2007 for mid-sized cars rented at Boston's Logan Airport:

Monday through Thursday	$80 per day
Friday through Sunday	$22 per day

Avis's actual daily costs of renting a car are the same whether the car is rented on a weekday or on a weekend. Why the difference in prices? One explanation is that there is a greater demand for cars on weekdays because of business activity. Faced with capacity limits, Avis charges peak-load prices at levels the market will bear.

A second explanation is that the rental rates are a form of price discrimination. On weekdays, demand for cars comes largely from business travelers, who need to rent cars and who are insensitive to prices. Higher rental rates on weekdays are profitable because they have little effect on demand. Weekend rental demand comes from pleasure travelers, who are price-sensitive. Lower rates stimulate demand from these individuals and increase Avis's operating income. Under either explanation, the pricing decision is not primarily driven by cost considerations.

Another example of considerations other than costs affecting prices occurs when the same product is sold in different countries. Consider software, books, and medicines produced in one country and sold globally. The prices charged in each country vary much more than the costs of delivering the product to each country. These price differences arise because of differences in the purchasing power of consumers in different countries (a form of price discrimination) and government restrictions that may limit the prices that can be charged.

Effects of Antitrust Laws on Pricing

Learning Objective 8

Explain the effects of antitrust laws on pricing

. . . antitrust laws attempt to counteract pricing below costs to drive out competitors or fixing prices artificially high to harm consumers

Legal considerations affect pricing decisions. Companies are not always free to charge whatever price they like. For example, under the U.S. Robinson-Patman Act, a manufacturer cannot price-discriminate between two customers if the intent is to lessen or prevent competition for customers. Two key features of price-discrimination laws are:

1. Price discrimination is permissible if differences in prices can be justified by differences in costs.
2. Price discrimination is illegal only if the intent is to lessen or prevent competition.

The price discrimination by airlines and car rental companies described earlier is legal because their practices do not hinder competition.

To comply with U.S. antitrust laws, such as the Sherman Act, the Clayton Act, the Federal Trade Commission Act, and the Robinson-Patman Act, pricing must not be predatory.[5] A company engages in **predatory pricing** when it deliberately prices below its costs in an effort to drive competitors out of the market and restrict supply, and then raises prices rather than enlarge demand.[6]

The U.S. Supreme Court established the following conditions to prove that predatory pricing has occurred:

- The predator company charges a price below an appropriate measure of its costs, and
- The predator company has a reasonable prospect of recovering in the future, through larger market share or higher prices, the money it lost by pricing below cost.

The Supreme Court has not specified the "appropriate measure of costs."[7]

Most courts in the United States have defined the "appropriate measure of costs" as the short-run marginal or average variable costs.[8] In *Adjustor's Replace-a-Car v. Agency Rent-a-Car,* Adjustor's (the plaintiff) claimed that it was forced to withdraw from the Austin and San Antonio, Texas, markets because Agency had engaged in predatory pricing.[9] To prove predatory pricing, Adjustor pointed to "the net loss from operations" in Agency's income statement, calculated after allocating Agency's headquarters overhead. The judge, however, ruled that Agency had not engaged in predatory pricing because the price it charged for a rental car never dropped below its average variable costs.

The Supreme Court decision in *Brooke Group v. Brown & Williamson Tobacco (BWT)* increased the difficulty of proving predatory pricing. The Court ruled that pricing

---

[5] Discussion of the Sherman Act and the Clayton Act is in A. Barkman and J. Jolley, "Cost Defenses for Antitrust Cases," *Management Accounting* 67 (no. 10): 37–40.

[6] For more details, see W. Viscusi, J. Harrington, and J. Vernon, *Economics of Regulation and Antitrust*, 4th ed. (Cambridge, MA: MIT Press, 2006); and J. L. Goldstein, "Single Firm Predatory Pricing in Antitrust Law: The Rose Acre Recoupment Test and the Search for an Appropriate Judicial Standard," *Columbia Law Review* 91 (1991): 1557–1592.

[7] *Brooke Group v. Brown & Williamson Tobacco*, 113 S. Ct. (1993); T. J. Trujillo, "Predatory Pricing Standards Under Recent Supreme Court Decisions and Their Failure to Recognize Strategic Behavior as a Barrier to Entry," *Iowa Journal of Corporation Law* (Summer 1994): 809–831.

[8] An exception is *McGahee v. Northern Propane Gas Co.* [858 F, 2d 1487 (1988)], in which the Eleventh Circuit Court held that prices below average total cost constitute evidence of predatory intent. For more discussion, see P. Areeda and D. Turner, "Predatory Pricing and Related Practices under Section 2 of Sherman Act," *Harvard Law Review* 88 (1975): 697–733. For an overview of case law, see W. Viscusi, J. Harrington, and J. Vernon, *Economics of Regulation and Antitrust*, 4th ed. (Cambridge, MA: MIT Press, 2006). See also the "Legal Developments" section of the *Journal of Marketing* for summaries of court cases.

[9] *Adjustor's Replace-a-Car, Inc. v. Agency Rent-a-Car*, 735 2d 884 (1984).

below average variable costs is not predatory if the company does not have a reasonable chance of later increasing prices or market share to recover its losses.[10] The defendant, BWT, a cigarette manufacturer, sold brand-name cigarettes and had 12% of the cigarette market. The introduction of generic cigarettes threatened BWT's market share. BWT responded by introducing its own version of generics priced below average variable cost, thereby making it difficult for generic manufacturers to continue in business. The Supreme Court ruled that BWT's action was a competitive response and not predatory pricing. That's because, given BWT's small 12% market share and the existing competition within the industry, it would be unable to later charge a monopoly price to recoup its losses.

Closely related to predatory pricing is dumping. Under U.S. laws, **dumping** occurs when a non-U.S. company sells a product in the United States at a price below the market value in the country where it is produced, and this lower price materially injures or threatens to materially injure an industry in the United States. If dumping is proven, an antidumping duty can be imposed under U.S. tariff laws equal to the amount by which the foreign price exceeds the U.S. price. Cases related to dumping have occurred in the cement, computer, lumber, steel, semiconductor, and sweater industries. In March 2007, the U.S. Commerce Department said it would place import duties of 10.9% to 20.4% on imports of coated Chinese paper. China could challenge the decision to the dispute settlement panel of the World Trade Organization (WTO), an international institution created with the goal of promoting and regulating trade practices among countries.

Another violation of antitrust laws is collusive pricing. **Collusive pricing** occurs when companies in an industry conspire in their pricing and production decisions to achieve a price above the competitive price and so restrain trade. For example, in 2002, the European Commission fined video-games manufacturer Nintendo 149 million euros for colluding with distributors to prevent the export of products to European Union countries where video game prices were low. In 2004, the U.S. Department of Justice fined Bayer AG $66 million for colluding with various companies to artificially regulate prices in the rubber chemicals market.

Problem for Self-Study

Reconsider the Astel Computer example (pp. 430–431). Astel's marketing manager realizes that a further reduction in price is necessary to sell 200,000 units of Provalue II. To maintain a target profitability of $16 million, or $80 per unit, Astel will need to reduce costs of Provalue II by $6 million, or $30 per unit. Astel targets a reduction of $4 million, or $20 per unit, in manufacturing costs, and $2 million, or $10 per unit, in marketing, distribution, and customer-service costs. The cross-functional team assigned to this task proposes the following changes to manufacture a different version of Provalue, called Provalue III:

1. Reduce direct materials and ordering costs by purchasing subassembled components rather than individual components.
2. Reengineer ordering and receiving to reduce ordering and receiving costs per order.
3. Reduce testing time and the labor and power required per hour of testing.
4. Develop new rework procedures to reduce rework costs per hour.

No changes are proposed in direct manufacturing labor cost per unit and in total machining costs.

[10] *Brooke Group v. Brown & Williamson Tobacco*, 113 S. Ct. (1993).

The following table summarizes the cost-driver quantities and the cost per unit of each cost driver for Provalue III compared with Provalue II.

	A	B	C	D	E	F	G	H	I	J	K	L	M	N
1			Manufacturing cost information						Manufacturing cost information					
2			for 200,000 units of Provalue II for 2010						for 200,000 units of Provalue III for 2010					
3	Cost Category	Cost Driver	Details of Budgeted Cost Driver Quantities				Budgeted Total Quantity of Cost Driver	Budgeted Cost per Unit of Cost Driver	Details of Budgeted Cost Driver Quantities				Budgeted Total Quantity of Cost Driver	Budgeted Cost per Unit of Cost Driver
4	(1)	(2)	(3)		(4)		(5)=(3)x(4)	(6)	(7)		(8)		(9)=(7)x(8)	(10)
5	Direct materials	No. of kits	1	kit per unit	200,000	units	200,000	$385	1	kit per unit	200,000	units	200,000	$375
6	Direct manuf. labor (DML)	DML hours	2.65	DML hours per unit	200,000	units	530,000	$ 20	2.65	DML hours per unit	200,000	units	530,000	$ 20
7	Direct machining (fixed)	Machine-hours					300,000	$ 38					300,000	$ 38
8	Ordering and receiving	No. of orders	50	orders per component	425	components	21,250	$ 80	50	orders per component	400	components	20,000	$ 60
9	Test and inspection	Testing-hours	15	testing-hours per unit	200,000	units	3,000,000	$ 2	14	testing-hours per unit	200,000	units	2,800,000	$ 1.70
10	Rework				6.5%	defect rate					6.5%	defect rate		
11		Rework-hours	2.5	rework-hours per defective unit	13,000[a]	defective units	32,500	$ 40	2.5	rework-hours per defective unit	13,000[a]	defective units	32,500	$ 32
12														
13	[a]6.5% defect rate x 200,000 units = 13,000 defective units													

Required

Will the proposed changes achieve Astel's targeted reduction of \$4 million, or \$20 per unit, in manufacturing costs for Provalue III? Show your computations.

Solution

Exhibit 12-7 presents the manufacturing costs for Provalue III based on the proposed changes. Manufacturing costs will decline from \$108 million, or \$540 per unit (Exhibit 12-5), to \$104 million, or \$520 per unit (Exhibit 12-7), and will achieve the target reduction of \$4 million, or \$20 per unit.

Exhibit 12-7

Target Manufacturing Costs of Provalue III for 2010 Based on Proposed Changes

	A	B	C	D
1		Budgeted		Budgeted
2		Manufacturing Costs		Manufacturing
3		for 200,000 Units		Cost per Unit
4		(1)		(2) = (1) ÷ 200,000
5	Direct manufacturing costs			
6	Direct material costs			
7	(200,000 kits x $375 per kit)	$ 75,000,000		$375.00
8	Direct manufacturing labor costs			
9	(530,000 DML-hours x $20 per hour)	10,600,000		53.00
10	Direct machining costs			
11	(300,000 machine-hours x $38 per machine-hour)	11,400,000		57.00
12	Direct manufacturing costs	97,000,000		485.00
13				
14	Manufacturing overhead costs			
15	Ordering and receiving costs			
16	(20,000 orders x $60 per order)	1,200,000		6.00
17	Testing and inspection costs			
18	(2,800,000 testing-hours x $1.70 per hour)	4,760,000		23.80
19	Rework costs			
20	(32,500 rework-hours x $32 per hour)	1,040,000		5.20
21	Manufacturing overhead costs	7,000,000		35.00
22	Total manufacturing costs	$104,000,000		$520.00

Decision Points

The following question-and-answer format summarizes the chapter's learning objectives. Each decision presents a key question related to a learning objective. The guidelines are the answers to that question.

Decision	Guidelines
1. What are the three major influences on pricing decisions?	Customers, competitors, and costs influence prices through their effects on demand and supply; customers and competitors affect demand, and costs affect supply.
2. How do short-run pricing decisions differ from long-run pricing decisions?	Short-run pricing decisions focus on a time horizon of less than a year and have no long-run implications. Long-run pricing decisions focus on a time horizon of a year or longer. The time horizon appropriate to a decision on pricing dictates which costs are relevant, how costs are managed, and the profit that must be earned.
3. How do companies determine target costs?	One approach to long-run pricing is to use a target price. Target price is the estimated price that potential customers are willing to pay for a product or service. Target operating income per unit is subtracted from the target price to determine target cost per unit. Target cost per unit is the estimated long-run cost of a product or service that when sold enables the company to achieve target operating income per unit. The challenge for the company is to make the cost improvements necessary through value-engineering methods to achieve the target cost.

4. Why is it important to distinguish cost incurrence from locked-in costs?	Cost incurrence describes when a resource is sacrificed. Locked-in costs are costs not yet incurred but which, based on decisions that have already been made, will be incurred in the future. To reduce costs, techniques such as value engineering are most effective *before* costs are locked in.
5. How do companies price products using the cost-plus approach?	The cost-plus approach to pricing adds a markup component to a cost base as the starting point for pricing decisions. Many different costs, such as full cost of the product or manufacturing cost, can serve as the cost base in applying the cost-plus formula. Prices are then modified on the basis of customers' reactions and competitors' responses. Therefore, the size of the "plus" is determined by the marketplace.
6. What are life-cycle budgeting and life-cycle costing, and when should companies use these techniques?	Life-cycle budgeting estimates and life-cycle costing tracks and accumulates the costs (and revenues) attributable to a product from its initial R&D to its final customer service and support. These life-cycle techniques are particularly important when (a) a high percentage of total life-cycle costs are incurred before production begins and revenues are earned over several years, and (b) a high fraction of the life-cycle costs are locked in at the R&D and design stages.
7. What are price discrimination and peak-load pricing?	Price discrimination is charging some customers a higher price for a given product or service than other customers. Peak-load pricing is charging a higher price for the same product or service when demand approaches physical-capacity limits. Under price discrimination and peak-load pricing, prices differ among market segments even though the cost of providing the product or service is approximately the same.
8. How do antitrust laws affect pricing?	To comply with antitrust laws, a company must not engage in predatory pricing, dumping, or collusive pricing, which lessen competition; put another company at a competitive disadvantage; or harm consumers.

TERMS TO LEARN

The chapter and the Glossary at the end of the book contain definitions of:

collusive pricing (**p. 448**)
cost incurrence (**p. 437**)
customer life-cycle costs (**p. 445**)
designed-in costs (**p. 437**)
dumping (**p. 448**)
life-cycle budgeting (**p. 443**)
life-cycle costing (**p. 443**)
locked-in costs (**p. 437**)
nonvalue-added cost (**p. 436**)
peak-load pricing (**p. 446**)
predatory pricing (**p. 447**)
price discrimination (**p. 446**)
product life cycle (**p. 443**)
target cost per unit (**p. 435**)
target operating income per unit (**p. 435**)
target price (**p. 434**)
target rate of return on investment (**p. 441**)
value-added cost (**p. 436**)
value engineering (**p. 436**)

ASSIGNMENT MATERIAL

Questions

12-1 What are the three major influences on pricing decisions?

12-2 "Relevant costs for pricing decisions are full costs of the product." Do you agree? Explain.

12-3 Give two examples of pricing decisions with a short-run focus.

12-4 How is activity-based costing useful for pricing decisions?

12-5 Describe two alternative approaches to long-run pricing decisions.

12-6 What is a target cost per unit?

12-7 Describe value engineering and its role in target costing.

12-8 Give two examples of a value-added cost and two examples of a nonvalue-added cost.

12-9 "It is not important for a company to distinguish between cost incurrence and locked-in costs." Do you agree? Explain.

12-10 What is cost-plus pricing?

12-11 Describe three alternative cost-plus pricing methods.

12-12 Give two examples in which the difference in the costs of two products or services is much smaller than the difference in their prices.

12-13 What is life-cycle budgeting?

12-14 What are three benefits of using a product life-cycle reporting format?

12-15 Define predatory pricing, dumping, and collusive pricing.

Exercises

12-16 Relevant-cost approach to pricing decisions, special order. The following financial data apply to the videotape production plant of the Dill Company for October 2009:

	Budgeted Manufacturing Cost per Videotape
Direct materials	$1.60
Direct manufacturing labor	0.90
Variable manufacturing overhead	0.70
Fixed manufacturing overhead	1.00
Total manufacturing cost	$4.20

Variable manufacturing overhead varies with the number of units produced. Fixed manufacturing overhead of $1 per tape is based on budgeted fixed manufacturing overhead of $150,000 per month and budgeted production of 150,000 tapes per month. The Dill Company sells each tape for $5.

Marketing costs have two components:

- Variable marketing costs (sales commissions) of 5% of revenues
- Fixed monthly costs of $65,000

During October 2009, Lyn Randell, a Dill Company salesperson, asked the president for permission to sell 1,000 tapes at $4.00 per tape to a customer not in Dill's normal marketing channels. The president refused this special order because the selling price was below the total budgeted manufacturing cost.

Required

1. What would have been the effect on monthly operating income of accepting the special order?
2. Comment on the president's "below manufacturing costs" reasoning for rejecting the special order.
3. What other factors should the president consider before accepting or rejecting the special order?

12-17 Relevant-cost approach to short-run pricing decisions. The San Carlos Company is an electronics business with eight product lines. Income data for one of the products (XT-107) for June 2009 are:

Revenues, 200,000 units at average price of $100 each		$20,000,000
Variable costs		
Direct materials at $35 per unit	$7,000,000	
Direct manufacturing labor at $10 per unit	2,000,000	
Variable manufacturing overhead at $6 per unit	1,200,000	
Sales commissions at 15% of revenues	3,000,000	
Other variable costs at $5 per unit	1,000,000	
Total variable costs		14,200,000
Contribution margin		5,800,000
Fixed costs		5,000,000
Operating income		$ 800,000

Abrams, Inc., an instruments company, has a problem with its preferred supplier of XT-107 components. This supplier has had a three-week labor strike. Abrams approaches the San Carlos sales representative, Sarah Holtz, about providing 3,000 units of XT-107 at a price of $75 per unit. Holtz informs the XT-107 product manager, Jim McMahon, that she would accept a flat commission of $8,000 rather than the usual 15% of revenues if this special order were accepted. San Carlos has the capacity to produce 300,000 units of XT-107 each month, but demand has not exceeded 200,000 units in any month in the past year.

Required

1. If the 3,000-unit order from Abrams is accepted, how much will operating income increase or decrease? (Assume the same cost structure as in June 2009.)
2. McMahon ponders whether to accept the 3,000-unit special order. He is afraid of the precedent that might be set by cutting the price. He says, "The price is below our full cost of $96 per unit. I think we should quote a full price, or Abrams will expect favored treatment again and again if we continue to do business with it." Do you agree with McMahon? Explain.

12-18 Short-run pricing, capacity constraints. Vermont Hills Dairy, maker of specialty cheeses, produces a soft cheese from the milk of Holstein cows raised on a special corn-based diet. One kilogram of soft cheese, which has a contribution margin of $8, requires 4 liters of milk. A well-known gourmet restaurant has asked Vermont Hills to produce 2,000 kilograms of a hard cheese from the same milk of Holstein cows. Knowing that the dairy has sufficient unused capacity, Elise Princiotti, owner of Vermont Hills, calculates the costs of making one kilogram of the desired hard cheese:

Milk (10 liters × $1.50 per liter)	$15
Variable direct manufacturing labor	5
Variable manufacturing overhead	3
Fixed manufacturing cost allocated	6
Total manufacturing cost	$29

Required

1. Suppose Vermont Hills can acquire all the Holstein milk that it needs. What is the minimum price per kilogram it should charge for the hard cheese?
2. Now suppose that the Holstein milk is in short supply. Every kilogram of hard cheese produced by Vermont Hills will reduce the quantity of soft cheese that it can make and sell. What is the minimum price per kilogram it should charge to produce the hard cheese?

12-19 Value-added, nonvalue-added costs. The Marino Repair Shop repairs and services machine tools. A summary of its costs (by activity) for 2009 is as follows:

a. Materials and labor for servicing machine tools	$800,000
b. Rework costs	75,000
c. Expediting costs caused by work delays	60,000
d. Materials-handling costs	50,000
e. Materials-procurement and inspection costs	35,000
f. Preventive maintenance of equipment	15,000
g. Breakdown maintenance of equipment	55,000

Required

1. Classify each cost as value-added, nonvalue-added, or in the gray area in between.
2. For any cost classified in the gray area, assume 65% is value-added and 35% is nonvalue-added. How much of the total of all seven costs is value-added and how much is nonvalue-added?
3. Marino is considering the following changes: (a) introducing quality-improvement programs whose net effect will be to reduce rework and expediting costs by 75% and materials and labor costs for servicing machine tools by 5%; (b) working with suppliers to reduce materials-procurement and inspection costs by 20% and materials-handling costs by 25%; and (c) increasing preventive-maintenance costs by 50% to reduce breakdown-maintenance costs by 40%. Calculate the effect of programs (a), (b), and (c) on value-added costs, nonvalue-added costs, and total costs. Comment briefly.

12-20 Target operating income, value-added costs, service company. Carasco Associates prepares architectural drawings to conform to local structural-safety codes. Its income statement for 2009 is:

Revenues	$680,000
Salaries of professional staff (8,000 hours × $50 per hour)	400,000
Travel	18,000
Administrative and support costs	160,000
Total costs	578,000
Operating income	$102,000

Following is the percentage of time spent by professional staff on various activities:

Making calculations and preparing drawings for clients	75%
Checking calculations and drawings	4
Correcting errors found in drawings (not billed to clients)	7
Making changes in response to client requests (billed to clients)	6
Correcting own errors regarding building codes (not billed to clients)	8
Total	100%

Assume administrative and support costs vary with professional-labor costs.

Required

Consider each requirement independently.

1. How much of the total costs in 2009 are value-added, nonvalue-added, or in the gray area in between? Explain your answers briefly. What actions can Carasco take to reduce its costs?

2. Suppose Carasco could eliminate all errors so that it did not need to spend any time making corrections and, as a result, could proportionately reduce professional-labor costs. Calculate Carasco's operating income for 2009.
3. Now suppose Carasco could take on as much business as it could complete, but it could not add more professional staff. Assume Carasco could eliminate all errors so that it does not need to spend any time correcting errors. Assume Carasco could use the time saved to increase revenues proportionately. Assume travel costs will remain at $18,000. Calculate Carasco's operating income for 2009.

12-21 Target prices, target costs, activity-based costing. Snappy Tiles is a small distributor of marble tiles. Snappy identifies its three major activities and cost pools as ordering, receiving and storage, and shipping, and it reports the following details for 2008:

Activity	Cost Driver	Quantity of Cost Driver	Cost per Unit of Cost Driver
1. Placing and paying for orders of marble tiles	Number of orders	500	$50 per order
2. Receiving and storage	Loads moved	4,000	$30 per load
3. Shipping of marble tiles to retailers	Number of shipments	1,500	$40 per shipment

For 2008, Snappy buys 250,000 marble tiles at an average cost of $3 per tile and sells them to retailers at an average price of $4 per tile. Assume Snappy has no fixed costs and no inventories.

Required

1. Calculate Snappy's operating income for 2008.
2. For 2009, retailers are demanding a 5% discount off the 2008 price. Snappy's suppliers are only willing to give a 4% discount. Snappy expects to sell the same quantity of marble tiles in 2009 as in 2008. If all other costs and cost-driver information remain the same, calculate Snappy's operating income for 2009.
3. Suppose further that Snappy decides to make changes in its ordering and receiving-and-storing practices. By placing long-run orders with its key suppliers, Snappy expects to reduce the number of orders to 200 and the cost per order to $25 per order. By redesigning the layout of the warehouse and reconfiguring the crates in which the marble tiles are moved, Snappy expects to reduce the number of loads moved to 3,125 and the cost per load moved to $28. Will Snappy achieve its target operating income of $0.30 per tile in 2009? Show your calculations.

12-22 Target costs, effect of product-design changes on product costs. Medical Instruments uses a manufacturing costing system with one direct-cost category (direct materials) and three indirect-cost categories:

a. Setup, production order, and materials-handling costs that vary with the number of batches
b. Manufacturing-operations costs that vary with machine-hours
c. Costs of engineering changes that vary with the number of engineering changes made

In response to competitive pressures at the end of 2008, Medical Instruments used value-engineering techniques to reduce manufacturing costs. Actual information for 2008 and 2009 is:

	2008	2009
Setup, production-order, and materials-handling costs per batch	$ 8,000	$ 7,500
Total manufacturing-operations cost per machine-hour	$ 55	$ 50
Cost per engineering change	$12,000	$10,000

The management of Medical Instruments wants to evaluate whether value engineering has succeeded in reducing the target manufacturing cost per unit of one of its products, HJ6, by 10%.

Actual results for 2008 and 2009 for HJ6 are:

	Actual Results for 2008	Actual Results for 2009
Units of HJ6 produced	3,500	4,000
Direct material cost per unit of HJ6	$1,200	$1,100
Total number of batches required to produce HJ6	70	80
Total machine-hours required to produce HJ6	21,000	22,000
Number of engineering changes made	14	10

Required

1. Calculate the manufacturing cost per unit of HJ6 in 2008.
2. Calculate the manufacturing cost per unit of HJ6 in 2009.
3. Did Medical Instruments achieve the target manufacturing cost per unit for HJ6 in 2009? Explain.
4. Explain how Medical Instruments reduced the manufacturing cost per unit of HJ6 in 2009.

12-23 Cost-plus target return on investment pricing. John Beck is the managing partner of a business that has just finished building a 60-room motel. Beck anticipates that he will rent these rooms for 16,000 nights next year (or 16,000 room-nights). All rooms are similar and will rent for the same price. Beck estimates the following operating costs for next year:

Variable operating costs	$4 per room-night
Fixed costs	
Salaries and wages	$177,000
Maintenance of building and pool	40,000
Other operating and administration costs	141,000
Total fixed costs	$358,000

The capital invested in the motel is $1,000,000. The partnership's target return on investment is 25%. Beck expects demand for rooms to be uniform throughout the year. He plans to price the rooms at full cost plus a markup on full cost to earn the target return on investment.

Required

1. What price should Beck charge for a room-night? What is the markup as a percentage of the full cost of a room-night?
2. Beck's market research indicates that if the price of a room-night determined in requirement 1 is reduced by 10%, the expected number of room-nights Beck could rent would increase by 10%. Should Beck reduce prices by 10%? Show your calculations.

12-24 Cost-plus, target pricing, working backward. (S. Sridhar, adapted) Waterbury, Inc., manufactures and sells RF17, a specialty raft used for whitewater rafting. In 2009, it reported the following:

	A	B
1		**2009**
2	Units produced and sold	20,000
3	Investment	$2,400,000
4	Full cost per unit	$ 300
5	Rate of return on investment	20%
6	Markup percentage on variable cost	50%

If you want to use Excel to solve this exercise, go to the Excel Lab at **www.prenhall.com/horngren/cost13e** and download the template for Exercise 12-24.

Required

1. What was the selling price in 2009? What was the percentage markup on full cost? What was the variable cost per unit?
2. Waterbury is considering raising its selling price to $348. However, at this price, its sales volume is predicted to fall by 10%. If Waterbury's cost structure (variable cost per unit and total fixed costs) remains unchanged and if its demand forecast is accurate, should it raise the selling price to $348?
3. In 2010, due to increased competition, Waterbury must reduce its selling price to $315 in order to sell 20,000 units. The manager of the rafts division reduces annual investment to $2,100,000 but still demands a 20% target rate of return on investment. If fixed costs cannot be changed in this time frame, what is the target variable cost per unit?

12-25 Life cycle product costing. Intentical Inc., manufactures game systems. Intentical has decided to create and market a new system with wireless controls and excellent video graphics. Intentical's managers are thinking of calling this system the Yew. Based on past experience they expect the total life cycle of the Yew to be four years, with the design phase taking about a year. They budget the following costs for the Yew:

		Total fixed costs over four years	Variable cost per unit
Year 1	R&D costs	$ 6,590,000	—
	Design costs	1,450,000	—
Years 2–4	Production	19,560,000	$50 per unit
	Marketing & distribution	5,242,000	10 per unit
	Customer service	2,900,000	—

Required

1. Suppose the managers at Intentical price the Yew game system at $110 per unit. How many units do they need to sell to break even?
2. The managers at Intentical are thinking of two alternative pricing strategies.
   a. Sell the Yew at $110 each from the outset. At this price they expect to sell 1,500,000 units over its life-cycle.

b. Boost the selling price of the Yew in Year 2 when it first comes out to $240 per unit. At this price they expect to sell 100,000 units in Year 2. In Years 3 and 4 drop the price to $110 per unit. The managers expect to sell 1,200,000 units in Years 3 and 4.

Which pricing strategy would you recommend? Explain.

3. What other factors should Intentical consider in choosing its pricing strategy?

Problems

12-26 Relevant-cost approach to pricing decisions. Stardom, Inc., cans peaches for sale to food distributors. All costs are classified as either manufacturing or marketing. Stardom prepares monthly budgets. The March 2009 budgeted absorption-costing income statement is as follows:

Revenues (1,000 crates × $100 a crate)	$100,000
Cost of goods sold	60,000
Gross margin	40,000
Marketing costs	30,000
Operating income	$ 10,000
Normal markup percentage: $40,000 ÷ $60,000 = 66.7% of absorption cost	

Monthly costs are classified as fixed or variable (with respect to the number of crates produced for manufacturing costs and with respect to the number of crates sold for marketing costs):

	Fixed	Variable
Manufacturing	$20,000	$40,000
Marketing	16,000	14,000

Stardom has the capacity to can 1,500 crates per month. The relevant range in which monthly fixed manufacturing costs will be "fixed" is from 500 to 1,500 crates per month.

Required

1. Calculate the markup percentage based on total variable costs.
2. Assume that a new customer approaches Stardom to buy 200 crates at $55 per crate for cash. The customer does not require any marketing effort. Additional manufacturing costs of $2,000 (for special packaging) will be required. Stardom believes that this is a one-time-only special order because the customer is discontinuing business in six weeks' time. Stardom is reluctant to accept this 200-crate special order because the $55-per-crate price is below the $60-per-crate absorption cost. Do you agree with this reasoning? Explain.
3. Assume that the new customer decides to remain in business. How would this longevity affect your willingness to accept the $55-per-crate offer? Explain.

12-27 Target rate of return on investment, activity-based costing. Electronic Arts (EA) distributes video games to retail stores and video-game parlors. It has a simple business model: Order the video games, catalog the games on EA's Web site, deliver and provide on-site support, and bill and collect from the customers. EA reported the following costs in April 2009:

Activity	Cost Driver	Quantity	Cost per Unit of Cost Driver
Ordering	Number of game vendors	40	$250 per vendor
Cataloging	Number of new titles	20	$100 per title
Delivery and support	Number of deliveries	400	$ 15 per delivery
Billing and collection	Number of customers	300	$ 50 per customer

In April 2009, EA purchased 12,000 video-game disks at an average cost of $15 per disk, and it sold them at an average price of $22 per disk. The catalog on the Web site and the customer interactions that occur during delivery are EA's main marketing inputs. EA incurs no other costs.

Required

1. Calculate EA's operating income for April 2009. If the monthly investment in EA is $300,000, what rate of return on investment does the business earn?
2. The current crop of game systems is maturing, and prices for games are beginning to decline. EA anticipates that from May onward, it will be able to sell 12,000 game disks each month for an average of $18 per disk, and it will have to pay vendors an average of $12 per disk. Assuming other costs are the same as in April, will EA be able to earn its 15% target rate of return on investment?
3. EA's small workforce gathers as a team and considers process improvements. They recommend "firing" the marginal vendors—those who need a lot of "hand holding" but whose titles are not very popular.

They agree that they should shift some of their resources from vendor relationships and cataloging to delivery and customer relationships. In May 2009, EA reports the following support costs:

Activity	Cost Driver	Quantity	Cost per Unit of Cost Driver
Ordering	Number of game vendors	30	$200 per vendor
Cataloging	Number of new titles	15	$100 per title
Delivery and support	Number of deliveries	450	$ 20 per delivery
Billing and collection	Number of customers	300	$ 50 per customer

At a selling price of $18 and a cost of $12 per disk, how many game disks must EA sell in May 2009 to earn its 15% target rate of return on investment?

12-28 Cost-plus, target pricing, working backward. The new CEO of Roile Manufacturing has asked for a variety of information about the operations of the firm from last year. The CEO is given the following information, but with some data missing:

Total sales revenue	?
Number of units produced and sold	500,000 units
Selling price	?
Operating income	$225,000
Total investment in assets	$2,500,000
Variable cost per unit	$2.50
Fixed costs for the year	$3,250,000

Required

1. Find (a) total sales revenue, (b) selling price, (c) rate of return on investment, and (d) markup percentage on full cost for this product.
2. The new CEO has a plan to reduce fixed costs by $250,000 and variable costs by $0.50 per unit. Using the same markup percentage as in requirement 1, calculate the new selling price.
3. Assume the CEO institutes the changes in requirement 2 including the new selling price, expecting to sell more units of product because of the lower price. However, the reduction in variable cost has resulted in lower product quality leading to 10% fewer units being sold compared to before the change. Calculate operating income (loss).

12-29 Target prices, target costs, value engineering, cost incurrence, locked-in costs, activity-based costing. Cutler Electronics makes a radio-cassette player, CE100, which has 80 components. Cutler sells 7,000 units each month for $70 each. The costs of manufacturing CE100 are $45 per unit, or $315,000 per month. Monthly manufacturing costs incurred are:

Direct material costs	$182,000
Direct manufacturing labor costs	28,000
Machining costs (fixed)	31,500
Testing costs	35,000
Rework costs	14,000
Ordering costs	3,360
Engineering costs (fixed)	21,140
Total manufacturing costs	$315,000

Cutler's management identifies the activity cost pools, the cost driver for each activity, and the cost per unit of the cost driver for each overhead cost pool as follows:

Manufacturing Activity	Description of Activity	Cost Driver	Cost per Unit of Cost Driver
1. Machining costs	Machining components	Machine-hour capacity	$4.50 per machine-hour
2. Testing costs	Testing components and final product (Each unit of CE100 is tested individually.)	Testing-hours	$2 per testing-hour
3. Rework costs	Correcting and fixing errors and defects	Units of CE100 reworked	$20 per unit
4. Ordering costs	Ordering of components	Number of orders	$21 per order
5. Engineering costs	Designing and managing of products and processes	Engineering-hour capacity	$35 per engineering-hour

Cutler's management views direct material costs and direct manufacturing labor costs as variable with respect to the units of CE100 manufactured. Over a long-run horizon, each of the overhead costs described in the preceding table varies, as described, with the chosen cost drivers.

The following additional information describes the existing design:

a. Testing and inspection time per unit is 2.5 hours.
b. 10% of the CE100s manufactured are reworked.
c. Cutler places two orders with each component supplier each month. Each component is supplied by a different supplier.
d. It currently takes 1 hour to manufacture each unit of CE100.

In response to competitive pressures, Cutler must reduce its price to $62 per unit and its costs by $8 per unit. No additional sales are anticipated at this lower price. However, Cutler stands to lose significant sales if it does not reduce its price. Manufacturing has been asked to reduce its costs by $6 per unit. Improvements in manufacturing efficiency are expected to yield a net savings of $1.50 per radio-cassette player, but that is not enough. The chief engineer has proposed a new modular design that reduces the number of components to 50 and also simplifies testing. The newly designed radio-cassette player, called "New CE100" will replace CE100.

The expected effects of the new design are as follows:

a. Direct material cost for the New CE100 is expected to be lower by $2.20 per unit.
b. Direct manufacturing labor cost for the New CE100 is expected to be lower by $0.50 per unit.
c. Machining time required to manufacture the New CE100 is expected to be 20% less, but machine-hour capacity will not be reduced.
d. Time required for testing the New CE100 is expected to be lower by 20%.
e. Rework is expected to decline to 4% of New CE100s manufactured.
f. Engineering-hours capacity will remain the same.

Assume that the cost per unit of each cost driver for CE100 continues to apply to New CE100.

Required

1. Calculate Cutler's manufacturing cost per unit of New CE100.
2. Will the new design achieve the per-unit cost-reduction targets that have been set for the manufacturing costs of New CE100? Show your calculations.
3. The problem describes two strategies to reduce costs: (a) improving manufacturing efficiency and (b) modifying product design. Which strategy has more impact on Cutler's costs? Why? Explain briefly.

12-30 Cost-plus, target return on investment pricing. Vend-o-licious makes candy bars for vending machines and sells them to vendors in cases of 30 bars. Although Vend-o-licious makes a variety of candy, the cost differences are insignificant, and the cases all sell for the same price.

Vend-o-licious has a total investment in capital of $13,000,000. It expects to sell 500,000 cases of candy next year, as it has had relatively constant sales over the past few years. Vend-o-licious requires a 10% target return on investment.

Expected costs for next year are:

Variable production costs	$3.50 per case
Variable marketing and distribution costs	$1.50 per case
Fixed production costs	$1,000,000
Fixed marketing and distribution costs	$700,000
Other fixed costs	$500,000

Vend-o-licious prices the cases of candy at full cost plus markup to generate profits equal to the target return on capital.

Required

1. What is the target operating income?
2. What is the selling price Vend-o-licious needs to charge to earn the target operating income? Calculate the markup percentage on full cost.
3. Vend-o-licious's closest competitor has just increased its candy case price to $15, although it sells 36 candy bars per case. Vend-o-licious is considering increasing its selling price to $14 per case. Assuming sales decrease by 5%, calculate Vend-o-licious' return on investment. Is increasing the selling price a good idea?

12-31 Cost-plus, time and materials. Mazzoli Brothers is an auto repair shop. Mazzoli's cost accounting system tracks two cost categories: direct labor (working on the cars) and direct materials (parts). Mazzoli uses a time-and-materials pricing system, with direct labor marked up 100% and direct materials marked up 50% to recover indirect costs of support staff, support materials, and shared machines and tools, and to earn a profit.

Johanna White brings her car to the shop. The head mechanic, Luke Bariess, concludes her car's problem is with the clutch plate. He considers two options: replace the clutch plate or repair it. The cost information available to Bariess follows:

	A	B	C	D
1		Labor		Materials
2	Repair option	3.5	hours	$ 40
3	Replace option	1.5	hours	$200
4	Markup	100%		50%
5				
6	Labor rate	$30	per labor-hour	

If you want to use Excel to solve this problem, go to the Excel Lab at **www.prenhall.com/horngren/cost13e** and download the template for Problem 12-31.

Required

1. Why might Mazzoli use different markup rates for direct materials and for direct labor?
2. If Bariess presents White with the replace or repair options, what price would he quote for each?
3. If the two options were equally safe and effective for the three years that White intends to use the car before junking it, which option would she choose?
4. If Bariess's objective is to maximize profits, which option would Bariess recommend to White? Is this the option chosen by White in requirement 3? Comment on your answers in requirements 3 and 4.

12-32 Cost-plus and market-based pricing. California Temps, a large labor contractor, supplies contract labor to building-construction companies. For 2009, California Temps has budgeted to supply 80,000 hours of contract labor. Its variable costs are $12 per hour, and its fixed costs are $240,000. Roger Mason, the general manager, has proposed a cost-plus approach for pricing labor at full cost plus 20%.

Required

1. Calculate the price per hour that California Temps should charge based on Mason's proposal.
2. The marketing manager supplies the following information on demand levels at different prices:

Price per Hour	Demand (Hours)
$16	120,000
17	100,000
18	80,000
19	70,000
20	60,000

   California Temps can meet any of these demand levels. Fixed costs will remain unchanged for all the demand levels. On the basis of this additional information, calculate the price per hour that California Temps should charge to maximize operating income.
3. Comment on your answers to requirements 1 and 2. Why are they the same or different?

12-33 Cost-plus and market-based pricing. (CMA, adapted) Best Test Laboratories evaluates the reaction of materials to extreme increases in temperature. Much of the company's early growth was attributable to government contracts, but recent growth has come from expansion into commercial markets. Two types of testing at Best Test are Heat Testing (HTT) and Arctic-condition Testing (ACT.) Currently, all of the budgeted operating costs are collected in a single overhead pool. All of the estimated testing-hours are also collected in a single pool. One rate per test-hour is used for both types of testing. This hourly rate is marked up by 45% to recover administrative costs and taxes, and to earn a profit.

Rick Shaw, Best Test's controller, believes that there is enough variation in the test procedures and cost structure to establish separate costing rates and billing rates at a 45% mark up. He also believes that the inflexible rate structure currently being used is inadequate in today's competitive environment. After analyzing the company data, he has divided operating costs into the following three cost pools:

Labor and supervision	$ 491,840
Setup and facility costs	402,620
Utilities	368,000
Total budgeted costs for the period	$1,262,460

Rick Shaw budgets 106,000 total test-hours for the coming period. This is also the cost driver for labor and supervision. The budgeted quantity of cost driver for setup and facility costs is 800 setup hours. The budgeted quantity of cost driver for utilities is 10,000 machine-hours.

Rick has estimated that HTT uses 60% of the testing hours, 25% of the setup hours, and half the machine-hours.

Required

1. Find the single rate for operating costs based on test-hours and the hourly billing rate for HTT and ACT.
2. Find the three activity-based rates for operating costs.

3. What will the billing rate for HTT and ACT be based on the activity-based costing structure? State the rates in terms of testing hours. Referring to both requirements 1 and 2, which rates make more sense for Best Test?
4. If Best Test's competition all charge $20 per hour for arctic testing, what can Best Test do to stay competitive?

12-34 Life-cycle costing. Fearless Furniture Manufacturing (FFM) has been manufacturing furniture for the home for over 30 years. George Fearless, the owner, has decided he would like to manufacture an executive desk that contains space for not only a laptop dock but also an MP3 player dock. Based on his experience with furniture, he believes the desk will be a popular item for 4 years, and then will be obsolete because technology will have changed again.

FFM expects the design phase to be very short; maybe four months. There is no R&D cost because the idea came from George, without any real research. Also, fixed production costs will not be high because FFM has excess capacity in the factory. The FFM accountants have developed the following budget for the new executive desk:

		Fixed	Variable
Months 1–4	Design costs	$700,000	—
Months 5–36	Production	$9,000	$225 per desk
	Marketing	3,000	—
	Distribution	2,000	$ 20 per desk
Months 37–52	Production	$9,000	$225 per desk
	Marketing	1,000	—
	Distribution	1,000	$ 22 per desk

The design cost is for the total period of 4 months. The fixed costs of production, marketing, and distribution are the expected costs PER month. Ignore time value of money.

Required

1. Assume FFM expects to make and sell 16,000 units in the first 32 months (Months 5–36) of production (500 units per month) and 4,800 units (300 per month) in the last 16 months (Months 37–52) of production. If FFM prices the desks at $500 each, how much profit will FFM make in total and on average per desk?
2. Suppose FFM is wrong about the demand for these executive desks, and after the first 36 months it stops making them altogether. It sells 16,000 desks for $400 each with the costs described for months 5–36, and then incurs no additional costs nor generates additional revenues. Will this have been a profitable venture for FFM?
3. Will your answer to requirement 2 change if FFM still must incur the estimated fixed production costs for the whole period through month 52, even if FFM stops making executive desks at the end of 36 months?

12-35 Airline pricing, considerations other than cost in pricing. Air Americo is about to introduce a daily round-trip flight from New York to Los Angeles and is determining how it should price its round-trip tickets.

The market research group at Air Americo segments the market into business and pleasure travelers. It provides the following information on the effects of two different prices on the number of seats expected to be sold and the variable cost per ticket, including the commission paid to travel agents:

		Number of Seats Expected to Be Sold	
Price Charged	**Variable Cost per Ticket**	**Business**	**Pleasure**
$ 500	$ 80	200	100
2,000	180	190	20

Pleasure travelers start their travel during one week, spend at least one weekend at their destination, and return the following week or thereafter. Business travelers usually start and complete their travel within the same work week. They do not stay over weekends.

Assume that round-trip fuel costs are fixed costs of $24,000 and that fixed costs allocated to the round-trip flight for airplane-lease costs, ground services, and flight-crew salaries total $188,000.

Required

1. If you could charge different prices to business travelers and pleasure travelers, would you? Show your computations.
2. Explain the key factor (or factors) for your answer in requirement 1.
3. How might Air Americo implement price discrimination? That is, what plan could the airline formulate so that business travelers and pleasure travelers each pay the price desired by the airline?

12-36 Ethics and pricing. Baker, Inc., is preparing to submit a bid for a ball-bearings order. Greg Lazarus, controller of the Bearings Division of Baker, has asked John Decker, the cost analyst, to prepare the bid. To determine the amount of the bid, Baker's policy is to mark up the full costs of the order by 10%. Lazarus tells Decker that he is keen on winning the bid and that the bid amount he calculates should be competitive.

Decker prepares the following costs for the bid:

Direct materials		$40,000
Direct manufacturing labor		10,000
Overhead costs		
Design and parts administration	$4,000	
Production order	5,000	
Setup	5,500	
Materials handling	6,500	
General and administration	9,000	
Total overhead costs		30,000
Full product costs		$80,000

All direct costs and 30% of overhead costs are incremental costs of the order.

Lazarus reviews the numbers and says, "Your costs are way too high. You have allocated too many overhead costs to this order. You know our fixed overhead is not going to change if we win this order and manufacture the bearings. Rework your numbers. You have got to make the costs lower."

Decker verifies that his numbers are correct. He knows that Lazarus wants this order because the additional revenues from the order would lead to a big bonus for Lazarus and the senior division managers. Decker knows that if he does not come up with a lower bid, Lazarus will be very upset.

Required

1. Using Baker's pricing policy and based on Decker's estimates, calculate the total amount Baker should bid for the ball-bearings order.
2. Calculate the incremental costs of the ball-bearing order. Why do you think Baker uses full costs of the order rather than incremental costs in its bidding decisions?
3. Evaluate whether Lazarus' suggestion to Decker to use lower cost numbers is unethical. Would it be unethical for Decker to change his analysis so that a lower cost can be calculated? What steps should Decker take to resolve this situation?

Collaborative Learning Problem

12-37 Target pricing, target cost, and value engineering. Avery, Inc., manufactures component parts. One product, TX40, has annual sales of 50,000 units. Avery sells TX40 for $40.60 per unit. Avery has two direct-cost categories (direct materials, direct manufacturing labor) and two activity-based indirect-cost categories (engineering and testing). All R&D and design costs are included in the engineering cost category. There are no marketing, distribution, or customer-service costs. The cost driver for engineering is engineer-hours, and the cost driver for testing is test-hours. Testing costs are variable costs. Engineering costs are fixed costs based on engineering capacity. Information on annual costs includes the following

Direct materials: $14.98 per unit
Direct manufacturing labor: $15 per direct manufacturing labor-hour
Engineering: $14 per engineer-hour (based on capacity of 25,000 engineering-hours)
Testing: $12 per test-hour
Each unit of TX40 requires 0.5 direct manufacturing labor-hour to produce and 0.25 test-hour to test.

Required

1. Calculate the full cost per unit of TX40 at the production level of 50,000 units.
2. What is the markup percentage on the full cost per unit of TX40?
3. The sales manager thinks that Avery can sell 10,000 more units at the $40.60 price if Avery spends $200,000 on marketing by putting advertisements in trade magazines. Avery will not need to do any additional engineering for these units. Is this a good idea?
4. If Avery spends an extra $200,000 on marketing but uses the same markup percentage on the full cost per unit as in requirement 2, calculate the new selling price.

13 Strategy, Balanced Scorecard, and Strategic Profitability Analysis

Learning Objectives

1. Recognize which of two generic strategies a company is using
2. Understand what comprises reengineering
3. Describe the four perspectives of the balanced scorecard
4. Analyze changes in operating income to evaluate strategy
5. Distinguish engineered costs from discretionary costs
6. Identify unused capacity and how to manage it

Olive Garden wants to know. So do Barnes and Noble, PepsiCo, and L.L. Bean. Even your local car dealer and transit authority are curious. They all want to know how well they are doing and how they score against the measures they strive to meet. The balanced scorecard can help them answer this question by evaluating key performance measures. Many companies have successfully used the balanced scorecard approach. KeyCorp, a Cleveland-based bank, is one of them.

Balanced Scorecard Helps Bank Hit New Profitability High[1]

In late 2000, KeyCorp hit a low that proved to be a springboard to a new beginning. The bank holding company was fighting off takeover rumors amid a plunging stock price. Drastic cost cuts sideswiped worker morale as customer gripes grew. Everyone knew the company needed a fresh start, and it happened.

Led by new Chief Executive Henry Meyer, Cleveland-based KeyCorp searched for better ways to gauge employee performance and raise accountability. KeyCorp also wanted to foster teamwork across its departments. After weighing various performance management systems, the bank's executives chose the *balanced scorecard.* "We were looking for a tool to help us dig under the financial numbers and understand cause-and-effect relationships," said Michele Seyranian, an executive vice president at KeyCorp who managed the new program. "We wanted to gain perspectives to help manage our employees, client expectations, our shareholders and internal processes."

The score card now plays a central role in employees' performance appraisals. From tellers to salespeople, staffers know they will be evaluated on how their contributions impact KeyCorp's stated objectives and targets. Department heads get scores on a 1 to 10 scale based on measures such as customer satisfaction surveys and client attrition statistics.

This discipline and transparency translates into bottom-line results. Internal surveys indicate that client retention rates gained

[1] *Source:* Reprinted from Morey Stettner, "Scorecard Gives Bank Its Best Shot," *Investor's Business Daily,* May 20, 2006, p. A11.

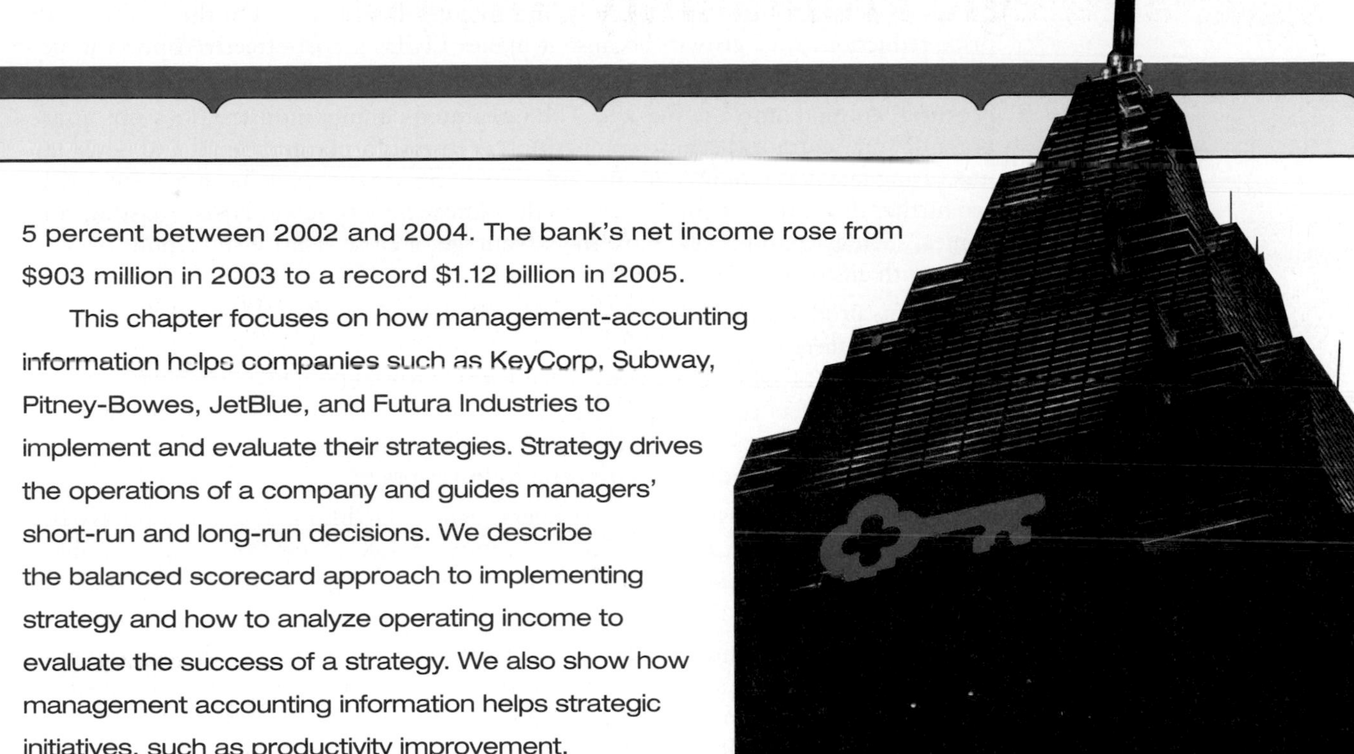

5 percent between 2002 and 2004. The bank's net income rose from $903 million in 2003 to a record $1.12 billion in 2005.

This chapter focuses on how management-accounting information helps companies such as KeyCorp, Subway, Pitney-Bowes, JetBlue, and Futura Industries to implement and evaluate their strategies. Strategy drives the operations of a company and guides managers' short-run and long-run decisions. We describe the balanced scorecard approach to implementing strategy and how to analyze operating income to evaluate the success of a strategy. We also show how management accounting information helps strategic initiatives, such as productivity improvement, reengineering, and downsizing.

What Is Strategy?

Strategy specifies how an organization matches its own capabilities with the opportunities in the marketplace to accomplish its objectives. In other words, strategy describes how an organization can create value for its customers while differentiating itself from its competitors. For example, Wal-Mart, the retail giant, creates value for its customers by locating stores in suburban and rural areas, and by offering low prices, a wide range of product categories, and few choices within each product category. Consistent with its strategy, Wal-Mart has developed the capability to keep costs down by aggressively negotiating low prices with its suppliers in exchange for high volumes and by maintaining a no-frills, cost-conscious environment.

In formulating its strategy, an organization must first thoroughly understand its industry. Industry analysis focuses on five forces: (1) competitors, (2) potential entrants into the market, (3) equivalent products, (4) bargaining power of customers, and (5) bargaining power of input suppliers.[2] The collective effect of these forces shapes an organization's profit potential. In general, profit potential decreases with greater competition, stronger potential entrants, products that are similar, and more-demanding customers and suppliers. We illustrate these five forces for Chipset, Inc., maker of linear integrated circuit devices (LICDs) used in modems and communication networks. Chipset produces a single specialized product, CX1. This standard, high-performance microchip can be used in multiple applications. Chipset designed CX1 with extensive input from customers.

1. **Competitors.** The CX1 model enjoys a reputation for superior features relative to competing products. However, severe competition exists with respect to price, timely

[2] M. Porter, *Competitive Strategy* (New York: Free Press, 1980); M. Porter, *Competitive Advantage* (New York: Free Press, 1985); and M. Porter, "What Is Strategy?" *Harvard Business Review* (November–December 1996): 61–78.

delivery, and quality. Companies in the industry have high fixed costs, and therefore pressures persist to use capacity fully and to cut selling prices. On the positive side, price reductions spur growth because it makes LICDs a cost-effective option in new applications such as digital subscriber lines (DSLs).

2. **Potential entrants into the market.** The integrated-circuits industry does not attract potential new entrants because competition keeps profit margins small and new manufacturing facilities require a lot of capital. Companies that have been making LICDs are further down the learning curve, so they know how to lower costs. Existing companies, such as Chipset, also have the advantage of close relationships built over the years with customers and suppliers.
3. **Equivalent products.** Chipset employs a technology that allows its customers to use CX1 to best meet their needs. CX1's flexible design is easily integrated into the end products, such as DSL networks, of Chipset's customers. This reduces the risk of equivalent products or new technologies replacing CX1 during the next few years. Such a risk is further reduced if Chipset continuously improves CX1's design and processes to reduce production costs and to lower prices.
4. **Bargaining power of customers.** Customers such as EarthLink and Verizon have bargaining power because each buys large quantities of CX1. Customers can also obtain microchips from other suppliers. Customers negotiate aggressively with Chipset to keep prices down.
5. **Bargaining power of input suppliers.** To deliver a superior product, Chipset purchases high-quality materials, such as silicon wafers, pins for connectivity, and plastic or ceramic packaging from its suppliers and employs skilled engineers, technicians, and manufacturing labor. Materials suppliers and employees have some bargaining power to demand higher prices and wages.

Learning Objective 1

Recognize which of two generic strategies a company is using

. . . product differentiation or cost leadership

In summary, strong competition and the bargaining powers of customers and suppliers put significant pressure on Chipset's selling prices. To respond to these challenges, Chipset must choose one of two basic strategies: *differentiating its product* or *achieving cost leadership*.

Product differentiation is an organization's ability to offer products or services perceived by its customers to be superior and unique relative to the products or services of its competitors. Hewlett-Packard has successfully differentiated its products in the electronics industry, as have Johnson & Johnson in the pharmaceutical industry and Coca-Cola in the soft drink industry. These companies have achieved differentiation through innovative product R&D, careful development and promotion of their brands, and the rapid push of products to market. Differentiation increases brand loyalty and the willingness of customers to pay higher prices.

Cost leadership is an organization's ability to achieve lower costs relative to competitors through productivity and efficiency improvements, elimination of waste, and tight cost control. Cost leaders in their respective industries include Wal-Mart (consumer retailing), Home Depot and Lowe's (building products), Texas Instruments (consumer electronics), and Emerson Electric (electric motors). These companies all provide products and services that are similar to—not differentiated from—those of their competitors, but they are provided at a lower cost to the customer. Lower selling prices, rather than unique products or services, provide a competitive advantage for these cost leaders.

What strategy should Chipset follow? To help it decide, Chipset develops the customer preference map shown in Exhibit 13-1. The *y*-axis describes various attributes of the product desired by customers. The *x*-axis describes how well Chipset and Visilog, a competitor of Chipset that follows a product-differentiation strategy, do along the various attributes desired by customers from 1 (poor) to 5 (very good). The map highlights the trade-offs in any strategy. Chipset's CX1 chip has an advantage in terms of price, scalability (the CX1 technology allows Chispet's customer to achieve different performance levels by simply altering the number of CX1 units in their product), and customer service. Visilog's chips are faster and more powerful and are customized for various applications such as different types of modems and communication networks.

CX1 is already somewhat differentiated from competing products. Differentiating CX1 further would be costly, but Chipset may be able to charge a higher price. Conversely,

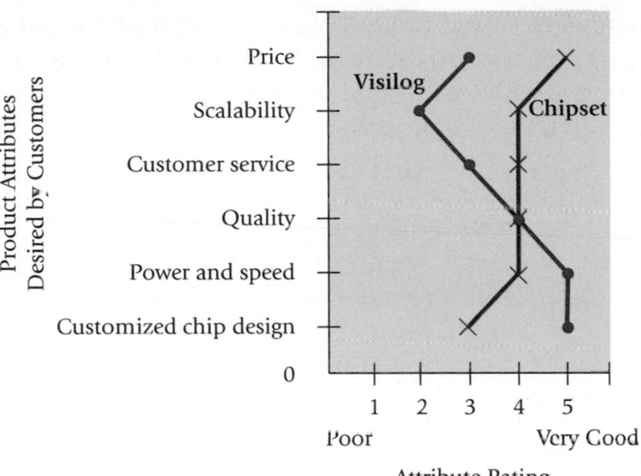

Exhibit 13-1

Customer Preference Map for LICDs

reducing the cost of manufacturing CX1 would allow the company to reduce its price and spur growth. Chipset considers designing new customized microchips for different applications but concludes that the scalability of CX1 provides a more cost-effective solution for meeting customer needs. Also, Chipset's current engineering staff is more skilled at making product and process improvements than at creatively designing new products and technologies. In addition, customers want Chipset to keep the current design of CX1 but lower its price. Chipset concludes that it should follow a cost-leadership strategy. Successful cost leadership also is expected to increase Chipset's market share and help the company grow.

To achieve its cost-leadership strategy, Chipset must improve its own internal capabilities. It must enhance quality and reengineer processes to downsize and eliminate excess capacity. At the same time, Chipset's management team does not want to make cuts in personnel that would hurt company morale and hinder future growth.

Building Internal Capabilities: Quality Improvement and Reengineering at Chipset

Learning Objective 2

Understand what comprises reengineering

. . . redesigning business processes to improve performance by reducing cost and improving quality

To improve product quality—that is, reduce defect rates and improve yields in its manufacturing process—Chipset must maintain process parameters within tight ranges. To achieve this goal, Chipset needs real-time data about manufacturing-process parameters, such as temperature and pressure, and more-effective process-control methods. Chipset must also train its workers in quality-management techniques to help them identify the causes of defects and ways to prevent them. Following this training, Chipset needs to empower its workers to make decisions and take actions that will improve quality.

A second element of Chipset's strategy is reengineering its order-delivery process. Some of Chipset's customers have complained about the time span between ordering products and receiving them. **Reengineering** is the fundamental rethinking and redesign of business processes to achieve improvements in critical measures of performance, such as cost, quality, service, speed, and customer satisfaction.[3] To illustrate reengineering, consider the order-delivery system at Chipset in 2008. When Chipset received an order from a customer, a copy was sent to manufacturing, where a production scheduler began planning the manufacturing of the ordered products. Frequently, a considerable amount of time elapsed before production began on the ordered product. After manufacturing was complete, CX1 chips moved to the Shipping Department, which matched the quantities of CX1 to be shipped against customer orders. Often, completed CX1 chips stayed in inventory until a truck became available for shipment. If the quantity to be shipped was less than the number of chips requested by the customer, a special shipment was made for the balance of the

[3] See M. Hammer and J. Champy, *Reengineering the Corporation: A Manifesto for Business Revolution* (New York: Harper, 1993); E. Ruhli, C. Treichler, and S. Schmidt, "From Business Reengineering to Management Reengineering—A European Study," *Management International Review* (1995): 361–371; and K. Sandberg, "Reengineering Tries a Comeback—This Time for Growth, Not Just for Cost Savings," *Harvard Management Update* (November 2001).

chips. Shipping documents moved to the Billing Department for issuing invoices. Special staff in the Accounting Department followed up with customers for payments.

The many transfers of CX1 chips and information across departments (sales, manufacturing, shipping, billing, and accounting) to satisfy a customer's order created delays. Furthermore, no single individual was responsible for fulfilling each customer order. A cross-functional team from the various departments has reengineered the order-delivery process for 2009. Under the new system, a customer-relationship manager is responsible for each customer and negotiates long-term contracts specifying quantities and prices. The customer-relationship manager works closely with the customer and with manufacturing to specify delivery schedules for CX1 one month in advance of shipment. The schedule of customer orders is sent electronically to manufacturing. Completed chips are shipped directly from the manufacturing plant to customer sites. Each shipment automatically triggers an invoice that the customer receives electronically. Customers then transfer funds electronically to Chipset's bank.

The experiences of many companies, such as AT&T, Banca di America e di Italia, Cigna Insurance, Cisco, Pepsi, and Siemens Nixdorf, indicate that the benefits from reengineering are most significant when it cuts across functional lines to focus on an entire business process (as in the Chipset example). Reengineering only the shipping or invoicing activity at Chipset rather than the entire order-delivery process would not be particularly beneficial. Successful reengineering efforts focus on changing roles and responsibilities, eliminating unnecessary activities and tasks, using information technology, and developing employee skills.

In summary, note the interrelatedness and consistency in Chipset's strategy—from (1) understanding customer preference maps to (2) deciding on a cost-leadership strategy to (3) building internal capabilities to achieve cost leadership. Take another look at Exhibit 13-1. Note how Chipset uses process engineering to improve its internal capabilities to help meet customer preferences for price, quality, and customer service—key elements for the success of Chipset's cost-leadership strategy. Chipset's next challenge is to effectively implement its strategy.

Strategy Implementation and the Balanced Scorecard

Management accountants design reports to help managers track progress in implementing strategy. Many organizations, such as Allstate Insurance, Bank of Montreal, BP, and Dow Chemical, have introduced a *balanced scorecard* approach to manage the implementation of their strategies.

The Balanced Scorecard

The **balanced scorecard** translates an organization's mission and strategy into a set of performance measures that provides the framework for implementing its strategy.[4] The balanced scorecard does not focus solely on achieving financial objectives. It also highlights the nonfinancial objectives that an organization must achieve to meet and sustain its financial objectives. The scorecard measures an organization's performance from four perspectives: (1) financial, (2) customer, (3) internal business processes, and (4) learning and growth. A company's strategy influences the measures it uses to track performance in each of these perspectives.

Why is this tool called a balanced scorecard? Because it balances the use of financial and nonfinancial performance measures to evaluate short-run and long-run performance in a single report. The balanced scorecard reduces managers' emphasis on short-run financial performance, such as quarterly earnings. That's because the key strategic nonfinancial

[4] See R. S. Kaplan and D. P. Norton, *The Balanced Scorecard* (Boston: Harvard Business School Press, 1996); R. S. Kaplan and D. P. Norton, *The Strategy-Focused Organization: How Balanced Scorecard Companies Thrive in the New Business Environment* (Boston: Harvard Business School Press, 2001); R. S. Kaplan and D. P. Norton, *Strategy Maps: Converting Intangible Assets into Tangible Outcomes* (Boston: Harvard Business School Press, 2004); R. S. Kaplan and D. P. Norton, *Alignment: Using the Balanced Scorecard to Create Corporate Synergies* (Boston: Harvard Business School Press, 2006).

and operational indicators, such as product quality and customer satisfaction, measure changes that a company is making for the long run. The financial benefits of these long-run changes may not appear immediately in short-run earnings; however, given the company's strategy, strong improvement in nonfinancial measures usually indicates the creation of future economic value. For example, an increase in customer satisfaction, as measured by customer surveys and repeat purchases, signals a strong likelihood of higher sales and income in the future. By balancing the mix of financial and nonfinancial measures, the balanced scorecard broadens management's attention to short-run *and* long-run performance. Never lose sight of the key point. In for-profit companies, the goal of the balanced scorecard is to improve a company's overall financial performance. Nonfinancial measures simply serve as leading indicators for the hard-to-measure long-run financial goals.

We illustrate the four perspectives of the balanced scorecard using the Chipset example. The measures Chipset's managers choose for each perspective relate to the action plans for furthering Chipset's cost leadership strategy: *improve quality* and *reengineer processes.*

Four Perspectives of the Balanced Scorecard

Learning Objective 3

Describe the four perspectives of the balanced scorecard

. . . financial, customer, internal business process, learning and growth

Exhibit 13-2 presents Chipset's balanced scorecard. It highlights the four perspectives of performance: financial, customer, internal business process, and learning and growth. At the beginning of 2009, the company's managers specify the objectives, measures, initiatives (necessary actions to achieve the objectives), and target performance (the first four columns of Exhibit 13-2).

Competitor benchmarks provide the basis for target performance levels for financial and nonfinancial measures. These benchmarks indicate the performance levels necessary to meet customer needs, compete effectively, and achieve financial goals. Chipset wants to use the balanced scorecard targets to drive the organization to higher levels of performance. Managers therefore set targets at a level of performance that is achievable, yet distinctly better than competitors. Chipset's managers complete the fifth column, reporting actual performance at the end of 2009. This column shows how well Chipset performed relative to target performance.

1. **Financial perspective.** This perspective evaluates the profitability of the strategy. Because cost reduction relative to competitors' costs and sales growth are Chipset's key strategic initiatives, the financial perspective focuses on how much of operating income results from reducing costs and selling more units of CX1.
2. **Customer perspective.** This perspective identifies targeted customer and market segments and measures the company's success in these segments. To monitor its growth objectives, Chipset uses measures such as market share in the communication-networks segment, number of new customers, and customer-satisfaction ratings.
3. **Internal-business-process perspective.** This perspective focuses on internal operations that create value for customers that, in turn, furthers the financial perspective by increasing shareholder value. Chipset determines internal-business-process improvement targets after benchmarking against its main competitors. As we discussed in Chapter 12, there are different sources of competitor cost analysis: published financial statements, prevailing prices, customers, suppliers, former employees, industry experts, and financial analysts. To estimate competitors' costs, Chipset also physically disassembles competitors' products and compares them with its own products and designs. The internal-business-process perspective comprises three subprocesses:
   - **Innovation process:** Creating products, services, and processes that will meet the needs of customers. This is a very important process for companies that follow a product-differentiation strategy. These companies must constantly design and develop innovative new products to remain competitive in the marketplace. Chipset focuses its innovation on processes and on improving its manufacturing technology and process controls to lower costs and improve quality.
   - **Operations process:** Producing and delivering existing products and services that will meet the needs of customers. Chipset's strategic initiatives are (a) improving manufacturing quality, (b) reducing delivery time to customers, and (c) meeting specified delivery dates.

Exhibit 13-2 The Balanced Scorecard for Chipset, Inc., for 2009

Objectives	Measures	Initiatives	Target Performance	Actual Performance
Financial Perspective				
Increase shareholder value	Operating income from productivity gain	Manage costs and unused capacity	$2,000,000	$2,012,500
	Operating income from growth	Build strong customer relationships	$3,000,000	$3,420,000
	Revenue growth		6%	6.48%[a]
Customer Perspective				
Increase market share	Market share in communication-networks segment	Identify future needs of customers	6%	7%
Increase customer satisfaction	Number of new customers	Identify new target-customer segments	1	1[b]
	Customer-satisfaction ratings	Increase customer focus of sales organization	90% of customers give top two ratings	87% of customers give top two ratings
Internal-Business-Process Perspective				
Improve postsales service	Service response time	Improve customer-service process	Within 4 hours	Within 3 hours
Improve manufacturing quality and productivity	Yield	Identify root causes of problems and improve quality	78%	79.3%
Reduce delivery time to customers	Order-delivery time	Reengineer order-delivery process	30 days	30 days
Meet specified delivery dates	On-time delivery	Reengineer order-delivery process	92%	90%
Improve processes	Number of major improvements in manufacturing and business processes	Organize teams from manufacturing and sales to modify processes	5	5
Improve manufacturing capability	Percentage of processes with advanced controls	Organize R&D/manufacturing teams to implement advanced controls	75%	75%
Learning-and-Growth Perspective				
Align employee and organization goals	Employee-satisfaction ratings	Employee participation and suggestions program to build teamwork	80% of employees give top two ratings	88% of employees give top two ratings
Empower workforce	Percentage of line workers empowered to manage processes	Have supervisors act as coaches rather than decision makers	85%	90%
Develop process skill	Percentage of employees trained in process and quality management	Employee training programs	90%	92%
Enhance information-system capabilities	Percentage of manufacturing processes with real-time feedback	Improve online and offline data gathering	80%	80%

[a](Revenues in 2009 – Revenues in 2008) ÷ Revenues in 2008 = ($28,750,000 – $27,000,000) ÷ $27,000,000 = 6.48%.

[b]Number of customers increased from seven to eight in 2009.

- **Postsales-service process:** Providing service and support to the customer after the sale of a product or service. Chipset monitors how quickly and accurately it is responding to customer-service requests.

4. **Learning-and-growth perspective.** This perspective identifies the capabilities the organization must excel at to achieve superior internal processes that create value for customers and shareholders. Chipset's learning and growth perspective emphasizes three capabilities: (1) information-system capabilities, measured by the percentage of manufacturing processes with real-time feedback; (2) employee capabilities, measured by the percentage of employees trained in process and quality management; and (3) motivation, measured by employee satisfaction and the percentage of manufacturing and sales employees (line employees) empowered to manage processes.

The arrows in Exhibit 13-2 indicate the *broad* cause-and-effect linkages—how gains in the learning-and-growth perspective lead to improvements in internal business processes, which lead to higher customer satisfaction and market share, and finally lead to superior financial performance. Note how the scorecard describes elements of Chipset's strategy implementation. Worker training and empowerment improve employee satisfaction and lead to manufacturing and business-process improvements that improve quality and reduce delivery time. The result is increased customer satisfaction and higher market share. These initiatives have been successful from a financial perspective. Chipset has earned significant operating income from its cost leadership strategy, and that strategy has also led to growth.

Many companies that implement the balanced scorecard also implement strategy maps to represent *more detailed* cause-and-effect relationships across various scorecard measures. Exhibit 13-3 presents a strategy map of the balanced scorecard measures in Exhibit 13-2. You can follow the arrows to see how a measure affects other measures. For example, percentage of line workers empowered to manage processes affects both employee satisfaction and number of major improvements in manufacturing and business processes. Employee satisfaction affects yield and major improvements in manufacturing and business processes. The latter affects yield, order-delivery time, on-time delivery, and service-response time, each of which improves customer satisfaction. Yield directly increases operating income from productivity and customer satisfaction that in turn drives revenue growth and operating income from growth.

Chipset operates in a knowledge-intensive business. To compete successfully, Chipset invests in its employees, implements new technology and process controls, improves quality, and reengineers processes. Doing these activities well enables Chipset to build capabilities and intangible assets, which are not recorded as assets in its financial books. The strategy map helps Chipset evaluate whether these intangible assets are generating financial returns.

Chipset could include many other cause-and-effect relationships in the strategy map in Exhibit 13-3. But, Chipset, like other companies implementing the balanced scorecard, focuses on only the relationships that it believes to be the most significant.

A major benefit of the balanced scorecard is that it promotes causal thinking. Think of the balanced scorecard as a *linked scorecard* or a *causal scorecard*. Managers must search for empirical evidence (rather than rely on faith alone) to test the validity and strength of the various connections. A causal scorecard enables a company to focus on the key drivers that steer the implementation of the strategy. Without convincing links, the scorecard loses much of its value.

Implementing a Balanced Scorecard

To successfully implement a balanced scorecard requires commitment and leadership from top management. At Chipset, the team building the balanced scorecard (headed by the vice president of strategic planning) conducted interviews with senior managers, probed executives about customers, competitors, and technological developments, and sought proposals for balanced scorecard objectives across the four perspectives. The team then met to discuss the responses and to build a prioritized list of objectives.

In a meeting with all senior managers, the team sought to achieve consensus on the scorecard objectives. Senior management was then divided into four groups, with each group responsible for one of the perspectives. In addition, each group broadened the base of inputs

Exhibit 13-3 Strategy Map for Chipset, Inc., for 2009

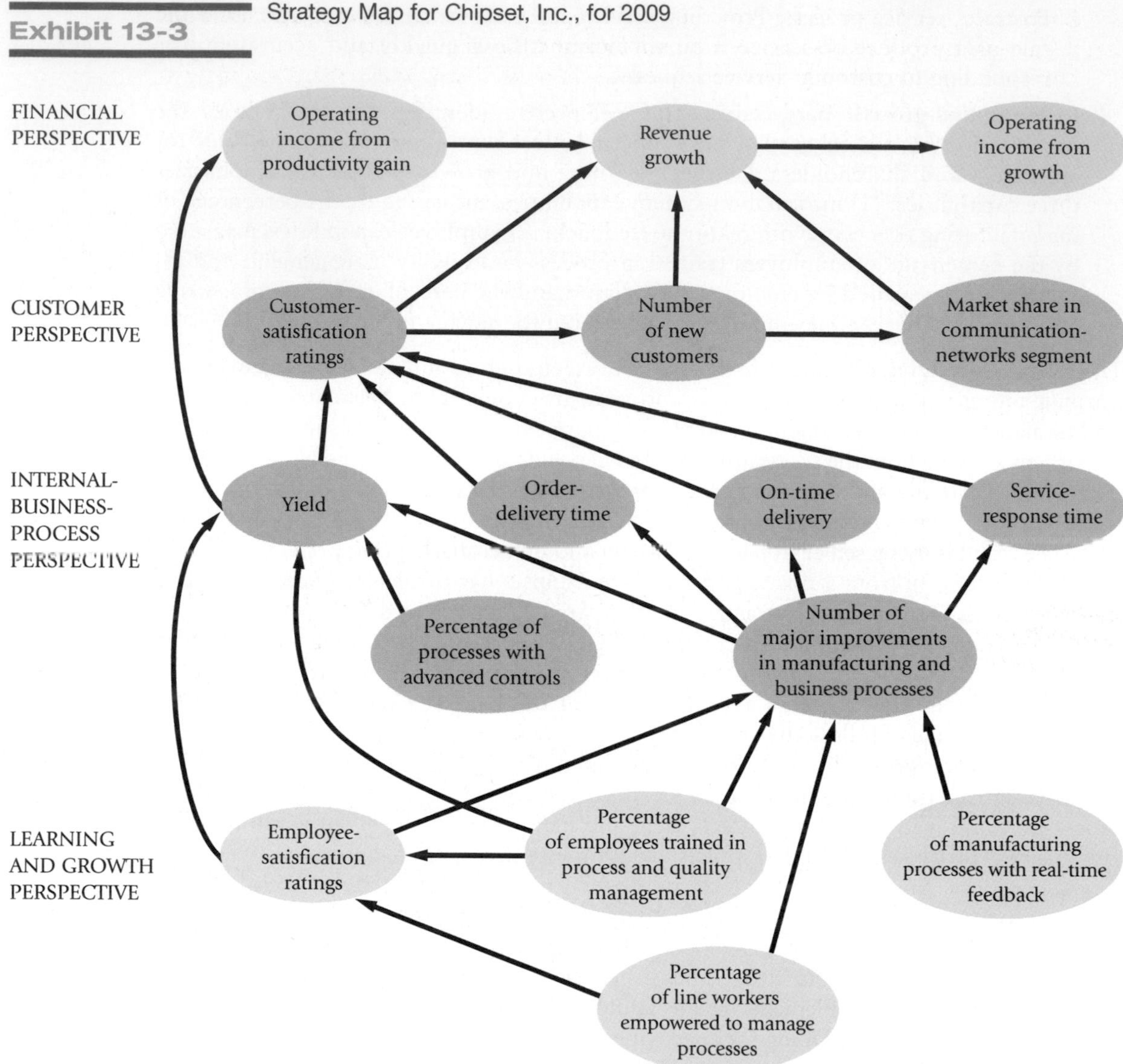

by including representatives from the next-lower levels of management and key functional managers. The groups identified measures for each objective and the sources of information for each measure. The groups then met to finalize scorecard objectives, measures, targets, and the initiatives to achieve the targets. Management accountants played an important role in the design and implementation of the balanced scorecard, particularly in determining measures to represent the realities of the business. This required management accountants to understand the economic environment of the industry, Chipset's customers and competitors, and internal business issues such as human resources, operations, and distribution.

Managers made sure that employees understood the scorecard and the scorecard process. The final balanced scorecard was communicated to all employees. Sharing the scorecard allowed engineers and operating personnel, for example, to understand the reasons for customer satisfaction and dissatisfaction and to make suggestions for improving internal processes directly aimed at satisfying customers and implementing Chipset's strategy. Too often, scorecards are seen by only a select group of managers. By limiting the scorecard's exposure, an organization loses the opportunity for widespread organization engagement and alignment.

Chipset, like Cigna Property and Casualty Insurance and Wells Fargo, also encourages each department to develop its own scorecard that ties into Chipset's main scorecard described in Exhibit 13-2. For example, the quality control department's scorecard has measures that its department managers use to improve quality—number of quality circles, statistical process control charts, Pareto diagrams, and root-cause analyses implemented (see Chapter 19, pp. 670–672 for more details.). Department scorecards help align actions that each department needs to perform to implement Chipset's strategy.

Companies frequently use balanced scorecards to evaluate and reward managerial performance and to thereby influence a manager's behavior. This use of the balanced scorecard motivates managers to give stronger consideration to nonfinancial drivers of performance and to thereby widen the performance management lens. Surveys indicate, however, that companies continue to assign more weight to the financial perspective (55%) than to the other perspectives—customer (19%), internal business process (12%), and learning and growth (14%). Companies cite several reasons for this—difficulty evaluating the relative importance of different measures, challenges in measuring and quantifying qualitative, nonfinancial data, and problems in compensating managers despite poor financial performance (see Chapter 23 for a more detailed discussion of performance evaluation). For the balanced scorecard to be effective, managers must view it as fairly assessing and rewarding all important aspects of a manager's performance.

Aligning the Balanced Scorecard to Strategy

Different strategies call for different scorecards. Recall Chipset's competitor Visilog, which follows a product-differentiation strategy by designing custom chips for modems and communication networks. Visilog designs its balanced scorecard to fit its strategy. For example, in the financial perspective, Visilog evaluates how much of its operating income comes from charging premium prices for its products. In the customer perspective, Visilog measures the percentage of its revenues from new products and new customers. In the internal-business-process perspective, Visilog measures the number of new products introduced and new product development time. In the learning-and-growth perspective, Visilog measures the development of advanced manufacturing capabilities to produce custom chips. Visilog also uses some of the measures described in Chipset's balanced scorecard in Exhibit 13-2. For example, revenue growth, customer satisfaction ratings, order-delivery time, on-time delivery, percentage of frontline workers empowered to manage processes, and employee-satisfaction ratings are also important measures under the product-differentiation strategy. The point is to align the balanced scorecard with company strategy.[5] Exhibit 13-4 presents some common measures found on company scorecards in the service, retail, and manufacturing sectors.

Features of a Good Balanced Scorecard

A well-designed balanced scorecard has several features:

1. It tells the story of a company's strategy, articulating a sequence of cause-and-effect relationships—the links among the various perspectives that align implementation of the strategy. In for-profit companies, each measure in the scorecard is part of a cause-and-effect chain leading to financial outcomes. Not-for-profit organizations design the cause-and-effect chain to achieve their strategic service objectives—for example, number of people no longer in poverty, or number of children still in school.
2. The balanced scorecard helps to communicate the strategy to all members of the organization by translating the strategy into a coherent and linked set of understandable and measurable operational targets. Guided by the scorecard, managers and employees take actions and make decisions to achieve the company's strategy. Companies that have distinct strategic business units (SBUs)—such as consumer products and pharmaceuticals at Johnson & Johnson—develop their balanced scorecards at the SBU level. Each SBU has its own unique strategy and implementation

[5] For simplicity, we have presented the balanced scorecard in the context of companies that have followed either a cost-leadership or a product-differentiation strategy. Of course, a company may have some products for which cost leadership is critical and other products for which product differentiation is important. The company will then develop separate scorecards to implement the different product strategies. In still other contexts, product differentiation may be of primary importance, but some cost leadership must also be achieved. The balanced scorecard measures would then be linked in a cause-and-effect way to this strategy.

Exhibit 13-4

Frequently Cited Balanced Scorecard Measures

Financial Perspective
Income measures: Operating income, gross margin percentage
Revenue and cost measures: Revenue growth, revenues from new products, cost reductions in key areas
Income and investment measures: Economic value added [a](EVA®), return on investment
Customer Perspective
Market share, customer satisfaction, customer-retention percentage, time taken to fulfill customers' requests, number of customer complaints
Internal-Business-Process Perspective
Innovation Process: Operating capabilities, number of new products or services, new-product development times, and number of new patents
Operations Process: Yield, defect rates, time taken to deliver product to customers, percentage of on-time deliveries, average time taken to respond to orders, setup time, manufacturing downtime
Postsales Service Process: Time taken to replace or repair defective products, hours of customer training for using the product
Learning-and-Growth Perspective
Employee measures: Employee education and skill levels, employee-satisfaction ratings, employee turnover rates, percentage of employee suggestions implemented, percentage of compensation based on individual and team incentives
Technology measures: Information system availability, percentage of processes with advanced controls

[a]This measures is described in Chapter 23.

goals; building separate scorecards allows each SBU to choose measures that help implement its distinctive strategy.

3. In for-profit companies, the balanced scorecard must motivate managers to take actions that eventually result in improvements in financial performance. Managers sometimes tend to focus too much on innovation, quality, and customer satisfaction as ends in themselves. For example, Xerox spent heavily to increase customer satisfaction without a resulting financial payoff. The company later discovered that a measure of customer loyalty, not general customer satisfaction, was a leading indicator of future financial performance. When financial and nonfinancial performance measures are properly linked, most, if not all, of the nonfinancial measures serve as leading indicators of lagging future financial performance. Some companies use statistical methods, such as regression analysis, to test the anticipated cause-and-effect relationships among various nonfinancial measures and financial measures. The data for this analysis can come from either time series data (collected over time) or cross-sectional data (collected, for example, across multiple stores of a retail chain). In the Chipset example, improvements in nonfinancial factors have, in fact, already led to improvements in financial factors.
4. The balanced scorecard limits the number of measures, identifying only the most critical ones. Chipset's scorecard, for example, has 16 measures, between 3 and 5 measures for each perspective. Limiting the number of measures focuses managers' attention on those that most affect strategy implementation. Using too many measures makes it difficult for managers to process relevant information.
5. The balanced scorecard highlights less-than-optimal trade-offs that managers may make when they fail to consider operational and financial measures together. For example, a company whose strategy is innovation and product differentiation could achieve superior short-run financial performance by reducing spending on R&D. A good balanced scorecard would signal that the short-run financial performance might have been achieved by taking actions that hurt future financial performance because a leading indicator of that performance, R&D spending and R&D output, has declined.

Pitfalls in Implementing a Balanced Scorecard

Pitfalls to avoid in implementing a balanced scorecard include the following:

1. Managers should not assume the cause-and-effect linkages are precise. They are merely hypotheses. Over time, a company must gather evidence of the strength and

timing of the linkages among the nonfinancial and financial measures. With experience, organizations should alter their scorecards to include those nonfinancial objectives and measures that are the best leading indicators (the causes) of financial performance (a lagging indicator or effect). Understanding that the scorecard evolves over time helps managers to avoid unproductively spending time and money trying to design the "perfect" scorecard at the outset. Furthermore, as the business environment and strategy change over time, the measures in the scorecard will also need to change.

2. Managers should not seek improvements across all of the measures all of the time. For example, strive for quality and on-time performance but not beyond a point at which further improvement in these objectives is so costly that it is inconsistent with long-run profit maximization. Cost-benefit considerations should always be a central element when designing a balanced scorecard.
3. Managers should not use only objective measures in the balanced scorecard. Chipset's balanced scorecard includes both objective measures (such as operating income from cost leadership, market share, and manufacturing yield) and subjective measures (such as customer- and employee-satisfaction ratings). When using subjective measures, though, management must be careful that the benefits of this potentially rich information are not lost by using measures that are inaccurate or that can be easily manipulated.
4. Despite challenges of measurement, top management should not ignore nonfinancial measures when evaluating managers and other employees. Managers tend to focus on what their performance is measured by. Excluding nonfinancial measures when evaluating performance will reduce the significance and importance that managers give to nonfinancial measures.

Evaluating the Success of Strategy and Implementation

To evaluate how successful Chipset's strategy and its implementation have been, its management compares the target- and actual-performance columns in the balanced scorecard (Exhibit 13-2). Chipset met most targets set on the basis of competitor benchmarks in 2009 itself. That's because, in the Chipset context, improvements in the learning and growth perspective quickly ripple through to the financial perspective. Chipset will continue to seek improvements on the targets it did not achieve, but meeting most targets suggests that the strategic initiatives that Chipset identified and measured for learning and growth resulted in improvements in internal business processes, customer measures, and financial performance.

How would Chipset know if it had problems in strategy implementation? If it did not meet its targets on the two perspectives that are more internally focused: learning and growth and internal business processes.

What if Chipset performed well on learning and growth and internal business processes, but customer measures and financial performance in this year and the next did not improve? Chipset's managers would then conclude that Chipset did a good job of implementation (the various internal nonfinancial measures it targeted improved) but that its strategy was faulty (there was no effect on customers or on long-run financial performance and value creation). Management failed to identify the correct causal links. It implemented the wrong strategy well! Management would then reevaluate the strategy and the factors that drive it.

Now what if Chipset performed well on its various nonfinancial measures, and operating income over this year and the next also increased? Chipset's managers might be tempted to declare the strategy a success because operating income increased. Unfortunately, management still cannot conclude with any confidence that Chipset successfully formulated and implemented its strategy. Why? Because operating income can increase simply because entire markets are expanding, not because a company's strategy has been successful. Also, changes in operating income might occur because of factors outside the strategy. For example, a company such as Chipset that has chosen a cost-leadership strategy may find that its operating-income increase instead resulted incidentally from, say, some degree of product differentiation. *Managers and management accountants need to evaluate the success of a strategy by linking the sources of operating-income increases to the strategy.*

For Chipset to conclude that it was successful in implementing its strategy, it must demonstrate that improvements in its financial performance and operating income over time resulted from achieving targeted cost savings and growth in market share. Fortunately, the top two rows of Chipset's balanced scorecard in Exhibit 13-2 show that operating-income gains from productivity ($2,012,500) and growth ($3,420,000) exceeded targets. The next section of this chapter describes how these numbers were calculated. To be sure that the strategy has been successful, Chipset's management would like to see similar gains in subsequent years.

Chipset's management accountants subdivide changes in operating income into components that can be identified with product differentiation, cost leadership, and growth. Why growth? Because successful cost leadership or product differentiation generally increases market share and helps a company to grow. Subdividing the change in operating income to evaluate the success of a strategy is conceptually similar to the variance analysis discussed in Chapters 7 and 8. One difference, however, is that management accountants compare actual operating performance over two different periods, not actual to budgeted numbers in the same time period as in variance analysis.[6]

Strategic Analysis of Operating Income

Learning Objective 4

Analyze changes in operating income to evaluate strategy

... growth, price recovery, and productivity

The following illustration explains how to subdivide the change in operating income from one period to *any* future period. The individual components describe company performance with regard to cost leadership, product differentiation, and growth.[7] We illustrate the analysis using data from 2008 and 2009 because Chipset implemented key elements of its strategy in late 2008 and early 2009 and expects the financial consequences of these strategies to appear in 2009. Suppose the financial consequences of these strategies had been expected to affect operating income in, say, 2010 only. Then we could just as easily have compared 2008 to 2010. If necessary, we could also have compared 2008 to 2009 and 2010 taken together.

Chipset's data for 2008 and 2009 follow.

	2008	2009
1. Units of CX1 produced and sold	1,000,000	1,150,000
2. Selling price	$27	$25
3. Direct materials (square centimeters of silicon wafers)	3,000,000	2,900,000
4. Direct material cost per square centimeter	$1.40	$1.50
5. Manufacturing processing capacity (in square centimeters of silicon wafer)	3,750,000	3,500,000
6. Conversion costs (all manufacturing costs other than direct material costs)	$16,050,000	$15,225,000
7. Conversion cost per unit of capacity (Row 6 ÷ Row 5)	$4.28	$4.35
8. R&D employees	40	39
9. R&D costs	$4,000,000	$3,900,000
10. R&D cost per employee (Row 9 ÷ Row 8)	$100,000	$100,000

Chipset provides the following additional information.

1. Conversion costs for each year depend on production capacity defined in terms of the quantity of square centimeters of silicon wafers that can be processed. Such costs do not vary with the actual quantity of silicon wafers processed. (Because direct manufacturing

[6] Other examples of focusing on actual performance over two periods rather than comparisons of actuals with budgets can be found in J. Hope and R. Fraser, *Beyond Budgeting* (Boston, MA: Harvard Business School Press, 2003).

[7] For other details, see R. Banker, S. Datar, and R. Kaplan, "Productivity Measurement and Management Accounting," *Journal of Accounting, Auditing and Finance* (1989): 528–554; and A. Hayzen and J. Reeve, "Examining the Relationships in Productivity Accounting," *Management Accounting Quarterly* (2000): 32–39.

labor costs are small and tied to capacity, that is, labor is not paid on a piece-rate basis, Chipset includes these costs together with manufacturing overhead costs in conversion costs rather than as a separate cost category.) To reduce conversion costs, management would have to reduce capacity by selling some of the manufacturing equipment and by reassigning manufacturing personnel to other tasks or laying them off.

2. At the start of each year, management uses its discretion to determine the amount of R&D work to be done. This work is independent of the actual quantity of CX1 produced and sold or silicon wafers processed.
3. Chipset's marketing and sales costs are small relative to the other costs. Chipset has fewer than 10 customers, each purchasing roughly the same quantities of CX1. Because of the highly technical nature of the product, Chipset uses a cross-functional team for its marketing and sales activities. Engineers from R&D work closely with customers to understand their needs regarding upgrades of CX1 and to market CX1 to them. Once a contract to supply chips is signed, the customer-relationship manager located in the manufacturing area is responsible for ensuring that quality products are delivered at the time agreed upon. This cross-functional approach ensures that, although marketing and sales costs are small, the entire Chipset organization remains focused on increasing customer satisfaction and market share. (The Problem for Self-Study at the end of this chapter describes a situation in which marketing, sales, and customer-service costs are significant.)
4. Chipset's asset structure is very similar in 2008 and 2009. Operating income for each year is as follows.

	2008	2009
Revenues		
($27 per unit × 1,000,000 units; $25 per unit × 1,150,000 units)	$27,000,000	$28,750,000
Costs		
Direct material costs		
($1.40/sq. cm. × 3,000,000 sq. cm.; $1.50/sq. cm. × 2,900,000 sq. cm.)	4,200,000	4,350,000
Conversion costs		
($4.28/sq. cm. × 3,750,000 sq. cm.; $4.35/sq. cm. × 3,500,000 sq. cm.)	16,050,000	15,225,000
R&D costs ($100,000 × 40 employees; $100,000 × 39 employees)	4,000,000	3,900,000
Total costs	24,250,000	23,475,000
Operating income	$ 2,750,000	$ 5,275,000
Change in operating income	$2,525,000 F	

The goal of Chipset's managers is to evaluate how much of the $2,525,000 increase in operating income was caused by the successful implementation of the company's cost-leadership strategy. To do this, management accountants analyze three main factors: growth, price recovery, and productivity.

The **growth component** measures the change in operating income attributable solely to the change in the quantity of output sold between 2008 and 2009.

The **price-recovery component** measures the change in operating income attributable solely to changes in Chipset's prices of inputs and outputs between 2008 and 2009. The price-recovery component measures change in output price compared with changes in input prices. A company that has successfully pursued a strategy of product differentiation will be able to increase its output price faster than the increase in its input prices, boosting profit margins and operating income: It will show a large positive price-recovery component.

The **productivity component** measures the change in costs attributable to a change in the quantity of inputs used in 2009 relative to the quantity of inputs that would have been used in 2008 to produce the 2009 output. The productivity component measures the amount by which operating income increases by using inputs efficiently to lower costs. A company that has successfully pursued a strategy of cost leadership will be able to produce a given quantity of output with a lower cost of inputs: It will show a large positive productivity component. Given Chipset's strategy of cost leadership, we expect the increase in operating income to be attributable to the productivity and growth components, not to price recovery. We now examine these three components in detail.

Growth Component of Change in Operating Income

The growth component of the change in operating income measures the increase in revenues minus the increase in costs from selling more units of CX1 in 2009 (1,150,000 units) than in 2008 (1,000,000 units), *assuming nothing else has changed*. That is, the growth-component calculations use 2008 output prices, input prices, efficiencies, and capacity relationships.

Revenue effect of growth

$$\text{Revenue effect of growth} = \left(\begin{array}{c}\text{Actual units of}\\ \text{output sold}\\ \text{in 2009}\end{array} - \begin{array}{c}\text{Actual units of}\\ \text{output sold}\\ \text{in 2008}\end{array}\right) \times \begin{array}{c}\text{Selling}\\ \text{price}\\ \text{in 2008}\end{array}$$

$$= (1{,}150{,}000 \text{ units} - 1{,}000{,}000 \text{ units}) \times \$27 \text{ per unit}$$

$$= \$4{,}050{,}000 \text{ F}$$

This component is favorable (F) because the increase in output sold in 2009 increases operating income. Components that decrease operating income are unfavorable (U).

Note that Chipset uses the 2008 price of CX1 here and focuses only on the increase in units sold between 2008 and 2009. That's because the objective of the revenue effect of the growth component is to isolate the increase in revenues between 2008 and 2009 due solely to the change in the units sold, *assuming* the 2008 selling price continues into 2009.

Cost effect of growth The cost effect of growth measures how much costs would have changed in 2008 if Chipset had produced 1,150,000 units of CX1 instead of 1,000,000 units. To measure the cost effect of growth, Chipset's managers distinguish variable costs such as direct material costs from fixed costs such as conversion costs and R&D costs. That's because as units produced (and sold) increase, variable costs increase proportionately but fixed costs, generally, do not change.

$$\begin{array}{c}\text{Cost effect of}\\ \text{growth for}\\ \text{variable costs}\end{array} = \left(\begin{array}{c}\text{Units of input}\\ \text{required to}\\ \text{produce 2009}\\ \text{output in 2008}\end{array} - \begin{array}{c}\text{Actual units of}\\ \text{input used}\\ \text{to produce}\\ \text{2008 output}\end{array}\right) \times \begin{array}{c}\text{Input}\\ \text{price}\\ \text{in 2008}\end{array}$$

$$\begin{array}{c}\text{Cost effect of}\\ \text{growth for}\\ \text{direct materials}\end{array} = \left(3{,}000{,}000 \text{ sq.cm.} \times \frac{1{,}150{,}000 \text{ units}}{1{,}000{,}000 \text{ units}} - 3{,}000{,}000 \text{ sq.cm.}\right) \times \$1.40 \text{ per sq.cm.}$$

$$= (3{,}450{,}000 \text{ sq.cm.} - 3{,}000{,}000 \text{ sq.cm.}) \times \$1.40 \text{ per sq.cm.} = \$630{,}000 \text{ U}$$

$$\begin{array}{c}\text{Cost effect of}\\ \text{growth for}\\ \text{fixed costs}\end{array} = \left(\begin{array}{c}\text{Actual units of capacity in}\\ \text{2008 if adquate to produce}\\ \text{2009 output in 2008}\\ \text{OR}\\ \text{If 2008 capacity inadequate}\\ \text{to produce 2009 output in 2008,}\\ \text{units of capacity required}\\ \text{to produce 2009 output in 2008}\end{array} - \begin{array}{c}\text{Actual units}\\ \text{of capacity}\\ \text{in 2008}\end{array}\right) \times \begin{array}{c}\text{Price per}\\ \text{unit of}\\ \text{capacity}\\ \text{in 2008}\end{array}$$

$$\begin{array}{c}\text{Cost effect of}\\ \text{growth for}\\ \text{conversion costs}\end{array} = (3{,}750{,}000 \text{ sq.cm.} - 3{,}750{,}000 \text{ sq.cm.}) \times \$4.28 \text{ per sq.cm.} = \$0$$

Conversion costs are fixed costs at a given level of capacity. Chipset has manufacturing capacity to process 3,750,000 square centimeters of silicon wafers in 2008 at a cost of $16,050,000, or $4.28 per square centimeter (rows 5, 6, and 7 of data on p. 474). To produce 1,150,000 units of output in 2008, Chipset would have needed to process 3,450,000 square centimeters of direct materials. Chipset has adequate capacity to produce 1,150,000 units, so no additional conversion cost capacity would be needed and conversion costs would not change.

$$\text{Cost effect of growth for R \& D costs} = (40 \text{ employees} - 40 \text{ employees}) \times \$100{,}000 \text{ per employee} = \$0$$

R&D costs are fixed discretionary costs that would not have changed in 2008 if Chipset had produced and sold more units of CX1.

In summary, the net increase in operating income attributable to growth equals:

Revenue effect of growth		$4,050,000 F
Cost effect of growth		
Direct material costs	$630,000 U	
Conversion costs	0	
R&D costs	0	630,000 U
Change in operating income due to growth		$3,420,000 F

Price-Recovery Component of Change in Operating Income

Assuming that the 2008 relationship between inputs and outputs continued in 2009, the price-recovery component of the change in operating income measures solely the effect of price changes on revenues and costs to produce and sell the 1,150,000 units of CX1 in 2009.

Revenue effect of price recovery

$$\begin{aligned}\text{Revenue effect of price recovery} &= \left(\text{Selling price in 2009} - \text{Selling price in 2008}\right) \times \text{Actual units of output sold in 2009} \\ &= (\$25 \text{ per unit} - \$27 \text{ per unit}) \times 1{,}150{,}000 \text{ units} \\ &= \$2{,}300{,}000 \text{ U}\end{aligned}$$

Note that the calculation focuses on revenue changes caused by changes in the selling price of CX1 between 2008 and 2009.

Cost effect of price recovery Chipset's management accountants calculate the cost effects of price recovery separately for variable costs and for fixed costs, just as they did when calculating the cost effect of growth.

$$\text{Cost effect of price recovery for variable costs} = \left(\text{Input price in 2009} - \text{Input price in 2008}\right) \times \text{Units of input required to produce 2009 output in 2008}$$

$$\text{Cost effect of price recovery for direct materials} = (\$1.50 \text{ per sq.cm.} - \$1.40 \text{ per sq.cm.}) \times 3{,}450{,}000 \text{ sq.} = \$345{,}000 \text{ U}$$

Recall that the direct materials of 3,450,000 square centimeters required to produce 2009 output in 2008 had already been calculated when computing the cost effect of growth (p. 476).

$$\text{Cost effect of price recovery for fixed costs} = \left(\text{Price per unit of capacity in 2009} - \text{Price per unit of capacity in 2008}\right) \times \begin{pmatrix}\text{Actual units of capacity in 2008, if adequate to produce 2009 output in 2008} \\ \text{OR} \\ \text{If 2008 capacity inadequate to produce 2009 output in 2008, units of capacity required to produce 2009 output in 2008}\end{pmatrix}$$

Cost effects of price recovery for fixed costs are:

Conversion costs: ($4.35 per sq. cm. − $4.28 per sq. cm.) × 3,750,000 sq. cm. = $262,500U

R&D costs: ($100,000 per employee − $100,000 per employee) × 40 employees = $0

Recall that the units of capacity in these calculations equal the 2008 capacity because adequate capacity is available in 2008 to produce 2009 output—3,750,000 sq. cm. of conversion capacity and 40 employees of R&D capacity. The detailed analyses of capacities were presented when computing the cost effect of growth (pp. 476–477).

In summary, the net decrease in operating income attributable to price recovery equals:

Revenue effect of price recovery		\$2,300,000 U
Cost effect of price recovery		
Direct material costs	\$345,000 U	
Conversion costs	262,500 U	
R&D costs	0	607,500 U
Change in operating income due to price recovery		\$2,907,500 U

The price-recovery analysis indicates that, even as the prices of its inputs increased, the selling prices of CX1 decreased and Chipset could not pass on input-price increases to its customers.

Productivity Component of Change in Operating Income

The productivity component of the change in operating income uses 2009 input prices to measure how costs have decreased as a result of using fewer inputs, a better mix of inputs, and/or less capacity to produce 2009 output, compared with the inputs and capacity that would have been used in 2008.

The productivity-component calculations use 2009 prices and output. That's because the productivity component isolates the change in costs between 2008 and 2009 caused solely by the change in the quantities, mix, and/or capacities of inputs.[8]

$$\text{Cost effect of productivity for variable costs} = \left(\begin{array}{c}\text{Actual units of input used}\\\text{to produce 2009 output}\end{array} - \begin{array}{c}\text{Units of input required to}\\\text{produce 2009 output in 2008}\end{array}\right) \times \begin{array}{c}\text{Input price}\\\text{in 2009}\end{array}$$

Using the 2009 data given on page 474 and the calculation of units of input required to produce 2009 output in 2008 when discussing the cost effects of growth (p. 476),

$$\text{Cost effect of productivity for direct materials} = (2{,}900{,}000 \text{ sq.cm.} - 3{,}450{,}000 \text{ sq. cm.}) \times \$1.50 \text{ per sq.cm}$$

$$= 550{,}000 \text{ sq.cm.} \times \$1.50 \text{ per sq. cm.} = \$825{,}000 \text{ F}$$

Chipset's quality and yield improvements reduced the quantity of direct materials needed to produce output in 2009 relative to 2008.

$$\text{Cost effect of productivity for fixed costs} = \left(\begin{array}{c}\text{Actual units of}\\\text{capacity}\\\text{in 2009}\end{array} - \begin{array}{c}\text{Actual units of capacity in}\\\text{2008, if adequate to produce}\\\text{2009 output in 2008}\\\text{OR}\\\text{If 2008 capacity inadequate}\\\text{to produce 2009 output in 2008,}\\\text{units of capacity required to}\\\text{produce 2009 output in 2008}\end{array}\right) \times \begin{array}{c}\text{Price per}\\\text{unit of}\\\text{capacity}\\\text{in 2009}\end{array}$$

[8] Note that the productivity-component calculation uses actual 2009 input prices, whereas its counterpart, the efficiency variance in Chapters 7 and 8, uses budgeted prices. (In effect, the budgeted prices correspond to 2008 prices). Year 2009 prices are used in the productivity calculation because Chipset wants its managers to choose input quantities to minimize costs in 2009 based on currently prevailing prices. If 2008 prices had been used in the productivity calculation, managers would choose input quantities based on irrelevant input prices that prevailed a year ago! Why does using budgeted prices in Chapters 7 and 8 not pose a similar problem? Because, unlike 2008 prices that describe what happened a year ago, budgeted prices represent prices that are expected to prevail in the current period. Moreover, budgeted prices can be changed, if necessary, to bring them in line with actual current-period prices.

Using the 2009 data given on page 474, and the analyses of capacity required to produce 2009 output in 2008 when discussing the cost effect of growth (pp. 476–477),

Cost effects of productivity for fixed costs are

Conversion costs: (3,500,000 sq. cm − 3,750,000 sq. cm.) × $4.35 per sq. cm. = $1,087,500 F

R&D costs: (39 employees − 40 employees) × $100,000 per employee = $100,000 F

Chipset's managers decreased manufacturing capacity in 2009 to 3,500,000 square centimeters. They did so by selling off old equipment and laying off workers. R&D capacity decreased because Chipset's managers did not replace an engineer who quit.

In summary, the net increase in operating income attributable to productivity equals

Cost effect of productivity	
Direct material costs	$ 825,000 F
Conversion costs	1,087,500 F
R&D costs	100,000 F
Change in operating income due to productivity	2,012,500 F

The productivity component indicates that Chipset was able to increase operating income by improving quality and productivity, eliminating capacity, and reducing costs. The appendix to this chapter examines partial and total factor productivity changes between 2008 and 2009 and describes how the management accountant can obtain a deeper understanding of Chipset's cost-leadership strategy. Note that the productivity component focuses exclusively on costs, so there is no revenue effect for this component.

Exhibit 13-5 summarizes the growth, price-recovery, and productivity components of the changes in operating income. Generally, companies that have been successful at cost leadership will show favorable productivity and growth components. Companies that have successfully differentiated their products will show favorable price-recovery and growth components. In Chipset's case, consistent with its strategy and its implementation, productivity contributed $2,012,500 to the increase in operating income, and growth contributed $3,420,000. Price-recovery contributed a $2,907,500 decrease in operating income, however, because, even as input prices increased, the selling price of CX1 decreased. Had Chipset been able to differentiate its product and charge a higher price, the price-recovery effects might have been less unfavorable or perhaps even favorable. As a result, Chipset's managers plan to evaluate some modest changes in product features that might help differentiate CX1 somewhat from competing products.

Further Analysis of Growth, Price-Recovery, and Productivity Components

As in all variance and profit analysis, Chipset's managers want to more closely analyze the change in operating income. Chipset's growth might have been helped, for example,

Exhibit 13-5 Strategic Analysis of Profitability

	Income Statement Amounts in 2008 (1)	Revenue and Cost Effects of Growth Component in 2009 (2)	Revenue and Cost Effects of Price-Recovery Component in 2009 (3)	Cost Effect of Productivity Component in 2009 (4)	Income Statement Amounts in 2009 (5) = (1) + (2) + (3) + (4)
Revenues	$27,000,000	$4,050,000 F	$2,300,000 U	—	$28,750,000
Costs	24,250,000	630,000 U	607,500 U	$2,012,500 F	23,475,000
Operating income	$ 2,750,000	$3,420,000 F	$2,907,500 U	$2,012,500 F	$ 5,275,000
			$2,525,000 F		
			Change in operating income		

by an increase in industry market size. Therefore, at least part of the increase in operating income may be attributable to favorable economic conditions in the industry rather than to any successful implementation of strategy. Some of the growth might also have come as a result of a management decision at Chipset to take advantage of its productivity gains by decreasing selling price. In this case, the increase in operating income from cost leadership must include the productivity gain, any increase in operating income from productivity-related growth in market share, and any decrease in operating income from lowering prices.

To illustrate these ideas, consider again the Chipset example and the following additional information.

- The market growth rate in the industry is 10% in 2009. Of the 150,000 (1,150,000 − 1,000,000) units of increased sales of CX1 between 2008 and 2009, 100,000 (0.10 × 1,000,000) units are due to an increase in industry market size (which Chipset should have benefited from regardless of its productivity gains), and the remaining 50,000 units are due to an increase in market share.
- During 2009, Chipset experienced a $1.35, or 5%, decline in the price of CX1 (0.05 × $27 = $1.35). Taking advantage of productivity gains, management reduced the price of CX1 by an additional $0.65, which led to the 50,000-unit increase in market share. [Recall that the total decrease in the price of CX1 is from $27 to $25, or $2 ($1.35 + $0.65).]

The effect of the industry-market-size factor on operating income (rather than any specific strategic actions) is:

Change in operating income due to growth in industry market size

$$\$3{,}420{,}000 \text{ (Exhibit 13-5, column 2)} \times \frac{100{,}000 \text{ units}}{150{,}000 \text{ units}} = \$2{,}280{,}000 \text{ F}$$

Lacking a differentiated product, Chipset experiences a $1.35 decline in output prices even while the prices of its inputs increase.

The effect of product differentiation on operating income is:

Change in operating income due to a decline in the selling price of CX1 (other than the strategic reduction in price included as part of the cost-leadership component) $1.35/unit × 1,150,000 units	$1,552,500 U
Change in prices of inputs (cost effect of price recovery)	607,500 U
Change in operating income due to product differentiation	$2,160,000 U

The effect of cost leadership on operating income is:

Productivity component	$2,012,500 F
Effect of strategic decision to reduce price ($0.65/unit × 1,150,000 units)	747,500 U
Growth in market share due to productivity improvement and strategic decision to reduce prices	
$3,420,000 (Exhibit 13-5, column 2) × $\frac{50{,}000 \text{ units}}{150{,}000 \text{ units}}$	1,140,000 F
Change in operating income due to cost leadership	$2,405,000 F

A summary of the change in operating income between 2008 and 2009 follows.

Change due to industry market size	$2,280,000 F
Change due to product differentiation	2,160,000 U
Change due to cost leadership	2,405,000 F
Change in operating income	$2,525,000 F

Under different assumptions of how the change in selling price affects the quantity of CX1 sold, the analysis will attribute different amounts to the different strategies. The point to understand is that, consistent with its cost-leadership strategy, the productivity gains of $2,012,500 Chipset made in 2009 were a big part of the increase in operating income in 2009. The Problem for Self-Study on page 485 describes the analysis of the growth, price-recovery, and productivity components for a company following a product-differentiation strategy. The Concepts in Action feature (p. 483) describes the unique challenges that dot-com companies face in choosing a profitable strategy.

Applying the Five-Step Decision-Making Framework to Strategy

We next briefly describe how the five-step decision-making framework, introduced in Chapter 1, is also useful in making decisions about strategy.

1. *Identify the problem and uncertainties.* The decision about what strategy Chipset must choose depends on resolving two uncertainties—whether Chipset can add value to its customers that its competitors cannot emulate, and whether Chipset can develop the necessary internal capabilities to add this value.
2. *Obtain information.* Chipset's managers develop customer preference maps to identify various product attributes desired by customers and the competitive advantage or disadvantage it has on each attribute relative to competitors. The managers also gather data on Chipset's internal capabilities. How good is Chipset's R&D capability in designing and developing innovative new products? How good are its process and marketing capabilities?
3. *Make predictions about the future.* Chipset's managers conclude that they will not be able to develop innovative new products in a cost-effective way. They believe that Chipset's strength lies in improving quality, reengineering processes, reducing costs, and delivering products faster to customers.
4. *Make decisions by choosing among alternatives.* Chipset's management decides to follow a cost leadership rather than a product differentiation strategy. It decides to introduce a balanced scorecard to align and measure its quality improvement and process reengineering efforts.
5. *Implement the decision, evaluate performance, and learn.* On its balanced scorecard, Chipset's managers compare actual and targeted performance and evaluate possible cause-and-effect relationships. They learn, for example, that increasing the percentage of processes with advanced controls improves yield. As a result, just as they had anticipated, productivity and growth initiatives result in increases in operating income in 2009. The one change Chipset's managers plan for 2010 is to make modest changes in product features that might help differentiate CX1 somewhat from competing products. In this way, feedback and learning help in the development of future strategies and implementation plans.

Downsizing and the Management of Capacity

Learning Objective 5

Distinguish engineered costs

. . . a cause-and-effect relationship exists between output produced and costs incurred

from discretionary costs

. . . no cause-and-effect relationship exists between output produced and costs incurred

As we saw in our discussion of the productivity component, fixed costs are tied to capacity. Unlike variable costs, fixed costs do not change automatically with changes in activity level (for example, fixed conversion costs do not change with changes in the quantity of silicon wafers started into production). How then can managers reduce capacity-based fixed costs? By measuring and managing unused capacity. **Unused capacity** is the amount of productive capacity available over and above the productive capacity employed to meet consumer demand in the current period. To understand unused capacity, it is necessary to distinguish *engineered costs* from *discretionary costs.*

Engineered costs result from a cause-and-effect relationship between the cost driver—output—and the (direct or indirect) resources used to produce that output. In the Chipset example, direct material costs are *direct engineered costs.* Conversion costs are an example of *indirect engineered costs.* Consider 2009. The output of 1,150,000 units of CX1 and the efficiency with which inputs are converted into outputs result in

2,900,000 square centimeters of silicon wafers being started into production. Manufacturing-conversion-cost resources used to produce 1,150,000 units of CX1 equal $12,615,000 ($4.35 per sq. cm. × 2,900,000 sq. cm.), assuming that the cost of resources used increases proportionately with the number of square centimeters of silicon wafers processed. Conversion costs ($15,225,000) are higher because these costs relate to the manufacturing capacity to process 3,500,000 square centimeters of silicon wafer ($4.35 per sq. cm. × 3,500,000 sq. cm. = $15,225,000). Although these costs are fixed in the short run, over the long run there is a cause-and-effect relationship between output and manufacturing capacity required (and conversion costs needed). Engineered costs can be variable or fixed in the short run.

Discretionary costs have two important features: (1) They arise from periodic (usually annual) decisions regarding the maximum amount to be incurred; and (2) they have no measurable cause-and-effect relationship between output and resources used. There is often a delay between when a resource is acquired and when it is used. Examples of discretionary costs include advertising, executive training, R&D, and corporate-staff department costs such as legal, human resources, and public relations. Unlike engineered costs, a noteworthy aspect of discretionary costs is that managers are seldom confident that the "correct" amounts are being spent. The founder of Lever Brothers, an international consumer-products company, once noted, "Half the money I spend on advertising is wasted; the trouble is, I don't know which half!" In the Chipset example, R&D costs are discretionary costs because there is no measurable cause-and-effect relationship between output of 1,150,000 units produced and the R&D resources needed or used.[9]

Exhibit 13-6 summarizes two key distinctions between engineered and discretionary costs: the type of process and the level of uncertainty represented in a cost.

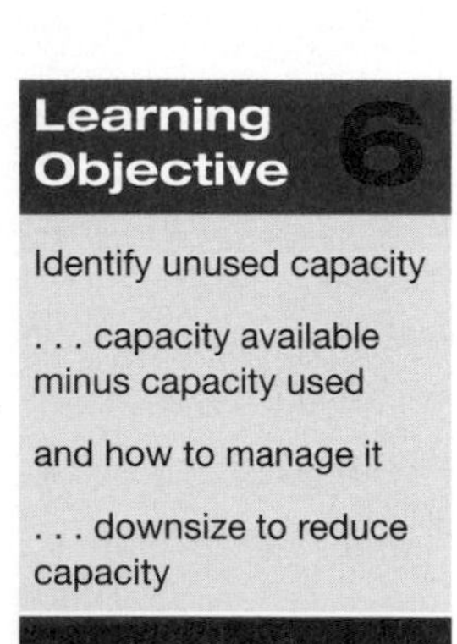

Learning Objective 6

Identify unused capacity

. . . capacity available minus capacity used

and how to manage it

. . . downsize to reduce capacity

Identifying Unused Capacity for Engineered and Discretionary Overhead Costs

How does the distinction between engineered and discretionary costs help a manager understand and manage unused capacity? Actually, each of these costs has a very different relationship to capacity. Consider engineered conversion costs. As shown in Exhibit 13-7, Chipset management indicates that manufacturing capacity can be added or reduced in increments to process 250,000 square centimeters of silicon wafers. At each level, conversion costs are fixed. For example, conversion costs are fixed at $13,050,000 if Chipset

Exhibit 13-6

Differences Between Engineered Costs and Discretionary Costs

	Engineered Costs (Examples: Manufacturing, Distribution)	Discretionary Costs (Examples: R&D, Advertising, Public Relations)
Type of process or activity	**a.** Detailed and physically observable **b.** Repetitive	**a.** Black box (knowledge of process is sketchy or unavailable) **b.** Nonrepetitive or nonroutine
Level of uncertainty (the possibility that actual costs will deviate from expected costs)	Moderate or small	Large

Source: This exhibit is a modification of one suggested by H. Itami.

[9] Managers also describe some costs as infrastructure costs—costs that arise from having property, plant, and equipment and a functioning organization. Examples are depreciation, long-run lease rental, and the acquisition of long-run technical capabilities. These costs are generally fixed costs because they are committed to and acquired before they are used. Infrastructure costs can be engineered or discretionary. For instance, manufacturing-overhead cost incurred at Chipset to acquire manufacturing capacity is an infrastructure cost that is an example of an engineered cost. In the long run, there is a cause-and-effect relationship between output and manufacturing-overhead costs needed to produce that output. R&D cost incurred to acquire technical capability is an infrastructure cost that is an example of a discretionary cost. There is no measurable cause-and-effect relationship between output and R&D cost incurred.

Concepts in Action

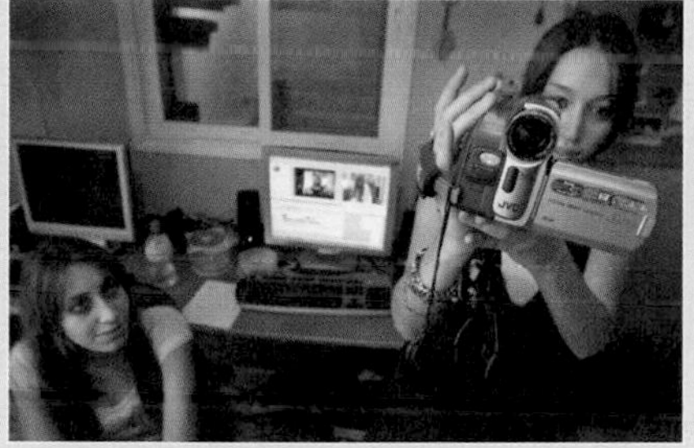

The Growth vs. Profitability Choice at YouTube

Competitive advantage comes from product differentiation or cost leadership. Successful implementation of these strategies helps a company to be profitable and to grow. Many Web start-ups pursue a strategy of short-run growth to build a customer-base, with the goal of later benefiting from such growth by either charging user fees or sustaining a free service for users supported by advertisers. However, during the 1990s dot-com boom (and subsequent bust), the most spectacular failures occurred in dot-com companies that followed the "get big fast" model but then failed to differentiate their products or reduce their costs.

Today, hundreds of Web 2.0 companies (second generation Web-based communities and hosted services), most notably YouTube, face this challenge. At YouTube, users can upload, view, and share digital video clips for free. This service allows users to easily contribute videos, avoid the technology limitations of sharing videos via email or FTP, and find others' clips using keywords (or tags). Additionally, many media companies upload their clips to YouTube to ensure greater distribution of their content. Within months, YouTube became the largest video-aggregation site on the Internet, and soon after was one of the Internet's busiest sites with more than 20 million users. In response to this phenomenal growth, search-engine giant Google purchased YouTube in November 2006 for $1.65 billion.

The question Google must answer is: How can YouTube be made profitable? Despite its rapid growth, YouTube generates very little revenue (mostly through advertising and charging companies to post their content). Moreover, the backbone of the YouTube service is supported by an estimated 45 terabytes of data storage—about 5,000 home computers' worth. It also requires several million dollars' worth of Internet bandwidth a month to transmit video files. The cost structure of YouTube means that the company must generate millions of dollars a month in revenue to sustain its operations over the long term. But how? Generally, there are three popular methods of online revenue generation:

1. Subscriptions: Many Internet sites, including Salesforce.com, charge users monthly subscription fees. Others such as business-networking site LinkedIn and sports-portal ESPN.com offer free access, but charge users for more advanced features and content.
2. Advertising: Popular sites including MySpace and Google provide Web site access free of charge, but include context-specific advertisements on all pages to generate income.
3. Transactions: Auction site eBay and payment-service PayPal earn revenue by collecting a percentage of individuals' transactions using their services.

In late 2007, YouTube began pursuing a unique advertising-based strategy. Careful not to alienate its users by making them watch commercials before their selected videos, YouTube rolled-out unobtrusive 10-second mini commercials at the bottom of its videos. Companies such as New Line Cinema, BMW, Fox, and Warner Brothers began advertising their new products and movies alongside selected videos chosen by the companies based on video topic, viewer demographics, and other factors. YouTube provides advertisers with a highly targeted and differentiated advertising opportunity. YouTube expects that this product differentiation will drive its future profitability.

Sources: YouTube Fact Sheet (July 2007), Available from YouTube. www.youtube.com/t/fact_sheet; H. Green, "YouTube: Waiting for the Payoff," *BusinessWeek*, September 18, 2006; L. Gomes, "Will All of Us Get Our 15 Minutes On a YouTube Video?" *The Wall Street Journal*, August 30, 2006; K. Delaney, "YouTube Sketches a Path to Profitability" *The Wall Street Journal*, June 29, 2006; A. Edgecliffe-Johnson, "Google Unveils YouTube Advertising Format," *Financial Times*, August 22, 2007.

wants enough capacity to process between 2,750,001 and 3,000,000 square centimeters of silicon wafers. If Chipset wants to process say, 3,100,000 square centimeters, it would need to increase its capacity to 3,250,000 square centimeters, an increase of 250,000 square centimeters of capacity at a cost of $1,087,500 ($4.35 per sq. cm. × 250,000 sq. cm.).

At the start of 2009, Chipset had capacity to process 3,750,000 square centimeters of silicon wafers. Quality and productivity improvements made during 2009 enabled Chipset to produce 1,150,000 units of CX1 by processing 2,900,000 square centimeters of silicon wafers. Chipset calculates its unused manufacturing capacity as 850,000 (3,750,000 − 2,900,000) square centimeters of silicon-wafer processing capacity at the beginning of 2009. At the 2009 conversion cost of $4.35 per square centimeter,

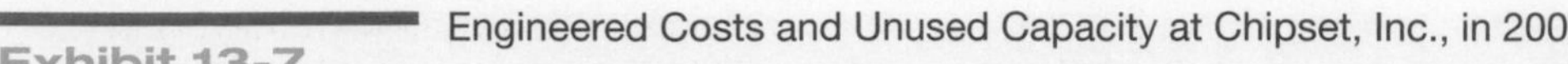

Exhibit 13-7 Engineered Costs and Unused Capacity at Chipset, Inc., in 2009

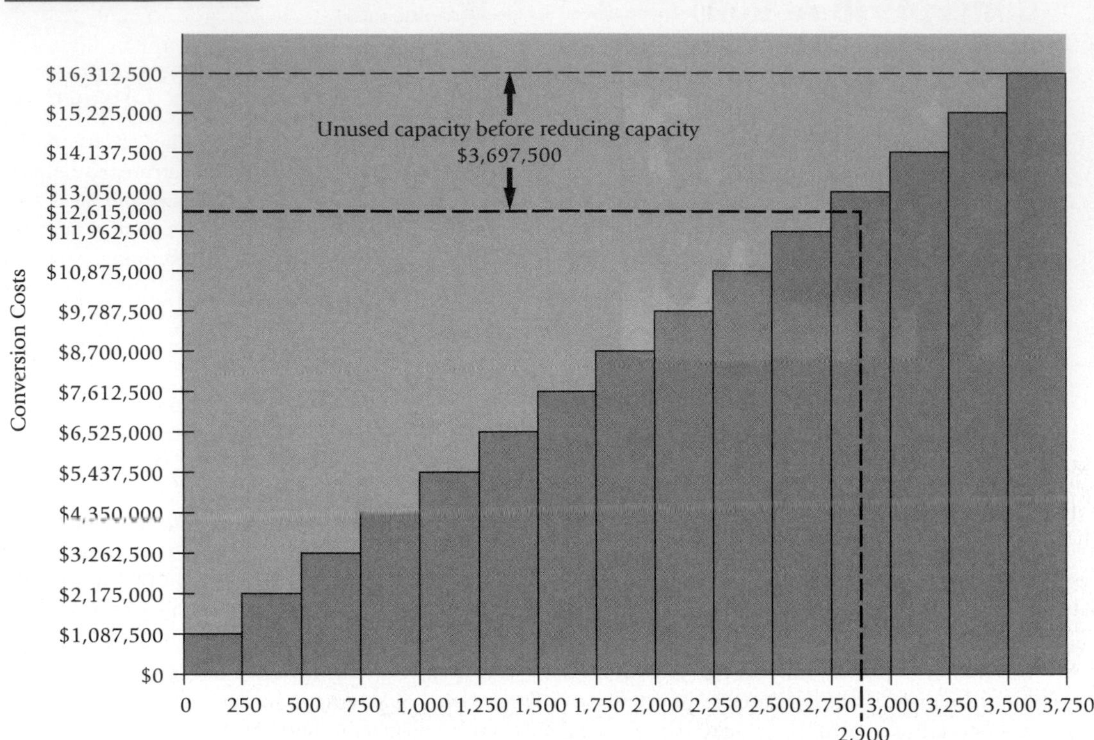

$$\text{Cost of unused capacity} = \text{Cost of capacity at the beginning of the year} - \text{Manufacturing resources used during the year}$$

$$= (3{,}750{,}000 \text{ sq. cm.} \times \$4.35 \text{ per sq. cm.}) - (2{,}900{,}000 \text{ sq. cm.} \times \$4.35 \text{ per sq. cm.})$$

$$= \$16{,}312{,}500 - \$12{,}615{,}000 = \$3{,}697{,}500$$

The absence of a cause-and-effect relationship makes identifying unused capacity for discretionary costs difficult. Management cannot determine the R&D resources used for the actual output produced to compare to R&D capacity. And without a measure of capacity used, it is not possible to compute unused capacity.

Managing Unused Capacity

What actions can Chipset management take when it identifies unused capacity? In general, it has two alternatives: Chipset can attempt to eliminate the unused capacity, or it can attempt to grow output to utilize the unused capacity.

In recent years, many companies have *downsized* in an attempt to eliminate their unused capacity. **Downsizing** (also called **rightsizing**) is an integrated approach of configuring processes, products, and people to match costs to the activities that need to be performed to operate effectively and efficiently in the present and future. Companies such as AT&T, Delta Airlines, General Motors, IBM, and Scott Paper have downsized to focus on their core businesses and have instituted organization changes to increase efficiency, reduce costs, and improve quality. However, downsizing often means eliminating jobs, which can adversely affect employee morale and the culture of a company. Downsizing is best done in the context of a company's overall strategy and by retaining individuals who have strong management, leadership, technical skills and experience.

Consider Chipset's alternatives with respect to its unused manufacturing capacity. Because it needed to process 2,900,000 square centimeters of silicon wafers in 2009, it could have reduced capacity to 3,000,000 square centimeters (recall, manufacturing capacity can be added or reduced only in increments of 250,000 sq. cm.), resulting in cost savings of $3,262,500 [(3,750,000 sq. cm. − 3,000,000 sq. cm.) × $4.35 per sq. cm.]. Chipset's strategy, however, was not only to reduce costs but also to grow its business. So early in 2009, Chipset reduced its manufacturing capacity by only 250,000 square centimeters—from 3,750,000 square centimeters to 3,500,000 square centimeters—saving $1,087,500 ($4.35 per sq. cm. × 250,000 sq. cm.). It retained some unused capacity for future growth. By avoiding greater reductions in capacity, it also maintained the morale of its skilled and capable workforce. The success of this strategy will depend on Chipset achieving the future growth it has projected.

Because identifying unused capacity for discretionary costs is difficult, downsizing or otherwise, managing this unused capacity is also difficult. Chipset's management uses judgment and discretion to reduce R&D costs by $100,000 in 2009. Its goal is to reduce R&D costs without significantly affecting the output of the R&D activity. Greater reductions in R&D costs could harm the business by slowing down needed product and process improvements. Chipset must meet its need for cost reductions without compromising quality, continuous improvement, and future growth.

Problem for Self-Study

Following a strategy of product differentiation, Westwood Corporation makes a high-end kitchen range hood, KE8. Westwood's data for 2008 and 2009 follow:

	2008	2009
1. Units of KE8 produced and sold	40,000	42,000
2. Selling price	$100	$110
3. Direct materials (square feet)	120,000	123,000
4. Direct material cost per square foot	$10	$11
5. Manufacturing capacity for KE8	50,000 units	50,000 units
6. Conversion costs	$1,000,000	$1,100,000
7. Conversion cost per unit of capacity (Row 6 ÷ Row 5)	$20	$22
8. Selling and customer-service capacity	30 customers	29 customers
9. Selling and customer-service costs	$720,000	$725,000
10. Cost per customer of selling and customer-service capacity (Row 9 ÷ Row 8)	$24,000	$25,000

Westwood produced no defective units and reduced direct material usage per unit of KE8 in 2009. Conversion costs in each year are tied to manufacturing capacity. Selling and customer service costs are related to the number of customers that the selling and service functions are designed to support. Westwood has 23 customers (wholesalers) in 2008 and 25 customers in 2009.

Required

1. Describe briefly the elements you would include in Westwood's balanced scorecard.
2. Calculate the growth, price-recovery, and productivity components that explain the change in operating income from 2008 to 2009.
3. Suppose during 2009, the market size for high-end kitchen range hoods grew 3% in terms of number of units and all increases in market share (that is, increases in the number of units sold greater than 3%) are due to Westwood's product-differentiation strategy. Calculate how much of the change in operating income from 2008 to 2009 is due to the industry-market-size factor, cost leadership, and product differentiation.
4. How successful has Westwood been in implementing its strategy? Explain.

Solution

1. The balanced scorecard should describe Westwood's product-differentiation strategy. Elements that should be included in its balanced scorecard are:
   - **Financial perspective** Increase in operating income from higher margins on KE8 and from growth

- **Customer perspective** Market share in the high-end market and customer satisfaction
- **Internal business process perspective** Manufacturing quality, order-delivery time, on-time delivery, new product features added, development time for new products, and improvements in manufacturing processes
- **Learning-and-growth perspective** Percentage of employees trained in process and quality management and employee satisfaction ratings

2. Operating income for each year is:

	2008	2009
Revenues		
($100 per unit × 40,000 units; $110 per unit × 42,000 units)	$4,000,000	$4,620,000
Costs		
Direct material costs		
($10 per sq. ft. × 120,000 sq. ft.; $11 per sq. ft. × 123,000 sq. ft.)	1,200,000	1,353,000
Conversion costs		
($20 per unit × 50,000 units; $22 per unit × 50,000 units)	1,000,000	1,100,000
Selling and customer-service cost		
($24,000 per customer × 30 customers; $25,000 per customer × 29 customers)	720,000	725,000
Total costs	2,920,000	3,178,000
Operating income	$1,080,000	$1,442,000
Change in operating income	$362,000 F	

Growth Component of Operating Income Change

$$\text{Revenue effect of growth} = \left(\begin{array}{c}\text{Actual units of}\\ \text{output sold}\\ \text{in 2009}\end{array} - \begin{array}{c}\text{Actual units of}\\ \text{output sold}\\ \text{in 2008}\end{array}\right) \times \begin{array}{c}\text{Selling}\\ \text{price}\\ \text{in 2008}\end{array}$$

$$= (42{,}000 \text{ units} - 40{,}000 \text{ units}) \times \$100 \text{ per unit} = \$200{,}000 \text{ F}$$

$$\begin{array}{c}\text{Cost effect}\\ \text{of growth for}\\ \text{variable costs}\end{array} = \left(\begin{array}{c}\text{Units of input}\\ \text{required to produce}\\ \text{2009 output in 2008}\end{array} - \begin{array}{c}\text{Actual units of input}\\ \text{used to produce}\\ \text{2008 output}\end{array}\right) \times \begin{array}{c}\text{Input}\\ \text{price}\\ \text{in 2008}\end{array}$$

$$\begin{array}{c}\text{Cost effect}\\ \text{of growth for}\\ \text{direct materials}\end{array} = \left(120{,}000 \text{ sq. ft} \times \frac{42{,}000 \text{ units}}{40{,}000 \text{ units}} - 120{,}000 \text{ sq. ft.}\right) \times \$10 \text{ per sq. ft.}$$

$$= (126{,}000 \text{ sq. ft.} - 120{,}000 \text{ sq. ft.}) \times \$10 \text{ per sq. ft.} = \$60{,}000 \text{ U}$$

$$\begin{array}{c}\text{Cost effect}\\ \text{of growth for}\\ \text{fixed costs}\end{array} = \left(\begin{array}{c}\text{Actual units of capacity in}\\ \text{2008, because adequate capacity}\\ \text{exists to produce 2009 output in 2008}\end{array} - \begin{array}{c}\text{Actual units}\\ \text{of capacity}\\ \text{in 2008}\end{array}\right) \times \begin{array}{c}\text{Price per}\\ \text{unit of}\\ \text{capacity}\\ \text{in 2008}\end{array}$$

Cost effects of growth for fixed costs are:

Conversion costs: (50,000 units − 50,000 units) × $20 per unit = $0

Selling and customer-service costs: (30 customers − 30 customers) × $24,000 per customer = $0

In summary, the net increase in operating income attributable to growth equals:

Revenue effect of growth		$200,000 F
Cost effect of growth		
Direct material costs	$60,000 U	
Conversion costs	0	
Selling and customer-service costs	0	60,000 U
Change in operating income due to growth		$140,000 F

Price-Recovery Component of Operating-Income Change

$$\begin{array}{c}\text{Revenue effect of}\\ \text{price recovery}\end{array} = \left(\begin{array}{c}\text{Selling price}\\ \text{in 2009}\end{array} - \begin{array}{c}\text{Selling price}\\ \text{in 2008}\end{array}\right) \times \begin{array}{c}\text{Actual units}\\ \text{of output}\\ \text{sold in 2009}\end{array}$$

$$= (\$110 \text{ per unit} - \$100 \text{ per unit}) \times 42{,}000 \text{ units} = \$420{,}000 \text{ F}$$

$$\begin{array}{c}\text{Cost effect of}\\ \text{price recovery}\\ \text{for variable costs}\end{array} = \left(\begin{array}{c}\text{Input}\\ \text{price}\\ \text{in 2009}\end{array} - \begin{array}{c}\text{Input}\\ \text{price}\\ \text{in 2008}\end{array}\right) \times \begin{array}{c}\text{Units of input}\\ \text{required to produce}\\ \text{2009 output in 2008}\end{array}$$

$$\text{Direct material costs: } (\$11 \text{ per sq. ft.} - \$10 \text{ per sq. ft.}) \times 126{,}000 \text{ sq. ft.} = \$126{,}000 \text{ U}$$

$$\begin{array}{c}\text{Cost effect of}\\ \text{price recovery}\\ \text{for fixed costs}\end{array} = \left(\begin{array}{c}\text{Price per}\\ \text{unit of}\\ \text{capacity}\\ \text{in 2009}\end{array} - \begin{array}{c}\text{Price per}\\ \text{unit of}\\ \text{capacity}\\ \text{in 2008}\end{array}\right) \times \begin{array}{c}\text{Actual units of capacity in}\\ \text{2008, because adequate capacity}\\ \text{exists to produce 2009 output in 2008}\end{array}$$

Cost effects of price recovery for fixed costs are:

$$\text{Conversion costs: } (\$22 \text{ per unit} - 20 \text{ per unit}) \times 50{,}000 \text{ units} = \$100{,}000 \text{ U}$$

$$\text{Selling and cust.-service costs: } (\$25{,}000 \text{ per cust.} - \$24{,}000 \text{ per cust.}) \times 30 \text{ customers} = \$30{,}000 \text{ U}$$

In summary, the net increase in operating income attributable to price recovery equals:

Revenue effect of price recovery		$420,000 F
Cost effect of price recovery		
Direct material costs	$126,000 U	
Conversion costs	100,000 U	
Selling and customer-service costs	30,000 U	256,000 U
Change in operating income due to price recovery		$164,000 F

Productivity Component of Operating-Income Change

$$\begin{array}{c}\text{Cost effect of}\\ \text{productivity for}\\ \text{variable costs}\end{array} = \left(\begin{array}{c}\text{Actual units of}\\ \text{input used to produce}\\ \text{2009 output}\end{array} - \begin{array}{c}\text{Units of input}\\ \text{required to produce}\\ \text{2009 output in 2008}\end{array}\right) \times \begin{array}{c}\text{Input}\\ \text{price in}\\ \text{2009}\end{array}$$

$$\begin{array}{l}\text{Cost effect of}\\ \text{productivity for}\\ \text{direct materials}\end{array} = (123{,}000 \text{ sq. ft.} - 126{,}000 \text{ sq. ft.}) \times \$11 \text{ per sq. ft.} = \$33{,}000 \text{ F}$$

$$\begin{array}{c}\text{Cost effect of}\\ \text{productivity for}\\ \text{fixed costs}\end{array} = \left(\begin{array}{c}\text{Actual units}\\ \text{of capacity}\\ \text{in 2009}\end{array} - \begin{array}{c}\text{Actual units of capacity in}\\ \text{2008, because adequate}\\ \text{capacity exists to produce}\\ \text{2009 output in 2008}\end{array}\right) \times \begin{array}{c}\text{Price per}\\ \text{unit of}\\ \text{capacity}\\ \text{in 2009}\end{array}$$

Cost effects of productivity for fixed costs are:

$$\text{Conversion costs: } (50{,}000 \text{ units} - 50{,}000 \text{ units}) \times \$22 \text{ per unit} = \$0$$

$$\text{Selling and customer-service costs: } (29 \text{ customers} - 30 \text{ customers}) \times \$25{,}000/\text{customer} = \$25{,}000\text{F}$$

In summary, the net increase in operating income attributable to productivity equals:

Cost effect of productivity:	
Direct material costs	$33,000 F
Conversion costs	0
Selling and customer-service costs	25,000 F
Change in operating income due to productivity	$58,000 F

A summary of the change in operating income between 2008 and 2009 follows:

	Income Statement Amounts in 2008 (1)	Revenue and Cost Effects of Growth Component in 2009 (2)	Revenue and Cost Effects of Price-Recovery Component in 2009 (3)	Cost Effect of Productivity Component in 2009 (4)	Income Statement Amounts in 2009 (5) = (1) + (2) + (3) + (4)
Revenue	$4,000,000	$200,000 F	$420,000 F	—	$4,620,000
Costs	2,920,000	60,000 U	256,000 U	$58,000 F	3,178,000
Operating income	$1,080,000	$140,000 F	$164,000 F	$58,000 F	$1,442,000
			362,000 F		

Change in operating income

3. *Effect of the industry-market-size factor on operating income* Of the increase in sales from 40,000 to 42,000 units, 3%, or 1,200 units (0.03 × 40,000), is due to growth in market size, and 800 units (2,000 − 1,200) are due to an increase in market share. The change in Westwood's operating income from the industry-market-size factor rather than specific strategic actions is:

$140,000 (column 2 of preceding table) $\times \dfrac{1{,}200 \text{ units}}{2{,}000 \text{ units}}$	$84,000 F

Effect of product differentiation on operating income

Increase in the selling price of KE8 (revenue effect of the price-recovery component)	$420,000 F
Increase in prices of inputs (cost effect of the price-recovery component)	256,000 U
Growth in market share due to product differentiation	
$140,000 (column 2 of preceding table) $\times \dfrac{800 \text{ units}}{2{,}000 \text{ units}}$	56,000 F
Change in operating income due to product differentiation	$220,000 F

Effect of cost leadership on operating income

Productivity component	$58,000 F

A summary of the net increase in operating income from 2008 to 2009 follows:

Change due to the industry-market-size factor	$ 84,000 F
Change due to product differentiation	220,000 F
Change due to cost leadership	58,000 F
Change in operating income	$362,000 F

4. The analysis of operating income indicates that a significant amount of the increase in operating income resulted from Westwood's successful implementation of its product-differentiation strategy. The company was able to continue to charge a premium price for KE8 while increasing market share. Westwood was also able to earn additional operating income from improving its productivity.

Decision Points

The following question-and-answer format summarizes the chapter's learning objectives. Each decision presents a key question related to a learning objective. The guidelines are the answer to that question.

Decision	Guidelines
1. What are two generic strategies a company can use?	Two generic strategies are product differentiation and cost leadership. Product differentiation is offering products and services that are perceived by customers as being superior and unique. Cost leadership is achieving low costs relative to competitors. A company chooses its strategy based on an understanding of customer preferences and its own internal capabilities, while differentiating itself from its competitors.
2. What is reengineering?	Reengineering is the rethinking of business processes, such as the order-delivery process, to improve critical performance measures such as cost, quality, and customer satisfaction.
3. How can an organization translate its strategy into a set of performance measures?	An organization can develop a balanced scorecard that provides the framework for a strategic measurement and management system. The balanced scorecard measures performance from four perspectives: (1) financial, (2) customer, (3) internal business processes, and (4) learning and growth. Organizations sometimes implement strategy maps to represent more detailed cause-and-effect relationships across various scorecard measures.
4. How can a company analyze changes in operating income to evaluate the success of its strategy?	To evaluate the success of its strategy, a company can subdivide the change in operating income into growth, price-recovery, and productivity components. The growth component measures the change in revenues and costs from selling more or less units, assuming no changes in prices of outputs and inputs or efficiencies. The price-recovery component measures changes in revenues and costs solely as a result of changes in the prices of outputs and inputs. The productivity component measures the decrease in costs from using fewer inputs, a better mix of inputs, and reducing capacity. A company is considered successful in implementing its strategy when changes in operating income align closely with its strategy.
5. How can a company distinguish engineered costs from discretionary costs?	Engineered costs result from a cause-and-effect relationship between output and the resources needed to produce that output. Discretionary costs arise from periodic (usually annual) management decisions regarding the amount to be incurred. Discretionary costs are not tied to a cause-and-effect relationship between inputs and outputs.
6. How can a company identify unused capacity, and if it is present, how can unused capacity be managed?	Identifying unused capacity is easier for engineered costs and more difficult for discretionary costs. Downsizing is an approach to managing unused capacity that matches costs to the activities that need to be performed to operate effectively.

APPENDIX: PRODUCTIVITY MEASUREMENT

Productivity measures the relationship between actual inputs used (both quantities and costs) and actual outputs produced. The lower the inputs for a given quantity of outputs or the higher the outputs for a given quantity of inputs, the higher the productivity. Measuring productivity improvements over time highlights the specific input-output relationships that contribute to cost leadership.

Partial Productivity Measures

Partial productivity, the most frequently used productivity measure, compares the quantity of output produced with the quantity of an individual input used. In its most common form, partial productivity is expressed as a ratio:

$$\text{Partial productivity} = \frac{\text{Quantity of output produced}}{\text{Quantity of input used}}$$

The higher the ratio, the greater the productivity.

Consider direct materials productivity at Chipset in 2009.

$$\begin{aligned}\text{Direct materials partial productivity} &= \frac{\text{Quantity of CX1 units produced during 2009}}{\text{Quantity of direct materials used to produce CX1 in 2009}} \\ &= \frac{1{,}150{,}000 \text{ units of CX1}}{2{,}900{,}000 \text{ sq. cm. of direct materials}} \\ &= 0.397 \text{ units of CX1 per sq. cm. of direct materials}\end{aligned}$$

Note direct materials partial productivity ignores Chipset's other inputs, manufacturing conversion capacity, and R&D. Partial-productivity measures become more meaningful when comparisons are made that examine productivity changes over time, either across different facilities or relative to a benchmark. Exhibit 13-8 presents partial-productivity measures for Chipset's inputs for 2009 and the comparable 2008 inputs that would have been used to produce 2009 output, using information from the productivity-component calculations on pages 478–479. These measures compare actual inputs used in 2009 to produce 1,150,000 units of CX1 with inputs that would have been used in 2009 had the input–output relationship from 2008 continued in 2009.

Evaluating Changes in Partial Productivities

Note how the partial-productivity measures differ for variable-cost and fixed-cost components. For variable-cost elements, such as direct materials, productivity improvements measure the reduction in input resources used to produce output (3,450,000 square centimeters of silicon wafers to 2,900,000 square centimeters). For fixed-cost elements such as manufacturing conversion capacity, partial productivity measures the reduction in overall capacity from 2008 to 2009 (3,750,000 square centimeters of silicon wafers to 3,500,000 square centimeters) regardless of the amount of capacity actually used in each period.

An advantage of partial-productivity measures is that they focus on a single input. As a result, they are simple to calculate and easily understood by operations personnel. Managers and operators examine these numbers to understand the reasons underlying productivity changes—better training of workers, lower labor turnover, better incentives, improved methods, or substitution of materials for labor. Isolating the relevant factors helps Chipset implement and sustain these practices in the future.

For all their advantages, partial-productivity measures also have serious drawbacks. Because partial productivity focuses on only one input at a time rather than on all inputs

Exhibit 13-8

Comparing Chipset's Partial Productivities in 2008 and 2009

Input (1)	Partial Productivity in 2009 (2)	Comparable Partial Productivity Based on 2008 Input–Output Relationships (3)	Percentage Change from 2008 to 2009 (4)
Direct materials	$\frac{1{,}150{,}000}{2{,}900{,}000} = 0.397$	$\frac{1{,}150{,}000}{3{,}450{,}000} = 0.333$	$\frac{0.397 - 0.333}{0.333} = 19.2\%$
Manufacturing conversion capacity	$\frac{1{,}150{,}000}{3{,}500{,}000} = 0.329$	$\frac{1{,}150{,}000}{3{,}750{,}000} = 0.307$	$\frac{0.329 - 0.307}{0.307} = 7.2\%$
R&D	$\frac{1{,}150{,}000}{39} = 29{,}487$	$\frac{1{,}150{,}000}{40} = 28{,}750$	$\frac{29{,}487 - 28{,}750}{28{,}750} = 2.6\%$

simultaneously, managers cannot evaluate the effect on overall productivity, if (say) manufacturing-conversion-capacity partial productivity increases while direct materials partial productivity decreases. Total factor productivity (TFP), or total productivity, is a measure of productivity that considers all inputs simultaneously.

Total Factor Productivity

Total factor productivity (**TFP**) is the ratio of the quantity of output produced to the costs of all inputs used based on current-period prices.

$$\text{Total factor productivity} = \frac{\text{Quantity of output produced}}{\text{Costs of all inputs used}}$$

TFP considers all inputs simultaneously and the trade-offs across inputs based on current input prices. Do not think of all productivity measures as physical measures lacking financial content—how many units of output are produced per unit of input. TFP is intricately tied to minimizing total cost—a financial objective.

Calculating and Comparing Total Factor Productivity

We first calculate Chipset's TFP in 2009, using 2009 prices and 1,150,000 units of output produced (based on information from the first part of the productivity-component calculations on pp. 478–479).

$$\begin{aligned}\text{Total factor productivity for 2009 using 2009 prices} &= \frac{\text{Quantity of output produced in 2009}}{\text{Costs of inputs used in 2009 based on 2009 prices}}\\ &= \frac{1{,}150{,}000}{(2{,}900{,}000 \times \$1.50) + (3{,}500{,}000 \times \$4.35) + (39 \times \$100{,}000)}\\ &= \frac{1{,}150{,}000}{\$23{,}475{,}000}\\ &= 0.048988 \text{ units of output per dollar of input cost}\end{aligned}$$

By itself, the 2009 TFP of 0.048988 units of CX1 per dollar of input costs is not particularly helpful. We need something to compare the 2009 TFP against. One alternative is to compare TFPs of other similar companies in 2009. However, finding similar companies and obtaining accurate comparable data are often difficult. Companies, therefore, usually compare their own TFPs over time. In the Chipset example, we use as a benchmark TFP calculated using the inputs that Chipset would have used in 2008 to produce 1,150,000 units of CX1 at 2009 prices (that is, we use the costs calculated from the second part of the productivity-component calculations on pp. 478–479). Why do we use 2009 prices? Because using the current year's prices in both calculations controls for input-price differences and focuses the analysis on adjustments the manager made in quantities of inputs in response to changes in prices.

$$\begin{aligned}\text{Benchmark TFP} &= \frac{\text{Quantity of output produced in 2009}}{\text{Costs of inputs that would have been used in 2008 to produce 2009 output}}\\ &= \frac{1{,}150{,}000}{(3{,}450{,}000 \times \$1.50) + (3{,}750{,}000 \times \$4.35) + (40 \times \$100{,}000)}\\ &= \frac{1{,}150{,}000}{\$25{,}487{,}500}\\ &= 0.045120 \text{ units of output per dollar of input cost}\end{aligned}$$

Using 2009 prices, TFP increased 8.6% [(0.048988 − 0.045120) ÷ 0.045120 = 0.086, or 8.6%] from 2008 to 2009. Note that the 8.6% increase in TFP also equals the $2,012,500 gain (Exhibit 13-5, column 4) divided by the $23,475,000 of actual costs incurred in

2009 (Exhibit 13-5, column 5). Total factor productivity increased because Chipset produced more output per dollar of input cost in 2009 relative to 2008, measured in both years using 2009 prices. The gain in TFP occurs because Chipset increases the partial productivities of individual inputs and, consistent with its strategy, seeks a combination of inputs to produce CX1 to lower its costs. Note that increases in TFP cannot be due to differences in input prices because we used 2009 prices to evaluate both the inputs that Chipset would have used in 2008 to produce 1,150,000 units of CX1 and the inputs actually used in 2009.

Using Partial and Total Factor Productivity Measures

A major advantage of TFP is that it measures the combined productivity of all inputs used to produce output and explicitly considers gains from using fewer physical inputs as well as substitution among inputs. Managers can analyze these numbers to understand the reasons for changes in TFP—for example, better human resource management practices, higher quality of materials, or improved manufacturing methods.

Although TFP measures are comprehensive, operations personnel find financial TFP measures more difficult to understand and less useful than physical partial-productivity measures. For example, companies that are more labor intensive than Chipset use manufacturing-labor partial-productivity measures. However, if productivity-based bonuses depend on gains in manufacturing-labor partial productivity alone, workers have incentives to substitute materials (and capital) for labor. This substitution improves their own productivity measure, while possibly decreasing the overall productivity of the company as measured by TFP. To overcome these incentive problems, some companies—for example, TRW, Eaton, and Whirlpool—explicitly adjust bonuses based on manufacturing-labor partial productivity for the effects of other factors such as investments in new equipment and higher levels of scrap. That is, they combine partial productivity with TFP-like measures.

Many companies such as Behlen Manufacturing, a steel fabricator, and Dell Computers use both partial productivity and total factor productivity to evaluate performance. *Partial productivity and TFP measures work best together because the strengths of one offset the weaknesses of the other.*

TERMS TO LEARN

This chapter and the Glossary at the end of the book contain definitions of:

balanced scorecard (**p. 466**)
cost leadership (**p. 464**)
discretionary costs (**p. 482**)
downsizing (**p. 484**)
engineered costs (**p. 481**)
growth component (**p. 475**)
partial productivity (**p. 490**)
price-recovery component (**p. 475**)
product differentiation (**p. 464**)
productivity (**p. 489**)
productivity component (**p. 475**)
reengineering (**p. 465**)
rightsizing (**p. 484**)
total factor productivity (TFP) (**p. 491**)
unused capacity (**p. 481**)

ASSIGNMENT MATERIAL

Questions

13-1 Define strategy.

13-2 Describe the five key forces to consider when analyzing an industry.

13-3 Describe two generic strategies.

13-4 What is a customer preference map and why is it useful?

13-5 What is reengineering?

13-6 What are four key perspectives in the balanced scorecard?

13-7 What is a strategy map?

13-8 Describe three features of a good balanced scorecard.

13-9 What are three important pitfalls to avoid when implementing a balanced scorecard?

13-10 Describe three key components in doing a strategic analysis of operating income.

13-11 Why might an analyst incorporate the industry-market-size factor and the interrelationships among the growth, price-recovery, and productivity components into a strategic analysis of operating income?

13-12 How does an engineered cost differ from a discretionary cost?

13-13 What is downsizing?

13-14 What is a partial-productivity measure?

13-15 "We are already measuring total factor productivity. Measuring partial productivities would be of no value." Do you agree? Comment briefly.

Exercises

13-16 Balanced scorecard. La Quinta Corporation manufactures corrugated cardboard boxes. It competes and plans to grow by selling high-quality boxes at a low price and by delivering them to customers quickly after receiving customers' orders. There are many other manufacturers who produce similar boxes. La Quinta believes that continuously improving its manufacturing processes and having satisfied employees are critical to implementing its strategy in 2009.

Required

1. Is La Quinta's 2009 strategy one of product differentiation or cost leadership? Explain briefly.
2. Mesa Corporation, a competitor of La Quinta, manufactures corrugated boxes with more designs and color combinations than La Quinta at a higher price. Mesa's boxes are of high quality but require more time to produce and so have longer delivery times. Draw a simple customer preference map as in Exhibit 13-1 for La Quinta and Mesa using the attributes of price, delivery time, quality, and design.
3. Indicate two measures you would expect to see under each perspective in La Quinta's balanced scorecard for 2009. Use a strategy map as in Exhibit 13-3 to explain your answer.

13-17 Analysis of growth, price-recovery, and productivity components (continuation of 13-16). An analysis of La Quinta's operating-income changes between 2008 and 2009 shows the following:

Operating income for 2008	$1,700,000
Add growth component	70,000
Deduct price-recovery component	(60,000)
Add productivity component	140,000
Operating income for 2009	$1,850,000

The industry market size for corrugated cardboard boxes did not grow in 2009, input prices did not change, and La Quinta reduced the prices of its boxes.

Required

1. Was La Quinta's gain in operating income in 2009 consistent with the strategy you identified in requirement 1 of Exercise 13-16?
2. Explain the productivity component. In general, does it represent savings in only variable costs, only fixed costs, or both variable and fixed costs?

13-18 Strategy, balanced scorecard, merchandising operation. Oceano & Sons buys T-shirts in bulk, applies its own trendsetting silk-screen designs, and then sells the T-shirts to a number of retailers. Oceano wants to be known for its trendsetting designs, and it wants every teenager to be seen in a distinctive Oceano T-shirt. Oceano presents the following data for its first two years of operations, 2008 and 2009.

File Edit View Insert Format Tools Data Window Help

	A	B	C
1		2008	2009
2	Number of T-shirts purchased	200,000	250,000
3	Number of T-shirts discarded	2,000	3,300
4	Number of T-shirts sold	198,000	246,700
5	Average selling price	$ 25.00	$ 26.00
6	Average cost per T-shirt	$ 10.00	$ 8.50
7	Administrative capacity (number of customers)	4,000	3,750
8	Administrative cost	$1,200,000	$1,162,500
9	Administrative cost per customer	$ 300	$ 310
10	Design staff	5	5
11	Total design costs	$ 250,000	$ 275,000
12	Design cost per employee	$ 50,000	$ 55,000

Administrative costs depend on the number of customers that Oceano has created capacity to support, not on the actual number of customers served. Oceano had 3,600 customers in 2008 and 3,500 customers in 2009. At the start of each year, management uses its discretion to determine the number of employees on the design staff for the year. The design staff and its costs have no direct relationship with the number of T-shirts purchased and sold or the number of customers to whom T-shirts are sold.

Required

1. Is Oceano's strategy one of product differentiation or cost leadership? Explain briefly.
2. Describe briefly the key elements Oceano should include in its balanced scorecard and the reasons it should do so.

13-19 Strategic analysis of operating income (continuation of 13-18). Refer to Exercise 13-18.

If you want to use Excel to solve this exercise, go to the Excel Lab at **www.prenhall.com/horngren/cost13e** and download the template for Exercise 13-18.

Required

1. Calculate Oceano's operating income in both 2008 and 2009.
2. Calculate the growth, price-recovery, and productivity components that explain the change in operating income from 2008 to 2009.
3. Comment on your answers in requirement 2. What do each of these components indicate?

13-20 Analysis of growth, price-recovery, and productivity components (continuation of 13-19). Refer to Exercise 13-19. Suppose that the market for silk-screened T-shirts grew by 10% during 2009. All other increases in Oceano's sales were the result of its own strategic actions.

If you want to use Excel to solve this exercise, go to the Excel Lab at **www.prenhall.com/horngren/cost13e** and download the template for Exercise 13-18.

Required

Calculate the change in operating income from 2008 to 2009 due to growth in market size, cost leadership, and product differentiation. How successful has Oceano been in implementing its strategy? Explain.

13-21 Identifying and managing unused capacity (continuation of 13-18). Refer to Exercise 13-18.

If you want to use Excel to solve this exercise, go to the Excel Lab at **www.prenhall.com/horngren/cost13e** and download the template for Exercise 13-18.

Required

1. Calculate the amount and cost of (a) unused administrative capacity and (b) unused design capacity at the beginning of 2009, based on information for 2009. If you are unable to calculate the amount and cost of a particular unused capacity, indicate why not.
2. Suppose Oceano can only add or reduce administrative capacity in increments of 200 customers. What is the maximum amount of costs that Oceano can save in 2009 by downsizing administrative capacity?
3. What factors, other than cost, should Oceano consider before it downsizes administrative capacity?

13-22 Strategy, balanced scorecard. Meredith Corporation makes a special-purpose machine, D4H, used in the textile industry. Meredith has designed the D4H machine for 2009 to be distinct from its competitors. It has been generally regarded as a superior machine. Meredith presents the following data for 2008 and 2009.

	2008	2009
1. Units of D4H produced and sold	200	210
2. Selling price	$40,000	$42,000
3. Direct materials (kilograms)	300,000	310,000
4. Direct material cost per kilogram	$8	$8.50
5. Manufacturing capacity in units of D4H	250	250
6. Total conversion costs	$2,000,000	$2,025,000
7. Conversion cost per unit of capacity	$8,000	$8,100
8. Selling and customer-service capacity	100 customers	95 customers
9. Total selling and customer-service costs	$1,000,000	$940,500
10. Selling and customer-service capacity cost per customer	$10,000	$9,900
11. Design staff	12	12
12. Total design costs	$1,200,000	$1,212,000
13. Design cost per employee	$100,000	$101,000

Meredith produces no defective machines, but it wants to reduce direct materials usage per D4H machine in 2009. Conversion costs in each year depend on production capacity defined in terms of D4H units that can be produced, not the actual units produced. Selling and customer-service costs depend on the number of customers that Meredith can support, not the actual number of customers it serves. Meredith has 75 customers in 2008 and 80 customers in 2009. At the start of each year, management uses its discretion to determine the number of design staff for the year. The design staff and its costs have no direct relationship with the quantity of D4H produced or the number of customers to whom D4H is sold.

Required

1. Is Meredith's strategy one of product differentiation or cost leadership? Explain briefly.
2. Describe briefly key elements that you would include in Meredith's balanced scorecard and the reasons for doing so.

13-23 Strategic analysis of operating income (continuation of 13-22). Refer to Exercise 13-22.

Required

1. Calculate the operating income of Meredith Corporation in 2008 and 2009.
2. Calculate the growth, price-recovery, and productivity components that explain the change in operating income from 2008 to 2009.
3. Comment on your answer in requirement 2. What do these components indicate?

13-24 Analysis of growth, price-recovery, and productivity components (continuation of 13-23). Suppose that during 2009, the market for Meredith's special-purpose machines grew by 3%. All increases in market share (that is, sales increases greater than 3%) are the result of Meredith's strategic actions.

Required

Calculate how much of the change in operating income from 2008 to 2009 is due to the industry-market-size factor, cost leadership, and product differentiation. How successful has Meredith been in implementing its strategy? Explain.

13-25 Identifying and managing unused capacity (continuation of 13-22). Refer to Exercise 13-22.

Required

1. Where possible, calculate the amount and cost of (a) unused manufacturing capacity, (b) unused selling and customer-service capacity, and (c) unused design capacity at the beginning of 2009, based on 2009 production. If you are unable to calculate the amount and cost of unused capacity, indicate why not.
2. Suppose Meredith can add or reduce its manufacturing capacity in increments of 30 units. What is the maximum amount of costs that Meredith could save in 2009 by downsizing manufacturing capacity?
3. Meredith, in fact, does not eliminate any of its unused manufacturing capacity. Why might Meredith not downsize?

13-26 Strategy, balanced scorecard, service company. Snyder Corporation is a small information-systems consulting firm that specializes in helping companies implement sales-management software. The market for Snyder's products is very competitive. To compete, Snyder must deliver quality service at a low cost. Snyder bills clients in terms of units of work performed, which depends on the size and complexity of the sales-management system. Snyder presents the following data for 2008 and 2009.

	2008	2009
1. Units of work performed	60	70
2. Selling price	$50,000	$48,000
3. Software-implementation labor-hours	30,000	32,000
4. Cost per software-implementation labor-hour	$60	$63
5. Software-implementation support capacity (in units of work)	90	90
6. Total cost of software-implementation support	$360,000	$369,000
7. Software-implementation support-capacity cost per unit of work	$4,000	$4,100
8. Number of employees doing software-development	3	3
9. Total software-development costs	$375,000	$390,000
10. Software-development cost per employee	$125,000	$130,000

Software-implementation labor-hour costs are variable costs. Software-implementation support costs for each year depend on the software-implementation support capacity (defined in terms of units of work) that Snyder chooses to maintain each year. It does not vary with the actual units of work performed that year. At the start of each year, management uses its discretion to determine the number of software-development employees. The software-development staff and costs have no direct relationship with the number of units of work performed.

Required

1. Is Snyder Corporation's strategy one of product differentiation or cost leadership? Explain briefly.
2. Describe key elements you would include in Snyder's balanced scorecard and your reasons for doing so.

13-27 Strategic analysis of operating income (continuation of 13-26). Refer to Exercise 13-26.

Required

1. Calculate the operating income of Snyder Corporation in 2008 and 2009.
2. Calculate the growth, price-recovery, and productivity components that explain the change in operating income from 2008 to 2009.
3. Comment on your answer in requirement 2. What do these components indicate?

13-28 Analysis of growth, price-recovery, and productivity components (continuation of 13-27). Suppose that during 2009 the market for implementing sales-management software increases by 5% and that Snyder experiences a 1% decline in selling prices. Assume that any further decreases in selling price and increases in market share are strategic choices by Snyder's management to implement their strategy.

Required

Calculate how much of the change in operating income from 2008 to 2009 is due to the industry-market-size factor, cost leadership, and product differentiation. How successful has Snyder been in implementing its strategy? Explain.

13-29 Identifying and managing unused capacity (continuation of 13-26). Refer to Exercise 13-26.

Required

1. Where possible, calculate the amount and cost of (a) unused software-implementation support capacity and (b) unused software-development capacity at the beginning of 2009, based on units of

work performed in 2009. If you are unable to calculate the amount and cost of unused capacity, indicate why not.

2. Suppose Snyder can add or reduce its software-implementation support capacity in increments of 15 units. What is the maximum amount of costs that Snyder could save in 2009 by downsizing software-implementation support capacity?
3. Snyder, in fact, does not eliminate any of its unused software-implementation support capacity. Why might Snyder not downsize?

Problems

13-30 Balanced scorecard and strategy. Dransfield Company manufactures an electronic component, ZP98. This component is significantly less expensive than similar products sold by Dransfield's competitors. Order-processing time is very short; however, approximately10% of products are defective and returned by the customer. Returns and refunds are handled promptly. Yorunt Manufacturing, Dransfield's main competitor, has a higher priced product with almost no defects, but a longer order-processing time.

Required

1. Draw a simple customer preference map for Dransfield and Yorunt using the attributes of price, quality, and delivery time. Use the format of Exhibit 13-1.
2. Is Dransfield's current strategy that of product differentiation or cost leadership?
3. Dransfield would like to improve quality without significantly increasing costs or order-processing time. Dransfield's managers believe the increased quality will increase sales. What elements should Dransfield include in its balanced scorecard?
4. Draw a strategy map like the one in Exhibit 13-3 to explain cause-and-effect relationships in Dransfield's balanced scorecard.

13-31 Strategic analysis of operating income (continuation of 13-30) Refer to Problem 13-30. Assume that in 2009, Dransfield has changed its processes and trained workers to recognize quality problems and fix them before products are finished and shipped to customers. Quality is now at an acceptable level. Cost per pound of materials is about the same as before, but conversion costs are higher, and Dransfield has raised its selling price in line with the market. Sales have increased and returns have decreased. Dransfield's managers attribute this to higher quality and a price that is still less than Yorunt's. Information about the current period (2009) and last period (2008) follows.

	2008	2009
1a. Units of ZP98 produced and sold	5,000	6,250
1b. Units of ZP98 returned	500	225
1c. Net sales in units	4,500	6,025
2. Selling price	$44	$50
3. Direct materials (pounds) used	2,500	3,125
4. Direct material cost per pound	$10	$10
5. Manufacturing capacity in units of ZP98	8,000	8,000
6. Total conversion costs	$128,000	$184,000
7. Conversion cost per unit of capacity	$16	$23
8. Selling and customer-service capacity	60 customers	60 customers
9. Total selling and customer-service costs	$4,000	$4,180
10. Selling and customer-service capacity cost per customer	$66.67	$69.67
11. Advertising staff	1	1
12. Total advertising costs	$20,000	$24,000
13. Advertising cost per employee	$20,000	$24,000

Conversion costs in each year depend on production capacity defined in terms of ZP98 units that can be produced, not the actual units produced. Selling and customer-service costs depend on the number of customers that Dransfield can support, not the actual number of customers it serves. Dransfield has 50 customers in 2008 and 60 customers in 2009. At the start of each year, management uses its discretion to determine the number of advertising staff for the year. Advertising staff and its costs have no direct relationship with the quantity of ZP98 units produced and sold or the number of customers who buy ZP98.

Required

1. Calculate operating income of Dransfield Company for 2008 and 2009.
2. Calculate the growth, price-recovery, and productivity components that explain the change in operating income from 2008 to 2009.
3. Comment on your answer in requirement 2. What do these components indicate?

13-32 Analysis of growth, price-recovery, and productivity components (continuation of 13-31) Suppose that during 2009, the market for ZP98 grew 8%. All increases in market share (that is, sales increases greater than 8%) are the result of Dransfield's strategic actions.

Required

Calculate how much of the change in operating income from 2008 to 2009 is due to the industry-market-size factor, product differentiation, and cost leadership. How does this relate to Dransfield's strategy and its success in implementation? Explain.

13-33 Identifying and managing unused capacity (continuation of 13-31) Refer to the information for Dransfield Company in 13-31.

Required

1. Calculate the amount and cost of unused capacity for:
   a. Manufacturing
   b. Sales and customer service
   c. Advertising

   If you are unable to calculate the amount and cost of unused capacity, explain why.
2. State two reasons Dransfield might downsize and two reasons they might not downsize.
3. Assume Dransfield has several product lines, of which ZP98 is only one. The manager for the ZP98 product line is evaluated on the basis of manufacturing and customer sales and service costs, but not advertising costs. The manager wants to increase capacity for customers because he thinks the market is growing, and this will cost an additional $1,098. However, the manager is not going to use this extra capacity immediately, so he classifies it as advertising cost rather than customer sales and service cost. How will the deliberate misclassification of this cost affect:
   a. the operating income overall?
   b. the growth, price-recovery, and productivity components?
   c. the evaluation of the ZP98 manager?

You are not required to calculate any numbers when answering requirement 3. Only discuss whether it will have a positive, negative, or no effect; and comment on the ethics of the manager's actions.

13-34 Balanced scorecard. Following is a random-order listing of perspectives, strategic objectives, and performance measures for the balanced scorecard.

Perspectives	**Performance Measures**
Internal business process	Percentage of defective-product units
Customer	Return on assets
Learning and growth	Number of patents
Financial	Employee turnover rate
Strategic Objectives	Net income
Acquire new customers	Customer profitability
Increase shareholder value	Percentage of processes with real-time feedback
Retain customers	Return on sales
Improve manufacturing quality	Average job-related training-hours per employee
Develop profitable customers	Return on equity
Increase proprietary products	Percentage of on-time deliveries by suppliers
Increase information-system capabilities	Product cost per unit
Enhance employee skills	Profit per salesperson
On-time delivery by suppliers	Percentage of error-free invoices
Increase profit generated by each salesperson	Customer cost per unit
Introduce new products	Earnings per share
Minimize invoice-error rate	Number of new customers
	Percentage of customers retained

Required

For each perspective, select those strategic objectives from the list that best relate to it. For each strategic objective, select the most appropriate performance measure(s) from the list.

13-35 Balanced scorecard. (R. Kaplan, adapted) Caltex, Inc., refines gasoline and sells it through its own Caltex Gas Stations. On the basis of market research, Caltex determines that 60% of the overall gasoline market consists of "service-oriented customers," medium- to high-income individuals who are willing to pay a higher price for gas if the gas stations can provide excellent customer service, such as a clean facility, a convenience store, friendly employees, a quick turnaround, the ability to pay by credit card, and high-octane premium gasoline. The remaining 40% of the overall market are "price shoppers" who look to buy the cheapest gasoline available. Caltex's strategy is to focus on the 60% of service-oriented customers. Caltex's balanced scorecard for 2009 follows. For brevity, the initiatives taken under each objective are omitted.

Objectives	Measures	Target Performance	Actual Performance
Financial Perspective			
Increase shareholder value	Operating-income changes from price recovery	$90,000,000	$95,000,000
	Operating-income changes from growth	$65,000,000	$67,000,000
Customer Perspective			
Increase market share	Market share of overall gasoline market	10%	9.8%
Internal-Business-Process Perspective			
Improve gasoline quality	Quality index	94 points	95 points
Improve refinery performance	Refinery-reliability index (%)	91%	91%
Ensure gasoline availability	Product-availability index (%)	99%	100%
Learning-and-Growth Perspective			
Increase refinery process capability	Percentage of refinery processes with advanced controls	88%	90%

Required

1. Was Caltex successful in implementing its strategy in 2009? Explain your answer.
2. Would you have included some measure of employee satisfaction and employee training in the learning-and-growth perspective? Are these objectives critical to Caltex for implementing its strategy? Why or why not? Explain briefly.
3. Explain how Caltex did not achieve its target market share in the total gasoline market but still exceeded its financial targets. Is "market share of overall gasoline market" the correct measure of market share? Explain briefly.
4. Is there a cause-and-effect linkage between improvements in the measures in the internal business-process perspective and the measure in the customer perspective? That is, would you add other measures to the internal-business-process perspective or the customer perspective? Why or why not? Explain briefly.
5. Do you agree with Caltex's decision not to include measures of changes in operating income from productivity improvements under the financial perspective of the balanced scorecard? Explain briefly.

13-36 Balanced scorecard. Lee Corporation manufactures various types of color laser printers in a highly automated facility with high fixed costs. The market for laser printers is competitive. The various color laser printers on the market are comparable in terms of features and price. Lee believes that satisfying customers with products of high quality at low costs is key to achieving its target profitability. For 2009, Lee plans to achieve higher quality and lower costs by improving yields and reducing defects in its manufacturing operations. Lee will train workers and encourage and empower them to take the necessary actions. Currently, a significant amount of Lee's capacity is used to produce products that are defective and cannot be sold. Lee expects that higher yields will reduce the capacity that Lee needs to manufacture products. Lee does not anticipate that improving manufacturing will automatically lead to lower costs because Lee has high fixed costs. To reduce fixed costs per unit, Lee could lay off employees and sell equipment, or it could use the capacity to produce and sell more of its current products or improved models of its current products.

Lee's balanced scorecard (initiatives omitted) for the just-completed fiscal year 2009 follows:

Objectives	Measures	Target Performance	Actual Performance
Financial Perspective			
Increase shareholder value	Operating-income changes from productivity improvements	$1,000,000	$400,000
	Operating-income changes from growth	$1,500,000	$600,000
Customer Perspective			
Increase market share	Market share in color laser printers	5%	4.6%
Internal-Business-Process Perspective			
Improve manufacturing quality	Yield	82%	85%
Reduce delivery time to customers	Order-delivery time	25 days	22 days
Learning-and-Growth Perspective			
Develop process skills	Percentage of employees trained in process and quality management	90%	92%
Enhance information-system capabilities	Percentage of manufacturing processes with real-time feedback	85%	87%

Required

1. Was Lee successful in implementing its strategy in 2009? Explain.
2. Is Lee's balanced scorecard useful in helping the company understand why it did not reach its target market share in 2009? If it is, explain why. If it is not, explain what other measures you might want to add under the customer perspective and why.
3. Would you have included some measure of employee satisfaction in the learning-and-growth perspective and new-product development in the internal-business-process perspective? That is, do you think employee satisfaction and development of new products are critical for Lee to implement its strategy? Why or why not? Explain briefly.
4. What problems, if any, do you see in Lee improving quality and significantly downsizing to eliminate unused capacity?

13-37 Partial productivity measurement. Guble Company manufactures wallets from fabric. In 2008, Guble made 2,500,000 wallets using 1,875,000 yards of fabric. In 2009, Guble plans to make 2,650,000 wallets and wants to make fabric use more efficient. At the same time, Guble wants to reduce capacity; capacity in 2008 was 3,000,000 wallets at a total cost of $9,000,000. Guble wants to reduce capacity to 2,800,000 wallets, at a total cost of $8,680,000 in 2009.

Suppose that in 2009 Guble makes 2,650,000 wallets, uses 1,669,500 yards of fabric, and reduces capacity to 2,800,000 units and costs to $8,680,000.

Required

1. Calculate the partial-productivity ratios for materials and conversion (capacity costs) for 2009, and compare them to a benchmark for 2008 calculated based on 2009 output.
2. How can Guble Company use the information from the partial-productivity calculations?

13-38 Total factor productivity (continuation of 13-37). Refer to the data for problem 13-38. Assume the fabric costs $4 per yard in 2009 and $4.10 per yard in 2008.

Required

1. Compute Guble Company's total factor productivity (TFP) for 2009.
2. Compare TFP for 2009 with a benchmark TFP for 2008 inputs based on 2009 output.
3. What additional information does TFP provide that partial productivity measures do not?

Collaborative Learning Problem

13-39 Strategic analysis of operating income. Halsey Company sells women's clothing. Halsey's strategy is to offer a wide selection of clothes and excellent customer service and to charge a premium price. Halsey presents the following data for 2009 and 2010. For simplicity, assume that each customer purchases one piece of clothing.

	2009	2010
1. Pieces of clothing purchased and sold	40,000	40,000
2. Average selling price	$60	$59
3. Average cost per piece of clothing	$40	$41
4. Selling and customer-service capacity	51,000 customers	43,000 customers
5. Selling and customer-service costs	$357,000	$296,700
6. Selling and customer-service capacity cost per customer (Line 5 ÷ Line 4)	$7 per customer	$6.90 per customer
7. Purchasing and administrative capacity	980 designs	850 designs
8. Purchasing and administrative costs	$245,000	$204,000
9. Purchasing and administrative capacity cost per distinct design (Line 8 ÷ Line 7)	$250 per design	$240 per design

Total selling and customer-service costs depend on the number of customers that Halsey has created capacity to support, not the actual number of customers that Halsey serves. Total purchasing and administrative costs depend on purchasing and administrative capacity that Halsey has created (defined in terms of the number of distinct clothing designs that Halsey can purchase and administer). Purchasing and administrative costs do not depend on the actual number of distinct clothing designs purchased. Halsey purchased 930 distinct designs in 2009 and 820 distinct designs in 2010.

At the start of 2010, Halsey planned to increase operating income by 10% over operating income in 2009.

Required

1. Is Halsey's strategy one of product differentiation or cost leadership? Explain.
2. Calculate Halsey's operating income in 2009 and 2010.
3. Calculate the growth, price-recovery, and productivity components of changes in operating income between 2009 and 2010.
4. Does the strategic analysis of operating income indicate Halsey was successful in implementing its strategy in 2010? Explain.

14 Cost Allocation, Customer-Profitability Analysis, and Sales-Variance Analysis

Learning Objectives

1. Identify four purposes for allocating costs to cost objects
2. Understand criteria to guide cost-allocation decisions
3. Discuss decisions faced when collecting costs in indirect cost pools
4. Discuss why a company's revenues can differ across customers purchasing the same product
5. Apply the concept of cost hierarchy to customer costing
6. Discuss why customer-level costs differ across customers
7. Subdivide the sales-volume variance into the sales-mix variance and the sales-quantity variance
8. Subdivide the sales-quantity variance into the market-share variance and the market-size variance

Companies desperately want to make their customers happy. But how far should they go to please them, and at what price? At what point are you better off not to do business with some customers at all? The following article explains why it's so important for managers to be able to figure out how profitable each of their customers is.

Minding the Store: Analyzing Customers, Best Buy Decides Not All Are Welcome[1]

Brad Anderson, chief executive officer of Best Buy Co., is embracing a heretical notion for a retailer. He wants to separate the "angels" among his 1.5 million daily customers from the "devils."

The angels are customers who boost profits at the consumer-electronics giant by snapping up high-definition televisions, portable electronics, and newly released DVDs without waiting for markdowns or rebates.The devils are its worst customers. They buy products, apply for rebates, return the purchases, then buy them back at returned-merchandise discounts. They load up on "loss leaders," severely discounted merchandise designed to boost store traffic, then flip the goods at a profit on eBay.

Best Buy found that its most desirable customers fell into five distinct groups: upper-income men, suburban mothers, small-business owners, young family men, and technology enthusiasts. For example, male technology enthusiasts, nicknamed Buzzes, are early adopters, interested in buying and showing off the latest gadgets. Each store analyzes the demographics of its local market, then focuses on two of these groups. For example, at stores popular with young Buzzes, Best Buy sets up videogame areas with leather chairs and game players hooked to mammoth, plasma-screen televisions.

Best Buy began working on ways to deter customers who drove profits down. It couldn't bar them from its stores. But starting in 2004 it began taking steps to put a stop to their most damaging practices. It began enforcing a restocking fee of 15% of the purchase price on returned merchandise. To discourage customers who return items

[1] *Source:* "Minding the Store: Analyzing Customers, Best Buy Decides Not All Are Welcome," *The Wall Street Journal,* November 8, 2004; "Best Buy Investor and Analyst Day: Customer Growth," Best Buy Inc; www.bestbuy.com Webcast Presentation August 9, 2007.

with the intention of repurchasing them at an "open-box" discount, it is experimenting with reselling them over the Internet, so the goods don't reappear in the store where they were originally purchased.

To determine which product, customer, program, or department is profitable, organizations must decide how to allocate costs. Television and newspaper stories about questionable cost-charging practices frequently focus on cost-allocation issues. In one case, a patient in a hospital was charged $17 for a quart of distilled water—$3.40 of direct costs and $13.60 of allocated costs. Much of the $13.60 was questionably related to the services provided to the patient.

In this chapter and the next, we provide insight into cost allocation. The emphasis in this chapter is on macro issues in cost allocation: allocation of costs to divisions, plants, and customers. Chapter 15 describes micro issues in cost allocation—allocating support-department costs to operating departments and allocating common costs to various cost objects—as well as revenue allocations.

Purposes of Cost Allocation

Learning Objective 1

Identify four purposes for allocating costs to cost objects

. . . to provide information for decisions, motivate managers, justify costs, and measure income

Indirect costs of a particular cost object are costs that are related to that cost object but cannot be traced to it in an economically feasible (cost-effective) way. These costs often comprise a large percentage of the overall costs assigned to such cost objects as products, customers, and distribution channels. Why do managers allocate indirect costs to these cost objects? Exhibit 14-1 illustrates four purposes of cost allocation.

Different set of costs are appropriate for the different purposes described in Exhibit 14-1. Consider costs in different business functions of the value chain.

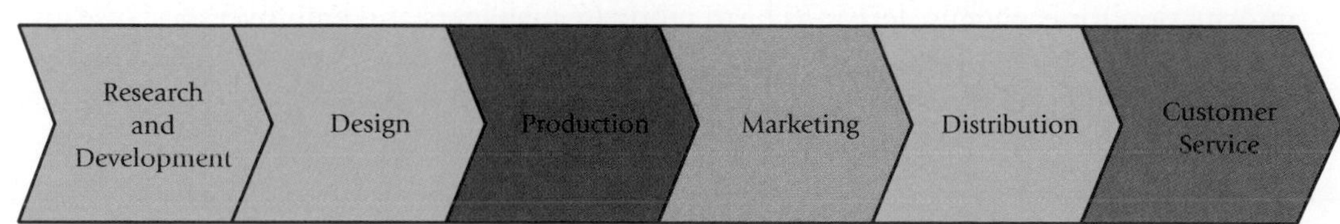

For some decisions related to the economic-decision purpose (for example, long-run product pricing), the costs in all six functions are relevant. For other decisions, particularly

Exhibit 14-1

Purposes of Cost Allocation

Purpose	Examples
1. To provide information for economic decisions	To decide whether to add a new airline flight To decide whether to manufacture a component part of a television set or to purchase it from another manufacturer To decide on the selling price for a customized product or service To evaluate the cost of available capacity used to support different products
2. To motivate managers and other employees	To encourage the design of products that are simpler to manufacture or less costly to service To encourage sales representatives to emphasize high-margin products or services
3. To justify costs or compute reimbursement amounts	To cost products at a "fair" price, often required by law and government defense contracts To compute reimbursement for a consulting firm based on a percentage of the cost savings resulting from the implementation of its recommendations
4. To measure income and assets	To cost inventories for reporting to external parties To cost inventories for reporting to tax authorities

short-run economic decisions (for example, make or buy decisions), costs from only one or two functions (for example, design and manufacturing) might be relevant.

For the motivation purpose, costs from more than one but not all business functions are often included to emphasize to decision makers how costs in different functions are related to one another. For example, to estimate product costs, product designers at companies such as Hitachi and Toshiba include costs of production, distribution, and customer service. The goal: to focus designers' attention on how different product-design choices affect total costs.

For the cost-reimbursement purpose, a particular contract will often stipulate what costs will be reimbursed. For instance, cost-reimbursement rules for U.S.-government contracts explicitly exclude marketing costs.

For the purpose of income and asset measurement for reporting to external parties under GAAP, only manufacturing costs (and product-design costs in some cases) are inventoriable and allocated to products. In the United States, R&D costs (in most industries), marketing, distribution, and customer-service costs are period costs that are expensed as they are incurred.

Criteria to Guide Cost-Allocation Decisions

Learning Objective 2

Understand criteria to guide cost-allocation decisions

. . . such as identifying factors that cause resources to be consumed

After identifying the purposes of cost allocation, managers and management accountants must decide how to allocate costs. This section describes the different criteria companies use to allocate costs.

Exhibit 14-2 presents four criteria used to guide cost-allocation decisions. These decisions affect both the number of indirect-cost pools and the cost-allocation base for each indirect-cost pool. We emphasize the superiority of the cause-and-effect and the benefits-received criteria, especially when the purpose of cost allocation is to provide information for economic decisions or to motivate managers and employees.[2] Cause and effect is the primary criterion used in activity-based costing (ABC) applications. ABC systems use the concept of a cost hierarchy to identify the cost drivers that best demonstrate

[2] The Federal Accounting Standards Advisory Board (which sets standards for management accounting for U.S.-government departments and agencies) recommends: "Cost assignments should be performed by: (a) directly tracing costs whenever feasible and economically practicable, (b) assigning costs on a cause-and-effect basis, and (c) allocating costs on a reasonable and consistent basis." (*FASAB*, 1995, p. 12)

Exhibit 14-2

Criteria for Cost-Allocation Decisions

1. **Cause and Effect.** Using this criterion, managers identify the variables that cause resources to be consumed. For example, managers may use hours of testing as the variable when allocating the costs of a quality-testing area to products. Cost allocations based on the cause-and-effect criterion are likely to be the most credible to operating personnel.
2. **Benefits Received.** Using this criterion, managers identify the beneficiaries of the outputs of the cost object. The costs of the cost object are allocated among the beneficiaries in proportion to the benefits each receives. Consider a corporatewide advertising program that promotes the general image of the corporation rather than any individual product. The costs of this program may be allocated on the basis of division revenues; the higher the revenues, the higher the division's allocated cost of the advertising program. The rationale behind this allocation is that divisions with higher revenues apparently benefited from the advertising more than divisions with lower revenues and, therefore, ought to be allocated more of the advertising costs.
3. **Fairness or Equity.** This criterion is often cited in government contracts when cost allocations are the basis for establishing a price satisfactory to the government and its suppliers. Cost allocation here is viewed as a "reasonable" or "fair" means of establishing a selling price in the minds of the contracting parties. For most allocation decisions, fairness is a matter of judgment rather than an operational criterion.
4. **Ability to Bear.** This criterion advocates allocating costs in proportion to the cost object's ability to bear costs allocated to it. An example is the allocation of corporate executive salaries on the basis of division operating income. The presumption is that the more-profitable divisions have a greater ability to absorb corporate headquarters' costs.

the cause-and-effect relationship between each activity and the costs in the related cost pool. The cost drivers are then chosen as cost-allocation bases.

Fairness and ability to bear are less-frequently-used and more problematic criteria than cause and effect or benefits received. Fairness is a difficult criterion on which to obtain agreement. What one party views as fair, another party may view as unfair.[3] For example, a university may view allocating a share of general administrative costs to government contracts as fair because general administrative costs are incurred to support all activities of the university. The government may view the allocation of such costs as unfair because the general administrative costs would have been incurred by the university regardless of whether the government contract existed. Perhaps the fairest way to resolve this issue is to understand, as well as possible, the cause-and-effect relationship between the government contract activity and general administrative costs. In other words, fairness is more a matter of judgment than an easily implementable choice criterion.

To get a sense of the issues that arise when using the ability-to-bear criterion, consider a product that consumes a large amount of indirect costs but whose selling price is currently below its direct costs. This product has no ability to bear any of the indirect costs it uses. If the indirect costs it consumes are allocated to other products, these other products are subsidizing the product that is losing money.

Most importantly, companies must weigh the costs and benefits when designing and implementing their cost allocations. Companies incur costs not only in collecting data but also in taking the time to educate managers about cost allocations. In general, the more complex the cost allocations, the higher these education costs.

The costs of designing and implementing complex cost allocations are highly visible. Unfortunately, the benefits from using well-designed cost allocations—enabling managers to make better-informed sourcing decisions, pricing decisions, cost-control decisions, and so on—are difficult to measure. Still, when making cost allocations, managers should consider the benefits as well as the costs. As costs of collecting and processing information decrease, companies are building more-detailed cost allocations.

[3] Kaplow and Shavell, for example, in a review of the legal literature, note that "notions of fairness are many and varied. They are analyzed and rationalized by different writers in different way, and they also typically depend upon the circumstances under consideration. Accordingly, it is not possible to identify a consensus view on these notions ..." See L. Kaplow and S. Shavell, "Fairness Versus Welfare," *Harvard Law Review* (February 2001); and L. Kaplow and S. Shavell, *Fairness Versus Welfare* (Boston: Harvard University Press, 2002).

Cost Allocation and Costing Systems

In this section, we focus on the first purpose of cost allocation: to provide information for economic decisions, such as pricing, by measuring the full costs of delivering products based on an ABC system.

Chapter 5 described how ABC systems define indirect-cost pools for different activities and use cost drivers as allocation bases to assign costs of indirect-cost pools to products—the second stage of cost allocation. In this section, we focus on the first stage of cost allocation—how costs are assigned to indirect-cost pools.

We will use Consumer Appliances, Inc. (CAI), to illustrate how costs incurred in different parts of a company can be assigned, and then reassigned, for costing products, services, customers, or contracts. CAI has two divisions; each has its own manufacturing plant. The Refrigerator Division has a plant in Minneapolis, and the Clothes Dryer Division has a plant in St. Paul. CAI's headquarters is in a separate location in Minneapolis. Each division manufactures and sells multiple products that differ in size and complexity.

CAI's management team collects costs at the following levels:

- **Corporate costs**—there are three major categories of corporate costs:
  1. **Treasury costs**—$900,000 of costs incurred for financing the construction of new assembly equipment in the two divisions. The cost of new assembly equipment is $5,200,000 in the Refrigerator Division and $3,800,000 in the Clothes Dryer Division.
  2. **Human-resource-management costs**—recruitment and ongoing employee training and development, $1,600,000.
  3. **Corporate-administration costs**—executive salaries, rent, and general administration costs, $5,400,000.
- **Division costs**—Each division has two direct-cost categories (direct materials and direct manufacturing labor) and seven indirect-cost pools—one cost pool each for the five activities (design, setup, manufacturing, distribution, and administration), one cost pool to accumulate facility costs, and one cost pool for the allocated corporate treasury costs. Exhibit 14-3 presents data for six of the division indirect-cost pools and cost-allocation bases. (In a later section, we describe how corporate treasury

Exhibit 14-3 Division Indirect-Cost Pools and Cost-Allocation Bases, CAI, Inc., for Refrigerator Division (R) and Clothes Dryer Division (CD)

Division Indirect-Cost Pools	Example of Costs		Total Indirect Costs	Cost Hierarchy Category	Cost-Allocation Base	Cause-and-Effect Relationship That Motivates Management's Choice of Allocation Base
Design	Design engineering salaries	(R) (CD)	$6,000,000 4,250,000	Product sustaining	Parts times cubic feet	Complex products (more parts and larger size) require greater design resources.
Setups of machines	Setup labor and equipment cost	(R) (CD)	$3,000,000 2,400,000	Batch level	Setup-hours	Overhead costs of the setup activity increase as setup-hours increase.
Manufacturing operations	Plant and equipment, energy	(R) (CD)	$25,000,000 18,750,000	Output unit level	Machine-hours	Manufacturing-operations overhead costs support machines and, hence, increase with machine usage.
Distribution	Shipping labor and equipment	(R) (CD)	$8,000,000 5,500,000	Output unit level	Cubic feet	Distribution-overhead costs increase with cubic feet of product shipped.
Administration	Division executive salaries	(R) (CD)	$1,000,000 800,000	Facility sustaining	Revenues	Weak relationship between division executive salaries and revenues, but justified by CAI on a benefits-received basis.
Facility	Annual building and space costs	(R) (CD)	$4,500,000 3,500,000	All	Square feet	Facility costs increase with square feet of space.

costs are allocated to each division to create the seventh division indirect-cost pool.) CAI identifies the cost hierarchy category for each cost pool—output-unit level, batch level, product-sustaining level, and facility-sustaining level (as described in Chapter 5, pp. 147–148).

Exhibit 14-4 presents an overview diagram of the allocation of corporate and division indirect costs to products of the Refrigerator Division. Note: The Clothes Dryer Division has its own seven indirect-cost pools used to allocate costs to products. These cost pools and cost-allocation bases parallel the indirect-cost pools and allocation bases for the Refrigerator Division.

Look first at the middle row of the exhibit, where you see "Division Indirect-Cost Pools," and scan the lower half. It is similar to Exhibit 5-3 (p. 150), which illustrates ABC systems using indirect-cost pools and cost drivers for different activities. A major difference in the lower half of Exhibit 14-4 is the cost pool called Facility Costs (far right, middle row), which accumulates all annual costs of buildings and furnishings (such as depreciation) incurred in the division. The arrows in Exhibit 14-4 indicate that CAI allocates facility costs to the five activity-cost pools. Recall from Exhibit 14-3 that CAI uses square feet area required for various activities (design, setup, manufacturing, distribution, and administration) to allocate these facility costs. These activity-cost pools then include the costs of the building and facilities needed to perform the various activities.

The costs in the six remaining indirect-cost pools (that is, after costs of the facility cost pool have been allocated to other cost pools) are allocated to products on the basis of cost drivers described in Exhibit 14-3. (We later describe how corporate treasury costs that have been allocated to divisions are further allocated to products.) These cost drivers are chosen as the cost-allocation bases because there is a cause-and-effect relationship between the cost drivers and the costs in the indirect-cost pool. A cost rate per unit is calculated for each cost-allocation base. Indirect costs are allocated to products on the basis of the total quantity of the cost allocation base for each activity used by the product.

Next focus on the upper half of Exhibit 14-4: how corporate costs are allocated to divisions and then to indirect-cost pools. Before getting into the details of the allocations, let's first consider some broader choices that CAI faces regarding the allocation of corporate costs.

Allocating Corporate Costs to Divisions and Products

Learning Objective 3

Discuss decisions faced when collecting costs in indirect-cost pools

. . . determining the number of cost pools and the costs to be included in each cost pool

CAI's management team has several choices to make when accumulating and allocating corporate costs to divisions.

1. Which corporate-cost categories should CAI allocate as indirect costs of the divisions? Should CAI allocate all corporate costs or only some of them?
   - Some companies allocate all corporate costs to divisions because corporate costs are incurred to support division activities. Allocating all corporate costs motivates division managers to examine how corporate costs are planned and controlled. Also, companies that want to calculate the full cost of products must allocate all corporate costs to indirect-cost pools of divisions.
   - Other companies do not allocate corporate costs to divisions because these costs are not controllable by division managers.
   - Still other companies allocate only those corporate costs, such as corporate human resources, that are widely perceived as causally related to division activities or that provide explicit benefits to divisions. These companies exclude corporate costs such as corporate donations to charitable foundations because division managers often have no say in making these decisions and because the benefits to the divisions are less evident or too remote. If a company decides not to allocate some or all corporate costs, this results in total company profitability being less than the sum of individual division or product profitabilities.

   For some decision purposes, allocating some but not all corporate costs to divisions may be the preferred alternative. Consider the performance evaluation of division managers. The controllability notion (see p. 198) is frequently used to

Exhibit 14-4 Overview Diagram of Allocation of Corporate and Division Indirect Costs to Products of the Refrigerator Division, CAI, Inc.

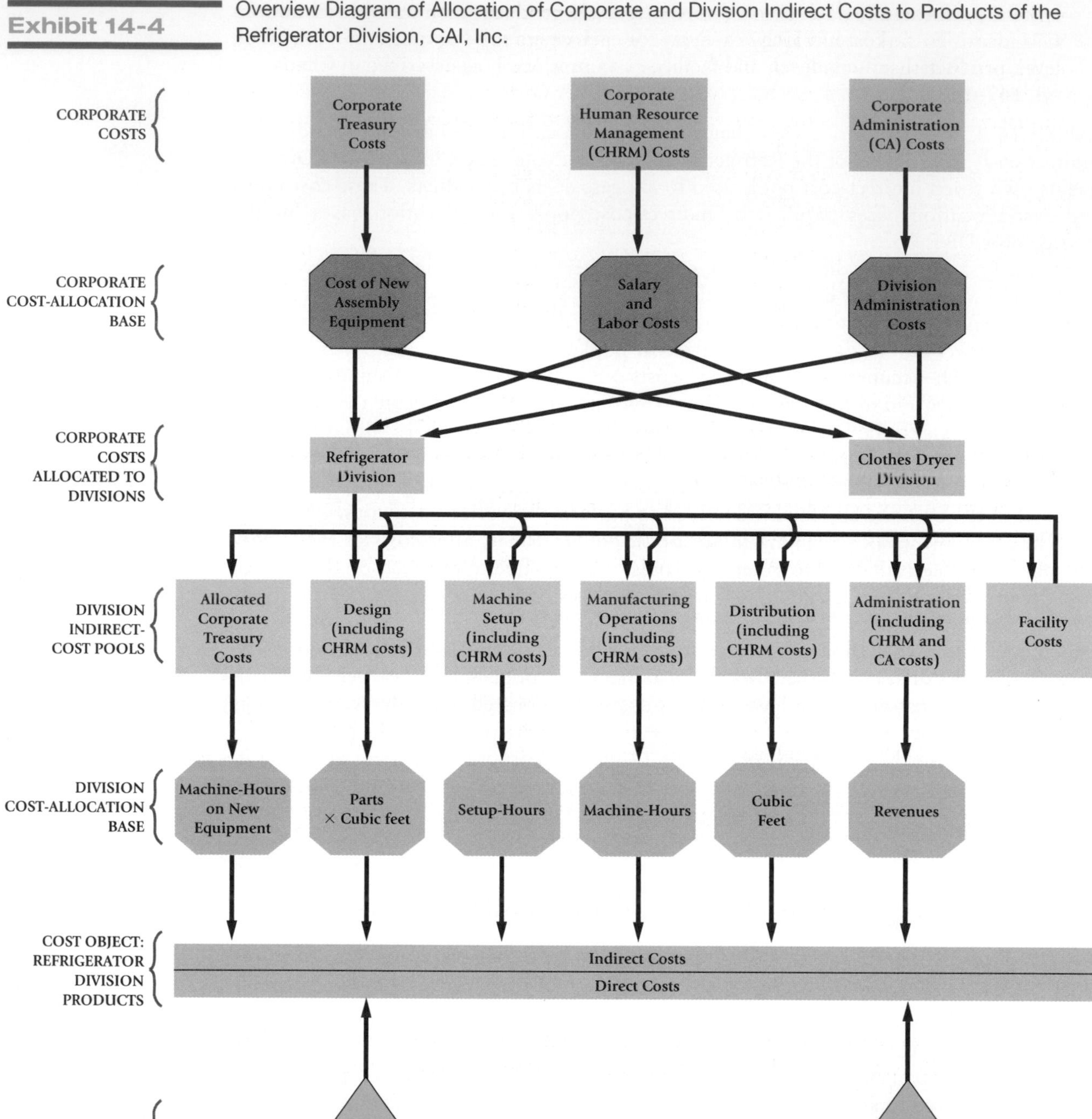

justify excluding some corporate costs from division reports. For example, salaries of the top management at corporate headquarters are often excluded from responsibility accounting reports of division managers. Although divisions tend to benefit from these corporate costs, division managers argue they have no say in ("are not responsible for") how much of these corporate resources they use or how much they cost. The contrary argument is that full allocation is justified because the divisions receive benefits from all corporate costs.

2. When allocating corporate costs to divisions, should CAI allocate only costs that vary with division activity or fixed costs as well? Companies allocate both variable and fixed costs to divisions and then to products because they use these product costs to

make long-run strategic decisions, such as which products they should sell and at what price. To make good long-run decisions, managers need to know the cost of all resources (whether variable or fixed) needed to produce products. Why? Because in the long run, more costs can be managed and fewer costs are regarded as fixed, and to survive and prosper in the long run, prices charged for products must exceed total costs (both variable and fixed).

Companies that allocate corporate costs to divisions must carefully identify relevant costs for specific decisions. Suppose a division is profitable before any corporate costs are allocated but "unprofitable" after allocation of corporate costs. Should the division be closed down? The relevant corporate costs in this case are not the allocated corporate costs but those corporate costs that will be saved if the division is closed. If division profits exceed the relevant corporate costs, the division should not be closed.

3. If CAI allocates corporate costs to divisions, how many cost pools should it use? One extreme is to aggregate all corporate costs into a single cost pool. The other extreme is to have numerous individual corporate cost pools. As discussed in Chapter 5, a major consideration is to construct **homogeneous cost pools** so that all of the costs in the cost pool have the same or a similar cause-and-effect or benefits-received relationship with the cost-allocation base.

For example, when allocating corporate costs to divisions, CAI can combine corporate administration costs and corporate human-resource-management costs into a single cost pool if both cost categories have the same or similar cause-and-effect relationship with the same cost-allocation base (say, number of employees in each division). If, however, each cost category has a cause-and-effect relationship with a different cost-allocation base (for example, number of employees in each division affects corporate human-resource-management costs, whereas revenues of each division affect corporate administration costs), CAI will prefer to maintain separate cost pools for each of these costs. Determining homogeneous cost pools requires judgment and should be revisited on a regular basis.

The benefit of using a multiple cost-pool system must be balanced against the costs of implementing it. Advances in information-gathering technology make it more likely that multiple cost-pool systems will pass the cost-benefit test.

Implementing Corporate Cost Allocations

After much discussion and debate, CAI's management team chooses to allocate all corporate costs to divisions. We now illustrate the allocation of corporate costs to divisions in CAI's ABC system.

The demands for corporate resources by the Refrigerator Division and the Clothes Dryer Division depend on the demands that each division's products place on these resources. The top half of Exhibit 14-4 graphically represents the allocations.

1. CAI allocates treasury costs to each division on the basis of the cost of new assembly equipment installed in each division (the cost driver of treasury costs). It allocates the \$900,000 of treasury costs as follows (using information from p. 504):

$$\text{Refrigerator Division: \$900,000} \times \frac{\$5{,}200{,}000}{\$5{,}200{,}000 + \$3{,}800{,}000} = \$520{,}000$$

$$\text{Clothes Dryer Division: \$900,000} \times \frac{\$3{,}800{,}000}{\$5{,}200{,}000 + \$3{,}800{,}000} = \$380{,}000$$

Each division then creates a *separate cost pool* consisting of the allocated corporate treasury costs and reallocates these costs to products on the basis of machine-hours used on the new equipment. Treasury costs are an output unit-level cost because they represent resources used on activities performed on each individual unit of a product.

2. CAI's analysis indicates that the demand for corporate human-resource-management (CHRM) costs for recruitment and training varies with total salary and labor costs in each division. Suppose salary and labor costs are \$44,000,000 in the Refrigerator

Division and \$36,000,000 in the Clothes Dryer Division. Then CHRM costs are allocated to the divisions as follows:

$$\text{Refrigerator Division: \$1,600,000} \times \frac{\$44,000,000}{\$44,000,000 + \$36,000,000} = \$880,000$$

$$\text{Clothes Dryer Division: \$1,600,000} \times \frac{\$36,000,000}{\$44,000,000 + \$36,000,000} = \$720,000$$

Each division reallocates the CHRM costs allocated to it to the indirect-cost pools—design, machine setup, manufacturing operations, distribution, and division administration (the allocated-corporate-treasury cost pool and the facility costs pool have no salary and labor costs, so no CHRM costs are allocated to them)—on the basis of total salary and labor costs of each indirect-cost pool. CHRM costs that are added to division indirect-cost pools are then allocated to products using the cost driver for the respective cost pool. Therefore, CHRM costs are product-sustaining costs (for the portion of CHRM costs allocated to the design cost pool), batch-level costs (for the portion of CHRM costs allocated to the machine-setup cost pool), output unit-level costs (for the portions of CHRM costs allocated to the manufacturing-operations and distribution cost pools), and facility sustaining costs (for the portion of CHRM costs allocated to the division-administration cost pool).

3. CAI allocates corporate administration costs to each division on the basis of division administration costs (Exhibit 14-3 shows the amounts of division administration costs) because corporate administration's main role is to support division administration.

$$\text{Refrigerator Division: \$5,400,000} \times \frac{\$1,000,000}{\$1,000,000 + \$800,000} = \$3,000,000$$

$$\text{Clothes Dryer Division: \$5,400,000} \times \frac{\$800,000}{\$1,000,000 + \$800,000} = \$2,400,000$$

Each division adds the allocated corporate-administration costs to the division-administration cost pool. The costs in this cost pool are facility-sustaining costs and do not have a cause-and-effect relationship with individual products produced and sold by each division. CAI's policy, however, is to allocate all costs to products so that CAI's division managers become aware of all costs incurred at CAI in their pricing and other decisions. It allocates the division-administration costs (including allocated corporate-administration costs) to products on the basis of product revenues (a benefits-received criterion).

The issues discussed in this section regarding divisions and products apply nearly identically to customers, as we shall show next. *Instructors and students who, at this point, want to explore more-detailed issues in cost allocation rather than focusing on how activity-based costing extends to customer profitability can skip ahead to Chapter 15.*

Customer Revenues and Customer Costs

Customer-profitability analysis is the reporting and analysis of revenues earned from customers and the costs incurred to earn those revenues. An analysis of customer differences in revenues and costs can provide insight into why differences exist in the operating income earned from different customers. Managers use this information to ensure that customers making large contributions to the operating income of a company receive a high level of attention from the company.

Consider Spring Distribution Company, which sells bottled water. It has two distribution channels: (1) a wholesale distribution channel, in which the wholesaler sells to supermarkets, drugstores, and other stores, and (2) a retail distribution channel for a small number of business customers. We focus mainly on customer-profitability analysis in Spring's retail distribution channel. The list selling price in this channel is \$14.40 per case (24 bottles). The full cost to Spring is \$12 per case. If every case is sold at list price in this distribution channel, Spring would earn a gross margin of \$2.40 per case.

Customer-Revenue Analysis

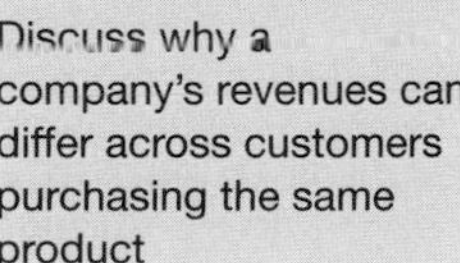

Learning Objective 4

Discuss why a company's revenues can differ across customers purchasing the same product

. . . revenues can differ because of differences in the quantity purchased and the price discounts given

Consider revenues from 4 of Spring's 10 retail customers in June 2009:

	A	B	C	D	E
1		CUSTOMER			
2		A	B	G	J
3	Cases sold	42,000	33,000	2,900	2,500
4	List selling price	$ 14.40	$ 14.40	$ 14.40	$ 14.40
5	Price discount	$ 0.96	$ 0.24	$ 1.20	$ 0.00
6	Invoice price	$ 13.44	$ 14.16	$ 13.20	$ 14.40
7	Revenues (Row 3 x Row 6)	$564,480	$467,280	$38,280	$36,000

Two variables explain revenue differences across these four customers: (1) the number of cases they purchased and (2) the magnitude of price discounting. A **price discount** is the reduction in selling price below list selling price to encourage customers to purchase more. Companies that record only the final invoice price in their information system cannot readily track the magnitude of their price discounting.[4]

Price discounts are a function of multiple factors, including the volume of product purchased (higher-volume customers receive higher discounts) and the desire to sell to a customer who might help promote sales to other customers. Discounts could also be because of poor negotiating by a salesperson or the unwanted effect of an incentive plan based only on revenues. At no time should price discounts run afoul of the law by way of price discrimination, predatory pricing, or collusive pricing (pp. 447–448). Price discounts can also be unethical, for example, when discounts are given by pharmaceutical representatives to doctors to encourage them to prescribe a particular drug.

Tracking price discounts by customer and by salesperson helps improve customer profitability. For example, Spring Distribution may decide to strictly enforce its volume-based price discounting policy. It may also require its salespeople to obtain approval for giving large discounts to customers who do not normally qualify for such discounts. In addition, Spring could track the future sales of customers who its salespeople have given sizable price discounts to because of their "high growth potential." For example, Spring should track future sales to Customer G to see if the $1.20-per-case discount translates into higher future sales.

Customer revenues are one element of customer profitability. The other element is customer costs.

Customer-Cost Analysis

Learning Objective 5

Apply the concept of cost hierarchy to customer costing

. . . such as assigning some costs to individual customers and other costs to distribution channels or to corporate-wide effects

We apply to customers the cost hierarchy discussed in the previous section and in Chapter 5. A **customer-cost hierarchy** categorizes costs related to customers into different cost pools on the basis of different types of cost drivers, or cost-allocation bases, or different degrees of difficulty in determining cause-and-effect or benefits-received relationships. Spring's ABC system focuses on customers rather than products. It has one direct cost—the cost of bottled water—and multiple indirect-cost pools. Spring identifies five categories of indirect costs in its customer cost hierarchy:

1. **Customer output unit-level costs**—costs of activities to sell each unit (case) to a customer. An example is product-handling costs of each case sold.
2. **Customer batch-level costs**—costs of activities related to a group of units (cases) sold to a customer. Examples are costs incurred to process orders or to make deliveries.

[4] Further analysis of customer revenues could distinguish gross revenues from net revenues. This approach highlights differences across customers in sales returns. Additional discussion of ways to analyze revenue differences across customers is in R. S. Kaplan and R. Cooper, *Cost and Effect* (Boston, MA: Harvard Business School Press, 1998, Chapter 10); and G. Cokins, *Activity-Based Cost Management: An Executive's Guide* (New York: John Wiley & Sons, 2001, Chapter 3).

3. **Customer-sustaining costs**—costs of activities to support individual customers, regardless of the number of units or batches of product delivered to the customer. Examples are costs of visits to customers or costs of displays at customer sites.
4. **Distribution-channel costs**—costs of activities related to a particular distribution channel rather than to each unit of product, each batch of product, or specific customers. An example is the salary of the manager of Spring's retail distribution channel.
5. **Corporate-sustaining costs**—costs of activities that cannot be traced to individual customers or distribution channels. Examples are top-management and general-administration costs.

Note from these descriptions that four of the five levels of Spring's cost hierarchy closely parallel the cost hierarchy described in Chapter 5, except that Spring focuses on *customers* whereas the cost hierarchy in Chapter 5 focused on *products*. Spring has one additional cost hierarchy category—distribution-channel costs—for the costs it incurs to support its wholesale and retail distribution channels.

Customer-Level Costs

Learning Objective 6

Discuss why customer-level costs differ across customers

. . . because different customers place different demands on a company's resources

Spring is particularly interested in analyzing *customer-level indirect costs*—costs incurred in the first three categories of the customer-cost hierarchy: customer output-unit-level costs, customer batch-level costs, and customer-sustaining costs. Spring wants to work with customers to reduce these costs. It believes customer actions will have less impact on distribution-channel and corporate-sustaining costs. The following table shows five activities (in addition to cost of goods sold) that Spring identifies as resulting in customer-level costs. The table indicates the cost drivers and cost-driver rates for each activity, as well as the cost-hierarchy category for each activity.

	G	H	I	J
1	**Activity Area**	**Cost Driver and Rate**		**Cost-Hierarchy Category**
2	Product handling	$0.50	per case sold	Customer output-unit-level costs
3	Order taking	$ 100	per purchase order	Customer batch-level costs
4	Delivery vehicles	$ 2	per delivery mile traveled	Customer batch-level costs
5	Rush deliveries	$ 300	per expedited delivery	Customer batch-level costs
6	Visits to customers	$ 80	per sales visit	Customer-sustaining costs

Information on the quantity of cost drivers used by each of four customers is:

	A	B	C	D	E
10		**CUSTOMER**			
11		**A**	**B**	**G**	**J**
12	Number of purchase orders	30	25	15	10
13	Number of deliveries	60	30	20	15
14	Miles traveled per delivery	5	12	20	6
15	Number of rush deliveries	1	0	2	0
16	Number of visits to customers	6	5	4	3

Exhibit 14-5 shows a customer-profitability analysis for the four retail customers using information on customer revenues previously presented (p. 509) and customer-level costs from the ABC system.

Spring Distribution can use the information in Exhibit 14-5 to work with customers to reduce the quantity of activities needed to support them. Consider a comparison of Customer G and Customer A. Customer G purchases only 7% of the cases that Customer A purchases (2,900 versus 42,000). Yet, compared with Customer A, Customer G uses one-half as many purchase orders, two-thirds as many visits to customers, one-third as many deliveries, and twice as many rush deliveries. By implementing charges for each of these services, Spring might be able to induce Customer G to make fewer but larger purchase orders, and require fewer customer visits, deliveries, and rush deliveries while looking to increase sales in the future.

Consider Owens and Minor, a distributor of medical supplies to hospitals. It strategically prices each of its services separately. For example, if a hospital wants a rush delivery or special packaging, Owens and Minor charges the hospital an additional price for each particular service. How have Owens and Minor's customers reacted? Hospitals that value these services continue to demand them and pay for them while hospitals that do not value these services drop them, saving Owens and Minor some costs. Owens and Minor's pricing strategy influences customer behavior in a way that increases its revenues or decreases its costs. See the Concepts in Action feature, p. 515 for another example of a company managing its customer profitability.

The ABC system also highlights a second opportunity for cost reduction: Spring can seek to reduce costs of each activity. For example, improving the efficiency of the ordering process (such as by having customers order electronically) can reduce costs even if customers place the same number of orders.

Exhibit 14-6 shows a monthly operating income statement for Spring Distribution. The customer-level operating income of Customers A and B in Exhibit 14-5 are shown in columns 8 and 9 of Exhibit 14-6. The format of Exhibit 14-6 is based on Spring's cost hierarchy. All costs incurred to serve customers are not included in customer-level costs and therefore are not allocated to customers in Exhibit 14-6. For example, distribution-channel costs such as the salary of the manager of the retail distribution channel are not included in customer-level costs and are not allocated to customers. Instead, these costs are identified as costs of the retail channel as a whole. That's because Spring's management believes that changes in customer behavior will not affect distribution-channel costs. These costs will be affected only by decisions pertaining to the whole channel, such as a decision to discontinue retail distribution. Another reason Spring does not allocate distribution-channel costs to customers is motivation. Spring's managers contend that salespersons responsible for managing individual customer accounts would lose motivation if their bonuses were affected by the allocation to customers of distribution-channel costs over which they had minimal influence.

Exhibit 14-5 Customer-Profitability Analysis for Four Retail Channel Customers of Spring Distribution for June 2009

File Edit View Insert Format Tools Data Window Help

	A	B	C	D	E
1			CUSTOMER		
2		A	B	G	J
3	Revenues at list price: $14.40 x 42,000; 33,000; 2,900; 2,500	$604,800	$475,200	$41,760	$36,000
4	Price discount: $0.96 x 42,000; $0.24 x 33,000; $1.20 x 2,900; $0 x 2,500	40,320	7,920	3,480	0
5	Revenues (at actual price)	564,480	467,280	38,280	36,000
6	Cost of goods sold: $12 x 42,000; 33,000; 2,900; 2,500	504,000	396,000	34,800	30,000
7	Gross margin	60,480	71,280	3,480	6,000
8	Customer-level operating costs				
9	Product handling $0.50 x 42,000; 33,000; 2,900; 2,500	21,000	16,500	1,450	1,250
10	Order taking $100 x 30; 25; 15; 10	3,000	2,500	1,500	1,000
11	Delivery vehicles $2 x (5 x 60); (12 x 30); (20 x 20); (6 x 15)	600	720	800	180
12	Rush deliveries $300 x 1; 0; 2; 0	300	0	600	0
13	Visits to customers $80 x 6; 5; 4; 3	480	400	320	240
14	Total customer-level operating costs	25,380	20,120	4,670	2,670
15	Customer-level operating income	$ 35,100	$ 51,160	$ (1,190)	$ 3,330

Exhibit 14-6 Income Statement of Spring Distribution for June 2009

	A	B	C	D	E	F	G	H	I	J	K	L	M
1			CUSTOMER DISTRIBUTION CHANNELS										
2			Wholesale Customers						Retail Customers				
3		Total	Total	A1	A2	A3	▪		Total	A[a]	B[a]	C	▪
4		(1) = (2) + (7)	(2)	(3)	(4)	(5)	(6)		(7)	(8)	(9)	(10)	(11)
5	Revenues (at actual prices)	$12,138,120	$10,107,720	$1,946,000	$1,476,000	▪	▪		$2,030,400	$564,480	$467,280	▪	▪
6	Customer-level costs	11,633,760	9,737,280	1,868,000	1,416,000	▪	▪		1,896,480	529,380[b]	416,120[b]	▪	▪
7	Customer-level operating income	504,360	370,440	$ 78,000	$ 60,000	▪	▪		133,920	$ 35,100	$ 51,160	▪	▪
8	Distribution-channel costs	160,500	102,500						58,000				
9	Distribution-channel-level operating income	343,860	$ 267,940						$ 75,920				
10	Corporate-sustaining costs	263,000											
11	Operating income	$ 80,860											
12													
13	[a]Full details are presented in Exhibit 14-5												
14	[b]Cost of goods sold + Total customer-level operating costs from Exhibit 14-5.												

Next, consider corporate-sustaining costs such as top-management and general-administration costs. Spring's managers have concluded that there is no cause-and-effect or benefits-received relationship between any cost-allocation base and corporate-sustaining costs. Consequently, allocation of corporate-sustaining costs serves no useful purpose in decision making, performance evaluation, or motivation. For example, suppose Spring allocated the $263,000 of corporate-sustaining costs to its distribution channels: $173,000 to the wholesale channel and $90,000 to the retail channel. Using information from Exhibit 14-6, the retail channel would then show a loss of $14,080 ($75,920 − $90,000).

If this same situation persisted in subsequent months, should Spring shut down the retail distribution channel? No, because if retail distribution were discontinued, corporate-sustaining costs would be unaffected. Allocating corporate-sustaining costs to distribution channels could give the misleading impression that the potential cost savings from discontinuing a distribution channel would be greater than the likely amount.

Some managers and management accountants advocate fully allocating all costs to customers and distribution channels so that (1) the sum of operating incomes of all customers in a distribution channel (segment) equals the operating income of the distribution channel and (2) the sum of the distribution-channel operating incomes equals company-wide operating income. These managers and management accountants argue that customers and products must eventually be profitable on a full-cost basis. In the previous example, CAI allocated all corporate and division-level costs to its refrigerator and clothes dryer products (see pp. 507–508). For some decisions, such as pricing, allocating all costs ensures that long-run prices are set at a level to cover the cost of all resources used to produce and sell products. Nevertheless, the value of the hierarchical format in Exhibit 14-6 is that it distinguishes among various degrees of objectivity when allocating costs, and it dovetails with the different levels at which decisions are made and performance is evaluated. The issue of when and what costs to allocate is another example of the "different costs for different purposes" theme emphasized throughout this book.

Customer-Profitability Profiles

Customer-profitability profiles provide a useful tool for managers. Exhibit 14-7 ranks Spring's 10 retail customers based on customer-level operating income. (Four of these customers are analyzed in Exhibit 14-5.)

Column 4, computed by adding the individual amounts in column 1, shows the cumulative customer-level operating income. For example, Customer C has a cumulative income of $107,330 in column 4. This $107,330 is the sum of $51,160 for Customer B, $35,100 for Customer A, and $21,070 for Customer C.

Exhibit 14-7 Customer-Profitability Analysis for Retail Channel Customers: Spring Distribution, June 2009

	A	B	C	D	E	F
1	**Customers Ranked on Customer-Level Operating Income**					
2						**Cumulative**
3						**Customer-Level**
4		**Customer-**				**Operating Income**
5		**Level**		**Customer-Level**	**Cumulative**	**as a % of Total**
6		**Operating**	**Customer**	**Operating Income**	**Customer-Level**	**Customer-Level**
7	**Customer**	**Income**	**Revenue**	**Divided by Revenue**	**Operating Income**	**Operating Income**
8	**Code**	**(1)**	**(2)**	**(3) = (1) ÷ (2)**	**(4)**	**(5) = (4) ÷ $133,920**
9	B	$ 51,160	$ 467,280	10.9%	$ 51,160	38%
10	A	35,100	564,480	6.2%	86,260	64%
11	C	21,070	255,640	8.2%	107,330	80%
12	D	17,580	277,000	6.3%	124,910	93%
13	F	7,504	123,500	6.1%	132,414	99%
14	J	3,330	36,000	9.3%	135,744	101%
15	E	3,176	193,000	1.6%	138,920	104%
16	G	-1,190	38,280	-3.1%	137,730	103%
17	H	-1,690	38,220	-4.4%	136,040	102%
18	I	-2,120	37,000	-5.7%	133,920	100%
19		$133,920	$2,030,400			
20						

Column 5 shows what percentage the $107,330 *cumulative* total for Customers B, A, and C is of the total customer-level operating income of $133,920 earned in the retail distribution channel from all 10 customers. The three most profitable customers contribute 80% of total customer-level operating income. These customers deserve the highest service and priority. In many companies, it is common for a small number of customers to contribute a high percentage of operating income. Microsoft uses the phrase "not all revenue dollars are endowed equally in profitability" to stress this point.

Column 3 shows the profitability per dollar of revenue by customer. This measure of customer profitability indicates that, although Customer A contributes the second-highest operating income, the profitability per dollar of revenue is lower because of high price discounts. Spring's goal is to increase profit margins for Customer A by decreasing the price discounts or saving customer-level costs while maintaining or increasing sales. Customer J has a high profit margin percentage but has lower total sales. Spring's challenge with Customer J is to maintain margins while increasing sales.

Managers often find the bar chart presentation in Exhibit 14-8 to be the most intuitive way to visualize customer profitability. The highly profitable customers clearly stand out. Moreover, the number of "unprofitable" customers and the magnitude of their losses are apparent. Spring's managers must explore ways to make unprofitable customers profitable. Exhibits 14-5 to 14-8 emphasize short-run customer profitability. Other factors managers should consider in deciding how to allocate resources among customers include:

- **Likelihood of customer retention.** The more likely a customer will continue to do business with a company, the more valuable the customer. Customers differ in their loyalty and their willingness to frequently "shop their business."
- **Potential for sales growth.** The higher the likely growth of the customer's industry and the customer's sales, the more valuable the customer. Customers to whom a company can cross-sell other products are more desirable.

Exhibit 14-8

Bar Chart of Customer-Level Operating Income for Spring Distribution's Retail Channel Customers in June 2009

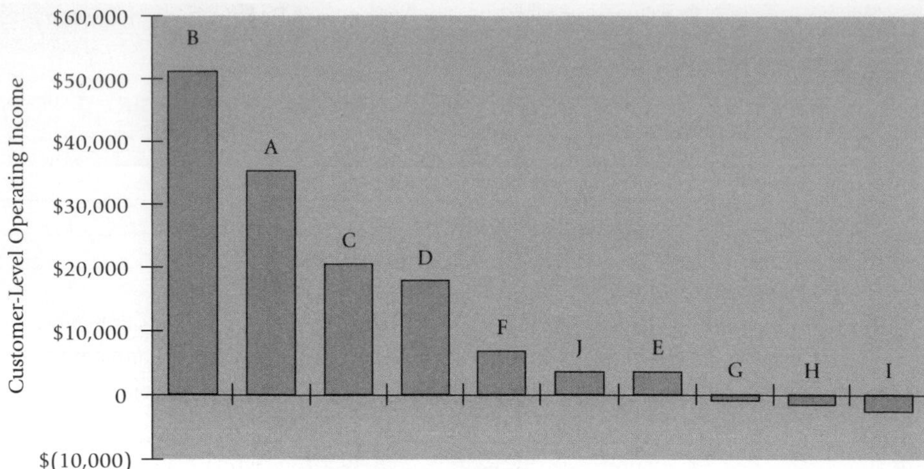

- **Long-run customer profitability.** This factor will be influenced by the first two factors specified and the cost of customer-support staff and special services required to retain customer accounts.
- **Increases in overall demand from having well-known customers.** Customers with established reputations help generate sales from other customers through product endorsements.
- **Ability to learn from customers.** Customers who provide ideas about new products or ways to improve existing products are especially valuable.

Managers should be cautious when deciding to discontinue customers in the short run. Consider Customer G in Exhibit 14-7. The long-run unprofitability of Customer G may provide misleading signals about Customer G's short-run profitability. Not all costs assigned to Customer G are variable in the short run. Discontinuing Customer G will not eliminate all the costs assigned to that customer in the short run.

Using the Five-Step Decision-Making Process to Manage Customer Profitability

The different types of customer analyses that we have just covered provide companies with key information to guide the allocation of resources across customers. Use the five-step decision-making process, introduced in Chapter 1, to think about how managers use these analyses to make customer-management decisions.

1. *Identify the problem and uncertainties.* The problem is how to manage and allocate resources across customers.
2. *Obtain information.* Managers identify past revenues generated by each customer and customer-level costs incurred in the past to support each customer.
3. *Make predictions about the future.* Managers estimate the revenues they expect from each customer and the customer-level costs they will incur in the future. In making these predictions, managers consider the effects that future price discounts will have on revenues, the effect that pricing for different services (such as rush deliveries) will have on the demand for these services by customers, and ways to reduce the cost of providing services.
4. *Make decisions by choosing among alternatives.* Managers use the customer-profitability profiles to identify the small set of customers who deserve the highest service and priority. They also identify ways to make less-profitable customers (for example, Spring's Customer G) more profitable. In making resource-allocation decisions, managers also

Concepts in Action

Customer Profitability at Verizon Wireless

Verizon Wireless, a leading wireless-communications service provider, offers cellular telephone service and wireless-data access to a broad range of businesses, government agencies, and individuals. Verizon Wireless uses cost accounting to price its various wireless service plans and to calculate overall customer profitability.

The costs of serving different wireless customers vary. Most business customers, for example, require reliable service during peak network usage periods (that is, standard business hours), and large amounts of wireless data bandwidth for email and Internet access on their PDA and BlackBerry handheld devices. In contrast, many individuals use their wireless phone extensively at night and on weekends and use features such as text messaging, digital pictures, music ringtones, and video games. Within each segment, customers differ in their amount of overall usage and geographic locations (urban versus rural).

Verizon Wireless considers the costs for each of these services when developing pricing plans and calculating customer profitability. Therefore, individuals using their phone service sparingly can select a less-expensive plan with limited minutes, for use mostly at night and on weekends, whereas more-demanding individuals and lucrative business customers can choose plans with more telephone minutes, secure wireless data bandwidth access, and guaranteed service reliability. . . for a price. In 2007, Verizon Wireless' base wireless plans range from $39.99 to $239.99 per month, with additional charges for data services, rural-area roaming, and music and game downloads. Business and government customers who use Verizon Wireless' services extensively are eligible for negotiated volume discounts.

Because of the range in prices, Verizon Wireless analyzes customer profitability to ensure that its prices cover the costs it incurs to provide services to its different customers. Verizon Wireless then uses customer-profitability analysis to determine where and how to expand its service network, design new pricing plans, offer new paid-download services, manage costs, and develop strategies to ensure that the company acquires and retains the most profitable customers. The result has been the highest customer-retention rate, wireless-network reliability, and overall profitability among wireless carriers.

Sources: S. Rosenbush, "Verizon's Wireless Wonder," *BusinessWeek* Online (August 27, 2004); C. Osborn, "Customer Retention: Can Wireless Data Make 'Em Stay Put?" in *The Future of Wireless: Business Strategies, Broadband Technologies, and Network Operations* (Chicago: International Engineering Consortium, 2004); J. Biln, *U.S. Wireless Carrier Data Services 3Q06-3Q07 Vendor Analysis: QView Summary and Analysis* (IDC, January 23, 2007); R. Dineen, *Verizon Communications* (HSBC, June 14, 2007); Verizon Wireless Web site, www.verizonwireless.com, accessed July 11, 2007.

consider long-term effects, such as the potential for future sales growth and the opportunity to leverage a particular customer account to make sales to other customers.

5. *Implement the decision, evaluate performance, and learn.* After the decision is implemented, managers compare actual results to predicted outcomes to evaluate the decision they made, its implementation, and ways in which they might improve profitability.

Sales Variances

The customer-profitability analysis in the previous section focused on the actual profitability of individual customers within a distribution channel (retail, for example) and their effect on Spring Distribution's profitability for June 2009. At a more-strategic level, however, recall that Spring operates in two different markets: wholesale and retail. The operating margins in the retail market are much higher than the operating margins in the wholesale market. In June 2009, Spring had budgeted to sell 80% of its cases to wholesalers and 20% to retailers. It actually sold more cases in total than it had budgeted, but its actual sales mix (in cases) was 84% to wholesalers and 16% to retailers. Regardless of the profitability of sales to individual customers within each of the retail and wholesale channels, Spring's actual operating income, relative to the master budget, is likely to be positively affected by the higher sales of cases and negatively affected by the shift in mix away from the more-profitable retail customers. Sales-quantity and sales-mix variances can identify the effect of each of these factors on Spring's profitability. Companies such as Cisco, GE, and Hewlett-Packard perform similar analyses because they sell their products through multiple distribution channels, for example, via the Internet, over the telephone, or in retail stores.

Spring classifies all customer-level costs as variable costs and distribution-channel and corporate-sustaining costs as fixed costs. To simplify the sales-variances analysis and calculations, we assume that all these variable costs are variable with respect to units (cases) sold. (This means, for example, that average batch sizes remain the same as the total cases sold vary.) Without this assumption, the analysis would become more complex and would have to be done using the ABC-variance analysis approach described in Chapter 7, pp. 242–244. The basic insights, however, would not change.

Budgeted and actual operating data for June 2009 are:

Budget Data for June 2009

	Selling Price (1)	Variable Cost per Unit (2)	Contribution Margin per Unit (3) = (1) − (2)	Sales Volume in Units (4)	Sales Mix (Based on Units) (5)	Contribution Margin (6) = (3) × (4)
Wholesale channel	$13.37	$12.88	$0.49	712,000	80%[a]	$348,880
Retail channel	14.10	13.12	0.98	178,000	20	174,440
Total				890,000	100%	$523,320

[a] Percentage of unit sales to wholesale channel = 712,000 units ÷ 890,000 total unit = 80%.

Actual Results for June 2009

	Selling Price (1)	Variable Cost per Unit (2)	Contribution Margin per Unit (3) = (1) − (2)	Sales Volume in Units (4)	Sales Mix (Based on Units) (5)	Contribution Margin (6) = (3) × (4)
Wholesale channel	$13.37	$12.88	$0.49	756,000	84%	$370,440
Retail channel	14.10	13.17	0.93	144,000	16	133,920
Total				900,000	100%	$504,360

The budgeted and actual fixed distribution-channel costs and corporate-sustaining costs are $160,500 and $263,000, respectively (see Exhibit 14-6, p. 512).

Recall that the levels of detail introduced in Chapter 7 included the static-budget variance (level 1), the flexible-budget variance (level 2), and the sales-volume variance (level 2). The sales-quantity and sales-mix variances are level 3 variances that subdivide the sales-volume variance.[5]

Static-Budget Variance

The *static-budget variance* is the difference between an actual result and the corresponding budgeted amount in the static budget. Our analysis focuses on the difference between actual and budgeted contribution margins (column 6 in the preceding tables). The total static-budget variance is $18,960 U (actual contribution margin of $504,360 − budgeted contribution margin of $523,320). Exhibit 14-9 (columns 1 and 3) uses the columnar format introduced in Chapter 7 to show detailed calculations of the static-budget variance. Managers can gain more insight about the static-budget variance by subdividing it into the flexible-budget variance and the sales-volume variance.

[5] The presentation of the variances in this chapter and the appendix draws on teaching notes prepared by J. K. Harris.

Exhibit 14-9 Flexible-Budget and Sales-Volume Variance Analysis of Spring Distribution for June 2009

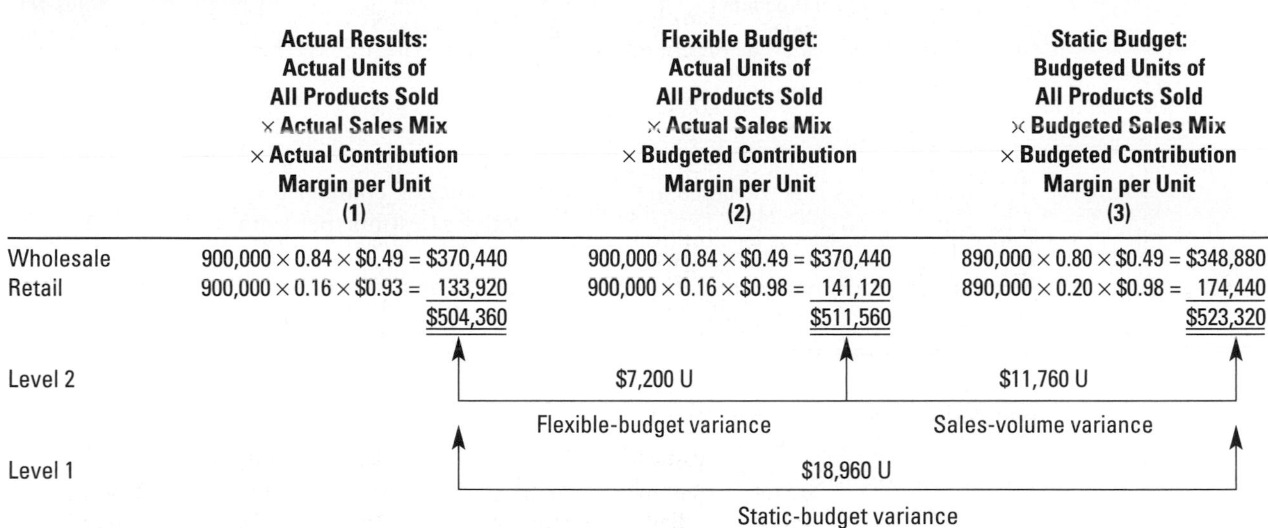

	Actual Results: Actual Units of All Products Sold × Actual Sales Mix × Actual Contribution Margin per Unit (1)	Flexible Budget: Actual Units of All Products Sold × Actual Sales Mix × Budgeted Contribution Margin per Unit (2)	Static Budget: Budgeted Units of All Products Sold × Budgeted Sales Mix × Budgeted Contribution Margin per Unit (3)
Wholesale	900,000 × 0.84 × \$0.49 = \$370,440	900,000 × 0.84 × \$0.49 = \$370,440	890,000 × 0.80 × \$0.49 = \$348,880
Retail	900,000 × 0.16 × \$0.93 = 133,920	900,000 × 0.16 × \$0.98 = 141,120	890,000 × 0.20 × \$0.98 = 174,440
	\$504,360	\$511,560	\$523,320

F = favorable effect on operating income; U = unfavorable effect on operating income.

Flexible-Budget Variance and Sales-Volume Variance

The *flexible-budget variance* is the difference between an actual result and the corresponding flexible-budget amount based on actual output level in the budget period. The flexible budget contribution margin is equal to budgeted contribution margin per unit times actual units sold of each product. Exhibit 14-9, column 2, shows the flexible-budget calculations. The flexible budget measures the contribution margin that Spring would have budgeted for the actual quantities of cases sold. The flexible-budget variance is the difference between columns 1 and 2 in Exhibit 14-9. The only difference between columns 1 and 2 is that actual units sold of each product is multiplied by actual contribution margin per unit in column 1 and budgeted contribution margin per unit in column 2. The \$7,200 U flexible-budget variance arises because actual contribution margin on retail sales of \$0.93 per case is lower than the budgeted amount of \$0.98 per case. Spring's management is aware that this difference of \$0.05 per case resulted from excessive price discounts, and they have taken action to reduce discounts in the future.

The *sales-volume variance* is the difference between a flexible-budget amount and the corresponding static-budget amount. In Exhibit 14-9, the sales-volume variance shows the effect on budgeted contribution margin of the difference between actual quantity of units sold and budgeted quantity of units sold. The sales-volume variance of \$11,760 U is the difference between columns 2 and 3 in Exhibit 14-9. Spring's managers can gain substantial insight into the sales-volume variance by subdividing it into the sales-mix variance and the sales-quantity variance.

Learning Objective 7

Subdivide the sales-volume variance into the sales-mix variance

. . . the variance arises because actual sales mix differs from budgeted sales mix

and the sales-quantity variance

. . . this variance arises because actual total unit sales differ from budgeted total unit sales

Sales-Mix and Sales-Quantity Variances

Exhibit 14-10 uses the columnar format to calculate the sales-mix variance and the sales-quantity variance. Refer to this exhibit when reading the following discussion of these two variances.

Sales-Mix Variance

The **sales-mix variance** is the difference between (1) budgeted contribution margin for the *actual sales mix* and (2) budgeted contribution margin for the *budgeted sales mix*. The formula and computations (using data from p. 516) are:

	Actual Units of All Products Sold	×	(Actual Sales-Mix Percentage − Budgeted Sales-Mix Percentage)	×	Budgeted Contribution Margin per Unit	=	Sales-Mix Variance
Wholesale	900,000 units	×	(0.84 − 0.80)	×	$0.49 per unit	=	$17,640 F
Retail	900,000 units	×	(0.16 − 0.20)	×	$0.98 per unit	=	35,280 U
Total sales-mix variance							$17,640 U

A favorable sales-mix variance arises for the wholesale channel because the 84% actual sales-mix percentage exceeds the 80% budgeted sales-mix percentage. In contrast, the retail channel has an unfavorable variance because the 16% actual sales-mix percentage is less than the 20% budgeted sales-mix percentage. The total sales-mix variance is unfavorable because actual sales mix shifted toward the less-profitable wholesale channel relative to budgeted sales mix.

The concept underlying the sales-mix variance is best explained in terms of budgeted contribution margin per composite unit of the sales mix. A **composite unit** is a hypothetical unit with weights based on the mix of individual units. For actual sales mix, the composite unit consists of 0.84 units of sales to the wholesale channel and 0.16 units of sales to the retail channel. For budgeted sales mix, the composite unit consists of 0.80 units of sales to the wholesale channel and 0.20 units of sales to the retail channel. In the following table, budgeted contribution margin per composite unit is computed in column 3 for actual mix and in column 5 for budgeted mix:

	Budgeted Contribution Margin per Unit (1)	Actual Sales-Mix Percentage (2)	Budgeted Contribution Margin per Composite Unit for Actual Mix (3) = (1) × (2)	Budgeted Sales-Mix Percentage (4)	Budgeted Contribution Margin per Composite Unit for Budgeted Mix (5) = (1) × (4)
Wholesale	$0.49	0.84	$0.4116	0.80	$0.3920
Retail	0.98	0.16	0.1568	0.20	0.1960
			$0.5684		$0.5880

Actual sales mix has a budgeted contribution margin per composite unit of $0.5684. Budgeted sales mix has a budgeted contribution margin per composite unit of $0.5880. Budgeted contribution margin per composite unit can be computed in another way by

Exhibit 14-10 Sales-Mix and Sales-Quantity Variance Analysis of Spring Distribution for June 2009

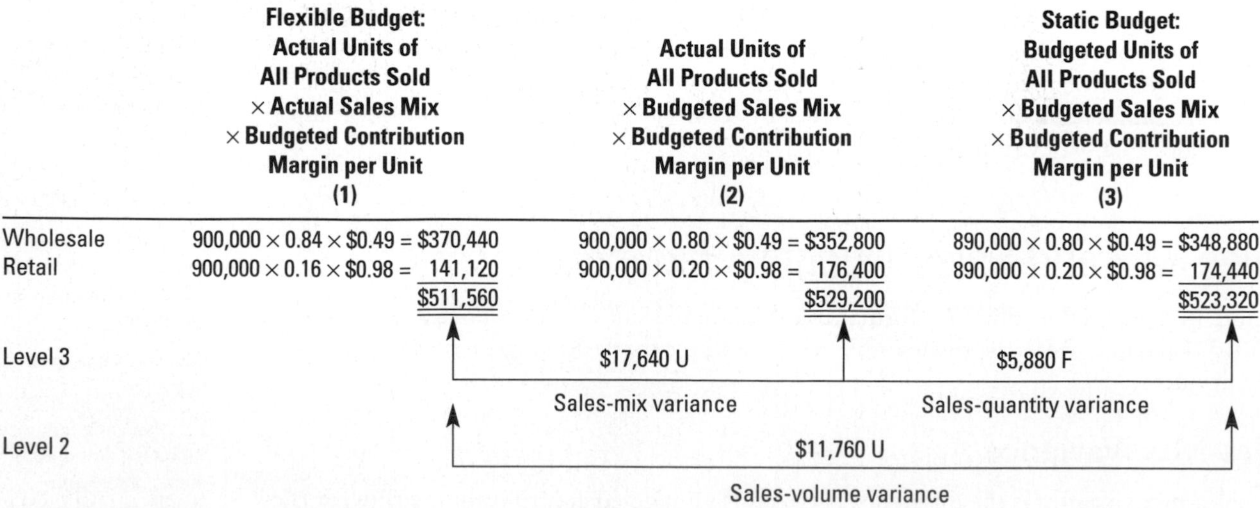

F = favorable effect on operating income; U = unfavorable effect on operating income.

dividing total budgeted contribution margin of \$523,320 by total budgeted units of 890,000 (p. 516): \$523,320 ÷ 890,000 units = \$0.5880 per unit. The effect of the sales-mix shift for Spring is to decrease budgeted contribution margin per composite unit by \$0.0196 (\$0.5880 − \$0.5684). For the 900,000 units actually sold, this decrease translates to a \$17,640 U sales-mix variance (\$0.0196 per unit × 900,000 units).

Managers should probe why the \$17,640 U total sales-mix variance occurred in June 2009. Is the shift in sales mix because, as the analysis in the previous section showed, profitable retail customers proved to be more difficult to find? Is it because of a competitor in the retail channel providing better service at a lower price? Or is it because the initial sales-volume estimates were made without adequate analysis of the potential market?

Sales-Quantity Variance

The **sales-quantity variance** is the difference between (1) budgeted contribution margin based on *actual units sold of all products* at the budgeted mix and (2) contribution margin in the static budget (which is based on *budgeted units of all products to be sold* at budgeted mix). The formula and computations (using data from p. 516) are:

	(Actual Units of All Products Sold	−	Budgeted Units of All Products Sold)	×	Budgeted Sales-Mix Percentages	×	Budgeted Contribution Margin per Unit	=	Sales-Quantity Variance
Wholesale	(900,000 units	−	890,000 units)	×	0.80	×	\$0.49 per unit	=	\$3,920 F
Retail	(900,000 units	−	890,000 units)	×	0.20	×	\$0.98 per unit	=	1,960 F
Total sales-quantity variance									\$5,880 F

This variance is favorable when actual units of all products sold exceed budgeted units of all products sold. Spring sold 10,000 more cases than were budgeted, resulting in a \$5,880 F total sales-quantity variance (also equal to budgeted contribution margin per composite unit for the budgeted sales mix times additional cases sold, \$0.5880 × 10,000). Managers would want to probe the reasons for the increase in sales. Did higher sales come as a result of a competitor's distribution problems? Better customer service? Or growth in the overall market? Further insight into the causes of the sales-quantity variance can be gained by analyzing changes in Spring's share of the total industry market and in the size of that market.

Market-Share and Market-Size Variances

Learning Objective 8

Subdivide the sales-quantity variance into the market-share variance

. . . the variance arises because actual market share differs from budgeted market share

. . . and the market-size variance

. . . this variance arises because actual market size differs from budgeted market size

Sales depend on overall demand for bottled water, as well as Spring's share of the market. Assume that Spring derived its total unit sales budget for June 2009 from a management estimate of a 25% market share and a budgeted industry market size of 3,560,000 units (0.25 × 3,560,000 units = 890,000 units). For June 2009, actual market size was 4,000,000 units and actual market share was 22.5% (900,000 units ÷ 4,000,000 units = 0.225 or 22.5%). Exhibit 14-11 shows the columnar presentation of how Spring's sales-quantity variance can be further subdivided into market-share and market-size variances.

Market-Share Variance

The **market-share variance** is the difference in budgeted contribution margin for actual market size in units caused solely by *actual market share* being different from *budgeted market share*. The formula for computing the market-share variance is:

$$\text{Market-share variance} = \begin{matrix}\text{Actual}\\ \text{market size}\\ \text{in units}\end{matrix} \times \left(\begin{matrix}\text{Actual}\\ \text{market}\\ \text{share}\end{matrix} - \begin{matrix}\text{Budgeted}\\ \text{market}\\ \text{share}\end{matrix}\right) \times \begin{matrix}\text{Budgeted}\\ \text{contribution margin}\\ \text{per composite unit}\\ \text{for budgeted mix}\end{matrix}$$

$$= 4{,}000{,}000 \text{ units} \times (0.225 - 0.25) \times \$0.5880 \text{ per unit}$$

$$= \$58{,}800 \text{ U}$$

Budgeted contribution margin per composite unit for budgeted mix (also called budgeted average contribution margin per unit) equal to \$0.5880 per unit was computed on p. 518.

Spring lost 2.5 market-share percentage points—from the 25% budgeted share to the actual share of 22.5%. The \$58,800 U market-share variance is the effect of the decline in contribution margin.

Market-Size Variance

The **market-size variance** is the difference in budgeted contribution margin at budgeted market share caused solely by *actual market size in units* being different from *budgeted market size in units*. The formula for computing the market-size variance is:

$$\text{Market-size variance} = \left(\begin{matrix}\text{Actual} \\ \text{market} \\ \text{size}\end{matrix} - \begin{matrix}\text{Budgeted} \\ \text{market} \\ \text{size}\end{matrix}\right) \times \begin{matrix}\text{Budgeted} \\ \text{market} \\ \text{share}\end{matrix} \times \begin{matrix}\text{Budgeted} \\ \text{contribution margin} \\ \text{per composite unit} \\ \text{for budgeted mix}\end{matrix}$$

$$= (4{,}000{,}000 \text{ units} - 3{,}560{,}000 \text{ units}) \times 0.25 \times \$0.5880 \text{ per unit}$$

$$= \$64{,}680 \text{ F}$$

The market-size variance is favorable because actual market size increased 12.4% [(4,000,000 − 3,560,000) ÷ 3,560,000 = 0.124, or 12.4%] compared to budgeted market size.

Managers should probe the reasons for the market-share and market-size variances for June 2009. Was the \$58,800 unfavorable market-share variance because of competitors providing better service and offering a lower price? Did Spring's products experience quality-control problems that were the subject of negative media coverage? Is the \$64,680 F market-size variance because of an increase in market size that can be expected to continue in the future? If yes, Spring has much to gain by attaining or exceeding its budgeted 25% market share.

Some companies place more emphasis on the market-share variance than the market-size variance when evaluating their managers. That's because they believe the market-size variance is influenced by economywide factors and shifts in consumer preferences that are outside the managers' control, whereas the market-share variance measures how well managers performed relative to their peers.

Exhibit 14-11 Market-Share and Market-Size Variance Analysis of Spring Distribution for June 2009

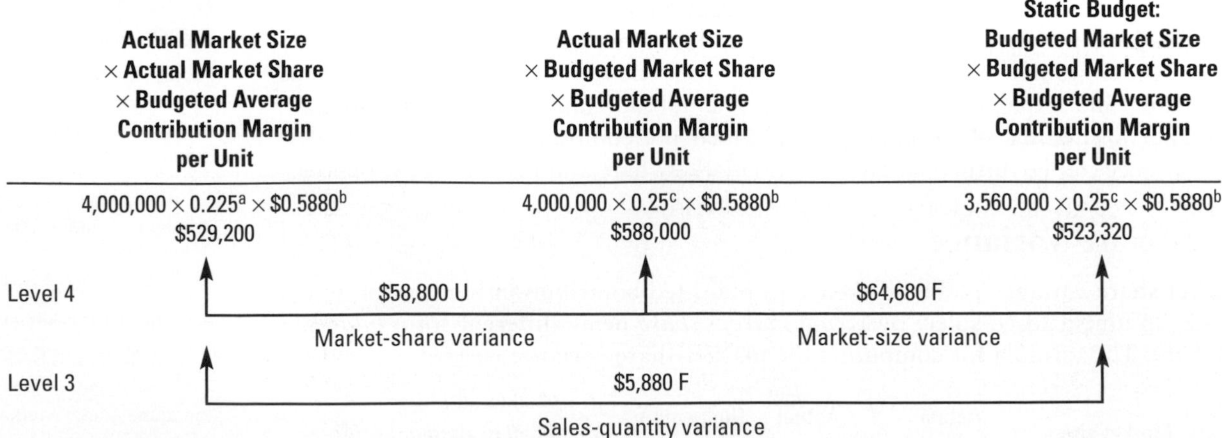

F = favorable effect on operating income; U = unfavorable effect on operating income.

[a] Actual market share: 900,000 units ÷ 4,000,000 units = 0.225, or 22.5%.

[b] Budgeted average contribution margin per unit: \$523,320 ÷ 890,000 units = \$0.5880 per unit.

[c] Budgeted market share: 890,000 units ÷ 3,560,000 units = 0.25, or 25%.

Be cautious when computing the market-size variance and the market-share variance. Reliable information on market size and market share is available for some, but not all, industries. The automobile, computer, and television industries are cases in which market-size and market-share statistics are widely available. In other industries, such as management consulting and personal financial planning, information about market size and market share is far less reliable.

Exhibit 14-12 presents an overview of the level 1 to level 4 variances. The appendix to this chapter describes mix and quantity variances for production inputs.

The sales-mix variance, sales-quantity variance, market-share variance, and market-size variance can also be calculated in a multiproduct company, in which each individual product has a different contribution margin per unit. The Problem for Self-Study calculates these level 3 and level 4 sales variances in a multiproduct company.

Exhibit 14-12 Overview of Variances for Spring Distribution for June 2009

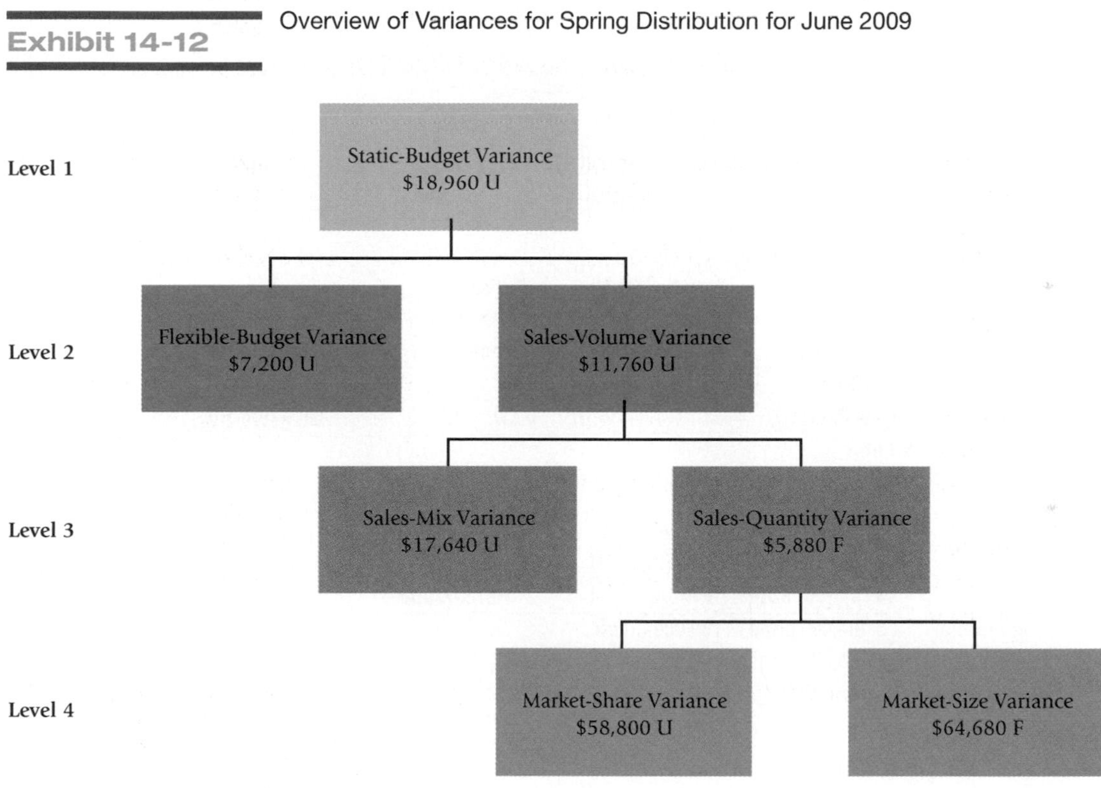

F = favorable effect on operating income; U = unfavorable effect on operating income

Problem for Self-Study

The Payne Company manufactures two types of vinyl flooring. Budgeted and actual operating data for 2009 are:

	Static Budget			Actual Results		
	Commercial	**Residential**	**Total**	**Commercial**	**Residential**	**Total**
Unit sales in rolls	20,000	60,000	80,000	25,200	58,800	84,000
Contribution margin	$10,000,000	$24,000,000	$34,000,000	$11,970,000	$24,696,000	$36,666,000

In late 2008, a marketing research firm estimated industry volume for commercial and residential vinyl flooring for 2009 at 800,000 rolls. Actual industry volume for 2009 was 700,000 rolls.

Required

1. Compute the sales-mix variance and the sales-quantity variance by type of vinyl flooring and in total. (Compute all variances in terms of contribution margins.)

2. Compute the market-share variance and the market-size variance.
3. What insights do the variances calculated in 1 and 2 provide about Payne Company's performance in 2009?

Solution

1. Actual sales-mix percentage:

Commercial = 25,200 ÷ 84,000 = 0.30, or 30%

Residential = 58,800 ÷ 84,000 = 0.70, or 70%

Budgeted sales-mix percentage:

Commercial = 20,000 ÷ 80,000 = 0.25, or 25%

Residential = 60,000 ÷ 80,000 = 0.75, or 75%

Budgeted contribution margin per unit:

Commercial = $10,000,000 ÷ 20,000 units = $500 per unit

Residential = $24,000,000 ÷ 60,000 units = $400 per unit

	Actual Units of All Products Sold	×	(Actual Sales-Mix Percentage − Budgeted Sales-Mix Percentage)	×	Budgeted Contribution Margin per Unit	=	Sales-Mix Variance
Commercial	84,000 units	×	(0.30 − 0.25)	×	$500 per unit	=	$2,100,000 F
Residential	84,000 units	×	(0.70 − 0.75)	×	$400 per unit	=	1,680,000 U
Total sales-mix variance							$ 420,000 F

	(Actual Units of All Products Sold − Budgeted Units of All Products Sold)	×	Budgeted Sales-Mix Percentage	×	Budgeted Contribution Margin per Unit	=	Sales-Quantity Variance
Commercial	(84,000 units − 80,000 units)	×	0.25	×	$500 per unit	=	$ 500,000 F
Residential	(84,000 units − 80,000 units)	×	0.75	×	$400 per unit	=	1,200,000 F
Total sales-quantity variance							$ 1,700,00 F

2. Actual market share = 84,000 ÷ 700,000 = 0.12, or 12%

Budgeted market share = 80,000 ÷ 800,000 units = 0.10, or 10%

Budgeted contribution margin per composite unit of budgeted mix = $34,000,000 ÷ 80,000 units = $425 per unit

Budgeted contribution margin per composite unit of budgeted mix can also be calculated as:

Commercial: $500 per unit × 0.25 =	$125
Residential: $400 per unit × 0.75 =	300
Budgeted contribution margin per composite unit	$425

$$\text{Market-share variance} = \text{Actual market size in units} \times \left(\text{Actual market share} - \text{Budgeted market share}\right) \times \text{Budgeted contribution margin per composite unit for budgeted mix}$$

$$= 700{,}000 \text{ units} \times (0.12 - 0.10) \times \$425 \text{ per unit}$$

$$= \$5{,}950{,}000 \text{ F}$$

$$\text{Market-size variance} = \left(\begin{array}{c}\text{Actual}\\ \text{market size}\\ \text{in units}\end{array} - \begin{array}{c}\text{Budgeted}\\ \text{market size}\\ \text{in units}\end{array}\right) \times \begin{array}{c}\text{Budgeted}\\ \text{market}\\ \text{share}\end{array} \times \begin{array}{c}\text{Budgeted}\\ \text{contribution margin}\\ \text{per composite unit}\\ \text{for budgeted mix}\end{array}$$

$$= (700{,}000 \text{ units} - 800{,}000 \text{ units}) \times 0.10 \times \$125 \text{ per unit}$$

$$= \$4{,}250{,}000 \text{ U}$$

Note that the algebraic sum of the market-share variance and the market-size variance is equal to the sales-quantity variance: $5,950,000 F + $4,250,000 U = $1,700,000 F.

3. Both the total sales-mix variance and the total sales-quantity variance are favorable. The favorable total sales-mix variance occurred because the actual mix comprised more of the higher-margin commercial vinyl flooring. The favorable total sales-quantity variance occurred because the actual total quantity of rolls sold exceeded the budgeted amount.

   The company's large favorable market-share variance is due to a 12% actual market share compared with a 10% budgeted market share. The market-size variance is unfavorable because the actual market size was 100,000 rolls less than the budgeted market size. Payne's performance in 2009 appears to be very good. Although overall market size declined, the company sold more units than budgeted by gaining market share.

Decision Points

The following question-and-answer format summarizes the chapter's learning objectives. Each decision presents a key question related to a learning objective. The guidelines are the answer to that question.

Decision	Guidelines
1. What are four purposes for allocating costs to cost objects?	Four purposes of cost allocation are (a) to provide information for economic decisions, (b) to motivate managers and other employees, (c) to justify costs or compute reimbursement amounts, and (d) to measure income and assets for reporting to external parties. Different cost allocations are appropriate for different purposes.
2. What criteria should managers use to guide cost-allocation decisions?	Managers should use the cause-and-effect and the benefits-received criteria to guide most cost-allocation decisions. Other criteria are fairness or equity and ability to bear.
3. What are two key decisions managers must make when collecting costs in indirect-cost pools?	Two key decisions related to indirect-cost pools are the number of indirect-cost pools to form and the individual cost items to be included in each cost pool to make homogeneous cost pools.
4. Why can revenues differ across customers purchasing the same product?	Revenues can differ because of differences in the quantity purchased and price discounts given from the list selling price.
5. What is the advantage of using a customer-cost hierarchy?	Customer-cost hierarchies highlight how different cost pools have different types of cost drivers and how some costs can be reliably assigned to individual customers whereas other costs can be reliably assigned only to distribution channels or to companywide activities.

6. Why do customer-level costs differ across customers?	Different customers place different demands on a company's resources in terms of processing purchase orders, making deliveries, and customer support. Companies should be aware of and devote sufficient resources to maintaining and expanding relationships with customers who contribute significantly to profitability. Customer-profitability reports often highlight that a small percentage of customers contributes a large percentage of operating income.
7. What are the two components of the sales-volume variance?	The two components are (a) the difference between actual sales mix and budgeted sales mix (the sales-mix variance) and (b) the difference between actual unit sales and budgeted unit sales (the sales-quantity variance).
8. What are the two components of the sales-quantity variance?	The two components are (a) the difference between actual share of the market attained and budgeted share (the market-share variance) and (b) the difference between actual market size in units and budgeted market size in units (the market-size variance).

APPENDIX: MIX AND YIELD VARIANCES FOR SUBSTITUTABLE INPUTS

The framework for calculating the sales-mix variance and the sales-quantity variance can also be used to analyze production-input variances in cases in which managers have some leeway in combining and substituting inputs. For example, Del Monte can combine material inputs (such as pineapples, cherries, and grapes) in varying proportions for its cans of fruit cocktail. Within limits, these individual fruits are *substitutable inputs* in making the fruit cocktail.

We illustrate how the efficiency variance discussed in Chapter 7 (p. 235) can be subdivided into variances that highlight the financial impact of input mix and input yield when inputs are substitutable. Consider Delpino Corporation, which makes tomato ketchup. Our example focuses on direct material inputs and substitution among three of these inputs. The same approach can also be used to examine substitutable direct manufacturing labor inputs.

To produce ketchup of a specified consistency, color, and taste, Delpino mixes three types of tomatoes grown in different regions: Latin American tomatoes (Latoms), California tomatoes (Caltoms), and Florida tomatoes (Flotoms). Delpino's production standards require 1.60 tons of tomatoes to produce 1 ton of ketchup; 50% of the tomatoes are budgeted to be Latoms, 30% Caltoms, and 20% Flotoms. The direct material inputs budgeted to produce 1 ton of ketchup are:

0.80 (50% of 1.6) ton of Latoms at $70 per ton	$ 56.00
0.48 (30% of 1.6) ton of Caltoms at $80 per ton	38.40
0.32 (20% of 1.6) ton of Flotoms at $90 per ton	28.80
Total budgeted cost of 1.6 tons of tomatoes	$123.20

Budgeted average cost per ton of tomatoes is $123.20 ÷ 1.60 tons = $77 per ton.

Because Delpino uses fresh tomatoes to make ketchup, no inventories of tomatoes are kept. Purchases are made as needed, so all price variances relate to tomatoes purchased and used. Actual results for June 2009 show that a total of 6,500 tons of tomatoes were used to produce 4,000 tons of ketchup:

3,250	tons of Latoms at actual cost of $70 per ton	$227,500
2,275	tons of Caltoms at actual cost of $82 per ton	186,550
975	tons of Flotoms at actual cost of $96 per ton	93,600
6,500	tons of tomatoes	507,650
Budgeted cost of 4,000 tons of ketchup at $123.20 per ton		492,800
Flexible-budget variance for direct materials		$ 14,850 U

Exhibit 14-13 Direct Materials Price and Efficiency Variances for the Delpino Corporation June 2009

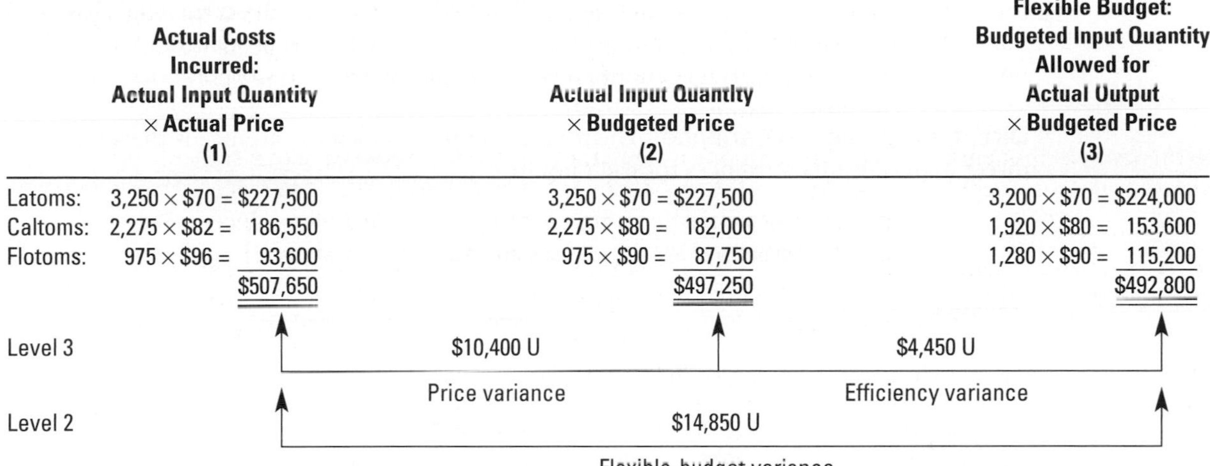

	Actual Costs Incurred: Actual Input Quantity × Actual Price (1)	Actual Input Quantity × Budgeted Price (2)	Flexible Budget: Budgeted Input Quantity Allowed for Actual Output × Budgeted Price (3)
Latoms:	3,250 × $70 = $227,500	3,250 × $70 = $227,500	3,200 × $70 = $224,000
Caltoms:	2,275 × $82 = 186,550	2,275 × $80 = 182,000	1,920 × $80 = 153,600
Flotoms:	975 × $96 = 93,600	975 × $90 = 87,750	1,280 × $90 = 115,200
	$507,650	$497,250	$492,800

Level 3: $10,400 U Price variance (between columns 1 and 2); $4,450 U Efficiency variance (between columns 2 and 3)

Level 2: $14,850 U Flexible-budget variance (between columns 1 and 3)

F = favorable effect on operating income; U = unfavorable effect on operating income.

Given the standard ratio of 1.60 tons of tomatoes to 1 ton of ketchup, 6,400 tons of tomatoes should be used to produce 4,000 tons of ketchup. At standard mix, quantities of each type of tomato required are:

Latoms:	0.50 × 6,400 = 3,200 tons
Caltoms:	0.30 × 6,400 = 1,920 tons
Flotoms:	0.20 × 6,400 = 1,280 tons

Direct Materials Price and Efficiency Variances

Exhibit 14-13 presents in columnar format the analysis of the flexible-budget variance for direct materials discussed in Chapter 7. The materials price and efficiency variances are calculated separately for each input material and then added together. The variance analysis prompts Delpino to investigate the unfavorable price and efficiency variances. Why did it pay more for tomatoes and use greater quantities than it had budgeted? Were actual market prices of tomatoes higher, in general, or could the Purchasing Department have negotiated lower prices? Did the inefficiencies result from inferior tomatoes or from problems in processing?

Direct Materials Mix and Direct Materials Yield Variances

Managers sometimes have discretion to substitute one material for another. The manager of Delpino's ketchup plant has some leeway in combining Latoms, Caltoms, and Flotoms without affecting the ketchup's quality. We will assume that to maintain quality, mix percentages of each type of tomato can only vary up to 5% from standard mix. For example, the percentage of Caltoms in the mix can vary between 25% and 35% (30% ± 5%). When inputs are substitutable, direct materials efficiency improvement relative to budgeted costs can come from two sources: (1) using a cheaper mix to produce a given quantity of output, measured by the direct materials mix variance, and (2) using less input to achieve a given quantity of output, measured by the direct materials yield variance.

Holding actual total quantity of all direct materials inputs used constant, the total **direct materials mix variance** is the difference between (1) budgeted cost for actual mix of actual total quantity of direct materials used and (2) budgeted cost of budgeted mix of actual total quantity of direct materials used. Holding budgeted input mix constant, the **direct materials yield variance** is the difference between (1) budgeted cost of direct materials based on actual total quantity of direct materials used and (2) flexible-budget cost of direct materials based on budgeted total quantity of direct materials allowed for actual output produced. Exhibit 14-14 presents the direct materials mix and yield variances for the Delpino Corporation.

Direct materials mix variance The total direct materials mix variance is the sum of the direct materials mix variances for each input:

$$\begin{matrix}\text{Direct}\\\text{materials}\\\text{mix variance}\\\text{for each input}\end{matrix} = \begin{matrix}\text{Actual total}\\\text{quantity of all}\\\text{direct materials}\\\text{inputs used}\end{matrix} \times \left(\begin{matrix}\text{Actual}\\\text{direct materials}\\\text{input mix}\\\text{percentage}\end{matrix} - \begin{matrix}\text{Budgeted}\\\text{direct materials}\\\text{input mix}\\\text{percentage}\end{matrix}\right) \times \begin{matrix}\text{Budgeted}\\\text{price of}\\\text{direct materials}\\\text{input}\end{matrix}$$

The direct materials mix variances are:

Latoms:	6,500 tons × (0.50 − 0.50) × $70 per ton	= 6,500 × 0.00 × $70	=	$ 0
Caltoms:	6,500 tons × (0.35 − 0.30) × $80 per ton	= 6,500 × 0.05 × $80	=	26,000 U
Flotoms:	6,500 tons × (0.15 − 0.20) × $90 per ton	= 6,500 × −0.05 × $90	=	29,250 F
Total direct materials mix variance				$ 3,250 F

The total direct materials mix variance is favorable because relative to the budgeted mix, Delpino substitutes 5% of the cheaper Caltoms for 5% of the more-expensive Flotoms.

Direct Materials Yield Variance The direct materials yield variance is the sum of the direct materials yield variances for each input:

$$\begin{matrix}\text{Direct}\\\text{materials}\\\text{yield variance}\\\text{for each input}\end{matrix} = \left(\begin{matrix}\text{Actual total}\\\text{quantity of}\\\text{all direct}\\\text{materials}\\\text{inputs used}\end{matrix} - \begin{matrix}\text{Budgeted total}\\\text{quantity of all}\\\text{direct materials}\\\text{inputs allowed}\\\text{for actual output}\end{matrix}\right) \times \begin{matrix}\text{Budgeted}\\\text{direct materials}\\\text{input mix}\\\text{percentage}\end{matrix} \times \begin{matrix}\text{Budgeted}\\\text{price of}\\\text{direct materials}\\\text{input}\end{matrix}$$

Exhibit 14-14 Total Direct Materials Yield and Mix Variances for the Delpino Corporation for June 2009

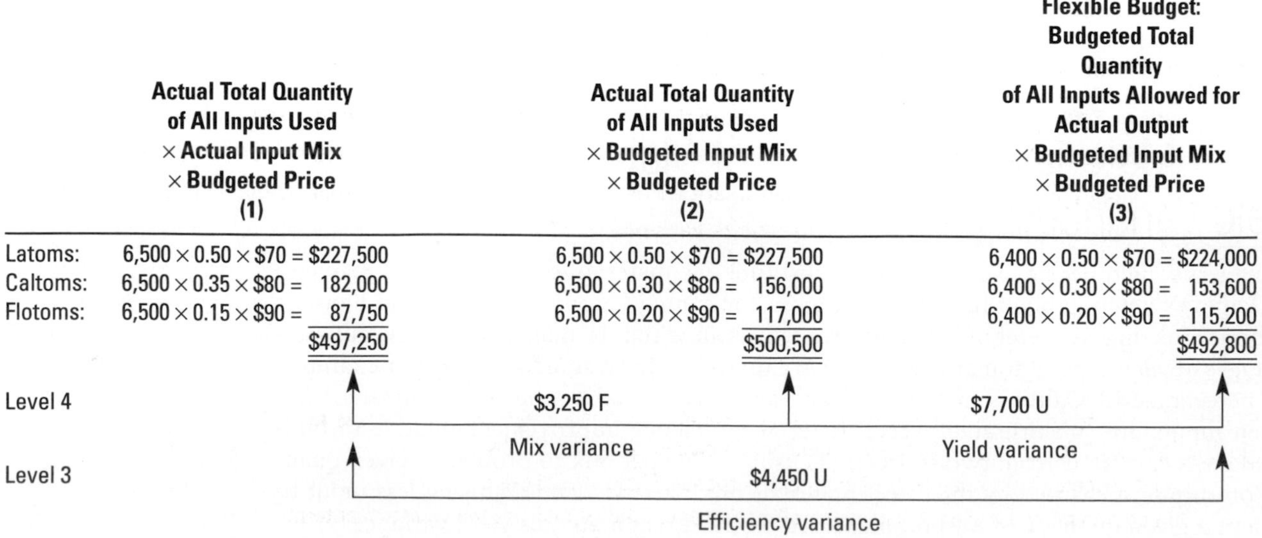

	Actual Total Quantity of All Inputs Used × Actual Input Mix × Budgeted Price (1)	Actual Total Quantity of All Inputs Used × Budgeted Input Mix × Budgeted Price (2)	Flexible Budget: Budgeted Total Quantity of All Inputs Allowed for Actual Output × Budgeted Input Mix × Budgeted Price (3)
Latoms:	6,500 × 0.50 × $70 = $227,500	6,500 × 0.50 × $70 = $227,500	6,400 × 0.50 × $70 = $224,000
Caltoms:	6,500 × 0.35 × $80 = 182,000	6,500 × 0.30 × $80 = 156,000	6,400 × 0.30 × $80 = 153,600
Flotoms:	6,500 × 0.15 × $90 = 87,750	6,500 × 0.20 × $90 = 117,000	6,400 × 0.20 × $90 = 115,200
	$497,250	$500,500	$492,800

F = favorable effect on operating income; U = unfavorable effect on operating income.

The direct materials yield variances are:

Latoms: (6,500 − 6,400) tons × 0.50 × $70 per ton	= 100 × 0.50 × $70	=	$3,500 U
Caltoms: (6,500 − 6,400) tons × 0.30 × $80 per ton	= 100 × 0.30 × $80	=	2,400 U
Flotoms: (6,500 − 6,400) tons × 0.20 × $90 per ton	= 100 × 0.20 × $90	=	1,800 U
Total direct materials yield variance			$7,700 U

The total direct materials yield variance is unfavorable because Delpino used 6,500 tons of tomatoes rather than the 6,400 tons that it should have used to produce 4,000 tons of ketchup. Holding the budgeted mix and budgeted prices of tomatoes constant, the budgeted cost per ton of tomatoes in the budgeted mix is $77 per ton. The unfavorable yield variance represents the budgeted cost of using 100 more tons of tomatoes, (6,500 − 6,400) tons × $77 per ton = $7,700 U. Delpino would want to investigate reasons for this unfavorable yield variance. For example, did the substitution of the cheaper Caltoms for Flotoms that resulted in the favorable mix variance also cause the unfavorable yield variance?

The direct materials variances computed in Exhibits 14-13 and 14-14 can be summarized as follows:

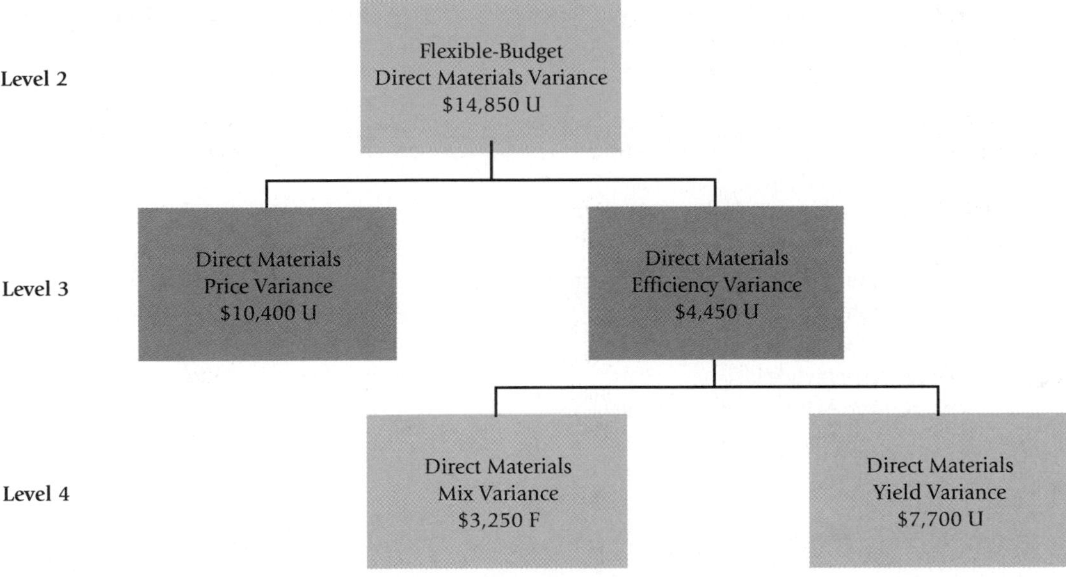

TERMS TO LEARN

This chapter and the Glossary at the end of the book contain definitions of:

composite unit **(p. 518)**
customer-cost hierarchy **(p. 509)**
customer-profitability analysis **(p. 508)**
direct materials mix variance **(p. 525)**
direct materials yield variance **(p. 526)**
homogeneous cost pool **(p. 507)**
market-share variance **(p. 519)**
market-size variance **(p. 520)**
price discount **(p. 509)**
sales-mix variance **(p. 517)**
sales-quantity variance **(p. 519)**

ASSIGNMENT MATERIAL

Questions

14-1 I am going to fo cus on the customers of my business and leave cost-allocation issues to my accountant." Do you agree with this comment by a division president? Why?

14-2 A given cost may be allocated for one or more purposes. List four purposes.

14-3 What criteria might be used to guide cost-allocation decisions? Which are the dominant criteria?

14-4 "A company should not allocate all of its corporate costs to its divisions." Do you agree? Explain.

14-5 "Once a company allocates corporate costs to divisions, these costs should not be reallocated to the indirect-cost pools of the division." Do you agree? Explain.

14-6 Why is customer-profitability analysis a vitally important topic to managers?

14-7 How can the extent of price discounting be tracked on a customer-by-customer basis?

14-8 "A customer-profitability profile highlights those customers who should be dropped to improve profitability." Do you agree? Explain.

14-9 Give examples of three different levels of costs in a customer-cost hierarchy.

14-10 Show how managers can gain insight into the causes of a sales-volume variance by subdividing the components of this variance.

14-11 How can the concept of a composite unit be used to explain why an unfavorable total sales-mix variance of contribution margin occurs?

14-12 Explain why a favorable sales-quantity variance occurs.

14-13 Distinguish between a market-share variance and a market-size variance.

14-14 Why might some companies not compute market-size and market-share variances?

14-15 Explain how the direct materials mix and yield variances provide additional information about the direct materials efficiency variance.

Exercises

14-16 Cost allocation in hospitals, alternative allocation criteria. Dave Meltzer vacationed at Lake Tahoe last winter. Unfortunately, he broke his ankle while skiing and spent two days at the Sierra University Hospital. Meltzer's insurance company received a $4,800 bill for his two-day stay. One item that caught Meltzer's attention was an $11.52 charge for a roll of cotton. Meltzer is a salesman for Johnson & Johnson and knows that the cost to the hospital of the roll of cotton is in the $2.20 to $3.00 range. He asked for a breakdown of the $11.52 charge. The accounting office of the hospital sent him the following information:

a. Invoiced cost of cotton roll	$ 2.40
b. Cost of processing of paperwork for purchase	0.60
c. Supplies-room management fee	0.70
d. Operating-room and patient-room handling costs	1.60
e. Administrative hospital costs	1.10
f. University teaching–related costs	0.60
g. Malpractice insurance costs	1.20
h. Cost of treating uninsured patients	2.72
i. Profit component	0.60
Total	$11.52

Meltzer believes the overhead charge is obscene. He comments, "There was nothing I could do about it. When they come in and dab your stitches, it's not as if you can say, 'Keep your cotton roll. I brought my own.'"

Required

1. Compute the overhead rate Sierra University Hospital charged on the cotton roll.
2. What criteria might Sierra use to justify allocation of the overhead items b through i in the preceding list? Examine each item separately and use the allocation criteria listed in Exhibit 14-2 (p. 503) in your answer.
3. What should Meltzer do about the $11.52 charge for the cotton roll?

14-17 Allocating Costs to Divisions. Gether Corporation manufactures appliances. It has four divisions: Refrigerator, Stove, Dishwasher, and Microwave oven. Each division is located in a different city and the headquarters is located in Oakland, California. Headquarters incurs a total of $14,255,000 in costs, none of which are direct costs of any of the divisions. Revenues, costs, and facility space for each division are as follows:

	Refrigerator	Stove	Dishwasher	Microwave oven
Revenue	$10,900,000	$18,800,000	$11,500,000	$6,780,000
Direct costs	5,700,000	10,400,000	6,200,000	3,220,000
Segment margin	$ 5,200,000	$ 8,400,000	$ 5,300,000	$3,560,000
Square feet of floor space occupied	130,000	90,000	80,000	100,000

Gether wants to allocate the indirect costs of headquarters on the basis of either square feet or segment margin for each division.

Required

1. Allocate the indirect headquarters costs to each division, first using square feet of space and then using segment margin as the allocation base. Calculate the division operating margins after each allocation in dollars and as a percentage of revenues.

2. Which allocation base do you prefer? Why?
3. Should any of the divisions be dropped based on your calculations? Why or why not?

14-18 Cost allocation to divisions. Rembrandt Hotel & Casino is situated on beautiful Lake Tahoe in Nevada. The complex includes a 300-room hotel, a casino, and a restaurant. As Rembrandt's new controller, you are asked to recommend the basis to be used for allocating fixed overhead costs to the three divisions in 2008. You are presented with the following income statement information for 2008:

	Hotel	Restaurant	Casino
Revenues	$16,425,000	$5,256,000	$12,340,000
Direct costs	9,819,260	3,749,172	4,248,768
Segment margin	$ 6,605,740	$1,506,828	$ 8,091,232

You are also given the following data on the three divisions:

	Hotel	Restaurant	Casino
Floor space (square feet)	80,000	16,000	64,000
Number of employees	200	50	250

You are told that you may choose to allocate indirect costs based on one of the following: direct costs, or square feet, or the number of employees. Total fixed overhead costs for 2008 was $14,550,000.

Required

1. Calculate division margins in percentage terms prior to allocating fixed overhead costs.
2. Allocate indirect costs to the three divisions using each of the three allocation bases suggested. For each allocation base, calculate division operating margins after allocations in dollars and as a percentage of revenues.
3. Discuss the results. How would you decide how to allocate indirect costs to the divisions? Why?
4. Would you recommend closing any of the three divisions (and possibly reallocating resources to other divisions) as a result of your analysis? If so, which division would you close and why?

14-19 Cost allocation to divisions. Lenzig Corporation has three divisions: Pulp, Paper, and Fibers. Lenzig's new controller, Ari Bardem, is reviewing the allocation of fixed corporate-overhead costs to the three divisions. He is presented with the following information for each division for 2009:

	A	B	C	D
1		Pulp	Paper	Fibers
2	Revenues	$8,500,000	$17,500,000	$24,000,000
3	Direct manufacturing costs	4,100,000	8,600,000	11,300,000
4	Division administrative costs	2,000,000	1,800,000	3,200,000
5	Division margin	$2,400,000	$ 7,100,000	$ 9,500,000
6				
7	Number of employees	350	250	400
8	Floor space (square feet)	35,000	24,000	66,000

Until now, Lenzig Corporation has allocated fixed corporate-overhead costs to the divisions on the basis of division margins. Bardem asks for a list of costs that comprise fixed corporate overhead and suggests the following new allocation bases:

	F	G	H
1	Fixed Corporate Overhead Costs		Suggested Allocation Bases
2	Human resource management	$1,800,000	Number of employees
3	Facility	2,700,000	Floor space (square feet)
4	Corporate Administration	4,500,000	Division administrative costs
5	Total	$9,000,000	

If you want to use Excel to solve this exercise, go to the Excel Lab at **www.prenhall.com/horngren/cost13e** and download the template for Exercise 14-19.

Required

1. Allocate 2009 fixed corporate-overhead costs to the three divisions using division margin as the allocation base. What is each division's operating margin percentage (division margin minus allocated fixed corporate-overhead costs as a percentage of revenues)?
2. Allocate 2009 fixed costs using the allocation bases suggested by Bardem. What is each division's operating margin percentage under the new allocation scheme?
3. Compare and discuss the results of requirements 1 and 2. If division performance is linked to operating margin percentage, which division would be most receptive to the new allocation scheme? Which division would be the least receptive? Why?
4. Which allocation scheme should Lenzig Corporation use? Why? How might Bardem overcome any objections that may arise from the divisions?

14-20 Customer profitability, customer-cost hierarchy. Ramish Electronics has only two retail and two wholesale customers. Information relating to each customer for 2009 follows (in thousands):

	A	B	C	D	E
1		Wholesale Customers		Retail Customers	
2		North America	South America	Big Sam	World
3		Wholesaler	Wholesaler	Stereo	Market
4	Revenues at list price	$420,000	$580,000	$130,000	$100,000
5	Discounts from list prices	30,000	40,000	7,000	500
6	Cost of goods sold	325,000	455,000	118,000	90,000
7	Delivery costs	450	650	200	125
8	Order processing costs	800	1,000	200	130
9	Costs of sales visits	5,600	5,500	2,300	1,350

Ramish's annual distribution-channel costs are $38 million for wholesale customers and $7 million for retail customers. Its annual corporate-sustaining costs, such as salary for top management and general-administration costs, are $65 million. There is no cause-and-effect or benefits-received relationship between any cost-allocation base and corporate-sustaining costs. That is, corporate-sustaining costs could be saved only if Ramish Electronics were to completely shut down.

If you want to use Excel to solve this exercise, go to the Excel Lab at **www.prenhall.com/horngren/cost13e** and download the template for Exercise 14-20.

Required

1. Calculate customer-level operating income using the format in Exhibit 14-5.
2. Prepare a customer-cost hierarchy report, using the format in Exhibit 14-6.
3. Ramish's management decides to allocate all corporate-sustaining costs to distribution channels: $51 million to the wholesale channel and $14 million to the retail channel. As a result, distribution channel costs are now $89 million ($38 million + $51 million) for the wholesale channel and $21 million ($7 million + $14 million) for the retail channel. Calculate the distribution-channel-level operating income. On the basis of these calculations, what actions, if any, should Ramish's managers take? Explain.

14-21 Customer profitability, service company. Instant Service (IS) repairs printers and photocopiers for five multisite companies in a tristate area. IS's costs consist of the cost of technicians and equipment that are directly traceable to the customer site and a pool of office overhead. Until recently, IS estimated customer profitability by allocating the office overhead to each customer based on share of revenues. For 2010, IS reported the following results:

	A	B	C	D	E	F	G
1		Avery	Okie	Wizard	Grainger	Duran	Total
2	Revenues	$260,000	$200,000	$322,000	$122,000	$212,000	$1,116,000
3	Technician and equipment cost	182,000	175,000	225,000	107,000	178,000	867,000
4	Office overhead allocated	31,859	24,507	39,457	14,949	25,978	136,750
5	Operating income	$ 46,141	$ 493	$ 57,543	$ 51	$ 8,022	$ 112,250

Tina Sherman, IS's new controller, notes that office overhead is more than 10% of total costs, so she spends a couple of weeks analyzing the consumption of office overhead resources by customers. She collects the following information:

	I	J	K
1	Activity Area	Cost Driver Rate	
2	Service call handling	$75	per service call
3	Parts ordering	$80	per web-base parts order
4	Billing and collection	$50	per bill (or reminder)
5	Customer database maintenance	$10	per service call

	A	B	C	D	E	F
8		Avery	Okie	Wizard	Grainger	Duran
9	Number of service calls	150	240	40	120	180
10	Number of web-based parts orders	120	210	60	150	150
11	Number of bills (or reminders)	30	90	90	60	120

If you want to use Excel to solve this exercise, go to the Excel Lab at **www.prenhall.com/horngren/cost13e** and download the template for Exercise 14-21.

Required

1. Compute customer-level operating income using the new information that Sherman has gathered.
2. Prepare exhibits for IS similar to Exhibits 14-7 and 14-8. Comment on the results.
3. What options should IS consider, with regard to individual customers, in light of the new data and analysis of office overhead?

14-22 Customer profitability, distribution. Figure Four is a distributor of pharmaceutical products. Its ABC system has five activities:

Activity Area	Cost Driver Rate in 2009
1. Order processing	$40 per order
2. Line-item ordering	$3 per line item
3. Store deliveries	$50 per store delivery
4. Carton deliveries	$1 per carton
5. Shelf-stocking	$16 per stocking-hour

Rick Flair, the controller of Figure Four, wants to use this ABC system to examine individual customer profitability within each distribution market. He focuses first on the Ma and Pa single-store distribution market. Two customers are used to exemplify the insights available with the ABC approach. Data pertaining to these two customers in August 2009 are as follows:

	Charleston Pharmacy	Chapel Hill Pharmacy
Total orders	13	10
Average line items per order	9	18
Total store deliveries	7	10
Average cartons shipped per store delivery	22	20
Average hours of shelf-stocking per store delivery	0	0.5
Average revenue per delivery	$2,400	$1,800
Average cost of goods sold per delivery	$2,100	$1,650

Required

1. Use the ABC information to compute the operating income of each customer in August 2009. Comment on the results and what, if anything, Flair should do.
2. Flair ranks the individual customers in the Ma and Pa single-store distribution market on the basis of monthly operating income. The cumulative operating income of the top 20% of customers is $55,680. Figure Four reports operating losses of $21,247 for the bottom 40% of its customers. Make four recommendations that you think Figure Four should consider in light of this new customer-profitability information.

14-23 Variance analysis, multiple products. The Detroit Penguins play in the American Ice Hockey League. The Penguins play in the Downtown Arena (owned and managed by the City of Detroit), which has a capacity of 15,000 seats (5,000 lower-tier seats and 10,000 upper-tier seats). The Downtown Arena charges the Penguins a per-ticket charge for use of their facility. All tickets are sold by the Reservation Network, which charges the Penguins a reservation fee per ticket. The Penguins' budgeted contribution margin for each type of ticket in 2010 is computed as follows:

	Lower-Tier Tickets	Upper-Tier Tickets
Selling price	$35	$14
Downtown Arena fee	10	6
Reservation Network fee	5	3
Contribution margin per ticket	$20	$ 5

The budgeted and actual average attendance figures per game in the 2010 season are:

	Budgeted Seats Sold	Actual Seats Sold
Lower tier	4,000	3,300
Upper tier	6,000	7,700
Total	10,000	11,000

There was no difference between the budgeted and actual contribution margin for lower-tier or upper-tier seats.

The manager of the Penguins was delighted that actual attendance was 10% above budgeted attendance per game, especially given the depressed state of the local economy in the past six months.

Required

1. Compute the sales-volume variance for each type of ticket and in total for the Detroit Penguins in 2010. (Calculate all variances in terms of contribution margins.)
2. Compute the sales-quantity and sales-mix variances for each type of ticket and in total in 2010.
3. Present a summary of the variances in requirements 1 and 2. Comment on the results.

14-24 Variance analysis, working backward. The Jinwa Corporation sells two brands of wine glasses: Plain and Chic. Jinwa provides the following information for sales in the month of June 2009:

Static-budget total contribution margin	$5,600
Budgeted units to be sold of all glasses	2,000 units
Budgeted contribution margin per unit of Plain	$2 per unit
Budgeted contribution margin per unit of Chic	$6 per unit
Total sales-quantity variance	$1,400 U
Actual sales-mix percentage of Plain	60%

All variances are to be computed in contribution-margin terms.

Required

1. Calculate the sales-quantity variances for each product for June 2009.
2. Calculate the individual-product and total sales-mix variances for June 2009. Calculate the individual-product and total sales-volume variances for June 2009.
3. Briefly describe the conclusions you can draw from the variances.

14-25 Variance analysis, multiple products. Soda-King manufactures and sells three soft drinks: Kola, Limor, and Orlem. Budgeted and actual results for 2009 are as follows:

	Budget for 2009			Actual for 2009		
Product	Selling Price	Variable Cost per Carton	Cartons Sold	Selling Price	Variable Cost per Carton	Cartons Sold
Kola	$6.00	$4.00	400,000	$6.20	$4.50	480,000
Limor	$4.00	$2.80	600,000	$4.25	$2.75	900,000
Orlem	$7.00	$4.50	1,500,000	$6.80	$4.60	1,620,000

Required

1. Compute the total sales-volume variance, the total sales-mix variance, and the total sales-quantity variance. (Calculate all variances in terms of contribution margin.) Show results for each product in your computations.
2. What inferences can you draw from the variances computed in requirement 1?

14-26 Market-share and market-size variances (continuation of 14-25). Soda-King prepared the budget for 2009 assuming a 10% market share based on total sales in the western region of the United States. The total soft drinks market was estimated to reach sales of 25 million cartons in the region. However, actual total sales volume in the western region was 24 million cartons.

Required Calculate the market-share and market-size variances for Soda-King in 2009. (Calculate all variances in terms of contribution margin.) Comment on the results.

Problems

14-27 Allocation of corporate costs to divisions. Dusty Rhodes, controller of Richfield Oil Company, is preparing a presentation to senior executives about the performance of its four divisions. Summary data (dollar amounts in millions) related to the four divisions for the most recent year are:

	A	B	C	D	E	F
1		DIVISIONS				
2		Oil & Gas Upstream	Oil & Gas Downstream	Chemical Products	Copper Mining	Total
3	Revenues	$ 8,000	$16,000	$4,800	$3,200	$32,000
4	Operating Costs	3,000	15,000	3,800	3,500	25,300
5	Operating Income	$ 5,000	$ 1,000	$1,000	$ (300)	$ 6,700
6						
7	Identifiable assets	$14,000	$ 6,000	$3,000	$2,000	$25,000
8	Number of employees	9,000	12,000	6,000	3,000	30,000

Under the existing accounting system, costs incurred at corporate headquarters are collected in a single cost pool ($3,228 million in the most recent year) and allocated to each division on the basis of its actual revenues. The top managers in each division share in a division-income bonus pool. Division income is defined as operating income less allocated corporate costs.

Rhodes has analyzed the components of corporate costs and proposes that corporate costs be collected in four cost pools. The components of corporate costs for the most recent year (dollar amounts in millions) and Rhodes' suggested cost pools and allocation bases are:

	A	B	C	D	E	F
11	Corporate Cost Category	Amount	Suggested Cost Pool	Suggested Allocation Base		
12	Interest on debt	$2,000	Cost Pool 1	Identifiable assets		
13	Corporate salaries	150	Cost Pool 2			
14	Accounting and control	110	Cost Pool 2			
15	General marketing	200	Cost Pool 2	Division Revenues		
16	Legal	140	Cost Pool 2			
17	Research and Development	200	Cost Pool 2			
18	Public affairs	203	Cost Pool 3	Positive Operating Income*		
19	Personnel and payroll	225	Cost Pool 4	Number of employees		
20	Total	$3,228				
21						
22	*Since Public Affairs cost includes the cost of public relations staff, lobbyists, and donations to					
23	environmental charities, Rhodes proposes that this cost be allocated using operating income (if positive)					
24	of divisions, with only divisions with positive operating income included in the allocation base.					

If you want to use Excel to solve this problem, go to the Excel Lab at **www.prenhall.com/horngren/cost13e** and download the template for Problem 14-27.

Required

1. Discuss two reasons why Richfield Oil should allocate corporate costs to each division.
2. Calculate the operating income of each division when all corporate costs are allocated based on revenues of each division.
3. Calculate the operating income of each division when all corporate costs are allocated using the four cost pools.
4. How do you think the new proposal will be received by the division managers? What are the strengths and weaknesses of Rhodes' proposal relative to the existing single-cost-pool method?

14-28 Cost allocation to divisions. Forber Bakery makes baked goods for grocery stores, and has three divisions: Bread, Cake, and Doughnuts. Each division is run and evaluated separately, but the main headquarters incurs costs that are indirect costs for the divisions. Costs incurred in the main headquarters are:

Human resources (HR) costs	$1,900,000
Accounting department costs	1,400,000
Rent and depreciation	1,200,000
Other	600,000
Total costs	$5,100,000

The Forber upper management currently allocates this cost to the divisions equally. One of the division managers has done some research on activity-based costing and proposes the use of different allocation bases for the different indirect costs—number of employees for HR costs, total revenues for accounting department costs, square feet of space for rent and depreciation costs, and equal allocation among the divisions of "other" costs. Information about the three divisions follows:

	Bread	Cake	Doughnuts
Total revenues	$20,900,000	$4,500,000	$13,400,000
Direct costs	14,500,000	3,200,000	7,250,000
Segment margin	$ 6,400,000	$1,300,000	$ 6,150,000
Number of employees	400	100	300
Square feet of space	10,000	4,000	6,000

Required

1. Allocate the indirect costs of Forber to each division equally. Calculate division operating income after allocation of headquarter costs.
2. Allocate headquarter costs to the individual divisions using the proposed allocation bases. Calculate the division operating income after allocation. Comment on the allocation bases used to allocate headquarter costs.
3. Which division manager do you think suggested this new allocation? Explain briefly. Which allocation do you think is "better?"

14-29 Customer profitability Ring Delights is a new company that manufactures custom jewelry. Ring Delights currently has six customers referenced by customer number: 01, 02, 03, 04, 05 and 06. Besides the costs of making the jewelry, the company has the following activities:

1. Customer orders. The salespeople, designers, and jewelry makers spend time with the customer. The cost driver rate is $40 per hour spent with a customer.
2. Customer fittings. Before the jewelry piece is completed the customer may come in to make sure it looks right and fits properly. Cost driver rate is $25 per hour.
3. Rush orders. Some customers want their jewelry quickly. The cost driver rate is $100 per rush order.
4. Number of customer return visits. Customers may return jewelry up to 30 days after the pickup of the jewelry to have something refitted or repaired at no charge. The cost driver rate is $30 per return visit.

Information about the six customers follows. Some customers purchased multiple items. The cost of the jewelry is 70% of the selling price.

Customer number	01	02	03	04	05	06
Sales revenue	$600	$4,200	$300	$2,500	$4,900	$700
Cost of item(s)	$420	$2,940	$210	$1,750	$3,430	$490
Hours spent on customer order	2	7	1	5	20	3
Hours on fittings	1	2	0	0	4	1
Number of rush orders	0	0	1	1	3	0
Number of return visits	0	1	0	1	5	1

Required

1. Calculate the customer-level operating income for each customer. Rank the customers in order of most to least profitable and prepare a customer profitability analysis, as in Exhibit 14-7.
2. Are any customers unprofitable? What is causing this? What should Ring Delights do with respect to these customers?

14-30 Customer profitability, distribution. Spring Distribution has decided to analyze the profitability of five new customers (see pp. 508–514). It buys bottled water at $12 per case and sells to retail customers at a list price of $14.40 per case. Data pertaining to the five customers are:

	Customer				
	P	Q	R	S	T
Cases sold	2,080	8,750	60,800	31,800	3,900
List selling price	$14.40	$14.40	$14.40	$14.40	$14.40
Actual selling price	$14.40	$14.16	$13.20	$13.92	$12.96
Number of purchase orders	15	25	30	25	30
Number of customer visits	2	3	6	2	3
Number of deliveries	10	30	60	40	20
Miles traveled per delivery	14	4	3	8	40
Number of expedited deliveries	0	0	0	0	1

Its five activities and their cost drivers are:

Activity	Cost Driver Rate
Order taking	$100 per purchase order
Customer visits	$80 per customer visit
Deliveries	$2 per delivery mile traveled
Product handling	$0.50 per case sold
Expedited deliveries	$300 per expedited delivery

Required

1. Compute the customer-level operating income of each of the five retail customers now being examined (P, Q, R, S, and T). Comment on the results.
2. What insights are gained by reporting both the list selling price and the actual selling price for each customer?
3. What factors should Spring Distribution consider in deciding whether to drop one or more of the five customers?

14-31 Customer profitability in a manufacturing firm. Bizzan Manufacturing makes a component they call P14-31. This component is manufactured only when ordered by a customer, so Bizzan keeps no inventory of P14-31. The list price is $100 per unit, but customers who place "large" orders receive a 10% discount on price. Currently, the salespeople decide whether an order is large enough to qualify for the discount. When the product is finished, it is packed in cases of 10. When a customer order is not a multiple of 10, Bizzan uses a full case to pack the partial amount left over (e.g. if Customer C orders 25 units, three cases will be required). Customers pick up the order so Bizzan incurs costs of holding the product in the warehouse until customer pick up. The customers are manufacturing firms; if the component needs to be exchanged or repaired, customers can come back within 10 days for free exchange or repair.

The full cost of manufacturing a unit of P14-31 is $80. In addition, Bizzan incurs customer-level costs. Customer-level cost-driver rates are:

Order taking	$380 per order
Product handling	$10 per case
Warehousing (holding finished product)	$55 per day
Rush order processing	$520 per rush order
Exchange and repair costs	$40 per unit

Information about Bizzan's five biggest customers follows:

	A	B	C	D	E
Number of units purchased	5,000	2,400	1,200	4,000	8,000
Discounts given	10%	0	10%	0	10% on half the units
Number of orders	10	12	48	16	12
Number of cases	500	240	144	400	812
Days in warehouse (total for all orders)	13	16	0	12	120
Number of rush orders	0	2	0	0	5
Number of units exchanged/repaired	0	30	5	20	95

The salesperson gave customer C a price discount because, although Customer C ordered only 1,200 units in total, only 12 orders (one per month) were placed. The salesperson wanted to reward customer C for repeat business. All customers except E ordered units in the same order size. Customer E's order quantity varied, so E got a discount some of the time but not all the time.

Required

1. Calculate the customer-level operating income for these five customers. Use the format in Exhibit 14-5. Prepare a customer profitability analysis by ranking the customers from most to least profitable, as in Exhibit 14-7
2. Discuss the results of your customer profitability analysis. Does Bizzan have unprofitable customers? Is there anything Bizzan should do differently with its five customers?

14-32 Variance analysis, sales-mix, and sales-quantity variances. Aussie Infonautics, Inc., produces handheld Windows CE™–compatible organizers. Aussie Infonautics markets three different handheld models. PalmPro is a souped-up version for the executive on the go; PalmCE is a consumer-oriented version; and PalmKid is a stripped-down version for the young adult market. You are Aussie Infonautics' senior vice president of marketing. The CEO has discovered that the total contribution margin came in lower than budgeted, and it is your responsibility to explain to him why actual results are different from the budget. Budgeted and actual operating data for the company's third quarter of 2010 are as follows:

Budgeted Operating Data, Third Quarter 2010

	Selling Price	Variable Cost per Unit	Contribution Margin per Unit	Sales Volume in Units
PalmPro	$379	$182	$197	12,500
PalmCE	269	98	171	37,500
PalmKid	149	65	84	50,000
				100,000

Actual Operating Data, Third Quarter 2010

	Selling Price	Variable Cost per Unit	Contribution Margin per Unit	Sales Volume in Units
PalmPro	$349	$178	$171	11,000
PalmCE	285	92	193	44,000
PalmKid	102	73	29	55,000
				110,000

Required

1. Compute the actual and budgeted contribution margins in dollars for each product and in total for the third quarter of 2010.
2. Calculate the actual and budgeted sales mixes for the three products for the third quarter of 2010.
3. Calculate total sales-volume, sales-mix, and sales-quantity variances for the third quarter of 2010. (Calculate all variances in terms of contribution margins.)
4. Given that your CEO is known to have temper tantrums, you want to be well prepared for this meeting. In order to prepare, write a paragraph or two comparing actual results to budgeted amounts.

14-33 Market-share and market-size variances (continuation of 14-32). Aussie Infonautics' senior vice president of marketing prepared his budget at the beginning of the third quarter assuming a 25% market share based on total sales. The total handheld-organizer market was estimated by Foolinstead Research to reach sales of 400,000 units worldwide in the third quarter. However, actual sales in the third quarter were 500,000 units.

Required

1. Calculate the market-share and market-size variances for Aussie Infonautics in the third quarter of 2010 (calculate all variances in terms of contribution margins).
2. Explain what happened based on the market-share and market-size variances.
3. Calculate the actual market size, in units, that would have led to no market-size variance (again using budgeted contribution margin per unit). Use this market-size figure to calculate the actual market share that would have led to a zero market-share variance.

14-34 Variance analysis, multiple products. Debbie's Delight, Inc., operates a chain of cookie stores. Budgeted and actual operating data of its three Chicago stores for August 2009 are as follows:

Budget for August 2009

	Selling Price per Pound	Variable Cost per Pound	Contribution Margin per Pound	Sales Volume in Pounds
Chocolate chip	$4.50	$2.50	$2.00	45,000
Oatmeal raisin	5.00	2.70	2.30	25,000
Coconut	5.50	2.90	2.60	10,000
White chocolate	6.00	3.00	3.00	5,000
Macadamia nut	6.50	3.40	3.10	15,000
				100,000

Actual for August 2009

	Selling Price per Pound	Variable Cost per Pound	Contribution Margin per Pound	Sales Volume in Pounds
Chocolate chip	$4.50	$2.60	$1.90	57,600
Oatmeal raisin	5.20	2.90	2.30	18,000
Coconut	5.50	2.80	2.70	9,600
White chocolate	6.00	3.40	2.60	13,200
Macadamia nut	7.00	4.00	3.00	21,600
				120,000

Debbie's Delight focuses on contribution margin in its variance analysis.

Required

1. Compute the total sales-volume variance for August 2009.
2. Compute the total sales-mix variance for August 2009.
3. Compute the total sales-quantity variance for August 2009.
4. Comment on your results in requirements 1, 2, and 3.

14-35 Market-share and market-size variances (continuation of 14-34). Debbie's Delight attains a 10% market share based on total sales of the Chicago market. The total Chicago market is expected to be 1,000,000 pounds in sales volume for August 2009. The actual total Chicago market for August 2009 was 960,000 pounds in sales volume.

Required

Compute the market-share and market-size variances for Debbie's Delight in August 2009. Calculate all variances in contribution-margin terms. Comment on the results.

14-36 Direct materials efficiency, mix and yield variances. Flavr-Wave Company makes candy. Their most popular product is the toe pop, a large lollipop shaped like a toe. The direct materials used in the toe pop are sugar, flavoring, and coloring. For each batch of 100 pops, the budgeted quantities and budgeted prices of direct materials are as follows:

	Quantity for One Batch	Price of Input
Sugar	7 cups	$1 per cup
Flavoring	2 cups	$3 per cup
Coloring	1 cup	$2 per cup

Changing the standard mix of direct material quantities slightly does not significantly affect the overall end product, particularly for the flavoring and coloring.

In the current period, Flavr-Wave made 2,300 toe pops in 23 batches with the following actual quantity, cost and mix of inputs:

	Actual Quantity	Actual Cost	Actual Mix (rounded)
Sugar	165 cups	$165	70%
Flavoring	45 cups	135	19%
Coloring	25 cups	50	11%
Total actual	235	$350	100%

Required

1. What is the budgeted cost of direct materials for the 2,300 toe pops?
2. Calculate the total direct materials efficiency variance.
3. Why is the total direct materials price variance zero?
4. Calculate the total direct materials mix and yield variances. What are these variances telling you about the 2,300 toe pops produced this period? Are the variances large enough to investigate?

14-37 Materials variances: price, efficiency, mix, and yield. PDS Manufacturing makes wooden furniture. One of their products is a wooden dresser. The exterior and some of the shelves are made of oak, a high quality wood, but the interior drawers are made of pine, a less expensive wood. The budgeted direct materials quantities and prices for one dresser are:

	Quantity	Price per Unit of Input	Cost for One Dresser
Oak	8 board feet	$6 per board foot	$48
Pine	12 board feet	2 per board foot	24

That is, each dresser is budgeted to use 20 board feet of wood, comprised of 40% oak and 60% pine, although sometimes more pine is used in place of oak with no obvious change in the quality or function of the dresser.

During the month of May, PDS manufactures 3,000 dressers. Actual direct materials costs are:

Oak (23,180 board feet)	$141,398
Pine (37,820 board feet)	68,076
Total actual direct materials cost	$209,474

Required

1. What is the budgeted cost of direct materials for 3,000 dressers?
2. Calculate the total direct materials price and efficiency variances.
3. For the 3,000 dressers, what is the total actual amount of oak and pine used? What is the actual direct materials input mix percentage? What is the budgeted amount of oak and pine that should have been used for the 3,000 dressers?

4. Calculate the total direct materials mix and yield variances. How do these numbers relate to the total direct materials efficiency variance? What do these variances tell you?

14-38 Customer profitability and ethics. Glat Corporation manufactures a product called the glat, which it sells to merchandising firms such as International House of Glats (IHoG,) Glats-R-Us (GRU,) Glat Marcus (GM,) Glat City (GC,) Good Glats (GG,) and Glat-mart (Gmart.) The list price of a glat is $40, and the full manufacturing costs are $30. Salespeople receive a commission on sales, but the commission is based on number of orders taken, not on sales revenue generated or number of units sold. Salespeople receive a commission of $20 per order (in addition to regular salary.)

Glat Corporation makes products based on anticipated demand. Glat Corporation carries an inventory of glats so rush orders do not result in any extra manufacturing costs over and above the $30 per glat. Glat Corporation ships finished product to the customer at no additional charge to the customer for either regular or expedited delivery. Glat incurs significantly higher costs for expedited deliveries than for regular deliveries.

Expected and actual customer-level cost driver rates are:

Order taking (excluding sales commission)	$28 per order
Product handling	$1 per unit
Delivery	$1 per mile driven
Expedited (rush) delivery	$300 per shipment

Because salespeople are paid $20 per order, they break up large orders into multiple smaller orders. This practice reduces the actual order taking cost by $16 per smaller order (from $28 per order to $12 per order) because the smaller orders are all written at the same time. This lower cost rate is not included in budgeted rates because salespeople create smaller orders without telling management or the accounting department. Also, salespeople offer customers discounts to entice them to place more orders; GRU and Gmart each receive a 5% discount off the list price of $40.

Information about Glat's clients follows:

	IHG	GRU	GM	GC	GG	Gmart
Total number of units purchased	200	540	300	100	400	1,000
Number of actual orders	2	12	2	2	4	10
Number of written orders per actual order	2	1*	3	2	4	2
Total number of miles driven to deliver all products	80	120	72	28	304	100
Number of expedited deliveries	0	4	0	0	1	3

*Because GRU places 12 separate orders, its order costs are $28 per order. All other orders are multiple smaller orders and so have actual order costs of $12 each.

Required

1. Using the information above, calculate the expected customer-level operating income for the six customers of Glat Corporation. Use the number of written orders at $28 each to calculate expected order costs.
2. Recalculate the customer-level operating income using the number of written orders but at their actual $12 cost per order instead of $28 (except for GRU, whose actual cost is $28 per order.) How will Glat Corporation evaluate customer-level operating cost performance this period?
3. Recalculate the customer-level operating income if salespeople had not broken up actual orders into multiple smaller orders. Don't forget to also adjust sales commissions.
4. How is the behavior of the salespeople affecting the profit of Glat Corporation? Is their behavior ethical? What could Glat Corporation do to change the behavior of the salespeople?

Collaborative Learning Problem

14-39 Cost allocation and decision making. Greenbold Manufacturing has four divisions named after its locations: Arizona, Colorado, Delaware, and Florida. Corporate headquarters is in Minnesota. Greenbold corporate headquarters incurs $5,600,000 per period, which is an indirect cost of the divisions. Corporate headquarters currently allocates this cost to the divisions based on the revenues of each division. The CEO has asked each division manager to suggest an allocation base for the indirect headquarters costs from among revenues, segment margin, direct costs, and number of employees. Below is relevant information about each division:

	Arizona	Colorado	Delaware	Florida
Revenues	$7,800,000	$8,500,000	$6,200,000	$5,500,000
Direct costs	5,300,000	4,100,000	4,300,000	4,600,000
Segment margin	$2,500,000	$4,400,000	$1,900,000	$ 900,000
Number of employees	2,000	4,000	1,500	500

Required

1. Allocate the indirect headquarters costs of Greenbold Manufacturing to each of the four divisions using revenues, direct costs, segment margin, and number of employees as the allocation bases. Calculate operating margins for each division after allocating headquarters costs.
2. Which allocation base do you think the manager of the Florida division would prefer? Explain.
3. What factors would you consider in deciding which allocation base Greenbold should use?
4. Suppose the Greenbold CEO decides to use direct costs as the allocation base. Should the Florida division be closed? Why or why not?

15 Allocation of Support-Department Costs, Common Costs, and Revenues

Learning Objectives

1. Distinguish the single-rate method from the dual-rate method
2. Understand how the uncertainty users face is affected by the choice between budgeted and actual cost-allocation rates
3. Allocate support-department costs using the direct method, the step down method, and the reciprocal method
4. Allocate common costs using the stand-alone method and the incremental method
5. Explain the importance of explicit agreement between contracting parties when the reimbursement amount is based on costs incurred
6. Understand how bundling of products gives rise to revenue-allocation issues
7. Allocate the revenues of a bundled product to the individual products in that bundle.

How a company allocates its overhead and internal support costs—costs related to marketing, advertising, and other internal services—among its various production departments or projects, can have a big impact on how profitable those departments or projects are. The allocation won't affect the firm's profit as a whole. However, it can make some departments and projects (and their managers) look better or worse than they should profit-wise, if the allocation isn't done properly.

As the following article shows, Hollywood movie studios allocate certain costs to the different films they produce. And these allocations, in turn, determine how profitable (or not) a film is. The problem is that how these allocations are made affects not just the people who work for the studio but also those outside of the firm—people like writers and others who have been promised a return on the film's net profits.

Is Hollywood Taking "Creative License" With Its Cost Allocations?[1]

Hollywood accounting can be every bit as creative as a good movie script. The hit movie *Forrest Gump,* which won the Academy Award for Best Picture of 1994, claimed a worldwide theatrical gross of $661 million through May of 1995. Yet, according to Paramount Studios, by the end of 1994, the film project had lost $62 million on a box-office gross of $382 million. It is just one of a string of hit movies to report a loss.

The production costs for a film represent only a fraction of the cost charged to the project. In addition, studios add charges for advertising and studio overhead, as well as promotion, distribution, and financing costs to the total cost of the project. Another significant portion of the cost is the payment made to *gross participants* on the basis of a percentage of the studio's gross revenues—not its net profits. Often, gross participants are star actors, directors, or producers.

If a film doesn't break even according to the studio's accounting, it creates a problem for people who have contracted with the studio as *net-profit participants.* Writers, for example, and actors who are considered minor talent are usually net-profit participants.

How can the studios be losing so much money on their most successful projects? At issue is the way the studios calculate the net profit. Critics argue that some of the costs, such as distribution fees,

[1] *Source:* Glenn Pfeiffer, Robert Capettini, and Gene Whittenburg, "Forrest Gump—Accountant—A Study of Accounting in the Motion Picture Industry," *Journal of Accounting Education,* Vol. 15, No. 3, pp. 319–334, 1997, Elsevier Science Ltd.; en.wikipedia.org/wiki/Hollywood_accounting (accessed 10/03/07).

are really studio profits disguised as costs. In addition, charges for overhead, such as studio and advertising overhead, are based on arbitrary allocations, which some have argued are much greater than the actual overhead costs attributable to the film.

Winston Groom, the author of *Forrest Gump,* was paid $350,000 for the movie rights to the book and was entitled to 3 percent of the film's net profits. When Paramount reported that the movie took a loss, Groom retained an attorney to try to get his fair share of the movie's true profits. Similar lawsuits have occurred in recent years in connection with blockbuster movies such as *Spider-Man* and *Lord of the Rings*.

Similar to the issues within the Hollywood studio accounting example, issues related to the allocation of corporate costs or the costs of support departments, as well as the apportionment of revenues when products are sold in bundles, are a perennial source of controversy within organizations. These concerns are common to managers at manufacturing companies such as Nestle, merchandising companies such as Staples, service companies such as Verizon, and universities such as New York University. This chapter focuses on several challenges that arise with regard to cost and revenue allocations.

Allocating Costs of a Support Department to Operating Departments

Learning Objective 1

Distinguish the single-rate method

. . . one rate for allocating costs in a cost pool

from the dual-rate method

. . . two rates for allocating costs in a cost pool—one for variable costs and one for fixed costs

Companies distinguish operating departments (and operating divisions) from support departments. An **operating department**, which is also called a **production department**, directly adds value to a product or service. A **support department**, which is also called a **service department**, provides the services that assist other internal departments (operating departments and other support departments) in the company. Examples of support departments are information systems and plant maintenance. Managers face two questions when allocating the costs of a support department to operating departments or divisions: (1) Should fixed costs of support departments be allocated to operating divisions? (2) If fixed costs are allocated, should variable and fixed costs be allocated in the same way? With regard to the first question, most companies believe that fixed costs of support departments should be allocated because the support department needs to incur fixed costs to provide operating divisions with the services they require. Depending on the answer to the second question, there are two approaches to allocating support-department costs: the *single-rate cost-allocation method* and the *dual-rate cost-allocation method.*

Single-Rate and Dual-Rate Methods

The **single-rate method** makes no distinction between fixed and variable costs. It allocates costs in each cost pool (support department in this section) to cost objects (operating divisions in this section) using the same rate per unit of a single allocation base. By contrast, the **dual-rate method** partitions the cost of each support department into two pools—a variable-cost pool and a fixed-cost pool—and allocates each using a different cost-allocation base. When using either the single-rate method or the dual-rate method, managers can allocate support-department costs to operating divisions based on (a) *budgeted* rate and hours *budgeted* to be used by operating divisions, or (b) *budgeted* rate and *actual* hours used by operating divisions. We illustrate each of these methods next.[2]

Consider the Central Computer Department of Sand Hill Company (SHC). This support department has two users, both operating divisions: the Microcomputer Division and the Peripheral Equipment Division. The following data relate to the 2009 budget:

Practical capacity	18,750 hours
Fixed costs of operating the computer facility in the 6,000-hour to 18,750-hour relevant range	$3,000,000
Budgeted long-run usage (quantity) in hours:	
Microcomputer Division	8,000 hours
Peripheral Equipment Division	4,000 hours
Total	12,000 hours
Budgeted variable cost per hour in the 6,000-hour to 18,750-hour relevant range	$200 per hour used
Actual usage in 2009 in hours:	
Microcomputer Division	9,000 hours
Peripheral Equipment Division	3,000 hours
Total	12,000 hours

The budgeted rates for Central Computer Department costs can be computed based on either the demand for computer services or the supply of computer services. We consider the allocation of Central Computer Department costs based first on the demand for (or usage of) computer services and then on the supply of computer services.

Allocation Based on the Demand for (or Usage of) Computer Services

We present the single-rate method followed by the dual-rate method.

Single-rate method In this method, a combined budgeted rate is used for fixed and variable costs. The rate is calculated as follows.

Budgeted usage	12,000 hours
Budgeted total cost pool: $3,000,000 + (12,000 hours × $200/hour)	$5,400,000
Budgeted total rate per hour: $5,400,000 ÷ 12,000 hours	$450 per hour used
Allocation rate for Microcomputer Division	$450 per hour used
Allocation rate for Peripheral Equipment Division	$450 per hour used

Note that the budgeted rate of $450 per hour is substantially higher than the $200 budgeted *variable* cost per hour. That's because the $450 rate includes an allocated amount of $250 per hour (budgeted fixed costs, $3,000,000, ÷ budgeted usage, 12,000 hours) for the *fixed* costs of operating the facility.

The single-rate method is generally employed in conjunction with option (b) mentioned earlier (budgeted rate and actual hours). Applying this to our example, SHC allocates Central Computer Department costs based on the budgeted rate and *actual* hours used by the operating divisions. The support costs allocated to the two divisions under this method are as follows:

[2] A third approach is to use the *actual* rate and *actual* hours used by operating divisions, but this is neither conceptually preferred nor widely used in practice. We explain why later in this section.

Microcomputer Division: 9,000 hours × $450 per hour	$4,050,000
Peripheral Equipment Division: 3,000 hours × $450 per hour	$1,350,000

A problem with the single-rate method is that it makes the $250 allocated fixed cost per hour of the Central Computer Department appear as a variable cost to users of that department. As a result, the operating divisions might take actions that could harm SHC as a whole. For example, suppose an external vendor offers the Microcomputer Division computer services at a rate of $340 per hour, at a time when the Central Computer Department has unused capacity. The Microcomputer Division's managers may be tempted to use this vendor because it would appear to decrease costs ($340 per hour instead of $450 per hour if it uses the Central Computer Department). In the short run, however, the fixed costs of the Central Computer Department remain unchanged in the relevant range (between 6,000 hours of usage and the practical capacity of 18,750 hours). SHC will therefore incur an additional cost of $140 per hour if the managers were to take this offer—the difference between the $340 external purchase price and the true internal variable cost of $200 of using the Central Computer Department.

Dual-rate method When the dual-rate method is used, allocation bases must be chosen for both the variable and fixed cost pools of the Central Computer Department. SHC allocates variable costs to each division based on the *budgeted* variable cost per hour of $200 for *actual* hours used by each division (option (b), as in the single-rate method above). SHC allocates fixed costs based on *budgeted* fixed costs per hour and the *budgeted* number of hours for each division (option (a) mentioned earlier). In effect, the fixed costs are assigned as a lump-sum based on the relative proportions of the central computing facilities expected to be used by the operating divisions. Given the budgeted usage of 8,000 hours for the Microcomputer Division and 4,000 hours for the Peripheral Equipment Division, the budgeted fixed-cost rate is $250 per hour ($3,000,000 ÷ 12,000 hours). The costs allocated to the Microcomputer Division in 2009 would be:

Fixed costs: $250 per hour × 8,000 (budgeted) hours	$2,000,000
Variable costs: $200 per hour × 9,000 (actual) hours	1,800,000
Total costs	$3,800,000

The costs allocated to the Peripheral Equipment Division in 2009 would be:

Fixed costs: $250 per hour × 4,000 (budgeted) hours	$1,000,000
Variable costs: $200 per hour × 3,000 (actual) hours	600,000
Total costs	$1,600,000

If you were to use the same option—either option (a), budgeted rates and budgeted hours of usage, or option (b), budgeted rates and actual hours of usage—throughout, the single-rate and dual-rate methods would yield identical results. However, this is not the case in the SHC example. Both fixed and variable costs are assigned jointly using option (b) in the single-rate method. Yet, variable costs are assigned using option (b) in the dual-rate method, while fixed costs are assigned using option (a). In other words, the final cost allocations under the two methods differ in the SHC example because the single-rate method allocates fixed costs of the support department based on actual usage of computer resources by the user divisions, whereas the dual-rate method allocates fixed costs based on budgeted usage.

We next consider the alternative approach of allocating Central Computer Department costs based on the capacity of computer services supplied.

Allocation Based on the Supply of Capacity

We illustrate this approach using the 18,750 hours of practical capacity of the Central Computer Department. The budgeted rate is then determined as follows:

Budgeted fixed-cost rate per hour, $3,000,000 ÷ 18,750 hours	$160 per hour
Budgeted variable-cost rate per hour	200 per hour
Budgeted total-cost rate per hour	$360 per hour

Using the same options for the single-rate and dual-rate methods as in the previous section, the support cost allocations to the operating divisions are as follows:

Single-rate method	
Microcomputer Division: \$360 per hour × 9,000 (actual) hours	\$3,240,000
Peripheral Equipment Division: \$360 per hour × 3,000 (actual) hours	1,080,000
Fixed costs of unused computer capacity:	
\$160 per hour × 6,750 hours[a]	1,080,000

[a] 6,750 hours = Practical capacity of 18,750 − (9,000 hours used by Microcomputer Division + 3,000 hours used by Peripheral Equipment Division).

Dual-rate method	
Microcomputer Division	
Fixed costs: \$160 per hour × 8,000 (budgeted) hours	\$1,280,000
Variable costs: \$200 per hour × 9,000 (actual) hours	1,800,000
Total costs	\$3,080,000
Peripheral Equipment Division	
Fixed costs: \$160 per hour × 4,000 (budgeted) hours	\$ 640,000
Variable costs: \$200 per hour × 3,000 (actual) hours	600,000
Total costs	\$1,240,000
Fixed costs of unused computer capacity:	
\$160 per hour × 6,750 hours[b]	\$1,080,000

[b] 6,750 hours = Practical capacity of 18,750 hours − (8,000 hours budgeted to be used by Microcomputer Division + 4,000 hours budgeted to be used by Peripheral Equipment Division).

When practical capacity is used to allocate costs, the single-rate and the dual-rate methods allocate, respectively, only the actual fixed-cost resources used or the budgeted fixed-cost resources to be used by the Microcomputer and Peripheral Equipment divisions. Unused Central Computer Department resources are highlighted but usually not allocated to the divisions. If, however, the slack in Central Computer Department resources was caused by one of the divisions—say, the Microcomputer Division, asking for Central Computer Department resources that it later did not need—the unused Central Computer Department resources would be allocated to the Microcomputer Division.

The advantage of using practical capacity to allocate costs is that it focuses management's attention on managing unused capacity (described in Chapter 9, pp. 315–316, and Chapter 13, pp. 482–485). Using practical capacity also avoids burdening the user divisions with the cost of unused capacity of the Central Computer Department. In contrast, when costs are allocated on the basis of the demand for computer services (either budgeted or actual usage), all \$3,000,000 of fixed costs, including the cost of unused capacity, are allocated to user divisions. If costs are used as a basis for pricing, then charging user divisions for unused capacity could result in the downward demand spiral (see p. 316).

There are benefits and costs of both the single-rate and dual-rate methods. One benefit of the single-rate method is the low cost to implement it. The single-rate method avoids the often-expensive analysis necessary to classify the individual cost items of a department into fixed and variable categories. However, the single-rate method makes the allocated fixed costs of the support department appear as variable costs to the operating divisions. Consequently, the single-rate method may lead division managers to make outsourcing decisions that are in their own best interest but that may hurt the organization as a whole.

A big benefit of the dual-rate method is that it signals to division managers how variable costs and fixed costs behave differently. This information guides division managers to make decisions that benefit the organization as a whole, as well as each division. For example, using a third-party computer provider that charges more than \$200 per hour would result in SHC being worse off than if its own Central Computer Department were used, because the latter has a variable cost of \$200 per hour. Under the dual-rate method, neither division manager has an incentive to pay more than \$200 per hour for an external provider because the internal charge for computer services is precisely that amount. By charging the fixed costs of resources budgeted to be used by the divisions as a lump-sum, the dual-rate method succeeds in removing fixed costs from the division managers' consideration when making marginal decisions regarding the outsourcing of services.

Budgeted Usage, Actual Usage, and Capacity-Level Allocation Bases

We have studied the dual-rate method under the assumption that fixed costs are assigned on the basis of budgeted usage. The choice between actual usage and budgeted usage for allocating fixed costs can affect a manager's behavior. We illustrate this next.

Consider the budget of $3,000,000 fixed costs at the Central Computer Department of SHC. Recall that budgeted usage is 8,000 hours for the Microcomputer Division and 4,000 hours for the Peripheral Equipment Division. Assume that actual usage by the Microcomputer Division is always equal to budgeted usage. We consider three cases: when actual usage by the Peripheral Equipment Division equals (Case 1), is greater than (Case 2), and is less than (Case 3) budgeted usage.

Allocation based on budgeted usage When budgeted usage is the allocation base, user divisions know their allocated costs in advance. In all three cases, regardless of actual usage, the fixed-cost allocations are the same (Exhibit 15-1, column 2). This information helps the user divisions with both short-run and long-run planning. Companies commit to infrastructure costs (such as the fixed costs of a support department) on the basis of a long-run planning horizon; budgeted usage measures the long-run demands of the user divisions for support-department services.

Allocating fixed costs on the basis of budgeted long-run usage may tempt some managers to underestimate their planned usage. Underestimating will result in their divisions bearing a lower percentage of fixed costs (assuming all other managers do not similarly underestimate their usage). To discourage such underestimates, some companies offer bonuses or other rewards—the carrot approach—to managers who make accurate forecasts of long-run usage. Other companies impose cost penalties—the stick approach—for underestimating long-run usage. For instance, a higher cost rate is charged after a division exceeds its budgeted usage.

Allocation based on actual usage Exhibit 15-1, column 3, presents the allocation of total fixed costs of $3,000,000 to each division when allocations are made on the basis of actual usage. Compare columns 2 and 3 in Exhibit 15-1. In Case 1, the fixed-cost allocation equals the budgeted amount. In Case 2, the fixed-cost allocation is $400,000 less to the Microcomputer Division than the amount based on budgeted usage ($1,600,000 versus $2,000,000). In Case 3, the fixed-cost allocation is $400,000 more to the Microcomputer Division than the amount based on budgeted usage ($2,400,000 versus $2,000,000). Why does the Microcomputer Division receive $400,000 more in costs in Case 3, even though its actual usage equals its budgeted usage? Because the total fixed costs of $3,000,000 are now spread over 2,000 fewer hours of actual total usage. In other words, the lower usage by the Peripheral Equipment Division leads to an increase in the fixed costs allocated to the

Exhibit 15-1 Effect of Variations in Actual Usage on Cost Allocation to Divisions

	(1) Actual Usage		(2) Budgeted Usage as Allocation Base		(3) Actual Usage as Allocation Base		(4) Practical Capacity-Based Allocations	
Case	Micro. Div.	Periph. Div.	Micro. Div.	Periph. Div.	Micro. Div.	Periph. Div.	Micro. Div.	Periph. Div.
1	8,000 hours	4,000 hours	$2,000,000[a]	$1,000,000[b]	$2,000,000[a]	$1,000,000[b]	$1,280,000[g]	$ 640,000[h]
2	8,000 hours	7,000 hours	$2,000,000[a]	$1,000,000[b]	$1,600,000[c]	$1,400,000[d]	$1,280,000[g]	$1,120,000[i]
3	8,000 hours	2,000 hours	$2,000,000[a]	$1,000,000[b]	$2,400,000[e]	$ 600,000[f]	$1,280,000[g]	$ 320,000[j]

[a] $\frac{8,000}{(8,000+4,000)} \times \$3,000,000$ [c] $\frac{8,000}{(8,000+7,000)} \times \$3,000,000$ [e] $\frac{8,000}{(8,000+2,000)} \times \$3,000,000$ [g] $8,000 \times \$160$ [i] $7,000 \times \$160$

[b] $\frac{4,000}{(8,000+4,000)} \times \$3,000,000$ [d] $\frac{7,000}{(8,000+7,000)} \times \$3,000,000$ [f] $\frac{2,000}{(8,000+2,000)} \times \$3,000,000$ [h] $4,000 \times \$160$ [j] $2,000 \times \$160$

Microcomputer Division. When allocations are based on actual usage, user divisions will not know their fixed cost allocations until the end of the budget period.

Allocation based on practical capacity As we have seen, an alternative to using measures of capacity demanded—budgeted usage or actual usage—is to allocate fixed costs of the Central Computer Department on the basis of the practical capacity supplied. The budgeted fixed-cost rate is \$160 per hour (budgeted fixed costs, \$3,000,000, ÷ practical capacity, 18,750 hours). Exhibit 15-1, column 4, shows the fixed costs allocated to the Microcomputer and Peripheral Equipment divisions using this approach.

There are three features of this approach: (1) each division is charged only for the computer-facility services it actually uses; (2) variations in actual usage in one division (the Peripheral Equipment Division) do not affect the costs allocated to the other division (the Microcomputer Division is allocated \$1,280,000 in all three cases); and (3) the costs of unused capacity of the Central Computer Department are highlighted and are not allocated to user divisions. In all three cases, because of the presence of slack capacity, the total amount of fixed costs allocated to the user divisions is less than the \$3,000,000 fixed costs of the Central Computer Department.

Budgeted versus Actual Rates

Learning Objective 2

Understand how the uncertainty users face is affected by the choice between budgeted cost-allocation rates

. . . there is no uncertainty because users know the rates at the start of the period

and actual cost-allocation rates

. . . there is uncertainty because users don't know the rates until the end of the period

The methods we have illustrated so far have all used budgeted rates to assign costs. An alternative approach is to employ the actual rates based on the costs realized during the period. This method is much less common because of the level of uncertainty it imposes on user divisions. When allocations are made using budgeted rates, managers of divisions to which costs are allocated know with certainty the rates to be used in that budget period. Users can then determine the amount of the service to request and—if company policy allows—whether to use the internal source or an external vendor. In contrast, when actual rates are used for cost allocation, user divisions will not know the rates to be used until the end of the budget period.

Budgeted rates also help motivate the manager of the supplier (support) department (for example, the Central Computer Department) to improve efficiency. During the budget period, the supplier department, not the user divisions, bears the risk of any unfavorable cost variances. That's because user divisions do not pay for any costs or inefficiencies of the supplier department that cause actual rates to exceed budgeted rates.

The manager of the supplier department would likely view the budgeted rates negatively if unfavorable cost variances occur due to price increases outside of his or her control. Some organizations try to identify these uncontrollable factors and relieve the supplier-department manager of responsibility for these variances. In other organizations, the supplier department and the user division agree to share the risk (through an explicit formula) of a large, uncontrollable increase in the prices of inputs used by the supplier department. This procedure avoids imposing the risk completely on either the supplier department (as when budgeted rates are used) or the user division (as in the case of actual rates).

For the rest of this chapter, we will continue to consider only allocation methods that employ budgeted rates.

Allocating Costs of Multiple Support Departments

We just examined general issues that arise when allocating costs from one support department to operating divisions. In this section, we examine the special cost-allocation problems that arise when two or more of the support departments whose costs are being allocated provide reciprocal support to each other as well as to operating departments. An example of reciprocal support is a Corporate Human Resource (HR) Department providing services to a Corporate Legal Department (such as advice about hiring attorneys) while the Corporate Legal Department provides services to the HR department (such as advice on compliance with labor laws). More-accurate support-department cost allocations result in more-accurate product, service, and customer costs.

Consider Castleford Engineering, which operates at practical capacity to manufacture engines used in electric-power generating plants. Castleford has two support departments and two operating departments in its manufacturing facility:

Support Departments	**Operating Departments**
Plant (and equipment) maintenance	Machining
Information systems	Assembly

The two support departments at Castleford provide reciprocal support to each other as well as support to the two operating departments. Costs are accumulated in each department for planning and control purposes. Exhibit 15-2 displays the data for this example. To understand the percentages in this exhibit, consider the Plant Maintenance Department. This support department provides a total of 20,000 hours of support work: 20% (4,000 ÷ 20,000 = 0.20) for the Information Systems Department, 30% (6,000 ÷ 20,000 = 0.30) for the Machining Department, and 50% (10,000 ÷ 20,000 = 0.50) for the Assembly Department.

We now examine three methods of allocating the costs of reciprocal support departments: *direct*, *step-down*, and *reciprocal*. To simplify the explanation and to focus on concepts, we use the single-rate method to allocate the costs of each support department using budgeted rates and budgeted hours used by the other departments. (The Problem for Self-Study illustrates the dual-rate method for allocating reciprocal support-department costs.)

Learning Objective 3

Allocate support-department costs using the direct method,

. . . allocate support-department costs directly to operating departments

the step-down method,

. . . partially allocates support-department costs to other support departments

and the reciprocal method

. . . fully allocates support-department costs to other support departments

Direct Method

The **direct method** allocates each support department's costs to operating departments only. The direct method does not allocate support-department costs to other support departments. Exhibit 15-3 illustrates this method using the data in Exhibit 15-2. The base used to allocate Plant Maintenance costs to the operating departments is the budgeted total maintenance labor-hours worked in the operating departments: 6,000 + 10,000 = 16,000 hours. This amount excludes the 4,000 hours of budgeted support time provided by Plant Maintenance to Information Systems. Similarly, the base used for allocation of Information Systems costs to the operating departments is 4,000 + 500 = 4,500 budgeted hours of computer time, which excludes the 500 hours of budgeted support time provided by Information Systems to Plant Maintenance.

An equivalent approach to implementing the direct method involves calculating a budgeted rate for each support department's costs. For example, the rate for Plant Maintenance Department costs is $6,300,000 ÷ 16,000 hours, or $393.75 per hour. The Machining Department is then allocated $2,362,500 ($393.75 per hour × 6,000 hours)

Exhibit 15-2 Data for Allocating Support-Department Costs at Castleford Engineering for 2009

File Edit View Insert Format Tools Data Window Help

	A	B	C	D	E	F	G
1		SUPPORT DEPARTMENTS			OPERATING DEPARTMENTS		
2		Plant Maintenance	Information Systems		Machining	Assembly	Total
3	Budgeted overhead costs						
4	before any interdepartment cost allocations	$6,300,000	$1,452,150		$4,000,000	$2,000,000	$13,752,150
5	Support work furnished:						
6	By Plant Maintenance						
7	Budgeted labor-hours	—	4,000		6,000	10,000	20,000
8	Percentage	—	20%		30%	50%	100%
9	By Information Systems						
10	Budgeted computer hours	500	—		4,000	500	5,000
11	Percentage	10%	—		80%	10%	100%

Exhibit 15-3 Direct Method of Allocating Support-Department Costs at Castleford Engineering for 2009

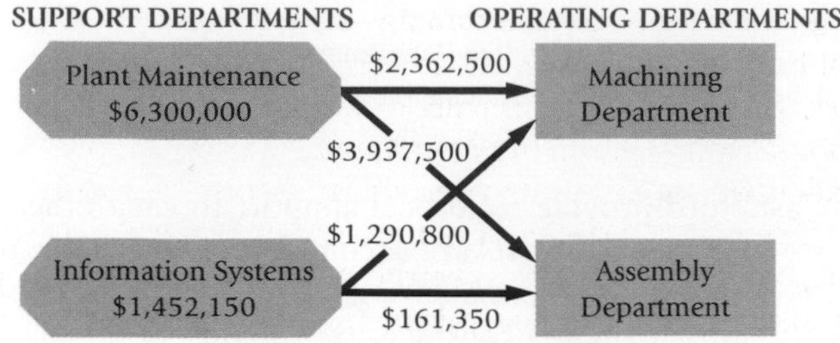

	A	B	C	D	E	F	G
1		SUPPORT DEPARTMENTS			OPERATING DEPARTMENTS		
2		Plant Maintenance	Information Systems		Machining	Assembly	Total
3	Budgeted overhead costs						
4	before any interdepartment cost allocations	$6,300,000	$1,452,150		$4,000,000	$2,000,000	$13,752,150
5	Allocation of Plant Maintenance (3/8, 5/8)[a]	(6,300,000)			2,362,500	3,937,500	
6	Allocation of Information Systems (8/9, 1/9)[b]		(1,452,150)		1,290,800	161,350	
7							
8	Total budgeted overhead of operating departments	$ 0	$ 0		$7,653,300	$6,098,850	$13,752,150
9							
10	[a] Base is (6,000 + 10,000), or 16,000 hours; 6,000 ÷ 16,000 = 3/8; 10,000 ÷ 16,000 = 5/8.						
11	[b] Base is (4,000 + 500), or 4,500 hours; 4,000 ÷ 4,500 = 8/9; 500 ÷ 4,500 = 1/9.						

while the Assembly Department is assigned $3,937,500 ($393.75 per hour × 10,000 hours). For ease of explanation throughout this section, we will use the fraction of the support-department services used by other departments, rather than calculate budgeted rates, to allocate support-department costs.

The direct method is widely practiced because of its ease of use. The benefit of the direct method is simplicity. There is no need to predict the usage of support-department services by other support departments. A disadvantage of the direct method is that it ignores information about reciprocal services provided among support departments and can therefore lead to inaccurate estimates of the cost of operating departments. We now examine a second approach, which partially recognizes the services provided among support departments.

Step-Down Method

Some organizations use the **step-down method**—also called the **sequential allocation method**—which allocates support-department costs to other support departments and to operating departments in a sequential manner that partially recognizes the mutual services provided among all support departments.

Exhibit 15-4 shows the step-down method. The Plant Maintenance costs of $6,300,000 are allocated first. Exhibit 15-2 shows that Plant Maintenance provides 20% of its services to Information Systems, 30% to Machining, and 50% to Assembly. Therefore, $1,260,000 is allocated to Information Systems (20% of $6,300,000), $1,890,000 to Machining (30% of $6,300,000), and $3,150,000 to Assembly (50% of $6,300,000). The Information Systems costs now total $2,712,150: budgeted costs of the Information Systems Department before any interdepartmental cost allocations, $1,452,150, plus $1,260,000 from the allocation of Plant Maintenance costs to the Information Systems Department. The $2,712,150 is then only allocated between the two operating departments based on the proportion of the Information Systems Department services provided to Machining and Assembly. From Exhibit 15-2, the Information Systems Department provides 80% of its services to Machining and 10% to Assembly, so \$2,410,800 (8/9 × \$2,712,150) is allocated to Machining and \$301,350 (1/9 × \$2,712,150) is allocated to Assembly.

Note that this method requires the support departments to be ranked (sequenced) in the order that the step-down allocation is to proceed. In our example, the costs of the Plant Maintenance Department were allocated first to all other departments, including the Information Systems Department. The costs of the Information Systems support department were allocated second, but only to the two operating departments. Different sequences will result in different allocations of support-department costs to operating departments—for example, if the Information Systems Department costs had been allocated first and the Plant Maintenance Department costs second. A popular step-down sequence begins with the support department that renders the highest percentage of its total services to *other support departments*. The sequence continues with the department that renders the next-highest percentage, and so on, ending with the support department that renders the lowest percentage.[3] In our example, costs of the Plant Maintenance Department were allocated first because it provides 20% of its services to the Information Systems Department, whereas the Information Systems Department provides only 10% of its services to the Plant Maintenance Department (see Exhibit 15-2).

Under the step-down method, once a support department's costs have been allocated, no subsequent support-department costs are allocated back to it. Once the Plant Maintenance

Exhibit 15-4 Step-Down Method of Allocating Support-Department Costs at Castleford Engineering for 2009

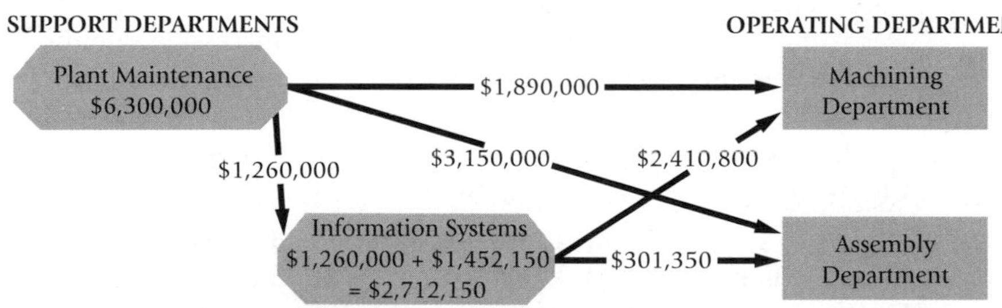

	A	B	C	D	E	F	G
1		SUPPORT DEPARTMENTS			OPERATING DEPARTMENTS		
2		Plant Maintenance	Information Systems		Machining	Assembly	Total
3	Budgeted overhead costs before any						
4	interdepartment cost allocations	\$6,300,000	\$1,452,150		\$4,000,000	\$2,000,000	\$13,752,150
5	Allocation of Plant Maintenance (2/10, 3/10, 5/10)[a]	(6,300,000)	1,260,000		1,890,000	3,150,000	
6			2,712,150				
7	Allocation of Information Systems (8/9, 1/9)[b]		(2,712,150)		2,410,800	301,350	
8							
9	Total budgeted overhead of operating departments	\$ 0	\$ 0		\$8,300,800	\$5,451,350	\$13,752,150
10							
11	[a] Base is (4,000 + 6,000 + 10,000), or 20,000 hours; 4,000 ÷ 20,000 = 2/10; 6,000 ÷ 20,000 = 3/10; 10,000 ÷ 20,000 = 5/10.						
12	[b] Base is (4,000 + 500), or 4,500 hours; 4,000 ÷ 4,500 = 8/9; 500 ÷ 4,500 = 1/9.						

[3] An alternative approach to selecting the sequence of allocations is to begin with the support department that renders the highest dollar amount of services to other support departments. The sequence ends with the allocation of the costs of the department that renders the lowest dollar amount of services to other support departments.

Department costs are allocated, it receives no further allocation from other (lower-ranked) support departments. The result is that the step-down method does not recognize the total services that support departments provide to one another. The reciprocal method fully recognizes all such services, as you will see next.

Reciprocal Method

The **reciprocal method** allocates support-department costs to operating departments by fully recognizing the mutual services provided among all support departments. For example, the Plant Maintenance Department maintains all the computer equipment in the Information Systems Department. Similarly, Information Systems provides database support for Plant Maintenance. The reciprocal method fully incorporates interdepartmental relationships into the support-department cost allocations.

Exhibit 15-5 presents one way to understand the reciprocal method. First, Plant Maintenance costs are allocated to all other departments, including the Information Systems support department (Information Systems, 20%; Machining, 30%; Assembly, 50%). The costs in the Information Systems Department then total \$2,712,150 (\$1,452,150 + \$1,260,000 from the first-round allocation), as in Exhibit 15-4. The \$2,712,150 is then allocated to all other departments that the Information Systems Department supports, including the Plant Maintenance support department—Plant Maintenance, 10%; Machining, 80%; and Assembly, 10% (see Exhibit 15-2). The Plant Maintenance costs that had been brought down to \$0 now have \$271,215 from the Information Systems Department allocation. These costs are again reallocated to all other departments, including Information Systems, in the same ratio that the Plant Maintenance costs were previously assigned. Now the Information Systems Department costs that had been brought down to \$0 have \$54,243 from the Plant Maintenance Department allocations. These costs are again allocated in the same ratio that the Information Systems Department costs were previously assigned. Successive rounds result in smaller and smaller amounts being allocated to and reallocated from the support departments until eventually all support-department costs are allocated to the operating departments.

An alternative way to implement the reciprocal method is to formulate and solve linear equations. This process requires three steps.

Step 1: Express Support Department Costs and Reciprocal Relationships in the Form of Linear Equations. Let *PM* be the *complete reciprocated costs* of Plant Maintenance and *IS* be the *complete reciprocated costs* of Information Systems. By **complete reciprocated costs**, we mean the support department's own costs plus any interdepartmental cost allocations. We then express the data in Exhibit 15-2 as follows:

$$PM = \$6{,}300{,}000 + 0.1IS \qquad (1)$$
$$IS = \$1{,}452{,}150 + 0.2PM \qquad (2)$$

The $0.1IS$ term in equation (1) is the percentage of the Information Systems services *used by* Plant Maintenance. The $0.2PM$ term in equation (2) is the percentage of Plant Maintenance services *used by* Information Systems. The complete reciprocated costs in equations (1) and (2) are sometimes called the **artificial costs** of the support departments.

Step 2: Solve the Set of Linear Equations to Obtain the Complete Reciprocated Costs of Each Support Department. Substituting equation (1) into (2):

$$\begin{aligned} IS &= \$1{,}452{,}150 + [0.2(\$6{,}300{,}000 + 0.1IS)] \\ IS &= \$1{,}452{,}150 + \$1{,}260{,}000 + 0.02IS \\ 0.98IS &= \$2{,}712{,}150 \\ IS &= \$2{,}767{,}500 \end{aligned}$$

Substituting this into equation (1):

$$\begin{aligned} PM &= \$6{,}300{,}000 + 0.1(\$2{,}767{,}500) \\ PM &= \$6{,}300{,}000 + \$276{,}750 = \$6{,}576{,}750 \end{aligned}$$

When there are more than two support departments with reciprocal relationships, software such as Excel can be used to calculate the complete reciprocated costs of each

Exhibit 15-5 Reciprocal Method of Allocating Support-Department Costs Using Repeated Iterations at Castleford Engineering for 2009

	A	B	C	D	E	F	G
1		SUPPORT DEPARTMENTS			OPERATING DEPARTMENTS		
2		Plant Maintenance	Information Systems		Machining	Assembly	Total
3	Budgeted overhead costs before any						
4	interdepartment cost allocations	$6,300,000	$1,452,150		$4,000,000	$2,000,000	$13,752,150
5	1st Allocation of Plant Maintenance (2/10, 3/10, 5/10)[a]	(6,300,000)	1,260,000		1,890,000	3,150,000	
6			2,712,150				
7	1st Allocation of Information Systems (1/10, 8/10, 1/10)[b]	271,215	(2,712,150)		2,169,720	271,215	
8	2nd Allocation of Plant Maintenance (2/10, 3/10, 5/10)[a]	(271,215)	54,243		81,364	135,608	
9	2nd Allocation of Information Systems (1/10, 8/10, 1/10)[b]	5,424	(54,243)		43,395	5,424	
10	3rd Allocation of Plant Maintenance (2/10, 3/10, 5/10)[a]	(5,424)	1,085		1,627	2,712	
11	3rd Allocation of Information Systems (1/10, 8/10, 1/10)[b]	109	(1,085)		867	109	
12	4th Allocation of Plant Maintenance (2/10, 3/10, 5/10)[a]	(109)	22		33	54	
13	4th Allocation of Information Systems (1/10, 8/10, 1/10)[b]	2	(22)		18	2	
14	4th Allocation of Plant Maintenance (2/10, 3/10, 5/10)[a]	(2)	0		1	1	
15							
16	Total budgeted overhead of operating departments	$ 0	$ 0		$8,187,025	$5,565,125	$13,752,150
17							
18	Total support department amounts allocated and reallocated (the numbers in parentheses in the first two columns):						
19	Plant Maintenance: $6,300,000 + $271,215 + $5,424 + $109 + $2 = $6,576,750						
20	Information Systems: $2,712,150 + $54,243 + $1,085 + $22 = $2,767,500						
21							
22	[a] Base is (4,000 + 6,000 + 10,000), or 20,000 hours; 4,000 ÷ 20,000 = 2/10; 6,000 ÷ 20,000 = 3/10; 10,000 ÷ 20,000 = 5/10.						
23	[b] Base is (500 + 4,000 + 500), or 5,000 hours; 500 ÷ 5,000 = 1/10; 4,000 ÷ 5,000 = 8/10; 500 ÷ 5,000 = 1/10.						

support department. The complete-reciprocated-cost figures also appear at the bottom of Exhibit 15-5 as the total amounts allocated and reallocated (subject to minor rounding differences).

Step 3: Allocate the Complete Reciprocated Costs of Each Support Department to All Other Departments (Both Support Departments and Operating Departments) on the Basis of the Usage Percentages (Based on Total Units of Service Provided to All Departments). Consider the Information Systems Department. The complete reciprocated costs of $2,767,500 are allocated as follows:

To Plant Maintenance (1/10) × $2,767,500	= $ 276,750
To Machining (8/10) × $2,767,500	= 2,214,000
To Assembly (1/10) × $2,767,500	= 276,750
Total	$2,767,500

Exhibit 15-6 presents summary data pertaining to the reciprocal method.

Castleford's $9,344,250 complete reciprocated costs of the support departments exceeds the budgeted amount of $7,752,150.

Support Department	Complete Reciprocated Costs	Budgeted Costs	Difference
Plant Maintenance	$6,576,750	$6,300,000	$ 276,750
Information Systems	2,767,500	1,452,150	1,315,350
Total	$9,344,250	$7,752,150	$1,592,100

Exhibit 15-6 Reciprocal Method of Allocating Support-Department Costs Using Linear Equations at Castleford Engineering for 2009

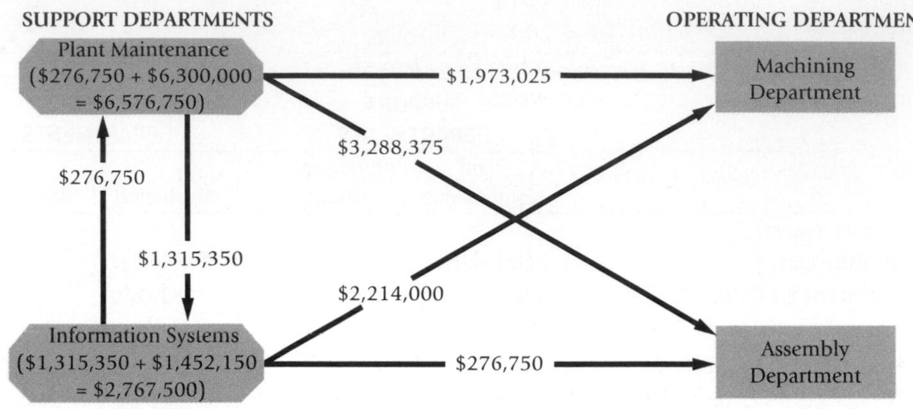

	A	B	C	D	E	F	G
1		SUPPORT DEPARTMENTS			OPERATING DEPARTMENTS		
2		Plant Maintenance	Information Systems		Machining	Assembly	Total
3	Budgeted overhead costs before any						
4	interdepartment cost allocations	$6,300,000	$1,452,150		$4,000,000	$2,000,000	$13,752,150
5	Allocation of Plant Maintenance (2/10, 3/10, 5/10)[a]	(6,576,750)	1,315,350		1,973,025	3,288,375	
6	Allocation of Information Systems (1/10, 8/10, 1/10)[b]	276,750	(2,767,500)		2,214,000	276,750	
7							
8	Total budgeted overhead of operating departments	$ 0	$ 0		$8,187,025	$5,565,125	$13,752,150
9							
10	[a] Base is (4,000 + 6,000 + 10,000), or 20,000 hours; 4,000 ÷ 20,000 = 2/10; 6,000 ÷ 20,000 = 3/10; 10,000 ÷ 20,000 = 5/10.						
11	[b] Base is (500 + 4,000 + 500), or 5,000 hours; 500 ÷ 5,000 = 1/10; 4,000 ÷ 5,000 = 8/10; 500 ÷ 5,000 = 1/10.						

Each support department's complete reciprocated cost is greater than the budgeted amount to take into account that the allocation of support costs will be made to all departments using its services and not just to operating departments. This step ensures that the reciprocal method fully recognizes all interrelationships among support departments, as well as relationships between support and operating departments. The difference between complete reciprocated costs and budgeted costs for each support department reflects the costs allocated among support departments. The total costs allocated to the operating departments under the reciprocal method are still only $7,752,150.

Overview of Methods

Assume that Castleford reallocates the total budgeted overhead costs of each operating department in Exhibits 15-3 through 15-6 to individual products on the basis of budgeted machine-hours for the Machining Department (18,000 hours) and budgeted direct labor-hours for the Assembly Department (25,000 hours). The budgeted overhead allocation rates (to the nearest dollar) for each operating department by allocation method are:

Support Department Cost-Allocation Method	Total Budgeted Overhead Costs After Allocation of All Support-Department Costs: Machining	Assembly	Budgeted Overhead Rate per Hour for Product-Costing Purposes: Machining (18,000 machine-hours)	Assembly (25,000 labor-hours)
Direct	$7,653,300	$6,098,850	$425	$244
Step-down	8,300,800	5,451,350	461	218
Reciprocal	8,187,025	5,565,125	455	223

These differences in budgeted overhead rates under the three support-department cost-allocation methods can, for example, affect the amount of costs Castleford is reimbursed for engines it manufactures under cost-reimbursement contracts. Consider a cost-reimbursement contract for a project that uses 200 machine-hours in the Machining Department and 50 direct labor-hours in the Assembly Department. The overhead costs allocated to this contract under the three methods would be:

Direct:	\$97,200 (\$425 per hour × 200 hours + \$244 per hour × 50 hours)
Step-down:	103,100 (\$461 per hour × 200 hours + \$218 per hour × 50 hours)
Reciprocal:	102,150 (\$455 per hour × 200 hours + \$223 per hour × 50 hours)

The amount of cost reimbursed to Castleford will differ depending on the method used to allocate support-department costs to the contract. Differences among the three methods' allocations increase (1) as the magnitude of the reciprocal allocations increases and (2) as the differences across operating departments' usage of each support department's services increase. Note that while the final allocations under the reciprocal method are in between those under the direct and step-down methods in our example, this is not true in general. To avoid disputes in cost-reimbursement contracts that require allocation of support-department costs, managers should always clarify the method to be used for allocation. For example, Medicare reimbursements and federal contracts with universities that pay for the recovery of indirect costs typically mandate use of the step-down method, with explicit requirements about the costs that can be included in the indirect cost pools.

The reciprocal method is conceptually the most precise method because it considers the mutual services provided among all support departments. The advantage of the direct and step-down methods is that they are simple to compute and understand relative to the reciprocal method. However, as computing power to perform repeated iterations (as in Exhibit 15-5) or to solve sets of simultaneous equations (as on pp. 550–552) increases, more companies find the reciprocal method easier to implement.

Another advantage of the reciprocal method is that it highlights the complete reciprocated costs of support departments and how these costs differ from budgeted or actual costs of the departments. Knowing the complete reciprocated costs of a support department is a key input for decisions about whether to outsource all the services that the support department provides.

Suppose all of Castleford's support-department costs are variable over the period of a possible outsourcing contract. Consider a third party's bid to provide, say, all the information systems services currently provided by Castleford's Information Systems Department. Do not compare the bid to the \$1,452,150 costs reported for the Information Systems Department. The complete reciprocated costs of the Information Systems Department, which include the services the Plant Maintenance Department provides the Information Systems Department, are \$2,767,500 to deliver 5,000 hours of computer time to all other departments at Castleford. The complete reciprocated costs for computer time are \$553.50 per hour (\$2,767,500 ÷ 5,000 hours). Other things being equal, a third party's bid to provide the same information services as Castleford's internal department at less than \$2,767,500, or \$553.50 per hour (even if much greater than \$1,452,150) would improve Castleford's operating income.

To see this point, note that the relevant savings from shutting down the Information Systems Department are \$1,452,150 of Information Systems Department costs *plus* \$1,315,350 of Plant Maintenance Department costs. By closing down the Information Systems Department, Castleford will no longer incur the 20% of reciprocated Plant Maintenance Department costs (equal to \$1,315,350) that were incurred to support the Information Systems Department. Therefore, the total cost savings are \$2,767,500 (\$1,452,150 + \$1,315,350).[4] Neither the direct nor the step-down methods can provide this relevant information for outsourcing decisions.

We now consider common costs, another special class of costs for which management accountants have developed specific allocation methods.

---

[4] Technical issues when using the reciprocal method in outsourcing decisions are discussed in R. S. Kaplan and A. A. Atkinson, *Advanced Management Accounting*, 3rd ed. (Upper Saddle River, NJ: Prentice Hall, 1998, pp. 73–81).

Allocating Common Costs

Learning Objective 4

Allocate common costs using the stand-alone method

. . . uses cost information of each user as a separate entity to allocate common costs

and the incremental method

. . . allocates common costs primarily to one user and the remainder to other users

A **common cost** is a cost of operating a facility, activity, or like cost object that is shared by two or more users. Common costs exist because each user obtains a lower cost by sharing than the separate cost that would result if such user were an independent entity.

The goal is to allocate common costs to each user in a reasonable way. Consider Jason Stevens, a graduating senior in Seattle who has been invited to a job interview with an employer in Albany. The round-trip Seattle–Albany airfare costs $1,200. A week later, Stevens is also invited to an interview with an employer in Chicago. The Seattle–Chicago round-trip airfare costs $800. Stevens decides to combine the two recruiting trips into a Seattle–Albany–Chicago–Seattle trip that will cost $1,500 in airfare. The $1,500 is a common cost that benefits both prospective employers. Two methods of allocating this common cost between the two prospective employers are the stand-alone method and the incremental method.

Stand-Alone Cost-Allocation Method

The **stand-alone cost-allocation method** determines the weights for cost allocation by considering each user of the cost as a separate entity. For the common-cost airfare of $1,500, information about the separate (stand-alone) round-trip airfares ($1,200 and $800) is used to determine the allocation weights:

$$\text{Albany employer:} \quad \frac{\$1{,}200}{\$1{,}200 + \$800} \times \$1{,}500 = 0.60 \times \$1{,}500 = \$900$$

$$\text{Chicago employer:} \quad \frac{\$800}{\$800 + \$1{,}200} \times \$1{,}500 = 0.40 \times \$1{,}500 = \$600$$

Advocates of this method often emphasize the fairness or equity criterion described in Exhibit 14-2 (p. 503). The method is viewed as reasonable because each employer bears a proportionate share of total costs in relation to the individual stand-alone costs.

Incremental Cost-Allocation Method

The **incremental cost-allocation method** ranks the individual users of a cost object in the order of users most responsible for the common cost and then uses this ranking to allocate cost among those users. The first-ranked user of the cost object is the *primary user* (also called the *primary party*) and is allocated costs up to the costs of the primary user as a stand-alone user. The second-ranked user is the *first incremental user* (*first incremental party*) and is allocated the additional cost that arises from two users instead of only the primary user. The third-ranked user is the *second incremental user* (*second incremental party*) and is allocated the additional cost that arises from three users instead of two users, and so on.

To see how this method works, consider again Jason Stevens and his $1,500 airfare cost. Assume the Albany employer is viewed as the primary party. Stevens's rationale is that he had already committed to go to Albany before accepting the invitation to interview in Chicago. The cost allocations would be:

Party	Costs Allocated	Cumulative Costs Allocated
Albany (primary)	$1,200	$1,200
Chicago (incremental)	300 ($1,500 − $1,200)	$1,500
Total	$1,500	

The Albany employer is allocated the full Seattle–Albany airfare. The unallocated part of the total airfare is then allocated to the Chicago employer. If the Chicago employer had been chosen as the primary party, the cost allocations would have been Chicago $800 (the stand-alone round-trip Seattle–Chicago airfare) and Albany $700 ($1,500 − $800). When there are more than two parties, this method requires them to be ranked from first to last (say, based on the date on which each employer invited the candidate to interview).

Under the incremental method, the primary party typically receives the highest allocation of the common costs. If the incremental users are newly formed companies or subunits, such as a new product line or a new sales territory, the incremental method may enhance their chances for short-run survival by assigning them a low allocation of the common costs. The difficulty with the method is that, particularly if a large common cost is involved, every user would prefer to be viewed as the incremental party!

One approach to sidestep disputes in such situations is to use the stand-alone cost-allocation method. Another approach is to use the *Shapley value*, which considers each party as first the primary party and then the incremental party. From the calculations shown earlier, the Albany employer is allocated $1,200 as the primary party and $700 as the incremental party, for an average of $950 [($1,200 + $700) ÷ 2]. The Chicago employer is allocated $800 as the primary party and $300 as the incremental party, for an average of $550 [($800 + 300) ÷ 2]. The Shapley value method allocates, to each employer, the average of the costs allocated as the primary party and as the incremental party—that is, $950 to the Albany employer and $550 to the Chicago employer.[5]

As our discussion suggests, allocating common costs is not clear-cut and can generate disputes. Whenever feasible, the rules for such allocations should be agreed on in advance. If this is not done, then, rather than blindly follow one method or another, managers should exercise judgment when allocating common costs. For instance, Stevens must choose an allocation method for his airfare cost that is acceptable to each prospective employer. He cannot, for example, exceed the maximum reimbursable amount of airfare for either firm. The next section discusses the role of cost data in various types of contracts, another area where disputes about cost allocation frequently arise.

Cost Allocations and Contracts

Many commercial contracts include clauses based on cost accounting information. For example:

- A contract between the Department of Defense and a company designing and assembling a new fighter plane specifies that the price paid for the plane is to be based on the contractor's direct and overhead costs plus a fixed fee.
- A contract between an energy-consulting firm and a hospital specifies that the consulting firm receive a fixed fee plus a share of the energy-cost savings that arise from implementing the consulting firm's recommendations.

Learning Objective 5

Explain the importance of explicit agreement between contracting parties when the reimbursement amount is based on costs incurred

. . . to avoid disputes regarding allowable cost items and how indirect costs should be allocated

Contract disputes often arise with respect to cost allocation. The areas of dispute between the contracting parties can be reduced by making the "rules of the game" explicit and in writing at the time the contract is signed. Such rules of the game include the definition of allowable cost items; the definitions of terms used, such as what constitutes direct labor; the permissible cost-allocation bases; and how to account for differences between budgeted and actual costs.

Contracting with the U.S. Government

The U.S. government reimburses most contractors in one of two main ways:

1. **The contractor is paid a set price without analysis of actual contract cost data.** This approach is used, for example, when there is competitive bidding, when there is adequate price competition, or when there is an established catalog with prices quoted for items sold in substantial quantities to the general public.
2. **The contractor is paid after analysis of actual contract cost data.** In some cases, the contract will explicitly state that the reimbursement amount is based on actual allowable costs plus a fixed fee.[6] This arrangement is called a *cost-plus contract*.

All contracts with U.S. government agencies must comply with cost accounting standards issued by the **Cost Accounting Standards Board (CASB)**. For government contracts, the

[5] For further discussion of the Shapley value, see J. Demski, "Cost Allocation Games," in S. Moriarity (Ed.), *Joint Cost Allocations* (University of Oklahoma Center for Economic and Management Research, 1981); L. Kruz and P. Bronisz, "Cooperative Game Solution Concepts to a Cost Allocation Problem," *European Journal of Operations Research* (vol. 122: 2000, 258–271).

CASB has the exclusive authority to make, put into effect, amend, and rescind cost accounting standards and interpretations. The standards are designed to achieve *uniformity and consistency* in regard to measurement, assignment, and allocation of costs to government contracts within the United States.[7]

In government contracting, there is a complex interplay of political considerations and accounting principles. Terms such as "fairness" and "equity," as well as cause and effect and benefits received, are often used in government contracts.

Fairness of Pricing

In many defense contracts, there is great uncertainty about the final cost to produce a new weapon or equipment. Such contracts are rarely subject to competitive bidding. The reason is that no contractor is willing to assume all the risk of receiving a fixed price for the contract and subsequently incurring high costs to fulfill it. Hence, setting a market-based fixed price for the contract fails to attract contractors, or requires a contract price that is too high from the government's standpoint. To address this issue, the government typically assumes a major share of the risk of the potentially high costs of completing the contract. Rather than relying on selling prices as ordinarily set by suppliers in the marketplace, the government negotiates contracts on the basis of *costs plus a fixed fee*. In costs-plus-fixed-fee contracts, which often involve billions of dollars, the allocation of a specific cost may be difficult to defend on the basis of any cause-and-effect reasoning. Nonetheless, the contracting parties may still view it as a "reasonable" or "fair" means to help establish a contract amount.

Some costs are "allowable;" others are "unallowable." An **allowable cost** is a cost that the contract parties agree to include in the costs to be reimbursed. Some contracts specify how allowable costs are to be determined. For example, only economy-class airfares are allowable in many U.S. government contracts. Other contracts identify cost categories that are unallowable. For example, the costs of lobbying activities and alcoholic beverages are not allowable costs in U.S. government contracts. However, the set of allowable costs is not always clear-cut. Contract disputes and allegations about overcharging the government arise from time to time (see Concepts in Action, p. 559).

Revenue Allocation and Bundled Products

Learning Objective 6

Understand how bundling of products

. . . two or more products sold for a single-price

gives rise to revenue-allocation issues

. . . allocating revenues to each product in the bundle to evaluate managers of individual products

Allocation issues can also arise when revenues from multiple products (for example, different software programs) are bundled together and sold at a single price. The methods for revenue allocation parallel those described for common-cost allocations.

Revenues are inflows of assets (almost always cash or accounts receivable) received for products or services provided to customers. Similar to cost allocation, **revenue allocation** occurs when revenues are related to a particular *revenue object* but cannot be traced to it in an economically feasible (cost-effective) way. A **revenue object** is anything for which a separate measurement of revenue is desired. Examples of revenue objects include products, customers, and divisions. We illustrate revenue-allocation issues for Supersoft Corporation, which develops, sells, and supports three software programs:

1. WordMaster, a word-processing program—current version is WordMaster 5.0, released 36 months ago (January 2007).

---

[6] The Federal Acquisition Regulation (FAR) includes the following definition of "allocability" (in FAR 31.201-4): A cost is allocable if it is assignable or chargeable to one or more cost objectives on the basis of relative benefits received or other equitable relationship. Subject to the foregoing, a cost is allocable to a Government contract if it:

- Is incurred specifically for the contract;
- Benefits both the contract and other work, and can be distributed to them in reasonable proportion to the benefits received; or
- Is necessary to the overall operation of the business, although a direct relationship to any particular cost objective cannot be shown.

AcqNet, "Federal Acquisition Regulation," issued March 2005; see www.acqnet.gov/far/current/pdf/FAR.book.pdf.

[7] Details on the Cost Accounting Standards Board are available at www.whitehouse.gov/omb/procurement/casb.html. The CASB is part of the Office of Federal Procurement Policy, U.S. Office of Management and Budget.

2. SpreadMaster, a spreadsheet program—current version is SpreadMaster 3.0, released 18 months ago (July 2008).
3. FinanceMaster, a budgeting and cash-management program—current version is FinanceMaster 1.0, released six months ago (July 2009) with a lot of favorable media attention.

Supersoft sells these three products individually as well as together as bundled products.

A **bundled product** is a package of two or more products (or services) that is sold for a single price but whose individual components may be sold as separate items at their own "stand-alone" prices. The price of a bundled product is typically less than the sum of the prices of the individual products sold separately. For example, banks often provide individual customers with a bundle of services from different departments (checking, safety-deposit box, and investment advisory) for a single fee. A resort hotel may offer, for a single amount per customer, a weekend package that includes services from its Lodging (the room), Food (the restaurant), and Recreational (golf and tennis) departments. When department managers have revenue or profit responsibilities for individual products, the bundled revenue must be allocated among the individual products in the bundle.[8]

Supersoft allocates revenues from its bundled product sales (called "suite sales") to individual products. Individual-product profitability is used to compensate software engineers, outside developers, and product managers responsible for developing and managing each product.

Revenue-Allocation Methods

Learning Objective 7

Allocate the revenues of a bundled product to the individual products in that bundle

. . . using the stand-alone method, the incremental method, or management judgment

How should Supersoft allocate suite revenues to individual products? Consider information pertaining to the three "stand-alone" and "suite" products in 2009:

	Selling Price	Manufacturing Cost per Unit
Stand-alone		
WordMaster	$125	$18
SpreadMaster	150	20
FinanceMaster	225	25
Suite		
Word + Spread	$220	
Word + Finance	280	
Finance + Spread	305	
Word + Finance + Spread	380	

Just as we saw in the section on common-cost allocations, the two main revenue-allocation methods are the stand-alone method and the incremental method.

Stand-Alone Revenue-Allocation Method

The **stand-alone revenue-allocation method** uses product-specific information on the products in the bundle as weights for allocating the bundled revenues to the individual products. The term *stand-alone* refers to the product as a separate (nonsuite) item. Consider the Word + Finance suite, which sells for $280. Three types of weights for the stand-alone method are as follows:

1. **Selling prices.** Using the individual selling prices of $125 for WordMaster and $225 for FinanceMaster, the weights for allocating the $280 suite revenues between the products are:

[8] Revenue-allocation issues also arise in external reporting. Statement of Position 97-2 (Software Revenue Recognition) states that with bundled products, revenue allocation "based on vendor-specific objective evidence of fair value" is required. The "price charged when the element is sold separately" is said to be "objective evidence of fair value." See American Institute of Certified Public Accountants, "Statement of Position 97-2" (Jersey City, NJ: AICPA, 1998).

$$\text{WordMaster:} \quad \frac{\$125}{\$125 + \$225} \times \$280 = 0.357 \times \$280 = \$100$$

$$\text{FinanceMaster:} \quad \frac{\$225}{\$125 + \$225} \times \$280 = 0.643 \times \$280 = \$180$$

2. **Unit costs.** This method uses the costs of the individual products (in this case, manufacturing cost per unit) to determine the weights for the revenue allocations.

$$\text{WordMaster:} \quad \frac{\$18}{\$18 + \$25} \times \$280 = 0.419 \times \$280 = \$117$$

$$\text{FinanceMaster:} \quad \frac{\$25}{\$18 + \$25} \times \$280 = 0.581 \times \$280 = \$163$$

3. **Physical units.** This method gives each product unit in the suite the same weight when allocating suite revenue to individual products. Therefore, with two products in the Word + Finance suite, each product is allocated 50% of the suite revenues.

$$\text{WordMaster:} \quad \frac{1}{1 + 1} \times \$280 = 0.50 \times \$280 = \$140$$

$$\text{FinanceMaster:} \quad \frac{1}{1 + 1} \times \$280 = 0.50 \times \$280 = \$140$$

These three approaches to determining weights for the stand-alone method result in very different revenue allocations to the individual products:

Revenue-Allocation Weights	WordMaster	FinanceMaster
Selling prices	$100	$180
Unit costs	117	163
Physical units	140	140

Which method is preferred? The selling prices method is best, because the weights explicitly consider the prices customers are willing to pay for the individual products. Weighting approaches that use revenue information better capture "benefits received" by customers than unit costs or physical units. The physical-units revenue-allocation method is used when any of the other methods cannot be used (such as when selling prices are unstable or unit costs are difficult to calculate for individual products).

Incremental Revenue-Allocation Method

The **incremental revenue-allocation method** ranks individual products in a bundle according to criteria determined by management—such as the product in the bundle with the most sales—and then uses this ranking to allocate bundled revenues to individual products. The first-ranked product is the *primary product* in the bundle. The second-ranked product is the *first incremental product*, the third-ranked product is the *second incremental product*, and so on.

How do companies decide on product rankings under the incremental revenue-allocation method? Some organizations survey customers about the importance of each of the individual products to their purchase decision. Others use data on the recent stand-alone sales performance of the individual products in the bundle. A third approach is for top managers to use their knowledge or intuition to decide the rankings.

Consider again the Word + Finance suite. Assume WordMaster is designated as the primary product. If the suite selling price exceeds the stand-alone price of the primary product, the primary product is allocated 100% of its *stand-alone* revenue. Because the suite price of $280 exceeds the stand-alone price of $125 for WordMaster, WordMaster is allocated revenues of $125, with the remaining revenue of $155 ($280 − $125) allocated to FinanceMaster:

Product	Revenue Allocated	Cumulative Revenue Allocated
WordMaster	$125	$125
FinanceMaster	155 ($280 − $125)	$280
Total	$280	

Concepts in Action

Contract Disputes over Reimbursable Costs for U.S. Government Agencies

Allegations about a contractor overcharging a government agency invariably make interesting copy for the media. The following four examples are from cases in which contractors "settled with the government without admitting wrongdoing with respect to the charges." The U.S. Department of Justice's Civil Division pursued these cases and negotiated the settlements on behalf of the federal government. These recent examples illustrate several types of cost disputes that arise in practice:

1. Ogilvy & Mather North America, one of the largest advertising agencies in the world, agreed to pay $1.8 million to resolve claims that the company overcharged the Office of National Drug Control Policy for labor costs on a contract to provide advertising services. Ogilvy & Mather had a cost-plus-fixed-fee contract in which the labor-hours were charged on the basis of time records reflecting the proportion of an employee's time spent on the contract. The government alleged that Ogilvy's labor charges were based on inaccurate timesheets submitted by employees and that the company's management did not exercise reasonable control to ensure that billings for labor were accurate.
2. Lockheed Martin, a leading defense contractor, agreed to pay the federal government $37.9 million to settle allegations that it inflated the cost of performing several Air Force contracts. The complaint alleged that a Lockheed Martin program-management team deliberately inflated costs in four cost-plus contract proposals for the purchase of navigation and targeting pods for military jets.
3. Northrop Grumman, another large defense contractor, paid $60 million to resolve allegations that it overcharged the government on Navy shipbuilding contracts. From 1994 to 1999, Newport News Shipbuilding (at the time an independent company, now a Northrop Grumman subsidiary) was alleged to have mischarged as Independent Research and Development (IR&D) its cost for the design and development of double-hulled tankers that the shipbuilder had already designed for commercial customers. Under federal regulations, costs may be charged only as IR&D to government contracts if the R&D is specifically incurred for the contract.
4. In 1991, Stanford University was accused of overcharging the federal government $200 million by inflating its indirect cost recovery rate for government contracts. Expenses related to furnishings and private gatherings in the university president's house, as well as a luxury yacht, were allegedly improperly included in the pool of indirect costs allocated to sponsored research. Stanford eventually reimbursed the government for $1.2 million to settle the claims, but the scandal led to the resignation of its president, as well as the forced lowering of its indirect recovery rates from 74% in 1990 to 55.5% in 1991. The rate has never exceeded 60% in all the years since.

Source: Press releases from the U.S. Department of Justice, Civil Division, Stanford GSB Case A-155A (Stanford University: Indirect Cost Recovery by Ratna Sarkar and Steve Huddart).

If the suite price is less than or equal to the stand-alone price of the primary product, the primary product is allocated 100% of the *suite* revenue. All other products in the suite receive no allocation of revenue.

Now suppose FinanceMaster is designated as the primary product and WordMaster as the first incremental product. Then, the incremental revenue-allocation method allocates revenues of the Word + Finance suite as:

Product	Revenue Allocated	Cumulative Revenue Allocated
FinanceMaster	$225	$225
WordMaster	55 ($280 − $225)	$280
Total	$280	

If Supersoft sells equal quantities of WordMaster and FinanceMaster, then the Shapley value method allocates to each product the average of the revenues allocated as the primary and first incremental products:

WordMaster:	(\$125 + \$ 55) ÷ 2 = \$180 ÷ 2 =	\$ 90
FinanceMaster:	(\$225 + \$155) ÷ 2 = \$380 ÷ 2 =	190
Total		\$280

But what if, in the most recent quarter, Supersoft sells 80,000 units of WordMaster and 20,000 units of FinanceMaster. Because Supersoft sells four times as many units of WordMaster, its managers believe that the sales of the Word + Finance suite are four times more likely to be driven by WordMaster as the primary product. The *weighted Shapley value method* takes this fact into account by weighting the revenue allocations when WordMaster is the primary product four times as much as when FinanceMaster is the primary product:

WordMaster:	(\$125 × 4 + \$ 55 × 1) ÷ (4 + 1) = \$555 ÷ 5 =	\$111
FinanceMaster:	(\$225 × 1 + \$155 × 4) ÷ (4 + 1) = \$845 ÷ 5 =	169
Total		\$280

When there are more than two products in the suite, the incremental revenue-allocation method allocates suite revenues sequentially. Assume WordMaster is the primary product in Supersoft's three-product suite (Word + Finance + Spread). FinanceMaster is the first incremental product, and SpreadMaster is the second incremental product. This suite sells for \$380. The allocation of the \$380 suite revenues proceeds as follows:

Product	Revenue Allocated	Cumulative Revenue Allocated
WordMaster	\$125	\$125
FinanceMaster	155 (\$280 − \$125)	\$280 (price of Word + Finance suite)
SpreadMaster	100 (\$380 − \$280)	\$380 (price of Word + Finance + Spread suite)
Total	\$380	

Now suppose WordMaster is the primary product, SpreadMaster is the first incremental product, and FinanceMaster is the second incremental product.

Product	Revenue Allocated	Cumulative Revenue Allocated
WordMaster	\$125	\$125
SpreadMaster	95 (\$220 − \$125)	\$220 (price of Word + Spread suite)
FinanceMaster	160 (\$380 − \$220)	\$380 (price of Word + Spread + Finance suite)
Total	\$380	

The ranking of the individual products in the suite determines the revenues allocated to them. Product managers at Supersoft likely would differ on how they believe their individual products contribute to sales of the suite products. In fact, each product manager would claim to be responsible for the primary product in the Word + Finance + Spread suite![9] Because the stand-alone revenue-allocation method does not require rankings of individual products in the suite, this method is less likely to cause debates among product managers.

Other Revenue-Allocation Methods

Management judgment not explicitly based on a specific formula is another method of revenue allocation. In one case, the president of a software company decided to issue a set of revenue-allocation weights after the managers of the three products in a bundled product could not agree among themselves on a set of weights. The weights chosen by the president were 45% for product A, 45% for product B, and 10% for product C. Factors the president considered included stand-alone selling prices (all three were very similar), stand-alone unit sales (A and B were over 10 times more than C), product ratings by independent experts, and consumer awareness. The product C manager complained that his 10% weighting drastically shortchanged the contribution of product C to suite revenues. The president responded that its inclusion in the suite greatly increased consumer

[9] Calculating the Shapley value mitigates this problem because each product is considered as a primary, first-incremental, and second-incremental product. Assuming equal weights on all products, the revenue allocated to each product is an average of the revenues calculated for the product under these different assumptions. In the above example, the interested reader can verify that this will result in the following revenue assignments: FinanceMaster, \$180; WordMaster, \$87.50; and SpreadMaster, \$112.50.

exposure to product C, with the result that product C's total revenues would be far larger (even with only 10% of suite revenues) than if it had not been included in the suite.

Problem for Self-Study

This problem illustrates how costs of two corporate support departments are allocated to operating divisions using the dual-rate method. Fixed costs are allocated using budgeted costs and budgeted hours used by other departments. Variable costs are allocated using actual costs and actual hours used by other departments.

Computer Horizons budgets the following amounts for its two central corporate support departments (legal and personnel) in supporting each other and the two manufacturing divisions, the Laptop Division (LTD) and the Work Station Division (WSD):

	A	B	C	D	E	F	G
1		SUPPORT			OPERATING		
2		Legal Department	Personnel Department		LTD	WSD	Total
3	BUDGETED USAGE						
4	Legal (hours)	—	250		1,500	750	2,500
5	(Percentages)	—	10%		60%	30%	100%
6	Personnel (hours)	2,500	—		22,500	25,000	50,000
7	(Percentages)	5%	—		45%	50%	100%
8							
9	ACTUAL USAGE						
10	Legal (hours)	—	400		400	1,200	2,000
11	(Percentages)	—	20%		20%	60%	100%
12	Personnel (hours)	2,000	—		26,600	11,400	40,000
13	(Percentages)	5%	—		66.50%	28.5%	100%
14	Budgeted fixed overhead costs before any						
15	interdepartment cost allocations	$360,000	$475,000		—	—	$835,000
16	Actual variable overhead costs before any						
17	interdepartment cost allocations	$200,000	$600,000		—	—	$800,000

Required

What amount of support-department costs for legal and personnel will be allocated to LTD and WSD using (a) the direct method, (b) the step-down method (allocating the Legal Department costs first), and (c) the reciprocal method using linear equations?

Solution

Exhibit 15-7 presents the computations for allocating the fixed and variable support-department costs. A summary of these costs follows:

	Laptop Division (LTD)	Work Station Division (WSD)
(a) Direct Method		
Fixed costs	$465,000	$370,000
Variable costs	470,000	330,000
	$935,000	$700,000
(b) Step-Down Method		
Fixed costs	$458,053	$376,947
Variable costs	488,000	312,000
	$946,053	$688,947
(c) Reciprocal Method		
Fixed costs	$462,513	$372,487
Variable costs	476,364	323,636
	$938,877	$696,123

Exhibit 15-7 Alternative Methods of Allocating Corporate Support-Department Costs to Operating Divisions of Computer Horizons: Dual-Rate Method

File Edit View Insert Format Tools Data Window Help

	A	B	C	D	E	F	G
20		**CORPORATE SUPPORT DEPARTMENTS**			**OPERATING DIVISIONS**		
21	**Allocation Method**	**Legal Department**	**Personnel Department**		**LTD**	**WSD**	**Total**
22	**A. DIRECT METHOD**						
23	Fixed Costs	$360,000	$475,000				
24	Legal (1,500 ÷ 2,250; 750 ÷ 2,250)	(360,000)			$240,000	$120,000	
25	Personnel (22,500 ÷ 47,500; 25,000 ÷ 47,500)		(475,000)		225,000	250,000	
26	Fixed support dept. cost allocated to operating divisions	$ 0	0		$465,000	$370,000	$835,000
27	Variable Costs	$200,000	$600,000				
28	Legal (400 ÷ 1,600; 1,200 ÷ 1,600)	(200,000)			$ 50,000	$150,000	
29	Personnel (26,600 ÷ 38,000; 11,400 ÷ 38,000)		(600,000)		420,000	180,000	
30	Variable support dept. cost allocated to operating divisions	$ 0	0		$470,000	$330,000	$800,000
31	**B. STEP-DOWN METHOD**						
32	(Legal Department First)						
33	Fixed Costs	$360,000	$475,000				
34	Legal (250 ÷ 2,500; 1,500 ÷ 2,500; 750 ÷ 2,500)	(360,000)	36,000		$216,000	$108,000	
35	Personnel (22,500 ÷ 47,500; 25,000 ÷ 47,500)		(511,000)		242,053	268,947	
36	Fixed support dept. cost allocated to operating divisions	$ 0	0		$458,053	$376,947	$835,000
37	Variable Costs	$200,000	$600,000				
38	Legal (400 ÷ 2,000; 400 ÷ 2,000; 1,200 ÷ 2,000)	(200,000)	40,000		$ 40,000	$120,000	
39	Personnel (26,600 ÷ 38,000; 11,400 ÷ 38,000)		(640,000)		448,000	192,000	
40	Variable support dept. cost allocated to operating divisions	$ 0	0		$488,000	$312,000	$800,000
41	**C. RECIPROCAL METHOD**						
42	Fixed Costs	$360,000	$475,000				
43	Legal (250 ÷ 2,500; 1,500 ÷ 2,500; 750 ÷ 2,500)	(385,678)[a]	38,568		$231,407	$115,703	
44	Personnel (2,500 ÷ 50,000; 22,500 ÷ 50,000; 25,000 ÷ 50,000)	25,678	(513,568)[a]		231,106	256,784	
45	Fixed support dept. cost allocated to operating divisions	$ 0	$ 0		$462,513	$372,487	$835,000
46	Variable Costs	$200,000	$600,000				
47	Legal (400 ÷ 2,000; 400 ÷ 2,000; 1,200 ÷ 2,000)	(232,323)[b]	46,465		$ 46,465	$139,393	
48	Personnel (2,000 ÷ 40,000; 26,600 ÷ 40,000; 11,400 ÷ 40,000)	32,323	(646,465)[b]		429,899	184,243	
49	Variable support dept. cost allocated to operating divisions	$ 0	$ 0		$476,364	$323,636	$800,000
50							

	A	B
51	[a] FIXED COSTS	[b] VARIABLE COSTS
52	Letting *LF* = Legal Department Fixed Costs, and *PF* = Personnel Department Fixed Costs, the simultaneous equations for the reciprocal method for fixed costs are	Letting *LF* = Legal Department Variable Costs, and *PV* = Personnel Department Variable Costs, the simultaneous equations for the reciprocal method for variable costs are
53	$LF = \$360{,}000 + 0.05\ PF$	$LV = \$200{,}000 + 0.05\ PV$
54	$PF = \$475{,}000 + 0.10\ LF$	$PV = \$600{,}000 + 0.20\ LV$
55	$LF = \$360{,}000 + 0.05\ (\$475{,}000 + 0.10\ LF)$	$LV = \$200{,}000 + 0.05\ (\$600{,}000 + 0.20\ LV)$
56	$LF = \$385{,}678$	$LV = \$232{,}323$
57	$PF = \$475{,}000 + 0.10\ (\$385{,}678) = \$513{,}568$	$PV = \$600{,}000 + 0.20\ (\$232{,}323) = \$646{,}465$

Decision Points

The following question-and-answer format summarizes the chapter's learning objectives. Each decision presents a key question related to a learning objective. The guidelines are the answer to that question.

Decision	Guidelines
1. Should managers use the single-rate or the dual-rate method?	The single-rate method aggregates fixed and variable costs and allocates them to objects using a single allocation base and rate. Under the dual-rate method, costs are grouped into separate variable cost and fixed cost pools; each pool uses a different cost-allocation base and rate. If costs can be easily separated into variable and fixed costs, the dual-rate method should be used because it provides better information for making decisions.
2. What factors should managers consider when deciding whether to use budgeted or actual cost allocation rates?	When cost allocations are made using budgeted rates, managers of divisions to which costs are allocated face no uncertainty about the rates to be used in that budget period. In contrast, when actual rates are used for cost allocation, managers do not know the rates until the end of the budget period. If actual rates are used, the efficiency of the supplier department affects the costs allocated to the user departments.
3. What methods can managers use to allocate costs of multiple support departments to operating departments?	The three methods managers can use are the direct, the step-down, and the reciprocal methods. The direct method allocates each support department's costs to operating departments without allocating a support department's costs to other support departments. The step-down method allocates support-department costs to other support departments and to operating departments in a sequential manner that partially recognizes the mutual services provided among all support departments. The reciprocal method fully recognizes mutual services provided among all support departments.
4. What methods can managers use to allocate common costs to two or more users?	Common costs are the costs of a cost object (such as operating a facility or performing an activity) that are shared by two or more users. The stand-alone cost-allocation method uses information pertaining to each user of the cost object to determine cost-allocation weights. The incremental cost-allocation method ranks individual users of the cost object and allocates common costs first to the primary user and then to the other incremental users. The Shapley value method considers each user, in turn, as the primary and the incremental user.
5. How can contract disputes over reimbursement amounts based on costs be reduced?	Disputes can be reduced by making the cost-allocation rules as explicit as possible and in writing at the time the contract is signed. These rules should include details such as the allowable cost items, the acceptable cost-allocation bases, and how differences between budgeted and actual costs are to be accounted for.
6. What is product bundling and why does it give rise to revenue-allocation issues?	Bundling occurs when a package of two or more products (or services) is sold for a single price. Revenue allocation of the bundled price is required when managers of the individual products in the bundle are evaluated on product revenue or product operating income.
7. What methods can managers use to allocate revenues of a bundled product to individual products in the package?	Revenues can be allocated for a bundled product using the stand-alone method, the incremental method, the Shapley value method, or management judgment.

TERMS TO LEARN

This chapter and the Glossary at the end of the book contain definitions of:

allowable cost (**p. 556**)
artificial costs (**p. 550**)
bundled product (**p. 557**)
common cost (**p. 554**)
complete reciprocated costs (**p. 550**)
Cost Accounting Standards Board (CASB) (**p. 555**)
direct method (**p. 547**)

ASSIGNMENT MATERIAL

Questions

15-1 Distinguish between the single-rate and the dual-rate methods.

15-2 Describe how the dual-rate method is useful to division managers in decision making.

15-3 How do budgeted cost rates motivate the support-department manager to improve efficiency?

15-4 Give examples of allocation bases used to allocate support-department cost pools to operating departments.

15-5 Why might a manager prefer that budgeted rather than actual cost-allocation rates be used for costs being allocated to his or her department from another department?

15-6 "To ensure unbiased cost allocations, fixed costs should be allocated on the basis of estimated long-run use by user-department managers." Do you agree? Why?

15-7 Distinguish among the three methods of allocating the costs of support departments to operating departments.

15-8 What is conceptually the most defensible method for allocating support-department costs? Why?

15-9 Distinguish between two methods of allocating common costs.

15-10 What role does the Cost Accounting Standards Board play when companies contract with the U.S. government?

15-11 What is one key way to reduce cost-allocation disputes that arise with government contracts?

15-12 Describe how companies are increasingly facing revenue-allocation decisions.

15-13 Distinguish between the stand-alone and the incremental revenue-allocation methods.

15-14 Identify and discuss arguments that individual product managers may put forward to support their preferred revenue-allocation method.

15-15 How might a dispute over the allocation of revenues of a bundled product be resolved?

Exercises

15-16 Single-rate versus dual-rate methods, support department. The Chicago power plant that services all manufacturing departments of MidWest Engineering has a budget for the coming year. This budget has been expressed in the following monthly terms:

Manufacturing Department	Needed at Practical Capacity Production Level (Kilowatt-Hours)	Average Expected Monthly Usage (Kilowatt-Hours)
Rockford	10,000	8,000
Peoria	20,000	9,000
Hammond	12,000	7,000
Kankakee	8,000	6,000
Total	50,000	30,000

The expected monthly costs for operating the power plant during the budget year are $15,000: $6,000 variable and $9,000 fixed.

Required

1. Assume that a single cost pool is used for the power plant costs. What budgeted amounts will be allocated to each manufacturing department if (a) the rate is calculated based on practical capacity and costs are allocated based on practical capacity and (b) the rate is calculated based on expected monthly usage and costs are allocated based on expected monthly usage?
2. Assume the dual-rate method is used with separate cost pools for the variable and fixed costs. Variable costs are allocated on the basis of expected monthly usage. Fixed costs are allocated on the basis of practical capacity. What budgeted amounts will be allocated to each manufacturing department? Why might you prefer the dual-rate method?

15-17 Single-rate method, budgeted versus actual costs and quantities. Chocolat Inc. is a producer of premium chocolate based in Palo Alto. The company has a separate division for each of its two products: dark chocolate and milk chocolate. Chocolat purchases ingredients from Wisconsin for its Dark Chocolate division and from Louisiana for its Milk Chocolate division. Both locations are the same distance from Chocolat's Palo Alto plant.

Chocolat Inc. operates a fleet of trucks as a cost center that charges the divisions for variable costs (drivers and fuel) and fixed costs (vehicle depreciation, insurance, and registration fees) of operating the fleet. Each division is evaluated on the basis of its operating income. For 2009, the trucking fleet had a practical capacity of 50 round-trips between the Palo Alto plant and the two suppliers. It recorded the following information:

	A	B	C
1		Budgeted	Actual
2	Costs of truck fleet	$115,000	$96,750
3	Number of round-trips for Dark Chocolate Division (Palo Alto plant -- Wisconsin)	30	30
4	Number of round-trips for Milk Chocolate Division (Palo Alto plant -- Louisiana)	20	15

If you want to use Excel to solve this exercise, go to the Excel Lab at **www.prenhall.com/horngren/cost13e** and download the template for Exercise 15-17.

Required

1. Using the single-rate method, allocate costs to the Dark Chocolate Division and the Milk Chocolate Division in these three ways.
   a. Calculate the budgeted rate per round-trip and allocate costs based on round-trips budgeted for each division.
   b. Calculate the budgeted rate per round-trip and allocate costs based on actual round-trips used by each division.
   c. Calculate the actual rate per round-trip and allocate costs based on actual round-trips used by each division.
2. Describe the advantages and disadvantages of using each of the three methods in requirement 1. Would you encourage Chocolat Inc. to use one of these methods? Explain and indicate any assumptions you made.

15-18 Dual-rate method, budgeted versus actual costs and quantities (continuation of 15-17). Chocolat, Inc. decides to examine the effect of using the dual-rate method for allocating truck costs to each round-trip. At the start of 2009, the budgeted costs were:

Variable cost per round-trip	$ 1,500
Fixed costs	$40,000

The actual results for the 45 round-trips made in 2009 were:

Variable costs	$60,750
Fixed costs	36,000
	$96,750

Assume all other information to be the same as in Exercise 15-17.

If you want to use Excel to solve this exercise, go to the Excel Lab at **www.prenhall.com/horngren/cost13e** and download the template for Exercise 15-17.

Required

1. Using the dual-rate method, what are the costs allocated to the Dark Chocolate Division and the Milk Chocolate Division when (a) variable costs are allocated using the budgeted rate per round-trip and actual round-trips used by each division and when (b) fixed costs are allocated based on the budgeted rate per round-trip and round-trips budgeted for each division?
2. From the viewpoint of the Dark Chocolate Division, what are the effects of using the dual-rate method rather than the single-rate methods?

15-19 Support-department cost allocation; direct and step-down methods. Phoenix Partners provides management consulting services to government and corporate clients. Phoenix has two support departments—Administrative Services (AS) and Information Systems (IS)—and two operating departments—Government Consulting (GOVT) and Corporate Consulting (CORP). For the first quarter of 2009, Phoenix's cost records indicate the following:

	A	B	C	D	E	F	G
1		SUPPORT			OPERATING		
2		AS	IS		GOVT	CORP	Total
3	Budgeted overhead costs before any						
4	interdepartment cost allocations	$600,000	$2,400,000		$8,756,000	$12,452,000	$24,208,000
5	Support work supplied by AS (Budgeted head count)	—	25%		40%	35%	100%
6	Support work supplied by IS (Budgeted computer time)	10%	—		30%	60%	100%

If you want to use Excel to solve this exercise, go to the Excel Lab at **www.prenhall.com/horngren/cost13e** and download the template for Exercise 15-19.

Required

1. Allocate the two support departments' costs to the two operating departments using the following methods:
   a. Direct method
   b. Step-down method (allocate AS first)
   c. Step-down method (allocate IS first)
2. Compare and explain differences in the support-department costs allocated to each operating department.
3. What approaches might be used to decide the sequence in which to allocate support departments when using the step-down method?

15-20 Support-department cost allocation, reciprocal method (continuation of 15-19). Refer to the data given in Exercise 15-19.

If you want to use Excel to solve this exercise, go to the Excel Lab at **www.prenhall.com/horngren/cost13e** and download the template for Exercise 15-19.

Required

1. Allocate the two support departments' costs to the two operating departments using the reciprocal method. Use (a) linear equations and (b) repeated iterations.
2. Compare and explain differences in requirement 1 with those in requirement 1 of Exercise 15-19. Which method do you prefer? Why?

15-21 Direct and step-down allocation. E-books, an online book retailer, has two operating departments—Corporate Sales and Consumer Sales—and two support departments—Human Resources and Information Systems. Each sales department conducts merchandising and marketing operations independently. E-books uses number of employees to allocate Human Resources costs and processing time to allocate Information Systems costs. The following data are available for September 2009:

	A	B	C	D	E	F
1		SUPPORT DEPARTMENTS			OPERATING DEPARTMENTS	
2		Human Resources	Information Systems		Corporate Sales	Consumer Sales
3	Budgeted costs incurred before any					
4	interdepartment cost allocations	$72,700	$234,400		$998,270	$489,860
5	Support work supplied by Human Resources Department					
6	Budgeted number of employees	—	21		42	28
7	Support work supplied by Information Systems Department					
8	Budgeted processing time (in minutes)	320	—		1,920	1,600

If you want to use Excel to solve this exercise, go to the Excel Lab at **www.prenhall.com/horngren/cost13e** and download the template for Exercise 15-21.

Required

1. Allocate the support departments' costs to the operating departments using the direct method.
2. Rank the support departments based on the percentage of their services provided to other support departments. Use this ranking to allocate the support departments' costs to the operating departments based on the step-down method.
3. How could you have ranked the support departments differently?

15-22 Reciprocal cost allocation (continuation of 15-21). Consider E-books again. The controller of E-books reads a widely used textbook that states that "the reciprocal method is conceptually the most defensible." He seeks your assistance.

If you want to use Excel to solve this exercise, go to the Excel Lab at **www.prenhall.com/horngren/cost13e** and download the template for Exercise 15-21.

Required

1. Describe the key features of the reciprocal method.
2. Allocate the support departments' costs (Human Resources and Information Systems) to the two operating departments using the reciprocal method.
3. In the case presented in this exercise, which method (direct, step-down, or reciprocal) would you recommend? Why?

15-23 Allocation of common costs. Mike and Ed are students at Berkeley College. They share an apartment that is owned by Ed. Ed is considering subscribing to an Internet provider that has the following packages available:

Package	Per Month
A. Internet access	$40
B. Phone services	20
C. Internet access + phone services	55

Mike spends most of his time on the Internet ("everything can be found online now"). Ed prefers to spend his time talking on the phone rather than using the Internet ("going online is a waste of time"). They agree that the purchase of the $55 total package is a "win–win" situation.

Required

1. Allocate the $55 between Mike and Ed using (a) the stand-alone cost-allocation method, (b) the incremental cost-allocation method, and (c) the Shapley value method.
2. Which method would you recommend they use and why?

15-24 Allocation of common costs. Sunny Gunn, a self-employed consultant near Sacramento, received an invitation to visit a prospective client in Baltimore. A few days later, she received an invitation to make a presentation to a prospective client in Chicago. She decided to combine her visits, traveling from Sacramento to Baltimore, Baltimore to Chicago, and Chicago to Sacramento.

Gunn received offers for her consulting services from both companies. Upon her return, she decided to accept the engagement in Chicago. She is puzzled over how to allocate her travel costs between the two clients. She has collected the following data for regular round-trip fares with no stopovers:

Sacramento to Baltimore	$1,400
Sacramento to Chicago	$1,100

Gunn paid $1,800 for her three-leg flight (Sacramento–Baltimore, Baltimore–Chicago, Chicago–Sacramento). In addition, she paid $30 each way for limousines from her home to Sacramento Airport and back when she returned.

Required

1. How should Gunn allocate the $1,800 airfare between the clients in Baltimore and Chicago using (a) the stand-alone cost-allocation method, (b) the incremental cost-allocation method, and (c) the Shapley value method?
2. Which method would you recommend Gunn use and why?
3. How should Gunn allocate the $60 limousine charges between the clients in Baltimore and Chicago?

15-25 Revenue allocation, bundled products. Yves Parfum Company blends and sells designer fragrances. It has a Men's Fragrances Division and a Women's Fragrances Division, each with different sales strategies, distribution channels, and product offerings. Yves is now considering the sale of a bundled product consisting of a men's cologne and a women's perfume. For the most recent year, Yves reported the following:

	A	B
1	**Product**	**Retail Price**
2	Monaco (men's cologne)	$ 80
3	Innocence (women's perfume)	120
4	L'Amour (Monaco + Innocence)	180

If you want to use Excel to solve this exercise, go to the Excel Lab at **www.prenhall.com/horngren/cost13e** and download the template for Exercise 15-25.

Required

1. Allocate revenue from the sale of each unit of L'Amour to Monaco and Innocence using:
   a. The stand-alone revenue-allocation method based on selling price of each product

b. The incremental revenue-allocation method, with Monaco ranked as the primary product
c. The incremental revenue-allocation method, with Innocence ranked as the primary product
d. The Shapley value method, assuming equal unit sales of Monaco and Innocence.

2. Of the four methods in requirement 1, which one would you recommend for allocating L'Amour's revenues to Monaco and Innocence? Explain.

15-26 Allocation of Common Costs. The cities of Albany, Troy and Schenectady are considering the implementation of a new program to handle disposal of hazardous waste to comply with a new, more stringent state law. Because of the close proximity of the three cities, a joint program has been suggested. The annual cost of separate programs and a joint program are:

City	Capacity	Cost
Albany	100,000 tons	$2,100,000
Troy	25,000 tons	$1,400,000
Schenectady	175,000 tons	$3,500,000
Joint Program	300,000 tons	$5,000,000

Required

1. Allocate the $5,000,000 cost of the joint program to each of the three cities using:
   a. The stand-alone method
   b. The incremental-allocation method (in the order of the most waste to the least waste).
2. How do you think the citizens of each community would feel about each of the two methods of allocation?

Problems

15-27 Single-rate, dual-rate, and practical capacity allocation. Beauty Department Store has a new promotional program that offers a free gift-wrapping service for its customers. Beauty's customer-service department has practical capacity to wrap 7,500 gifts at a budgeted fixed cost of $6,750 each month. The budgeted variable cost to gift wrap an item is $0.50. Although the service is free to customers, a gift-wrapping service cost allocation is made to the department where the item was purchased. The customer-service department reported the following for the most recent month:

	A	B	C	D
1	Department	Actual Number of Gifts Wrapped	Budgeted Number of Gifts to be Wrapped	Practical Capacity Available for Gift-Wrapping
2	Women's Face Wash	2,100	2,475	2,625
3	Men's Face Wash	750	825	938
4	Fragrances	1,575	1,800	1,969
5	Body Wash	525	450	656
6	Hair Products	1,050	1,200	1,312
7	Total	6,000	6,750	7,500

If you want to use Excel to solve this problem, go to the Excel Lab at **www.prenhall.com/horngren/cost13e** and download the template for Problem 15-27.

Required

1. Using the single-rate method, allocate gift-wrapping costs to different departments in these three ways.
   a. Calculate the budgeted rate based on the budgeted number of gifts to be wrapped and allocate costs based on the budgeted use (of gift-wrapping services).
   b. Calculate the budgeted rate based on the budgeted number of gifts to be wrapped and allocate costs based on actual usage.
   c. Calculate the budgeted rate based on the practical gift-wrapping capacity available and allocate costs based on actual usage.
2. Using the dual-rate method, compute the amount allocated to each department when (a) the fixed-cost rate is calculated using budgeted costs and the practical gift-wrapping capacity, (b) fixed costs are allocated based on budgeted usage of gift-wrapping services, and (c) variable costs are allocated using the budgeted variable-cost rate and actual usage.
3. Comment on your results in requirements 1 and 2. Discuss the advantages of the dual-rate method.

15-28 Revenue allocation. Lee Shu-yu Inc. produces and sells DVDs to business people and students who are planning extended stays in China. It has been very successful with two DVDs: Beginning Mandarin and Conversational Mandarin. It is introducing a third DVD, Reading Chinese Characters. It has decided to market its new DVD in two different packages grouping the Reading Chinese Characters DVD with each of the other two language DVDs. Information about the separate DVDs and the packages follow.

DVD	Selling Price
Beginning Mandarin (BegM)	$60
Conversational Mandarin (ConM)	$50
Reading Chinese Characters (RCC)	$40
BegM + RCC	$90
ConM + RCC	$72

Required

1. Using the selling prices, allocate revenues from the BegM + RCC package to each DVD in that package using **(a)** the stand-alone method **(b)** the incremental method, in either order **(c)** the Shapley value method.
2. Using the selling prices, allocate revenues from the ConM + RCC package to each DVD in that package using **(a)** the stand-alone method **(b)** the incremental method, in either order **(c)** the Shapley value method.
3. Which method is most appropriate for allocating revenues among the DVDs? Why?

15-29 Fixed cost allocation. Three restaurants in a downtown area of a large city have decided to share a valet service and parking lot for their customers. The cost of the service and lot is $10,000 per month. The owners of the restaurants need to decide how to divide the $10,000 cost. The actual usage, planned usage, and practical capacity in the month of May was:

Restaurant	Actual Parking Spots Used	Planned Parking Spots	Practical Capacity Parking Spots
A	1,500	1,600	2,000
B	1,400	1,300	1,500
C	1,300	1,100	1,500

Required

1. Allocate the fixed cost to each restaurant using actual, planned, and capacity usage measures.
2. In this situation, which method of allocation makes the most sense?

15-30 Allocating costs of support departments; step-down and direct methods. The Central Valley Company has prepared department overhead budgets for budgeted-volume levels before allocations as follows:

Support departments:		
Building and grounds	$10,000	
Personnel	1,000	
General plant administration	26,090	
Cafeteria: operating loss	1,640	
Storeroom	2,670	$ 41,400
Operating departments:		
Machining	$34,700	
Assembly	48,900	83,600
Total for support and operating departments		$125,000

Management has decided that the most appropriate inventory costs are achieved by using individual-department overhead rates. These rates are developed after support-department costs are allocated to operating departments.

Bases for allocation are to be selected from the following:

Department	Direct Manufacturing Labor-Hours	Number of Employees	Square Feet of Floor Space Occupied	Manufacturing Labor-Hours	Number of Requisitions
Building and grounds	0	0	0	0	0
Personnel[a]	0	0	2,000	0	0
General plant administration	0	35	7,000	0	0
Cafeteria: operating loss	0	10	4,000	1,000	0
Storeroom	0	5	7,000	1,000	0
Machining	5,000	50	30,000	8,000	2,000
Assembly	15,000	100	50,000	17,000	1,000
Total	20,000	200	100,000	27,000	3,000

[a]Basis used is number of employees.

Required

1. Using the step-down method, allocate support-department costs. Develop overhead rates per direct manufacturing labor-hour for machining and assembly. Allocate the costs of the support departments in the order given in this problem. Use the allocation base for each support department you think is most appropriate.
2. Using the direct method, rework requirement 1.
3. Based on the following information about two jobs, determine the total overhead costs for each job by using rates developed in (a) requirement 1 and (b) requirement 2.

	Direct Manufacturing Labor-Hours	
	Machining	Assembly
Job 88	18	2
Job 89	3	17

4. The company evaluates the performance of the operating department managers on the basis of how well they managed their total costs, including allocated costs. As the manager of the Machining Department, which allocation method would you prefer from the results obtained in requirements 1 and 2? Explain.

15-31 Support-department cost allocations; single-department cost pools; direct, step-down, and reciprocal methods. The Manes Company has two products. Product 1 is manufactured entirely in Department X. Product 2 is manufactured entirely in Department Y. To produce these two products, the Manes Company has two support departments: A (a materials-handling department) and B (a power-generating department).

An analysis of the work done by departments A and B in a typical period follows:

	Used By			
Supplied By	A	B	X	Y
A	—	100	250	150
B	500	—	100	400

The work done in Department A is measured by the direct labor-hours of materials-handling time. The work done in Department B is measured by the kilowatt-hours of power. The budgeted costs of the support departments for the coming year are:

	Department A (Materials Handling)	Department B (Power Generation)
Variable indirect labor and indirect materials costs	$ 70,000	$10,000
Supervision	10,000	10,000
Depreciation	20,000	20,000
	$100,000	$40,000
	+ Power costs	+ Materials-handling costs

The budgeted costs of the operating departments for the coming year are $1,500,000 for Department X and $800,000 for Department Y.

Supervision costs are salary costs. Depreciation in Department B is the straight-line depreciation of power-generation equipment in its nineteenth year of an estimated 25-year useful life; it is old, but well-maintained, equipment.

Required

1. What are the allocations of costs of support departments A and B to operating departments X and Y using (a) the direct method, (b) the step-down method (allocate Department A first), (c) the step-down method (allocate Department B first), and (d) the reciprocal method?
2. An outside company has offered to supply all the power needed by the Manes Company and to provide all the services of the present power department. The cost of this service will be $40 per kilowatt-hour of power. Should Manes accept? Explain.

15-32 Common costs. Wright Inc. and Brown Inc. are two small clothing companies that are considering leasing a dyeing machine together. The companies estimated that in order to meet production, Wright needs the machine for 900 hours and Brown needs it for 600 hours. If each company rents the machine on its own, the fee will be $40 per hour of usage. If they rent the machine together, the fee will decrease to $32 per hour of usage.

Required

1. Calculate Wright's and Brown's respective share of fees under the stand-alone cost-allocation method.
2. Calculate Wright's and Brown's respective share of fees using the incremental cost-allocation method. Assume Wright to be the primary party.

3. Calculate Wright's and Brown's respective share of fees using the Shapley value method.
4. Which method would you recommend Wright and Brown use to share the fees?

15-33 Stand-alone revenue allocation. Funland is an amusement park complex in southern Florida. Funland is divided into three autonomous divisions: a water park, a superhero theme park with rides, and an animal park. In addition to selling a daily entrance ticket for each park, Funland has decided to sell a three-day ticket that would allow entrance into each of the parks for one day. The ticket selling price and the costs associated with each entrant into a park are:

Park	Ticket Price	Daily Cost Per Entrant
Water Park	$40	$15
Superhero Theme Park	$60	$25
Animal Park	$20	$10
Three-day ticket	$90	

Required

1. Allocate the revenue from the three-day ticket to each park using the stand-alone method based on ticket price.
2. Allocate the revenue from the three-day ticket to each park using the stand-alone method based on cost per entrant.
3. Allocate the revenue from the three-day ticket to each park using the stand-alone method based on physical units (that is, number of tickets received for each park).
4. Which basis of allocation makes the most sense in this situation? Explain your answer.

15-34 Effect of demand (continuation of 15-33). The director of the water park, Lori Lemaris, is upset with the allocation of the revenues for the three-day ticket. Because of her hard work, and Florida's hot weather in June, July, and August, the water park is always sold out. She does not think it is equitable for her park to receive less than the full entrance ticket price. The president of Funland, Kent Clark, agrees with Lori.

Required

1. How would the allocations in requirements 1, 2, and 3 of problem 15-33 differ if the water park gets its full ticket price?
2. If the director of the superhero theme park raises the same argument, Funland could not handle the situation in the same way. Why?
3. In light of requirement 2, how would you suggest Kent handle the problem?

Collaborative Learning Problem

15-35 Revenue allocation, bundled products. Heavenly Resorts operates a five-star hotel with a world-recognized championship golf course. Heavenly has a decentralized management structure, with three divisions:

- Lodging (rooms, conference facilities)
- Food (restaurants and in-room service)
- Recreation (golf course, tennis courts, and so on)

Starting next month, Heavenly Resorts will offer a two-day, two-person "getaway package" for $1,000.
This deal includes:

- Two nights' stay for two in an ocean-view room—separately priced at $800 ($400 per night for two).
- Two rounds of golf—separately priced at $375 ($187.50 per round). One person can do two rounds, or two people can do one round each.
- Candlelight dinner for two at the exclusive Heavenly Resorts Restaurant—separately priced at $200 ($100 per person).

Jenny Lee, president of the Recreation Division, recently asked the CEO of Heavenly Resorts how her division would share in the $1,000 revenue from the package. The golf course was operating at 100% capacity. Under the getaway-package rules, participants who booked one week in advance were guaranteed access to the golf course. Lee noted that every "getaway" booking would displace $375 of golf bookings. She emphasized that the high demand reflected the devotion of her team to keeping the golf course rated one of the "Best 10 Courses in the World" by *Golf Monthly*. As an aside, she also noted that the Lodging and Food divisions had to turn away customers during only "peak-season events such as the New Year's period."

Required

1. Using selling prices, allocate the $1,000 getaway-package revenue to the three divisions using:
   a. The stand-alone revenue-allocation method
   b. The incremental revenue-allocation method (with Recreation first, then Lodging, and then Food)
2. What are the pros and cons of the two methods in requirement 1?

16 Cost Allocation: Joint Products and Byproducts

Learning Objectives

1. Identify the splitoff point in a joint-cost situation
2. Distinguish joint products from byproducts
3. Explain why joint costs are allocated to individual products
4. Allocate joint costs using four methods
5. Explain why the sales value at splitoff method is preferred when allocating joint costs
6. Explain why joint costs are irrelevant in a sell-or-process-further decision
7. Account for byproducts using two methods

Many companies, such as dairies, produce and sell two or more products simultaneously. Similarly, some companies, such as healthcare providers, sell or provide multiple services. The question is: How should these companies allocate costs to "joint" products and services? Knowing how to allocate joint product costs isn't something that just companies need to understand. It's something the government has to deal with, too—especially when it comes to paying millions of dollars to companies that provide goods and services to U.S. taxpayers.

Medicare Dissects the Costs Allocated to Organ Donations[1]

Each year, thousands of organ and tissue donors and their families courageously give the gift of hope and life to thousands of people in need in the United States. Organ procurement organizations (OPOs), transplant centers, and medical professionals play a vital role in this gift. Many organ recipients are Medicare patients, and the key question for Medicare is: What does it cost OPOs to procure these organs?

Here's how the program works: Medicare reimburses an OPO a certain amount of money based on the type of organ transplanted into a Medicare patient. But to calculate this charge, the program requires organs to equally share the "joint" product costs incurred when multiple organs are recovered from a single donor—costs such as operating room time and medications required to preserve the donor's organs. If the joint costs are not allocated to the various "organ centers" properly, the result is that the cost of acquiring specific organs is misrepresented to Medicare, as well as to third-party payers.

A key principle is that all general costs must be allocated to all organs that the OPO intends to procure, regardless of whether the OPO actually recovers the organ for transplant. For example, if a lung and kidney donation is planned, but the surgeon discovers during the operation that the lung is not viable for donation, then a portion of the joint costs must still be assigned to the lung transplant—otherwise

[1] *Sources:* Department of Health and Human Services Centers for Medicare & Medicaid Services, "Ruling No.: CMS-1543-R," December 21, 2006; Department of Health and Human Services, Office of Inspector General, "Review of Organ Acquisition Costs Claimed by Certified Transplant Centers (A-09-05-00034)," September 28, 2006; and Jim Warren, "CMS Enforcement of Rule Covering Organ Acquisition Fees Could Shut Down Some OPOs, Transplant Centers," *Transplant News,* April 28, 2003.

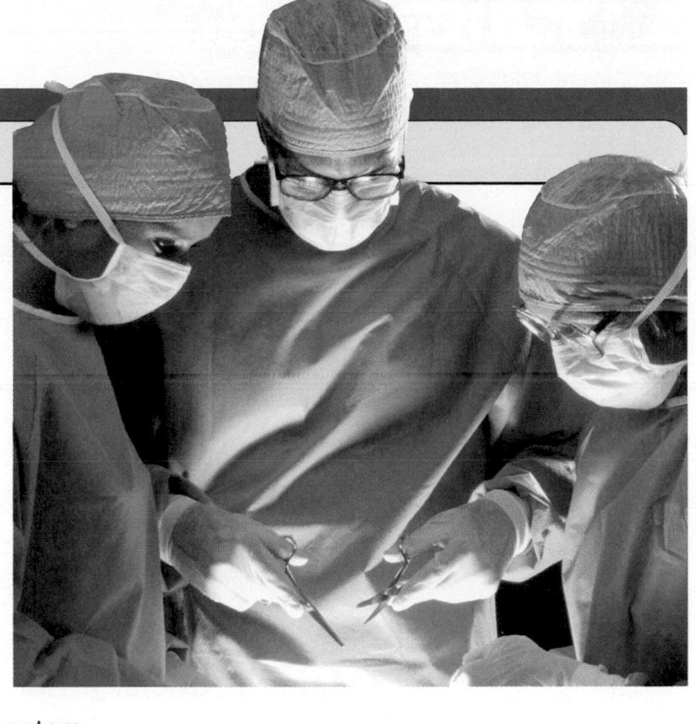

the kidney recipient would bear the full cost of the operation. This is a big problem for Medicare because the majority of kidneys donated in the United States—62 percent—are transplanted into Medicare patients.

While precise estimates of the misallocation of costs are unavailable, one Medicare audit at 11 centers found that of $80 million in organ acquisition costs, almost $47 million were unallowable and unsupported costs. As a result of such findings, Medicare issued specific guidelines in 2006 for cost allocations in OPOs and transplant centers.

Accounting concerns similar to those in the Medicare example are also present when companies such as ExxonMobil simultaneously produce crude oil, natural gas, and raw liquefied petroleum gas (LPG) from petroleum, in a single process. This chapter examines methods for allocating costs to joint products. We also examine how cost numbers appropriate for one purpose, such as external reporting, may not be appropriate for other purposes, such as decisions about the further processing of joint products.

Joint-Cost Basics

Learning Objective 1

Identify the splitoff point in a joint-cost situation

. . . the point at which two or more products become separately identifiable

Joint costs are the costs of a production process that yields multiple products simultaneously. Consider the distillation of coal, which yields coke, natural gas, and other products. The costs of this distillation are joint costs. The **splitoff point** is the juncture in a joint production process when two or more products become separately identifiable. An example is the point at which coal becomes coke, natural gas, and other products. **Separable costs** are all costs—manufacturing, marketing, distribution, and so on—incurred beyond the splitoff point that are assignable to each of the specific products identified at the splitoff point. At or beyond the splitoff point, decisions relating to the sale or further processing of each identifiable product can be made independently of decisions about the other products.

Industries abound in which a production process simultaneously yields two or more products, either at the splitoff point or after further processing. Exhibit 16-1 presents examples of joint-cost situations in diverse industries. In each of these examples, no individual product can be produced without the accompanying products appearing, although in some cases the proportions can be varied. The focus of joint costing is on allocating costs to individual products at the splitoff point.

Exhibit 16-1

Examples of Joint-Cost Situations

Industry	Separable Products at the Splitoff Point
Agriculture and Food Processing Industries	
Cocoa beans	Cocoa butter, cocoa powder, cocoa drink mix, tanning cream
Lambs	Lamb cuts, tripe, hides, bones, fat
Hogs	Bacon, ham, spare ribs, pork roast
Raw milk	Cream, liquid skim
Lumber	Lumber of varying grades and shapes
Turkeys	Breast, wings, thighs, drumsticks, digest, feather meal, and poultry meal
Extractive Industries	
Coal	Coke, gas, benzol, tar, ammonia
Copper ore	Copper, silver, lead, zinc
Petroleum	Crude oil, natural gas
Salt	Hydrogen, chlorine, caustic soda
Chemical Industries	
Raw LPG (liquefied petroleum gas)	Butane, ethane, propane
Crude oil	Gasoline, kerosene, benzene, naphtha
Semiconductor Industry	
Fabrication of silicon-wafer chips	Memory chips of different quality (as to capacity), speed, life expectancy, and temperature tolerance

Main Products, Joint Products, and Byproducts

Learning Objective 2

Distinguish joint products

. . . products with high sales values

from byproducts

. . . products with low sales values

The outputs of a joint production process can be classified into two general categories: outputs with a positive sales value and outputs with a zero sales value.[2] For example, offshore processing of hydrocarbons yields oil and natural gas, which have positive sales value, and it also yields water, which has zero sales value and is recycled back into the ocean. The term **product** describes any output that has a positive total sales value (or an output that enables a company to avoid incurring costs, such as an intermediate chemical product used as input in another process). The total sales value can be high or low.

When a joint production process yields one product with a high total sales value, compared with total sales values of other products of the process, that product is called a **main product**. When a joint production process yields two or more products with high total sales values compared with the total sales values of other products, if any, those products are called **joint products**. The products of a joint production process that have low total sales values compared with the total sales value of the main product or of joint products are called **byproducts**.

Consider some examples. If timber (logs) is processed into standard lumber and wood chips, standard lumber is a main product and wood chips are the byproduct. That's because standard lumber has a high total sales value compared with wood chips. If, however, logs are processed into fine-grade lumber, standard lumber, and wood chips, fine-grade lumber and standard lumber are joint products, and wood chips are the byproduct. That's because both fine-grade lumber and standard lumber have high total sales values when compared with wood chips.

Distinctions among main products, joint products, and byproducts are not so definite in practice. For example, some companies may classify kerosene obtained when refining crude oil as a byproduct because they believe kerosene has a low total sales value relative to the total sales values of gasoline and other products. Other companies may classify kerosene as a joint product because they believe kerosene has a high total sales value relative to the total sales values of gasoline and other products. Moreover, the classification of products—main, joint, or byproduct—can change over time, especially for products such as lower-grade semiconductor chips, whose market prices can increase or decrease by, say, 30% or more in a year. When prices of lower-grade chips are high, they are considered joint products together with higher-grade chips; when prices of lower-grade chips fall considerably, they are considered byproducts. Be sure you understand how a specific company classifies products and uses terms.

[2] Some outputs of a joint production process have "negative" revenue when their disposal costs (such as the costs of handling nonsalable toxic substances that require special disposal procedures) are considered. These disposal costs should be added to the joint production costs that are allocated to joint or main products.

Why Allocate Joint Costs?

Some of the contexts that require joint costs to be allocated to individual products or services are:

- Computation of inventoriable costs and cost of goods sold for financial accounting purposes and reports for income tax authorities
- Computation of inventoriable costs and cost of goods sold for internal reporting purposes (Such reports are used in division-profitability analysis, and they affect evaluation of division managers' performance.)
- Cost reimbursement for companies that have a few, but not all, of their products or services reimbursed under cost-plus contracts with, say, a government agency
- Insurance-settlement computations for damage claims made on the basis of cost information of jointly produced products
- Rate regulation for one or more of the jointly produced products or services that are subject to price regulation[3]
- Litigation in which costs of joint products are key inputs

Learning Objective 3

Explain why joint costs are allocated to individual products

. . . to calculate cost of goods sold and inventory, and for reimbursements under cost-plus contracts and other types of claims

Approaches to Allocating Joint Costs

Two approaches are used to allocate joint costs.

- **Approach 1.** Allocate joint costs using *market-based* data such as revenues. This chapter illustrates three methods that use this approach:
  1. Sales value at splitoff method
  2. Net realizable value (NRV) method
  3. Constant gross-margin percentage NRV method
- **Approach 2.** Allocate joint costs using *physical measures*, such as the weight (say, kilograms), quantity (say, physical units) or volume (say, cubic feet) of the joint products.

Learning Objective 4

Allocate joint costs using four methods

. . . sales value at splitoff, physical measure, net realizable value (NRV), and constant gross-margin percentage NRV

In preceding chapters, we used the cause-and-effect and benefits-received criteria for guiding cost-allocation decisions (see Exhibit 14-2, p. 503). Joint costs do not have a cause-and-effect relationship with individual products because the production process simultaneously yields multiple products. Using the benefits-received criterion leads to a preference for methods under approach 1 because revenues are, in general, a better indicator of benefits received than physical measures. Mining companies, for example, receive more benefits from 1 ton of gold than they do from 10 tons of coal.

In the simplest joint production process, the joint products are sold at the splitoff point without further processing. Example 1, which follows, illustrates the two methods that apply in this case: the sales value at splitoff method and the physical-measure method. Then we introduce joint production processes that yield products that require further processing beyond the splitoff point. Example 2 illustrates the NRV method and the constant-gross margin percentage NRV method. To help you focus on key concepts, we use numbers and amounts in all examples in this chapter that are much smaller than the numbers that are typically found in practice.

The exhibits in this chapter use the following symbols to distinguish a joint or main product from a byproduct:

Joint Product or Main Product

Byproduct

[3] See J. Crespi and J. Harris, "Joint Cost Allocation Under the Natural Gas Act: An Historical Review," *Journal of Extractive Industries Accounting* (Summer 1993): 133–142. Also see International Accounting Standards Committee Foundation, *IASC Issues Paper: Extractive Industries* (London, United Kingdom: IASB, 2000).

To compare methods, we report gross-margin percentages for individual products under each method.

Example 1: Farmers' Dairy purchases raw milk from individual farms and processes it until the splitoff point, when two products—cream and liquid skim—emerge. These two products are sold to an independent company, which markets and distributes them to supermarkets and other retail outlets.

In May 2009, Farmers' Dairy processes 110,000 gallons of raw milk. During processing, 10,000 gallons are lost due to evaporation and spillage, yielding 25,000 gallons of cream and 75,000 gallons of liquid skim. Summary data follow.

	A	B	C
1		**Joint Costs**	
2	Joint costs (costs of 110,000 gallons raw milk and processing to splitoff point)	$400,000	
3			
4		**Cream**	**Liquid Skim**
5	Beginnning inventory (gallons)	0	0
6	Production (gallons)	25,000	75,000
7	Sales (gallons)	20,000	30,000
8	Ending inventory (gallons)	5,000	45,000
9	Selling price per gallon	$ 8	$ 4

Exhibit 16-2 depicts the basic relationships in this example.

How much of the $400,000 joint costs should be allocated to the cost of goods sold of 20,000 gallons of cream and 30,000 gallons of liquid skim, and how much should be allocated to the ending inventory of 5,000 gallons of cream and 45,000 gallons of liquid skim? In the following sections we illustrate how the sales value at splitoff method and the physical-measure method allocate the $400,000 in joint costs to joint products.

Sales Value at Splitoff Method

The **sales value at splitoff method** allocates joint costs to joint products on the basis of the relative total sales value at the splitoff point. Using this method for Example 1, Exhibit 16-3, Panel A, shows how joint costs are allocated to individual products to calculate cost per gallon of cream and liquid skim for valuing ending inventory. This method uses the sales value of the *entire production of the accounting period* (25,000 gallons of

Exhibit 16-2

Example 1: Overview of Farmers' Dairy

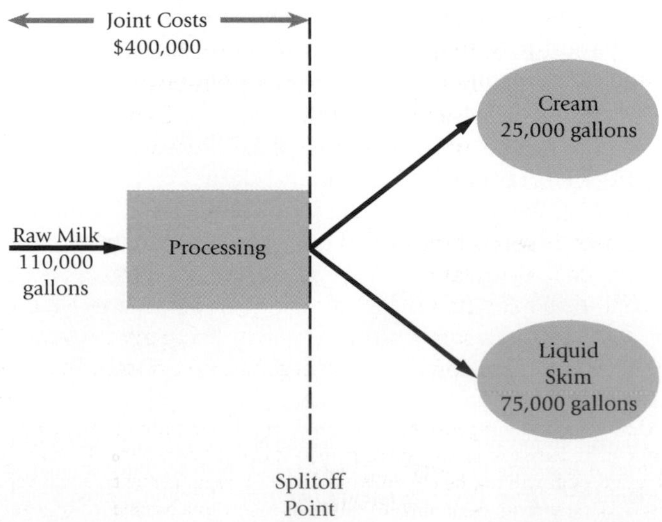

Exhibit 16-3 Joint-Cost Allocation and Product-Line Income Statement Using Sales Value at Splitoff Method: Farmers' Dairy for May 2009

	A	B	C	D
1	**PANEL A: Allocation of Joint Costs Using Sales Value at Splitoff Method**	**Cream**	**Liquid Skim**	**Total**
2	Sales value of total production at splitoff point			
3	(25,000 gallons x $8 per gallon; 75,000 gallons x $4 per gallon)	$200,000	$300,000	$500,000
4	Weighting ($200,000 ÷ $500,000; $300,000 ÷ 500,000)	0.40	0.60	
5	Joint costs allocated (0.40 x $400,000; 0.60 x $400,000)	$160,000	$240,000	$400,000
6	Joint production cost per gallon			
7	($160,000 ÷ 25,000 gallons; $240,000 ÷ 75,000 gallons)	$ 6.40	$ 3.20	
8				
9	**PANEL B: Product-Line Income Statement Using Sales Value at Splitoff Method for May 2009**	**Cream**	**Liquid Skim**	**Total**
10	Revenues (20,000 gallons x $8 per gallon; 30,000 gallons x $4 per gallon)	$160,000	$120,000	$280,000
11	Cost of goods sold (joint costs)			
12	Production costs (0.40 x $400,000; 0.60 x $400,000)	160,000	240,000	400,000
13	Deduct ending inventory (5,000 gallons x $6.40 per gallon; 45,000 gallons x $3.20 per gallon)	32,000	144,000	176,000
14	Cost of goods sold (joint costs)	128,000	96,000	224,000
15	Gross margin	$ 32,000	$ 24,000	$ 56,000
16	Gross margin percentage ($32,000 ÷ $160,000; $24,000 ÷ $120,000; $56,000 ÷ $280,000)	20%	20%	20%

cream and 75,000 gallons of liquid skim), not just the quantity sold (20,000 gallons of cream and 30,000 gallons of liquid skim). The reason is that the joint costs were incurred on all units produced, not just the portion sold during the current period. Exhibit 16-3, Panel B, presents the product-line income statement using the sales value at splitoff method. Note that the sales value at splitoff method allocates joint costs to each product in proportion to sales value of total production (cream: $160,000 ÷ $200,000 = 80%; liquid skim: $240,000 ÷ $300,000 = 80%). Therefore, the gross-margin percentage for each product manufactured in May 2009 is the same: 20%.[4]

Note how the sales value at splitoff method follows the benefits-received criterion of cost allocation: Costs are allocated to products in proportion to their revenue-generating power (their expected revenues). This method is both straightforward and intuitive. The cost-allocation base (total sales value at splitoff) is expressed in terms of a common denominator (the amount of revenues) that is systematically recorded in the accounting system. To use this method, selling prices must exist for all products at the splitoff point.

Physical-Measure Method

The **physical-measure method** allocates joint costs to joint products on the basis of a *comparable* physical measure such as the relative weight, quantity, or volume at the splitoff point. In Example 1, the $400,000 joint costs produced 25,000 gallons of cream and 75,000 gallons of liquid skim. Using the number of gallons produced as the physical measure, Exhibit 16-4, Panel A, shows how joint costs are allocated to individual products to calculate the cost per gallon of cream and liquid skim.

Because the physical-measure method allocates joint costs on the basis of the number of gallons, cost per gallon is the same for both products. Exhibit 16-4, Panel B, presents the product-line income statement using the physical-measure method. The gross-margin percentages are 50% for cream and 0% for liquid skim.

Under the benefits-received criterion, the physical-measure method is much less desirable than the sales value at splitoff method. This is because the physical measure of the individual products may have no relationship to their respective revenue-generating abilities. Consider a gold mine that extracts ore containing gold, silver, and lead. Use of a common physical measure (tons) would result in almost all costs being allocated to lead—the product that weighs the most but has the lowest revenue-generating power. In this case, the method

[4] Suppose Farmers' Dairy has beginning inventory of cream and liquid milk in May 2009. Suppose further that when this inventory is sold, Farmers' earns a gross margin different from 20%. Then the gross-margin percentage for cream and liquid skim will not be the same. The gross-margin percentage will depend on how much of the sales of each product came from beginning inventory and how much came from current-period production.

Exhibit 16-4 Joint-Cost Allocation and Product-Line Income Statement Using Physical-Measure Method: Farmers' Dairy for May 2009

	A	B	C	D
1	**PANEL A: Allocation of Joint Costs Using Physical-Measure Method**	**Cream**	**Liquid Skim**	**Total**
2	Physical measure of total production (gallons)	25,000	75,000	100,000
3	Weighting (25,000 gallons ÷ 100,000 gallons; 75,000 gallons ÷ 100,000 gallons)	0.25	0.75	
4	Joint costs allocated (0.25 x $400,000; 0.75 x $400,000)	$100,000	$300,000	$400,000
5	Joint production cost per gallon ($100,000 ÷ 25,000 gallons; $300,000 ÷ 75,000 gallons)	$ 4.00	$ 4.00	
6				
7	**PANEL B: Product-Line Income Statement Using Physical-Measure Method for May 2009**	**Cream**	**Liquid Skim**	**Total**
8	Revenues (20,000 gallons x $8 per gallon; 30,000 gallons x $4 per gallon)	$160,000	$120,000	$280,000
9	Cost of goods sold (joint costs)			
10	Production costs (0.25 x $400,000; 0.75 x $400,000)	100,000	300,000	400,000
11	Deduct ending inventory (5,000 gallons x $4 per gallon; 45,000 gallons x $4 per gallon)	20,000	180,000	200,000
12	Cost of goods sold (joint costs)	80,000	120,000	200,000
13	Gross margin	$ 80,000	$ 0	$ 80,000
14	Gross margin percentage ($80,000 ÷ $160,000; $0 ÷ $120,000; $80,000 ÷ $280,000)	50%	0%	28.6%

of cost allocation is inconsistent with the main reason that the mining company is incurring mining costs—to earn revenues from gold and silver, not lead. When a company uses the physical-measure method in a product-line income statement, products that have a high sales value per ton—for example, gold and silver—would show a large "profit," and products that have a low sales value per ton—for example, lead—would show sizable losses.

Obtaining comparable physical measures for all products is not always straightforward. Consider the joint costs of producing oil and natural gas; oil is a liquid and gas is a vapor. To use a physical measure, the oil and gas need to be converted to the energy equivalent for oil and gas, British thermal units (BTUs). Using some physical measures to allocate joint costs may require assistance from technical personnel outside of accounting.

Determining which products of a joint process to include in a physical-measure computation can greatly affect the allocations to those products. Outputs with no sales value (such as dirt in gold mining) are always excluded. Although many more tons of dirt than gold are produced, costs are not incurred to produce outputs that have zero sales value. Byproducts are also often excluded from the denominator used in the physical-measure method because of their low sales values relative to the joint products or the main product. The general guideline for the physical-measure method is to include only the joint-product outputs in the weighting computations.

Net Realizable Value (NRV) Method

In many cases, products are processed beyond the splitoff point to bring them to a marketable form or to increase their value above their selling price at the splitoff point. For example, when crude oil is refined, the gasoline, kerosene, benzene, and naphtha must be processed further before they can be sold. To illustrate, let's extend the Farmers' Dairy example.

Example 2: Assume the same data as in Example 1 except that both cream and liquid skim can be processed further:

- Cream → Buttercream: 25,000 gallons of cream are further processed to yield 20,000 gallons of buttercream at additional processing costs of $280,000. Buttercream, which sells for $25 per gallon, is used in the manufacture of butter-based products.
- Liquid Skim → Condensed Milk: 75,000 gallons of liquid skim are further processed to yield 50,000 gallons of condensed milk at additional processing costs of $520,000. Condensed milk sells for $22 per gallon.
- Sales during May 2009 were 12,000 gallons of buttercream and 45,000 gallons of condensed milk.

Exhibit 16-5 Example 2: Overview of Farmers' Dairy

PANEL A: Graphical Presentation of Process for Example 2

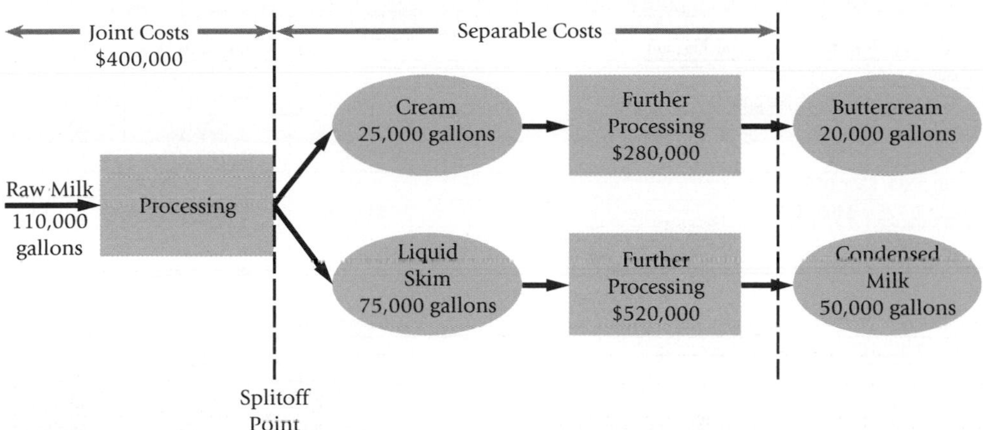

PANEL B: Data for Example 2

	A	B	C	D	E
1		Joint Costs		Buttercream	Condensed Milk
2	Joint costs (costs of 110,000 gallons raw milk and processing to splitoff point)	$400,000			
3	Separable cost of processing 25,000 gallons cream into 20,000 gallons buttercream			$280,000	
4	Separable cost of processing 75,000 gallons liquid skim into 50,000 gallons condensed milk				$520,000
5					
6		Cream	Liquid Skim	Buttercream	Condensed Milk
7	Beginning inventory (gallons)	0	0	0	0
8	Production (gallons)	25,000	75,000	20,000	50,000
9	Transfer for further processing (gallons)	25,000	75,000		
10	Sales (gallons)			12,000	45,000
11	Ending inventory (gallons)	0	0	8,000	5,000
12	Selling price per gallon	$ 8	$ 4	$ 25	$ 22

Exhibit 16-5, Panel A, depicts how (a) raw milk is converted into cream and liquid skim in the joint production process, and (b) how cream is separately processed into buttercream and liquid skim is separately processed into condensed milk. Panel B shows the data for Example 2.

The **net realizable value (NRV) method** allocates joint costs to joint products on the basis of relative NRV—final sales value minus separable costs. The NRV method is typically used in preference to the sales value at splitoff method only when selling prices for one or more products at splitoff do not exist. Using this method for Example 2, Exhibit 16-6, Panel A, shows how joint costs are allocated to individual products to calculate cost per gallon of buttercream and condensed milk.

Exhibit 16-6, Panel B presents the product-line income statement using the NRV method. Gross-margin percentages are 22.0% for buttercream and 26.4% for condensed milk.

The NRV method is often implemented using simplifying assumptions. For example, even though companies may frequently change the number of processing steps beyond the splitoff point, they assume a specific set of such steps when implementing the NRV method. Also, even when selling prices of joint products vary frequently, companies implement the NRV method using a given set of selling prices throughout the accounting period.

Exhibit 16-6 Joint-Cost Allocation and Product-Line Income Statement Using NRV Method: Farmers' Dairy for May 2009

	A	B	C	D
1	**PANEL A: Allocation of Joint Costs Using Net Realizable Value Method**	**Buttercream**	**Condensed Milk**	**Total**
2	Final sales value of total production during accounting period			
3	(20,000 gallons x $25 per gallon; 50,000 gallons x $22 per gallon)	$500,000	$1,100,000	$1,600,000
4	Deduct separable costs	280,000	520,000	800,000
5	Net realizable value at splitoff point	$220,000	$ 580,000	$ 800,000
6	Weighting ($220,000 ÷ $800,000; $580,000 ÷ $800,000)	0.275	0.725	
7	Joint costs allocated (0.275 x $400,000; 0.725 x $400,000)	$110,000	$ 290,000	$ 400,000
8	Production cost per gallon			
9	([$110,000 + $280,000] ÷ 20,000 gallons; [$290,000 + $520,000] ÷ 50,000 gallons)	$ 19.50	$ 16.20	
10				
11	**PANEL B: Product-Line Income Statement Using Net Realizable Value Method for May 2009**	**Buttercream**	**Condensed Milk**	**Total**
12	Revenues (12,000 gallons x $25 per gallon; 45,000 gallons x $22 per gallon)	$300,000	$ 990,000	$1,290,000
13	Cost of goods sold			
14	Joint costs (0.275 x $400,000; 0.725 x $400,000)	110,000	290,000	400,000
15	Separable costs	280,000	520,000	800,000
16	Production costs	390,000	810,000	1,200,000
17	Deduct ending inventory (8,000 gallons x $19.50 per gallon; 5,000 gallons x $16.20 per gallon)	156,000	81,000	237,000
18	Cost of goods sold	234,000	729,000	963,000
19	Gross margin	$ 66,000	$ 261,000	$ 327,000
20	Gross margin percentage ($66,000 ÷ $300,000; $261,000 ÷ $990,000; $327,000 ÷ $1,290,000)	22.0%	26.4%	25.3%

Constant Gross-Margin Percentage NRV Method

The **constant gross-margin percentage NRV method** allocates joint costs to joint products in such a way that each individual product achieves an identical gross-margin percentage. The method works backward in that the overall gross margin is computed first. Then, for each product, this gross-margin percentage and any separable costs are deducted from the final sales value of production in order to back into the joint cost allocation for that product. The method can be broken down into three discrete steps. Exhibit 16-7, Panel A, shows these steps for allocating the $400,000 joint costs between buttercream and condensed milk in the Farmers' Dairy example. As we describe each step, refer to Exhibit 16-7, Panel A, for an illustration of the step.

Step 1: Compute overall gross margin percentage. The overall gross-margin percentage for all joint products together is first calculated. This is based on the final sales value of *total production* during the accounting period, not the *total revenues* of the period. Note, Exhibit 16-7, Panel A, uses $1,600,000, the final expected sales value of the entire output of buttercream and condensed milk, not the $1,290,000 in actual sales revenue for the month of May.

Step 2: Compute total production costs for each product. The gross margin (in dollars) for each product is computed by multiplying the overall gross-margin percentage by the product's final sales value of total production. The difference between the final sales value of total production and the gross margin then yields the total production costs that the product must bear.

Step 3: Compute allocated joint costs. As the final step, the separable costs for each product are deducted from the total production costs that the product must bear to obtain the joint-cost allocation for that product.

Exhibit 16-7, Panel B, presents the product-line income statement for the constant gross-margin percentage NRV method.

The constant gross-margin percentage NRV method is the only method of allocating joint costs under which products may receive negative allocations. This may be required in order to bring the gross-margin percentages of relatively unprofitable products up to the overall average. The constant gross-margin percentage NRV method also differs from the other two market-based joint-cost-allocation methods described earlier in another fundamental way. Neither the sales value at splitoff method nor the NRV method takes account of profits earned either before or after the splitoff point when allocating the joint costs. In

Exhibit 16-7 Joint-Cost Allocation and Product-Line Income Statement Using Constant Gross-Margin Percentage NRV Method: Farmers' Dairy for May 2009

	A	B	C	D
1	**PANEL A: Allocation of Joint Costs Using Constant Gross-Margin Percentage NRV Method**			
2	**Step 1**			
3	Final sales value of total production during accounting period: (20,000 gallons x \$25 per gallon) + (50,000 gallons x \$22 per gallon)	\$1,600,000		
4	Deduct joint and separable costs (\$400,000 + \$280,000 + \$520,000)	1,200,000		
5	Gross margin	\$ 400,000		
6	Gross margin percentage (\$400,000 ÷ \$1,600,000)	25%		
7		**Buttercream**	**Condensed Milk**	**Total**
8	**Stop 2**			
9	Final sales value of total production during accounting period: (20,000 gallons x \$25 per gallon; 50,000 gallons x \$22 per gallon)	\$ 500,000	\$1,100,000	\$1,600,000
10	Deduct gross margin, using overall gross-margin percentage (25% x \$500,000; 25% x \$1,100,000)	125,000	275,000	400,000
11	Total production costs	375,000	825,000	1,200,000
12	**Step 3**			
13	Deduct separable costs	280,000	520,000	800,000
14	Joint costs allocated	\$ 95,000	\$ 305,000	\$ 400,000
15				
16	**PANEL B: Product-Line Income Statement Using Constant Gross-Margin Percentage NRV Method for May 2009**	**Buttercream**	**Condensed Milk**	**Total**
17	Revenues (12,000 gallons x \$25 per gallon; 45,000 gallons x \$22 per gallon)	\$ 300,000	\$ 990,000	\$1,290,000
18	Cost of goods sold			
19	Joint costs (from Panel A)	95,000	305,000	400,000
20	Separable costs	280,000	520,000	800,000
21	Production costs	375,000	825,000	1,200,000
22	Deduct ending inventory			
23	(8,000 gallons x \$18.75 per gallon[a]; 5,000 gallons x \$16.50 per gallon[b])	150,000	82,500	232,500
24	Cost of goods sold	225,000	742,500	967,500
25	Gross margin	\$ 75,000	\$ 247,500	\$ 322,500
26	Gross margin percentage (\$75,000 ÷ 300,000; \$247,500 ÷ \$990,000; \$322,500 ÷ \$1,290,000)	25%	25%	25%
27				
28	[a]Total production costs of buttercream ÷ Total production of buttercream = \$375,000 ÷ 20,000 gallons = \$18.75 per gallon.			
29	[b]Total production costs of condensed milk ÷ Total production of condensed milk = \$825,000 ÷ 50,000 gallons = \$16.50 per gallon.			

contrast, the constant gross-margin percentage NRV method allocates both joint costs and profits: gross margin is allocated to the joint products in order to determine the joint-cost allocations so that the resulting gross-margin percentage for each product is the same.

Choosing a Method

Learning Objective 5

Explain why the sales value at splitoff method is preferred when allocating joint costs

. . . because it objectively measures the benefits received by each product

Which method of allocating joint costs should be used? The sales value at splitoff method is preferable when selling-price data exist at splitoff (even if further processing is done). Reasons for using the sales value at splitoff method include:

1. **Measurement of the value of the joint products at the splitoff point.** Sales value at splitoff is the best measure of the benefits received as a result of joint processing relative to all other methods of allocating joint costs. It is a meaningful basis for allocating joint costs because generating revenues is the reason why a company incurs joint costs in the first place.
2. **No anticipation of subsequent management decisions.** The sales value at splitoff method does not require information on the processing steps after splitoff, if there is further processing. In contrast, the NRV and constant gross-margin percentage NRV methods require information on (a) the specific sequence of further processing decisions, (b) the separable costs of further processing, and (c) the point at which individual products will be sold.
3. **Availability of a common basis to allocate joint costs to products.** The sales value at splitoff method (as well as other market-based methods) has a common basis to allocate joint costs to products, which is revenue. In contrast, the physical-measure at

splitoff method may lack an easily identifiable common basis to allocate joint costs to individual products.

4. **Simplicity.** The sales value at splitoff method is simple. In contrast, the NRV and constant gross-margin percentage NRV methods can be complex for processing operations having multiple products and multiple splitoff points. This complexity increases when management makes frequent changes in the specific sequence of post-splitoff processing decisions or in the point at which individual products are sold.

When selling prices of all products at the splitoff point are unavailable, the NRV method is commonly used because it attempts to approximate sales value at splitoff by subtracting from selling prices separable costs incurred after the splitoff point. The NRV method assumes that all the markup or profit margin is attributable to the joint process and none of the markup is attributable to the separable costs. Profit, however, is attributable to all phases of production and marketing, not just the joint process. More of the profit may be attributable to the joint process if the separable process is relatively routine, whereas more of the profit may be attributable to the separable process if the separable process uses a special patented technology. Despite its complexities, the NRV method is used when selling prices at splitoff are not available as it provides a better measure of benefits received compared with the constant gross-margin percentage NRV method or the physical-measure method.

The main advantage of the constant gross-margin percentage NRV method is that it is relatively easy to implement. This method treats the joint products as though they comprise a single product by calculating an aggregate gross-margin percentage, applying this gross-margin percentage to each product, and backing out the joint costs allocated to each product. This method avoids the complexities inherent in the NRV method to measure the benefits received by each of the joint products at the splitoff point. The main issue with the constant gross-margin percentage NRV method is the assumption that all products have the same ratio of cost to sales value. Such a situation is very uncommon, for example, when companies produce multiple products that do not involve joint costs.

Although there are difficulties in using the physical-measure method—such as lack of congruence with the benefits-received criterion—there are instances when it may be preferred. Consider rate or price regulation. Market-based measures are difficult to use in this context because using selling prices as a basis for setting prices (rates) and at the same time using selling prices to allocate the costs on which prices (rates) are based leads to circular reasoning. To avoid this dilemma, the physical-measure method is useful in rate regulation.

Not Allocating Joint Costs

The preceding methods for allocating joint costs to individual products are somewhat arbitrary, so some companies do not allocate joint costs to products. Instead, they carry their inventories at NRV. Income on each product is recognized when production is completed. Some industries that use variations of this no-allocation approach include meatpacking, canning, and mining.

Accountants do not ordinarily record inventories at NRV because carrying inventory at NRV recognizes income *before* sales are made. In response, some companies using this no-allocation approach carry their inventories at NRV minus an estimated operating income margin. When any end-of-period inventories are sold in the next period, cost of goods sold will be NRV minus the estimated operating income margin on these products shown in prior period's ending inventory.

Explain why joint costs are irrelevant in a sell-or-process-further decision

. . . because joint costs are the same whether or not further processing occurs

Irrelevance of Joint Costs for Decision Making

Chapter 11 introduced the concepts of *relevant revenues*—expected future revenues that differ among alternative courses of action—and *relevant costs*—expected future costs that differ among alternative courses of action. These concepts can be applied to decisions on whether a joint product or main product should be sold at the splitoff point or processed further.

Sell-or-Process-Further Decisions

Consider Farmers' Dairy's decision to either sell the joint products, cream and liquid skim, at the splitoff point or to further process them into buttercream and condensed milk. The decision to incur additional costs for further processing should be based on the incremental operating income attainable beyond the splitoff point. Example 2 assumed it was profitable for both cream and liquid skim to be further processed into buttercream and condensed milk, respectively. The incremental analysis for the decision to process further is:

Further Processing Cream into Buttercream	
Incremental revenues	
($25/gallon × 20,000 gallons) − ($8/gallon × 25,000 gallons)	$300,000
Deduct incremental processing costs	280,000
Increase in operating income from buttercream	$ 20,000
Further Processing Liquid Skim into Condensed Milk	
Incremental revenues	
($22/gallon × 50,000 gallons) − ($4/gallon × 75,000 gallons)	$800,000
Deduct incremental processing costs	520,000
Increase in operating income from condensed milk	$280,000

In this example, operating income increases for both products, so the manager decides to process cream into buttercream and liquid skim into condensed milk. *The $400,000 joint costs incurred before the splitoff point are irrelevant in deciding whether to process further.* Why? Because the joint costs of $400,000 are the same whether the products are sold at the splitoff point or processed further.

Incremental costs are the additional costs incurred for an activity, such as further processing. *Do not assume all separable costs in joint-cost allocations are always incremental costs.* Some separable costs may be fixed costs, such as lease costs on buildings where the further processing is done; some separable costs may be sunk costs, such as depreciation on the equipment that converts cream into buttercream; and some separable costs may be allocated costs, such as corporate costs allocated to the condensed milk operations. None of these costs will differ between the alternatives of selling products at the splitoff point or processing further; therefore, they are irrelevant.

Joint-Cost Allocation and Performance Evaluation

The potential conflict between cost concepts used for decision making and cost concepts used for evaluating the performance of managers could also arise in sell-or-process-further decisions. To see how, let us continue with Example 2. Suppose *allocated* fixed corporate and administrative costs of further processing cream into buttercream equal $30,000 and that these costs will be allocated only to buttercream and to the manager's product-line income statement if buttercream is produced. How might this policy affect the decision to process further?

As we have seen, on the basis of incremental revenues and incremental costs, Farmers' operating income will increase by $20,000 if it processes cream into buttercream. However, producing the buttercream also results in an additional charge for allocated fixed costs of $30,000. If the manager is evaluated on a full-cost basis (that is, after allocating all costs), processing cream into buttercream will lower the manager's performance-evaluation measure by $10,000 (incremental operating income, $20,000 − allocated fixed costs, $30,000). Therefore, the manager may be tempted to sell cream at splitoff and not process it into buttercream.

A similar conflict can also arise with respect to production of joint products. Consider again Example 1. Suppose Farmers' Dairy has the option of selling raw milk at a profit of $20,000. From a decision-making standpoint, Farmers' would maximize operating income by processing raw milk into cream and liquid skim because the total revenues from selling both joint products ($500,000, p. 577) exceed the joint costs ($400,000, p. 576) by

$100,000. (This amount is greater than the $20,000 Farmers' Dairy would make if it sold the raw milk instead of processing it.) Suppose, however, the cream and liquid-skim product lines are managed by different managers, each of whom is evaluated based on a product-line income statement. If the physical-measure method of joint-cost allocation is used and the selling price per gallon of liquid skim falls below $4.00 per gallon, the liquid-skim product line will show a loss (from Exhibit 16-4, p. 578, revenues will be less than $120,000, but cost of goods sold will be unchanged at $120,000). The manager of the liquid-skim line will prefer, from his performance-evaluation standpoint, to not produce liquid skim but rather to sell the raw milk.

This conflict between decision making and performance evaluation is less severe if Farmers' Dairy uses any of the market-based methods of joint-cost allocations—sales value at splitoff, NRV, or constant gross-margin percentage NRV. That's because each of these methods allocates costs using revenues, which generally leads to a positive income for each joint product.

Pricing Decisions

Should the joint costs allocated to the joint products be used in making pricing decisions for joint products? No. Why? Because there is no cause-and-effect relationship that identifies the resources demanded by each joint product that can then be used as a basis for pricing. Today in much of joint-costing, selling prices (through their effects on benefits received) drive joint-cost allocations. Cost allocations do not drive pricing.

Accounting for Byproducts

Learning Objective 7

Account for byproducts using two methods

. . . recognize in financial statements at time of production or at time of sale

Joint production processes may yield not only joint products and main products but also byproducts. Although byproducts have low total sales values compared with total sales values of joint or main products, the presence of byproducts in a joint production process can affect the allocation of joint costs. Let's consider a two-product example consisting of a main product and a byproduct.

Example 3: The Westlake Corporation processes timber into fine-grade lumber and wood chips that are used as mulch in gardens and lawns. Information about these products follows:

- Fine-grade lumber (the main product)—sells for $6 per board foot (b.f.)
- Wood chips (the byproduct)—sells for $1 per cubic foot (c.f.)

Data for July 2009 are:

	Beginning Inventory	Production	Sales	Ending Inventory
Fine-grade lumber (b.f.)	0	50,000	40,000	10,000
Wood chips (c.f.)	0	4,000	1,200	2,800

Joint manufacturing costs for these products in July 2009 were $250,000, comprising $150,000 for direct materials and $100,000 for conversion costs. Both products are sold at the splitoff point without further processing, as Exhibit 16-8 shows.

We present two byproduct accounting methods: the production method and the sales method. The production method recognizes byproducts in the financial statements at the time production is completed. The sales method delays recognition of byproducts until the time of sale.[5] Exhibit 16-9 presents the income statement of Westlake Corporation under both methods.

[5] For a discussion of joint cost allocation and byproduct accounting methods, see P. D. Marshall and R. F. Dombrowski, "A Small Business Review of Accounting for Primary Products, Byproducts and Scrap," *The National Public Accountant* (February/March 2003): 10–13.

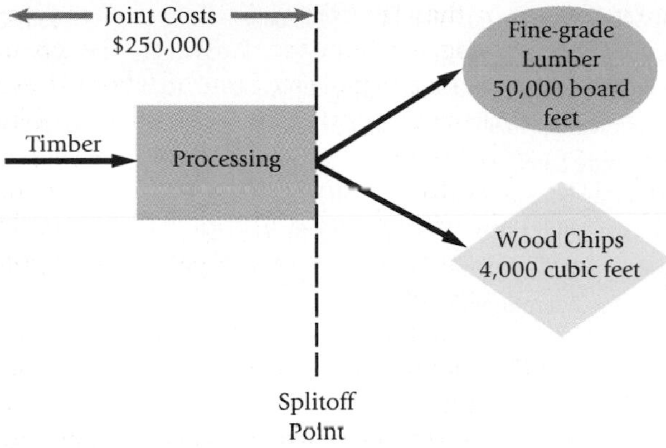

Exhibit 16-8

Example 3: Overview of Westlake Corporation

Production Method: Byproducts Recognized at Time Production Is Completed

This method recognizes the byproduct in the financial statements—the 4,000 cubic feet of wood chips—in the month it is produced, July 2009. The NRV from the byproduct produced is offset against the costs of the main product (see Concepts in Action, p. 587). The following journal entries illustrate the production method:

1. Work in Process	150,000	
Accounts Payable		150,000
To record direct materials purchased and used in production during July.		
2. Work in Process	100,000	
Various accounts such as Wages Payable and Accumulated Depreciation		100,000
To record conversion costs in the production process during July; examples include energy, manufacturing supplies, all manufacturing labor, and plant depreciation.		
3. Byproduct Inventory—Wood Chips (4,000 c.f. × $1 per c.f.)	4,000	
Finished Goods—Fine-grade Lumber ($250,000 − $4,000)	246,000	
Work in Process ($150,000 + $100,000)		250,000
To record cost of goods completed during July.		

Exhibit 16-9

Income Statements of Westlake Corporation for July 2009 Using the Production and Sales Methods for Byproduct Accounting

	Production Method	Sales Method
Revenues		
Main product: Fine-grade lumber (40,000 b.f. × $6 per b.f.)	$240,000	$240,000
Byproduct: Wood chips (1,200 c.f. × $1 per c.f.)	—	1,200
Total revenues	240,000	241,200
Cost of goods sold		
Total manufacturing costs	250,000	250,000
Deduct byproduct revenue (4,000 c.f. × $1 per c.f.)	(4,000)	—
Net manufacturing costs	246,000	250,000
Deduct main-product inventory	(49,200)[a]	(50,000)[b]
Cost of goods sold	196,800	200,000
Gross margin	$ 43,200	$ 41,200
Gross-margin percentage ($43,200 ÷ $240,000; $41,200 ÷ $241,200)	18.00%	17.08%
Inventoriable costs (end of period):		
Main product: Fine-grade lumber	$ 49,200	$ 50,000
Byproduct: Wood chips (2,800 c.f. × $1 per c.f.)[c]	2,800	0

[a](10,000 ÷ 50,000) × net manufacturing cost = (10,000 ÷ 50,000) × $246,000 = $49,200.

[b](10,000 ÷ 50,000) × total manufacturing cost = (10,000 ÷ 50,000) × $250,000 = $50,000.

[c]Recorded at selling prices.

		Debit	Credit
4a.	Cost of Goods Sold [(40,000 b.f. ÷ 50,000 b.f.) × $246,000]	196,800	
	Finished Goods—Fine-grade Lumber		196,800
	To record the cost of the main product sold during July.		
4b.	Cash or Accounts Receivable (40,000 b.f. × $6 per b.f.)	240,000	
	Revenues—Fine-grade Lumber		240,000
	To record the sales of the main product during July.		
5.	Cash or Accounts Receivable (1,200 c.f. × $1 per c.f.)	1,200	
	Byproduct Inventory—Wood Chips		1,200
	To record the sales of the byproduct during July.		

The production method reports the byproduct inventory of wood chips in the balance sheet at its $1 per cubic foot selling price [(4,000 cubic feet − 1,200 cubic feet) × $1 per cubic foot = $2,800].

One variation of this method would be to report byproduct inventory at its NRV reduced by a normal profit margin ($2,800 − 20% × $2,800 = $2,240, assuming a normal profit margin of 20%).[6] When byproduct inventory is sold in a subsequent period, the income statement will match the selling price, $2,800, with the "cost" reported for the byproduct inventory, $2,240, resulting in a byproduct operating income of $560 ($2,800 − $2,240).

Sales Method: Byproducts Recognized at Time of Sale

This method makes no journal entries for byproducts until they are sold. Revenues of the byproduct are reported as a revenue item in the income statement at the time of sale. These revenues are either grouped with other sales, included as other income, or are deducted from cost of goods sold. In the Westlake Corporation example, byproduct revenues in July 2009 are $1,200 (1,200 cubic feet × $1 per cubic foot) because only 1,200 cubic feet of wood chips are sold in July (of the 4,000 cubic feet produced). The journal entries are:

		Debit	Credit
1. and 2.	*Same as for the production method.*		
	Work in Process	150,000	
	Accounts Payable		150,000
	Work in Process	100,000	
	Various accounts such as Wages Payable and Accumulated Depreciation		100,000
3.	Finished Goods—Fine-grade Lumber	250,000	
	Work in Process		250,000
	To record cost of main product completed during July.		
4a.	Cost of Goods Sold [(40,000 b.f. ÷ 50,000 b.f.) × $250,000]	200,000	
	Finished Goods—Fine-grade Lumber		200,000
	To record the cost of the main product sold during July.		
4b.	Same as for the production method.		
	Cash or Accounts Receivable (40,000 b.f. × $6 per b.f.)	240,000	
	Revenues—Fine-grade Lumber		240,000
5.	Cash or Accounts Receivable	1,200	
	Revenues—Wood Chips		1,200
	To record the sales of the byproduct during July.		

Which method should a company use? The production method is conceptually correct in that it is consistent with the matching principle. This method recognizes byproduct inventory in the accounting period in which it is produced and simultaneously reduces the cost

[6] One way to make this calculation is to assume all products have the same "normal" profit margin like the constant gross-margin percentage NRV method. Alternatively, the company might allow products to have different profit margins based on an analysis of the margins earned by other companies that sell these products individually.

Concepts in Action

Chicken Processing: Costing of Joint Products and Byproducts

Chicken-processing operations provide examples in which joint and byproduct costing issues arise. White breast meat, the highest revenue-generating product, is obtained from the front part of the bird; dark meat from the back part. Other edible products include chicken wings and giblets. There are many inedible products that have a diverse set of uses. For example, poultry feathers are used in bedding and sporting goods.

Poultry companies use individual-product cost information for several purposes. One purpose is in customer-profitability analysis. Customers (such as supermarkets and fast-food restaurants) differ greatly in the mix of products they purchase. Individual-product cost data enable companies to determine differences in individual-customer profitability. A subset of products is placed into frozen storage, which creates a demand for individual-product cost information for inventory valuation.

Companies differ in how they cost individual products. Consider two of the largest U.S. companies: Southern Poultry and Golden State Poultry (disguised names).

Southern Poultry classifies white breast meat as the single main product in its costing system. All other products are classified as byproducts. Selling prices of the many byproducts are used to reduce the chicken-processing costs that are allocated to the main product. White breast meat is often further processed into many individual products (such as trimmed chicken and marinated chicken). The separable cost of this further processing is added to the cost per pound of deboned white breast meat to obtain the cost of further-processed products.

Golden State Poultry classifies any product sold to a retail outlet as a joint product. Such products include breast fillets, half-breasts, thighs, whole legs, and wings. Products not sold to a retail outlet are classified as byproducts. Revenue that will be earned from byproducts is offset against the chicken-processing cost before that cost is allocated among the joint products. Average selling prices of products sold to retail outlets are used to allocate net chicken-processing cost to the individual joint products. Distribution costs of transporting the chicken products from the processing plants to retail outlets are not taken into account when determining weights for joint-cost allocation.

Source: Adapted from conversations with executives of Southern Poultry and Golden State Poultry.

of manufacturing the main or joint products, thereby better matching the revenues and expenses from selling the main product. However, the sales method is simpler and is often used in practice, primarily on the grounds that the dollar amounts of byproducts are immaterial. Then again, the sales method permits managers to "manage" reported earnings by timing when they sell byproducts. Managers may store byproducts for several periods and give revenues and income a "small boost" by selling byproducts accumulated over several periods when revenues and profits from the main product or joint products are low.

Problem for Self-Study

Inorganic Chemicals (IC) processes salt into various industrial products. In July 2009, IC incurred joint costs of $100,000 to purchase salt and convert it into two products: caustic soda and chlorine. Although there is an active outside market for chlorine, IC processes all 800 tons of chlorine it produces into 500 tons of PVC (polyvinyl chloride), which is then sold. There were no beginning or ending inventories of salt, caustic soda, chlorine, or PVC in July. Information for July 2009 production and sales follows:

	A	B	C	D
1		Joint Costs		PVC
2	Joint costs (costs of salt and processing to splitoff point)	$100,000		
3	Separable cost of processing 800 tons chlorine into 500 tons PVC			$20,000
4				
5		Caustic Soda	Chlorine	PVC
6	Beginning inventory (tons)	0	0	0
7	Production (tons)	1,200	800	500
8	Transfer for further processing (tons)		800	
9	Sales (tons)	1,200		500
10	Ending inventory (tons)	0	0	0
11	Selling price per ton in active outside market (for products not actually sold)		$ 75	
12	Selling price per ton for products sold	$ 50		$ 200

Required

1. Allocate the joint costs of $100,000 between caustic soda and PVC under (a) the sales value at splitoff method and (b) the physical-measure method.
2. Allocate the joint costs of $100,000 between caustic soda and PVC under the NRV method.
3. Under the three allocation methods in requirements 1 and 2, what is the gross-margin percentage of (a) caustic soda and (b) PVC?
4. Lifetime Swimming Pool Products offers to purchase 800 tons of chlorine in August 2009 at $75 per ton. Assume all other production and sales data are the same for August as they were for July. This sale of chlorine to Lifetime would mean that no PVC would be produced by IC in August. How would accepting this offer affect IC's August 2009 operating income?

Solution

The following picture provides a visual illustration of the main facts in this problem.

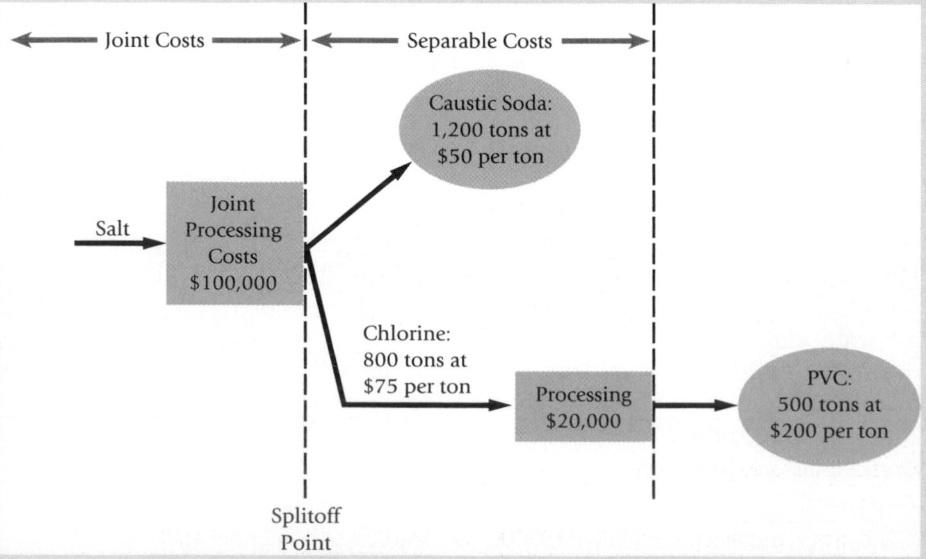

Note that caustic soda is sold as is while chlorine, despite having a market value at splitoff, is sold only in processed form as PVC. The goal is to allocate the joint costs of $100,000 to the final products—caustic soda and PVC. However, since PVC exists only in the form of chlorine at the splitoff point, we use chlorine's sales value and physical measure as the basis for allocating joint costs to PVC under the sales value at splitoff and physical measure at splitoff methods. Detailed calculations are shown below.

1a. Sales value at splitoff method

	A	B	C	D
1	**Allocation of Joint costs using Sales Value at Splitoff Method**	**Caustic Soda**	**PVC / Chlorine**	**Total**
2	Sales value of total production at splitoff point			
3	(1,200 tons x $50 per ton; 800 x $75 per ton)	$60,000	$60,000	$120,000
4	Weighting ($60,000 ÷ $120,000; $60,000 ÷ $120,000)	0.50	0.50	
5	Joint costs allocated (0.50 x $100,000; 0.50 x $100,000)	$50,000	$50,000	$100,000

1b. Physical-measure method

	A	B	C	D
8	**Allocation of Joint Costs using Physical-Measure Method**	**Caustic Soda**	**PVC / Chlorine**	**Total**
9	Physical measure of total production (tons)	1,200	800	2,000
10	Weighting (1,200 tons ÷ 2,000 tons; 800 tons ÷ 2,000 tons)	0.60	0.40	
11	Joint cost allocated (0.60 x $100,000; 0.40 x $100,000)	$60,000	$40,000	$100,000

2. Net realizable value (NRV) method

	A	B	C	D
14	**Allocation of Joint Costs using Net Realizable Value Method**	**Caustic Soda**	**PVC**	**Total**
15	Final sales value of total production during accounting period			
16	(1,200 tons x $50 per ton; 500 tons x $200 per ton)	$60,000	$100,000	$160,000
17	Deduct separable costs to complete and sell	0	20,000	20,000
18	Net realizable value at splitoff point	$60,000	$ 80,000	$140,000
19	Weighting ($60,000 ÷ $140,000; $80,000 ÷ $140,000)	3/7	4/7	
20	Joint costs allocated (3/7 x $100,000; 4/7 x $100,000)	$42,857	$ 57,143	$100,000

3a. Gross-margin percentage of caustic soda

	A	B	C	D
23	**Caustic Soda**	**Sales Value at Splitoff Point**	**Physical Measure**	**NRV**
24	Revenues (1,200 tons x $50 per ton)	$60,000	$60,000	$60,000
25	Cost of goods sold (joint costs)	50,000	60,000	42,857
26	Gross margin	$10,000	$ 0	$17,143
27	Gross margin percentage ($10,000 ÷ $60,000; $0 ÷ $60,000; $17,143 ÷ $60,000)	16.67%	0.00%	28.57%

3b. Gross-margin percentage of PVC

	A	B	C	D
30	PVC	Sales Value at Splitoff Point	Physical Measure	NRV
31	Revenues (500 tons x $200 per ton)	$100,000	$100,000	$100,000
32	Cost of goods sold			
33	Joint costs	50,000	40,000	57,143
34	Separable costs	20,000	20,000	20,000
35	Cost of goods sold	70,000	60,000	77,143
36	Gross margin	$ 30,000	$ 40,000	$ 22,857
37	Gross margin percentage ($30,000 ÷ $100,000; $40,000 ÷ $100,000; $22,857 ÷ $100,000)	30.00%	40.00%	22.86%

4.

A	B
Incremental revenue from processing 800 tons of chlorine into 500 tons of PVC	
(500 tons x $200 per ton) – (800 tons x $75 per ton)	$40,000
Incremental cost of processing 800 tons of chlorine into 500 tons of PVC	20,000
Incremental operating income from further processing	$20,000

If IC sells 800 tons of chlorine to Lifetime Swimming Pool Products instead of further processing it into PVC, its August 2009 operating income will be reduced by $20,000.

Decision Points

The following question-and-answer format summarizes the chapter's learning objectives. Each decision presents a key question related to a learning objective. The guidelines are the answer to that question.

Decision	Guidelines
1. What are a joint cost and a splitoff point?	A joint cost is the cost of a single production process that yields multiple products simultaneously. The splitoff point is the juncture in a joint production process when the products become separately identifiable.
2. How do joint products differ from byproducts?	Joint products have high total sales values at the splitoff point. A byproduct has a low total sales value at the splitoff point compared with the total sales value of a joint or main product. Products can change from byproducts to joint products when their total sales values significantly increase or change from joint products to byproducts when their total sales values significantly decrease.
3. Why are joint costs allocated to individual products?	The purposes for allocating joint costs to products include inventory costing for financial accounting and internal reporting, cost reimbursement, insurance settlements, rate regulation, and product-cost litigation.
4. What methods can be used to allocate joint costs to individual products?	The methods to allocate joint costs to products are the sales value at splitoff, NRV, constant gross-margin percentage NRV, and physical-measure methods.

5. When is the sales value at splitoff method used for allocating joint costs to individual products and why?

The sales value at splitoff method is used when market prices exist at splitoff because using revenues is consistent with the benefits-received criterion, it does not anticipate subsequent management decisions on further processing, and it is simple.

6. Are joint costs relevant in a sell-or-process-further decision?

No, joint costs and how they are allocated are irrelevant in deciding whether to process further because joint costs are the same regardless of whether further processing occurs.

7. What methods can be used to account for byproducts and which of them is preferable?

The production method recognizes byproducts in financial statements at the time of production, whereas the sales method recognizes byproducts in financial statements at the time of sale. The production method is conceptually superior, but the sales method is often used in practice because dollar amounts of byproducts are immaterial.

TERMS TO LEARN

This chapter and the Glossary at the end of the book contain definitions of:

byproducts **(p. 574)**
constant gross-margin percentage NRV method **(p. 580)**
joint costs **(p. 573)**
joint products **(p. 574)**
main product **(p. 574)**
net realizable value (NRV) method **(p. 579)**
physical-measure method **(p. 577)**
product **(p. 574)**
sales value at splitoff method **(p. 576)**
separable costs **(p. 573)**
splitoff point **(p. 573)**

ASSIGNMENT MATERIAL

Questions

16-1 Give two examples of industries in which joint costs are found. For each example, what are the individual products at the splitoff point?

16-2 What is a joint cost? What is a separable cost?

16-3 Distinguish between a joint product and a byproduct.

16-4 Why might the number of products in a joint-cost situation differ from the number of outputs? Give an example.

16-5 Provide three reasons for allocating joint costs to individual products or services.

16-6 Why does the sales value at splitoff method use the sales value of the total production in the accounting period and not just the revenues from the products sold?

16-7 Describe a situation in which the sales value at splitoff method cannot be used but the NRV method can be used for joint-cost allocation.

16-8 Distinguish between the sales value at splitoff method and the NRV method.

16-9 Give two limitations of the physical-measure method of joint-cost allocation.

16-10 How might a company simplify its use of the NRV method when final selling prices can vary sizably in an accounting period and management frequently changes the point at which it sells individual products?

16-11 Why is the constant gross-margin percentage NRV method sometimes called a "joint-cost-allocation and a profit-allocation" method?

16-12 "Managers must decide whether a product should be sold at splitoff or processed further. The sales value at splitoff method of joint-cost allocation is the best method for generating the information managers need for this decision." Do you agree? Explain.

16-13 "Managers should consider only additional revenues and separable costs when making decisions about selling at splitoff or processing further." Do you agree? Explain.

16-14 Describe two major methods to account for byproducts.

16-15 Why might managers seeking a monthly bonus based on attaining a target operating income prefer the sales method of accounting for byproducts rather than the production method?

Exercises

16-16 Joint-cost allocation, insurance settlement. Quality Chicken grows and processes chickens. Each chicken is disassembled into five main parts. Information pertaining to production in July 2009 is:

Parts	Pounds of Product	Wholesale Selling Price per Pound When Production Is Complete
Breasts	100	$0.55
Wings	20	0.20
Thighs	40	0.35
Bones	80	0.10
Feathers	10	0.05

Joint cost of production in July 2009 was $50.

A special shipment of 40 pounds of breasts and 15 pounds of wings has been destroyed in a fire. Quality Chicken's insurance policy provides reimbursement for the cost of the items destroyed. The insurance company permits Quality Chicken to use a joint-cost-allocation method. The splitoff point is assumed to be at the end of the production process.

Required

1. Compute the cost of the special shipment destroyed using
   a. Sales value at splitoff method
   b. Physical-measure method (pounds of finished product)
2. What joint-cost-allocation method would you recommend Quality Chicken use? Explain.

16-17 Joint products and byproducts (continuation of 16-16). Quality Chicken is computing the ending inventory values for its July 31, 2009, balance sheet. Ending inventory amounts on July 31 are 15 pounds of breasts, 4 pounds of wings, 6 pounds of thighs, 5 pounds of bones, and 2 pounds of feathers.

Quality Chicken's management wants to use the sales value at splitoff method. However, they want you to explore the effect on ending inventory values of classifying one or more products as a byproduct rather than a joint product.

Required

1. Assume Quality Chicken classifies all five products as joint products. What are the ending inventory values of each product on July 31, 2009?
2. Assume Quality Chicken uses the production method of accounting for byproducts. What are the ending inventory values for each joint product on July 31, 2009, assuming breasts and thighs are the joint products and wings, bones, and feathers are byproducts?
3. Comment on differences in the results in requirements 1 and 2.

16-18 Net realizable value method. Convad Company is one of the world's leading corn refiners. It produces two joint products—corn syrup and corn starch—using a common production process. In July 2009, Convad reported the following production and selling-price information:

File Edit View Insert Format Tools Data Window Help

	A	B	C	D
1		Corn Syrup	Corn Starch	Joint Costs
2	Joint costs (costs of processing corn to splitoff point)			$325,000
3	Separable cost of processing beyond splitoff point	$375,000	$93,750	
4	Beginning inventory (cases)	0	0	
5	Production and Sales (cases)	12,500	6,250	
6	Ending inventory (cases)	0	0	
7	Selling price per case	50	$ 25	

If you want to use Excel to solve this exercise, go to the Excel Lab at **www.prenhall.com/horngren/cost13e** and download the template for Exercise 16-18.

Required

Allocate the $325,000 joint costs using the NRV method.

16-19 Alternative joint-cost-allocation methods, further-process decision. The Wood Spirits Company produces two products—turpentine and methanol (wood alcohol)—by a joint process. Joint costs amount to $120,000 per batch of output. Each batch totals 10,000 gallons: 25% methanol and 75% turpentine. Both products are processed further without gain or loss in volume. Separable processing costs are methanol, $3 per gallon; turpentine, $2 per gallon. Methanol sells for $21 per gallon. Turpentine sells for $14 per gallon.

Required

1. How much of the joint costs per batch will be allocated to turpentine and to methanol, assuming that joint costs are allocated based on the number of gallons at splitoff point?
2. If joint costs are allocated on an NRV basis, how much of the joint costs will be allocated to turpentine and to methanol?
3. Prepare product-line income statements per batch for requirements 1 and 2. Assume no beginning or ending inventories.

4. The company has discovered an additional process by which the methanol (wood alcohol) can be made into a pleasant-tasting alcoholic beverage. The selling price of this beverage would be $60 a gallon. Additional processing would increase separable costs $9 per gallon (in addition to the $3 per gallon separable cost required to yield methanol). The company would have to pay excise taxes of 20% on the selling price of the beverage. Assuming no other changes in cost, what is the joint cost applicable to the wood alcohol (using the NRV method)? Should the company produce the alcoholic beverage? Show your computations.

16-20 Alternative methods of joint-cost allocation, ending inventories. The Darl Company operates a simple chemical process to convert a single material into three separate items, referred to here as X, Y, and Z. All three end products are separated simultaneously at a single splitoff point.

Products X and Y are ready for sale immediately upon splitoff without further processing or any other additional costs. Product Z, however, is processed further before being sold. There is no available market price for Z at the splitoff point.

The selling prices quoted here are expected to remain the same in the coming year. During 2009, the selling prices of the items and the total amounts sold were:

- X—120 tons sold for $1,500 per ton
- Y—340 tons sold for $1,000 per ton
- Z—475 tons sold for $700 per ton

The total joint manufacturing costs for the year were $400,000. Darl spent an additional $200,000 to finish product Z.

There were no beginning inventories of X, Y, or Z. At the end of the year, the following inventories of completed units were on hand: X, 180 tons; Y, 60 tons; Z, 25 tons. There was no beginning or ending work in process.

Required

1. Compute the cost of inventories of X, Y, and Z for balance sheet purposes and the cost of goods sold for income statement purposes as of December 31, 2009, using the following joint cost allocation methods:
   a. NRV method
   b. Constant gross-margin percentage NRV method.
2. Compare the gross-margin percentages for X, Y, and Z using the two methods given in requirement 1.

16-21 Joint-cost allocation, process further. Sinclair Oil & Gas, a large energy conglomerate, jointly processes purchased hydrocarbons to generate three nonsaleable intermediate products: ICR8, ING4, and XGE3. These intermediate products are further processed separately to produce Crude Oil, Natural Gas Liquids (NGL) and Natural Gas (measured in liquid equivalents). An overview of the process and results for August 2009 are shown here (Note: The numbers are small to keep the focus on key concepts):

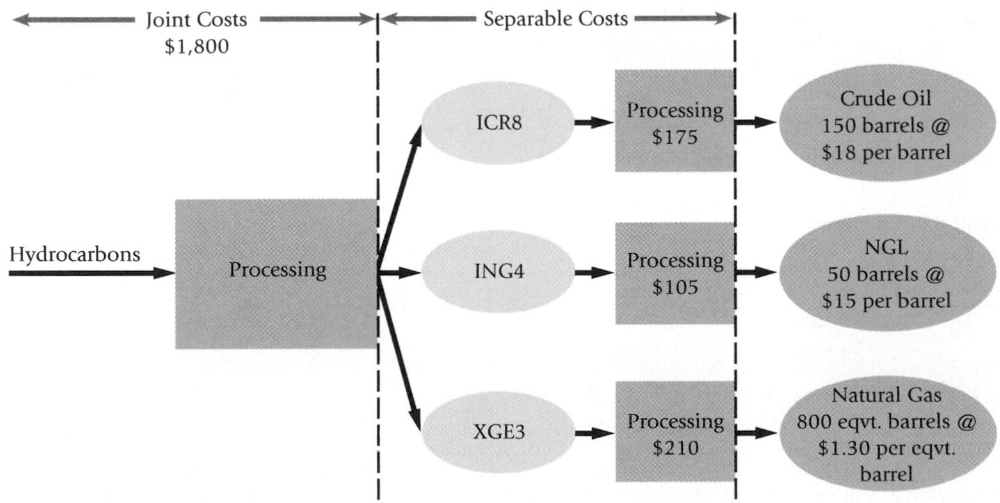

A new federal law has recently been passed that taxes crude oil at 30% of operating income. No new tax is to be paid on natural gas liquid or natural gas. Starting August 2009, Sinclair Oil & Gas must report a separate product-line income statement for crude oil. One challenge facing Sinclair Oil & Gas is how to allocate the joint cost of producing the three separate saleable outputs. Assume no beginning or ending inventory.

Required

1. Allocate the August 2009 joint cost among the three products using
   a. Physical-measure method
   b. NRV method.
2. Show the operating income for each product using the methods in requirement 1.

3. Discuss the pros and cons of the two methods to Sinclair Oil & Gas for making decisions about product emphasis (pricing, sell-or-process further decisions, and so on).
4. Draft a letter to the taxation authorities on behalf of Sinclair Oil & Gas that justifies the joint-cost-allocation method you recommend Sinclair use.

16-22 Joint-cost allocation, sales value, physical measure, NRV methods. Instant Foods produces two types of microwavable products—beef-flavored ramen and shrimp-flavored ramen. The two products share common inputs such as noodle and spices. The production of ramen results in a waste product referred to as stock, which Instant dumps at negligible costs in a local drainage area. In June 2009, the following data were reported for the production and sales of beef-flavored and shrimp-flavored ramen:

	A	B	C
1		Joint Costs	
2	Joint costs (costs of noodles, spices, and other inputs and processing to splitoff point)	$240,000	
3			
4		Beef Ramen	Shrimp Ramen
5	Beginning inventory (tons)	0	0
6	Production (tons)	10,000	20,000
7	Sales (tons)	10,000	20,000
8	Selling price per ton	$ 10	$ 15

Due to the popularity of its microwavable products, Instant decides to add a new line of products that targets dieters. These new products are produced by adding a special ingredient to dilute the original ramen and are to be sold under the names Special B and Special S, respectively. The following is the monthly data for all the products:

	A	B	C	D	E
11		Joint Costs		Special B	Special S
12	Joint costs (costs of noodles, spices, and other inputs and processing to splitoff point)	$240,000			
13	Separable costs of processing 10,000 tons of Beef Ramen into 12,000 tons of Special B			$48,000	
14	Separable cost of processing 20,000 tons of Shrimp Ramen into 24,000 tons of Special S				$168,000
15					
16		Beef Ramen	Shrimp Ramen	Special B	Special S
17	Beginning inventory (tons)	0	0	0	0
18	Production (tons)	10,000	20,000	12,000	24,000
19	Transfer for further processing (tons)	10,000	20,000		
20	Sales (tons)			12,000	24,000
21	Selling price per ton	$ 10	$ 15	$ 18	$ 25

If you want to use Excel to solve this exercise, go to the Excel Lab at **www.prenhall.com/horngren/cost13e** and download the template for Exercise 16-22.

Required

1. Calculate Instant's gross-margin percentage for Special B and Special S when joint costs are allocated using:
   a. Sales value at splitoff method
   b. Physical-measure method
   c. Net realizable value method
2. Recently, Instant discovered that the stock it is dumping can be sold to cattle ranchers at $5 per ton. In a typical month with the production levels shown above, 4,000 tons of stock are produced and can be sold by incurring marketing costs of $10,800. Sherrie Dong, a management accountant, points out that

treating the stock as a joint product and using the sales value at splitoff method, the stock product would lose about $2,228 each month, so it should not be sold. How did Dong arrive at that final number, and what do you think of her analysis? Should Instant sell the stock?

16-23 Joint cost allocation: sell immediately or process further. Iowa Soy Products (ISP) buys soy beans and processes them into other soy products. Each ton of soy beans that ISP purchases for $300 can be converted for an additional $200 into 500 lbs of soy meal and 100 gallons of soy oil. A pound of soy meal can be sold at splitoff for $1 and soy oil can be sold in bulk for $4 per gallon.

ISP can process the 500 lbs of soy meal into 600 lbs of soy cookies at an additional cost of $300. Each pound of soy cookies can be sold for $2 per pound. The 100 gallons of soy oil can be packaged at a cost of $200 and made into 400 quarts of Soyola. Each quart of Soyola can be sold for $1.25.

Required

1. Allocate the joint cost to the cookies and the Soyola using the
   a. Sales value at splitoff method; and
   b. NRV method.
2. Should ISP have processed each of the products further? What effect does the allocation method have on this decision?

16-24 Accounting for a main product and a byproduct. (Cheatham and Green, adapted) Yum, Inc. is a producer of potato chips. A single production process at Yum, Inc. yields potato chips as the main product and a byproduct that can also be sold as a snack. Both products are fully processed by the splitoff point, and there are no separable costs.

For September 2009, the cost of operations is $480,000. Production and sales data are as follows:

	Production (in Pounds)	Sales (in Pounds)	Selling Price per Pound
Main product: Potato Chips	40,000	32,000	$20
Byproduct	8,000	5,600	$ 5

There were no beginning inventories on September 1, 2009.

1. What is the gross margin for Yum, Inc. under the production method and the sales method of byproduct accounting?
2. What are the inventory costs reported in the balance sheet on September 30, 2009, for the main product and byproduct under the two methods of byproduct accounting in requirement 1?

16-25 Joint costs and byproducts. (W. Crum) Royston, Inc. is a large food processing company. It processes 120,000 pounds of peanuts in the Peanuts Department at a cost of $160,000 to yield 10,000 pounds of product A, 60,000 pounds of product B, and 20,000 pounds of product C.

- Product A is processed further in the Salting Department to yield 10,000 pounds of salted peanuts at a cost of $20,000 and sold for $10 per pound.
- Product B (Raw Peanuts) is sold without further processing at $2 per pound.
- Product C is considered a byproduct and is processed further in the Paste Department to yield 20,000 pounds of peanut butter at a cost of $10,000 and sold for $3 per pound.

The company wants to make a gross margin of 10% of revenues on product C and needs to allow 25% of revenues for marketing costs on product C. An overview of operations follows:

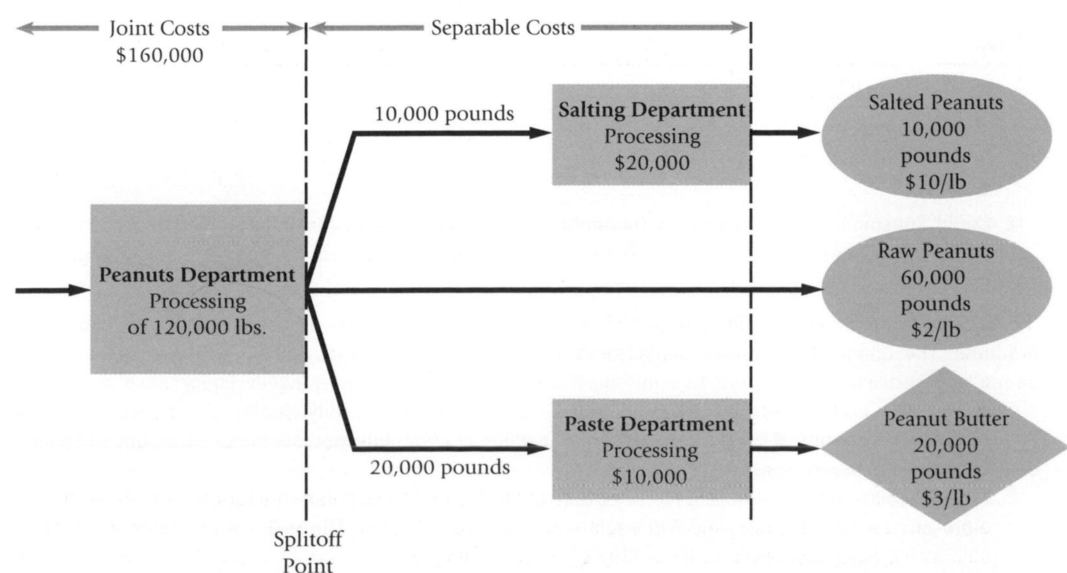

Required

1. Compute unit costs per pound for products A, B, and C, treating C as a byproduct. Use the NRV method for allocating joint costs. Deduct the NRV of the byproduct produced from the joint cost of products A and B.
2. Compute unit costs per pound for products A, B, and C, treating all three as joint products and allocating joint costs by the NRV method.

Problems

16-26 Accounting for a byproduct. Washington Oceanic Water (WOW) desalinates and bottles sea water. The desalinated water is in high demand from a large group of environmentally conscious people on the west coast of the United States. During March, WOW processes 1,000 gallons of sea water and obtains 800 gallons of drinking water and 50 pounds of sea salt (the rest of the sea water evaporates in the desalinization process). Processing the 1,000 gallons of water costs WOW $1,500. WOW sells 600 gallons of the desalinated water in 2-gallon containers for $8 per container. In addition, WOW sells 40 pounds of sea salt for $1.20 per pound. Due to the relatively small proportion of sea salt, WOW has decided to treat it as a byproduct.

Required

1. Assuming WOW accounts for the byproduct using the production method, what is the inventoriable cost for each product and WOW's gross margin?
2. Assuming WOW accounts for the byproduct using the sales method, what is the inventoriable cost for each product and WOW's gross margin?
3. Discuss the difference between the two methods of accounting for byproducts.

16-27 Alternative methods of joint-cost allocation, product-mix decisions. The Sunshine Oil Company buys crude vegetable oil. Refining this oil results in four products at the splitoff point: A, B, C, and D. Product C is fully processed by the splitoff point. Products A, B, and D can individually be further refined into Super A, Super B, and Super D. In the most recent month (December), the output at the splitoff point was:

- Product A, 300,000 gallons
- Product B, 100,000 gallons
- Product C, 50,000 gallons
- Product D, 50,000 gallons

The joint costs of purchasing and processing the crude vegetable oil were $100,000. Sunshine had no beginning or ending inventories. Sales of product C in December were $50,000. Products A, B, and D were further refined and then sold. Data related to December are:

	Separable Processing Costs to Make Super Products	Revenues
Super A	$200,000	$300,000
Super B	80,000	100,000
Super D	90,000	120,000

Sunshine had the option of selling products A, B, and D at the splitoff point. This alternative would have yielded the following revenues for the December production:

- Product A, $50,000
- Product B, $30,000
- Product D, $70,000

Required

1. Compute the gross-margin percentage for each product sold in December, using the following methods for allocating the $100,000 joint costs:

   a. Sales value at splitoff
   b. Physical-measure
   c. NRV

2. Could Sunshine have increased its December operating income by making different decisions about the further processing of products A, B, or D? Show the effect on operating income of any changes you recommend.

16-28 Comparison of alternative joint-cost-allocation methods, further-processing decision, chocolate products. The Chocolate Factory manufactures and distributes chocolate products. It purchases cocoa beans and processes them into two intermediate products: Chocolate-powder liquor base and Milk-chocolate liquor base. These two intermediate products become separately identifiable at a single splitoff point. Every 1,500 pounds of cocoa beans yields 60 gallons of chocolate-powder liquor base and 90 gallons of milk-chocolate liquor base.

The chocolate-powder liquor base is further processed into chocolate powder. Every 60 gallons of chocolate-powder liquor base yield 600 pounds of chocolate powder. The milk-chocolate liquor base is further processed into milk chocolate. Every 90 gallons of milk-chocolate liquor base yield 1,020 pounds of milk chocolate.

Production and sales data for August 2009 are (assume no beginning inventory):

- Cocoa beans processed, 15,000 pounds
- Costs of processing cocoa beans to splitoff point (including purchase of beans), $30,000

	Production	Sales	Selling Price	Separable Processing Costs
Chocolate powder	6,000 pounds	6,000 pounds	$4 per pound	$12,750
Milk chocolate	10,200 pounds	10,200 pounds	$5 per pound	$26,250

Chocolate Factory fully processes both of its intermediate products into chocolate powder or milk chocolate. There is an active market for these intermediate products. In August 2009, Chocolate Factory could have sold the chocolate-powder liquor base for $21 a gallon and the milk-chocolate liquor base for $26 a gallon.

Required

1. Calculate how the joint costs of $30,000 would be allocated between chocolate powder and milk chocolate under the following methods:
   a. Sales value at splitoff
   b. Physical-measure (gallons)
   c. NRV
   d. Constant gross-margin percentage NRV
2. What are the gross-margin percentages of chocolate powder and milk chocolate under each of the methods in requirement 1?
3. Could Chocolate Factory have increased its operating income by a change in its decision to fully process both of its intermediate products? Show your computations.

16-29 Joint-cost allocation, process further or sell. (CMA, adapted) Sonimad Sawmill, Inc. (SSI), purchases logs from independent timber contractors and processes the logs into three types of lumber products:

- Studs for residential buildings (walls, ceilings)
- Decorative pieces (fireplace mantels, beams for cathedral ceilings)
- Posts used as support braces (mine support braces, braces for exterior fences on ranch properties)

These products are the result of a joint sawmill process that involves removal of bark from the logs, cutting the logs into a workable size (ranging from 8 to 16 feet in length), and then cutting the individual products from the logs.

The joint process results in the following costs of products for a typical month:

Direct materials (rough timber logs)	$ 500,000
Debarking (labor and overhead)	50,000
Sizing (labor and overhead)	200,000
Product cutting (labor and overhead)	250,000
Total joint costs	$1,000,000

Product yields and average sales values on a per-unit basis from the joint process are as follows:

Product	Monthly Output of Materials at Splitoff Point	Fully Processed Selling Price
Studs	75,000 units	$ 8
Decorative pieces	5,000 units	100
Posts	20,000 units	20

The studs are sold as rough-cut lumber after emerging from the sawmill operation without further processing by SSI. Also, the posts require no further processing beyond the splitoff point. The decorative pieces must be planed and further sized after emerging from the sawmill. This additional processing costs $100,000 per month and normally results in a loss of 10% of the units entering the process. Without this planing and sizing process, there is still an active intermediate market for the unfinished decorative pieces in which the selling price averages $60 per unit.

Required

1. Based on the information given for Sonimad Sawmill, allocate the joint processing costs of $1,000,000 to the three products using:
   a. Sales value at splitoff method
   b. Physical-measure method (volume in units)
   c. NRV method
2. Prepare an analysis for Sonimad Sawmill that compares processing the decorative pieces further, as they currently do, with selling them as a rough-cut product immediately at splitoff.

3. Assume Sonimad Sawmill announced that in six months it will sell the unfinished decorative pieces at splitoff due to increasing competitive pressure. Identify at least three types of likely behavior that will be demonstrated by the skilled labor in the planing-and-sizing process as a result of this announcement. Include in your discussion how this behavior could be influenced by management.

16-30 Joint-cost allocation. Elsie Dairy Products Corp buys one input, full-cream milk, and refines it in a churning process. From each gallon of milk Elsie produces two cups (one pound) of butter and two quarts (8 cups) of buttermilk. During May 2008, Elsie bought 10,000 gallons of milk for $15,000. Elsie spent another $5,000 on the churning process to separate the milk into butter and buttermilk. Butter could be sold immediately for $2 per pound and buttermilk could be sold immediately for $1.50 per quart.

Elsie chooses to process the butter further into spreadable butter by mixing it with canola oil, incurring an additional cost of $0.50 per pound. This process results in 2 tubs of spreadable butter for each pound of butter processed. Each tub of spreadable butter sells for $2.50.

Required

1. Allocate the $20,000 joint cost to the spreadable butter and the buttermilk using the
   a. Physical-measure method (using cups) of joint cost allocation
   b. Sales value at splitoff method of joint cost allocation
   c. NRV method of joint cost allocation
   d. Constant gross margin percentage NRV method of joint cost allocation
2. Each of these measures has advantages and disadvantages; what are they?
3. Some claim that the sales value at split off method is the best method to use. Discuss the logic behind this claim.

16-31 Further processing decision (continuation of 16-30). Elsie has decided that buttermilk may sell better if it was marketed for baking and sold in pints. This would involve additional packaging at an incremental cost of $0.25 per pint. Each pint could be sold for $0.90. (Note: 1 quart = 2 pints)

1. If Elsie uses the sales value at splitoff method, what combination of products should Elsie sell to maximize profits?
2. If Elsie uses the physical-measure method, what combination of products should Elsie sell to maximize profits?
3. Explain the effect that the different cost allocation methods have on the decision to sell the products at split off or to process them further.

16-32 Joint-cost allocation with a byproduct. The Cumberland Mine is a small mine that extracts coal in West Virginia. Each ton of coal mined is 40% Grade A coal, 40% Grade B coal, and 20% coal tar. All output is sold immediately to a local utility. In May, Cumberland mined 1,000 tons of coal. It spent $10,000 on the mining process. Grade A coal sells for $100 per ton. Grade B coal sells for $60 per ton. Cumberland gets one-quarter of a vat of coal tar from each ton of coal tar processed. The coal tar sells for $60 per vat. Cumberland treats Grade A and Grade B coal as joint products, and treats coal tar as a byproduct.

Required

1. Assume that Cumberland allocates the joint costs to Grade A and Grade B coal using the sales value at splitoff method and accounts for the byproduct using the production method. What is the inventoriable cost for each product and Cumberland's gross margin?
2. Assume that Cumberland allocates the joint costs to Grade A and Grade B coal using the sales value at splitoff method and accounts for the byproduct using the sales method. What is the inventoriable cost for each product and Cumberland's gross margin?
3. Discuss the difference between the two methods of accounting for byproducts, focusing on what conditions are necessary to use each method.

16-33 Byproduct-costing journal entries (continuation of 16-32). Cumberland's accountant needs to record the information about the joint and byproducts in the general journal, but is not sure what the entries should be. Cumberland Mine has hired you as a consultant to help its accountant.

Required

1. Show journal entries at the time of production and at the time of sale assuming Cumberland accounts for the byproduct using the production method.
2. Show journal entries at the time of production and at the time of sale assuming Cumberland accounts for the byproduct using the sales method.

16-34 Process further or sell, byproduct. (CMA, adapted) Newcastle Mining Company (NMC) mines coal, puts it through a one-step crushing process, and loads the bulk raw coal onto river barges for shipment to customers.

NMC's management is currently evaluating the possibility of further processing the raw coal by sizing and cleaning it and selling it to an expanded set of customers at higher prices. The option of building a new sizing and cleaning plant is ruled out as being financially infeasible. Instead, Amy Kimbell, a mining engineer, is asked to explore outside-contracting arrangements for the cleaning and sizing process. Kimbell puts together the following summary:

	A	B	C
1	Selling price of raw coal	$ 27	per ton
2	Cost of producing raw coal	$ 22	per ton
3	Selling price of sized and cleaned coal	$ 36	per ton
4	Annual raw coal output	10,000,000	tons
5	Percentage of material weight loss in sizing/cleaning coal	6%	
6			
7		**Incremental Costs of Sizing & Cleaning Processes**	
8	Direct labor	$800,000	per year
9	Supervisory personnel	$200,000	per year
10	Heavy equipment: rental, operating, maintenance costs	$ 25,000	per month
11	Contract sizing and cleaning	$ 3.50	per ton of raw coal
12	Outbound rail freight	$ 240	per 60-ton rail car

Kimbell also learns that 75% of the material loss that occurs in the cleaning and sizing process can be salvaged as coal fines, which can be sold to steel manufacturers for their furnaces. The sale of coal fines is erratic and NMC may need to stockpile it in a protected area for up to one year. The selling price of coal fine ranges from $15 to $24 per ton and costs of preparing coal fines for sale range from $2 to $4 per ton.

If you want to use Excel to solve this problem, go to the Excel Lab at **www.prenhall.com/horngren/cost13e** and download the template for Problem 16-34.

Required

1. Prepare an analysis to show whether it is more profitable for NMC to continue selling raw bulk coal or to process it further through sizing and cleaning. (Ignore coal fines in your analysis.)
2. How would your analysis be affected if the cost of producing raw coal could be held down to $20 per ton?
3. Now consider the potential value of the coal fines and prepare an addendum that shows how their value affects the results of your analysis prepared in requirement 1.

16-35 Accounting for a byproduct. Sanjana's Silk Shirts (SSS) hand-makes blouses and sells them to high-end department stores. SSS buys bolts of silk for $300 each. Out of each bolt it gets 30 blouses, which it sells for $90 each. SSS's new manager has suggested taking the scraps left after cutting out the blouses and using them to make scarves. By carefully cutting the blouses, SSS can produce 6 scarves from each bolt, which it can sell for $25 each. During September, SSS buys 50 bolts of silk and spends an additional $10,000 on the cutting and sewing process. By the end of the month, SSS sells 1200 blouses and 260 scarves made from these bolts. Because the scarves are lower in value than the blouses, SSS decides to treat the scarves as a byproduct.

Required

1. Assuming SSS accounts for the byproduct using the production method, what is the inventoriable cost of each product and SSS's gross margin?
2. Assuming SSS accounts for the byproduct using the sales method, what is the inventoriable cost of each product and SSS's gross margin?
3. Show all journal entries for the month of September assuming SSS accounts for the byproduct using (a) the production method and (b) the sales method.

Collaborative Learning Problem

16-36 Joint Cost Allocation. Memory Manufacturing Company (MMC) produces memory modules in a two-step process: chip fabrication and module assembly.

In chip fabrication, each batch of raw silicon wafers yields 500 *standard* chips and 500 *deluxe* chips. Chips are classified as standard or deluxe on the basis of their density (the number of memory bits on each chip). Standard chips have 500 memory bits per chip, and deluxe chips have 1,000 memory bits per chip. Joint costs to process each batch are $24,000.

In module assembly, each batch of standard chips is converted into standard memory modules at a separately identified cost of $1,000 and then sold for $8,500. Each batch of deluxe chips is converted into deluxe memory modules at a separately identified cost of $1,500 and then sold for $25,000.

Required

1. Allocate joint costs of each batch to deluxe modules and standard modules using (a) the NRV method, (b) the constant gross-margin percentage NRV method, and (c) the physical-measure method, based on the number of memory bits. Which method should MMC use?
2. MMC can process each batch of 500 standard memory modules to yield 400 DRAM modules at an additional cost of $1,600. The selling price per DRAM module would be $26. Assume MMC uses the physical-measure method. Should MMC sell the standard memory modules or the DRAM modules?

17 Process Costing

Learning Objectives

1. Identify the situations in which process-costing systems are appropriate
2. Describe the five steps in process costing
3. Calculate equivalent units and understand how to use them
4. Use the weighted-average method of process costing
5. Use the first-in, first-out (FIFO) method of process costing
6. Incorporate standard costs into process-costing systems
7. Apply process-costing methods to situations with transferred-in costs

Companies that produce identical or similar units of a product or service, for example, an oil-refining company, often use process costing. A key part of process costing is valuing inventory—determining how many units of the product the firm has on hand and at the end of an accounting reporting period, evaluating the units' stages of completion, and assigning costs to the units. There are different methods for doing this, each of which can result in different profits. Once a company chooses a method, accounting rules generally require the company to continue to use it over time. However, companies do sometimes change inventory policies and, in the case of Shell, the change occurred at an opportune time, when the firm was reeling from allegations of questionable accounting practices elsewhere in its operations.

Faulty Accounting Forces Shell to Restate Its Earnings[1]

The Royal/Dutch Shell Group—or often just Shell—revealed in 2004 that the company had overstated its proven oil and gas reserves by nearly one-fifth, which resulted in its having to restate its earnings downward by approximately $432 million. Shell also reported that other accounting improprieties, related to its treatment of exploration costs and some gas contracts, had resulted in profits being overstated by an additional $156 million between 2000 and 2002. But even after correcting these overstatements, Shell's reported profits for those years rose. How could that have happened?

At the time Shell downgraded its reserves, Shell switched the accounting method used to cost its North American inventory to the *First-in-First-Out (FIFO)* method. There were two stated rationales for this change. The first was to have a single accounting policy for inventories worldwide: Shell used *FIFO* to cost its inventory everywhere other than North America. Second, Shell was preparing to adopt International Financial Reporting Standards (IFRS) in 2005, under which *FIFO* is the prescribed method for valuing inventories.

Assigning costs to inventory is a critical part of process costing, and a company's choice of method can result in different profits. Under *FIFO*, Shell used the cost of the oldest crude in its inventory to calculate

[1] *Source:* Stephen Taub, "Royal Dutch Shell to Pay $350 Million," *CFO.com,* April 11, 2007; Heather Timmons, "Ousted Shell Chairman Assails Regulators," *The New York Times,* September 17, 2004; "Shell To Pay $150 Million in Settlements on Reserves," *The New York Times,* August 25, 2004; The Associated Press, "Shell says it overstated profit by $432 million," July 6, 2004; Reuters (London), "Shell profit jumps as refining shines," July 26, 2007.

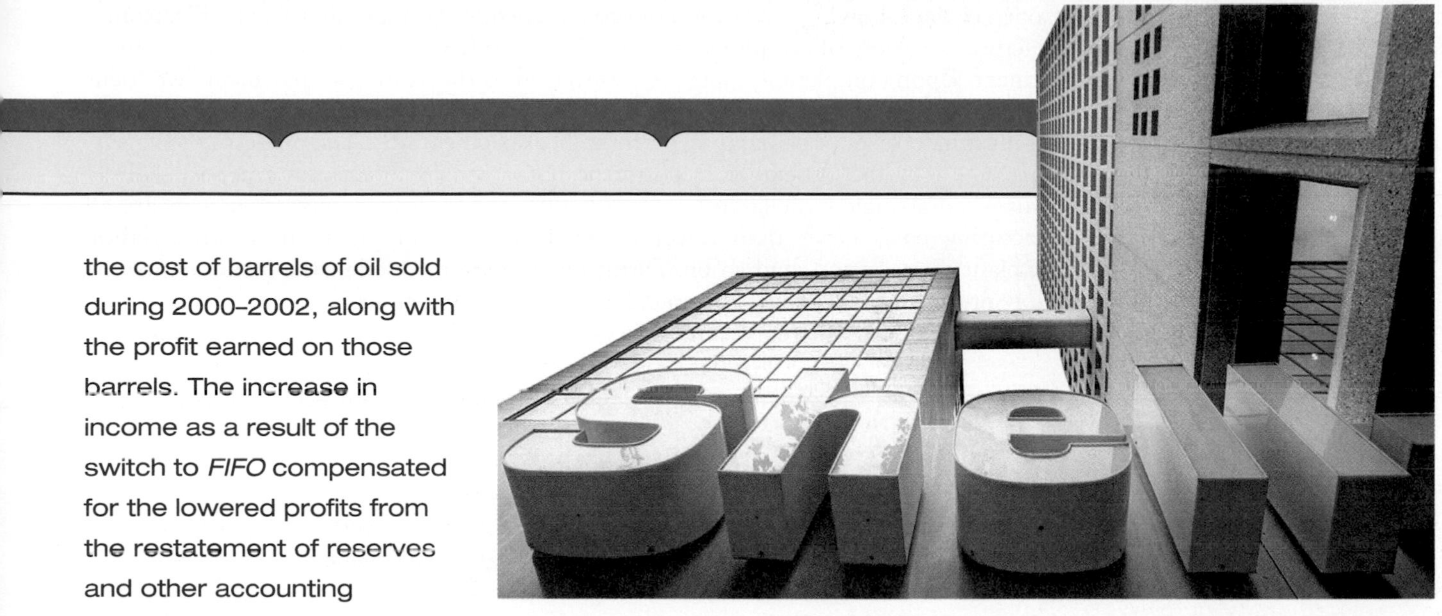

the cost of barrels of oil sold during 2000–2002, along with the profit earned on those barrels. The increase in income as a result of the switch to *FIFO* compensated for the lowered profits from the restatement of reserves and other accounting adjustments.

Companies such as Shell, pharmaceutical products manufacturer GlaxoSmithKline, and juice maker Nantucket Nectars, produce many identical or similar units of a product using mass-production techniques. The focus of these companies on individual production processes gives rise to process costing. This chapter describes how companies use process costing methods to determine the costs of products or services and to value inventory and cost of goods sold (using methods like FIFO).

Illustrating Process Costing

Learning Objective 1

Identify the situations in which process-costing systems are appropriate

. . . when masses of identical or similar units are produced

Before we examine process costing in more detail, let's briefly compare job costing and process costing. Job-costing and process-costing systems are best viewed as ends of a continuum:

Job-costing system	Process-costing system
Distinct, identifiable units of a product or service (for example, custom-made machines and houses)	Masses of identical or similar units of a product or service (for example, food or chemical processing)

In a *process-costing system*, the unit cost of a product or service is obtained by assigning total costs to many identical or similar units. In other words, unit costs are calculated by dividing total costs incurred by the number of units of output from the production process. In a manufacturing process-costing setting, each unit receives the same or similar amounts of direct material costs, direct manufacturing labor costs, and indirect manufacturing costs (manufacturing overhead).

The main difference between process costing and job costing is the *extent of averaging* used to compute unit costs of products or services. In a job-costing system, individual jobs use different quantities of production resources, so it would be incorrect to cost each job at the same average production cost. In contrast, when identical or similar units of products or services are mass-produced, not processed as individual jobs, process costing is used to calculate an average production cost for all units produced. Some processes such as clothes manufacturing have aspects of both process costing (cost per unit of each operation, such as cutting or sewing, is identical) and job costing (different materials are used in different batches of clothing, say, wool versus cotton). The appendix to this chapter describes "hybrid" costing systems that combine elements of both job and process costing.

Consider the following illustration of process costing: Suppose that Pacific Electronics manufactures a variety of cell phone models. These models are assembled in the Assembly Department. Upon completion, units are transferred to the Testing Department. We focus on the Assembly Department process for one model, SG-40. All units of SG-40 are identical and must meet a set of demanding performance specifications. The process-costing system for SG-40 in the Assembly Department has a single direct-cost category—direct materials—and a single indirect-cost category—conversion costs. Conversion costs are all manufacturing costs other than direct material costs, including manufacturing labor, energy, plant depreciation, and so on. Direct materials are added at the beginning of the Assembly process. Conversion costs are added evenly during assembly.

The following graphic represents these facts:

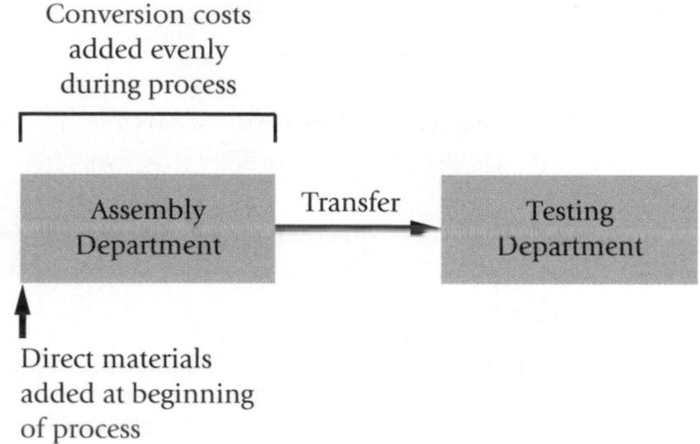

Process-costing systems separate costs into cost categories according to *when costs are introduced into the process*. Often, as in our Pacific Electronics example, only two cost classifications—direct materials and conversion costs—are necessary to assign costs to products. Why only two? Because *all* direct materials are added to the process at one time and all conversion costs generally are added to the process evenly through time. If, however, two different direct materials were added to the process at different times, two different direct-materials categories would be needed to assign these costs to products. Similarly, if manufacturing labor costs were added to the process at a different time from when the other conversion costs were added, an additional cost category—direct manufacturing labor costs—would be needed to separately assign these costs to products.

We will use the production of the SG-40 component in the Assembly Department to illustrate process costing in three cases, starting with the simplest case and introducing additional complexities in subsequent cases:

- **Case 1**—Process costing with zero beginning and zero ending work-in-process inventory of SG-40 (that is, all units are started and fully completed within the accounting period). *This case presents the most basic concepts of process costing and illustrates the feature of averaging of costs.*
- **Case 2**—Process costing with zero beginning work-in-process inventory but some ending work-in-process inventory of SG-40 (that is, some units of SG-40 started during the accounting period are incomplete at the end of the period). *This case introduces the concept of equivalent units and the five steps of process costing.*
- **Case 3**—Process costing with both some beginning and some ending work-in-process inventory of SG-40. *This case adds more complexity and illustrates the effect of weighted-average and first-in, first-out (FIFO) cost flow assumptions on cost of units completed and cost of work-in-process inventory.*

Case 1: Process Costing with Zero Beginning and Zero Ending Work-in-Process Inventory

On January 1, 2009, there was no beginning inventory of SG-40 units in the Assembly Department. During January, Pacific Electronics started, completely assembled, and transferred out to the Testing Department 400 units.

Data for the Assembly Department for January 2009 are:

Physical Units for January 2009	
Work in process, beginning inventory (January 1)	0 units
Started during January	400 units
Completed and transferred out during January	400 units
Work in process, ending inventory (January 31)	0 units

Physical units refer to the number of output units, whether complete or incomplete. In January 2009, all 400 physical units started were completed.

Total Costs for January 2009	
Direct material costs added during January	$32,000
Conversion costs added during January	24,000
Total Assembly Department costs added during January	$56,000

Pacific Electronics records direct material costs and conversion costs in the Assembly Department as these costs are incurred. By averaging, assembly cost of SG-40 is $56,000 ÷ 400 units = $140 per unit, itemized as follows:

Direct material cost per unit ($32,000 ÷ 400 units)	$ 80
Conversion cost per unit ($24,000 ÷ 400 units)	60
Assembly Department cost per unit	$140

Case 1 shows that in a process-costing system, average unit costs are calculated by dividing total costs in a given accounting period by total units produced in that period. Because each unit is identical, we assume all units receive the same amount of direct material costs and conversion costs. Case 1 applies whenever a company produces a homogeneous product or service but has no incomplete units when each accounting period ends, which is a common situation in service-sector organizations. For example, a bank can adopt this process-costing approach to compute the unit cost of processing 100,000 customer deposits, each similar to the other, made in a month.

Case 2: Process Costing with Zero Beginning but Some Ending Work-in-Process Inventory

In February 2009, Pacific Electronics places another 400 units of SG-40 into production. Because all units placed into production in January were completely assembled, there is no beginning inventory of partially completed units in the Assembly Department on February 1. Some customers order late, so not all units started in February are completed by the end of the month. Only 175 units are completed and transferred to the Testing Department.

Data for the Assembly Department for February 2009 are:

	A	B	C	D	E
1		Physical Units (SG-40s) (1)	Direct Materials (2)	Conversion Costs (3)	Total Costs (4) = (2) + (3)
2	Work in process, beginning inventory (February 1)	0			
3	Started during February	400			
4	Completed and transferred out during February	175			
5	Work in process, ending inventory (February 28)	225			
6	Degree of completion of ending work in process		100%	60%	
7	Total costs added during February		$32,000	$18,600	$50,600

The 225 partially assembled units as of February 28, 2009, are fully processed with respect to direct materials. That's because all direct materials in the Assembly Department are added at the beginning of the assembly process. Conversion costs, however, are added evenly during assembly. Based on the work completed relative to the total work required to complete the SG-40 units still in process at the end of February, an Assembly Department supervisor estimates that the partially assembled units are, on average, 60% complete with respect to conversion costs.

The accuracy of the completion estimate of conversion costs depends on the care, skill, and experience of the estimator and the nature of the conversion process. Estimating the degree of completion is usually easier for direct material costs than for conversion costs. That's because the quantity of direct materials needed for a completed unit and the quantity of direct materials in a partially completed unit can be measured more accurately. In contrast, the conversion sequence usually consists of a number of basic operations for a specified number of hours, days, or weeks for various steps in the production process. The degree of completion for conversion costs depends on the proportion of the total conversion costs needed to complete one unit or one batch of production that has already been incurred on the units still in process. It is a challenge for management accountants to make this estimate accurately. Because of these uncertainties, department supervisors and line managers—individuals most familiar with the process—often make conversion cost estimates. Still, in some industries, such as semiconductor manufacturing, no exact estimate is possible or, as in the textile industry, vast quantities in process make the task of estimation costly. In these cases, it is necessary to assume that all work in process in a department is complete to some degree with respect to conversion costs (for example, one-third, one-half, or two-thirds complete).

Learning Objective 2

Describe the five steps in process costing

. . . to assign total costs to units completed and to units in work in process

The point to understand here is that a partially assembled unit is not the same as a fully assembled unit. Faced with some fully assembled units and some partially assembled units, we require a common metric that will enable us to compare the work done in each category and, more important, obtain a total measure of work done. The concept we will use in this regard is that of *equivalent units*. We will explain this notion in greater detail next as part of the set of five steps required to calculate (1) the cost of fully assembled units in February 2009 and (2) the cost of partially assembled units still in process at the end of that month, for Pacific Electronics. The five steps of process costing are:

Step 1: Summarize the flow of physical units (of output).

Step 2: Compute output in terms of equivalent units.

Step 3: Summarize total costs to account for.

Step 4: Compute cost per equivalent unit.

Step 5: Assign total costs to units completed and to units in ending work in process.

Physical Units and Equivalent Units (Steps 1 and 2)

Learning Objective 3

Calculate equivalent units

. . . output units adjusted for incomplete units

and understand how to use them

. . . to calculate cost per equivalent unit

Step 1 tracks physical units of output. Recall that physical units are the number of output units, whether complete or incomplete. Where did physical units come from? Where did they go? The physical-units column of Exhibit 17-1 tracks where the physical units came from (400 units started) and where they went (175 units completed and transferred out, and 225 units in ending inventory).

Because not all 400 physical units are fully completed, output in step 2 is computed in *equivalent units*, not in *physical units*. To see what we mean by equivalent units, let's say that during a month, 50 physical units were started but not completed by the end of the month. These 50 units in ending inventory are estimated to be 70% complete with respect to conversion costs. Let's examine those units from the perspective of the conversion costs already incurred to get the units to be 70% complete. Suppose we put all the conversion costs represented in the 70% into making fully completed units. How many units could have been 100% complete by the end of the month? The answer: 35 units. Why? Because 70% of conversion costs incurred on 50 incomplete units could have been incurred to make 35 (0.70×50) complete units by the end of the month. That is, if all the conversion-cost input in the 50 units in inventory had been used to make completed output units, the company would have produced 35 completed units (also called *equivalent units*) of output.

Equivalent units is a derived amount of output units that (1) takes the quantity of each input (factor of production) in units completed and in incomplete units of work in process and (2) converts the quantity of input into the amount of completed output units that could

	A	B	C	D
1		(Step 1)	(Step 2)	
2			Equivalent Units	
3	Flow of Production	Physical Units	Direct Materials	Conversion Costs
4	Work in process, beginning	0		
5	Started during current period	400		
6	To account for	400		
7	Completed and transferred out during current period	175	175	175
8	Work in process, ending[a]	225		
9	(225 x 100%; 225 x 60%)		225	135
10	Accounted for	400		
11	Work done in current period only		400	310
12				
13	[a]Degree of completion in this department; direct materials, 100%; conversion costs, 60%.			

Exhibit 17-1

Steps 1 and 2: Summarize Output in Physical Units and Compute Output in Equivalent Units for Assembly Department of Pacific Electronics for February 2009

be produced with that quantity of input. Note that equivalent units are calculated separately for each input (such as direct materials and conversion costs). Moreover, every completed unit, by definition, is comprised of one equivalent unit of each input required to make it. This chapter focuses on equivalent-unit calculations in manufacturing settings. But, equivalent-unit concepts are also found in nonmanufacturing settings. For example, universities convert their part-time student enrollments into "full-time student equivalents."

When calculating equivalent units in step 2, focus on quantities. Disregard dollar amounts until after equivalent units are computed. In the Pacific Electronics example, all 400 physical units—the 175 fully assembled units and the 225 partially assembled units—are 100% complete with respect to direct materials because all direct materials are added in the Assembly Department at the start of the process. Therefore, Exhibit 17-1 shows output as 400 *equivalent units* for direct materials: 175 equivalent units for the 175 physical units assembled and transferred out, and 225 equivalent units for the 225 physical units in ending work-in-process inventory.

The 175 fully assembled units are also completely processed with respect to conversion costs. The partially assembled units in ending work in process are 60% complete (on average). Therefore, conversion costs in the 225 partially assembled units are *equivalent* to conversion costs in 135 (60% of 225) fully assembled units. Hence, Exhibit 17-1 shows output as 310 *equivalent units* with respect to conversion costs: 175 equivalent units for the 175 physical units assembled and transferred out and 135 equivalent units for the 225 physical units in ending work-in-process inventory.

Calculation of Product Costs (Steps 3, 4, and 5)

Exhibit 17-2 shows steps 3, 4, and 5. Together, they are called the *production cost worksheet.* Step 3 summarizes total costs to account for. Because the beginning balance of work-in-process inventory is zero on February 1, total costs to account for (that is, the total charges or debits to the Work in Process—Assembly account) consist only of costs added during February: direct materials of $32,000 and conversion costs of $18,600, for a total of $50,600.

Step 4 in Exhibit 17-2 calculates cost per equivalent unit separately for direct materials and for conversion costs by dividing direct material costs and conversion costs added during February by the related quantity of equivalent units of work done in February (as calculated in Exhibit 17-1).

To see the importance of using equivalent units in unit-cost calculations, compare conversion costs for January and February 2009. Total conversion costs of $18,600 for the 400 units worked on during February are lower than the conversion costs of $24,000 for the 400 units worked on in January. However, in this example, the conversion costs to fully assemble a unit are $60 in both January and February. Total conversion costs are lower in February because fewer equivalent units of conversion-costs work were completed in February (310) than in January (400). Using physical units instead of equivalent

Exhibit 17-2 Steps 3, 4, and 5: Summarize Total Costs to Account For, Compute Cost per Equivalent Unit, and Assign Total Costs to Units Completed and to Units in Ending Work in Process for Assembly Department of Pacific Electronics for February 2009

	A	B	C	D	E
1			**Total Production Costs**	**Direct Materials**	**Conversion Costs**
2	**(Step 3)**	Costs added during February	$50,600	$32,000	$18,600
3		Total costs to account for	$50,600	$32,000	$18,600
4					
5	**(Step 4)**	Costs added in current period	$50,600	$32,000	$18,600
6		Divide by equivalent units of work done in current period (Exhibit 17-1)		÷ 400	÷ 310
7		Cost per equivalent unit		$ 80	$ 60
8					
9	**(Step 5)**	Assignment of costs:			
10		Completed and transferred out (175 units)	$24,500	(175[a] x $80) +	(175[a] x $60)
11		Work in process, ending (225 units):	26,100	(225[b] x $80) +	(135[b] x $60)
12		Total costs accounted for	$50,600	$32,000 +	$18,600
13					
14	[a]Equivalent units completed and transferred out from Exhibit 17-1, step 2.				
15	[b]Equivalent units in ending work in process from Exhibit 17-1, step 2.				

units in the per-unit calculation would have led to the erroneous conclusion that conversion costs per unit declined from $60 in January to $46.50 ($18,600 ÷ 400 units) in February. This incorrect costing might have prompted Pacific Electronics to presume that greater efficiencies in processing had been achieved and to lower the price of SG-40, for example, when in fact costs had not declined.

Step 5 in Exhibit 17-2 assigns these costs to units completed and transferred out and to units still in process at the end of February 2009. The idea is to attach dollar amounts to the equivalent output units for direct materials and conversion costs of (a) units completed and (b) ending work in process, as calculated in Exhibit 17-1, step 2. *Equivalent output units for each input are multiplied by cost per equivalent unit, as calculated in step 4 of Exhibit 17-2.* For example, costs assigned to the 225 physical units in ending work-in-process inventory are:

Direct material costs of 225 equivalent units (Exhibit 17-1, step 2) × $80 cost per equivalent unit of direct materials calculated in step 4	$18,000
Conversion costs of 135 equivalent units (Exhibit 17-1, step 2) × $60 cost per equivalent unit of conversion costs calculated in step 4	8,100
Total cost of ending work-in-process inventory	$26,100

Note that total costs to account for in step 3 ($50,600) equal total costs accounted for in step 5.

Journal Entries

Journal entries in process-costing systems are similar to the entries made in job-costing systems with respect to direct materials and conversion costs. The main difference is that, in process costing, there is one Work-in-Process account for each process—in our example, Work in Process—Assembly and Work in Process—Testing. Pacific Electronics purchases direct materials as needed. These materials are delivered directly to the Assembly Department. Using amounts from Exhibit 17-2, summary journal entries for February are:

1. Work in Process—Assembly	32,000	
Accounts Payable Control		32,000
To record direct materials purchased and used in production during February.		
2. Work in Process—Assembly	18,600	
Various accounts such as Wages Payable Control and Accumulated Depreciation		18,600
To record conversion costs for February; examples include energy, manufacturing supplies, all manufacturing labor, and plant depreciation.		
3. Work in Process—Testing	24,500	
Work in Process—Assembly		24,500
To record cost of goods completed and transferred from Assembly to Testing during February.		

Exhibit 17-3 shows a general framework for the flow of costs through T-accounts. Notice how entry 3 for $24,500 follows the physical transfer of goods from the Assembly to the Testing Department. The T-account Work in Process—Assembly shows February 2009's ending balance of $26,100, which is the beginning balance of Work in Process—Assembly in March 2009.

Case 3: Process Costing with Some Beginning and Some Ending Work-in-Process Inventory

At the beginning of March 2009, Pacific Electronics had 225 partially assembled SG-40 units in the Assembly Department. It started production of another 275 units in March. Data for the Assembly Department for March are:

	A	B	C	D	E
1		Physical Units (SG-40s) (1)	Direct Materials (2)	Conversion Costs (3)	Total Costs (4) = (2) + (3)
2	Work in process, beginning inventory (March 1)	225	$18,000[a]	$8,100[a]	$26,100
3	Degree of completion of beginning work in process		100%	60%	
4	Started during March	275			
5	Completed and transferred out during March	400			
6	Work in process, ending inventory (March 31)	100			
7	Degree of completion of ending work in process		100%	50%	
8	Total costs added during March		$19,800	$16,380	$36,180
9					
10					
11	[a]Work in process, beginning inventory (equals work in process, ending inventory for February)				
12	Direct materials: 225 physical units x 100% completed x $80 per unit = $18,000				
13	Conversion costs: 225 physical units x 60% completed x $60 per unit = $8,100				

Pacific Electronics now has incomplete units in both beginning work-in-process inventory and ending work-in-process inventory for March 2009. We can still use the five steps described earlier to calculate (1) cost of units completed and transferred out and (2) cost of ending work in process. To assign costs to each of these categories, however, we first need to choose an inventory-valuation method. We next describe the five-step approach for two important methods—the weighted-average method and the first-in, first-out method. These different valuation methods produce different amounts for cost of units completed and for ending work in process when the unit cost of inputs changes from one period to the next.

Exhibit 17-3

Flow of Costs in a Process-Costing System for Assembly Department of Pacific Electronics for February 2009

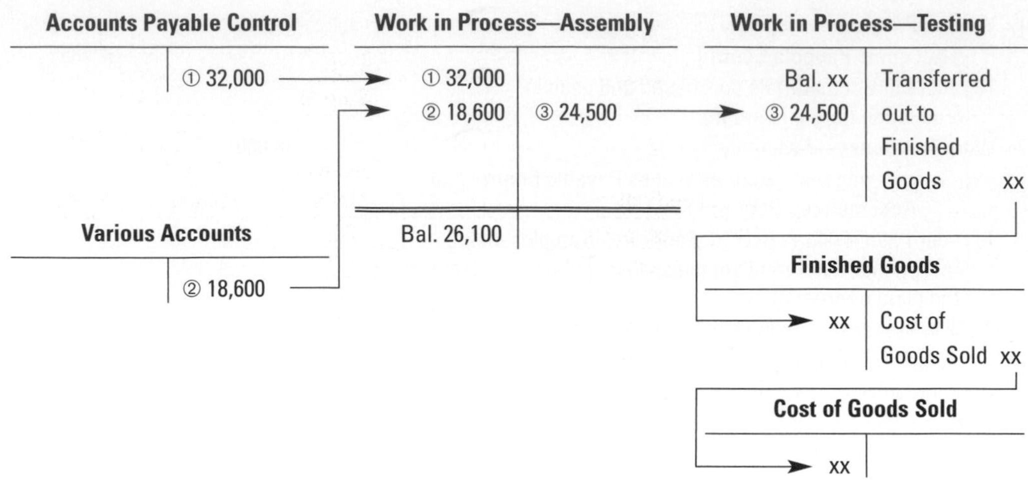

Weighted-Average Method

Learning Objective 4

Use the weighted-average method of process costing

. . . assigns costs based on total costs and equivalent units completed to date

The **weighted-average process-costing method** calculates cost per equivalent unit of all *work done to date* (regardless of the accounting period in which it was done) and assigns this cost to equivalent units completed and transferred out of the process and to equivalent units in ending work-in-process inventory. The weighted-average cost is the total of all costs entering the Work in Process account (whether they are from beginning work in process or from work started during the current period) divided by total equivalent units of work done to date. We now describe the weighted-average method using the five-step procedure introduced on p. 604.

Step 1: Summarize the Flow of Physical Units. The physical-units column of Exhibit 17-4 shows where the units came from—225 units from beginning inventory and 275 units started during the current period—and where they went—400 units completed and transferred out and 100 units in ending inventory.

Step 2: Compute Output in Terms of Equivalent Units. The weighted-average cost of inventory is calculated by merging together the costs of beginning inventory and the manufacturing costs of a period and dividing by the total number of units in beginning inventory and units produced during the accounting period. We apply the same concept here except that calculating the units—in this case equivalent units—is done differently. We use the relationship shown in the equation below.

Equivalent units in beginning work in process	+	Equivalent units of work done in current period	=	Equivalent units completed and transferred out in current period	+	Equivalent units in ending work in process

Although we are interested in calculating the sum of equivalent units in beginning work in process and equivalent units of work done in the current period, it is easier to calculate this sum using the right-hand side of the preceding equation: (1) equivalent units completed and transferred out in the current period plus (2) equivalent units in ending work in process. *Note that the stage of completion of the current-period beginning work in process is not used in this computation.*

The equivalent-units columns in Exhibit 17-4 show equivalent units of work done to date: 500 equivalent units of direct materials and 450 equivalent units of conversion costs. All completed and transferred-out units are 100% complete as to both direct materials and conversion costs. Partially completed units in ending work in process are 100% complete as to direct materials, because direct materials are introduced at the beginning of the process, and 50% complete as to conversion costs, based on estimates made by the Assembly Department manager.

Step 3: Summarize Total Costs to Account For. Exhibit 17-5 presents step 3. Total costs to account for in March 2009 are described in the example data on page 607: beginning work in process, \$26,100 (direct materials, \$18,000, plus conversion costs, \$8,100), plus

Exhibit 17-4

Steps 1 and 2: Summarize Output in Physical Units and Compute Output in Equivalent Units Using Weighted-Average Method of Process Costing for Assembly Department of Pacific Electronics for March 2009

	A	B	C	D
1		(Step 1)	(Step 2)	
2			Equivalent Units	
3	Flow of Production	Physical Units	Direct Materials	Conversion Costs
4	Work in process, beginning (given, p. 607)	225		
5	Started during current period (given, p. 607)	275		
6	To account for	500		
7	Completed and transferred out during current period	400	400	400
8	Work in process, ending[a] (given, p. 607)	100		
9	(100 x 100%; 100 x 50%)		100	50
10	Accounted for	500		
11	Work done to date		500	450
12				
13	[a]Degree of completion in this department; direct materials, 100%; conversion costs, 50%.			

costs added during March, $36,180 (direct materials, $19,800, plus conversion costs, $16,380). The total of these costs is $62,280.

Step 4: Compute Cost per Equivalent Unit. Exhibit 17-5, step 4, shows the computation of weighted-average cost per equivalent unit for direct materials and conversion costs. Weighted-average cost per equivalent unit is obtained by dividing the sum of costs for beginning work in process plus costs for work done in the current period by total equivalent units of work done to date. When calculating weighted-average conversion cost per equivalent unit in Exhibit 17-5, for example, we divide total conversion costs, $24,480 (beginning work in process, $8,100, plus work done in current period, $16,380), by total equivalent units of work done to date, 450 (equivalent units of conversion costs in

Exhibit 17-5

Steps 3, 4 and 5: Summarize Total Costs to Account For, Compute Cost per Equivalent Unit, and Assign Total Costs to Units Completed and to Units in Ending Work in Process Using Weighted-Average Method of Process Costing for Assembly Department of Pacific Electronics for March 2009

	A	B	C	D		E
1			Total Production Costs	Direct Materials		Conversion Costs
2	(Step 3)	Work in process, beginning (given, p. 607)	$26,100	$18,000		$ 8,100
3		Costs added in current period (given, p. 607)	36,180	19,800		16,380
4		Total costs to account for	$62,280	$37,800		$24,480
5						
6	(Step 4)	Costs incurred to date		$37,800		$24,480
7		Divide by equivalent units of work done to date (Exhibit 17-4)		÷ 500		÷ 450
8		Cost per equivalent unit of work done to date		$ 75.60		$ 54.40
9						
10	(Step 5)	Assignment of costs:				
11		Completed and transferred out (400 units)	$52,000	(400[a] x $75.60)	+	(400[a] x $54.40)
12		Work in process, ending (100 units):	10,280	(100[b] x $75.60)	+	(50[a] x $54.40)
13		Total costs accounted for	$62,280	$37,800	+	$24,480
14						
15	[a]Equivalent units completed and transferred out from Exhibit 17-4, step 2.					
16	[b]Equivalent units in ending work in process from Exhibit 17-4, step 2.					

beginning work in process and in work done in current period), to obtain weighted-average cost per equivalent unit of $54.40.

Step 5: Assign Total Costs to Units Completed and to Units in Ending Work in Process. Step 5 in Exhibit 17-5 takes the equivalent units completed and transferred out and equivalent units in ending work in process calculated in Exhibit 17-4, step 2, and assigns dollar amounts to them using the weighted-average cost per equivalent unit for direct materials and conversion costs calculated in step 4. For example, total costs of the 100 physical units in ending work in process are:

Direct materials:	
100 equivalent units × weighted-average cost per equivalent unit of $75.60	$ 7,560
Conversion costs:	
50 equivalent units × weighted-average cost per equivalent unit of $54.40	2,720
Total costs of ending work in process	$10,280

The following table summarizes total costs to account for ($62,280) and how they are accounted for in Exhibit 17-5. The arrows indicate that the costs of units completed and transferred out and units in ending work in process are calculated using weighted-average total costs obtained after merging costs of beginning work in process and costs added in the current period.

Costs to Account For			Costs Accounted for Calculated on a Weighted-Average Basis	
Beginning work in process	$26,100	→	Completed and transferred out	$52,000
Costs added in current period	36,180	→	Ending work in process	10,280
Total costs to account for	$62,280		Total costs accounted for	$62,280

Before proceeding, review Exhibits 17-4 and 17-5 to check your understanding of the weighted-average method. Note: Exhibit 17-4 deals with only physical and equivalent units, not costs. Exhibit 17-5 shows the cost amounts.

Using amounts from Exhibit 17-5, the summary journal entries under the weighted-average method for March 2009 at Pacific Electronics are:

1. Work in Process—Assembly	19,800	
Accounts Payable Control		19,800
To record direct materials purchased and used in production during March.		
2. Work in Process—Assembly	16,380	
Various accounts such as Wages Payable Control and Accumulated Depreciation		16,380
To record conversion costs for March; examples include energy, manufacturing supplies, all manufacturing labor, and plant depreciation.		
3. Work in Process—Testing	52,000	
Work in Process—Assembly		52,000
To record cost of goods completed and transferred from Assembly to Testing during March.		

The T-account Work in Process—Assembly, under the weighted-average method, shows:

Work in Process—Assembly

Beginning inventory, March 1	26,100	③ Completed and transferred out to Work in Process—Testing	52,000
① Direct materials	19,800		
② Conversion costs	16,380		
Ending inventory, March 31	10,280		

First-In, First-Out Method

The **first-in, first-out (FIFO) process-costing method** (1) assigns the cost of the previous accounting period's equivalent units in beginning work-in-process inventory to the first units completed and transferred out of the process; and (2) assigns the cost of equivalent units worked on during the *current* period first to complete beginning inventory, next to start and complete new units, and finally to units in ending work-in-process inventory. The FIFO method assumes that the earliest equivalent units in work in process are completed first.

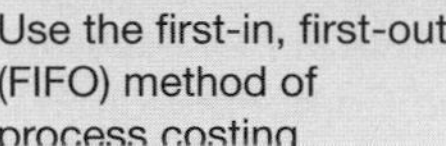

Use the first-in, first-out (FIFO) method of process costing

. . . to assign costs based on costs and equivalent units of work done in the current period

A distinctive feature of the FIFO process-costing method is that work done on beginning inventory before the current period is kept separate from work done in the current period. Costs incurred and units produced in the current period are used to calculate cost per equivalent unit of work done in the current period. In contrast, equivalent-unit and cost-per-equivalent-unit calculations under the weighted-average method *merge* units and costs in beginning inventory with units and costs of work done in the current period.

We now describe the FIFO method using the five-step procedure introduced on p. 604.

Step 1: Summarize the Flow of Physical Units. Exhibit 17-6, step 1, traces the flow of physical units of production. The following observations help explain the calculation of physical units under the FIFO method for Pacific Electronics.

- The first physical units assumed to be completed and transferred out during the period are 225 units from beginning work-in-process inventory.
- The March data on page 607 indicate that 400 physical units were completed during March. The FIFO method assumes that of these 400 units, 175 units (400 units − 225 units from beginning work-in-process inventory) must have been started and completed during March.
- Ending work-in-process inventory consists of 100 physical units—the 275 physical units started minus the 175 units that were started and completed.
- The physical units "to account for" equal the physical units "accounted for" (500 units).

Step 2: Compute Output in Terms of Equivalent Units. Exhibit 17-6 also presents the computations for step 2 under the FIFO method. *The equivalent-unit calculations for each cost category focus on equivalent units of work done in the current period (March) only.*

Under the FIFO method, equivalent units of work done in March on the beginning work-in-process inventory equal 225 physical units times *the percentage of work remaining to be done in March to complete these units*: 0% for direct materials, because beginning work in process is 100% complete with respect to direct materials, and 40% for conversion costs, because beginning work in process is 60% complete with respect to conversion costs. The results are 0 (0% × 225) equivalent units of work for direct materials and 90 (40% × 225) equivalent units of work for conversion costs.

The equivalent units of work done on the 175 physical units started and completed equals 175 units times 100% for both direct materials and conversion costs, because all work on these units is done in the current period.

The equivalent units of work done on the 100 units of ending work in process equal 100 physical units times 100% for direct materials (because all direct materials for these units are added in the current period) and 50% for conversion costs (because 50% of conversion-costs work on these units is done in the current period).

Step 3: Summarize Total Costs to Account For. Exhibit 17-7 presents step 3 and summarizes total costs to account for in March 2009 (beginning work in process and costs added in the current period) of $62,280, as described in the example data (p. 607).

Step 4: Compute Cost per Equivalent Unit. Exhibit 17-7 shows the step 4 computation of cost per equivalent unit for *work done in the current period only* for direct materials and conversion costs. For example, conversion cost per equivalent unit of $52 is obtained by dividing current-period conversion costs of $16,380 by current-period conversion-costs equivalent units of 315.

Step 5: Assign Total Costs to Units Completed and to Units in Ending Work in Process. Exhibit 17-7 shows the assignment of costs under the FIFO method. Costs of work done in the current period are assigned (1) first to the additional work done to complete the beginning work in process, then (2) to work done on units started and completed during the current period, and finally (3) to ending work in process. *Step 5 takes each quantity of equivalent units calculated in Exhibit 17-6, step 2, and assigns dollar amounts to them (using the cost-per-equivalent-unit calculations in step 4).* The goal is to use the cost of work done in the current period to determine total costs of all units completed from beginning inventory and from work started and completed in the current period, and costs of ending work in process.

Exhibit 17-6

Steps 1 and 2: Summarize Output in Physical Units and Compute Output in Equivalent Units Using FIFO Method of Process Costing for Assembly Department of Pacific Electronics for March 2009

	A	B	C	D
1		(Step 1)	(Step 2)	
2			Equivalent Units	
3	Flow of Production	Physical Units	Direct Materials	Conversion Costs
4	Work in process, beginning (given, p. 607)	225	(work done before current period)	
5	Started during current period (given, p. 607)	275		
6	To account for	500		
7	Completed and transferred out during current period:			
8	From beginning work in process[a]	225		
9	[225 x (100% - 100%); 225 x (100% - 60%)]		0	90
10	Started and completed	175[b]		
11	(175 x 100%; 175 x 100%)		175	175
12	Work in process, ending[c] (given, p. 607)	100		
13	(100 x 100%; 100 x 50%)		100	50
14	Accounted for	500		
15	Work done in current period only		275	315
16				
17	[a]Degree of completion in this department; direct materials, 100%; conversion costs, 60%.			
18	[b]400 physical units completed and transferred out minus 225 physical units completed and			
19	transferred out from beginning work-in-process inventory.			
20	[c]Degree of completion in this department: direct materials, 100%; conversion costs, 50%.			

Of the 400 completed units, 225 units are from beginning inventory and 175 units are started and completed during March. The FIFO method starts by assigning the costs of beginning work-in-process inventory of $26,100 to the first units completed and transferred out. As we saw in step 2, an additional 90 equivalent units of conversion costs are needed to complete these units in the current period. Current-period conversion cost per equivalent unit is $52, so $4,680 (90 equivalent units × $52 per equivalent unit) of additional costs are incurred to complete beginning inventory. Total production costs for units in beginning inventory are $26,100 + $4,680 = $30,780. The 175 units started and completed in the current period consist of 175 equivalent units of direct materials and 175 equivalent units of conversion costs. These units are costed at the cost per equivalent unit in the current period (direct materials, $72, and conversion costs, $52) for a total production cost of $21,700 [175 × ($72 + $52)].

Under FIFO, ending work-in-process inventory comes from units that were started but not fully completed during the current period. Total costs of the 100 partially assembled physical units in ending work in process are:

Direct materials:	
100 equivalent units × $72 cost per equivalent unit in March	$7,200
Conversion costs:	
50 equivalent units × $52 cost per equivalent unit in March	2,600
Total cost of work in process on March 31	$9,800

The following table summarizes total costs to account for and costs accounted for of $62,280 in Exhibit 17-7. Notice how under the FIFO method, the layers of beginning work in process and costs added in the current period are kept separate. The arrows indicate where the costs in each layer go—that is, to units completed and transferred out or to ending work in process. Be sure to include costs of beginning work in process ($26,100) when calculating costs of units completed from beginning inventory.

Exhibit 17-7 Steps 3, 4 and 5: Summarize Total Costs to Account For, Compute Cost per Equivalent Unit, and Assign Total Costs to Units Completed and to Units in Ending Work in Process Using FIFO Method of Process Costing for Assembly Department of Pacific Electronics for March 2009

	A	B	C	D		E
1			Total Production Costs	Direct Material		Conversion Costs
2	(Step 3)	Work in process, beginning (given, p. 607)	$26,100	$18,000		$ 8,100
3		Costs added in current period (given, p. 607)	36,180	19,800		16,380
4		Total costs to account for	$62,280	$37,800		$24,480
5						
6	(Step 4)	Costs added in current period		$19,800		$16,380
7		Divide by equivalent units of work done in current period (Exhibit 17-6)		÷ 275		÷ 315
8		Cost per equivalent unit of work done in current period		$ 72		$ 52
9						
10	(Step 5)	Assignment of costs:				
11		Completed and transferred out (400 units):				
12		Work in process, beginning (225 units)	$26,100	$18,000	+	$8,100
13		Costs added to beginning work in process in current period	4,680	(0[a] x $72)	+	(90[a] x $52)
14		Total from beginning inventory	30,780			
15		Started and completed (175 units)	21,700	(175[b] x $72)	+	(175[b] x $52)
16		Total costs of units completed and transferred out	52,480			
17		Work in process, ending (100 units):	9,800	(100[c] x $72)	+	(50[c] x $52)
18		Total costs accounted for	$62,280	$37,800	+	$24,480
19						
20	[a]Equivalent units used to complete beginning work in process from Exhibit 17-6, step 2.					
21	[b]Equivalent units started and completed from Exhibit 17-6, step 2.					
22	[c]Equivalent units in ending work in process from Exhibit 17-6, step 2.					

Costs to Account for		Costs Accounted for Calculated on a FIFO Basis	
		Completed and transferred out	
Beginning work in process	$26,100	Beginning work in process	$26,100
Costs added in current period	36,180	Used to complete beginning work in process	4,680
		Started and completed	21,700
		Completed and transferred out	52,480
		Ending work in process	9,800
Total costs to account for	$62,280	Total costs accounted for	$62,280

Before proceeding, review Exhibits 17-6 and 17-7 to check your understanding of the FIFO method. Note: Exhibit 17-6 deals with only physical and equivalent units, not costs. Exhibit 17-7 shows the cost amounts.

The journal entries under the FIFO method are identical to the journal entries under the weighted-average method except for one difference. The entry to record the cost of goods completed and transferred out would be $52,480 under the FIFO method instead of $52,000 under the weighted-average method.

Only rarely is an application of pure FIFO ever encountered in process costing. That's because FIFO is applied within a department to compile the cost of units *transferred out*, but as a practical matter, units *transferred in* during a given period usually are carried at a single average unit cost. For example, the average cost of units transferred out of the Assembly Department is $52,480 ÷ 400 units = $131.20 per SG-40 unit. The Assembly Department uses FIFO to distinguish between monthly batches of production. The succeeding department, Testing, however, costs these units (which consist of costs incurred in both February and March) at one average unit cost ($131.20 in this illustration). If this averaging were not done, the attempt to track costs on a pure FIFO basis throughout a series of processes would be cumbersome. As a result, the FIFO method should really be called a *modified* or *department* FIFO method.

Comparison of Weighted-Average and FIFO Methods

Consider the summary of the costs assigned to units completed and to units still in process under the weighted-average and FIFO process-costing methods in our example for March 2009:

	Weighted Average (from Exhibit 17-5)	**FIFO (from Exhibit 17-7)**	**Difference**
Cost of units completed and transferred out	$52,000	$52,480	+$480
Work in process, ending	10,280	9,800	−$480
Total costs accounted for	$62,280	$62,280	

The weighted-average ending inventory is higher than the FIFO ending inventory by $480, or 4.9% ($480 ÷ $9,800 = 0.049, or 4.9%). This would be a significant difference when aggregated over the many thousands of products that Pacific Electronics makes. When completed units are sold, the weighted-average method in our example leads to a lower cost of goods sold and, therefore, higher operating income and higher income taxes than the FIFO method. To see why the weighted-average method yields a lower cost of units completed, recall the data on page 607. Direct material cost per equivalent unit in beginning work-in-process inventory is $80, and conversion cost per equivalent unit in beginning work-in-process inventory is $60. These costs are greater, respectively, than the $72 direct materials cost and the $52 conversion cost per equivalent unit of work done during the current period. The current-period costs could be lower due to a decline in the prices of direct materials and conversion-cost inputs, or as a result of Pacific Electronics becoming more efficient in its processes by using smaller quantities of inputs per unit of output, or both.

For the Assembly Department, FIFO assumes that (1) all the higher-cost units from the previous period in beginning work in process are the first to be completed and transferred out of the process and (2) ending work in process consists of only the lower-cost current-period units. The weighted-average method, however, smooths out cost per equivalent unit by assuming that (1) more of the lower-cost units are completed and transferred out and (2) some of the higher-cost units are placed in ending work in process. The decline in the current-period cost per equivalent unit results in a lower cost of units completed and transferred out and a higher ending work-in-process inventory under the weighted-average method compared with FIFO.

Cost of units completed and, hence, operating income, can differ materially between the weighted-average and FIFO methods when (1) direct material or conversion cost per equivalent unit varies significantly from period to period and (2) physical-inventory levels of work in process are large in relation to the total number of units transferred out of the process. As companies move toward long-term procurement contracts that reduce differences in unit costs from period to period and reduce inventory levels, the difference in cost of units completed under the weighted-average and FIFO methods will decrease.[2]

[2] For example, suppose beginning work-in-process inventory for March were 125 physical units (instead of 225), and suppose costs per equivalent unit of work done in the current period (March) were direct materials, $75, and conversion costs, $55. Assume that all other data for March are the same as in our example. In this case, the cost of units completed and transferred out would be $52,833 under the weighted-average method and $53,000 under the FIFO method. The work-in-process ending inventory would be $10,417 under the weighted-average method and $10,250 under the FIFO method (calculations not shown). These differences are much smaller than in the chapter example. The weighted-average ending inventory is higher than the FIFO ending inventory by only $167 ($10,417 − $10,250), or 1.6% ($167 ÷ $10,250 = 0.016, or 1.6%), compared with 4.9% higher in the chapter example.

Managers use information from process-costing systems to aid them in pricing and product-mix decisions and to provide them with feedback about their performance. FIFO provides managers with information about changes in costs per unit from one period to the next. Managers can use this information to adjust selling prices based on current conditions (for example, based on the $72 direct material cost and $52 conversion cost in March). They can also more easily evaluate performance in the current period compared with a budget or relative to performance in the previous period (for example, recognizing the decline in both unit direct material and conversion costs relative to the prior period). By focusing on work done and costs of work done during the current period, the FIFO method provides useful information for these planning and control purposes.

The weighted-average method merges unit costs from different accounting periods, obscuring period-to-period comparisons. For example, the weighted-average method would lead managers at Pacific Electronics to make decisions based on the $75.60 direct materials and $54.40 conversion costs, rather than the costs of $72 and $52 prevailing in the current period. Advantages of the weighted-average method, however, are its relative computational simplicity and its reporting of a more-representative average unit cost when input prices fluctuate markedly from month to month.

Activity-based costing plays a significant role in our study of job costing, but how is activity-based costing related to process costing? Each process—assembly, testing, and so on—can be considered a different (production) activity. However, no additional activities need to be identified within each process. That's because products are homogeneous and use resources of each process in a uniform way. The bottom line: activity-based costing has less applicability in process-costing environments.

Standard-Costing Method of Process Costing

Learning Objective 6

Incorporate standard costs into process-costing systems

. . . use standard costs as the cost per equivalent unit

This section assumes that you have studied Chapters 7 and 8. Instructors and students who wish to skip this section can go directly to the section on Transferred-In Costs in Process Costing, page 619, without any loss of continuity.

Companies that use process-costing systems produce masses of identical or similar units of output. In such companies, it is fairly easy to set standards for quantities of inputs needed to produce output. Standard cost per input unit can then be multiplied by input quantity standards to develop standard cost per output unit.

The weighted-average and FIFO methods become very complicated when used in process industries that produce a wide variety of similar products. For example, a steel-rolling mill uses various steel alloys and produces sheets of various sizes and finishes. The different types of direct materials used and the operations performed are few, but used in various combinations, they yield a wide variety of products. Similarly, complex conditions are frequently found, for example, in plants that manufacture rubber products, textiles, ceramics, paints, and packaged food products. In each of these cases, if the broad averaging procedure of *actual* process costing were used, the result would be inaccurate costs for each product. Therefore, the standard-costing method of process costing is widely used in these industries.

Under the standard-costing method, teams of design and process engineers, operations personnel, and management accountants work together to determine *separate* standard costs per equivalent unit on the basis of different technical processing specifications for each product. Identifying standard costs for each product overcomes the disadvantage of costing all products at a single average amount, as under actual costing.

Computations Under Standard Costing

We return to the Assembly Department of Pacific Electronics, but this time we use standard costs. Assume the same standard costs apply in February and March of 2009. Data for the Assembly Department are:

File Edit View Insert Format Tools Data Window Help

	A	B	C	D	E
1		Physical Units (SG-40s) (1)	Direct Materials (2)	Conversion Costs (3)	Total Costs (4) = (2) + (3)
2	Standard cost per unit		$ 74	$ 54	
3	Work in process, beginning inventory (March 1)	225			
4	Degree of completion of beginning work in process		100%	60%	
5	Beginning work in process inventory at standard costs		$16,650[a]	$ 7,290[a]	$23,940
6	Started during March	275			
7	Completed and transferred out during March	400			
8	Work in process, ending inventory (March 31)	100			
9	Degree of completion of ending work in process		100%	50%	
10	Actual total costs added during March		$19,800	$16,380	$36,180
11					
12	[a]Work in process, beginning inventory at standard costs				
13	Direct materials: 225 physical units x 100% completed x $74 per unit = $16,650				
14	Conversion costs: 225 physical units x 60% completed x $54 per unit = $7,290				

We illustrate the standard-costing method of process costing using the five-step procedure introduced earlier (p. 604).

Exhibit 17-8 presents steps 1 and 2. These steps are identical to the steps described for the FIFO method in Exhibit 17-6 because, as in FIFO, the standard-costing method also assumes that the earliest equivalent units in beginning work in process are completed first. Work done in the current period for direct materials is 275 equivalent units. Work done in the current period for conversion costs is 315 equivalent units.

Exhibit 17-9 describes steps 3, 4, and 5. In step 3, total costs to account for (that is, the total debits to Work in Process—Assembly) differ from total debits to Work in Process—Assembly under the actual-cost-based weighted-average and FIFO methods. That's because, as in all standard-costing systems, the debits to the Work-in-Process account are at standard costs, rather than actual costs. These standard costs total $61,300 in

Exhibit 17-8

Steps 1 and 2: Summarize Output in Physical Units and Compute Output in Equivalent Units Using Standard-Costing Method of Process Costing for Assembly Department of Pacific Electronics for March 2009

File Edit View Insert Format Tools Data Window Help

	A	B	C	D
1		(Step 1)	(Step 2)	
2			Equivalent Units	
3	Flow of Production	Physical Units	Direct Materials	Conversion Costs
4	Work in process, beginning (given, p. 616)	225		
5	Started during current period (given, p. 616)	275		
6	To account for	500		
7	Completed and transferred out during current period:			
8	From beginning work in process[a]	225		
9	[225 x (100% - 100%); 225 x (100% - 60%)]		0	90
10	Started and completed	175[b]		
11	(175 x 100%; 175 x 100%)		175	175
12	Work in process, ending[c] (given, p. 616)	100		
13	(100 x 100%; 100 x 50%)		100	50
14	Accounted for	500		
15	Work done in current period only		275	315
16				
17	[a]Degree of completion in this department; direct materials, 100%; conversion costs, 60%.			
18	[b]400 physical units completed and transferred out minus 225 physical units completed and transferred out from beginning work-in-process inventory.			
19	[c]Degree of completion in this department: direct materials, 100%; conversion costs, 50%.			

Exhibit 17-9. In step 4, costs per equivalent unit are standard costs: direct materials, $74, and conversion costs, $54. *Therefore, costs per equivalent unit do not have to be computed as they were for the weighted-average and FIFO methods.*

Exhibit 17-9, step 5, assigns total costs to units completed and transferred out and to units in ending work-in-process inventory, as in the FIFO method. Step 5 assigns amounts of standard costs to equivalent units calculated in Exhibit 17-8. These costs are assigned (1) first to complete beginning work-in-process inventory, (2) next to start and complete new units, and (3) finally to start new units that are in ending work-in-process inventory. Note how the $61,300 total costs accounted for in step 5 of Exhibit 17-9 equal total costs to account for.

Accounting for Variances

Process-costing systems using standard costs record actual direct material costs in Direct Materials Control and actual conversion costs in Conversion Costs Control (similar to Manufacturing Overhead Control in Chapter 8). In the journal entries that follow, the first two journal entries record these *actual costs*. In entries 3 and 4a, the Work-in-Process—Assembly account accumulates direct material costs and conversion costs at *standard costs*. Entries 3 and 4b isolate total variances. The final entry transfers out completed goods at standard costs.

Exhibit 17-9 Steps 3, 4, and 5: Summarize Total Costs to Account For, Compute Cost per Equivalent Unit, and Assign Total Costs to Units Completed and to Units in Ending Work in Process Using Standard-Costing Method of Process Costing for Assembly Department of Pacific Electronics for March 2009

	A	B	C	D	E	F	G
1			Total Production Costs	Direct Materials		Conversion Costs	
2	(Step 3)	Work in process, beginning (given, p. 616)					
3		Direct materials, 225 x $74; Conversion costs, 135 x $54	$23,940	$16,650		$ 7,290	
4		Costs added in current period at standard costs					
5		Direct materials, 275 x $74; Conversion costs, 315 x $54	37,360	20,350		17,010	
6		Total costs to account for	$61,300	$37,000		$24,300	
7							
8	(Step 4)	Standard cost per equivalent unit (given, p. 616)		$ 74		$ 54	
9							
10	(Step 5)	Assignment of costs at standard costs:					
11		Completed and transferred out (400 units):					
12		Work in process, beginning (225 units)	$23,940	$16,650	+	$ 7,290	
14		Costs added to beginning work in process in current period	4,860	(0[a] x $74)	+	(90[a] x $54)	
15		Total from beginning inventory	28,800				
16		Started and completed (175 units)	22,400	(175[b] x $74)	+	(175[b] x $54)	
17		Total costs of units completed and transferred out	51,200				
18		Work in process, ending (100 units):	10,100	(100[c] x $74)	+	(50[c] x $54)	
19		Total costs accounted for	$61,300	$37,000	+	$24,300	
20							
21	Summary of variances for current performance:						
22	Costs added in current period at standard costs (see step 3 above)			$20,350		$17,010	
23	Actual costs incurred (given, p. 616)			$19,800		$16,380	
24	Variance			$ 550	F	$ 630	F
25							
26	[a]Equivalent units used to complete beginning work in process from Exhibit 17-8, step 2.						
27	[b]Equivalent units started and completed from Exhibit 17-8, step 2.						
28	[c]Equivalent units in ending work in process from Exhibit 17-8, step 2.						

	Debit	Credit
1. Assembly Department Direct Materials Control (at actual costs)	19,800	
Accounts Payable Control		19,800
To record direct materials purchased and used in production during March. This cost control account is debited with actual costs.		
2. Assembly Department Conversion Costs Control (at actual costs)	16,380	
Various accounts such as Wages Payable Control and Accumulated Depreciation		16,380
To record Assembly Department conversion costs for March. This cost control account is debited with actual costs.		
Entries 3, 4, and 5 use standard cost amounts from Exhibit 17-9.		
3. Work in Process—Assembly (at standard costs)	20,350	
Direct Materials Variances		550
Assembly Department Direct Materials Control		19,800
To record standard costs of direct materials assigned to units worked on and total direct materials variances.		
4a. Work in Process—Assembly (at standard costs)	17,010	
Assembly Department Conversion Costs Allocated		17,010
To record conversion costs allocated at standard rates to the units worked on during March.		
4b. Assembly Department Conversion Costs Allocated	17,010	
Conversion Costs Variances		630
Assembly Department Conversion Costs Control		16,380
To record total conversion costs variances.		
5. Work in Process—Testing (at standard costs)	51,200	
Work in Process—Assembly (at standard costs)		51,200
To record standard costs of units completed and transferred out from Assembly to Testing.		

Exhibit 17-10

Flow of Standard Costs in a Process-Costing System for Assembly Department of Pacific Electronics for March 2009

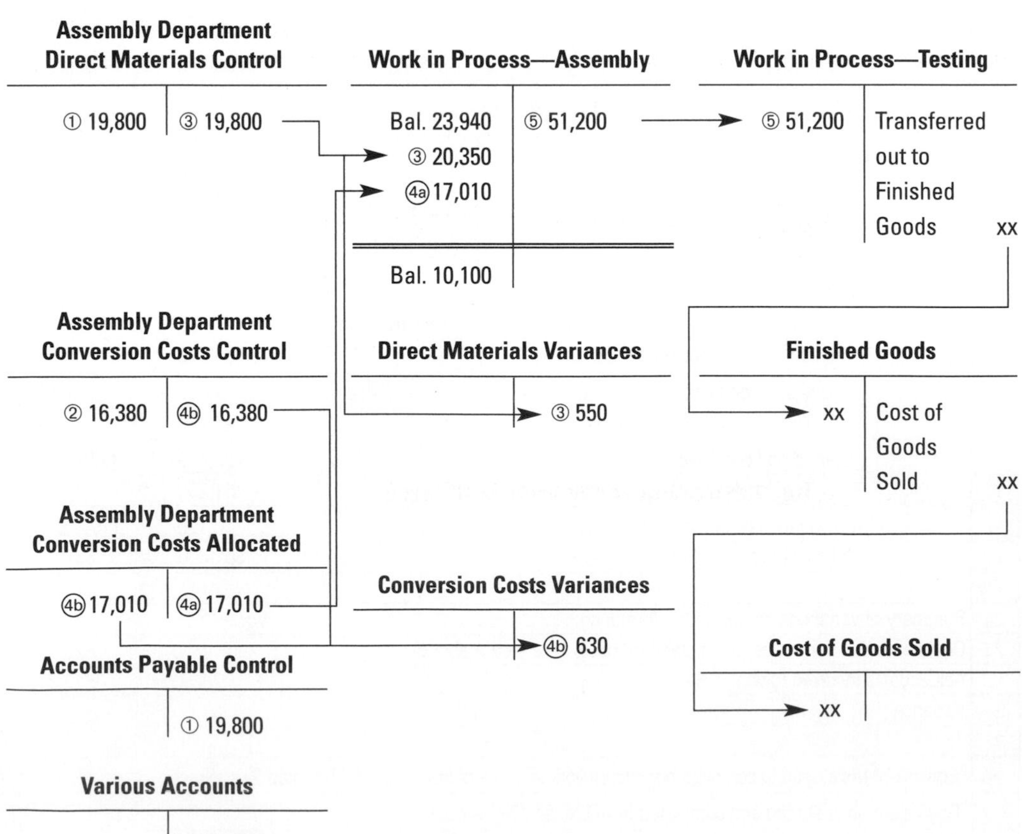

Variances arise under standard costing, as in entries 3 and 4b. That's because the standard costs assigned to products on the basis of work done in the current period do not equal actual costs incurred in the current period. Variances can be analyzed in little or great detail for planning and control purposes, as described in Chapters 7 and 8. Sometimes direct materials price variances are isolated at the time direct materials are purchased and only efficiency variances are computed in entry 3. Exhibit 17-10 shows how the costs flow through the general-ledger accounts under standard costing.

Transferred-In Costs in Process Costing

Learning Objective 7

Apply process-costing methods to situations with transferred-in costs

. . . using weighed-average and FIFO methods

Many process-costing systems have two or more departments or processes in the production cycle. As units move from department to department, the related costs are also transferred by monthly journal entries. **Transferred-in costs** (also called **previous-department costs**) are costs incurred in previous departments that are carried forward as the product's cost when it moves to a subsequent process in the production cycle. If standard costs are used, accounting for such transfers is simple. However, if the weighted-average or FIFO method is used, the accounting becomes more complex.

We now extend our Pacific Electronics example to the Testing Department. As the assembly process is completed, the Assembly Department of Pacific Electronics immediately transfers SG-40 units to the Testing Department. In Testing, units receive additional direct materials at the *end* of the process, crating and other packing materials to prepare units for shipment. Conversion costs are added evenly during the Testing Department's process. As units are completed in Testing, they are immediately transferred to Finished Goods. Computation of Testing Department costs consists of transferred-in costs, as well as direct materials and conversion costs that are added in Testing.

The following diagram represents these facts:

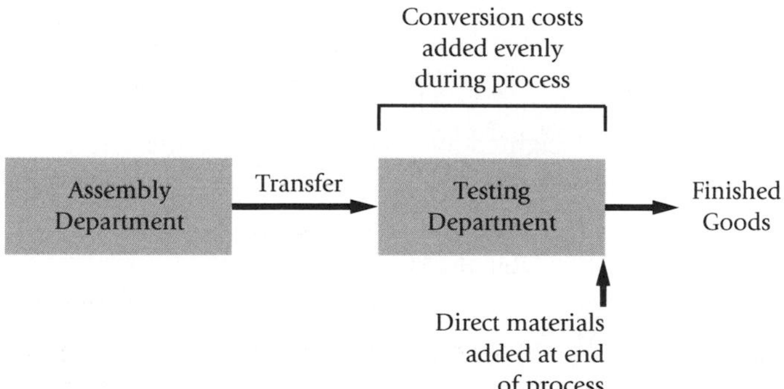

Data for the Testing Department for March 2009 are:

	A	B	C	D	E
1		Physical Units (SG-40s)	Transferred-in Costs	Direct Materials	Conversion Costs
2	Work in process, beginning inventory (March 1)	240	$33,600	$ 0	$18,000
3	Degree of completion of beginning work in process		100%	0%	62.5%
4	Transferred in during March	400			
5	Completed and transferred out during March	440			
6	Work in process, ending inventory (March 31)	200			
7	Degree of completion of ending work in process		100%	0%	80%
8	Total costs added during March				
9	Direct materials and conversion costs			$13,200	$48,600
10	Transferred in (Weighted-average from Exhibit 17-5)[a]		$52,000		
11	Transferred in (FIFO from Exhibit 17-7)[a]		$52,480		
12					
13	[a]The transferred-in costs during March are different under the weighted-average method (Exhibit 17-5) and the FIFO method (Exhibit 17-7). In our example, beginning work-in-process inventory, $51,600 ($33,600 + $0 + $18,000) is the same under both the weighted-average and FIFO inventory methods because we assume costs per equivalent unit to be the same in both January and February. If costs per equivalent unit had been different in the two months, work-in-process inventory at the end of February (beginning of March) would be costed differently under the weighted-average and FIFO methods. The basic approach to process costing with transferred-in costs, however, would still be the same as what we describe in this section.				

Transferred-in costs are treated as if they are a separate type of direct material added at the beginning of the process. When successive departments are involved, transferred units from one department become all or a part of the direct materials of the next department; however, they are called transferred-in costs, not direct material costs.

Transferred-In Costs and the Weighted-Average Method

To examine the weighted-average process-costing method with transferred-in costs, we use the five-step procedure described earlier (p. 604) to assign costs of the Testing Department to units completed and transferred out and to units in ending work in process.

Exhibit 17-11 shows steps 1 and 2. The computations are similar to the calculations of equivalent units under the weighted-average method for the Assembly Department in Exhibit 17-4, but here we also have transferred-in costs as an additional input. All units,

Exhibit 17-11 Steps 1 and 2: Summarize Output in Physical Units and Compute Output in Equivalent Units Using Weighted-Average Method of Process Costing for Testing Department of Pacific Electronics for March 2009

	A	B	C	D	E
1		(Step 1)		(Step 2)	
2				Equivalent Units	
3	Flow of Production	Physical Units	Transferred-in Costs	Direct Materials	Conversion Costs
4	Work in process, beginning (given, p. 620)	240			
5	Transferred in during current period (given, p. 620)	400			
6	To account for	640			
7	Completed and transferred out during current period	440	440	440	440
8	Work in process, ending[a] (given, p. 620)	200			
9	(200 x 100%; 200 x 0%; 200 x 80%)		200	0	160
10	Accounted for	640			
11	Work done to date		640	440	600
12					
13	[a]Degree of completion in this department; transferred-in costs, 100%; direct materials, 0%; conversion costs, 80%.				

Exhibit 17-12 Steps 3, 4, and 5: Summarize Total Costs to Account For, Compute Cost per Equivalent Unit, and Assign Total Costs to Units Completed and to Units in Ending Work in Process Using Weighted-Average Method of Process Costing for Testing Department of Pacific Electronics for March 2009

	A	B	C	D	E	F
1			Total Production Costs	Transferred-in Costs	Direct Materials	Conversion Costs
2	(Step 3)	Work in process, beginning (given, p. 620)	$ 51,600	$33,600	$ 0	$18,000
3		Costs added in current period (given, p. 620)	113,800	52,000	13,200	48,600
4		Total costs to account for	$165,400	$85,600	$13,200	$66,600
5						
6	(Step 4)	Costs incurred to date		$85,600	$13,200	$66,600
7		Divide by equivalent units of work done to date (Exhibit 17-11)		÷ 640	÷ 440	÷ 600
8		Cost per equivalent unit of work done to date		$133.75	$ 30.00	$111.00
9						
10	(Step 5)	Assignment of costs:				
11		Completed and transferred out (440 units)	$120,890	(440[a] x $133.75)	+ (440[a] x $30)	+ (440[a] x $111)
12		Work in process, ending (200 units):	44,510	(200[b] x $133.75)	+ (0[b] x $30)	+ (160[b] x $111)
13		Total costs accounted for	$165,400	$85,600	+ $13,200	+ $66,600
14						
15	[a]Equivalent units completed and transferred out from Exhibit 17-11, step 2.					
16	[b]Equivalent units in ending work in process from Exhibit 17-11, step 2.					

whether completed and transferred out during the period or in ending work in process, are fully completed as to transferred-in costs carried forward from the previous process. But direct material costs have a zero degree of completion in both beginning and ending work-in-process inventories because, in Testing, direct materials are introduced at the *end* of the process.

Exhibit 17-12 describes steps 3, 4, and 5 for the weighted-average method. Beginning work in process and work done in the current period are combined for purposes of computing cost per equivalent unit for transferred-in costs, direct material costs, and conversion costs.

The journal entry for the transfer from Testing to Finished Goods (see Exhibit 17-12) is:

Finished Goods Control	120,890	
Work in Process—Testing		120,890
To record cost of goods completed and transferred from Testing to Finished Goods.		

Entries in the Work in Process—Testing account (see Exhibit 17-12) are:

Work in Process—Testing

Beginning inventory, March 1	51,600	Transferred out	120,890
Transferred-in costs	52,000		
Direct materials	13,200		
Conversion costs	48,600		
Ending inventory, March 31	44,510		

Transferred-In Costs and the FIFO Method

To examine the FIFO process-costing method with transferred-in costs, we again use the five-step procedure. Exhibit 17-13 shows steps 1 and 2. Other than considering transferred-in costs, computations of equivalent units are the same as under the FIFO method for the Assembly Department shown in Exhibit 17-6.

Exhibit 17-14 describes steps 3, 4, and 5. In step 3, total costs to account for of $165,880 under the FIFO method differs from the corresponding amount under the weighted-average method of $165,400. That's because of different costs of completed

Exhibit 17-13 Steps 1 and 2: Summarize Output in Physical Units and Compute Output in Equivalent Units Using FIFO Method of Process Costing for Testing Department of Pacific Electronics for March 2009

	A	B	C	D	E
1		(Step 1)		(Step 2)	
2				Equivalent Units	
3	Flow of Production	Physical Units	Transferred-in Costs	Direct Materials	Conversion Costs
4	Work in process, beginning (given, p. 620)	240	(work done before current period)		
5	Transferred in during current period (given, p. 620)	400			
6	To account for	640			
7	Completed and transferred out during current period:				
8	From beginning work in process[a]	240			
9	[240 x (100% - 100%); 240 x (100% - 0%); 240 x (100% - 62.5%)]		0	240	90
10	Started and completed	200[b]			
11	(200 x 100%; 200 x 100%; 200 x 100%)		200	200	200
12	Work in process, ending[c] (given, p. 620)	200			
13	(200 x 100%; 200 x 0%; 200 x 80%)		200	0	160
14	Accounted for	640			
15	Work done in current period only		400	440	450
16					
17	[a]Degree of completion in this department: Transferred-in costs, 100%; direct materials, 0%; conversion costs, 62.5%.				
18	[b]440 physical units completed and transferred out minus 240 physical units completed and transferred out from beginning				
19	work-in-process inventory.				
20	[c]Degree of completion in this department: Transferred-in costs, 100%; direct materials, 0%; conversion costs, 80%.				

units transferred in from the Assembly Department under the two methods—$52,480 under FIFO and $52,000 under weighted average. Cost per equivalent unit for the current period in step 4 is calculated on the basis of costs transferred in and work done in the current period only. Step 5 then accounts for the total costs of $165,880 by assigning them to the units transferred out and those in ending work in process. Again, other than considering transferred-in costs, the calculations mirror those under the FIFO method for the Assembly Department shown in Exhibit 17-7.

The journal entry for the transfer from Testing to Finished Goods (see Exhibit 17-14) is:

Finished Goods Control	122,360	
Work in Process—Testing		122,360
To record cost of goods completed and transferred from Testing to Finished Goods.		

Entries in the Work in Process—Testing account (see Exhibit 17-14) are:

Work in Process—Testing

Beginning inventory, March 1	51,600	Transferred out	122,360
Transferred-in costs	52,480		
Direct materials	13,200		
Conversion costs	48,600		
Ending inventory, March 31	43,520		

Remember that in a series of interdepartmental transfers, each department is regarded as separate and distinct for accounting purposes. All costs transferred in during a given accounting period are carried at the same unit cost, as described when discussing modified FIFO (p. 614), whether previous departments used the weighted-average method or the FIFO method.

Exhibit 17-14 Steps 3, 4, and 5: Summarize Total Costs to Account For, Compute Cost per Equivalent Unit, and Assign Total Costs to Units Completed and to Units in Ending Work in Process Using FIFO Method of Process Costing for Testing Department of Pacific Electronics for March 2009

	A	B	C	D		E		F
1			Total Production Costs	Transferred-in Cost		Direct Material		Conversion Costs
2	(Step 3)	Work in process, beginning (given, p. 620)	$ 51,600	$33,600		$ 0		$18,000
3		Costs added in current period (given, p. 620)	114,280	52,480		13,200		48,600
4		Total costs to account for	$165,880	$86,080		$13,200		$66,600
5								
6	(Step 4)	Costs added in current period		$52,480		$13,200		$48,600
7		Divide by equivalent units of work done in current period (Exhibit 17-13)		÷ 400		÷ 440		÷ 450
8		Cost per equivalent unit of work done in current period		$131.20		$ 30		$ 108
9								
10	(Step 5)	Assignment of costs:						
11		Completed and transferred out (440 units)						
12		Work in process, beginning (240 units)	$ 51,600	$33,600	+	$0	+	$18,000
13		Costs added to beginning work in process in current period	16,920	(0[a] x $131.20)	+	(240[a] x $30)	+	(90[a] x $108)
14		Total from beginning inventory	68,520					
15		Started and completed (200 units)	53,840	(200[b] x $131.20)	+	(200[b] x $30)	+	(200[b] x $108)
16		Total costs of units completed and transferred out	122,360					
17		Work in process, ending (200 units):	43,520	(200[c] x $131.20)	+	(0[c] x $30)	+	(160[c] x $108)
18		Total costs accounted for	$165,880	$86,080	+	$13,200	+	$66,600
19								
20	[a]Equivalent units used to complete beginning work in process from Exhibit 17-13, step 2.							
21	[b]Equivalent units started and completed from Exhibit 17-13, step 2.							
22	[c]Equivalent units in ending work in process from Exhibit 17-13, step 2.							

Points to Remember About Transferred-In Costs

Some points to remember when accounting for transferred-in costs are:

1. Be sure to include transferred-in costs from previous departments in your calculations.
2. In calculating costs to be transferred on a FIFO basis, do not overlook costs assigned in the previous period to units that were in process at the beginning of the current period but are now included in the units transferred. For example, do not overlook the $51,600 in Exhibit 17-14.
3. Unit costs may fluctuate between periods. Therefore, transferred units may contain batches accumulated at different unit costs. For example, the 400 units transferred in at $52,480 in Exhibit 17-14 using the FIFO method consist of units that have different unit costs of direct materials and conversion costs when these units were worked on in the Assembly Department (see Exhibit 17-7). Remember, however, that when these units are transferred to the Testing Department, they are costed at *one average unit cost* of $131.20 ($52,480 ÷ 400 units), as in Exhibit 17-14.
4. Units may be measured in different denominations in different departments. Consider each department separately. For example, unit costs could be based on kilograms in the first department and liters in the second department. Accordingly, as units are received in the second department, their measurements must be converted to liters.

Concepts in Action

Hybrid Costing for Customized Shoes at Adidas

Adidas has been designing and manufacturing athletic footwear for more than 80 years. Although shoemakers have long individually crafted shoes for professional athletes, Adidas took this concept a step further when it initiated the *mi adidas* program. *Mi adidas* gives customers throughout North America, Europe, and Asia the opportunity to create shoes to their exact personal specifications for function, fit, and aesthetics. *Mi adidas* is available in 100 U.S. retail stores and at specialized mobile units that travel to major sporting events, such as the Boston Marathon. In October 2006, Adidas opened its first Mi Innovation center in Paris, its largest store in the world.

The process works as follows: The customer goes to a *mi adidas* station, where a salesperson develops an in-depth customer profile, a 3-D computer scanner develops a scan of the customer's feet, and the customer selects from among 90 to 100 different styles and colors for his modularly designed shoe. During the three step, 30-minute high-tech process, *mi adidas* experts take customers through the "mi fit", "mi performance" and "mi design" phases, resulting in a customized shoe to fit their needs. The resulting data are transferred to an Adidas plant, where small, multiskilled teams produce the customized shoe. The measuring and fitting process is free, but purchasing your own specially made shoes costs between $40 and $65 on top of the normal retail price, depending on the style.

Historically, costs associated with individually customized products have fallen into the domain of job costing. Adidas, however, uses a hybrid-costing system—job costing for the material and customizable components that customers choose and process costing to account for the conversion costs of production. The cost of making each pair of shoes is calculated by accumulating all production costs and dividing by the number of shoes made. In other words, even though each pair of shoes is different, the conversion cost of each pair is assumed to be the same.

The combination of customization with certain features of mass production is called mass customization. It is the consequence of being able to digitize information that individual customers indicate is important to them. Various products that companies are now able to customize within a mass-production setting (for example, personal computers, blue jeans, bicycles) still require job costing of materials and considerable human intervention. However, as manufacturing systems become flexible, companies are also using process costing to account for the standardized conversion costs.

Sources: "The 'mi adidas' Mass Customization Initiative," IMD case number IMD159; N. Tait, "How 'mi adidas' Provides Personalized Style, Fit," *Apparel* (January 1, 2004); M. Kamenev, "Adidas' High Tech Footwear," *BusinessWeek.com* (November 3, 2006).

Hybrid Costing Systems

Product-costing systems do not always fall neatly into either job-costing or process-costing categories. Consider Ford Motor Company. Automobiles may be manufactured in a continuous flow (suited to process costing), but individual units may be customized with a special combination of engine size, transmission, music system, and so on (which requires job costing). A **hybrid-costing system** blends characteristics from both job-costing and process-costing systems. Product-costing systems often must be designed to fit the particular characteristics of different production systems. Many production systems are a hybrid: They have some features of custom-order manufacturing and other features of mass-production manufacturing. Manufacturers of a relatively wide variety of closely related standardized products (for example, televisions, dishwashers, and washing machines) tend to use hybrid-costing systems. The Concepts in Action feature (p. 624) describes a hybrid-costing system at Adidas. The appendix to this chapter explains *operation costing*, a common type of hybrid-costing system.

Problem for Self-Study

Allied Chemicals operates a thermo-assembly process as the second of three processes at its plastics plant. Direct materials in thermo-assembly are added at the end of the process. Conversion costs are added evenly during the process. The following data pertain to the Thermo Assembly Department for June 2009:

	A	B	C	D	E
1		Physical Units	Transferred-in Costs	Direct Materials	Conversion Costs
2	Work in process, beginning inventory	50,000			
3	Degree of completion of beginning work in process		100%	0%	80%
4	Transferred in during current period	200,000			
5	Completed and transferred out during current period	210,000			
6	Work in process, ending inventory	?			
7	Degree of completion of ending work in process		100%	0%	40%

Compute equivalent units under (1) the weighted-average method and (2) the FIFO method. **Required**

Solution

1. The weighted-average method uses equivalent units of work done to date to compute cost per equivalent unit. The calculations of equivalent units follow:

	A	B	C	D	E
1		(Step 1)	(Step 2)		
2			Equivalent Units		
3	Flow of Production	Physical Units	Transferred-in Costs	Direct Materials	Conversion Costs
4	Work in process, beginning (given)	50,000			
5	Transferred in during current period (given)	200,000			
6	To account for	250,000			
7	Completed and transferred out during current period	210,000	210,000	210,000	210,000
8	Work in process, ending[a]	40,000[b]			
9	(40,000 x 100%; 40,000 x 0%; 40,000 x 40%)		40,000	0	16,000
10	Accounted for	250,000			
11	Work done to date		250,000	210,000	226,000
12					
13	[a]Degree of completion in this department: Transferred-in costs, 100%; direct materials, 0%; conversion costs, 40%.				
14	[b]250,000 physical units to account for minus 210,000 physical units completed and transferred out				

2. The FIFO method uses equivalent units of work done in the current period only to compute cost per equivalent unit. The calculations of equivalent units follow:

	A	B	C	D	E
1		(Step 1)		(Step 2)	
2				Equivalent Units	
3	Flow of Production	Physical Units	Transferred-in Costs	Direct Materials	Conversion Costs
4	Work in process, beginning (given)	50,000			
5	Transferred in during current period (given)	200,000			
6	To account for	250,000			
7	Completed and transferred out during current period:				
8	From beginning work in process[a]	50,000			
9	[50,000 x (100% - 100%); 50,000 x (100% - 0%); 50,000 x (100% - 80%)]		0	50,000	10,000
10	Started and completed	160,000[b]			
11	(160,000 x 100%; 160,000 x 100%; 160,000 x 100%)		160,000	160,000	160,000
12	Work in process, ending[c]	40,000[d]			
13	(40,000 x 100%; 40,000 x 0%; 40,000 x 40%)		40,000	0	16,000
14	Accounted for	250,000			
15	Work done in current period only		200,000	210,000	186,000
16					
17	[a]Degree of completion in this department: Transferred-in costs, 100%; direct materials, 0%; conversion costs, 80%.				
18	[b]210,000 physical units completed and transferred out minus 50,000 physical units completed and transferred out from beginning work-in-process inventory.				
19	[c]Degree of completion in this department: Transferred-in costs, 100%; direct materials, 0%; conversion costs, 40%.				
20	[d]250,000 physical units to account for minus 210,000 physical units completed and transferred out.				

Decision Points

The following question-and-answer format summarizes the chapter's learning objectives. Each decision presents a key question related to a learning objective. The guidelines are the answer to that question.

Decision	Guidelines
1. Under what conditions is a process-costing system used?	A process-costing system is used to determine cost of a product or service when masses of identical or similar units are produced. Industries using process-costing systems include food, textiles, and oil refining.
2. What are the five steps in a process-costing system to assign costs to units completed and to units in ending work in process?	The five steps in a process-costing system are (1) summarize the flow of physical units of output, (2) compute output in terms of equivalent units, (3) summarize total costs to account for, (4) compute cost per equivalent unit, and (5) assign total costs to units completed and to units in ending work in process.
3. What are equivalent units and what role do they play in the process-costing sequence?	Equivalent units is a derived amount of output units that (a) takes the quantity of each input (factor of production) in units completed or in incomplete units in work in process and (b) converts the quantity of input into the amount of completed output units that could be made with that quantity of input. Equivalent-unit calculations are necessary when all physical units of output are not uniformly completed during an accounting period.
4. What is the weighted-average method of process costing?	The weighted-average method computes unit costs by dividing total costs in the work-in-process account (whether from beginning work in process or from work started during the period) by total equivalent units completed to date, and it assigns this average cost to units completed and to units in ending work-in-process inventory.

5. What is the first-in, first-out method of process costing?	The first-in, first-out (FIFO) method computes unit costs based on costs incurred during the current period and equivalent units of work done in the current period. It assigns the costs of beginning work-in-process inventory to the first units completed, and it assigns costs of the equivalent units worked on during the current period first to complete beginning inventory, next to start and complete new units, and finally to units in ending work-in-process inventory.
6. How does the standard-costing method simplify process costing?	Under this method, standard costs serve as the cost per equivalent unit for assigning cost to units completed and to units in ending work-in-process inventory.
7. How are the weighted-average and FIFO process-costing methods applied to transferred-in costs?	The weighted-average method computes transferred-in costs per unit by dividing total transferred-in costs to date by total equivalent transferred-in units completed to date, and it assigns this average cost to units completed and to units in ending work-in-process inventory. The FIFO method computes transferred-in costs per unit based on costs transferred in during the current period and equivalent units of transferred-in costs of work done in the current period. The FIFO method assigns transferred-in costs in beginning work in process to units completed and costs transferred in during the current period first to complete beginning inventory, next to start and complete new units, and finally to units in ending work-in-process inventory.

APPENDIX: OPERATION COSTING

This appendix describes operation costing and uses an example to illustrate it.

Overview of Operation-Costing Systems

An **operation** is a standardized method or technique that is performed repetitively, often on different materials, resulting in different finished goods. Multiple operations are usually conducted within a department. For instance, a suit maker may have a cutting operation and a hemming operation within a single department. The term *operation*, however, is often used loosely. It may be a synonym for a department or process. For example, some companies may call their finishing department a finishing process or a finishing operation.

An **operation-costing system** is a hybrid-costing system applied to batches of similar, but not identical, products. Each batch of products is often a variation of a single design, and it proceeds through a sequence of operations. Within each operation, all product units are treated exactly alike, using identical amounts of the operation's resources. A key point is that each batch does not necessarily move through the same operations as other batches. Batches are also called production runs.

Consider a company that makes suits. Management may select a single basic design for every suit to be made. Depending on specifications, each batch of suits varies somewhat from other batches. One batch may use wool; another batch, cotton. One batch may require special hand stitching; another batch, machine stitching. Other products manufactured in batches are semiconductors, textiles, and shoes.

An operation-costing system uses work orders that specify the needed direct materials and step-by-step operations. Product costs are compiled for each work order. Direct materials that are unique to different work orders are specifically identified with the appropriate work order, as in job costing. Each unit is assumed to use an identical amount of conversion costs for a given operation. For each operation, a single average conversion cost per unit is therefore calculated, as in process costing, by dividing total conversion costs by all units passing through that operation. This cost is then assigned to each unit passing through a given operation. Units that do not pass through an operation are not allocated any costs of that operation. Our examples assume only two cost categories—direct materials and conversion costs—but operation costing can have more than two cost categories. Costs in each category are identified with specific work orders using job-costing or process-costing methods as appropriate.

Managers find operation costing useful in cost management because operation costing focuses on control of physical processes, or operations, of a given production system. For example, in clothing manufacturing, managers are concerned with fabric waste, how many fabric layers that can be cut at one time, and so on. Operation costing measures, in financial terms, how well managers have controlled physical processes.

Illustration of an Operation-Costing System

Baltimore Company, a clothing manufacturer, produces two lines of blazers for department stores. Wool blazers use better-quality materials and undergo more operations than polyester blazers. Operations information on work order 423 for 50 wool blazers and work order 424 for 100 polyester blazers is:

	Work Order 423	**Work Order 424**
Direct materials	Wool	Polyester
	Satin full lining	Rayon partial lining
	Bone buttons	Plastic buttons
Operations		
1. Cutting cloth	Use	Use
2. Checking edges	Use	Do not use
3. Sewing body	Use	Use
4. Checking seams	Use	Do not use
5. Machine sewing of collars and lapels	Do not use	Use
6. Hand sewing of collars and lapels	Use	Do not use

Cost data for these work orders, started and completed in March 2009, are:

	Work Order 423	**Work Order 424**
Number of blazers	50	100
Direct material costs	$ 6,000	$3,000
Conversion costs allocated:		
Operation 1	580	1,160
Operation 2	400	—
Operation 3	1,900	3,800
Operation 4	500	—
Operation 5	—	875
Operation 6	700	—
Total manufacturing costs	$10,080	$8,835

As in process costing, all product units in any work order are assumed to consume identical amounts of conversion costs of a particular operation. Baltimore's operation-costing system uses a budgeted rate to calculate the conversion costs of each operation. The budgeted rate for Operation 1 (amounts assumed) is:

$$\begin{aligned}\text{Operation 1 budgeted conversion-cost rate for 2009} &= \frac{\text{Operation 1 budgeted conversion costs for 2009}}{\text{Operation 1 budgeted product units for 2009}}\\ &= \frac{\$232{,}000}{20{,}000\text{ units}}\\ &= \$11.60\text{ per unit}\end{aligned}$$

Budgeted conversion costs of Operation 1 include labor, power, repairs, supplies, depreciation, and other overhead of this operation. If some units have not been completed (so all units in Operation 1 have not received the same amounts of conversion costs), the conversion-cost rate is computed by dividing budgeted conversion costs by *equivalent units* of conversion costs, as in process costing.

As goods are manufactured, conversion costs are allocated to the work orders processed in Operation 1 by multiplying the $11.60 conversion cost per unit by the number of units processed. Conversion costs of Operation 1 for 50 wool blazers (work order 423) are $11.60 per blazer × 50 blazers = $580; and for 100 polyester blazers (work order 424) are $11.60 per blazer × 100 blazers = $1,160. If work order 424 had contained 75 blazers, its total costs in Operation 1 would be $870 ($11.60 per blazer × 75 blazers). When equivalent units are used to calculate the conversion-cost rate, costs are allocated to work orders by multiplying conversion cost per equivalent unit by number of equivalent units in the work order. Direct material costs of $6,000 for the 50 wool blazers (work order 423) and $3,000 for the 100 polyester blazers (work order 424) are specifically identified with each order, as in job costing. Remember the basic point in operation costing: Operation unit costs are assumed to be the same regardless of the work order, but direct material costs vary across orders when the materials for each work order vary.

Journal Entries

Actual conversion costs for Operation 1 in March 2009—assumed to be $24,400, including actual costs incurred for work order 423 and work order 424—are entered into a Conversion Costs Control account:

1. Conversion Costs Control	24,400	
Various accounts (such as Wages Payable Control and Accumulated Depreciation)		24,400

Summary journal entries for assigning costs to polyester blazers (work order 424) follow. Entries for wool blazers would be similar. Of the $3,000 of direct materials for work order 424, $2,975 are used in Operation 1, and the remaining $25 of materials are used in another operation. The journal entry to record direct materials used for the 100 polyester blazers in March 2009 is:

2. Work in Process, Operation 1	2,975	
Materials Inventory Control		2,975

The journal entry to record the allocation of conversion costs to products uses the budgeted rate of $11.60 per blazer times the 100 polyester blazers processed, or $1,160:

3. Work in Process, Operation 1	1,160	
Conversion Costs Allocated		1,160

The journal entry to record the transfer of the 100 polyester blazers (at a cost of $2,975 + $1,160) from Operation 1 to Operation 3 (polyester blazers do not go through Operation 2) is:

4. Work in Process, Operation 3	4,135	
Work in Process, Operation 1		4,135

After posting these entries, the Work in Process, Operation 1, account appears as follows:

Work in Process, Operation 1

② Direct materials	2,975	④ Transferred to Operation 3	4,135
③ Conversion costs allocated	1,160		
Ending inventory, March 31	0		

Costs of the blazers are transferred through the operations in which blazers are worked on and then to finished goods in the usual manner. Costs are added throughout the fiscal year in the Conversion Costs Control account and the Conversion Costs Allocated account. Any overallocation or underallocation of conversion costs is disposed of in the same way as overallocated or underallocated manufacturing overhead in a job-costing system. (See pp. 115–119.)

TERMS TO LEARN

This chapter and the Glossary at the end of the book contain definitions of:

ASSIGNMENT MATERIAL

Questions

17-1 Give three examples of industries that use process-costing systems.

17-2 In process costing, why are costs often divided into two main classifications?

17-3 Explain equivalent units. Why are equivalent-unit calculations necessary in process costing?

17-4 What problems might arise in estimating the degree of completion of semiconductor chips in a semiconductor plant?

17-5 Name the five steps in process costing when equivalent units are computed.

17-6 Name the three inventory methods commonly associated with process costing.

17-7 Describe the distinctive characteristic of weighted-average computations in assigning costs to units completed and to units in ending work in process.

17-8 Describe the distinctive characteristic of FIFO computations in assigning costs to units completed and to units in ending work in process.

17-9 Why should the FIFO method be called a modified or department FIFO method?

17-10 Identify a major advantage of the FIFO method for purposes of planning and control.

17-11 Identify the main difference between journal entries in process costing and job costing.

17-12 "The standard-costing method is particularly applicable to process-costing situations." Do you agree? Why?

17-13 Why should the accountant distinguish between transferred-in costs and additional direct material costs for each subsequent department in a process-costing system?

17-14 "Transferred-in costs are those costs incurred in the preceding accounting period." Do you agree? Explain.

17-15 "There's no reason for me to get excited about the choice between the weighted-average and FIFO methods in my process-costing system. I have long-term contracts with my materials suppliers at fixed prices." Do you agree with this statement made by a plant controller? Explain.

Exercises

17-16 Equivalent units, zero beginning inventory. Nihon, Inc. is a manufacturer of digital cameras. It has two departments: Assembly and Testing. In January 2009, the company incurred $750,000 on direct materials and $798,000 on conversion costs, for a total manufacturing cost of $1,548,000.

Required

1. Assume there was no beginning inventory of any kind on January 1, 2009. During January, 10,000 cameras were placed into production and all 10,000 were fully completed at the end of the month. What is the unit cost of an assembled camera in January?
2. Assume that during February 10,000 cameras are placed into production. Further assume the same total assembly costs for January are also incurred in February, but only 9,000 cameras are fully completed at the end of the month. All direct materials have been added to the remaining 1,000 cameras. However, on average, these remaining 1,000 cameras are only 50% complete as to conversion costs. (a) What are the equivalent units for direct materials and conversion costs and their respective costs per equivalent unit for February? (b) What is the unit cost of an assembled camera in February 2009?
3. Explain the difference in your answers to requirements 1 and 2.

17-17 Journal entries (continuation of 17-16). Refer to requirement 2 of Exercise 17-16.

Required

Prepare summary journal entries for the use of direct materials and incurrence of conversion costs. Also prepare a journal entry to transfer out the cost of goods completed. Show the postings to the Work-in-Process account.

17-18 Zero beginning inventory, materials introduced in middle of process. Roary Chemicals has a Mixing Department and a Refining Department. Its process-costing system in the Mixing Department has two direct materials cost categories (Chemical P and Chemical Q) and one conversion costs pool. The following data pertain to the Mixing Department for July 2009:

Units	
Work in process, July 1	0
Units started	50,000
Completed and transferred to Refining Department	35,000
Costs	
Chemical P	$250,000
Chemical Q	70,000
Conversion costs	135,000

Chemical P is introduced at the start of operations in the Mixing Department, and Chemical Q is added when the product is three-fourths completed in the Mixing Department. Conversion costs are added evenly during the process. The ending work in process in the Mixing Department is two-thirds complete.

Required

1. Compute the equivalent units in the Mixing Department for July 2009 for each cost category.
2. Compute (a) the cost of goods completed and transferred to the Refining Department during July and (b) the cost of work in process as of July 31, 2009.

17-19 Weighted-average method, equivalent units. Consider the following data for the Assembly Division of Fenton Watches, Inc.:

The Assembly Division uses the weighted-average method of process costing.

	Physical Units (Watches)	Direct Materials	Conversion Costs
Beginning work in process (May 1)[a]	80	$ 493,360	$ 91,040
Started in May 2009	500		
Completed during May 2009	460		
Ending work in process (May 31)[b]	120		
Total costs added during May 2009		$3,220,000	$1,392,000

[a]Degree of completion: direct materials, 90%; conversion costs, 40%.
[b]Degree of completion: direct materials, 60%; conversion costs, 30%.

Required

Compute equivalent units for direct materials and conversion costs. Show physical units in the first column of your schedule.

17-20 Weighted-average method, assigning costs (continuation of 17-19).

Required

For the data in Exercise 17-19, summarize total costs to account for, calculate cost per equivalent unit for direct materials and conversion costs, and assign total costs to units completed (and transferred out) and to units in ending work in process.

17-21 FIFO method, equivalent units. Refer to the information in Exercise 17-19. Suppose the Assembly Division at Fenton Watches, Inc., uses the FIFO method of process costing instead of the weighted-average method.

Required

Compute equivalent units for direct materials and conversion costs. Show physical units in the first column of your schedule.

17-22 FIFO method, assigning costs (continuation of 17-21).

Required

For the data in Exercise 17-19, use the FIFO method to summarize total costs to account for, calculate cost per equivalent unit for direct materials and conversion costs, and assign total costs to units completed (and transferred out) and to units in ending work in process.

17-23 Standard-costing method, assigning costs. Bucky's Boxes makes boxes for moving. It sells its boxes to Home Depot, U-Haul, and major national moving companies. Because of the simple nature of the production process, Bucky uses standard costing. The following information for July 2010 is available.

Bucky's Boxes Company
Standard Costing
For the Month Ended July 31, 2010

	Physical Units	Direct Materials	Conversion Costs
Standard cost per equivalent unit		$1.30	$2.10
Work in process, beginning inventory (July 1)	185,000	$240,500	$97,125
Degree of completion of beginning work in process		100%	25%
Started during July	465,000		
Completed and transferred out	512,000		
Work in process, ending inventory (July 31)	138,000		
Degree of completion of ending work in process		100%	80%
Actual total costs added during July		$607,500	$1,207,415

Required

1. Compute equivalent units for each cost category.
2. Summarize total costs to account for and assign total costs to units completed and transferred out and to units in ending work in process.

17-24 Weighted-average method, assigning costs. Bio Doc Corporation is a biotech company based in Milpitas. It makes a cancer-treatment drug in a single processing department. Direct materials are added at the start of the process. Conversion costs are added evenly during the process. Bio Doc uses the weighted-average method of process costing. The following information for July 2008 is available.

	Physical Units	Equivalent Units: Direct Materials	Equivalent Units: Conversion Costs
Work in process, July 1	12,500[a]	12,500	8,750
Started during July	50,000		
Completed and transferred out during July	42,500	42,500	42,500
Work in process, July 31	20,000[b]	20,000	10,000

[a]Degree of completion: direct materials, 100%; conversion costs, 70%.
[b]Degree of completion: direct materials, 100%; conversion costs, 50%.

Total Costs for July 2008		
Work in process, beginning		
Direct materials	$75,000	
Conversion costs	87,500	$162,500
Direct materials added during July		350,000
Conversion costs added during July		463,750
Total costs to account for		$976,250

Required

1. Calculate cost per equivalent unit for direct materials and conversion costs.
2. Summarize total costs to account for, and assign total costs to units completed (and transferred out) and to units in ending work in process.

17-25 FIFO method, assigning costs.

Required Do Exercise 17-24 using the FIFO method. Note that you first need to calculate the equivalent units of work done in the current period (for direct materials and conversion costs) to complete beginning work in process, to start and complete new units, and to produce ending work in process.

17-26 Standard-costing method, assigning costs. Refer to the information in Exercise 17-24. Suppose Bio Doc determines standard costs of $6.60 per equivalent unit for direct materials and $10.40 per equivalent unit for conversion costs for both beginning work in process and work done in the current period.

Required

1. Do Exercise 17-24 using the standard-costing method. Note that you first need to calculate the equivalent units of work done in the current period (for direct materials and conversion costs) to complete beginning work in process, to start and complete new units, and to produce ending work in process.
2. Compute the total direct materials and conversion costs variances for July 2008.

17-27 Transferred-in costs, weighted-average method. Asaya Clothing, Inc. is a manufacturer of winter clothes. It has a Knitting Department and a Finishing Department. This exercise focuses on the Finishing Department. Direct materials are added at the end of the process. Conversion costs are added evenly during the process. Asaya uses the weighted-average method of process costing. The following information for June 2009 is available.

	A	B	C	D	E
1		Physical Units (tons)	Transferred-in Costs	Direct Materials	Conversion Costs
2	Work in process, beginning inventory (June 1)	75	$ 75,000	$ 0	$30,000
3	Degree of completion, beginning work in process		100%	0%	60%
4	Transferred in during June	135			
5	Completed and transferred out during June	150			
6	Work in process, ending inventory (June 30)	60			
7	Degree of completion, ending work in process		100%	0%	75%
8	Total costs added during June		$142,500	$37,500	$78,000

If you want to use Excel to solve this exercise, go to the Excel Lab at **www.prenhall.com/horngren/cost13e** and download the template for Exercise 17-27.

Required

1. Calculate equivalent units of transferred-in costs, direct materials, and conversion costs.
2. Summarize total costs to account for, and calculate the cost per equivalent unit for transferred-in costs, direct materials, and conversion costs.
3. Assign total costs to units completed (and transferred out) and to units in ending work in process.

17-28 Transferred-in costs, FIFO method. Refer to the information in Exercise 17-27. Suppose that Asaya uses the FIFO method instead of the weighted-average method in all of its departments. The only changes to Exercise 17-27 under the FIFO method are that total transferred-in costs of beginning work in process on June 1 are $60,000 (instead of $75,000) and total transferred-in costs added during June are $130,800 (instead of $142,500).

If you want to use Excel to solve this exercise, go to the Excel Lab at **www.prenhall.com/horngren/cost13e** and download the template for Exercise 17-27.

Required

Do Exercise 17-27 using the FIFO method. Note that you first need to calculate equivalent units of work done in the current period (for transferred-in costs, direct materials, and conversion costs) to complete beginning work in process, to start and complete new units, and to produce ending work in process.

17-29 Standard-costing method. Ozumo's Gardening makes several different kinds of mulch. Its busy period is in the summer months. In August, the controller suddenly quit due to a stress-related disorder. He took with him the standard costing results for RoseBark, Ozumo's highest quality mulch. The controller had already completed the assignment of costs to finished goods and work in process, but Ozumo does not know standard costs or the completion levels of inventory. The following information is available:

Ozumo's Gardening
Standard Costing Calculations for RoseBark
For the Month Ended August 31, 2009

	Physical Units (Yards of Mulch)	Equivalent Units (yards) Direct Materials	Conversion Costs
Complete beginning work in process	965,000	—	434,250
Start and complete	845,000	845,000	845,000
Start ending work in process	1,817,000	1,817,000	1,090,200
		2,662,000	2,369,450
Units to account for	3,627,000		

	Costs
Cost of units completed from beginning work in process	$ 7,671,750
Cost of new units started and completed	6,717,750
Cost of units completed in August	14,389,500
Cost of ending work in process	12,192,070
Total costs accounted for	$ 26,581,570

Required

1. Completion percentages of beginning work in process with respect to the two inputs
2. Completion percentages of ending work in process with respect to the two inputs
3. Standard costs per unit for the two inputs
4. Cost of beginning work in process inventory

Problems

17-30 Weighted-average method. Larsen Company manufactures car seats in its San Antonio plant. Each car seat passes through the Assembly Department and the Testing Department. This problem focuses on the Assembly Department. The process-costing system at Larsen Company has a single direct-cost category (direct materials) and a single indirect-cost category (conversion costs). Direct materials are added at the beginning of the process. Conversion costs are added evenly during the process. When the Assembly Department finishes work on each car seat, it is immediately transferred to Testing.

Larsen Company uses the weighted-average method of process costing. Data for the Assembly Department for October 2009 are:

	Physical Units (Car Seats)	Direct Materials	Conversion Costs
Work in process, October 1[a]	5,000	$ 1,250,000	$ 402,750
Started during October 2009	20,000		
Completed during October 2009	22,500		
Work in process, October 31[b]	2,500		
Total costs added during October 2009		$4,500,000	$2,337,500

[a]Degree of completion: direct materials, ?%; conversion costs, 60%.
[b]Degree of completion: direct materials, ?%; conversion costs, 70%.

Required

1. For each cost category, compute equivalent units in the Assembly Department. Show physical units in the first column of your schedule.
2. For each cost category, summarize total Assembly Department costs for October 2009 and calculate the cost per equivalent unit.
3. Assign total costs to units completed and transferred out and to units in ending work in process.

17-31 Journal entries (continuation of 17-30).

Required Prepare a set of summarized journal entries for all October 2009 transactions affecting Work in Process—Assembly. Set up a T-account for Work in Process—Assembly and post your entries to it.

17-32 FIFO method (continuation of 17-30).

Required Do Problem 17-30 using the FIFO method of process costing. Explain any difference between the cost per equivalent unit in the Assembly Department under the weighted-average method and the FIFO method.

17-33 Transferred-in costs, weighted average method (related to 17-30 to 17-32). Larsen Company, as you know, is a manufacturer of car seats. Each car seat passes through the Assembly Department and Testing Department. This problem focuses on the Testing Department. Direct materials are added when the Testing Department process is 90% complete. Conversion costs are added evenly during the Testing Department's process. As work in Assembly is completed, each unit is immediately transferred to Testing. As each unit is completed in Testing, it is immediately transferred to Finished Goods.

Larsen Company uses the weighted-average method of process costing. Data for the Testing Department for October 2009 are:

	Physical Units (Car Seats)	Transferred-In Costs	Direct Materials	Conversion Costs
Work in process, October 1[a]	7,500	$2,932,500	$ 0	$ 835,460
Transferred in during October 2009	?			
Completed during October 2009	26,300			
Work in process, October 31[b]	3,700			
Total costs added during October 2009		$7,717,500	$9,704,700	$3,955,900

[a]Degree of completion: transferred-in costs, ?%; direct materials, ?%; conversion costs, 70%.
[b]Degree of completion: transferred-in costs, ?%; direct materials, ?%; conversion costs, 60%.

Required

1. What is the percentage of completion for (a) transferred-in costs and direct materials in beginning work-in-process inventory, and (b) transferred-in costs and direct materials in ending work-in-process inventory?
2. For each cost category, compute equivalent units in the Testing Department. Show physical units in the first column of your schedule.
3. For each cost category, summarize total Testing Department costs for October 2009, calculate the cost per equivalent unit, and assign total costs to units completed (and transferred out) and to units in ending work in process.
4. Prepare journal entries for October transfers from the Assembly Department to the Testing Department and from the Testing Department to Finished Goods.

17-34 Transferred-in costs, FIFO method (continuation of 17-33). Refer to the information in Problem 17-33. Suppose that Larsen Company uses the FIFO method instead of the weighted-average method in all of its departments. The only changes to Problem 17-33 under the FIFO method are that total transferred-in costs of beginning work in process on October 1 are $2,881,875 (instead of $2,932,500) and that total transferred-in costs added during October are $7,735,250 (instead of $7,717,500).

Required

Using the FIFO process-costing method, do Problem 17-33.

17-35 Weighted-average method. Porter Handcraft is a manufacturer of picture frames for large retailers. Every picture frame passes through two departments: the Assembly Department and the Finishing Department. This problem focuses on the Assembly Department. The process-costing system at Porter has a single direct-cost category (direct materials) and a single indirect-cost category (conversion costs). Direct materials are added when the Assembly Department process is 10% complete. Conversion costs are added evenly during the Assembly Department's process.

Porter uses the weighted-average method of process costing. Consider the following data for the Assembly Department in April 2009:

	Physical Unit (Frames)	Direct Materials	Conversion Costs
Work in process, April 1[a]	75	$ 1,775	$ 135
Started during April 2009	550		
Completed during April 2009	500		
Work in process, April 30[b]	125		
Total costs added during April 2009		$17,600	$10,890

[a]Degree of completion: direct materials, 100%; conversion costs, 40%.
[b]Degree of completion: direct materials, 100%; conversion costs, 20%.

Required

Summarize total Assembly Department costs for April 2009, and assign total costs to units completed (and transferred out) and to units in ending work in process.

17-36 Journal entries (continuation of 17-35).

Required

Prepare a set of summarized journal entries for all April transactions affecting Work in Process—Assembly. Set up a T-account for Work in Process—Assembly and post your entries to it.

17-37 FIFO method (continuation of 17-35).

Required

Do Problem 17-35 using the FIFO method of process costing. If you did Problem 17-35, explain any difference between the cost of work completed and transferred out and the cost of ending work in process in the Assembly Department under the weighted-average method and the FIFO method.

17-38 Transferred-in costs, weighted-average method. Publish, Inc. has two departments: Printing and Binding. Each department has one direct-cost category (direct materials) and one indirect-cost category (conversion costs). This problem focuses on the Binding Department. Books that have undergone the printing process are immediately transferred to the Binding Department. Direct material is added when the binding process is 80% complete. Conversion costs are added evenly during binding operations. When those operations are done, the books are immediately transferred to Finished Goods. Publish, Inc. uses the weighted-average method of process costing. The following is a summary of the April 2009 operations of the Binding Department.

File Edit View Insert Format Tools Data Window Help

	A	B	C	D	E
1		Physical Units (books)	Transferred-in Costs	Direct Materials	Conversion Costs
2	Beginning work in process	900	$ 32,775	$ 0	$15,000
3	Degree of completion, beginning work in process		100%	0%	40%
4	Transferred in during April 2009	2,700			
5	Completed and transferred out during April	3,000			
6	Ending work in process (April 30)	600			
7	Degree of completion, ending work in process		100%	0%	60%
8	Total costs added during April		$144,000	$26,700	$69,000

If you want to use Excel to solve this problem, go to the Excel Lab at **www.prenhall.com/horngren/cost13e** and download the template for Problem 17-38.

Required

1. Summarize total Binding Department costs for April 2009, and assign these costs to units completed (and transferred out) and to units in ending work in process.
2. Prepare journal entries for April transfers from the Printing Department to the Binding Department and from the Binding Department to Finished Goods.

17-39 Transferred-in costs, FIFO method. Refer to the information in Problem 17-38. Suppose that Publish, Inc. uses the FIFO method instead of the weighted-average method in all of its departments. The only changes to Problem 17-38 under the FIFO method are that total transferred-in costs of beginning work in process on April 1 are $27,855 (instead of $32,775) and that total transferred-in costs added during April are $141,750 (instead of $144,000).

If you want to use Excel to solve this problem, go to the Excel Lab at **www.prenhall.com/horngren/cost13e** and download the template for Problem 17-38.

Required

1. Using the FIFO process-costing method, do Problem 17-38.
2. If you did Problem 17-38, explain any difference between the cost of work completed and transferred out and the cost of ending work in process in the Binding Department under the weighted-average method and the FIFO method.

17-40 Transferred-in costs, weighted-average and FIFO methods. Frito-Lay, Inc., manufactures convenience foods, including potato chips and corn chips. Production of corn chips occurs in four departments: Cleaning, Mixing, Cooking, and Drying and Packaging. Consider the Drying and Packaging Department, where direct materials (packaging) are added at the end of the process. Conversion costs are added evenly during the process. The accounting records of a Frito-Lay plant provide the following information for corn chips in its Drying and Packaging Department during a weekly period (week 37):

	Physical Units (Cases)	Transferred-In Costs	Direct Materials	Conversion Costs
Beginning work in process[a]	1,250	$29,000	$ 0	$ 9,060
Transferred in during week 37 from Cooking Department	5,000			
Completed during week 37	5,250			
Ending work in process, week 37[b]	1,000			
Total costs added during week 37		$96,000	$25,200	$38,400

[a]Degree of completion: transferred-in costs, 100%; direct materials, ?%; conversion costs, 80%.
[b]Degree of completion: transferred-in costs, 100%; direct materials, ?%; conversion costs, 40%.

Required

1. Using the weighted-average method, summarize the total Drying and Packaging Department costs for week 37, and assign total costs to units completed (and transferred out) and to units in ending work in process.
2. Assume that the FIFO method is used for the Drying and Packaging Department. Under FIFO, the transferred-in costs for work-in-process beginning inventory in week 37 are $28,920 (instead of $29,000 under the weighted-average method), and the transferred-in costs during week 37 from the Cooking Department are $94,000 (instead of $96,000 under the weighted-average method). All other data are unchanged. Summarize the total Drying and Packaging Department costs for week 37, and assign total costs to units completed and transferred out and to units in ending work in process using the FIFO method.

17-41 Standard-costing with beginning and ending work in process. Paquita's Pearls Company (PPC) is a manufacturer of knock off jewelry. Paquita attends Fashion Week in New York City every September and February to gauge the latest fashion trends in jewelry. She then makes trendy jewelry at a fraction of the cost of those designers who participate in Fashion Week. This Fall's biggest item is triple-stranded pearl necklaces. Because of her large volume, Paquita uses process costing to account for her production. In October, she had started some of the triple strands. She continued to work on those in November. Costs and output figures are as follows:

Paquita's Pearls Company
Process Costing
For the Month Ended November 30, 2010

	Units	Direct Materials	Conversion Costs
Standard cost per unit		$2.50	$10.00
Work in process, beginning inventory (Nov. 1)	25,000	$62,500	$187,500
Degree of completion of beginning work in process		100%	75%
Started during November	126,250		
Completed and transferred out	125,000		
Work in process, ending inventory (Nov. 30)	26,250		
Degree of completion of ending work in process		100%	50%
Total costs added during November		$327,500	$1,207,415

Required

1. Compute equivalent units for direct materials and conversion costs. Show physical units in the first column of your schedule.
2. Compute the total standard costs of pearls transferred out in November and the total standard costs of the November 30 inventory of work in process.
3. Compute the total November variances for direct materials and conversion costs.

Collaborative Learning Problem

17-42 Operation costing (chapter appendix). Farkas Shoes, a high-end shoe manufacturer, produces two lines of shoes for women. The shoes are identical in design, but differ in the materials used and the trim added to the shoes. The basic shoes are made from a synthetic leather, have a synthetic insole, and have plain buttons decorating the upper. The elaborate shoes are made from genuine leather, have a special insole, and have creative buttons applied to the upper. Each shoe is assumed to use an identical amount of conversion costs for a given operation. Work orders 10399 and 10400 are representative work orders for the two types of shoes.

Farkas Shoes
Selected Work Orders
For the month ended 28 Feb 2009

	Work order 10399	Work order 10400
Quantity (pairs of shoes)	1,000	150
Direct Materials	Syn Leather	Gen Leather
	Syn Insole	FitDry Insole
	Plain Buttons	Creative Buttons
Operations		
1. Cut leather	Use	Use
2. Shape leather	Use	Use
3. Treat leather	Do not use	Use
4. Sew shoe	Use	Use
5. Machine application of buttons	Use	Do not use
6. Hand application of buttons	Do not use	Use

Selected budget information for February follows:

	Basic	Elaborate	Total
Units	30,000	2,250	32,250
Direct material costs	$390,000	$63,000	$453,000

Budgeted conversion costs for each operation for February follow:

Operation 1	$145,125	Operation 4	$67,725
Operation 2	58,050	Operation 5	13,500
Operation 3	4,275	Operation 6	2,025

Required

1. Using budgeted pairs of shoes as the denominator, calculate the budgeted conversion-cost rates for each of the six operations.
2. Using the information in requirement 1, calculate the budgeted cost of goods manufactured for the two February work orders.
3. Based on the two representative work orders for February, calculate the budgeted cost of each pair of shoes.

18 Spoilage, Rework, and Scrap

Learning Objectives

1. Distinguish among different types of spoilage, rework, and scrap
2. Account for spoilage in process costing using the weighted-average method
3. Account for spoilage in process costing using the first-in, first-out (FIFO) method
4. Account for spoilage in process costing using the standard-costing method
5. Account for spoilage in job costing
6. Account for rework in job costing
7. Account for scrap

When a product doesn't meet specifications but is subsequently repaired and sold, it is called rework. Firms try to minimize rework, and similarly, spoilage and scrap during production. Why? Because higher-than-normal levels of spoilage and scrap can have a significant negative effect on a company's profits. And rework can cause substantial production delays, as the following article shows.

Rework Delays Airbus[1]

The largest passenger plane ever built, the Airbus A380, has been a $6 billion headache for its European manufacturer, Airbus. A380 customers have endured one delay after another and are now wrestling with whether to stick with the A380 or bail out and order planes from archrival Boeing instead.

FedEx has already done just that, stunning Airbus in November 2006 by canceling a $3 billion order for ten planes and striking a $3.5 billion deal with Boeing for ten new 777s. The blow was the latest in a series of setbacks for the audacious $14 billion project to launch a 555-passenger aircraft—setbacks that have caused the once-highflying company to lose its lead over Boeing. Now, even as Airbus engineers in France and Germany race to sort out the wiring problems that sparked the delays, Airbus co-chief commercial officer John Leahy is waging just as critical a battle. His mission: Stop other A380 customers from heading for the exits. With 165 firm orders in place by October 2007, Airbus remains well shy of its break-even point.

"We think it's a great plane," says Mark Giuffre, a spokesman for UPS, whose order for ten A380 freighters has been pushed back from 2009 to mid-2010. "But we're concerned about [Airbus'] ability to make the proposed delivery schedule."

On a wintry January day in 2007 in Hamburg ... top Airbus execs in suits and ties joined workers ... to celebrate the final wiring of an A380 destined for Singapore Airlines .... While the first Singapore jet's problems have been solved, another 20 planes will have to be flown from the company's Toulouse factory to Hamburg, where ill-fitting

[1] *Source:* Nelson D. Schwartz, "Big Plane, Big Problems," *Fortune*, March 1, 2007; Michelle Dunlop, "Airbus delivers first A380 today, more than a year late," *HeraldNet*, October 15, 2007 (www.heraldnet.com/article/20071015/NEWS01/710150041&news01ad=1 accessed October 23, 2007).

wiring is ripped out and painstakingly replaced. Not until the end of 2008 will new software systems allow engineers in Toulouse and Hamburg to work together and avoid any rewiring.

Like Airbus, companies are increasingly focused on improving the quality of, and reducing the defects in, their products, services, and activities. A rate of defects regarded as normal in the past is no longer tolerable. In this chapter, we focus on three types of costs that arise as a result of defects—spoilage, rework, and scrap—and ways to account for them. We also describe how to determine (1) cost of products, (2) cost of goods sold, and (3) inventory values when spoilage, rework, and scrap occur.

Terminology

Learning Objective 1

Distinguish among spoilage,

. . . unacceptable units of production

rework,

. . . unacceptable units of production subsequently repaired

and scrap

. . . leftover material

The terms used in this chapter may seem familiar, but be sure you understand them in the context of management accounting.

Spoilage is units of production—whether fully or partially completed—that do not meet the specifications required by customers for good units and that are discarded or sold at reduced prices. Some examples of spoilage are defective shirts, jeans, shoes, and carpeting sold as "seconds," or defective aluminum cans sold to aluminum manufacturers for remelting to produce other aluminum products.

Rework is units of production that do not meet the specifications required by customers but which are subsequently repaired and sold as good finished units. For example, defective units of products (such as pagers, computers, and telephones) detected during or after the production process but before units are shipped to customers can sometimes be reworked and sold as good products.

Scrap is residual material that results from manufacturing a product. It has low sales value compared with the total sales value of the product. Examples are short lengths from woodworking operations, edges from plastic molding operations, and frayed cloth and end cuts from suit-making operations.

Some amounts of spoilage, rework, or scrap are inherent in many production processes. For example, semiconductor manufacturing is so complex and delicate that some spoiled units are commonly produced; usually, the spoiled units cannot be reworked. In the manufacture of high-precision machine tools, spoiled units can be reworked to meet standards, but only at a considerable cost. And in the mining industry, companies process ore that contains varying amounts of valuable metals and rock. Some amount of rock, which is scrap, is inevitable.

Different Types of Spoilage

Accounting for spoilage aims to determine the magnitude of spoilage costs and to distinguish between costs of normal and abnormal spoilage.[2] To manage, control, and reduce

[2] The helpful suggestions of Samuel Laimon, University of Saskatchewan, are gratefully acknowledged.

spoilage costs, companies need to highlight them, not bury them as an unidentified part of the costs of good units manufactured.

To illustrate normal and abnormal spoilage, consider Mendonza Plastics, which makes plastic casings for the iMac computer using plastic injection molding. In January 2008, Mendonza incurs costs of $615,000 to produce 20,500 units. Of these 20,500 units, 20,000 are good units and 500 are spoiled units. Mendonza has no beginning inventory and no ending inventory that month. Of the 500 spoiled units, 400 units are spoiled because the injection molding machines are unable to manufacture good casings 100% of the time. That is, these units are spoiled even though the machines were run carefully and efficiently. The remaining 100 units are spoiled because of machine breakdowns and operator errors.

Normal Spoilage

Normal spoilage is spoilage inherent in a particular production process. In particular, it arises even when the process is operated in an efficient manner. The costs of normal spoilage are typically included as a component of the costs of good units manufactured because good units cannot be made without also making some units that are spoiled. There is a tradeoff between the speed of production and the normal spoilage rate. Management makes a conscious decision about how many units to produce per hour with the understanding that at the rate decided on, a certain level of spoilage is almost unavoidable. This justifies including the cost of normal spoilage in the cost of the good units completed. At Mendonza Plastics, the 400 units spoiled because of the limitations of injection molding machines and despite efficient operating conditions are considered normal spoilage. The calculations are as follows:

Manufacturing cost per unit, $615,000 ÷ 20,500 units = $30	
Manufacturing costs of good units alone, $30 per unit × 20,000 units	$600,000
Normal spoilage costs, $30 per unit × 400 units	12,000
Manufacturing costs of good units completed (includes normal spoilage)	$612,000

$$\text{Manufacturing cost per good unit} = \frac{\$612{,}000}{20{,}000 \text{ units}} = \$30.60$$

Because normal spoilage is the spoilage related to the good units produced, normal spoilage rates are computed by dividing units of normal spoilage by total *good units completed*, not total *actual units started* in production. At Mendonza Plastics, the normal spoilage rate is therefore computed as 400 ÷ 20,000 = 0.02.

Abnormal Spoilage

Abnormal spoilage is spoilage that is not inherent in a particular production process and would not arise under efficient operating conditions. At Mendonza, the 100 units spoiled because of machine breakdowns and operator errors are abnormal spoilage. Abnormal spoilage is usually regarded as avoidable and controllable. Line operators and other plant personnel generally can decrease or eliminate abnormal spoilage by identifying the reasons for machine breakdowns, operator errors, and the like, and by taking steps to prevent their recurrence. To highlight the effect of abnormal spoilage costs, companies calculate the units of abnormal spoilage and record the cost in the Loss from Abnormal Spoilage account, which appears as a separate line item in the income statement. At Mendonza, the loss from abnormal spoilage is $3,000 ($30 per unit × 100 units).

Issues about accounting for spoilage arise in both process-costing and job-costing systems. We first present the accounting for spoilage in process-costing systems.

Process Costing and Spoilage

How do process-costing systems account for spoiled units? We have already said that units of abnormal spoilage should be counted and recorded separately in a Loss from Abnormal Spoilage account. But what about units of normal spoilage? The correct method is to count these units when computing output units—physical or equivalent—in a process-costing system. The following example and discussion illustrate this approach.

Count All Spoilage

Example 1: Chipmakers, Inc., manufactures computer chips for television sets. All direct materials are added at the beginning of the production process. To highlight issues that arise with normal spoilage, we assume no beginning inventory and focus only on direct material costs. The following data are available for May 2008.

	A	B	C
1		Physical Units	Direct Materials
2	Work in process, beginning inventory (May 1)	0	
3	Started during May	10,000	
4	Good units completed and transferred out during May	5,000	
5	Units spoiled (all normal spoilage)	1,000	
6	Work in process, ending inventory (May 31)	4,000	
7	Degree of completion of ending work in process		100%
8	Direct material costs added in May		$270,000

Spoilage is detected upon completion of the process and has zero net disposal value.

An **inspection point** is the stage of the production process at which products are examined to determine whether they are acceptable or unacceptable units. Spoilage is typically assumed to occur at the stage of completion where inspection takes place. As a result, the spoiled units in our example are assumed to be 100% complete with respect to direct materials.

Exhibit 18-1 calculates and assigns cost per unit of direct materials. Overall, Chipmakers generated 10,000 equivalent units of output: 5,000 equivalent units in good units completed (5,000 physical units × 100%), 4,000 units in ending work in process (4,000 physical units × 100%), and 1,000 equivalent units in normal spoilage (1,000 physical units × 100%). Given total direct material costs of $270,000 in May, this yields an equivalent-unit cost of $27. The total cost of good units completed and transferred out, which includes the cost of normal spoilage, is then $162,000 (6,000 equivalent units × $27), while the ending work in process is assigned a cost of $108,000 (4,000 equivalent units × $27).

Exhibit 18-1

Effect of Recognizing Equivalent Units in Spoilage for Direct Material Costs Chipmakers, Inc., for May 2008

	A	B
1		Approach Counting Spoiled Units When Computing Output in Equivalent Units
2	Costs to account for	$270,000
3	Divide by equivalent units of output	÷ 10,000
4	Cost per equivalent unit of output	$ 27
5	Assignment of costs:	
6	Good units completed (5,000 units x $27 per unit)	$135,000
7	Add normal spoilage (1,000 units x $27 per unit)	27,000
8	Total costs of good units completed and transferred out	162,000
9	Work in process, ending (4,000 units x $27 per unit)	108,000
10	Costs accounted for	$270,000

There are two noteworthy features of this approach. First, the 4,000 units in ending work in process are not assigned any of the costs of normal spoilage. This is appropriate because the units have not yet been inspected. While the units in ending work in process undoubtedly include some that will be detected as spoiled when inspected, these units will only be identified when the units are completed in the subsequent accounting period. At that time, costs of normal spoilage will be assigned to the good units completed in that period. Second, the approach used in Exhibit 18-1 delineates the cost of normal spoilage as $27,000. By highlighting the magnitude of this cost, the approach helps to focus management's attention on the potential economic benefits of reducing spoilage.

Five-Step Procedure for Process Costing with Spoilage

Example 2: Anzio Company manufactures a recycling container in its Forming Department. Direct materials are added at the beginning of the production process. Conversion costs are added evenly during the production process. Some units of this product are spoiled as a result of defects, which are detectable only upon inspection of finished units. Normally, spoiled units are 10% of the finished output of good units. That is, for every 10 good units produced, there is 1 unit of normal spoilage. Summary data for July 2008 are:

File Edit View Insert Format Tools Data Window Help

	A	B	C	D	E
1		Physical Units (1)	Direct Materials (2)	Conversion Costs (3)	Total Costs (4) = (2) + (3)
2	Work in process, beginning inventory (July 1)	1,500	$12,000	$ 9,000	$ 21,000
3	Degree of completion of beginning work in process		100%	60%	
4	Started during July	8,500			
5	Good units completed and transferred out during July	7,000			
6	Work in process, ending inventory (July 31)	2,000			
7	Degree of completion of ending work in process		100%	50%	
8	Total costs added during July		$76,500	$89,100	$165,600
9	Normal spoilage as a percentage of good units	10%			
10	Degree of completion of normal spoilage		100%	100%	
11	Degree of completion of abnormal spoilage		100%	100%	

The five-step procedure for process costing used in Chapter 17 needs only slight modification to accommodate spoilage.

Step 1: Summarize the Flow of Physical Units. Identify the number of units of both normal and abnormal spoilage.

$$\text{Total Spoilage} = \left(\text{Units in beginning work-in-process inventory} + \text{Units started}\right) - \left(\text{Good units completed and transferred out} + \text{Units in ending work-in-process inventory}\right)$$

$$= (1{,}500 + 8{,}500) - (7{,}000 + 2{,}000)$$
$$= 10{,}000 - 9{,}000$$
$$= 1{,}000 \text{ units}$$

Recall that normal spoilage is 10% of good output at Anzio Company. Therefore, normal spoilage = 10% of the 7,000 units of *good* output = 700 units.

$$\text{Abnormal spoilage} = \text{Total spoilage} - \text{Normal spoilage}$$
$$= 1{,}000 \text{ units} - 700 \text{ units}$$
$$= 300 \text{ units}$$

Step 2: Compute Output in Terms of Equivalent Units. Compute equivalent units for spoilage in the same way we compute equivalent units for good units. As illustrated above, all spoiled units are included in the computation of output units. Because Anzio's inspection point is at the completion of production, the same amount of work will have been done on each spoiled and each completed good unit.

Step 3: Summarize Total Costs to Account For. The total costs to account for are all the costs debited to Work in Process. The details for this step are similar to step 3 in Chapter 17.

Step 4: Compute Cost per Equivalent Unit. This step is similar to step 4 in Chapter 17.

Step 5: Assign Total Costs to Units Completed, to Spoiled Units, and to Units in Ending Work in Process. This step now includes computation of the cost of spoiled units and the cost of good units.

We illustrate these five steps of process costing for the weighted-average, FIFO, and standard-costing methods.

Weighted-Average Method and Spoilage

Learning Objective 2

Account for spoilage in process costing using the weighted-average method

. . . spoilage cost based on total costs and equivalent units completed to date

Exhibit 18-2, Panel A, presents steps 1 and 2 to calculate equivalent units of work done to date and includes calculations of equivalent units of normal and abnormal spoilage. Exhibit 18-2, Panel B, presents steps 3, 4, and 5 (together called the production-cost worksheet).

Step 3 summarizes total costs to account for. Step 4 presents cost-per-equivalent-unit calculations using the weighted-average method. Note how, for each cost category, costs of beginning work in process and costs of work done in the current period are totaled and divided by equivalent units of all work done to date to calculate the weighted-average cost per equivalent unit. Step 5 assigns total costs to completed units, normal and abnormal spoiled units, and ending inventory by multiplying the equivalent units calculated in step 2 by the cost per equivalent unit calculated in step 4. Also note that the \$13,825 costs of normal spoilage are added to the costs of the related good units completed and transferred out.

$$\text{Cost per good unit completed and transferred out of the process} = \frac{\text{Total costs transferred out (including normal spoilage)}}{\text{Number of good units produced}}$$

$$= \$152{,}075 \div 7{,}000 \text{ good units} = \$21.725 \text{ per good unit}$$

This amount is not equal to \$19.75 per good unit, the sum of the \$8.85 cost per equivalent unit of direct materials plus the \$10.90 cost per equivalent unit of conversion costs. That's because the cost per good unit equals the sum of the direct material and conversion costs per equivalent unit, \$19.75, plus a share of normal spoilage, \$1.975 (\$13,825 ÷ 7,000 good units), for a total of \$21.725 per good unit. The \$5,925 costs of abnormal spoilage are charged to the Loss from Abnormal Spoilage account and do not appear in the costs of good units.[3]

FIFO Method and Spoilage

Learning Objective 3

Account for spoilage in process costing using the first-in, first-out (FIFO) method

. . . spoilage cost based on costs of current period and equivalent units of work done in current period

Exhibit 18-3, Panel A, presents steps 1 and 2 using the FIFO method, which focuses on equivalent units of work done in the current period. Exhibit 18-3, Panel B, presents steps 3, 4, and 5. Note how when assigning costs, the FIFO method keeps the costs of the beginning work in process separate and distinct from the costs of work done in the current period. All spoilage costs are assumed to be related to units completed during this period, using the unit costs of the current period.[4]

---

[3] The actual costs of spoilage (and rework) are often greater than the costs recorded in the accounting system because the opportunity costs of disruption of the production line, storage, and lost contribution margins are not recorded in accounting systems. Chapter 19 discusses these opportunity costs from the perspective of cost management.

[4] To simplify calculations under FIFO, spoiled units are accounted for as if they were started in the current period. Although some of the beginning work in process probably did spoil, all spoilage is treated as if it came from current production.

Exhibit 18-2 Weighted-Average Method of Process Costing with Spoilage
Forming Department of the Anzio Company for July 2008

PANEL A: Steps 1 and 2—Summarize Output in Physical Units and Compute Equivalent Units

	A	B	C	D	E
1			(Step 1)	(Step 2)	
2				Equivalent Units	
3		Flow of Production	Physical Units	Direct Materials	Conversion Costs
4		Work in process, beginning (given, p. 642)	1,500		
5		Started during current period (given, p. 642)	8,500		
6		To account for	10,000		
7		Good units completed and transferred out during current period	7,000	7,000	7,000
8		Normal spoilage[a]	700		
9		(700 x 100%; 700 x 100%)		700	700
10		Abnormal spoilage[b]	300		
11		(300 x 100%; 300 x 100%)		300	300
12		Work in process, ending[c] (given, p. 642)	2,000		
13		(2,000 x 100%; 2,000 x 50%)		2,000	1,000
14		Accounted for	10,000		
15		Work done to date		10,000	9,000
16					
17	[a]Normal spoilage is 10% of good units transferred out: 10% x 7,000 = 700 units. Degree of completion of normal spoilage				
18	in this department: direct materials, 100%; conversion costs, 100%.				
19	[b]Abnormal spoilage = Total spoilage – Normal spoilage = 1,000 – 700 = 300 units. Degree of completion of abnormal spoilage				
20	in this department: direct materials, 100%; conversion costs, 100%.				
21	[c]Degree of completion in this department: direct materials, 100%; conversion costs, 50%.				

PANEL B: Steps 3, 4, and 5—Summarize Total Costs to Account For, Compute Cost per Equivalent Unit, and Assign Total Costs to Units Completed, to Spoiled Units, and to Units in Ending Work in Process

			Total Production Costs	Direct Materials		Conversion Costs
23						
24	(Step 3)	Work in process, beginning (given, p. 642)	$ 21,000	$12,000		$ 9,000
25		Costs added in current period (given, p. 642)	165,600	76,500		89,100
26		Total costs to account for	$186,600	$88,500		$98,100
27	(Step 4)	Costs incurred to date		$88,500		$98,100
28		Divided by equivalent units of work done to date		÷10,000		÷ 9,000
29		Cost per equivalent unit		$ 8.85		$ 10.90
30	(Step 5)	Assignment of costs:				
31		Good units completed and transferred out (7,000 units)				
32		Costs before adding normal spoilage	$138,250	(7,000[d] x $8.85)	+	(7,000[d] x $10.90)
33		Normal spoilage (700 units)	13,825	(700[d] x $8.85)	+	(700[d] x $10.90)
34	(A)	Total costs of good units completed and transferred out	152,075			
35	(B)	Abnormal spoilage (300 units)	5,925	(300[d] x $8.85)	+	(300[d] x $10.90)
36	(C)	Work in process, ending (2,000 units)	28,600	(2,000[d] x $8.85)	+	(1,000[d] x $10.90)
37	(A)+(B)+(C)	Total costs accounted for	$186,600	$88,500	+	$98,100
38						
39	[d]Equivalent units of direct materials and conversion costs calculated in step 2 in Panel A.					

Exhibit 18-3 First-In, First-Out (FIFO) Method of Process Costing with Spoilage
Forming Department of the Anzio Company for July 2008

PANEL A: Steps 1 and 2—Summarize Output in Physical Units and Compute Equivalent Units

	A	B	C	D	E
1			(Step 1)	(Step 2)	
2				Equivalent Units	
3		Flow of Production	Physical Units	Direct Materials	Conversion Costs
4		Work in process, beginning (given, p. 642)	1,500		
5		Started during current period (given, p. 642)	8,500		
6		To account for	10,000		
7		Good units completed and transferred out during current period:			
8		From beginning work in process[a]	1,500		
9		[1,500 x (100% –100%); 1,500 x (100% –60%)]		0	600
10		Started and completed	5,500[b]		
11		(5,500 x 100%; 5,500 x 100%)		5,500	5,500
12		Normal spoilage[c]	700		
13		(700 x 100%; 700 x 100%)		700	700
14		Abnormal spoilage[d]	300		
15		(300 x 100%; 300 x 100%)		300	300
16		Work in process, ending[e] (given, p. 642)	2,000		
17		(2,000 x 100%; 2,000 x 50%)		2,000	1,000
18		Accounted for	10,000		
19		Work done in current period only		8,500	8,100
20					
21	[a]Degree of completion in this department: direct materials, 100%; conversion costs, 60%.				
22	[b]7,000 physical units completed and transferred out minus 1,500 physical units completed and transferred out from beginning				
23	work-in-process inventory.				
24	[c]Normal spoilage is 10% of good units transferred out: 10% x 7,000 = 700 units. Degree of completion of normal spoilage				
25	in this department: direct materials, 100%; conversion costs, 100%.				
26	[d]Abnormal spoilage = Actual spoilage – Normal spoilage = 1,000 – 700 = 300 units. Degree of completion of abnormal spoilage				
27	in this department: direct materials, 100%; conversion costs, 100%.				
28	[e]Degree of completion in this department: direct materials, 100%; conversion costs, 50%.				

PANEL B: Steps 3, 4, and 5—Summarize Total Costs to Account For, Compute Cost per Equivalent Unit, and Assign Total Costs to Units Completed, to Spoiled Units, and to Units in Ending Work in Process

			Total Production Costs	Direct Materials		Conversion Costs
30						
31	(Step 3)	Work in process, beginning (given, p. 642)	$ 21,000	$12,000		$ 9,000
32		Costs added in current period (given, p. 642)	165,600	76,500		89,100
33		Total costs to account for	$186,600	$88,500		$98,100
34	(Step 4)	Costs added in current period		$76,500		$89,100
35		Divided by equivalent units of work done in current period		÷ 8,500		÷ 8,100
36		Cost per equivalent unit		$ 9.00		$ 11.00
37	(Step 5)	Assignment of costs:				
38		Good units completed and transferred out (7,000 units)				
39		Work in process, beginning (1,500 units)	$ 21,000	$12,000	+	$9,000
40		Costs added to beginning work in process in current period	6,600	(0[f] x $9)	+	(600[f] x $11)
41		Total from beginning inventory before normal spoilage	27,600			
42		Started and completed before normal spoilage (5,500 units)	110,000	(5,500[f] x $9)	+	(5,500[f] x $11)
43		Normal spoilage (700 units)	14,000	(700[f] x $9)	+	(700[f] x $11)
44	(A)	Total costs of good units completed and transferred out	151,600			
45	(B)	Abnormal spoilage (300 units)	6,000	(300[f] x $9)	+	(300[f] x $11)
46	(C)	Work in process, ending (2,000 units)	29,000	(2,000[f] x $9)	+	(1,000[f] x $11)
47	(A)+(B)+(C)	Total costs accounted for	$186,600	$88,500	+	$98,100
48						
49						
50						
51	[f]Equivalent units of direct materials and conversion costs calculated in step 2 in Panel A.					

Standard-Costing Method and Spoilage

Learning Objective 4

Account for spoilage in process costing using the standard-costing method

. . . spoilage cost based on standard cost as the cost per equivalent unit

This section assumes you have studied the standard-costing method in Chapter 17 (pp. 615–619). Instructors and students who wish to skip this section can go directly to the section on Job Costing and Spoilage, page 648, without any loss of continuity.

The standard-costing method simplifies the computations for normal and abnormal spoilage. To illustrate, suppose Anzio Company develops the following standard costs per unit for work done in the Forming Department in July 2008:

Direct materials	$ 8.50
Conversion costs	10.50
Total manufacturing cost	$19.00

Assume the same standard costs per unit also apply to the beginning inventory: 1,500 (1,500 × 100%) equivalent units of direct materials and 900 (1,500 × 60%) equivalent units of conversion costs. Hence, the beginning inventory at standard costs is:

Direct materials, 1,500 units × $8.50 per unit	$12,750
Conversion costs, 900 units × $10.50 per unit	9,450
Total manufacturing costs	$22,200

Exhibit 18-4, Panel A, presents steps 1 and 2 for calculating physical and equivalent units. These steps are the same as for the FIFO method described in Exhibit 18-3. Exhibit 18-4, Panel B, presents steps 3, 4, and 5.

The costs to account for in step 3 are at standard costs and, hence, they differ from the costs to account for under the weighted-average and FIFO methods, which are at actual costs. In step 4, cost per equivalent unit is simply the standard cost: $8.50 per unit for direct materials and $10.50 per unit for conversion costs. The standard-costing method makes calculating equivalent-unit costs unnecessary, so it simplifies process costing. Step 5 assigns standard costs to units completed (including normal spoilage), to abnormal spoilage, and to ending work-in-process inventory by multiplying the equivalent units calculated in step 2 by the standard costs per equivalent unit presented in step 4. Variances can then be measured and analyzed in the manner described in Chapter 17 (pp. 617–619).[5]

Journal Entries

The information from Panel B in Exhibits 18-2, 18-3, and 18-4 supports the following journal entries to transfer good units completed to finished goods and to recognize the loss from abnormal spoilage.

	Weighted Average		FIFO		Standard Costs	
Finished Goods	152,075		151,600		146,300	
Work in Process—Forming		152,075		151,600		146,300
To record transfer of good units completed in July.						
Loss from Abnormal Spoilage	5,925		6,000		5,700	
Work in Process—Forming		5,925		6,000		5,700
To record abnormal spoilage detected in July.						

[5] For example, from Exhibit 18-4, Panel B, the standard costs for July are direct materials used, 8,500 × $8.50 = $72,250, and conversion costs, 8,100 × $10.50 = $85,050. From page 642, the actual costs added during July are direct materials, $76,500, and conversion costs, $89,100, resulting in a direct materials variance of $72,250 − $76,500 = $4,250 U and a conversion costs variance of $85,050 − $89,100 = $4,050 U. These variances could then be subdivided further as in Chapters 7 and 8; the abnormal spoilage would be part of the efficiency variance.

Exhibit 18-4 Standard-Costing Method of Process Costing with Spoilage Forming Department of the Anzio Company for July 2008

PANEL A: Steps 1 and 2—Summarize Output in Physical Units and Compute Equivalent Units

	A	B	C	D	E
1			(Step 1)	(Step 2)	
2				Equivalent Units	
3		Flow of Production	Physical Units	Direct Materials	Conversion Costs
4		Work in process, beginning (given, p. 642)	1,500		
5		Started during current period (given, p. 642)	8,500		
6		To account for	10,000		
7		Good units completed and transferred out during current period:			
8		From beginning work in process[a]	1,500		
9		[1,500 x (100% –100%); 1,500 x (100% –60%)]		0	600
10		Started and completed	5,500[b]		
11		(5,500 x 100%; 5,500 x 100%)		5,500	5,500
12		Normal spoilage[c]	700		
13		(700 x 100%; 700 x 100%)		700	700
14		Abnormal spoilage[d]	300		
15		(300 x 100%; 300 x 100%)		300	300
16		Work in process, ending[e] (given, p. 642)	2,000		
17		(2,000 x 100%; 2,000 x 50%)		2,000	1,000
18		Accounted for	10,000		
19		Work done in current period only		8,500	8,100
20					
21	[a]Degree of completion in this department: direct materials, 100%; conversion costs, 60%.				
22	[b]7,000 physical units completed and transferred out minus 1,500 physical units completed and transferred out from beginning				
23	work-in-process inventory.				
24	[c]Normal spoilage is 10% of good units transferred out: 10% x 7,000 = 700 units. Degree of completion of normal spoilage in this				
25	department: direct materials, 100%; conversion costs, 100%.				
26	[d]Abnormal spoilage = Actual spoilage – Normal spoilage = 1,000 – 700 = 300 units. Degree of completion of abnormal spoilage in this				
27	department: direct materials, 100%; conversion costs, 100%.				
28	[e]Degree of completion in this department: direct materials, 100%; conversion costs, 50%.				

PANEL B: Steps 3, 4, and 5—Summarize Total Costs to Account For, Compute Cost per Equivalent Unit, and Assign Total Costs to Units Completed, to Spoiled Units, and to Units in Ending Work in Process

	A	B	C	D	E
30			Total Production Costs	Direct Materials	Conversion Costs
31	(Step 3)	Work in process, beginning (given, p. 646)	$ 22,200	(1,500 x $8.50)	(900 x $10.50)
32		Costs added in current period at standard prices	157,300	(8,500 x $8.50)	(8,100 x $10.50)
33		Total costs to account for	$179,500	$85,000	$94,500
34	(Step 4)	Standard costs per equivalent unit (given, p. 646)	$ 19.00	$ 8.50	$ 10.50
35	(Step 5)	Assignment of costs at standard costs:			
36		Good units completed and transferred out (7,000 units)			
37		Work in process, beginning (1,500 units)	$ 22,200	(1,500 x $8.50)	+ (900 x $10.50)
38		Costs added to beginning work in process in current period	6,300	(0[f] x $8.50)	+ (600[f] x $10.50)
39		Total from beginning inventory before normal spoilage	28,500		
40		Started and completed before normal spoilage (5,500 units)	104,500	(5,500[f] x $8.50)	+ (5,500[f] x $10.50)
41		Normal spoilage (700 units)	13,300	(700[f] x $8.50)	+ (700[f] x $10.50)
42	(A)	Total costs of good units completed and transferred out	146,300		
43	(B)	Abnormal spoilage (300 units)	5,700	(300[f] x $8.50)	+ (300[f] x $10.50)
44	(C)	Work in process, ending (450 units)	27,500	(2,000[f] x $8.50)	+ (1,000[f] x $10.50)
45	(A)+(B)+(C)	Total costs accounted for	$179,500	$85,000	+ $94,500
46					
47	[f]Equivalent units of direct materials and conversion costs calculated in step 2 in Panel A.				

Inspection Points and Allocating Costs of Normal Spoilage

Our Anzio Company example assumes inspection occurs upon completion of the units. However, spoilage might actually occur at various stages of the production process, although it is typically detected only at one or more inspection points. The cost of spoiled units is assumed to equal all costs incurred in producing spoiled units up to the point of inspection. When spoiled goods have a disposal value (for example, carpeting sold as "seconds"), the net cost of spoilage is computed by deducting the disposal value from the costs of the spoiled goods that have been accumulated up to the inspection point. The unit costs of normal and abnormal spoilage are the same when the two are detected at the same inspection point. However, situations may arise when abnormal spoilage is detected at a different point from normal spoilage. Consider shirt manufacturing. Normal spoilage in the form of defective shirts is identified upon inspection at the end of the production process. Now suppose a faulty machine causes many defective shirts to be produced at the halfway point of the production process. These defective shirts are abnormal spoilage and occur at a different point in the production process from normal spoilage. In such cases, the unit cost of abnormal spoilage, which is based on costs incurred up to the halfway point of the production process, differs from the unit cost of normal spoilage, which is based on costs incurred through the end of the production process.

Costs of abnormal spoilage are separately accounted for as losses of the accounting period in which they are detected. However, recall that normal spoilage costs are added to the costs of good units, which raises an additional issue: Should normal spoilage costs be allocated between completed units and ending work-in-process inventory? *The common approach is to presume that normal spoilage occurs at the inspection point in the production cycle and to allocate its cost over all units that have passed that point during the accounting period.* In the Anzio Company example, spoilage is assumed to occur when units are inspected at the end of the production process, so no costs of normal spoilage are allocated to ending work in process.

The costs of normal spoilage are allocated to units in ending work in process—in addition to completed units—if the units in ending work in process have passed the inspection point. For example, if the inspection point is at the halfway point of production, then any ending work in process that is at least 50% complete would be allocated a full measure of normal spoilage costs, and those spoilage costs would be calculated on the basis of all costs incurred up to the inspection point. But if ending work in process is less than 50% complete, no normal spoilage costs would be allocated to it. The appendix to this chapter contains a discussion of spoilage when units are inspected at different points in the production process.

Early and frequent inspections prevent any further direct materials and conversion costs being wasted on units that are already spoiled. If inspection can occur when units are 80% (rather than 100%) complete as to conversion costs and spoilage occurs prior to the 80% point, a company can avoid incurring the final 20% of conversion costs on the spoiled units.

Job Costing and Spoilage

Account for spoilage in job costing

. . . normal spoilage assigned directly or indirectly to job; abnormal spoilage written off as a loss of the period

The concepts of normal and abnormal spoilage also apply to job-costing systems. Abnormal spoilage is separately identified so companies can work to eliminate it altogether. Costs of abnormal spoilage are not considered to be inventoriable costs and are written off as costs of the accounting period in which the abnormal spoilage is detected. Normal spoilage costs in job-costing systems—as in process-costing systems—are inventoriable costs, although increasingly companies are tolerating only small amounts of spoilage as normal. When assigning costs, job-costing systems generally distinguish *normal spoilage attributable to a specific job from normal spoilage common to all jobs.*

We describe accounting for spoilage in job costing using the following example.

Example 3: In the Hull Machine Shop, 5 aircraft parts out of a job lot of 50 aircraft parts are spoiled. Costs assigned prior to the inspection point are $2,000 per part. Our presentation here and in subsequent sections focuses on how the $2,000 cost per part is accounted for. When the spoilage is detected, the spoiled goods are inventoried at $600 per part, the net disposal value.

Normal spoilage attributable to a specific job When normal spoilage occurs because of the specifications of a particular job, that job bears the cost of the spoilage minus the disposal value of the spoilage. The journal entry to recognize disposal value (items in parentheses indicate subsidiary ledger postings) is:

Materials Control (spoiled goods at current net disposal value):		
5 units × $600 per unit	3,000	
Work-in-Process Control (specific job): 5 units × $600 per unit		3,000

Note, the Work-in-Process Control (specific job) has already been debited (charged) $10,000 for the spoiled parts (5 spoiled parts × $2,000 per part). The net cost of normal spoilage = $7,000 ($10,000 − $3,000), which is an additional cost of the 45 (50 − 5) good units produced. Therefore, total cost of the 45 good units is $97,000: $90,000 (45 units × $2,000 per unit) incurred to produce the good units plus the $7,000 net cost of normal spoilage. Cost per good unit is $2,155.56 ($97,000 ÷ 45 good units).

Normal spoilage common to all jobs In some cases, spoilage may be considered a normal characteristic of the production process. The spoilage inherent in production will, of course, occur when a specific job is being worked on. But the spoilage is not attributable to, and hence is not charged directly to, the specific job. Instead, the spoilage is allocated indirectly to the job as manufacturing overhead because the spoilage is common to all jobs. The journal entry is:

Materials Control (spoiled goods at current disposal value):		
5 units × $600 per unit	3,000	
Manufacturing Overhead Control (normal spoilage):		
($10,000 − $3,000)	7,000	
Work-in-Process Control (specific job): 5 units × $2,000 per unit		10,000

When normal spoilage is common to all jobs, the budgeted manufacturing overhead rate includes a provision for normal spoilage cost. Normal spoilage cost is spread, through overhead allocation, over all jobs rather than allocated to a specific job.[6] For example, if Hull produced 140 good units from all jobs in a given month, the $7,000 of normal spoilage overhead costs would be allocated at the rate of $50 per good unit ($7,000 ÷ 140 good units). Normal spoilage overhead costs allocated to the 45 good units in the job would be $2,250 ($50 × 45 good units). Total cost of the 45 good units is $92,250: $90,000 (45 units × $2,000 per unit) incurred to produce the good units plus $2,250 of normal spoilage overhead costs. Cost per good unit is $2,050 ($92,250 ÷ 45 good units).

Abnormal spoilage If the spoilage is abnormal, the net loss is charged to the Loss from Abnormal Spoilage account. Unlike normal spoilage costs, abnormal spoilage costs are not included as a part of the cost of good units produced. Total cost of the 45 good units is $90,000 (45 units × $2,000 per unit). Cost per good unit is $2,000 ($90,000 ÷ 45 good units).

Materials Control (spoiled goods at current disposal value):		
5 units × $600 per unit	3,000	
Loss from Abnormal Spoilage ($10,000 − $3,000)	7,000	
Work-in-Process Control (specific job): 5 units × $2,000 per unit		10,000

Even though, for external reporting purposes, abnormal spoilage costs are written off in the accounting period and are not linked to specific jobs or units, companies often identify the particular reasons for abnormal spoilage, and, when appropriate, link abnormal spoilage with specific jobs or units for cost management purposes.

---

[6] Note that costs already assigned to products are charged back to Manufacturing Overhead Control, which generally accumulates only costs incurred, not both costs incurred and costs already assigned.

Job Costing and Rework

Learning Objective 6

Account for rework in job costing

. . . normal rework assigned directly or indirectly to job; abnormal rework written off as a loss of the period

Rework is units of production that are inspected, determined to be unacceptable, repaired, and sold as acceptable finished goods. We again distinguish (1) normal rework attributable to a specific job, (2) normal rework common to all jobs, and (3) abnormal rework.

Consider the Hull Machine Shop data in Example 3 on page 648. Assume the five spoiled parts are reworked. The journal entry for the $10,000 of total costs (the details of these costs are assumed) assigned to the five spoiled units before considering rework costs is:

Work-in-Process Control (specific job)	10,000	
Materials Control		4,000
Wages Payable Control		4,000
Manufacturing Overhead Allocated		2,000

Assume the rework costs equal $3,800 (comprising $800 direct materials, $2,000 direct manufacturing labor, and $1,000 manufacturing overhead).

Normal rework attributable to a specific job If the rework is normal but occurs because of the requirements of a specific job, the rework costs are charged to that job. The journal entry is:

Work-in-Process Control (specific job)	3,800	
Materials Control		800
Wages Payable Control		2,000
Manufacturing Overhead Allocated		1,000

Normal rework common to all jobs When rework is normal and not attributable to a specific job, the costs of rework are charged to manufacturing overhead and are spread, through overhead allocation, over all jobs.

Manufacturing Overhead Control (rework costs)	3,800	
Materials Control		800
Wages Payable Control		2,000
Manufacturing Overhead Allocated		1,000

Abnormal rework If the rework is abnormal, it is recorded by charging abnormal rework to a loss account.

Loss from Abnormal Rework	3,800	
Materials Control		800
Wages Payable Control		2,000
Manufacturing Overhead Allocated		1,000

Accounting for rework in a process-costing system also requires abnormal rework to be distinguished from normal rework. Process costing accounts for abnormal rework in the same way as job costing. Accounting for normal rework follows the accounting described for normal rework common to all jobs (units) because masses of identical or similar units are being manufactured.

Costing rework focuses managers' attention on the resources wasted on activities that would not have to be undertaken if the product had been made correctly. The cost of rework prompts managers to seek ways to reduce rework, for example, by designing new products or processes, training workers, or investing in new machines. To eliminate rework and to simplify the accounting, some companies set a standard of zero rework. All rework is then treated as abnormal and is written off as a cost of the current period.

Accounting for Scrap

Learning Objective 7

Account for scrap

. . . reduces cost of job either at time of sale or at time of production

Scrap is residual material that results from manufacturing a product; it has low total sales value compared with the total sales value of the product. No distinction is made between normal and abnormal scrap because no cost is assigned to scrap. The only distinction made is between scrap attributable to a specific job and scrap common to all jobs.

There are two aspects of accounting for scrap:

1. Planning and control, including physical tracking
2. Inventory costing, including when and how scrap affects operating income

Initial entries to scrap records are commonly in physical terms. In various industries, companies quantify items such as stamped-out metal sheets or edges of molded plastic parts by weighing, counting, or some other measure. Scrap records not only help measure efficiency, but also help keep track of scrap, and so reduce the chances of theft. Companies use scrap records to prepare periodic summaries of the amounts of actual scrap compared with budgeted or standard amounts. Scrap is either sold or disposed of quickly or it is stored for later sale, disposal, or reuse.

Careful tracking of scrap often extends into the accounting records. Many companies maintain a distinct account for scrap costs somewhere in their accounting system. The issues here are similar to the issues in Chapter 16 regarding the accounting for byproducts:

- When should the value of scrap be recognized in the accounting records—at the time scrap is produced or at the time scrap is sold?
- How should revenues from scrap be accounted for?

To illustrate, we extend our Hull example. Assume the manufacture of aircraft parts generates scrap and that the scrap from a job has a net sales value of $900.

Recognizing Scrap at the Time of Its Sale

When the dollar amount of scrap is immaterial, the simplest accounting is to record the physical quantity of scrap returned to the storeroom and to regard scrap sales as a separate line item in the income statement. In this case, the only journal entry is:

Sale of scrap:	Cash or Accounts Receivable	900	
	Scrap Revenues		900

When the dollar amount of scrap is material and the scrap is sold quickly after it is produced, the accounting depends on whether the scrap is attributable to a specific job or is common to all jobs.

Scrap attributable to a specific job Job-costing systems sometimes trace scrap revenues to the jobs that yielded the scrap. This method is used only when the tracing can be done in an economically feasible way. For example, the Hull Machine Shop and its customers, such as the U.S. Department of Defense, may reach an agreement that provides for charging specific jobs with all rework or spoilage costs and then crediting these jobs with all scrap revenues that arise from the jobs. The journal entry is:

Scrap returned to storeroom:	No journal entry. [Notation of quantity received and related job entered in the inventory record]		
Sale of scrap:	Cash or Accounts Receivable	900	
	Work-in-Process Control		900
	Posting made to specific job cost record.		

Unlike spoilage and rework, there is no cost assigned to the scrap, so no distinction is made between normal and abnormal scrap. All scrap revenues, whatever the amount, are credited to the specific job. Scrap revenues reduce the costs of the job.

Scrap common to all jobs The journal entry in this case is:

Scrap returned to storeroom:	No journal entry. [Notation of quantity received and related job entered in the inventory record]		
Sale of scrap:	Cash or Accounts Receivable	900	
	Manufacturing Overhead Control		900
	Posting made to subsidiary ledger—"Sales of Scrap" column on department cost record.		

Scrap is not linked with any particular job or product. Instead, all products bear production costs without any credit for scrap revenues except in an indirect manner: Expected scrap revenues are considered when setting the budgeted manufacturing overhead rate. Thus, the budgeted overhead rate is lower than it would be if the overhead budget had not been reduced by expected scrap revenues. This method of accounting for scrap is also used in process costing when the dollar amount of scrap is immaterial. That's because the scrap in process costing is common to the manufacture of all the identical or similar units produced (and cannot be identified with specific units).

Recognizing Scrap at the Time of Its Production

Our preceding illustrations assume that scrap returned to the storeroom is sold quickly, so it is not assigned an inventory cost figure. Sometimes, as in the case with edges of molded plastic parts, the value of scrap is not immaterial, and the time between storing it and selling or reusing it can be long. In these situations, the company assigns an inventory cost to scrap at a conservative estimate of its net realizable value so that production costs and related scrap revenues are recognized in the same accounting period. Some companies tend to delay sales of scrap until its market price is considered attractive. Volatile price fluctuations are typical for scrap metal. In these cases, it's not easy to determine some "reasonable inventory value."

Scrap attributable to a specific job The journal entry in the Hull example is:

Scrap returned to storeroom:	Materials Control	900	
	Work-in-Process Control		900

Scrap common to all jobs The journal entry in this case is:

Scrap returned to storeroom:	Materials Control	900	
	Manufacturing Overhead Control		900

Observe that the Materials Control account is debited in place of Cash or Accounts Receivable. When the scrap is sold, the journal entry is:

Sale of scrap:	Cash or Accounts Receivable	900	
	Materials Control		900

Scrap is sometimes reused as direct material rather than sold as scrap. In this case, Materials Control is debited at its estimated net realizable value and then credited when the scrap is reused. For example, the entries when the scrap is common to all jobs are:

Scrap returned to storeroom:	Materials Control	900	
	Manufacturing Overhead Control		900
Reuse of scrap:	Work-in-Process Control	900	
	Materials Control		900

Concepts in Action

Managing Waste and Environmental Costs at Toyota

Toyota Motor Corporation, which is set to become the world's largest automotive manufacturer in 2007, builds and sells a wide range of vehicles under the Toyota, Lexus, and Scion brands. Toyota has done a wonderful job of reducing waste and environmental costs. Shoichiro Toyoda, honorary chairman and former president of Toyota Motor Corporation, defined waste as "anything other than the minimum amount of equipment, materials, parts, space, and workers' time which are absolutely essential to add value to the product." Scrap, generated from wasted materials and parts, poses additional problems because of its impact on the environment. Domestic and international environmental laws dictate that scrap materials be disposed of in an environmentally friendly way; therefore, they add to the cost of generating waste.

Toyota regards environmental preservation and improvement as a top-priority management issue. The company seeks to reduce the environmental burden at every stage of a car's lifecycle, from production, distribution, and use to disposal and recycling. It feeds the information learned from recycling processes back to the design stage in order to produce easy-to-recycle cars. Consistent with its corporate culture and the recommendations of the U.S. Environmental Protection Agency and Japanese Ministry of the Environment, Toyota focuses on source reduction (avoidance of waste altogether, rather than disposal and treatment of waste) as the best way to achieve profitability and environmental performance. For example, at its California-based NUMMI joint venture with GM, more than 175,000 gallons of purge solvent used to clean paint lines was previously disposed of as hazardous waste but is now reclaimed for reuse in the plant; furthermore, Toyota is looking to implement the use of more effective water-based paints in order to eventually eliminate the use of paint solvents in the production process. Toyota and its subsidiary companies have crafted environmental-action guidelines, which include the following:

- Develop and provide clean products with minimal environmental impact
- Promote waste reduction and resource conservation actions to achieve zero emissions
- Support and accelerate the creation of environmental management systems
- Actively participate in public environmental-waste reduction efforts as a responsible corporate citizen

Thus far, the results have been remarkable. Currently, 99% of all scrap metal generated by Toyota plants is recycled; Toyota vehicles are 85% recyclable; combustible waste has been reduced 87% since 1990; and Toyota has achieved zero landfill at its manufacturing facilities in North America as a whole. Overall, these efforts have resulted in tremendous cost savings. For example, in 2006 alone, the use of returnable shipping containers saved Toyota $5.8 million in packaging costs and eliminated nearly 7 million pounds of wood and 2.7 million pounds of cardboard. Not satisfied with these results, Toyota plans to further reduce costs by achieving zero landfill at Vehicle Design Facilities, reducing compensated waste (nonhazardous waste plus materials Toyota pays to be recycled) to 30 kg per vehicle, achieving a 90% recycling rate at U.S. Toyota Logistics Services by fiscal year 2011, and achieving the highest fuel-efficiency performance in all vehicle classes in all countries and regions.

Sources: Forbes.com, www.forbes.com/markets/feeds/afx/2006/12/22/afx3277462.html; Toyota North America Environmental Report, 2006, available at: a230.g.akamai.net/7/230/2320/v001/toyota.download.akamai.com/2320/toyota/media/about/2006envrep.pdf; Toyota Motor Corporation, *Sustainability Report 2006: Towards a New Future for People, Society and the Planet,* August 2006, available at: www.toyota.co.jp/en/environmental_rep/06/download/pdf/e_report06.pdf; Toyota Motor Corporation, "About Toyota: Environmental Commitment—Manufacturing—How Does Toyota Help the Environment," www.toyota.com/about/environment/manufacturing/help_environment.html, Toyota Motor Corporation Web site, accessed February 20, 2007.

Accounting for scrap under process costing is like the accounting under job costing when scrap is common to all jobs. That's because the scrap in process costing is common to the manufacture of masses of identical or similar units.

Managers focus their attention on ways to reduce scrap and to use it more profitably, especially when the cost of scrap is high (see Concepts in Action on p. 653). For example, General Motors has redesigned its plastic injection molding processes to reduce the scrap plastic that must be broken away from its molded products. General Motors also regrinds and reuses the plastic scrap as direct material, saving substantial input costs.

Problem for Self-Study

Burlington Textiles has some spoiled goods that had an assigned cost of $40,000 and zero net disposal value.

Required Prepare a journal entry for each of the following conditions under (a) process costing (Department A) and (b) job costing:

1. Abnormal spoilage of $40,000
2. Normal spoilage of $40,000 regarded as common to all operations
3. Normal spoilage of $40,000 regarded as attributable to specifications of a particular job

Solution

(a) Process Costing			(b) Job Costing		
1. Loss from Abnormal Spoilage	40,000		Loss from Abnormal Spoilage	40,000	
Work in Process—Dept. A		40,000	Work-in-Process Control (specific job)		40,000
2. No entry until units are completed and transferred out. Then the normal spoilage costs are transferred as part of the cost of good units.			Manufacturing Overhead Control	40,000	
			Work-in-Process Control (specific job)		40,000
Work in Process—Dept. B	40,000				
Work in Process—Dept. A		40,000			
3. Not applicable			No entry. Normal spoilage cost remains in Work-in-Process Control (specific job)		

Decision Points

The following question-and-answer format summarizes the chapter's learning objectives. Each decision presents a key question related to a learning objective. The guidelines are the answer to that question.

Decision	Guidelines
1. What are spoilage, rework, and scrap?	Spoilage is units of production that do not meet the specifications required by customers for good units and that are discarded or sold at reduced prices. Spoilage is generally divided into normal spoilage, which is inherent to a particular production process, and abnormal spoilage, which arises because of inefficiency in operations. Rework is unacceptable units that are subsequently repaired and sold as acceptable finished goods. Scrap is residual material that results from manufacturing a product; it has low total sales value compared with the total sales value of the product.
2. How does the weighted-average method of process costing calculate the costs of good units and spoilage?	The weighted-average method combines costs in beginning inventory with costs of the current period when determining the costs of good units (which include normal spoilage) and the costs of abnormal spoilage, which are written off as a loss of the accounting period.
3. How does the FIFO method of process costing calculate the costs of good units and spoilage?	The FIFO method keeps separate the costs in beginning inventory from the costs of the current period when determining the costs of good units (which include normal spoilage) and the costs of abnormal spoilage, which are written off as a loss of the accounting period.

4. How does the standard-costing method of process costing calculate the costs of good units and spoilage?	The standard-costing method uses standard costs to determine the costs of good units (which include a normal spoilage amount) and the costs of abnormal spoilage, which are written off as a loss of the accounting period.
5. How do job-costing systems account for spoilage?	Normal spoilage specific to a job is assigned to that job, or when common to all jobs, is allocated as part of manufacturing overhead. Cost of abnormal spoilage is written off as a loss of the accounting period.
6. How do job-costing systems account for rework?	Completed reworked units should be indistinguishable from non-reworked good units. Normal rework specific to a job is assigned to that job, or when common to all jobs, is allocated as part of manufacturing overhead. Cost of abnormal rework is written off as a loss of the accounting period.
7. How is scrap accounted for?	Scrap is recognized in the accounting records either at the time of its sale or at the time of its production. Sale of scrap, if immaterial, is often recognized as other revenue. If not immaterial, sale of scrap or its net realizable value reduces the cost of a specific job or, when common to all jobs, reduces Manufacturing Overhead Control.

APPENDIX: INSPECTION AND SPOILAGE AT VARIOUS STAGES OF COMPLETION IN PROCESS COSTING

How does inspection at various stages of completion affect the amount of normal and abnormal spoilage? Consider the Forging Department of Dana Corporation, a manufacturer of automobile parts. Direct materials are added at the start of production in the Forging Department. Conversion costs are added evenly during the process. We will assume that all units in work in process inventory are at the same stage of completion.

Consider three different cases: Inspection occurs at (1) the 20%, (2) the 50%, or (3) the 100% completion stage. A total of 8,000 units are spoiled in all three cases. Normal spoilage is computed on the basis of the number of *good units* that pass the inspection point *during the current period.* Assume that normal spoilage is 10% of the good units passing inspection. The following data are for October 2009. Note how the number of units of normal and abnormal spoilage change, depending on when inspection occurs.

	Physical Units: Stage of Completion at Which Inspection Occurs		
Flow of Production	**20%**	**50%**	**100%**
Work in process, beginning[a]	11,000	11,000	11,000
Started during October	74,000	74,000	74,000
To account for	85,000	85,000	85,000
Good units completed and transferred out			
(85,000 – 8,000 spoiled – 16,000 ending)	61,000	61,000	61,000
Normal spoilage	6,600[b]	7,700[c]	6,100[d]
Abnormal spoilage (8,000 – normal spoilage)	1,400	300	1,900
Work in process, ending[e]	16,000	16,000	16,000
Accounted for	85,000	85,000	85,000

[a]Degree of completion in this department: direct materials, 100%; conversion costs, 25%.
[b]10% × (74,000 units started – 8,000 units spoiled), because only the units started passed the 20% completion inspection point in the current period. Beginning work in process is excluded from this calculation because, being 25% complete at the start of the period, it passed the inspection point in the previous period.
[c]10% × (85,000 units – 8,000 units spoiled), because all units passed the 50% completion inspection point in the current period.
[d]10% × 61,000, because 61,000 units are fully completed and inspected in the current period.
[e]Degree of completion in this department: direct materials, 100%; conversion costs, 75%.

The following diagram shows the flow of physical units for October and illustrates the normal spoilage numbers in the table. Note that 61,000 good units are completed and transferred out—11,000 from beginning work in process and 50,000 started and completed during the period—and 16,000 units are in ending work in process.

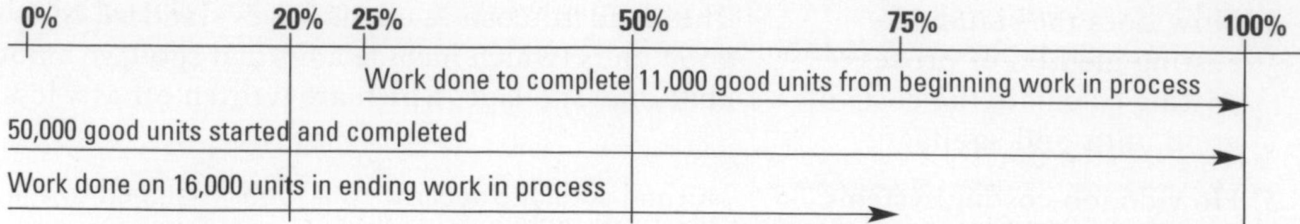

To see the number of units passing each inspection point, consider in the diagram the vertical lines at the 20%, 50%, and 100% inspection points. Note that the vertical line at 20% crosses two horizontal lines—50,000 good units started and completed and 16,000 units in ending work in process—for a total of 66,000 good units. (The 20% vertical line does not cross the line representing work done on the 11,000 good units completed from beginning work in process because these units are already 25% complete at the start of the period and, hence, are not inspected this period.) Normal spoilage equals 10% of 66,000 = 6,600 units. Similarly, the vertical line at the 50% point crosses all three horizontal lines, indicating that 11,000 + 50,000 + 16,000 = 77,000 good units pass this point. Normal spoilage in this case is 10% of 77,000 = 7,700 units. At the 100% point, normal spoilage = 10% of 61,000 (11,000 + 50,000) good units = 6,100 units.

Exhibit 18-5 shows the computation of equivalent units under the weighted-average method, assuming inspection at the 50% completion stage. The calculations depend on the direct materials and conversion costs incurred to get the units to this inspection point. The spoiled units have a full measure of direct materials and a 50% measure of conversion costs. Calculations of costs per equivalent unit and the assignment of total costs to units completed and to ending work in process are similar to calculations in previous illustrations in this chapter. Because ending work in process has passed the inspection point in this example, these units bear normal spoilage costs, just like the units that have been completed and transferred out. For example, conversion costs for units completed and transferred out include conversion costs for 61,000 good units produced plus 50% × (10% × 61,000) = 0.50 × 6,100 = 3,050 equivalent units of normal spoilage. *We multiply by 50% to obtain equivalent units of normal spoilage because conversion costs are only 50% complete at the inspection point.* Conversion costs of equivalent units in ending work in process include conversion costs of 75% of 16,000 = 12,000 equivalent good units plus 50% × (10% × 16,000) = 0.50 × 1,600 = 800 equivalent units of normal spoilage. We take 10% of 16,000 because 16,000 good units currently in ending work in process passed the inspection point. Thus, the equivalent units of normal spoilage accounted for are 3,050 equivalent units related to units completed and transferred out

Exhibit 18-5

Steps 1 and 2: Computing Equivalent Units with Spoilage Using Weighted-Average Method of Process Costing with Inspection at 50% of Completion for Forging Department of the Dana Corporation for October 2009

		(Step 2) Equivalent Units	
Flow of Production	**(Step 1) Physical Units**	**Direct Materials**	**Conversion Costs**
Work in process, beginning[a]	11,000		
Started during current period	74,000		
To account for	85,000		
Good units completed and transferred out	61,000	61,000	61,000
Normal spoilage	7,700		
(7,700 × 100%; 7,700 × 50%)		7,700	3,850
Abnormal spoilage	300		
(300 × 100%; 300 × 50%)		300	150
Work in process, ending[b]	16,000		
(16,000 × 100%; 16,000 × 75%)		16,000	12,000
Accounted for	85,000		
Total work done to date		85,000	77,000

[a]Degree of completion: direct materials, 100%; conversion costs, 25%.
[b]Degree of completion: direct materials, 100%; conversion costs, 75%.

plus 800 equivalent units related to units in ending work in process, for a total of 3,850 equivalent units, as shown in Exhibit 18-5.

TERMS TO LEARN

This chapter and the Glossary at the end of the book contain definitions of:

abnormal spoilage (**p. 640**)
inspection point (**p. 641**)
normal spoilage (**p. 640**)
rework (**p. 639**)
scrap (**p. 639**)
spoilage (**p. 639**)

ASSIGNMENT MATERIAL

Questions

18-1 Why is there an unmistakable trend in manufacturing to improve quality?

18-2 Distinguish among spoilage, rework, and scrap.

18-3 "Normal spoilage is planned spoilage." Discuss.

18-4 "Costs of abnormal spoilage are losses." Explain.

18-5 "What has been regarded as normal spoilage in the past is not necessarily acceptable as normal spoilage in the present or future." Explain.

18-6 "Units of abnormal spoilage are inferred rather than identified." Explain.

18-7 "In accounting for spoiled units, we are dealing with cost assignment rather than cost incurrence." Explain.

18-8 "Total input includes abnormal as well as normal spoilage and is, therefore, inappropriate as a basis for computing normal spoilage." Do you agree? Explain.

18-9 "The inspection point is the key to the allocation of spoilage costs." Do you agree? Explain.

18-10 "The unit cost of normal spoilage is the same as the unit cost of abnormal spoilage." Do you agree? Explain.

18-11 "In job costing, the costs of normal spoilage that occur while a specific job is being done are charged to the specific job." Do you agree? Explain.

18-12 "The costs of rework are always charged to the specific jobs in which the defects were originally discovered." Do you agree? Explain.

18-13 "Abnormal rework costs should be charged to a loss account, not to manufacturing overhead." Do you agree? Explain.

18-14 When is a company justified in inventorying scrap?

18-15 How do managers use information about scrap?

Exercises

18-16 Normal and abnormal spoilage in units. The following data, in physical units, describe a grinding process for January:

Work in process, beginning	19,000
Started during current period	150,000
To account for	169,000
Spoiled units	12,000
Good units completed and transferred out	132,000
Work in process, ending	25,000
Accounted for	169,000

Inspection occurs at the 100% completion stage. Normal spoilage is 5% of the good units passing inspection.

Required

1. Compute the normal and abnormal spoilage in units.
2. Assume that the equivalent-unit cost of a spoiled unit is $10. Compute the amount of potential savings if all spoilage were eliminated, assuming that all other costs would be unaffected. Comment on your answer.

18-17 Weighted-average method, spoilage, equivalent units. (CMA, adapted) Consider the following data for November 2009 from Gray Manufacturing Company, which makes silk pennants and uses a process-costing system. All direct materials are added at the beginning of the process, and conversion costs are added evenly during the process. Spoilage is detected upon inspection at the completion of the process. Spoiled units are disposed of at zero net disposal value. Gray Manufacturing Company uses the weighted-average method of process costing.

	Physical Units (Pennants)	Direct Materials	Conversion Costs
Work in process, November 1[a]	1,000	$ 1,423	$ 1,110
Started in November 2009	?		
Good units completed and transferred out during November 2009	9,000		
Normal spoilage	100		
Abnormal spoilage	50		
Work in process, November 30[b]	2,000		
Total costs added during November 2009		$12,180	$27,750

[a]Degree of completion: direct materials, 100%; conversion costs, 50%.
[b]Degree of completion: direct materials, 100%; conversion costs, 30%.

Required Compute equivalent units for direct materials and conversion costs. Show physical units in the first column of your schedule.

18-18 Weighted-average method, assigning costs (continuation of 18-17).

Required For the data in Exercise 18-17, summarize total costs to account for, calculate the cost per equivalent unit for direct materials and conversion costs, and assign total costs to units completed and transferred out (including normal spoilage), to abnormal spoilage, and to units in ending work in process.

18-19 FIFO method, spoilage, equivalent units. Refer to the information in Exercise 18-17. Suppose Gray Manufacturing Company uses the FIFO method of process costing instead of the weighted-average method.

Required Compute equivalent units for direct materials and conversion costs. Show physical units in the first column of your schedule.

18-20 FIFO method, assigning costs (continuation of 18-19).

Required For the data in Exercise 18-17, use the FIFO method to summarize total costs to account for, calculate the cost per equivalent unit for direct materials and conversion costs, and assign total costs to units completed and transferred out (including normal spoilage), to abnormal spoilage, and to units in ending work in process.

18-21 Weighted-average method, spoilage. Appleton Company makes wooden toys in its Forming Department, and it uses the weighted-average method of process costing. All direct materials are added at the beginning of the process, and conversion costs are added evenly during the process. Spoiled units are detected upon inspection at the end of the process and are disposed of at zero net disposal value. Summary data for August 2009 are

File Edit View Insert Format Tools Data Window Help

	A	B	C	D
1		Physical Units	Direct Materials	Conversion Costs
2	Work in process, beginning inventory (August 1)	2,000	$17,700	$10,900
3	Degree of completion of beginning work in process		100%	50%
4	Started during August	10,000		
5	Good units completed and transferred out during August	9,000		
6	Work in process, ending inventory (August 31)	1,800		
7	Degree of completion of ending work in process		100%	75%
8	Total costs added during August		$81,300	$93,000
9	Normal spoilage as a percentage of good units	10%		
10	Degree of completion of normal spoilage		100%	100%
11	Degree of completion of abnormal spoilage		100%	100%

If you want to use Excel to solve this exercise, go to the Excel Lab at **www.prenhall.com/horngren/cost13e** and download the template for Exercise 18-21.

Required

1. For each cost category, calculate equivalent units. Show physical units in the first column of your schedule.

2. Summarize total costs to account for, calculate cost per equivalent unit for each cost category, and assign total costs to units completed and transferred out (including normal spoilage), to abnormal spoilage, and to units in ending work in process.

18-22 Standard costing method, spoilage, journal entries. Aaron, Inc., is a manufacturer of vents for water heaters. The company uses a process-costing system to account for its work-in-process inventories. When Job 512 was being processed in the machining department, a piece of sheet metal was off center in the bending machine and two vents were spoiled. Because this problem occurs periodically, it is considered normal spoilage and is consequently recorded as an overhead cost. Because this step comes first in the procedure for making the vents, the only costs incurred were $250 for direct materials. Assume the sheet metal cannot be sold, and its cost has been recorded in work-in-process inventory.

Required

Prepare the journal entries to record the spoilage incurred.

18-23 Recognition of loss from spoilage. Arokia Electronics manufactures cell phone models in its Walnut Creek plant. Suppose the company provides you with the following information regarding operations for September 2009:

Total cell phones manufactured	10,000
Phones rejected as spoiled units	500
Total manufacturing cost	$209,000

Assume the spoiled units have no disposal value.

Required

1. What is the unit cost of making the 10,000 cell phones?
2. What is the total cost of the 500 spoiled units?
3. If the spoilage is considered normal, what is the increase in the unit cost of good phones manufactured as a result of the spoilage?
4. If the spoilage is considered abnormal, prepare the journal entries for the spoilage incurred.

18-24 Weighted-average method, spoilage. Chipcity is a fast-growing manufacturer of computer chips. Direct materials are added at the start of the production process. Conversion costs are added evenly during the process. Some units of this product are spoiled as a result of defects not detectable before inspection of finished goods. Spoiled units are disposed of at zero net disposal value. Chipcity uses the weighted-average method of process costing.

Summary data for September 2008 are:

	A	B	C	D
1		Physical Units (Computer Chips)	Direct Materials	Conversion Costs
2	Work in process, beginning inventory (September 1)	600	$ 96,000	$ 15,300
3	Degree of completion of beginning work in process		100%	30%
4	Started during September	2,550		
5	Good units completed and transferred out during September	2,100		
6	Work in process, ending inventory (September 30)	450		
7	Degree of completion of ending work in process		100%	40%
8	Total costs added during September		$567,000	$230,400
9	Normal spoilage as a percentage of good units	15%		
10	Degree of completion of normal spoilage		100%	100%
11	Degree of completion of abnormal spoilage		100%	100%

If you want to use Excel to solve this exercise, go to the Excel Lab at **www.prenhall.com/horngren/cost13e** and download the template for Exercise 18-24.

Required

1. For each cost category, compute equivalent units. Show physical units in the first column of your schedule.
2. Summarize total costs to account for, calculate cost per equivalent unit for each cost category, and assign total costs to units completed and transferred out (including normal spoilage), to abnormal spoilage, and to units in ending work in process.

18-25 FIFO method, spoilage. Refer to the information in Exercise 18-24. If you want to use Excel to solve this exercise, go to the Excel Lab at **www.prenhall.com/horngren/cost13e** and download the template for Exercise 18-24.

Required Do Exercise 18-24 using the FIFO method of process costing.

18-26 Standard-costing method, spoilage. Refer to the information in Exercise 18-24. Suppose Chipcity determines standard costs of $200 per equivalent unit for direct materials and $75 per equivalent unit for conversion costs for both beginning work in process and work done in the current period.

If you want to use Excel to solve this exercise, go to the Excel Lab at **www.prenhall.com/horngren/cost13e** and download the template for Exercise 18-24.

Required Do Exercise 18-24 using the standard-costing method.

18-27 Spoilage and job costing. (L. Bamber) Bamber Kitchens produces a variety of items in accordance with special job orders from hospitals, plant cafeterias, and university dormitories. An order for 2,500 cases of mixed vegetables costs $6 per case: direct materials, $3; direct manufacturing labor, $2; and manufacturing overhead allocated, $1. The manufacturing overhead rate includes a provision for normal spoilage. Consider each requirement independently.

Required

1. Assume that a laborer dropped 200 cases. Suppose part of the 200 cases could be sold to a nearby prison for $200 cash. Prepare a journal entry to record this event. Calculate and explain briefly the unit cost of the remaining 2,300 cases.
2. Refer to the original data. Tasters at the company reject 200 of the 2,500 cases. The 200 cases are disposed of for $400. Assume that this rejection rate is considered normal. Prepare a journal entry to record this event, and:
   a. Calculate the unit cost if the rejection is attributable to exacting specifications of this particular job.
   b. Calculate the unit cost if the rejection is characteristic of the production process and is not attributable to this specific job.
   c. Are unit costs the same in requirements 2a and 2b? Explain your reasoning briefly.
3. Refer to the original data. Tasters rejected 200 cases that had insufficient salt. The product can be placed in a vat, salt can be added, and the product can be reprocessed into jars. This operation, which is considered normal, will cost $200. Prepare a journal entry to record this event and:
   a. Calculate the unit cost of all the cases if this additional cost was incurred because of the exacting specifications of this particular job.
   b. Calculate the unit cost of all the cases if this additional cost occurs regularly because of difficulty in seasoning.
   c. Are unit costs the same in requirements 3a and 3b? Explain your reasoning briefly.

18-28 Reworked units, costs of rework. White Goods assembles washing machines at its Auburn plant. In February 2009, 60 tumbler units that cost $44 each (from a new supplier who subsequently went bankrupt) were defective and had to be disposed of at zero net disposal value. White Goods was able to rework all 60 washing machines by substituting new tumbler units purchased from one of its existing suppliers. Each replacement tumbler cost $50.

Required

1. What alternative approaches are there to account for the material cost of reworked units?
2. Should White Goods use the $44 tumbler or the $50 tumbler to calculate the cost of materials reworked? Explain.
3. What other costs might White Goods include in its analysis of the total costs of rework due to the tumbler units purchased from the (now) bankrupt supplier?

18-29 Scrap, job costing. The Mendoza Company has an extensive job-costing facility that uses a variety of metals. Consider each requirement independently.

Required

1. Job 372 uses a particular metal alloy that is not used for any other job. Assume that scrap is material in amount and sold for $490 quickly after it is produced. Prepare the journal entry.
2. The scrap from Job 372 consists of a metal used by many other jobs. No record is maintained of the scrap generated by individual jobs. Assume that scrap is accounted for at the time of its sale. Scrap totaling $4,000 is sold. Prepare two alternative journal entries that could be used to account for the sale of scrap.
3. Suppose the scrap generated in requirement 2 is returned to the storeroom for future use, and a journal entry is made to record the scrap. A month later, the scrap is reused as direct material on a subsequent job. Prepare the journal entries to record these transactions.

Problems

18-30 Weighted-average method, spoilage. The Boston Company is a food-processing company based in San Francisco. It operates under the weighted-average method of process costing and has two departments: Cleaning and Packaging. For the Cleaning Department, conversion costs are added evenly during the process, and direct materials are added at the beginning of the process. Spoiled units are detected upon inspection at the end of the process and are disposed of at zero net disposal value. All completed work is transferred to the Packaging Department. Summary data for May follow:

File Edit View Insert Format Tools Data Window Help

	A	B	C	D
1	**The Boston Company: Cleaning Department**	**Physical Units**	**Direct Materials**	**Conversion Costs**
2	Work in process, beginning inventory (May 1)	2,500	$ 2,500	$ 2,000
3	Degree of completion of beginning work in process		100%	80%
4	Started during May	22,500		
5	Good units completed and transferred out during May	18,500		
6	Work in process, ending inventory (May 31)	4,000		
7	Degree of completion of ending work in process		100%	25%
8	Total costs added during May		$22,500	$20,000
9	Normal spoilage as a percentage of good units	10%		
10	Degree of completion of normal spoilage		100%	100%
11	Degree of completion of abnormal spoilage		100%	100%

If you want to use Excel to solve this problem, go to the Excel Lab at **www.prenhall.com/horngren/cost13e** and download the template for Problem 18-30.

Required

For the Cleaning Department, summarize total costs to account for, and assign total costs to units completed and transferred out (including normal spoilage), to abnormal spoilage, and to units in ending work in process. Carry unit-cost calculations to four decimal places when necessary. Calculate final totals to the nearest dollar. (Problem 18-32 explores additional facets of this problem.)

18-31 FIFO method, spoilage. Refer to the information in Problem 18-30. If you want to use Excel to solve this problem, go to the Excel Lab at **www.prenhall.com/horngren/cost13e** and download the template for Problem 18-30.

Required

Do Problem 18-30 using the FIFO method of process costing. (Problem 18-33 explores additional facets of this problem.)

18-32 Weighted-average method, Packaging Department (continuation of 18-30). In Boston Company's Packaging Department, conversion costs are added evenly during the process, and direct materials are added at the end of the process. Spoiled units are detected upon inspection at the end of the process and are disposed of at zero net disposal value. All completed work is transferred to the next department. The transferred-in costs for May equal the total cost of good units completed and transferred out in May from the Cleaning Department, which were calculated in Problem 18-30 using the weighted-average method of process costing. Summary data for May follow.

File Edit View Insert Format Tools Data Window Help

	A	B	C	D	E
1	**The Boston Company: Packaging Department**	**Physical Units**	**Transferred-in Costs**	**Direct Materials**	**Conversion Costs**
2	Work in process, beginning inventory (May 1)	7,500	$16,125	$ 0	$ 6,125
3	Degree of completion of beginning work in process		100%	0%	80%
4	Started during May	18,500			
5	Good units completed and transferred out during May	15,000			
6	Work in process, ending inventory (May 31)	10,000			
7	Degree of completion of ending work in process		100%	0%	25%
8	Total costs added during May		?	$1,600	$12,375
9	Normal spoilage as a percentage of good units	5%			
10	Degree of completion of normal spoilage			100%	100%
11	Degree of completion of abnormal spoilage			100%	100%

If you want to use Excel to solve this problem, go to the Excel Lab at **www.prenhall.com/horngren/cost13e** and download the template for Problem 18-32.

Required

For the Packaging Department, use the weighted-average method to summarize total costs to account for and assign total costs to units completed and transferred out (including normal spoilage), to abnormal spoilage, and to units in ending work in process.

18-33 FIFO method, Packaging Department (continuation of 18-31). Refer to the information in Problem 18-32 except for the transferred-in costs for May, which equal the total cost of good units completed and transferred out in May from the Cleaning Department, which were calculated in Problem 18-31 using the FIFO method of process costing.

If you want to use Excel to solve this problem, go to the Excel Lab at **www.prenhall.com/horngren/cost13e** and download the template for Problem 18-32.

Required For the Packaging Department, use the FIFO method to summarize total costs to account for, and assign total costs to units completed and transferred out (including normal spoilage), to abnormal spoilage, and to units in ending work in process.

18-34 Job-costing spoilage and scrap. (F. Mayne) Santa Cruz Metal Fabricators, Inc., has a large job, No. 2734, that calls for producing various ore bins, chutes, and metal boxes for enlarging a copper concentrator. The following charges were made to the job in November 2009:

Direct materials	$40,400
Direct manufacturing labor	22,600
Manufacturing overhead	11,300

The contract with the customer called for the total price to be based on a cost-plus approach. The contract defined cost to include direct materials, direct manufacturing labor costs, and manufacturing overhead to be allocated at 50% of direct manufacturing labor costs. The contract also provided that the total costs of all work spoiled were to be removed from the billable cost of the job and that the benefits from scrap sales were to reduce the billable cost of the job.

1. In accordance with the stated terms of the contract, prepare journal entries for the following two items:
   a. A cutting error was made in production. The up-to-date job cost record for this batch of work showed materials of $975, direct manufacturing labor of $600, and allocated overhead of $300. Because fairly large pieces of metal were recoverable, the company believed their value was $800 and that the materials recovered could be used on other jobs. The spoiled work was sent to the warehouse.
   b. Small pieces of metal cuttings and scrap in November 2009 amounted to $1,995, which was the price quoted by a scrap dealer. No journal entries were made with regard to the scrap until the price was quoted by the scrap dealer. The scrap dealer's offer was immediately accepted.
2. Consider normal and abnormal spoilage. Suppose the contract described above had contained the clause "a normal spoilage allowance of 1% of the job costs will be included in the billable costs of the job."
   a. Is this clause specific enough to define exactly how much spoilage is normal and how much is abnormal? Explain.
   b. Repeat requirement 1a with this "normal spoilage of 1%" clause in mind. You should be able to provide two slightly different journal entries.

18-35 Spoilage in job costing. Whitefish Machine Shop is a manufacturer of motorized carts for vacation resorts.

Peter Cruz, the plant manager of Whitefish, obtains the following information for Job #10 in August 2007. A total of 40 units were started, and 5 spoiled units were detected and rejected at final inspection, yielding 35 good units. The spoiled units were considered to be normal spoilage. Costs assigned prior to the inspection point are $1,000 per unit. The current disposal price of the spoiled units is $200 per unit. When the spoilage is detected, the spoiled goods are inventoried at $200 per unit.

Required

1. What is the normal spoilage rate?
2. Prepare the journal entries to record the normal spoilage, assuming:
   a. The spoilage is related to a specific job.
   b. The spoilage is common to all jobs.
   c. The spoilage is considered to be abnormal spoilage.

18-36 Rework in job costing, journal entry (continuation of 18-35). Assume that the 5 spoiled units of Whitefish Machine Shop's Job #10 can be reworked for a total cost of $1,800. A total cost of $5,000 associated with these units has already been assigned to Job #10 before the rework.

Required Prepare the journal entries for the rework, assuming:

a. The rework is related to a specific job.
b. The rework is common to all jobs.
c. The rework is considered to be abnormal.

18-37 Scrap at time of sale or at time of production, journal entries (continuation of 18-35). Assume that Job #10 of Whitefish Machine Shop generates normal scrap with a total sales value of $300 (it is assumed that the scrap returned to the storeroom is sold quickly).

Prepare the journal entries for the recognition of scrap, assuming: **Required**

a. The value of scrap is immaterial and scrap is recognized at the time of sale.
b. The value of scrap is material, is related to a specific job and is recognized at the time of sale.
c. The value of scrap is material, is common to all jobs and is recognized at the time of sale.
d. The value of scrap is material, scrap is recognized as inventory at the time of production and is recorded at its net realizable value.

18-38 Physical units, inspection at various stages of completion (chapter appendix). Normal spoilage is 6% of the good units passing inspection in a forging process. In March, a total of 10,000 units were spoiled. Other data include: units started during March, 120,000; work in process, beginning, 14,000 units (20% completed for conversion costs); and work in process, ending, 11,000 units (70% completed for conversion costs).

Using the format on page 655, compute the normal and abnormal spoilage in units, assuming the inspection point is at (a) the 15% stage of completion, (b) the 40% stage of completion, and (c) the 100% stage of completion. **Required**

18-39 Weighted-average method, inspection at 80% completion (chapter appendix). (A. Atkinson) The Kim Company is a furniture manufacturer with two departments: molding and finishing. The company uses the weighted-average method of process costing. In August, the following data were recorded for the Finishing Department:

Units of beginning work in process inventory	12,500
Percentage completion of beginning work in process units	25%
Cost of direct materials in beginning work in process	$0
Units started	87,500
Units completed	62,500
Units in ending inventory	25,000
Percentage completion of ending work in process units	95%
Spoiled units	12,500
Total costs added during current period:	
Direct materials	$819,000
Direct manufacturing labor	$794,500
Manufacturing overhead	$770,000
Work in process, beginning:	
Transferred-in costs	$103,625
Conversion costs	$52,500
Cost of units transferred in during current period	$809,375

Conversion costs are added evenly during the process. Direct material costs are added when production is 90% complete. The inspection point is at the 80% stage of production. Normal spoilage is 10% of all good units that pass inspection. Spoiled units are disposed of at zero net disposal value.

For August, summarize total costs to account for, and assign these costs to units completed and transferred out (including normal spoilage), to abnormal spoilage, and to units in ending work in process. **Required**

Collaborative Learning Problem

18-40 Job costing, rework. Solutions Corporation is a manufacturer of computer chips based in San Jose. It manufactures two types of computer chips, CS1 and CS2. The costs of manufacturing each CS1 chip, excluding rework costs, are direct materials, $60; direct manufacturing labor, $12; and manufacturing overhead, $38. Defective units are sent to a separate rework area. Rework costs per CS1 chip are direct materials, $12; direct manufacturing labor, $9; and manufacturing overhead, $15.

In August 2008, Solutions manufactured 1,000 CS1 and 500 CS2 chips. Eighty of the CS1 chips and none of the CS2 chips required rework. Solutions classifies 50 of the CS1 chips reworked as normal rework caused by inherent problems in its production process that only coincidentally occurred during the production of CS1. Hence the rework costs for these 50 CS1 chips are normal rework costs not specifically attributable to the CS1 product. Solutions classifies the remaining 30 units of CS1 chips reworked as abnormal rework. Solutions allocates manufacturing overhead on the basis of machine-hours required to manufacture CS1 and CS2. Each CS1 or CS2 chip requires the same number of machine-hours.

Required

1. Prepare journal entries to record the accounting for the cost of the spoiled chips and for rework.
2. What were the total rework costs of CS1 chips in August 2008?

19 Balanced Scorecard: Quality, Time, and the Theory of Constraints

Learning Objectives

1. Explain the four cost categories in a costs-of-quality program
2. Provide examples of nonfinancial quality measures of customer satisfaction in the balanced scorecard
3. Use three methods to identify quality problems
4. Identify relevant costs and benefits of quality improvement programs
5. Describe the benefits of financial and nonfinancial measures of quality
6. Describe customer-response time and explain why delays happen and their costs
7. Apply the three measures in the theory of constraints
8. Explain how to manage bottlenecks

To satisfy ever-increasing customer expectations, managers need to find cost-effective ways to continuously improve the quality of their products and services and shorten response times. This requires trading off the costs of achieving these improvements and the benefits from higher performance on these dimensions. When companies do not meet customer expectations, the losses can be substantial, as the following article about JetBlue shows. Of the many direct costs associated with this service failure, which ones are connected to compensating customers for the current failure and which do you think are expenditures to prevent this problem from recurring? What are some of the indirect costs of this service failure?

JetBlue Plans Overhaul after Snafus Irk Customers[1]

JetBlue Airways Corp. has long strived to set itself apart from traditional domestic airlines. The airline has enjoyed a strong customer-service record, attracting fewer consumer complaints, such as mishandled bags, than most of its competitors. But a days-long operational meltdown forced the discounter to swallow changes that will make it a bit more like its "legacy" rivals.

JetBlue found itself in the cross hairs in February 2007 when a snow-and-ice storm barreled into the New York area. JetBlue, whose main hub is at New York's John F. Kennedy International Airport, canceled about half of its 502 daily flights that day; but not until about 10 planes were stranded for up to 10 hours before passengers were evacuated into airport buses. The carrier, which has made a virtue of not canceling flights because it thinks passengers would prefer to get to their destination even if late, cut some flights from its schedule, but that was too little, too late. Pilots and flight attendants were out of position or had run out of duty time, meaning they had to rest before they could work again. Or, they couldn't be reached because the carrier's crew call-in desk was overwhelmed. JetBlue's terminal at JFK became crowded with angry customers and piled-up baggage.

Despite its best efforts, JetBlue couldn't catch up to the cascade of miscues. It promised full refunds and free round-trip tickets to all passengers trapped on a plane for more than three hours.

[1] *Source:* Susan Carey and Dagmar Aalund, "JetBlue Plans Overhaul as Snafus Irk Customers," *The Wall Street Journal*, February 20, 2007.

To avoid these problems in the future, JetBlue planned to upgrade its crew-communications system to allow pilots and flight attendants to send Internet messages about their location and availability; double or triple the number of employees trained in crew-scheduling duties; double the number of reservationists available in critical situations; and train about 1,300 workers in emergency airport duties in case they are needed.

As the JetBlue example illustrates, customers the world over are becoming less tolerant of poor quality and long response times. But improving quality and speed is hard work. This chapter describes how a balanced scorecard approach helps managers and management accountants to improve quality, customer-response time and throughput.

We present this chapter in three parts. Part One is Quality as a Competitive Tool, Part Two is Time as a Competitive Tool, and Part Three is Theory of Constraints and Throughput Contribution Analysis. The presentation is modular so that you can omit a part or explore these topics in any order.

PART ONE: QUALITY AS A COMPETITIVE TOOL

We begin by introducing different aspects of quality and then describe how quality measures appear on the balanced scorecard. The American Society for Quality defines **quality** as the total features and characteristics of a product or a service made or performed according to specifications to satisfy customers at the time of purchase and during use. Many companies throughout the world—for example, Cisco Systems and Motorola in the United States and Canada, British Telecom in the United Kingdom, Fujitsu and Toyota in Japan, Crysel in Mexico, and Samsung in South Korea—have emphasized quality as an important strategic initiative. Service quality has also become increasingly important in nonprofit sectors such as health care and government. For example, Kaiser Permanente, a leading nonprofit health insurer, pays bonuses to its doctors based on patient satisfaction. That's because a quality focus reduces costs and increases customer satisfaction. Several high-profile awards—the Malcolm Baldrige National Quality Award in the United States, the Deming Prize in Japan, and the Premio Nacional de Calidad in Mexico—are given to companies that have produced high-quality products and services.

International quality standards have also emerged. ISO 9000, developed by the International Organization for Standardization, is a set of five international standards for quality management adopted by more than 85 countries. ISO 9000 enables companies to effectively document and certify the elements of their production processes that lead to quality. To ensure that their suppliers deliver high-quality products at competitive costs, companies such as DuPont and General Electric require their suppliers to obtain ISO 9000 certification. Documenting evidence of quality through ISO 9000 has become a necessary condition for competing in the global marketplace.

Focusing on the quality of a product or service will generally build expertise in producing it, lower the costs of providing it, create higher satisfaction for customers using it, and generate higher future revenues for the company selling it. In some cases, the benefit of better quality is in preserving revenues, not generating higher revenues. A company that does not invest in quality improvement while competitors are doing so will likely suffer a decline in its market share, revenues, and profits. In addition, product or service quality problems can cause serious losses, as they did at JetBlue.

As corporations' responsibilities toward the environment grow, managers are applying the quality management and measurement practices discussed in this chapter to find cost-effective ways to reduce the environmental and economic costs of air pollution, wastewater, oil spills, and hazardous waste disposal. Under the U.S. Clean Air Act, costs of environmental damage can be extremely high. Exxon paid $125 million in fines and restitution on top of $1 billion in civil payments for the Exxon Valdez oil spill, which harmed the Alaskan coast. An environmental management standard, ISO 14000, encourages organizations to pursue environmental goals vigorously by developing (1) environmental management systems to reduce environmental costs and (2) environmental auditing and performance-evaluation systems to review and provide feedback on environmental goals.

We focus on two basic aspects of quality: design quality and conformance quality. **Design quality** refers to how closely the characteristics of a product or service meet the needs and wants of customers. Suppose customers of photocopying machines want copiers that combine copying, faxing, scanning, and electronic printing. Photocopying machines that fail to meet these customer needs fail in the quality of their designs. If customers of a bank want online banking services, then not providing these services would be a design-quality failure.

Conformance quality is the performance of a product or service relative to its design and product specifications. For example, if a part breaks on a new car, it fails to satisfy conformance quality. A bank that deposits a customer's check into the wrong account fails on conformance quality.

To ensure that performance will achieve customer satisfaction, companies must first design products or services to satisfy customers through design quality. They must then meet design specifications through conformance quality. The following diagram illustrates that actual performance can fall short of customer satisfaction because of design-quality failure and because of conformance-quality failure.

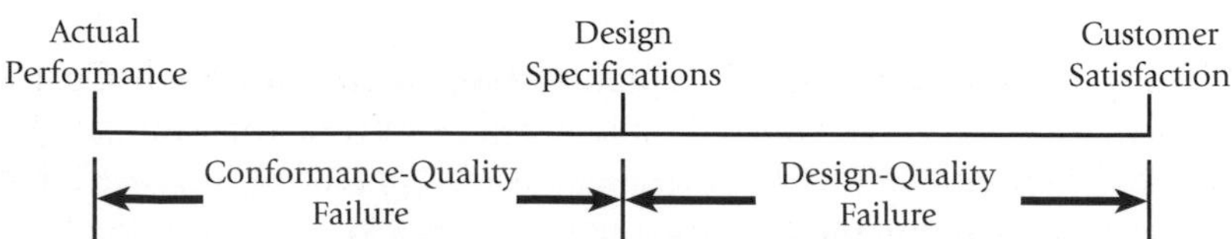

We illustrate the issues in managing quality—computing the costs of quality, identifying quality problems, and taking actions to improve quality—using Photon Corporation. Photon makes many products; however, we'll focus on Photon's photocopying machines, which earned an operating income of $24 million on revenues of $300 million (from sales of 20,000 copiers) in 2008.

Recall from Chapter 13 the four perspectives of the balanced scorecard: financial, customer, internal business process, and learning and growth. We now present the financial measures of quality and, in particular, the costs of conformance quality. The (financial) costs of poor design quality are mainly the opportunity costs of future sales lost if Photon does not design a product that customers want. These opportunity costs are difficult to measure objectively. Photon measures design quality only in its customer perspective.

The Financial Perspective: Costs of Quality

Learning Objective 1

Explain the four cost categories in a costs-of-quality program

. . . prevention, appraisal, internal failure, and external failure costs

The financial perspective of Photon's balanced scorecard includes measures such as revenue growth and operating income—financial measures that are likely to be affected by quality improvement programs. In addition, Photon measures costs of quality. **Costs of quality (COQ)** are the costs incurred to prevent, or the costs arising as a result of, the production of a low-quality product. Costs of quality are classified into four categories; examples for each category are listed in Exhibit 19-1.

1. **Prevention costs**—costs incurred to preclude the production of products that do not conform to specifications.
2. **Appraisal costs**—costs incurred to detect which of the individual units of products do not conform to specifications.
3. **Internal failure costs**—costs incurred on defective products before they are shipped to customers.
4. **External failure costs**—costs incurred on defective products after they are shipped to customers.

The items in Exhibit 19-1 come from all business functions of the value chain, and they are broader than the internal failure costs of spoilage, rework, and scrap described in Chapter 18.

An important role for management accountants is preparing costs-of-quality reports for managers. Photon determines the costs of quality of its photocopying machines by adapting the seven-step activity-based costing approach described in Chapter 5.

Step 1: Identify the Product That Is the Chosen Cost Object. The cost object is the photocopying machine that Photon made and sold in 2008. Photon's goal is to calculate the total costs of quality of these 20,000 machines.

Step 2: Identify the Direct Costs of Quality of the Product. Direct costs include employees such as inspectors and workers in repair areas who are dedicated to a product line. The photocopying machines have no direct costs of quality because no inspection or repair workers are dedicated to the photocopying machines.

Step 3: Select the Activities and Cost-Allocation Bases to Use for Allocating Indirect Costs of Quality to the Product. Column 1 of Exhibit 19-2, Panel A, classifies the activities that result in prevention, appraisal, and internal and external failure costs, and it indicates in parentheses the business functions of the value chain in which these costs occur. For example, the inspection activity results in appraisal costs and occurs in the manufacturing function. Photon identifies the number of inspection-hours as the cost-allocation base for the inspection activity. (To avoid details not needed to explain the concepts here, we do not provide information on the total quantities of each cost-allocation base.)

Step 4: Identify the Indirect Costs of Quality Associated with Each Cost-Allocation Base. These are the total costs (variable and fixed) incurred for each of the costs-of-quality activities, such as inspections, in all of Photon's operations. (To avoid details not needed to understand the points described here, we do not provide information about these total costs.)

Exhibit 19-1

Items Pertaining to Costs-of-Quality Reports

Prevention Costs	Appraisal Costs	Internal Failure Costs	External Failure Costs
Design engineering	Inspection	Spoilage	Customer support
Process engineering	Online product manufacturing and process inspection	Rework	Manufacturing/ process engineering for external failures
Supplier evaluations	Product testing	Scrap	Warranty repair costs
Preventive equipment maintenance		Machine repairs	Liability claims
Quality training		Manufacturing/ process engineering on internal failures	
Testing of new materials			

Exhibit 19-2 Analysis of Activity-Based Costs of Quality (COQ) for Photocopying Machines at Photon Corporation

File Edit View Insert Format Tools Data Window Help

	A	B	C	D	E	F	G
1	**PANEL A: COQ REPORT**						**Percentage of**
2		**Cost Allocation**		**Quantity of Cost**		**Total**	**Revenues**
3	**Cost of Quality and Value-Chain Category**	**Rate[a]**		**Allocation Base**		**Costs**	**(5) = (4) ÷**
4	**(1)**	**(2)**		**(3)**		**(4) = (2) x (3)**	**$300,000,000**
5	*Prevention costs*						
6	Design engineering (R&D/Design)	$ 80	per hour	40,000	hours	$ 3,200,000	1.1%
7	Process engineering (R&D/Design)	$ 60	per hour	45,000	hours	2,700,000	0.9%
8	Total prevention costs					5,900,000	2.0%
9	*Appraisal costs*						
10	Inspection (Manufacturing)	$ 40	per hour	240,000	hours	9,600,000	3.2%
11	Total appraisal costs					9,600,000	3.2%
12	*Internal failure costs*						
13	Rework (Manufacturing)	$100	per hour	100,000	hours	10,000,000	3.3%
14	Total internal failure costs					10,000,000	3.3%
15	*External failure costs*						
16	Customer support (Marketing)	$ 50	per hour	12,000	hours	600,000	0.2%
17	Transportation (Distribution)	$240	per load	3,000	loads	720,000	0.2%
18	Warranty repair (Customer service)	$110	per hour	120,000	hours	13,200,000	4.4%
19	Total external failure costs					14,520,000	4.8%
20	Total costs of quality					$40,020,000	13.3%
21							
22	[a]Amounts assumed.						
23							
24	**PANEL B: OPPORTUNITY COST ANALYSIS**						
25						**Total Estimated**	**Percentage**
26						**Contribution**	**of Revenues**
27	**Cost of Quality Category**					**Margin Lost**	**(3) = (2) ÷**
28	**(1)**					**(2)**	**$300,000,000**
29	*External failure costs*						
30	Estimated forgone contribution margin						
31	and income on lost sales					$12,000,000[b]	4.0%
32	Total external failure costs					$12,000,000	4.0%
33							
34	[b]Calculated as total revenues minus all variable costs (whether output-unit, batch, product-sustaining, or facility-sustaining) on						
35	lost sales in 2008. If poor quality causes Photon to lose sales in subsequent years as well, the opportunity costs will be						
36	even greater.						

Step 5: Compute the Rate per Unit of Each Cost-Allocation Base. For each activity, total costs (identified in step 4) are divided by total quantity of the cost-allocation base (calculated in step 3) to compute rate per unit of each cost-allocation base. Column 2 of Exhibit 19-2, Panel A, shows these rates (without supporting calculations).

Step 6: Compute the Indirect Costs of Quality Allocated to the Product. Photon first determines the quantity of each cost-allocation base used by the photocopying machines (column 3 of Panel A). For example, photocopying machines use 240,000 inspection-hours. The indirect costs of quality of the photocopying machines, shown in column 4, Panel A, equal the total quantity of the cost-allocation base used by the photocopying machines for each activity (column 3) multiplied by the cost-allocation rate from step 5 (column 2). For example, quality-related inspection costs for the photocopying machines are \$9,600,000 (\$40 per hour × 240,000 inspection-hours).

Step 7: Compute the Total Costs of Quality by Adding All Direct and Indirect Costs of Quality Assigned to the Product. Photon's total costs of quality in the COQ report for photocopying machines is \$40.02 million (bottom of column 4, Panel A), or 13.3% of current revenues (bottom of column 5).

The largest costs-of-quality items are frequently the opportunity costs of the contribution margin and income forgone from lost sales, lost production, and lower prices that result from poor quality. However, these opportunity costs are not recorded in financial accounting systems. Instead, companies often estimate the opportunity costs of poor quality using marketing research on the probability that customers who experience or hear about quality problems will stop buying the product or service. Photon's Market Research Department estimates lost sales of 2,000 photocopying machines in 2008 because of external failures. The forgone contribution margin and operating income of \$12 million (Exhibit 19-2, Panel B) measures the financial costs of estimated sales lost because of quality problems. Total costs of quality, including opportunity costs, equal \$52.02 million (\$40.02 million in Panel A + \$12 million in Panel B), or 17.3% of current revenues. Opportunity costs account for 23.1% (\$12 million ÷ \$52.02 million) of Photon's total costs of quality.

The COQ report and the opportunity-cost analysis highlight Photon's high internal and external failure costs. But even before the opportunity cost of lost sales appears in the financial perspective of its balanced scorecard, Photon uses nonfinancial measures to determine how its customers are reacting to the quality of its photocopiers. For example, a customer who is not satisfied with a photocopier may tell others about its problems and may decide not to buy Photon's photocopies in the future, but the resulting revenue losses will not show up for some time. Without completing both analyses (financial and nonfinancial), Photon would limit the potential to identify and reduce its high internal and external failure costs.

The Customer Perspective: Nonfinancial Measures of Customer Satisfaction

Learning Objective 2

Provide examples of nonfinancial quality measures of customer satisfaction in the balanced scorecard

. . . market share, number of customer complaints, on-time delivery rate

Nonfinancial balanced scorecard measures of customer satisfaction relating to quality include measures of both design quality and conformance quality. Management accountants are usually responsible for maintaining and presenting these nonfinancial measures.

Similar to Unilever, Federal Express, and TiVo, Photon measures customer satisfaction over time. Some measures are:

- Market research information on customer preferences for and customer satisfaction with specific product features (to measure design quality)
- Market share
- Percentage of customers that give high ratings for customer satisfaction
- Number of defective units shipped to customers as a percentage of total units shipped
- Number of customer complaints (Companies estimate that for every customer who actually complains, there are 10 to 20 others who have had bad experiences with the product or service but did not complain.)
- Percentage of products that fail soon after delivery
- Delivery delays (difference between the scheduled delivery date and the date requested by the customer)
- On-time delivery rate (percentage of shipments made on or before the scheduled delivery date)

Photon's management monitors whether these numbers improve or deteriorate over time. If improvement occurs, management can be more confident about operating income being strong in future years. For example, improvements in design quality should lead to future revenue growth. Reducing defects and improving conformance quality should decrease the number of problems experienced by customers, leading to higher customer satisfaction. Higher satisfaction, in turn, should lead to increased future revenues due to higher customer retention and loyalty and positive word-of-mouth advertising. If, however, customer-satisfaction numbers deteriorate, costs of quality will be higher in the future as current and potential customers buy from competitors.

Because many of the quality-related factors that influence customer satisfaction are influenced by the quality of Photon's internal business process, the company must improve these processes to satisfy its customers and to achieve better financial performance. Even though a particular customer measure's assumptions and methodology may be open to challenge, managers benefit from monitoring changes in the measures over time.

The Internal-Business-Process Perspective: Analyzing Quality Problems and Improving Quality

Learning Objective 3

Use three methods to identify quality problems

. . . control charts, Pareto diagrams, and cause-and-effect diagrams

To enhance the quality of work done inside the company, Photon's managers analyze and identify quality problems with the goal of reducing failures. Three techniques we consider for identifying and analyzing quality problems are control charts, Pareto diagrams, and cause-and-effect diagrams.

Control Charts

Statistical quality control (SQC), which is also called statistical process control (SPC), is a formal means of distinguishing between random and nonrandom variations in an operating process. Random variations occur, for example, when power surges or chance fluctuations in temperature cause defective products to be produced in a chemical process. Nonrandom variations occur when defective products are produced as a result of a systematic problem such as inaccurate temperature readings. A **control chart**, one of the tools in SQC, is a graph of a series of successive observations of a particular step, procedure, or operation taken at regular intervals of time. Each observation is plotted relative to specified ranges that represent the limits within which observations are expected to fall. Only those observations outside the control limits are ordinarily regarded as nonrandom and worth investigating.

Exhibit 19-3 presents control charts for the daily defect rates observed at Photon's three photocopying-machine production lines. Defect rates in the prior 60 days for each production line were assumed to provide a good basis from which to calculate the distribution of daily defect rates. The arithmetic mean (μ, read mu) and standard deviation (σ, read sigma) are the two parameters of the distribution that are used in the control charts in Exhibit 19-3. On the basis of experience, the company decides that any observation outside the $\mu \pm 2\sigma$ range should be investigated.

For production line A, all observations are within the range of $\mu \pm 2\sigma$, so management believes no investigation is necessary. For production line B, the last two observations signal that an out-of-control occurrence is highly likely. Given the $\pm 2\sigma$ rule, both observations would be investigated. Production line C illustrates a process that would not prompt an investigation under the $\pm 2\sigma$ rule but that may well be out of control. That's because the last eight observations show a clear direction, and the last six are getting further and further away from the mean. This could be due to the tooling on a machine beginning to wear out. As the tooling deteriorates further, the trend is likely to persist until the production line is no longer in statistical control. Statistical procedures have been developed using the trend as well as the variation to evaluate whether a process is out of control.

Exhibit 19-3 Statistical Quality Control Charts: Daily Defect Rate for Photocopying Machines at Photon Corporation

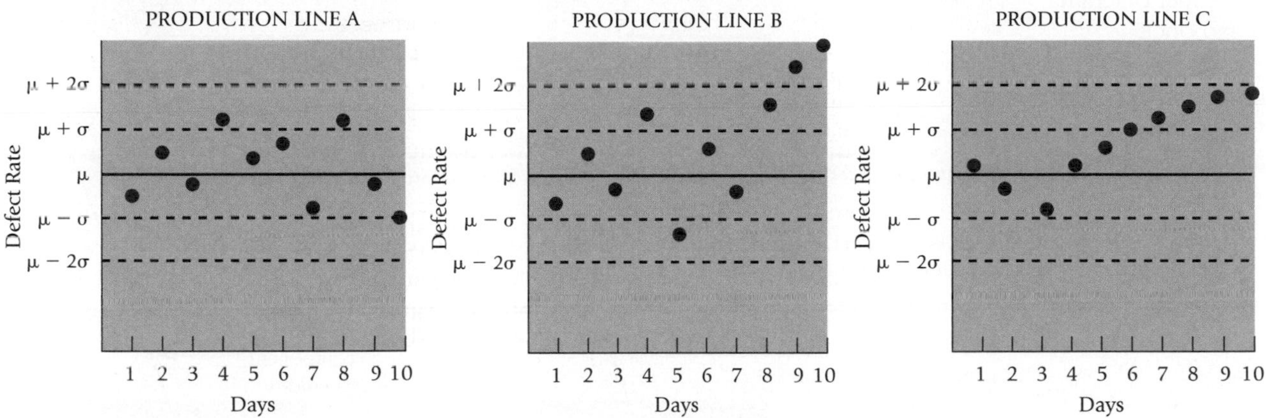

Pareto Diagrams

Observations outside control limits serve as inputs for Pareto diagrams. A **Pareto diagram** is a chart that indicates how frequently each type of defect occurs, ordered from the most frequent to the least frequent. Exhibit 19-4 presents a Pareto diagram of quality problems with respect to Photon's photocopying machines. Fuzzy and unclear copies are the most frequently recurring problem. Fuzzy and unclear copies result in high rework costs. Sometimes fuzzy and unclear copies occur at customer sites and result in high warranty and repair costs and low customer satisfaction.

Cause-and-Effect Diagrams

The most frequently recurring and costly problems identified by the Pareto diagram are analyzed using cause-and-effect diagrams. A **cause-and-effect diagram** identifies potential causes of defects using a diagram that resembles the bone structure of a fish (hence, cause-and-effect diagrams are also called *fishbone diagrams*).[2] Exhibit 19-5 presents the cause-and-effect diagram describing potential reasons why fuzzy and unclear copies occur. The "backbone" of the diagram represents the problem being examined. The large "bones" coming off the backbone represent the main categories of potential causes of failure. The exhibit identifies four of these: human factors, methods and design factors, machine-related factors, and materials and components factors. Additional arrows or

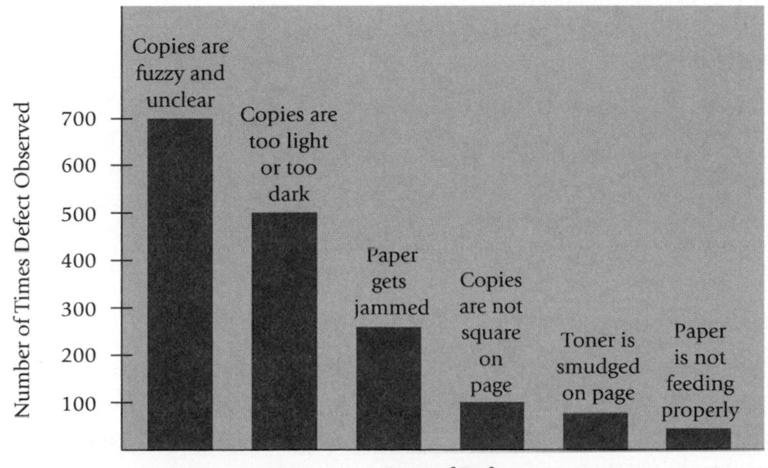

Exhibit 19-4

Pareto Diagram for Photocopying Machines at Photon Corporation

[2] See P. Clark, "Getting the Most from Cause-and-Effect Diagrams," *Quality Progress* (June 2000).

Exhibit 19-5

Cause-and-Effect Diagram for Fuzzy and Unclear Photocopies at Photon Corporation

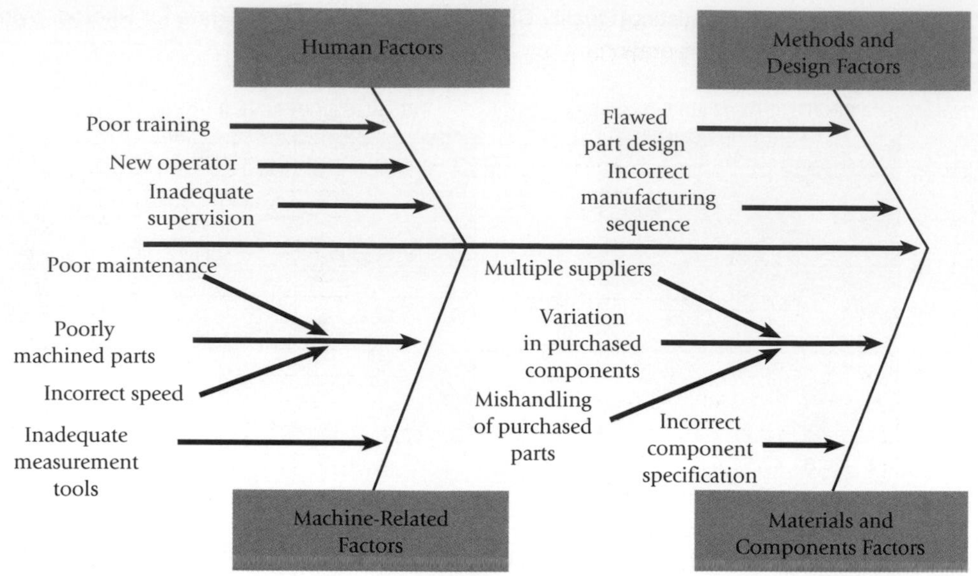

bones are added to provide more-detailed reasons for each higher-level cause. For example, the two potential causes of material and component problems are variation in purchased components and incorrect component specification. The root causes of variation in purchased components, in turn, are the use of multiple suppliers and mishandling of purchased parts. Improvements in purchased components, and resulting improvements in copy quality, will require Photon to address these two root causes.

The analysis of quality problems is aided by automated equipment and computers that record the number and types of defects and the operating conditions that existed at the time the defects occurred. Using these inputs, computer programs simultaneously prepare control charts, Pareto diagrams, and cause-and-effect diagrams.

Relevant Costs and Benefits of Evaluating Quality Improvement

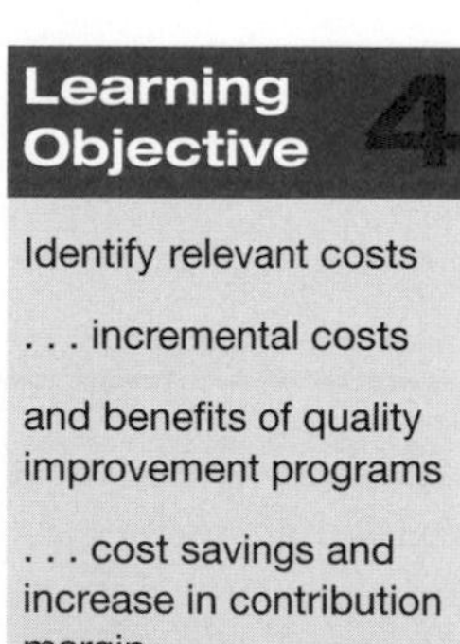

Identify relevant costs

. . . incremental costs

and benefits of quality improvement programs

. . . cost savings and increase in contribution margin

Analysis of Photon's cause-and-effect diagram reveals that the steel frame (or chassis) of the copier is often mishandled as it travels from a supplier's warehouse to Photon's plant. The frame must be produced to within very precise specifications or else copier components (such as drums, mirrors, and lenses) will not fit exactly on the frame. Mishandling during transport causes the frame to vary from manufacturing specifications, which results in the copier producing fuzzy and unclear copies.

The team of engineers working to solve this problem offers two solutions: (1) further inspect the frames immediately on delivery or (2) redesign and strengthen the frames and their shipping containers to better withstand mishandling during transportation.

To evaluate each alternative versus the status quo, management identifies the relevant costs and benefits for each solution. The key question is *how total costs and total revenues will change under each alternative solution*. Remember, relevant-cost and relevant-revenue analysis ignores allocated amounts, as explained in Chapter 11.

Photon considers only a one-year time horizon over which to analyze each solution because it plans to introduce a completely new line of copiers at the end of the year. The new line will be so different that the choice of either the inspection or the redesign alternative will have no effect on the sales of copiers in future years.

Exhibit 19-6 shows the relevant costs and benefits for each alternative.

1. **Estimated incremental costs:** \$400,000 for the inspection alternative; \$460,000 for the redesign alternative.
2. **Cost savings from less rework, customer support, and repairs.** Exhibit 19-6, line 10 shows that reducing rework results in savings of \$40 per hour. Exhibit 19-2, Panel A,

Exhibit 19-6 Estimated Effects of Quality-Improvement Actions on Costs of Quality for Photocopying Machines at Photon Corporation

	A	B	C	D	E	F	G	H	I	J
1				Relevant Costs and Benefits of						
2				Further Inspecting Incoming Frames				Redesigning Frames		
3	Relevant Items	Relevant Benefit per Unit		Quantity		Total Benefits		Quantity		Total Benefits
4	(1)	(2)		(3)		(4)		(5)		(6)
5	Additional inspection and testing costs					$ (400,000)				
6	Additional process engineering costs									$ (300,000)
7	Additional design engineering costs									(160,000)
8										
9						(2) x (3)				(2) x (5)
10	Savings in rework costs	$ 40	per hour	24,000	hours	$ 960,000		32,000	hours	$1,280,000
11	Savings in customer-support costs	$ 20	per hour	2,000	hours	40,000		2,800	hours	56,000
12	Savings in transportation costs for repair parts	$ 180	per load	500	loads	90,000		700	loads	126,000
13	Savings in warranty repair costs	$ 45	per hour	20,000	hours	900,000		28,000	hours	1,260,000
14	Total contribution margin from additional sales	$6,000	per copier	250	copiers	1,500,000		300	copiers	1,800,000
15										
16	Net cost savings and additional contribution margin					$3,090,000				$4,062,000
17										
18	Difference in favor of redesigning frames (J16) – (F16)						$972,000			

column 2, line 13, shows total rework cost per hour of $100. Why the difference? Because Photon concludes that as it improves quality, it will save only the $40 variable cost per rework-hour, not the $60 fixed cost per rework-hour.

Exhibit 19-6, line 10, shows the inspection alternative is expected to eliminate 24,000 rework-hours and therefore save variable costs of $960,000 ($40 per hour × 24,000 rework-hours). The redesign alternative (Exhibit 19-6, line 10) is expected to eliminate 32,000 rework-hours and therefore save variable costs of $1,280,000 ($40 per rework-hour × 32,000 rework-hours). Exhibit 19-6 also shows expected variable-cost savings in customer support, transportation, and warranty repair for the two alternatives.

3. **Increased contribution margin from higher sales as a result of building a reputation for quality and performance (Exhibit 19-6, line 14):** $1,500,000 for 250 copiers under the inspection alternative and $1,800,000 for 300 copiers under the redesign alternative. This benefit is important because quality improvements cannot always be translated into lower costs. For example, laying off workers (as a result of quality improvements) to reduce costs can adversely affect the morale of employees and limit future quality initiatives. Management should always look for opportunities to generate higher revenues, not just cost reductions, from quality improvements.

Exhibit 19-6 shows that both the inspection and the redesign alternatives yield net benefits relative to the status quo. However, the net benefits from the redesign alternative are expected to be $972,000 greater.

Note how making improvements in internal business processes affects the COQ numbers reported in the financial perspective of the balanced scorecard. In our example, redesigning the frame increases prevention costs (design and process engineering), decreases internal failure costs (rework), and decreases external failure costs (warranty repairs). COQ reports provide more insight about quality improvements when managers compare trends over time. In successful quality programs, companies decrease total costs of quality as a percentage of revenues and the sum of internal and external failure costs as a percentage of total costs of quality. Many companies, such as Hewlett-Packard, go further and believe they should eliminate all failure costs and have zero defects.

We now describe the nonfinancial quality-related measures Photon uses for the internal-business-process perspective in its balanced scorecard.

Nonfinancial Measures of Internal-Business-Process Quality

Photon measures internal-business-process quality using the following nonfinancial measures:

- Percentage of defective products
- Average time taken to repair photocopying machines at customer sites
- Percentage of reworked products
- Number of different types of defects analyzed using control charts, Pareto diagrams, and cause-and-effect diagrams
- Number of design and process changes made to improve design quality or reduce costs of quality

Photon's managers believe that improving these measures will lead to greater customer satisfaction, lower costs of quality, and better financial performance.

The Learning-and-Growth Perspective for Quality Improvements

What are the drivers of internal-business-process quality? Photon measures the following factors in the learning-and-growth perspective in the balanced scorecard:

- Employee turnover (ratio of number of employees who leave the company to the average total number of employees)
- Employee empowerment (ratio of the number of processes in which employees have the right to make decisions without consulting supervisors to the total number of processes)
- Employee satisfaction (ratio of employees indicating high satisfaction ratings to the total number of employees surveyed)
- Employee training (percentage of employees trained in different quality-enhancing methods)

Improvements in these measures are expected to lead to improvements in internal business-process, customer, and financial measures. As shown in the cause-and-effect diagram in Exhibit 19-5 (p. 672), two of the root human factor causes of fuzzy and unclear copies are poor training and new operators. Photon believes that increased employee training and lower employee turnover will therefore reduce the number of defective products and increase customer satisfaction, leading to better financial performance. These quality-related balanced scorecard measures are particularly informative when managers examine trends and relationships (across the learning and growth, the internal business process, and the customer and financial perspectives) over time as they seek to improve performance. To provide information on trends, management accountants must review the nonfinancial measures for accuracy and consistency.

Learning Objective 5

Describe the benefits of financial measures of quality

. . . evaluate trade-offs among different categories of costs of quality

and nonfinancial measures of quality

. . . identify problem areas, highlight leading indicators of future performance

Evaluating Quality Performance

Financial (COQ) and nonfinancial measures of quality in the balanced scorecard have different advantages.

Advantages of COQ Measures

- Consistent with the attention-directing role of management accounting, COQ measures focus managers' attention on the costs of poor quality.
- Total COQ provides a measure of quality performance for evaluating trade-offs among prevention costs, appraisal costs, internal failure costs, and external failure costs.

- COQ measures assist in problem solving by comparing costs and benefits of different quality-improvement programs and setting priorities for cost reduction.

Advantages of Nonfinancial Measures of Quality

- Nonfinancial measures of quality are often easy to quantify and understand.
- Nonfinancial measures direct attention to physical processes and hence help managers identify the precise problem areas that need improvement.
- Nonfinancial measures, such as number of defects, provide immediate short-run feedback on whether quality-improvement efforts are succeeding.
- Nonfinancial measures such as measures of customer satisfaction and employee satisfaction are useful indicators of long-run future performance.

COQ measures and nonfinancial measures complement each other. Without financial quality measures, companies could be spending more money on improving nonfinancial quality measures than it is worth. Without nonfinancial quality measures, quality problems might not be identified until it is too late. As a result, most organizations use both types of measures to gauge quality performance. McDonald's, for example, evaluates employees and individual franchisees on multiple measures of quality and customer satisfaction. A mystery shopper—an outside party contracted by McDonald's to evaluate restaurant performance—scores individual restaurants on quality, cleanliness, service, and value. A restaurant's performance on these dimensions is evaluated over time and against other restaurants. In its balanced scorecard, Photon evaluates whether improvements in various nonfinancial quality measures eventually lead to improvements in financial measures. By doing this, the company ensures that its quality improvement efforts are achieving success and improving profits.

PART TWO: TIME AS A COMPETITIVE TOOL

Companies increasingly view time as a driver of strategy.[3] Conducting business correctly and quickly helps increase revenues and decrease costs. For example, CapitalOne has increased business on its Web site by promising home-loan approval decisions in thirty minutes or less. Companies such as AT&T, General Electric, and Wal-Mart attribute not only higher revenues but also lower costs to doing things faster and on time. They cite, for example, the need to carry less inventory because of their ability to respond rapidly to customer demands.

Companies need to measure time to manage it properly. In this section, we focus on *operational measures of time*, which reveal how quickly companies respond to customers' demands for their products and services and their reliability in meeting scheduled delivery dates. Two common operational measures of time are customer-response time and on-time performance. We will also show how companies can measure the causes and costs of delays.

Learning Objective 6

Describe customer-response time

. . . time between receipt of customer order and product delivery

and explain why delays happen and their costs

. . . uncertainty about the timing of customer orders and limited capacity lead to lower revenues and higher inventory carrying costs

Customer-Response Time and On-Time Performance

Customer-response time is how long it takes from the time a customer places an order for a product or service to the time the product or service is delivered to the customer. Fast responses to customers are of strategic importance in industries such as construction, banking, car rental, and fast food. Some companies, such as Airbus, have to pay penalties to compensate their customers for lost revenues and profits (such as from being unable to operate flights) as a result of delays in delivering products to them.

[3] See K. Eisenhardt and S. Brown, "Time Pacing: Competing in Strategic Markets That Won't Stand Still," *Harvard Business Review* (March–April 1998); and T. Willis and A. Jurkus, "Product Development: An Essential Ingredient of Time-Based Competition," *Review of Business* (2001).

Exhibit 19-7 describes the components of customer-response time. In the case of Airbus, *receipt time* is how long it takes the Marketing Department to specify to the Manufacturing Department the exact requirements in the customer's order. **Manufacturing cycle time** (also called **manufacturing lead time**) is how long it takes from the time an order is received by Manufacturing to the time a finished good is produced. Manufacturing cycle time is the sum of waiting time and manufacturing time for an order. An aircraft order received by Airbus may need to wait because the required equipment is busy processing earlier orders. *Delivery time* is how long it takes to deliver a completed order to a customer.

Some companies evaluate their response time improvement efforts using a measure called **manufacturing cycle efficiency (MCE)**:

$$\text{MCE} = (\text{Value-Added manufacturing time} \div \text{Manufacturing cycle time})$$

Note that this measure includes only manufacturing time, and does not include the waiting time before the order is received by Manufacturing. As discussed in Chapter 12, value-added manufacturing activities are tasks that, if eliminated, would reduce the actual or perceived value or utility the customer receives from using the product, such as the time actually spent assembling the product. The rest of manufacturing cycle time represents nonvalue-added activities that, if eliminated, would not reduce the actual or perceived value or utility customers obtain from using the product. Examples of nonvalue-added cycle time include the time the product spends waiting for parts or for the next stage in the production process, being inspected or repaired, and being moved. By identifying and minimizing the sources of nonvalue-added cycle time, companies can increase customer responsiveness while reducing costs.

Similar measures apply to service industries as well. Consider a 40-minute doctor's office visit, of which 9 minutes is spent on administrative tasks such as filling out forms, 20 minutes is spent waiting in the reception area and examination room, and 11 minutes is spent with a nurse or doctor. The service cycle efficiency for this visit equals 11 ÷ 40, or 0.275. In other words, only 27.5% of the time in the office added value to the customer. Minimizing nonvalue-added cycle time in their medical delivery processes has allowed hospitals such as Alle-Kiski Medical Center in Pennsylvania to treat more patients in less time.

On-time performance is delivery of a product or service by the time it is scheduled to be delivered. Consider Federal Express, which specifies a price per package and a next-day delivery time of 10:30 A.M. for its overnight courier service. Federal Express measures on-time performance by how often it meets its stated delivery time of 10:30 A.M. On-time performance increases customer satisfaction. Commercial airlines gain loyal passengers as a result of consistent on-time service. But there is a trade-off between customer-response time and on-time performance. Deliberately scheduling longer customer-response times, such as airlines lengthening scheduled arrival times, makes achieving on-time performance easier—but it could displease customers!

Time Drivers and Costs of Time

Managing customer-response time and on-time performance requires understanding the causes and costs of delays. Delays can occur, for example, at a machine in a manufacturing plant or at a checkout counter in a store.

Exhibit 19-7

Components of Customer-Response Time

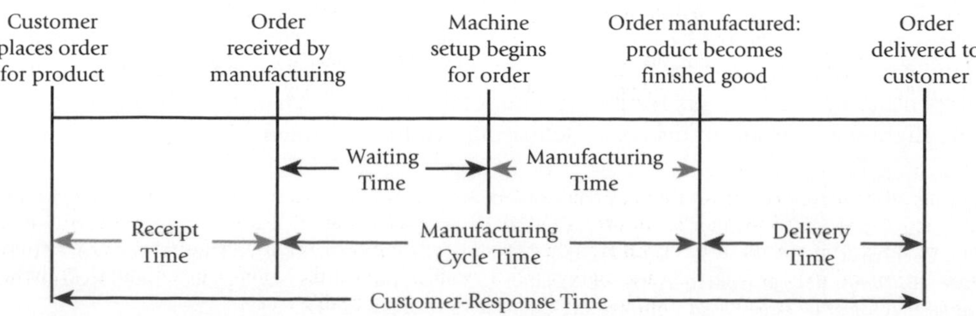

Uncertainty and Bottlenecks as Drivers of Time

A **time driver** is any factor that causes a change in the speed of an activity when the factor changes. Two time drivers we consider are:

1. **Uncertainty about when customers will order products or services.** For example, the more randomly Airbus receives orders for its airplanes, the more likely queues will form and delays will occur.
2. **Bottlenecks due to limited capacity.** A **bottleneck** occurs in an operation when the work to be performed approaches or exceeds the capacity available to do it. For example, a bottleneck results and causes delays when products that must be processed at a particular machine arrive while the machine is being used to process other products. Bottlenecks can also occur on the Internet, for example, when many people try to view a company's Web site at the same time (see Concepts in Action, p. 678).

Consider Falcon Works (FW), which uses one turning machine to convert steel bars into a special gear for planes. FW makes this gear, which is its only product, only after customers have ordered it. To focus on manufacturing lead time, we assume FW's receipt time and delivery time are minimal. FW's strategy is to differentiate itself from competitors by offering faster delivery. The company is examining opportunities to increase profits without sacrificing the competitive advantage provided by shorter customer-response times. It examines these opportunities using the five-step decision-making process introduced in Chapter 1.

Step 1. Identify the problem and uncertainties. FW is considering whether to introduce a second product, a piston for pumps. The primary uncertainty is how the introduction of a second product will affect manufacturing lead times for gears.

Step 2. Obtain information. FW begins investigating the potential effect of pistons on manufacturing lead times by gathering data on gear manufacturing times. FW typically receives 30 orders for gears, but it could receive 10, 30, or 50 orders. Each order is for 1,000 units and takes 100 hours of manufacturing time (8 hours of setup time to clean and prepare the machine, and 92 hours of processing time). Annual capacity of the machine is 4,000 hours. If FW receives the 30 orders it expects, the total amount of manufacturing time required on the machine is 3,000 hours (100 hours per order × 30 orders), which is within the available machine capacity of 4,000 hours. Even though capacity utilization is not strained, queues and delays can still occur. That's because uncertainty about when FW's customers will place their orders can cause an order to be received while the machine is processing an earlier order.

Step 3. Make predictions about the future. FW needs to make assumptions about the pattern of customer orders and how the orders will be processed. In the single-product case (when FW is only making gears), **average waiting time**, the average amount of time that an order will wait in line before the machine is set up and the order is processed, equals:[4]

$$\frac{\begin{array}{c}\text{Annual average}\\ \text{number of}\\ \text{orders for gears}\end{array} \times \left(\begin{array}{c}\text{Manufacturing}\\ \text{time per order}\\ \text{for gears}\end{array}\right)^2}{2 \times \left[\begin{array}{c}\text{Annual machine}\\ \text{capacity}\end{array} - \left(\begin{array}{c}\text{Annual average number}\\ \text{of orders for gears}\end{array} \times \begin{array}{c}\text{Manufacturing}\\ \text{time per order for gears}\end{array}\right)\right]}$$

$$= \frac{30 \times (100)^2}{2 \times [4{,}000 - (30 \times 100)]} = \frac{30 \times 10{,}000}{2 \times (4{,}000 - 3{,}000)} = \frac{300{,}000}{2 \times 1{,}000} = \frac{300{,}000}{2{,}000} = 150 \text{ hours per order (for gears)}$$

[4] The technical assumptions are (a) that customer orders for the product follow a Poisson distribution with a mean equal to the expected number of orders (30 in our example), and (b) that orders are processed on a first-in, first-out (FIFO) basis. The Poisson arrival pattern for customer orders has been found to be reasonable in many real-world settings. The FIFO assumption can be modified. Under the modified assumptions, the basic queuing and delay effects will still occur, but the precise formulas will be different.

Concepts in Action

Overcoming Bottlenecks on the Internet

In 2007, Deloitte & Touche reported that the unrelenting growth in Internet traffic is beginning to overwhelm the Internet's backbone and threatens the flow of broadband traffic. Could this be true? While the Internet will not collapse tomorrow, exponential growth in Web usage in recent years already causes many users to suffer from online bottlenecks. These bottlenecks are caused when too many people try to view the same information on a computer server at the same time. They affect all users, but these bottlenecks are most harmful to companies buying and selling their products and services over the Internet.

As companies become increasingly reliant on e-commerce and time-sensitive information sharing, the inability of a company to handle all the traffic on its Web site can become a serious problem. One study found that more than 40% of online shoppers abandon a transaction if the site they are on is responding too slowly. The costs can be much larger. In recent years, a three-day outage forced ESPN to compensate some of its 260,000 online fantasy baseball players. Wal-Mart, Disney, and Amazon.com lost millions of dollars in sales in 2006 because of Web site crashes on the busiest U.S. shopping day of the year: the day after Thanksgiving. And, in 2007, a two-day crash of voice-over IP (VoIP) telephone service, Skype, reduced the value of eBay, its parent company, stock by more than $1 billion.

To relieve these bottlenecks and avoid their negative consequences, companies have developed technologies that use remote caching (storing duplicated data) and remote mirroring. Storing, or caching, seldom-updated content on remote servers is one way to reduce network traffic. Social-networking site MySpace, for example, stores its static content on Akamai's third-party global network, which consists of over 15,000 servers. When someone accesses the MySpace Web site, the caching system routes each individual request for content to servers that are geographically closer to the user, so the request travels a shorter distance along the Internet for faster page loading and transaction processing.

Remote mirroring allows a company to copy (or "mirror") huge databases in many different geographically remote locations. Using redundant arrays of inexpensive disks (RAID) technology, backup databases are copied via the Internet on computer-storage devices. Each extra copy not only serves as a backup in the event of system crashes, but it also relieves traffic congestion on the Internet by allowing remote mirroring technology to instantly reroute Web traffic around trouble spots to data sites that have much less traffic and faster response times.

Remote caching and remote mirroring allow companies to efficiently relieve bottleneck constraints, increase capacity, and improve customer-response time. As Internet traffic increases exponentially with voice-over IP (VoIP) telephone service and hundreds of millions of new users from developing countries logging on for the first time, these technologies will be critical to ensuring the stability, operability, and profitability of many of the Internet's most popular sites.

Sources: *Risk Management* (May 2001); *The Wall Street Journal* (March 20, 2001); *Business Wire* (October 4, 1999); and a poll conducted by www.esearch.com in 1999; "Downtime and Lost Revenue," *NetSource America*, www.netsourceamerica.com/networth1.html, accessed September 17, 2004; T. Wilson, "The Cost of Downtime," NMSalert.com, cms.nmsalert.com/website-monitoring-articles/downtime-costs-website, accessed September 17, 2004; Riley, D., "EBay Sees $1 Billion Knocked Off Market Cap; Skype Outages Continue," Techcrunch.com (August 16, 2007), www.techcrunch.com/2007/08/16/ebay-sees-1-billion-knocked-off-market-cap-as-skype-outages-continue/, accessed September 10, 2007; "Customer Story: MySpace," Akamai Technologies, Inc., www.akamai.com/html/customers/myspace.html, accessed September 10, 2007; *Telecommunications Predictions: TMT Trends 2007*. Deloitte Touche Tohmatsu (January 2007); Schuman, E., "Black Friday Turns Servers Dark at Wal-Mart, Macy's," eWeek.com, www.eweek.com/article2/0,1759,2063540,00.asp?kc=EWRSS03119TX1K0000594, accessed September 12, 2007; "If You're Going To Plan Online Doorbusters, Shouldn't You Plan Ahead For The Traffic?" Techdirt.com, techdirt.com/articles/20061127/003219.shtml, accessed September 12, 2007.

Therefore, the average manufacturing lead time for an order is 250 hours (150 hours of average waiting time + 100 hours of manufacturing time). Note that manufacturing time per order is a squared term in the numerator. It indicates the disproportionately large impact manufacturing time has on waiting time. The longer the manufacturing time, the much greater the chance that the machine will be in use when an order arrives, leading to longer delays. The denominator in this formula is a measure of the unused capacity, or cushion. The smaller the unused capacity, the greater the chance that the machine is processing an earlier order, and the greater the delays.

Our formula describes only the *average* waiting time. A particular order might arrive when the machine is free, in which case manufacturing will start immediately. In another situation, FW may receive an order while two other orders are waiting to be processed, which means the delay will be longer than 150 hours.

In considering whether to produce a second product, pistons, FW makes the following predictions: It expects to receive 10 orders for pistons, each order for 800 units, in the coming year. Each order will take 50 hours of manufacturing time, comprising 3 hours for setup and 47 hours of processing. Expected demand for FW's gears will be unaffected by whether FW introduces piston products.

Average waiting time *before* machine setup begins is determined using the following formula, which is an extension of the preceding formula for the single-product case.

$$\frac{\left[\text{Annual average number of orders for gears} \times \left(\text{Manufacturing time per order for gears}\right)^2\right] + \left[\text{Annual average number of orders for pistons} \times \left(\text{Manufacturing time per order for pistons}\right)^2\right]}{2 \times \left[\text{Annual machine capacity} - \left(\text{Annual average number of orders for gears} \times \text{Manufacturing time per order for gears}\right) - \left(\text{Annual average number of orders for pistons} \times \text{Manufacturing time per order for pistons}\right)\right]}$$

$$= \frac{[30 \times (100)^2] + [10 \times (50)^2]}{2 \times [4{,}000 - (30 \times 100) - (10 \times 50)]} = \frac{(30 \times 10{,}000) + (10 \times 2{,}500)}{2 \times (4{,}000 - 3{,}000 - 500)}$$

$$= \frac{300{,}000 + 25{,}000}{2 \times 500} = \frac{325{,}000}{1{,}000} = 325 \text{ hours per order (for gears } \textit{and} \text{ pistons)}$$

Introducing pistons causes average waiting time for an order to more than double, from 150 hours to 325 hours. That's because introducing pistons causes unused capacity to shrink, increasing the probability that, at any point in time, new orders will arrive while current orders are being manufactured or waiting to be manufactured. Average waiting time is very sensitive to the shrinking of unused capacity.

With the addition of another product, average manufacturing lead time for a gear order is now 425 hours (325 hours of average waiting time + 100 hours of manufacturing time), and for a piston order 375 hours (325 hours of average waiting time + 50 hours of manufacturing time). Note that a piston order spends 86.7% (325 ÷ 375) of its manufacturing lead time just waiting for manufacturing to start!

Step 4. Make decisions by choosing among alternatives. Given the anticipated effects on manufacturing lead time of adding pistons, should FW introduce pistons? FW would likely ask its management accountant to evaluate the profitability of a new product, given capacity constraints. The management accountant needs to identify and analyze the relevant revenues and relevant costs of adding the piston product and, in particular, to evaluate the cost effects of the resulting delays on all products. The rest of this section continues to focus on Step 4. While we do not cover Step 5 in this particular example, we discuss using the balanced scorecard to evaluate and learn from time-based performance later in the chapter.

Relevant Revenues and Costs of Time

To determine the relevant revenues and costs of adding pistons under Step 4, consider the following additional information:

Product	Annual Average Number of Orders	Average Selling Price per Order If Average Manufacturing Lead Time per Order Is		Direct Material Cost per Order	Inventory Carrying Cost per Order per Hour
		Less Than 300 Hours	More Than 300 Hours		
Gears	30	$22,000	$21,500	$16,000	$1.00
Pistons	10	10,000	9,600	8,000	0.50

Manufacturing lead times affect both revenues and costs in our example. Revenues are affected because customers are willing to pay a higher price for faster delivery. On the cost side, direct material costs and inventory carrying costs are the only costs that will be affected by introducing pistons (all other costs are unaffected, and hence irrelevant). Inventory carrying costs consist of the opportunity costs of investment tied up in inventory (see Chapter 11, pp. 399–400) and the relevant costs of storage, such as space rental, spoilage, deterioration, and materials handling. Companies usually calculate inventory carrying costs on a per-unit, per-year basis. To simplify calculations, we express inventory carrying costs on a per-order, per-hour basis. As in most companies, we assume FW acquires direct materials at the time the order is received by manufacturing, and, therefore, incurs inventory carrying costs for the duration of the manufacturing lead time.

Exhibit 19-8 presents relevant revenues and relevant costs for the "introduce pistons" and "do not introduce pistons" alternatives. Interestingly, the decision is to not introduce pistons, even though pistons have a positive contribution margin of $1,600 ($9,600 – $8,000) per order. Also, FW has the capacity to process pistons (even if it produces pistons, FW will, on average, use only 3,500 of the available 4,000 machine-hours). So why is FW better off to not introduce pistons? *Because of the negative effects that producing pistons will have on the existing product, gears.* The following table presents the *costs of time*—that is, the expected loss in revenues and expected increase in carrying costs as a result of delays caused by using machine capacity to manufacture pistons.

	Effect of Increasing Average Manufacturing Lead Time		Expected Loss in Revenues Plus Expected Increase in Carrying Costs of Introducing Pistons
Product	Expected Loss in Revenues for Gears (1)	Expected Increase in Carrying Costs for All Products (2)	(3) = (1) + (2)
Gears	$15,000[a]	$5,250[b]	$20,250
Pistons	—	1,875[c]	1,875
Total	$15,000	$7,125	$22,125

[a]($22,000 – $21,500) per order × 30 expected orders = $15,000.
[b](425 – 250) hours per order × $1.00 per hour × 30 expected orders = $5,250.
[c](375 – 0) hours per order × $0.50 per hour × 10 expected orders = $1,875.

Introducing pistons causes the average manufacturing lead time of gears to increase from 250 hours to 425 hours. The cost of longer manufacturing lead times is an increase in inventory carrying costs of gears and a decrease in gear revenues (caused by average manufacturing lead time for gears exceeding 300 hours). The expected costs of longer lead times from introducing pistons, $22,125, exceeds the expected contribution margin of $16,000 ($1,600 per order × 10 expected orders) from selling pistons by $6,125 (the difference calculated in Exhibit 19-8).

Our simple setting illustrates that when demand uncertainty is high, some unused capacity is desirable.[5] Increasing the capacity of a bottleneck resource reduces manufacturing lead times and delays. One way to increase capacity is to reduce the time required for setups and processing via more-efficient setups and processing. Another way to increase capacity is to invest in new equipment, such as flexible manufacturing systems that can be programmed to switch quickly from producing one product to producing another. Delays can also be reduced through careful scheduling of orders on machines—for example, by batching similar jobs together for processing.

Learning Objective 7

Apply the three measures in the theory of constraints

. . . throughput contribution, investments, and operating costs

PART THREE: THEORY OF CONSTRAINTS AND THROUGHPUT-CONTRIBUTION ANALYSIS

In this section, we consider products that are made from multiple parts and processed on multiple machines. With multiple parts and machines, dependencies arise among operations—that is, some operations cannot be started until parts from the preceding operation

[5] Other complexities, such as analyzing a network of machines, priority scheduling, and allowing for uncertainty in processing times, are beyond the scope of this book. In these cases, the basic queuing and delay effects persist, but the precise formulas are more complex.

Exhibit 19-8

Determining Expected Relevant Revenues and Relevant Costs for Falcon Works' Decision to Introduce Pistons

Relevant Items	Alternative 1: Introduce Pistons (1)	Alternative 2: Do Not Introduce Pistons (2)	Difference (3) = (1) – (2)
Expected revenues	$741,000[a]	$660,000[b]	$ 81,000
Expected variable costs	560,000[c]	480,000[d]	(80,000)
Expected inventory carrying costs	14,625[e]	7,500[f]	(7,125)
Expected total costs	574,625	487,500	(87,125)
Expected revenues minus expected costs	$166,375	$172,500	$ (6,125)

[a]($21,500 × 30) + ($9,600 × 10) = $741,000; average manufacturing lead time will be more than 300 hours.

[b]($22,000 × 30) = $660,000; average manufacturing lead time will be less than 300 hours.

[c]($16,000 × 30) + ($8,000 × 10) = $560,000.

[d]$16,000 × 30 = $480,000.

[e](Average manufacturing lead time for gears × Unit carrying cost per order for gears × Expected number of orders for gears) + (Average manufacturing lead time for pistons × Unit carrying cost per order for pistons × Expected number of orders for pistons) = (425 × $1.00 × 30) + (375 × $0.50 × 10) = $12,750 + $1,875 = $14,625.

[f]Average manufacturing lead time for gears × Unit carrying cost per order for gears × Expected number of orders for gears = 250 × $1.00 × 30 = $7,500.

are available. Furthermore, some operations are bottlenecks (have limited capacity), and others are not.

Managing Bottlenecks

Learning Objective 8

Explain how to manage bottlenecks

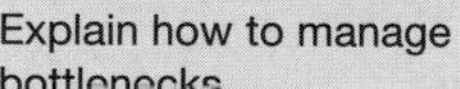

. . . keep bottlenecks busy and increase their efficiency and capacity

The **theory of constraints (TOC)** describes methods to maximize operating income when faced with some bottleneck and some nonbottleneck operations.[6] The TOC defines three measures:

1. **Throughput contribution** equals revenues minus the direct material costs of the goods sold.
2. *Investments* equal the sum of materials costs in direct materials, work-in-process, and finished goods inventories; R&D costs; and costs of equipment and buildings.
3. *Operating costs* equal all costs of operations (other than direct materials) incurred to earn throughput contribution. Operating costs include salaries and wages, rent, utilities, depreciation, and the like.

The objective of TOC is to increase throughput contribution while decreasing investments and operating costs. *TOC considers a short-run time horizon and assumes that operating costs are fixed costs.* The steps in managing bottleneck operations are:

Step 1: Recognize that the bottleneck operation determines throughput contribution of the entire system.

Step 2: Identify the bottleneck operation by identifying operations with large quantities of inventory waiting to be worked on.

Step 3: Keep the bottleneck operation busy and subordinate all nonbottleneck operations to the bottleneck operation. That is, the needs of the bottleneck operation determine the production schedule of the nonbottleneck operations.

Step 3 represents one of the concepts described in Chapter 11: To maximize operating income, the plant must maximize contribution margin (in this case, throughput contribution) of the constrained or bottleneck resource (see pp. 400–401). For this reason, step 3 suggests that the bottleneck machine must always be kept running. It should not be waiting

[6] See E. Goldratt and J. Cox, *The Goal* (New York: North River Press, 1986); E. Goldratt, *The Theory of Constraints* (New York: North River Press, 1990); E. Noreen, D. Smith, and J. Mackey, *The Theory of Constraints and Its Implications for Management Accounting* (New York: North River Press, 1995); and M. Woeppel, *Manufacturers' Guide to Implementing the Theory of Constraints* (Boca Raton, FL: Lewis Publishing, 2000).

for jobs. To achieve this objective, companies often maintain a small buffer inventory of jobs waiting for the bottleneck machine. The bottleneck machine sets the pace for all nonbottleneck machines. For example, production schedulers instruct workers at nonbottleneck machines to not produce more output than can be processed by the bottleneck machine. Producing more nonbottleneck output only creates excess inventory; it does not increase throughput contribution.

Step 4: Take actions to increase the efficiency and capacity of the bottleneck operation: The objective is to increase the difference between throughput contribution and the incremental costs of increasing efficiency and capacity. The management accountant's role in step 4 is calculating throughput contribution, identifying relevant and irrelevant costs, and preparing cost–benefit analyses of alternative actions.

We illustrate step 4 using data from Cardinal Industries (CI). CI manufactures car doors in two operations: stamping and pressing.

	Stamping	Pressing
Capacity per hour	20 units	15 units
Annual capacity (6,000 hours of capacity available in each operation)		
6,000 hours × 20 units/hour; 6,000 hours × 15 units/hour)	120,000 units	90,000 units
Annual production and sales	90,000 units	90,000 units
Other fixed operating costs (excluding direct materials)	$720,000	$1,080,000
Other fixed operating costs per unit produced ($720,000 ÷ 90,000 units; $1,080,000 ÷ 90,000 units)	$8 per unit	$12 per unit

Each door sells for $100 and has a direct material cost of $40. Variable costs in other functions of the value chain—R&D, design of products and processes, marketing, distribution, and customer service—are negligible. CI's output is constrained by the capacity of 90,000 units in the pressing operation. What can CI do to relieve the bottleneck constraint of the pressing operation? Desirable actions include:

1. **Eliminate idle time at the bottleneck operation (time when the pressing machine is neither being set up to process products nor actually processing products).** CI is considering permanently positioning two workers at the pressing operation to unload finished units as soon as one batch of units is processed and to set up the machine to process the next batch. Suppose the annual cost of this action is $48,000 and the effect is to increase bottleneck output by 1,000 doors per year. Should CI incur the additional costs? Yes, because CI's throughput contribution increases by $60,000 [(selling price per door, $100 − direct material cost per door, $40) × 1,000 doors], which exceeds the additional cost of $48,000. All other costs are irrelevant.
2. **Process only those parts or products that increase throughput contribution, not parts or products that will remain in finished goods or spare parts inventories.** Making products that remain in inventory does not increase throughput contribution.
3. **Shift products that do not have to be made on the bottleneck machine to nonbottleneck machines or to outside processing facilities.** Suppose Spartan Corporation, an outside contractor, offers to press 1,500 doors at $15 per door from stamped parts that CI supplies. Spartan's quoted price is greater than CI's own operating costs in the Pressing Department of $12 per door. Should CI accept the offer? Yes, because pressing is the bottleneck operation. Getting additional doors pressed by Spartan increases throughput contribution by $90,000 [($100 − $40) per door × 1,500 doors], while relevant costs increase by $22,500 ($15 per door × 1,500 doors). The fact that CI's unit cost is less than Spartan's quoted price is irrelevant in the analysis.

   Suppose Gemini Industries, another outside contractor, offers to stamp 2,000 doors from direct materials that CI supplies at $6 per door. Gemini's price is lower than CI's operating cost of $8 per door in the Stamping Department. Should CI accept the offer? No, because other operating costs are fixed costs. CI will not save any costs by subcontracting the stamping operations. Total costs will be greater by $12,000 ($6 per door × 2,000 doors) under the subcontracting alternative. Stamping more doors will not increase throughput contribution, which is constrained by pressing capacity.

4. **Reduce setup time and processing time at bottleneck operations (for example, by simplifying the design or reducing the number of parts in the product).** Suppose CI can reduce setup time at the pressing operation by incurring additional costs of $55,000 a year. Suppose further that reducing setup time enables CI to press 2,500 more doors a year. Should CI incur the costs to reduce setup time? Yes, because throughput contribution increases by $150,000 [($100 − $40) per door × 2,500 doors], which exceeds the additional costs incurred of $55,000. Will CI find it worthwhile to incur costs to reduce machining time at the nonbottleneck stamping operation? No. Other operating costs will increase, but throughput contribution will remain unchanged because bottleneck capacity has not increased.
5. **Improve the quality of parts or products manufactured at the bottleneck operation.** Poor quality is often more costly at a bottleneck operation than it is at a nonbottleneck operation. The cost of poor quality at a nonbottleneck operation is the cost of materials wasted. If CI produces 1,000 defective doors at the stamping operation, the cost of poor quality is $40,000 (direct material cost per door, $40, × 1,000 doors). No throughput contribution is forgone because stamping has unused capacity. Despite the defective production, stamping can produce and transfer 90,000 good-quality doors to the pressing operation. At a bottleneck operation, the cost of poor quality is the cost of materials wasted *plus* the opportunity cost of lost throughput contribution. Bottleneck capacity not wasted in producing defective units could be used to generate additional throughput contribution. If CI produces 1,000 defective units at the pressing operation, the cost of poor quality is the lost revenue of $100,000, or alternatively stated, direct material costs of $40,000 (direct material cost per door, $40, × 1,000 doors) plus forgone throughput contribution of $60,000 [($100 − $40) per door × 1,000 doors].

   The high cost of poor quality at the bottleneck operation means that bottleneck time should not be wasted processing units that are defective. That is, inspection should be done before processing parts at the bottleneck operation to ensure that only good-quality units are transferred to the bottleneck operation. Furthermore, quality-improvement programs should place special emphasis on minimizing defects at bottleneck machines.

If the actions in step 4 are successful, the capacity of the pressing operation will increase and eventually exceed the capacity of the stamping operation. The bottleneck will then shift to the stamping operation. CI would then focus continuous-improvement actions on increasing stamping efficiency and capacity. For example, the contract with Gemini Industries to stamp 2,000 doors at $6 per door from direct material supplied by CI becomes attractive then. That's because throughput contribution will increase by ($100 − $40) per door × 2,000 doors = $120,000, while costs will increase by $12,000 ($6 per door × 2,000 doors).

The theory of constraints emphasizes management of bottleneck operations as the key to improving performance of production operations as a whole. It focuses on short-run maximization of throughput contribution—revenues minus direct material costs of goods sold. Because TOC regards operating costs as difficult to change in the short run, it does not identify individual activities and drivers of costs. TOC is, therefore, less useful for the long-run management of costs. Activity-based costing (ABC) systems, however, take a longer-run perspective when more costs can be managed; the focus is on improving processes by eliminating nonvalue-added activities and reducing the costs of performing value-added activities. ABC systems, therefore, are more useful for long-run pricing, long-run cost control and profit planning, and capacity management. The short-run TOC emphasis on maximizing throughput contribution by managing bottlenecks complements the long-run strategic-cost-management focus of ABC.[7]

[7] For an excellent evaluation of TOC, operations management, cost accounting, and the relationship between TOC and activity-based costing, see A. Atkinson, "*Cost Accounting, the Theory of Constraints, and Costing,*" (Issue Paper, CMA Canada, December 2000).

Balanced Scorecard and Time-Related Measures

The balanced scorecard can play a key role in the final step of the five-step decision-making process (implementing the decision, evaluating performance, and learning). This is achieved by tracking changes in time-based measures and determining whether these changes affect financial performance. Based on this information, decisions and plans can be modified as required to achieve the company's goals. In this section, we use the balanced scorecard to summarize how financial and nonfinancial measures of time relate to one another. We classify these measures under the four perspectives of the balanced scorecard—financial, customer, internal business processes, and learning and growth. Managers use the balanced scorecard measures to reduce delays and to increase throughput of their bottleneck operations.

Financial measures

Revenue losses or price discounts attributable to delays

Carrying cost of inventories

Throughput contribution minus operating costs

Customer measures

Customer-response time (the time it takes to fulfill a customer order)

On-time performance (delivering a product or service by the scheduled time)

Internal-business-process measures

Average manufacturing time for key products

Manufacturing cycle efficiency for key processes

Idle time at bottleneck operations

Defective units produced at bottleneck operations

Average reduction in setup time and processing time at bottleneck operations

Learning-and-growth measures

Employee satisfaction

Number of employees trained in managing bottleneck operations

Note the cause-and-effect linkages across these measures. For example, better employee training leads to better management of bottleneck operations, which in turn leads to better customer-response times and higher revenues and throughput contributions. Managers use time-related measures in the balanced scorecard to help them identify actions that improve customer-response times and create long-run competitive advantage. For example, The Bell Group, a designer and manufacturer of equipment for the jewelry industry, used the theory of constraints to select measures in the four balanced scorecard categories. Based on TOC analysis, the company determined that a key financial measure was improving throughput contribution by 18% for a specific product line. In the customer perspective, the company set a goal of a two-day turn-around time on all orders for the product. To achieve this goal, the internal-business-process measure was the amount of time a bottleneck machine operated, with a goal of running 22 hours per day, six days a week. Finally, in the learning perspective, the company focused on training new employees to carry out nonbottleneck operations in order to free experienced employees to operate the bottleneck machine. The Bell Group's emphasis on time-related measures in its balanced scorecard has allowed the company to substantially increase manufacturing throughput and slash response times, leading to higher revenues and increased profits.[8]

[8] "The Bell Group Uses the Balanced Scorecard with the Theory of Constraints to Keep Strategic Focus," FastTrack.roundtable.com, fasttrack.roundtable.com/app/content/knowledgesource/item/197, accessed May 15, 2007.

Problem for Self-Study

The Sloan Moving Corporation transports household goods from one city to another within the continental United States. It measures quality of service in terms of (a) time required to transport goods, (b) on-time delivery (within two days of agreed-upon delivery date), and (c) number of lost or damaged shipments. Sloan is considering investing in a new scheduling-and-tracking system costing $160,000 per year, which should help it improve performance with respect to items (b) and (c). The following information describes Sloan's current performance and the expected performance if the new system is implemented:

	Current Performance	Expected Future Performance
On-time delivery performance	85%	95%
Variable cost per carton lost or damaged	$60	$60
Fixed cost per carton lost or damaged	$40	$40
Number of cartons lost or damaged per year	3,000 cartons	1,000 cartons

Sloan expects each percentage point increase in on-time performance to increase revenue by $20,000 per year. Sloan's contribution margin percentage is 45%.

Required

1. Should Sloan acquire the new system? Show your calculations.
2. Sloan is very confident about the cost savings from fewer lost or damaged cartons as a result of introducing the new system. Calculate the minimum amount of increase in revenues needed for Sloan to invest in the new system.

Solution

1. Additional costs of the new scheduling-and-tracking system are $160,000 per year. Additional annual benefits of the new scheduling-and-tracking system are:

Additional annual revenues from a 10% improvement in on-time performance, from 85% to 95%, $20,000 per 1% × 10 percentage points	$200,000
45% contribution margin from additional annual revenues (0.45 × $200,000)	$ 90,000
Decrease in costs per year from fewer cartons lost or damaged (only variable costs are relevant) [$60 per carton × (3,000 − 1,000) cartons]	120,000
Total additional benefits	$210,000

Because the benefits of $210,000 exceed the costs of $160,000, Sloan should invest in the new system.

2. As long as Sloan earns a contribution margin of $40,000 (to cover incremental costs of $160,000 minus relevant variable-cost savings of $120,000) from additional annual revenues, investing in the new system is beneficial. This contribution margin corresponds to additional revenues of $40,000 ÷ 0.45 = $88,889.

Decision Points

The following question-and-answer format summarizes the chapter's learning objectives. Each decision presents a key question related to a learning objective. The guidelines are the answer to that question.

Decision	Guidelines
1. What are the four cost categories of a costs-of-quality program?	Four cost categories in a costs-of-quality program are prevention costs (costs incurred to preclude the production of products that do not conform to specifications), appraisal costs (costs incurred to detect which of the individual units of products do not conform to specifications), internal failure costs (costs incurred on defective products before they are shipped to customers), and external failure costs (costs incurred on defective products after they are shipped to customers).
2. What nonfinancial quality measures of customer satisfaction can managers use in their balanced scorecards?	Nonfinancial quality measures of customer satisfaction that managers can use in their balanced scorecards include number of customer complaints and percentage of defective units shipped to customers.
3. What methods can managers use to identify quality problems and improve quality?	Three methods to identify quality problems and to improve quality are (a) control charts, to distinguish random from nonrandom variations in an operating process; (b) Pareto diagrams, to indicate how frequently each type of failure occurs; and (c) cause-and-effect diagrams, to identify potential causes of failure.
4. How do managers identify the relevant costs and benefits of quality improvement programs?	The relevant costs of quality improvement programs are the incremental costs to implement the quality program. The relevant benefits are the cost savings and the estimated increase in contribution margin from the higher revenues that result from quality improvements.
5. Why should managers use both financial and nonfinancial measures of quality?	Financial measures are helpful to evaluate trade-offs among prevention costs, appraisal costs, and failure costs. Nonfinancial measures identify problem areas that need improvement and serve as indicators of future long-run performance.
6. What is customer-response time? What are the reasons for and the costs of delays?	Customer-response time is how long it takes from the time a customer places an order for a product or service to the time the product or service is delivered to the customer. Delays occur because of (a) uncertainty about when customers will order products or services and (b) bottlenecks due to limited capacity. Bottlenecks are operations at which the work to be performed approaches or exceeds available capacity. Costs of delays include lower revenues and increased inventory carrying costs.
7. What three measures do managers need to implement the theory of constraints?	The three measures in the theory of constraints are (1) throughput contribution (equal to revenues minus direct material costs of the goods sold); (2) investments (equal to the sum of materials costs in direct materials, work-in-process, and finished goods inventories along with R&D costs and costs of equipment and buildings); and (3) operating costs (equal to all operating costs, other than direct material costs, incurred to earn throughput contribution).
8. What are the steps managers can take to manage bottlenecks?	The four steps in managing bottlenecks are (1) recognize that the bottleneck operation determines throughput contribution, (2) identify the bottleneck, (3) keep the bottleneck busy and subordinate all nonbottleneck operations to the bottleneck operation, and (4) increase bottleneck efficiency and capacity.

TERMS TO LEARN

This chapter and the Glossary at the end of the book contain definitions of:

appraisal costs (**p. 667**)
average waiting time (**p. 677**)
bottleneck (**p. 677**)
cause-and-effect diagram (**p. 671**)
conformance quality (**p. 666**)
control chart (**p. 670**)
costs of quality (COQ) (**p. 667**)
customer-response time (**p. 675**)
design quality (**p. 666**)
external failure costs (**p. 667**)
internal failure costs (**p. 667**)
manufacturing cycle efficiency (MCE) (**p. 676**)
manufacturing cycle time (**p. 676**)
manufacturing lead time (**p. 676**)
on-time performance (**p. 676**)
Pareto diagram (**p. 671**)
prevention costs (**p. 667**)
quality (**p. 665**)
theory of constraints (TOC) (**p. 681**)
throughput contribution (**p. 681**)
time driver (**p. 677**)

ASSIGNMENT MATERIAL

Questions

19-1 Describe two benefits of improving quality.

19-2 How does conformance quality differ from design quality? Explain.

19-3 Name two items classified as prevention costs.

19-4 Distinguish between internal failure costs and external failure costs.

19-5 Describe three methods that companies use to identify quality problems.

19-6 "Companies should focus on financial measures of quality because these are the only measures of quality that can be linked to bottom-line performance." Do you agree? Explain.

19-7 Give two examples of nonfinancial measures of customer satisfaction relating to quality in a balanced scorecard.

19-8 Give two examples of nonfinancial measures of internal-business-process quality in a balanced scorecard.

19-9 Distinguish between customer-response time and manufacturing lead time.

19-10 "There is no trade-off between customer-response time and on-time performance." Do you agree? Explain.

19-11 Give two reasons why delays occur.

19-12 "Companies should always make and sell all products whose selling prices exceed variable costs." Assuming fixed costs are irrelevant, do you agree? Explain.

19-13 Describe the three main measures used in the theory of constraints.

19-14 Describe the four key steps in managing bottleneck operations.

19-15 Describe three ways to improve the performance of a bottleneck operation.

Exercises

19-16 Costs of quality. (CMA, adapted) Costen, Inc., produces cell phone equipment. Jessica Tolmy, Costen's president, decided to devote more resources to the improvement of product quality after learning that her company had been ranked fourth in product quality in a 2008 survey of cell phone users. Costen's quality-improvement program has now been in operation for two years, and the cost report shown here has recently been issued.

	A	B	C	D	E
1	Semi-annual COQ report, Costen, Inc.				
2	(In thousands)				
3		6/30/2009	12/31/2009	6/30/2010	12/31/2010
4	Prevention costs				
5	Machine maintenance	$ 440	$ 440	$ 390	$ 330
6	Supplier training	20	100	50	40
7	Design reviews	50	214	210	200
8	Total prevention costs	510	754	650	570
9	Appraisal costs				
10	Incoming inspections	108	123	90	63
11	Final testing	332	332	293	203
12	Total appraisal costs	440	455	383	266
13	Internal failure costs				
14	Rework	231	202	165	112
15	Scrap	124	116	71	67
16	Total internal failure costs	355	318	236	179
17	External failure costs				
18	Warranty repairs	165	85	72	68
19	Customer returns	570	547	264	188
20	Total external failure costs	735	632	336	256
21	Total quality costs	$2,040	$2,159	$1,605	$1,271
22					
23	Total revenues	$8,240	$9,080	$9,300	$9,020

If you want to use Excel to solve this exercise, go to the Excel Lab at **www.prenhall.com/horngren/cost13e** and download the template for Exercise 19-16.

Required

1. For each period, calculate the ratio of each COQ category to revenues and to total quality costs.
2. Based on the results of requirement 1, would you conclude that Costen's quality program has been successful? Prepare a short report to present your case.
3. Based on the 2008 survey, Jessica Tolmy believed that Costen had to improve product quality. In making her case to Costen management, how might Tolmy have estimated the opportunity cost of not implementing the quality-improvement program?

19-17 Costs of quality analysis. Safe Rider produces car seats for children from newborn to 2 years old. The company is worried because one of its competitors has recently come under public scrutiny because of product failure. Historically, Safe Rider's only problem with its car seats was stitching in the straps. The problem can usually be detected and repaired during an internal inspection. The cost of the inspection is $5, and the repair cost is $1. All 100,000 car seats were inspected last year and 5% were found to have problems with the stitching in the straps during the internal inspection. Another 2% of the 100,000 car seats had problems with the stitching, but the internal inspection did not discover them. Defective units that were sold and shipped to customers needed to be shipped back to Safe Rider and repaired. Shipping costs are $10, and repair costs are $1. However, the out-of-pocket costs (shipping and repair) are not the only costs of defects not discovered in the internal inspection. For 20% of the external failures, negative word of mouth will result in a loss of sales, lowering the following year's sales by $500 for each of the 20% of units with external failures.

Required

1. Calculate appraisal cost.
2. Calculate internal failure cost.
3. Calculate out-of-pocket external failure cost.
4. Determine the opportunity cost associated with the external failures.
5. What are the total costs of quality?
6. Safe Rider is concerned with the high up-front cost of inspecting all 100,000 units. It is considering an alternative internal inspection plan that will cost only $1.50 per car seat inspected. During the internal inspection, the alternative technique will detect only 2.5% of the 100,000 car seats that have stitching problems. The other 4.5% will be detected after the car seats are sold and shipped. What are the total costs of quality for the alternative technique?
7. What factors other than cost should Safe Rider consider before changing inspection techniques?

19-18 Costs of quality, ethical considerations. Refer to information in Exercise 19-17 in answering this question. Safe Rider has discovered a more serious problem with the plastic core of its car seats. An accident can cause the plastic in some of the seats to crack and break, resulting in serious injuries to the occupant. It is estimated that this problem will affect about 200 car seats in the next year. This problem could be corrected by using a higher quality of plastic that would increase the cost of every car seat produced by $25. If this problem is not corrected, Safe Rider estimates that out of the 200 accidents, customers will realize that the problem is due to a defect in the seats in only two cases. Safe Rider's legal team has estimated that each of these two accidents would result in a lawsuit that could be settled for about $750,000. All lawsuits settled would include a confidentiality clause, so Safe Rider's reputation would not be affected.

Required

1. Assuming that Safe Rider expects to sell 100,000 car seats next year, what would be the cost of increasing the quality of all 100,000 car seats?
2. What will be the total cost of the lawsuits next year if the problem is not corrected?
3. Safe Rider has decided not to increase the quality of the plastic because the cost of increasing the quality exceeds the benefits (saving the cost of lawsuits). What do you think of this decision? (Note: Because of the confidentiality clause, the decision will have no effect on Safe Rider's reputation.)
4. Are there any other costs or benefits that Safe Rider should consider?

19-19 Nonfinancial measures of quality and time. Worldwide Cell Phones (WCP) has developed a cell phone that can be used anywhere in the world (even countries like Japan that have a relatively unique cell phone system). WCP has been receiving complaints about the phone. For the past two years, WCP has been test marketing the phones and gathering nonfinancial information related to actual and perceived aspects of the phone's quality. They expect that, given the lack of competition in this market, increasing the quality of the phone will result in higher sales and thereby higher profits.

Quality data for 2009 and 2010 include the following:

	2009	2010
Cell phones produced and shipped	2,000	10,000
Number of defective units shipped	100	400
Number of customer complaints	150	250
Units reworked before shipping	120	700
Manufacturing lead time	15 days	16 days
Average customer response time	30 days	28 days

Required

1. For each year, 2009 and 2010, calculate:
   a. Percentage of defective units shipped.
   b. Customer complaints as a percentage of units shipped.
   c. Percentage of units reworked during production.
   d. Manufacturing lead time as a percentage of total time from order to delivery.
2. Referring to the information computed in requirement 1, explain whether WCP's quality and timeliness have improved.
3. Why would manufacturing lead time have increased while customer response time decreased? (It may be useful to first describe what is included in each time measurement—see Exhibit 19-7, p. 676).

19-20 Quality improvement, relevant costs, relevant revenues. TechnoPrint manufactures and sells 20,000 high-technology printing presses each year. The variable and fixed costs of rework and repair are as follows:

	A	B	C	D
1		Variable Cost	Fixed Cost	Total Cost
2	Rework cost per hour	$ 80	$120	$200
3	Repair costs			
4	Customer support cost per hour	40	60	100
5	Transportation cost per load	360	120	480
6	Warranty repair cost per hour	90	130	220

TechnoPrint's current presses have a quality problem that causes variations in the shade of some colors. Its engineers suggest changing a key component in each press. The new component will cost $55 more than the old one. In the next year, however, TechnoPrint expects that with the new component it will (1) save 12,875 hours of rework, (2) save 900 hours of customer support, (3) move 200 fewer loads, (4) save 7,000 hours of warranty repairs, and (5) sell an additional 150 printing presses, for a total contribution margin of $1,800,000. TechnoPrint believes that even as it improves quality, it will not be able to save any of the fixed costs of rework or repair. TechnoPrint uses a one-year time horizon for this decision, because it plans to introduce a new press at the end of the year.

If you want to use Excel to solve this exercise, go to the Excel Lab at **www.prenhall.com/horngren/cost13e** and download the template for Exercise 19-20.

Required

1. Should TechnoPrint change to the new component? Show your calculations.
2. Suppose the estimate of 150 additional printing presses sold is uncertain. What is the minimum number of additional printing presses that TechnoPrint needs to sell to justify adopting the new component?

19-21 Nonfinancial quality measures, on-time delivery. Checkers Pizza promises to deliver pizzas in twenty-five minutes or less. If pizzas are not delivered on time, then the customer receives $5 off the price of the order. Some store managers, who receive bonuses based on store profits, believe that the guarantee is a win-win situation for Checkers. Because the average pizza sells for $9 but has a marginal cost of $2.25, the store makes a profit no matter what the delivery time. If a pizza is delivered on time, then the store earns $6.75 ($9 − $2.25) per pizza. If a pizza is delivered late, then the store still earns $1.75 ($9 − $5 − $2.25) per pizza. If more than one pizza is ordered, then Checkers makes even more money because it only gives one $5 discount per order.

The head of the Checkers chain is worried that this perceived win-win situation may encourage a complacent attitude in store managers with respect to on-time deliveries. While short-run profits are still earned with late deliveries, repeated late deliveries could lead to annoyance on the part of customers and eventually to a loss of customers. Therefore, the Checkers corporate headquarters has decided to gather information about late deliveries and customer satisfaction. It has developed a survey that asks delivery customers to rate their satisfaction based on three attributes: delivery service, value for money, and overall satisfaction with Checkers. Responses can range from 1 to 5, where 1 is "Awful" and 5 is "Excellent." The following responses were gathered from stores in a single city.

	Store 1	Store 2	Store 3	Store 4
Percentage of deliveries that were late	10%	5%	12%	25%
Average rating of delivery service	4	4.5	3.8	2
Average rating of value received	3.5	4.1	3.5	1.5
Average overall satisfaction with Checkers	3.6	4	3	2

Required

1. Examine the relationship between the percentage of deliveries that were late and average responses to the three survey questions. Do the data provide any support for Checkers headquarters' concerns?
2. Using the high-low method discussed in Chapter 10 (pp. 346–347), estimate the effect of changes in the late delivery percentage on average overall satisfaction with Checkers. Use the customer satisfaction score as the dependent variable. Based on this analysis, compute the impact of a change from 5% late deliveries to 7% late deliveries on overall customer satisfaction.
3. What factors would Checkers need to consider when determining whether the delivery guarantee is actually beneficial for the company?

19-22 Waiting time, service industry. The registration advisors at a small midwestern university (SMU) help 4,000 students develop each of their class schedules and register for classes each semester. Each advisor works for 10 hours a day during the registration period. SMU currently has 10 advisors. While advising an individual student can take anywhere from 2 to 30 minutes, it takes an average of 12 minutes per student. During the registration period, the 10 advisors see an average of 300 students a day.

Required

1. Using the formula on p. 677, calculate how long the average student will have to wait in the advisor's office before being advised.
2. The head of the registration advisors would like to increase the number of students seen each day, because at 300 students a day it would take 14 working days to see all of the students. This is a problem because the registration period lasts for only two weeks (10 working days). If the advisors could advise 400 students a day, it would take only two weeks (10 days). However, they want to make sure that the waiting time is not excessive. What would be the average waiting time if 400 students were seen each day?
3. SMU wants to know the effect of reducing the average advising time on the average wait time. If SMU can reduce the average advising time to 10 minutes, what would be the average waiting time if 400 students were seen each day?

19-23 Waiting time, cost considerations, customer satisfaction. Refer to the information presented in Exercise 19-22. The head of the registration advisors at SMU has decided that the advisors must finish their advising in two weeks and therefore must advise 400 students a day. However, the average waiting time given a 12-minute advising period will result in student complaints, as will reducing the average advising time to 10 minutes. SMU is considering two alternatives:

A. Hire two more advisors for the two-week (10-working day) advising period. This will increase the available number of advisors to 12 and therefore lower the average waiting time.

B. Increase the number of days that the advisors will work during the two-week registration period to 6 days a week. If SMU increases the number of days worked to six per week, then the 10 advisors need only see 350 students a day to advise all of the students in two weeks.

Required

1. What would the average wait time be under each alternative described above?
2. If advisors earn $100 per day, which alternative would be cheaper for SMU (assume that if advisors work 6 days in a given work week, they will be paid time and a half for the sixth day)?
3. From a student satisfaction point of view, which of the two alternatives would be preferred? Why?

19-24 Manufacturing cycle time, manufacturing cycle efficiency. (CMA, adapted) Torrance Manufacturing evaluates the performance of its production managers based on a variety of factors, including cost, quality, and cycle time. The following information relates to the average amount of time needed to complete an order for its one product:

■ Wait time:	
From order being placed to start of production	8 days
From start of production to completion	6 days
■ Inspection time	2 days
■ Process time	4 days
■ Move time	2 days

Required

1. Compute the manufacturing cycle efficiency for an order.
2. Compute the manufacturing cycle time (or lead time) for an order.

19-25 Theory of constraints, throughput contribution, relevant costs. The Mayfield Corporation manufactures filing cabinets in two operations: machining and finishing. It provides the following information:

	Machining	Finishing
Annual capacity	100,000 units	80,000 units
Annual production	80,000 units	80,000 units
Fixed operating costs		
(excluding direct materials)	$640,000	$400,000
Fixed operating costs per unit produce		
($640,000 ÷ 80,000; $400,000 ÷ 80,000)	$8 per unit	$5 per unit

Each cabinet sells for $72 and has direct material costs of $32 incurred at the start of the machining operation. Mayfield has no other variable costs. Mayfield can sell whatever output it produces. The following requirements refer only to the preceding data. There is no connection between the requirements.

Required

1. Mayfield is considering using some modern jigs and tools in the finishing operation that would increase annual finishing output by 1,000 units. The annual cost of these jigs and tools is $30,000. Should Mayfield acquire these tools? Show your calculations.
2. The production manager of the Machining Department has submitted a proposal to do faster setups that would increase the annual capacity of the Machining Department by 10,000 units and would cost $5,000 per year. Should Mayfield implement the change? Show your calculations.
3. An outside contractor offers to do the finishing operation for 12,000 units at $10 per unit, double the $5 per unit that it costs Mayfield to do the finishing in-house. Should Mayfield accept the subcontractor's offer? Show your calculations.
4. The Hunt Corporation offers to machine 4,000 units at $4 per unit, half the $8 per unit that it costs Mayfield to do the machining in-house. Should Mayfield accept Hunt's offer? Show your calculations.

19-26 Theory of constraints, throughput contribution, quality. Refer to the information in Exercise 19-25 in answering the following requirements. There is no connection between the requirements.

Required

1. Mayfield produces 2,000 defective units at the machining operation. What is the cost to Mayfield of the defective items produced? Explain your answer briefly.
2. Mayfield produces 2,000 defective units at the finishing operation. What is the cost to Mayfield of the defective items produced? Explain your answer briefly.

Problems

19-27 Quality improvement, relevant costs, and relevant revenues. The Thomas Corporation sells 300,000 V262 valves to the automobile and truck industry. Thomas has a capacity of 110,000 machine-hours and can produce 3 valves per machine-hour. V262's contribution margin per unit is $8. Thomas sells only 300,000 valves because 30,000 valves (10% of the good valves) need to be reworked. It takes 1 machine-hour to rework 3 valves, so 10,000 hours of capacity are used in the rework process. Thomas's rework costs are $210,000. Rework costs consist of:

- Direct materials and direct rework labor (variable costs): $3 per unit
- Fixed costs of equipment, rent, and overhead allocation: $4 per unit

Thomas's process designers have developed a modification that would maintain the speed of the process and ensure 100% quality and no rework. The new process would cost $315,000 per year. The following additional information is available:

- The demand for Thomas's V262 valves is 370,000 per year.
- The Jackson Corporation has asked Thomas to supply 22,000 T971 valves (another product) if Thomas implements the new design. The contribution margin per T971 valve is $10. Thomas can make two T971 valves per machine-hour with 100% quality and no rework.

Required

1. Suppose Thomas's designers implement the new design. Should Thomas accept Jackson's order for 22,000 T971 valves? Show your calculations.
2. Should Thomas implement the new design? Show your calculations.
3. What nonfinancial and qualitative factors should Thomas consider in deciding whether to implement the new design?

19-28 Quality improvement, relevant costs, and relevant revenues. The Tan Corporation uses multicolor molding to make plastic lamps. The molding operation has a capacity of 200,000 units per year. The demand for lamps is very strong. Tan will be able to sell whatever output quantities it can produce at $40 per lamp.

Tan can start only 200,000 units into production in the Molding Department because of capacity constraints on the molding machines. If a defective unit is produced at the molding operation, it must be scrapped at a net disposal value of zero. Of the 200,000 units started at the molding operation, 30,000 defective units (15%) are produced. The cost of a defective unit, based on total (fixed and variable) manufacturing costs incurred up to the molding operation, equals $25 per unit, as follows:

Direct materials (variable)	$16 per unit
Direct manufacturing labor, setup labor, and materials-handling labor (variable)	3 per unit
Equipment, rent, and other allocated overhead, including inspection and testing costs on scrapped parts (fixed)	6 per unit
Total	$25 per unit

Tan's designers have determined that adding a different type of material to the existing direct materials would result in no defective units being produced, but it would increase the variable costs by $4 per lamp in the Molding Department.

Required

1. Should Tan use the new material? Show your calculations.
2. What nonfinancial and qualitative factors should Tan consider in making the decision?

19-29 Statistical quality control, airline operations. Jetrans Airlines operates daily round-trip flights on the London–Los Angeles route using a fleet of three 747s: the Spirit of Atlanta, the Spirit of Boston, and the Spirit of Sacramento. The budgeted quantity of fuel for each round-trip flight is the 12-month mean (average) round-trip fuel consumption of 200 gallon-units, with a standard deviation of 20 gallon-units. A gallon-unit is 1,000 gallons.

Using a statistical quality control (SQC) approach, Shirley Watson, the Jetrans operations manager, investigates any round-trip with fuel consumption that is greater than two standard deviations from the mean. In October, Watson receives the following report for round-trip fuel consumption for the three planes on the London–Los Angeles route:

	A	B	C	D
1		Spirit of	Spirit of	Spirit of
2		Atlanta	Boston	Sacramento
3	Flight	(gallons-units)	(gallons-units)	(gallons-units)
4	1	208	206	194
5	2	187	188	208
6	3	194	192	221
7	4	202	214	208
8	5	211	184	242
9	6	215	226	234
10	7	216	198	249
11	8	218	212	227
12	9	221	202	232
13	10	232	186	244

If you want to use Excel to solve this problem, go to the Excel Lab at **www.prenhall.com/horngren/cost13e** and download the template for Problem 19-29.

Required

1. Using the $\pm 2\sigma$ rule, what variance-investigation decisions would be made?
2. Present SQC charts for round-trip fuel usage for each of the three 747s in October. What inferences can you draw from the charts?
3. Some managers propose that Jetrans Airlines present its SQC charts in monetary terms rather than in physical-quantity terms (gallon-units). What are the advantages and disadvantages of using monetary fuel costs rather than gallon-units in the SQC charts?

19-30 Compensation linked with profitability, waiting time, and quality measures. Mid-Atlantic Healthcare operates two medical groups, one in Philadelphia and one in Baltimore. The semi-annual bonus plan for each medical group's president has three components:

a. Profitability performance. Add 1% of operating income.
b. Average patient waiting time. Add $50,000 if the average waiting time for a patient to see a doctor after the scheduled appointment time is less than 15 minutes. If average patient waiting time is more than 15 minutes, add nothing.
c. Patient satisfaction performance. Deduct $50,000 if patient satisfaction (measured using a survey asking patients about their satisfaction with their doctor and their overall satisfaction with Mid-Atlantic Healthcare) falls below 70 on a scale from 0 (lowest) to 100 (highest). No additional bonus is awarded for satisfaction scores of 70 or more.

Semi-annual data for 2009 for the Philadelphia and Baltimore groups are as follows:

	A	B	C
1		**January-June**	**July-December**
2	**Philadelphia**		
3	Operating income	$10,650,000	$10,600,000
4	Average waiting time	14 minutes	16 minutes
5	Patient satisfaction	79	82
6			
7	**Baltimore**		
8	Operating income	$ 9,000,000	$ 950,000
9	Average waiting time	17 minutes	14.5 minutes
10	Patient satisfacation	66	70

If you want to use Excel to solve this problem, go to the Excel Lab at **www.prenhall.com/horngren/cost13e** and download the template for Problem 19-30.

Required

1. Compute the bonuses paid in each half year of 2009 to the Philadelphia and Baltimore medical group presidents.
2. Discuss the validity of the components of the bonus plan as measures of profitability, waiting time performance, and patient satisfaction. Suggest one shortcoming of each measure and how it might be overcome (by redesign of the plan or by another measure).
3. Why do you think Mid-Atlantic Healthcare includes measures of both operating income and waiting time in its bonus plan for group presidents? Give one example of what might happen if waiting time was dropped as a performance measure.

19-31 Waiting times, manufacturing lead times. The SRG Corporation uses an injection molding machine to make a plastic product, Z39. SRG makes products only after receiving firm orders from its customers. SRG estimates that it will receive 50 orders for Z39 (each order is for 1,000 units) during the coming year. Each order of Z39 will take 80 hours of machine time. The annual capacity of the machine is 5,000 hours.

Required

1. Calculate (a) the average amount of time that an order for Z39 will wait in line before it is processed and (b) the average manufacturing lead time per order for Z39.
2. SRG is considering introducing a new product, Y28. SRG expects it will receive 25 orders of Y28 (each order for 200 units) in the coming year. Each order of Y28 will take 20 hours of machine time. The average demand for Z39 will be unaffected by the introduction of Y28. Calculate (a) the average waiting time for an order received and (b) the average manufacturing lead time per order for each product, if SRG introduces Y28.

19-32 Waiting times, relevant revenues, and relevant costs (continuation of 19-31). SRG is still deciding whether it should introduce Y28. The following table provides information on selling prices, variable costs, and inventory carrying costs for Z39 and Y28. SRG will incur additional variable costs and inventory carrying costs for Y28 only if it introduces Y28. Fixed costs equal to 40% of variable costs are allocated to all products produced and sold during the year.

Product	Annual Average Number of Orders	Selling Price per Order If Average Manufacturing Lead Time per Order Is		Variable Cost per Order	Inventory Carrying Cost per Order per Hour
		Less Than 320 Hours	More Than 320 Hours		
Z39	50	$27,000s	$26,500	$15,000	$0.75
Y28	25	8,400	8,000	5,000	0.25

Required

1. Should SRG manufacture and sell Y28? Show your calculations.
2. Should SRG manufacture and sell Y28 if the data in Problem 19-31 are changed as follows: Selling price per order is $6,400, instead of $8,400, if average manufacturing lead time per order is less than 320 hours; and $6,000, instead of $8,000, if average manufacturing lead time per order is more than 320 hours? All other data for Y28 are the same.

19-33 Manufacturing lead times, relevant revenues, and relevant costs. The Brandt Corporation makes wire harnesses for the aircraft industry. Brandt is uncertain about when and how many customer orders will be received. The company makes harnesses only after receiving firm orders from its customers. Brandt has recently purchased a new machine to make two types of wire harnesses, one for Boeing airplanes (B7) and the other for Airbus Industries airplanes (A3). The annual capacity of the new machine is 6,000 hours. The following information is available for next year:

Customer	Annual Average Number of Orders	Manufacturing Time Required	Selling Price per Order If Average Manufacturing Lead Time per Order Is		Variable Cost per Order	Inventory Carrying Cost per Order per Hour
			Less Than 200 Hours	More Than 200 Hours		
B7	125	40 hours	$15,000	$14,400	$10,000	$0.50
A3	10	50 hours	13,500	12,960	9,000	0.45

Required

1. Calculate the average manufacturing lead times per order (a) if Brandt manufactures only B7 and (b) if Brandt manufactures both B7 and A3.
2. Even though A3 has a positive contribution margin, Brandt's managers are evaluating whether Brandt should (a) make and sell only B7 or (b) make and sell both B7 and A3. Which alternative will maximize Brandt's operating income? Show your calculations.
3. What other factors should Brandt consider in choosing between the alternatives in requirement 2?

19-34 Theory of constraints, throughput contribution, relevant costs. Colorado Industries manufactures electronic testing equipment. Colorado also installs the equipment at customers' sites and ensures that it functions smoothly. Additional information on the Manufacturing and Installation Departments is as follows (capacities are expressed in terms of the number of units of electronic testing equipment):

	Equipment Manufactured	Equipment Installed
Annual capacity	400 units per year	300 units per year
Equipment manufactured and installed	300 units per year	300 units per year

Colorado manufactures only 300 units per year because the Installation Department has only enough capacity to install 300 units. The equipment sells for $40,000 per unit (installed) and has direct material costs of $15,000. All costs other than direct material costs are fixed. The following requirements refer only to the preceding data. There is no connection between the requirements.

Required

1. Colorado's engineers have found a way to reduce equipment manufacturing time. The new method would cost an additional $50 per unit and would allow Colorado to manufacture 20 additional units a year. Should Colorado implement the new method? Show your calculations.
2. Colorado's designers have proposed a change in direct materials that would increase direct material costs by $2,000 per unit. This change would enable Colorado to install 320 units of equipment each year. If Colorado makes the change, it will implement the new design on all equipment sold. Should Colorado use the new design? Show your calculations.
3. A new installation technique has been developed that will enable Colorado's engineers to install 10 additional units of equipment a year. The new method will increase installation costs by $50,000 each year. Should Colorado implement the new technique? Show your calculations.

4. Colorado is considering how to motivate workers to improve their productivity (output per hour). One proposal is to evaluate and compensate workers in the Manufacturing and Installation Departments on the basis of their productivities. Do you think the new proposal is a good idea? Explain briefly.

19-35 Theory of constraints, throughput contribution, quality, relevant costs. Aardee Industries manufactures pharmaceutical products in two departments: Mixing and Tablet-Making. Additional information on the two departments follows. Each tablet contains 0.5 gram of direct materials.

	Mixing	Tablet Making
Capacity per hour	150 grams	200 tablets
Monthly capacity		
(2,000 hours available in each department)	300,000 grams	400,000 tablets
Monthly production	200,000 grams	390,000 tablets
Fixed operating costs (excluding direct materials)	$16,000	$39,000
Fixed operating cost per tablet		
($16,000 ÷ 200,000 grams; $39,000 ÷ 390,000 tablets)	$0.08 per gram	$0.10 per tablet

The Mixing Department makes 200,000 grams of direct materials mixture (enough to make 400,000 tablets) because the Tablet-Making Department has only enough capacity to process 400,000 tablets. All direct material costs are incurred in the Mixing Department. Aardee incurs $156,000 in direct material costs. The Tablet-Making Department manufactures only 390,000 tablets from the 200,000 grams of mixture processed; 2.5% of the direct materials mixture is lost in the tablet-making process. Each tablet sells for $1. All costs other than direct material costs are fixed costs. The following requirements refer only to the preceding data. There is no connection between the requirements.

Required

1. An outside contractor makes the following offer: If Aardee will supply the contractor with 10,000 grams of mixture, the contractor will manufacture 19,500 tablets for Aardee (allowing for the normal 2.5% loss of the mixture during the tablet-making process) at $0.12 per tablet. Should Aardee accept the contractor's offer? Show your calculations.
2. Another company offers to prepare 20,000 grams of mixture a month from direct materials Aardee supplies. The company will charge $0.07 per gram of mixture. Should Aardee accept the company's offer? Show your calculations.
3. Aardee's engineers have devised a method that would improve quality in the Tablet-Making Department. They estimate that the 10,000 tablets currently being lost would be saved. The modification would cost $7,000 a month. Should Aardee implement the new method? Show your calculations.
4. Suppose that Aardee also loses 10,000 grams of mixture in its Mixing Department. These losses can be reduced to zero if the company is willing to spend $9,000 per month in quality-improvement methods. Should Aardee adopt the quality-improvement method? Show your calculations.
5. What are the benefits of improving quality in the Mixing Department compared with improving quality in the Tablet-Making Department?

19-36 Theory of constraints, contribution margin, sensitivity analysis. Low Tech Toys (LTT) produces dolls in two processes: molding and assembly. LTT is currently producing two models: Chatty Chelsey and Talking Tanya. Production in the Molding Department is limited by the amount of materials available. Production in the Assembly Department is limited by the amount of trained labor available. The only variable costs are materials in the Molding Department and labor in the Assembly Department. Following are the requirements and limitations by doll model and department.

	Molding Materials	Assembly Time	Selling Price
Chatty Chelsey	1.5 pounds per doll	20 minutes per doll	$35 per doll
Talking Tanya	2 pounds per doll	30 minutes per doll	$45 per doll
Materials/Labor Available	30,000 pounds	8,400 hours	
Cost	$10 per pound	$12 per hour	

Required

1. If LTT sold only one type of doll, which doll would it produce? How many of these dolls would it make and sell?
2. If LTT sells two Chatty Chelseys for each Talking Tanya, how many dolls of each type would it produce and sell? What would be the total contribution margin?
3. If LTT sells two Chatty Chelseys for each Talking Tanya, how much would production and contribution margin increase if the Molding Department could buy 10 more pounds of materials for $10 per pound?
4. If LTT sells two Chatty Chelseys for each Talking Tanya, how much would production and contribution margin increase if the Assembly Department could get 10 more labor hours at $12 per hour?

19-37 Quality improvement, Pareto diagram, cause-and-effect diagram. The Murray Corporation manufactures, sells, and installs photocopying machines. Murray has placed heavy emphasis on reducing defects and failures in its production operations. Murray wants to apply the same total quality management principles to manage its accounts receivable.

Required

1. On the basis of your knowledge and experience, what would you classify as failures in accounts receivable?
2. Give examples of prevention activities that could reduce failures in accounts receivable.
3. Draw a Pareto diagram of the types of failures in accounts receivable and a cause-and-effect diagram of possible causes of one type of failure in accounts receivable.

19-38 Ethics and quality. Information from a quality report for 2009 prepared by Lindsey Williams, assistant controller of Citocell, a manufacturer of electric motors, is as follows:

Revenues	$10,000,000
Inspection of production	$ 90,000
Warranty liability	$ 260,000
Product testing	$ 210,000
Scrap	$ 230,000
Design engineering	$ 200,000
Percentage of customer complaints	5%
On-time delivery rate	93%

Davey Evans, the plant manager of Citocell, is eligible for a bonus if the total costs of quality as a percentage of revenues are less than 10%, the percentage of customer complaints is less than 4%, and the on-time delivery rate exceeds 92%. Evans is unhappy about the customer complaints of 5% because, when preparing her report, Williams actually surveyed customers regarding customer satisfaction. Evans expected Williams to be less proactive and to wait for customers to complain. Evans's concern with Williams's approach is that it introduces subjectivity into the results and also fails to capture the seriousness of customers' concerns. "When you wait for a customer to complain, you know he is complaining because it is something important. When you do customer surveys, customers mention whatever is on their mind, even if it is not terribly important."

John Roche, the controller, asks Williams to see him. He tells her about Evans's concerns. "I think Davey has a point. See what you can do." Williams is confident that the customer complaints are genuine and that customers are concerned about quality and service. She believes it is important for Citocell to be proactive and obtain systematic and timely customer feedback, and then to use this information to make improvements. She is also well aware that Citocell has not done customer surveys in the past, and that, except for her surveys, Evans would probably be eligible for the bonus. She is confused about how to handle Roche's request.

Required

1. Calculate the ratio of each cost-of-quality category (prevention, appraisal, internal failure, and external failure) to revenues in 2009. Are the total costs of quality as a percentage of revenues less than 10%?
2. Would it be unethical for Williams to modify her analysis? What steps should Williams take to resolve this situation?

Collaborative Learning Problem

19-39 Quality improvement, theory of constraints. The Wellesley Corporation makes printed cloth in two departments: Weaving and Printing. Direct material costs are Wellesley's only variable costs. The demand for Wellesley's cloth is very strong. Wellesley can sell whatever output quantities it produces at $1,250 per roll to a distributor who markets, distributes, and provides customer service for the product. Wellesley provides the following information.

	Weaving	Printing
Monthly capacity	10,000 rolls	15,000 rolls
Monthly production	9,500 rolls	8,550 rolls
Direct material cost per roll of cloth processed at each operation	$500	$100
Fixed operating costs	$2,850,000	$427,500
Fixed operating cost per roll ($2,850,000 ÷ 9,500 rolls; $427,500 ÷ 8,550 rolls)	$300 per roll	$50 per roll

Wellesley can start only 10,000 rolls of cloth in the Weaving Department because of capacity constraints of the weaving machines. If the Weaving Department produces defective cloth, the cloth must be scrapped and yields zero net disposal value. Of the 10,000 rolls of cloth started in the Weaving Department, 500 (5%)

defective rolls are produced. The cost of a defective roll, based on total (fixed and variable) manufacturing cost per roll incurred up to the end of the weaving operation, equals $785 per roll, as follows:

Direct material cost per roll (variable)	$500
Fixed operating cost per roll ($2,850,000 ÷ 10,000 rolls)	285
Total manufacturing cost per roll in Weaving Department	$785

The good rolls from the Weaving Department (called gray cloth) are sent to the Printing Department. Of the 9,500 good rolls started at the printing operation, 950 (10%) defective rolls are produced and scrapped at zero net disposal value. The cost of a defective roll based on total (fixed and variable) manufacturing cost per unit incurred up to the end of the printing operation, equals $930 per roll, calculated as follows:

Total manufacturing cost per roll in Weaving Department		$785
Printing Department manufacturing cost per roll		
Direct material cost per roll (variable)	$100	
Fixed operating cost per roll ($427,500 ÷ 9,500 rolls)	45	
Total manufacturing cost per roll in Printing Department		145
Total manufacturing cost per roll		$930

The Wellesley Corporation's total monthly sales of printed cloth equal the Printing Department's output.

Each requirement refers only to the preceding data. There is no connection between the requirements.

Required

1. The Printing Department is considering buying 5,000 additional rolls of gray cloth from an outside supplier at $900 per roll. The Printing Department manager is concerned that the cost of purchasing the gray cloth is much higher than Wellesley's cost of manufacturing it. The quality of the gray cloth acquired from the outside supplier is very similar to that manufactured in-house. The Printing Department expects that 10% of the rolls obtained from the outside supplier will result in defective products. Should the Printing Department buy the gray cloth from the outside supplier? Show your calculations.
2. Wellesley's engineers have developed a method that would lower the Printing Department's rate of defective products to 6% at the printing operation. Implementing the new method would cost $350,000 per month. Should Wellesley implement the change? Show your calculations.
3. The design engineering team has proposed a modification that would lower the Weaving Department's rate of defective products to 3%. The modification would cost the company $175,000 per month. Should Wellesley implement the change? Show your calculations.

20 Inventory Management, Just-in-Time, and Simplified Costing Methods

Learning Objectives

1. Identify six categories of costs associated with goods for sale
2. Balance ordering costs with carrying costs using the economic-order-quantity (EOQ) decision model
3. Identify and reduce conflicts that can arise between the EOQ decision model and models used for performance evaluation
4. Use a supply-chain approach to inventory management
5. Distinguish materials requirements planning (MRP) systems from just-in-time (JIT) systems for manufacturing
6. Identify the features of a just-in-time production system
7. Use backflush costing
8. Describe different ways backflush costing can simplify traditional inventory-costing systems
9. Understand the principles of lean accounting

Suppose you could receive a large quantity discount for a product that you regularly use. However, the discount requires you to buy enough of the product to last for a year and necessitates a large up-front expenditure. Would you take the quantity discount? Companies face similar decisions. That's because firms pay a price for tying up money in inventory sitting on their shelves or elsewhere. Consequently, companies like Best Buy and Chrysler are utilizing more-sophisticated methods than ever before to better manage their inventories.

Best Buy and Chrysler Use New Technology to Proactively Manage Their Inventories[1]

The trend in retailing for suppliers to take over responsibility of in-store inventories presents challenges as well as opportunities, says Bob Schwartz, Chief Information Officer at Panasonic Corporation of North America. This "push" model replaces the old "pull" one in which Panasonic would just wait until it got an order from Best Buy Co., for example, and then fill it. Here's how the push model works: Best Buy collects information on sales of Panasonic items at its stores' checkout stations and sends it to a unit of i2 Technologies Inc. in India. (Panasonic has outsourced supply chain analytics, such as forecasting, to I2.) I2 then sends manufacturing recommendations back to Panasonic, where they become the basis for factory schedules.

Another trend is the move by manufacturers to just-in-time inventories. Chrysler, for example, has 15 assembly plants in North America. Parts and supplies stream in from 2,000 locations, with each plant off-loading some 600 truckloads a day. Inventory levels inside the plants are measured in "a couple of hours." The company has a "central tracking group" to monitor and respond around the clock to automated alerts that signal glitches in the supply chain. Supply analysts in the tracking group use a "production control portal" that extends to multiple systems, including those of suppliers and shippers. "It tells you the status of a part and whether it's a potential shortage or if there's any advance notice of a potential problem," says Joe Bulat, director of IT for global procurement and supply systems. "If suppliers

[1] *Source:* Gary Anthes, "It's All Global Now," *Computerworld,* February 20, 2006.

exceed their shipping tolerances, we send out alerts indicating a shipment should have been made and was not."

Those "tolerances," already small, will shrink even further. At the company's new assembly plant in Belvidere, Ill., an on-site supplier will operate an "inbound parts sequencing center" that will take just-in-time inventory to new low levels. It will send parts to production operators in the plant in the exact sequence needed and at the precise time they are needed.

Inventory management is important because materials costs often account for more than 40% of total costs of manufacturing companies and more than 70% of total costs in merchandising companies. In this chapter we describe the components of inventory costs, relevant costs for different inventory-related decisions, and planning and control systems for managing inventory.

Inventory Management in Retail Organizations

Inventory management includes planning, coordinating, and controlling activities related to the flow of inventory into, through, and out of an organization. Consider this breakdown of operations for three major retailers for which cost of goods sold constitutes their largest cost item.

	Kroger	Costco	Wal-Mart
Revenues	100.0%	100.0%	100.0%
Deduct costs:			
Cost of goods sold	75.8%	87.7%	75.8%
Selling and administration costs	18.9%	9.5%	18.4%
Other costs, interest, and taxes	3.6%	1.0%	2.2%
Total costs	98.3%	98.2%	96.4%
Net income	1.7%	1.8%	3.6%

The percentages of net income to revenues are very low. This means that improving the purchase and management of goods for sale can cause dramatic percentage increases in net income.

Costs Associated with Goods for Sale

Managing inventories to increase net income requires companies to effectively manage costs that fall into the following six categories:

Learning Objective 1

Identify six categories of costs associated with goods for sale

. . . purchasing, ordering, carrying, stockout, quality, and shrinkage

1. **Purchasing costs**—the cost of goods acquired from suppliers, including incoming freight costs. These costs usually make up the largest cost category of goods for sale. Discounts for various purchase-order sizes and supplier credit terms affect purchasing costs.
2. **Ordering costs**—the costs of preparing and issuing purchase orders, receiving and inspecting the items included in the orders, and matching invoices received, purchase orders, and delivery records to make payments. Ordering costs include the cost of obtaining purchase approvals, as well as other special processing costs.
3. **Carrying costs**—the costs that arise while holding an inventory of goods for sale. Carrying costs include the opportunity cost of the investment tied up in inventory (see Chapter 11, pp. 399–400) and the costs associated with storage, such as space rental, insurance, obsolescence, and spoilage.
4. **Stockout costs**—the costs that result when a company runs out of a particular item for which there is customer demand—a *stockout*—and the company must act quickly to meet that demand or suffer the costs of not meeting it. A company may respond to a stockout by expediting an order from a supplier, which can be expensive because of additional ordering costs plus any associated transportation costs. Or the company may lose sales due to the stockout. In this case, the opportunity cost of the stockout includes lost contribution margin on the sale not made plus any contribution margin lost on future sales due to customer ill will.
5. **Costs of Quality**—the costs that result when features and characteristics of a product or service are not in conformance with customer specifications. There are four categories of quality costs—prevention costs, appraisal costs, internal failure costs, and external failure costs—described in Chapter 19.
6. **Shrinkage costs**—the costs that result from theft by outsiders, embezzlement by employees, misclassifications, and clerical errors. Shrinkage is measured by the difference between (a) the cost of the inventory recorded on the books in the absence of theft and other incidents just mentioned, and (b) the cost of inventory when physically counted. Shrinkage can often be an important measure of management performance. Consider, for example, the grocery business, where operating income percentages hover around two percent. With such small margins, it is easy to see why one of a store manager's prime responsibilities is controlling inventory shrinkage. A \$1,000 increase in shrinkage will erase the operating income from sales of \$50,000 (2% × \$50,000 = \$1,000).

Note that not all inventory costs are available in financial accounting systems. For example, opportunity costs are seldom recorded in these systems and are a significant component in several of these cost categories.

Information-gathering technology increases the reliability and timeliness of inventory information and reduces costs in the six cost categories. For example, bar-coding technology allows a scanner to record purchases and sales of individual units. As soon as a unit is scanned, an instantaneous record of inventory movements is created that helps in the management of purchasing, carrying, and stockout costs. In the next several sections, we consider how relevant costs are computed for different inventory-related decisions in merchandising companies.

Learning Objective 2

Balance ordering costs with carrying costs using the economic-order-quantity (EOQ) decision model

. . . choose the inventory quantity per order to minimize costs

Economic-Order-Quantity Decision Model

The first decision in managing goods for sale is *how much to order* of a given product. The **economic order quantity** (**EOQ**) is a decision model that, under a given set of assumptions, calculates the optimal quantity of inventory to order. The simplest version of an EOQ model assumes there are only ordering and carrying costs. It also assumes:

- The same quantity is ordered at each reorder point.
- Demand, ordering costs, and carrying costs are known with certainty. The **purchase-order lead time**—the time between placing an order and its delivery—is also known with certainty.

- Purchasing cost per unit is unaffected by the quantity ordered. This assumption makes purchasing costs irrelevant to determining EOQ because purchasing costs of all units acquired will be the same, regardless of the order size in which the units are ordered.
- No stockouts occur. The basis for this assumption is that the costs of stockouts are so high that managers maintain adequate inventory to prevent them.
- In deciding on the size of a purchase order, managers consider costs of quality and shrinkage costs only to the extent that these costs affect ordering or carrying costs.

Given these assumptions, EOQ analysis ignores purchasing costs, stockout costs, quality costs, and shrinkage costs. EOQ is the order quantity that minimizes the relevant ordering and carrying costs (that is, the ordering and carrying costs affected by the quantity of inventory ordered):

$$\text{Relevant total costs} = \text{Relevant ordering costs} + \text{Relevant carrying costs}$$

Let's consider an example to see how EOQ analysis works. CD World is an independent electronics store that sells blank compact disks. CD World purchases the CDs from Sontek at $14 a package (each package contains 10 disks). Sontek pays for all incoming freight. No inspection is necessary at CD World because Sontek supplies quality merchandise. CD World's annual demand is 13,000 packages, at a rate of 250 packages per week. CD World requires a 15% annual rate of return on investment. The purchase-order lead time is two weeks. Relevant ordering cost per purchase order is $200.

Relevant carrying cost per package per year is:

Required annual return on investment, 0.15 × $14	$2.10
Relevant insurance, materials handling, breakage, shrinkage, and so on, per year	3.10
Total	$5.20

What is the EOQ of packages of disks? The formula for the EOQ model is:

$$EOQ = \sqrt{\frac{2DP}{C}}$$

where

D = Demand in units for a specified period (one year in this example)
P = Relevant ordering cost per purchase order
C = Relevant carrying cost of one unit in stock for the time period used for D (one year)

The formula indicates that EOQ increases with higher demand and/or higher ordering costs and decreases with higher carrying costs.

For CD World:

$$EOQ = \sqrt{\frac{2 \times 13{,}000 \times \$200}{\$5.20}} = \sqrt{1{,}000{,}000} = 1{,}000 \text{ packages}$$

Purchasing 1,000 packages per order minimizes total relevant ordering and carrying costs. Therefore, the number of deliveries each period (one year in this example) is:

$$\frac{D}{EOQ} = \frac{13{,}000}{1{,}000} = 13 \text{ deliveries}$$

The annual relevant total costs (RTC) for any order quantity, Q, can then be calculated as follows:

$$RTC = \text{Annual relevant ordering costs} + \text{Annual relevant carrying costs}$$
$$= \left(\text{Number of purchase orders per year} \times \text{Relevant ordering cost per purchase order}\right) + \left(\text{Average inventory in units} \times \text{Annual relevant carrying cost per unit}\right)$$
$$= \left(\frac{D}{Q} \times P\right) + \left(\frac{Q}{2} \times C\right)$$
$$= \frac{DP}{Q} + \frac{QC}{2}$$

In this formula, Q can be any order quantity, not just the EOQ.

When $Q = 1{,}000$ units,

$$RTC = \frac{13{,}000 \times \$200}{1{,}000} + \frac{1{,}000 \times \$5.20}{2}$$
$$= \$2{,}600 + \$2{,}600 = \$5{,}200$$

Exhibit 20-1 graphs the annual relevant total costs of ordering (DP/Q) and carrying inventory ($QC/2$) under various order sizes (Q), and it illustrates the trade-off between these two types of costs. The larger the order quantity, the lower the annual relevant ordering costs, but the higher the annual relevant carrying costs. *Annual relevant total costs are at a minimum at the EOQ at which the relevant ordering and carrying costs are equal.*

When to Order, Assuming Certainty

The second decision in managing goods for sale is *when to order* a given product. The **reorder point** is the quantity level of inventory on hand that triggers a new purchase order. The reorder point is simplest to compute when both demand and purchase-order lead time are known with certainty:

$$\text{Reorder point} = \text{Number of units sold per unit of time} \times \text{Purchase-order lead time}$$

Exhibit 20-1 Graphic Analysis of Ordering Costs and Carrying Costs for Compact Disks at CD World

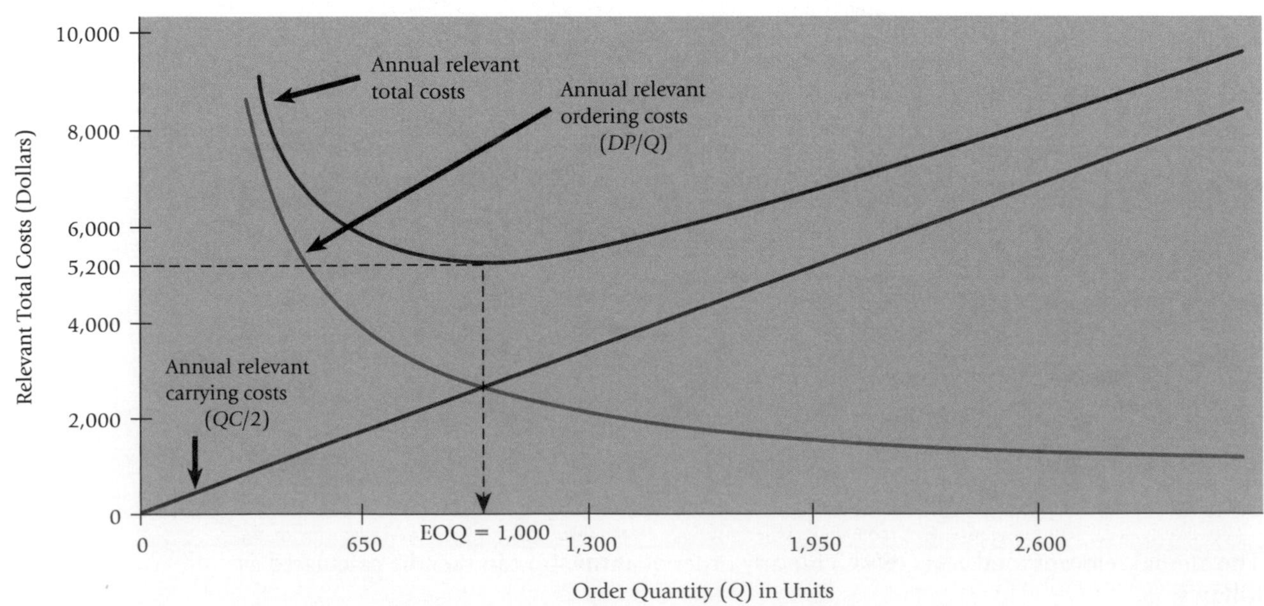

In our CD World example, we choose one week as the unit of time in the reorder-point formula:

Economic order quantity	1,000 packages
Number of units sold per week	250 packages per week
Purchase-order lead time	2 weeks

Reorder point = 250 packages per week × 2 weeks = 500 packages

CD World will order 1,000 packages each time inventory stock falls to 500 packages.[2] The graph in Exhibit 20-2 shows the behavior of the inventory level of compact disk packages, assuming demand occurs uniformly during each week. If purchase order lead time is two weeks, a new order will be placed when the inventory level falls to 500 packages, so the 1,000 packages ordered will be received at the precise time that inventory reaches zero.

Safety Stock

We have assumed that demand and purchase-order lead time are known with certainty. Retailers who are uncertain about demand, lead time, or the quantity that suppliers can provide, hold safety stock. **Safety stock** is inventory held at all times regardless of the quantity of inventory ordered using the EOQ model. Safety stock is used as a buffer against unexpected increases in demand, uncertainty about lead time, and unavailability of stock from suppliers. Suppose that in the CD World example, the only uncertainty is about demand. CD World's managers expect demand to be 250 packages per week, but they feel that a maximum demand of 400 packages per week may occur. If CD World's managers decide costs of stockouts are prohibitively high, they may decide to hold a safety stock of 300 packages. The 300 packages equal the maximum excess demand of 150 (400 − 250) packages per week times the two weeks of purchase-order lead time. Note that the computation of safety stock hinges on demand forecasts. CD World's managers will have some notion—usually based on experience—of the range of weekly demand.

Exhibit 20-2

Inventory Level of Compact Disks at CD World[a]

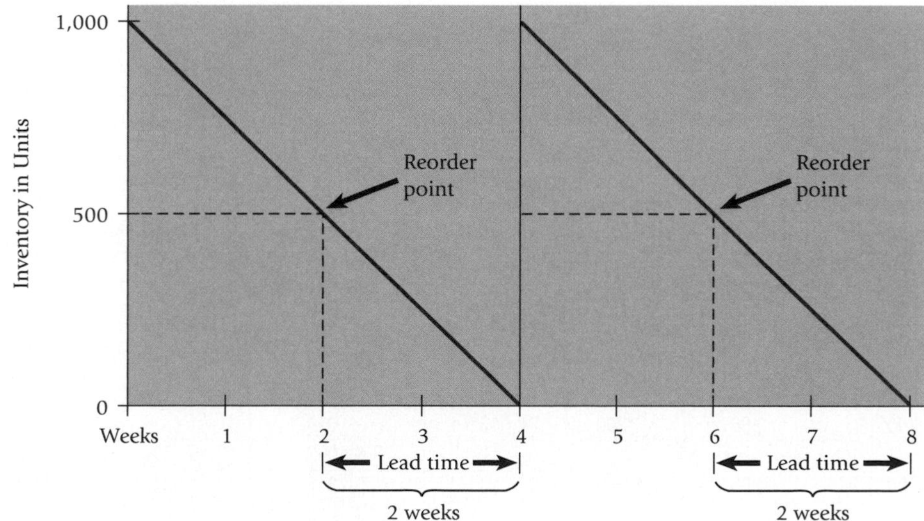

[a] This exhibit assumes that demand and purchase-order lead time are certain:
Demand = 250 CD packages per week
Purchase-order lead time = 2 weeks

[2] This handy but special formula does not apply when receipt of the order fails to increase inventory to the reorder-point quantity (for example, when lead time is three weeks and the order is a one-week supply). In these cases, orders will overlap.

A frequency distribution based on prior daily or weekly levels of demand forms the basis for computing safety-stock levels. Assume that one of the following levels of demand will occur over the two-week purchase-order lead time at CD World.

Total Demand for 2 Weeks	200 Units	300 Units	400 Units	500 Units	600 Units	700 Units	800 Units
Probability (sums to 1.00)	0.06	0.09	0.20	0.30	0.20	0.09	0.06

We see that 500 units is the most likely level of demand for two weeks because it has the highest probability of occurrence. We see also a 0.35 probability that demand will be 600, 700, or 800 packages (0.20 + 0.09 + 0.06 = 0.35).

If a customer wants to buy compact disks and the store has none in stock, CD World can "rush" them to the customer at an additional cost to CD World of $4 per package. The relevant stockout costs in this case are $4 per package. The optimal safety-stock level is the quantity of safety stock that minimizes the sum of annual relevant stockout and carrying costs. Note that CD World will place 13 orders per year and will incur the same ordering costs whatever level of safety stock it chooses. Therefore, ordering costs are irrelevant for the safety-stock decision. Recall that the relevant carrying cost for CD World is $5.20 per unit per year.

Exhibit 20-3 tabulates annual relevant total stockout and carrying costs when the reorder point is 500 units. We need only consider safety-stock levels of 0, 100, 200, and 300 units, because demand will exceed the 500 units of stock available at reordering by 0 if demand is 500, by 100 if demand is 600, by 200 if demand is 700, and by 300 if demand is 800. As Exhibit 20-3 shows, annual relevant total stockout and carrying costs would be the lowest ($1,352) when a safety stock of 200 packages is maintained. Therefore, 200 units is the optimal safety-stock level. Consider the 200 units of safety stock as extra stock that CD World maintains. For example, CD World's total inventory of compact disks at the time of reordering its EOQ of 1,000 units would be 700 units (the reorder point of 500 units plus safety stock of 200 units).

Exhibit 20-3 Computation of Safety Stock for CD World When Reorder Point Is 500 Units

File Edit View Insert Format Tools Data Window Help

	A	B	C	D	E	F	G	H	I
1	Safety	Demand							
2	Stock	Levels			Relevant	Number of	Expected	Relevant	Relevant
3	Level	Resulting	Stockout	Probability	Stockout	Orders	Stockout	Carrying	Total
4	in Units	in Stockouts	in Units[a]	of Stockout	Costs[b]	per Year[c]	Costs[d]	Costs[e]	Costs
5	(1)	(2)	(3) = (2) - 500 - (1)	(4)	(5) = (3) x $4	(6)	(7) = (4) x (5) x (6)	(8) = (1) x $5.20	(9) = (7) + (8)
6	0	600	100	0.20	$ 400	13	$1,040		
7		700	200	0.09	800	13	936		
8		800	300	0.06	1,200	13	936		
9							$2,912	$ 0	$2,912
10	100	700	100	0.09	400	13	$ 468		
11		800	200	0.06	800	13	624		
12							$1,092	$ 520	$1,612
13	200	800	100	0.06	400	13	$ 312	$1,040	$1,352
14	300	-	-	-	-	-	$ 0[f]	$1,560	$1,560
15									

16 [a]Demand level resulting in stockouts – Inventory available during lead time (excluding safety stock), 500 units – Safety stock.

17 [b]Stockout in units x Relevant stockout costs of $4.00 per unit.

18 [c]Annual demand, 13,000 ÷ 1,000 EOQ = 13 orders per year.

19 [d]Probability of stockout x Relevant stockout costs x Number of orders per year.

20 [e]Safety stock x Annual relevant carrying costs of $5.20 per unit (assumes that safety stock is on hand at all times and that there is no overstocking

21 caused by decreases in expected usage).

22 [f]At a safety stock level of 300 units, no stockout will occur and, hence, expected stockout costs = $0.

Estimating Inventory-Related Relevant Costs and Their Effects

As in earlier chapters, we need to determine which costs are relevant when making and evaluating inventory-management decisions. We next describe the estimates that need to be made to calculate the annual relevant carrying costs of inventory, stockout costs, and ordering costs.

Considerations in Obtaining Estimates of Relevant Costs

Relevant inventory carrying costs consist of the *relevant incremental costs* plus the *relevant opportunity cost of capital*.

What are the *relevant incremental costs* of carrying inventory? Only those costs of the purchasing company—for example, warehouse rent, warehouse workers' salaries, costs of obsolescence, costs of shrinkage, and costs of breakage—that change with the quantity of inventory held. Salaries paid to clerks, stockkeepers, and materials handlers are irrelevant if they are unaffected by changes in inventory levels. Suppose, however, that as inventories increase (decrease), total salary costs increase (decrease) as clerks, stockkeepers, and materials handlers are added (transferred to other activities or laid off). In this case, salaries paid are relevant costs of carrying inventory. Similarly, costs of storage space owned that cannot be used for other profitable purposes when inventories decrease are irrelevant. But if the space has other profitable uses, or if total rental cost is tied to the amount of space occupied, storage costs are relevant costs of carrying inventory.

What is the *relevant opportunity cost of capital*? It is the return forgone by investing capital in inventory rather than elsewhere. It is calculated as the required rate of return multiplied by the per-unit costs that (a) vary with the number of units purchased and (b) are incurred at the time the units are received. (Examples of these per-unit costs are the price of units purchased, incoming freight, and incoming inspection.) Opportunity costs are not computed on investments (say, in buildings) if these investments are unaffected by changes in inventory levels.

In the case of stockouts, calculating the relevant opportunity cost requires an estimate of lost contribution margin on sales lost because of a stockout, as well as lost contribution margin on future sales lost because of customer ill will resulting from the stockout.

Relevant ordering costs are only those ordering costs that change with the number of orders placed (for example, costs of preparing and issuing purchase orders and receiving and inspecting materials).

Cost of a Prediction Error

Predicting relevant costs is difficult and seldom flawless, which raises the question, What is the cost when actual relevant costs differ from the estimated relevant costs used for decision making?

Let's revisit the CD World example. Suppose relevant ordering costs per purchase order are \$100, instead of the \$200 estimate we used earlier. We can calculate the cost of this "prediction" error using a three-step approach.

Step 1: Compute the Monetary Outcome from the Best Action That Could Be Taken, Given the *Actual* Amount of the Cost Input (Cost per Purchase Order). Using D = 13,000 packages, P = \$100, and C = \$5.20,

$$EOQ = \sqrt{\frac{2DP}{C}}$$

$$= \sqrt{\frac{2 \times 13{,}000 \times \$100}{\$5.20}} = \sqrt{500{,}000}$$

$$= 707 \text{ packages (rounded)}$$

Annual relevant total costs when EOQ = 707 packages are:

$$RTC = \frac{DP}{Q} + \frac{QC}{2}$$
$$= \frac{13{,}000 \times \$100}{707} + \frac{707 \times \$5.20}{2}$$
$$= \$1{,}839 + \$1{,}838 = \$3{,}677$$

Step 2: Compute the Monetary Outcome from the Best Action Based on the Incorrect *Predicted* Amount of the Cost Input (Cost per Purchase Order). When the relevant ordering cost per purchase order is predicted to be \$200, the best action is to purchase 1,000 packages in each order (p. 701). Annual relevant total costs using this order quantity when D = 13,000 packages, P = \$100, and C = \$5.20 are:

$$RTC = \frac{13{,}000 \times \$100}{1{,}000} + \frac{1{,}000 \times \$5.20}{2}$$
$$= \$1{,}300 + \$2{,}600 = \$3{,}900$$

Step 3: Compute the Difference Between the Monetary Outcomes from step 1 and step 2.

	Monetary Outcome
Step 1	\$3,677
Step 2	3,900
Difference	\$ (223)

The cost of the prediction error, \$223, is less than 7% of the relevant total costs of \$3,677. Note that the annual relevant-total-costs curve in Exhibit 20-1 is somewhat flat over the range of order quantities from 650 to 1,300 units. *The square root in the EOQ model reduces the sensitivity of the ordering decision to errors in predicting its parameters.*

In the next section, we consider a planning-and-control and performance-evaluation issue that frequently arises when managing inventory.

Conflict Between the EOQ Decision Model and Managers' Performance Evaluation

Learning Objective 3

Identify and reduce conflicts that can arise between the EOQ decision model and models used for performance evaluation

. . . so managers can take actions that are in the best interest of the company as a whole

What happens if the order quantity calculated based on the EOQ decision model differs from the order quantity that managers making inventory-management decisions would choose to make their own performance look best? For example, because there are no opportunity costs recorded in financial accounting systems, conflicts may arise between the EOQ model's optimal order quantity and the order quantity that purchasing managers (who are evaluated on financial accounting numbers) will regard as optimal. As a result of ignoring some carrying costs (the opportunity costs), managers will be inclined to purchase larger lot sizes of materials than the lot sizes calculated according to the EOQ model. To achieve congruence between the EOQ decision model and managers' performance evaluations, companies such as Wal-Mart design performance-evaluation models that charge managers responsible for managing inventory levels with carrying costs that include a required return on investment.

Just-in-Time Purchasing

Just-in-time (JIT) purchasing is the purchase of materials (or goods) so that they are delivered just as needed for production (or sales). Consider JIT purchasing for Hewlett-Packard's (HP's) manufacture of computer printers. HP has long-term agreements with suppliers for the major components of its printers. Each supplier is required to make frequent deliveries of small orders directly to the production floor, based on the production schedule that HP gives its suppliers. Because HP holds very little inventory, a supplier who does not deliver components on time, or who delivers components that fail to meet agreed-upon quality standards, can cause an HP assembly plant not to meet its own scheduled deliveries for printers. Suppliers may sometimes fail to deliver products on time because of scheduling problems in their own plants, work stoppages, a strike, or contractual disputes. Generally, however, suppliers work hard to keep their commitments in order to build productive, long-term relationships with their customers.

JIT Purchasing and EOQ Model Parameters

Companies moving toward JIT purchasing to reduce their costs of carrying inventories (parameter C in the EOQ model) say that, in the past, carrying costs have actually been much greater than estimated because costs of warehousing, handling, shrinkage, and capital have not been fully identified. At the same time, the cost of placing a purchase order (parameter *P* in the EOQ model) is decreasing because:

- Companies are establishing long-term purchasing agreements that define price and quality terms over an extended period. Individual purchase orders covered by those agreements require no additional negotiation regarding price or quality.
- Companies are using electronic links to place purchase orders at a cost that is estimated to be a small fraction of the cost of placing orders by telephone or by mail.
- Companies are using purchase-order cards (similar to consumer credit cards such as VISA and MasterCard). As long as purchasing personnel stay within preset total and individual-transaction dollar limits, traditional labor-intensive procurement-approval procedures are not required.

Exhibit 20-4 tabulates the sensitivity of CD World's EOQ (p. 701) to changes in carrying and ordering costs. Exhibit 20-4 supports JIT purchasing because, as relevant carrying costs increase and relevant ordering costs per purchase order decrease, EOQ decreases and ordering frequency increases.

Relevant Costs of JIT Purchasing

JIT purchasing is not guided solely by the EOQ model. The EOQ model is designed only to emphasize the trade-off between relevant carrying and ordering costs. However, inventory management also includes purchasing costs, stockout costs, costs of quality, and shrinkage costs. We next present the calculation of relevant costs in a JIT purchasing decision.

CD World has recently established an Internet business-to-business purchase-order link with Sontek. CD World triggers a purchase order for compact disks by a single computer entry. Payments are made electronically for batches of deliveries, rather than for each individual delivery. These changes reduce the ordering cost from \$200 to only \$2 per purchase order! CD World will use the Internet purchase-order link whether or not it shifts to JIT purchasing. CD World is negotiating to have Sontek deliver 100 packages of disks 130 times per year (5 times every 2 weeks), instead of delivering 1,000 packages 13 times per year, as shown in Exhibit 20-1. Sontek is willing to make these frequent deliveries, but it would add \$0.02 to the price per compact disk. CD World's required rate of return on investment remains at 15%. Assume the annual relevant carrying cost of insurance, materials handling, shrinkage, breakage, and the like remains at \$3.10 per package per year.

Also assume that CD World incurs no stockout costs under its *current* purchasing policy, because demand and purchase-order lead times during each four-week period are

Exhibit 20-4

Sensitivity of EOQ to Variations in Relevant Ordering and Carrying Costs for CD World

File Edit View Insert Format Tools Data Window Help

	A	B	C	D	E	F	G
1				Economic Order Quantity in Units			
2				At Different Ordering and Carrying Costs			
3	Annual Demand (D) =	13,000	units				
4							
5	Relevant Carrying Costs			Relevant Ordering Costs per Purchase Order (P)			
6	Per Package per Year (C)			\$ 200	\$150	\$100	\$ 30
7	\$ 5.20			1,000	866	707	387
8	7.00			862	746	609	334
9	10.00			721	624	510	279
10	15.00			589	510	416	228

Exhibit 20-5 Annual Relevant Costs of Current Purchasing Policy and JIT Purchasing Policy for CD World

File Edit View Insert Format Tools Data Window Help

	A	B	C	D	E	F	G	H	I	J
1						Relevant Costs Under				
2		Current Purchasing Policy					JIT Purchasing Policy			
3	Relevant Items	Relevant Cost Per Unit		Quantity Per Year	Total Costs		Relevant Cost Per Unit		Quantity Per Year	Total Costs
4	(1)	(2)		(3)	(4) = (2) x (3)		(5)		(6)	(7) = (5) x (6)
5	Purchasing costs	$14.00	per unit	13,000	$182,000		$14.02	per unit	13,000	$182,260
6	Ordering costs	2.00	per order	13	26		2.00	per order	130	260
7	Opportunity carrying costs	2.10[a]	per unit of average inventory per year	500[b]	1,050		2.10[a]	per unit of average inventory per year	50[c]	105
8	Other carrying costs (insurance, materials handling, and so on)	3.10	per unit of average inventory per year	500[b]	1,550		3.10	per unit of average inventory per year	50[c]	155
9	Stockout costs	4.00	per unit	0	0		4.00	per unit	150	600
10	Total annual relevant costs				$184,626					$183,380
11	Annual difference in favor of JIT purchasing					$1,246				
12										
13	[a]Purchasing cost per unit x 0.15 per year									
14	[b]Order quantity ÷ 2 = 1,000 ÷ 2 = 500 units									
15	[c]Order quantity ÷ 2 = 100 ÷ 2 = 50 units									

known with certainty. CD World is concerned that lower inventory levels from implementing JIT purchasing will lead to more stockouts. That's because demand variations and delays in supplying disks are more likely in the short time intervals between orders delivered under JIT purchasing. Sontek has flexible manufacturing processes that enable it to respond rapidly to changing demand patterns. Nevertheless, CD World expects to incur stockout costs on 150 compact disk packages per year under the JIT purchasing policy. When a stockout occurs, CD World must rush-order compact disk packages from another supplier at an additional cost of $4 per package. Should CD World implement the JIT purchasing option of 130 deliveries per year? Exhibit 20-5 compares CD World's relevant costs under the current purchasing policy and the JIT policy, and it shows net cost savings of $1,246 per year by shifting to a JIT purchasing policy.

Supplier Evaluation and Relevant Costs of Quality and Timely Deliveries

Companies that implement JIT purchasing choose their suppliers carefully and develop long-term supplier relationships. Some suppliers are better positioned than others to support JIT purchasing. For example, Frito-Lay, a supplier of potato chips and other snack foods, has a corporate strategy that emphasizes service, consistency, freshness, and quality of the delivered products. As a result, the company makes more-frequent deliveries to retail outlets than many of its competitors.

What are the relevant costs when choosing suppliers? Consider again CD World. Denton Corporation, another supplier of disks, offers to supply all of CD World's compact disk needs at a price of $13.80 per package—less than Sontek's price of $14.02—under the same JIT delivery terms that Sontek offers. Denton proposes an Internet purchase-order link identical to Sontek's link, making CD World's ordering cost $2 per purchase order. CD World's relevant cost of insurance, materials handling, breakage, and the like would be $3.00 per package per year if it purchases from Denton, versus $3.10 if it purchases from Sontek. Should CD World buy from Denton? To answer, we need to consider the relevant costs of quality and delivery performance.

CD World has used Sontek in the past and knows that Sontek will deliver quality disks on time. In fact, CD World does not even inspect the compact disk packages that Sontek supplies and therefore incurs zero inspection costs. Denton, however, does not

Exhibit 20-6 Annual Relevant Costs of Purchasing From Sontek and Denton

File Edit View Insert Format Tools Data Window Help

	A	B	C	D	E	F	G	H	I	J
1					Relevant Cost of Purchasing From					
2			Sontek					Denton		
3	Relevant Items	Relevant Cost Per Unit		Quantity Per Year	Total Costs		Relevant Cost Per Unit		Quantity Per Year	Total Costs
4	(1)	(2)		(3)	(4) = (2) x (3)		(5)		(6)	(7) = (5) x (6)
5	Purchasing costs	$14.02	per unit	13,000	$182,260		$13.80	per unit	13,000	$179,400
6	Ordering costs	2.00	per order	130	260		2.00	per order	130	260
7	Inspection costs	0.05	per unit	0	0		0.05	per unit	13,000	650
8	Opportunity carrying costs	2.10[a]	per unit of average inventory per year	50[b]	105		2.07[a]	per unit of average inventory per year	50[b]	103
9	Other carrying costs (insurance, materials handling, and so on)	3.10	per unit of average inventory per year	50[b]	155		3.00	per unit of average inventory per year	50[b]	150
10	Customer return costs	10.00	per unit returned	0	0		10.00	per unit returned	325[c]	3,250
11	Stockout costs	4.00	per unit	150	600		4.00	per unit	360	1,440
12	Total annual relevant costs				$183,380					$185,253
13	Annual difference in favor of Sontek					$1,873				
14										
15	[a]Purchasing cost per unit x 0.15 per year									
16	[b]Order quantity ÷ 2 = 100 ÷ 2 = 50 units									
17	[c]2.5% of units returned x 13,000 units									

enjoy such a sterling reputation for quality. CD World anticipates the following negative aspects of using Denton:

- Inspection cost of $0.05 per package.
- Average stockouts of 360 packages per year requiring rush orders at an additional cost of $4 per package.
- Product returns of 2.5% of all packages sold due to poor compact disk quality. CD World estimates an additional cost of $10 to handle each returned package.

Exhibit 20-6 shows the relevant costs of purchasing from Sontek and Denton. Even though Denton is offering a lower price per package, there is a net cost savings of $1,873 per year by purchasing disks from Sontek. Selling Sontek's high-quality compact disks also enhances CD World's reputation and increases customer goodwill, which could lead to higher sales and profitability in the future.

JIT Purchasing, Planning and Control, and Supply-Chain Analysis

Learning Objective 4

Use a supply-chain approach to inventory management

... by coordinating the flow of inventory and information from initial sources of materials to delivery of products to consumers

The levels of inventories held by retailers are influenced by the demand patterns of their customers and supply relationships with their distributors and manufacturers, the suppliers to their manufacturers, and so on. *Supply chain* describes the flow of goods, services, and information from the initial sources of materials and services to the delivery of products to consumers, regardless of whether those activities occur in the same organization or in other organizations. Retailers should purchase inventories on a JIT basis only if activities throughout the supply chain are properly planned, coordinated, and controlled.

Procter and Gamble's (P&G's) experience with its Pampers product illustrates the gains from supply-chain coordination. Retailers selling Pampers encountered variability in weekly demand because families purchased disposable diapers randomly. Anticipating even more demand variability and lacking information about available inventory with P&G, retailers' orders to P&G became more variable. Trade promotions made the situation worse because retailers took advantage of lower prices to stock up for the future. Similarly, the high variability of orders at P&G translated into more variability of orders at P&G's suppliers. This resulted in high levels of inventory at all stages in the supply chain.

So how did P&G respond to these problems? By sharing information and planning and coordinating activities throughout the supply chain. The retailers began to share daily sales information about Pampers with P&G and P&G's suppliers. Sharing sales information reduced the level of uncertainty that P&G and its suppliers had about retail demand for Pampers. This reduction in demand uncertainty, combined with the sharing of inventory data throughout the supply chain, led to (1) fewer stockouts at the retail level, (2) reduced manufacture of Pampers not immediately needed by retailers, (3) fewer manufacturing orders that had to be "rushed" or "expedited," and (4) lower inventories held by each company in the supply chain. The benefits of supply chain coordination at P&G have been so great that retailers such as Wal-Mart have contracted with P&G to manage Wal-Mart's retail inventories on a just-in-time basis. This practice is called *supplier- or vendor-managed inventory*. Supply-chain management, however, is not without its challenges such as sharing accurate, timely, and relevant information about sales, inventory, and sales forecasts. These challenges arise because of problems of communication, trust, incompatible information systems and limited people and financial resources.

We now turn our attention to inventory management in manufacturing companies. Managers at manufacturing companies have also developed numerous systems to plan and implement production and inventory activities within their plants. We consider two widely used types of systems: materials requirements planning (MRP) and just-in-time (JIT) production.

Inventory Management and MRP

Learning Objective 5

Distinguish materials requirements planning (MRP) systems

. . . manufacturing products based on demand forecasts

from just-in-time (JIT) systems for manufacturing

. . . manufacturing products only upon receiving customer orders

Materials requirements planning (MRP) is a "push-through" system that manufactures finished goods for inventory on the basis of demand forecasts. MRP uses (1) demand forecasts for final products; (2) a bill of materials detailing the materials, components, and subassemblies for each final product; and (3) the quantities of materials, components, and product inventories to determine the necessary outputs at each stage of production. Taking into account the lead time required to purchase materials and to manufacture components and finished products, a master production schedule specifies the quantity and timing of each item to be produced. Once production starts as scheduled, the output of each department is pushed through the production line whether or not it is needed. This "push through" can sometimes result in an accumulation of inventory when workstations receive work they are not yet ready to process.

Inventory management is a challenge in an MRP system. One reason for unsuccessful attempts to implement MRP systems has been a failure to collect and update inventory records. The management accountant aids in MRP by maintaining accurate records of inventory and its costs. For example, after becoming aware of the full costs of carrying finished goods inventory in its MRP system, National Semiconductor contracted with Federal Express to airfreight its microchips from a central location in Singapore to customer sites worldwide, instead of storing products at geographically dispersed warehouses. The change enabled National to move products from plant to customer in 4 days rather than 45 days and to reduce distribution costs from 2.6% to 1.9% of revenues. These benefits subsequently led National to outsource all its shipping activities to Federal Express, including shipments between its own plants in the United States, Scotland, and Malaysia.

The management accountant must also estimate setup costs and downtime costs for production runs. *Costs of setting up a production run are analogous to ordering costs in the EOQ model.* When the costs of setting up machines are high—as in the case of a blast furnace in a steel mill—processing larger batches of materials and incurring larger inventory carrying costs is cheaper because it reduces the number of setups that must be made. Similarly, when the downtime costs are high, there are sizable benefits from maintaining continuous production.

MRP is a push-through approach. We now consider JIT production, a "demand-pull" approach, which is used by companies such as Toyota in the automobile industry, Dell in the computer industry, and Braun in the appliance industry.

Inventory Management and JIT Production

Learning Objective 

Identify the features of a just-in-time production system

. . . for example, organizing work in manufacturing cells, improving quality, reducing manufacturing lead time

Just-in-time (JIT) production, which is also called **lean production**, is a "demand-pull" manufacturing system that manufactures each component in a production line as soon as, and only when, needed by the next step in the production line. In a JIT production line, manufacturing activity at any particular workstation is prompted by the need for that workstation's output at the following workstation. Demand triggers each step of the production process, starting with customer demand for a finished product at the end of the process and working all the way back to the demand for direct materials at the beginning of the process. In this way, demand pulls an order through the production line. The demand-pull feature of JIT production systems achieves close coordination among workstations. It smooths the flow of goods, despite low quantities of inventory. JIT production systems aim to simultaneously (1) meet customer demand in a timely manner (2) with high-quality products and (3) at the lowest possible total cost.

A JIT production system has these features:

- Production is organized in **manufacturing cells**, a grouping of all the different types of equipment used to make a given product. Materials move from one machine to another, and various operations are performed in sequence, minimizing materials-handling costs.
- Workers are hired and trained to be multiskilled and capable of performing a variety of operations and tasks, including minor repairs and routine equipment maintenance.
- Defects are aggressively eliminated. Because of the tight links between workstations in the production line and the minimal inventories at each workstation, defects arising at one workstation quickly affect other workstations in the line. JIT creates an urgency for solving problems immediately and eliminating the root causes of defects as quickly as possible. Low levels of inventories allow workers to trace problems to and solve problems at earlier workstations in the production process, where the problems likely originated.
- *Setup time*—the time required to get equipment, tools, and materials ready to start the production of a component or product—is reduced. Simultaneously, *manufacturing lead time*—the time from when an order is received by manufacturing until it becomes a finished good—is also reduced. Reducing setup time makes production in smaller batches economical, which in turn reduces inventory levels. Reducing manufacturing lead time enables a company to respond faster to changes in customer demand (see Concepts in Action, p. 712).
- Suppliers are selected on the basis of their ability to deliver quality materials in a timely manner. Most companies implementing *JIT production* also implement *JIT purchasing*. JIT plants expect JIT suppliers to make timely deliveries of high-quality goods directly to the production floor.

We next present a relevant-cost analysis for deciding whether to implement a JIT production system.

Financial Benefits of JIT and Relevant Costs

Early advocates saw the benefit of JIT production as lower carrying costs of inventory. But there are other benefits of lower inventories: heightened emphasis on improving quality by eliminating the specific causes of rework, scrap, and waste, and lower manufacturing lead times. In computing the relevant benefits and costs of reducing inventories in JIT production systems, the cost analyst should take into account all benefits and all costs.

Consider Hudson Corporation, a manufacturer of brass fittings. Hudson is considering implementing a JIT production system. To implement JIT production, Hudson must incur \$100,000 in annual tooling costs to reduce setup times. Hudson expects that JIT will reduce average inventory by \$500,000 and that relevant costs of insurance, storage, materials handling, and setup will decline by \$30,000 per year. The company's required rate of return on inventory investments is 10% per year. Should Hudson implement a JIT production system?

Concepts in Action

After the Encore: Just-in-Time Live Concert CDs

Each year, hundreds of thousands of music fans flock to concerts to see bands such as the piano-based rock band Keane. Although many of them stop by the merchandise stand to pick up a T-shirt or poster after the show ends, they increasingly have another option . . . buying a multiple-CD set that contains a professional recording of the entire concert they just saw! Just-in-time production, enabled by recent advances in digital audio and CD-burning technology, now allows fans to relive the live concert experience, as soon as 10 minutes after the final chord is played!

Live concert recordings have long been hampered by production and distribution difficulties. Traditionally, fans could only hear these recordings via unofficial "bootleg" cassettes or CDs. Occasionally, artists would release official live albums between studio releases. But due to the remastering and album-production process, these recordings took months, if not years, to reach fans. Further, live albums typically sold few copies, and retail outlets that profit from volume-driven merchandise turnover were somewhat reluctant to carry them.

Enter instant concert recordings. Organizations such as Instant Live and DiscLive, employ microphones, recording and audio mixing hardware and software, and an army of high-speed CD burners to produce concert recordings during the show. As soon as each song is complete, engineers burn that track onto hundreds of CDs. At the end of the show, they have to burn only one last song on each CD. Once completed, the CD sets are packaged and rushed to merchandise stands throughout the venue for instant sale.

There are, of course, some limitations to this technology. With such a quick turnaround time, engineers cannot edit or remaster any aspect of the show. Therefore, any mistake during the show remains on the final CD. Also, although just-in-time live recordings work successfully in smaller venues, the logistics for arenas, amphitheatres, and stadiums are much more difficult. Dozens of additional employees and hundreds of costly, top-of-the-line CD burners are needed to meet the demands of larger crowds. Despite these concerns, the benefits of this new technology include sound-quality assurance, near-immediate production turnaround, and low finished-goods carrying costs. Further, these recordings can also be distributed through retailers and artist Web sites, making live recordings more accessible than ever. With such opportunities, it's no wonder that bands such as Keane augment their existing CD sales with just-in-time recordings. All of Keane's shows in its 2006 UK tour were recorded live and were still available for sale as limited-edition CDs in 2007, through Concert Live.

Sources: S. Chartrand, "How to Take the Concert Home," *The New York Times,* May 3, 2004; S. Humphries, "Get Your Official 'Bootleg' Here," *Christian Science Monitor,* November 21, 2003; S. Knopper, "Live Discs a Hit with Fans," *Rolling Stone,* November 7, 2003; S. Galupo, "Death of the Live Concert Album?" *Washington Times,* July 9, 2004; en.wikipedia.org/wiki/Keane, accessed September 28, 2007.

On the basis of the information provided, we would be tempted to say no. That's because annual relevant cost savings in carrying costs amount to \$80,000 [(10% of \$500,000) + \$30,000)], which is less than the additional annual tooling costs of \$100,000.

Our analysis, however, is incomplete. We have not considered the other benefits of lower inventories in JIT production. Hudson estimates that implementing JIT will improve quality and reduce rework on 500 units each year, resulting in savings of \$50 per unit. Also, better quality and faster delivery will allow Hudson to charge \$2 more per unit on the 20,000 units that it sells each year. The annual relevant quality and delivery benefits from JIT and lower inventory levels equal \$65,000 [(rework savings, \$50/unit × 500 units) + (additional contribution margin, \$2/unit × 20,000 units)]. Total annual relevant benefits and cost savings equal \$145,000 (\$80,000 + \$65,000), which exceeds annual JIT implementation costs of \$100,000. Therefore, Hudson should implement a JIT production system.

JIT in Service Industries

JIT purchasing and production methods can be applied in service industries as well. For example, inventories and supplies, and the associated labor costs to manage them, represent more than a third of the costs in most hospitals. As a result, inventory cost reductions have been a primary target for cost reduction. By implementing a JIT purchasing and distribution system, Eisenhower Memorial Hospital in Palm Springs, California, reduced its inventories and supplies by 90 percent in 18 months. McDonald's has adapted JIT production practices to making hamburgers.[3] Before, McDonald's precooked a batch of hamburgers that were placed under heat lamps to stay warm until ordered. If the hamburgers didn't sell within a specified period of time, they were thrown out. This had several consequences. First, inventory holding costs were high because each batch included safety stock to make sure McDonald's didn't run out of hamburgers and force customers to wait. Second, spoilage costs were high because many unsold hamburgers were thrown out. Third, the quality of hamburgers deteriorated the longer they sat under the heat lamps. Finally, customers placing a special order for a hamburger had to wait a long time for the hamburger to be cooked. Today, the use of new technology (including an innovative bun toaster) and JIT production practices allow McDonald's to cook hamburgers only when they are ordered, significantly reducing inventory holding and spoilage costs. More importantly, JIT has improved customer satisfaction by increasing the quality of hamburgers and reducing the time needed for special orders.

We next turn our attention to planning and control in JIT production systems.

Enterprise Resource Planning (ERP) Systems[4]

The success of a JIT production system hinges on the speed of information flows from customers to manufacturers to suppliers. Information flows are a problem for large companies that have fragmented information systems spread over dozens of unlinked computer systems, making planning and control more difficult. Many companies are implementing Enterprise Resource Planning (ERP) systems to improve these information flows. An ERP system is an integrated set of software modules covering accounting, distribution, manufacturing, purchasing, human resources, and other functions. Instead of concentrating on specific functions separately, ERP uses a single database that collects data and feeds it into all of these software applications, thereby allowing integrated, real-time information sharing and providing visibility to the company's business processes as a whole. For example, using an ERP system, a salesperson can generate a contract for a customer in Germany, verify the customer's credit limits, and place a production order. The system then uses this same information to schedule manufacturing in, say, Brazil, requisition materials from inventory, order components from suppliers, and schedule shipments. At the same time, it credits sales commissions to the salesperson and records all the costing and financial accounting information. All of this is done quickly and with no redundant information sharing or data entry.

ERP systems give lower-level managers, workers, customers, and suppliers access to detailed and timely operating information. This benefit, coupled with tight coordination across business functions of the value chain, enables ERP systems to shift manufacturing and distribution plans rapidly in response to changes in supply and demand. Companies believe that an ERP system is essential to support JIT initiatives because of the effect it has on lead times. Using an ERP system, Autodesk, a maker of computer-aided design software, reduced order lead time from 2 weeks to 1 day; Fujitsu reduced lead time from 18 to 1.5 days. ERP systems also help in forecasting demand and in doing materials requirements planning as part of their operations and logistics modules.

Although the tight coupling of systems throughout a company streamlines administrative and financial processes and saves costs, it can also make a system large and unwieldy. Because of its complexity, suppliers of ERP systems such as SAP and Oracle provide software packages that are standard, but that can be customized, although at considerable cost. Without some customization, unique and distinctive features that confer strategic advantage will not be available. The challenge when implementing ERP systems is to strike the right balance between standard systems and systems that for strategic reasons are designed to be unique.

---

[3] Charles Atkinson, "McDonald's, A Guide to the Benefits of JIT," *Inventory Management Review*, inventorymanagementreview.org/2005/11/mcdonalds_a_gui.html, accessed May 2, 2007.

[4] For an excellent discussion, see T. H. Davenport, "Putting the Enterprise into the Enterprise System," *Harvard Business Review*, July–August 1998; also see A. Cagilo, "Enterprise Resource Planning Systems and Accountants: Towards Hybridization?" *European Accounting Review*, May 2003.

Performance Measures and Control in JIT Production

In addition to personal observation, which is easier in a JIT environment because the lack of inventory makes problems and performance issues more visible, the following list describes measures managers use to evaluate and control JIT production and how these measures are expected to be affected by JIT.

1. Financial performance measures, such as inventory turnover ratio (Cost of goods sold $\div$ Average inventory), which is expected to increase
2. Nonfinancial performance measures of time, inventory, and quality, such as:
   - Manufacturing lead time, expected to decrease
   - Units produced per hour, expected to increase
   - Number of days of inventory on hand, expected to decrease

$$\frac{\text{Total setup time for machines}}{\text{Total manufacturing time}}\text{, expected to decrease}$$

$$\frac{\text{Number of units requiring rework or scrap}}{\text{Total number of units started and completed}}\text{, expected to decrease}$$

Personal observation and nonfinancial performance measures provide the most timely, intuitive, and easy to understand measures of manufacturing performance. Rapid, meaningful feedback is critical because the lack of inventories in a demand-pull system makes it urgent to detect and solve problems quickly. JIT measures can also be incorporated into the balanced scorecard. As discussed in Chapters 13 and 19, a balanced scorecard contains four perspectives: financial, customer, internal business process, and learning and growth. A key component of JIT production is employees who are multiskilled and well-trained in a variety of tasks. Improvements in these learning and growth measures should lead to improvements in internal business process measures such as the time, inventory, and quality measures above. As JIT improves operational performance, customer satisfaction should also improve due to greater flexibility, responsiveness, and quality. Finally, improvements in all these measures should lead to better financial performance as a result of lower purchasing, inventory holding, and quality costs, and higher revenues.

Effect of JIT Systems on Product Costing

By reducing materials handling, warehousing, and inspection, JIT systems reduce overhead costs. JIT systems also aid in direct tracing of some costs usually classified as indirect. For example, the use of manufacturing cells makes it cost-effective to trace materials handling and machine operating costs to specific products or product families made in these cells. These costs then become direct costs of those products. Also, the use of multiskilled workers in these cells allows the costs of setup, maintenance, and quality inspection to be traced as direct costs. These changes have prompted some companies using JIT to adopt simplified product costing methods that dovetail with JIT production and that are less costly to operate than the traditional costing systems described in Chapters 4, 7, 8, and 17. We examine two of these methods: backflush costing and lean accounting.

Backflush Costing

Learning Objective 7
Use backflush costing
. . . to delay recording some journal entries to later in the production and sales cycle

Organizing manufacturing in cells, reducing defects and manufacturing lead time, and ensuring timely delivery of materials, enables purchasing, production, and sales to occur in quick succession with minimal inventories. The absence of inventories makes choices about cost-flow assumptions (such as weighted-average or first-in, first-out) or inventory-costing methods (such as absorption or variable costing) unimportant: All manufacturing costs of the accounting period flow directly into cost of goods sold. The rapid conversion of direct materials into finished goods that are immediately sold greatly simplifies the costing system.

Simplified Normal or Standard Costing

Traditional normal and standard-costing systems (Chapters 4, 7, 8, and 17) use **sequential tracking**, which is a costing system in which recording of the journal entries occurs in the same order as actual purchases and progress in production. Costs are tracked sequentially as products pass through each of the following four stages:

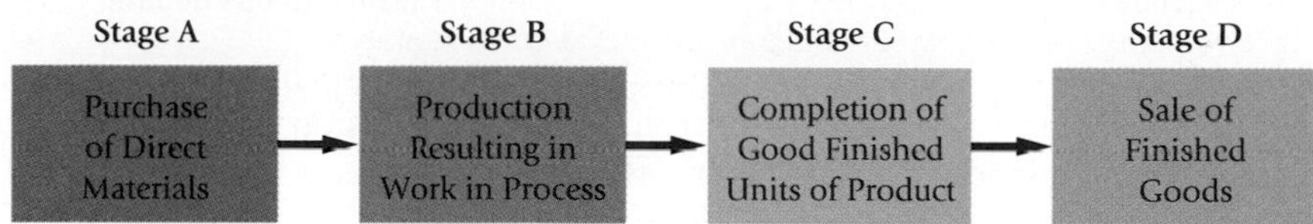

A sequential-tracking costing system has four *trigger points*, corresponding to stages A, B, C, and D. A **trigger point** is a stage in the cycle from purchase of direct materials (stage A) to sale of finished goods (stage D) at which journal entries are made in the accounting system.

An alternative approach to sequential tracking is backflush costing. **Backflush costing** is a costing system that omits recording some of the journal entries relating to the stages from purchase of direct materials to the sale of finished goods. When journal entries for one or more stages are omitted, the journal entries for a subsequent stage use normal or standard costs to work backward to "flush out" the costs in the cycle for which journal entries were *not* made. When inventories are minimal, as in JIT production systems, backflush costing simplifies the costing system without losing much information.

Learning Objective 8

Describe different ways backflush costing can simplify traditional inventory-costing systems

. . . for example, by not recording journal entries for work in process, purchase of materials, or production of finished goods

The following examples illustrate backflush costing. They differ in the number and placement of trigger points:

	Number of Journal-Entry Trigger Points	Location in Cycle When Journal Entries Are Made
Example 1	3	Stage A. Purchase of direct materials
		Stage C. Completion of good finished units of product
		Stage D. Sale of finished goods
Example 2	2	Stage A. Purchase of direct materials
		Stage D. Sale of finished goods
Example 3	2	Stage C. Completion of good finished units of product
		Stage D. Sale of finished goods

In all three examples, there are no journal entries in the accounting system for work in process (stage B) because JIT production results in minimal work in process.

We illustrate backflush costing using data from Silicon Valley Computer (SVC), which produces keyboards for personal computers. We assume the following information for SVC for the month of April.

- There are no beginning inventories of direct materials. Moreover, there is zero beginning and ending work in process.
- SVC has only one direct manufacturing cost category (direct materials) and one indirect manufacturing cost category (conversion costs). All manufacturing labor costs are included in conversion costs.
- From its bill of materials and an operations list (description of operations to be undergone), SVC determines that the standard direct material cost per keyboard unit is $19 and the standard conversion cost is $12.
- SVC purchases $1,950,000 of direct materials. To focus on the basic concepts, we assume SVC has no direct materials variances. Actual conversion costs equal $1,260,000. SVC produces 100,000 good keyboard units and sells 99,000 units.
- Any underallocated or overallocated conversion costs are written off to cost of goods sold at the end of April.

Example 1: Trigger points at purchase of direct materials (stage A), completion of good finished units of product (stage C), and sale of finished goods (stage D) In this example, SVC has two inventory accounts:

Type	Account Title
Combined materials inventory and materials in work in process	Inventory: Materials and In-Process Control
Finished goods	Finished Goods Control

Trigger point 1 occurs when materials are purchased. These costs increase (are debited to) Inventory: Materials and In-Process Control. Actual conversion costs are recorded as incurred under backflush costing, just as in other costing systems, and they increase (are debited to) Conversion Costs Control. Conversion costs are allocated to products at trigger point 2—the transfer of units to Finished Goods Control. Trigger point 3 occurs at the time finished goods are sold.

SVC uses the following steps to assign costs to units sold and to inventories.

Step 1: Record Direct Materials Purchased During the Accounting Period.

Entry (a)	Inventory: Materials and In-Process Control	1,950,000	
	Accounts Payable Control		1,950,000

Step 2: Record Conversion Costs Incurred During the Accounting Period.

Entry (b)	Conversion Costs Control	1,260,000	
	Various accounts (such as Wages Payable Control)		1,260,000

Step 3: Determine the Number of Good Finished Units Manufactured During the Accounting Period. 100,000 good units were manufactured in April.

Step 4: Compute the Normal or Standard Cost per Finished Unit. The standard cost is \$31 (\$19 direct materials + \$12 conversion costs) per unit.

Step 5: Record the Cost of Good Finished Units Completed During the Accounting Period. 100,000 units × \$31 per unit = \$3,100,000.

Entry (c)	Finished Goods Control	3,100,000	
	Inventory: Materials and In-Process Control		1,900,000
	Conversion Costs Allocated		1,200,000

Step 5 gives backflush costing its name. Costs have not been recorded sequentially with the flow of product along its production route through work in process and finished goods. Instead, the output trigger point reaches back and pulls the standard direct material costs from Inventory: Materials and In-Process Control and the standard conversion costs for manufacturing the finished goods.

Step 6: Record the Standard Cost of Goods Sold During the Accounting Period. Standard cost of 99,000 units sold in April (99,000 units × \$31 per unit = \$3,069,000):

Entry (d)	Cost of Goods Sold	3,069,000	
	Finished Goods Control		3,069,000

Step 7: Record Underallocated or Overallocated Conversion Costs. Actual conversion costs may be underallocated or overallocated in an accounting period. Chapter 4 (pp. 115–119) discussed various ways to dispose of underallocated or overallocated manufacturing overhead costs. Companies that use backflush costing typically have low inventories, so proration of underallocated or overallocated conversion costs between finished goods and cost of goods sold is seldom necessary. Many companies write off underallocated or overallocated conversion costs to cost of goods sold only at the end of the fiscal year. Other companies, like SVC, make the write-off monthly. The journal entry to dispose of the difference between actual conversion costs incurred and standard conversion costs allocated is:

Entry (e)	Conversion Costs Allocated	1,200,000	
	Cost of Goods Sold	60,000	
	Conversion Costs Control		1,260,000

The April 30 ending inventory balances are:

Inventory: Materials and In-Process Control ($1,950,000 − $1,900,000)	$50,000
Finished Goods Control, 1,000 units × $31/unit ($3,100,000 − $3,069,000)	31,000
Total	$81,000

Exhibit 20-7, Panel A (p. 718), presents the journal entries for this example. Exhibit 20-8, Panel A (p. 719), provides a general-ledger overview of this version of backflush costing.

The elimination of the typical Work-in-Process account reduces the amount of detail in the accounting system. Units on the production line may still be tracked in physical terms, but there is "no assignment of costs" to specific work orders while they are in the production cycle. In fact, there are no work orders or labor-time records in the accounting system. International Paper uses a method similar to Example 1 in its specialty papers plant.

The three trigger points to make journal entries in Example 1 will lead SVC's backflush costing system to report costs that are similar to the costs reported under sequential tracking when SVC has minimal work-in-process inventory. In Example 1, any inventories of direct materials or finished goods are recognized in SVC's backflush costing system when they first appear (as would be done in a costing system using sequential tracking).

Accounting for Variances

Accounting for variances between actual and standard costs is basically the same under all standard-costing systems. The procedures are described in Chapters 7 and 8. Suppose that in Example 1, we now assume SVC had an unfavorable direct materials price variance of $42,000. Then entry (a) would be:

Inventory: Materials and In-Process Control	1,950,000	
Direct Materials Price Variance	42,000	
Accounts Payable Control		1,992,000

Direct material costs are often a large proportion of total manufacturing costs, sometimes well over 60%. Consequently, many companies will at least measure the direct materials efficiency variance in total by physically comparing what remains in direct materials inventory against what should remain based on the output of finished goods for the accounting period. In our example, suppose that such a comparison showed an unfavorable materials efficiency variance of $30,000. The journal entry would be:

Direct Materials Efficiency Variance	30,000	
Inventory: Materials and In-Process Control		30,000

The underallocated or overallocated conversion costs are split into various overhead variances (spending variance, efficiency variance, and production-volume variance), as explained in Chapter 8. Each variance is closed to cost of goods sold, if immaterial in amount.

Example 2: Trigger points are purchase of direct materials (stage A) and sale of finished goods (stage D) This example uses the SVC data to illustrate a backflush costing system that differs more from a sequential-tracking costing system than the backflush costing system in Example 1. This example and Example 1 have the same first trigger point, purchase of direct materials. But the second trigger point in Example 2 is the sale, not the completion, of finished units. Toyota's cost accounting system at its Kentucky plant is similar to this example. There are two justifications for this accounting system:

1. To remove the incentive for managers to produce for inventory. Because finished goods inventory includes conversion costs, managers can increase operating income by producing more units than are sold. Having trigger point 2 as the sale instead of the completion of production eliminates a manager's incentive to produce for inventory by recording conversion costs as period costs instead of inventoriable costs.
2. To get managers more focused on selling units.

In this example, there is only one inventory account: direct materials, whether they are in storerooms, in process, or in finished goods.

Exhibit 20-7 Journal Entries in Backflush Costing

PANEL A, EXAMPLE 1: Three Trigger Points—Purchase of Direct Materials, Completion of Good Finished Units, and Sale of Finished Goods

Transactions			
(a) Purchase of direct materials[a]	Inventory: Materials and In-Process Control	1,950,000	
	Accounts Payable Control		1,950,000
(b) Incur conversion costs	Conversion Costs Control	1,260,000	
	Various Accounts		1,260,000
(c) Completion of good finished units[a]	Finished Goods Control	3,100,000	
	Inventory: Materials and In-Process Control		1,900,000
	Conversion Costs Allocated		1,200,000
(d) Sale of finished goods[a]	Cost of Goods Sold	3,069,000	
	Finished Goods Control		3,069,000
(e) Underallocated or overallocated conversion costs	Conversion Costs Allocated	1,200,000	
	Cost of Goods Sold	60,000	
	Conversion Costs Control		1,260,000

PANEL B, EXAMPLE 2: Two Trigger Points—Purchase of Direct Materials and Sale of Finished Goods

Transactions			
(a) Purchase of direct materials[a]	Inventory Control	1,950,000	
	Accounts Payable Control		1,950,000
(b) Incur conversion costs	Conversion Costs Control	1,260,000	
	Various Accounts		1,260,000
(c) Completion of good finished units	No entry		
(d) Sale of finished goods[a]	Cost of Goods Sold	3,069,000	
	Inventory Control		1,881,000
	Conversion Costs Allocated		1,188,000
(e) Underallocated or overallocated conversion costs	Conversion Costs Allocated	1,188,000	
	Cost of Goods Sold	72,000	
	Conversion Costs Control		1,260,000

PANEL C, EXAMPLE 3: Two Trigger Points—Completion of Good Finished Units and Sale of Finished Goods

Transactions			
(a) Purchase of direct materials	No entry		
(b) Incur conversion costs	Conversion Costs Control	1,260,000	
	Various Accounts		1,260,000
(c) Completion of good finished units[a]	Finished Goods Control	3,100,000	
	Accounts Payable Control		1,900,000
	Conversion Costs Allocated		1,200,000
(d) Sale of finished goods[a]	Cost of Goods Sold	3,069,000	
	Finished Goods Control		3,069,000
(e) Underallocated or overallocated conversion costs	Conversion Costs Allocated	1,200,000	
	Cost of Goods Sold	60,000	
	Conversion Costs Control		1,260,000

[a]A trigger point.

Type	Account Title
Combines direct materials inventory and any direct materials in work-in-process and finished goods inventories	Inventory Control

Exhibit 20-7, Panel B, presents the journal entries for Example 2. The two trigger points are represented by transactions (a) and (d). Entry (a) is prompted by the same trigger point 1 as in Example 1, the purchase of direct materials. Entry (b) for the conversion costs incurred is recorded in the same way as in Example 1. Trigger point 2 is the sale of finished goods (not the completion of finished units, as in Example 1), so there is no entry corresponding to entry (c) of Example 1. The cost of finished units is computed only when finished goods are sold [which corresponds to entry (d) of Example 1]: 99,000 units

Exhibit 20-8 General-Ledger Overview of Backflush Costing

PANEL A, EXAMPLE 1: Three Trigger Points—Purchase of Direct Materials, Completion of Finished Goods, and Sale of Finished Goods

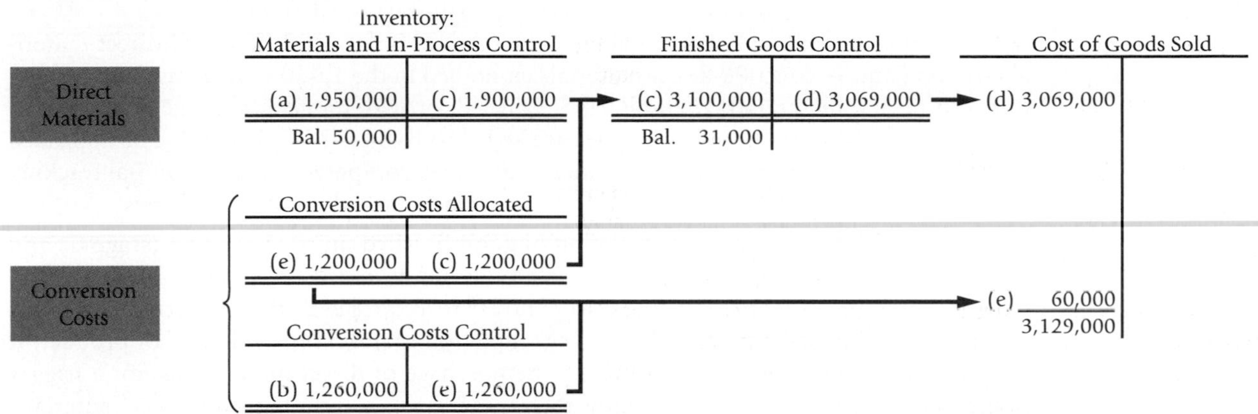

PANEL B, EXAMPLE 2: Two Trigger Points—Purchase of Direct Materials and Sale of Finished Goods

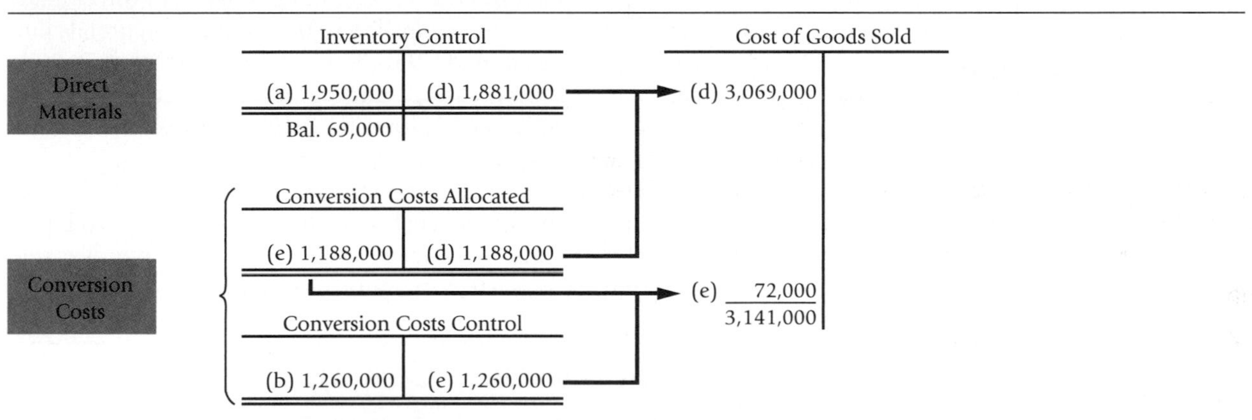

PANEL C, EXAMPLE 3: Two Trigger Points—Completion of Finished Goods and Sale of Finished Goods

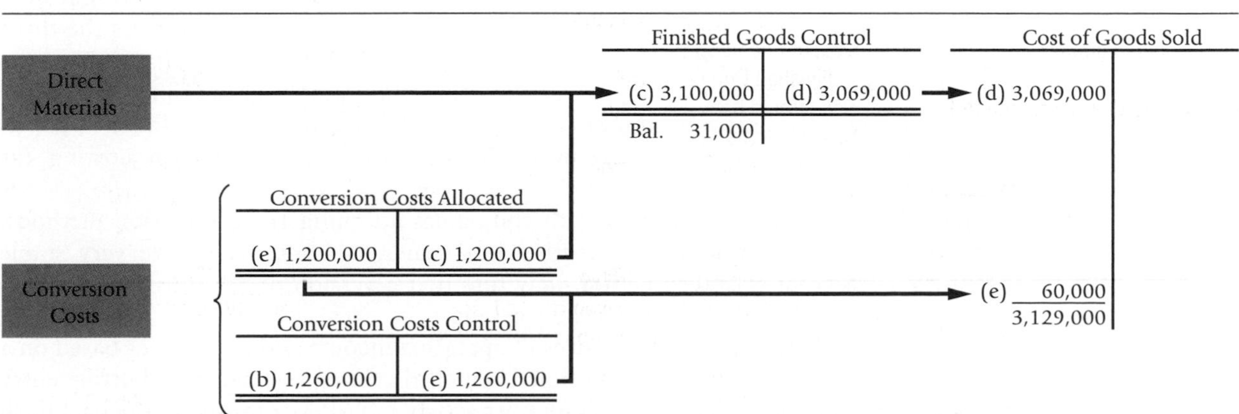

sold × \$31 per unit = \$3,069,000, which is composed of direct material costs (99,000 units × \$19 per unit = \$1,881,000) and conversion costs allocated (99,000 units × \$12 per unit = \$1,188,000).

No conversion costs are inventoried. That is, compared with Example 1, Example 2 does not assign \$12,000 (\$12 per unit × 1,000 units) of conversion costs to finished goods inventory. Hence, Example 2 allocates $12,000 less in conversion costs to inventory relative to the conversion costs allocated to inventory in Example 1. Of the $1,260,000 in conversion costs, $1,188,000 is allocated at standard cost to the units sold. The remaining $72,000 ($1,260,000 − $1,188,000) of conversion costs is underallocated. Entry (e) in Exhibit 20-7, Panel B, presents the journal entry if SVC, like many companies, writes off these underallocated costs monthly as additions to cost of goods sold.

The April 30 ending balance of Inventory Control is $69,000 ($50,000 direct materials still on hand + $19,000 direct materials embodied in the 1,000 units manufactured but not sold during the period). Exhibit 20-8, Panel B, provides a general-ledger overview of this version of backflush costing. Entries are keyed to Exhibit 20-7, Panel B. The approach described in Example 2 closely approximates the costs computed using sequential tracking when a company holds minimal work-in-process and finished goods inventories.

Example 3: Trigger points are completion of good finished units of product (stage C) and sale of finished goods (stage D) This example has two trigger points. Exhibit 20-7, Panel C, presents the journal entries. In contrast to Example 2, the first trigger point in Example 3 is delayed until stage C, SVC's completion of good finished units of product. It is represented by transaction (c). Because the purchase of direct materials is not a trigger point, there is no entry corresponding to transaction (a)—purchase of direct materials. Exhibit 20-8, Panel C, provides a general-ledger overview of this version of backflush costing. Entries are keyed to Exhibit 20-7, Panel C.

Compare entry (c) in Exhibit 20-7, Panel C, with entries (a) and (c) in Exhibit 20-7, Panel A. The simpler version in Example 3 ignores the $1,950,000 purchases of direct materials [shown in entry (a) of Example 1]. At the end of April, $50,000 of direct materials purchased have not yet been placed into production ($1,950,000 − $1,900,000 = $50,000), nor have the cost of those direct materials been entered into the inventory-costing system. The Example 3 version of backflush costing is suitable for a JIT production system in which both direct materials inventory and work-in-process inventory are minimal.

Extending Example 3, backflush costing systems could use the sale of finished goods as the only trigger point. This version of backflush costing is most suitable for a JIT production system with minimal direct materials, work-in-process, and finished goods inventories. That's because this backflush costing system maintains no inventory accounts.

Special Considerations in Backflush Costing

The accounting procedures illustrated in Examples 1, 2, and 3 do not strictly adhere to generally accepted accounting principles (GAAP). For example, work in process inventory, which is an asset, exists although it is not recognized in the financial statements. Advocates of backflush costing, however, cite the generally accepted accounting principle of materiality in support of the various versions of backflush costing. As the three examples illustrate, backflush costing can approximate the costs that would be reported under sequential tracking by varying the number of trigger points and where they are located. If significant amounts of direct materials inventory or finished goods inventory exist, adjusting entries can be incorporated into backflush costing (as explained below).

Backflush costing is not restricted to companies adopting JIT production methods. Companies that have short manufacturing lead times, or those that have very stable inventory levels from period to period, may find that a version of backflush costing will report cost numbers similar to sequential tracking.

Suppose there are material differences in operating income and inventories based on a backflush costing system and a conventional standard-costing system. An adjusting entry can be recorded to make the backflush number satisfy GAAP. For example, the backflush entries in Example 2 would result in expensing all conversion costs to Cost of Goods Sold ($1,188,000 at standard costs + $72,000 write-off of underallocated conversion costs = $1,260,000). But suppose conversion costs were regarded as sufficiently material in amount to be included in Inventory Control. Then entry (e), closing the Conversion Costs accounts, would change as follows:

Original entry (e)	Conversion Costs Allocated	1,188,000	
	Cost of Goods Sold	72,000	
	Conversion Costs Control		1,260,000
Revised entry (e)	Conversion Costs Allocated	1,188,000	
	Inventory Control (1,000 units × $12)	12,000	
	Cost of Goods Sold	60,000	
	Conversion Costs Control		1,260,000

Critics say backflush costing leaves no audit trails—the ability of the accounting system to pinpoint the uses of resources at each step of the production process. However, the absence of large amounts of materials inventory and work-in-process inventory means managers can keep track of operations by personal observations, computer monitoring, and nonfinancial measures.

What are the implications of JIT and backflush costing systems for activity-based costing (ABC) systems? Simplifying the production process, as in a JIT system, makes more of the costs direct and reduces the extent of overhead cost allocations. Simple ABC systems are often adequate for companies implementing JIT. These simple ABC systems work well with backflush costing. Costs from ABC systems yield more-accurate budgeted conversion cost per unit for different products in the backflush costing system. The activity-based cost information is also useful for product costing, decision making, and cost management.

Lean Accounting

Learning Objective 9

Understand the principles of lean accounting

. . . focus on costing value streams rather than products, and limit arbitrary allocations

Another approach for simplified product costing in JIT (or lean production) systems is *lean accounting*. Successful JIT production requires companies to focus on the entire value chain from suppliers to manufacturers to customers in order to reduce inventories, lead times, and waste. The emphasis on improvements throughout the value chain has led some JIT companies to develop organizational structures and costing systems that focus on **value streams**, which represent all the value-added activities needed to design, manufacture, and deliver a given product or product line to customers. For example, a value stream can include the activities needed to develop and engineer products, advertise and market these products, process orders, purchase and receive materials, manufacture and ship orders, bill customers, and collect payments. The focus on value streams is aided by the use of manufacturing cells in JIT systems that group together the operations needed to make a given product or product line.

Lean accounting is a costing method that supports creating value for the customer by costing the entire value stream, not individual products or departments, thereby eliminating waste in the accounting process.[5] If multiple, related products are made in a single value stream, product costs for the individual products are not computed. Actual costs are directly traced to the value stream and standard costs and variances are not computed. Direct tracing of costs is easy because companies using lean accounting dedicate resources to individual value streams. Moreover, many lean accounting systems expense the costs of all purchased materials in the period in which they are bought to signal that direct material and work-in-process inventory need to be reduced. Facility costs (such as depreciation, property taxes, and leases) are allocated to value streams based on the square footage used by each value stream to encourage managers to use less space for holding and moving inventory. Unused facility costs are not allocated to value streams. Instead, these costs are treated as plant or business unit expenses. Excluding unused facility costs from value stream costs increases the visibility of unused capacity costs, and creates incentives to reduce these costs or to find alternative uses for capacity (see Chapter 13, pp. 481–485). Common costs such as corporate or support department costs that cannot reasonably be assigned to value streams are also excluded from value stream costs.

Lean accounting is much simpler than traditional product costing. Why? Because it requires little overhead allocation when computing actual product costs by value stream.

[5] See B. Baggaley, "Costing by Value Stream," *Journal of Cost Management* (May–June 2003).

Compared to traditional product costing methods, the focus on value streams and costs is consistent with the emphasis of JIT and lean production on improvements in the value chain from suppliers to customers. Moreover, the practices that lean accounting encourages, such as reducing direct material and work-in-process inventories, using less space and eliminating unused capacity support the goals of JIT production.

A potential limitation of lean accounting is that it does not compute costs for individual products. Critics charge that this limits its usefulness for decision making. Proponents of lean accounting argue that the lack of individual product costs is not a problem because most decisions are made at the product line level rather than the individual product level, and that pricing decisions are based on the value created for the customer and not product costs. Another criticism is that lean accounting excludes certain support costs and unused capacity costs. As a result, the decisions based on only value stream costs will look profitable because they do not consider all costs. Supporters argue that lean accounting overcomes this problem by adding a large markup on value stream costs to compensate for these excluded costs. A final criticism is that lean accounting, like backflush costing, does not correctly account for inventories under generally accepted accounting principles (GAAP). However, proponents are quick to point out that in lean accounting environments, work in process and finished goods inventories are immaterial from an accounting perspective.

Problems for Self-Study

Problem 1

Lee Company has a Singapore plant that manufactures MP3 players. One component is an XT chip. Expected demand is for 5,200 of these chips in March 2009. Lee estimates the ordering cost per purchase order to be $250. The monthly carrying cost for one unit of XT in stock is $5.

Required

1. Compute the EOQ for the XT chip.
2. Compute the number of deliveries of XT in March 2009.

Solution

$$EOQ = \sqrt{\frac{2 \times 5{,}200 \times \$250}{\$5}}$$
$$= 721 \text{ chips (rounded)}$$

$$\text{Number of deliveries} = \frac{5{,}200}{721}$$
$$= 8 \text{ (rounded)}$$

Problem 2

Littlefield Company uses a backflush costing system with three trigger points:

- Purchase of direct materials
- Completion of good finished units of product
- Sale of finished goods

There are no beginning inventories. Information for April 2009 is:

Direct materials purchased	$880,000	Conversion costs allocated	$ 400,000
Direct materials used	$850,000	Costs transferred to finished goods	$1,250,000
Conversion costs incurred	$422,000	Cost of goods sold	$1,190,000

Required

1. Prepare journal entries for April (without disposing of underallocated or overallocated conversion costs). Assume there are no direct materials variances.
2. Under an ideal JIT production system, how would the amounts in your journal entries differ from the journal entries in requirement 1?

Solution

1. Journal entries for April are:

Entry (a)	Inventory: Materials and In-Process Control	880,000	
	Accounts Payable Control		880,000
	(direct materials purchased)		
Entry (b)	Conversion Costs Control	422,000	
	Various accounts (such as Wages Payable Control)		422,000
	(conversion costs incurred)		
Entry (c)	Finished Goods Control	1,250,000	
	Inventory: Materials and In-Process Control		850,000
	Conversion Costs Allocated		400,000
	(standard cost of finished goods completed)		
Entry (d)	Cost of Goods Sold	1,190,000	
	Finished Goods Control		1,190,000
	(standard costs of finished goods sold)		

2. Under an ideal JIT production system, if the manufacturing lead time per unit is very short, there could be zero inventories at the end of each day. Entry (c) would be $1,190,000 finished goods production [to match finished goods sold in entry (d)], not $1,250,000. If the Marketing Department could only sell goods costing $1,190,000, the JIT production system would call for direct materials purchases and conversion costs of lower than $880,000 and $422,000, respectively, in entries (a) and (b).

Decision Points

The following question-and-answer format summarizes the chapter's learning objectives. Each decision presents a key question related to a learning objective. The guidelines are the answer to that question.

Decision	Guidelines
1. What are the six categories of costs associated with goods for sale?	The six categories are purchasing costs (costs of goods acquired from suppliers), ordering costs (costs of preparing a purchase order and receiving goods), carrying costs (costs of holding inventory of goods for sale), stockout costs (costs arising when a customer demands a unit of product and that unit is not on hand), costs of quality (prevention, appraisal, internal failure, and external failure costs), and shrinkage costs (the costs resulting from theft by outsiders, embezzlement by employees, misclassifications, and clerical errors).
2. How do managers use the EOQ decision model?	The economic-order-quantity (EOQ) decision model calculates the optimal quantity of inventory to order by balancing ordering costs and carrying costs. The larger the order quantity, the higher the annual carrying costs and the lower the annual ordering costs. The EOQ model includes costs recorded in the financial accounting system as well as opportunity costs not recorded in the financial accounting system.
3. How can companies reduce the conflict between the EOQ decision model and models used for performance evaluation?	The opportunity cost of investment tied up in inventory is a key input in the EOQ decision model. Many companies include opportunity costs when evaluating managers so that the EOQ decision model is consistent with the performance-evaluation model.

4. What is a supply chain, and what is the benefit of supply-chain analysis?	The supply chain describes the flow of goods, services, and information from the initial sources of materials and services to the delivery of products to consumers, regardless of whether those activities occur in the same organization or in other organizations. Using supply-chain analysis allows companies to coordinate their activities and reduce inventories throughout the supply chain.
5. How do materials requirements planning (MRP) systems differ from just-in-time (JIT) production systems?	Materials requirements planning (MRP) systems use a "push-through" approach that manufactures finished goods for inventory on the basis of demand forecasts. Just-in-time (JIT) production systems use a "demand-pull" approach in which goods are manufactured only to satisfy customer orders.
6. What are the features of a JIT production system?	Five features of a JIT production system are (a) organizing production in manufacturing cells, (b) hiring and training multiskilled workers, (c) emphasizing total quality management, (d) reducing manufacturing lead time and setup time, and (e) building strong supplier relationships.
7. What is backflush costing?	Backflush costing delays recording some of the journal entries (and omits others) relating to the cycle from purchase of direct materials to the sale of finished goods.
8. How does backflush costing simplify inventory costing?	Traditional inventory-costing systems use sequential tracking, in which recording of the journal entries occurs in the same order as actual purchases and progress in production. Most backflush costing systems do not record journal entries for the work-in-process stage of production. Some backflush costing systems also do not record entries for either the purchase of direct materials or the completion of finished goods.
9. How is lean accounting different from traditional costing methods?	Lean accounting costs value streams rather than products. Unused capacity costs and costs that cannot be easily traced to value streams are not allocated.

TERMS TO LEARN

This chapter and the Glossary at the end of the book contain definitions of:

backflush costing (**p. 715**)
carrying costs (**p. 700**)
economic order quantity (EOQ) (**p. 700**)
inventory management (**p. 699**)
just-in-time (JIT) production (**p. 711**)
just-in-time (JIT) purchasing (**p. 706**)
lean accounting (**p. 721**)
lean production (**p. 711**)
manufacturing cells (**p. 711**)
materials requirements planning (MRP) (**p. 710**)
ordering costs (**p. 700**)
purchasing costs (**p. 700**)
purchase-order lead time (**p. 700**)
reorder point (**p. 702**)
safety stock (**p. 703**)
sequential tracking (**p. 715**)
shrinkage costs (**p. 700**)
stockout costs (**p. 700**)
trigger point (**p. 715**)
value stream (**p. 721**)

ASSIGNMENT MATERIAL

Questions

20-1 Why do better decisions regarding the purchasing and managing of goods for sale frequently cause dramatic percentage increases in net income?

20-2 Name six cost categories that are important in managing goods for sale in a retail company.

20-3 What assumptions are made when using the simplest version of the economic-order-quantity (EOQ) decision model?

20-4 Give examples of costs included in annual carrying costs of inventory when using the EOQ decision model.

20-5 Give three examples of opportunity costs that typically are not recorded in accounting systems, although they are relevant when using the EOQ model.

20-6 What are the steps in computing the cost of a prediction error when using the EOQ decision model?

20-7 Why might goal-congruence issues arise when an EOQ model is used to guide decisions on how much to order?

20-8 Describe JIT purchasing and its benefits.

20-9 What are three factors causing reductions in the cost to place purchase orders for materials?

20-10 "You should always choose the supplier who offers the lowest price per unit." Do you agree? Explain.

20-11 What is supply-chain analysis, and how can it benefit manufacturers and retailers?

20-12 What are the main features of JIT production?

20-13 Distinguish inventory-costing systems using sequential tracking from those using backflush costing.

20-14 Describe three different versions of backflush costing.

20-15 Discuss the differences between lean accounting and traditional cost accounting.

Exercises

20-16 Economic order quantity for retailer. Fan Base (FB) operates a megastore featuring sports merchandise. It uses an EOQ decision model to make inventory decisions. It is now considering inventory decisions for its Los Angeles Galaxy soccer jerseys product line. This is a highly popular item. Data for 2009 are:

Expected annual demand for Galaxy jerseys	10,000
Ordering cost per purchase order	$200
Carrying cost per year	$7 per jersey

Each jersey costs FB $40 and sells for $80. The $7 carrying cost per jersey per year comprises the required return on investment of $4.80 (12% × $40 purchase price) plus $2.20 in relevant insurance, handling, and theft-related costs. The purchasing lead time is 7 days. FB is open 365 days a year.

Required

1. Calculate the EOQ.
2. Calculate the number of orders that will be placed each year.
3. Calculate the reorder point.

20-17 Economic order quantity, effect of parameter changes (continuation of 20-16). Athletic Textiles (AT) manufactures the Galaxy jerseys that Fan Base (FB) sells to its customers. AT has recently installed computer software that enables its customers to conduct "one-stop" purchasing using state-of-the-art Web site technology. FB's ordering cost per purchase order will be $30 using this new technology.

Required

1. Calculate the EOQ for the Galaxy jerseys using the revised ordering cost of $30 per purchase order. Assume all other data from Exercise 20-16 are the same. Comment on the result.
2. Suppose AT proposes to "assist" FB. AT will allow FB customers to order directly from the AT Web site. AT would ship directly to these customers. AT would pay $10 to FB for every Galaxy jersey purchased by one of FB's customers. Comment qualitatively on how this offer would affect inventory management at FB. What factors should FB consider in deciding whether to accept AT's proposal?

20-18 EOQ for a retailer. The Cloth Center sells fabrics to a wide range of industrial and consumer users. One of the products it carries is denim cloth, used in the manufacture of jeans and carrying bags. The supplier for the denim cloth pays all incoming freight. No incoming inspection of the denim is necessary because the supplier has a track record of delivering high-quality merchandise. The purchasing officer of the Cloth Center has collected the following information:

Annual demand for denim cloth	20,000 yards
Ordering cost per purchase order	$160
Carrying cost per year	20% of purchase costs
Safety-stock requirements	None
Cost of denim cloth	$8 per yard

The purchasing lead time is 2 weeks. The Cloth Center is open 250 days a year (50 weeks for 5 days a week).

Required

1. Calculate the EOQ for denim cloth.
2. Calculate the number of orders that will be placed each year.
3. Calculate the reorder point for denim cloth.

20-19 EOQ for manufacturer. Lakeland Company, which produces lawn mowers, purchases 18,000 units of a rotor blade part each year at a cost of $60 per unit. Lakeland requires a 15% annual rate of return on investment. In addition, the relevant carrying cost (for insurance, materials handling, breakage, and so on) is $6 per unit per year. The relevant ordering cost per purchase order is $150.

Required

1. Calculate Lakeland's EOQ for the rotor blade part.

2. Calculate Lakeland's annual relevant ordering costs for the EOQ calculated in requirement 1.
3. Calculate Lakeland's annual relevant carrying costs for the EOQ calculated in requirement 1.
4. Assume that demand is uniform throughout the year and known with certainty so that there is no need for safety stocks. The purchase-order lead time is half a month. Calculate Lakeland's reorder point for the rotor blade part.

20-20 Sensitivity of EOQ to changes in relevant ordering and carrying costs. Alyia Company's annual demand for Model X253 is 10,000 units. Alyia is unsure about the relevant carrying cost per unit per year and the relevant ordering cost per purchase order. This table presents six possible combinations of carrying and ordering costs.

Relevant Carrying Cost per Unit per Year	Relevant Ordering Cost per Purchase Order
$10	$300
$10	$200
$15	$300
$15	$200
$20	$300
$20	$200

Required

1. Determine EOQ for Alyia for each of the relevant ordering and carrying-cost alternatives.
2. How does your answer to requirement 1 give insight into the impact on EOQ of changes in relevant ordering and carrying costs?

20-21 Inventory management and the balanced scorecard. Devin Sports Cars (DSC) has implemented a balanced scorecard to measure and support its just-in-time production system. In the learning and growth category, DSC measures the percentage of employees who are cross-trained to perform a wide variety of production tasks. Internal business process measures are inventory turns and on-time delivery. The customer perspective is measured using a customer satisfaction measure, and financial performance using operating income. DSC estimates that if it can increase the percentage of cross-trained employees by 5%, the resulting increase in labor productivity will reduce inventory-related costs by $100,000 per year and shorten delivery times by 10%. The 10% reduction in delivery times, in turn, is expected to increase customer satisfaction by 5%, and each 1% increase in customer satisfaction is expected to increase revenues by 2% due to higher prices.

Required

1. Assume that budgeted revenues in the coming year are $5,000,000. Ignoring the costs of training, what is the expected increase in operating income in the coming year if the number of cross-trained employees is increased by 5%?
2. What is the most DSC would be willing to pay to increase the percentage of cross-trained employees if it is only interested in maximizing operating income in the coming year?
3. What factors other than short-term profits should DSC consider when assessing the benefits from employee cross-training?

20-22 JIT production, relevant benefits, relevant costs. The Champion Hardware Company manufactures specialty brass door handles at its Lynchburg plant. Champion is considering implementing a JIT production system. The following are the estimated costs and benefits of JIT production.

a. Annual additional tooling costs would be $100,000.
b. Average inventory would decline by 80% from the current level of $1,000,000.
c. Insurance, space, materials-handling and setup costs, which currently total $300,000 annually, would decline by 25%.
d. The emphasis on quality inherent in JIT production would reduce rework costs by 30%. Champion currently incurs $200,000 in annual rework costs.
e. Improved product quality under JIT production would enable Champion to raise the price of its product by $4 per unit. Champion sells 40,000 units each year.

Champion's required rate of return on inventory investment is 15% per year.

Required

1. Calculate the net benefit or cost to Champion if it adopts JIT production at the Lynchburg plant.
2. What nonfinancial and qualitative factors should Champion consider when making the decision to adopt JIT production?
3. Suppose Champion implements JIT production at its Lynchburg plant. Give examples of performance measures Champion could use to evaluate and control JIT production. What would be the benefit of Champion implementing an enterprise resource planning (ERP) system?

20-23 Backflush costing and JIT production. Road Warrior Corporation assembles handheld computers that have scaled-down capabilities of laptop computers. Each handheld computer takes 6 hours to assemble. Road Warrior uses a JIT production system and a backflush costing system with three trigger points:

- Purchase of direct materials
- Completion of good finished units of product
- Sale of finished goods

There are no beginning inventories of materials or finished goods. The following data are for August 2008:

Direct materials purchased	$2,754,000	Conversion costs incurred	$723,600
Direct materials used	$2,733,600	Conversion costs allocated	$750,400

Road Warrior records direct materials purchased and conversion costs incurred at actual costs. When finished goods are sold, the backflush costing system "pulls through" standard direct material cost ($102 per unit) and standard conversion cost ($28 per unit). Road Warrior produced 26,800 finished units in August 2008 and sold 26,400 units. The actual direct material cost per unit in August 2008 was $102, and the actual conversion cost per unit was $27.

Required

1. Prepare summary journal entries for August 2008 (without disposing of under- or overallocated conversion costs).
2. Post the entries in requirement 1 to T-accounts for applicable Inventory: Materials and In-Process Control, Finished Goods Control, Conversion Costs Control, Conversion Costs Allocated, and Cost of Goods Sold.
3. Under an ideal JIT production system, how would the amounts in your journal entries differ from those in requirement 1?

20-24 Backflush costing, two trigger points, materials purchase and sale (continuation of 20-23). Assume the same facts as in Exercise 20-23, except that Road Warrior now uses a backflush costing system with the following two trigger points:

- Purchase of direct materials
- Sale of finished goods

The Inventory Control account will include direct materials purchased but not yet in production, materials in work in process, and materials in finished goods but not sold. No conversion costs are inventoried. Any under- or overallocated conversion costs are written off monthly to Cost of Goods Sold.

Required

1. Prepare summary journal entries for August, including the disposition of under- or overallocated conversion costs.
2. Post the entries in requirement 1 to T-accounts for Inventory Control, Conversion Costs Control, Conversion Costs Allocated, and Cost of Goods Sold.

20-25 Backflush costing, two trigger points, completion of production and sale (continuation of 20-23). Assume the same facts as in Exercise 20-23, except now Road Warrior uses only two trigger points, the completion of good finished units of product and the sale of finished goods. Any under- or overallocated conversion costs are written off monthly to Cost of Goods Sold.

Required

1. Prepare summary journal entries for August, including the disposition of under- or overallocated conversion costs.
2. Post the entries in requirement 1 to T-accounts for Finished Goods Control, Conversion Costs Control, Conversion Costs Allocated, and Cost of Goods Sold.

Problems

20-26 Effect of different order quantities on ordering costs and carrying costs, EOQ. Koala Blue, a retailer of bed and bath linen, sells 234,000 packages of Mona Lisa designer sheets each year. Koala Blue incurs an ordering cost of $81 per purchase order placed with Mona Lisa Enterprises and an annual carrying cost of $11.70 per package. Liv Carrol, purchasing manager at Koala Blue, seeks your help: She wants to understand how ordering and carrying costs vary with order quantity.

File Edit View Insert Format Tools Data Window Help

	A	B	C	D	E	F
1				Scenario		
2		1	2	3	4	5
3	Annual demand (packages)	234,000	234,000	234,000	234,000	234,000
4	Cost per purchase order	$ 81	$ 81	$ 81	$ 81	$ 81
5	Carrying cost per package per year	$ 11.70	$ 11.70	$ 11.70	$ 11.70	$ 11.70
6	Quantity (packages) per purchase order	900	1,500	1,800	2,100	2,700
7	Number of purchase orders per year					
8	Annual relevant ordering costs					
9	Annual relevant carrying costs					
10	Annual total relevant costs of ordering and carrying inventory					

If you want to use Excel to solve this problem, go to the Excel Lab at **www.prenhall.com/horngren/cost13e** and download the template for Problem 20-26.

Required

1. Complete the preceding table for Liv Carrol. What is the EOQ? Comment on your results.
2. Mona Lisa is about to introduce a Web-based ordering system for its customers. Liv Carrol estimates that Koala Blue's ordering costs will be reduced to $49 per purchase order. Calculate the new EOQ and the new annual relevant costs of ordering and carrying inventory.
3. Liv Carrol estimates that Koala Blue will incur a cost of $2,000 to train its two purchasing assistants to use the new Mona Lisa system. Help Liv Carrol present a case to upper management showing that Koala Blue will be able to recoup its training costs within the first year of adoption.

20-27 EOQ, uncertainty, safety stock, reorder point. Clarkson Shoe Co. produces and sells excellent quality walking shoes. After production, the shoes are distributed to 20 warehouses around the country. Each warehouse services approximately 100 stores in its region. Clarkson uses an EOQ model to determine the number of pairs of shoes to order for each warehouse from the factory. Annual demand for Warehouse OR2 is approximately 120,000 pairs of shoes. The ordering cost is $250 per order. The annual carrying cost of a pair of shoes is $2.40 per pair.

Required

1. Use the EOQ model to determine the optimal number of pairs of shoes per order.
2. Assume each month consists of approximately 4 weeks. If it takes 1 week to receive an order, at what point should warehouse OR2 reorder shoes?
3. Although OR2's average monthly demand is 10,000 pairs of shoes (120,000 ÷ 12 months), demand each month may vary from the average by up to 20%. To handle the variation in demand Clarkson has decided that OR2 should maintain enough safety stock to cover any demand level. How much safety stock should Warehouse OR2 hold? How will this affect the reorder point and reorder quantity?
4. What is the total relevant ordering and carrying costs with safety stock and without safety stock?

20-28 MRP, EOQ and JIT. MacroHard Corp produces J-Pods, music players that can download thousands of songs. MacroHard forecasts that demand in 2010 will be 48,000 J-Pods. The variable production cost of each J-Pod is $50. Due to the large $50,000 cost per setup, MacroHard plans to produce J-Pods once a month in batches of 4,000 each. The carrying cost of a unit in inventory is $20 per year.

Required

1. Using an MRP system, what is the annual cost of producing and carrying J-Pods in inventory? (Assume that, on average, half of the units produced in a month are in inventory.)
2. A new manager at MacroHard has suggested that the company use the EOQ model to determine the optimal batch size to produce. (To use the EOQ model, MacroHard needs to treat the setup cost in the same way it would treat ordering cost in a traditional EOQ model.) Determine the optimal batch size and number of batches. Round up the number of batches to the nearest whole number. What would be the annual cost of producing and carrying J-Pods in inventory if it uses the optimal batch size?
3. MacroHard is also considering switching from an MRP system to a JIT system. This will result in producing to demand in batch sizes of 500 J-Pods. The frequency of production batches will force MacroHard to reduce setup time and will result in a reduction in setup cost. The new setup cost will be $5,000 per setup. What is the annual cost of producing and carrying J-Pods in inventory under the JIT system?
4. Compare the models analyzed in the previous parts of the problem. What are the advantages and disadvantages of each?

20-29 Effect of management evaluation criteria on EOQ model. Computers 4 U is an online company that sells computers to individual consumers. The annual demand for one model that will be shipped from the northeast distribution center is estimated to be 500,000 computers. The ordering cost is $800 per order. The cost of carrying a computer in inventory is $50 per year, which includes $20 in opportunity cost of investment. The average purchase cost of a computer is $200.

Required

1. Compute the optimal order quantity using the EOQ model.
2. Compute the number of orders per year and the annual relevant total cost of ordering and holding inventory.
3. Assume that the benchmark that is used to evaluate distribution center managers includes only the out-of-pocket costs incurred (that is, managers' evaluations do not include the opportunity cost of investment tied up in holding inventory). If the manager makes the EOQ decision based upon the benchmark, the order quantity would be calculated using a carrying cost of $30 not $50. How would this affect the EOQ amount and the actual annual relevant cost of ordering and carrying inventory?
4. What will the inconsistency between the actual carrying cost and the benchmark used to evaluate managers cost the company? Why do you think the company currently excludes the opportunity costs from the calculation of the benchmark? What could the company do to encourage the manager to make decisions more congruent with the goal of reducing total inventory costs?

20-30 Effect of EOQ ordering on supplier costs (continuation of Problem 20-29). IMBest Computers supplies computers to Computers 4 U. Terry Moore, the president of IMBest, is pleased to hear that Computers 4 U will be ordering 500,000 computers. Moore has asked his accounting and production departments to team up and determine the best production schedule to meet Computers 4 U's desired delivery schedule. Assume that the computers would be ordered in batches of 2,000 and that there would be 250 orders annually. Because Computers 4 U's employees work a 5-day work week for 50 weeks a year, they would expect to receive an order every day. They have developed the following two production alternatives:

A. IMBest could produce the 10,000 units demanded per week (2,000 × 5) in one large run on Mondays. Shipments would be made each day. If this option is chosen then IMBest would only have to set up the machines once a week, but would incur carrying cost to hold the computers in inventory until Computers 4 U's desired delivery date.

B. IMBest could rearrange its production schedule during the week and produce 2,000 computers each day of the week, totaling 10,000 computers per week. Shipments would be made at the end of each production day. If it chooses this alternative, then it will incur setup costs every day, but carrying costs would be negligible and are assumed to be zero.

Required

1. If setup costs are $1,000 per setup and carrying costs are $50 per computer per year, what would be the annual cost of each alternative?
2. How much would carrying costs have to increase before the preferred alternative would change?

20-31 JIT purchasing, relevant benefits, relevant costs. (CMA, adapted) The Margro Corporation is an automotive supplier that uses automatic turning machines to manufacture precision parts from steel bars. Margro's inventory of raw steel averages $600,000. John Oates, president of Margro, and Helen Gorman, Margro's controller, are concerned about the costs of carrying inventory. The steel supplier is willing to supply steel in smaller lots at no additional charge. Gorman identifies the following effects of adopting a JIT inventory program to virtually eliminate steel inventory:

- Without scheduling any overtime, lost sales due to stockouts would increase by 35,000 units per year. However, by incurring overtime premiums of $40,000 per year, the increase in lost sales could be reduced to 20,000 units per year. This would be the maximum amount of overtime that would be feasible for Margro.
- Two warehouses currently used for steel bar storage would no longer be needed. Margro rents one warehouse from another company under a cancelable leasing arrangement at an annual cost of $60,000. The other warehouse is owned by Margro and contains 12,000 square feet. Three-fourths of the space in the owned warehouse could be rented for $1.50 per square foot per year. Insurance and property tax costs totaling $14,000 per year would be eliminated.

Margro's required rate of return on investment is 20% per year. Margro's budgeted income statement for the year ending December 31, 2008 (in thousands) is as follows:

Revenues (900,000 units)		$10,800
Cost of goods sold		
Variable costs	$4,050	
Fixed costs	1,450	
Total costs of goods sold		5,500
Gross margin		5,300
Marketing and distribution costs		
Variable costs	$ 900	
Fixed costs	1,500	
Total marketing and distribution costs		2,400
Operating income		$ 2,900

Required

1. Calculate the estimated dollar savings (loss) for the Margro Corporation that would result in 2008 from the adoption of JIT purchasing.
2. Identify and explain other factors that Margro should consider before deciding whether to adopt JIT purchasing.

20-32 Supply chain effects on total relevant inventory cost. Cow Spot Computer Co. outsources the production of motherboards for its computers. It has narrowed down its choice of suppliers to two companies: Maji and Induk. Maji is an older company with a good reputation, while Induk is a newer company with cheaper prices. Given the difference in reputation, 5% of the motherboards will be inspected if they are purchased from Maji, but 25% of the motherboards will be inspected if they are purchased from Induk. The following data refers to costs associated with Maji and Induk.

	Maji	Induk
Number of orders per year	50	50
Annual motherboards demanded	10,000	10,000
Price per motherboard	$93	$90
Ordering cost per order	$10	$8
Inspection cost per unit	$5	$5
Average inventory level	100 units	100 units
Expected number of stockouts	100	300
Stockout cost (cost of rush order) per stockout	$5	$8
Units returned by customers for replacing motherboards	50	500
Cost of replacing each motherboard	$25	$25
Required annual return on investment	10%	10%
Other carrying cost per unit per year	$2.50	$2.50

Required

1. What is the relevant cost of purchasing from Maji and Induk?
2. What factors other than cost should Cow Spot consider?

20-33 Backflush costing and JIT production. The Acton Corporation manufactures electrical meters. For August, there were no beginning inventories of direct materials and no beginning or ending work in process. Acton uses a JIT production system and backflush costing with three trigger points for making entries in the accounting system:

- Purchase of direct materials—debited to Inventory: Materials and In-Process Control
- Completion of good finished units of product—debited to Finished Goods Control
- Sale of finished goods

Acton's August standard cost per meter is direct material, $25; and conversion cost, $20. The following data apply to August manufacturing:

Direct materials purchased	$550,000	Number of finished units manufactured	21,000
Conversion costs incurred	$440,000	Number of finished units sold	20,000

Required

1. Prepare summary journal entries for August (without disposing of under- or overallocated conversion costs). Assume no direct materials variances.
2. Post the entries in requirement 1 to T-accounts for Inventory: Materials and In-Process Control, Finished Goods Control, Conversion Costs Control, Conversion Costs Allocated, and Cost of Goods Sold.

20-34 Backflush, two trigger points, materials purchase and sale (continuation of 20-33). Assume that the second trigger point for Acton Corporation is the sale—rather than the completion—of finished goods. Also, the inventory account is confined solely to direct materials, whether these materials are in a storeroom, in work in process, or in finished goods. No conversion costs are inventoried. They are allocated to the units sold at standard costs. Any under- or overallocated conversion costs are written off monthly to Cost of Goods Sold.

Required

1. Prepare summary journal entries for August, including the disposition of under- or overallocated conversion costs. Assume no direct materials variances.
2. Post the entries in requirement 1 to T-accounts for Inventory Control, Conversion Costs Control, Conversion Costs Allocated, and Cost of Goods Sold.

20-35 Backflush, two trigger points, completion of production and sale (continuation of 20-33). Assume the same facts as in Problem 20-33 except now there are only two trigger points: the completion of good finished units of product and the sale of finished goods.

Required

1. Prepare summary journal entries for August, including the disposition of under- or overallocated conversion costs. Assume no direct materials variances.
2. Post the entries in requirement 1 to T-accounts for Finished Goods Control, Conversion Costs Control, Conversion Costs Allocated, and Cost of Goods Sold.

20-36 Lean Accounting. Flexible Security Devices (FSD) has introduced a just-in-time production process and is considering the adoption of lean accounting principles to support its new production philosophy. The company has two product lines: Mechanical Devices and Electronic Devices. Two individual products are made in each line. The company's traditional cost accounting system allocates all plant-level overhead costs to individual products. Product-line overhead costs are traced directly to product lines, and then allocated to the two individual products in each line. Equipment costs are directly traced to products. The latest accounting report using traditional cost accounting methods included the following information (in thousands of dollars).

	Mechanical Devices		Electronic Devices	
	Product A	Product B	Product C	Product D
Sales	$700	$500	$900	$450
Direct material (based on quantity used)	200	100	250	75
Direct manufacturing labor	150	75	200	60
Equipment costs	90	125	200	100
Allocated product-line overhead	110	60	125	50
Allocated plant-level overhead	50	35	80	25
Operating income	$100	$105	$ 45	$140

FSD has determined that each of the two product lines represents a distinct value stream. It has also determined that $120,000 of the allocated plant-level overhead costs represents occupancy costs. Product A occupies 20% of the plant's square footage, Product B occupies 20%, Product C occupies 30%, and Product D occupies 15%. The remaining square footage is occupied by plant administrative functions or is not being used. Finally, FSD has decided that direct material should be expensed in the period it is purchased, rather than when the material is used. According to purchasing records, direct material purchase costs during the period were:

	Mechanical Devices		Electronic Devices	
	Product A	Product B	Product C	Product D
Direct material (purchases)	$190	$125	$250	$90

Required

1. What are the cost objects in FSD's lean accounting system? Which of FSD's costs would be excluded when computing operating income for these cost objects?
2. Compute operating income for the cost objects identified in requirement 1 using lean accounting principles. Why does operating income differ from the operating income computed using traditional cost accounting methods?

Collaborative Learning Problem

20-37 Backflushing. The following conversation occurred between Brian Richardson, plant manager at Glendale Engineering, and Charles Cheng, plant controller. Glendale manufactures automotive component parts, such as gears and crankshafts, for automobile manufacturers. Richardson has been very enthusiastic about implementing JIT and about simplifying and streamlining production and other business processes.

"Charles," Richardson began, "I would like to substantially simplify our accounting in the new JIT environment. Can't we just record one journal entry at the time we ship products to our customers? I don't want to have our staff spending time tracking inventory from one stage to the next, when we have as little inventory as we do."

"Brian," Cheng said, "I think you are right about simplifying the accounting, but we still have a fair amount of direct materials and finished goods inventory that varies from period to period, depending on the demand for specific products. Doing away with all inventory accounting may be a problem."

"Well," Richardson replied, "you know my desire to simplify, simplify, simplify. I know that there are some costs of oversimplifying, but I believe that, in the long run, simplification pays dividends. Why don't you and your staff study the issues involved, and I will put it on the agenda for our next management meeting."

Required

1. What version of backflush costing would you recommend that Cheng adopt? Remember Richardson's desire to simplify the accounting as much as possible. Develop support for your recommendation.
2. Think about the three versions of backflush costing shown in Exhibit 20-8 (p. 719). These versions differ with respect to the number and types of trigger points used. Suppose your goal of implementing backflush costing is to simplify the accounting, but only if it closely matches the sequential-tracking approach. Which version of backflush costing would you propose if:
   a. Glendale had no direct materials and no work-in-process inventories but did have finished goods inventory?
   b. Glendale had no work in process and no finished goods inventories but did have direct materials inventory?
   c. Glendale had no direct materials, no work-in-process, and no finished goods inventories?
3. Backflush costing has its critics. In an article in the magazine *Management Accounting* titled "Beware of the New Accounting Myths," R. Calvasina, E. Calvasina, and G. Calvasina state:

   > The periodic (backflush) system has never been reflective of the reporting needs of a manufacturing system. In the highly standardized operating environments of the present JIT era, the appropriate system to be used is a perpetual accounting system based on an up-to-date, realistic set of standard costs. For management accountants to backflush on an actual cost basis is to return to the days of the outdoor privy (toilet).

   Comment on this statement.

21 Capital Budgeting and Cost Analysis

Learning Objectives

1. Recognize the multiyear focus of capital budgeting
2. Understand the five stages of capital budgeting for a project
3. Use and evaluate the two main discounted cash flow (DCF) methods: the net present value (NPV) method and the internal rate-of-return (IRR) method
4. Use and evaluate the payback method
5. Use and evaluate the accrual accounting rate-of-return (AARR) method
6. Identify and reduce conflicts from using DCF for capital budgeting decisions and accrual accounting for performance evaluation
7. Identify relevant cash inflows and outflows for capital budgeting decisions

A firm's accountants play an important role when it comes to deciding the major expenditures, or investments, a company should make. They, along with top executives, have to figure out how and when to best allocate the firm's scarce financial resources among alternative opportunities to create future value for the company. But because it's hard to know what the future holds and what projects will ultimately cost, this can be a challenging task. It's one that companies like Chevron constantly confront. To meet this challenge, Chevron has developed a framework for making project-related capital budgeting decisions. This chapter explains the different methods managers use to get the "biggest bang" for the firm's "buck" in terms of the projects they undertake.

Chevron Pumps Up Its Capital Budget[1]

Chevron Corp will spend $19.6 billion in 2007 drilling new oil and natural gas wells, building offshore platforms, and upgrading gasoline refineries, a 22.5 percent increase over 2006. Chevron has been under pressure from investors to increase oil production worldwide after several low-production years. Lawmakers are also pressuring U.S. oil companies to increase their spending to boost crude and natural-gas supplies to lower prices for consumers.

One problem Chevron faces is that the companies it hires to drill wells and install rigs have raised their fees. In fact, as oil prices have doubled, so have the rents for the most advanced deepwater drilling. To get the few rigs available, producers like Chevron are signing contracts committing to pay more than $500,000 a day for multiple years to use rigs offered by drillers. Labor and equipment expenses are soaring as producers compete for drilling rigs and work crews.

Other factors constraining oil production at Chevron are instability in oil-producing countries like Nigeria and efforts by Russia and Venezuela to take control of energy projects undertaken by foreign companies.

To manage these complex capital investments, Chevron developed the Chevron Project Development and Execution Process

[1] *Sources:* Ian McKinnon, "Petro-Canada Plans C$26.2 Billion Oil-Sands Project," *Bloomberg.com,* June 27, 2007; "Chevron Boosts Capital Budget: Energy Giant Invests in Oil, Gas Production amid Records Profits," *San Francisco Chronicle,* December 8, 2006; Joe Carroll and Dan Lonkevich, "Chevron to Raise Capital Spending to $19.6 Billion," *Bloomberg.com,* December 7, 2006; Dennis J. Cohen and Judd Kuehn, "Value Added Project Management: Doing the Project Right Is Not Enough," *SMG White Paper,* Strategic Management Group, Inc., 2005.

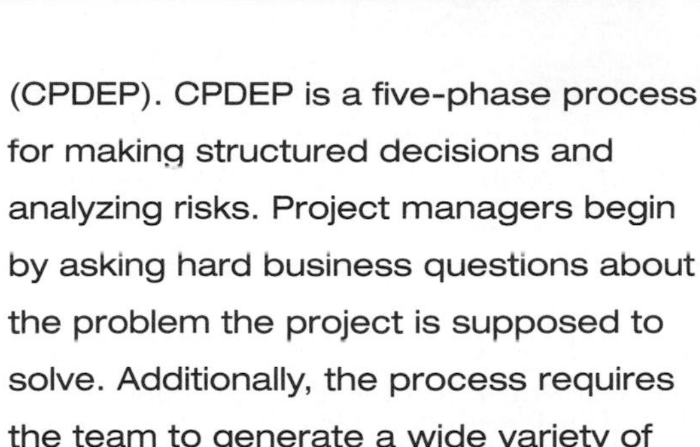

(CPDEP). CPDEP is a five-phase process for making structured decisions and analyzing risks. Project managers begin by asking hard business questions about the problem the project is supposed to solve. Additionally, the process requires the team to generate a wide variety of alternatives from both a technical and business perspective. A key aspect of the CPDEP framework is to evaluate the specific return that the project will earn over time and the economic value it will create for the company.

Managers at companies such as Chevron, Apple, Toyota, Microsoft, Sony, and Banana Republic constantly face challenging investment decisions. In this chapter, we introduce several capital budgeting methods used to evaluate long-term investment projects. These methods help managers choose the projects that will contribute the most value to their organizations.

Two Dimensions of Cost Analysis

Learning Objective 1

Recognize the multiyear focus of capital budgeting

. . . capital budgeting decisions consider revenues and costs over long periods

Unlike the majority of accounting where cost analysis is performed on a period-by-period basis, in choosing investments, managers are selecting among multiple projects, each of which may span several periods. Exhibit 21-1 illustrates these two different, yet intersecting, dimensions of cost analysis: (1) horizontally across, as the *project dimension*, and (2) vertically upward, as the *accounting-period dimension*. Each project is represented as a horizontal rectangle starting and ending at different times and stretching over time spans longer than one year. The vertical rectangle for the 2009 accounting period, for example, represents the dimension of income determination and routine annual planning and control that cuts across all projects that are ongoing that year.

Capital budgeting analyzes each project by considering all the lifespan cash flows from its initial investment through its termination. It is analogous therefore to life-cycle budgeting and costing (Chapter 12, pp. 443–445). For example, when Volvo considers a new-car project it begins by estimating all potential revenues from the new car as well as any costs that will be incurred along its life cycle, which may be as long as 10 years. Only after examining the potential costs and benefits across all of the business functions in the value chain, from R&D to customer service, across the entire lifespan of the new-car project, does Volvo decide whether the new model is a wise investment.

Exhibit 21-1

The Project and Time Dimensions of Capital Budgeting

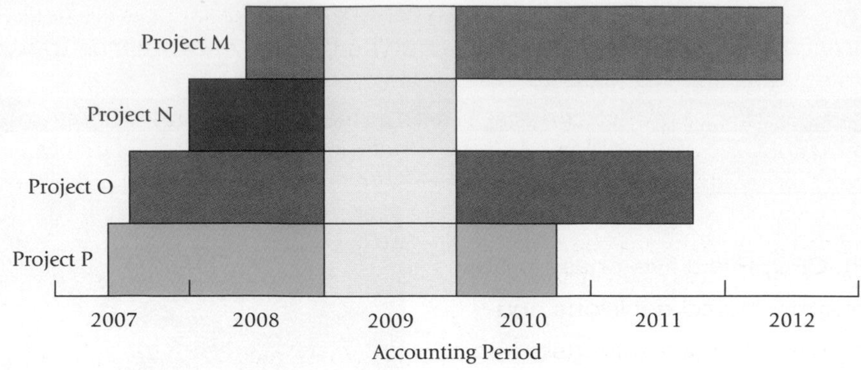

Stages of Capital Budgeting

Learning Objective 2

Understand the five stages of capital budgeting for a project

. . . identify projects, obtain information, make predictions, make decisions, and implement the decision, evaluate performance, and learn

Capital budgeting is the process of making long-run planning decisions for investments in projects. It is both a decision-making and a control tool. Like the five-step decision process that we have emphasized throughout this book, there are five stages to the capital budgeting process:

Stage 1: Identify Projects *Identify potential capital investments that agree with the organization's strategy.* For example, when the Microsoft Office group sought a strategy of product differentiation, it listed possible upgrades and changes from its present offering. Alternatively, a strategy of cost leadership could be promoted by projects that improve productivity and efficiency. In the case of a manufacturer of computer hardware, such a project could include the outsourcing of certain components to lower-cost contract manufacturing facilities located overseas. Identifying which types of capital projects to invest in is largely the responsibility of senior line managers.

Stage 2: Obtain Information *Gather information from all parts of the value chain to evaluate alternative projects.* Returning to the new car example at Volvo, in this stage, marketing is queried for potential revenue numbers, the plant manager is asked about assembly time, and suppliers are asked about prices and the availability of key components. Some projects may even be rejected at this stage. For example, suppose Volvo learns that the car simply cannot be built using existing plants. It may then opt to cancel the project altogether.

Stage 3: Make Predictions *Forecast all potential cash flows attributable to the alternative projects.* Capital investment projects generally involve substantial initial outlays, which are recouped over time through annual cash inflows and the disposal values from the termination of the project. As a result, they require the firm to make forecasts of cash flows several years into the future. BMW, for example, estimates yearly cash flows and sets its investment budgets accordingly using a 12-year planning horizon. Because of the greater uncertainty associated with these predictions, firms typically analyze a wide range of possible scenarios.

Stage 4: Make Decisions by Choosing Among Alternatives *Determine which investment yields the greatest benefit and the least cost to the organization.* Using the quantitative information obtained in stage 3, the firm uses any one of several capital budgeting methodologies to determine which project best meets organizational goals. While capital budgeting calculations are typically limited to financial information, managers use their judgment and intuition to factor in qualitative information as well.

Stage 5: Implement the Decision, Evaluate Performance, and Learn Given the complexities of capital investment decisions and the long time horizons they span, this stage can be separated into two phases:

- *Obtain funding and make the investments selected in stage 4.* Sources of funding include internally generated cash flow as well as equity and debt securities sold in capital markets. Making capital investments is often an arduous task, laden with the purchase of many different goods and services. If Volvo opts to build a new car, it must order steel, aluminum, paint, and so on. If some of the supplies are not available according to plan, managers must revisit and determine the economic feasibility of substituting the missing material with alternative inputs.

- *Track realized cash flows, compare against estimated numbers, and revise plans if necessary*. As the cash outflows and inflows begin to accumulate, managers can verify whether the predictions made in stage 3 agree with the actual flows of cash from the project. When the BMW group initially released the new Mini, realized sales were substantially higher than the original demand estimates. BMW responded by manufacturing more cars to meet the higher demand. It also decided to expand the Mini line to include convertibles.

To illustrate capital budgeting, consider Top-Spin tennis racquets. Top-Spin was one of the first major tennis-racquet producers to introduce graphite in its racquets. This allowed Top-Spin to produce some of the lightest and stiffest racquets in the market. However, new carbon-fiber impregnated racquets are even lighter and stiffer than their graphite counterparts. Top-Spin has always been an innovator in the tennis-racquet industry, and wants to stay that way and so in stage 1 it identifies the carbon fiber racquet project. In the information gathering stage (stage 2), the company learns that it could feasibly begin using carbon-fiber in its racquets as early as 2008 if it replaces one of its graphite forming machines with a carbon-fiber weaving machine. After collecting additional data, Top-Spin begins to forecast future cash flows if it invests in the new machine (stage 3). Top-Spin estimates that it can purchase a carbon-fiber weaving machine with a useful life of 5 years for a net after-tax initial investment of $379,100, which is calculated as follows:

Cost of new machine	$390,000
Investment in working capital (supplies and spare parts for new machine)	9,000
Cash flow from disposing of existing machine (after-tax)	(19,900)
Net initial investment for new machine	$379,100

The machine is believed to have no terminal disposal value after 5 years; however, at the end of year 5, the $9,000 in working capital is returned. Managers estimate that by introducing carbon-fiber impregnated racquets, operating cash inflows (cash revenues minus cash operating costs) will increase by $100,000 (after tax) in the first four years and $91,000 in year 5. To simplify the analysis, suppose that all cash flows occur at the end of each year. Note that cash flow at the end of year 5 also increases by $100,000, $91,000 in operating cash inflows and $9,000 in working capital. Management next calculates the costs and benefits of the proposed project (stage 4). This chapter discusses four capital budgeting methods to analyze financial information:

1. Net present value (NPV)
2. Internal rate of return (IRR)
3. Payback
4. Accrual accounting rate of return (AARR)

Both the NPV and IRR methods use discounted cash flows.

Learning Objective 3

Use and evaluate the two main discounted cash flow (DCF) methods: the net present value (NPV) method and the internal rate-of-return (IRR) method

. . . to explicitly consider all project cash flows and the time value of money

Discounted Cash Flow

Discounted cash flow (DCF) methods measure all expected future *cash* inflows and outflows of a project discounted back to the present period. The key feature of DCF methods is the **time value of money,** which means that a dollar (or any other monetary unit) received today is worth more than a dollar received at any future time. The reason is that $1 received today can be invested at, say, 10% per year so that it grows to $1.10 at the end of one year. The time value of money is the opportunity cost (the return of $0.10 forgone per year) from not having the money today. In this example, $1 received one year from now is worth $1 ÷ 1.10 = $0.9091 today. In this way, discounted cash flow methods explicitly weight cash flows by the time value of money. So in our example, $100 received one year from now will be weighted by 0.9091 to yield a discounted cash flow of $90.91, which is today's value of that $100 next year. Note that DCF focuses exclusively on *cash* inflows and outflows rather than on operating income as determined by accrual accounting.

The compound interest tables and formulas used in DCF analysis are in Appendix B, pages 836–842. If you are unfamiliar with compound interest, do not proceed until you have studied Appendix B. The tables in Appendix B will be used frequently in this chapter.

The two DCF methods we describe are the net present value (NPV) method and the internal rate-of-return (IRR) method. Both DCF methods use what is called the **required rate of return (RRR)**, the minimum acceptable annual rate of return on an investment. The RRR is internally set, usually by upper management, and typically reflects the return that an organization could expect to receive elsewhere for an investment of comparable risk. The RRR is also called the **discount rate**, **hurdle rate**, **cost of capital**, or **opportunity cost of capital**. Suppose the CFO at Top-Spin has set the required rate of return for the firm's investments at 8% per year.

Net Present Value Method

The **net present value (NPV) method** calculates the expected monetary gain or loss from a project by discounting all expected future cash inflows and outflows back to the present point in time using the required rate of return. To use the NPV method, apply the following three steps:

Step 1: Draw a Sketch of Relevant Cash Inflows and Outflows. The right side of Exhibit 21-2 shows arrows that depict the cash flows of the new carbon-fiber machine. *Note that parentheses denote relevant cash outflows throughout all exhibits in Chapter 21.* The sketch helps the decision maker visualize and organize the data in a systematic way. Note, Exhibit 21-2 includes the outflow for the acquisition of the new machine at the start of year 1 (also referred to as end of year 0). The NPV method specifies cash flows regardless of the source of the cash flows, such as from operations, purchase or sale of equipment, or investment in or recovery of working capital. *Do not* inject accrual-accounting concepts such as sales made on credit or noncash expenses into the determination of cash inflows and outflows.

Step 2: Discount the Cash Flows Using the Correct Compound Interest Table from Appendix B and Sum Them. In our example, we can discount each year's cash flow separately using Table 2, or we can compute the present value of an annuity, a series of equal cash flows at equal time intervals, using Table 4. Both tables are in Appendix B. If we use Table 2, we find the discount factors for periods 1 through 5 under the 8% column. Approach 1 in Exhibit 21-2 uses the five discount factors. To obtain the present value amount, multiply each discount factor by the corresponding amount represented by the arrow on the right in Exhibit 21-2 (−$379,100 × 1.000; $100,000 × 0.926; and so on to $100,000 × 0.681). Because the investment in the new machine produces an annuity, we may also use Table 4. Under Approach 2, we find that the annuity factor for five periods under the 8% column is 3.993, which is the sum of the five discount factors used in Approach 1. We multiply the uniform annual cash inflow by this factor to obtain the present value of the inflows ($399,300 = $100,000 × 3.993). Subtracting the initial investment then reveals the NPV of the project as $20,200 ($20,200 = $399,300 − $379,100).

Step 3: Make the Project Decision on the Basis of the Calculated NPV. If NPV is zero or positive, financial considerations suggest that the project should be accepted; its expected rate of return equals or exceeds the required rate of return. If NPV is negative, the project should be rejected; its expected rate of return is below the required rate of return.

Exhibit 21-2 calculates an NPV of $20,200 at the required rate of return of 8% per year. The project is acceptable based on financial information. The cash flows from the project are adequate (1) to recover the net initial investment in the project and (2) to earn a return greater than 8% per year on the investment tied up in the project over its useful life.

Managers must also weigh nonfinancial factors such as the effect that purchasing the machine will have on Top-Spin's brand. This is a nonfinancial factor because the financial benefits that accrue from Top-Spin's brand are very difficult to estimate. Nevertheless,

Exhibit 21-2 Net Present Value Method: Top-Spin's Carbon-Fiber Machine

File Edit View Insert Format Tools Data Window Help

	A	B	C	D	E	F	G	H	I
1			Net initial investment	$379,100					
2			Useful life	5 years					
3			Annual cash inflow	$100,000					
4			Required rate of return	8%					
5									
6		Present Value	Present Value of		Sketch of Relevant Cash Flows at End of Each Year				
7		of Cash Flow	$1 Discounted at 8%	0	1	2	3	4	5
8	**Approach 1: Discounting Each Year's Cash Flow Separately**[a]								
9	Net initial investment	$(379,100) ←	1.000 ←	$(379,100)					
10		92,600 ←	0.926 ←		$100,000				
11		85,700 ←	0.857 ←			$100,000			
12	Annual cash inflow	79,400 ←	0.794 ←				$100,000		
13		73,500 ←	0.735 ←					$100,000	
14		68,100 ←	0.681 ←						$100,000
15	NPV if new machine purchased	$ 20,200							
16									
17	**Approach 2: Using Annuity Table**[b]								
18	Net initial investment	$(379,100) ←	1.000 ←	$(379,100)					
19					$100,000	$100,000	$100,000	$100,000	$100,000
20									
21	Annual cash inflow	399,300 ←	3.993 ←						
22	NPV if new machine purchased	$ 20,200							
23									
24	*Note:* Parentheses denote relevant cash outflows throughout all exhibits in Chapter 21.								
25	[a] Present values from Table 2, Appendix B at the end of the book. For example, $0.857 = 1 \div (1.08)^2$.								
26	[b] Annuity present value from Table 4, Appendix B. The annuity table value of 3.993 is the sum of the individual discount rates								
27	0.926 + 0.857 + 0.794 + 0.735 + 0.681, subject to rounding.								

managers must consider brand effects before reaching a final decision. Suppose, for example, that the NPV of the carbon-fiber machine is negative. Management may still decide to buy the machine if it maintains Top-Spin's technological image and helps sell other Top-Spin products.

Pause here. Do not proceed until you understand what you see in Exhibit 21-2. Compare approach 1 with approach 2 in Exhibit 21-2 to see how Table 4 in Appendix B merely aggregates the present value factors of Table 2. That is, the fundamental table is Table 2. Table 4 simply reduces calculations when there is an annuity.

Internal Rate-of-Return Method

The **internal rate-of-return (IRR) method** calculates the discount rate at which an investment's present value of all expected cash inflows equals the present value of its expected cash outflows. That is, the IRR is the discount rate that makes NPV = $0. Exhibit 21-3 presents the cash flows and shows the calculation of NPV using a 10% annual discount rate for Top-Spin's carbon-fiber project. At a 10% discount rate, the NPV of the project is $0. Therefore, IRR is 10% per year.

How do managers determine the discount rate that yields NPV = $0? In most cases, managers or analysts solving capital budgeting problems use a calculator or computer program to provide the internal rate of return. The following trial-and-error approach can also provide the answer.

Step 1: Use a discount rate and calculate the project's NPV.

Step 2: If the calculated NPV is less than zero, use a lower discount rate. (A *lower* discount rate will *increase* NPV. Remember that we are trying to find a discount rate for

Exhibit 21-3 Internal Rate-of-Return Method: Top-Spin's Carbon-Fiber Machine[a]

File Edit View Insert Format Tools Data Window Help

	A	B	C	D	E	F	G	H	I
1			Net initial investment	$379,100					
2			Useful life	5 years					
3			Annual cash inflow	$100,000					
4			Annual discount rate	10%					
5									
6		**Present Value**	**Present Value of**	**Sketch of Relevant Cash Flows at End of Each Year**					
7		**of Cash Flow**	**$1 Discounted at 10%**	**0**	**1**	**2**	**3**	**4**	**5**
8	**Approach 1: Discounting Each Year's Cash Flow Separately[b]**								
9	Net initial investment	$(379,100) ←	1.000 ←	$(379,100)					
10		90,900 ←	0.909 ←		$100,000				
11		82,600 ←	0.826 ←			$100,000			
12	Annual cash inflow	75,100 ←	0.751 ←				$100,000		
13		68,300 ←	0.683 ←					$100,000	
14		62,100 ←	0.621 ←						$100,000
15	NPV if new machine purchased[c]	$ 0							
16	(the zero difference proves that								
17	the internal rate of return is 10%)								
18									
19	**Approach 2: Using Annuity Table**								
20	Net initial investment	$(379,100) ←	1.000 ←	$(379,100)					
21					$100,000	$100,000	$100,000	$100,000	$100,000
22									
23	Annual cash inflow	379,100 ←	3.791[d] ←						
24	NPV if new machine purchased	$ 0							
25									
26	*Note: Parentheses denote relevant cash outflows throughout all exhibits in Chapter 21.*								
27	[a]The internal rate of return is computed by methods explained on pp. 737–738.								
28	[b]Present values from Table 2, Appendix B at the end of the book.								
29	[c]Sum is $(100) due to rounding. We round to $0.								
30	[d]Annuity present value from Table 4, Appendix B. The annuity table value of 3.791 is the sum of the individual discount rates								
31	0.909 + 0.826 + 0.751 + 0.683 + 0.621, subject to rounding.								

which NPV = $0.) If NPV is greater than zero, use a higher discount rate to lower NPV. Keep adjusting the discount rate until NPV = $0. In the Top-Spin example, a discount rate of 8% yields an NPV of +$20,200 (see Exhibit 21-2). A discount rate of 12% yields an NPV of −$18,600 (3.605, the present value annuity factor from Table 4, × $100,000 minus $379,100). Therefore, the discount rate that makes NPV = $0 must lie between 8% and 12%. We use 10% and get NPV = $0. Hence, the IRR is 10% per year.

The step-by-step computations of internal rate of return are easier when the cash inflows are constant, as in our example. Information from Exhibit 21-3 can be expressed by:

$$\$379{,}100 = \text{Present value of annuity of } \$100{,}000 \text{ at } X\% \text{ per year for 5 years}$$

Or, what factor F in Table 4 (Appendix B) will satisfy this equation?

$$\$379{,}100 = \$100{,}000F$$
$$F = \$379{,}100 \div \$100{,}000 = 3.791$$

On the five-period line of Table 4, find the percentage column that is closest to 3.791. It is exactly 10%. If the factor (F) falls between the factors in two columns, straight-line interpolation is used to approximate IRR. This interpolation is illustrated in the Problem for Self-Study (pp. 752–753).

A project is accepted only if IRR equals or exceeds required rate of return (RRR). In the Top-Spin example, the carbon-fiber machine has an IRR of 10%, which is greater than the RRR of 8%. On the basis of financial factors, Top-Spin should invest in the new machine. In general, the NPV and IRR decision rules result in consistent project acceptance

with shorter payback periods (projects that are more liquid) to projects with longer payback periods, if all other things are equal. Projects with shorter payback periods give an organization more flexibility because funds for other projects become available sooner. Also, managers are less confident about cash flow predictions that stretch far into the future, again favoring shorter payback periods.

Unlike the NPV and IRR methods where management selected a RRR, under the payback method, management chooses a cutoff period for a project. Projects with a payback period that is less than the cutoff period are considered acceptable, and those with a payback period that is longer than the cutoff period are rejected. Japanese companies favor the payback method over other methods and use cutoff periods ranging from three to five years depending on the risks involved with the project. In general, modern risk management calls for using shorter cutoff periods, the riskier the project. If Top-Spin's cutoff period under the payback method is three years, it will reject the new machine.

The payback method is easy to understand. As in DCF methods, the payback method is not affected by accrual accounting conventions such as depreciation. Payback is a useful measure when (1) preliminary screening of many proposals is necessary, (2) interest rates are high, and (3) the expected cash flows in later years of a project are highly uncertain. That's because, under these conditions, companies give much more weight to cash flows in early periods of a capital budgeting project and to recovering the investments they have made.

Two weaknesses of the payback method are that (1) it fails to explicitly incorporate the time value of money and (2) it does not consider a project's cash flows after the payback period. Consider an alternative to the $379,100 carbon-fiber machine. Another carbon-fiber machine, with a three-year useful life and no terminal disposal value, requires only a $300,000 net initial investment and will also result in cash inflows of $100,000 per year. First, compare the payback periods:

$$\text{Machine 1} = \frac{\$379{,}100}{\$100{,}000} = 3.8 \text{ years}$$

$$\text{Machine 2} = \frac{\$300{,}000}{\$100{,}000} = 3.0 \text{ years}$$

The payback criterion favors machine 2, with the shorter payback. If the cutoff period were three years, machine 1 would fail to meet the payback criterion.

Consider next the NPV of the two investment options using Top-Spin's 8% required rate of return for the carbon-fiber machine investment. At a discount rate of 8%, the NPV of machine 2 is –$42,300 (2.577, the present value annuity factor for three years at 8% per year from Table 4, times $100,000 = $257,700 minus net initial investment of $300,000). Machine 1, as we know, has a positive NPV of $20,200 (from Exhibit 21-2). The NPV criterion suggests Top-Spin should acquire machine 1. Machine 2, with a negative NPV, would fail to meet the NPV criterion.

The payback method gives a different answer from the NPV method in this example because the payback method ignores cash flows after the payback period and ignores the time value of money. Another problem with the payback method is that choosing too short a cutoff period for project acceptance may promote the selection of only short-lived projects. An organization will tend to reject long-run, positive-NPV projects. Despite these differences, companies find it useful to look at both NPV and payback when making capital investment decisions.

Nonuniform Cash Flows

When cash flows are not uniform, as is most often the case, the payback computation takes a cumulative form: The cash flows over successive years are accumulated until the amount of net initial investment is recovered. Assume that Venture Law Group is considering the purchase of videoconferencing equipment for $150,000. The equipment is expected to provide a total cash savings of $380,000 over the next five years, due to reduced travel costs and more effective use of associates' time. The cash savings occur uniformly throughout each year, but nonuniformly across years.

Year	Cash Savings	Cumulative Cash Savings	Net Initial Investment Unrecovered at End of Year
0	—	—	$150,000
1	$ 50,000	$ 50,000	100,000
2	60,000	110,000	40,000
3	80,000	190,000	—
4	90,000	280,000	—
5	100,000	380,000	—

It is clear from the chart that payback occurs during the third year. Straight-line interpolation within the third year reveals that the final \$40,000 needed to recover the \$150,000 investment (that is, \$150,000 − \$110,000 recovered by the end of year 2) will be achieved halfway through year 3 (in which \$80,000 of cash savings occur):

$$\text{Payback period} = 2 \text{ years} + \left(\frac{\$40{,}000}{\$80{,}000} \times 1 \text{ year}\right) = 2.5 \text{ years}$$

The videoconferencing example has a single cash outflow of \$150,000 in year 0. When a project has multiple cash outflows occurring at different points in time, these outflows are added to obtain a total cash-outflow figure for the project. No adjustment is made for the time value of money when adding these cash outflows in computing the payback period.

Accrual Accounting Rate-of-Return Method

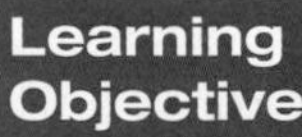

Learning Objective 5

Use and evaluate the accrual accounting rate-of-return (AARR) method

. . . after-tax operating income divided by investment

We now consider a fourth method for analyzing the financial aspects of capital budgeting projects. The **accrual accounting rate of return (AARR)** method divides the average annual (accrual accounting) income of a project by a measure of the investment in it. The ratio is also called the **accounting rate of return**. We illustrate AARR for the Top-Spin example using the project's net initial investment as the amount in the denominator:

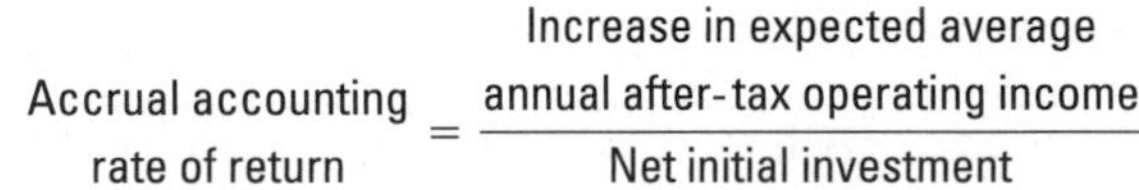

$$\text{Accrual accounting rate of return} = \frac{\text{Increase in expected average annual after-tax operating income}}{\text{Net initial investment}}$$

If Top-Spin purchases the new carbon-fiber machine, the increase in expected average after-tax annual operating cash inflows is \$98,200. This amount is the expected after-tax total operating cash inflows of \$491,000 (\$100,000 for four years and \$91,000 in year 5) ÷ 5 years. The new machine results in additional depreciation deductions of \$70,000 per year (\$78,000 − \$8,000, see p. 744). The net initial investment is \$379,100. The AARR on net initial investment is:

$$AARR = \frac{\$98{,}200 - \$70{,}000}{\$379{,}100} = \frac{\$28{,}200 \text{ per year}}{\$379{,}100} = 0.074, \text{ or } 7.4\% \text{ per year}$$

AARR of 7.4% per year indicates the average rate at which a dollar of investment generates after-tax operating income. AARR on the new carbon-fiber machine is low for two reasons: (1) using net initial investment makes the denominator larger than it would be using average level of investment, and (2) annual depreciation must be deducted from annual operating income in the numerator. Many companies calculate AARR using an average level of investment to recognize that the book value of the investment declines over time. In its simplest form, average investment for Top-Spin (with terminal disposal value of machine equal to \$0 and terminal recovery of working capital equal to \$9,000) is

$$\text{Average investment over five years} = \frac{\text{Net initial investment} + \text{returned working capital}}{2}$$

$$= \frac{\$379{,}100 + \$9{,}000}{2} = \$194{,}050$$

$$AARR = \frac{\$28{,}200}{\$194{,}050} = 0.145, \text{ or } 14.5\% \text{ per year}$$

Our point here is that companies vary in how they calculate AARR. There is no uniformly preferred approach. Be sure you understand how AARR is defined in each individual situation. Projects whose AARR exceeds a specified hurdle required rate of return are regarded as acceptable (the higher the AARR, the better the project is considered to be).

The AARR method is similar to the IRR method in that both methods calculate a rate of return percentage. The AARR method calculates return using operating-income numbers after considering accruals and taxes, whereas the IRR method calculates return on the basis of after-tax cash flows and the time value of money. Because cash flows and time value of money are central to capital budgeting decisions, the IRR method is regarded as better than the AARR method.

AARR computations are easy to understand, and they use numbers reported in the financial statements. AARR gives managers an idea of how the accounting numbers they will report in the future will be affected if a project is accepted. Unlike the payback method, which ignores cash flows after the payback period, the AARR method considers income earned *throughout* a project's expected useful life. Unlike the NPV method, the AARR method uses accrual accounting income numbers, it does not track cash flows, and it ignores the time value of money. Critics cite these arguments as drawbacks of the AARR method.

Evaluating Managers and Goal-Congruence Issues

Learning Objective 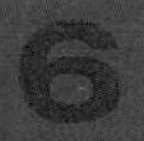

Identify and reduce conflicts from using DCF for capital budgeting decisions and accrual accounting for performance evaluation

. . . an acceptable project can decrease operating income in its early years

Companies frequently report NPV, IRR, payback, and AARR on the forms they use for evaluating capital investment decisions. When different methods lead to different rankings of projects, finance theory suggests that more weight be given to the NPV method. That's because the assumptions made by the NPV method are most consistent with making decisions that maximize company value. Corporate finance texts discuss these issues in more detail.

Capital budgeting decisions made using the NPV method might not be consistent with decisions that would be made if AARR were used for performance evaluation. Consider the manager of the racquet production plant at Top-Spin. The NPV method indicates that the manager should purchase the carbon-fiber machine because it has a positive NPV of $20,200. But suppose top management at Top-Spin uses AARR for judging performance. The plant manager may then reject purchasing the carbon-fiber machine if the AARR of 7.4% on the net initial investment reduces the AARR of the entire plant and negatively affects the department's reported performance.

There is an inconsistency between using the NPV method as best for capital budgeting decisions and then using a different method to evaluate performance. This inconsistency means managers are tempted to make capital budgeting decisions on the basis of the method by which they are being evaluated. Such temptations become more pronounced if managers are frequently transferred (or promoted), or if their bonuses are affected by the level of year-to-year accrual income.[3] This conflict can be reduced by evaluating managers on a project-by-project basis and by looking at how well managers achieve the amounts and timing of forecasted cash flows.

Note that another conflict between decision making and performance evaluation persists even if a company uses AARR for both purposes. If the AARR on the carbon-fiber machine exceeds the minimum required AARR but is below the current AARR of the production plant, the manager may still be tempted to reject purchasing the carbon-fiber

[3] Managers are often interested in how accepting a project will affect a bonus plan that is based on reported annual accrual accounting numbers. Do not assume that the AARR computed by the formula on page 742 is the appropriate number to use in examining the effect that adoption of a project will have on a manager's bonus plan. It is necessary to examine on a year-by-year basis how the AARR is computed when determining bonuses. For example, the numerator in the formula is the "increase in expected average annual after-tax operating income." This average increase need not be the same each year during a project. Assume that the president of Top-Spin receives an annual $50,000 lump-sum bonus if the AARR on assets exceeds 8% in that year. Project A has an AARR over its five-year life of 10% and an NPV of $20,000. Project B has an AARR over its five-year life of 9% and an NPV of $18,000. Project A has cash inflows in years 1 and 5 but zero cash inflows in years 2, 3, and 4. Project B has equal cash inflows in years 1 through 5. It could well be that the president would receive higher bonuses with project B—the project with a lower NPV.

machine. That's because the lower AARR of the carbon-fiber machine will reduce the AARR of the entire plant and hurt the manager's reported performance. Chapter 23 describes how performance evaluation models such as economic value added (EVA®) help achieve greater congruency with decision-making models.

Relevant Cash Flows in Discounted Cash Flow Analysis

Learning Objective 7

Identify relevant cash inflows and outflows for capital budgeting decisions

. . . the differences in expected future cash flows resulting from the investment

We have so far examined methods for evaluating long-term projects in settings where the expected future cash flows of interest were assumed to be known. But one of the biggest challenges in capital budgeting, particularly DCF analysis, is determining which cash flows are relevant in making an investment selection. Relevant cash flows are the differences in expected future cash flows as a result of making the investment. In the Top-Spin example, the relevant cash flows are the differences in expected future cash flows between continuing to use the old technology or updating its technology with the purchase of a new machine. *When reading this section, focus on identifying expected future cash flows and the differences in expected future cash flows.*

To illustrate relevant cash flow analysis, consider a more complex version of the Top-Spin example with these additional assumptions:

- Top-Spin is a profitable company. The income tax rate is 40% of operating income each year.
- The before-tax additional operating cash inflows from the carbon-fiber machine are $120,000 in years 1 through 4 and $105,000 in year 5.
- For tax purposes, Top-Spin uses the straight-line depreciation method and assumes no terminal disposal value.
- Gains or losses on the sale of depreciable assets are taxed at the same rate as ordinary income.
- The tax effects of cash inflows and outflows occur at the same time that the cash inflows and outflows occur.
- Top-Spin uses an 8% required rate of return for discounting after-tax cash flows.

Summary data for the machines are:

	Old Graphite Machine	New Carbon-Fiber Machine
Purchase price	—	$390,000
Current book value	$40,000	—
Current disposal value	6,500	Not applicable
Terminal disposal value 5 years from now	0	0
Annual depreciation	8,000[a]	78,000[b]
Working capital required	6,000	15,000

[a] $40,000 ÷ 5 years = $8,000 annual depreciation.
[b] $390,000 ÷ 5 years = $78,000 annual depreciation.

Relevant After-Tax Flows

We use the concepts of differential cost and differential revenue introduced in Chapter 11. We compare (1) the after-tax cash outflows as a result of replacing the old machine with (2) the additional after-tax cash inflows generated from using the new machine rather than the old machine.

It is important first to understand how income taxes affect cash flows in each year. Income taxes are a fact of life for most corporations and individuals. As Benjamin Franklin said, "Two things in life are certain: death and taxes." Exhibit 21-5 shows how investing in the new machine will affect Top-Spin's cash flow from operations and its income taxes in year 1. Recall that Top-Spin will generate $120,000 in before-tax additional operating cash

Exhibit 21-5

Effect on Cash Flow from Operations, Net of Income Taxes, in Year 1 for Top-Spin's Investment in the New Carbon-Fiber Machine

PANEL A: Two Methods Based on the Income Statement

C	Operating cash inflows from investment in machine	$120,000
D	Additional depreciation deduction	70,000
OI	Increase in operating income	50,000
T	Income taxes (Income tax rate $t \times OI$) = 40% × $50,000	20,000
NI	Increase in net income	$ 30,000
	Increase in cash flow from operations, net of income taxes	
	Method 1: $C - T$ = $120,000 – $20,000 = $100,000 or	
	Method 2: $NI + D$ = $30,000 + $70,000 = $100,000	

PANEL B: Item-by-Item Method

	Effect of cash operating flows	
C	Operating cash inflows from investment in machine	$120,000
$t \times C$	Deduct income tax cash outflow at 40%	48,000
$C - (t \times C) = (1 - t) \times C$	After-tax cash flow from operations (excluding the depreciation effect)	72,000
	Effect of depreciation	
D	Additional depreciation deduction, $70,000	
$t \times D$	Income tax cash savings from additional depreciation deduction at 40% × $70,000	28,000
$(1 - t) \times C + (t \times D) = C - (t \times C) + (t \times D)$	Cash flow from operations, net of income taxes	$100,000

inflows by investing in the new machine (p. 744), but it will record additional depreciation of $70,000 ($78,000 − $8,000) for tax purposes.

Panel A shows that the year 1 cash flow from operations, net of income taxes, equals $100,000, using two methods based on the income statement. The first method focuses on cash items only, the $120,000 operating cash inflows minus income taxes of $20,000. The second method starts with the $30,000 increase in net income (calculated after subtracting the $70,000 additional depreciation deductions for income tax purposes) and adds back that $70,000, because depreciation is an operating cost that reduces net income but is a noncash item itself.

Panel B of Exhibit 21-5 describes a third method that we will use frequently to compute cash flow from operations, net of income taxes. The easiest way to interpret the third method is to think of the government as a 40% (equal to the tax rate) partner in Top-Spin. Each time Top-Spin obtains operating cash inflows, C, its income is higher by C, so it will pay 40% of the operating cash inflows (0.40C) in taxes. This results in additional after-tax cash operating flows of C − 0.40C, which in this example is $120,000 − (0.40 × $120,000) = $72,000, or $120,000 × (1 − 0.40) = $72,000.

To achieve the higher operating cash inflows, C, Top-Spin incurs higher depreciation charges, D, from investing in the new machine. Depreciation costs do not directly affect cash flows because depreciation is a noncash cost, but higher depreciation cost *lowers* Top-Spin's taxable income by D, saving income tax cash outflows of 0.40*D*, which in this example is 0.40 × $70,000 = $28,000.

Letting t = tax rate, cash flow from operations, net of income taxes, in this example equals the operating cash inflows, C, minus the tax payments on these inflows, $t \times C$, plus the tax savings on depreciation deductions, $t \times D$: $120,000 − (0.40 × $120,000) + (0.40 × $70,000) = $120,000 − $48,000 + $28,000 = $100,000.

By the same logic, each time Top-Spin has a gain on the sale of assets, G, it will show tax outflows, $t \times G$; and each time Top-Spin has a loss on the sale of assets, L, it will show tax benefits or savings, $t \times L$.

Categories of Cash Flows

A capital investment project typically has three categories of cash flows: (1) net initial investment in the project, which includes the acquisition of assets and any associated additions to working capital, minus the after-tax cash flow from the disposal of existing assets; (2) after-tax cash flow from operations (including income tax cash savings from annual depreciation deductions); and (3) after-tax cash flow from terminal disposal of an asset and recovery of working capital. We use the Top-Spin example to discuss these three categories.

As you work through the cash flows in each category, refer to Exhibit 21-6. This exhibit sketches the relevant cash flows for Top-Spin's decision to purchase the new machine as described in items 1 through 3 here. Note that the total relevant cash flows for each year equal the relevant cash flows used in Exhibits 21-2 and 21-3 to illustrate the NPV and IRR methods.

1. **Net Initial Investment** Three components of net-initial-investment cash flows are (a) cash outflow to purchase the machine, (b) cash outflow for working capital, and (c) after-tax cash inflow from current disposal of the old machine.

   1a. *Initial machine investment.* These outflows, made for purchasing plant and equipment, occur at the beginning of the project's life and include cash outflows for transporting and installing the equipment. In the Top-Spin example, the $390,000 cost (including transportation and installation) of the carbon-fiber machine is an outflow in year 0. These cash flows are relevant to the capital budgeting decision because they will be incurred only if Top-Spin decides to purchase the new machine.

   1b. *Initial working-capital investment.* Initial investments in plant and equipment are usually accompanied by additional investments in working capital. These additional investments take the form of current assets, such as accounts receivable and inventories, minus current liabilities, such as accounts payable. Working-capital investments are similar to plant and equipment investments in that they require cash.

   The Top-Spin example assumes a $9,000 additional investment in working capital (for supplies and spare-parts inventory) if the new machine is acquired. The additional working-capital investment is the difference between working capital required to operate the new machine ($15,000) and working capital required to

Exhibit 21-6 Relevant Cash Inflows and Outflows for Top-Spin's Carbon-Fiber Machine

	A	B	C	D	E	F	G	H
1				Sketch of Relevant Cash Flows at End of Year				
2			0	1	2	3	4	5
3	1a.	Initial machine investment	$(390,000)					
4	1b.	Initial working-capital investment	(9,000)					
5	1c.	After-tax cash flow from current disposal						
6		of old machine	19,900					
7	Net initial investment		(379,100)					
8	2a.	Annual after-tax cash flow from operations						
9		(excluding the depreciation effect)		$ 72,000	$ 72,000	$ 72,000	$ 72,000	$ 63,000
10	2b.	Income tax cash savings from annual						
11		depreciation deductions		28,000	28,000	28,000	28,000	28,000
12	3a.	After-tax cash flow from terminal disposal						
13		of machine						0
14	3b.	After-tax cash flow from recovery of						
15		working capital						9,000
16	Total relevant cash flows,							
17		as shown in Exhibits 21-2 and 21-3	$(379,100)	$ 100,000	$100,000	$100,000	$100,000	$100,000
18								

operate the old machine ($6,000). The $9,000 additional investment in working capital is a cash outflow in year 0 and is returned at the end of year 5.

1c. *After-tax cash flow from current disposal of old machine.* Any cash received from disposal of the old machine is a relevant cash inflow (in year 0). That's because it is an expected future cash flow that differs between the alternatives of investing and not investing in the new machine. Only if Top-Spin invests in the new carbon-fiber machine, will it dispose of the old machine for $6,500. Recall that the book value (which is original cost minus accumulated depreciation) of the old equipment is irrelevant to the decision (Chapter 11, p. 405). It is a past, or sunk, cost. Nothing can change what was originally paid.

To calculate the tax consequences of disposing of the old machine, we compute the gain or loss on disposal:

Current disposal value of old machine (given, p. 744)	$ 6,500
Deduct current book value of old machine (given, p. 744)	40,000
Loss on disposal of machine	$(33,500)

Any loss on the sale of assets lowers taxable income and results in tax savings. The after-tax cash flow from disposal of the old machine equals:

Current disposal value of old machine	$ 6,500
Tax savings on loss (0.40 × $33,500)	13,400
After-tax cash inflow from current disposal of old machine	$19,900

The sum of items **1a**, **1b**, and **1c** appears in Exhibit 21-6 as the year 0 net initial investment for the new carbon-fiber machine equal to $379,100 (initial machine investment, $390,000, plus additional working-capital investment, $9,000, minus after-tax cash inflow from current disposal of the old machine, $19,900).

2. Cash Flow from Operations This category includes the difference between each year's cash flow from operations under the two alternatives. Organizations make capital investments to generate future cash inflows. These inflows may result from savings in operating costs, or, as for Top-Spin, from producing and selling additional goods. Annual cash flow from operations can be net outflows in some years. BP makes periodic upgrades to its oil extraction equipment, and in years of upgrades, cash flow from operations tends to be negative for the site being upgraded, albeit in the long-run such upgrades are NPV positive. Always focus on cash flow from operations, not on revenues and expenses under accrual accounting.

Top-Spin's additional operating cash inflows—$120,000 in each of the first four years and $105,000 in the fifth year—are relevant because they are expected future cash flows that will differ between the alternatives of investing and not investing in the new machine. The after-tax effects of these cash flows follow.

2a. *Annual after-tax cash flow from operations (excluding the depreciation effect).* The 40% tax rate reduces the benefit of the $120,000 additional operating cash inflows for years 1 through 4 with the new carbon-fiber machine. After-tax cash flow (excluding the depreciation effect) is:

Annual cash flow from operations with new machine	$120,000
Deduct income tax payments (0.40 × $120,000)	48,000
Annual after-tax cash flow from operations	$ 72,000

For year 5, the after-tax cash flow (excluding the depreciation effect) is:

Annual cash flow from operations with new machine	$105,000
Deduct income tax payments (0.40 × $105,000)	42,000
Annual after-tax cash flow from operations	$ 63,000

Exhibit 21-6, item **2a**, shows the $72,000 amounts for each of the years 1 through 4 and $63,000 for year 5.

To reinforce the idea about focusing on cash flows, consider the following additional fact about the Top-Spin example. Suppose the total plant overhead costs will not change whether the new machine is purchased or the old machine is kept. The production plant's overhead costs are allocated to individual machines—Top-Spin has several—on the basis of the labor costs for operating each machine. Because the new carbon-fiber machine would have lower labor costs, overhead costs allocated to it would be $30,000 less than the amount allocated to the machine it would replace. How should Top-Spin incorporate the decrease in allocated overhead costs of $30,000 in the relevant cash flow analysis?

To answer that question, we need to ask, "Do *total* overhead costs decrease at Top-Spin's production plant as a result of acquiring the new machine?" In our example, they do not. Total overhead costs of the production plant remain the same whether or not the new machine is acquired. *Only the overhead costs allocated to individual machines change.* The overhead costs allocated to the new machine are $30,000 less than the amount allocated to the machine it would replace. This $30,000 difference in overhead would be allocated to *other* machines in the department. That is, no cash flow savings in total overhead would occur. Therefore, the $30,000 should not be included as part of annual cash savings from operations.

Next consider the effects of depreciation. *The depreciation line item is itself irrelevant in DCF analysis.* That's because it's a noncash allocation of costs, whereas DCF is based on inflows and outflows of *cash*. In DCF methods, the initial cost of equipment is regarded as a *lump-sum* outflow of cash in year 0. Deducting depreciation expenses from operating cash inflows would result in counting the lump-sum amount twice. *However, depreciation results in income tax cash savings. These tax savings are a relevant cash flow.*

2b. *Income tax cash savings from annual depreciation deductions.* Tax deductions for depreciation, in effect, partially offset the cost of acquiring the new carbon-fiber machine. The following table calculates the income tax cash savings from the additional depreciation deductions each year as a result of acquiring the new machine.

Year	Depreciation Deduction on New Carbon-Fiber Machine (p. 744)	Depreciation Deduction on Old Graphite Machine (p. 744)	Difference in Depreciation Deduction	Income Tax Rate	Increase in Income Tax Cash Savings from Depreciation Deductions with New Carbon-Fiber Machine
1	$78,000	$8,000	$70,000	40%	$28,000
2	78,000	8,000	70,000	40%	28,000
3	78,000	8,000	70,000	40%	28,000
4	78,000	8,000	70,000	40%	28,000
5	78,000	8,000	70,000	40%	28,000

Exhibit 21-6, item **2b**, shows these $28,000 amounts for years 1 through 5.[4]

For economic-policy reasons, usually to encourage (or in some cases, discourage) investments, tax laws specify which depreciation methods and which depreciable lives are permitted. Suppose the government permitted accelerated depreciation to be used, allowing for higher depreciation deductions in earlier years. If allowable, should Top-Spin use accelerated depreciation? Yes, because there is a general rule in tax planning for profitable companies such as Top-Spin: When there is a legal choice, take the depreciation (or any other deduction)

[4] If Top-Spin were a nonprofit foundation not subject to income taxes, cash flow from operations would equal $120,000 in years 1 through 4 and $105,000 in year 5. The revenues would not be reduced by 40%, nor would there be income tax cash savings from the depreciation deduction.

sooner rather than later. Doing so causes the (cash) income tax savings to occur earlier, which increases the project's NPV.

3. **Terminal Disposal of Investment** The disposal of the new investment generally increases cash inflow when the project terminates. Errors in forecasting terminal disposal value are seldom critical for long-duration projects because the present value of amounts to be received in the distant future is usually small. Two components of the terminal disposal value of an investment are (a) after-tax cash flow from terminal disposal of machines and (b) after-tax cash flow from recovery of working capital.

3a. *After-tax cash flow from terminal disposal of machines.* At the end of the useful life of the project, the machine's terminal disposal value may be $0 or an amount considerably less than the net initial investment. The relevant cash inflow is the difference in expected after-tax cash inflow from terminal disposal at the end of five years under the two alternatives of purchasing the new machine or keeping the old machine.

Although the old machine has a positive terminal disposal value today (year 0), in year 5, it will have a zero terminal value. As such, both the existing and the new machines have zero after-tax cash inflow from terminal disposal in year 5. Hence, the difference in after-tax cash inflow from terminal disposal is also $0.

To better illustrate the tax effects from terminal disposal, consider a different example. Suppose that Nestle upgrades a conveyer belt in its chocolate-bar plant. Furthermore, assume that the conveyer belt is projected to work for 5 years, after which it has a market disposal value of $5,000, and an accounting book value of $2,000. The approach for computing the terminal inflow (illustrated below for the Nestle example) is identical to that for calculating the after-tax cash flow from current disposal:

Terminal disposal value of new conveyor belt at end of year 5	$5,000
Deduct book value of new conveyor belt at end of year 5	2,000
Gain (or loss) on disposal of new conveyor belt	$3,000
Terminal disposal value of new conveyor belt at end of year 5	$5,000
Deduct taxes paid on gain (add taxes saved on loss), 0.40 × $3,000	1,200
After-tax cash inflow from terminal disposal of new conveyor belt	$3,800

3b. *After-tax cash flow from terminal recovery of working-capital investment.* The initial investment in working capital is usually fully recouped when the project is terminated. At that time, inventories and accounts receivable necessary to support the project are no longer needed. Top-Spin receives cash equal to the book value of its working capital. Thus, there is no gain or loss on working capital and, hence, no tax consequences. The relevant cash inflow is the difference in the expected working capital recovered under the two alternatives. At the end of year 5, Top-Spin recovers $15,000 cash from working capital if it invests in the new carbon-fiber machine versus $6,000 if it continues to use the old machine. The relevant cash inflow at the end of year 5 if Top-Spin invests in the new machine is thus $9,000 ($15,000 − $6,000).

Some capital investment projects *reduce* working capital. Assume that a computer-integrated manufacturing (CIM) project with a seven-year life will reduce inventories and, hence, working capital by $20 million from, say, $50 million to $30 million. This reduction will be represented as a $20 million cash *inflow* for the project in year 0. At the end of seven years, the recovery of working capital will show a relevant incremental cash *outflow* of $20 million. That's because, at the end of year 7, the company recovers only $30 million of working capital under CIM, rather than the $50 million of working capital it would have recovered had it not implemented CIM.

Exhibit 21-6 shows items **3a** and **3b** in the year 5 column. The relevant cash flows in Exhibit 21-6 serve as inputs for the four capital budgeting methods described earlier in the chapter.

Managing the Project

The first dimension of stage 5 of capital budgeting is implementing the decision. We do not consider the different financing options (refer to a text on corporate finance). By implementing the decision we mean managing the project. There are two aspects of managing a project: management control of the investment activity itself and management control of the project as a whole.

Capital budgeting projects, such as purchasing a carbon-fiber machine or videoconferencing equipment, are easier to implement than projects that involve building shopping malls or manufacturing plants. The building projects are more complex, so monitoring and controlling the investment schedules and budgets are critical to successfully completing the investment activity. This leads to the second dimension of stage 5 in the capital budgeting process: evaluate performance and learn.

A post-investment audit provides management with feedback about the performance of a project, so management can compare actual results to the costs and benefits expected at the time the project was selected. Suppose actual outcomes (such as additional operating cash flows from the new carbon-fiber machine in the Top-Spin example) are much lower than expected. Management must then investigate to determine if this result occurred because the original estimates were overly optimistic or because of implementation problems. Either of these explanations is a concern.

Optimistic estimates may result in the acceptance of a project that should have been rejected. To discourage optimistic estimates, companies such as DuPont maintain records comparing actual results to the estimates made by individual managers when seeking approval for capital investments. Post-investment audits punish inaccurate estimates, and therefore discourage unrealistic forecasts. This prevents managers from overstating project cash inflows and accepting projects that should never have been undertaken. Implementation problems, such as weak project management, poor quality control, or inadequate marketing are also a concern. Post-investment audits help to alert senior management to these problems so that they can be quickly corrected.

However, post-investment audits require thoughtfulness and care. They should be done only after project outcomes have stabilized because performing audits too early may yield misleading feedback. Obtaining actual results to compare against estimates is often not easy. For example, additional revenues from the new carbon-fiber technology may not be comparable to the estimated revenues because in any particular season, the rise or decline of a tennis star can greatly affect the popularity of the sport and the subsequent demand for racquets. A better evaluation would look at the average revenues across a couple of seasons.

Strategic Considerations in Capital Budgeting

A company's strategy is the source of its strategic capital budgeting decisions. Strategic decisions by United Airlines, Westin Hotels, Federal Express, and Pizza Hut to expand in Europe and Asia required capital investments to be made in several countries (see also Concepts in Action feature, p. 751). The strategic decision by Barnes & Noble to support book sales over the Internet required capital investments creating barnesandnoble.com and an Internet infrastructure. News Corp.'s decision to enlarge its online presence resulted in a large investment to purchase MySpace, and additional supporting investments to integrate MySpace with the firm's pre-existing assets. Pfizer's decision to develop its cholesterol-reducing drug Lipitor led to major investments in R&D and marketing. Toyota's decision to offer a line of hybrids across both its Toyota and Lexus platforms required start-up investments to form a hybrid division and ongoing investments to fund the division's continuing research efforts.

Capital investment decisions that are strategic in nature require managers to consider a broad range of factors that may be difficult to estimate. Consider some of the difficulties of justifying investments made by companies such as Mitsubishi, Sony, and Audi

Concepts in Action

Globalizing Capital Budgeting at AES Corporation

AES Corporation, a Fortune 500 company, is a leading global electricity producer with more than $30 billion in assets stretched across 27 countries and 5 continents. Despite impressive international growth throughout the company's 20-year history, the global economic downturn that began in late 2000 devastated AES. The devaluation of key South American currencies, adverse changes in energy regulatory environments, and declines in energy prices weakened AES's cash flow and ability to service debt. As a result, AES stock collapsed and its market capitalization fell nearly 95%, from $28 billion in December 2000 to $1.6 billion just two years later.

In response, the AES board of directors asked Rob Venerus, director of the company's new Corporate Analysis & Planning Group, to develop a new methodology for evaluating capital budgeting projects. Historically, capital budgeting at AES was fairly straightforward. Early in the company's history, a relatively simple model was developed, and a 12% discount rate was applied to all projects, regardless of geographic location. This model remained unchanged through the years, despite rapid expansion into new international markets that required advanced financial-analysis methods. For example, when AES entered countries such as Brazil and Argentina, the model failed to properly adjust the required rate of return to account for higher risk, such as regulatory and currency risk. Another factor that created fundamental difficulties for applying this model overseas was an ever-increasing complexity in the financing of international operations.

To overhaul the capital budgeting process so that managers could evaluate each international investment as a distinct opportunity with unique risks, Venerus knew he would have to calculate a cost of capital for each of the many diverse AES businesses. These businesses included power plant construction, energy generation, and power distribution. As a starting point, he considered 15 representative projects from various countries and derived a weighted average cost of capital (WACC) for each project. This involved measuring all of the constituent parts for the projects: the cost of debt, the target capital structure, the local-country tax rates, and an appropriate cost of equity.

During this process Venerus knew he had to find a way to capture the country-specific risks in foreign markets. He developed an approach with two parts. First, he calculated a cost of debt and a cost of equity for each of the 15 projects using U.S. market data. Second, he added the difference between the yield on local government bonds and the yield on corresponding U.S. Treasury bonds to both the cost of debt and the cost of equity. Venerus and his team believed that this difference, or "sovereign spread," approximated the incremental borrowing costs (and market risk) in the local country.

These efforts provided AES with a more sophisticated way to think about capital budgeting risk and its cost of capital around the world. As a global company with operations in countries that were significantly different from the United States, this framework helped AES more accurately evaluate capital projects and protect against overleveraging its assets, which almost imploded the company in 2002. Although subsequent changes to the model's calculations and methodology were made, this process helped AES regain its financial footing through the reevaluation and restructuring of existing capital projects while ensuring that the company selected only new capital projects that met these revised criteria. So far, the company has been successful! By 2004, AES was projecting long-term financial stability. In the past five years, the stock price of AES has risen by over 600% and the company now projects annual earnings per share growth between 14% and 20% in the 2007–2011 period.

Sources: Based on "Globalizing the Cost of Capital and Capital Budgeting at AES," Harvard Business School Case No. 9-204-109; "AES Provides Guidance Through 2011" (BusinessWire: May 25, 2007), GoogleFinance: June 8, 2007; and discussions with the case writer and company management.

in computer-integrated manufacturing (CIM) technology. In CIM, computers give instructions that quickly and automatically set up and run equipment to manufacture many different products. Quantifying these benefits requires some notion of how quickly consumer-demand will change in the future. CIM technology also increases worker knowledge of, and experience with automation; however, the benefit of this knowledge and experience is difficult to measure. Managers must develop judgment and intuition to make these decisions.

Customer Value and Capital Budgeting

The same framework used to evaluate investment projects can also be used to evaluate customers. Consider Potato Supreme, which makes potato products for sale to retail outlets. It is currently analyzing two of its customers: Shine Stores and Always Open. Potato Supreme predicts the following cash flow from operations, net of income taxes (in thousands), from each customer account for the next five years:

	2008	2009	2010	2011	2012
Shine Stores	$1,450	$1,305	$1,175	$1,058	$ 950
Always Open	690	1,160	1,900	2,950	4,160

Which customer is more valuable to Potato Supreme? Looking at only the current period, 2008, Shine Stores provides more than double the cash flow compared to Always Open ($1,450 versus $690). A different picture emerges, however, when looking over the entire five-year horizon. Potato Supreme anticipates Always Open's orders to increase; meanwhile, it expects Shine Stores' orders to decline. Using Potato Supreme's 10% RRR, the NPV of the Always Open customer is $7,610, compared to $4,591 for Shine Stores (computations not shown). Note how NPV captures in its estimate of customer value the future growth of Always Open. Potato Supreme uses this information to allocate more resources and salespersons to service the Always Open account. Potato Supreme can also use NPV calculations to examine the effects of alternative ways of increasing customer loyalty and retention, such as introducing frequent-purchaser cards.

A comparison of year-to-year changes in customer NPV estimates highlights whether managers have been successful in maintaining long-run profitable relationships with their customers. Suppose the NPV of Potato Supreme's customer base declines 15% in one year. Management can then examine the reasons for the decline, such as aggressive pricing by competitors, and devise new-product development and marketing strategies for the future.

Capital One, a financial-services company, uses NPV to estimate the value of different credit-card customers. Cellular telephone companies such as Cellular One and Verizon Wireless attempt to sign up customers for multiple years of service. The objective is to prevent "customer churn," customers switching frequently from one company to another. The higher the probability of customer churn, the lower the NPV of the customer.

Investment in Research and Development

Companies such as GlaxoSmithKline in the pharmaceutical industry and Intel in the semiconductor industry regard R&D projects as important strategic investments. The distant payoffs from R&D investments, however, are more uncertain than other investments such as new equipment. On the positive side, R&D investments are often staged: as time unfolds, companies can increase or decrease the resources committed to a project based on how successful it has been up to that point. This option feature of R&D investments—called real options—is an important aspect of R&D investments and increases the NPV of these investments. That's because a company can limit its losses when things are going badly and take advantage of new opportunities when things are going well.

Problem for Self-Study

PART A

Returning to the Top-Spin carbon-fiber machine project, assume that Top-Spin is a *nonprofit organization* and that the expected additional operating cash inflows are $130,000 in years 1 through 4 and $121,000 in year 5. Using data from page 744, the net initial investment is $392,500 (new machine, $390,000 plus additional working capital, $9,000 minus terminal disposal value of old machine, $6,500). All other facts are unchanged: a five-year useful life, no terminal disposal value, and an 8% RRR. Year 5 cash inflows are $130,000, which includes a $9,000 recovery of working capital.

Required

Calculate the following:
1. Net present value
2. Internal rate of return
3. Payback
4. Accrual accounting rate of return on net initial investment

Solution

1. $NPV = (\$130{,}000 \times 3.993) - \$392{,}500$
$= \$519{,}090 - \$392{,}500 = \$126{,}590$

2. There are several approaches to computing IRR. One is to use a calculator with an IRR function. This approach gives an IRR of 19.6%. Another approach is to use Table 4 in Appendix B at the end of the text:

$$\$392{,}500 = \$130{,}000F$$

$$F = \frac{\$392{,}500}{\$130{,}000} = 3.019$$

On the five-period line of Table 4, the column closest to 3.019 is 20%. To obtain a more-accurate number, use straight-line interpolation:

	Present Value Factors	
18%	3.127	3.127
IRR	—	3.019
20%	2.991	—
Difference	0.136	0.108

$$IRR = 18\% + \frac{0.108}{0.136}(2\%) = 19.6\% \text{ per year}$$

3. $$\text{Payback period} = \frac{\text{Net initial investment}}{\text{Uniform increase in annual future cash flows}}$$
$$= \$392{,}500 \div \$130{,}000 = 3.0 \text{ years}$$

4. $$AARR = \frac{\text{Increase in expected average annual operating income}}{\text{Net initial investment}}$$

$$\text{Increase in expected average annual operating cash inflows} = [(\$130{,}000 \times 4) + \$121{,}000] \div 5 \text{ years}$$
$$= \$641{,}000 \div 5 = \$128{,}200$$

$$\text{Increase in annual depreciation} = \$70{,}000\ (\$78{,}000 - \$8{,}000, \text{ see p. 744})$$

$$\text{Increase in expected average annual operating income} = \$128{,}200 - \$70{,}000 = \$58{,}200$$

$$AARR = \frac{\$58{,}200}{\$392{,}500} = 14.8\% \text{ per year}$$

PART B

Assume that Top-Spin is subject to income tax at a 40% rate. All other information from Part A is unchanged. Compute the NPV of the new carbon-fiber machine project.

Solution

To save space, Exhibit 21-7 shows the calculations using a format slightly different from the format used in this chapter. Item **2a** is where the new $130,000 cash flow assumption affects the NPV analysis (compared to Exhibit 21-6). All other amounts in Exhibit 21-7 are identical to the corresponding amounts in Exhibit 21-6. For years 1 through 4, after-tax cash flow (excluding the depreciation effect) is:

Annual cash flow from operations with new machine	$130,000
Deduct income tax payments (0.40 × $130,000)	52,000
Annual after-tax cash flow from operations	$ 78,000

For year 5, after-tax cash flow (excluding the depreciation effect) is:

Annual cash flow from operations with new machine	$121,000
Deduct income tax payments (0.40 × $121,000)	48,400
Annual after-tax cash flow from operations	$ 72,600

NPV in Exhibit 21-7 is $46,610. As computed in Part A, NPV when there are no income taxes is $126,590. The difference in these two NPVs illustrates the impact of income taxes in capital budgeting analysis.

Exhibit 21-7 Net Present Value Method Incorporating Income Taxes: Top-Spin's Carbon-Fiber Machine with Revised Annual Cash Flow from Operations

	A	B	C	D	E	F	G	H	I	J
1			**Present**	**Present Value of**						
2			**Value of**	**$1 Discounted at**	**Sketch of Relevant Cash Flows at End of Year**					
3			**Cash Flow**	**8%**	0	1	2	3	4	5
4	**1a.**	Initial machine investment	$(390,000)	← 1.000 ←	$(390,000)					
5										
6	**1b.**	Initial working-capital investment	(9,000)	← 1.000 ←	$ (9,000)					
7	**1c.**	After-tax cash flow from current								
8		disposal of old machine	19,900	← 1.000 ←	$ 19,900					
9	Net initial investment		(379,100)							
10	**2a.**	Annual after-tax cash flow from								
11		operations (excluding the depreciation effect)								
12		Year 1	72,228	← 0.926 ←		$78,000				
13		Year 2	66,846	← 0.857 ←			$78,000			
14		Year 3	61,932	← 0.794 ←				$78,000		
15		Year 4	57,330	← 0.735 ←					$78,000	
16		Year 5	49,441	← 0.681 ←						$72,600
17	**2b.**	Income tax cash savings from annual								
18		depreciation deductions								
19		Year 1	25,928	← 0.926 ←		$28,000				
20		Year 2	23,996	← 0.857 ←			$28,000			
21		Year 3	22,232	← 0.794 ←				$28,000		
22		Year 4	20,580	← 0.735 ←					$28,000	
23		Year 5	19,068	← 0.681 ←						$28,000
24	**3.**	After-tax cash flow from								
25		**a.** Terminal disposal of machine	0	← 0.681 ←						$ 0
26		**b.** Recovery of working capital	6,129	← 0.681 ←						$ 9,000
27	NPV if new machine purchased		$ 46,610							
28										

Decision Points

The following question-and-answer format summarizes the chapter's learning objectives. Each decision presents a key question related to a learning objective. The guidelines are the answer to that question.

Decision	Guidelines
1. Over what time horizon is capital budgeting done?	Capital budgeting is long-run planning for proposed investment projects. The life of a project is usually longer than one year, so capital budgeting decisions consider cash inflows and outflows over long periods. In contrast, accrual accounting measures income on a year-by-year basis.
2. What are the five stages of capital budgeting?	The five stages of capital budgeting are: 1) Identify projects: identify potential capital investments that agree with the organization's strategy; 2) Obtain information: gather information from all parts of the value chain to evaluate alternative projects; 3) Make predictions: forecast all potential cash flows attributable to the alternative projects; 4) Make decisions by choosing among alternatives: determine which investment yields the greatest benefit and the least cost to the organization; and 5) Implement the decision, evaluate performance, and learn: Obtain funding and make the investments selected in stage 4; track realized cash flows, compare against estimated numbers, and revise plans if necessary.
3. What are the two main discounted cash flow (DCF) methods? What are their advantages?	The two main DCF methods are the net present value (NPV) method and the internal rate-of-return (IRR) method. The NPV method calculates the expected net monetary gain or loss from a project by discounting to the present all expected future cash inflows and outflows, using the required rate of return. A project is acceptable in financial terms if it has a positive NPV. The IRR method computes the rate of return (also called the discount rate) at which the present value of expected cash inflows from a project equals the present value of expected cash outflows from the project. A project is acceptable in financial terms if its IRR exceeds the required rate of return. DCF is the best approach to capital budgeting. It explicitly includes all project cash flows and recognizes the time value of money. The NPV method is the preferred DCF method.
4. What is the payback method? What are its two main weaknesses?	The payback method measures the time it will take to recoup, in the form of cash inflows, the total cash amount invested in a project. The payback method neglects both cash flows after the payback period and the time value of money.
5. What is the accrual accounting rate-of-return (AARR) method? What is its limitation?	The accrual accounting rate of return (AARR) divides an accrual accounting measure of average annual income from a project by an accrual accounting measure of its investment. AARR considers profitability but does not consider the time value of money.
6. What conflicts can arise between using DCF methods for capital budgeting decisions and accrual accounting for performance evaluation? How can these conflicts be reduced?	Using accrual accounting to evaluate the performance of a manager may create conflicts with using DCF methods for capital budgeting. Frequently, the decision made using a DCF method will not report good "operating income" results in the project's early years under accrual accounting. For this reason, managers are tempted to not use DCF methods even though the decisions based on them would be in the best interests of the company as a whole over the long run. This conflict can be reduced by evaluating managers on a project-by-project basis and by looking at their ability to achieve the amounts and timing of forecasted cash flows.

7. What are the relevant cash inflows and outflows for capital budgeting decisions? How should accrual accounting concepts be considered?

Relevant cash inflows and outflows in DCF analysis are the differences in expected future cash flows as a result of making the investment. Only cash inflows and outflows matter; accrual accounting concepts are irrelevant for DCF methods. For example, the income taxes saved as a result of depreciation deductions are relevant because they decrease cash outflows, but the depreciation itself is a noncash item.

APPENDIX: CAPITAL BUDGETING AND INFLATION

The Top-Spin example (Exhibits 21-2 to 21-6) does not include adjustments for inflation in the relevant revenues and costs. **Inflation** is the decline in the general purchasing power of the monetary unit, such as dollars. An inflation rate of 10% per year means that an item bought for $100 at the beginning of the year will cost $110 at the end of the year.

Why is it important to account for inflation in capital budgeting? Because declines in the general purchasing power of the monetary unit will inflate future cash flows above what they would have been in the absence of inflation. These inflated cash flows will cause the project to look better than it really is unless the analyst recognizes that the inflated cash flows are measured in dollars that have less purchasing power than the dollars that were initially invested. When analyzing inflation, distinguish real rate of return from nominal rate of return:

Real rate of return is the rate of return demanded to cover investment risk if there is no inflation. The real rate is made up of two elements: (a) a risk-free element (that's the pure rate of return on risk-free long-term government bonds when there is no expected inflation) and (b) a business-risk element (that's the risk premium demanded for bearing risk).

Nominal rate of return is the rate of return demanded to cover investment risk and the decline in general purchasing power of the monetary unit as a result of expected inflation. The nominal rate is made up of three elements: (a) a risk-free element when there is no expected inflation, (b) a business-risk element, and (c) an inflation element. Items (a) and (b) make up the real rate of return to cover investment risk. The inflation element is the premium above the real rate. The rates of return earned in the financial markets are nominal rates, because investors want to be compensated both for the investment risks they take and for the expected decline in the general purchasing power, as a result of inflation, of the money they get back.

Assume that the real rate of return for investments in high-risk cellular data-transmission equipment at Network Communications is 20% per year and that the expected inflation rate is 10% per year. Nominal rate of return is:

$$\begin{aligned}\text{Nominal rate} &= (1 + \text{Real rate})(1 + \text{Inflation rate}) - 1\\ &= (1 + 0.20)(1 + 0.10) - 1\\ &= (1.20 \times 1.10) - 1 = 1.32 - 1 = 0.32, \text{ or } 32\%\end{aligned}$$

Nominal rate of return is related to the real rate of return and the inflation rate:

Real rate of return	0.20
Inflation rate	0.10
Combination (0.20 × 0.10)	0.02
Nominal rate of return	0.32

Note the nominal rate, 0.32, is slightly higher than 0.30, the real rate (0.20) plus the inflation rate (0.10). That's because the nominal rate recognizes that inflation of 10% also decreases the purchasing power of the real rate of return of 20% earned during the year. The combination component represents the additional compensation investors seek for the decrease in the purchasing power of the real return earned during the year because of inflation.[5]

Net Present Value Method and Inflation

When incorporating inflation into the NPV method, the key is *internal consistency*. There are two internally consistent approaches:

1. **Nominal approach**—predicts cash inflows and outflows in nominal monetary units *and* uses a nominal rate as the required rate of return
2. **Real approach**—predicts cash inflows and outflows in real monetary units *and* uses a real rate as the required rate of return

We will limit our discussion to the simpler nominal approach. Consider an investment that is expected to generate sales of 100 units and a net cash inflow of $1,000 ($10 per unit) each year for two years *absent inflation*. Assume cash flows occur at the end of each year. If inflation of 10% is expected each year, net cash inflows from the sale of each unit would be $11 ($10 × 1.10) in year 1 and $12.10 ($11 × 1.10, or $10 × $(1.10)^2$) in year 2, resulting in net cash inflows of $1,100 in year 1 and $1,210 in year 2. The net cash inflows of $1,100 and $1,210 are nominal cash inflows because they include the effects of inflation. *Nominal cash flows are the cash flows that are recorded in the accounting system.* The cash inflows of $1,000 each year are real cash flows. The accounting system does not record these cash flows. The nominal approach is easier to understand and apply because it uses nominal cash flows from accounting systems and nominal rates of return from financial markets.

Assume that Network Communications can purchase equipment to make and sell a cellular data-transmission product at a net initial investment of $750,000. It is expected to have a four-year useful life and no terminal disposal value. An annual inflation rate of 10% is expected over this four-year period. Network Communications requires an after-tax nominal rate of return of 32% (see p. 756). The following table presents the predicted amounts of real (that's assuming no inflation) and nominal (that's after considering cumulative inflation) net cash inflows from the equipment over the next four years (excluding the $750,000 investment in the equipment and before any income tax payments):

Year (1)	Before-Tax Cash Inflows in Real Dollars (2)	Cumulative Inflation Rate Factor[a] (3)	Before-Tax Cash Inflows in Nominal Dollars (4) = (2) × (3)
1	$500,000	$(1.10)^1 = 1.1000$	$550,000
2	600,000	$(1.10)^2 = 1.2100$	726,000
3	600,000	$(1.10)^3 = 1.3310$	798,600
4	300,000	$(1.10)^4 = 1.4641$	439,230

[a] 1.10 = 1.00 + 0.10 inflation rate.

We continue to make the simplifying assumption that cash flows occur at the end of each year. The income tax rate is 40%. For tax purposes, the cost of the equipment will be depreciated using the straight-line method.

Exhibit 21-8 shows the calculation of NPV using cash flows in nominal dollars and using a nominal discount rate. The calculations in Exhibit 21-8 include the net initial machine investment, annual after-tax cash flows from operations (excluding the depreciation effect), and income tax cash savings from annual depreciation deductions. The NPV is $202,513 and, based on financial considerations alone, Network Communications should purchase the equipment.

[5] The real rate of return can be expressed in terms of the nominal rate of return as follows:

$$\text{Real rate} = \frac{1 + \text{Nominal rate}}{1 + \text{Inflation rate}} - 1 = \frac{1 + 0.32}{1 + 0.10} - 1 = 0.20, \text{ or } 20\%$$

Exhibit 21-8 Net Present Value Method Using Nominal Approach to Inflation for Network Communication's New Equipment

File Edit View Insert Format Tools Data Window Help

	A	B	C	D	E	F	G	H	I	J	K	L
1						Present	Present Value					
2						Value of	Discount Factor[a] at	Sketch of Relevant Cash Flows at End of Each Year				
3						Cash Flow	32%	0	1	2	3	4
4	1.	Net initial investment										
5		Year	Investment Outflows									
6		0	$(750,000)			$(750,000)	← 1.000 ←	$(750,000)				
7	2a.	Annual after-tax cash flow from										
8		operations (excluding the depreciation effect)										
9			Annual		Annual							
10			Before-Tax	Income	After-Tax							
11			Cash Flow	Tax	Cash Flow							
12		Year	from Operations	Outflows	from Operations							
13		(1)	(2)	(3) = 0.40 x (2)	(4) = (2) - (3)							
14		1	$550,000	$220,000	$330,000	250,140	← 0.758 ←		$330,000			
15		2	726,000	290,400	435,600	250,034	← 0.574 ←			$435,600		
16		3	798,600	319,440	479,160	208,435	← 0.435 ←				$479,160	
17		4	439,230	175,692	263,538	86,704	← 0.329 ←					$263,538
18						795,313						
19	2b.	Income tax cash savings from annual										
20		depreciation deductions										
21		Year	Depreciation	Tax Cash Savings								
22		(1)	(2)	(3) = 0.40 x (2)								
23		1	$187,500[b]	$75,000		56,850	← 0.758 ←		$ 75,000			
24		2	187,500	75,000		43,050	← 0.574 ←			$ 75,000		
25		3	187,500	75,000		32,625	← 0.435 ←				$ 75,000	
26		4	187,500	75,000		24,675	← 0.329 ←					$ 75,000
27						157,200						
28	NPV if new equipment purchased					$ 202,513						
29												
30												

31 [a]The nominal discount rate of 32% is made up of the real rate of return of 20% and the inflation rate of 10% [(1 + 0.20) (1 + 1.10)] – 1 = 0.32.

32 [b]$750,000 ÷ 4 = $187,500

TERMS TO LEARN

This chapter and the Glossary at the end of the book contain definitions of:

accounting rate of return (**p. 742**)
accrual accounting rate of return (AARR) (**p. 742**)
capital budgeting (**p. 734**)
cost of capital (**p. 736**)
discount rate (**p. 736**)
discounted cash flow (DCF) methods (**p. 735**)
hurdle rate (**p. 736**)
inflation (**p. 756**)
internal rate-of-return (IRR) method (**p. 737**)
net present value (NPV) method (**p. 736**)
nominal rate of return (**p. 756**)
opportunity cost of capital (**p. 736**)
payback method (**p. 740**)
real rate of return (**p. 756**)
required rate of return (RRR) (**p. 736**)
time value of money (**p. 735**)

ASSIGNMENT MATERIAL

Questions

21-1 "Capital budgeting has the same focus as accrual accounting." Do you agree? Explain.

21-2 List and briefly describe each of the five stages in capital budgeting.

21-3 What is the essence of the discounted cash flow methods?

21-4 "Only quantitative outcomes are relevant in capital budgeting analyses." Do you agree? Explain.

21-5 How can sensitivity analysis be incorporated in DCF analysis?

21-6 What is the payback method? What are its main strengths and weaknesses?

21-7 Describe the accrual accounting rate-of-return method. What are its main strengths and weaknesses?

21-8 "The trouble with discounted cash flow methods is that they ignore depreciation." Do you agree? Explain.

21-9 "Let's be more practical. DCF is not the gospel. Managers should not become so enchanted with DCF that strategic considerations are overlooked." Do you agree? Explain.

21-10 "All overhead costs are relevant in NPV analysis." Do you agree? Explain.

21-11 Bill Watts, president of Western Publications, accepts a capital budgeting project proposed by Division X. This is the division in which the president spent his first 10 years with the company. On the same day, the president rejects a capital budgeting project proposal from Division Y. The manager of Division Y is incensed. She believes that the Division Y project has an internal rate of return at least 10 percentage points higher than the Division X project. She comments, "What is the point of all our detailed DCF analysis? If Watts is panting over a project, he can arrange to have the proponents of that project massage the numbers so that it looks like a winner." What advice would you give the manager of Division Y?

21-12 Distinguish different categories of cash flows to be considered in an equipment-replacement decision by a taxpaying company.

21-13 Describe three ways income taxes can affect the cash inflows or outflows in a motor-vehicle-replacement decision by a taxpaying company.

21-14 How can capital budgeting tools assist in evaluating a manager who is responsible for retaining customers of a cellular telephone company?

21-15 Distinguish the nominal rate of return from the real rate of return.

Exercises

21-16 Exercises in compound interest, no income taxes. To be sure that you understand how to use the tables in Appendix B at the end of this book, solve the following exercises. Ignore income tax considerations. The correct answers, rounded to the nearest dollar, appear on pages 766–767.

Required

1. You have just won $5,000. How much money will you accumulate at the end of 10 years if you invest it at 6% compounded annually? At 14%?
2. Ten years from now, the unpaid principal of the mortgage on your house will be $89,550. How much do you need to invest today at 6% interest compounded annually to accumulate the $89,550 in 10 years?
3. If the unpaid mortgage on your house in 10 years will be $89,550, how much money do you need to invest at the end of each year at 6% to accumulate exactly this amount at the end of the tenth year?
4. You plan to save $5,000 of your earnings at the end of each year for the next 10 years. How much money will you accumulate at the end of the tenth year if you invest your savings compounded at 12% per year?
5. You have just turned 65 and an endowment insurance policy has paid you a lump sum of $200,000. If you invest the sum at 6%, how much money can you withdraw from your account in equal amounts at the end of each year so that at the end of 10 years (age 75) there will be nothing left?
6. You have estimated that for the first 10 years after you retire you will need a cash inflow of $50,000 at the end of each year. How much money do you need to invest at 6% at your retirement age to obtain this annual cash inflow? At 20%?
7. The following table shows two schedules of prospective operating cash inflows, each of which requires the same net initial investment of $10,000 now:

Year	Annual Cash Inflows	
	Plan A	Plan B
1	$ 1,000	$ 5,000
2	2,000	4,000
3	3,000	3,000
4	4,000	2,000
5	5,000	1,000
Total	$15,000	$15,000

The required rate of return is 6% compounded annually. All cash inflows occur at the end of each year. In terms of net present value, which plan is more desirable? Show your computations.

21-17 Capital budgeting methods, no income taxes. Riverbend Company runs hardware stores in a tri-state area. Riverbend's management estimates that if it invests $160,000 in a new computer system, it can save $60,000 in annual cash operating costs. The system has an expected useful life of 5 years and no terminal disposal value. The required rate of return is 12%. Ignore income tax issues in your answers. Assume all cash flows occur at year-end except for initial investment amounts.

Required

1. Calculate the following for the new computer system:
   a. Net present value
   b. Payback period
   c. Internal rate of return
   d. Accrual accounting rate of return based on the net initial investment (assume straight-line depreciation)
2. What other factors should Riverbend consider in deciding whether to purchase the new computer system?

21-18 Capital budgeting methods, no income taxes. City Hospital, a non-profit organization, estimates that it can save $28,000 a year in cash operating costs for the next 10 years if it buys a special-purpose eye-testing machine at a cost of $110,000. No terminal disposal value is expected. City Hospital's required rate of return is 14%. Assume all cash flows occur at year-end except for initial investment amounts.

Required

1. Calculate the following for the special-purpose eye-testing machine:
   a. Net present value
   b. Payback period
   c. Internal rate of return
   d. Accrual accounting rate of return based on net initial investment (Assume straight-line depreciation.)
2. What other factors should City Hospital consider in deciding whether to purchase the special-purpose eye-testing machine?

21-19 Capital budgeting, income taxes. Assume the same facts as in Exercise 21-18 except that City Hospital is a taxpaying entity. The income tax rate is 30% for all transactions that affect income taxes.

Required

1. Do requirement 1 of Exercise 21-18.
2. How would your computations in requirement 1 be affected if the special-purpose machine had a $10,000 terminal disposal value at the end of 10 years? Assume depreciation deductions are based on the $110,000 purchase cost and zero terminal disposal value using the straight-line method. Answer briefly in words without further calculations.

21-20 Capital budgeting with uneven cash flows, no income taxes. Southern Cola is considering the purchase of a special-purpose bottling machine for $23,000. It is expected to have a useful life of 4 years with no terminal disposal value. The plant manager estimates the following savings in cash operating costs:

Year	Amount
1	$10,000
2	8,000
3	6,000
4	5,000
Total	$29,000

Southern Cola uses a required rate of return of 16% in its capital budgeting decisions. Ignore income taxes in your analysis. Assume all cash flows occur at year-end except for initial investment amounts.

Required

Calculate the following for the special-purpose bottling machine:

1. Net present value
2. Payback period
3. Internal rate of return
4. Accrual accounting rate of return based on net initial investment (Assume straight-line depreciation. Use the average annual savings in cash operating costs when computing the numerator of the accrual accounting rate of return.)

21-21 Comparison of projects, no income taxes. (CMA, adapted) New Bio Corporation is a rapidly growing biotech company that has a required rate of return of 12%. It plans to build a new facility in Santa Clara County. The building will take two years to complete. The building contractor offered New Bio a choice of three payment plans, as follows:

- **Plan I** Payment of $375,000 at the time of signing the contract and $4,425,000 upon completion of the building. The end of the second year is the completion date.
- **Plan II** Payment of $1,500,000 at the time of signing the contract and $1,500,000 at the end of each of the two succeeding years.
- **Plan III** Payment of $150,000 at the time of signing the contract and $1,500,000 at the end of each of the three succeeding years.

Required

1. Using the net present value method, calculate the comparative cost of each of the three payment plans being considered by New Bio.

2. Which payment plan should New Bio choose? Explain.
3. Discuss the financial factors, other than the cost of the plan, and the nonfinancial factors that should be considered in selecting an appropriate payment plan.

21-22 Payback and NPV methods, no income taxes. (CMA, adapted) Andrews Construction is analyzing its capital expenditure proposals for the purchase of equipment in the coming year. The capital budget is limited to $6,000,000 for the year. Lori Bart, staff analyst at Andrews, is preparing an analysis of the three projects under consideration by Corey Andrews, the company's owner.

	A	B	C	D
1		**Project A**	**Project B**	**Project C**
2	**Projected cash outflow**			
3	Net initial investment	$3,000,000	$1,500,000	$4,000,000
4				
5	**Projected cash inflows**			
6	Year 1	$1,000,000	$ 400,000	$2,000,000
7	Year 2	1,000,000	900,000	2,000,000
8	Year 3	1,000,000	800,000	200,000
9	Year 4	1,000,000		100,000
10				
11	Required rate of return	10%	10%	10%

If you want to use Excel to solve this exercise, go to the Excel Lab at **www.prenhall.com/horngren/cost13e** and download the template for Exercise 21-22.

Required

1. Because the company's cash is limited, Andrews thinks the payback method should be used to choose between the capital budgeting projects.
   a. What are the benefits and limitations of using the payback method to choose between projects?
   b. Calculate the payback period for each of the three projects. Ignore income taxes. Using the payback method, which projects should Andrews choose?
2. Bart thinks that projects should be selected based on their NPVs. Assume all cash flows occur at the end of the year except for initial investment amounts. Calculate the NPV for each project. Ignore income taxes.
3. Which projects, if any, would you recommend funding? Briefly explain why.

21-23 DCF, accrual accounting rate of return, working capital, evaluation of performance, no income taxes. Century Lab plans to purchase a new centrifuge machine for its New Hampshire facility. The machine costs $137,500 and is expected to have a useful life of eight years, with a terminal disposal value of $37,500. Savings in cash operating costs are expected to be $31,250 per year. However, additional working capital is needed to keep the machine running efficiently. The working capital must continually be replaced, so an investment of $10,000 needs to be maintained at all times, but this investment is fully recoverable (will be "cashed in") at the end of the useful life. Century Lab's required rate of return is 14%. Ignore income taxes in your analysis. Assume all cash flows occur at year-end except for initial investment amounts.

Required

1. Calculate net present value.
2. Calculate internal rate of return.
3. Calculate accrual accounting rate of return based on net initial investment. Assume straight-line depreciation.
4. You have the authority to make the purchase decision. Why might you be reluctant to base your decision on the DCF methods?

21-24 New equipment purchase, income taxes. Anna's Bakery plans to purchase a new oven for its store. The oven has an estimated useful life of 4 years. The estimated pretax cash flows for the oven are as shown in the table that follows, with no anticipated change in working capital. Anna's Bakery has a 12% after-tax required rate of return and a 40% income tax rate. Assume depreciation is calculated on a straight-line basis for tax purposes using the initial oven investment and estimated terminal disposal value of the oven. Assume all cash flows occur at year-end except for initial investment amounts.

If you want to use Excel to solve this exercise, go to the Excel Lab at **www.prenhall.com/horngren/cost13e** and download the template for Exercise 21-24.

Required

1. Calculate (a) net present value, (b) payback period, and (c) internal rate of return.
2. Compare and contrast the capital budgeting methods in requirement 1.

	A	B	C	D	E	F
1		Relevant Cash Flows at End of Each Year				
2		0	1	2	3	4
3	Initial machine investment	$(88,000)				
4	Annual cash flow from operations (excluding the depreciation effect)		$36,000	$36,000	$36,000	$36,000
5	Cash flow from terminal disposal of machine					$ 8,000

21-25 New equipment purchase, income taxes. Innovation, Inc. is considering the purchase of a new industrial electric motor to improve efficiency at its Fremont plant. The motor has an estimated useful life of 5 years. The estimated pretax cash flows for the motor are shown in the table that follows, with no anticipated change in working capital. Innovation has a 12% after-tax required rate of return and a 40% income tax rate. Assume depreciation is calculated on a straight-line basis for tax purposes. Assume all cash flows occur at year-end except for initial investment amounts.

	A	B	C	D	E	F	
1		Relevant Cash Flows at End of Each Year					
2		0	1	2	3	4	5
3	Initial motor investment	$(62,500)					
4	Annual cash flow from operations (excluding the depreciation effect)		$31,250	$31,250	$31,250	$31,250	$31,250
5	Cash flow from terminal disposal of motor						$ 0

If you want to use Excel to solve this exercise, go to the Excel Lab at **www.prenhall.com/horngren/cost13e** and download the template for Exercise 21-25.

Required

1. Calculate (a) net present value, (b) payback period, and (c) internal rate of return.
2. Compare and contrast the capital budgeting methods in requirement 1.

21-26 Selling a plant, income taxes. (CMA, adapted) The Crossroad Company is an international clothing manufacturer. Its Santa Monica plant will become idle on December 31, 2008. Peter Laney, the corporate controller, has been asked to look at three options regarding the plant.

- Option 1: The plant, which has been fully depreciated for tax purposes, can be sold immediately for $340,000.
- Option 2: The plant can be leased to the Austin Corporation, one of Crossroad's suppliers, for four years. Under the lease terms, Austin would pay Crossroad $96,000 rent per year (payable at year-end) and would grant Crossroad a $18,960 annual discount off the normal price of fabric purchased by Crossroad (assume discount received at year-end for each of the four years). Austin would bear all of the plant's ownership costs. Crossroad expects to sell this plant for $80,000 at the end of the four-year lease.
- Option 3: The plant could be used for four years to make souvenir jackets for the Olympics. Fixed overhead costs (a cash outflow) before any equipment upgrades are estimated to be $8,000 annually for the four-year period. The jackets are expected to sell for $42 each. Variable cost per unit is expected to be $33. The following production and sales of jackets are expected: 2009, 8,000 units; 2010, 12,000 units; 2011, 16,000 units; 2012, 4,000 units. In order to manufacture the jackets, some of the plant equipment would need to be upgraded at an immediate cost of $60,000. The equipment would be depreciated using the straight-line depreciation method and zero terminal disposal value over the four years it would be in use. Because of the equipment upgrades, Crossroad could sell the plant for $120,000 at the end of four years. No change in working capital would be required.

Crossroad treats all cash flows as if they occur at the end of the year, and it uses an after-tax required rate of return of 12%. Crossroad is subject to a 40% tax rate on all income, including capital gains.

Required

1. Calculate net present value of each of the options and determine which option Crossroad should select using the NPV criterion.
2. What nonfinancial factors should Crossroad consider before making its choice?

Problems

21-27 Equipment replacement, no income taxes. Pro Chips is a manufacturer of prototype chips based in Dublin, Ireland. Next year, in 2010, Pro Chips expects to deliver 552 prototype chips at an average price of $80,000. Pro Chips' marketing vice president forecasts growth of 60 prototype chips per year through 2016. That is, demand will be 552 in 2010, 612 in 2011, 672 in 2012, and so on.

The plant cannot produce more than 540 prototype chips annually. To meet future demand, Pro Chips must either modernize the plant or replace it. The old equipment is fully depreciated and can be sold for $3,600,000 if the plant is replaced. If the plant is modernized, the costs to modernize it are to be capitalized and depreciated over the useful life of the updated plant. The old equipment is retained as part of the modernize alternative. The following data on the two options are available:

	Modernize	Replace
Initial investment in 2010	$33,600,000	$58,800,000
Terminal disposal value in 2016	$6,000,000	$14,400,000
Useful life	7 years	7 years
Total annual cash operating costs per prototype chip	$62,000	$56,000

Pro Chips uses straight-line depreciation, assuming zero terminal disposal value. For simplicity, we assume no change in prices or costs in future years. The investment will be made at the beginning of 2010, and all transactions thereafter occur on the last day of the year. Pro Chips' required rate of return is 12%.

There is no difference between the modernize and replace alternatives in terms of required working capital. Pro Chips has a special waiver on income taxes until 2016.

Required

1. Sketch the cash inflows and outflows of the modernize and replace alternatives over the 2010 to 2016 period.
2. Calculate payback period for the modernize and replace alternatives.
3. Calculate net present value of the modernize and replace alternatives.
4. What factors should Pro Chips consider in choosing between the alternatives?

21-28 Equipment replacement, income taxes (continuation of 21-27). Assume the same facts as in Problem 21-27, except that the plant is located in Austin, Texas. Pro Chips has no special waiver on income taxes. It pays a 30% tax rate on all income. Proceeds from sales of equipment above book value are taxed at the same 30% rate.

Required

1. Sketch the after-tax cash inflows and outflows of the modernize and replace alternatives over the 2010 to 2016 period.
2. Calculate net present value of the modernize and replace alternatives.
3. Suppose Pro Chips is planning to build several more plants. It wants to have the most advantageous tax position possible. Pro Chips has been approached by Spain, Malaysia, and Australia to construct plants in their countries. Use the data in Problem 21-27 and this problem to briefly describe in qualitative terms the income tax features that would be advantageous to Pro Chips.

21-29 DCF, sensitivity analysis, no income taxes. (CMA, adapted) Landom Corporation is an international manufacturer of fragrances for women. Management at Landom is considering expanding the product line to men's fragrances. From the best estimates of the marketing and production managers, annual sales (all for cash) for this new line is 1,000,000 units at $25 per unit; cash variable cost is $10 per unit; cash fixed costs is $5,000,000 per year. The investment project requires $30,000,000 of cash outflow and has a project life of 5 years.

At the end of the five-year useful life, there will be no terminal disposal value. Assume all cash flows occur at year-end except for initial investment amounts.

Men's fragrance is a new market for Landom, and management is concerned about the reliability of the estimates. The controller has proposed applying sensitivity analysis to selected factors. Ignore income taxes in your computations. Landom's required rate of return on this project is 14%.

Required

1. Calculate the net present value of this investment proposal.
2. Calculate the effect on the net present value of the following two changes in assumptions. (Treat each item independently of the other.)
   - **a.** 5% reduction in the selling price
   - **b.** 5% increase in the variable cost per unit
3. Discuss how management would use the data developed in requirements 1 and 2 in its consideration of the proposed capital investment.

21-30 NPV, IRR, and sensitivity analysis. Crumbly Cookie Company is considering expanding by buying a new (additional) machine that costs $42,000, has zero terminal disposal value and a 10-year useful life. It expects the annual increase in cash revenues from the expansion to be $23,000 per year. It expects additional annual cash costs to be $16,000 per year. Its cost of capital is 6%. Ignore taxes.

Required

1. Calculate the net present value and internal rate of return for this investment.
2. Assume the finance manager of Crumbly Cookie Company is not sure about the cash revenues and costs. The revenues could be anywhere from 10% higher to 10% lower than predicted. Assume cash costs are still $16,000 per year. What are NPV and IRR at the high and low points for revenue?
3. The finance manager thinks that costs will vary with revenues, and if the revenues are 10% higher, the costs will be 7% higher. If the revenues are 10% lower, the costs will be 10% lower. Recalculate the NPV and IRR at the high and low revenue points with this new cost information.
4. The finance manager has decided that the company should earn 2% more than the cost of capital on any project. Recalculate the original NPV in requirement 1 using the new discount rate and evaluate the investment opportunity.
5. Discuss how the changes in assumptions have affected the decision to expand.

21-31 Payback, even and uneven cash flows. You have the opportunity to expand your business by purchasing new equipment for $159,000. You expect to incur cash fixed costs of $96,000 per year to use this new equipment, and you expect to incur cash variable costs in the amount of 10% of cash revenues.

Required

1. Calculate the payback period for this investment assuming you will generate $140,000 in cash revenues every year.
2. Assume you expect the following cash revenue stream for this investment:

Year 1	$ 90,000
Year 2	115,000
Year 3	130,000
Year 4	155,000
Year 5	170,000
Year 6	180,000
Year 7	140,000
Year 8	125,000
Year 9	80,000

Based on this estimated revenue stream, what is the payback period for this investment?

21-32 Replacement of a machine, income taxes, sensitivity. (CMA, adapted) The Smacker Company is a family-owned business that produces fruit jam. The company has a grinding machine that has been in use for three years. On January 1, 2009, Smacker is considering the purchase of a new grinding machine. Smacker has two options: (1) continue using the old machine or (2) sell the old machine and purchase a new machine. The seller of the new machine isn't offering a trade-in. The following information has been obtained:

File Edit View Insert Format Tools Data Window Help

	A	B	C
1		**Old Machine**	**New Machine**
2	Initial purchase cost of machines	$120,000	$180,000
3	Useful life from acquisition date (years)	7	4
4	Terminal disposal value at the end of useful life on		
5	Dec. 31, 2012, assumed for depreciation purposes	$ 15,000	$ 30,000
6	Expected annual cash operating costs:		
7	Variable cost per can of jam	$ 0.20	$ 0.14
8	Total fixed costs	$ 22,500	$ 21,000
9	Depreciation method for tax purposes	Straight line	Straight line
10	Estimated disposal value of machine:		
11	January 1, 2009	$ 60,000	$180,000
12	December 31, 2012	$ 10,500	$ 30,000
13	Expected cans of jam made and sold each year	450,000	450,000

Smacker is subject to a 40% income tax rate. Assume that any gain or loss on the sale of machines is treated as an ordinary tax item and will affect the taxes paid by Smacker in the year in which it occurs. Smacker's after-tax required rate of return is 16%. Assume all cash flows occur at year-end except for initial investment amounts.

If you want to use Excel to solve this problem, go to the Excel Lab at **www.prenhall.com/horngren/cost13e** and download the template for Problem 21-32.

Required

1. You have been asked whether Smacker should buy the new machine. To help in your analysis, calculate the following:
   a. One-time after-tax cash effect of disposing of the old machine on January 1, 2009
   b. Annual recurring after-tax cash operating savings from using the new machine (variable and fixed)
   c. Cash tax savings due to differences in annual depreciation of the old machine and the new machine
   d. Difference in after-tax cash flow from terminal disposal of new machine and old machine
2. Use your calculations in requirement 1 and the net present value method to determine whether Smacker should use the old machine or acquire the new machine.
3. How much more or less would the recurring after-tax cash operating savings of the new machine need to be for Smacker to earn exactly the 16% after-tax required rate of return? Assume that all other data about the investment do not change.

21-33 NPV and AARR, goal-congruence issues. Nate Stately, a manager of the Plate Division for the Great Slate Manufacturing company, has the opportunity to expand the division by investing in additional machinery costing $320,000. He would depreciate the equipment using the straight-line method, and expects it to have no residual value. It has a useful life of six years. The firm mandates a required rate of return of 10% on investments. Nate estimates annual net cash inflows for this investment of $100,000 before taxes, and an investment in working capital of $5,000. Tax rate is 40%.

Required

1. Calculate the net present value of this investment.
2. Calculate the accrual accounting rate of return for this investment.
3. Should Nate accept the project? Will Nate accept the project if his bonus depends on achieving an accrual accounting rate of return of 10%? How can this conflict be resolved?

21-34 Recognizing cash flows for capital investment projects. Ludmilla Quagg owns a fitness center and is thinking of replacing the old Fit-O-Matic machine with a brand new Flab-Buster 3000. The old Fit-O-Matic has a historical cost of $50,000 and accumulated depreciation of $46,000, but has a trade-in value of $5,000. It currently costs $1,200 per month in utilities and another $10,000 a year in maintenance to run the Fit-O-Matic. Ludmilla feels that the Fit-O-Matic can be used for another 10 years, after which it would have no salvage value.

The Flab-Buster 3000 would reduce the utilities costs by 30% and cut the maintenance cost in half. The Flab-Buster 3000 costs $98,000, has a ten-year life, and an expected disposal value of $10,000 at the end of its useful life.

Ludmilla charges customers $10 per hour to use the fitness center. Replacing the fitness machine will not affect the price of service or the number of customers she can serve.

Ludmilla also looked at replacing the Fit-O-Matic with a Walk-N-Pull Series 3, which costs $78,000. However, she prefers the Flab-Buster 3000.

Required

1. Ludmilla wants to evaluate the Flab-Buster 3000 project using capital budgeting techniques, but does not know how to begin. To help her, read through the problem and separate the cash flows into four groups: (1) net initial investment cash flows, (2) cash flow savings from operations, (3) cash flows from terminal disposal of investment, and (4) cash flows not relevant to the capital budgeting problem.
2. Assuming a tax rate of 40%, a required rate of return of 8%, and straight-line depreciation over remaining useful life of machines, should Ludmilla buy the Flab-Buster 3000?

21-35 Recognizing cash flows for capital investment projects, NPV. Met-All Manufacturing manufactures over 20,000 different products made from metal, including building materials, tools, and furniture parts. The manager of the furniture parts division has proposed that his division expand into bicycle parts as well. The furniture parts division currently generates cash revenues of $4,700,000 and incurs cash costs of $3,600,000, with an investment in assets of $12,090,000. One-fourth of the cash costs are direct labor.

The manager estimates that the expansion of the business will require an investment in working capital of $45,000. Because the company already has a facility, there would be no additional rent or purchase costs for a building, but the project would generate an additional $390,000 in annual cash overhead. Moreover, the manager expects annual materials cash costs for bicycle parts to be $1,700,000, and labor for the bicycle parts to be about the same as the labor cash costs for furniture parts.

The Controller of Met-All, working with various managers, estimates that the expansion would require the purchase of equipment with a $5,000,000 cost and an expected disposal value of $400,000 at the end of its 10-year useful life. Depreciation would occur on a straight-line basis.

The CFO of Met-All determines the firm's cost of capital as 12%. The CFO's salary is $460,000 per year. Adding another division will not change that. The CEO asks for a report on expected revenues for the project, and is told by the marketing department that it might be able to achieve cash revenues of $3,750,000 annually from bicycle parts. Met-All Manufacturing has a tax rate of 30%.

Required

1. Separate the cash flows into four groups: (1) net initial investment cash flows, (2) cash flows from operations, (3) cash flows from terminal disposal of investment, and (4) cash flows not relevant to the capital budgeting problem.
2. Calculate the NPV of the expansion project and comment on your analysis.

21-36 NPV and inflation. Cost-Less Foods is considering replacing all of its old cash registers with new ones. The old registers are fully depreciated and have no disposal value. The new registers cost $600,000 (in total). Because the new registers are more efficient than the old registers, Cost-Less will have annual incremental cash savings from using the new registers in the amount of $140,000 per year. The registers have a six-year useful life, and are depreciated using the straight-line method with no disposal value. Cost-Less requires a 10% real rate of return. Ignore taxes.

Required

1. Given the information above, what is the net present value of the project?
2. Assume the $140,000 cost savings is in current real dollars, and the inflation rate is 5.5%. Find the NPV of the project assuming inflation.
3. Should Cost-Less buy the new cash registers?

21-37 NPV, inflation and taxes (continuation of 21-36). Refer to the information in the preceding problem, but now assume that the tax rate is 30% and that you are not ignoring taxes.

Required

1. Calculate the NPV of the project without inflation.
2. Calculate the NPV of the project with inflation.
3. Should Cost-Less buy the new cash registers?

Collaborative Learning Problem

21-38 Net present value, Internal Rate of Return, Sensitivity Analysis. Francesca Freed wants a Burg-N-Fry franchise. The buy-in is $500,000. Burg-N-Fry headquarters tells Francesca that typical annual operating costs are $160,000 (cash) and that she can bring in "as much as" $260,000 in cash revenues per year. Burg-N-Fry headquarters also wants her to pay 10% of her revenues to them per year. Francesca wants to earn at least 8% on the investment, because she has to borrow the $500,000 at a cost of 6%. Use a 12-year window, and ignore taxes.

Required

1. Find the NPV and IRR of this investment, given the information that Burg-N-Fry has given Francesca.
2. Francesca is nervous about the "as much as" statement from Burg-N-Fry, and worries that the cash revenues will be lower than $260,000. Repeat requirement 1 using revenues of $240,000 and $220,000.
3. Francesca thinks she should try to negotiate a lower payment to the Burg-N-Fry headquarters, and also thinks that if revenues are lower than $260,000, her costs might also be lower by about $10,000. Repeat requirement 2 using $150,000 as annual cash operating cost and a payment to Burg-N-Fry of only 6% of sales revenues.
4. Discuss how the sensitivity analysis will affect Francesca's decision to buy the franchise. Why don't you have to recalculate the internal rate of return if you change the desired (discount) interest rate?

Answers to Exercises in Compound Interest (Exercise 21-16)

The general approach to these exercises centers on a key question: Which of the four basic tables in Appendix B should be used? No computations should be made until this basic question has been answered with confidence.

1. **From Table 1.** The $5,000 is the present value P of your winnings. Their future value S in 10 years will be:

$$S = P(1 + r)^n$$

The conversion factor, $(1 + r)^n$, is on line 10 of Table 1.

$$\text{Substituting at 6\%: } S = 5{,}000\,(1.791) = \$8{,}955$$
$$\text{Substituting at 14\%: } S = 5{,}000\,(3.707) = \$18{,}535$$

2. **From Table 2.** The $89,550 is a future value. You want the present value of that amount. $P = S \div (1 + r)^n$. The conversion factor, $1 \div (1 + r)^n$, is on line 10 of Table 2. Substituting,

$$P = \$89{,}550\,(0.558) = \$49{,}969$$

3. **From Table 3.** The $89,550 is a future value. You are seeking the uniform amount (annuity) to set aside annually. Note that $1 invested each year for 10 years at 6% has a future value of $13.181 after 10 years, from line 10 of Table 3.

$$S_n = \text{Annual deposit } (F)$$
$$\$89{,}550 = \text{Annual deposit } (13.181)$$
$$\text{Annual deposit} = \frac{\$89{,}550}{13.181} = \$6{,}794$$

4. **From Table 3.** You need to find the future value of an annuity of $5,000 per year. Note that $1 invested each year for 10 years at 12% has a future value of $17.549 after 10 years.

$$S_n = \$5{,}000F, \text{ where } F \text{ is the conversion factor}$$
$$S_n = \$5{,}000\,(17.549) = \$87{,}745$$

5. **From Table 4.** When you reach age 65, you will get $200,000, a present value at that time. You need to find the annuity that will exactly exhaust the invested principal in 10 years. To pay yourself $1 each year for 10 years when the interest rate is 6% requires you to have $7.360 today, from line 10 of Table 4.

$$P_n = \text{Annual withdrawal } (F)$$
$$\$200{,}000 = \text{Annual withdrawal } (7.360)$$
$$\text{Annual withdrawal} = \frac{\$200{,}000}{7.360} = \$27{,}174$$

6. **From Table 4.** You need to find the present value of an annuity for 10 years.

At 6%:
$$P_n = \text{Annual withdrawal } (F)$$
$$P_n = \$50{,}000\,(7.360)$$
$$P_n = \$368{,}000$$

At 20%:
$$P_n = \$50{,}000\,(4.192)$$
$$P_n = \$209{,}600, \text{ a much lower figure}$$

7. Plan B is preferable. The NPV of plan B exceeds that of plan A by $980 ($3,126 − $2,146):

		Plan A		Plan B	
Year	**PV Factor at 6%**	**Cash Inflows**	**PV of Cash Inflows**	**Cash Inflows**	**PV of Cash Inflows**
0	1.000	$(10,000)	$(10,000)	$(10,000)	$(10,000)
1	0.943	1,000	943	5,000	4,715
2	0.890	2,000	1,780	4,000	3,560
3	0.840	3,000	2,520	3,000	2,520
4	0.792	4,000	3,168	2,000	1,584
5	0.747	5,000	3,735	1,000	747
			$ 2,146		$ 3,126

Even though plans A and B have the same total cash inflows over the five years, plan B is preferred because it has greater cash inflows occurring earlier.

22 Management Control Systems, Transfer Pricing, and Multinational Considerations

Learning Objectives

1. Describe a management control system and its three key properties
2. Describe the benefits and costs of decentralization
3. Explain transfer prices and four criteria used to evaluate them
4. Calculate transfer prices using three methods
5. Illustrate how market-based transfer prices promote goal congruence in perfectly competitive markets
6. Understand how to avoid making suboptimal decisions when transfer prices are based on full cost plus a markup
7. Describe the range over which two divisions negotiate the transfer price when there is unused capacity
8. Apply a general guideline for determining a minimum transfer price
9. Incorporate income tax considerations in multinational transfer pricing

Transfer pricing is the price one subunit of a company charges for the services it provides another subunit of the same company. Top management uses transfer prices (1) to focus managers' attention on the performance of their own subunits and (2) to plan and coordinate the actions of different subunits to maximize the company's income as a whole. But transfer pricing can also be contentious because managers of different subunits often have very different preferences about how transfer prices should be set. For example, some managers prefer the prices be based on market prices. Others prefer the prices be based on costs alone. Controversy also arises when multinational corporations seek to reduce their overall income tax burden by charging high transfer prices to units located in countries with high tax rates. Many countries, including the United States, attempt to restrict this practice, as the following article shows.

Transfer Pricing Leads Symantec to $1 Billion Dispute with the IRS[1]

Symantec Corp., a large U.S. software company, is in a $1 billion court dispute with the Internal Revenue Service [IRS] involving dealings among two affiliated companies. The IRS is seeking more than $757 million in back taxes owed by Veritas Software Corp., a company acquired by Symantec in 2005. The IRS is also seeking $303 million in penalties. The fight is over the company's formula for "transfer pricing," a complex set of rules determining how companies set prices, fees, and cost-allocation arrangements between their operations in different tax jurisdictions.

In Symantec's case, the dispute is over the fees and cost-allocation arrangements between Veritas and an Irish subsidiary. Ireland has emerged as a popular tax haven for U.S. technology companies. The IRS contends that licensing fees paid by the Irish subsidiary to Veritas in the U.S. were too low, and that Veritas charged the U.S. business with too much of the cost of developing certain technology. Both had the effect of increasing the income of Veritas's subsidiary in Ireland at the expense of income in the U.S., consequently lowering the U.S. tax bills in 2000 and 2001.

[1] *Source:* Jesse Drucker, "Symantec Is in $1 Billion IRS Dispute," *The Wall Street Journal,* June 29, 2006; "Michael Hickens, "Symantec Rebuts IRS Claims," Internetnews.com, June 29, 2006 (www.internetnews.com/bus-news/article.php/3617341); and C. Williams, "Symantec squares up to the IRS over $1bn tax demand," *The Register (UK)* (June 30, 2006).

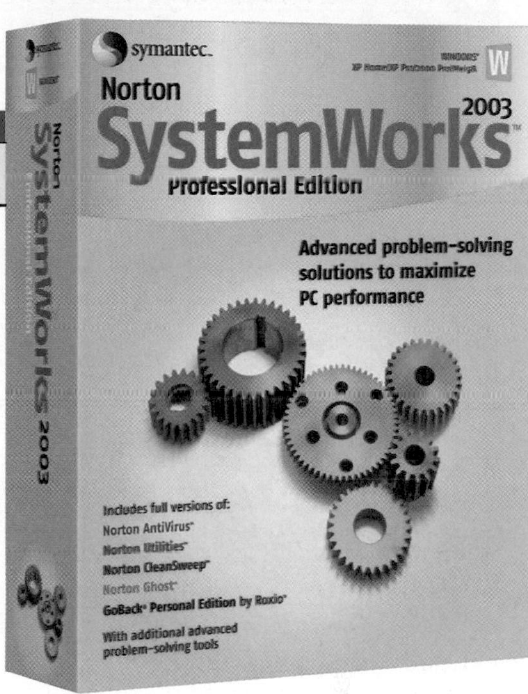

Symantec, however, maintains that it acted appropriately. The company claims that the IRS erred in several calculations, including its allocation of taxable income, cost sharing with regards to stock-based compensation, and other inter-company allocations. In a statement, the company claimed: "We believe we have done everything to cooperate with the IRS to resolve this issue in good faith. We do not agree with the IRS petition."

Though not all companies face multinational tax concerns, transfer-pricing issues are common to many companies. In these companies, transfer pricing is part of the larger management control system. This chapter develops the links between strategy, organization structure, management control systems, and accounting information. We'll examine the benefits and costs of centralized and decentralized organization structures, and we'll look at the pricing of products or services transferred between subunits of the same company. We emphasize how accounting information, such as costs, budgets, and prices, helps in planning and coordinating actions of subunits. Some of the material in the chapter is "softer" than material in other chapters—that is, it includes relatively few numbers. Nevertheless, the concepts are important for management accountants to understand.

Management Control Systems

A **management control system** is a means of gathering and using information to aid and coordinate the planning and control decisions throughout an organization and to guide the behavior of its managers and other employees. Some companies design their management control system around the concept of the balanced scorecard (see Chapter 13 for details). Consider Exxon-Mobil. Its management control system contains financial and nonfinancial information in each of the four perspectives of the balanced scorecard.

1. **Financial perspective**—for example, stock price, net income, return on investment, cash flow from operations, and cost per gallon of gasoline.
2. **Customer perspective**—for example, customer satisfaction, time taken to respond to customer requests for products, customers' repeat purchases, and market share in key market segments.
3. **Internal-business-process perspective**—for example, on-time delivery of gasoline from refineries to retail stations, gasoline quality, refinery downtime, number of days lost due to accidents and environmental problems, speed of service at retail stations, friendliness of employees, and stocking of convenience stores.

Learning Objective 1

Describe a management control system

. . . gathers information for planning and control decisions

and its three key properties

. . . aligns with strategy, supports organizational responsibility of managers, and motivates employees

4. **Learning-and-growth perspective**—for example, employee satisfaction, absenteeism, information systems capabilities, and number of processes with real-time feedback.

The target performance levels are based on competitor benchmarks, which indicate the performance levels necessary to meet customer needs, compete effectively, and achieve financial goals. Well-designed management control systems use information both from within the company, such as net income and employee satisfaction, and from outside the company, such as stock price and customer satisfaction.

Management control systems consist of formal and informal control systems. The formal management control system of a company includes explicit rules, procedures, performance measures, and incentive plans that guide the behavior of its managers and other employees. The formal control system is comprised of several systems. For example, the management accounting system provides information regarding costs, revenues, and income. The human resources systems provide information on recruiting, training, absenteeism, and accidents; and quality systems provide information on yield, defective products, and late deliveries to customers.

The informal management control system includes shared values, loyalties, and mutual commitments among members of the company, company culture, and the unwritten norms about acceptable behavior for managers and other employees. Examples of company slogans that reinforce values and loyalties are "At Ford, Quality Is Job 1," and "At Home Depot, Low Prices Are Just the Beginning."

Evaluating Management Control Systems

To be effective, management control systems should be closely aligned with the company's strategies and goals. Two examples of strategies at Exxon-Mobil are (1) providing innovative products and services to increase market share in key customer segments (by targeting customers who are willing to pay more for faster service, better facilities, and well-stocked convenience stores) and (2) reducing costs and targeting price-sensitive customers. Suppose Exxon-Mobil decides, wisely or unwisely, to provide innovative products and services. The management control system must then reinforce this goal, and Exxon-Mobil should tie managers' rewards to achieving the targeted measures.

Management control systems should also be designed to support the organizational responsibilities of individual managers. Different levels of management at Exxon-Mobil need different kinds of information to perform their tasks. For example, top management needs stock-price information to evaluate how much shareholder value the company has created. Stock price, however, is less important for line managers supervising individual refineries. They are more concerned with obtaining information about on-time delivery of gasoline, equipment downtime, product quality, number of days lost to accidents and environmental problems, cost per gallon of gasoline, and employee satisfaction. Similarly, marketing managers are more concerned with information about service at gas stations, customer satisfaction, and market share.

Effective management control systems should also motivate managers and other employees. **Motivation** is the desire to attain a selected goal (the *goal-congruence* aspect) combined with the resulting pursuit of that goal (the *effort* aspect).

Goal congruence exists when individuals and groups work toward achieving the organization's goals—that is, managers working in their own best interest take actions that align with the overall goals of top management. Suppose the goal of Exxon-Mobil's top management is to maximize operating income. If the management control system evaluates the refinery manager *only* on the basis of costs, the manager may be tempted to make decisions that minimize cost but overlook product quality or timely delivery to retail stations, which will likely not maximize operating income of the company as a whole. In this case, the management control system will not achieve goal congruence.

Effort is exertion toward achieving a goal. Effort goes beyond physical exertion, such as a worker producing at a faster rate, to include both physical and mental actions. Management control systems motivate managers and other employees to exert effort through a variety of rewards tied to the achievement of goals. These rewards can be monetary (such as cash, shares of company stock, use of a company car, or membership in a club) or nonmonetary (such as power or pride in working for a successful company).

Organization Structure and Decentralization

Management control systems must fit an organization's structure. An organization whose structure is decentralized has additional issues to consider for its management control system to be effective.

Decentralization is the freedom for managers at lower levels of the organization to make decisions. **Autonomy** is the degree of freedom to make decisions. The greater the freedom, the greater the autonomy. As we discuss the issues of decentralization and autonomy, we use the term subunit to refer to any part of an organization. A subunit may be a large division, such as the Refining Division of Exxon-Mobil, or a small group, such as a two-person advertising department of a local clothing chain.

Total decentralization means minimum constraints and maximum freedom for managers at the lowest levels of an organization to make decisions and to take actions. Total centralization means maximum constraints and minimum freedom for managers at the lowest levels of an organization to make decisions. Companies' organization structures fall somewhere in between these two extremes because there are both benefits and costs of decentralization.

Learning Objective 2

Describe the benefits of decentralization

. . . responsiveness to customers, faster decision making, management development

and the costs of decentralization

. . . loss of control, duplication of activities

Benefits of Decentralization

How much decentralization is optimal? Managers try to choose the degree of decentralization that maximizes benefits over costs. From a practical standpoint, top management can seldom quantify either the benefits or the costs of decentralization. Still, the cost-benefit approach helps them focus on the issues.

Supporters of decentralizing decision making and granting responsibilities to managers of subunits advocate the following benefits:

1. **Creates greater responsiveness to local needs.** Good decisions cannot be made without good information. Compared with top managers, subunit managers are better informed about their customers, competitors, suppliers, and employees, as well as about local factors that affect performance, such as ways to decrease costs, improve quality, and be responsive to customers. Eastman Kodak reports that two advantages of decentralization are an "increase in the company's knowledge of the marketplace and improved service to customers."
2. **Leads to gains from faster decision making.** Decentralization speeds decision making, creating a competitive advantage over centralized organizations. Centralization slows decision making as responsibility for decisions creeps upward through layer after layer of management. Interlake, a manufacturer of materials handling equipment, cites this benefit of decentralization: "We have distributed decision-making powers more broadly to the cutting edge of product and market opportunity." Interlake's materials-handling equipment must often be customized to fit customers' needs. Delegating decision making to the sales force allows Interlake to respond faster to changing customer requirements.
3. **Increases motivation of subunit managers.** Subunit managers are more motivated and committed when they can exercise initiative. Johnson & Johnson, a highly decentralized company, maintains that "Decentralization = Creativity = Productivity."
4. **Assists management development and learning.** Giving managers more responsibility helps develop an experienced pool of management talent to fill higher-level management positions. The company also learns which people are not management material. According to Tektronix, an electronics instruments company: "Decentralized units provide a training ground for general managers and a visible field of combat where product champions can fight for their ideas."

5. **Sharpens the focus of subunit managers.** In a decentralized setting, the manager of a small subunit has a concentrated focus. Also, top management, relieved of the burden of day-to-day operating decisions, can spend more time and effort on strategic planning for the entire organization.

Costs of Decentralization

Advocates of more-centralized decision making point to the following costs of decentralizing decision making:

1. **Leads to suboptimal decision making, which arises when a decision's benefit to one subunit is more than offset by the costs or loss of benefits to the organization as a whole.** This cost arises because top management has given up control over decision making.

   Suboptimal decision making—also called **incongruent decision making** or **dysfunctional decision making**—is most likely to occur when the subunits in the company are highly interdependent, such as when the end product of one subunit is used or sold by another subunit. For example, a manufacturing manager evaluated on the basis of manufacturing costs may be unresponsive to requests from marketing to schedule a rush order for a customer if altering production schedules will increase manufacturing costs. From the company's viewpoint, however, supplying the product to the customer may be preferred both because the customer is willing to pay a premium price and because the company expects the customer to place many orders in the future. Suboptimal decision making also occurs when subunit managers do not have the necessary skills to do their jobs.
2. **Focuses manager's attention on the subunit rather than the company as a whole.** Individual subunit managers may regard themselves as competing with managers of other subunits in the same company as if they were external rivals. Consequently, managers may be unwilling to share information or to assist when another subunit faces an emergency. Also, subunit managers may use information they have about local conditions to further their own self-interest rather than to help achieve the company's goals. For example, they may not disclose the full potential for sales for fear of missing their goal or so they can reduce the effort they need to exert.
3. **Increases costs of gathering information.** Managers may spend too much time obtaining information about different subunits of the company in order to coordinate their actions.
4. **Results in duplication of activities.** Several individual subunits of the company may undertake the same activity separately. For example, there may be a duplication of staff functions (accounting, human resources, and legal) if a company is highly decentralized. Centralizing these functions helps to consolidate, streamline, and use fewer resources for these activities.

Comparison of Benefits and Costs

To choose an organization structure that will implement a company's strategy, top managers must compare the benefits and costs of decentralization, often on a function-by-function basis. Surveys of U.S. and European companies report that the decisions made most frequently at the decentralized level and least frequently at the corporate level are related to product mix and product advertising. In these areas, subunit managers develop their own operating plans and performance reports and make faster decisions based on local information. Decisions related to the type and source of long-term financing and income taxes are made least frequently at the decentralized level and most frequently at the corporate level. Corporate managers have better information about financing terms in different markets and can obtain the best terms. Centralizing income tax strategies allows the organization to trade off and manage income in a subunit with losses in others. The benefits of decentralization are generally greater when companies face uncertainties in their environments, require detailed local knowledge for performing various jobs, and have few interdependencies among divisions.

Decentralization in Multinational Companies

Multinational companies—companies that operate in multiple countries—are often decentralized because centralized control of a company with subunits around the world is often physically and practically impossible. Also, language, customs, cultures, business practices, rules, laws, and regulations vary significantly across countries. Decentralization enables managers in different countries to make decisions that exploit their knowledge of local business and political conditions and to deal with uncertainties in their individual environments. For example, Philips, a global electronics company headquartered in the Netherlands, delegates marketing and pricing decisions for its television business in the Indian and Singaporean markets to the managers in those countries. Multinational corporations often rotate managers between foreign locations and corporate headquarters. Job rotation combined with decentralization helps develop managers' abilities to operate in the global environment.

There are drawbacks to decentralizing multinational companies. One of the most important is the lack of control and the resulting risks. Barings PLC, a British investment banking firm, went bankrupt and had to be sold when one of its traders in Singapore caused the firm to lose more than £1 billion on unauthorized trades that were not detected until after the trades were made. Similarly, a trader at Sumitomo Corporation racked up \$2.6 billion in copper-trading losses because poor controls failed to detect the magnitude of the trader's activities. Multinational corporations that implement decentralized decision making usually design their management control systems to measure and monitor division performance. Information and communications technology helps the flow of information for reporting and control.

Choices About Responsibility Centers

To measure the performance of subunits in centralized or decentralized companies, the management control system uses one or a mix of the four types of responsibility centers presented in Chapter 6:

1. *Cost center*—the manager is accountable for costs only.
2. *Revenue center*—the manager is accountable for revenues only.
3. *Profit center*—the manager is accountable for revenues and costs.
4. *Investment center*—the manager is accountable for investments, revenues, and costs.

Centralization or decentralization is not mentioned in the descriptions of these centers because each type of responsibility center can be found in either centralized or decentralized companies.

A common misconception is that *profit center*—and, in some cases, *investment center*—is a synonym for a decentralized subunit, and *cost center* is a synonym for a centralized subunit. *Profit centers can be coupled with a highly centralized organization, and cost centers can be coupled with a highly decentralized organization.* For example, managers in a division organized as a profit center may have little freedom in making decisions. They may need to obtain approval from corporate headquarters for every expenditure over, say, \$10,000 and may be forced to do what the central staff wants. In another company, divisions may be organized as cost centers, but their managers may have great latitude on capital expenditures and on where to purchase materials and services. In short, the labels "profit center" and "cost center" are independent of the degree of centralization or decentralization in a company.

Transfer Pricing

In decentralized organizations, much of the decision-making power resides in its individual subunits. In these cases, the management control system often uses *transfer prices* to coordinate the actions of the subunits and to evaluate their performance.

Learning Objective 3

Explain transfer prices

. . . price one subunit charges another for product

and four criteria used to evaluate them

. . . goal congruence, management effort, subunit performance evaluation, and subunit autonomy

A **transfer price** is the price one subunit (department or division) charges for a product or service supplied to another subunit of the same organization. If, for example, a car manufacturer has a separate division that manufactures engines, the transfer price is the price the engine division charges when it transfers engines to the car assembly division. The transfer price creates revenues for the selling subunit (the engine division in our example) and purchase costs for the buying subunit (the assembly division in our example), affecting each subunit's operating income. These operating incomes can be used to evaluate subunits' performances and to motivate their managers. The product or service transferred between subunits of an organization is called an **intermediate product**. This product may either be further worked on by the receiving subunit (as in the engine example) or, if transferred from production to marketing, sold to an external customer.

In one sense, transfer pricing is a curious phenomenon. Activities within an organization are clearly nonmarket in nature; products and services are not bought and sold as they are in open-market transactions. Yet, establishing prices for transfers among subunits of a company has a distinctly market flavor. The rationale for transfer prices is that subunit managers (such as the manager of the engine division), when making decisions, need only focus on how their decisions will affect their subunit's performance without evaluating their impact on companywide performance. In this sense, transfer prices ease the subunit managers' information-processing and decision-making tasks. In a well-designed transfer-pricing system, a manager focuses on optimizing subunit performance (the performance of the engine division) and in so doing optimizes the performance of the company as a whole.

As in all management control systems, transfer prices should help achieve a company's strategies and goals and fit its organization structure. We describe four criteria to evaluate transfer pricing. (1) Transfer prices should promote goal congruence. (2) They should motivate a high level of management effort. Subunits selling a product or service should be motivated to hold down their costs; subunits buying the product or service should be motivated to acquire and use inputs efficiently. (3) The transfer price should help top management evaluate the performance of individual subunits. (4) If top management favors a high degree of decentralization, transfer prices should preserve a high degree of subunit autonomy in decision making. That is, a subunit manager seeking to maximize the operating income of the subunit should have the freedom to transact with other subunits of the company (on the basis of transfer prices) or to transact with external parties.

There are three methods for determining transfer prices:

Learning Objective 4

Calculate transfer prices using three methods

. . . market-based, cost-based, negotiated

1. **Market-based transfer prices.** Top management may choose to use the price of a similar product or service publicly listed in, say, a trade association Web site. Also, top management may select, for the internal price, the external price that a subunit charges to outside customers.
2. **Cost-based transfer prices.** Top management may choose a transfer price based on the cost of producing the product in question. Examples include variable production cost, variable and fixed production costs, and full cost of the product. Full cost of the product includes all production costs plus costs from other business functions (R&D, design, marketing, distribution, and customer service). The cost used in cost-based transfer prices can be actual cost or budgeted cost. Sometimes, the cost-based transfer price includes a markup or profit margin that represents a return on subunit investment.
3. **Negotiated transfer prices.** In some cases, the subunits of a company are free to negotiate the transfer price between themselves and then to decide whether to buy and sell internally or deal with external parties. Subunits may use information about costs and market prices in these negotiations, but there is no requirement that the chosen transfer price bear any specific relationship to either cost or market-price data. Negotiated transfer prices are often employed when market prices are volatile and change constantly. The negotiated transfer price is the outcome of a bargaining process between selling and buying subunits.

To see how each of the three transfer-pricing methods works and to see the differences among them, we examine transfer pricing at Horizon Petroleum against the four criteria of promoting goal congruence, motivating management effort, evaluating subunit performance, and preserving subunit autonomy (if desired).

An Illustration of Transfer Pricing

Horizon Petroleum has two divisions, each operating as a profit center. The Transportation Division purchases crude oil in Matamoros, Mexico, and transports it from Matamoros to Houston, Texas. The Refining Division processes crude oil into gasoline. For simplicity, we assume gasoline is the only salable product the Houston refinery makes and that it takes two barrels of crude oil to yield one barrel of gasoline.

Variable costs in each division are variable with respect to a single cost driver: barrels of crude oil transported by the Transportation Division, and barrels of gasoline produced by the Refining Division. The fixed cost per unit is based on the budgeted annual fixed costs and practical capacity of crude oil that can be transported by Transportation, and the budgeted fixed costs and practical capacity of gasoline that can be produced by Refining. Horizon Petroleum reports all costs and revenues of its non-U.S. operations in U.S. dollars using the prevailing exchange rate.

- The Transportation Division has obtained rights to certain oil fields in the Matamoros area. It has a long-term contract to purchase crude oil produced from these fields at $72 per barrel. The division transports the oil to Houston and then "sells" it to the Refining Division. The pipeline from Matamoros to Houston has the capacity to carry 40,000 barrels of crude oil per day.
- The Refining Division has been operating at capacity (30,000 barrels of crude oil a day), using oil supplied by Horizon's Transportation Division (an average of 10,000 barrels per day) and oil bought from another producer and delivered to the Houston refinery (an average of 20,000 barrels per day at $85 per barrel).
- The Refining Division sells the gasoline it produces to outside parties at $190 per barrel.

Exhibit 22-1 summarizes Horizon Petroleum's variable and fixed costs per barrel of crude oil in the Transportation Division and variable and fixed costs per barrel of gasoline in the Refining Division, the external market prices of buying crude oil, and the external market price of selling gasoline. What's missing in the exhibit is the actual transfer price from the Transportation Division to the Refining Division. This transfer price will vary depending on the transfer-pricing method used. Transfer prices from the Transportation Division to the Refining Division under each of the three methods are:

1. Market-based transfer price of $85 per barrel of crude oil based on the competitive market price in Houston.
2. Cost-based transfer prices at, say, 105% of full cost, where full cost is the cost of the crude oil purchased in Matamoros plus the Transportation Division's own variable and fixed costs: $1.05 \times (\$72 + \$1 + \$3) = \$79.80$.
3. Negotiated transfer price of $82.50 per barrel of crude oil, which is between the market-based and cost-based transfer prices.

Exhibit 22-2 presents division operating incomes per 100 barrels of crude oil purchased under each transfer-pricing method. Transfer prices create income for the selling division and corresponding costs for the buying division that cancel out when division results are consolidated for the company as a whole. The exhibit assumes all three transfer-pricing methods yield transfer prices that are in a range that does not cause division managers to change the business relationships shown in Exhibit 22-1. That is, Horizon Petroleum's total operating income from purchasing, transporting, and refining the 100 barrels of crude oil and selling the 50 barrels of gasoline is the same, $1200, *regardless of the internal transfer prices used.*

$$\text{Operating income} = \text{Revenues} - \text{Cost of crude oil purchases in Matamoros} - \text{Transportation Division costs} - \text{Refining Division costs}$$

$$= (\$190 \times 50 \text{ barrels of gasoline}) - (\$72 \times 100 \text{ barrels of crude oil}) - (\$4 \times 100 \text{ barrels of crude oil}) - (\$14 \times 50 \text{ barrels of gasoline})$$

$$= \$9{,}500 - \$7{,}200 - \$400 - \$700 = \$1{,}200$$

Exhibit 22-1 Operating Data for Horizon Petroleum

	A	B	C	D	E	F	G	H
1								
2				**Transportation Division**				
3	Contract price per barrel of crude oil supplied in Matamoros =			Variable cost per barrel of crude oil	$1			
4		$72	→	Fixed cost per barrel of crude oil	3			
5				Full cost per barrel of crude oil	$4			
6				↓				
7								
8				Barrels of crude oil transferred				
9				↓				
10								
11				**Refining Division**				
12	Market price per barrel of crude oil supplied to Houston refinery =			Variable cost per barrel of gasoline	$ 8		Market price per barrel of gasoline sold to external parties =	
13		$85	→	Fixed cost per barrel of gasoline	6	→		$190
14				Full cost per barrel of gasoline	$14			
15								

Note further that under all three methods, summing the two division operating incomes equals Horizon Petroleum's total operating income of $1,200. By keeping total operating income the same, we focus attention on the effects of different transfer-pricing methods on the operating income of each division. Subsequent sections of this chapter show that different transfer-pricing methods can cause managers to take different actions leading to different total operating incomes.

Consider the two methods in the first two columns of Exhibit 22-2. The operating income of the Transportation Division is $520 more ($900 − $380) if transfer prices are based on market prices rather than on 105% of full cost. The operating income of the Refining Division is $520 more ($820 − $300) if transfer prices are based on 105% of full cost rather than market prices. If the Transportation Division's sole criterion were to maximize its own division operating income, it would favor transfer prices at market prices. In contrast, the Refining Division would prefer transfer prices at 105% of full cost to maximize its own division operating income. The transfer price of $82.50 negotiated by the Transportation and Refining Division managers is between the 105% of full cost and market-based transfer prices and splits the $1,200 of operating income almost equally between the divisions ($650 for the Transportation Division and $550 for the Refining Division). It's not surprising that subunit managers take considerable interest in setting transfer prices, especially those managers whose compensation or promotion directly depends on subunit operating income. To reduce the excessive focus of subunit managers on their own subunits, many companies compensate subunit managers on the basis of both subunit and companywide operating incomes.

We next examine market-based, cost-based, and negotiated transfer prices in more detail. We show how the choice of transfer-pricing method combined with managers' sourcing decisions can determine the size of the companywide operating-income pie itself.

Learning Objective 5

Illustrate how market-based transfer prices promote goal congruence in perfectly competitive markets

. . . division managers transacting internally are motivated to take the same actions as if they were transacting externally

Market-Based Transfer Prices

Transferring products or services at market prices generally leads to optimal decisions when three conditions are satisfied: (1) The market for the intermediate product is perfectly competitive, (2) interdependencies of subunits are minimal, and (3) there are no additional costs or benefits to the company as a whole from buying or selling in the external market instead of transacting internally.

Exhibit 22-2 Division Operating Income of Horizon Petroleum for 100 Barrels of Crude Oil Under Alternative Transfer-Pricing Methods

File Edit View Insert Format Tools Data Window Help

	A	B	C	D	E	F	G	H
1	**Production and Sales Data**							
2	Barrels of crude oil transferred =	100						
3	Barrels of gasoline sold =	50						
4								
5		**Internal Transfers**			**Internal Transfers at**		**Internal Transfers at**	
6		**at Market Price of**			**105% of Full Cost =**		**Negotiated Price of**	
7		**$85**			**$79.80**		**$82.50**	
8		**per barrel**			**per barrel**		**per barrel**	
9	**Transportation Division**							
10	Revenues, $85, $79.80, $82.50 x 100 barrels of crude oil	$8,500			$7,980		$8,250	
11	Costs							
12	Crude oil purchase costs,							
13	$72 x 100 barrels of crude oil	7,200			7,200		7,200	
14	Division variable costs,							
15	$1 x 100 barrels of crude oil	100			100		100	
16	Division fixed costs,							
17	$3 x 100 barrels of crude oil	300			300		300	
18	Total division costs	7,600			7,600		7,600	
19	Division operating income	$ 900			$ 380		$ 650	
20								
21	**Refining Division**							
22	Revenues, $190 x 50 barrels of gasoline	$9,500			$9,500		$9,500	
23	Costs							
24	Transferred-in costs, $85, $79.80, $82.50							
25	x 100 barrels of crude oil	8,500	←		7,980	←	8,250	←
26	Division variable costs,							
27	$8 x 50 barrels of gasoline	400			400		400	
28	Division fixed costs,							
29	$6 x 50 barrels of gasoline	300			300		300	
30	Total division costs	9,200			8,680		8,950	
31	Division operating income	$ 300			$ 820		$ 550	
32								
33	Operating income of both divisions together	$1,200			$1,200		$1,200	

Perfectly-Competitive-Market Case

A **perfectly competitive market** exists when there is a homogeneous product with buying prices equal to selling prices and no individual buyers or sellers can affect those prices by their own actions. By using market-based transfer prices in perfectly competitive markets, a company can (1) promote goal congruence, (2) motivate management effort, (3) evaluate subunit performance, and (4) preserve subunit autonomy.

Consider Horizon Petroleum again. Assume there is a perfectly competitive market for crude oil in the Houston area. As a result, the Transportation Division can sell and the Refining Division can buy as much crude oil as each wants at $85 per barrel. Horizon would prefer its managers to buy or sell crude oil internally. Think about the decisions that Horizon's division managers would make if each had the autonomy to sell or buy crude oil externally. If the transfer price between Horizon's Transportation and Refining Divisions is set below $85, the manager of the Transportation Division will be motivated to sell all crude oil to external buyers in the Houston area at $85 per barrel. If the transfer price is set above $85, the manager of the Refining Division will be motivated to purchase all crude oil requirements from external suppliers. Only a $85 transfer price will motivate the Transportation Division and the Refining Division to buy and sell internally. That's because neither division profits by buying or selling in the external market.

Suppose Horizon evaluates division managers on the basis of their individual division's operating income. The Transportation Division will sell, either internally or externally, as much crude oil as it can profitably transport, and the Refining Division will buy, either internally or externally, as much crude oil as it can profitably refine. A $85-per-barrel transfer price achieves goal congruence—the actions that maximize each division's operating income are also the actions that maximize operating income of Horizon Petroleum as a whole. Furthermore, because the transfer price is not based on costs, it motivates each division manager to exert management effort to maximize his or her own division's operating income. Market prices also serve to evaluate the economic viability and profitability of each division individually. For example, if under market-based transfer prices, the Refining Division consistently shows small or negative profits, Horizon may decide to shut down the Refining Division and simply transport and sell the oil to other refineries in the Houston area.

Distress Prices

When supply outstrips demand, market prices may drop well below their historical averages. If the drop in prices is expected to be temporary, these low market prices are sometimes called "distress prices." Deciding whether a current market price is a distress price is often difficult. The market prices of several agricultural commodities, such as wheat and oats, have stayed for many years at what many people initially believed were temporary distress levels!

Which transfer price should be used for judging performance if distress prices prevail? Some companies use the distress prices themselves, but others use long-run average prices, or "normal" market prices. In the short run, the manager of the selling subunit should supply the product or service at the distress price as long as it exceeds the *incremental costs* of supplying the product or service. If the distress price is used as the transfer price, the selling division will show a loss because the distress price will not exceed the *full cost* of the division. If the long-run average market price is used, forcing the manager to buy internally at a price above the current market price will hurt the buying division's short-run operating income. But the long-run average market price will provide a better measure of the long-run profitability and viability of the supplier division. Of course, if the price remains low in the long run, the company should use the low market price as the transfer price. If this price is lower than the variable and fixed costs that can be saved if manufacturing facilities are shut down, the production facilities of the selling subunit should be sold, and the buying subunit should purchase the product from an external supplier.

If markets are not perfectly competitive, selling prices affect the quantity of product sold. If the selling division sells its product in the external market, the selling division manager would choose a price and quantity combination that would maximize the division's operating income. If the transfer price is set at this selling price, the buying division may find that acquiring the product is too costly and results in a loss. It may decide not to purchase the product. Yet, from the point of view of the company as a whole, it may well be that profits are maximized if the selling division transfers the product to the buying division for further processing and sale. When markets are not perfectly competitive, using market-based transfer prices can lead to goal incongruence.

Learning Objective 6

Understand how to avoid making suboptimal decisions when transfer prices are based on full cost plus a markup

. . . in situations when buying divisions regard the fixed costs and the markup as variable costs

Cost-Based Transfer Prices

Cost-based transfer prices are helpful when market prices are unavailable, inappropriate, or too costly to obtain—for example, when markets are not perfectly competitive, when the product is specialized, or when the internal product is different from the products available externally in terms of quality and customer service.

Full-Cost Bases

In practice, many companies use transfer prices based on full cost. To approximate market prices, cost-based transfer prices are sometimes set at full cost plus a margin. These transfer prices, however, can lead to suboptimal decisions. Suppose Horizon Petroleum makes internal transfers at 105% of full cost. Recall that the Refining Division purchases, on average, 20,000 barrels of crude oil per day from a local Houston supplier, who delivers the crude oil to the refinery at a price of $85 per barrel. To reduce crude oil costs, the Refining Division has located an independent producer in Matamoros—Gulfmex Corporation—that is willing to sell 20,000 barrels of crude oil per day at $79 per barrel, delivered to Horizon's pipeline in Matamoros. Given Horizon's organization structure, the Transportation Division would purchase the 20,000 barrels of crude oil in Matamoros from Gulfmex, transport it to Houston, and then sell it to the Refining Division. The pipeline has unused capacity and can ship the 20,000 barrels per day at its variable cost of $1 per barrel without affecting the shipment of the 10,000 barrels of crude oil per day acquired under its existing long-term contract arrangement. Will Horizon Petroleum incur lower costs by purchasing crude oil from Gulfmex in Matamoros or by purchasing crude oil from the Houston supplier? Will the Refining Division show lower crude oil purchasing costs by acquiring oil from Gulfmex or by acquiring oil from its current Houston supplier?

The following analysis shows that Horizon Petroleum's operating income would be maximized by purchasing oil from Gulfmex. The analysis compares the incremental costs in both divisions under the two alternatives. The analysis assumes the fixed costs of the Transportation Division will be the same regardless of the alternative chosen. That is, the Transportation Division cannot save any of its fixed costs if it does not transport Gulfmex's 20,000 barrels of crude oil per day.

- **Alternative 1:** Buy 20,000 barrels from the Houston supplier at $85 per barrel. Total costs to Horizon Petroleum are 20,000 barrels × $85 per barrel = $1,700,000.
- **Alternative 2:** Buy 20,000 barrels in Matamoros at $79 per barrel and transport them to Houston at a variable cost of $1 per barrel. Total costs to Horizon Petroleum are 20,000 barrels × ($79 + $1) per barrel = $1,600,000.

There is a reduction in total costs to Horizon Petroleum of $100,000 ($1,700,000 − $1,600,000) by acquiring oil from Gulfmex.

Suppose the Transportation Division's transfer price to the Refining Division is 105% of full cost. The Refining Division will see its reported division costs increase if the crude oil is purchased from Gulfmex:

$$\text{Transfer price} = 1.05 \times \left(\begin{array}{c}\text{Purchase price}\\ \text{from}\\ \text{Gulfmex}\end{array} + \begin{array}{c}\text{Variable cost per unit}\\ \text{of Transportation}\\ \text{Division}\end{array} + \begin{array}{c}\text{Fixed cost per unit}\\ \text{of Transportation}\\ \text{Division}\end{array}\right)$$

$$= 1.05 \times (\$79 + \$1 + \$3) = 1.05 \times \$83 = \$87.15 \text{ per barrel}$$

- **Alternative 1:** Buy 20,000 barrels from Houston supplier at $85 per barrel. Total costs to Refining Division are 20,000 barrels × $85 per barrel = $1,700,000.
- **Alternative 2:** Buy 20,000 barrels from the Transportation Division of Horizon Petroleum that were purchased from Gulfmex. Total costs to Refining Division are 20,000 barrels × $87.15 per barrel = $1,743,000.

As a profit center, the Refining Division can maximize its short-run division operating income by purchasing from the Houston supplier at $1,700,000.

The Refining Division looks at each barrel that it obtains from the Transportation Division as a variable cost of $87.15 per barrel; if 10 barrels are transferred, it costs the Refining Division $871.50; if 100 barrels are transferred, it costs $8,715. In fact, the variable cost per barrel is $80 ($79 to purchase the oil from Gulfmex plus $1 to transport it to Houston). The remaining $7.15 ($87.15 − $80) per barrel is the Transportation Division's fixed cost and markup. *The full cost plus a markup transfer-pricing method causes the Refining Division to regard the fixed cost (and the 5% markup) of the Transportation Division as a variable cost and leads to goal incongruence.*

Should Horizon's top management interfere and force the Refining Division to buy from the Transportation Division? Top management interference would undercut the philosophy of decentralization, so Horizon's top management would probably view the decision by the Refining Division to purchase crude oil from external suppliers as an inevitable cost of decentralization and not interfere. Of course, some interference may occasionally be necessary to prevent costly blunders. But recurring interference and constraints would simply transform Horizon from a decentralized company into a centralized company.

What transfer price will promote goal congruence for both the Transportation and Refining divisions? The minimum transfer price is $80 per barrel. A transfer price below $80 does not provide the Transportation Division with an incentive to purchase crude oil from Gulfmex in Matamoros because it is below the Transportation Division's incremental costs. The maximum transfer price is $85 per barrel. A transfer price above $85 will cause the Refining Division to purchase crude oil from the external market rather than from the Transportation Division. A transfer price between the minimum and maximum transfer prices of $80 and $85 will promote goal congruence: Each division will increase its own reported operating income while increasing Horizon Petroleum's operating income if the Refining Division purchases crude oil from Gulfmex in Matamoros. For example, a transfer price based on the full costs of $83 without a markup will achieve goal congruence; the Transportation Division will show no operating income and will be evaluated as a cost center.

In the absence of a market-based transfer price, senior management at Horizon Petroleum cannot easily determine the profitability of the investment made in the Transportation Division and hence whether Horizon should keep or sell the pipeline. Furthermore, if the transfer price had been based on the actual costs of the Transportation Division, it would provide the division with no incentive to control costs. That's because all cost inefficiencies of the Transportation Division would get passed along as part of the actual full-cost transfer price. However, surveys indicate that, despite the limitations, managers generally prefer to use full-cost-based transfer prices. That's because these transfer prices represent relevant costs for long-run decisions, they facilitate external pricing based on variable and fixed costs, and they are the least costly to administer.

Using full-cost-based transfer prices requires an allocation of each subunit's fixed costs to products. Full-cost transfer pricing raises many issues. How are indirect costs allocated to products? Have the correct activities, cost pools, and cost-allocation bases been identified? Should the chosen fixed-cost rates be actual or budgeted? The issues here are similar to the issues that arise in allocating fixed costs, which were introduced in Chapter 14. Many companies determine the transfer price based on budgeted rates and practical capacity because it overcomes the problem of inefficiencies in actual costs and costs of unused capacity getting passed along to the buying division.

Variable-Cost Bases

Transferring 20,000 barrels of crude oil from the Transportation Division to the Refining Division at the variable cost of $80 per barrel achieves goal congruence, as shown in the preceding section. The Refining Division would buy from the Transportation Division because the Transportation Division's variable cost is less than the $85 price charged by external suppliers. Setting the transfer price equal to the variable cost has other benefits. Knowledge of the variable cost per barrel of crude oil is very helpful to the Refining Division for many decisions such as the short-run pricing decisions discussed in Chapters 11 and 12. However, at the $80-per-barrel transfer price, the Transportation Division would record an operating loss, and the Refining Division would show large profits because it would be charged only for the variable costs of the Transportation Division. One approach to addressing this problem is to have the Refining Division make a lump-sum transfer payment to cover fixed costs and generate some operating income for the Transportation Division while the Transportation Division continues to make transfers at variable cost. The fixed payment is the price the Refining Division pays for using the capacity of the

Transportation Division. The income earned by each division can then be used to evaluate the performance of each division and its manager.

Prorating the Difference Between Maximum and Minimum Transfer Prices

An alternative cost-based approach is for Horizon Petroleum to choose a transfer price that splits, on some fair basis, the $5 difference between the $85-per-barrel maximum transfer price the Refining Division is willing to pay and the $80-per-barrel minimum transfer price the Transportation Division wants to receive. Suppose Horizon Petroleum allocates the $5 difference on the basis of the budgeted variable costs of the two divisions. Using the data in Exhibit 22-1 (p. 776), variable costs are as follows:

Transportation Division's variable costs to transport 100 barrels of crude oil ($1 × 100)	$100
Refining Division's variable costs to refine 100 barrels of crude oil and produce 50 barrels of gasoline ($8 × 50)	400
Total variable costs	$500

Of the $5 difference, the Transportation Division gets to keep ($100 ÷ $500) × $5.00 = $1.00, and the Refining Division gets to keep ($400 ÷ $500) × $5.00 = $4.00. That is, the transfer price is $81 per barrel of crude oil ($79 purchase cost + $1 variable cost + $1 that the Transportation Division gets to keep). This approach is a budgeted variable-cost-plus transfer price. The "plus" indicates the setting of a transfer price above variable cost.

To decide on the $1 and $4 allocations of the $5 contribution to total company operating income per barrel, the divisions must share information about their variable costs. In effect, each division does not operate (at least for this transaction) in a totally decentralized manner. Furthermore, each division has an incentive to overstate its variable costs to receive a more-favorable transfer price.

Dual Pricing

There is seldom a single cost-based transfer price that simultaneously meets the criteria of promoting goal congruence, motivating management effort, evaluating subunit performance, and preserving subunit autonomy. As a result, some companies choose **dual pricing,** using two separate transfer-pricing methods to price each transfer from one subunit to another. An example of dual pricing arises when the selling division receives a full-cost-based price and the buying division pays the market price for the internally transferred products. Assume Horizon Petroleum purchases crude oil from Gulfmex in Matamoros at $79 per barrel. One way of recording the journal entry for the transfer between the Transportation Division and the Refining Division is:

1. Debit the Refining Division (the buying division) with the market-based transfer price of $85 per barrel of crude oil.
2. Credit the Transportation Division (the selling division) with the 105%-of-full-cost transfer price of $87.15 per barrel of crude oil.
3. Debit a corporate cost account for the $2.15 ($87.15 − $85) per barrel difference between the two transfer prices.

The dual-pricing system promotes goal congruence because it makes the Refining Division no worse off if it purchases the crude oil from the Transportation Division rather than from the external supplier at $85 per barrel. The Transportation Division receives a corporate subsidy. In dual pricing, the operating income for Horizon Petroleum as a whole is less than the sum of the operating incomes of the divisions.

Dual pricing is not widely used in practice even though it reduces the goal incongruence associated with a pure cost-based transfer-pricing method. One concern with dual pricing is that it leads to problems in computing the taxable income of subunits located in different tax jurisdictions, such as in our example, where the Transportation Division is taxed in

Mexico while the Refining Division is taxed in the United States. A second concern is that dual pricing insulates managers from the frictions of the marketplace because costs, not market prices, affect the revenues of the supplying division.

Negotiated Transfer Prices

Learning Objective 7

Describe the range over which two divisions negotiate the transfer price when there is unused capacity

. . . from variable cost to market price of the product transferred

Negotiated transfer prices result from a bargaining process between selling and buying subunits. Consider again Horizon Petroleum. As we saw earlier, the Transportation Division has unused capacity it can use to transport oil from Matamoros to Houston at an incremental cost of $80 per barrel of crude oil. Horizon Petroleum as a whole maximizes operating income if the Refining Division purchases crude oil from the Transportation Division rather than from the Houston market (incremental cost per barrel of $80 versus price per barrel of $85). Both divisions would be interested in transacting with each other (and achieve goal congruence) if the transfer price is between $80 and $85.

Where between $80 and $85 will the transfer price per barrel be set? Under a negotiated transfer price, the answer depends on several things: the bargaining strengths of the two divisions; information the Transportation Division has about the price minus incremental marketing costs of supplying crude oil to outside refineries; and the information the Refining Division has about its other available sources of crude oil. Negotiations become particularly sensitive because Horizon Petroleum can now evaluate each division's performance on the basis of division operating income. The price negotiated by the two divisions will, in general, have no specific relationship to either costs or market price. But cost and price information is often the starting point in the negotiation process.

Consider the following situation: Suppose the Refining Division receives an order to supply specially processed gasoline. The Refining Division will profit from this order only if the Transportation Division can supply crude oil at a price not exceeding $82 per barrel. Suppose the incremental cost to purchase and supply crude oil is $80 per barrel. In this case, the transfer price that would benefit both divisions must be greater than $80 but less than $82. Negotiations would allow the two divisions to achieve an acceptable transfer price. By contrast, a rule-based transfer price, such as a market-based price of $85 or a 105% of full-cost-based price of $87.15, would result in Horizon passing up a profitable opportunity.

A negotiated transfer price strongly preserves division autonomy. It also has the advantage that each division manager is motivated to put forth effort to increase division operating income. Its disadvantage is the time and energy spent on the negotiations.

A General Guideline for Transfer-Pricing Situations

Learning Objective 8

Apply a general guideline for determining a minimum transfer price

. . . incremental cost plus opportunity cost of supplying division

Exhibit 22-3 summarizes the properties of the different transfer-pricing methods using the criteria described in this chapter. As the exhibit indicates, it is difficult for a transfer-pricing method to meet all criteria. Market conditions, the goal of the transfer-pricing system, and the criteria of promoting goal congruence, motivating management effort, evaluating subunit performance, and preserving subunit autonomy (if desired) must all be considered simultaneously. The transfer price a company will eventually choose depends on the economic circumstances and the decision at hand. Surveys of company practice indicate that the full-cost-based transfer price is generally the most frequently used transfer-pricing method around the world, followed by market-based transfer price and negotiated transfer price.

The following general guideline (formula) is a helpful first step in setting a minimum transfer price in many situations:

$$\text{Minimum transfer price} = \begin{array}{c}\text{Incremental cost}\\ \text{per unit}\\ \text{incurred up}\\ \text{to the point of transfer}\end{array} + \begin{array}{c}\text{Opportunity cost}\\ \text{per unit}\\ \text{to the selling subunit}\end{array}$$

Exhibit 22-3

Comparison of Different Transfer-Pricing Methods

Criteria	Market-Based	Cost-Based	Negotiated
Achieves goal congruence	Yes, when markets are competitive	Often, but not always	Yes
Motivates management effort	Yes	Yes, when based on budgeted costs; less incentive to control costs if transfers are based on actual costs	Yes
Useful for evaluating subunit performance	Yes, when markets are competitive	Difficult unless transfer price exceeds full cost and even then is somewhat arbitrary	Yes, but transfer prices are affected by bargaining strengths of the buying and selling divisions
Preserves subunit autonomy	Yes, when markets are competitive	No, because it is rule-based	Yes, because it is based on negotiations between subunits
Other factors	Market may not exist, or markets may be imperfect or in distress	Useful for determining full cost of products and services; easy to implement	Bargaining and negotiations take time and may need to be reviewed repeatedly as conditions change

Incremental cost in this context means the additional cost of producing and transferring the product or service. Opportunity cost here is the maximum contribution margin forgone by the selling subunit if the product or service is transferred internally. For example, if the selling subunit is operating at capacity, the opportunity cost of transferring a unit internally rather than selling it externally is equal to the market price minus variable cost. That's because by transferring a unit internally, the subunit forgoes the contribution margin it could have obtained by selling the unit in the external market. We distinguish incremental cost from opportunity cost because the financial accounting system typically records incremental cost but not opportunity cost. The guideline measures a *minimum* transfer price because it represents the selling unit's cost of transferring the product. We illustrate the general guideline in some specific situations using data from Horizon Petroleum.

1. **A perfectly competitive market for the intermediate product exists, and the selling division has no unused capacity.** If the market for crude oil in Houston is perfectly competitive, the Transportation Division can sell all the crude oil it transports to the external market at $85 per barrel, and it will have no unused capacity. The Transportation Division's incremental cost (as shown in Exhibit 22-1, p. 776) is $73 per barrel (purchase cost of $72 per barrel plus variable transportation cost of $1 per barrel) for oil purchased under the long-term contract or $80 per barrel (purchase cost of $79 plus variable transportation cost of $1) for oil purchased at current market prices from Gulfmex. The Transportation Division's opportunity cost per barrel of transferring the oil internally is the contribution margin per barrel forgone by not selling the crude oil in the external market: $12 for oil purchased under the long-term contract (market price, $85, minus variable cost, $73) and $5 for oil purchased from Gulfmex (market price, $85, minus variable cost, $80). In either case,

$$\begin{aligned}\text{Minimum transfer price per barrel} &= \text{Incremental cost per barrel} + \text{Opportunity cost per barrel}\\ &= \$73 + \$12 = \$85\\ &\text{or}\\ &= \$80 + \$5 = \$85\end{aligned}$$

2. **An intermediate market exists that is not perfectly competitive, and the selling division has unused capacity.** In markets that are not perfectly competitive, capacity utilization can only be increased by decreasing prices. Unused capacity exists because decreasing prices is often not worthwhile—it decreases operating income.

If the Transportation Division has unused capacity, its opportunity cost of transferring the oil internally is zero because the division does not forgo any external sales or contribution margin from internal transfers. In this case,

$$\frac{\text{Minimum transfer price}}{\text{per barrel}} = \frac{\text{Incremental cost}}{\text{per barrel}} = \begin{array}{c}\text{\$73 per barrel for oil purchased under the}\\ \text{long-term contract or \$80 per barrel for}\\ \text{oil purchased from Gulfmex in Matamoros}\end{array}$$

In general, when markets are not perfectly competitive, the potential to influence demand and operating income through prices complicates the measurement of opportunity costs. The transfer price depends on constantly changing levels of supply and demand. There is not just one transfer price. Rather, the transfer prices for various quantities supplied and demanded depend on the incremental costs and opportunity costs of the units transferred.

3. **No market exists for the intermediate product.** This situation would occur for the Horizon Petroleum case if the crude oil transported by the Transportation Division could be used only by the Houston refinery (due to, say, its high tar content) and would not be wanted by external parties. Here, the opportunity cost of supplying crude oil internally is zero because the inability to sell crude oil externally means no contribution margin is forgone. For the Transportation Division of Horizon Petroleum, the minimum transfer price under the general guideline is the incremental cost per barrel (either $73 or $80). As in the previous case, any transfer price between the incremental cost and $85 will achieve goal congruence.

Multinational Transfer Pricing and Tax Considerations

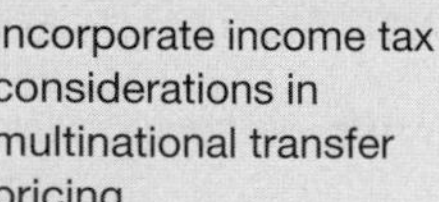

Incorporate income tax considerations in multinational transfer pricing

. . . set transfer prices to minimize tax payments to the extent permitted by tax authorities

Transfer prices often have tax implications. Tax factors include not only income taxes, but also payroll taxes, customs duties, tariffs, sales taxes, value-added taxes, environment-related taxes, and other government levies. Our aim here is to highlight tax factors, and in particular income taxes, as important considerations in determining transfer prices.

Consider the Horizon Petroleum data in Exhibit 22-2 (p. 777). Assume that the Transportation Division based in Mexico pays Mexican income taxes at 30% of operating income and that the Refining Division based in the United States pays income taxes at 20% of operating income. Horizon Petroleum would minimize its total income tax payments with the 105%-of-full-cost transfer-pricing method, as shown in the following table, because this method minimizes income reported in Mexico, where income is taxed at a higher rate than in the United States.

	Operating Income for 100 Barrels of Crude Oil			Income Tax on 100 Barrels of Crude Oil		
Transfer-Pricing Method	Transportation Division (Mexico) (1)	Refining Division (U.S.) (2)	Total (3) = (1) + (2)	Transportation Division (Mexico) (4) = 0.30 × (1)	Refining Division (U.S.) (5) = 0.20 × (2)	Total (6) = (4) + (5)
Market price	$900	$300	$1,200	$270	$ 60	$330
105% of full costs	380	820	1,200	114	164	278
Negotiated price	650	550	1,200	195	110	305

Income tax considerations raise additional issues. Tax issues may conflict with other objectives of transfer pricing. Suppose the market for crude oil in Houston is perfectly competitive. In this case, the market-based transfer price achieves goal congruence, provides incentives for management effort, and helps Horizon to evaluate the economic profitability of the Transportation Division. But it is costly from the perspective of income taxes. To minimize income taxes, Horizon would favor using 105% of full cost for tax reporting. Tax laws in the United States and Mexico, however, constrain this option. In particular, the Mexican tax authorities, aware of Horizon's incentives to minimize income

Concepts in Action

U.S. Internal Revenue Service, Japanese National Tax Agency, and Transfer-Pricing Disputes

Tax authorities and government officials across the globe pay close attention to taxes paid by multinational companies operating within their boundaries. At the heart of the issue are the transfer prices that companies use to transfer products from one country to another. Over time, the U.S. Internal Revenue Service (IRS) and the Japanese National Tax Agency (NTA) have been among the most active agencies pursuing international transfer-pricing disputes.

For example, in 1993, the IRS investigated and concluded that Nissan Motor Company had understated U.S. taxes by setting transfer prices on passenger cars and trucks imported from Japan at "unrealistically" high levels. Nissan argued that it had maintained low margins in the United States to increase long-run market share in a very competitive market. Eventually, Nissan agreed to pay the IRS $170 million, but the company suffered no loss. That's because the Japanese NTA refunded Nissan the full amount of the IRS payment.

Conversely, in May 1994, Japan's NTA alleged that Coca-Cola Corporation had underreported its taxable income in Japan by charging "excessive" transfer prices to its local subsidiary for materials and concentrate imported from the parent company and by levying "excessive" royalty payments on its Japanese subsidiary for the use of its brand name and sales and marketing expertise. The NTA pointed out that the royalties paid by Coca-Cola's Japanese subsidiary were higher than those paid by other companies in the same industry. It also said that the Japanese subsidiary paid royalties even for products it had developed on its own. The NTA imposed taxes and penalties of $150 million. Coca-Cola filed a complaint with the IRS, charging that the levying of the Japanese tax resulted in the same income being taxed twice, because Coca-Cola had already paid tax on this income in the United States. This complaint led to negotiations between Japanese and U.S. tax authorities to decide which country gets to tax Coca-Cola's Japanese income. In a 1998 compromise settlement, Japan's NTA reduced its tax levy against Coca-Cola from $150 million to $50 million. For its part, the IRS reduced Coca-Cola's income tax liability by the amount of taxes paid in Japan.

In 2000, Japan's NTA and the IRS had to settle another dispute regarding transfer prices. This time Coca-Cola's Japanese subsidiary had to record an additional $450 million in taxable income from 1993 through 1999, which meant that it owed approximately $170 million in back taxes and penalties. To avoid double taxation, the IRS refunded Coca-Cola the taxes paid in Japan.

Historically, disputes arose between governments over what constituted a "fair" transfer price because of the absence of an easily observable market price for the transferred product. In 2003, the United States and Japan signed a new tax treaty that, among other things, stipulates that future transfer-pricing disputes be addressed in accordance with the Organization for Economic Cooperation and Development's *Transfer Pricing Guidelines*, which advocate the use of a more transparent "arm's length" transfer-pricing protocol.

While this development has eased many previous U.S.-Japan disputes, the IRS and NTA remain actively engaged in transfer-pricing disputes with other nations. In 2006, U.K.-based pharmaceutical manufacturer GlaxoSmithKline agreed to pay the IRS $3.4 billion stemming from a transfer-pricing dispute regarding disputed profits from 1989 through 2000. Meanwhile, the Japanese NTA brought a $243 million action against Sony in 2006 for allegedly transferring part of the company's income subject to Japanese tax to its U.S. subsidiaries. While Sony paid the back taxes to the NTA, the company asked the IRS and NTA to hold talks to ensure Sony avoids double taxation on the revenue in question.

Sources: Adapted from C. Pass, "Transfer Pricing in Multinational Companies," *Management Accounting* (September 1994); "Coca-Cola Gets 10 Billion Yen Reprieve in Back Taxes," *Yomiuri Shimbun* (February 24, 1998); *Financial Times* (September 3, 1999); and *Daily Yomiuri* (February 24, 1998, and April 30, 2000); Morrison & Foerster, LLP, *New United States-Japan Tax Treaty Enters into Force: New Withholding Rates Take Effect on July 1, 2004*, April 2004; K. Reed, "GSK Pays 'Biggest Tax Settlement in US History'," *Accountancy Age*, September 11, 2006; and "Sony Ordered to Pay 27.9 Billion Yen in Extra Tax, to File Objection," *Kyodo News International*, July 1, 2006.

taxes by reducing the income reported in Mexico, would challenge any attempts to shift income to the Refining Division through an unreasonably low transfer price (see also Concepts in Action).

Section 482 of the U.S. Internal Revenue Code governs taxation of multinational transfer pricing. Section 482 requires that transfer prices between a company and its foreign division or subsidiary, for both tangible and intangible property, equal the price that would be charged by an unrelated third party in a comparable transaction. Regulations related to Section 482 recognize that transfer prices can be market-based or cost-plus-based, where the plus represents margins on comparable transactions.[2]

If the market for crude oil in Houston is perfectly competitive, Horizon would be required to calculate taxes using the market price of $85 for transfers from the Transportation Division to the Refining Division. Horizon might successfully argue that the transfer price should be set below the market price because the Transportation Division incurs no marketing and distribution costs when selling crude oil to the Refining Division. For example, if marketing and distribution costs equal $2 per barrel. Horizon could set the transfer price at $83 ($85 − $2) per barrel, the selling price net of marketing and distribution costs. Under the U.S. Internal Revenue Code, Horizon could obtain advanced approval of the transfer-pricing arrangements from the tax authorities, called an *advanced pricing agreement* (*APA*). The APA is a binding agreement for a specified number of years. The goal of the APA program is to avoid costly transfer-pricing disputes between taxpayers and tax authorities.

To meet multiple transfer-pricing objectives, such as minimizing income taxes, achieving goal congruence, and motivating management effort, a company may choose to keep one set of accounting records for tax reporting and a second set for internal management reporting. The difficulty here is that tax authorities may interpret two sets of books as meaning the company manipulated its reported taxable income to avoid tax payments. To avoid the problems caused by maintaining two sets of books, companies that choose tax-minimizing transfer-pricing strategies often use other management control techniques.

Consider a U.S. company that makes high-end data storage machines that it sells through its own sales organization in different countries. To minimize taxes, suppose the U.S. company sets a very high transfer price. Setting a high transfer price lowers the operating income of the sales organization in each country, even though the country sales organization has no say or control in determining the transfer price. To neutralize this negative effect on operating income, the company evaluates sales managers only on revenues minus marketing costs incurred in their respective countries. That is, the transfer prices incurred to acquire the product by the sales organizations in the countries are added back to the operating income of the sales organizations for performance-evaluation purposes. The difficulty with this approach is that it creates incentives for the sales organization in each country to maximize revenue per dollar of marketing costs rather than actual operating income per dollar of marketing costs. Corporate managers must then step in and specify product priorities based on the full product profitability information available to them.

Additional factors that arise in multinational transfer pricing include tariffs and customs duties levied on imports of products into a country. The issues here are similar to income tax considerations; companies will have incentives to lower transfer prices for products imported into a country to reduce tariffs and customs duties charged on those products.

In addition to the motivations for choosing transfer prices already described, multinational transfer prices are sometimes influenced by restrictions that some countries place on dividend- or income-related payments to parties outside their national borders. By increasing the prices of goods or services transferred into divisions in these countries, companies can seek to increase the cash paid out of these countries without violating dividend- or income-related restrictions.

---

[2] R. Feinschreiber (Ed.), *Transfer Pricing Handbook*, 3rd ed. (New York: John Wiley & Sons, 2002); L. Eden, *Taxing Multinationals: Transfer Pricing and Corporate Income Taxation in North America* (Toronto: University of Toronto Press, 1998); M. Levey, "Transfer Pricing—What Next?" *International Financial Law Review* (June 2001); J. Henshall, S. Wrappe, and K. Chung, "Transfer Pricing," *International Tax Review* (April 2001).

Problem for Self-Study

The Pillercat Corporation is a highly decentralized company. Each division manager has full authority for sourcing decisions and selling decisions. The Machining Division of Pillercat has been the major supplier of the 2,000 crankshafts that the Tractor Division needs each year.

The Tractor Division, however, has just announced that it plans to purchase all its crankshafts in the forthcoming year from two external suppliers at $200 per crankshaft. The Machining Division of Pillercat recently increased its selling price for the forthcoming year to $220 per unit (from $200 per unit in the current year).

Juan Gomez, manager of the Machining Division, feels that the 10% price increase is justified. It results from a higher depreciation charge on some new specialized equipment used to manufacture crankshafts and an increase in labor costs. Gomez wants the president of Pillercat Corporation to force the Tractor Division to buy all its crankshafts from the Machining Division at the price of $220. The following table summarizes the key data.

File Edit View Insert Format Tools Data Window Help

	A	B
1	Number of crankshafts purchased by Tractor Division	2,000
2	External supplier's market price per crankshaft	$ 200
3	Variable cost per crankshaft in Machining Division	$ 190
4	Fixed cost per crankshaft in Machining Division	$ 20

Required

1. Compute the advantage or disadvantage in terms of annual operating income to the Pillercat Corporation as a whole if the Tractor Division buys crankshafts internally from the Machining Division under each of the following cases:
   a. The Machining Division has no alternative use for the facilities used to manufacture crankshafts.
   b. The Machining Division can use the facilities for other production operations, which will result in annual cash operating savings of $29,000.
   c. The Machining Division has no alternative use for its facilities, and the external supplier drops the price to $185 per crankshaft.
2. As the president of Pillercat, how would you respond to Juan Gomez's request that you force the Tractor Division to purchase all of its crankshafts from the Machining Division? Would your response differ according to the three cases described in requirement 1? Explain.

Solution

1. Computations for the Tractor Division buying crankshafts internally for one year under cases **a**, **b**, and **c** are:

	A	B	C	D
1			Case	
2		a	b	c
3	Number of crankshafts purchased by Tractor Division	2,000	2,000	2,000
4	External supplier's market price per crankshaft	$ 200	$ 200	$ 185
5	Variable cost per crankshaft in Machining Division	$ 190	$ 190	$ 190
6	Opportunity costs of the Machining Division supplying crankshafts to the Tractor Division	-	$ 29,000	-
7				
8	Total purchase costs if buying from an external supplier			
9	(2,000 shafts x $200, $200, $185 per shaft)	$400,000	$400,000	$370,000
10	Incremental cost of buying from the Machining Division			
11	(2,000 shafts x $190 per shaft)	380,000	380,000	380,000
12	Total opportunity costs of the Machining Division	-	29,000	-
13	Total relevant costs	380,000	409,000	380,000
14	Annual operating income advantage (disadvantage) to			
15	Pillercat of buying from the Machining Division	$ 20,000	$ (9,000)	$ (10,000)

The general guideline that was introduced in the chapter (p. 782) as a first step in setting a transfer price can be used to highlight the alternatives:

	A	B	C	D	E	F	G
1	Case	Incremental Cost per Unit Incurred to Point of Transfer	+	Opportunity Cost per Unit to the Supplying Division	=	Transfer Price	External Market Price
2	a	$190	+	$0	=	$190.00	$200
3	b	$190	+	$14.50[a]	=	$204.50	$200
4	c	$190	+	$0	=	$190.00	$185
5							
6	[a]Opportunity cost	=	Total opportunity	÷	Number of	= $29,000 ÷ 2,000 = $14.50	
7	per unit		costs		crankshafts		

Comparing transfer price to external-market price, the Tractor Division will maximize annual operating income of Pillercat Corporation as a whole by purchasing from the Machining Division in case **a** and by purchasing from the external supplier in cases **b** and **c**.

2. Pillercat Corporation is a highly decentralized company. If no forced transfer were made, the Tractor Division would use an external supplier, a decision that would be in the best interest of the company as a whole in cases **b** and **c** of requirement 1 but not in case **a**.

   Suppose in case **a**, the Machining Division refuses to meet the price of $200. This decision means that the company will be $20,000 worse off in the short run. Should top management interfere and force a transfer at $200? This interference would undercut the philosophy of decentralization. Many top managements would not interfere because they would view the $20,000 as an inevitable cost of a suboptimal decision that can occur under decentralization. But how high must this cost be before the temptation to interfere would be irresistible? $30,000? $40,000?

   Any top management interference with lower-level decision making weakens decentralization. Of course, Pillercat's management may occasionally interfere to prevent costly mistakes. But recurring interference and constraints would hurt Pillercat's attempts to operate as a decentralized company.

Decision Points

The following question-and-answer format summarizes the chapter's learning objectives. Each decision presents a key question related to a learning objective. The guidelines are the answer to that question.

Decision	Guidelines
1. What is a management control system and how should it be designed?	A management control system is a means of gathering and using information to aid and coordinate the planning and control decisions throughout the organization and to guide the behavior of managers and other employees. Effective management control systems (a) are closely aligned to the organization's strategy, (b) support the organizational responsibilities of individual managers, and (c) motivate managers and other employees to give effort to achieve the organization's goals.
2. What are the benefits and costs of decentralization?	The benefits of decentralization include (a) greater responsiveness to local needs, (b) gains from faster decision making, (c) increased motivation of subunit managers, (d) greater management development and learning, and (e) sharpened focus of subunit managers. The costs of decentralization include (a) suboptimal decision making, (b) excessive focus on the subunit rather than the company as a whole, (c) increased costs of information gathering, and (d) duplication of activities.
3. What is a transfer price, and what is it intended to achieve?	A transfer price is the price one subunit charges for a product or service supplied to another subunit of the same organization. Transfer prices seek to (a) promote goal congruence, (b) motivate management effort, (c) help evaluate subunit performance, and (d) preserve subunit autonomy (if desired).
4. What methods can be used to calculate transfer prices?	Transfer prices can be (a) market-based, (b) cost-based, or (c) negotiated. Different transfer-pricing methods produce different revenues and costs for individual subunits, and hence, different operating incomes for the subunits.
5. What transfer price should be used if the market for the product to be transferred is perfectly competitive?	In perfectly competitive markets, there is no unused capacity, and division managers can buy and sell as much of a product or service as they want at the market price. Setting the transfer price at the market price motivates division managers to transact internally and to take exactly the same actions as they would if they were transacting in the external market.
6. What problems can arise when full cost plus a markup is used as a transfer price?	A transfer price based on full cost plus a markup may lead to suboptimal decisions because it leads the buying division to regard the fixed costs and the markup of the selling division as a variable cost. The buying division may then purchase products from an external supplier expecting savings in costs that, in fact, will not occur.
7. What is the range over which two divisions will negotiate a transfer price when there is unused capacity?	When there is unused capacity, the transfer-price range for negotiations generally lies between the minimum price at which the selling division is willing to sell (its variable cost per unit) and the maximum price the buying division is willing to pay (the price at which the product is available from external suppliers).
8. What is the general guideline for determining a minimum transfer price?	The general guideline states that the minimum transfer price equals the incremental cost per unit incurred up to the point of transfer plus the opportunity cost per unit to the selling division resulting from transferring products or services internally.
9. What are the income tax considerations when determining transfer prices?	Transfer prices can reduce income tax payments by reporting more income in low-tax-rate countries and less income in high-tax-rate countries. However, tax regulations of different countries restrict the transfer prices that companies can use.

TERMS TO LEARN

This chapter and the Glossary at the end of the book contain definitions of:

autonomy (**p. 771**)
decentralization (**p. 771**)
dual pricing (**p. 781**)
dysfunctional decision making (**p. 772**)
effort (**p. 770**)
goal congruence (**p. 770**)
incongruent decision making (**p. 772**)
intermediate product (**p. 774**)
management control system (**p. 769**)
motivation (**p. 770**)
perfectly competitive market (**p. 777**)
suboptimal decision making (**p. 772**)
transfer price (**p. 774**)

ASSIGNMENT MATERIAL

Questions

22-1 What is a management control system?

22-2 Describe three criteria you would use to evaluate whether a management control system is effective.

22-3 What is the relationship among motivation, goal congruence, and effort?

22-4 Name three benefits and two costs of decentralization.

22-5 "Organizations typically adopt a consistent decentralization or centralization philosophy across all their business functions." Do you agree? Explain.

22-6 "Transfer pricing is confined to profit centers." Do you agree? Explain.

22-7 What are the three methods for determining transfer prices?

22-8 What properties should transfer-pricing systems have?

22-9 "All transfer-pricing methods give the same division operating income." Do you agree? Explain.

22-10 Under what conditions is a market-based transfer price optimal?

22-11 What is one potential limitation of full-cost-based transfer prices?

22-12 Give two reasons why the dual-pricing system of transfer pricing is not widely used.

22-13 "Cost and price information play no role in negotiated transfer prices." Do you agree? Explain.

22-14 "Under the general guideline for transfer pricing, the minimum transfer price will vary depending on whether the supplying division has unused capacity or not." Do you agree? Explain.

22-15 How should managers consider income tax issues when choosing a transfer-pricing method?

Exercises

22-16 Management control systems, balanced scorecard. Greystone Corporation manufactures stone tiles for kitchen counters and floors. Its strategy is to manufacture high quality products at reasonable prices, and to rapidly deliver products following sales. Greystone sells to both hardware stores and contractors. To avoid holding large inventories of finished goods, Greystone manufactures products based on orders from customers. The factory set up enables workers to perform multiple functions, including receiving orders, running different machines, inspecting for quality, packaging, and shipping the final product.

Required Given Greystone's strategy, describe the financial and nonfinancial measures that you would include in its balanced scorecard-based management control system.

22-17 Cost centers, profit centers, decentralization, transfer prices. Fenster Corporation manufactures windows with wood and metal frames. Fenster has three departments: Glass, Wood, and Metal. The Glass Department makes the window glass and sends it to either the Wood or Metal Department where the glass is framed. The window is then sold. Upper management sets the production schedules for the three departments and evaluates them on output quantity, cost variances, and product quality.

Required

1. Are the three departments cost centers, revenue centers, or profit centers?
2. Are the three departments centralized or decentralized?
3. Can a centralized department be a profit center? Why or why not?
4. Suppose the upper management of Fenster Corporation decides to let the three departments set their own production schedules, buy and sell products in the external market, and have Wood and Metal negotiate with Glass for the glass panes using a transfer price.
   a. Will this change your answers to requirements 1 and 2?
   b. How would you recommend upper management evaluate the three departments if this change is made?

22-18 Decentralization, goal congruence, responsibility centers. Hexton Chemicals consists of seven independent operating divisions. The operating divisions are assisted by a number of support groups, such as R&D, human resources, and environmental management. The environmental-management group consists of 20 environmental engineers. These engineers must seek business from the operating divisions—that is, the projects they work on must be mutually agreed to and paid for by one of the operating divisions. Under Hexton's rules, the environmental group is required to charge the operating divisions for environmental services at cost.

Required

1. Is the environmental-management group centralized or decentralized?
2. What type of responsibility center is the environmental-management group?
3. What benefits and problems do you see in structuring the environmental-management group in this way? Does it lead to goal congruence and motivation? Explain.

22-19 Multinational transfer pricing, effect of alternative transfer-pricing methods, global income tax minimization. User Friendly Computer, Inc., with headquarters in San Francisco, manufactures and sells a desktop computer. User Friendly has three divisions, each of which is located in a different country:

a. China Division—manufactures memory devices and keyboards
b. South Korea Division—assembles desktop computers using internally manufactured parts and memory devices and keyboards from the China Division
c. U.S. Division—packages and distributes desktop computers

Each division is run as a profit center. The costs for the work done in each division for a single desktop computer are as follows:

China Division:	Variable cost = 1,000 yuan
	Fixed cost = 1,800 yuan
South Korea Division:	Variable cost = 360,000 won
	Fixed cost = 480,000 won
U.S. Division:	Variable cost = $100
	Fixed cost = $200

- Chinese income tax rate on China Division's operating income: 40%
- South Korean income tax rate on South Korea Division's operating income: 20%
- U.S. income tax rate on U.S. Division's operating income: 30%

Each desktop computer is sold to retail outlets in the United States for $3,200. Assume that the current foreign exchange rates are:

8 yuan = $1 U.S.
1,200 won = $1 U.S.

Both the China and the South Korea divisions sell part of their production under a private label. The China Division sells the comparable memory/keyboard package used in each User Friendly desktop computer to a Chinese manufacturer for 3,600 yuan. The South Korea Division sells the comparable desktop computer to a South Korean distributor for 1,560,000 won.

Required

1. Calculate the after-tax operating income per unit earned by each division under the following transfer-pricing methods: (a) market price, (b) 200% of full cost, and (c) 300% of variable cost. (Income taxes are not included in the computation of the cost-based transfer prices.)
2. Which transfer-pricing method(s) will maximize the after-tax operating income per unit of User Friendly Computer?

22-20 Transfer-pricing methods, goal congruence. British Columbia Lumber has a Raw Lumber Division and a Finished Lumber Division. The variable costs are:

- Raw Lumber Division: $100 per 100 board-feet of raw lumber
- Finished Lumber Division: $125 per 100 board-feet of finished lumber

Assume that there is no board-feet loss in processing raw lumber into finished lumber. Raw lumber can be sold at $200 per 100 board-feet. Finished lumber can be sold at $275 per 100 board-feet.

Required

1. Should British Columbia Lumber process raw lumber into its finished form? Show your calculations.
2. Assume that internal transfers are made at 110% of variable cost. Will each division maximize its division operating-income contribution by adopting the action that is in the best interest of British Columbia Lumber as a whole? Explain.
3. Assume that internal transfers are made at market prices. Will each division maximize its division operating-income contribution by adopting the action that is in the best interest of British Columbia Lumber as a whole? Explain.

22-21 Effect of alternative transfer-pricing methods on division operating income. (CMA, adapted) Ajax Corporation has two divisions. The Mining Division makes toldine, which is then transferred to the Metals Division. The toldine is further processed by the Metals Division and is sold to customers at a price of $150 per unit. The Mining Division is currently required by Ajax to transfer its total yearly output of 200,000 units of toldine to the Metals Division at 110% of full manufacturing cost. Unlimited quantities of toldine can be purchased and sold on the outside market at $90 per unit.

The following table gives the manufacturing cost per unit in the Mining and Metals divisions for 2009:

	Mining Division	Metals Division
Direct material cost	$12	$ 6
Direct manufacturing labor cost	16	20
Manufacturing overhead cost	32[a]	25[b]
Total manufacturing cost per unit	$60	$51

[a] Manufacturing overhead costs in the Mining Division are 25% fixed and 75% variable.
[b] Manufacturing overhead costs in the Metals Division are 60% fixed and 40% variable.

Required

1. Calculate the operating incomes for the Mining and Metals divisions for the 200,000 units of toldine transferred under the following transfer-pricing methods: (a) market price and (b) 110% of full manufacturing cost.
2. Suppose Ajax rewards each division manager with a bonus, calculated as 1% of division operating income (if positive). What is the amount of bonus that will be paid to each division manager under the transfer-pricing methods in requirement 1? Which transfer-pricing method will each division manager prefer to use?
3. What arguments would Brian Jones, manager of the Mining Division, make to support the transfer-pricing method that he prefers?

22-22 Transfer pricing, general guideline, goal congruence. (CMA, adapted). Quest Motors, Inc., operates as a decentralized multidivision company. The Tivo Division of Quest Motors purchases most of its airbags from the Airbag Division. The Airbag Division's incremental cost for manufacturing the airbags is $90 per unit. The Airbag Division is currently working at 80% of capacity. The current market price of the airbags is $125 per unit.

Required

1. Using the general guideline presented in the chapter, what is the minimum price at which the Airbag Division would sell airbags to the Tivo Division?
2. Suppose that Quest Motors requires that whenever divisions with unused capacity sell products internally, they must do so at the incremental cost. Evaluate this transfer-pricing policy using the criteria of goal congruence, evaluating division performance, motivating management effort, and preserving division autonomy.
3. If the two divisions were to negotiate a transfer price, what is the range of possible transfer prices? Evaluate this negotiated transfer-pricing policy using the criteria of goal congruence, evaluating division performance, motivating management effort, and preserving division autonomy.
4. Do you prefer the transfer-pricing policy in requirement 2 or requirement 3? Explain your answer briefly.

22-23 Multinational transfer pricing, global tax minimization. The Mornay Company manufactures telecommunications equipment at its plant in Toledo, Ohio. The company has marketing divisions throughout the world. A Mornay marketing division in Vienna, Austria, imports 1,000 units of Product 4A36 from the United States. The following information is available:

U.S. income tax rate on the U.S. division's operating income	40%
Austrian income tax rate on the Austrian division's operating income	44%
Austrian import duty	10%
Variable manufacturing cost per unit of Product 4A36	$350
Full manufacturing cost per unit of Product 4A36	$500
Selling price (net of marketing and distribution costs) in Austria	$750

Suppose the U.S. and Austrian tax authorities only allow transfer prices that are between the full manufacturing cost per unit of $500 and a market price of $650, based on comparable imports into Austria. The Austrian import duty is charged on the price at which the product is transferred into Austria. Any import duty paid to the Austrian authorities is a deductible expense for calculating Austrian income taxes due.

Required

1. Calculate the after-tax operating income earned by the U.S. and Austrian divisions from transferring 1,000 units of Product 4A36 (a) at full manufacturing cost per unit and (b) at market price of comparable imports. (Income taxes are not included in the computation of the cost-based transfer prices.)

2. Which transfer price should the Mornay Company select to minimize the total of company import duties and income taxes? Remember that the transfer price must be between the full manufacturing cost per unit of $500 and the market price of $650 of comparable imports into Austria. Explain your reasoning.

22-24 Multinational transfer pricing, goal congruence (continuation of 22-23). Suppose that the U.S. division could sell as many units of Product 4A36 as it makes at $600 per unit in the U.S. market, net of all marketing and distribution costs.

Required

1. From the viewpoint of the Mornay Company as a whole, would after-tax operating income be maximized if it sold the 1,000 units of Product 4A36 in the United States or in Austria? Show your computations.
2. Suppose division managers act autonomously to maximize their division's after-tax operating income. Will the transfer price calculated in requirement 2 of Exercise 22-23 result in the U.S. division manager taking the actions determined to be optimal in requirement 1 of this exercise? Explain.
3. What is the minimum transfer price that the U.S. division manager would agree to? Does this transfer price result in the Mornay Company as a whole paying more import duty and taxes than the answer to requirement 2 of Exercise 22-23? If so, by how much?

22-25 Transfer-pricing dispute. The Allison-Chambers Corporation, manufacturer of tractors and other heavy farm equipment, is organized along decentralized product lines, with each manufacturing division operating as a separate profit center. Each division manager has been delegated full authority on all decisions involving the sale of that division's output both to outsiders and to other divisions of Allison-Chambers. Division C has in the past always purchased its requirement of a particular tractor-engine component from Division A. However, when informed that Division A is increasing its selling price to $150, Division C's manager decides to purchase the engine component from external suppliers.

Division C can purchase the component for $135 per unit in the open market. Division A insists that, because of the recent installation of some highly specialized equipment and the resulting high depreciation charges, it will not be able to earn an adequate return on its investment unless it raises its price. Division A's manager appeals to top management of Allison-Chambers for support in the dispute with Division C and supplies the following operating data:

C's annual purchases of the tractor-engine component	1,000 units
A's variable cost per unit of the tractor-engine component	$120
A's fixed cost per unit of the tractor-engine component	$ 20

Required

1. Assume that there are no alternative uses for internal facilities of Division A. Determine whether the company as a whole will benefit if Division C purchases the component from external suppliers for $135 per unit. What should the transfer price for the component be set at so that division managers acting in their own divisions' best interests take actions that are in the best interest of the company as a whole?
2. Assume that internal facilities of Division A would not otherwise be idle. By not producing the 1,000 units for Division C, Division A's equipment and other facilities would be used for other production operations that would result in annual cash-operating savings of $18,000. Should Division C purchase from external suppliers? Show your computations.
3. Assume that there are no alternative uses for Division A's internal facilities and that the price from outsiders drops $20. Should Division C purchase from external suppliers? What should the transfer price for the component be set at so that division managers acting in their own divisions' best interests take actions that are in the best interest of the company as a whole?

22-26 Transfer-pricing problem (continuation of 22-25). Refer to Exercise 22-25. Assume that Division A can sell the 1,000 units to other customers at $155 per unit, with variable marketing cost of $5 per unit.

Required

Determine whether Allison-Chambers will benefit if Division C purchases the 1,000 units from external suppliers at $135 per unit. Show your computations.

Problems

22-27 General guideline, transfer pricing. The Shamrock Company manufactures and sells television sets. Its Assembly Division (AD) buys television screens from the Screen Division (SD) and assembles the TV sets. The SD, which is operating at capacity, incurs an incremental manufacturing cost of $80 per screen. The SD can sell all its output to the outside market at a price of $120 per screen, after incurring a variable marketing and distribution cost of $5 per screen. If the AD purchases screens from outside suppliers at a price of $120 per screen, it will incur a variable purchasing cost of $3 per screen. Shamrock's division managers can act autonomously to maximize their own division's operating income.

Required

1. What is the minimum transfer price at which the SD manager would be willing to sell screens to the AD?
2. What is the maximum transfer price at which the AD manager would be willing to purchase screens from the SD?

3. Now suppose that the SD can sell only 80% of its output capacity of 10,000 screens per month on the open market. Capacity cannot be reduced in the short run. The AD can assemble and sell more than 10,000 TV sets per month.
   a. What is the minimum transfer price at which the SD manager would be willing to sell screens to the AD?
   b. From the point of view of Shamrock's management, how much of the SD output should be transferred to the AD?
   c. What transfer-pricing policy will achieve the outcome desired in requirement 3b?

22-28 Pertinent transfer price. Europa, Inc., has two divisions, A and B, which manufacture expensive bicycles. Division A produces the bicycle frame, and Division B assembles the rest of the bicycle onto the frame. There is a market for both the subassembly and the final product. Each division has been designated as a profit center. The transfer price for the subassembly has been set at the long-run average market price. The following data are available for each division:

Selling price for final product	$300
Long-run average selling price for intermediate product	200
Incremental cost per unit for completion in Division B	150
Incremental cost per unit in Division A	120

The manager of Division B has made the following calculation:

Selling price for final product		$300
Transferred-in cost per unit (market)	$200	
Incremental cost per unit for completion	150	350
Contribution (loss) on product		$(50)

Required

1. Should transfers be made to Division B if there is no unused capacity in Division A? Is the market price the correct transfer price? Show your computations.
2. Assume that Division A's maximum capacity for this product is 1,000 units per month and sales to the intermediate market are now 800 units. Should 200 units be transferred to Division B? At what transfer price? Assume that for a variety of reasons, Division A will maintain the $200 selling price indefinitely. That is, Division A is not considering lowering the price to outsiders even if idle capacity exists.
3. Suppose Division A quoted a transfer price of $150 for up to 200 units. What would be the contribution to the company as a whole if a transfer were made? As manager of Division B, would you be inclined to buy at $150? Explain.

22-29 Pricing in imperfect markets (continuation of 22-28). Refer to Problem 22-28.

Required

1. Suppose the manager of Division A has the option of (a) cutting the external price to $195, with the certainty that sales will rise to 1,000 units or (b) maintaining the external price of $200 for the 800 units and transferring the 200 units to Division B at a price that would produce the same operating income for Division A. What transfer price would produce the same operating income for Division A? Is that price consistent with that recommended by the general guideline in the chapter so that the resulting decision would be desirable for the company as a whole?
2. Suppose that if the selling price for the intermediate product were dropped to $195, sales to external parties could be increased to 900 units. Division B wants to acquire as many as 200 units if the transfer price is acceptable. For simplicity, assume that there is no external market for the final 100 units of Division A's capacity.
   a. Using the general guideline, what is (are) the minimum transfer price(s) that should lead to the correct economic decision? Ignore performance-evaluation considerations.
   b. Compare the total contributions under the alternatives to show why the transfer price(s) recommended lead(s) to the optimal economic decision.

22-30 Effect of alternative transfer-pricing methods on division operating income. Crango Products is a cranberry cooperative that operates two divisions: a Harvesting Division and a Processing Division. Currently, all of Harvesting's output is converted into cranberry juice by the Processing Division, and the juice is sold to large beverage companies that produce cranberry juice blends. The Processing Division has a yield of 500 gallons of juice per 1,000 pounds of cranberries. Cost and market price data for the two divisions are as follows:

	A	B	C	D	E
1	**Harvesting Division**			**Processing Division**	
2	Variable cost per pound of cranberries	$0.10		Variable processing cost per gallon of juice produced	$0.20
3	Fixed cost per pound of cranberries	$0.25		Fixed cost per gallon of juice produced	$0.40
4	Selling price per pound of cranberries in outside market	$0.60		Selling price per gallon of juice	$2.10

If you want to use Excel to solve this problem, go to the Excel Lab at **www.prenhall.com/horngren/cost13e** and download the template for Problem 22-30.

Required

1. Compute Crango's operating income from harvesting 400,000 pounds of cranberries during June 2009 and processing them into juice.
2. Crango rewards its division managers with a bonus equal to 5% of operating income. Compute the bonus earned by each division manager in June 2009 for each of the following transfer pricing methods:
   a. 200% of full cost
   b. Market price
3. Which transfer-pricing method will each division manager prefer? How might Crango resolve any conflicts that may arise on the issue of transfer pricing?

22-31 Goal-congruence problems with cost-plus transfer-pricing methods, dual-pricing system (continuation of 22-30). Assume that Pat Borges, CEO of Crango, had mandated a transfer price equal to 200% of full cost. Now he decides to decentralize some management decisions and sends around a memo that states: "Effective immediately, each division of Crango is free to make its own decisions regarding the purchase of direct materials and the sale of finished products."

If you want to use Excel to solve this problem, go to the Excel Lab at **www.prenhall.com/horngren/cost13e** and download the template for Problem 22-30.

Required

1. Give an example of a goal-congruence problem that will arise if Crango continues to use a transfer price of 200% of full cost and Borges's decentralization policy is adopted.
2. Borges feels that a dual transfer-pricing policy will improve goal congruence. He suggests that transfers out of the Harvesting Division be made at 200% of full cost and transfers into the Processing Division be made at market price. Compute the operating income of each division under this dual transfer pricing method when 400,000 pounds of cranberries are harvested during June 2009 and processed into juice.
3. Why is the sum of the division operating incomes computed in requirement 2 different from Crango's operating income from harvesting and processing 400,000 pounds of cranberries?
4. Suggest two problems that may arise if Crango implements the dual transfer prices described in requirement 2.

22-32 Multinational transfer pricing, global tax minimization. Industrial Diamonds, Inc., based in Los Angeles, has two divisions:

- South African Mining Division, which mines a rich diamond vein in South Africa
- U.S Processing Division, which polishes raw diamonds for use in industrial cutting tools

The Processing Division's yield is 50%: It takes 2 pounds of raw diamonds to produce 1 pound of top-quality polished industrial diamonds. Although all of the Mining Division's output of 4,000 pounds of raw diamonds is sent for processing in the United States, there is also an active market for raw diamonds in South Africa. The foreign exchange rate is 7 ZAR (South African Rand) = $1 U.S. The following information is known about the two divisions:

	A	B	C
1	**South African Mining Division**		
2	Variable cost per pound of raw diamonds	560	ZAR
3	Fixed cost per pound of raw diamonds	1,540	ZAR
4	Market price per pound of raw diamonds	3,150	ZAR
5	Tax rate	18%	
6			
7	**U.S. Processing Division**		
8	Variable cost per pound of polished diamonds	150	U.S. dollars
9	Fixed cost per pound of polished diamonds	700	U.S. dollars
10	Market price per pound of polished diamonds	5,000	U.S. dollars
11	Tax rate	30%	

If you want to use Excel to solve this problem, go to the Excel Lab at **www.prenhall.com/horngren/cost13e** and download the template for Problem 22-32.

Required

1. Compute the annual pre-tax operating income, in U.S. dollars, of each division under the following transfer-pricing methods: (a) 200% of full cost and (b) market price.
2. Compute the after-tax operating income, in U.S. dollars, for each division under the transfer-pricing methods in requirement 1. (Income taxes are not included in the computation of cost-based transfer price, and Industrial Diamonds does not pay U.S. income tax on income already taxed in South Africa.)
3. If the two division managers are compensated based on after-tax division operating income, which transfer-pricing method will each prefer? Which transfer-pricing method will maximize the total after-tax operating income of Industrial Diamonds?
4. In addition to tax minimization, what other factors might Industrial Diamonds consider in choosing a transfer-pricing method?

22-33 International transfer pricing, taxes, goal congruence. Argone Division of Gemini Corporation is located in the United States. Its effective income tax rate is 20%. Another division of Gemini, Calcia, is located in Canada, where the income tax rate is 38%. Calcia manufactures, among other things, an intermediate product for Argone called IP-2007. Calcia operates at capacity and makes 20,000 units of IP-2007 for Argone each period, at a variable cost of $80 per unit. Assume that there are no outside customers for IP-2007. Because the IP-2007 must be shipped from Canada to the United States, it costs Calcia an additional $2 per unit to ship the IP-2007 to Argone. There are no direct fixed costs for IP-2007. Calcia also manufactures other products.

A product similar to IP-2007 that Argone could use as a substitute is available in the United States for $100 per unit.

Required

1. What is the minimum and maximum transfer price that would be acceptable to Argone and Calcia for IP-2007, and why?
2. What transfer price would minimize income taxes for Gemini Corporation as a whole? Would Calcia and Argone want to be evaluated on operating income using this transfer price?
3. Suppose Gemini uses the transfer price from requirement 2, and each division is evaluated on its own after-tax division operating income. Now suppose Calcia has an opportunity to sell 10,000 units of IP-2007 to an outside customer for $95 each. Calcia will not incur shipping costs because the customer is nearby and offers to pay for shipping. Assume that if Calcia accepts the special order, Argone will have to buy 10,000 units of the substitute product in the United States at $100 per unit.
   a. Will accepting the special order maximize after-tax operating income for Gemini Corporation as a whole?
   b. Will Argone want Calcia to accept this special order? Why or why not?
   c. Will Calcia want to accept this special order? Explain.
   d. Suppose Gemini Corporation wants to operate in a decentralized manner. What transfer price should Gemini set for IP-2007 so that each division acting in its own best interest takes actions with respect to the special order that are in the best interests of Gemini Corporation as a whole?

22-34 Transfer pricing, goal congruence. The Orsilo Corporation makes and sells 10,000 multisystem music players each year. Its Assembly Division purchases components from other divisions of Orsilo or from external suppliers and assembles the multisystem music players. In particular, the Assembly Division can purchase the CD player from the Compact Disc Division of Orsilo or from Johnson Corporation. Johnson agrees to meet all of Orsilo's quality requirements and is currently negotiating with the Assembly Division to supply 10,000 CD players at a price between $38 and $45 per CD player.

A critical component of the CD player is the head mechanism that reads the disc. To ensure the quality of its multisystem music players, Orsilo requires that if Johnson wins the contract to supply CD players, it must purchase the head mechanism from Orsilo's Compact Disc Division for $20 each.

The Compact Disc Division can manufacture at most 12,000 CD players annually. It also manufactures as many additional head mechanisms as can be sold. The incremental cost of manufacturing the head mechanism is $15 per unit. The incremental cost of manufacturing a CD player (including the cost of the head mechanism) is $25 per unit, and any number of CD players can be sold for $35 each in the external market.

Required

1. What are the incremental costs minus revenues from sale to external buyers for the company as a whole if the Compact Disc Division transfers 10,000 CD players to the Assembly Division and sells the remaining 2,000 CD players on the external market?
2. What are the incremental costs minus revenues from sales to external buyers for the company as a whole if the Compact Disc Division sells 12,000 CD players on the external market and the Assembly Division accepts Johnson's offer at (a) $38 per CD player or (b) $45 per CD player?
3. What is the minimum transfer price per CD player at which the Compact Disc Division would be willing to transfer 10,000 CD players to the Assembly Division?
4. Suppose that the transfer price is set to the minimum computed in requirement 3 plus $1, and the division managers at Orsilo are free to make their own profit-maximizing sourcing and selling decisions.

Now, Johnson offers 10,000 CD players for $40.50 each.

a. What decisions will the managers of the Compact Disc Division and Assembly Division make?

b. Are these decisions optimal for Orsilo as a whole?

c. Based on this exercise, at what price would you recommend the transfer price be set?

22-35 Transfer pricing, goal congruence, ethics. Whengon Manufacturing makes electronic hearing aids. Department A manufactures 10,000 units of part HR-7 and Department B uses this part to make the finished product. HR-7 is a specific part for a patented product that cannot be purchased or sold outside of Whengon, so there is no outside demand for this part. Variable costs of making HR-7 are $12 per unit. Fixed costs directly traced to HR-7 equal $30,000.

Upper management has asked the two departments to negotiate a transfer price for HR-7. The manager of Department A, Henry Lasker, is worried that Department B will insist on using variable cost as the transfer price because Department A has excess capacity. Lasker asks Joe Bedford, his management accountant, to show more costs as variable costs and fewer costs as fixed costs. Lasker says, "There are gray areas when distinguishing between fixed and variable costs. I think the variable cost of making HR-7 is $14 per unit."

Required

1. If Lasker is correct, calculate the benefit to Department A from showing a variable cost of $14 per unit rather than $12 per unit.
2. What cost-based transfer price mechanism would you propose for HR-7? Explain briefly.
3. Evaluate whether Lasker's comment to Bedford about the variable cost of HR-7 is ethical. Would it be ethical for Bedford to revise the variable cost per unit? What steps should Bedford take to resolve the situation?

Collaborative Learning Problem

22-36 Transfer pricing, utilization of capacity. (J. Patell, adapted) The California Instrument Company (CIC) consists of the Semiconductor Division and the Process-Control Division, each of which operates as an independent profit center. The Semiconductor Division employs craftsmen who produce two different electronic components: the new high-performance Super-chip and an older product called Okay-chip. These two products have the following cost characteristics:

	Super-chip	Okay-chip
Direct materials	$ 2	$1
Direct manufacturing labor, 2 hours × $14; 0.5 hour × $14	28	7

Annual overhead in the Semiconductor Division totals $400,000, all fixed. Due to the high skill level necessary for the craftsmen, the Semiconductor Division's capacity is set at 50,000 hours per year.

One customer orders a maximum of 15,000 Super-chips per year, at a price of $60 per chip. If CIC cannot meet this entire demand, the customer curtails its own production. The rest of the Semiconductor Division's capacity is devoted to the Okay-chip, for which there is unlimited demand at $12 per chip.

The Process-Control Division produces only one product, a process-control unit, with the following cost structure:

- Direct materials (circuit board): $60
- Direct manufacturing labor (5 hours × $10): $50

Fixed overhead costs of the Process-Control Division are $80,000 per year. The current market price for the control unit is $132 per unit.

A joint research project has just revealed that a single Super-chip could be substituted for the circuit board currently used to make the process-control unit. Using Super-chip would require an extra one hour of labor per control unit for a new total of six hours per control unit.

Required

1. Calculate the contribution margin per hour of selling Super-chip and Okay-chip. If no transfers of Super-chip are made to the Process-Control Division, how many Super-chips and Okay-chips should the Semiconductor Division sell? Show your computations.
2. The Process-Control Division expects to sell 5,000 process-control units this year. From the viewpoint of California Instruments as a whole, should 5,000 Super-chips be transferred to the Process-Control Division to replace circuit boards? Show your computations.
3. If demand for the process-control unit is certain to be 5,000 units but its *price is uncertain*, what should the transfer price of Super-chip be to ensure that the division managers' actions maximize operating income for CIC as a whole? (All other data are unchanged.)
4. If demand for the process-control unit is certain to be 12,000 units, but its *price is uncertain*, what should the transfer price of Super-chip be to ensure that the division managers' actions maximize operating income for CIC as a whole? (All other data are unchanged.)

23 Performance Measurement, Compensation, and Multinational Considerations

Learning Objectives

1. Select financial and nonfinancial performance measures to use in a balanced scorecard
2. Design an accounting-based performance measure
3. Analyze return on investment (ROI) using the DuPont method
4. Use the residual-income (RI) measure and understand its advantages
5. Describe the economic value added (EVA®) method
6. Contrast current-cost and historical-cost asset-measurement methods
7. Indicate the difficulties that occur when the performance of divisions operating in different countries is compared
8. Understand the roles of salaries and incentives when rewarding managers
9. Describe the four levers of control and why they are necessary

At the end of this school term, you're going to receive a grade that represents a measure of your performance in this course. Your grade will likely consist of four elements—homework, quizzes, exams, and class participation. Do some of these elements better reflect your knowledge of the material than others? Would the relative weights placed on the various elements when determining your final grade influence how much effort you expend to improve performance on the different elements? Organizations go through a similar process. What measures should be used to evaluate managers' performance, and how should different measures be weighted? What is clear is that what gets measured and rewarded is what gets done. The following article about the resignation of Home Depot CEO Bob Nardelli in 2007 demonstrates as much. Home Depot's board changed Nardelli's pay package to emphasize the company's accounting performance rather than its stock performance. By accounting performance measures, such as revenues and profits, Nardelli performed solidly: earnings per share, for example, climbed sharply under his watch. Nevertheless, Home Depot's stock price declined.

Retooling CEO Compensation at Home Depot[1]

After CEO Bob Nardelli pulled down $38.1 million from his last yearly contract, angry investors were promising an ugly fight at the company's annual meeting in May 2007. When board members asked Nardelli to more closely tie his future stock awards to shareholder gains, he refused, according to people familiar with the matter. Things came to a head at a board meeting on Jan. 2, 2007, leading to Home Depot's stunning announcement the next day that Nardelli would resign.

Judged solely by certain company financial measures, Nardelli should have enjoyed acclaim for transforming Home Depot from a faltering retail chain into an earnings juggernaut. Driven by a housing and home improvement boom, sales soared from $46 billion in 2000, the year Nardelli took over, to $81.5 billion in 2005, an average annual growth rate of 12%. Profits more than doubled, to $5.8 billion that year.

During the current housing slowdown, however, Home Depot's financials eroded. The CEO's reputation also suffered because of Wall Street's affection for Home Depot's smaller archrival, Lowe's

[1] *Source:* Brian Grow, "Behind the Flameout of Controversial CEO Bob Nardelli," *BusinessWeek*, January 4, 2007.

Companies, whose stock price had soared more than 200% since 2000, while Home Depot's shares declined 6%.

Possibly more devastating to his chances of a longer reign at Home Depot, Nardelli alienated customers just as thoroughly as he did employees. Staffing cuts led to persistent complaints that there weren't enough workers in Home Depot's stores to help do-it-yourself customers. In 2005, Home Depot slipped to last among major U.S. retailers in the University of Michigan's annual American Consumer Satisfaction Index.

Companies measure and reward performance to motivate managers to achieve company strategies and goals. As the Home Depot example illustrates, however, if the measures are inappropriate or incomplete, managers may improve their performance evaluations and increase compensation without achieving company goals. This chapter discusses the general design, implementation, and uses of performance measures, part of the final step in the decision-making process.

Financial and Nonfinancial Performance Measures

Many organizations are increasingly presenting financial and nonfinancial performance measures for their subunits in a single report called the *balanced scorecard* (Chapter 13). Different organizations stress different measures in their scorecards, but the measures are always derived from a company's strategy. Consider the case of Hospitality Inns, a chain of hotels. Hospitality Inns' strategy is to provide excellent customer service and to charge a higher room rate than its competitors. Hospitality Inns uses the following measures in its balanced scorecard:

Learning Objective 1

Select financial performance measures

. . . such as return on investment, residual income

and nonfinancial performance measures to use in a balanced scorecard

. . . such as customer-satisfaction, number of defects

1. **Financial perspective**—stock price, net income, return on sales, return on investment, economic value added
2. **Customer perspective**—market share in different geographic locations, customer satisfaction, average number of repeat visits
3. **Internal-business-process perspective**—customer-service time for making reservations, for check-in, and in restaurants; cleanliness of hotel and room, quality of room service; time taken to clean rooms; quality of restaurant experience; number of new services provided to customers (fax, wireless Internet, video games); time taken to plan and build new hotels

4. **Learning-and-growth perspective**—employee education and skill levels, employee satisfaction, employee turnover, hours of employee training, and information-system availability

As in all balanced scorecard implementations, the goal is to make improvements in the learning-and-growth perspective that will lead to improvements in the internal-business-process perspective that, in turn, will result in improvements in the customer and financial perspectives. Hospitality Inns also uses balanced scorecard measures to evaluate and reward the performance of its managers.

Some performance measures, such as the time it takes to plan and build new hotels, have a long time horizon. Other measures, such as time taken to check in or quality of room service, have a short time horizon. In this chapter, we focus on *organization subunits'* most widely used performance measures that cover an intermediate-to-long time horizon. These are internal financial measures based on accounting numbers routinely reported by organizations. In later sections, we describe why companies use both financial and nonfinancial measures to evaluate performance.

Designing accounting-based performance measures requires six steps:

Learning Objective 2

Design an accounting-based performance measure

. . . to achieve top management's goals, measure subunit performance, and motivate managers

Step 1: Choose Performance Measures That Align with Top Management's Financial Goals. For example, is operating income, net income, return on assets, or revenues the best measure of a subunit's financial performance?

Step 2: Choose the Time Horizon of Each Performance Measure in Step 1. For example, should performance measures, such as return on assets, be calculated for one year or for a multiyear period?

Step 3: Choose a Definition of the Components in Each Performance Measure in Step 1. For example, should assets be defined as total assets or net assets (total assets minus total liabilities)?

Step 4: Choose a Measurement Alternative for Each Performance Measure in Step 1. For example, should assets be measured at historical cost or current cost?

Step 5: Choose a Target Level of Performance. For example, should all subunits have identical targets, such as the same required rate of return on assets?

Step 6: Choose the Timing of Feedback. For example, should performance reports be sent to top management daily, weekly, or monthly?

These six steps need not be done sequentially. The issues considered in each step are interdependent, and top management will often proceed through these steps several times before deciding on one or more accounting-based performance measures. The answers to the questions raised at each step depend on top management's beliefs about how well each alternative measure fulfills the behavioral criteria discussed in Chapter 22: promoting goal congruence, motivating management effort, evaluating subunit performance, and preserving subunit autonomy.

Choosing Among Different Performance Measures: Step 1

Companies commonly use four measures to evaluate the economic performance of their subunits. We illustrate these measures for Hospitality Inns.

Hospitality Inns owns and operates three hotels—one each in San Francisco, Chicago, and New Orleans. Exhibit 23-1 summarizes data for each hotel for 2011. At present, Hospitality Inns does not allocate the total long-term debt of the company to the three separate hotels. The exhibit indicates that the New Orleans hotel generates the highest operating income, $510,000, compared with Chicago's $300,000 and San Francisco's $240,000. But does this comparison mean the New Orleans hotel is the most "successful"? The main weakness of comparing operating incomes alone is that differences in *the size of the investment* in each hotel are ignored. **Investment** refers to the resources or

Exhibit 23-1

Financial Data for Hospitality Inns for 2011 (in Thousands)

	A	B	C	D	E
1		San Francisco Hotel	Chicago Hotel	New Orleans Hotel	Total
2	Hotel revenues	$1,200,000	$1,400,000	$3,185,000	$5,785,000
3	Hotel variable costs	310,000	375,000	995,000	1,680,000
4	Hotel fixed costs	650,000	725,000	1,680,000	3,055,000
5	Hotel operating income	$ 240,000	$ 300,000	$ 510,000	1,050,000
6	Interest costs on long-term debt at 10%				450,000
7	Income before income taxes				600,000
8	Income taxes at 30%				180,000
9	Net income				$ 420,000
10	Net book value at the end of 2011:				
11	Current assets	$ 400,000	$ 500,000	$ 660,000	$1,560,000
12	Long-term assets	600,000	1,500,000	2,340,000	4,440,000
13	Total assets	$1,000,000	$2,000,000	$3,000,000	$6,000,000
14	Current liabilities	$ 50,000	$ 150,000	$ 300,000	$ 500,000
15	Long-term debt				4,500,000
16	Stockholders' equity				1,000,000
17	Total liabilities and stockholders' equity				$6,000,000
18					

assets used to generate income. The question is not, How large is operating income? Rather, it is, How large is operating income in relation to the investment made to earn it?

Three of the approaches to measuring performance include a measure of investment: return on investment, residual income, and economic value added. A fourth approach, return on sales, does not measure investment.

Return on Investment

Learning Objective 3

Analyze return on investment (ROI) using the DuPont method

. . . calculate return on sales and investment turnover

Return on investment (ROI) is an accounting measure of income divided by an accounting measure of investment.

$$\text{Return on investment} = \frac{\text{Income}}{\text{Investment}}$$

Return on investment is the most popular approach to measure performance. ROI is popular for two reasons: it blends all the ingredients of profitability—revenues, costs, and investment—into a single percentage; and it can be compared with the rate of return on opportunities elsewhere, inside or outside the company. Like any single performance measure, however, ROI should be used cautiously and in conjunction with other measures.

ROI is also called the *accounting rate of return* or the *accrual accounting rate of return* (Chapter 21, pp. 742–743). Managers usually use the term ROI when evaluating the performance of an organization subunit such as a division and the term accrual accounting rate of return when using an ROI measure to evaluate a project. Companies vary in the way they define income in the numerator and investment in the denominator of the ROI calculation. Some companies use operating income for the numerator; others prefer to calculate ROI on an after-tax basis and use net income. Some companies use total assets in the denominator; others prefer to focus on only those assets financed by long-term debt and stockholders' equity and use total assets minus current liabilities.

Consider the ROIs of each of the three Hospitality hotels in Exhibit 23-1. For our calculations, we use the operating income of each hotel for the numerator and total assets of each hotel for the denominator.

Using these ROI figures, the San Francisco hotel appears to make the best use of its total assets.

Hotel	Operating Income	÷	Total Assets	=	ROI
San Francisco	$240,000	÷	$1,000,000	=	24%
Chicago	$300,000	÷	$2,000,000	=	15%
New Orleans	$510,000	÷	$3,000,000	=	17%

Each hotel manager can increase ROI, for example, by increasing revenues or decreasing costs (each of which increases the numerator), or by decreasing investment (which decreases the denominator). A hotel manager can increase ROI even when operating income decreases by reducing total assets by a greater percentage. Suppose, for example, that operating income of the Chicago hotel decreases by 4% from $300,000 to $288,000 [$300,000 × (1 − 0.04)] and total assets decrease by 10% from $2,000,000 to $1,800,000 [$2,000,000 × (1 − 0.10)]. The ROI of the Chicago hotel would then increase from 15% to 16% ($288,000 ÷ $1,800,000).

ROI can provide more insight into performance when it is represented as two components:

$$\frac{\text{Income}}{\text{Investment}} = \frac{\text{Income}}{\text{Revenues}} \times \frac{\text{Revenues}}{\text{Investment}}$$

which is also written as,

$$ROI = \text{Return on sales} \times \text{Investment turnover}$$

This approach is known as the *DuPont method of profitability analysis*. The DuPont method recognizes the two basic ingredients in profit-making: increasing income per dollar of revenues and using assets to generate more revenues. An improvement in either ingredient without changing the other increases ROI.

Assume that top management at Hospitality Inns adopts a 30% target ROI for the San Francisco hotel. How can this return be attained? We illustrate the DuPont method for the San Francisco hotel and show how this method can be used to describe three alternative ways in which the San Francisco hotel can increase its ROI from 24% to 30%.

	Operating Income (1)	Revenues (2)	Total Assets (3)	Operating Income / Revenues (4) = (1) ÷ (2)	×	Revenues / Total Assets (5) = (2) ÷ (3)	=	Operating Income / Total Assets (6) = (4) × (5)
Current ROI	$240,000	$1,200,000	$1,000,000	20%	×	1.2	=	24%
Alternatives								
A. Decrease assets (such as receivables), keeping revenues and operating income per dollar of revenue constant	$240,000	$1,200,000	$800,000	20%	×	1.5	=	30%
B. Increase revenues (via higher occupancy rate), keeping assets and operating income per dollar of revenue constant	$300,000	$1,500,000	$1,000,000	20%	×	1.5	=	30%
C. Decrease costs (via, say, efficient maintenance) to increase operating income per dollar of revenue, keeping revenue and assets constant	$300,000	$1,200,000	$1,000,000	25%	×	1.2	=	30%

Other alternatives, such as increasing the selling price per room, could increase both the revenues per dollar of total assets and the operating income per dollar of revenues. ROI makes clear the benefits that managers can obtain by reducing their investment in current or long-term assets. Some managers know the need to boost revenues or to control costs, but they pay less attention to reducing their investment base. Reducing the investment base means decreasing idle cash, managing credit judiciously, determining proper inventory levels, and spending carefully on long-term assets.

Residual Income

Learning Objective 4

Use the residual income (RI) measure

. . . income minus a dollar amount for required return on investment

and understand its advantages

. . . motivates managers to act in the best interest of the company as a whole.

Residual income (RI) is an accounting measure of income minus a dollar amount for required return on an accounting measure of investment.

$$\text{Residual income } (RI) = \text{Income} \times (\text{Required rate of return} \times \text{Investment})$$

Required rate of return multiplied by the investment is the *imputed cost of the investment*. **Imputed costs** are costs recognized in particular situations but not incorporated in financial accounting records.

Suppose Hospitality Inns' investments are financed 50% by long-term debt and 50% by stockholders' equity. Long-term debt has an interest cost of 10% per year, which is booked in Hospitality Inn's financial accounting records under accrual accounting procedures. Hospitality Inns' stockholders' equity has a cost of 14% per year. This 14% represents the opportunity cost to equity investors of investing in Hospitality Inns—the return forgone by not investing in other equity securities of similar risk. The cost of equity, like all opportunity costs, is not booked in Hospitality Inns' financial accounting records. It is an imputed cost that is, nevertheless, a real economic cost of the amount of investment financed by equity. The weighted-average cost of capital for investments in Hospitality Inns is (50% × cost of debt) + (50% × cost of equity) = (0.50 × 10%) + (0.50 × 14%) = 5% + 7% = 12%. This is the required rate of return used when calculating RI for Hospitality Inns. A large component of this required rate of return is an imputed cost.

Assume each hotel faces similar risks. Hospitality Inns defines RI for each hotel as operating income minus the required rate of return of 12% of total assets:

Hotel	Operating Income	−	Required Rate of Return	×	Investment	=	Residual Income
San Francisco	$240,000	−	(12%	×	$1,000,000)	=	$120,000
Chicago	$300,000	−	(12%	×	$2,000,000)	=	$ 60,000
New Orleans	$510,000	−	(12%	×	$3,000,000)	=	$150,000

Given the 12% required annual rate of return, the New Orleans hotel has the best RI.

Some companies favor the RI measure because managers will concentrate on maximizing an absolute amount, such as dollars of RI, rather than a percentage, such as ROI. The objective of maximizing RI means that as long as a subunit earns a return in excess of the required return for investments, that subunit should continue to invest.

The objective of maximizing ROI may induce managers of highly profitable subunits to reject projects that, from the viewpoint of the company as a whole, should be accepted. Suppose Hospitality Inns is considering upgrading room features and furnishings at the San Francisco hotel. The upgrade will increase operating income of the San Francisco hotel by $70,000 and increase its total assets by $400,000. The ROI for the expansion is 17.5% ($70,000 ÷ $400,000), which is attractive to Hospitality Inns because it exceeds the required rate of return of 12%. By making this expansion, however, the San Francisco hotel's ROI will decrease:

$$\text{Preupgrade } ROI = \frac{\$240{,}000}{\$1{,}000{,}000} = 0.24, \text{ or } 24\%$$

$$\text{Postupgrade } ROI = \frac{\$240{,}000 + \$70{,}000}{\$1{,}000{,}000 + \$400{,}000} = \frac{\$310{,}000}{\$1{,}400{,}000} = 0.221, \text{ or } 22.1\%$$

The annual bonus paid to the San Francisco manager may decrease if ROI affects the bonus calculation and the upgrading option is selected. Consequently, the manager may shun the expansion. In contrast, if the annual bonus is a function of RI, the San Francisco manager will favor the expansion:

$$\text{Preupgrade } RI = \$240{,}000 - (0.12 \times \$1{,}000{,}000) = \$120{,}000$$
$$\text{Postupgrade } RI = \$310{,}000 - (0.12 \times \$1{,}400{,}000) = \$142{,}000$$

Goal congruence (ensuring that subunit managers work toward achieving the company's goals) is more likely using RI rather than ROI as a measure of the subunit manager's performance.

Economic Value Added[2]

Learning Objective 5

Describe the economic value added (EVA®) method

. . . a variation of residual income using after-tax amounts

Economic value added is a specific type of RI calculation that is used by many companies. **Economic value added (EVA®)** equals after-tax operating income *minus* the (after-tax) weighted-average cost of capital *multiplied* by total assets minus current liabilities.

$$\text{Economic value added } (EVA) = \text{After-tax operating income} - \left[\text{Weighted-average cost of capital} \times \left(\text{Total assets} - \text{Current liabilities}\right)\right]$$

EVA substitutes the following numbers in the RI calculations: (1) Income equal to after-tax operating income, (2) required rate of return equal to the (after-tax) weighted-average cost of capital, and (3) investment equal to total assets minus current liabilities.[3]

We use the Hospitality Inns data in Exhibit 23-1 to illustrate the basic EVA calculations. The weighted-average cost of capital (WACC) equals the *after-tax* average cost of all the long-term funds used by Hospitality Inns. The company has two sources of long-term funds: (a) long-term debt with a market value and book value of \$4.5 million issued at an interest rate of 10%, and (b) equity capital that also has a market value of \$4.5 million (but a book value of \$1 million).[4] Because interest costs are tax-deductible and the income tax rate is 30%, the after-tax cost of debt financing is $0.10 \times (1 - \text{Tax rate}) = 0.10 \times (1 - 0.30) = 0.10 \times 0.70 = 0.07$, or 7%. The cost of equity capital is the opportunity cost to investors of not investing their capital in another investment that is similar in risk to Hospitality Inns. Hospitality Inns' cost of equity capital is 14%.[5] The WACC computation, which uses market values of debt and equity, is:

$$
\begin{aligned}
WACC &= \frac{(7\% \times \text{Market value of debt}) + (14\% \times \text{Market value of equity})}{\text{Market value of debt} + \text{Market value of equity}} \\
&= \frac{(0.07 \times \$4{,}500{,}000) + (0.14 \times \$4{,}500{,}000)}{\$4{,}500{,}000 + \$4{,}500{,}000} \\
&= \frac{\$945{,}000}{\$9{,}000{,}000} = 0.105, \text{ or } 10.5\%
\end{aligned}
$$

The company applies the same WACC to all its hotels because each hotel faces similar risks.

Total assets minus current liabilities (see Exhibit 23-1) can also be computed as:

$$
\begin{aligned}
\text{Total assets} - \text{Current liabilities} &= \text{Long-term assets} + \text{Current assets} - \text{Current liabilities} \\
&= \text{Long-term assets} + \text{Working capital}
\end{aligned}
$$

where

$$\text{Working capital} = \text{Current assets} - \text{Current liabilities}$$

After-tax hotel operating income is:

$$\text{Hotel operating income} \times (1 - \text{Tax rate}) = \text{Hotel operating income} \times (1 - 0.30) = \text{Hotel operating income} \times 0.70$$

---

[2] S. O'Byrne and D. Young, *EVA and Value-Based Management: A Practical Guide to Implementation* (New York: McGraw-Hill, 2000); J. Stein, J. Shiely, and I. Ross, *The EVA Challenge: Implementing Value Added Change in an Organization* (New York: John Wiley and Sons, 2001).

[3] When implementing EVA, companies make several adjustments to the operating income and asset numbers reported under generally accepted accounting principles (GAAP). For example, when calculating EVA, costs such as R&D, restructuring costs, and leases that have long-run benefits are recorded as assets (which are then amortized), rather than as current operating costs. The goal of these adjustments is to obtain a better representation of the economic assets, particularly intangible assets, used to earn income. Of course, the specific adjustments applicable to a company will depend on its individual circumstances.

[4] The market value of Hospitality Inns' equity exceeds book value because book value, based on historical cost, does not measure the current value of the company's assets and because various intangible assets, such as the company's brand name, are not shown at current value in the balance sheet under GAAP.

[5] For details on calculating cost of equity capital adjusted for risk, see J. Van Horne, *Financial Management and Policy*, 12th ed. (Upper Saddle River, NJ: Prentice Hall, 2002).

EVA calculations for Hospitality Inns are as follows:

Hotel	After-Tax Operating Income	−	[WACC ×	(Total Assets	−	Current Liabilities)]	=	EVA
San Francisco	$240,000 × 0.70	−	[10.50% ×	($1,000,000	−	$50,000)]	=	$68,250
Chicago	$300,000 × 0.70	−	[10.50% ×	($2,000,000	−	$150,000)]	=	$15,750
New Orleans	$510,000 × 0.70	−	[10.50% ×	($3,000,000	−	$300,000)]	=	$73,500

The New Orleans hotel has the highest EVA. Economic value added, like residual income, charges managers for the cost of their investments in long-term assets and working capital. Value is created only if after-tax operating income exceeds the cost of investing the capital. To improve EVA, managers can, for example, (a) earn more after-tax operating income with the same capital, (b) use less capital to earn the same after-tax operating income, or (c) invest capital in high-return projects.

Managers in companies such as Briggs and Stratton, Coca-Cola, CSX, Equifax, and FMC use the estimated impact on EVA to guide their decisions. Division managers find EVA helpful because it allows them to incorporate the cost of capital, which is generally only available at the companywide level, into decisions at the division level. Comparing the actual EVA achieved to the estimated EVA is useful for evaluating performance and providing feedback to managers about performance. CSX, a railroad company, credits EVA for decisions such as to run trains with three locomotives instead of four and to schedule arrivals just in time for unloading rather than having trains arrive at their destination several hours in advance. The result? Higher income because of lower fuel costs and lower capital investments in locomotives.

Return on Sales

The income-to-revenues ratio (or sales ratio)—often called *return on sales (ROS)*—is a frequently used financial performance measure. ROS is one component of ROI in the DuPont method of profitability analysis. To calculate ROS for each of Hospitality's hotels, we divide operating income by revenues:

Hotel	Operating Income	÷	Revenues (Sales)	=	ROS
San Francisco	$240,000	÷	$1,200,000	=	20.0%
Chicago	$300,000	÷	$1,400,000	=	21.4%
New Orleans	$510,000	÷	$3,185,000	=	16.0%

The Chicago hotel has the highest ROS, but its performance is rated worse than the other hotels using measures such as ROI, RI, and EVA.

Comparing Performance Measures

The following table summarizes the performance of each hotel and ranks it (in parentheses) under each of the four performance measures:

Hotel	ROI	RI	EVA	ROS
San Francisco	24% (1)	$120,000 (2)	$68,250 (2)	20.0% (2)
Chicago	15% (3)	$ 60,000 (3)	$15,750 (3)	21.4% (1)
New Orleans	17% (2)	$150,000 (1)	$73,500 (1)	16.0% (3)

The RI and EVA rankings are the same. They differ from the ROI and ROS rankings. Consider the ROI and RI rankings for the San Francisco and New Orleans hotels. The New Orleans hotel has a smaller ROI. Although its operating income is only slightly more than twice the operating income of the San Francisco hotel—$510,000 versus $240,000—its total assets are three times as large—$3 million versus $1 million. The New Orleans hotel has a higher RI because it earns a higher income after covering the required rate of return on investment of 12%. The high ROI of the San Francisco hotel indicates that its assets are being used efficiently. Even though each dollar invested in the New Orleans hotel does not give the same return as the San Francisco hotel, this large investment creates considerable value because its return exceeds the required rate of return. The Chicago hotel has the highest ROS but the lowest ROI. The high ROS indicates that the Chicago hotel has the lowest cost structure per dollar of revenues of all of Hospitality Inns' hotels. The reason for Chicago's low ROI is that it generates very low revenues per dollar of assets invested. Is any one method better than the others for measuring performance? No, because each evaluates a different aspect of performance.

ROS measures how effectively costs are managed. To evaluate overall aggregate performance, ROI, RI, or EVA measures are more appropriate than ROS because they consider both income and investment. ROI indicates which investment yields the highest return. RI and EVA measures overcome some of the goal-congruence problems of ROI. Some managers favor EVA because it explicitly considers tax effects while (pretax) RI measures do not. Other managers favor (pretax) RI because it is easier to calculate and because, in most cases, it leads to the same conclusions as EVA. Generally, companies use multiple financial measures to evaluate performance.

Choosing the Time Horizon of the Performance Measures: Step 2

Step 2 of designing accounting-based performance measures is choosing the time horizon of the performance measures. The ROI, RI, EVA, and ROS calculations represent the results for a single period, one year in our example. Managers could take actions that cause short-run increases in these measures but that conflict with the long-run interest of the company. For example, managers may curtail R&D and plant maintenance in the last three months of a fiscal year to achieve a target level of annual operating income. For this reason, many companies evaluate subunits on the basis of ROI, RI, EVA, and ROS over multiple years.

Another reason to evaluate subunits over multiple years is that the benefits of actions taken in the current period may not show up in short-run performance measures, such as the current year's ROI or RI. For example, an investment in a new hotel may adversely affect ROI and RI in the short run but benefit ROI and RI in the long run.

A multiyear analysis highlights another advantage of the RI measure: Net present value of all cash flows over the life of an investment equals net present value of the RIs.[6] This characteristic means that if managers use the net present value method to make investment decisions (as advocated in Chapter 21), then using multiyear RI to evaluate managers' performances achieves goal congruence.

Another way to motivate managers to take a long-run perspective is by compensating them on the basis of changes in the market price of the company's stock. That's because stock prices incorporate the expected future effects of current decisions.

[6] We are grateful to S. Reichelstein for pointing out this equality. To see the equivalence, suppose the $400,000 investment in the San Francisco hotel increases operating income by $70,000 per year as follows: Increase in operating cash flows of $150,000 each year for five years minus depreciation of $80,000 ($400,000 ÷ 5) per year, assuming straight-line depreciation and $0 terminal disposal value. Depreciation reduces the investment amount by $80,000 each year. Assuming a required rate of return of 12%, net present values of cash flows and residual incomes are as follows:

Year	0	1	2	3	4	5	Net Present Value
(1) Cash flow	−$400,000	$150,000	$150,000	$150,000	$150,000	$150,000	
(2) Present value of $1 discounted at 12%	1	0.89286	0.79719	0.71178	0.63552	0.56743	
(3) Present value: (1) × (2)	−$400,000	$133,929	$119,578	$106,767	$ 95,328	$ 85,114	$140,716
(4) Operating income		$ 70,000	$ 70,000	$ 70,000	$ 70,000	$ 70,000	
(5) Assets at start of year		$400,000	$320,000	$240,000	$160,000	$ 80,000	
(6) Capital charge: (5) × 12%		$ 48,000	$ 38,400	$ 28,800	$ 19,200	$ 9,600	
(7) Residual income: (4) − (6)		$ 22,000	$ 31,600	$ 41,200	$ 50,800	$ 60,400	
(8) Present value of RI: (7) × (2)		$ 19,643	$ 25,191	$ 29,325	$ 32,284	$ 34,273	$140,716

Choosing Alternative Definitions for Performance Measures: Step 3

To illustrate step 3 of designing accounting-based performance measures, we consider four alternative definitions of investment that companies use:

1. **Total assets available**—includes all assets, regardless of their intended purpose.
2. **Total assets employed**—total assets available minus the sum of idle assets and assets purchased for future expansion. For example, if the New Orleans hotel in Exhibit 23-1 has unused land set aside for potential expansion, total assets employed by the hotel would exclude the cost of that land.
3. **Total assets employed minus current liabilities**—total assets excluding assets financed by short-term creditors. One negative feature of defining investment in this way is that it may encourage subunit managers to use an excessive amount of short-term debt because short-term debt reduces the amount of investment.
4. **Stockholders' equity**—calculated by assigning liabilities among subunits and deducting these amounts from the total assets of each subunit. One drawback of this method is that it combines operating decisions made by hotel managers with financing decisions made by top management.

Companies that use ROI or RI generally define investment as the total assets available. When top management directs a subunit manager to carry extra or idle assets, total assets employed can be more informative than total assets available. Companies that adopt EVA define investment as total assets employed minus current liabilities. The most common rationale for using total assets employed minus current liabilities is that the subunit manager often influences decisions on current liabilities of the subunit.

Choosing Measurement Alternatives for Performance Measures: Step 4

Learning Objective 6

Contrast current-cost

. . . cost today of purchasing an asset

and historical-cost asset-measurement methods

. . . original cost of an asset minus accumulated depreciation

To design accounting-based performance measures, we must consider different ways to measure assets included in the investment calculations. Should assets be measured at historical cost or current cost? Should gross book value (that is, original cost) or net book value (original cost minus accumulated depreciation) be used for depreciable assets?

Current Cost

Current cost is the cost of purchasing an asset today identical to the one currently held, or the cost of purchasing an asset that provides services like the one currently held if an identical asset cannot be purchased. Of course, measuring assets at current costs will result in different ROIs than the ROIs calculated on the basis of historical costs.

We illustrate the current-cost ROI calculations using the data for Hospitality Inns (Exhibit 23-1) and then compare current-cost-based ROIs and historical-cost-based ROIs. Assume the following information about the long-term assets of each hotel:

	San Francisco	Chicago	New Orleans
Age of facility in years (at end of 2011)	8	4	2
Gross book value (original cost)	$1,400,000	$2,100,000	$2,730,000
Accumulated depreciation	$ 800,000	$ 600,000	$ 390,000
Net book value (at end of 2011)	$ 600,000	$1,500,000	$2,340,000
Depreciation for 2011	$ 100,000	$ 150,000	$ 195,000

Hospitality Inns assumes a 14-year estimated useful life, zero terminal disposal value for the physical facilities, and straight-line depreciation.

An index of construction costs indicating how the cost of construction has changed over the eight-year period that Hospitality Inns has been operating (2003 year-end = 100) is:

Year	2004	2005	2006	2007	2008	2009	2010	2011
Construction cost index	110	122	136	144	152	160	174	180

Earlier in this chapter, we computed an ROI of 24% for San Francisco, 15% for Chicago, and 17% for New Orleans (p. 802). One possible explanation of the high ROI for the San Francisco hotel is that its long-term assets are expressed in 2003 construction-price levels—prices that prevailed eight years ago—and the long-term assets for the Chicago and New Orleans hotels are expressed in terms of higher, more-recent construction-price levels, which depress ROIs for these two hotels.

Exhibit 23-2 illustrates a step-by-step approach for incorporating current-cost estimates of long-term assets and depreciation expense into the ROI calculation. We make these calculations to approximate what it would cost today to obtain assets that would produce the same expected operating income that the subunits currently earn. (Similar adjustments to represent the current costs of capital employed and depreciation expense can also be made in the RI and EVA calculations.) The current-cost adjustment reduces the ROI of the San Francisco hotel by more than half.

	Historical-Cost ROI	Current-Cost ROI
San Francisco	24%	10.8%
Chicago	15%	11.1%
New Orleans	17%	14.7%

Adjusting assets to recognize current costs negates differences in the investment base caused solely by differences in construction-price levels. Compared with historical-cost ROI, current-cost ROI better measures the current economic returns from the investment. If Hospitality Inns were to invest in a new hotel today, investing in one like the New Orleans hotel offers the best ROI.

Current cost estimates may be difficult to obtain for some assets. Why? Because the estimate requires a company to consider, in addition to increases in price levels, technological advances and processes that could reduce the current cost of assets needed to earn today's operating income.

Long-Term Assets: Gross or Net Book Value?

Historical cost of assets is often used to calculate ROI. There has been much discussion about whether gross book value or net book value of assets should be used. Using the data in Exhibit 23-1 (p. 801), we calculate ROI using net and gross book values of plant and equipment as follows:

	Operating Income (from Exhibit 23-1) (1)	Net Book Value of Total Assets (from Exhibit 23-1) (2)	Accumulated Depreciation (from p. 807) (3)	Gross Book Value of Total Assets (4)=(2)+(3)	2011 ROI Using Net Book Value of Total Assets (calculated earlier) (5)=(1) ÷ (2)	2011 ROI Using Gross Book Value of Total Assets (6)=(1) ÷ (4)
San Francisco	$240,000	$1,000,000	$800,000	$1,800,000	24%	13.3%
Chicago	$300,000	$2,000,000	$600,000	$2,600,000	15%	11.5%
New Orleans	$510,000	$3,000,000	$390,000	$3,390,000	17%	15.0%

Using gross book value, the 13.3% ROI of the older San Francisco hotel is lower than the 15.0% ROI of the newer New Orleans hotel. Those who favor using gross book value claim it enables more-accurate comparisons of ROI across subunits. For example, using gross-book-value calculations, the return on the original plant-and-equipment investment is higher for the newer New Orleans hotel than for the older San Francisco hotel. This difference probably reflects the decline in earning power of the San Francisco hotel. Using the net book value masks this decline in earning power because the constantly decreasing investment base results in a higher ROI for the San Francisco hotel—24% in this example.

Exhibit 23-2 ROI for Hospitality Inns: Computed Using Current-Cost Estimates as of the End of 2011 for Depreciation Expense and Long-Term Assets

File Edit View Insert Format Tools Data Window Help

	A	B	C	D	E	F	G	H	I	J
1	**Step 1:** Restate long-term assets from gross book value at historical cost to gross book value at current cost as of the end of 2011.									
2		**Gross book value of long-term assets at historical cost**	**x**	**(Construction cost index in 2011**	**÷**	**Construction cost index in year of construction)**	**=**	**Gross book value of long-term assets at current cost at end of 2011**		
3	San Francisco	$1,400,000	x	(180	÷	100)	=	$2,520,000		
4	Chicago	$2,100,000	x	(180	÷	144)	=	$2,625,000		
5	New Orleans	$2,730,000	x	(180	÷	160)	=	$3,071,250		
6										
7	**Step 2:** Derive net book value of long-term assets at current cost as of the end of 2011 (Assume estimated useful life of each hotel is 14 years.)									
8		**Gross book value of long-term assets at current cost at end of 2011**	**x**	**(Estimated remaining useful life**	**÷**	**Estimated total useful life)**	**=**	**Net book value of long-term assets at current cost at end of 2011**		
9	San Francisco	$2,520,000	x	(6	÷	14)	=	$1,080,000		
10	Chicago	$2,625,000	x	(10	÷	14)	=	$1,875,000		
11	New Orleans	$3,071,250	x	(12	÷	14)	=	$2,632,500		
12										
13	**Step 3:** Compute current cost of total assets in 2011 (Assume current assets of each hotel are expressed in 2011 dollars.)									
14		**Current assets at end of 2011 (from Exhibit 23-1)**	**+**	**Long-term assets from Step 2 above**	**=**	**Current cost of total assets at end of 2011**				
15	San Francisco	$400,000	+	$1,080,000	=	$1,480,000				
16	Chicago	$500,000	+	$1,875,000	=	$2,375,000				
17	New Orleans	$660,000	+	$2,632,500	=	$3,292,500				
18										
19	**Step 4:** Compute current-cost depreciation expense in 2011 dollars.									
20		**Gross book value of long-term assets at current cost at end of 2011 (from Step 1)**	**÷**	**Estimated total useful life**	**=**	**Current-cost depreciation expense in 2011 dollars**				
21	San Francisco	$2,520,000	÷	14	=	$180,000				
22	Chicago	$2,625,000	÷	14	=	$187,500				
23	New Orleans	$3,071,250	÷	14	=	$219,375				
24										
25	**Step 5:** Compute 2011 operating income using 2011 current-cost depreciation expense.									
26		**Historical-cost operating income**	**–**	**(Current-cost depreciation expense in 2011 dollars (from Step 4)**	**–**	**Historical-cost depreciation expense)**	**=**	**Operating income for 2011 using current-cost depreciation expense in 2011 dollars**		
27	San Francisco	$240,000	–	($180,000	–	$100,000)	=	$160,000		
28	Chicago	$300,000	–	($187,500	–	$150,000)	=	$262,500		
29	New Orleans	$510,000	–	($219,375	–	$195,000)	=	$485,625		
30										
31	**Step 6:** Compute ROI using current-cost estimates for long-term assets and depreciation expense.									
32		**Operating income for 2011 using current-cost depreciation expense in 2011 dollars (from Step 5)**	**÷**	**Current cost of total assets at end of 2011 (from step 3)**	**=**	**ROI using current-cost estimate**				
33	San Francisco	$160,000	÷	$1,480,000	=	10.8%				
34	Chicago	$262,500	÷	$2,375,000	=	11.1%				
35	New Orleans	$485,625	÷	$3,292,500	=	14.7%				

This higher rate may mislead decision makers into thinking that the earning power of the San Francisco hotel has not decreased.

The proponents of using net book value as an investment base maintain it is less confusing because (1) it is consistent with the amount of total assets shown in the conventional balance sheet, and (2) it is consistent with income computations that include deductions for depreciation expense. Surveys report net book value to be the dominant measure of assets used by companies for internal performance evaluation.

Choosing Target Levels of Performance: Step 5

We next consider target-setting for accounting-based measures of performance against which actual performance can be compared. Historical-cost-based accounting measures are usually inadequate for evaluating economic returns on new investments, and in some cases, they create disincentives for expansion. Despite these problems, historical-cost ROIs can be used to evaluate current performance by establishing *target* ROIs. For Hospitality Inns, we need to recognize that the hotels were built in different years, which means they were built at different construction-price levels. Top management could adjust the target historical-cost-based ROIs accordingly, say, by setting San Francisco's ROI at 26%, Chicago's at 18%, and New Orleans' at 19%.

This useful alternative of comparing actual results with target or budgeted performance is frequently overlooked. The budget should be carefully negotiated with full knowledge of historical-cost accounting pitfalls. *Companies should tailor a budget to a particular subunit, a particular accounting system, and a particular performance measure.* For example, many problems of asset valuation and income measurement can be resolved if top management can get subunit managers to focus on what is attainable in the forthcoming budget period—whether ROI, RI, or EVA is used and whether the financial measures are based on historical cost or some other measure, such as current cost.

A popular way to establish targets is to set continuous improvement targets. If a company is using EVA as a performance measure, top management can evaluate operations on year-to-year changes in EVA, rather than on absolute measures of EVA. Evaluating performance on the basis of *improvements* in EVA makes the initial method of calculating EVA less important.

In establishing targets for financial performance measures, companies using the balanced scorecard simultaneously determine targets in the customer, internal-business-process, and learning-and-growth perspectives. For example, Hospitality Inns will establish targets for employee training and employee satisfaction, customer-service time for reservations and check-in, quality of room service, and customer satisfaction that each hotel must reach to achieve its ROI and EVA targets.

Choosing the Timing of Feedback: Step 6

The final step in designing accounting-based performance measures is the timing of feedback. Timing of feedback depends largely on (a) how critical the information is for the success of the organization, (b) the specific level of management receiving the feedback, and (c) the sophistication of the organization's information technology. For example, hotel managers responsible for room sales want information on the number of rooms sold (rented) on a daily or weekly basis. That's because a large percentage of hotel costs are fixed costs, so achieving high room sales and taking quick action to reverse any declining sales trends are critical to the financial success of each hotel. Supplying managers with daily information about room sales is much easier if Hospitality Inns has a computerized room-reservation and check-in system. Top management, however, may look at information about daily room sales only on a monthly basis. In some instances, for example because of concern about the low sales-to-total-assets ratio of the Chicago hotel, they may want the information weekly.

The timing of feedback for measures in the balanced scorecard varies. For example, human resources managers at each hotel measure employee satisfaction annually because satisfaction is best measured over a longer horizon. However, housekeeping-department managers measure the quality of room service over much shorter time horizons, such as a week. That's because poor levels of performance in these areas for even a short period of time can harm a hotel's reputation for a long period. Moreover, housekeeping problems can be detected and resolved over a short time period.

Performance Measurement in Multinational Companies

Learning Objective 7

Indicate the difficulties that occur when the performance of divisions operating in different countries is compared

. . . adjustments needed for differences in inflation rates and changes in exchange rates

Our discussion so far has focused on performance evaluation of different divisions of a company operating within a single country. We next discuss the additional difficulties created when the performance of divisions of a company operating in different countries is compared. Several issues arise.[7]

- The economic, legal, political, social, and cultural environments differ significantly across countries.
- Governments in some countries may limit selling prices of, and impose controls on, a company's products. For example, some countries in Asia, Latin America, and Eastern Europe impose tariffs and custom duties to restrict imports of certain goods.
- Availability of materials and skilled labor, as well as costs of materials, labor, and infrastructure (power, transportation, and communication), may also differ significantly across countries.
- Divisions operating in different countries account for their performance in different currencies. Issues of inflation and fluctuations in foreign-currency exchange rates affect performance measures.

As a result of these differences, adjustments need to be made to compare performance measures across countries.

Calculating the Foreign Division's ROI in the Foreign Currency

Suppose Hospitality Inns invests in a hotel in Mexico City. The investment consists mainly of the costs of buildings and furnishings. Also assume:

- The exchange rate at the time of Hospitality's investment on December 31, 2010, is 10 pesos = $1.
- During 2011, the Mexican peso suffers a steady decline in its value. The exchange rate on December 31, 2011, is 15 pesos = $1.
- The average exchange rate during 2011 is [(10 + 15) ÷ 2] = 12.5 pesos = $1.
- The investment (total assets) in the Mexico City hotel is 30,000,000 pesos.
- The operating income of the Mexico City hotel in 2011 is 6,000,000 pesos.

What is the historical-cost-based ROI for the Mexico City hotel in 2011?

To answer, Hospitality Inns' managers first have to determine: Should they calculate the ROI in pesos or in dollars? If they calculate the ROI in dollars, what exchange rate should they use? The managers may also be interested in how the ROI of Hospitality Inns Mexico City (HIMC) compares with the ROI of Hospitality Inns New Orleans (HINO),

[7] See M. Z. Iqbal, *International Accounting—A Global Perspective* (Cincinnati: South-Western College Publishing, 2002).

which is also a relatively new hotel of approximately the same size. The answers to these questions yield information that will be helpful when making future investment decisions.

$$\text{HIMC's } ROI \text{ (calculated using pesos)} = \frac{\text{Operating income}}{\text{Total assets}} = \frac{6{,}000{,}000 \text{ pesos}}{30{,}000{,}000 \text{ pesos}} = 0.20, \text{ or } 20\%$$

HIMC's ROI of 20% is higher than HINO's ROI of 17% (p. 802). Does this mean that HIMC outperformed HINO based on the ROI criterion? Not necessarily. That's because HIMC operates in a very different economic environment than HINO.

The peso has declined in value relative to the dollar in 2011. This decline has led to higher inflation in Mexico than in the United States. As a result of the higher inflation in Mexico, HIMC will charge higher prices for its hotel rooms, which will increase HIMC's operating income and lead to a higher ROI. Inflation clouds the real economic returns on an asset and makes historical-cost-based ROI higher. Differences in inflation rates between the two countries make a direct comparison of HIMC's peso-denominated ROI with HINO's dollar-denominated ROI misleading.

Calculating the Foreign Division's ROI in U.S. Dollars

One way to make a comparison of historical-cost-based ROIs more meaningful is to restate HIMC's performance in U.S. dollars. But what exchange rate should be used to make the comparison meaningful? Assume operating income was earned evenly throughout 2011. Hospitality Inns' managers should use the average exchange rate of 12.5 pesos = \$1 to convert operating income from pesos to dollars: 6,000,000 pesos ÷ 12.5 pesos per dollar = \$480,000. The effect of dividing the operating income in pesos by the higher pesos-to-dollar exchange rate prevailing during 2011, rather than the 10 pesos = \$1 exchange rate prevailing on December 31, 2010, is that any increase in operating income in pesos as a result of inflation during 2011 is eliminated when converting back to dollars.

At what rate should HIMC's total assets of 30,000,000 pesos be converted? The 10 pesos = \$1 exchange rate prevailing when the assets were acquired on December 31, 2010. That's because HIMC's assets are recorded in pesos at the December 31, 2010, cost, and they are not revalued as a result of inflation in Mexico in 2011. Because the cost of assets in HIMC's financial accounting records is unaffected by subsequent inflation, the exchange rate prevailing when the assets were acquired should be used to convert the assets into dollars. Using exchange rates after December 31, 2010, would be incorrect because these exchange rates incorporate the higher inflation in Mexico in 2011. Total assets are converted to 30,000,000 pesos ÷ 10 pesos per dollar = \$3,000,000.

Then,

$$\text{HIMCs } ROI \text{ (calculated using dollars)} = \frac{\text{Operating income}}{\text{Total assets}} = \frac{\$480{,}000}{\$3{,}000{,}000} = 0.16, \text{ or } 16\%$$

As we have discussed, these adjustments make the historical-cost-based ROIs of the Mexico City and New Orleans hotels comparable because they negate the effects of any differences in inflation rates between the two countries. HIMC's ROI of 16% is less than HINO's ROI of 17%.

Residual income calculated in pesos suffers from the same problems as ROI calculated using pesos. Calculating HIMC's RI in dollars adjusts for changes in exchange rates and makes for more-meaningful comparisons with Hospitality's other hotels:

$$\begin{aligned}\text{HIMC's } RI &= \$480{,}000 - (0.12 \times \$3{,}000{,}000)\\ &= \$480{,}000 - \$360{,}000 = \$120{,}000\end{aligned}$$

which is also less than HINO's RI of \$150,000. In interpreting HIMC's and HINO's ROI and RI, keep in mind that they are historical-cost-based calculations. They do, however, pertain to relatively new hotels.

Distinction Between Managers and Organization Units[8]

Our focus has been on how to evaluate the performance of a subunit of a company, such as a division. However, is evaluating the performance of a subunit manager the same as evaluating the performance of the subunit? If the subunit performed well, does it mean the manager performed well? In this section, we argue that the performance evaluation of a *manager* should be distinguished from the performance evaluation of that manager's *subunit*. For example, companies often put the most skillful division manager in charge of the division producing the poorest economic return in an attempt to improve it. The division may take years to show improvement. Furthermore, the manager's efforts may result merely in bringing the division up to a minimum acceptable ROI. The division may continue to be a poor performer in comparison with other divisions, but it would be a mistake to conclude from the poor performance of the division that the manager is performing poorly. The division's performance may be adversely affected by economic conditions over which the manager has no control.

As another example, consider again the Hospitality Inn Mexico City (HIMC) hotel. Suppose, despite the high inflation in Mexico, HIMC could not increase room prices because of price-control regulations imposed by the government. HIMC's performance in dollar terms would be very poor because of the decline in the value of the peso. But should top management conclude from HIMC's poor performance that the HIMC manager performed poorly? Probably not. That's because most likely the poor performance of HIMC is largely the result of regulatory factors beyond the manager's control.

In the following sections, we show the basic principles for evaluating the performance of an individual subunit manager. These principles apply to managers at all organization levels. Later sections consider examples at the individual-worker level and the top-management level. We illustrate these principles using the RI performance measure.

The Basic Trade-Off: Creating Incentives versus Imposing Risk

Learning Objective 8

Understand the roles of salaries and incentives when rewarding managers

. . . balancing risk and performance-based rewards

How the performance of managers and other employees is measured and evaluated affects their rewards. Compensation arrangements range from a flat salary with no direct performance-based incentive (or bonus), as in the case of many government employees, to rewards based on only performance, as in the case of real estate agents who receive no salary and are compensated via commissions paid on the properties they sell. Most managers' total compensation includes some combination of salary and performance-based incentive. In designing compensation arrangements, we need to consider the *trade-off between creating incentives and imposing risk*. We illustrate this trade-off in the context of our Hospitality Inns example.

Sally Fonda owns the Hospitality Inns chain of hotels. Roger Brett manages the Hospitality Inns San Francisco (HISF) hotel. Assume Fonda uses RI to measure performance. To improve RI, Fonda would like Brett to increase sales, control costs, provide prompt and courteous customer service, and reduce working capital. But even if Brett did all those things, high RI is not guaranteed. That's because HISF's RI is affected by many factors beyond Fonda's and Brett's control, such as a recession in the San Francisco economy or an earthquake that might negatively affect HISF. Or, there could be other uncontrollable factors, such as road construction near competing hotels, that might have a positive effect on HISF's RI. Uncontrollable factors make HISF's profitability uncertain and, therefore, risky.

As an entrepreneur, Fonda expects to bear risk. But Brett does not like being subject to risk. One way of "insuring" Brett against risk is to pay Brett a flat salary, regardless of the actual amount of RI earned. All the risk would then be borne by Fonda. This arrangement creates a problem, however, because Brett's effort is difficult to monitor. The absence of performance-based compensation means that Brett has no direct incentive to

[8] The presentations here draw (in part) from teaching notes prepared by S. Huddart, N. Melumad, and S. Reichelstein.

work harder or to undertake extra physical and mental effort beyond what is necessary to retain his job or to uphold his own personal values.

Moral hazard describes a situation in which an employee prefers to exert less effort (or to report distorted information) compared with the effort (or accurate information) desired by the owner because the employee's effort (or validity of the reported information) cannot be accurately monitored and enforced.[9] In some repetitive jobs, such as in electronic assembly, a supervisor can monitor the workers' actions, and the moral-hazard problem may not arise. However, a manager's job is to gather and interpret information and to exercise judgment on the basis of the information obtained. Monitoring a manager's effort is more difficult.

Paying no salary and rewarding Brett *only* on the basis of some performance measure—RI in our example—raises different concerns. In this case, Brett would be motivated to strive to increase RI because his rewards would increase with increases in RI. But compensating Brett on RI also subjects him to risk. That's because HISF's RI depends not only on Brett's effort, but also on factors such as local economic conditions over which Brett has no control.

Brett does not like being subject to risk. To compensate Brett for taking risk, Fonda must pay him extra compensation. That is, using performance-based bonuses will cost Fonda more money, *on average*, than paying Brett a flat salary. Why "on average"? Because Fonda's compensation payment to Brett will vary with RI outcomes. When averaged over these outcomes, the RI-based compensation will cost Fonda more than paying Brett a flat salary. The motivation for having some salary and some performance-based bonus in compensation arrangements is to balance the benefit of incentives against the extra cost of imposing risk on the manager.

Intensity of Incentives and Financial and Nonfinancial Measurements

What affects the intensity of incentives? That is, how large should the incentive component of a manager's compensation be relative to the salary component? To answer these questions, we need to understand how much the performance measure is affected by actions the manager takes to further the owner's objectives.

Preferred performance measures are those that are sensitive to or that change significantly with the manager's performance. They do not change much with changes in factors that are beyond the manager's control. Sensitive performance measures motivate the manager as well as limit the manager's exposure to risk, reducing the cost of providing incentives. Less-sensitive performance measures are not affected by the manager's performance and fail to induce the manager to improve. The more that owners have sensitive performance measures available to them, the more they can rely on incentive compensation for their managers.

The salary component of compensation dominates when performance measures that are sensitive to managers' actions are not available. This is the case, for example, for some corporate staff and government employees. A high salary component, however, does not mean incentives are completely absent. Promotions and salary increases do depend on some overall measure of performance, but the incentives are less direct. The incentive component of compensation is high when sensitive performance measures are available and when monitoring the employee's effort is difficult, such as in real estate agencies.

In evaluating Brett, Fonda uses measures from multiple perspectives of the balanced scorecard because nonfinancial measures on the balanced scorecard—employee satisfaction and the time taken for check-in, cleaning rooms, and providing room service—are more sensitive to Brett's actions. Financial measures such as RI are less sensitive to Brett's actions because they are affected by external factors such as local economic conditions beyond Brett's control. Residual income may be a very good measure of the economic viability of the hotel, but it is only a partial measure of Brett's performance.

---

[9] The term *moral hazard* originated in insurance contracts to represent situations in which insurance coverage caused insured parties to take less care of their properties than they might otherwise. One response to moral hazard in insurance contracts is the system of deductibles (that is, the insured pays for damages below a specified amount).

Another reason for using nonfinancial measures in the balanced scorecard is that these measures follow Hospitality Inns' strategy and are drivers of future performance. Evaluating managers on these nonfinancial measures motivates them to take actions that will sustain long-run performance. Therefore, evaluating performance in all four perspectives of the balanced scorecard promotes both short- and long-run actions.

Benchmarks and Relative Performance Evaluation

Owners often use financial and nonfinancial benchmarks to evaluate performance. Benchmarks representing "best practice" may be available inside or outside an organization. For HISF, benchmarks could be from similar hotels, either within or outside the Hospitality Inns chain. Suppose Brett has responsibility for revenues, costs, and investments. In evaluating Brett's performance, Fonda would want to use as a benchmark a hotel of a similar size influenced by the same uncontrollable factors—for example, location, demographic trends, and economic conditions—that affect HISF. If all these factors were the same, *differences* in performances of the two hotels would occur only because of differences in the two managers' performances. Benchmarking, which is also called *relative performance evaluation*, filters out the effects of the common uncontrollable factors.

Can the performance of two managers responsible for running similar operations within a company be benchmarked against each other? Yes, but this approach could create a problem: The use of these benchmarks may reduce incentives for these managers to help one another. That's because a manager's performance-evaluation measure improves either by doing a better job or as a result of the other manager doing poorly. When managers do not cooperate, the company suffers. In this case, using internal benchmarks for performance evaluation may not lead to goal congruence.

Performance Measures at the Individual Activity Level

There are two issues when evaluating performance at the individual-activity level:

1. Designing performance measures for activities that require multiple tasks
2. Designing performance measures for activities done in teams

Performing Multiple Tasks

Most employees perform more than one task as part of their jobs. Marketing representatives sell products, provide customer support, and gather market information. Manufacturing workers are responsible for both the quantity and quality of their output. Employers want employees to allocate their time and effort intelligently among various tasks or aspects of their jobs.

Consider mechanics at an auto repair shop. Their jobs have two distinct aspects: repair work—performing more repair work generates more revenues for the shop—and customer satisfaction—the higher the quality of the job, the more likely the customer will be pleased. If the employer wants an employee to focus on both aspects, then the employer must measure and compensate performance on both aspects.

Suppose that the employer can easily measure the quantity, but not the quality, of auto repairs. If the employer rewards workers on a by-the-job rate, which pays workers only on the basis of the number of repairs actually performed, mechanics will likely increase the number of repairs they make and quality will likely suffer. Sears experienced this problem when it introduced by-the-job rates for its mechanics. To resolve the problem, Sears' managers took three steps to motivate workers to balance both quantity and quality: (1) They dropped the by-the-job rate system and paid mechanics an hourly salary, a step that deemphasized the quantity of repairs. Management determined mechanics' bonuses, promotions, and pay increases on the basis of an assessment of each mechanic's overall performance regarding quantity and quality of repairs. (2) Sears evaluated employees, in part, using data such as customer-satisfaction surveys, the number of dissatisfied customers, and the number of customer complaints. (3) Finally, Sears used staff from an independent outside agency to randomly monitor whether the repairs performed were of high quality.

Team-Based Compensation Arrangements

Many manufacturing, marketing, and design problems can be resolved when employees with multiple skills, knowledge, experiences, and perceptions pool their talents. A team achieves better results than individual employees acting alone.[10] Companies reward individuals on a team based on team performance. Such team-based incentives encourage individuals to help one another as they strive toward a common goal.

The specific forms of team-based compensation vary across companies. Colgate Palmolive rewards teams on the basis of each team's performance. Novartis, the Swiss pharmaceutical company, rewards teams on companywide performance—a certain amount of team-based bonuses are paid only if the company reaches certain goals. To encourage the development of team skills, Tennessee Eastman, a chemical manufacturer, rewards team members using a checklist of team skills, such as communication and willingness to help one another. Whether team-based compensation is desirable depends, to a large extent, on the culture and management style of a particular organization. For example, one criticism of team-based compensation, especially in the United States, is that incentives for individual employees to excel are diminished, harming overall performance. Another problem is how to manage team members who are not productive contributors to the team's success but who, nevertheless, share in the team's rewards.

Executive Performance Measures and Compensation

The principles of performance evaluation described in the previous sections also apply to executive compensation plans. These plans are based on both financial and nonfinancial performance measures and consist of a mix of (1) base salary; (2) annual incentives, such as a cash bonus based on achieving a target annual RI; (3) long-run incentives, such as stock options (described later in this section) based on stock performance over, say, a five-year period; and (4) other benefits, such as medical benefits, pensions plans, and life insurance.

Well-designed plans use a compensation mix that balances risk (the effect of uncontrollable factors on the performance measure and hence compensation) with short-run and long-run incentives to achieve the organization's goals. For example, evaluating performance on the basis of annual EVA sharpens an executive's short-run focus. And using EVA and stock option plans over, say, five years motivates the executive to take a long-run view as well.

Stock options give executives the right to buy company stock at a specified price (called the exercise price) within a specified period. Suppose that on September 16, 2008, Hospitality Inns gave its CEO the option to buy 200,000 shares of the company's stock at any time before June 30, 2016, at the September 16, 2008, market price of $49 per share. Let's say Hospitality Inns' stock price rises to $69 per share on March 24, 2014, and the CEO exercises his options on all 200,000 shares. The CEO would earn $20 ($69 − $49) per share on 200,000 shares, or $4 million. If Hospitality Inns' stock price stays below $49 during the entire period, the CEO will simply forgo his right to buy the shares. By linking CEO compensation to increases in the company's stock price, the stock option plan motivates the CEO to improve the company's long-run performance and stock price. (See also the Concepts in Action feature, p. 818.)[11]

The Securities and Exchange Commission (SEC) requires detailed disclosures of the compensation arrangements of top-level executives. In complying with these rules in 2007, Hilton Hotels, for example, disclosed a compensation table showing the salaries, bonuses,

[10] *Teams That Click: The Results-Driven Manager Series* (Boston: Harvard Business School Press, 2004).

[11] Although stock options can improve incentives by linking CEO pay to improvements in stock price, they have been criticized for promoting improper or illegal activities by CEOs to increase the options' value. See J. Fox, "Sleazy CEOs Have Even More Options Tricks," www.money.cnn.com/2006/11/13/magazines/fortune/options_scandals.fortune/index.htm, accessed September 5, 2007.

stock options, other stock awards, and other compensation earned by its top five executives during the 2004, 2005, and 2006 fiscal years. Hilton also disclosed the peer companies that it uses to set executive pay and conduct performance comparisons. These include competitors in the hospitality industry, as well as similarly sized companies in other industries with strong brands and multiple locations. Investors use this information to evaluate the relationship between compensation and performance across companies generally, across companies of similar sizes, and across companies operating in similar industries.

The SEC rules also require companies to disclose the principles underlying their executive compensation plans and the performance criteria—such as profitability, revenue growth, and market share—used in determining compensation. In its financial statements, Hilton Hotels described some of these principles as supporting a unified company culture and brands across the globe, providing clear communication of performance expectations and reward opportunities, and linking pay to performance that drives stockholder value creation. Hilton uses corporate earnings as one performance criteria to determine annual incentives for all of its executives. In addition, each executive has an individual scorecard of financial and nonfinancial performance measures. The company's board of directors creates the overall strategic direction of the company. Individual and strategic goals for executives are then established to support the overall company goals but are tailored to each executive's area of control.

Strategy and Levers of Control[12]

Learning Objective 9

Describe the four levers of control and why they are necessary

. . . boundary, belief, and interactive control systems counterbalance diagnostic control systems

Given the management accounting focus of this book, this chapter has emphasized the role of quantitative financial and nonfinancial performance-evaluation measures that companies use to implement their strategies. These measures—such as ROI, RI, EVA, customer satisfaction, and employee satisfaction—monitor critical performance variables that help managers track progress toward achieving a company's strategic goals. Because these measures help diagnose whether a company is performing to expectations, they are collectively called **diagnostic control systems**. Companies motivate managers to achieve goals by holding them accountable for and by rewarding them for meeting these goals. The concern, however, is that the pressure to perform may cause managers to cut corners and misreport numbers to make their performance look better than it is, as happened at companies such as Enron, WorldCom, Tyco, and Health South. To prevent unethical behavior, companies need to balance the push for performance resulting from diagnostic control systems, the first of four levers of control, with three other levers: *boundary systems, belief systems,* and *interactive control systems.*

Boundary systems describe standards of behavior and codes of conduct expected of all employees, especially actions that are off-limits. Ethical behavior on the part of managers is paramount. In particular, numbers that subunit managers report should not be tainted by "cooking the books." They should be free of, for example, overstated assets, understated liabilities, fictitious revenues, and understated costs.

Codes of business conduct signal appropriate and inappropriate individual behaviors. The following is from Caterpillar Tractor's "Code of Worldwide Business Conduct and Operating Principles":

> *The law is a floor. Ethical business conduct should normally exist at a level well above the minimum required by law. Caterpillar employees shall not accept costly entertainment or gifts (excepting mementos and novelties of nominal value) from dealers, suppliers and others with whom we do business. And we won't tolerate circumstances that produce, or reasonably appear to produce, conflict between personal interests of an employee and interests of the company.*

Division managers often cite enormous pressure from top management "to make the budget" as excuses or rationalizations for not adhering to ethical accounting policies and procedures. A healthy amount of motivational pressure is desirable, as long as the "tone

[12] For a more-detailed discussion see R. Simons, *Levers of Control: How Managers Use Innovative Control Systems to Drive Strategic Renewal* (Boston: Harvard Business School Press, 1995).

Concepts in Action

CEO Compensation and Company Performance

Over the years, CEO compensation has been a hot-button issue for many publicly traded companies, their shareholders, the general public, and the government. The recent wave of corporate scandals has only intensified the scrutiny placed on the large salaries, stock-option grants, and other executive perks given to corporate heads. The following table summarizes the 2006 compensation for the highest-paid CEOs of Forbes 500 companies:

CEO	Company	Total Compensation	Salary	Bonus	Value of Stock Options Exercised in 2006	Other (Including Vested Restricted Stock) in 2006
Steven Jobs	Apple	$646,600,000	0.0%	0.0%	0.0%	100.0%
Ray Irani	Occidental Petroleum	$321,640,000	0.4%	0.9%	84.0%	14.7%
Barry Diller	IAC/InterActiveCorp	$295,140,000	0.3%	1.1%	98.3%	0.3%
William Foley II	Fidelity National Financial	$179,560,000	0.3%	11.9%	85.9%	1.9%
Terry Semel	Yahoo!	$174,200,000	0.3%	0.0%	99.7%	0.0%

These large amounts are primarily due to the exercise or sale of previously granted stock options or restricted stock, whose value is directly linked to a company's stock-price performance. CEOs with stock-heavy packages, such as Steven Jobs of Apple, earn very high compensation if their companies perform well. In contrast, the following table outlines the 2006 compensation for the lowest-paid Forbes 500 CEOs.

CEO	Company	Total Compensation	Salary	Bonus	Value of Stock Options Exercised in 2006	Other (Including Vested Restricted Stock) in 2006
Richard Kinder	Kinder Morgan	$ 0	0.0%	0.0%	0.0%	0.0%
Warren Buffett	Berkshire Hathaway	$100,000	100.0%	0.0%	0.0%	0.0%
Richard Fairbank	CapitalOne	$150,000	0.0%	0.0%	0.0%	100.0%
John Busksbaum	General Growth Properties	$240,000	69.7%	0.0%	0.0%	30.3%
John Delaney	CapitalSource	$410,000	42.5%	0.0%	0.0%	57.5%

The lowest-paid Forbes 500 CEOs received no compensation from bonuses, the exercise of stock options, or the vesting of restricted stock, though Richard Kinder already owns 17.9% of Kinder Morgan stock and Warren Buffett owns 31% of Berkshire Hathaway stock.

This raises an interesting question: Does a company's performance differ depending on how a CEO is compensated? Most shareholders, analysts, and boards of directors believe that linking compensation to performance motivates CEOs, attracts talent, and is seen as fair. But changes are coming. As a result of external pressures and strengthened demand for results, boards of directors and their compensation committees are making modifications in the structure of CEO compensation packages. Many companies, such as General Electric and Microsoft, are moving away from granting stock options, rebalancing the long-term incentive mix, and reigning in overall pay while strengthening the link between pay and performance.

Source: "Special Report: CEO Compensation," Forbes.com, May 3, 2007, www.forbes.com/2007/05/03/highest-paid-ceos-lead-07ceo-cz_sd_0503ceo_land.html, accessed June 12, 2007.

from the top" and the code of conduct simultaneously communicate the absolute need for all managers to behave ethically at all times. Managers should train employees to behave ethically. They should promptly and severely reprimand unethical conduct, regardless of the benefits that might accrue to the company from unethical actions. Some companies, such as Lockheed-Martin, emphasize ethical behavior by routinely evaluating employees against a business code of ethics.

Many organizations also set explicit boundaries precluding actions that harm the environment. Environmental violations (such as water and air pollution) carry heavy fines and prison terms under the laws of the United States and other countries. But in many companies, environmental responsibilities extend beyond legal requirements.

Socially responsible companies set aggressive environmental goals and measure and report their performance against them. German, Swiss, Dutch, and Scandinavian companies report on environmental performance as part of a larger set of social responsibility disclosures (such as employee welfare and community development activities). Some companies, such as DuPont, make environmental performance a line item on every employee's salary appraisal report. Duke Power Company appraises employees on their performance in reducing solid waste, cutting emissions and discharges, and implementing environmental plans. The result? Duke Power has met all its environmental goals.

Belief systems articulate the mission, purpose, and core values of a company. They describe the accepted norms and patterns of behavior expected of all managers and employees with respect to one another, shareholders, customers, and communities. Johnson & Johnson describes its values and norms in its credo statement:

> *We believe our first responsibility is to the doctors, nurses and patients, to mothers and fathers and all others who use our products and services. . . . Everything we do must be of high quality.*
>
> *We are responsible to our employees. . . . We must respect their dignity and recognize their merit. They must have a sense of security in their jobs. . . . We must be mindful of ways to help our employees fulfill their family responsibilities. . . . We must provide competent management, and their actions must be just and ethical.*
>
> *We are responsible to the communities in which we live. . . . We must support good works and charities and bear our fair share of taxes. . . . We must encourage civic improvements and better health and education.*
>
> *Our final responsibility is to our stockholders. Business must make a sound profit . . . . We must experiment with new ideas. . . develop innovative programs and pay for mistakes.*

Johnson & Johnson's credo is intended to inspire all managers and other employees to do their best. Belief systems play to employees' intrinsic motivations.

Intrinsic motivation is the desire to achieve self-satisfaction from good performance regardless of external rewards such as bonuses or promotion. Intrinsic motivation comes from being given greater responsibility, doing interesting and creative work, having pride in doing that work, establishing commitment to the organization, and developing personal bonds with coworkers. High intrinsic motivation enhances performance because managers and workers have a sense of achievement in doing something important, feel satisfied with their jobs, and see opportunities for personal growth.

Interactive control systems are formal information systems that managers use to focus organization attention and learning on key strategic issues. Managers use interactive control systems to create an ongoing dialogue around these key issues and to personally involve themselves in subordinates' decision-making activities. An excessive focus on diagnostic control systems and critical performance variables can cause an organization to ignore emerging threats and opportunities—changes in technology, customer preferences, regulations, and industry competition that can undercut a business. Interactive control systems help prevent this problem by highlighting and tracking strategic uncertainties that businesses face, such as the emergence of digital imaging in the case of Kodak and Fujifilm, airline deregulation in the case of American Airlines and Southwest Airlines, and the shift in customer preferences for mini- and microcomputers in the case of IBM. The key to this control lever is frequent face-to-face communications regarding these critical uncertainties. The result is ongoing discussion and debate about assumptions and action plans. New strategies emerge from the dialogue and debate surrounding the interactive process. Interactive control systems force busy managers to step back from the actions needed to manage the business today and to shift their focus forward to positioning the organization for the opportunities and threats of tomorrow.

Measuring and rewarding managers for achieving critical performance variables is an important driver of corporate performance. But these diagnostic control systems must be counterbalanced by the other levers of control—boundary systems, belief systems, and interactive control systems—to ensure that proper business ethics, inspirational values, and attention to future threats and opportunities are not sacrificed while achieving business results.

Problems for Self-Study

The Baseball Division of Home Run Sports manufactures and sells baseballs. Assume production equals sales. Budgeted data for February 2008 are:

Current assets	$ 400,000
Long-term assets	600,000
Total assets	$1,000,000
Production output	200,000 baseballs per month
Target ROI (Operating income ÷ Total assets)	30%
Fixed costs	$400,000 per month
Variable cost	$4 per baseball

Required

1. Compute the minimum selling price per baseball necessary to achieve the target ROI of 30%.
2. Using the selling price from requirement 1, separate the target ROI into its two components using the DuPont method.
3. Compute the RI of the Baseball Division for February 2008, using the selling price from requirement 1. Home Run Sports uses a required rate of return of 12% on total division assets when computing division RI.
4. In addition to her salary, Pamela Stephenson, the division manager, receives 3% of the monthly RI of the Baseball Division as a bonus. Compute Stephenson's bonus. Why do you think Stephenson is rewarded using both salary and a performance-based bonus? Stephenson does not like bearing risk.

Solution

1.

$$\begin{aligned}
\text{Target operating income} &= 30\% \text{ of } \$1{,}000{,}000 \text{ of total assets}\\
&= \$300{,}000\\
\text{Let } P &= \text{Selling price}\\
\text{Revenues} - \text{Variabe costs} - \text{Fixed costs} &= \text{Operating income}\\
200{,}000P - (200{,}000 \times \$4) - \$400{,}000 &= \$300{,}000\\
200{,}000P &= \$300{,}000 + \$800{,}000 + \$400{,}000\\
&= \$1{,}500{,}000\\
P &= \$7.50 \text{ per baseball}
\end{aligned}$$

Proof:		
	Revenues, 200,000 baseballs × $7.50/baseball	$1,500,000
	Variable costs, 200,000 baseballs × $4/baseball	800,000
	Contribution margin	700,000
	Fixed costs	400,000
	Operating income	$ 300,000

2. The DuPont method describes ROI as the product of two components: return on sales (income ÷ revenues) and investment turnover (revenues ÷ investment).

$$\frac{\text{Income}}{\text{Revenues}} \times \frac{\text{Revenues}}{\text{Investment}} = \frac{\text{Income}}{\text{Investment}}$$

$$\frac{\$300{,}000}{\$1{,}500{,}000} \times \frac{\$1{,}500{,}000}{\$1{,}000{,}000} = \frac{\$300{,}000}{\$1{,}000{,}000}$$

$$0.2 \times 1.5 = 0.30, \text{ or } 30\%$$

3.

$$\begin{aligned}
RI &= \text{Operating income} - \text{Required return on investment}\\
&= \$300{,}000 - (0.12 \times \$1{,}000{,}000)\\
&= \$300{,}000 - \$120{,}000\\
&= \$180{,}000
\end{aligned}$$

4. Stephenson's bonus $= 3\%$ of RI
$= 0.03 \times \$180{,}000 = \$5{,}400$

The Baseball Division's RI is affected by many factors, such as general economic conditions, beyond Stephenson's control. These uncontrollable factors make the Baseball Division's profitability uncertain and risky. Because Stephenson does not like bearing risk, paying her a flat salary, regardless of RI, would shield her from this risk. But there is a moral-hazard problem with this compensation arrangement. Because Stephenson's effort is difficult to monitor, the absence of performance-based compensation will provide her with no incentive to undertake extra physical and mental effort beyond what is necessary to retain her job or to uphold her personal values.

Paying no salary and rewarding Stephenson only on the basis of RI provides her with incentives to work hard but also subjects her to excessive risk because of uncontrollable factors that will affect RI and hence Stephenson's compensation. A compensation arrangement based only on RI would be more costly for Home Run Sports because it would have to compensate Stephenson for taking on uncontrollable risk. A compensation arrangement that consists of both a salary and an RI-based performance bonus balances the benefits of incentives against the extra costs of imposing uncontrollable risk

Decision Points

The following question-and-answer format summarizes the chapter's learning objectives. Each decision presents a key question related to a learning objective. The guidelines are the answer to that question.

Decision	Guidelines
1. What financial and nonfinancial performance measures do companies use in their balanced scorecards?	Financial measures such as return on investment and residual income measure aspects of both manager performance and organization-subunit performance. In many cases, financial measures are supplemented with nonfinancial measures of performance from the customer, internal-business-process, and learning-and-growth perspectives of the balanced scorecard—for example, customer-satisfaction, quality of products and services, and employee satisfaction.
2. What are the steps in designing an accounting-based performance measure?	The steps are (1) choose performance measures that align with top management's financial goals, (2) choose the time horizon of each performance measure, (3) choose a definition of the components in each performance measure, (4) choose a measurement alternative for each performance measure, (5) choose a target level of performance, and (6) choose the timing of feedback.
3. How does the DuPont method analyze return on investment?	The DuPont method describes return on investment (ROI) as the product of two components: income divided by revenues (return on sales) and revenues divided by investment (investment turnover). For example, ROI can be increased by increasing revenues, decreasing costs, and decreasing investment.
4. What is residual income and what are its advantages?	Residual income (RI) is income minus a dollar amount of required return on investment. RI is designed to overcome some of the limitations of ROI. For example, RI is more likely than ROI to promote goal congruence. ROI may induce managers of highly profitable divisions to reject projects (because accepting the project reduces ROI) even though the project should be accepted from the perspective of the company as a whole.
5. What is economic value added?	Economic value added (EVA) is a variation of the RI calculation. It equals after-tax operating income minus the product of (after-tax) weighted-average cost of capital and total assets minus current liabilities.

6. Should companies use the current cost or the historical cost of assets to measure performance?	Current cost of an asset is the cost now of purchasing an asset identical to the one currently held. Historical-cost asset-measurement methods generally consider net book value of the assets, which is original cost minus accumulated depreciation. Historical-cost measures are often inadequate for measuring economic returns. Current-cost measures are better. More generally, however, problems in any performance measure can be overcome by emphasizing budgets and targets that stress continuous improvement.
7. How can companies compare the performance of divisions operating in different countries?	Comparing the performance of divisions operating in different countries is difficult because of legal, political, social, economic, and currency differences. ROI and RI calculations for subunits operating in different countries need to be adjusted for differences in inflation between the two countries and changes in exchange rates.
8. Why are managers compensated based on a mix of salary and incentives?	Companies create incentives by rewarding managers on the basis of performance. But managers face risks because factors beyond their control may also affect their performance. Owners choose a mix of salary and incentive compensation to trade off the incentive benefit against the cost of imposing risk.
9. What are the four levers of control, and why does a company need to implement them?	The four levers of control are diagnostic control systems, boundary systems, belief systems, and interactive control systems. Implementing the four levers of control helps a company simultaneously strive for performance, behave ethically, inspire employees, and respond to strategic threats and opportunities.

TERMS TO LEARN

This chapter and the Glossary at the end of the book contain definitions of:

belief systems (**p. 819**)
boundary systems (**p. 817**)
current cost (**p. 807**)
diagnostic control systems (**p. 817**)
economic value added (EVA®) (**p. 804**)
imputed costs (**p. 803**)
interactive control systems (**p. 819**)
investment (**p. 800**)
moral hazard (**p. 814**)
residual income (RI) (**p. 803**)
return on investment (ROI) (**p. 801**)

ASSIGNMENT MATERIAL

Questions

23-1 Give examples of financial and nonfinancial performance measures that can be found in each of the four perspectives of the balanced scorecard.

23-2 What are the six steps in designing accounting-based performance measures?

23-3 What factors affecting ROI does the DuPont method of profitability analysis highlight?

23-4 "RI is not identical to ROI, although both measures incorporate income and investment into their computations." Do you agree? Explain.

23-5 Describe EVA.

23-6 Give three definitions of investment used in practice when computing ROI.

23-7 Distinguish between measuring assets based on current cost and historical cost.

23-8 What special problems arise when evaluating performance in multinational companies?

23-9 Why is it important to distinguish between the performance of a manager and the performance of the organization subunit for which the manager is responsible? Give an example.

23-10 Describe moral hazard.

23-11 "Managers should be rewarded only on the basis of their performance measures. They should be paid no salary." Do you agree? Explain.

23-12 Explain the role of benchmarking in evaluating managers.

23-13 Explain the incentive problems that can arise when employees must perform multiple tasks as part of their jobs.

23-14 Describe two disclosures required by the SEC with respect to executive compensation.

23-15 Describe the four levers of control.

Exercises

23-16 ROI, comparisons of three companies. (CMA, adapted) Return on investment (ROI) is often expressed as follows:

$$\frac{\text{Income}}{\text{Investment}} = \frac{\text{Income}}{\text{Revenues}} \times \frac{\text{Revenues}}{\text{Investment}}$$

Required

1. What advantages are there in the breakdown of the computation into two separate components?
2. Fill in the following blanks:

	Companies in Same Industry		
	A	**B**	**C**
Revenues	$1,000,000	$500,000	?
Income	$ 100,000	$ 50,000	?
Investment	$ 500,000	?	$5,000,000
Income as a percentage of revenues	?	?	0.5%
Investment turnover	?	?	2
ROI	?	1%	?

After filling in the blanks, comment on the relative performance of these companies as thoroughly as the data permit.

23-17 Analysis of return on invested assets, comparison of two divisions, DuPont method. Learning World, Inc. has two divisions: Test Preparation and Language Arts. Results (in millions) for the past three years are partially displayed here:

	A	B	C	D	E	F	G
1		Operating Income	Operating Revenues	Total Assets	Operating Income/ Operating Revenues	Operating Revenues/ Total Assets	Operating Income/ Total Assets
2	Test Preparation Division						
3	2008	$ 680	$ 7,960	$1920	?	?	?
4	2009	840	?	?	10%	?	42%
5	2010	1,160	?	?	11%	5	?
6	Language Arts Department						
7	2008	$ 620	$ 2,360	$1,280	?	?	?
8	2009	?	3,000	1,800	22%	?	?
9	2010	?	?	2,340	?	2	25%
10	Learning World Inc.						
11	2008	$1,300	$10,320	$3,200	?	?	?
12	2009	?	?	?	?	?	?
13	2010	?	?	?	?	?	?

If you want to use Excel to solve this exercise, go to the Excel Lab at **www.prenhall.com/horngren/cost13e** and download the template for Exercise 23-17.

Required

1. Complete the table by filling in the blanks.
2. Use the DuPont method of profitability analysis to explain changes in the operating-income-to-total-assets ratios over the 2008 through 2010 period for each division and for Learning World as a whole. Comment on the results.

23-18 ROI and RI. (D. Kleespie, adapted) The Outdoor Sports Company produces a wide variety of outdoor sports equipment. Its newest division, Golf Technology, manufactures and sells a single product: AccuDriver, a golf club that uses global positioning satellite technology to improve the accuracy of golfers' shots. The demand for AccuDriver is relatively insensitive to price changes. The following data are available for Golf Technology, which is an investment center for Outdoor Sports:

Total annual fixed costs	$30,000,000
Variable cost per AccuDriver	$ 500
Number of AccuDrivers sold each year	150,000
Average operating assets invested in the division	$48,000,000

Required

1. Compute Golf Technology's ROI if the selling price of AccuDrivers is $720 per club.
2. If management requires an ROI of at least 25% from the division, what is the minimum selling price that the Golf Technology Division should charge per AccuDriver club?
3. Assume that Outdoor Sports judges the performance of its investment centers on the basis of RI rather than ROI. What is the minimum selling price that Golf Technology should charge per AccuDriver if the company's required rate of return is 20%?

23-19 ROI and RI with manufacturing costs. Superior Motor Company makes electric cars and has only two products, the Simplegreen and the Superiorgreen. To produce the Simplegreen, Superior Motor employed assets of $13,500,000 at the beginning of the period, and $13,400,000 of assets at the end of the period. Other costs to manufacture the Simplegreen include:

Direct materials	$3,000 per unit
Setup	$1,300 per setup hour
Production	$415 per machine hour

General administration and selling costs total $7,340,000 for the period. In the current period, Superior Motor produced 10,000 Simplegreen cars using 6,000 setup hours and 175,200 machine hours. Superior Motor sold these cars for $12,000 each.

Required

1. Assuming that Superior Motor defines investment as average assets during the period, what is the return on investment for the Simplegreen division?
2. Calculate the residual income for the Simplegreen if Superior Motor has a required rate of return of 12% on investments.

23-20 Financial and nonfinancial performance measures, goal congruence. (CMA, adapted) Summit Equipment specializes in the manufacture of medical equipment, a field that has become increasingly competitive. Approximately two years ago, Ben Harrington, president of Summit, decided to revise the bonus plan (based, at the time, entirely on operating income) to encourage division managers to focus on areas that were important to customers and that added value without increasing cost. In addition to a profitability incentive, the revised plan includes incentives for reduced rework costs, reduced sales returns, and on-time deliveries. Bonuses are calculated and awarded semiannually on the following basis: A base bonus is calculated at 2% of operating income; this amount is then adjusted as follows:

a. (i) Reduced by excess of rework costs over and above 2% of operating income
   (ii) No adjustment if rework costs are less than or equal to 2% of operating income
b. (i) Increased by $5,000 if more than 98% of deliveries are on time, and by $2,000 if 96% to 98% of deliveries are on time
   (ii) No adjustment if on-time deliveries are below 96%
c. (i) Increased by $3,000 if sales returns are less than or equal to 1.5% of sales
   (ii) Decreased by 50% of excess of sales returns over 1.5% of sales

Note: If the calculation of the bonus results in a negative amount for a particular period, the manager simply receives no bonus, and the negative amount is not carried forward to the next period.

Results for Summit's Charter Division and Mesa Division for 2009, the first year under the new bonus plan, follow. In 2008, under the old bonus plan, the Charter Division manager earned a bonus of $27,060 and the Mesa Division manager, a bonus of $22,440.

	Charter Division		Mesa Division	
	January 1, 2009 to June 30, 2009	July 1, 2009 to Dec. 31, 2009	January 1, 2009 to June 30, 2009	July 1, 2009 to Dec. 31, 2009
Revenues	$4,200,000	$4,400,000	$2,850,000	$2,900,000
Operating income	$462,000	$440,000	$342,000	$406,000
On-time delivery	95.4%	97.3%	98.2%	94.6%
Rework costs	$11,500	$11,000	$6,000	$8,000
Sales returns	$84,000	$70,000	$44,750	$42,500

Required

1. Why did Harrington need to introduce these new performance measures? That is, why does Harrington need to use these performance measures in addition to the operating-income numbers for the period?
2. Calculate the bonus earned by each manager for each six-month period and for 2009.
3. What effect did the change in the bonus plan have on each manager's behavior? Did the new bonus plan achieve what Harrington desired? What changes, if any, would you make to the new bonus plan?

23-21 Goal incongruence and ROI. Bleefl Corporation manufactures furniture in several divisions, including the Patio Furniture division. The manager of the Patio Furniture division plans to retire in two years. The manager receives a bonus based on the division's ROI, which is currently 11%.

One of the machines that the Patio Furniture division uses to manufacture the furniture is rather old, and the manager must decide whether to replace it. The new machine would cost $30,000 and would last 10 years. It would have no salvage value. The old machine is fully depreciated and has no trade-in value. Bleefl uses straight-line depreciation for all assets. The new machine, being new and more efficient, would save the company $5,000 per year in cash operating costs. The only difference between cash flow and net income is depreciation. The internal rate of return of the project is approximately 11%. Bleefl Corporation's weighted average cost of capital is 6%. Bleefl is not subject to any income taxes.

Required

1. Should Bleefl Corporation replace the machine? Why or why not?
2. Assume that "investment" is defined as average net long-term assets after depreciation. Compute the project's ROI for each of its first five years. If the Patio Furniture manager is interested in maximizing his bonus, would he replace the machine before he retires? Why or why not?
3. What can Bleefl do to entice the manager to replace the machine before retiring?

23-22 ROI, RI, EVA. Performance Auto Company operates a New Car Division (that sells high performance sports cars) and a Performance Parts Division (that sells performance improvement parts for family cars). Some division financial measures for 2008 are as follows:

	A	B	C
1		New Car Division	Performance Parts Division
2	Total assets	$33,000,000	$28,500,000
3	Current liabilities	$ 6,600,000	$ 8,400,000
4	Operating income	$ 2,475,000	$ 2,565,000
5	Required rate of return	12%	12%

If you want to use Excel to solve this exercise, go to the Excel Lab at **www.prenhall.com/horngren/cost13e** and download the template for Exercise 23-22.

Required

1. Calculate return on investment (ROI) for each division using operating income as a measure of income and total assets as a measure of investment.
2. Calculate residual income (RI) for each division using operating income as a measure of income and total assets minus current liabilities as a measure of investment.
3. William Abraham, the New Car Division manager, argues that the Performance Parts Division has "loaded up on a lot of short-term debt" to boost its RI. Calculate an alternative RI for each division that is not sensitive to the amount of short-term debt taken on by the Performance Parts Division. Comment on the result.
4. Performance Auto Company, whose tax rate is 40%, has two sources of funds: long-term debt with a market value of $18,000,000 at an interest rate of 10%, and equity capital with a market value of $12,000,000 and a cost of equity of 15%. Applying the same weighted-average cost of capital (WACC) to each division, calculate EVA for each division.
5. Use your preceding calculations to comment on the relative performance of each division.

23-23 ROI, RI, measurement of assets. (CMA, adapted) Carter Corporation recently announced a bonus plan to be awarded to the manager of the most profitable division. The three division managers are to choose whether ROI or RI will be used to measure profitability. In addition, they must decide whether investment will be measured using gross book value or net book value of assets. Carter defines income as operating income and investment as total assets. The following information is available for the year just ended:

Division	Gross Book Value of Assets	Accumulated Depreciation	Operating Income
Radnor	$1,200,000	$645,000	$142,050
Easttown	1,140,000	615,000	137,550
Marion	750,000	420,000	92,100

Carter uses a required rate of return of 10% on investment to calculate RI.

Required Each division manager has selected a method of bonus calculation that ranks his or her division Number 1. Identify the method for calculating profitability that each manager selected, supporting your answer with appropriate calculations. Comment on the strengths and weaknesses of the methods chosen by each manager.

23-24 Multinational performance measurement, ROI, RI. The Grandlund Corporation manufactures similar products in the United States and Norway. The U.S. and Norwegian operations are organized as decentralized divisions. The following information is available for 2011; ROI is calculated as operating income divided by total assets:

	U.S. Division	Norwegian Division
Operating income	?	8,100,000 kroner
Total assets	$8,000,000	52,500,000 kroner
ROI	15%	?

Both investments were made on December 31, 2010. The exchange rate at the time of Grandlund's investment in Norway on December 31, 2010, was 6 kroner = $1. During 2011, the Norwegian Kroner increased steadily in value so that the exchange rate on December 31, 2011, is 7 kroner = $1. The average exchange rate during 2011 is [(6 + 7) ÷ 2] = 6.5 kroner = $1.

Required

1. **a.** Calculate the U.S. division's operating income for 2011.
   b. Calculate the Norwegian division's ROI for 2011 in kroner.
2. Top management wants to know which division earned a better ROI in 2011. What would you tell them? Explain your answer.
3. Which division do you think had the better RI performance? Explain your answer. The required rate of return on investment (calculated in U.S. dollars) is 12%.

23-25 ROI, RI, EVA and Performance Evaluation. Eva Manufacturing makes fashion products and competes on the basis of quality and leading-edge designs. The company has $3,000,000 invested in assets in its clothing manufacturing division. After-tax operating income from sales of clothing this year is $600,000. The cosmetics division has $10,000,000 invested in assets and an after-tax operating income this year of $1,600,000. Income for the clothing division has grown steadily over the last few years. The weighted average cost of capital for Eva is 10% and the previous period's after-tax return on investment for each division was 15%. The CEO of Eva has told the manager of each division that the division that "performs best" this year will get a bonus.

Required

1. Calculate the ROI and residual income for each division of Eva Manufacturing, and briefly explain which manager will get the bonus. What are the advantages and disadvantages of each measure?
2. The CEO of Eva Manufacturing has recently heard of another measure similar to residual income called EVA. The CEO has the accountant calculate EVA adjusted incomes of Clothing and Cosmetics, and finds that the adjusted after-tax operating incomes are $720,000 and $1,430,000, respectively. Also, the Clothing Division has $400,000 of current liabilities, while the Cosmetics Division has only $200,000 of current liabilities. Using the above information, calculate EVA, and discuss which division manager will get the bonus.
3. What nonfinancial measures could Eva use to evaluate divisional performances?

23-26 Risk sharing, incentives, benchmarking, multiple tasks. The Dexter Division of AMCO sells car batteries. AMCO's corporate management gives Dexter management considerable operating and investment autonomy in running the division. AMCO is considering how it should compensate Jim Marks, the general manager of the Dexter Division. Proposal 1 calls for paying Marks a fixed salary. Proposal 2 calls for paying Marks no salary and compensating him only on the basis of the division's ROI, calculated based on operating income before any bonus payments. Proposal 3 calls for paying Marks some salary and some bonus based on ROI. Assume that Marks does not like bearing risk.

Required

1. Evaluate the three proposals, specifying the advantages and disadvantages of each.
2. Suppose that AMCO competes against Tiara Industries in the car battery business. Tiara is approximately the same size as the Dexter Division and operates in a business environment that is similar to Dexter's. The top management of AMCO is considering evaluating Marks on the basis of Dexter's ROI minus Tiara's ROI. Marks complains that this approach is unfair because the performance of another company, over which he has no control, is included in his performance-evaluation measure. Is Marks's complaint valid? Why or why not?
3. Now suppose that Marks has no authority for making capital-investment decisions. Corporate management makes these decisions. Is ROI a good performance measure to use to evaluate Marks? Is ROI a good measure to evaluate the economic viability of the Dexter Division? Explain.
4. Dexter's salespersons are responsible for selling and providing customer service and support. Sales are easy to measure. Although customer service is important to Dexter in the long run, it has not yet implemented customer-service measures. Marks wants to compensate his sales force only on the

basis of sales commissions paid for each unit of product sold. He cites two advantages to this plan: (a) It creates strong incentives for the sales force to work hard, and (b) the company pays salespersons only when the company itself is earning revenues. Do you like his plan? Why or why not?

Problems

23-27 Residual Income and EVA; timing issues. Doorwhistle Company makes doorbells. It has a weighted average cost of capital of 8%, and total assets of $5,690,000. Doorwhistle has current liabilities of $700,000. Its operating income for the year was $649,000. Doorwhistle does not have to pay any income taxes. One of the expenses for accounting purposes was a $100,000 advertising campaign. The entire amount was deducted this year, although the Doorwhistle CEO believes the beneficial effects of this advertising will last four years.

Required

1. Calculate residual income, assuming Doorwhistle defines investment as total assets.
2. Calculate EVA for the year. Adjust both the assets and operating income for advertising assuming that for the purposes of economic value added the advertising is capitalized and amortized on a straight-line basis over four years.
3. Discuss the difference between the outcomes of requirements 1 and 2 and which measure is preferred.

23-28 ROI performance measures based on historical cost and current cost. Nature's Elixir Corporation operates three divisions that process and bottle natural fruit juices. The historical-cost accounting system reports the following information for 2008:

	Passion Fruit Division	Kiwi Fruit Division	Mango Fruit Division
Revenues	$1,000,000	$1,400,000	$2,200,000
Operating costs			
(excluding plant depreciation)	600,000	760,000	1,200,000
Plant depreciation	140,000	200,000	240,000
Operating income	$ 260,000	$ 440,000	$ 760,000
Current assets	$ 400,000	$ 500,000	$ 600,000
Long-term assets—plant	280,000	1,800,000	2,640,000
Total assets	$ 680,000	$2,300,000	$3,240,000

Nature's Elixir estimates the useful life of each plant to be 12 years, with no terminal disposal value. The straight-line depreciation method is used. At the end of 2008, the Passion Fruit plant is 10 years old, the Kiwi Fruit plant is 3 years old, and the Mango Fruit plant is 1 year old. An index of construction costs over the 10-year period that Nature's Elixir has been operating (1998 year-end = 100) is:

1998	2005	2007	2008
100	136	160	170

Given the high turnover of current assets, management believes that the historical-cost and current-cost measures of current assets are approximately the same.

1. Compute the ROI ratio (operating income to total assets) of each division using historical-cost measures. Comment on the results.
2. Use the approach in Exhibit 23-2 (p. 809) to compute the ROI of each division, incorporating current-cost estimates as of 2008 for depreciation expense and long-term assets. Comment on the results.
3. What advantages might arise from using current-cost asset measures as compared with historical-cost measures for evaluating the performance of the managers of the three divisions?

23-29 Evaluating managers, ROI, DuPont method, value-chain analysis of cost structure. Peach Computer Corporation is the largest personal computer company in the world. The CEO of Peach is retiring, and the board of directors is considering external candidates to fill the position. The board's top two choices are CEOs Peter Diamond (current CEO of NetPro) and Norma Provan (current CEO of On Point). As a board member on the search committee, you collect the following information (in millions):

	A	B	C	D	E
1		NetPro		On Point	
2		2007	2008	2007	2008
3	Revenues	$ 600.0	$ 480.0	$300.0	$525.0
4	Costs				
5	R&D	71.2	40.2	35.9	76.1
6	Production	132.6	145.6	107.6	128.2
7	Marketing and distribution	173.2	193.7	96.4	153.8
8	Customer service	65.5	40.0	30.4	67.6
9	Total costs	442.5	419.5	270.3	425.7
10	Operating income	$ 157.5	$ 60.5	$ 29.7	$ 99.3
11	Total assets	$540.00	$510.0	$240.0	$360.0

In early 2009, a leading computer magazine gave On Point's main product five stars, its highest rating. NetPro's main product received three stars, down from five stars a year earlier. In the same article, On Point's new products received praise; NetPro's new products were judged as "mediocre."

If you want to use Excel to solve this problem, go to the Excel Lab at **www.prenhall.com/horngren/cost13e** and download the template for Problem 23-29.

Required

1. Use the DuPont method to calculate NetPro's and On Point's ROIs in 2007 and 2008. Comment on the results. What can you tell from the DuPont analysis that you might have missed from calculating ROI itself?
2. Compute the percentage of costs in each of the four business-function cost categories for NetPro and On Point in 2007 and 2008. Comment on the results.
3. Relate the results of requirements 1 and 2 to the comments made by the computer magazine. Of Diamond and Provan, whom would you suggest to be the new CEO of Peach?

23-30 ROI, RI and Multinational Firms. Konekopf Corporation has a division in the United States, and another in France. The investment in the French assets was made when the exchange rate was $1.20 per euro. The average exchange rate for the year was $1.30 per euro. The exchange rate at the end of the fiscal year was $1.38 per euro. Income and investment for the two divisions are:

	United States	France
Investment in assets	$3,490,000	2,400,000 euros
Income for current year	$ 383,900	266,400 euros

Required

1. The required return for Konekopf is 10%. Calculate ROI and RI for the two divisions. For the French division, calculate these measures using both dollars and euros. Which division is doing better?
2. What are the advantages and disadvantages of translating the French division information from euros to dollars?

23-31 Multinational firms, differing risk, comparison of profit, ROI and RI. Zzwuig Multinational, Inc. has divisions in the United States, Germany, and New Zealand. The U.S. division is the oldest and most established of the three, and has a cost of capital of 6%. The German division was started three years ago when the exchange rate for euros was 1 euro = $1.25. Although it is a large and powerful division of Zzwuig Inc., its cost of capital is 10%. The New Zealand division was started this year, when the exchange rate was 1 New Zealand Dollar (NZD) = $0.64. Its cost of capital is 13%. Average exchange rates for the current year are 1 euro = $1.32 and 1 NZD = $0.67. Other information for the three divisions includes:

	United States	Germany	New Zealand
Long term assets	$14,845,000	9,856,000 euros	9,072,917 NZD
Operating revenues	$10,479,000	5,200,000 euros	4,800,000 NZD
Operating expenses	$ 7,510,000	3,600,000 euros	3,500,000 NZD
Income tax rate	40%	30%	20%

Required

1. Translate the German and New Zealand information into dollars to make the divisions comparable. Find the after-tax operating income for each division and compare the profits.
2. Calculate ROI using after-tax operating income. Compare among divisions.

3. Use after-tax operating income and the individual cost of capital of each division to calculate residual income and compare.
4. Redo requirement 2 using pretax operating income instead of net income. Why is there a big difference, and what does it mean for performance evaluation?

23-32 ROI, RI, DuPont method, investment decisions, balanced scorecard. News Mogul Group has two major divisions: Print and Internet. Summary financial data (in millions) for 2008 and 2009 are as follows:

	A	B	C	D	E	F	G	H	I
1		Operating Income			Revenues			Total Assets	
2		2008	2009		2008	2009		2008	2009
3	Print	$3,780	$4,620		$18,900	$19,320		$18,400	$20,500
4	Internet	546	672		25,200	26,880		11,340	12,600

The two division managers' annual bonuses are based on division ROI (defined as operating income divided by total assets). If a division reports an increase in ROI from the previous year, its management is automatically eligible for a bonus; however, the management of a division reporting a decline in ROI has to present an explanation to the News Mogul Group board and is unlikely to get any bonus.

Carol Mays, manager of the Print Division, is considering a proposal to invest $800 million in a new computerized news reporting and printing system. It is estimated that the new system's state-of-the-art graphics and ability to quickly incorporate late-breaking news into papers will increase 2010 division operating income by $120 million. News Mogul Group uses a 15% required rate of return on investment for each division.

If you want to use Excel to solve this problem, go to the Excel Lab at **www.prenhall.com/horngren/cost12e** and download the template for Problem 23-32.

Required

1. Use the DuPont method of profitability analysis to explain differences in 2009 ROIs between the two divisions. Use 2009 total assets as the investment base.
2. Why might Mays be less than enthusiastic about accepting the investment proposal for the new system, despite her belief in the benefits of the new technology?
3. Murdoch Turner, CEO of News Mogul Group, is considering a proposal to base division executive compensation on division RI.
   a. Compute the 2009 RI of each division.
   b. Would adoption of an RI measure reduce Mays' reluctance to adopt the new computerized system investment proposal?
4. Turner is concerned that the focus on annual ROI could have an adverse long-run effect on News Mogul Group's customers. What other measurements, if any, do you recommend that Turner use? Explain briefly.

23-33 Division managers' compensation, levers of control (continuation of 23-32). Murdoch Turner seeks your advice on revising the existing bonus plan for division managers of News Mogul Group. Assume division managers do not like bearing risk. Turner is considering three ideas:

- Make each division manager's compensation depend on division RI.
- Make each division manager's compensation depend on companywide RI.
- Use benchmarking, and compensate division managers on the basis of their division's RI minus the RI of the other division.

Required

1. Evaluate the three ideas Turner has put forth using performance-evaluation concepts described in this chapter. Indicate the positive and negative features of each proposal.
2. Turner is concerned that the pressure for short-run performance may cause managers to cut corners. What systems might Turner introduce to avoid this problem? Explain briefly.
3. Turner is also concerned that the pressure for short-run performance might cause managers to ignore emerging threats and opportunities. What system might Turner introduce to prevent this problem? Explain briefly.

23-34 Executive compensation, balanced scorecard. Community Bank recently introduced a new bonus plan for its business unit executives. The company believes that current profitability and customer satisfaction levels are equally important to the bank's long-term success. As a result, the new plan awards a bonus equal to 1% of salary for each 1% increase in net income or 1% increase in the company's customer satisfaction index. For example, increasing net income from $3 million to $3.3 million (or 10% from its initial value) leads to a bonus of 10% of salary, while increasing the bank's customer satisfaction index from 70 to 73.5 (or 5% from its initial value) leads to a bonus of 5% of salary. There is no bonus penalty when net income or customer satisfaction declines. In 2008 and 2009, Community Bank's three business units reported the following performance results:

	Retail Banking		Business Banking		Credit Cards	
	2008	**2009**	**2008**	**2009**	**2008**	**2009**
Net income	$2,800,000	$3,220,000	$2,900,000	$3,016,000	$2,750,000	$2,722,500
Customer satisfaction	73	73	70	75.6	69	79.35

Required

1. Compute the bonus as a percent of salary earned by each business unit executive in 2009.
2. What factors might explain the different improvement rates for net income and customer satisfaction in the three units?
3. Community Bank's board of directors is concerned that the 2009 bonus awards may not actually reflect the executives' overall performance. In particular, it is concerned that executives can earn large bonuses by doing well on one performance dimension but underperforming on the other. What changes can it make to the bonus plan to prevent this from happening in the future? Explain briefly.

23-35 Ethics, manager's performance evaluation. (A. Spero, adapted) Hamilton Semiconductors manufactures specialized chips that sell for $20 each. Hamilton's manufacturing costs consist of variable cost of $2 per chip and fixed costs of $9,000,000. Hamilton also incurs $400,000 in fixed marketing costs each year.

Hamilton calculates operating income using absorption costing—that is, Hamilton calculates manufacturing cost per unit by dividing total manufacturing costs by actual production. Hamilton costs all units in inventory at this rate and expenses the costs in the income statement at the time when the units in inventory are sold. Next year, 2011, appears to be a difficult year for Hamilton. It expects to sell only 500,000 units. The demand for these chips fluctuates considerably, so Hamilton usually holds minimal inventory.

Required

1. Calculate Hamilton's operating income in 2011 (a) if Hamilton manufactures 500,000 units and (b) if Hamilton manufactures 600,000 units.
2. Would it be unethical for Randy Jones, the general manager of Hamilton Semiconductors, to produce more units than can be sold in order to show better operating results? Jones's compensation has a bonus component based on operating income. Explain your answer.
3. Would it be unethical for Jones to ask distributors to buy more product than they need? Hamilton follows the industry practice of booking sales when products are shipped to distributors. Explain your answer.

23-36 Ethics, levers of control. (R. Madison, adapted, *Strategic Finance*, January 2000). United Forest Products (UFP) is a large timber and wood processing plant. UFP's performance-evaluation system pays its managers substantial bonuses if the company achieves annual budgeted profit numbers. In the last quarter of 2009, Amy Kimbell, UFP's controller, noted a slight increase in output and a significant decrease in the purchase cost of raw timber.

One day when Kimbell was at the log yard where timber is received and scaled (weighed and checked for quality) to determine what UFP pays for it, she noted that a timber contractor was quite aggravated when he was given the scale report (board feet and quality). When she asked one of the scale employees what was bothering the contractor, he revealed that the scalers had received instructions from their supervisors to deliberately "lowball" evaluations of timber quantity and quality. This reduced the price paid to timber suppliers, which also reduced direct material costs, helping UFP to meet its profit target.

1. What should Kimbell do? You may want to refer to *Standards of Ethical Conduct for Management Accountants and Resolution of Ethical Conflict*, pp. 16–17.
2. Which lever of control is UFP emphasizing? What changes, if any, should be made?

Collaborative Learning Problem

23-37 ROI, RI, division manager's compensation, balanced scorecard. Key information for the Peoria Division (PD) of Barrington Industries for 2009 follows.

Revenues	$15,000,000
Operating income	$ 1,800,000
Total assets	$10,000,000

PD's managers are evaluated and rewarded on the basis of ROI defined as operating income divided by total assets. Barrington Industries expects its divisions to increase ROI each year.

Next year, 2010, appears to be a difficult year for PD. PD had planned a new investment to improve quality but, in view of poor economic conditions, has postponed the investment. ROI for 2010 was certain to decrease if PD had made the investment.

Management is now considering ways to meet its target ROI of 20% for next year. It anticipates revenues to be steady at $15,000,000 in 2010.

Required

1. Calculate PD's return on sales (ROS) and ROI for 2009.
2. a. By how much would PD need to cut costs in 2010 to achieve its target ROI of 20%, assuming no change in total assets between 2009 and 2010?
   b. By how much would PD need to decrease total assets in 2010 to achieve its target ROI of 20%, assuming no change in operating income between 2009 and 2010?
3. Calculate PD's RI in 2009 assuming a required rate of return on investment of 15%.
4. PD wants to increase RI by 50% in 2010. Assuming it could cut costs by $45,000 in 2010, by how much would PD need to decrease total assets in 2010?
5. Barrington Industries is concerned that the focus on cost cutting, asset sales, and no new investments will have an adverse long-run effect on PD's customers. Yet Barrington wants PD to meet its financial goals. What other measurements, if any, do you recommend that Barrington use? Explain briefly.

Appendix A: Recommended Readings

The literature of cost accounting and related areas is vast and varies. The following books illustrate recent publications that capture current developments:

- Ansari, S., J. Bell, and CAM-I Target Cost Core Group, *Target Costing: The Next Frontier in Strategic Cost Management.* Homewood, IL: Irwin McGraw-Hill, 1997.
- Brimson, J., *Activity Accounting: An Activity-Based Costing Approach.* New York: John Wiley & Sons, 1997.
- Cheffers, M., and M. Pakaluk, *Understanding Accounting Ethics, 2nd Edition.* Manchaug, MA: Allen David Press, 2007.
- Connell, R., *Measuring Customer and Service Profitability in the Finance Sector.* London, U.K.: Chapman & Hall, 1996.
- Cooper, R., and R. Kaplan, *The Design of Cost Management Systems.* Upper Saddle River, NJ: Prentice Hall, 1999.
- Gray, R., and J. Bebbington, *Accounting for the Environment, 2nd Edition.* Thousand Oaks, CA: Sage Publications, 2002.
- Johnson, H., *Relevance Regained.* New York: Free Press, 1992.
- Kaplan, R., and S. Anderson, *Time-Driven Activity-Based Costing: A Simpler and More Powerful Path to Higher Profits.* Boston: Harvard Business School Press, 2007.
- Miller, J., *Implementing Activity-Based Management.* New York: John Wiley & Sons, 1996.
- Oliver, L., *Designing Strategic Cost Systems.* New York: John Wiley & Sons, 2004.
- Player, S., and D. Keys, *Activity-Based Management.* New York: MasterMedia Limited, 1995.
- Shank. J., and V. Govindarajan, *Strategic Management Accounting.* New York: Free Press, 1993.
- Simons, R., *Performance Measurement and Control Systems for Implementing Strategy.* Upper Saddle River, NJ: Prentice Hall, 2000.
- Young, S., and S. O'Byrne, *EVA and Value-Based Management.* Columbus, OH: McGraw-Hill, 2000.

Books of readings related to cost or management accounting include:

- Aly, I., ed., *Readings in Management Accounting.* Dubuque, Iowa: Kendall/Hunt, 1995.
- Bhimani, A., ed., *Contemporary Issues in Management Accounting.* New York: Oxford University Press, 2006.
- Bhimani, A., ed., *Management Accounting in the Digital Economy.* New York: Oxford University Press, 2004.
- Brinker, B., ed., *Emerging Practices in Cost Management.* Boston: Warren, Gorham, and Lamont, 1995.
- Ratnatunga, J., J. Miller, N. Mudalige, and A. Sohalled, eds., *Issues in Strategic Management Accounting.* Sydney, Australia: Harcourt Brace Jovanovich, 1993.
- Young, M., ed., *Readings in Management Accounting, 4th Edition.* Upper Saddle River, NJ: Prentice Hall, 2003.

The Harvard Business School series in accounting and control offers important contributions to the cost accounting literature, including:

- Anthony, R., *The Management Control Function*. Boston: Harvard Business School Press, 1998.
- Berliner, C., and J. Brimson, eds., *Cost Management for Today's Advanced Manufacturing: The CAMI Conceptual Design*. Boston: Harvard Business School Press, 1988.
- Bruns, W., ed., *Performance Measurement, Evaluation, and Incentives*. Boston: Harvard Business School Press, 1992.
- Cooper, R., *When Lean Enterprises Collide*. Boston: Harvard Business School Press, 1995.
- Hope, J., *Reinventing the CFO: How Financial Managers Can Transform Their Roles and Add Greater Value*. Boston: Harvard Business School Press, 2006.
- Hope, J., and R. Fraser, *Beyond Budgeting: How Managers Can Break Free from the Annual Performance Trap*. Boston: Harvard Business School Press, 2003.
- Johnson, H., and R. Kaplan, *Relevance Lost: The Rise and Fall of Management Accounting*. Boston: Harvard Business School Press, 1987.
- Kaplan, R., ed., *Measures for Manufacturing Excellence*. Boston: Harvard Business School Press, 1990.
- Kaplan, R., and R. Cooper, *Cost and Effect*. Boston: Harvard Business School Press, 1998.
- Kaplan, R., and D. Norton, *The Balanced Scorecard*. Boston: Harvard Business School Press, 1996.
- Kaplan, R., and D. Norton, *The Strategy-Focused Organization: How Balanced Scorecard Companies Thrive in the New Business Environment*. Boston: Harvard Business School Press, 2001.
- Kaplan, R., and D. Norton, *Strategy Maps: Converting Intangible Assets into Tangible Outcomes*. Boston: Harvard Business School Press, 2004.
- Kaplan, R., and D. Norton, *Alignment: Using the Balanced Scorecard to Create Corporate Synergies*. Boston: Harvard Business School Press, 2006.
- Kim, W., and R. Mauborgne, *Blue Ocean Strategy: How to Create Uncontested Market Space and Make the Competition Irrelevant*. Boston: Harvard Business School Press, 2005.
- Simons, R., *Levers of Control*. Boston: Harvard Business School Press, 1995.

Productivity Press publishes many books with a global focus on cost and management accounting, including:

- Cooper, R., and R. Slagmulder, *Target Costing and Value Engineering*. Portland, OR: Productivity Press, 1997.
- Maskall, B., and B. Baggaley, *Practical Lean Accounting: A Proven System for Measuring and Managing the Lean Enterprise*. Portland, OR: Productivity Press, 2003.
- Monden, Y., *Cost Reduction Systems: Target Costing and Kaizen Costing*. Portland, OR: Productivity Press, 2003.
- Sakurai, M. *Integrated Cost Management*. Portland, OR: Productivity Press, 1996.
- Thurn, W., *Maximizing Profit: How to Measure the Financial Impact of Manufacturing Decisions*. Portland, OR: Productivity Press, 2002.

The Institute of Management Accountants formerly published monographs and books covering cost accounting topics, such as:

- Atkinson, A., J. Hamburg, and C. Ittner, *Linking Quality to Profits*. Montvale, NJ: Institute of Management Accountants and Milwaukee, WI: ASQC Quality Press, 1994.

- Cooper, R., R. Kaplan, L. Maisel, E. Morrissey, and R. Oehm, *Implementing Activity-Based Cost Management: Moving from Analysis to Action*. Montvale, NJ: Institute of Management Accountants, 1993.
- Epstein, M., *Measuring Corporate Environmental Performance*. Montvale, NJ: Institute of Management Accountants, 1995.
- Klammer, T., *Managing Strategic and Capital Investment Decisions*. Burr Ridge, IL: Irwin and Montvale, NJ: Institute of Management Accountants, 1994.
- Martinson, O., *Cost Accounting in the Service Industry*. Montvale, NJ: Institute of Management Accountants, 1994.
- Noreen, E., D. Smith, and J. Mackey, *The Theory of Constraints and Its Implications for Management Accounting*. Great Barrington, MA: North River Press, 1995.

The Financial Executives Research Foundation publishes monographs and books concerning topics of interest to financial executives, such as:

- de Mesa Graziano, C., *Enron and the Powers Report: An Examination of Business and Accounting Failures*. Morristown, NJ: Financial Executives Research Foundation, 2002.
- Jablonski, S., *Changing Roles of Financial Management*. Morristown, NJ: Financial Executives Research Foundation, 2004.
- Najarian, G., *Understanding Different Cost Accounting Solutions*. Morristown, NJ: Financial Executives Research Foundation, 2007.

The Chartered Institute of Management Accountants, London, U.K., publishes monographs and books, including:

- Burns, J., M. Ezzamel, and R. Scapens, *Challenge of Management Accounting Change*. London, U.K.: Chartered Institute of Management Accountants, 2003.
- Doyle, D., *Cost Control: A Strategic Guide*. London, U.K.: Chartered Institute of Management Accountants, 2002.
- Drury, C., ed., *Management Accounting Handbook*. London, U.K.: Butterworth Heinemann and Chartered Institute of Management Accountants, 1997.
- Drury, C., and M. Tayles, *Cost System Design and Profitability Analysis in UK Companies*. London, U.K.: Chartered Institute of Management Accountants, 2000.
- Ezzamel, M., C. Green, S. Lilley, and H. Willmott, *Changing Managers and Managing Change*. London, U.K.: Chartered Institute of Management Accountants, 1995.
- Friedman, A., and S. Lylne, *Activity Based Techniques: The Real Life Consequences*. London, U.K.: Chartered Institute of Management Accountants, 1995.
- Mackay, A., *A Practitioners' Guide to the Balanced Scorecard*. London, U.K.: Chartered Institute of Management Accountants, 2004.
- McLaren, J., *Implementing the EVA Business Philosophy: Management Accounting Evidence from New Zealand*. London, U.K.: Chartered Institute of Management Accountants, 2005.
- Murphy, C., J. Currie, M. Fahy, and W. Golden, *Deciding the Future: Management Accountants as Decision Support Personnel*. London, U.K.: Chartered Institute of Management Accountants, 1995.

Elsevier B.V. publishes *Advances in Management Accounting* on an annual basis. It is edited by M. Epstein and J. Lee and includes a broad cross-section of research articles and case studies.

Case books on cost and management accounting include:

- Allen, B., E. Brownlee, M. Haskins, L. Lynch, J. Rotch, *Cases in Management Accounting and Control Systems*, 4th Edition. Upper Saddle River, NJ: Prentice Hall, 2004.
- Shank, J., *Cases in Cost Management: A Strategic Emphasis*, 2nd Edition. Mason, OH: South-Western College Publishing, 2000.

The following are detailed annotated bibliographies of the cost management and accounting research literatures:

- Bentley, H., *Bibliography of Works on Accounting by American Authors*. Mansfield Centre, CT: Martino Publishing, 1998.
- Brown, L., J. Gardner, and M. Vasarhelyi, *Accounting Research Directory: Database of Accounting Literature*. Princeton, NJ: Markus Wiener Publishers, 1994.
- Clancy, D., *Annotated Management Accounting Readings*. Management Accounting Section of the American Accounting Association, 1986.
- Klemstine, C., and M. Maher, *Management Accounting Research: 1926–1983*. New York: Garland Publishing, 1984.

Two journals bearing on management accounting are published by sections of the American Accounting Association, 7171 Bessie Drive, Sarasota, FL 34233: *Journal of Management Accounting Research* and *Behavioral Research in Accounting*.

Professional associations that specialize in serving members with cost and management accounting interests include:

- *Institute of Management Accountants*, 10 Paragon Drive, Montvale, NJ 07645. Publishes the *Strategic Finance* and *Management Accounting Quarterly* journals.
- *Financial Executives International*, 200 Campus Drive, Florham Park, NJ 07932. Publishes *Financial Executive*.
- *Society of Cost Estimating and Analysis*, 101 South Whiting Street, Suite 201, Alexandria, VA 22304. Publishes the *Journal of Cost Analysis & Management* and monographs on topics related to cost estimation and price analysis in government and industry.
- *The Institute of Internal Auditors*, 249 Maitland Avenue, Altamonte Springs, FL 32701. Publishes *The Internal Auditor* journal. Also publishes monographs on topics related to internal control.
- *Certified Management Accountants of Canada*, One Robert Speck Parkway, Suite 1400, Mississauga, Ontario L4Z 3M3. Publishes the *CMA Magazine*.
- *The Chartered Institute of Management Accountants*, 26 Chapter Street, London, SW1P 4NP. Publishes the *Financial Management* journal. Also publishes monographs covering cost and management accounting topics.

In many countries, individuals with cost and management accounting interests belong to professional bodies that serve members with financial reporting and taxation, as well as cost and management accounting, interests.

Appendix B: Notes on Compound Interest and Interest Tables

Interest is the cost of using money. It is the rental charge for funds, just as renting a building and equipment entails a rental charge. When the funds are used for a period of time, it is necessary to recognize interest as a cost of using the borrowed ("rented") funds. This requirement applies even if the funds represent ownership capital and if interest does not entail an outlay of cash. Why must interest be considered? Because the selection of one alternative automatically commits a given amount of funds that could otherwise be invested in some other alternative.

Interest is generally important, even when short-term projects are under consideration. Interest looms correspondingly larger when long-run plans are studied. The rate of interest has significant enough impact to influence decisions regarding borrowing and investing funds. For example, $100,000 invested now and compounded annually for 10 years at 8% will accumulate to $215,900; at 20%, the $100,000 will accumulate to $619,200.

Interest Tables

Many computer programs and pocket calculators are available that handle computations involving the time value of money. You may also turn to the following four basic tables to compute interest.

Table 1—Future Amount of $1

Table 1 shows how much $1 invested now will accumulate in a given number of periods at a given compounded interest rate per period. Consider investing $1,000 now for three years at 8% compound interest. A tabular presentation of how this $1,000 would accumulate to $1,259.70 follows:

Year	Interest per Year	Cumulative Interest Called Compound Interest	Total at End of Year
0	$ —	$ —	$1,000.00
1	80.00 (0.08 × $1,000)	80.00	1,080.00
2	86.40 (0.08 × $1,080)	166.40	1,166.40
3	93.30 (0.08 × $1,166.40)	259.70	1,259.70

This tabular presentation is a series of computations that could appear as follows, where S is the future amount and the subscripts 1, 2, and 3 indicate the number of time periods.

$$S_1 = \$1{,}000(1.08)^1 = \$1.080$$
$$S_2 = \$1{,}080(1.08) = \$1{,}000(1.08)^2 = \$1{,}166.40$$
$$S_3 = \$1{,}166.40 \times (1.08) = \$1{,}000(1.08)^3 = \$1{,}259.70$$

The formula for the "amount of 1," often called the "future value of $1" or "future amount of $1," can be written

$$S = P(1 + r)^n$$
$$S = \$1{,}000(1 + .08)^3 = \$1{,}259.70$$

S is the future value amount; P is the present value, \$1,000 in this case; r is the rate of interest; and n is the number of time periods.

Fortunately, tables make key computations readily available. A facility in selecting the *proper* table will minimize computations. Check the accuracy of the preceding answer using Table 1, p. 839.

Table 2—Present Value of \$1

In the previous example, if \$1,000 compounded at 8% per year will accumulate to \$1,259.70 in 3 years, then \$1,000 must be the present value of \$1,259.70 due at the end of 3 years. The formula for the present value can be derived by reversing the process of *accumulation* (finding the future amount) that we just finished.

If $$S - P(1 + r)^n$$

then $$P = \frac{S}{(1 + r)^n}$$

$$P = \frac{\$1{,}259.70}{(1.08)^3} = \$1{,}000$$

Use Table 2, p. 840, to check this calculation.

When accumulating, we advance or roll forward in time. The difference between our original amount and our accumulated amount is called *compound interest.* When discounting, we retreat or roll back in time. The difference between the future amount and the present value is called *compound discount.* Note the following formulas (where P = \$1,000):

$$\text{Compound interest} = P[(1 + r)^n - 1] = \$259.70$$

$$\text{Compound discount} = S\left[1 - \frac{1}{(1 + r)^n}\right] = \$259.70$$

Table 3—Amount of Annuity of \$1

An (ordinary) *annuity* is a series of equal payments (receipts) to be paid (or received) at the end of successive periods of equal length. Assume that \$1,000 is invested at the end of each of 3 years at 8%:

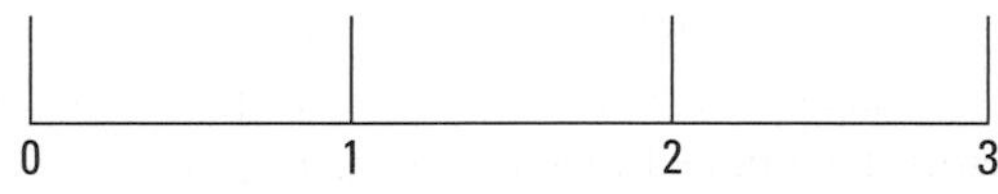

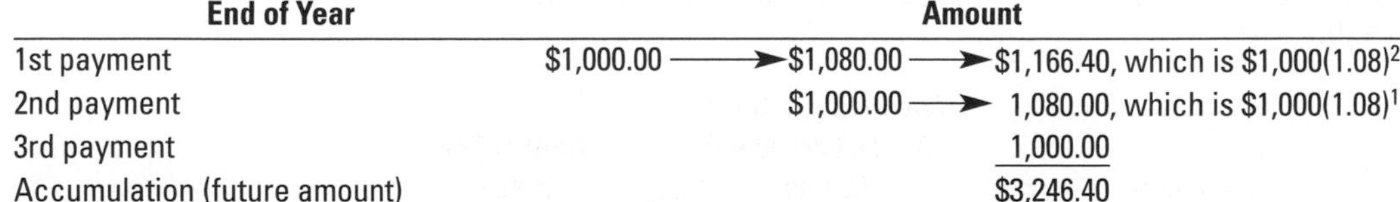

End of Year		Amount	
1st payment	\$1,000.00 ⟶	\$1,080.00 ⟶	\$1,166.40, which is \$1,000(1.08)^2
2nd payment		\$1,000.00 ⟶	1,080.00, which is \$1,000(1.08)^1
3rd payment			1,000.00
Accumulation (future amount)			\$3,246.40

The preceding arithmetic may be expressed algebraically as the amount of an ordinary annuity of \$1,000 for 3 years = \$1,000$(1 + r)^2$ + \$1,000$(1 + r)^1$ + \$1,000.

We can develop the general formula for S_n, the amount of an ordinary annuity of \$1, by using the example above as a basis:

1. $S_n = 1 + (1 + r)^1 + (1 + r)^2$
2. Substitute: $S_n = 1 + (1.08)^1 + (1.08)^2$
3. Multiply (2) by $(1 + r)$: $(1.08)S_n = (1.08)^1 + (1.08)^2 + (1.08)^3$
4. Subtract (2) from (3): Note that all terms on the right-hand side are removed except $(1.08)^3$ in equation (3) and 1 in equation (2). $1.08S_n - S_n = (1.08)^3 - 1$

5. Factor (4): $S_n(1.08 - 1) = (1.08)^3 - 1$

6. Divide (5) by (1.08 − 1): $S_n = \dfrac{(1.08)^3 - 1}{1.08 - 1} = \dfrac{(1.08)^3 - 1}{.08}$

7. The general formula for the amount of an ordinary annuity of \$1 becomes: $S_n = \dfrac{(1 + r)^n - 1}{r}$ or $\dfrac{\text{Compound interest}}{\text{Rate}}$

This formula is the basis for Table 3, p. 841. Look at Table 3 or use the formula itself to check the calculations.

Table 4—Present Value of an Ordinary Annuity of \$1

Using the same example as for Table 3, we can show how the formula of P_n, *the present value of an ordinary annuity*, is developed.

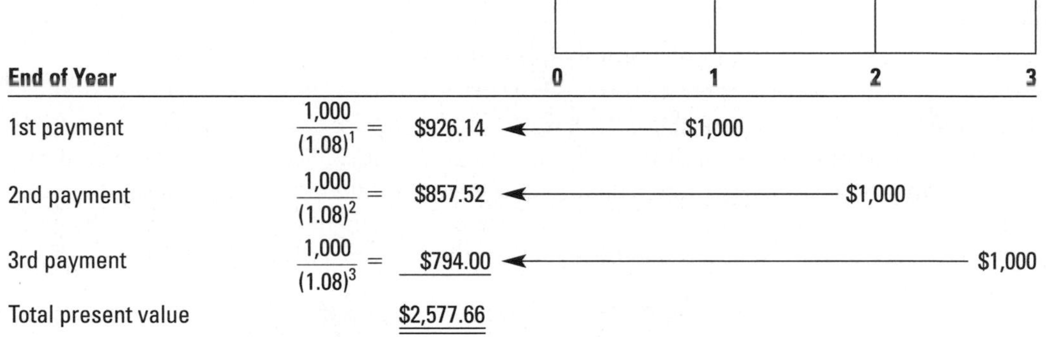

End of Year			0	1	2	3
1st payment	$\dfrac{1{,}000}{(1.08)^1}$ =	\$926.14	←	\$1,000		
2nd payment	$\dfrac{1{,}000}{(1.08)^2}$ =	\$857.52	←		\$1,000	
3rd payment	$\dfrac{1{,}000}{(1.08)^3}$ =	\$794.00	←			\$1,000
Total present value		\$2,577.66				

For the general case, the present value of an ordinary annuity of \$1 may be expressed as:

1. $P_n = \dfrac{1}{1 + r} + \dfrac{1}{(1 + r)^2} + \dfrac{1}{(1 + r)^3}$

2. Substitute $P_n = \dfrac{1}{1.08} + \dfrac{1}{(1.08)^2} + \dfrac{1}{(1.08)^3}$

3. Multiply by $\dfrac{1}{1.08}$: $P_n\dfrac{1}{1.08} = \dfrac{1}{(1.08)^2} + \dfrac{1}{(1.08)^3} + \dfrac{1}{(1.08)^4}$

4. Subtract (3) from (2): $P_n - P_n\dfrac{1}{1.08} = \dfrac{1}{1.08} - \dfrac{1}{(1.08)^4}$

5. Factor: $P_n\left(1 - \dfrac{1}{(1.08)}\right) = \dfrac{1}{1.08}\left[1 - \dfrac{1}{(1.08)^3}\right]$

6. or $P_n\left(\dfrac{.08}{1.08}\right) = \dfrac{1}{1.08}\left[1 - \dfrac{1}{(1.08)^3}\right]$

7. Multiply by $\dfrac{1.08}{.08}$: $P_n = \dfrac{1}{.08}\left[1 - \dfrac{1}{(1.08)^3}\right]$

The general formula for the present value of an annuity of \$1.00 is:

$$P_n = \frac{1}{r}\left[1 - \frac{1}{(1 + r)^n}\right] = \frac{\text{Compound discount}}{\text{Rate}}$$

Solving, $P_n = \dfrac{.2062}{.08} = 2.577$

The formula is the basis for Table 4, p. 842. Check the answer in the table. The present value tables, Tables 2 and 4, are used most frequently in capital budgeting.

The tables for annuities are not essential. With Tables 1 and 2, compound interest and compound discount can readily be computed. It is simply a matter of dividing either of these by the rate to get values equivalent to those shown in Tables 3 and 4.

Table 1

Compound Amount of $1.00 (The Future Value of $1.00)

$S = P(1 + r)^n$. In this table $P = \$1.00$

Periods	2%	4%	6%	8%	10%	12%	14%	16%	18%	20%	22%	24%	26%	28%	30%	32%	40%	Periods
1	1.020	1.040	1.060	1.080	1.100	1.120	1.140	1.160	1.180	1.200	1.220	1.240	1.260	1.280	1.300	1.320	1.400	1
2	1.040	1.082	1.124	1.166	1.210	1.254	1.300	1.346	1.392	1.440	1.488	1.538	1.588	1.638	1.690	1.742	1.960	2
3	1.061	1.125	1.191	1.260	1.331	1.405	1.482	1.561	1.643	1.728	1.816	1.907	2.000	2.097	2.197	2.300	2.744	3
4	1.082	1.170	1.262	1.360	1.464	1.574	1.689	1.811	1.939	2.074	2.215	2.364	2.520	2.684	2.856	3.036	3.842	4
5	1.104	1.217	1.338	1.469	1.611	1.762	1.925	2.100	2.288	2.488	2.703	2.932	3.176	3.436	3.713	4.007	5.378	5
6	1.126	1.265	1.419	1.587	1.772	1.974	2.195	2.436	2.700	2.986	3.297	3.635	4.002	4.398	4.827	5.290	7.530	6
7	1.149	1.316	1.504	1.714	1.949	2.211	2.502	2.826	3.185	3.583	4.023	4.508	5.042	5.629	6.275	6.983	10.541	7
8	1.172	1.369	1.594	1.851	2.144	2.476	2.853	3.278	3.759	4.300	4.908	5.590	6.353	7.206	8.157	9.217	14.758	8
9	1.195	1.423	1.689	1.999	2.358	2.773	3.252	3.803	4.435	5.160	5.987	6.931	8.005	9.223	10.604	12.166	20.661	9
10	1.219	1.480	1.791	2.159	2.594	3.106	3.707	4.411	5.234	6.192	7.305	8.594	10.086	11.806	13.786	16.060	28.925	10
11	1.243	1.539	1.898	2.332	2.853	3.479	4.226	5.117	6.176	7.430	8.912	10.657	12.708	15.112	17.922	21.199	40.496	11
12	1.268	1.601	2.012	2.518	3.138	3.896	4.818	5.936	7.288	8.916	10.872	13.215	16.012	19.343	23.298	27.983	56.694	12
13	1.294	1.665	2.133	2.720	3.452	4.363	5.492	6.886	8.599	10.699	13.264	16.386	20.175	24.759	30.288	36.937	79.371	13
14	1.319	1.732	2.261	2.937	3.797	4.887	6.261	7.988	10.147	12.839	16.182	20.319	25.421	31.691	39.374	48.757	111.120	14
15	1.346	1.801	2.397	3.172	4.177	5.474	7.138	9.266	11.974	15.407	19.742	25.196	32.030	40.565	51.186	64.359	155.568	15
16	1.373	1.873	2.540	3.426	4.595	6.130	8.137	10.748	14.129	18.488	24.086	31.243	40.358	51.923	66.542	84.954	217.795	16
17	1.400	1.948	2.693	3.700	5.054	6.866	9.276	12.468	16.672	22.186	29.384	38.741	50.851	66.461	86.504	112.139	304.913	17
18	1.428	2.026	2.854	3.996	5.560	7.690	10.575	14.463	19.673	26.623	35.849	48.039	64.072	85.071	112.455	148.024	426.879	18
19	1.457	2.107	3.026	4.316	6.116	8.613	12.056	16.777	23.214	31.948	43.736	59.568	80.731	108.890	146.192	195.391	597.630	19
20	1.486	2.191	3.207	4.661	6.727	9.646	13.743	19.461	27.393	38.338	53.358	73.864	101.721	139.380	190.050	257.916	836.683	20
21	1.516	2.279	3.400	5.034	7.400	10.804	15.668	22.574	32.324	46.005	65.096	91.592	128.169	178.406	247.065	340.449	1171.356	21
22	1.546	2.370	3.604	5.437	8.140	12.100	17.861	26.186	38.142	55.206	79.418	113.574	161.492	228.360	321.184	449.393	1639.898	22
23	1.577	2.465	3.820	5.871	8.954	13.552	20.362	30.376	45.008	66.247	96.889	140.831	203.480	292.300	417.539	593.199	2295.857	23
24	1.608	2.563	4.049	6.341	9.850	15.179	23.212	35.236	53.109	79.497	118.205	174.631	256.385	374.144	542.801	783.023	3214.200	24
25	1.641	2.666	4.292	6.848	10.835	17.000	26.462	40.874	62.669	95.396	144.210	216.542	323.045	478.905	705.641	1033.590	4499.880	25
26	1.673	2.772	4.549	7.396	11.918	19.040	30.167	47.414	73.949	114.475	175.936	268.512	407.037	612.998	917.333	1364.339	6299.831	26
27	1.707	2.883	4.822	7.988	13.110	21.325	34.390	55.000	87.260	137.371	214.642	332.955	512.867	784.638	1192.533	1800.927	8819.764	27
28	1.741	2.999	5.112	8.627	14.421	23.884	39.204	63.800	102.967	164.845	261.864	412.864	646.212	1004.336	1550.293	2377.224	12347.670	28
29	1.776	3.119	5.418	9.317	15.863	26.750	44.693	74.009	121.501	197.814	319.474	511.952	814.228	1285.550	2015.381	3137.935	17286.737	29
30	1.811	3.243	5.743	10.063	17.449	29.960	50.950	85.850	143.371	237.376	389.758	634.820	1025.927	1645.505	2619.996	4142.075	24201.432	30
35	2.000	3.946	7.686	14.785	28.102	52.800	98.100	180.314	327.997	590.668	1053.402	1861.054	3258.135	5653.911	9727.860	16599.217	130161.112	35
40	2.208	4.801	10.286	21.725	45.259	93.051	188.884	378.721	750.378	1469.772	2847.038	5455.913	10347.175	19426.689	36118.865	66520.767	700037.697	40

Table 2 ***(Place a clip on this page for easy reference.)***

Present Value of $1.00

$P = \frac{S}{(1+r)^n}$. In this table S = $1.00.

Periods	2%	4%	6%	8%	10%	12%	14%	16%	18%	20%	22%	24%	26%	28%	30%	32%	40%	Periods
1	0.980	0.962	0.943	0.926	0.909	0.893	0.877	0.862	0.847	0.833	0.820	0.806	0.794	0.781	0.769	0.758	0.714	1
2	0.961	0.925	0.890	0.857	0.826	0.797	0.769	0.743	0.718	0.694	0.672	0.650	0.630	0.610	0.592	0.574	0.510	2
3	0.942	0.889	0.840	0.794	0.751	0.712	0.675	0.641	0.609	0.579	0.551	0.524	0.500	0.477	0.455	0.435	0.364	3
4	0.924	0.855	0.792	0.735	0.683	0.636	0.592	0.552	0.516	0.482	0.451	0.423	0.397	0.373	0.350	0.329	0.260	4
5	0.906	0.822	0.747	0.681	0.621	0.567	0.519	0.476	0.437	0.402	0.370	0.341	0.315	0.291	0.269	0.250	0.186	5
6	0.888	0.790	0.705	0.630	0.564	0.507	0.456	0.410	0.370	0.335	0.303	0.275	0.250	0.227	0.207	0.189	0.133	6
7	0.871	0.760	0.665	0.583	0.513	0.452	0.400	0.354	0.314	0.279	0.249	0.222	0.198	0.178	0.159	0.143	0.095	7
8	0.853	0.731	0.627	0.540	0.467	0.404	0.351	0.305	0.266	0.233	0.204	0.179	0.157	0.139	0.123	0.108	0.068	8
9	0.837	0.703	0.592	0.500	0.424	0.361	0.308	0.263	0.225	0.194	0.167	0.144	0.125	0.108	0.094	0.082	0.048	9
10	0.820	0.676	0.558	0.463	0.386	0.322	0.270	0.227	0.191	0.162	0.137	0.116	0.099	0.085	0.073	0.062	0.035	10
11	0.804	0.650	0.527	0.429	0.350	0.287	0.237	0.195	0.162	0.135	0.112	0.094	0.079	0.066	0.056	0.047	0.025	11
12	0.788	0.625	0.497	0.397	0.319	0.257	0.208	0.168	0.137	0.112	0.092	0.076	0.062	0.052	0.043	0.036	0.018	12
13	0.773	0.601	0.469	0.368	0.290	0.229	0.182	0.145	0.116	0.093	0.075	0.061	0.050	0.040	0.033	0.027	0.013	13
14	0.758	0.577	0.442	0.340	0.263	0.205	0.160	0.125	0.099	0.078	0.062	0.049	0.039	0.032	0.025	0.021	0.009	14
15	0.743	0.555	0.417	0.315	0.239	0.183	0.140	0.108	0.084	0.065	0.051	0.040	0.031	0.025	0.020	0.016	0.006	15
16	0.728	0.534	0.394	0.292	0.218	0.163	0.123	0.093	0.071	0.054	0.042	0.032	0.025	0.019	0.015	0.012	0.005	16
17	0.714	0.513	0.371	0.270	0.198	0.146	0.108	0.080	0.060	0.045	0.034	0.026	0.020	0.015	0.012	0.009	0.003	17
18	0.700	0.494	0.350	0.250	0.180	0.130	0.095	0.069	0.051	0.038	0.028	0.021	0.016	0.012	0.009	0.007	0.002	18
19	0.686	0.475	0.331	0.232	0.164	0.116	0.083	0.060	0.043	0.031	0.023	0.017	0.012	0.009	0.007	0.005	0.002	19
20	0.673	0.456	0.312	0.215	0.149	0.104	0.073	0.051	0.037	0.026	0.019	0.014	0.010	0.007	0.005	0.004	0.001	20
21	0.660	0.439	0.294	0.199	0.135	0.093	0.064	0.044	0.031	0.022	0.015	0.011	0.008	0.006	0.004	0.003	0.001	21
22	0.647	0.422	0.278	0.184	0.123	0.083	0.056	0.038	0.026	0.018	0.013	0.009	0.006	0.004	0.003	0.002	0.001	22
23	0.634	0.406	0.262	0.170	0.112	0.074	0.049	0.033	0.022	0.015	0.010	0.007	0.005	0.003	0.002	0.002	0.000	23
24	0.622	0.390	0.247	0.158	0.102	0.066	0.043	0.028	0.019	0.013	0.008	0.006	0.004	0.003	0.002	0.001	0.000	24
25	0.610	0.375	0.233	0.146	0.092	0.059	0.038	0.024	0.016	0.010	0.007	0.005	0.003	0.002	0.001	0.001	0.000	25
26	0.598	0.361	0.220	0.135	0.084	0.053	0.033	0.021	0.014	0.009	0.006	0.004	0.002	0.002	0.001	0.001	0.000	26
27	0.586	0.347	0.207	0.125	0.076	0.047	0.029	0.018	0.011	0.007	0.005	0.003	0.002	0.001	0.001	0.001	0.000	27
28	0.574	0.333	0.196	0.116	0.069	0.042	0.026	0.016	0.010	0.006	0.004	0.002	0.002	0.001	0.001	0.000	0.000	28
29	0.563	0.321	0.185	0.107	0.063	0.037	0.022	0.014	0.008	0.005	0.003	0.002	0.001	0.001	0.000	0.000	0.000	29
30	0.552	0.308	0.174	0.099	0.057	0.033	0.020	0.012	0.007	0.004	0.003	0.002	0.001	0.001	0.000	0.000	0.000	30
35	0.500	0.253	0.130	0.068	0.036	0.019	0.010	0.006	0.003	0.002	0.001	0.001	0.000	0.000	0.000	0.000	0.000	35
40	0.453	0.208	0.097	0.046	0.022	0.011	0.005	0.003	0.001	0.001	0.000	0.000	0.000	0.000	0.000	0.000	0.000	40

Table 3

Compound Amount of Annuity of $1.00 in Arrears* (Future Value of Annuity)

$$S_n = \frac{(1 - r)^n - 1}{r}$$

Periods	2%	4%	6%	8%	10%	12%	14%	16%	18%	20%	22%	24%	26%	28%	30%	32%	40%	Periods
1	1.000	1.000	1.000	1.000	1.000	1.000	1.000	1.000	1.000	1.000	1.000	1.000	1.000	1.000	1.000	1.000	1.000	1
2	2.020	2.040	2.060	2.080	2.100	2.120	2.140	2.160	2.180	2.200	2.220	2.240	2.260	2.280	2.300	2.320	2.400	2
3	3.060	3.122	3.184	3.246	3.310	3.374	3.440	3.506	3.572	3.640	3.708	3.778	3.848	3.918	3.990	4.062	4.360	3
4	4.122	4.246	4.375	4.506	4.641	4.779	4.921	5.066	5.215	5.368	5.524	5.684	5.848	6.016	6.187	6.362	7.104	4
5	5.204	5.416	5.637	5.867	6.105	6.353	6.610	6.877	7.154	7.442	7.740	8.048	8.368	8.700	9.043	9.398	10.946	5
6	6.308	6.633	6.975	7.336	7.716	8.115	8.536	8.977	9.442	9.930	10.442	10.980	11.544	12.136	12.756	13.406	16.324	6
7	7.434	7.898	8.394	8.923	9.487	10.089	10.730	11.414	12.142	12.916	13.740	14.615	15.546	16.534	17.583	18.696	23.853	7
8	8.583	9.214	9.897	10.637	11.436	12.300	13.233	14.240	15.327	16.499	17.762	19.123	20.588	22.163	23.858	25.678	34.395	8
9	9.755	10.583	11.491	12.488	13.579	14.776	16.085	17.519	19.086	20.799	22.670	24.712	26.940	29.369	32.015	34.895	49.153	9
10	10.950	12.006	13.181	14.487	15.937	17.549	19.337	21.321	23.521	25.959	28.657	31.643	34.945	38.593	42.619	47.062	69.814	10
11	12.169	13.486	14.972	16.645	18.531	20.655	23.045	25.733	28.755	32.150	35.962	40.238	45.031	50.398	56.405	63.122	98.739	11
12	13.412	15.026	16.870	18.977	21.384	24.133	27.271	30.850	34.931	39.581	44.874	50.895	57.739	65.510	74.327	84.320	139.235	12
13	14.680	16.627	18.882	21.495	24.523	28.029	32.089	36.786	42.219	48.497	55.746	64.110	73.751	84.853	97.625	112.303	195.929	13
14	15.974	18.292	21.015	24.215	27.975	32.393	37.581	43.672	50.818	59.196	69.010	80.496	93.926	109.612	127.913	149.240	275.300	14
15	17.293	20.024	23.276	27.152	31.772	37.280	43.842	51.660	60.965	72.035	85.192	100.815	119.347	141.303	167.286	197.997	386.420	15
16	18.639	21.825	25.673	30.324	35.950	42.753	50.980	60.925	72.939	87.442	104.935	126.011	151.377	181.868	218.472	262.356	541.988	16
17	20.012	23.698	28.213	33.750	40.545	48.884	59.118	71.673	87.068	105.931	129.020	157.253	191.735	233.791	285.014	347.309	759.784	17
18	21.412	25.645	30.906	37.450	45.599	55.750	68.394	84.141	103.740	128.117	158.405	195.994	242.585	300.252	371.518	459.449	1064.697	18
19	22.841	27.671	33.760	41.446	51.159	63.440	78.969	98.603	123.414	154.740	194.254	244.033	306.658	385.323	483.973	607.472	1491.576	19
20	24.297	29.778	36.786	45.762	57.275	72.052	91.025	115.380	146.628	186.688	237.989	303.601	387.389	494.213	630.165	802.863	2089.206	20
21	25.783	31.969	39.993	50.423	64.002	81.699	104.768	134.841	174.021	225.026	291.347	377.465	489.110	633.593	820.215	1060.779	2925.889	21
22	27.299	34.248	43.392	55.457	71.403	92.503	120.436	157.415	206.345	271.031	356.443	469.056	617.278	811.999	1067.280	1401.229	4097.245	22
23	28.845	36.618	46.996	60.893	79.543	104.603	138.297	183.601	244.487	326.237	435.861	582.630	778.771	1040.358	1388.464	1850.622	5737.142	23
24	30.422	39.083	50.816	66.765	88.497	118.155	158.659	213.978	289.494	392.484	532.750	723.461	982.251	1332.659	1806.003	2443.821	8032.999	24
25	32.030	41.646	54.865	73.106	98.347	133.334	181.871	249.214	342.603	471.981	650.955	898.092	1238.636	1706.803	2348.803	3226.844	11247.199	25
26	33.671	44.312	59.156	79.954	109.182	150.334	208.333	290.088	405.272	567.377	795.165	1114.634	1561.682	2185.708	3054.444	4260.434	15747.079	26
27	35.344	47.084	63.706	87.351	121.100	169.374	238.499	337.502	479.221	681.853	971.102	1383.146	1968.719	2798.706	3971.778	5624.772	22046.910	27
28	37.051	49.968	68.528	95.339	134.210	190.699	272.889	392.503	566.481	819.223	1185.744	1716.101	2481.586	3583.344	5164.311	7425.699	30866.674	28
29	38.792	52.966	73.640	103.966	148.631	214.583	312.094	456.303	669.447	984.068	1447.608	2128.965	3127.798	4587.680	6714.604	9802.923	43214.343	29
30	40.568	56.085	79.058	113.263	164.494	241.333	356.787	530.312	790.948	1181.882	1767.081	2640.916	3942.026	5873.231	8729.985	12940.859	60501.081	30
35	49.994	73.652	111.435	172.317	271.024	431.663	693.573	1120.713	1816.652	2948.341	4783.645	7750.225	12527.442	20188.966	32422.868	51869.427	325400.279	35
40	60.402	95.026	154.762	259.057	442.593	767.091	1342.025	2360.757	4163.213	7343.858	12936.535	22728.803	39792.982	69377.460	120392.883	207874.272	1750091.741	40

*Payments (or receipts) at the end of each period.

Table 4 ***(Place a clip on this page for easy reference.)***

Present Value of Annuity $1.00 in Arrears*

$$P_n = \frac{1}{r}\left[1 - \frac{1}{(1+r)^n}\right]$$

Periods	2%	4%	6%	8%	10%	12%	14%	16%	18%	20%	22%	24%	26%	28%	30%	32%	40%	Periods
1	0.980	0.962	0.943	0.926	0.909	0.893	0.877	0.862	0.847	0.833	0.820	0.806	0.794	0.781	0.769	0.758	0.714	1
2	1.942	1.886	1.833	1.783	1.736	1.690	1.647	1.605	1.566	1.528	1.492	1.457	1.424	1.392	1.361	1.331	1.224	2
3	2.884	2.775	2.673	2.577	2.487	2.402	2.322	2.246	2.174	2.106	2.042	1.981	1.923	1.868	1.816	1.766	1.589	3
4	3.808	3.630	3.465	3.312	3.170	3.037	2.914	2.798	2.690	2.589	2.494	2.404	2.320	2.241	2.166	2.096	1.849	4
5	4.713	4.452	4.212	3.993	3.791	3.605	3.433	3.274	3.127	2.991	2.864	2.745	2.635	2.532	2.436	2.345	2.035	5
6	5.601	5.242	4.917	4.623	4.355	4.111	3.889	3.685	3.498	3.326	3.167	3.020	2.885	2.759	2.643	2.534	2.168	6
7	6.472	6.002	5.582	5.206	4.868	4.564	4.288	4.039	3.812	3.605	3.416	3.242	3.083	2.937	2.802	2.677	2.263	7
8	7.325	6.733	6.210	5.747	5.335	4.968	4.639	4.344	4.078	3.837	3.619	3.421	3.241	3.076	2.925	2.786	2.331	8
9	8.162	7.435	6.802	6.247	5.759	5.328	4.946	4.607	4.303	4.031	3.786	3.566	3.366	3.184	3.019	2.868	2.379	9
10	8.983	8.111	7.360	6.710	6.145	5.650	5.216	4.833	4.494	4.192	3.923	3.682	3.465	3.269	3.092	2.930	2.414	10
11	9.787	8.760	7.887	7.139	6.495	5.938	5.453	5.029	4.656	4.327	4.035	3.776	3.543	3.335	3.147	2.978	2.438	11
12	10.575	9.385	8.384	7.536	6.814	6.194	5.660	5.197	4.793	4.439	4.127	3.851	3.606	3.387	3.190	3.013	2.456	12
13	11.348	9.986	8.853	7.904	7.103	6.424	5.842	5.342	4.910	4.533	4.203	3.912	3.656	3.427	3.223	3.040	2.469	13
14	12.106	10.563	9.295	8.244	7.367	6.628	6.002	5.468	5.008	4.611	4.265	3.962	3.695	3.459	3.249	3.061	2.478	14
15	12.849	11.118	9.712	8.559	7.606	6.811	6.142	5.575	5.092	4.675	4.315	4.001	3.726	3.483	3.268	3.076	2.484	15
16	13.578	11.652	10.106	8.851	7.824	6.974	6.265	5.668	5.162	4.730	4.357	4.033	3.751	3.503	3.283	3.088	2.489	16
17	14.292	12.166	10.477	9.122	8.022	7.120	6.373	5.749	5.222	4.775	4.391	4.059	3.771	3.518	3.295	3.097	2.492	17
18	14.992	12.659	10.828	9.372	8.201	7.250	6.467	5.818	5.273	4.812	4.419	4.080	3.786	3.529	3.304	3.104	2.494	18
19	15.678	13.134	11.158	9.604	8.365	7.366	6.550	5.877	5.316	4.843	4.442	4.097	3.799	3.539	3.311	3.109	2.496	19
20	16.351	13.590	11.470	9.818	8.514	7.469	6.623	5.929	5.353	4.870	4.460	4.110	3.808	3.546	3.316	3.113	2.497	20
21	17.011	14.029	11.764	10.017	8.649	7.562	6.687	5.973	5.384	4.891	4.476	4.121	3.816	3.551	3.320	3.116	2.498	21
22	17.658	14.451	12.042	10.201	8.772	7.645	6.743	6.011	5.410	4.909	4.488	4.130	3.822	3.556	3.323	3.118	2.498	22
23	18.292	14.857	12.303	10.371	8.883	7.718	6.792	6.044	5.432	4.925	4.499	4.137	3.827	3.559	3.325	3.120	2.499	23
24	18.914	15.247	12.550	10.529	8.985	7.784	6.835	6.073	5.451	4.937	4.507	4.143	3.831	3.562	3.327	3.121	2.499	24
25	19.523	15.622	12.783	10.675	9.077	7.843	6.873	6.097	5.467	4.948	4.514	4.147	3.834	3.564	3.329	3.122	2.499	25
26	20.121	15.983	13.003	10.810	9.161	7.896	6.906	6.118	5.480	4.956	4.520	4.151	3.837	3.566	3.330	3.123	2.500	26
27	20.707	16.330	13.211	10.935	9.237	7.943	6.935	6.136	5.492	4.964	4.524	4.154	3.839	3.567	3.331	3.123	2.500	27
28	21.281	16.663	13.406	11.051	9.307	7.984	6.961	6.152	5.502	4.970	4.528	4.157	3.840	3.568	3.331	3.124	2.500	28
29	21.844	16.984	13.591	11.158	9.370	8.022	6.983	6.166	5.510	4.975	4.531	4.159	3.841	3.569	3.332	3.124	2.500	29
30	22.396	17.292	13.765	11.258	9.427	8.055	7.003	6.177	5.517	4.979	4.534	4.160	3.842	3.569	3.332	3.124	2.500	30
35	24.999	18.665	14.498	11.655	9.644	8.176	7.070	6.215	5.539	4.992	4.541	4.164	3.845	3.571	3.333	3.125	2.500	35
40	27.355	19.793	15.046	11.925	9.779	8.244	7.105	6.233	5.548	4.997	4.544	4.166	3.846	3.571	3.333	3.125	2.500	40

*Payments (or receipts) at the end of each period.

Appendix C: Cost Accounting in Professional Examinations

This appendix describes the role of cost accounting in professional examinations. We use professional examinations in the United States, Canada, Australia, Japan, and the United Kingdom to illustrate the role. A conscientious reader who has solved a representative sample of the problems at the end of the chapters will be well prepared for the professional examination questions dealing with cost accounting. This appendix aims to provide perspective, instill confidence, and encourage readers to take the examination.

American Professional Examinations

Many American readers may eventually take the Certified Public Accountant (CPA) examination or the Certified Management Accountant (CMA) examination. Certification is important to professional accountants for many reasons, such as:

1. Recognition of achievement and technical competence by fellow accountants and by users of accounting services
2. Increased self-confidence in one's professional abilities
3. Membership in professional organizations offering programs of career-long education
4. Enhancement of career opportunities
5. Personal satisfaction

The CPA certificate is issued by individual states; it is necessary to obtain a state's license to practice as a Certified Public Accountant. A prominent feature of public accounting is the use of independent (external) auditors to give assurance about the reliability of the financial statements supplied by managers. These auditors are called Certified Public Accountants in the United States and Chartered Accountants in many other English-speaking nations. The major U.S. professional association in the private sector that regulates the quality of external auditing is the American Institute of Certified Public Accountants (AICPA).

The CMA designation is offered by the Institute of Management Accountants (IMA). The IMA is the largest association of management accountants in the world. The major objective of the CMA certification is to enhance the development of the management accounting profession. In particular, focus is placed on the modern role of the management accountant as an active contributor to, and a participant in, management. The CMA designation is gaining increased stature in the business community as a credential parallel to the CPA designation.

The CMA examination is given in a computer-based format and has four parts. The questions are carefully constructed multiple-choice and written-response questions that test all levels of cognitive skills. The CMA exam consists of:

Part 1: Business Analysis

- Global Business
- Internal Controls
- Quantitative Methods
- Financial Statement Analysis
- Business Economics

Part 2: Management Accounting and Reporting

- Budget Preparation
- Cost Management
- Information Management
- Performance Measurement
- External Financial Reporting

Part 3: Strategic Management

- Strategic Planning
- Strategic Marketing
- Corporate Finance
- Decision Analysis
- Investment Decision Analysis

Part 4: Business Application

- All topics from Parts 1, 2, and 3, plus:
- Organization Management
- Organization Communication
- Behavioral Issues
- Ethical Considerations

A person who has successfully completed the U.S. CPA examination is exempt from Part 1. For more information, visit the IMA Web site at www.imanet.org.

Cost/management accounting questions are prominent in the CMA examination. The CPA examinations also include such questions, although they are less extensive than questions regarding financial accounting, auditing, and business law. This book includes many questions and problems used in past CMA and CPA examinations. In addition, a supplement to this book, *Student Guide and Review Manual* [John K. Harris (Upper Saddle River, NJ: Prentice Hall, 2009)], contains over 100 CMA and CPA questions and explanatory answers. Careful study of appropriate topics in this book will give candidates sufficient background for succeeding in the cost accounting portions of the professional examinations.

The IMA publishes *Strategic Finance* monthly. Each issue includes advertisements for courses that help students prepare for the CMA examination.

Canadian Professional Examinations

Three professional accounting designations are available in Canada:

Designation	Sponsoring Organization
Certified Management Accountant (CMA)	Certified Management Accountants of Canada (CMA)
Certified General Accountant (CGA)	Certified General Accountants' Association (CGA)
Chartered Accountant (CA)	Canadian Institute of Chartered Accountants (CICA)

The Society of Management Accountants (SMA) represents over 38,000 certified management accountants employed throughout Canadian business, industry, and government.

The CMA Entrance Examination is a one-day examination covering four topics: management accounting (35–40% of the exam), corporate finance (15–20%), financial accounting (35–40%), and taxation (5–10%). It consists entirely of multiple-choice questions and problem-based groups of multiple-choice questions, i.e., several questions based on a common scenario.

The SMA publishes *CMA Management* monthly. This magazine includes details of courses that assist students in preparing for the CMA exam.

Australian Professional Examinations

CPA Australia is the largest body representing accountants in Australia. Their professional designation is termed a CPA (Certified Practicing Accountant). The basic entry requirement for Associate membership in the Society is having an approved Bachelors degree. Associates of the Society can advance to CPA status by passing the CPA program and having the required amount of work experience. There are three compulsory core segments in the program: Reporting and Professional Practice, Corporate Governance and Accountability, and Business Strategy and Leadership. Candidates must also take three of nine elective subjects. These subjects are assurance services and auditing, financial accounting, financial reporting and disclosure, financial risk management, insolvency and reconstruction, knowledge management, personal financial planning and superannuation, strategic management accounting, and taxation.

The strategic management accounting segment topics include:

1. Management accounting: supporting the value creation process
2. Creating organizational value
3. Managing performance measures
4. Techniques for managing value
5. Project management

INTHEBLACK, published monthly, includes advertisements for courses that help students prepare for the CPA examination.

The Institute of Chartered Accountants in Australia (ICAA) offers the Chartered Accountant (CA) certification that has membership requirements including passing five modules: Financial Accounting and Reporting, Management Accounting and Analysis, Audit and Assurance, Taxation, and Ethics and Business Application.

The *Management Accounting & Analysis* module includes topics such as forecasting and budgeting with decision tools, investment analysis tools and techniques, risk management, strategic planning and analysis, ethics, and performance reporting.

Japanese Professional Examinations

There are two major Japanese management accounting organizations—Japanese Industrial Management and Accounting Association (JIMMA) and Enterprise Management Association. The JIMMA is the oldest, largest, and most authoritative accounting organization of its kind in Japan. It directs a School of Cost Control and a School of Corporate Tax Accounting. There are two courses in the School of Cost Control—Preparatory Course and Cost Control Course. These courses are taught by university professors and executives from member corporations. The Enterprise Management Association is the Japanese chapter of the U.S.-based Institute of Management Accountants.

The Japanese Institute of Certified Public Accountants (JICPA) is the organization of the CPA profession in Japan. The CPA exam, conducted by the Certified Public Accountants Board, consists of three stages. The second stage covers cost accounting.

United Kingdom Professional Examinations

The Chartered Institute of Management Accountants (CIMA) is the largest professional management accounting body in the United Kingdom. CIMA provides a wide range of services to members in commerce, education, government, and the accounting profession. The syllabus for the CIMA examination consists of three learning streams:

- *Business Management*: includes papers on organizational management and information systems, integrated management, and business strategy
- *Management Accounting*: includes papers on performance evaluation, decision making, and risk control and strategy
- *Financial Management*: includes papers on financial accounting and tax principles, financial analysis, and financial strategy.

Management Accounting, published monthly by CIMA, includes details of courses assisting students in preparing for their examinations. Management accounting topics are also covered by several other professional bodies. The syllabus for the examinations of the Chartered Association of Certified Accountants (ACCA) has three distinct parts. Skills examined include information for control, decision making, management, strategy, reporting, taxation, and overall strategic financial management.

Other accounting bodies include the Institute of Chartered Accountants in England and Wales (ICAEW) and the Institute for Chartered Accountants of Scotland (ICAS). Both Institutes have requirements that cover proficiency in "general management" topics as well as professional accounting topics.

Glossary

Abnormal spoilage. Spoilage that would not arise under efficient operating conditions; it is not inherent in a particular production process. (640)

Absorption costing. Method of inventory costing in which all variable manufacturing costs and all fixed manufacturing costs are included as inventoriable costs. (301)

Account analysis method. Approach to cost function estimation that classifies various cost accounts as variable, fixed, or mixed with respect to the identified level of activity. Typically, qualitative rather than quantitative analysis is used when making these cost-classification decisions. (343)

Accounting rate of return. See *accrual accounting rate-of-return (AARR)*. (742)

Accrual accounting rate of return (AARR). Divides an accrual accounting measure of average annual income of a project by an accrual accounting measure of its investment. Also called *accounting rate of return* or *return on investment (ROI)*. (742)

Activity. An event, task, or unit of work with a specified purpose. (144)

Activity-based budgeting (ABB). Budgeting approach that focuses on the budgeted cost of the activities necessary to produce and sell products and services. (191)

Activity-based costing (ABC). Approach to costing that focuses on individual activities as the fundamental cost objects. It uses the costs of these activities as the basis for assigning costs to other cost objects such as products or services. (144)

Activity-based management (ABM). Method of management decision-making that uses activity-based costing information to improve customer satisfaction and profitability. (152)

Actual cost. Cost incurred (a historical or past cost), as distinguished from a budgeted or forecasted cost. (27)

Actual costing. A costing system that traces direct costs to a cost object by using the actual direct-cost rates times the actual quantities of the direct-cost inputs and allocates indirect costs based on the actual indirect-cost rates times the actual quantities of the cost allocation bases. (101)

Actual indirect-cost rate. Actual total indirect costs in a cost pool divided by the actual total quantity of the cost-allocation base for that cost pool. (104)

Adjusted allocation-rate approach. Restates all overhead entries in the general ledger and subsidiary ledgers using actual cost rates rather than budgeted cost rates. (116)

Allowable cost. Cost that parties to a contract agree to include in the costs to be reimbursed. (556)

Appraisal costs. Costs incurred to detect which of the individual units of products do not conform to specifications. (667)

Artificial costs. See *complete reciprocated costs*. (550)

Autonomy. The degree of freedom to make decisions. (771)

Average cost. See *unit cost*. (35)

Average waiting time. The average amount of time that an order will wait in line before the machine is set up and the order is processed. (677)

Backflush costing. Costing system that omits recording some of the journal entries relating to the stages from purchase of direct material to the sale of finished goods. (715)

Balanced scorecard. A framework for implementing strategy that translates an organization's mission and strategy into a set of performance measures. (466)

Batch-level costs. The costs of activities related to a group of units of products or services rather than to each individual unit of product or service. (147)

Belief systems. Lever of control that articulates the mission, purpose, norms of behaviors, and core values of a company intended to inspire managers and other employees to do their best. (819)

Benchmarking. The continuous process of comparing the levels of performance in producing products and services and executing activities against the best levels of performance in competing companies or in companies having similar processes. (244)

Book value. The original cost minus accumulated depreciation of an asset. (405)

Bottleneck. An operation where the work to be performed approaches or exceeds the capacity available to do it. (677)

Boundary systems. Lever of control that describes standards of behavior and codes of conduct expected of all employees, especially actions that are off-limits. (817)

Breakeven point. Quantity of output sold at which total revenues equal total costs, that is where the operating income is zero. (66)

Budget. Quantitative expression of a proposed plan of action by management for a specified period and an aid to coordinating what needs to be done to implement that plan. (10)

Budgetary slack. The practice of underestimating budgeted revenues, or overestimating budgeted costs, to make budgeted targets more easily achievable. (199)

Budgeted cost. Predicted or forecasted cost (future cost) as distinguished from an actual or historical cost. (27)

Budgeted indirect-cost rate. Budgeted annual indirect costs in a cost pool divided by the budgeted annual quantity of the cost allocation base. (108)

Budgeted performance. Expected performance or a point of reference to compare actual results. (225)

Bundled product. A package of two or more products (or services) that is sold for a single price, but whose individual components may be sold as separate items at their own "stand-alone" prices. (557)

Business function costs. The sum of all costs (variable and fixed) in a particular business function of the value chain. (391)

Byproducts. Products from a joint production process that have low total sales values compared with the total sales value of the main product or of joint products. (574)

Capital budgeting. The making of long-run planning decisions for investments in projects. (734)

Carrying costs. Costs that arise while holding inventory of goods for sale. (700)

Cash budget. Schedule of expected cash receipts and disbursements. (205)

Cause-and-effect diagram. Diagram that identifies potential causes of defects. Four categories of potential causes of failure are human factors, methods and design factors, machine-related factors, and materials and components factors. Also called a *fishbone diagram*. (671)

Certified in Financial Management (CFM). Certifies that the holder has met the admission criteria and demonstrated the competency of technical knowledge in financial management required by the *Institute of Management Accountants*. (15)

Certified Management Accountant (CMA). Certifies that the holder has met the admission criteria and demonstrated the competency of technical knowledge in management accounting required by the *Institute of Management Accountants*. (15)

Chief financial officer (CFO). Executive responsible for overseeing the financial operations of an organization. Also called *finance director*. (13)

Choice criterion. Objective that can be quantified in a decision model. (81)

Coefficient of determination (r^2). Measures the percentage of variation in a dependent variable explained by one or more independent variables. (364)

Collusive pricing. Companies in an industry conspire in their pricing and production decisions to achieve a price above the competitive price and so restrain trade. (448)

Common cost. Cost of operating a facility, activity, or like cost object that is shared by two or more users. (554)

Complete reciprocated costs. The support department's own costs plus any interdepartmental cost allocations. Also called the *artificial costs* of the support department. (550)

Composite unit. Hypothetical unit with weights based on the mix of individual units. (518)

Conference method. Approach to cost function estimation on the basis of analysis and opinions about costs and their drivers gathered from various departments of a company (purchasing, process engineering, manufacturing, employee relations, and so on). (342)

Conformance quality. Refers to the performance of a product or service relative to its design and product specifications. (666)

Constant. The component of total cost that, within the relevant range, does not vary with changes in the level of the activity. Also called *intercept*. (338)

Constant gross-margin percentage NRV method. Method that allocates joint costs to joint products in such a way that the overall gross-margin percentage is identical for the individual products. (580)

Constraint. A mathematical inequality or equality that must be satisfied by the variables in a mathematical model. (411)

Continuous Budget. See *rolling budget*. (185)

Contribution income statement. Income statement that groups costs into variable costs and fixed costs to highlight the contribution margin. (63)

Contribution margin. Total revenues minus total variable costs. (62)

Contribution margin per unit. Selling price minus the variable cost per unit. (63)

Contribution margin percentage. Contribution margin per unit divided by selling price. Also called *contribution margin ratio*. (63)

Contribution margin ratio. See *contribution margin percentage*. (63)

Control. Taking actions that implement the planning decisions, deciding how to evaluate performance, and providing feedback and learning that will help future decision making. (10)

Control chart. Graph of a series of successive observations of a particular step, procedure, or operation taken at regular intervals of time. Each observation is plotted relative to specified ranges that represent the limits within which observations are expected to fall. (670)

Controllability. Degree of influence that a specific manager has over costs, revenues, or related items for which he or she is responsible. (198)

Controllable cost. Any cost that is primarily subject to the influence of a given responsibility center manager for a given period. (198)

Controller. The financial executive primarily responsible for management accounting and financial accounting. Also called *chief accounting officer*. (13)

Conversion costs. All manufacturing costs other than direct material costs. (42)

Cost. Resource sacrificed or forgone to achieve a specific objective. (27)

Cost accounting. Measures, analyzes, and reports financial and nonfinancial information relating to the costs of acquiring or using resources in an organization. It provides information for both management accounting and financial accounting. (4)

Cost Accounting Standards Board (CASB). Government agency that has the exclusive authority to make, put into effect, amend, and rescind cost accounting standards and interpretations thereof designed to achieve uniformity and consistency in regard to measurement, assignment, and allocation of costs to government contracts within the United States. (555)

Cost accumulation. Collection of cost data in some organized way by means of an accounting system. (27)

Cost allocation. Assignment of indirect costs to a particular cost object. (28)

Cost-allocation base. A factor that links in a systematic way an indirect cost or group of indirect costs to a cost object. (98)

Cost-application base. Cost-allocation base when the cost object is a job, product, or customer. (98)

Cost assignment. General term that encompasses both (1) tracing accumulated costs that have a direct relationship to a cost object and (2) allocating accumulated costs that have an indirect relationship to a cost object. (28)

Cost-benefit approach. Approach to decision-making and resource allocation based on a comparison of the expected benefits from attaining company goals and the expected costs. (12)

Cost center. Responsibility center where the manager is accountable for costs only. (197)

Cost driver. A variable, such as the level of activity or volume, that causally affects costs over a given time span. (32)

Cost estimation. The attempt to measure a past relationship based on data from past costs and the related level of an activity. (340)

Cost function. Mathematical description of how a cost changes with changes in the level of an activity relating to that cost. (337)

Cost hierarchy. Categorization of indirect costs into different cost pools on the basis of the different types of cost drivers, or cost-allocation bases, or different degrees of difficulty in determining cause-and-effect (or benefits received) relationships. (147)

Cost incurrence. Describes when a resource is consumed (or benefit forgone) to meet a specific objective. (437)

Cost leadership. Organization's ability to achieve lower costs relative to competitors through productivity and efficiency improvements, elimination of waste, and tight cost control. (464)

Cost management. The approaches and activities of managers to use resources to increase value to customers and to achieve organizational goals. (5)

Cost object. Anything for which a measurement of costs is desired. (27)

Cost of capital. See *required rate of return (RRR)*. (736)

Cost of goods manufactured. Cost of goods brought to completion, whether they were started before or during the current accounting period. (39)

Cost pool. A grouping of individual cost items. (98)

Cost predictions. Forecasts about future costs. (340)

Cost tracing. Describes the assignment of direct costs to a particular cost object. (28)

Costs of quality (COQ). Costs incurred to prevent, or the costs arising as a result of, the production of a low-quality product. (667)

Cost-volume-profit (CVP) analysis. Examines the behavior of total revenues, total costs, and operating income as changes occur in the units sold, the selling price, the variable cost per unit, or the fixed costs of a product. (61)

Cumulative average-time learning model. Learning curve model in which the cumulative average time per unit declines by a constant percentage each time the cumulative quantity of units produced doubles. (355)

Current cost. Asset measure based on the cost of purchasing an asset today identical to the one currently held, or the cost of purchasing an asset that provides services like the one currently held if an identical asset cannot be purchased. (807)

Customer-cost hierarchy. Hierarchy that categorizes costs related to customers into different cost pools on the basis of different types of cost drivers, or cost-allocation bases, or different degrees of difficulty in determining cause-and-effect or benefits-received relationships. (509)

Customer life-cycle costs. Focuses on the total costs incurred by a customer to acquire, use, maintain, and dispose of a product or service. (445)

Customer-profitability analysis. The reporting and analysis of revenues earned from customers and the costs incurred to earn those revenues. (508)

Customer-response time. Duration from the time a customer places an order for a product or service to the time the product or service is delivered to the customer. (675)

Customer service. Providing after-sale support to customers. (6)

Decentralization. The freedom for managers at lower levels of the organization to make decisions. (771)

Decision model. Formal method for making a choice, often involving both quantitative and qualitative analyses. (387)

Decision table. Summary of the alternative actions, events, outcomes, and probabilities of events in a decision model. (82)

Degree of operating leverage. Contribution margin divided by operating income at any given level of sales. (73)

Denominator level. The denominator in the budgeted fixed overhead rate computation. (268)

Denominator-level variance. See *production-volume variance*. (270)

Dependent variable. The cost to be predicted. (344)

Design of products, services, or processes. The detailed planning and engineering of products, services, or processes. (6)

Design quality. Refers to how closely the characteristics of a product of service meet the needs and wants of customers. (666)

Designed-in costs. See *locked-in costs*. (437)

Diagnostic control systems. Lever of control that monitors critical performance variables that help managers track progress toward achieving a company's strategic goals. Managers are held accountable for meeting these goals. (817)

Differential cost. Difference in total cost between two alternatives. (395)

Differential revenue. Difference in total revenue between two alternatives. (395)

Direct costing. See *variable costing*. (301)

Direct costs of a cost object. Costs related to the particular cost object that can be traced to that object in an economically feasible (cost-effective) way. (28)

Direct manufacturing labor costs. Include the compensation of all manufacturing labor that can be traced to the cost object (work in process and then finished goods) in an economically feasible way. (37)

Direct material costs. Acquisition costs of all materials that eventually become part of the cost object (work in process and then finished goods), and that can be traced to the cost object in an economically feasible way. (36)

Direct materials inventory. Direct materials in stock and awaiting use in the manufacturing process. (36)

Direct materials mix variance. The difference between (1) budgeted cost for actual mix of the actual total quantity of direct materials used and (2) budgeted cost of budgeted mix of the actual total quantity of direct materials used. (525)

Direct materials yield variance. The difference between (1) budgeted cost of direct materials based on the actual total quantity of direct materials used and (2) flexible-budget cost of direct materials based on the budgeted total quantity of direct materials allowed for the actual output produced. (526)

Direct method. Cost allocation method that allocates each support department's costs to operating departments only. (547)

Discount rate. See *required rate of return (RRR)*. (736)

Discounted cash flow (DCF) methods. Capital budgeting methods that measure all expected future cash inflows and outflows of a project as if they occurred at the present point in time. (735)

Discretionary costs. Arise from periodic (usually annual) decisions regarding the maximum amount to be incurred and have no measurable cause-and-effect relationship between output and resources used. (482)

Distribution. Delivering products or services to customers. (6)

Downsizing. An integrated approach of configuring processes, products, and people to match costs to the activities that need to be performed to operate effectively and efficiently in the present and future. Also called *rightsizing*. (484)

Downward demand spiral. Pricing context where prices are raised to spread capacity costs over a smaller number of output units. Continuing reduction in the demand for products that occurs when the prices of competitors' products are not met and, as demand drops further, higher and higher unit costs result in more and more reluctance to meet competitors' prices. (316)

Dual pricing. Approach to transfer pricing using two separate transfer-pricing methods to price each transfer from one subunit to another. (781)

Dual-rate method. Allocation method that classifies costs in each cost pool into two pools (a variable-cost pool and a fixed-cost pool) with each pool using a different cost-allocation base. (542)

Dumping. Under U.S. laws, occurs when a non-U.S. company sells a product in the United States at a price below the market value in the country where it is produced, and this lower price materially injures or threatens to materially injure an industry in the United States. (448)

Dysfunctional decision making. See *suboptimal decision making*. (772)

Economic order quantity (EOQ). Decision model that calculates the optimal quantity of inventory to order under a set of assumptions. (700)

Economic value added (EVA®). After-tax operating income minus the (after-tax) weighted average cost of capital multiplied by total assets minus current liabilities. (804)

Effectiveness. The degree to which a predetermined objective or target is met. (241)

Efficiency. The relative amount of inputs used to achieve a given output level. (241)

Efficiency variance. The difference between actual input quantity used and budgeted input quantity allowed for actual output, multiplied by budgeted price. Also called *usage variance*. (233)

Effort. Exertion toward achieving a goal. (770)

Engineered costs. Costs that result from a cause-and-effect relationship between the cost driver, output, and the (direct or indirect) resources used to produce that output. (481)

Equivalent units. Derived amount of output units that (a) takes the quantity of each input (factor of production) in units completed and in incomplete units of work in process and (b) converts the quantity of input into the amount of completed output units that could be produced with that quantity of input. (604)

Event. A possible relevant occurrence in a decision model. (82)

Expected monetary value. See *expected value*. (83)

Expected value. Weighted average of the outcomes of a decision with the probability of each outcome serving as the weight. Also called *expected monetary value*. (83)

Experience curve. Function that measures the decline in cost per unit in various business functions of the value chain, such as manufacturing, marketing, distribution, and so on, as the amount of these activities increases. (354)

External failure costs. Costs incurred on defective products after they are shipped to customers. (667)

Facility-sustaining costs. The costs of activities that cannot be traced to individual products or services but support the organization as a whole. (148)

Factory overhead costs. See *indirect manufacturing costs*. (37)

Favorable variance. Variance that has the effect of increasing operating income relative to the budgeted amount. Denoted F. (227)

Finance director. See *chief financial officer (CFO)*. (13)

Financial accounting. Measures and records business transactions and provides financial statements that are based on generally accepted accounting principles. It focuses on reporting to external parties such as investors and banks. (4)

Financial budget. Part of the master budget that focuses on how operations and planned capital outlays affect cash. It is made up of the capital expenditures budget, the cash budget, the budgeted balance sheet, and the budgeted statement of cash flows. (186)

Financial planning models. Mathematical representations of the relationships among operating activities, financial activities, and other factors that affect the master budget. (194)

Finished goods inventory. Goods completed but not yet sold. (36)

First-in, first-out (FIFO) process-costing method. Method of process costing that assigns the cost of the previous accounting period's equivalent units in beginning work-in-process inventory to the first units completed and transferred out of the process, and assigns the cost of equivalent units worked on during the current period first to complete beginning inventory, next to start and complete new units, and finally to units in ending work-in-process inventory. (610)

Fixed cost. Cost that remains unchanged in total for a given time period, despite wide changes in the related level of total activity or volume. (30)

Fixed overhead flexible-budget variance. The difference between actual fixed overhead costs and fixed overhead costs in the flexible budget. (269)

Fixed overhead spending variance. Same as the fixed overhead flexible-budget variance. The difference between actual fixed overhead costs and fixed overhead costs in the flexible budget. (269)

Flexible budget. Budget developed using budgeted revenues and budgeted costs based on the actual output in the budget period. (228)

Flexible-budget variance. The difference between an actual result and the corresponding flexible-budget amount based on the actual output level in the budget period. (228)

Full costs of the product. The sum of all variable and fixed costs in all business functions of the value chain (R&D, design, production, marketing, distribution, and customer service). (391)

Goal congruence. Exists when individuals and groups work toward achieving the organization's goals. Managers working in their own best interest take actions that align with the overall goals of top management. (770)

Gross margin percentage. Gross margin divided by revenues. (79)

Growth component. Change in operating income attributable solely to the change in the quantity of output sold between one period and the next. (475)

High-low method. Method used to estimate a cost function that uses only the highest and lowest observed values of the cost driver within the relevant range and their respective costs. (346)

Homogeneous cost pool. Cost pool in which all the costs have the same or a similar cause-and-effect or benefits-received relationship with the cost-allocation base. (507)

Hurdle rate. See *required rate of return (RRR)*. (736)

Hybrid-costing system. Costing system that blends characteristics from both job-costing systems and process-costing systems. (624)

Idle time. Wages paid for unproductive time caused by lack of orders, machine breakdowns, material shortages, poor scheduling, and the like. (44)

Imputed costs. Costs recognized in particular situations but not incorporated in financial accounting records. (803)

Incongruent decision making. See *suboptimal decision making*. (772)

Incremental cost. Additional total cost incurred for an activity. (395)

Incremental cost-allocation method. Method that ranks the individual users of a cost object in the order of users most responsible for the common cost and then uses this ranking to allocate cost among those users. (554)

Incremental revenue. Additional total revenue from an activity. (395)

Incremental revenue-allocation method. Method that ranks individual products in a bundle according to criteria determined by management (for example, sales), and then uses this ranking to allocate bundled revenues to the individual products. (558)

Incremental unit-time learning model. Learning curve model in which the incremental time needed to produce the last unit declines by a constant percentage each time the cumulative quantity of units produced doubles. (355)

Independent variable. Level of activity or cost driver used to predict the dependent variable (costs) in a cost estimation or prediction model. (344)

Indirect costs of a cost object. Costs related to the particular cost object that cannot be traced to that object in an economically feasible (cost-effective) way. (28)

Indirect manufacturing costs. All manufacturing costs that are related to the cost object (work in process and then finished goods) but that cannot be traced to that cost object in an economically feasible way. Also called *manufacturing overhead costs* and *factory overhead costs*. (37)

Industrial engineering method. Approach to cost function estimation that analyzes the relationship between inputs and outputs in physical terms. Also called *work measurement method*. (342)

Inflation. The decline in the general purchasing power of the monetary unit, such as dollars. (756)

Input-price variance. See *price variance*. (233)

Insourcing. Process of producing goods or providing services within the organization rather than purchasing those same goods or services from outside vendors. (393)

Inspection point. Stage of the production process at which products are examined to determine whether they are acceptable or unacceptable units. (641)

Institute of Management Accountants (IMA). A professional accounting organization. It is the largest association of management accountants in the United States. (15)

Interactive control systems. Formal information systems that managers use to focus organization attention and learning on key strategic issues. (819)

Intercept. See *constant*. (338)

Intermediate product. Product transferred from one subunit to another subunit of an organization. This product may either be further worked on by the receiving subunit or sold to an external customer. (774)

Internal failure costs. Costs incurred on defective products before they are shipped to customers. (667)

Internal rate-of-return (IRR) method. Capital budgeting discounted cash flow (DCF) method that calculates the discount rate at which the present value of expected cash inflows from a project equals the present value of its expected cash outflows. (737)

Inventoriable costs. All costs of a product that are considered as assets in the balance sheet when they are incurred and that become cost of goods sold only when the product is sold. (37)

Inventory management. Planning, coordinating, and controlling activities related to the flow of inventory into, through, and out of an organization. (699)

Investment. Resources or assets used to generate income. (800)

Investment center. Responsibility center where the manager is accountable for investments, revenues, and costs. (197)

Job. A unit or multiple units of a distinct product or service. (99)

Job-cost record. Source document that records and accumulates all the costs assigned to a specific job, starting when work begins. Also called *job-cost sheet.* (101)

Job-cost sheet. See *job-cost record.* (101)

Job-costing system. Costing system in which the cost object is a unit or multiple units of a distinct product or service called a job. (99)

Joint costs. Costs of a production process that yields multiple products simultaneously. (573)

Joint products. Two or more products that have high total sales values compared with the total sales values of other products yielded by a joint production process. (574)

Just-in-time (JIT) production. Demand-pull manufacturing system in which each component in a production line is produced as soon as, and only when, needed by the next step in the production line. Also called *lean production.* (711)

Just-in-time (JIT) purchasing. The purchase of materials (or goods) so that they are delivered just as needed for production (or sales). (706)

Kaizen budgeting. Budgetary approach that explicitly incorporates continuous improvement anticipated during the budget period into the budget numbers. (195)

Labor-time record. Source document that contains information about the amount of labor time used for a specific job in a specific department. (102)

Lean accounting. Costing method that supports creating value for the customer by costing the entire value stream, not individual products or departments, thereby eliminating waste in the accounting process. (721)

Lean production. See *just-in-time (JIT) production.* (711)

Learning. Involves managers examining past performance and systematically exploring alternative ways to make better-informed decisions and plans in the future. (10)

Learning curve. Function that measures how labor-hours per unit decline as units of production increase because workers are learning and becoming better at their jobs. (353)

Life-cycle budgeting. Budget that estimates the revenues and business function costs of the value chain attributable to each product from initial R&D to final customer service and support. (443)

Life-cycle costing. System that tracks and accumulates business function costs of the value chain attributable to each product from initial R&D to final customer service and support. (443)

Line management. Managers (for example, in production, marketing, or distribution) who are directly responsible for attaining the goals of the organization. (13)

Linear cost function. Cost function in which the graph of total costs versus the level of a single activity related to that cost is a straight line within the relevant range. (338)

Linear programming (LP). Optimization technique used to maximize an objective function (for example, contribution margin of a mix of products), when there are multiple constraints. (411)

Locked-in costs. Costs that have not yet been incurred but, based on decisions that have already been made, will be incurred in the future. Also called *designed-in costs.* (437)

Main product. Product from a joint production process that has a high total sales value compared with the total sales values of all other products of the joint production process. (574)

Make-or-buy decisions. Decisions about whether a producer of goods or services will insource (produce goods or services within the firm) or outsource (purchase them from outside vendors). (393)

Management accounting. Measures, analyzes, and reports financial and nonfinancial information that helps managers make decisions to fulfill the goals of an organization. It focuses on internal reporting. (4)

Management by exception. Practice of focusing management attention on areas not operating as expected and giving less attention to areas operating as expected. (225)

Management control system. Means of gathering and using information to aid and coordinate the planning and control decisions throughout an organization and to guide the behavior of its managers and employees. (769)

Manufacturing cells. Grouping of all the different types of equipment used to make a given product. (711)

Manufacturing cycle efficiency (MCE). Value-added manufacturing time divided by manufacturing cycle time. (676)

Manufacturing cycle time. See *manufacturing lead time.* (676)

Manufacturing lead time. Duration between the time an order is received by manufacturing to the time a finished good is produced. Also called *manufacturing cycle time.* (676)

Manufacturing overhead allocated. Amount of manufacturing overhead costs allocated to individual jobs, products, or services based on the budgeted rate multiplied by the actual quantity used of the cost-allocation base. Also called *manufacturing overhead applied.* (111)

Manufacturing overhead applied. See *manufacturing overhead allocated.* (111)

Manufacturing overhead costs. See *indirect manufacturing costs.* (37)

Manufacturing-sector companies. Companies that purchase materials and components and convert them into various finished goods. (36)

Margin of safety. Amount by which budgeted (or actual) revenues exceed breakeven revenues. (71)

Marketing. Promoting and selling products or services to customers or prospective customers. (6)

Market-share variance. The difference in budgeted contribution margin for actual market size in units caused solely by actual market share being different from budgeted market share. (519)

Market-size variance. The difference in budgeted contribution margin at the budgeted market share caused solely by actual market size in units being different from budgeted market size in units. (520)

Master budget. Expression of management's operating and financial plans for a specified period (usually a fiscal year) and includes a set of budgeted financial statements. Also called *pro forma statements*. (183)

Master-budget capacity utilization. The expected level of capacity utilization for the current budget period (typically one year). (314)

Materials requirements planning (MRP). Push-through system that manufactures finished goods for inventory on the basis of demand forecasts. (710)

Materials-requisition record. Source document that contains information about the cost of direct materials used on a specific job and in a specific department. (101)

Merchandising-sector companies. Companies that purchase and then sell tangible products without changing their basic form. (36)

Mixed cost. A cost that has both fixed and variable elements. Also called a *semivariable cost*. (338)

Moral hazard. Describes situations in which an employee prefers to exert less effort (or to report distorted information) compared with the effort (or accurate information) desired by the owner because the employee's effort (or validity of the reported information) cannot be accurately monitored and enforced. (814)

Motivation. The desire to attain a selected goal (the goal-congruence aspect) combined with the resulting pursuit of that goal (the effort aspect). (770)

Multicollinearity. Exists when two or more independent variables in a multiple regression model are highly correlated with each other. (371)

Multiple regression. Regression model that estimates the relationship between the dependent variable and two or more independent variables. (348)

Net income. Operating income plus nonoperating revenues (such as interest revenue) minus nonoperating costs (such as interest cost) minus income taxes. (68)

Net present value (NPV) method. Capital budgeting discounted cash flow (DCF) method that calculates the expected monetary gain or loss from a project by discounting all expected future cash inflows and outflows to the present point in time, using the required rate of return. (736)

Net realizable value (NRV) method. Method that allocates joint costs to joint products on the basis of final sales value minus separable costs of total production of the joint products during the accounting period. (579)

Nominal rate of return. Made up of three elements: (a) a risk-free element when there is no expected inflation, (b) a business-risk element, and (c) an inflation element. (756)

Nonlinear cost function. Cost function in which the graph of total costs based on the level of a single activity is not a straight line within the relevant range. (352)

Nonvalue-added cost. A cost that, if eliminated, would not reduce the actual or perceived value or utility (usefulness) customers obtain from using the product or service. (436)

Normal capacity utilization. The level of capacity utilization that satisfies average customer demand over a period (say, 2–3 years) that includes seasonal, cyclical, and trend factors. (314)

Normal costing. A costing system that traces direct costs to a cost object by using the actual direct-cost rates times the actual quantities of the direct-cost inputs and that allocates indirect costs based on the budgeted indirect-cost rates times the actual quantities of the cost-allocation bases. (108)

Normal spoilage. Spoilage inherent in a particular production process that arises even under efficient operating conditions. (640)

Objective function. Expresses the objective to be maximized (for example, operating income) or minimized (for example, operating costs) in a decision model (for example, a linear programming model). (411)

On-time performance. Delivering a product or service by the time it is scheduled to be delivered. (676)

One-time-only special order. Orders that have no long-run implications. (390)

Operating budget. Budgeted income statement and its supporting budget schedules. (186)

Operating department. Department that directly adds value to a product or service. Also called a *production department* in manufacturing companies. (541)

Operating income. Total revenues from operations minus cost of goods sold and operating costs (excluding interest expense and income taxes). (40)

Operating leverage. Effects that fixed costs have on changes in operating income as changes occur in units sold and hence in contribution margin. (73)

Operation. A standardized method or technique that is performed repetitively, often on different materials, resulting in different finished goods. (627)

Operation-costing system. Hybrid-costing system applied to batches of similar, but not identical, products. Each batch of products is often a variation of a single design, and it proceeds through a sequence of operations, but each batch does not necessarily move through the same operations as other batches. Within each operation, all product units use identical amounts of the operation's resources. (627)

Opportunity cost. The contribution to operating income that is forgone or rejected by not using a limited resource in its next-best alternative use. (396)

Opportunity cost of capital. See *required rate of return (RRR)*. (736)

Ordering costs. Costs of preparing, issuing, and paying purchase orders, plus receiving and inspecting the items included in the orders. (700)

Organization structure. Arrangement of lines of responsibility within the organization. (197)

Outcomes. Predicted economic results of the various possible combinations of actions and events in a decision model. (82)

Output unit-level costs. The costs of activities performed on each individual unit of a product or service. (147)

Outsourcing. Process of purchasing goods and services from outside vendors rather than producing the same goods or providing the same services within the organization. (393)

Overabsorbed indirect costs. See *overallocated indirect costs.* (116)

Overallocated indirect costs. Allocated amount of indirect costs in an accounting period is greater than the actual (incurred) amount in that period. Also called *overapplied indirect costs* and *overabsorbed indirect costs.* (116)

Overapplied indirect costs. See *overallocated indirect costs.* (116)

Overtime premium. Wage rate paid to workers (for both direct labor and indirect labor) in excess of their straight-time wage rates. (43)

Pareto diagram. Chart that indicates how frequently each type of defect occurs, ordered from the most frequent to the least frequent. (671)

Partial productivity. Measures the quantity of output produced divided by the quantity of an individual input used. (490)

Payback method. Capital budgeting method that measures the time it will take to recoup, in the form of expected future cash flows, the net initial investment in a project. (740)

Peak-load pricing. Practice of charging a higher price for the same product or service when the demand for it approaches the physical limit of the capacity to produce that product or service. (446)

Perfectly competitive market. Exists when there is a homogeneous product with buying prices equal to selling prices and no individual buyers or sellers can affect those prices by their own actions. (777)

Period costs. All costs in the income statement other than cost of goods sold. (37)

Physical-measure method. Method that allocates joint costs to joint products on the basis of the relative weight, volume, or other physical measure at the splitoff point of total production of these products during the accounting period. (577)

Planning. Selecting organization goals, predicting results under various alternative ways of achieving those goals, deciding how to attain the desired goals, and communicating the goals and how to attain them to the entire organization. (9)

Practical capacity. The level of capacity that reduces theoretical capacity by unavoidable operating interruptions such as scheduled maintenance time, shutdowns for holidays, and so on. (313)

Predatory pricing. Company deliberately prices below its costs in an effort to drive out competitors and restrict supply and then raises prices rather than enlarge demand. (447)

Prevention costs. Costs incurred to preclude the production of products that do not conform to specifications. (667)

Previous department costs. See *transferred-in costs.* (619)

Price discount. Reduction in selling price below list selling price to encourage increases in customer purchases. (509)

Price discrimination. Practice of charging different customers different prices for the same product or service. (446)

Price-recovery component. Change in operating income attributable solely to changes in prices of inputs and outputs between one period and the next. (475)

Price variance. The difference between actual price and budgeted price multiplied by actual quantity of input. Also called *input-price variance* or *rate variance.* (233)

Prime costs. All direct manufacturing costs. (42)

Pro forma statements. Budgeted financial statements. (183)

Probability. Likelihood or chance that an event will occur. (82)

Probability distribution. Describes the likelihood (or the probability) that each of the mutually exclusive and collectively exhaustive set of events will occur. (82)

Process-costing system. Costing system in which the cost object is masses of identical or similar units of a product or service. (99)

Product. Any output that has a positive total sales value (or an output that enables an organization to avoid incurring costs). (574)

Product cost. Sum of the costs assigned to a product for a specific purpose. (45)

Product-cost cross-subsidization. Costing outcome where one undercosted (overcosted) product results in at least one other product being overcosted (undercosted). (138)

Product differentiation. Organization's ability to offer products or services perceived by its customers to be superior and unique relative to the products or services of its competitors. (464)

Product life cycle. Spans the time from initial R&D on a product to when customer service and support is no longer offered for that product. (443)

Product-mix decisions. Decisions about which products to sell and in what quantities. (400)

Product overcosting. A product consumes a low level of resources but is reported to have a high cost per unit. (138)

Product-sustaining costs. The costs of activities undertaken to support individual products regardless of the number of units or batches in which the units are produced. (147)

Product undercosting. A product consumes a high level of resources but is reported to have a low cost per unit. (138)

Production. Acquiring, coordinating, and assembling resources to produce a product or deliver a service. (6)

Production department. See *operating department.* (541)

Production-denominator level. The denominator in the budgeted manufacturing fixed overhead rate computation. (268)

Production-volume variance. The difference between budgeted fixed overhead and fixed overhead allocated on the basis of actual output produced. Also called *denominator-level variance.* (270)

Productivity. Measures the relationship between actual inputs used (both quantities and costs) and actual outputs produced; the lower the inputs for a given quantity of outputs or the higher the outputs for a given quantity of inputs, the higher the productivity. (489)

Productivity component. Change in costs attributable to a change in the quantity of inputs used in the current period relative to the quantity of inputs that would have been used in the prior period to produce the quantity of current period output. (475)

Profit center. Responsibility center where the manager is accountable for revenues and costs. (197)

Proration. The spreading of underallocated manufacturing overhead or overallocated manufacturing overhead among ending work in process, finished goods, and cost of goods sold. (117)

Purchase-order lead time. The time between placing an order and its delivery. (700)

Purchasing costs. Cost of goods acquired from suppliers including incoming freight or transportation costs. (700)

PV graph. Shows how changes in the quantity of units sold affect operating income. (67)

Qualitative factors. Outcomes that are difficult to measure accurately in numerical terms. (389)

Quality. The total features and characteristics of a product made or a service performed according to specifications to satisfy customers at the time of purchase and during use. (665)

Quantitative factors. Outcomes that are measured in numerical terms. (389)

Rate variance. See *price variance.* (233)

Real rate of return. The rate of return demanded to cover investment risk (with no inflation). It has a risk-free element and a business-risk element. (756)

Reciprocal method. Cost allocation method that fully recognizes the mutual services provided among all support departments. (550)

Reengineering. The fundamental rethinking and redesign of business processes to achieve improvements in critical measures of performance, such as cost, quality, service, speed, and customer satisfaction. (465)

Refined costing system. Costing system that reduces the use of broad averages for assigning the cost of resources to cost objects (jobs, products, services) and provides better measurement of the costs of indirect resources used by different cost objects—no matter how differently various cost objects use indirect resources. (143)

Regression analysis. Statistical method that measures the average amount of change in the dependent variable associated with a unit change in one or more independent variables. (348)

Relevant costs. Expected future costs that differ among alternative courses of action being considered. (388)

Relevant range. Band of normal activity level or volume in which there is a specific relationship between the level of activity or volume and the cost in question. (32)

Relevant revenues. Expected future revenues that differ among alternative courses of action being considered. (388)

Reorder point. The quantity level of inventory on hand that triggers a new purchase order. (702)

Required rate of return (RRR). The minimum acceptable annual rate of return on an investment. Also called the *discount rate*, *hurdle rate*, *cost of capital*, or *opportunity cost of capital.* (736)

Research and development. Generating and experimenting with ideas related to new products, services, or processes. (6)

Residual income (RI). Accounting measure of income minus a dollar amount for required return on an accounting measure of investment. (803)

Residual term. The vertical difference or distance between actual cost and estimated cost for each observation in a regression model. (348)

Responsibility accounting. System that measures the plans, budgets, actions, and actual results of each responsibility center. (197)

Responsibility center. Part, segment, or subunit of an organization whose manager is accountable for a specified set of activities. (197)

Return on investment (ROI). An accounting measure of income divided by an accounting measure of investment. See also *accrual accounting rate of return.* (801)

Revenue allocation. The allocation of revenues that are related to a particular revenue object but cannot be traced to it in an economically feasible (cost-effective) way. (556)

Revenue center. Responsibility center where the manager is accountable for revenues only. (197)

Revenue driver. A variable, such as volume, that causally affects revenues. (65)

Revenue object. Anything for which a separate measurement of revenue is desired. (556)

Revenues. Inflows of assets (usually cash or accounts receivable) received for products or services provided to customers. (37)

Rework. Units of production that do not meet the specifications required by customers for finished units that are subsequently repaired and sold as good finished units. (639)

Rightsizing. See *downsizing.* (484)

Rolling budget. Budget or plan that is always available for a specified future period by adding a period (month, quarter or year) to the period that just ended. Also called *continuous budget.* (185)

Safety stock. Inventory held at all times regardless of the quantity of inventory ordered using the EOQ model. (703)

Sales mix. Quantities of various products or services that constitute total unit sales. (75)

Sales-mix variance. The difference between (1) budgeted contribution margin for the actual sales mix, and (2) budgeted contribution margin for the budgeted sales mix. (517)

Sales-quantity variance. The difference between (1) budgeted contribution margin based on actual units sold of all products at the budgeted-mix and (2) contribution margin in the static budget (which is based on the budgeted units of all products to be sold at the budgeted mix). (519)

Sales value at splitoff method. Method that allocates joint costs to joint products on the basis of the relative total sales value at the splitoff point of the total production of these products during the accounting period. (576)

Sales-volume variance. The difference between a flexible-budget amount and the corresponding static-budget amount. (228)

Scrap. Residual material left over when making a product. (639)

Selling-price variance. The difference between the actual selling price and the budgeted selling price multiplied by the actual units sold. (230)

Semivariable cost. See *mixed cost.* (338)

Sensitivity analysis. A what-if technique that managers use to examine how an outcome will change if the original predicted data are not achieved or if an underlying assumption changes. (71)

Separable costs. All costs (manufacturing, marketing, distribution, and so on) incurred beyond the splitoff point that are assignable to each of the specific products identified at the splitoff point. (573)

Sequential allocation method. See *step-down method.* (548)

Sequential tracking. Approach in a product-costing system in which recording of the journal entries occurs in the same order as actual purchases and progress in production. (715)

Service department. See *support department.* (541)

Service-sector companies. Companies that provide services or intangible products to their customers. (36)

Service-sustaining costs. The costs of activities undertaken to support individual services. (147)

Shrinkage costs. Costs that result from theft by outsiders, embezzlement by employees, misclassifications, and clerical errors. (700)

Simple regression. Regression model that estimates the relationship between the dependent variable and one independent variable. (348)

Single-rate method. Allocation method that allocates costs in each cost pool to cost objects using the same rate per unit of a single allocation base. (542)

Slope coefficient. Coefficient term in a cost estimation model that indicates the amount by which total cost changes when a one-unit change occurs in the level of activity within the relevant range. (338)

Source document. An original record that supports journal entries in an accounting system. (101)

Specification analysis. Testing of the assumptions of regression analysis. (365)

Splitoff point. The juncture in a joint-production process when two or more products become separately identifiable. (573)

Spoilage. Units of production that do not meet the specifications required by customers for good units and that are discarded or sold at reduced prices. (639)

Staff management. Staff (such as management accountants and human resources managers) who provide advice and assistance to line management. (13)

Stand-alone cost-allocation method. Method that uses information pertaining to each user of a cost object as a separate entity to determine the cost-allocation weights. (554)

Stand-alone revenue-allocation method. Method that uses product-specific information on the products in the bundle as weights for allocating the bundled revenues to the individual products. (557)

Standard. A carefully determined price, cost, or quantity that is used as a benchmark for judging performance. It is usually expressed on a per unit basis. (232)

Standard cost. A carefully determined cost of a unit of output. (232)

Standard costing. Costing system that traces direct costs to output produced by multiplying the standard prices or rates by the standard quantities of inputs allowed for actual outputs produced and allocates overhead costs on the basis of the standard overhead-cost rates times the standard quantities of the allocation bases allowed for the actual outputs produced. (262)

Standard error of the estimated coefficient. Regression statistic that indicates how much the estimated value of the coefficient is likely to be affected by random factors. (364)

Standard error of the regression. Statistic that measures the variance of residuals in a regression analysis. (364)

Standard input. A carefully determined quantity of input required for one unit of output. (232)

Standard price. A carefully determined price that a company expects to pay for a unit of input. (232)

Static budget. Budget based on the level of output planned at the start of the budget period. (226)

Static-budget variance. Difference between an actual result and the corresponding budgeted amount in the static budget. (227)

Step cost function. A cost function in which the cost remains the same over various ranges of the level of activity, but the cost increases by discrete amounts (that is, increases in steps) as the level of activity changes from one range to the next. (353)

Step-down method. Cost allocation method that partially recognizes the mutual services provided among all support departments. Also called *sequential allocation method.* (548)

Stockout costs. Costs that result when a company runs out of a particular item for which there is customer demand. The company must act to meet that demand or suffer the costs of not meeting it. (700)

Strategic cost management describes cost management that specifically focuses on strategic issues. (5)

Strategy. Specifies how an organization matches its own capabilities with the opportunities in the marketplace to accomplish its objectives. (5)

Suboptimal decision making. Decisions in which the benefit to one subunit is more than offset by the costs or loss of benefits to the organization as a whole. Also called *incongruent decision making* or *dysfunctional decision making.* (772)

Sunk costs. Past costs that are unavoidable because they cannot be changed no matter what action is taken. (389)

Super-variable costing. See *throughput costing.* (309)

Supply chain. Describes the flow of goods, services, and information from the initial sources of materials and services to the delivery of products to consumers, regardless of whether those activities occur in the same organization or in other organizations. (7)

Support department. Department that provides the services that assist other internal departments (operating departments and other support departments) in the company. Also called a *service department.* (541)

Target cost per unit. Estimated long-run cost per unit of a product or service that enables the company to achieve its target operating income per unit when selling at the target price.

Target cost per unit is derived by subtracting the target operating income per unit from the target price. (435)

Target operating income per unit. Operating income that a company aims to earn per unit of a product or service sold. (435)

Target price. Estimated price for a product or service that potential customers will pay. (434)

Target rate of return on investment. The target annual operating income that an organization aims to achieve divided by invested capital. (441)

Theoretical capacity. The level of capacity based on producing at full efficiency all the time. (313)

Theory of constraints (TOC). Describes methods to maximize operating income when faced with some bottleneck and some nonbottleneck operations. (681)

Throughput contribution. Revenues minus the direct material costs of the goods sold. (681)

Throughput costing. Method of inventory costing in which only variable direct material costs are included as inventoriable costs. Also called *super-variable costing.* (309)

Time driver. Any factor in which a change in the factor causes a change in the speed of an activity. (677)

Time value of money. Takes into account that a dollar (or any other monetary unit) received today is worth more than a dollar received at any future time. (735)

Total factor productivity (TFP). The ratio of the quantity of output produced to the costs of all inputs used, based on current period prices. (491)

Total-overhead variance. The sum of the flexible-budget variance and the production-volume variance. (277)

Transfer price. Price one subunit (department or division) charges for a product or service supplied to another subunit of the same organization. (774)

Transferred-in costs. Costs incurred in previous departments that are carried forward as the product's costs when it moves to a subsequent process in the production cycle. Also called *previous department costs.* (619)

Trigger point. Refers to a stage in the cycle from purchase of direct materials to sale of finished goods at which journal entries are made in the accounting system. (715)

Uncertainty. The possibility that an actual amount will deviate from an expected amount. (72)

Underabsorbed indirect costs. See *underallocated indirect costs.* (116)

Underallocated indirect costs. Allocated amount of indirect costs in an accounting period is less than the actual (incurred) amount in that period. Also called *underapplied indirect costs* or *underabsorbed indirect costs.* (116)

Underapplied indirect costs. See *underallocated indirect costs.* (116)

Unfavorable variance. Variance that has the effect of decreasing operating income relative to the budgeted amount. Denoted U. (227)

Unit cost. Cost computed by dividing total cost by the number of units. Also called *average cost.* (35)

Unused capacity. The amount of productive capacity available over and above the productive capacity employed to meet consumer demand in the current period. (481)

Usage variance. See *efficiency variance.* (233)

Value-added cost. A cost that, if eliminated, would reduce the actual or perceived value or utility (usefulness) customers obtain from using the product or service. (436)

Value chain. The sequence of business functions in which customer usefulness is added to products or services of a company. (6)

Value engineering. Systematic evaluation of all aspects of the value chain, with the objective of reducing costs and achieving a quality level that satisfies customers. (436)

Value stream. All valued-added activities needed to design, manufacture, and deliver a given product or product line to customers. (721)

Variable cost. Cost that changes in total in proportion to changes in the related level of total activity or volume. (30)

Variable costing. Method of inventory costing in which only all variable manufacturing costs are included as inventoriable costs. Also called *direct costing.* (300)

Variable overhead efficiency variance. The difference between the actual quantity of variable overhead cost-allocation base used and budgeted quantity of variable overhead cost-allocation base that should have been used to produce actual output, multiplied by budgeted variable overhead cost per unit of cost-allocation base. (264)

Variable overhead flexible-budget variance. The difference between actual variable overhead costs incurred and flexible-budget variable overhead amounts. (264)

Variable overhead spending variance. The difference between actual variable overhead cost per unit and budgeted variable overhead cost per unit of the cost-allocation base, multiplied by actual quantity of variable overhead cost-allocation base used for actual output. (265)

Variance. The difference between actual result and expected performance. (225)

Weighted-average process-costing method. Method of process costing that assigns the equivalent-unit cost of the work done to date (regardless of the accounting period in which it was done) to equivalent units completed and transferred out of the process and to equivalent units in ending work-in-process inventory. (608)

Work-in-process inventory. Goods partially worked on but not yet completed. Also called *work in progress.* (36)

Work in progress. See *work-in-process inventory.* (36)

Work-measurement method. See *industrial-engineering method.* (342)

Author Index

Company Index

Subject Index

D